BLUE RIBBON
COLLEGE BASKETBALL
YEARBOOK

Edited By
Chris Wallace

CONTRIBUTORS

American South: Bobby Dower
Atlantic Coast: Happy Fine & Chris Simko
Atlantic 10: Joe Lunardi
Big East: Happy Fine & Bob Herzog
Big Eight: Jim Thomas
Big Sky: Chris Havel
Big Ten: Jason Brist & Happy Fine
Big West: Jim Hague
Colonial Athletic Association: Chris Dortch & Happy Fine
East Coast: Bill Stetka
ECAC North Atlantic: Happy Fine & Jim Hague
Independents: Happy Fine
Ivy League: Mike Bradley
Mid-Eastern Athletic: Bill Stetka

Metro: Ron Higgins
Metro Atlantic: Happy Fine
Mid-American: Joe Menzer
Mid-Continent: Pete Dougherty
Midwestern Collegiate: John Sonderegger
Missouri Valley: Jim Ruppert
Northeast: Happy Fine & Jim Hague
Ohio Valley: Tom Woods
Pacific-10: Jack Rickard
Patriot: Happy Fine
Southern: Chris Dortch
Southland: Bobby Dower
Southeastern: Scooter Hobbs
Southwest: David McNabb
Southwest Athletic: Joe Planas

Sun Belt: John Packett
Trans America Athletic: Jack Mitchell
West Coast: Barry Zepel
Western Athletic: Dennis Latta
Eastern Teams: Mike Bradley, Happy Fine & Bill Stetka
Southern Teams: Chris Dortch
High School: Bob Gibbons
Junior College: Rick Ball
Small Colleges: Chuck Mistovich
Women's Division I: Joe Smith
Girls' High School: Russ Walburn
European: Richard Kaner

BANTAM BOOKS
NEW YORK · TORONTO · LONDON · SYDNEY · AUCKLAND

BLUE RIBBON COLLEGE BASKETBALL YEARBOOK
A Bantam Book / December 1990

ISBN 0-553-34997-X

Published simultaneously in the United States and Canada

Bantam Books are published by Bantam Books, a division of Bantam Double-
day Dell Publishing Group, Inc. Its trademark, consisting of the words "Bantam
Books" and the portrayal of a rooster, is Registered in U.S. Patent and Trademark Office in other countries. Marca Registrada, Bantam Books, 666 Fifth
Avenue, New York, New York 10103.

PRINTED IN THE UNITED STATES OF AMERICA

0 9 8 7 6 5 4 3 2 1

ASSOCIATE EDITORS — Happy Fine & Joe Lunardi
EXECUTIVE ASSISTANT — Diane Swiger
COPY EDITING — Debra Craig

SECRETARIAL SERVICES — Kathy Howes, Joyce Golden & Exeter Word Processing
TYPESETTING: Cold Comp — Pittsburgh, Pa.

PHOTO CREDITS:
*Buffington - Page 328; Ron Fried - Page 325; Steve Grieco HS
Headshots - Page 345-351; Kevin W. Reece - Page 333; Al Thielmans
- Page 350 (John Smith)*

TABLE OF CONTENTS

TEAM INDEX

NATION'S BEST

Last April 2, in McNichols Arena in Denver, the UNLV Runnin' Rebels put forth the most dominating display ever seen in the championship game of the NCAA tournament. UNLV won its first Division I national men's basketball championship by 30 points, 103-73 against Duke, in what was the largest margin defeat in the history of the event. In the last decade, the championship game has usually been a close affair but the Runnin' Rebels turned the 1990 championship into a total runaway before halftime, reminiscent of most Super Bowls.

In late July, UNLV was barred from defending its national championship by the NCAA. The decision was the final chapter of the NCAA's 13-year joust with UNLV coach Jerry Tarkanian.

The decision was truly a travesty of justice as all of the current Runnin' Rebels were in elementary school when UNLV was placed on probation in 1977 and ordered to suspend Tarkanian for two years. It certainly isn't their fight but they definitely received the blunt of the punishment.

UNLV will not get a chance to defend its national championship. If the Runnin' Rebels had defended their championship, they would have been the first team since UCLA in 1973 to win back-to-back titles. UNLV will appeal the decision but is not expected to win.

Even though UNLV is barred from post-season play, the Runnin' Rebels will be the best team in the nation this year. They also have a chance to be one of the best ever in the history of college basketball. For that reason, *Blue Ribbon* will still rank UNLV among the Final Four projections. The teams we believe will be Indianapolis Bound for the Final Four are Arizona, Arkansas, Michigan State and North Carolina.

For those of you reading *Blue Ribbon* for the first time, we have never used the traditional Top 20 in our previous nine editions. The talent level and competitiveness in college basketball is too strong all throughout the country to just feature a small number of teams. Instead, we give major attention to 40 teams and list them alphabetically within three groups.

The first grouping is the *Final Four Bound* selections. The second grouping, of 12 teams, is *The Next Wave*. Those 12 teams we predict will be in the Final 16 of the NCAA tournament next March. The final grouping among the Nation's Best is *Rough Customers*. This consists of a group of 23 teams who should be strong and viable on the national front.

FINAL FOUR BOUND

ARIZONA	MICHIGAN STATE	UNLV
ARKANSAS	NORTH CAROLINA	

THE NEXT WAVE

ALABAMA	LSU	SYRACUSE
DUKE	OHIO STATE	TEXAS
GEORGIA TECH	OKLAHOMA	UCLA
INDIANA	PITT	VIRGINIA

ROUGH CUSTOMERS

CALIFORNIA-SANTA BARBARA	LONG BEACH STATE	NOTRE DAME
CINCINNATI	KANSAS	OKLAHOMA STATE
CLEMSON	KENTUCKY	PRINCETON
CONNECTICUT	LOUISVILLE	ST. JOHN'S
DePAUL	MISSISSIPPI STATE	SOUTHERN MISSISSIPPI
EAST TENNESSEE STATE	NEW MEXICO	STANFORD
GEORGETOWN	NEW MEXICO STATE	TEMPLE
GEORGIA		WYOMING

★ CONFERENCE WINNERS ★

AMERICAN SOUTH: Louisiana Tech
ATLANTIC COAST: North Carolina
ATLANTIC 10: Temple
BIG EAST: Pitt
BIG EIGHT: Oklahoma
BIG SKY: Idaho
BIG SOUTH: Coastal Carolina
BIG TEN: Michigan State
BIG WEST: UNLV
COLONIAL ATHLETIC: James Madison
EAST COAST: Bucknell

ECAC NORTH ATLANTIC: Northeastern
IVY LEAGUE: Princeton
MID-EASTERN ATHLETIC: Coppin State
METRO: Southern Mississippi
METRO ATLANTIC: La Salle
MID-AMERICAN: Bowling Green
MID-CONTINENT: Wisconsin-Green Bay
MIDWESTERN COLLEGIATE: Marquette
MISSOURI VALLEY: Creighton
NORTHEAST: Marist
OHIO VALLEY: Murray State

PACIFIC-10: Arizona
PATRIOT: Fordham
SOUTHERN: East Tennessee State
SOUTHLAND: Northeast Louisiana
SOUTHEASTERN: LSU
SOUTHWEST: Arkansas
SOUTHWEST ATHLETIC: Southern University
SUN BELT: South Florida
TRANS AMERICA ATHLETIC: Stetson
WEST COAST: University of San Diego
WESTERN ATHLETIC: Wyoming

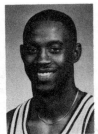

ANDERSON

JOHNSON

O'NEAL

OWENS

S. SMITH

AUGMON

LAETTNER

MONROE

MOURNING

WILLIAMS

DAVIS

DAY

MAYBERRY

MUTOMBO

D. SMITH

Blue Ribbon
ALL-AMERICA TEAM

CROTTY

STEVE SMITH — Michigan State
(Player of the Year)

LONGLEY

FIRST TEAM
Kenny Anderson, Sophomore . Georgia Tech
Larry Johnson, Senior . . . . UNLV
Shaquille O'Neal, Sophomore . . . . LSU
Billy Owens, Junior . . . . Syracuse
Steve Smith, Senior . . . . Michigan State

SECOND TEAM
Stacey Augmon, Senior . . . . UNLV
Christian Laettner, Junior . . . . Duke
Rodney Monroe, Senior . . . . N.C. State
Alonzo Mourning, Junior . . . . . Georgetown
Walt Williams, Junior . . . . Maryland

THIRD TEAM
Dale Davis, Senior . . . . Clemson
Todd Day, Junior . . . . Arkansas
Lee Mayberry, Junior . . . . Arkansas
Dikembe Mutombo, Junior . . . . Georgetown
Doug Smith, Senior . . . . Missouri

FOURTH TEAM
John Crotty, Senior . . . . Virginia
Luc Longley, Senior . . . . New Mexico
Mark Macon, Senior . . . . Temple
Bryant Stith, Junior . . . . Virginia
Clarence Weatherspoon, Junior . . So. Miss.

MACON

FIFTH TEAM
Chris Gatling, Senior . . . . Old Dominion
Anderson Hunt, Junior . . . . UNLV
Mark Randall, Senior . . . . Kansas
Brian Shorter, Senior . . . . Pitt
Chris Smith, Junior . . . . Connecticut

STITH

WEATHERSPOON

GATLING

HUNT

RANDALL

SHORTER

C. SMITH

5

BLUE RIBBON
HONORABLE MENTION ALL-AMERICA TEAM

Mark Alberts, Senior, Akron
Darwyn Alexander, Junior, Oklahoma State
Victor Alexander, Senior, Iowa State
Eric Anderson, Junior, Indiana
Greg Anthony, Senior, UNLV
Anthony Avent, Senior, Seton Hall
Mark Baker, Junior, Ohio State
Louis Banks, Senior, Cincinnati
Ronnie Battle, Sophomore, Auburn
Tanoka Beard, Sophomore, Boise State
Tony Bennett, Junior, Wisconsin-Green Bay
Alex Blackwell, Junior, Monmouth
David Booth, Junior, DePaul
Willie Brand, Senior, Texas-Arlington
Terrell Brandon, Junior, Oregon
Kevin Brooks, Senior, Southwestern Louisiana
Marc Brown, Senior, Siena
Randy Brown, Senior, New Mexico State
Cameron Burns, Senior, Mississippi State
Steve Carney, Senior, Northeastern
Greg Carter, Senior, Mississippi State
Perry Carter, Senior, Ohio State
Darrin Chancellor, Senior, Southern Mississippi
Livingston Chatman, Senior, Florida
Calbert Cheaney, Sophomore, Indiana
Melvin Cheatum, Senior, Alabama
Michael Christian, Senior, Tulane
Rod Cole, Senior, Georgia
Ronnie Coleman, Senior, Southern California
Locksley Collie, Senior, Texas
Chris Corchiani, Senior, North Carolina State
Anthony Dade, Junior, Louisiana Tech
Dwayne Davis, Senior, Florida
Terry Dehere, Sophomore, Seton Hall
Greg Dennis, Senior, East Tennessee State
Jean Derouillere, Senior, Kansas State
Radenko Dobras, Junior, South Florida
Scott Draud, Senior, Vanderbilt
Darrell Dumas, Senior, Stetson
Earl Duncan, Senior, Rutgers
Robert Dykes, Senior, George Mason
LaPhonso Ellis, Junior, Notre Dame
Bruce Evans, Junior, Furman
Roy Fisher, Senior, California
Will Flemons, Sophomore, Texas Tech
Alphonso Ford, Sophomore, Mississippi Valley State
Rick Fox, Senior, North Carolina
Carlos Funchess, Senior, Northeast Louisiana
Keith Gailes, Senior, Loyola
Chad Gallagher, Senior, Creighton

Josh Grant, Junior, Utah
Gary Gray, Senior, California-Santa Barbara
Sean Green, Senior, Iona
Litterial Green, Junior, Georgia
Tom Gugliotta, Junior, North Carolina State
John Gwynn, Senior, Connecticut
Reggie Hanson, Senior, Kentucky
Lucious Harris, Sophomore, Long Beach State
Bob Harstad, Senior, Creighton
Jim Havrilla, Junior, Western Michigan
Brian Hendrick, Sophomore, California
Donald Hodge, Junior, Temple
Cornelius Holden, Junior, Louisville
Steve Hood, Senior, James Madison
Robert Horry, Junior, Alabama
Allan Houston, Sophomore, Tennessee
Byron Houston, Junior, Oklahoma State
Stephen Howard, Junior, DePaul
Keith Hughes, Senior, Rutgers
Bobby Hurley, Sophomore, Duke
Reggie Isaac, Senior, Coppin State
Mike Iuzzolino, Senior, St. Francis
Jim Jackson, Sophomore, Ohio State
Ralph James, Senior, Harvard
Daron Jenkins, Senior, Southern Mississippi
Mister Jennings, Senior, East Tennessee State
Popeye Jones, Junior, Murray State
Anthony Jones, Senior, Northeast Louisiana
Adam Keefe, Junior, Stanford
Andy Kennedy, Senior, Alabama-Birmingham
Chris King, Junior, Wake Forest
Derrick Kirce, Senior, Tennessee-Chattanooga
Reggie Law, Senior, Jacksonville
Geoff Lear, Junior, Pepperdine
Eric Leslie, Senior, Rhode Island
Damon Lopez, Senior, Fordham
Terrell Lowery, Junior, Loyola Marymount
George Lynch, Sophomore, North Carolina
Kevin Lynch, Senior, Minnesota
Dan Lyttle, Senior, Pacific
Don MacLean, Junior, UCLA
Sterling Mahan, Senior, Southern Illinois
Barry Manning, Senior, South Carolina
Bobby Martin, Senior, Pitt
Darrick Martin, Junior, UCLA
Jason Matthews, Senior, Pitt
Marlon Maxey, Junior, UTEP
Jim McCoy, Junior, Massachusetts
Oliver Miller, Junior, Arkansas
Sean Miller, Junior, Pitt
Chris Mills, Sophomore, Arizona
Harold Miner, Freshman, Southern California

Aaron Mitchell, Senior, Southwestern Louisiana
Matt Muehlebach, Senior, Arizona
Kit Mueller, Senior, Princeton
Eric Murdock, Senior, Providence
Tracy Murray, Sophomore, UCLA
Lorenzo Neely, Senior, Eastern Michigan
Doug Overton, Senior, La Salle
Damon Patterson, Senior, Oklahoma
Anthony Peeler, Senior, Missouri
Elliott Perry, Senior, Memphis State
Michael Polite, Senior, Florida State
Darelle Porter, Senior, Pitt
Trevor Powell, Senior, Marquette
Darryl Reid, Senior, Southwest Missouri State
Joe Rhett, Junior, South Carolina
Rob Robbins, Senior, New Mexico
Keir Rogers, Senior, Loyola
Sean Rooks, Junior, Arizona
Tom Savage, Senior, Rutgers
James Scott, Senior, Arkansas-Little Rock
Brent Scott, Sophomore, Rice
Malik Sealy, Senior, St. John's
Willie Simms, Senior, Wisconsin
Reginald Slater, Junior, Wyoming
LaBradford Smith, Senior, Louisville
Larry Stewart, Senior, Coppin State
John Taft, Senior, Marshall
Donnell Thomas, Senior, Northern Illinois
Chandler Thompson, Senior, Ball State
Anthony Tucker, Junior, Wake Forest
Craig Upchurch, Senior, Houston
Shaun Vandiver, Senior, Colorado
Clinton Venable, Senior, Bowling Green
Rod Wade, Junior, Arkansas-Little Rock
Jamal Walker, Senior, Xavier
Robert Werdann, Junior, St. John's
Carlos Williams, Sophomore, Brown
Henry Williams, Junior, North Carolina Charlotte
Travis Williams, Senior, South Carolina State
Corey Williams, Junior, Oklahoma State
Brian Williams, Junior, Arizona
Desi Wilson, Senior, Fairleigh Dickinson
Marshall Wilson, Senior, Georgia
Stevie Wise, Senior, Colorado
Joey Wright, Senior, Texas
Joe Wylie, Senior, Miami of Florida
Kendall Youngblood, Junior, Utah State

FINAL FOUR BOUND

(March 30 & April 1, 1990 —
Hoosier Dome, Indianapolis, Indiana)

Arizona

Arkansas

Michigan State

North Carolina

*UNLV

*UNLV has been barred from defending its national championship by the NCAA.
The Runnin' Rebels are going to appeal, after press-time, but whether they are
allowed into the NCAA tournament or not, UNLV is the premier college basketball team in the country.

ARIZONA

LAST SEASON: 25-7
CONFERENCE RECORD: 15-3
STARTERS LOST: 1
STARTERS RETURNING: 4
CONFERENCE: PACIFIC-10
LOCATION: TUCSON, AZ
HOME FLOOR: McKALE
 CENTER (13,477)
NICKNAME: WILDCATS
COLORS: CARDINAL AND NAVY

★ COACH'S PROFILE ★

LUTE OLSON (Record at Arizona, 162-62. Career record, 353-155) In seven years in Tucson, Olson has completely rejuvenated the Arizona basketball program and put it on a different level not only in the Pacific-10 Conference but nationally. The year before Olson arrived, Arizona was 4-24 overall and 1-17 in the Pacific-10. His first Arizona team also lost its top four scorers and rebounders from the previous season. From those humble beginnings, ashes might be an apt description. Olson has made Arizona a conference power with four Pacific-10 titles (1986, 1988, 1989 and 1990). Arizona has also won three conference post-season tournaments. Under Olson, the Wildcats have averaged more than 23 victories per season, have winning records against all nine Pacific-10 opponents, are 92-14 in McKale Center and a consistent figure in the Top 20. He led Arizona to the 1988 Final Four in Kansas City and No. 1 rankings that season and in 1989.

Olson has certainly been recognized for his efforts. He was named Pacific-10 Coach of the Year on three occasions and National Coach of the Year by two national magazines in 1988.

The Arizona media guide begins its Olson biography this way: "It's really simple. Arizona could not have a better basketball coach than Lute Olson . . . he puts champions on the court and packs citizens in the stands."

When Olson took over at Arizona he told the fans to get their season tickets while they could because in a few years they would be unavailable. That statement has proven true as the last few years Arizona season tickets have been sold out and some have reportedly been scalped for as much as $5,000 each. Olson has succeeded in turning Tucson into one of college basketball's true hot beds.

His first Arizona team finished 11-17 but won six of its last eight conference games. Although he faced a severe personnel shortage when he came to Arizona, Olson was able to do some 11th hour recruiting that netted him two junior college players —Eddie Smith and Pete Williams —and he also spotted a good shooting guard in a California summer league who had not been offered any major Division I scholarships. That sleeper was Steve Kerr who turned out to be an integral part of Olson's rebuilding process and is now considered one of the all-time Arizona greats.

Olson's stabilization effort in his first year at Arizona allowed him to convince a few more quality players to come to Tucson. He also was the beneficiary of some extremely fortunate geographical circumstances. At that time, a hot shot prospect was coming up in Tucson's Cholla HS. That prospect was none other than Sean Elliott and he wanted to stay close to home and signed with the Wildcats. Elliott not only turned out to be the best player in Arizona history but he capped a brilliant career in 1988-89 by winning the Wooden Award given annually to college basketball's player of the year. Five other publications and polls also named Elliott their player of the year that season.

He is a selective recruiter and has been able to get his type of player at Arizona. Olson not only looks at the athletic ability and basketball skill, but intangibles. After a prospect visits the Arizona campus, Olson polls his current players to see whether they would like to have that player in the program. Since he came to Arizona in 1983, his players have given unfavorable reports about two recruits and neither were offered scholarships.

"We're very, very thorough before we bring them to campus," said Olson. "If they get here and there is something we don't know, they have done a good job of fooling us."

On the recruiting front, Olson has been able to make serious inroads in southern California, and the Wildcats can now compete on equal footing in that prime recruiting territory with UCLA, UNLV and the great programs from around the nation who regularly come in to raid. On this year's roster, seven Wildcats are either from southern California or have ties to the area. Also, Olson has tried to occasionally pick up a prospect outside of the Wildcats normal recruiting area and has gone back to the midwest for players. Last year signed his first prospect from New York City, highly regarded guard Khalid Reeves.

Arizona's emergence as a national power has helped enhance the image of western basketball which took a serious beating in the early to mid-80s. At that time the flagship program of western basketball, UCLA, was going through difficult times. It became fashionable for the best players in the west to look elsewhere. However, over the last few years that talent drain has slowed and Arizona's success has contributed greatly to the west's rise.

"Over the last few years we haven't had any of the top players in the West leave," Olson told the *Denver Post*. "We definitely turned it around. We're still behind, but the gap has been closed further. The exposure for UCLA and our program is excellent. We have seven network games this year. Kids don't have to travel across the country and freeze their behinds to play basketball."

The 56-year-old Olson was born on a farm near Mayville, N.D. When he was a toddler, his father died from a stroke, and eight months later his older brother was killed in a farm accident. His mother moved the family off the farm and into town. Olson became an excellent athlete at Central HS in Grand Forks, N.D., and went to college at small Augsburg College in Minnesota. He attended Augsburg because it was a Lutheran school and his mother wanted her son to attend a religious institution. He had to work as a janitor and on a construction crew during the summer to pay his way through school as Augsburg did not have athletic scholarships. He was a forward in basketball, a tight end and tackle in football and a pitcher in baseball and still graduated with a B+ academic average.

His first coaching job was at Mahnomen, Minn., HS. After spending a year there in 1958 Olson moved to Two Harbors (Minn.) HS where he stayed for three years. He headed west in 1963 and became the head coach at Western HS in Anaheim, Calif. He spent a year at Western before moving a few miles south to Anaheim Lora HS. From there he went on to Huntington Beach Marina HS where Olson coached for four years and compiled a 48-8 record over his last two seasons.

In 1970, he moved to the collegiate ranks as head coach at Long Beach City College. His 1971 team won the California state junior college championship. Olson was 104-20 at Long Beach City College and won three Metro Conference titles.

In 1973, Olson succeeded Jerry Tarkanian at Long Beach State. The fact that Olson followed Tarkanian is ironic because today as they are now major rivals. Olson went 24-2 in his only season at Long Beach State. From there he went to Iowa where Olson spent nine years rebuilding the Hawkeye program. His first Iowa team was 10-16, however, the Hawkeyes rose to 19-10 in his second year. His third Iowa team was 20-7 and by his fifth year, the Hawkeyes earned an NCAA tournament bid. That began a five-year streak of NCAA tournament participation. During that period Iowa won at least 21 games per season.

The highlight of his career at Iowa came in 1980 when Olson took the Hawkeyes to the Final Four. During their run to the Final Four, Iowa overcame a 16-point deficit in the finals of the East Region at Philadelphia against John Thompson's first mighty Georgetown team.

He was twice named Big Ten coach of the year and won one conference title. During his tenure, the Iowa program enjoyed unprecedented popularity. The Hawkeyes developed one of the most extensive in-state television networks for their games and season tickets were split so that more fans could see the Hawkeyes. A fund raising drive was begun that eventually led to the completion of Iowa's current facility, Carver-Hawkeye Arena.

Olson projects a fatherly yet stylish image on the sideline. With his silver hair and good looks, some writers have called Olson the "Cary Grant of College Basketball."

He is by all appearances, a man who has it made. Not only has Olson turned a terrible Arizona program into a Pacific-10 and national power, but he has also constructed a lifestyle fit for a king. Olson lives off one of the fairways of the picturesque Vantana Canyon Gulf Course in the hills overlooking Tucson. Most of his children and grandchildren live in Tucson. He is able to get away frequently for vacations in Maui, Coronado Island near San Diego, and other desirable locales. Olson also can vacation with peace of mind knowing he has built a Top Five program at Arizona in just seven years.

★ PLAYERS NOT RETURNING ★

JUD BUECHLER (6-6, F, 14.9 ppg, 8.3 rpg, 129 assists, 12 blocked shots, 40 steals) Buechler was the heart and soul of Arizona's Pacific-10 regular season and conference championship team. He led the Wildcats in scoring and rebounding last year. Buechler was second in minutes played, third in field goal percentage (.538), third in assists (129) and second in steals (40). He was also one of the better defensive players in the country. His versatility was extremely important to Arizona. Buechler could guard inside players or high scorers on the perimeter, go inside to rebound, hit the outside shot and score in the clutch down low. He did it all for Arizona and moved out of the shadow of Sean Elliott and Anthony Cook with his strong senior performance.

He was a second round choice of the Seattle SuperSonics and later was traded to the New Jersey Nets. Buechler was very impressive over the summer and should have a long and successful NBA career. Olson will have as much difficulty replacing Buechler as he has anyone other than Sean Elliott. Not only did Buechler contribute in every facet of the game plus provide considerable leadership, he was a plugging worker who set the tone for the other Wildcats. He gradually worked his way through the program and eventually had great success. One Arizona insider wonders what the Wildcats will do in the future without players like Buechler. Olson has been able to recruit a more highly regarded caliber player in the last few years. While those players have big time talent and reputations, they also come with high expectations. While the Wildcats certainly will be very talented, they won't be as tough and gritty without Buechler.

BRIAN DAVID (6-9, C, 2.4 ppg, 1.7 rpg, 6 assists, 9 blocked shots, 5 steals) David made his biggest contribution as a senior. He started three games and averaged 10 minutes per game for the Wildcats. He made 28-of-61 field goals (.459) and 19-of-27 free throws (.704). David was a hard working inside player who could take up space in the middle, rebound and score when needed. He provided some depth in the pivot but can be replaced.

HARVEY MASON (6-3, G, 4.0 ppg, 1.3 rpg, 44 assists, 9 blocked shots, 19 steals) Mason's senior year ended after 23 games due a knee injury. He started 15 games and averaged 19 minutes per game before being injured. He was one of Arizona's best defensive guards. While Mason was not a great scorer during his college career, he certainly played a key role coming off the bench.

With the addition of highly regarded freshman Khalid Reeves, the loss of Mason should not be crucial to Arizona.

★ RETURNING PLAYERS ★

MATT MUEHLEBACH (6-2, 185 lbs., SR, G, #24, 11.3 ppg, 2.9 rpg, 181 assists, 3 blocked shots, 41 steals, Rockhurst HS/Stilwell, Kan.) Muehlebach is Arizona's only senior this season. He has had a steady rise during his career in Tucson. Muehlebach averaged 1.5 points per game as a freshman, started 22 games as a sophomore and averaged 7.6 points and started all 32 games last year and his offensive production rose to 11.3 points per game. His 181 assists in 1989-90 were the fourth highest total in Arizona history. He also led Arizona in three-point shooting connecting on 66-of-152 treys (.434). Muehlebach also led Arizona in steals with 41 and free throw shooting (62-of-76 for .816). He spent roughly half of his time at shooting guard last year and his 5.7 assists per game average shows Muehlebach's ability to get the ball where it needs to go.

Some of his better scoring games last year were 20 points against California, 22 vs. Stanford and 21 in the regular season ending blowout of Oregon State. In the first round of the Pacific-10 tournament, in Tempe, Ariz., Muehlebach pulled down 11 rebounds. He was named to the Pacific-10 all-tournament team and shared the event's most outstanding player award with Jud Buechler. Muehlebach for the second straight year was named to the first-team Pacific-10 All-Academic squad.

Muehlebach is a versatile guard who can play either backcourt spot. He not only is a good shooter both from long distance and at the line, but Muehlebach is also a quality defender. As a sophomore he held Stanford All-America Todd Lichti to just five shots and 11 points in an Arizona victory in Tucson and to just eight shots and 11 points in the Pacific-10 tournament. He takes care of the ball and had only 58 turnovers in 908 minutes as a sophomore and 63 ballhandling misques in 1,083 minutes as a junior. Muehlebach is the smart, controlled type of guard Olson has always preferred.

Throughout his career, Muehlebach has been a big winner. Arizona is 89-14 during his career. In high school he led Rockhurst HS of Kansas City, Mo., to the 1987 Missouri state title. During his junior year at Bishop O'Dowd HS, in Oakland, Calif., he almost singlehandedly led the Dragons past the nation's No. 1 team, Los Angeles Crenshaw, before losing, 70-69, in the California state championship game.

MATT OTHICK (6-2, 175 lbs., JR, G, #12, 8.7 ppg, 2.1 rpg, 141 assists, 1 blocked shot, 32 steals, Bishop Gorman HS/Las Vegas, Nev.) Othick started 17 games as a sophomore and averaged 26 minutes per game. From the floor he made 72-of-178 field goals (.404) and from three-point range he was 47-of-128 (.367). Othick connected on 86-of-110 free throws (.782). He was second on the team behind Matt Muehlebach in assists and handled the point guard duties for Arizona.

He played his best basketball in the final weeks of the season, averaging more than 10 points and nearly seven assists per game in the last 10 games. He injured his ankle late in the season and hobbled a bit for the final weeks of the year, but recovered over the summer.

He had 17 points against Penn State, 18 vs. Oregon and reached double figures in 17 games.

He originally signed with New Mexico but asked out of his letter of intent when Lobo coach Gary Colson was fired. He then orally committed to hometown UNLV before changing his mind in the summer and entering Arizona. Othick's father, Roland, was a college basketball coach at Eastern New Mexico, North Texas State and Wichita State before entering private business.

He has good quickness, is disciplined and possesses outstanding court sense. Othick was a member of the five-man Pacific-10 all-freshman team and a key reserve in his first year at Arizona. He had only 70 turnovers for an average of just over two per game last year.

He is a capable player except when matched up against the top athletic, quick guards in the country who can harass defensively. He did not play well in Arizona's first round loss to Alabama in the NCAA tournament. Othick scored only five points in that loss.

"We hurt them," said Alabama coach Wimp Sanderson, "because we were able to play their guards aggressively, almost overplay them because we had better athletes out there. (Arizona's guards) are outstanding shooters and we made them move. Once they had to dribble and move, their percentages went down."

He will get a challenge for playing time this year from freshman guard Khalid Reeves is not a true point guard but can play both backcourt spots.

SEAN ROOKS (6-11, 245 lbs., JR, C, #45, 12.7 ppg, 4.9 rpg, 31 assists, 49 blocked shots, 14 steals, Fontana HS/Fontana, Calif.) Rooks is Arizona's top returning scorer. He has the best inside game of any Wildcat. He started only six games last year but was on the court an average of 22 minutes per game. Rooks made 140-of-263 field goals (.532) and was 114-of-161 (.708) from the line. He tied with freshman Ed Stokes for the team lead in blocked shots.

Rooks had 20 points in the season opening win over Michigan. He also had 19 against nationally ranked Purdue, 18 five times (UCLA, Oklahoma, Southern California, Washington State and Southern California) and had 24 points and nine rebounds in a home victory over UCLA.

Rooks is a poor and inconsistent rebounder for his size. He had 12 and 17 rebounds in two of Arizona's first four games, but only rebounded in double figures once more the rest of the season. The key to his future, besides better rebounding and defense, is staying in shape. Olson has not always been happy with Rooks' work habits. He appeared to be a more conscientious worker over the summer and should benefit from a good showing in the tryouts for the U.S. National team. Rooks advanced through the first round of the tryouts in Colorado Springs last May. Duke coach Mike Krzyzewski, the U.S. National team coach, commented on how Rooks' weight distribution was much more proportional. Duke had played Arizona in each of Rooks' first two years. Rooks was one of 25 players invited to the second stage of the trials at Duke. He was cut after the second stage but the experience should certainly help him this year. In the final night of the trials in an open public scrimmage, Rooks scored 14 points, grabbed a game-high 13 rebounds and blocked five shots. He was active, an intimidator on defense and ran the court well.

Inside Sports has ranked Rooks and Williams as the No. 3 "New Duos of Doom," a ranking of the top inside tandems in college basketball.

CASEY SCHMIDT (6-5, 185 lbs., SO, G, #11, 2.0 ppg, 0.8 rpg, 11 assists, Valparaiso HS/Valparaiso, Ind.) As a freshman Schmidt came off the bench to play in 28 games for a total of 172 minutes. He averaged six minutes per game. Schmidt came to Arizona known as a great outside shooter. However, in his limited playing time as a freshman he made only 17-of-58 field goals (.293) and 13-of-44 three-pointers (.295). Schmidt was accurate from the free throw line connecting on 9-of-10 (.900).

He is smart, unselfish and competitive. Schmidt has a great attitude but is going to have trouble getting more action unless he shoots the lights out. Freshman guard Khalid Reeves will certainly play a great deal and Kentucky transfer Chris Mills is the most talented player on the team and can also play in the backcourt.

Schmidt is one of only two players on the Arizona roster not from the west.

ED STOKES (7-0, 245 lbs., SO, F/C, #41, 8.0 ppg, 4.6 rpg, 7 assists, 49 blocked shots, 15 steals, St. Bernard HS/Los Angeles, Calif.) Arizona has the strongest inside game in the Pacific-10 with its trio of sophomore Ed Stokes, junior Sean Rooks and junior Brian Williams. Stokes went from the bench to start the final 16 games of the 1989-90 season. He was more consistent overall than either Rooks or Williams. Stokes still has a great deal to learn but his progress as a freshman was pleasing to Olson.

Stokes needs to develop more emotion and intensity. He also has to get stronger in the upper body and keep refining his inside offensive game. However, he has excellent quickness and shotblocking ability. Stokes tied Rooks for the team lead in blocked shots with 49 last year. He made 94-of-159 field goals (.599) but was just 44-of-78 (.564) from the line. His progress was remarkable considering Stokes didn't even play the first two games of the year. He did not score in eight games through the middle of the season before having an impressive run at the end. Stokes had 14 points and nine rebounds in a home win over UCLA, 12 points and 10 rebounds against rival Arizona State, 18 points vs. California, 15 points and nine rebounds in the Pacific-10 tournament semifinals against Stanford and 12 points and 12 rebounds in the opening round of the conference tournament over Southern California. He closed the season with 17 points and five rebounds in Arizona's second round loss in the NCAA tournament to Alabama.

He has impressive speed and overall physical ability. His father played college basketball and is now an orthopedic surgeon in Los Angeles.

If he continues to develop and gain more intensity, there is no reason why Stokes cannot be the best big man Arizona has ever produced.

BRIAN WILLIAMS (6-11, 242 lbs., JR, C/F, #21, 10.6 ppg, 5.7 rpg, 14 assists, 41 blocked shots, 19 steals, St. Monica's HS/Fresno, Calif.) When Williams transferred from Maryland and came west to Arizona he was billed as a potential superman. He supposedly was great in practices in the year he sat out at Arizona. Some Arizona insiders felt that he could even be a national player of the year in successive years. Well, Williams quickly proved to have feet of clay as he was mediocre in his first year at Arizona. Williams started 27 games and averaged 22 minutes per game. He was fourth on the team in scoring and second in rebounding. Williams was basically second in rebounding because of the senior Jud Buechler, Arizona had no other consistent rebounders. If he is to reach the vast potential predicted when he came out of St. Monica HS in Santa Monica, Calif., and during his only year at Maryland, Williams must spend more time on his game in the off-season.

Williams did not prove to be the great intimidator expected as he only blocked 41 shots and averaged a little more than a block per game. He reached double figures in rebounding four times. Williams had 18 points and 10 rebounds against Southern California, 28 points and seven rebounds in Arizona's opening round win in the NCAA tournament vs. South Florida and 13 rebounds in the championship game of the Pacific-10 tournament when Arizona defeated UCLA. He also scored 21 points against Washington State, 20 vs. rival Arizona State and 19 at Oregon. In 12 games, Williams failed to reach double figures. In three games, including the season ending loss to Alabama in the NCAA tournament, he failed to score.

He started the year at center and then moved to power forward. Williams was affected by a nagging knee problem and could not play effectively through two games in a three day period. In addition, he did not play in the summer of 1989 due to a stress fracture in his left foot. His conditioning was set back.

Williams may begin to benefit from being in the Arizona program for a third year. Dating back to his early days in high school, Williams had never played at the same school for more than a year. He played at three different high schools because his father, a member of the Platters singing group, moved frequently. He then spent one year at Maryland before leaving for Arizona. Olson is the fifth coach Williams has played for since his sophomore year in high school.

At Maryland, Williams averaged 12.5 points and six rebounds per game and blocked 36 shots as a freshman. He was rated as the nation's No. 1 high school player in 1987 by *The Sporting News*.

There is no doubt that he has outstanding physical ability. Williams can run the court and will get off his feet quickly to block shots and score in bunches when on his game. However, he has never been a consistent, dominating force so far on the high school or collegiate level. Olson is not happy with Williams' development. Since he already has two potential big time inside players in Rooks and Stokes, Olson can afford to withhold playing time from Williams if he does not work hard enough.

When Williams transferred to Arizona there was talk he might play a year or two and leave early for the NBA. That option is not as likely now as Williams has to have a great final two years to become a high first round draft choice.

WAYNE WOMACK (6-8, 210 lbs., JR, F, #30, 6.8 ppg, 3.9 rpg, 21 assists, 12 blocked shots, 11 steals, John Muir HS/Pasadena, Calif.) Womack started 12 games for Arizona last year and averaged 19 minutes per game. He started 12 games early in the season before Olson went to a bigger threesome up front. This season he figures to be in for playing time at both power and small forward.

His defense could earn Womack significant playing time if Olson wants to get more quickness in the lineup. He has worked hard and Olson knows what he has in Womack.

He has excellent quickness, speed and leaping ability. Womack can block shots and score inside, but his perimeter offensive skills are lacking. That puts Womack in a tough situation. At power forward, Arizona has bigger players who can do what Womack can do inside and on the perimeter there are more skilled player such as Kentucky transfer Chris Mills.

Statistically, his best game last year was 20 points and 12 rebounds against Miami (Fla.). Womack also scored 21 points against California and had 18 vs. Arizona State. However, he only reached double figures once in the last 19 games. In two NCAA tournament games, Womack had one point and two rebounds. That was surprising considering he scored 19 points and grabbed 16 rebounds in Arizona's semifinal and final wins (against Stanford and UCLA, respectively) in the Pacific-10 tournament.

He worked harder than any Wildcat in the off-season and should fit in well with Olson's new emphasis on an up-tempo style. After watching Womack in pre-season drills, many observers believe he will play a key role this year.

★ NEWCOMERS ★

TONY CLARK (6-8, 205 lbs., FR, F/G, #34, 43.7 ppg, 11.0 rpg, 4.0 apg, 3.3 blpg, 2.3 stpg, Christian HS/El Cajon, Calif.) If the Arizona players have any sense, they will try to befriend Tony Clark. Clark was the No. 2 overall pick in the 1990 amateur baseball draft, by the Detroit Tigers, and signed a contract reportedly worth around $400,000. Clark certainly ought to be able to come up with some spare change for his teammates now and then and let them borrow his car. He now has to pay his way to Arizona instead of accepting a basketball scholarship but that shouldn't be a problem.

Clark led the state of California in scoring last year with a 43.7 average. He was a first-team All-State selection and the player of the year in the San Diego area for two straight years. He was ranked as the No. 7 quick forward in the country by Van Coleman's *National Recruiters Cage Letter*. He was generally considered one of the Top 75 high school players in the country. Clark averaged over 30 points per game in his high school career and scored a San Diego CIF-record 2,549 points. He had a high game in high school of 64 points.

As a high school baseball player, Clark was sensational. He hit .543 and had 11 home runs and 21 RBIs in only 16 games last season. He is a switch hitting outfielder/shortstop/pitcher. Arizona assistant coach Jessie Evans still talks about how the first time he saw Clark play a baseball game, the opposing team intentionally walked him with the bases loaded. The next time he came to bat, the score was 5-4, so they had to pitch to him and Clark hit a home run. Later he came in and pitched in relief and won the game.

"He can play in the major leagues in two years, three years full-time," said Ed Patterson, Clark's baseball coach at Christian HS in El Cajon, Calif.

Clark was such a highly regarded prospect that Detroit Tigers' President Bo Schembechler and general manager Bill Lajoie visited him to determine how serious he was about baseball. It was Schembechler's first recruiting trip since leaving his previous position as the football coach at Michigan. Clark played in the Tigers' minor league system last year and hit around .200. He did not have a great season but supposedly it takes awhile for most prospects to adjust to professional baseball.

Reportedly, his contract with the Tigers allows Clark to attend Arizona and play basketball for three years before becoming a full-time baseball player.

As a basketball player, Clark is considered a superb outside shooter with three-point range. He is a powerful leaper, dribbles and passes well and is blessed with outstanding lateral quickness. He was considered the third best prospect in California at the end of last season behind UCLA's freshman Ed O'Bannon and Shon Tarver. Olson will try Clark out at both second guard and small forward. He will add more quickness to Arizona on the perimeter position which is something the Wildcats lacked last year and ultimately led to their downfall in the NCAA tournament.

KEVIN FLANAGAN (6-9, 235 lbs., FR, F, #51, 18.0 ppg, 11.0 rpg, Torrey Pines HS/Del Mar, Calif.) Flanagan was redshirted last year. As a senior at Torrey Pines HS, he was the co-MVP of the Palomar League and played on a 31-1 team. Flanagan is a rugged player around the basket who can defend and rebound. He is definitely a banger type rather than a swift athlete.

Flanagan will probably see limited action this year. Arizona is strong up front so there doesn't appear to be a great deal of room for him.

DERON JOHNSON (6-6, 175 lbs., FR, F/G, #23, 29.4 ppg, 13.0 rpg, Sunnyside HS/Tucson, Ariz.) Like Kevin Flanagan, Johnson redshirted his first year at Arizona. In practice he showed he can score and Olson was impressed with Johnson's defensive quickness. He has the size and quickness to defend at either the off-guard or small forward spots.

Johnson was the 1989 Arizona player of the year and was also considered a college prospect as wide receiver in football. He shot 69 percent from the floor during his senior year and scored a total 2,108 points in his high school career. Johnson was such an athletic, prolific scorer that he drew comparisons to another former Tucson high school star, Sean Elliott. Those comparisons are not fair as Johnson is not another Elliott but he is a talented left-handed shooter who can help give the Wildcats more quickness on the perimeter.

While he was a high scorer in high school, Johnson's role at Arizona, at least initially, will probably be defensive-oriented. If he can play strong and consistent defense, he can find a spot in what looks to be a nine-man playing rotation this year. Arizona is going to be more versatile and quicker on the perimeter and Johnson could play a key role there.

CHRIS MILLS (6-6, 210 lbs., SO, F/G, #42, Fairfax HS/Los Angeles, Calif.) While Arizona will probably never have another player the caliber of Sean Elliott, the Wildcats have a more reasonable facsimile this year in Kentucky transfer Chris Mills. As a freshman two years ago at Kentucky, Mills was second on the team in scoring (14.3 ppg), assists (92), blocked shots (26) and steals (45). He led Kentucky in rebounding with an 8.7 average. Mills made .484 of his field goal attempts and was 17-of-54 (31.5 percent) from three-point range. He played very well as a freshman considering the circumstances. Mills played on the worst Kentucky team in decades, the Wildcats were 13-19 that year, and he had to overcome an immense amount of controversy that dogged him before he even enrolled at Kentucky.

In April 1988, a story broke concerning a package shipped from the Kentucky basketball office, via Emery Air Freight, to Mills' home in Los Angeles. Reportedly, the package broke open at an Emery warehouse in Los Angeles and $1,000 in cash and a video tape fell out. Both Mills and the Kentucky basketball staff denied knowledge of the cash, but it wasn't long before the story was picked up and reported nationwide. The package was one of several major problems the Kentucky staff had to deal with that year and eventually the Wildcats went on probation.

"I know some people will be skeptical, but based on the information we were given by the NCAA enforcement people, Chris was not involved," Olson told *Inside Sports*. "We received very strong assurances. I feel comfortable with Chris. And after all, it's Chris we're dealing with (not Kentucky).

"I think he will fit in well here. Our program will be a good thing for him, in terms of getting to see Chris for what he really is. And I don't think he was given that opportunity at Kentucky."

Mills was one of the most highly regarded players to come out of the Los Angeles area in years. He was a first-team High School All-America as a senior at Fairfax HS and averaged 31.5 points, 14.6 rebounds, and three assists as a senior. He was unanimously considered the best high school player on the west coast in 1988.

"The strongest part of Chris' game right now is his mental approach, his understanding of it," said Fairfax coach Harvey Kitani. "For a high school player, I haven't seen a guy as smart as him in some time. His game is so complete, and he understands it from a coach's standpoint."

He displayed that same complete, all-around game at Kentucky. Mills can score from the perimeter or inside, put the ball on the floor, pass and rebound. He is a true multi-dimensional threat. The year's layoff didn't seem to hinder Mills last spring when he tried out for the U.S. National team. He played well in the first round of the tryouts at Colorado Springs and was one of 25 players, along with teammate Sean Rooks, to advance to the second round of the tryouts at Duke. Mills didn't make the final cut, but the experience should help him for the upcoming year.

"Mills was somewhat of a surprise . . . with someone who sat out a year, you can anticipate them not being a sharp," U.S. National team coach Mike Krzyzewski told Jon Wilner of the *Arizona Daily Star*. "He just came on throughout the trials to where he was a legitimate choice, we believe he has a chance to get even better throughout the summer."

The Arizona coaches were pleased with Mills' defense and work habits in practice last year. He is definitely going to be an immediate starter either at small forward or at big guard. Mills' flexibility means the Arizona backcourt will be stronger and deeper this year. Also, Arizona is much quicker, bigger and talented on the perimeter than last year. With Arizona's already formidable inside game now supplemented by an improved and more athletic perimeter game, the Wildcats are going to be very difficult to beat.

KHALID REEVES (6-3, 185 lbs., FR, G, #4, 28.6 ppg, 8.0 rpg, 5.1 apg, Christ the King HS/Middle Village, N.Y.) One of the by-products of the rise of the Arizona program under Lute Olson has been a stronger presence on the national recruiting front. That was evidenced as Olson reached into New York City to sign his first player from the Big Apple. And he just didn't sign any player, Olson came away with arguably the finest guard in the city last year in a year where the senior class was the best it had been in New York in well over a decade.

Reeves was the MVP of the McDonald's East-West Classic in Indianapolis last year. He had 22 points, 10 steals, seven rebounds and six assists. He was also a second-team *Parade Magazine* All-America pick and a *Basketball Times* second-team All-America selection. Reeves was a two-time first-team All-New York City selection by *The Daily News*. Reeves was the MVP of the 1989 New York state tournament. In all, Reeves earned MVP honors in three tournaments as a junior and one as a senior.

''I think he'll end up as an off-guard in college, but he can play both positions,'' said Christ the King coach Bob Oliva.

Reeves is Christ the King's all-time leading scorer with 1,676 career points. He had a 51-point game as a senior and made 70 percent of his shots. Esteemed New York observer, Tom Konchalski of *HSBI Report*, has predicted that Reeves is a future NBA player.

Last season he was the MVP of the Windy City Classic in Chicago and averaged 26 points in three games. One Chicago sportswriter who saw Reeves play in the Windy City Classic thought he was the best high school guard he'd ever seen. In early scrimmage games before the beginning of pre-season practice, Reeves was the talk of the Arizona team because of his all-around game and ability to blow by any defender. He is going to make a big difference in the Arizona backcourt. Reeves is a better athlete than last year's starting guards, Matt Muehlebach and Matt Othick. He is also more talented than those two and is the best pure guard Olson has ever signed at Arizona.

★ QUESTIONS ★

Can Olson replace the intangibles and all-around contributions of Jud Buechler?
Is this the year Brian Williams begins living up to his vast potential?

★ STRENGTHS ★

Lute Olson! In his seven years at Arizona, Olson has brought an unprecedented level of conference and national success plus excitement. He is a great coach and worth several points to Arizona in every game.

The best inside game in the Pacific-10 and maybe the country! In Sean Rooks, Ed Stokes and Brian Williams, Arizona should be absolutely dominant virtually every game up front.

Improved athletic ability, talent and depth on the perimeter!

More overall depth!

Improved speed and quickness! Olson believes this Arizona team has more speed and quickness than any he has ever coached.

Improved defense! Arizona has shotblockers inside and more defensive quickness than ever. Look for Arizona to use more full court pressure defense this year.

★ BLUE RIBBON ANALYSIS ★

After Arizona was bombed out of the NCAA tournament in the second round by Alabama, Wildcat coach Lute Olson said he wished he could begin practice for next year the following day. While Arizona was certainly successful last year, finishing 25-7 and the regular season and tournament champions in the Pacific-10, Olson knew that this year the Wildcats should be even stronger.

''We look at (next season's) team as one that should be better than this team was, and a year after that we'll certainly be a team in the upper echelon of college basketball, just as next year's team will be,'' Olson told Greg Hansen of the *Arizona Daily Star*.

The Wildcats will miss leading scorer and rebounder Jud Buechler, who also contributed a winning attitude in addition to his scoring and rebounding. If Buechler's intangibles and defense can be replaced, Arizona should be much improved in 1990-91. The starting backcourt of Matt Muehlebach and Matt Othick return as do a trio of inside players — Sean Rooks, Ed Stokes and Brian Williams —who could give Arizona the strongest inside game in the country. Junior forward Wayne Womack is an excellent athlete who worked hard in the off-season and should be ready to contribute even more this year.

What should make Arizona a much improved team this year is the presence of four key newcomers on the perimeter. Kentucky transfer Chris Mills is the second best talent Olson has brought to Arizona outside of the school's best ever

player, Sean Elliott. Mills was by far Arizona's most impressive player in practices last year and he literally can do it all. He looked good in the off-season in the tryouts for the U.S. National team. Mills had an excellent freshman year at Kentucky despite playing in the midst of unrelenting controversy due to the Wildcats' problems with the NCAA. Freshman guard Khalid Reeves is not only Olson's first recruit from New York City, but the best pure guard he has ever signed at Arizona. Reeves had a great career at Christ the King HS in Middle Village, N.Y., in the Queens Burrough of New York City. Tony Clark, a 6-8 freshman swingman from the San Diego area, is such an outstanding athlete that he was the No. 2 overall pick in the last major league baseball draft and signed a contract reportedly worth around $400,000 with the Detroit Tigers. Clark will add even more quickness, versatility and size on the perimeter for Arizona. Redshirt freshman Deron Johnson was a big high school scorer at Tucson Sunnyside HS and Olson is impressed with his defensive quickness.

In the three biggest losses Arizona has suffered in the Olson Era —against Oklahoma in the 1988 Final Four, to UNLV in the semifinals of the 1989 West Region, and last year in the second round of the NCAA tournament to Alabama —the Wildcats' lack of great athletic ability on the perimeter has been exploited. Strong, quick pressure defense got to the Arizona guards and caused the Wildcats shooting percentage to plunge in each of those three losses. In Arizona's last three losses in the NCAA tournament, the Wildcats have averaged 16.4 points below their season scoring average. That should not happen this year as the newcomers make Arizona an entirely different team out front.

''It will be a team with a lot of athletes,'' said Olson. ''Particularly when you look at the perimeter spots.

''It's exciting. We'll obviously have more flexibility in what we do. We'll have the quickness to get out and pressure more on defense and to get up and down the court more consistently.''

Olson may use as many as nine players regularly. The Wildcats will be more up-tempo offensively this year and stronger defensively because of the added quickness on the perimeter.

If it all comes together as expected, Arizona could be so good they're illegal. In September, several members of the Wildcats' 1988 Final Four team —Sean Elliott, Steve Kerr, Tom Tolbert, Anthony Cook and Buechler —were back in town. For a week they scrimmaged against this year's varsity. Crowds of over 3,000 would show up each day for the informal pickup games. The former Wildcats rarely were able to beat this year's team.

Arizona should win its fifth Pacific-10 title under Olson. The Wildcats will be Final Four bound this March.

LAST SEASON		1990-91 ARIZONA SCHEDULE		
#Michigan	82-75	Nov.	14	#Austin Peay
@Oregon	63-68		26	Western Illinois
@Oregon State	61-84	Dec.	1	Long Beach State
Northern Arizona	84-37		5	@Northern Arizona
Miami (FL)	83-53		8	@LSU
##Penn State	74-55		23	Providence
##Purdue	85-66	27 & 29		##Fiesta Bowl
California	71-70OT			Classic
Washington	65-51	Jan.	3	@Washington
Washington State	81-61		5	@Washington State
@Southern California	90-75		10	Southern California
@UCLA	67-73		12	UCLA
@Arizona State	70-61		16	@Arizona State
Oklahoma	78-74		19	@Villanova
Stanford	68-61		24	@Stanford
@Pitt	92-100		26	@California
@Washington State	86-62		31	Washington State
@Washington	75-60	Feb.	2	Washington
Southern California	95-70		7	@Southern
UCLA	83-74			California
Arizona State	71-50		10	@UCLA
@UNLV	87-95		13	Arizona State
@California	93-68		17	*Georgia Tech
@Stanford	80-61		21	California
@Duke	76-78		24	Duke
Oregon	84-58		26	Stanford
Oregon State	87-60		28	@Oregon State
*Southern California	80-57	Mar.	2	@Oregon
*Stanford	85-61		7	Oregon State
*UCLA	94-78		9	Oregon
**South Florida	79-67			
**Alabama	55-77			

@ Road Games
# Hall of Fame Classic, Springfield, MA
Valley Bank Fiesta Bowl Classic, Tucson, AZ
* Pacific-10 Tournament, Tempe, AZ
** NCAA Tournament, Long Beach, CA

@ Road Games
# Dodge NIT. If Arizona defeats Austin Peay, the Wildcats will play a second round game on Nov. 16. The semifinals and finals of the tournament will be held on Nov. 21 & 23 at Madison Square Garden, New York, NY.
Tucson, AZ (Iowa State, Pepperdine & Temple)
* Meadowlands Arena, East Rutherford, NJ

NOTES: If Arizona gets by Austin Peay, the Wildcats will play the winner of Brigham Young vs. East Tennessee State in Tucson on Nov. 16 . . . Arizona's opening round opponent in the Fiesta Bowl Classic is Pepperdine . . . The Feb. 17 matchup with Georgia Tech, in the Meadowlands, is the ''Hoops That Help'' game. $50,000 of the proceeds will be donated to homeless shelters in Tucson and Atlanta. The remaining proceeds are to go to homeless shelters in Newark, N.J. and New York City.

ARKANSAS

LAST SEASON: 30-5
CONFERENCE RECORD: 14-2
STARTERS LOST: 2
STARTERS RETURNING: 3
CONFERENCE: SOUTHWEST (SWC)
LOCATION: FAYETTEVILLE, AR
HOME FLOORS: BARNHILL
  ARENA (9,000), FAYETTEVILLE;
  BARTON COLISEUM (7,800),
  LITTLE ROCK;
  CONVENTION CENTER (7,400),
  PINE BLUFF
NICKNAME: RAZORBACKS
COLORS: CARDINAL AND WHITE

★ COACH'S PROFILE ★

NOLAN RICHARDSON (Record at Arkansas, 107-51. Career record, includes high school, 436-181) Last season was one of sweet redemption for Arkansas coach Nolan Richardson. In his fifth year at Arkansas, Richardson put the Razorbacks in the Final Four for the first time since 1978. Richardson came to Arkansas in 1985, replacing the hugely successful and popular Eddie Sutton. After his first two teams at Arkansas were 12-16 and 19-14, Richardson was second guessed throughout the whole state. The Arkansas fans wanted to change to Sutton's slower, surer pace and Richardson was regularly booed in Arkansas' Barnhill Arena. But after he started to get his players into the program, Arkansas began to surge quickly. The Razorbacks have won 21, 25 and 30 games in the last three years with Richardson's players and his philosophy firmly established.

"Eddie Sutton (who went from Arkansas to Kentucky) is a great coach. But he had recruited players to play his halfcourt style," Richardson told John Bannon of USA Today. "I come in and it's like we weren't even talking the same language."

Richardson also had to deal with more adversity than what he faced on the court. About the same time Richardson left Tulsa to take the Arkansas job, his daughter Yvonne was diagnosed with leukemia. His first inclination was to the turn the Arkansas opportunity down and remain in Tulsa but Yvonne made her dad reconsider. She told her father that the Arkansas position was too big of an opportunity to pass up and that she was strong enough to fight her battle, even if he wouldn't always be around.

"She always told me that if I ever got a gymnasium on campus and a good program and a decent chance to recruit, that I could win big," Richardson said. "Arkansas offered me that opportunity."

Yvonne Richardson had to go to Minneapolis for treatment and her father was understandably distracted through her ordeal. Her condition worsened and finally on January 22, 1987, she passed away.

"She's the reason I'm still coaching today," Richardson said. "It's like I tell my players. Life is not promised to you. Nothing is. If you don't use what you've got today, you don't have to worry about tomorrow. You may not be here."

"My daughter taught me that there are more important things than the dribble or the jump shot or the fans," he told Anthony Cotton of The Washington Post.

"There were times when I thought about chucking it in . . . One time I thought about taking a leave of absence, but she wouldn't hear of it. She had heard me speak to people who were hospitalized and she told me that I wasn't doing the things I had talked about and believed in.

"I never felt threatened about losing my job; I'd always been a winner and I thought I could win at Arkansas if I got the chance. So I sat down with the people in the athletic department and told (athletic director) Frank Broyles if he didn't think I could turn the program, he should get someone else."

Richardson certainly knows what its like to be a pioneer. He is the first black men's head coach of any kind in the Southwest Conference. He was also the first black coach of a desegregated high school in Texas. He was the first black coach of a desegregated junior college in Texas and he was the first black coach in a major college in Oklahoma.

Richardson was born in Los Angeles and grew up in El Paso, Tex. He played college basketball at Texas Western for legendary coach Don Haskins. He graduated in 1963 and was one of the greatest players in Texas Western (now UTEP) history. Following graduation, Richardson spent a year with the San Diego Chargers of the AFL and played a season with the Dallas Chaperrals of the ABA before entering the coaching profession. He probably is the only current Division I head basketball coach who ever played both professional football and basketball.

His first coaching position was at Bowie HS in El Paso. He coached at Bowie for 10 years and his record was 190-80. Richardson was named coach of the year in El Paso three times. He then went on to Western Texas JC and compiled a three-year record of 101-13. His final team at Western Texas, featuring current San Antonio Spur Paul Pressey, was 37-0 and won the national junior college championship. Many junior college experts believe that team may have been the finest ever

in the history of junior college basketball.

In 1981, Richardson took over the struggling Tulsa program. He was successful from the start and in his first game at Tulsa, the Golden Hurricane beat defending national champion Louisville. Tulsa went on to a 26-7 record his first year and won the NIT championship. Richardson was 24-6, 19-12, 27-4 and 23-8 over his final four years at Tulsa. Three of his Tulsa teams played in the NCAA tournament.

"Kids today care about two things," he told the USA Today. "They want to be on TV and they want to run when they are."

He has always been an up-tempo, pressure defense coach. Last year the Razorbacks averaged 95.9 points per game, sixth nationally. Arkansas was the highest scoring outfit in the Final Four, not UNLV.

"I have problems trying to matchup with anybody; I rarely look at scouting reports," he told Anthony Cotton of The Washington Post. "We press, play some zones, try to do whatever will make it difficult on the other team.

"We just don't want it to be a half-court game. I'm not into chess matches; I'm not very good at that. . . . I don't try to prepare kids for a certain team. I want them to be aware of what's going on, but I'm more concerned with how we play, how hard we're playing."

He has great rapport with his players, is a disciplinarian and recruits well. Richardson has recruited very well in Memphis, has successfully dipped into the junior college ranks and has been a recruiting presence in the neighboring states of Oklahoma and Texas. He basically recruits regionally unless there's an overwhelming reason to go national.

"I think if we conducted a study on the influence of Nolan Richardson in Northwest Arkansas, it would be noticeable," Gordon Morgan, a black professor of Sociology at Arkansas told Steve Wieberg of USA Today. "It's like a rock thrown in a pond. A ring goes out.

"Whenever Richardson's name comes up, I think it has a positive effect on race relations because of his visibility."

Richardson serves on the boards of many charities. He is involved in the Ronald McDonald houses in Little Rock, Tulsa and Minneapolis where families of children being treated for cancer can stay. He has donated proceeds from Arkansas' annual series of Red-White pre-season games to charities.

"When I went to Arkansas, I wanted to become . . . not just a basketball coach, but a guy who would help the state progress . . . become a part of that community," Richardson told Wieberg.

"Personally, I think it's great that in five years we've been able to put the program together and get into the Final Four," Richardson said. "After all the obstacles we had to go through to get to this point, a lot of things have been accomplished."

And a lot more will be accomplished. Richardson is just beginning to build what will become a continually, nationally prominent program at Arkansas. He'll be back in the Final Four, we expect that to happen this year, and he is going to be recognized before long as one of the premier coaches in the country.

★ PLAYERS NOT RETURNING ★

MARIO CREDIT (6-9, C, 9.4 ppg, 3.9 rpg, 13 assists, 10 blocked shots, 31 steals) Last year we predicted that Credit would have to have a big year for Arkansas to reach the Final Four. Well, that did not prove true as he slacked off as a senior but the Razorbacks still won 30 games and made it to McNichols Arena in Denver for the Final Four. Credit was replaced by Oliver Miller as Arkansas' top inside threat.

Credit was a good scorer down low, but an erratic rebounder. He also was extremely inconsistent throughout his career. He had the tools but just never developed them. His departure is not a big loss as newcomers Isiah Morris and Roosevelt Wallace will capably replace Credit.

MICHAEL HOGUE (6-8, F, 2.8 ppg, 1.8 rpg, 3 assists) Hogue played in only five games for a total of 47 minutes last year as a redshirt freshman. He was 6-of-12 from the field. Hogue was not a key factor. He transferred to Southwest Missouri Baptist College.

LENZIE HOWELL (6-4, F, 13.9 ppg, 5.4 rpg, 64 assists, 10 blocked shots, 34 steals) Howell was the starting forward for Arkansas. He was a steady hand who was undersized for a forward in big time basketball but got the job done. He was third on the team in scoring and rebounding.

"He's the kind of kid who does all the little things you need," Texas coach Tom Penders told Steve Wieberg of USA Today. "He's a great follow-up shooter. He's a great rebounder. He seems to always be where the ball is."

He wasn't pretty but he got the job done game after game. Howell was a big winner and a Nolan Richardson type player. While Arkansas is still an extremely talented team, finding someone to do the dirty work with the consistency of Howell may be a problem. He will be missed.

LARRY MARKS (6-7, F, 3.7 ppg, 2.4 rpg, 5 assists, 5 blocked shots, 5 steals) Marks came off the bench last year to average eight minutes per game. He had a final year of eligibility remaining but became academically ineligible over the summer.

Marks was a good shooter and a factor on the boards. He was one of many players who gave Arkansas tremendous depth. He would have had a role on this year's team, but the newcomers can replace Marks' contribution.

CANNON WHITBY (6-0, G, 1.3 ppg, 0.4 rpg, 15 assists, 5 steals) Whitby was a limited contributor last year. He played in 23 games for an average of five minutes per game. He came to Arkansas billed as a great perimeter shooter, but last year made only 9-of-40 field goals (22.5 percent) and was just 6-of-28 (21.4 percent) from three-point distance. As the Arkansas program got better under Richardson and the quality of the athletes improved, Whitby was not able to keep pace. He is not a major loss.

★ RETURNING PLAYERS ★

ARLYN BOWERS (5-10, 175 lbs., SR, G, #20, 5.5 ppg, 1.8 rpg, 83 assists, 40 steals, Southside HS/Memphis, Tenn.) Bowers started 25 games at guard for the Razorbacks last year. He and starting point guard Lee Mayberry give Arkansas one of the quickest backcourts in the country. Bowers uses his exceptional quickness well on the defensive end of the floor. He also passes well.

Bowers made 63-of-165 field goals (38.2 percent) and was 11-of-34 (32.4 percent) from three-point range last year. From the line Bowers made 54-of-68 free throws (79.4 percent). He averaged 21 minutes per game last year.

His value to Arkansas was evidenced in the championship game of the Midwest Region against Texas last year. Bowers didn't attempt a shot against Texas and was credited with no steals. However, when the game was on the line he twice came up with loose balls in key situations.

"Arlyn is the unsung hero," Richardson told Dave Maraniss of *The Washington Post*. "He's the one guy no one will remember. But the coaching staff will."

SHAWN DAVIS (6-9, 225 lbs., JR, C, #44, 0.0 ppg, 3.0 rpg, Maud HS/Maud, Tex.) Davis appeared in only three games for a total of 16 minutes last year. He missed all five field goal attempts and scored one point on the year. He did get nine rebounds in his 16 minutes of action.

In 1988-89, Davis played in just 17 games for a total of 95 minutes. He suffered a broken ankle early in pre-season drills last year and didn't make it back until after January. He's not likely to be a major factor on this deep and talented Arkansas team.

TODD DAY (6-8, 200 lbs., JR, F, #10, 19.5 ppg, 5.4 rpg, 89 assists, 33 blocked shots, 82 steals, Hamilton HS/Memphis, Tenn.) As a sophomore, Day emerged as one of the premier forwards in college basketball. He finished his sophomore campaign as Arkansas' leading scorer with his 19.5 average, which placed him fourth in the Southwest Conference. He was a consensus first-team All-Southwest Conference selection last year. Day also was Arkansas' second-leading rebounder. He was the MVP of the Southwest Conference tournament.

"The six-foot-eight small forward, who really plays as a third guard, has a sort of all-around talent and intensity that allows him to help his team even when playing below par," wrote David Maraniss in *The Washington Post*.

His 684 points last year were the third-highest single-season total in Arkansas history. Day already has 1,109 career points, which ranks 11th in Arkansas history. He set an Arkansas school record with his 71 three-pointers last year. His biggest shot of the year was the winning basket that gave Arkansas an 86-84 win over Dayton in the second round of the NCAA tournament.

For the year, Day made 237-of-483 field goals (.491) and 71-of-176 three-pointers (.403). He connected on 139-of-183 free throws (.760). He had 83 turnovers against 89 assists. Day averaged 29 minutes per game last year.

The Sporting News named Day "Most Versatile" in its season ending national awards. "Positioning is merely a designation in the scorebook for the jack-of-all-trades Todd Day of Arkansas," said *The Sporting News*.

"Day is bright lights, high-fives and taunting fingers," wrote Stephen Caldwell in *The Sporting News*.

"I'm not the kind of person who really gets after it day in and day out," Day told *The Sporting News*. "It seems like in the games, when I see the lights and the fans, that's when I play my best . . . I just play with a lot of emotion. The things I do, I don't try to do them to be fancy. If I want to make a behind-the-back pass and I think that's the only way I can get it there, then I'll try it. I'm not trying to be spectacular.

"And when I'm into the flow of the game, I might run my mouth. But it's all a part of trying to win. If I feel I can take a player's game away from him by talking to him, then I'll do that. A lot of times, if I start talking, they'll double team me, and that leaves Lee (Mayberry) open."

As a freshman Day played both small and power forward for Arkansas. He definitely considers himself a guard and with his ballhandling skill, ability to create an open shot and stick the long range jumper, who's to argue?

"(Day) thrives on fans and competition. You can see he steps up another level. It's not that he doesn't work hard. It just brings out more of him when it's game time," Richardson told *The Sporting News*.

"If you had two Todds, you'd probably have a problem. Todd's mentality is to score. And he needs the ball to score. . ."

Over the summer he made and played a key role for the U.S. National team that won the Silver Medal in the Goodwill Games in Seattle and the Bronze at the World Basketball Championship in Argentina. The U.S. team had its share of high

profile offensive players and Day became the team's defensive stopper.

"The best defense I had was from a Yugoslavian player (Valimir Perasovic)," said Brazilian star Oscar Schmidt, one of the foremost scorers in the world. "But this guy (Day), he plays very correct defense."

The experience of being a defensive stopper certainly will help Day this year. If his defense improves as expected this year, Day could be a first-team All-America by the end of the season.

CLYDE FLETCHER (6-6, 205 lbs., JR, F, #33, Whitehaven HS/Memphis, Tenn. & Westark JC/Fort Smith, Ark.) Flether underwent shoulder surgery prior to last season, later injured a knee and played in four early games for a total of 37 minutes. He redshirted and is expected to be at full strength this year.

In his four appearances last season, Fletcher averaged 3.0 points and 1.3 rebounds. He was a high school teammate of Ron Huery at Whitehaven HS in Memphis. Fletcher signed with Arkansas while in high school, wasn't eligible as a freshman and went to Westark JC for two years. He averaged 21.0 points and 12.0 rebounds and was an All-Conference player at Westark.

He has been injury prone and has underwent surgery six times.

Fletcher is aggressive, athletic and extremely physical. He should help Arkansas improve on a -3.0 rebounding margin.

DARRELL HAWKINS (6-5, 200 lbs., JR, F, #21, 4.1 ppg, 1.8 rpg, 31 assists, 3 blocked shots, 13 steals, Waller HS/Prairie View, Tex.) Hawkins came off the bench and averaged 10 minutes of playing time per game last year. He shot the ball well, making 59-of-111 field goals (.532) and he connected on 1-of-2 three-pointers. From the line Hawkins was 24-of-32 (75.0 percent). He showed great improvement in pre-season drills last year and earned more playing time as a result.

Hawkins was a high school center who had to make the transition to a more perimeter-oriented role in college. He is an aggressive offensive rebounder and an excellent athlete.

With the graduation of starting forward Lenzie Howell, Hawkins could be a more important player for the Razorbacks this year. He has waited his turn and is ready to step up.

RON HUERY (6-7, 200 lbs., SR, F, #31, 10.0 ppg, 3.0 rpg, 82 assists, 16 blocked shots, 37 steals, Whitehaven HS/Memphis, Tenn.) Huery returned to the Razorbacks last season after sitting out the 1988-89 season. He was suspended indefinitely prior to the 1988-89 season by Richardson. He had earlier been suspended from playing for the first semester (1988-89) by the Arkansas judiciary board because of an on-campus incident where he allegedly pointed a gun at the head of another student during a fraternity party. Huery also got into trouble in his home town of Memphis for driving while intoxicated, illegal possession of a gun, and driving at excessive speed with a flat tire. A warrant was even issued for his arrest for failing to appear at a hearing. Obviously, Huery was out of control off the court.

Since being reinstated last year, Huery has stayed off the police blotter and is now a member in good standing of the Arkansas team. Last season he started six games and averaged 21 minutes per game. Huery was Arkansas' fifth-leading scorer and assists man. He made 119-of-257 field goals (47.3 percent) and 17-of-52 three-pointers (32.7 percent).

As a sophomore in 1987-88, Huery averaged 13.4 points, four rebounds, handed out 72 assists, stole the ball 51 times and blocked 16 shots. He was an All-Southwest Conference performer. As a freshman, Huery was the only rookie in the Southwest Conference to average in double figures (11.7 ppg) and he was the named the conference's newcomer of the year.

Huery was a great high school player in Memphis and a key recruit for Richardson. He was the MVP of the Capital Classic and scored 28 points in that game. He led Whitehaven HS to a Tennessee state title and was named the state's Mr. Basketball.

Last year he handled the ball better and had almost a 2:1 assists to turnover ratio. As a sophomore, before his suspension, Huery had more turnovers than assists. His perimeter shooting improved.

He is now clearly overshadowed by Todd Day and Lee Mayberry but keep an eye on Huery this season. He is a gifted player who made impressive strides in his first year back in the program after being suspended. Now that his problems are far behind him and he has been back for a year, Huery could be a very productive fifth-year senior.

WARREN LINN (6-5, 190 lbs., SO, F, #3, 0.5 ppg, 0.3 rpg, 1 assist, 1 blocked shot, 1 steal, Metro Christian HS/Tulsa, Okla.) Linn played in 19 games for a total of 74 minutes last year as a freshman. He made 4-of-17 field goals (23.5 percent) and 1-of-4 three-pointers (25.0 percent). Linn canned one of his two free throws. He was redshirted in 1988-89 by Richardson.

Linn was considered an outstanding perimeter shooter when Richardson recruited him. He also has good height and strength for his position. Linn will probably be a spot player again this year as the Arkansas depth chart is simply loaded.

LEE MAYBERRY (6-2, 170 lbs., JR, G, #11, 14.5 ppg, 2.9 rpg, 183 assists, 7 blocked shots, 66 steals, Rogers HS/Tulsa, Okla.) Mayberry is one of the elite point guards in the college ranks. He shared Southwest Conference player of the year honors last year with Texas' Travis Mays (the 14th overall pick in the NBA draft by the Sacramento Kings). Mayberry's most impressive stat was his assists-to-turnover ratio. Arkansas was sixth in the nation in scoring last year and Mayberry averaged 32 minutes per game. Yet, he had 183 assists with only 59 turnovers for an assists-to-turnover ratio of 3:1. That mark was the best in the nation. His 183 assists were the second highest single-season total ever at Arkansas.

Heading into his junior year, Mayberry has already dished out 318 assists, only 23 shy of the Arkansas school record and 184 away from breaking into the Southwest Conference's Top Five in career assists. He led the nation for most of the 1989-90 season in three-point percentage before finishing the season fourth. Mayberry led the Southwest Conference in three-point field goal percentage. He made 65-of-129 treys (.504). From the field Mayberry made 193-of-381 field goals (.507).

"They are two exceptionally good players," Richardson told Stephen Caldwell of *The Sporting News* about his junior backcourt of Day and Mayberry. "I'd rather have them than any other guards. That's the only way I can answer that. There are guys who can do some more things. But I don't think there are any two who can do as many things as those two can do together . . . Lee tries to keep everyone involved. Todd needs a player like Lee. Lee is the kind of guy who can get his and help somebody else get theirs."

"As players, Mayberry and Day have plenty in common. They are both mechanically sound. They both have good basketball instincts. They both play the game in a seemingly effortless manner. And they both have an unmistakable aura of confidence. But all of this is displayed in very different ways, for they take almost opposite approaches to the game . . . Mayberry is confident and cocky, but it often is tough to resist the urge to take his pulse," Caldwell wrote in *The Sporting News*.

Mayberry plays the same no matter the opponent and is one of the most consistent players in college basketball. He earned All-Tournament honors at both the 1990 Southwest Conference tournament and the NCAA Midwest Region. Mayberry has led Arkansas in minutes played over the last two years.

Richardson's recruitment of Mayberry has to be considered an "inside job." Mayberry grew up in Tulsa when Richardson was the coach of the Tulsa Golden Hurricanes. He attended Richardson's camp and even played basketball in the coach's driveway. Mayberry's sister eventually married Richardson's son so how much chance do you think another school had to sign him?

Mayberry joined Day on the U.S. National team that played in the Goodwill Games in Seattle and the World Basketball Championship in Buenos Aires, Argentina.

OLIVER MILLER (6-9, 265 lbs., JR, C, #25, 11.1 ppg, 6.3 rpg, 49 assists, 85 blocked shots, 41 steals, Southwest HS/Fort Worth, Tex.) Miller could be the premier big man in the Southwest Conference this year. He alternated at center last year but played more than senior starter Mario Credit. His 85 blocked shots ranked second in the Southwest Conference. Miller's 85 blocked shots tied the Arkansas school record held by former Razorback Andrew Lang (Phoenix Suns). He has 145 career blocks in just two seasons.

Miller also led the Southwest Conference in field goal percentage at .639 (152-of-238). He led Arkansas in rebounding and earned all-tournament honors in both the Southwest Conference tournament and the NCAA Midwest Region.

Against Texas in the finals of the Midwest Region, Miller had nine points and 11 rebounds. However, his play in the final minutes on the defensive end was a major reason why Arkansas was able to hold the Longhorns at bay and advance to the Final Four.

"The Big O played a phenomenal game," said Richardson after the Texas game. "Just because you get behind our front line doesn't mean the big horse isn't going to be there. He's an intimidating force in there. It's not always the blocked shot. He alters shots . . . you can get on him, and I usually do, but when the chips are down, the Big O usually cashes in."

Miller had 49 assists against 77 turnovers but he is a talented passer. He has had trouble controlling his weight and ballooned up to 300 pounds prior to last season before it was discovered he had a thyroid problem. Miller's weight problem has lessened with the discovery. He has great timing as a shotblocker and is a very talented player. Miller is a fun loving, talkative type who yuks it up with opponents.

Miller has the ability to step up and become a factor on the national level this year.

ERNIE MURRY (6-1, 175 lbs., SR, G, #14, 4.0 ppg, 1.2 rpg, 49 assists, 1 blocked shot, 24 steals, Wabbaseka HS/Wabbaseka, Ark. & Mississippi County, Ark. JC) Murry walked-on to the Arkansas program last year and was impressive in pre-season. He played two years at Mississippi County JC and signed with Nicholls State (La.) but didn't attend that school and sat out the 1988-89 season. His high school coach contacted the Arkansas staff and asked if Murry could try out. He exceeded expectations and even started a game.

Murry averaged 11 minutes per game. He was 48-of-118 from the floor (.407) and 20-of-59 (33.9 percent) from three-point range. Murry made 21-of-35 free throws (60.0 percent). He had 49 assists against only 27 turnovers.

Murry is an excellent defensive guard. He can run the club in the half court setting or push the ball on the break. With All-America Lee Mayberry, senior Arlyn Bowers and Murry, Arkansas has as much quickness, on both ends of the floor, and depth in the backcourt as any team in country.

★ NEWCOMERS ★

RAY BIGGERS (6-8, 215 lbs., FR, F, #24, 21.0 ppg, Kincaid HS/Houston, Tex.) Biggers faced limited competition in his private school league but his physical ability is so exceptional he should quickly adjust to major college basketball. He was ranked as the No. 5 senior in Texas last season by *Hoop Scoop*.

He is already a dedicated weight lifter and has the low body fat of a model. Biggers is a high level runner and jumper, reminiscent of the great athletes Houston

in the Phi Slama Jamma era. Presently, he is more of a power forward but the Arkansas coaches believe in time he can play both forward spots. He does everything reasonably well, as far as his skills are concerned, but nothing outstanding. Biggers' contribution will come in the future.

KEN BILEY (6-6, 210 lbs., FR, F, #23, 23.1 ppg, Pine Bluff HS/Pine Bluff, Ark.) Of the Arkansas freshmen, Biley is considered the most likely to play immediately. He reminds the Arkansas staff of departed starting forward Lenzie Howell because of his hard working, blue collar ways. In fact, Biley was unquestionably the hardest working Razorback in pre-season drills.

He goes after every loose ball and contests all rebounds. Biley is a quick, springy athlete who nickels and dimes opponents, wearing them down in the process.

Last season he led Pine Bluff HS to the Arkansas state title and earned state player of the year honors. *All-Star Sports* ranked Biley as the No. 48 senior in the nation last spring.

The Razorbacks are deep and experienced but Biley will find a way to get playing time this year.

ELMER MARTIN (6-7, 210 lbs., FR, F, #40, Fairley HS/Memphis, Tenn.) Martin is a probable redshirt. He seriously injured a knee in the summer of 1989, did not play as a senior, and is not expected to practice until late December or in January. He had major reconstruction surgery.

Before his injury, Martin was ranked the No. 2 player in Memphis behind Anfernee Hardaway, a Memphis State recruit whom many experts thought was the top senior in the country last season. He led the city of Memphis in rebounding as a junior. Martin is a long, lanky, greyhound type who can also block shots.

He probably won't be ready for a major contribution until late next season, at the earliest.

Martin is one of five Memphis natives on the Arkansas roster.

ISIAH MORRIS (6-9, 230 lbs., JR, F/C, #35, 12.7 ppg, Huguenot HS/Richmond, Va. & San Jacinto JC/Pasadena, Tex.) Morris was brought in as a replacement for departed center/forward Mario Credit. Morris is a better player than Credit and should get the job done. He was an honorable mention JC All-America in *Basketball Weekly*. *All Star Sports* ranked Morris the No. 8 JC signee.

He was one of only three players to reach double figures, 14 points, for the Texas team at the NJCAA Texas/USA All-Star game in Midland, Texas. Morris played for a well-balanced San Jacinto team that finished 30-4 and seventh in the national junior college tournament.

The Richmond, Va., native is from the same JC program as former Arkansas starting forward Lenzie Howell. He is from the same home town as Paul Pressey, the San Antonio Spur who played for Richardson at Tulsa.

Morris is a good rebounder and inside scorer plus can run the floor with the Razorbacks. He can put the ball on the floor and shoot outside. He should be a defensive presence in the lane as well. The Arkansas coaching staff feels Morris reminds them of former Oklahoma star Harvey Grant.

With the additions of Morris, Virginia Union transfer Roosevelt Wallace and Clyde Fletcher, who redshirted last season, Arkansas will be a much better rebounding team.

DAVOR RIMAC (6-7, 200 lbs., FR, F, #22, 27.0 ppg, Yugoslavia — Fayetteville HS/Fayetteville, Ark.) Rimac is a Yugoslavian who is very familiar with Richardson and the Arkansas program. His father coached David Brown, who Richardson coached at Tulsa, in Switzerland. Rimac's father wanted his son to play in America and sent him to Richardson's basketball camp on the Arkansas campus. Rimac stayed in Fayetteville, lived with the Richardsons for a year and attended Fayetteville HS. He was expected to return home to Yugoslavia but stayed for his senior year.

Rimac had a great high school career. He had several 40 plus scoring games. Already, Rimac is considered one of Arkansas' best shooters. He is a fluid athlete, passes well and is fundamentally sound. All he needs is more strength, experience against high level competition and to become accustomed to the high speed at which Arkansas plays the game.

He was a first-team All-Arkansas pick. His game is sound and steady. After a few years in the program, Rimac could become a key figure for the Razorbacks.

ROOSEVELT WALLACE (6-7, 235 lbs., JR, F, #34, Shaw HS/Cleveland, Ohio) Wallace sat out the 1989-90 season after transferring to Arkansas from Division II power Virginia Union in Richmond, Va. As a sophomore, Wallace averaged 13 points and seven rebounds for a nationally ranked, 26-4 conference champion (CIAA). As a freshman, he averaged 10 points and six rebounds for a 27-4, CIAA champion. He played in the shadow of 6-9 center Terry Davis, who played last year for the Miami Heat, and 6-4 guard A.J. English, the top Division II player last season and a second round choice of the Washington Bullets.

At Cleveland Shaw HS, Wallace averaged 23 points and 13 rebounds as a senior. He was an All-Ohio selection.

Wallace is a strong rebounder and can score well in the low post. He has excellent strength and bulk plus can shoot from middle distance. Richardson expects an immediate boost to the Arkansas front line from Wallace. Although he played at a Division II school, Wallace competed in arguably the strongest small college league (CIAA) in the nation. He is the cousin of Chicago Bull Charles Oakley.

★ QUESTIONS ★

Rebounding? Arkansas was outrebounded by an average of three boards per game last year. However, Morris, Fletcher and Wallace could turn that weakness into a strength.

★ STRENGTHS ★

Todd Day and Lee Mayberry! Day and Mayberry are among the four best players in the country at their respective positions. They are two of the all-time greats at Arkansas.

Nolan Richardson! After a tough beginning at Arkansas, Richardson has his type of players and the results are apparent. He is one of the premier coaches in college basketball.

Defensive quickness in the backcourt!

Offensive firepower! Arkansas averaged 95.6 ppg last year, sixth nationally, and four of the top six scorers are back.

Team speed and quickness!

★ BLUE RIBBON ANALYSIS ★

After winning 30 games and advancing to the Final Four, Arkansas coach Nolan Richardson is still hungry for more.

"I'm still hungry," Richardson said. "We want to continue what we've built on. We want to win the Southwest Conference regular season and tournament championships again. We want to go back to the Final Four. We want to win the national

championship. But we need to stay hungry to get there."

Returning are four starters including point guard Lee Mayberry and swingman Todd Day. Both Mayberry and Day rank among the four best players in college basketball at their respective positions. They played on the U.S. National team over the summer.

Junior center Oliver Miller blocked 85 shots last year and led Arkansas in rebounding. Miller is an underrated talent who could be dominating this season.

Guards Arlyn Bowers and Ernie Murry apply great defensive pressure. Senior swingman Ron Huery averaged 10.0 ppg last season after missing the 1989-90 season for disciplinary reasons. Huery is a talented scorer who could blossom.

Newcomers Isiah Morris and Roosevelt Wallace plus Clyde Fletcher, who played in four games before injuring a knee, will make Arkansas a better rebounding team.

"We have guys who are accustomed to winning," Richardson said. "They have a winning feeling and tradition. That's why we're playing such a tough schedule. We don't have any sweethearts on there. Besides the regular season, we're also playing Vanderbilt in the pre-season NIT and have the possibilities of playing Oklahoma and Duke."

Arkansas also faces UNLV, in Fayetteville, in February. The Razorbacks have improved every season under Richardson. It will be difficult to improve on 30 victories, however, Arkansas can still be a better team. The Razorbacks averaged 95.6 ppg last year and are again lethal offensively. Arkansas is deep, talented, experienced and quick defensively. With expected improved rebounding and interior offensive play, there are no glaring weaknesses.

Arkansas should win a third straight Southwest Conference crown and return to the Final Four.

LAST SEASON

#Samford (AL)	97-67	@Baylor	77-82
##Oregon	102-75	@Texas Christian	79-81
@South Alabama	105-90	Southern Methodist	77-46
#Mississippi	90-76	Texas A&M	114-100
U.S. International (CA)	166-101	Rice	104-80
Missouri	88-89	###Southern Methodist	84-61
Bethune-Cookman (FL)	91-61	###Baylor	115-75
##VMI	92-61	###Houston	96-84
##Delaware State	117-75	*Princeton	68-64
@UNLV	101-93	*Dayton	86-84
@Houston	82-78	**North Carolina	96-73
@Texas Tech	92-75	**Texas	88-85
Baylor	99-84	***Duke	97-83
Texas Christian	93-79		
@Southern Methodist	80-61	@ Road Games	
@Texas A&M	100-84	# Pine Bluff, AR	
Houston	100-89	## Little Rock, AR	
Texas	109-100	### SWC Tournament, Dallas, TX	
@Alabama-Birmingham	109-95	* NCAA Tournament, Austin, TX	
@Rice	70-66	** NCAA Tournament, Dallas, TX	
@Texas	103-96OT	*** Final Four, Denver, CO	
Texas Tech	100-77		

1990-91 ARKANSAS SCHEDULE

Nov.	14	#Vanderbilt	Feb.	13	Texas Tech
	27	##Mississippi College		16	Texas Christian
Dec.	1	Kansas State		20	@Southern Methodist
	5	###Louisiana Tech		23	@Texas A&M
	8	@Missouri		26	Baylor
	11	South Alabama	Mar.	3	@Texas
	22	@Oregon		7-10	*SWC Tournament
	29	###Jackson State (MS)			
	31	##Northeast Louisiana	@ Road Games		
Jan.	2	@Rice	# Dodge NIT. If Arkansas defeats Vanderbilt, the Razorbacks will play a second round game on Nov. 16. The semifinals and finals of the tournament will be held on Nov. 21 & 23 at Madison Square Garden, New York, NY.		
	6	Houston			
	10	Texas			
	12	@Texas Tech			
	15	@Texas Christian			
	19	Southern Methodist	## Pine Bluff, AR		
	21	@Florida State	### Little Rock, AR		
	23	Texas A&M	* Dallas, TX		
	26	@Baylor			
	30	Alabama-Birmingham			
Feb.	2	Rice			
	7	@Houston			
	10	UNLV			

NOTES: Arkansas is expected to face the winner of Oklahoma vs. New Orleans, at an undecided location, if the Razorbacks defeat Vanderbilt in the first round of the Dodge NIT . . . the big news at Arkansas in the off-season was the Razorbacks' move to the SEC. Arkansas joins the SEC in basketball next year. "The fans told us, in every way possible that we

ought to go," said Chancellor Dan Ferritor . . . Arkansas' top high school signee 6-3 guard Clinton McDaniel of Booker T. Washington in Tulsa, Okla., is not academically eligible but has enrolled in school and should play next year . . . Richardson has owned Texas coach Tom Penders. In the two years Penders has been at Texas, Richardson is a perfect 6-0 against him.

MICHIGAN STATE

LAST SEASON: 28-6
CONFERENCE RECORD: 15-3
STARTERS LOST: 2
STARTERS RETURNING: 3
CONFERENCE: BIG TEN
LOCATION: EAST LANSING, MI
HOME FLOOR: BRESLIN
    CENTER (15,138)
NICKNAME: SPARTANS
COLORS: GREEN AND WHITE

is beginning his 15th season at Michigan State. Heathcote is the all-time winningest coach in Michigan State history. He led Michigan State to its first ever national championship in 1979 and has racked up three Big Ten titles. He has put Michigan State in the NCAA tournament five times in his 14 years.

"All he's concerned about is making sure his program is the best it can be and that his kids go to class and graduate," said California-Santa Barbara coach Jerry Pimm, a long time friend of Heathcote. "He cares about the things you're supposed to care about.

"The think I like about Jud is that he's not hung up on awards or being the winningest coach of all time or anything like that."

Heathcote took over for Gus Ganakas in 1976 and he promptly laid a strong dose of direction and discipline on the Spartans. "We couldn't believe the change. And at the time, we didn't enjoy it," said former Michigan State player Gregory Kelser.

His first Michigan State team was 12-15. Then Heathcote took advantage of an almost divine geographical blessing. It so happened that nearby Lansing Everett HS had a blossoming star by the name of Earvin "Magic" Johnson. Not too many college coaches are fortunate enough to have arguably the greatest basketball player of all-time growing up almost in their backyard and Heathcote

★ COACH'S PROFILE ★

JUD HEATHCOTE (Record at Michigan State, 242-170. Career record, 322-233) Ranking second behind Indiana's Bob Knight in longevity in the Big Ten, Heathcote made the most of that fortune by successfully recruiting Johnson. Johnson only stayed two years at Michigan State but he certainly made his presence felt. The Spartans went 25-5 and 26-6, won and shared Big Ten titles and took the 1979 NCAA title in Salt Lake City. The 1979 national championship remains Heathcote's crowning achievement. To this day, Heathcote enjoys reminiscing about the 1979 championship team. He still calls Johnson ''Earvin'' even though he has gained fame as ''Magic.''

''I remember when Earvin was thinking about going pro and people were writing that he was too slow and he couldn't shoot and that there no position in the NBA for a 6-9 point guard,'' Heathcote said. ''Finally I told him, 'Earvin, there's only two people in the world who know how good you are, that's me and you.' Nobody has ever done as much for a basketball team as Earvin Johnson did for us in 1979.''

After Johnson left, Heathcote wasn't able to sustain the program at a high level. Michigan State was 12-15, 13-14 and 12-16 in the three years following Johnson's early departure for the NBA. Finally he got things turned around and Michigan State put together a 17-13, 16-12, 19-10 and 23-8 seasons. During the lean times no one questioned Heathcote's coaching acumen, but his recruiting was criticized. Michigan State's Jennison Field House was antiquated by big time standards and that certainly didn't help Heathcote's recruiting efforts. He also was criticized for not being a high profile salesman like his rival, former Michigan coach Bill Frieder. Heathcote is a gritty, old-fashioned guy and is not a high profile salesman.

''I can't tell five separate kids they're my No. 1 recruit, it's just too dishonest,'' Heathcote said.

Since the 1979 national championship season, Heathcote has led Michigan State as far as the Final 16 of the NCAA tournament only to be knocked out in controversial endings in the region semifinals. Ironically, both controversial endings, in 1986 and last year, were the result of questionable officiating decisions that concerned the game clock. In 1986, Michigan State was ahead of Kansas in the semifinals of the Midwest Region at Kemper Arena in Kansas City. In the last minute of that game, the game clock malfunctioned and several seconds were lost. Kansas made up a deficit and went on to win the game and later advanced to the Final Four. Then last year history repeated itself in the semifinals of the Southeast Region at the Superdome in New Orleans. Michigan State led Georgia Tech by two points with five seconds left. Georgia Tech's freshman guard Kenny Anderson dribbled downcourt, veered to the left of the key to avoid three Spartan defenders and went up for a jumper. Television replays showed that Anderson's shot, which was good, was clearly launched after time had expired. However, there was another question concerning whether the shot was a three-pointer or not, he launched it right on the line, and the game officials disagreed as to whether or not it was a three-pointer. Finally, the officials decided that Anderson's shot was a two-pointer and there was no questioning on the floor as to whether his shot had been released before the buzzer. Georgia Tech went on to win the game 81-80 in overtime. Once again, the ides of March were not exactly in Michigan State's corner.

''In crucial games, I'm not so sure we shouldn't be using replay,'' Heathcote said, ''because you've got an awful lot at stake here in a game like this.''

The 62-year-old Heathcote grew up in Manchester, Wash., twelve miles by boat from Seattle. His father, a teacher and coach, died of diphtheria when Heathcote was three. He basically grew up with his high school coaches as father figures. He was the first nine-letter recipient in his high school's history and Heathcote was also ranked fifth in his senior class academically.

''Even with my Alzheimer's I can remember being obsessed with athletics as early as fifth or sixth grade,'' Heathcote told Jack Ebling of the Lansing State Journal. ''I wanted to be a teacher and a coach from ninth grade on. For some reason, I never waivered. . .

''It became an obsession not just to play, but to win. I matured very early. I was six-foot-one and a half, 193 pounds as a sophomore in high school. I started every game in every sport for three years, was our first all-state player and even had my number retired. Now, I see they've unretired it.''

He joined the Navy after high school and trained to become a pilot. After his stint in the Navy, Heathcote accepted a basketball scholarship to Washington State. He spent five years at Washington State and earned degrees in math and education. He was a hardnosed defensive specialist and excellent stationary shooter in college.

After college, his first head coaching job was at West Valley HS in Spokane, Wash. Heathcote taught math and coached basketball for 14 years. He won five conference championships at West Valley and was hired as an assistant at Washington State by coach Marv Harshman. Heathcote was the freshman coach at Washington State and he was 99-9 in that post over a five-year period.

''He's overly candid, even when it hurts him,'' Harshman told Ebling. ''He and Bob Knight have a lot in common. They're both misunderstood. Parents used and call and say their sons were coming home. And I'd say, 'Just give it a semester, and he'll die for that guy!' Jud has established more loyalty among players than any coach I've ever known.''

In 1971, he moved on to Montana. Heathcote was 80-53 in five years at Montana. The athletic director at Montana was Joe Kearney, who later went on to become the athletic director at Michigan State.

''He's a negative-type coach, but a great motivator. It takes at least a year to get used to all the cursing and swearing. I was as close to leaving as anyone could get —a signature away. Now, I'm glad I stayed. I've learned how to deal with a boss,'' former Michigan State forward Ken Redfield told Ebling.

He is definitely a perfectionist and a strong believer in a fundamental approach

to the game. However, he takes time in practice to work on individual skills and some of the normal shots that appear in the major college game, such as fadeaway jumpers and certain maneuvers off the dribble, that most coaches never work on individually. He definitely is very tough and demanding and spares no feelings among his staff or players. But Heathcote knows when its time to switch and be more low key around his team. He is known as one of the innovators of the match-up zone defense but will switch strategy when he feels it necessary without a great deal of prodding. For example, last year Michigan State didn't play man-to-man defense the first month and a half of the season. The Spartans were playing at Indiana and were down 8-0, 37 seconds into the game. Heathcote called a time out and changed immediately to man-to-man defense and Michigan State rarely went back to the matchup that season. He just felt at that point that the Spartans didn't have the proper personnel for the matchup and it was time to switch.

He is known as a great guard coach. Remember, prior to Magic Johnson no 6-9 player had that degree of freedom. Even though he is a tough, throwback coach with a traditional set of values, Heathcote has always let his best guards have complete free reign. He let Johnson loose, gave Sam Vincent freedom, and guided Scott Skiles to a great year in 1985-86 that resulted in Michigan State finishing an unexpected third in the Big Ten and advancing to the Final 16. Last year, he did it again as Michigan State guards Kirk Manns and Steve Smith had great years. There is no doubt that most Michigan State players show significant improvement throughout their careers.

''He's the same demanding man he was when I got here,'' said Manns. ''He's always looking for improvement. And he accepts nothing less. As a result, I've matured mentally. I've grown up a lot.''

This year Heathcote should have his best team since 1979. However, Michigan State has seemed to be most successful operating out of an underdog pose when little was expected. This year the expectations will be high as nine lettermen are returning including national Player of the Year candidate Steve Smith. We have a hunch that ol' Jud will be back in the Final Four this year.

Michigan State opened up the plush 15,100-seat Jack Breslin Student Event Center last year. The lack of a modern facility certainly hurt Michigan State in recruiting, but now that the new facility is open Heathcote may start to have some of the most talented teams he has ever enjoyed at Michigan State.

''We struggled recruiting,'' Heathcote told Marty Strasen of Basketball Weekly. ''We used to bring everybody in here and brag about the school and the league and academics, then we'd go apologize for Jennison Field House (Michigan State's home court for 50 years). Now, there are no apologies.

''Kids make comparisons. You bring 'em into (the Breslin Center), they're going to be impressed. You bring them into Jennison Field House, they're going to be depressed.

''I think this is a solid program year-to-year now in terms of recruiting. We're not up there where Michigan has been the last three or four years or where Indiana is always, but we're an emerging program that should have some stability at the upper level for a number of years.''

★ PLAYERS NOT RETURNING ★

JESSE HALL (6-3, 200 lbs., SR, G, #23, 1.0 ppg, 1.1 rpg, 7 assists, 1 blocked shot, 3 steals) Hall was a highly regarded player when he signed with Michigan State but his impact was limited. Last year his role decreased significantly. Hall started seven games as a sophomore in 1988-89 and played in 31 games. He not only didn't start a game but played in only 17. His field goal attempts decreased from 95 to 26 and Hall took only 5 three-point field goals after launching 29 as a sophomore.

He transferred to Southern Illinois —Edwardsville.

KIRK MANNS (6-1, G, 15.3 ppg, 1.8 rpg, 56 assists, 1 blocked shot, 15 steals) Manns was simply terrific as a senior. He did suffer a broken foot which kept him out of three games and out of the starting lineup for seven games. Manns led the Big Ten in three-point shooting. He made 81-of-178 threes (.455) and was second on the team in scoring behind Steve Smith. For awhile last season, Manns was the leading scorer in the Big Ten. He was named to the second-team All-Big Ten squad by United Press International and the Associated Press named him third-team All-Big Ten.

Before the season it was questionable that Manns would even be a starter as a senior. However, he lost weight and was hungrier as a senior. His terrific outside shooting and scoring overshadowed the fact that Manns improved the other facets of his game —ballhandling, rebounding and defending —and became more than a one-dimensional shooter.

When Manns went to the sideline with a broken foot, Mark Montgomery filled in and gained valuable experience. There is no way Heathcote can totally replace Manns' perimeter shooting and scoring, but he can get some solid guard play at the other backcourt position alongside Steve Smith. Look for Montgomery to step up and play well and two freshmen, Andy Penick and Kris Weshinskey, are good perimeter shooters who could also help replace Manns.

DAVE MUELLER (6-9, C, 0.3 ppg, 0.5 rpg) Mueller played in only 17 games for a total of 35 minutes last year. He was not a key player in terms of productivity or impact on games, but Mueller played a role in practice. He was very happy with his role and did a solid job off the court. Mueller was a rarity, a senior who has a rather limited role but is still a happy camper.

His intangibles will be missed.

KEN REDFIELD (6-7, F, 11.6 ppg, 6.8 rpg, 106 assists, 5 blocked shots, 44 steals) Redfield is a key loss for Michigan State. He was third on the team in scoring and led the Spartans in rebounding. Redfield also was second in assists and topped the Spartans in steals.

In addition to his scoring, rebounding and passing contributions, Redfield was also unquestionably the finest defensive player in the Big Ten. He checked everyone from Iowa center Les Jepsen to Michigan guard Rumeal Robinson and did an outstanding job. He was an outstanding athlete who came to Michigan State at the age of 17 and probably should have been redshirted. He was somewhat disappointing until his senior year when Redfield finally put it all together. He is expected to be replaced by either 6-7 sophomore Dwayne Stephens or 6-7 junior Parish Hickman.

TODD WOLFE (6-5, F, 2.1 ppg, 1.2 rpg, 11 assists, 1 blocked shot, 3 steals) Wolfe statistically had a better year as a junior and never got his confidence as a senior. He was considered an outstanding shooter, yet made only 24-of-66 (.364) of his field goal attempts and 7-of-25 (.280) from three-point range. He was too easily affected when adversity struck.

Wolfe was a member of a hard working Michigan State senior class that had a great deal to do with the Spartans' success. However, he is not a key loss.

★ RETURNING PLAYERS ★

JEFF CASLER (6-0, 175 lbs., SR, G, #22, 0.8 ppg, 0.4 rpg, 9 assists, 3 steals, St. John's HS/St. John's, Mich. & Lansing CC/Lansing, Mich.) Casler played in 17 games, starting two last year and saw 90 minutes of action. He made 5-of-7 field goals (.714) and was 3-of-4 (.750) from three-point range.

Casler is one of the older players in Division I basketball. He is 26-years-old and went to work after graduating from high school instead of immediately attending college. He grew up a short distance from East Lansing. Casler attended Lansing CC and was the MVP of the Division II junior college tournament.

He is married and the father of a small boy. Casler lives over an hour and a half drive from the Michigan State campus. He has tremendous self-discipline and could be a bigger factor this year. Casler is strong, gutty, shoots well off the dribble and is a smart point guard. He also defends well and could see considerable action if the highly touted freshman guards Andy Penick and Kris Weshinskey are not ready.

PARISH HICKMAN (6-7, 210 lbs., JR, F, #42, 6.3 ppg, 4.4 rpg, 25 assists, 9 blocked shots, 17 steals, Bishop Borgess HS/Detroit, Mich.) Hickman is a possibility to replace graduated forward Ken Redfield in the starting lineup. Last season he started 12 games and was fifth on the team in scoring and fourth in rebounding. There is no doubt that when he puts it altogether, Hickman is one of the best players on the team but consistency has been his problem.

He has decent range on his jumper, can rebound and is an excellent athlete. Against Georgia Tech, he had 10 tough rebounds, a season-high, in 25 minutes. Hickman scored in double figures on nine occasions and connected on 50 percent or better of his field goal attempts in 22 games. He made .545 of his field goal attempts on the year. He scored a career-high of 15 points against Eastern Michigan and tied Matt Steigenga for the team's scoring lead against Princeton with 14 points while also pulling down a team-high nine rebounds. Hickman was needled constantly by his teammates last year for missing three dunks in a row at Ohio State. He was in the starting lineup before 6-10 center Mike Peplowski became healthy. If his playing time is to expand this year, Heathcote believes Hickman must be able to learn to play facing the basket.

"Parish is much stronger than last year; but whether or not he can play away from the basket is still a question," Heathcote told Gordon Trowbridge of the *Lansing State Journal*. "Right now, he's still a center. Maybe later, he'll learn to play away from the post."

MARK MONTGOMERY (6-2, 170 lbs., JR, G, #11, 3.6 ppg, 2.0 rpg, 97 assists, 7 blocked shots, 25 steals, Southgate Aquinas HS/Inkster, Mich.) Last season Montgomery played in all 34 games, 13 as a starter, and started the last seven games of the season. He will get the first crack at the starting guard spot Kirk Manns held for most of last season.

Montgomery dished out a season-high nine assists against Murray State in Michigan State's opening game in the NCAA tournament. His best scoring effort was a 13-point game against Michigan. He shot 51 percent from the floor (26-of-51) over the last nine games. Montgomery finished tied for second on the team in steals. For the year he made 44-of-101 field goals (.436) and 12-of-32 (.375) three-point field goals. His foul shooting was poor, 22-of-44 (.550). He was a member of the Big Ten All-Academic team.

He is very quick and passes well. Montgomery needs to improve defensively and also has to develop a consistent shot. He has made some big shots in his career, but the consistency has been missing. He did make all 5 three-pointers against Illinois last year but basically his lack of consistent perimeter shooting was a concern for Heathcote all year long.

Despite the inconsistency, Heathcote detected an increase of confidence from Montgomery and believes he is ready to handle increased responsibility this year. He was a highly regarded high school player who was an important part of Michigan State's much heralded 1988 recruiting class. This year Montgomery will be a key player for the Spartans. It is doubtful that Michigan State can reach the Final Four without a good season from him.

MIKE PEPLOWSKI (6-10, 270 lbs., SO, C, #54, 5.3 ppg, 5.8 rpg, 19 assists, 10 blocked shots, 7 steals, De LaSalle HS/Detroit, Mich.) This season the Big Ten could see a much improved Mike Peplowski. During his senior year in high school Peplowski blew out a knee. Over the next two years he had four knee operations and Peplowski redshirted the 1988-89 season to rehabilitate his knee. It wasn't until after the fourth operation, last November, that Peplowski finally began to regain much of his past mobility and confidence.

"I really don't know what it is now," Peplowski told Jack Ebling of the *Lansing State Journal* last March. "People say I'm playing with a lot more confidence. I just know I feel a lot better. I'd forgotten how I used to play, diving all over the floor.

"I've lived a structured life and I've always been a basketball player and an entertainer," he said. "Everywhere I go, people ask me how tall I am and if I play basketball. I was so afraid I'd have to say, 'I used to play. But then I had this really bad injury. . .'"

Peplowski started 23 of the 28 games he played in. He finished third on the squad in rebounding and finished third in field goal percentage (.546). He had four games with 10 or more rebounds including a season-high 12 against Northwestern in an 84-68 win to clinch the tie for the Big Ten title for Michigan State. He led or tied for the team's rebounding lead in nine games, including an 11-board effort against California-Santa Barbara in the NCAA tournament. He scored a season-high 12 points against Iowa. Peplowski played 30 minutes against Minnesota and contributed nine points and 11 rebounds in a 75-73 overtime win. He shot 50 percent or better from the field in 21 games.

He is a free spirit who has a tattoo reading "Pure Bred" and a design of a Polish eagle on his ankle. Peplowski has always been huge. He will never be a great jumper and needs to further refine his post moves. One of his main strengths is an infectious enthusiasm, however, he sometimes gets so emotional and so high strung that he commits silly fouls. Peplowski has to work to keep his weight down and stay in shape.

Last year his role was mainly to clog the middle on defense and rebound. This year Heathcote plans on getting Peplowski more involved in the offense.

STEVE SMITH (6-6, 195 lbs., SR, G, #21, 20.2 ppg, 7.0 rpg, 150 assists, 17 blocked shots, 25 steals, Pershing HS/Detroit, Mich.) Michigan State's surprising run to the Big Ten title and the Final 16 of the NCAA tournament was keyed by many players. Seniors Kirk Manns and Ken Redfield played well all season long and various other Spartans came to the forefront when needed. Jud Heathcote turned in one of his best coaching efforts and everything seemed to fall in place for the Spartans. However, Michigan State also discovered that it has a true star in Steve Smith. Late in the season, Smith was sensational as Michigan State clinched the Big Ten title and won two games in the NCAA tournament before losing a controversial decision in overtime to Georgia Tech. Smith led the Spartans in scoring in the last eight games of the season. During that run he had 21 points against Indiana, 36 vs. rival Michigan, 39 in an overtime win at Minnesota, 23 at Northwestern, 22 in the Big Ten title clinching victory over Purdue, 22 in Michigan State's first round win in the NCAA tournament against Murray State, 21 in the second round vs. California-Santa Barbara and he closed the season with 32 points in the Spartans' heartbreaking loss to Georgia Tech.

He was named the Big Ten MVP by the *Chicago Tribune*. *The Sporting News* placed Smith on its first-team All-America squad. Both the *Associated Press* and the *United Press International* named Smith to their first-team All-Big Ten squads as well. He was named the Big Ten's player of the week on three occasions. Smith is the Player of the Year in the tenth edition of *Blue Ribbon College Basketball Yearbook*.

"Early in the year, we seemed to have a different hero every night," Heathcote said. "Down the stretch we kept having the same hero, and his name was Steve Smith."

Smith started the Big Ten portion of the season slowly because he broke his left hand before conference play started. Playing almost completely right handed, he struggled for several games and Michigan State was 5-3 heading into a road game with league leading and unbeaten Purdue. He led the Spartans to an upset and led all scorers with 22 points. Michigan State was just two games out with nine to play and the Spartans swept the rest of their Big Ten schedule and won the conference championship.

"Wearing ridiculously yet stylist baggy shorts, he jaws with opponents constantly, staring wild-eyed at players who try unsuccessfully to stop him. Pointing out who his next victim will be. Yet he is respected around the league and he delivers," wrote Kevin Roberts in *The Washington Post*.

Smith led Michigan State in scoring in 19 games. He recorded 14 games with 20 or more points and five outings with 30 or more points. His 39-point outburst against Minnesota was a career-high and he had the winning jumper with 29 seconds remaining in overtime that sparked Michigan State to a 75-73 win. He shot 50 percent or better from the field in 21 contests, including 14 of his last 17 appearances. He also paced the Spartans in rebounding in 14 games and had double-digit outings. Overall, he scored in double figures in 29 of 31 games and in 35 of his last 38 games dating back to the 1988-89 campaign. He was the MVP of the Great Alaska Shootout after establishing a tournament record for assists while ending up tied for third in scoring with 69 points. Smith finished tied for fourth among Big Ten players in scoring, seventh in field goal percentage (.535), 10th in assists (3.7 apg) and 12th in rebounding (5.7 rpg). Entering into this season he has 1,511 career points and stands seventh on the Michigan State all-time scoring list. He has also dished out 344 assists as a Spartan, good for fourth place on the school's all-time list.

"It is certainly a plus to have a 'go-to' player in all clutch situations and Steve savors those situations and thrives on it," Heathcote said. "We want to use that to our advantage."

Smith's game has already drawn comparisons to former Michigan State all-time great Magic Johnson. "He (Johnson) was a hero of mine when I was in middle school," Smith told Jack Saylor of the *Detroit Free Press*. "I really look up to him, and he's one of the reasons I picked Michigan State."

Smith was only 5-8 when he started high school and played all positions at Pershing HS. Even though as a senior he averaged a triple-double 26 points, 12 rebounds and 10 assists, Smith was not highly recruited. Besides Michigan State, he visited only two schools —Missouri and Detroit.

Concerning the Magic Johnson comparison, Heathcote said, "I see bits and pieces out there, but I compare no one to Magic. Steve has the same kind of versatile game as Earvin, but that's as far as I go."

Smith is a big time ballhandler and knows how to protect the ball from smaller guards. He can score from the outside, back his man down low in the lane, score on the break and put points on the boards in various ways. He is underrated defensively and had some key defensive stops at crucial junctures in big games last year.

Smith is extremely confident after last year's great run but he has not slacked up. He is not satisfied with his game and worked so hard in the off-season that one Michigan State insider said, "I have never seen anyone come close in terms of work ethic." He put more emphasis on weight training and is much stronger. He is also expected to graduate on time.

Smith is becoming more assertive as a leader and has always been a big winner. He is quiet and shy off the court, but once a game begins he becomes effervescent and talkative.

"You watch Steve play and you know he's from Detroit," said Leroy Haywood, older brother of former NBA all-star Spencer Haywood and the director of Detroit's Hawthorne Recreation Center, told Bryan Burwell of the *Detroit News*. "Yeah, you can tell. Detroit hoops are all about pride, competition and survival. Watch Steve play and you see all that."

Everything is in place for Steve Smith to have an absolutely sensational senior season. He worked hard in the off-season to prevent a let down, is extremely motivated and should be able to put the Spartans on his shoulders and carry them through tough times. Smith should definitely be one of the first five picks in the upcoming NBA draft. It will be interesting to see who is the best guard in the country at the end of the season, Smith or Georgia Tech sophomore Kenny Anderson.

MATT STEIGENGA (6-7, 220 lbs., JR, F, #35, 10.4 ppg, 3.5 rpg, 65 assists, 30 blocked shots, 22 steals, South Christian HS/Grand Rapids, Mich.) This is a big year for Steigenga. He has to come through and become much more consistent if Michigan State is to repeat as Big Ten champs and advance to the Final Four. No one doubts that Steigenga has the ability to be one of the best in the Big Ten, but he just hasn't been able to put it all together in his first two years at Michigan State.

Steigenga has started 66 of 67 games during his collegiate career. He ranked fourth on the team in scoring (10.4 ppg) while posting a team-high 30 blocked shots. Steigenga led the Big Ten in blocks (1.2 blpg) in conference games. He led Michigan State in field goal percentage (.587). Steigenga reached double figures in 21 games last year including a career-high 20 points against San Jose State. He closed out the season shooting 50 percent or better from the field in 26 games, including 15 of his last 18. He led Michigan State in scoring in four games including 17-point efforts against Illinois and Ohio State. His five blocks against Purdue in a 64-53 road win was the second best effort by a Big Ten player last year.

He was named to the All-Tournament team at the Great Alaska Shootout (44 points in three games) and the MVP of the Spartan Oldsmobile Classic (34 points, 12 rebounds in two games). He grabbed a season-high seven rebounds in games against Detroit and Princeton. He was named to the GTE/COSIDA Academic All-America third-team with a 3.42 GPA in general business last year.

He is one of the better athletes in the Big Ten. Steigenga is a tremendous leaper who can run the court. He admits his jumping ability gets him out of difficult situations.

"He's a fabulous athlete," said teammate Mike Peplowski. "Everything he does, he's good at. He has all the tools."

"I love the fast break," Steigenga said. "I love the running game, and I want it to end with a dunk if I can."

He played center in high school and during his freshman year at Michigan State when Peplowski was on the sidelines. Last year he moved back to his natural forward spot.

A former Michigan Mr. Basketball award winner, Steigenga was considered one of the Top 25 high school players in 1988. He was the focal point of Michigan State's prize recruiting class that year. He has shown flashes of his enormous potential so far. Basically, the game has just come easy for Steigenga. If he can improve his ballhandling and outside shooting and gain much needed consistency, Steigenga could be a major force this year. If he is, Michigan State will walk away with the Big Ten title and advance to the Final Four team.

DWAYNE STEPHENS (6-7, 215 lbs., SO, F, #31, 4.3 ppg, 3.0 rpg, 27 assists, 1 blocked shot, 6 steals, Ferndale HS/Ferndale, Mich.) Stephens played in all 34 games last year and was the most consistent Spartan off the bench. He will long be remembered at Michigan State for his big steal and subsequent basket with 20 seconds remaining against Purdue that clinched the Big Ten title for the Spartans.

He finished second on the team in field goal percentage (57.7 percent) and

averaged 15.6 minutes per game. Stephens came on strong during the second half of the season and played a season-high 29 minutes against Murray State in the NCAA tournament and responded with 12 points and five rebounds. He earned *Basketball Weekly* third-team freshman All-America honors.

Stephens scored a season-high 18 points against Detroit. He hit all five field goal attempts against Wisconsin en route to 11 points.

"D.J. plays very good defense," Heathcote told Jack Ebling of the *Lansing State Journal*. "Most freshmen can come in and play offense. Very seldom can they come in and play defense as well. But from Day One, he was one of our smartest defensive players."

Stephens does many things well. He has good court sense, handles himself well under pressure, rebounds and is confident in his ability. He must improve his range and diversify his offensive game.

While Parish Hickman has more experience, Stephens could be the eventual replacement for forward Ken Redfield in the Spartans' starting lineup. Redfield was the Big Ten Defensive Player of the Year last year and Stephens has the same potential. He could blossom this year.

JON ZULAUF (6-6, 200 lbs., SO, F, #25, 0.7 ppg, 0.1 rpg, 4 assists, 1 steal, Port Huron HS/Port Huron, Mich.) Zulauf played in 19 games for 72 minutes last year. He made only 6-of-21 field goals (.286) but is considered a promising outside shooter with three-point range. He possesses excellent work ethic and is a tremendous leaper.

He grabbed four rebounds in eight minutes against Furman. Zulauf has a lot of things going for him but he is not confident. His brother, Jay Zulauf, played at Bowling Green and is now at Marquette.

Zulauf could surprise and see more action this year. He is talented, athletic and could give Michigan State a boost off the bench.

★ NEWCOMERS ★

MATT HOFKAMP (6-10, 230 lbs., FR, C, #44, Ionia HS/Ionia, Mich.) Hofkamp redshirted last year at Michigan State. He has good skills, shoots the ball well for his size, but is not yet ready to be a major contributor. He must get stronger and tougher plus gain more confidence.

Hofkamp was an All-Michigan selection two years ago at Ionia HS. He was considered one of the better pivot prospects in the midwest. This year he will provide support help behind Mike Peplowski.

ANDY PENICK (6-2, 180 lbs., FR, G, #12, 28.5 ppg, 5.0 rpg, 8.0 apg, 5.0 stpg, Pleasure Ridge Park HS/Louisville, Ky.) Penick was considered one of the two best players in Kentucky last year along with Dwayne Morton, from Louisville Central HS and now sitting out this year at Louisville. Tom Goins of *Hoop Scoop* ranked Penick the top senior in Kentucky last year.

"Tremendous passing and ball handling skills. Tough 'D'. Combine his mental 'toughness' and aggressiveness with his quick release on the shot and you have the best guard to come out of Kentucky since Rex Chapman. Great shooter," said Goins.

Penick not only has outstanding skills but he has a toughness about him that almost borders on cockiness.

"Penick is an outstanding combination guard in the Jeff Lebo mold, although he's quicker and more athletic than the former UNC star. Andy is one of the premier shooters in the prep ranks . . . he is a fiery, intense competitor, and a very intelligent basketball player. Coach Dale Mabrey praises Penick's savvy, character, attitude, ballhandling and passing skills," wrote Bob Gibbons in *All Star Sports*.

Gibbons ranked Penick the No. 60 senior in the nation at the conclusion of last season.

If Penick can come in and quickly acclimate himself to Heathcote's system, he could see significant playing time as a freshman. He is a better shooter than Mark Montgomery, who figures to inherit Kirk Manns' starting backcourt spot. Heathcote is not the easiest coach for a freshman to play for, but Penick may be tough enough to hang in and fight through the tough times to emerge as a key factor.

SHAWN RESPERT (6-3, 170 lbs., FR, G, #24, 22.1 ppg, Bishop Borgess HS/Redford, Mich.) Respert was one of the top seniors in the always talent packed state of Michigan last year. He is coming off a knee injury and may be slowed as a freshman.

Respert is an average shooter but is a gifted athlete who played strong defense in high school. He was ranked the No. 6 player in Michigan by *Hoop Scoop*.

Respert will probably be a deep reserve this year as he goes into pre-season drills behind freshman Andy Penick and Kris Weshinskey.

KRIS WESHINSKEY (6-3, 175 lbs., FR, G, #3, Purcellville HS/Purcellville, Va.) Weshinskey is coming home. He lived in Okemos, Mich., a suburban area of East Lansing before moving to Virginia for his final two years in high school. He could be a surprise for the Spartans this year. He is an excellent perimeter shooter, quick with the ball, smart and has impressive speed and leaping ability.

"The guy who made the biggest name for himself was 6-3 Kris Weshinskey . . . who is comparable to Bill McCaffrey (Duke) in many ways. Much stronger than McCaffrey, Weshinskey is a great shooter who is impossible to defend because he'll drill it in your face if you don't guard him and he's so quick that he goes right around smaller guards if they come out and defend him. He also has incredible jumping ability and hang time and he dunked one in (Anthony) Pell's (freshman at Villanova) face that will be remembered as one of the top plays of the summer.

No where to be found before this session, Weshinskey now ranks among our Top 50 in the nation and promises to move higher before he's through,'' said *Hoop Scoop* publisher Clark Francis after watching Weshinskey at the Five Star Camp in Honesdale, Pa., in the summer of 1989.

Weshinskey and Penick give Heathcote two outstanding freshman guards. Respert also could be a good one before his career at Michigan State is over.

★ QUESTIONS ★

The consistency of the front line? Michigan State needs more consistency up front, especially from Matt Steigenga.

Perimeter shooting? Now that Kirk Manns is gone, Heathcote must find some more perimeter shooting to take some of the load off of superstar Steve Smith. The best candidates for that additional perimeter shooting are freshman guard Andy Penick and Kris Weshinskey.

The performance of Matt Steigenga and Mark Montgomery? These two juniors are talented but have been up and down throughout their careers. Both have to come through if the Spartans are to repeat as Big Ten champs and make a strong run at the Final Four.

The health of center Mike Peplowski? Peplowski played his best ball at the end of the season, however, he underwent four knee surgeries in the last four years and must watch his weight.

★ STRENGTHS ★

Steve Smith! Smith is *Blue Ribbon's* national player of the year. He was absolutely sensational down the stretch as Michigan State clinched the Big Ten title last year. He is undoubtedly the finest player at Michigan State since Magic Johnson.

Jud Heathcote! He is one of the best coaches around.

Inescapable hunger because of the controversial loss to Georgia Tech! The Spartans are still upset about how they were knocked out of the semifinals of the Southeast Region on Georgia Tech star Kenny Anderson's jumper which was clearly launched after the buzzer. That loss should be a motivating factor for Michigan State all year.

Rebounding! Michigan State outrebounded opponents in 13 of 18 Big Ten games last year. For the year the Spartans outrebounded opponents by nine boards per game.

Experience! The Spartans gained significant experience in learning how to win key games last year. They won 10 games down the stretch to take the Big Ten title. Included in that streak were some major road victories.

Defense! Heathcote is one of the finest defensive coaches in the country. Last year Michigan State held opponents to a mere .426 field goal percentage and just 68.5 points per game.

★ BLUE RIBBON ANALYSIS ★

Optimism is understandably high at Michigan State this year. The Spartans won a school record 28 games last year and brought home their first Big Ten championship since 1979 when an effervescent sophomore named Magic Johnson was ruling the court at Jennison Field House. Michigan State also advanced the Sweet 16 of the NCAA tournament before losing on a controversial call at the buzzer when Georgia Tech Kenny Anderson's last second shot, which was definitely launched after the buzzer, was ruled good and the Yellow Jackets took out the Spartans by one point in overtime.

Nine lettermen are returning, including senior guard Steve Smith who was absolutely sensational in the second half of last season. Smith is undoubtedly the finest player at Michigan State since Johnson left early for the pros in 1979. He is not only the best in the Big Ten, but in our opinion is the best in the country this year. The Spartans have a deep and experienced bench and a great deal of flexibility.

''We have a tremendous nucleus returning for this year and have excellent players,'' said Michigan State coach Jud Heathcote, the 1989-90 Kodak coach of the year. ''Of course, there is the realization that teams will be pointing towards us and be better prepared for MSU than last year. We certainly won't sneak up on anyone as we may have done last year. We'll have to rise to the occasion and play up to our ability.''

Smith is capable of carrying Michigan State a long way by himself. However, if the Spartans are to get to the Final Four, then junior forward Matt Steigenga, sophomore center Mike Peplowski and junior guard Mark Montgomery will have to pick up their scoring and take some of the load off Smith. Sophomore forward Dwayne Stephens and junior forward Parish Hickman are two other key players who should play key roles. Stephens has the potential to become the Big Ten defensive player of the year and Hickman has outstanding ability but has yet to put everything together. He is a fierce rebounder at both ends of the floor.

Freshman guards Andy Penick, Shawn Respert and Kris Weshinskey all come highly regarded and could get valuable playing time in the backcourt if Montgomery slips. Penick and Weshinskey are big time perimeter shooters who could complement Smith well.

Michigan State was an outstanding rebounding team last year, outrebounding foes by over nine per game and the Spartans are always tough defensively. Michigan State is still angry over the loss to Georgia Tech and that should be a motivating factor all season long.

Everything came together down the stretch for Michigan State as the Spartans won 10 straight games to take the Big Ten title. Smith was absolutely devastating during that run and has worked hard over the summer and is eager to improve on last year's sensational showing.

The high expectations in East Lansing should be met. Michigan State has a true superstar in Smith and what should be a strong supporting cast. The Big Ten is also down as several traditional conference powers such as Michigan and Illinois are not up to their usual strength. The Spartans will win their second straight Big Ten title.

The Final Four will be held in Indianapolis. What would a Final Four in the midwest be without a Big Ten representative? Look for the Spartans to be in Indianapolis for the Final Four. Michigan State hasn't been back to the Final Four since taking the national championship in 1979. The pieces are certainly in place for a return trip to college basketball's premier event by Heathcote's Spartans.

LAST SEASON

#Auburn	92-79	@Purdue	64-53
#Texas A&M	87-85	Wisconsin	60-57
#Kansas State	73-68	@Ohio State	84-75
Nebraska	80-69	@Iowa	80-70
@Furman	84-63	Illinois	70-63
Austin Peay	88-76	Indiana	72-66
@Illinois-Chicago	57-55	Michigan	78-70
Detroit	94-65	@Minnesota	75-73OT
Bowling Green	79-81	@Northwestern	84-68
@Evansville	80-66	Purdue	72-70
Eastern Michigan	87-73	*Murray State	75-71OT
##San Jose State	88-61	*California-Santa Barbara	62-58
##Princeton	51-49	**Georgia Tech	80-81OT
@Wisconsin	64-61	@ Road Games	
Ohio State	78-68	# Great Alaska Shootout, Anchorage, AK	
Iowa	87-80		
@Illinois	64-73	## Spartan Oldsmobile Classic, East Lansing, MI	
Northwestern	91-80		
@Indiana	75-57	* NCAA Tournament, Knoxville, TN	
@Michigan	63-65	** NCAA Tournament, New Orleans, LA	
Minnesota	74-79		

NOTES: Michigan State will open up with George Mason in the first round of the Spartan Oldsmobile Classic . . . the Dec. 15 game at the Palace in Auburn Hills with defending national champion UNLV will not only be telecast live by ABC, but part of the proceeds will go to charity in the Detroit and Las Vegas areas . . . Michigan State has an outstanding center prospect sitting out this year who will be eligible next season. Anthony Miller, 6-9,

1990-91 MICHIGAN STATE SCHEDULE

Nov.	23	Furman		14	@Northwestern
	28	@Nebraska		16	Illinois
Dec.	1	@Bowling Green		23	Purdue
	8	@Detroit		25	@Minnesota
	13	@Cincinnati		28	Indiana
	15	#UNLV	Mar.	3	@Ohio State
	18	Evansville		9 or 10	@Michigan
	20	Central Michigan			
	28-29	##Spartan Oldsmobile Classic	@ Road Games		
Jan.	3	Michigan	# The Palace, Auburn Hills, MI		
	5	@Iowa	## East Lansing, MI (Coastal Carolina, George Mason & Louisiana Tech)		
	10	Wisconsin			
	12	Northwestern			
	17	@Illinois			
	19	Minnesota			
	23	@Purdue			
	26	@Indiana			
	31	Ohio State			
Feb.	7	Iowa			
	9	@Wisconsin			

from Benton Harbor, Mich., was Mr. Basketball in the state of Michigan last year. He scored 23 points with eight rebounds and led the East team to victory in the Dapper Dan Roundball Classic in Pittsburgh last year. ''He runs the floor well and is a tenacious offensive rebounder,'' said Benton Harbor coach Paul Wilhite. ''His best days are ahead of him. With hard work, he'll be a pro some day.''

NORTH CAROLINA

LAST SEASON: 21-13
CONFERENCE RECORD: 8-6
STARTERS LOST: 2
STARTERS RETURNING: 3
CONFERENCE: ATLANTIC
    COAST (ACC)
LOCATION: CHAPEL HILL, NC
HOME FLOOR: DEAN E. SMITH
    STUDENT ACTIVITY CENTER
    (21,572)
NICKNAME: TAR HEELS
COLORS: CAROLINA BLUE AND WHITE

★ COACH'S PROFILE ★

DEAN SMITH (Record at North Carolina, 688-203) Smith, along with Bob Knight —the reigning icon among college basketball coaches, probably suffered through his most difficult season since way back in 1961 when he took over at North Carolina and fought his way out of Frank McGuire's shadow. It is a tribute to what Smith has wrought, that a temporary run of adversity worth little notice in most other programs should be deemed deserving of national attention in the case of North Carolina.

When the school has been ranked in the end-of-the season Top 20 for 20 consecutive years, then doesn't make it, that's news. When a team foregos the absolutely mind-boggling record of being out of the weekly Top 20 polls only three times since the 1984-85 season, it's absence will be more than duly noted. Not often do programs have standards to meet like 19 (now 20) consecutive 20-win seasons, nine consecutive Top 10 finishes, 25 straight first Division ACC finishes or 19 years in a row of hitting at least 51 percent of its field goal attempts.

Smith's reaction late in the season (even the Tar Heels recovery to a 17-11 record at the time was considered disappointing to many) was to put things in perspective. His first point was that North Carolina's killer early season schedule yielded losses to Missouri, Alabama, Georgetown, Iowa and Colorado State.

"Had we scheduled differently, we'd still be in single-digit losses at this period," Smith said. "We need to improve in all areas, but if shots drop, we wouldn't be getting all these questions. We shouldn't be so drastic in won or lost. I don't think I've changed whether we're winning a lot or losing a lot, nor do I think I should. There's a lot more important things in the world."

Eventually, North Carolina redeemed its season to a considerable degree by making the Final 16 for the 10th straight time, the longest such on-going streak in college basketball. It was the way the Tar Heels made it —knocking out Oklahoma, the No. 1 team in the country — that expunged some demons. Said Smith: "We usually play well against teams that shoot quickly."

North Carolina proved that by derailing the runaway Loyola Marymount express in the 1988 NCAA tournament. Noting the presence of four ACC teams in the Final 16 and the conference's 9-1 record at the time, Smith said: "We've proven we're a pretty good team that played all season in a pretty good league."

The reason "pretty good" is considered pretty bad at North Carolina —in Chapel Hill any basketball cup half full is considered half empty—is the unparalleled long-term success Smith has carved out while building North Carolina into the nation's marquee program.

"They say North Carolina is having a down year. There are a lot of people in this business who'd like to be as down as that son-of-a-gun," said Duke coach Mike Krzyzewski.

Smith's accomplishments have been well documented. He has guided North Carolina to seven Final Fours, he coached North Carolina to a national championship in 1982 and also was the head coach of the Gold Medal winning U.S. Olympic team in 1976. Until the last two seasons, Smith's North Carolina teams have had at least one first-team All-ACC player every year since 1962. He has recorded seven 25 or more victory campaigns. Most importantly, he has developed a system and a program that stands over the course of time rather than piles up short-lived accomplishments.

The Smith system at North Carolina starts in the recruiting process. North Carolina's recruiting style is understated. Smith does not promise any recruit a starting job and isn't the high profile salesman many in the profession are. Occasionally, it will cost him a recruit, like Georgia Tech's Kenny Anderson, but over the course of time he gets his type of player. Smith makes few appearances at summer camps, AAU tournaments and the like, so when he does go out to see a recruit play, it is very noticeable.

Freshmen at North Carolina, whether they are Michael Jordan or Scott Cherry, have to learn the system and to play the Tar Heel way before getting a big role. Freshmen also carry the equipment on the road. North Carolina players acknowledge the man who passed the ball after a score, the bench stands up en mass to congratulate any player who comes off the floor and no one attends a North Carolina practice without written permission from Smith. Visitors to practice sit in a certain area high above the floor and a team manager will come up to the section and take their permission slip. At North Carolina, no staff member speaks to the press or pro scouts except Smith.

Smith is also extremely loyal to his former players. His former players have not only gone on to do well in the pros but have been successful in many endeavors, including private business, coaching, teaching, the law, medicine, the armed forces, religion, etc. Smith proudly points to the long and impressive list of basketball alumni and their current occupations in the Tar Heel's media guide. Former North Carolina players consider themselves part of an extended family and are also fiercely loyal to Smith. Every summer North Carolina's players in the pros come back to Chapel Hill for pick-up games.

Smith has an extremely high graduation rate in his program. He also has advised any player who looked to be a certain high first round draft pick, usually in the first five, to go pro early. Among those Smith advised to leave North Carolina with eligibility remaining were Michael Jordan, James Worthy and J.R. Reid.

He introduced the four corner stall, which is not seen anymore due to the 45-second shot clock, to college basketball. He was also one of the first coaches to use defenses that relied heavily on trapping. Smith was also one of the first college coaches to substitute players for offensive and defensive situations during the final moments of close games.

He is a native of Emporia, Kan., and attended Kansas University on an academic scholarship. He played freshman football and varsity basketball and baseball for the Jayhawks. Smith was a member of Kansas' 1952 national championship team and the 1953 runners-up.

After graduating from Kansas, he became an assistant basketball and golf coach at Air Force in 1958, then went on to North Carolina as an assistant to Frank McGuire the next year. He became North Carolina's head coach in 1961.

Smith was not successful initially. After one road loss early in his career, the team returned to Chapel Hill to see Smith hung in effigy in a tree. Obviously, he has gained a lot more respect since then.

He also has a social conscience. Smith participated in some lunch counter sit-ins during the civil rights movement of the '60s. He gives half his sneaker money back to North Carolina for academic scholarships. He has always been quietly active in religion and politics. He cultivates a fatherly image and never smokes or drinks in front of his players.

He has been criticized in recent years for failing to get the Tar Heels to the Final Four since 1982. Critics wondered how Smith could not win a national championship or make it to the Final Four with a Michael Jordan and Sam Perkins in the lineup. While pointing for the Final Four has become commonplace among coaches of major programs in the last decade, Smith still builds for the long haul. He won't compromise his system or principals for a short term run. Smith doesn't necessarily always believe that the best team wins the NCAA championship.

"The idea of this (NCAA) tournament is not necessarily to find the best team," Smith said. "If it was, we'd be playing best-of-five or best-of-seven series. The idea is to find a champion. Sometimes that may not be the best team."

North Carolina has been stung by some criticism recently that the Tar Heels have slipped and nearby Duke has gained considerable ground. After all, Duke has been in four of the last five Final Fours and Blue Devil coach Mike Krzyzewski has put together great recruiting class after great recruiting class. We'll get a chance to see in the next few years just how true that opinion is. North Carolina has a freshman class that many recruiting experts believe is one of the greatest of the modern era.

★ PLAYERS NOT RETURNING ★

JEFF DENNY (6-4, G, 2.0 ppg, 0.7 rpg, 40 assists, 7 steals) Denny got his scholarship to North Carolina after Rex Chapman turned the Tar Heels down to go to Kentucky. He wanted to be a Tar Heel more than anything and accomplished that goal. Denny never became a big time player, but he was a useful reserve for North Carolina towards the end of his career. He hustled, scored a bit at times and moved the ball around on the offense. Denny won't be hard to replace. He wasn't a great, but he certainly got a great deal out of his college career.

KEVIN MADDEN (6-5, F/G, 10.1 ppg, 4.7 rpg, 58 assists, 7 blocked shots, 27 steals) After averaging 14.6 ppg as a junior, it was hoped Madden would finally fulfill a lot of the high expectations held for him coming out of high school. Madden, although contributing some solid minutes at times, was not the consistent factor the Tar Heels needed. He did some of the little things like screening well, but his turnovers (65) exceeded his assists (58) and he was not consistently productive.

Madden twisted his right knee severely during practice following North Carolina's upset in the second round of the NCAA tournament over Oklahoma and missed the Tar Heel's season-ending loss to Arkansas in the Final 16. He was not quick enough and never shot well enough to play permanently on the perimeter where he would have been more valuable. Madden's strengths were rebounding and inside scoring. He was all too often a forward trying to play guard.

Madden can be adequately replaced.

SCOTT WILLIAMS (6-10, C, 14.3 ppg, 7.3 rpg, 25 assists, 41 blocked shots, 36 steals) Williams' senior season was spent alternating between keeping the walls from sometimes crumbling around a team searching for identity and not dominating in situations he should have often enough. He wound up North Carolina's leading rebounder and shotblocker and second leading scorer. Williams was a major cog on a team that shook off a bundle of early disappointment and gradually rose to respectability, then another Final 16 finish.

He ranked fifth in the ACC in blocked shots. His size, shotblocking ability and overall defense could be significantly missed. He had a good career but not what was expected coming out of high school. Williams was a big time High School All-America at Wilson HS in Hacienda Heights, Calif. He was Smith's first recruit from the west coast. All too often, Williams seemed to struggle with himself.

Williams was not selected in the NBA draft but he did sign as a free agent with the Chicago Bulls.

★ RETURNING PLAYERS ★

SCOTT CHERRY (6-3, 175 lbs., SO, G, #11, 0.3 ppg, 0.1 rpg, 2 assists, 1 blocked shot, 1 steal, Central Catholic HS/Saratoga Springs, N.Y.) Cherry played in eight games last year for the Tar Heels as a freshman. He did not get much of an opportunity to show off his long range shooting skills, as he only attempted seven shots from the field. Cherry was considered an outstanding shooter in high school.

This season Cherry will compete for more playing time in the backcourt. Those minutes may be tough to come by, however, as North Carolina returns solid backcourt veterans and also has some talented freshmen. If he improved his ballhandling enough during the summer, Cherry could put himself in a position to be a quality reserve this year and his outside shooting could be an asset.

PETE CHILCUTT (6-10, 235 lbs., SR, F, #32, 9.0 ppg, 6.6 rpg, 47 assists, 20 blocked shots, 41 steals, Tuscaloosa Academy/Eutaw, Ala.) Chilcutt is one of three starters from last year's team returning to Chapel Hill this season. He improved his numbers from 6.9 ppg and 5.4 rpg in his sophomore season and 9.0 and 6.6 averages in the two categories as a junior. He finished tied for 12th in the ACC in rebounding last year. Chilcutt has shown over the course of his career an ability to both handle himself against physical players inside and to shoot the ball with finesse and range over much smaller players. He has long been likened by ACC followers to former Duke star forward Mark Alarie, who graduated in 1986 and is now with the Washington Bullets.

Chilcutt, even though he has shown steady improvement throughout his career, still has not reached a high level of production offensively, and his game still lacks consistency. His skills are good enough to make him a double-digit scorer every night but he has not yet shown that kind of output as a Tar Heel.

His defensive game has also improved, and with his quick hands he was responsible for 41 thefts last year. He is not blessed with quick feet, however, and he has to overcome this negative by working tirelessly on sound positioning. Chilcutt is rarely caught out of position down low and he has matured to the point where tough, physical contact among the big players in the paint no longer intimidate him.

Chilcutt will be looked to by Smith to provide senior leadership to this young, but talented, Tar Heel team. As an important part of this leadership, Chilcutt must also contribute more points offensively and assert himself as a major force, both inside and outside. He shot over 51 percent from the field for last season and he even connected on 12-of-30 three-point attempts (40 percent). He has great versatility for a player who is 6-10 and Chilcutt has one more collegiate season to build his own reputation.

HUBERT DAVIS (6-4 1/2, 177 lbs., JR, G, #40, 9.6 ppg, 1.8 rpg, 31 assists, 6 blocked shots, 33 steals, Lake Braddock HS/Burke, Va.) Davis was one of the Tar Heel's top reserves last season as a sophomore and he even started on several occasions. He played in all 34 games and was fourth on the club in shots attempted and total points scored. He connected on close to 45 percent of these attempts, including 40 percent from three-point range, while almost tripling his scoring output from his freshman year. Davis is a streaky scorer who has the ability to be a more consistent outside force and who can improve his offensive moves off the dribble. With his long arms and outstanding leaping ability, Davis should be able to drive to the basket if the outside shot is not there and score against virtually anybody.

He is a nephew of former North Carolina star and current Denver Nugget Walter Davis. Hubert may have the opportunity to be a starter for the Tar Heels this season, as he and sophomore Henrik Rodl will be the two experienced off-guards returning for Dean Smith. Davis' long arms and quick feet are also strong defensive weapons, and he used them to snatch 33 steals from opponents last year. With some more muscle added to his lanky frame, Davis could become an excellent rebounder from his guard position and would help the Tar Heels recoup some of the lost rebounds Kevin Madden took with him after graduation. Madden averaged close to five rebounds per game from his wing guard position last season.

Davis, while he did not come out of high school with a can't-miss reputation has improved his game to the point where he is a valuable contributor to the Tar Heels as he enters his junior season. He is an excellent athlete who is smooth both with and without the ball. He has the mentality of a good scorer, and with more consistency on his outside shot. Davis should become one of North Carolina's most reliable and well rounded offensive forces.

RICK FOX (6-7 1/2, 231 lbs., SR, F, #44, 16.2 ppg, 4.6 rpg, 84 assists, 6 blocked shots, 54 steals, Nassau, Bahamas & Warsaw Community HS/Warsaw, Ind.) Fox had an outstanding all-around season in 1989-90 for the Tar Heels. He was a third-team All-ACC selection as he finished 11th in the league in scoring, seventh in steals, sixth in field goal percentage (52.2 percent) and second in three-point percentage (43.8 percent). Fox may have been not only North Carolina's most versatile player, but possibly the most complete player in the ACC last year. There will be a great deal of pressure on Fox to improve on his outstanding numbers from a year ago, however, this year's extremely young team will heavily rely on him.

Smith can talk for a long time on the subject of Rick Fox. "Rick has really improved defensively and his confidence and his shooting has increased a great deal," said Smith. "His passing judgment is what we hoped it would be and he is an excellent competitor. He only learned how to play the game at a late age, but he has come on and improved rapidly."

Fox has gotten better and better in each of his previous three seasons in Chapel Hill. Last year, he added a long range shooting touch to his already vast arsenal of talents. Fox was given the opportunity to play on the perimeter quite a bit, and he responded by hitting almost 44 percent of his three-point tries, far away leading North Carolina in that category. His second place finish among ACC three-point shooters was even more impressive when one considers the fact that Fox shot a higher percentage from long range than highly publicized scorers Dennis Scott at Georgia Tech and Phil Henderson at Duke.

Fox continues to be a solid defender as well. He led North Carolina with 59 steals last season and he is rarely caught out of position by an offensive player. He is quick and agile enough to guard a player man-to-man on the perimeter and strong and determined enough to play in the back of a 2-1-2 or 2-3 zone and challenge players three or four inches taller.

The crowning achievement for Fox last year came in North Carolina's second round NCAA tournament game against highly ranked Oklahoma. North Carolina was expected, after an up and down season, to be disposed of easily by the high-flying Sooners. But as the final seconds ticked down, there was Rick Fox making a great drive to the basket and scoring on a twisting, off-balance layup while getting fouled. This clutch three-point play won the game for the Tar Heels, 79-77.

Fox will be looked to for the same kind of heroics throughout 1990-91. He, along with fellow seniors Pete Chilcutt and King Rice, must lead the team's youngsters both on and off the floor. And if he has the kind of senior year he is capable of, Fox will challenge for ACC player of the year and All-America honors, and the Tar Heels will be at, or certainly near, the top of the ACC.

KENNY HARRIS (6-2, 180 lbs., SO, G, #4, 1.8 ppg, 0.4 rpg, 12 assists, 5 steals, Petersburg HS/Petersburg, Va.) Harris received spot playing time last season as a freshman. He contributed most of his time as a backup point guard to King Rice, but he also gained experience at the second guard position. Harris has better scoring skills at this point in his college career than Rice had, but he must physically mature and prove that he can handle the ACC style of play on both ends of the floor.

Harris took 23 three-point shots last season and he made eight of them. He can provide the Tar Heels with some long range shooting off the bench and his ballhandling and passing skills are more than adequate. Harris will be in competition for playing time at point guard with freshman Derrick Phelps, a High School All-America from Christ the King HS in Middle Village, N.Y. Harris will need to shoot the ball consistently and develop his man-to-man defensive game in order to stay ahead of the slick ballhandling Phelps on the depth chart.

GEORGE LYNCH (6-7, 210 lbs., SO, F, #34, 8.6 ppg, 5.4 rpg, 34 assists, 14 blocked shots, 37 steals, Roanoke, Va. & Flint Hill HS/Falls Church, Va.) Lynch entered North Carolina last year ranked as one of the Top 10 freshmen in the country by many talent evaluators. He did not disappoint as he immediately contributed to the Tar Heels off the bench and became a valuable member of the team despite his rookie status. If not for the superhuman first season Kenny Anderson had for Georgia Tech, Lynch would have had a good chance of being the ACC's Rookie of the Year. He was selected to the All-ACC freshman team and he will most likely gain many more honors in the conference before his career ends.

Lynch's bread and butter is the inside game. He thrives on the defensive and offensive glass, collecting rebounds over taller players time after time. His quick feet and strong body put him in the great rebounding position, and once there, he lets his powerful hands and tireless work ethic do the rest. He simply has the great rebounder's mentality that every missed shot which comes off the rim is rightfully his to grab. Lynch grabbed quite a few of those missed shots last season as his total of 103 placed him third on the team.

He is also a sound offensive player who excels, you guessed it, inside. He has a quick first step which he uses to gain advantage along the baseline and to free himself up crossing the lane. His turnaround jumper is accurate and he also gained confidence in his jump hook as last season progressed. For the year Lynch shot a solid 52 percent from the field and he proved that he could not be intimidated once he got into the lane.

In 1990-91, with North Carolina's tremendous physical size in both the sophomore and freshman classes (four players 6-9 or taller, including two seven-footers), Smith will be asking Lynch to make an adjustment in his role. Lynch will be moved outside this year, and he will see extensive playing time at small forward. This will be a major adjustment for Lynch offensively, as he has always been an inside scorer, but his defensive responsibilities will not be altered dramatically. After all, Lynch did play a good deal of perimeter defense against opposing small forwards as a freshman.

This move to small forward is one which will take advantage of Lynch's versatility and athleticism. However, it is widely believed that the switch may be a temporary one to allow some of the younger players to get acclimated to the North Carolina system and that Lynch, by January or February, will be back in his customary position of banging away at power forward.

KING RICE (6-1, 191 lbs., SR, G, #21, 9.2 ppg, 2.0 rpg, 217 assists, 54 steals, Binghamton HS/Binghamton, N.Y.) Rice had his most consistent and effective season as the Tar Heel's floor general last year. He was excellent as a defender all year and he made intelligent choices in running the offense. Rice handed out 217 assists in 34 games last season, numbers which were good enough to place him fifth in the ACC in that category. Rice's assists-to-turnover ratio continued to be outstanding as it once again was better than 2:1 (217 assists to 101 turnovers). His sophomore ratio was also slightly better than 2:1 so Rice has shown consistency and responsibility handling the ball over the last two years.

In a conference filled with outstanding point guards, Rice has often been seen as the outsider. He was an excellent football player in high school, and his 190-plus pound frame makes Rice look somewhat out of character in a basketball uniform. Well, Rice certainly has proven that he belongs on the basketball court, as he enters his senior year he looks to rise to new heights among the league's floor leaders. He is an excellent complementary player and knows his limitations and will not try to do too much.

His major attribute has always been his defensive ability. Rice is the Tar Heels' foremost perimeter defender and he is like a bulldog when he goes nose-to-nose with the likes of Kenny Anderson and Chris Corchiani. He is physically stronger than any point guard in the ACC, and this strength allows him to keep his opponents from getting too far out of check. He combines strength with quick feet to cut off even the most talented penetrators before they can get into the lane and create.

His biggest problem, and it certainly has been well documented in Tar Heel country, is perimeter shooting. He is barely over 40 percent from the floor in his career (.406 last year from the field, including .309 from three-point range) and as a result he often finds himself facing sloughing defenses and packed-in zones daring him to shoot the open jumper. Rice has, on occasion, though, put these shooting woes behind him and made clutch shots to win games. Most notably, he made a buzzer-beater in last year's season opening win over James Madison in the Maui Classic. The Tar Heels rallied from 12 points down late in that game and the comeback was capped by Rice's last-second heroics.

This year Rice will be looked to for senior leadership. However, he will have to stay away from off-the-floor incidents which have plagued him in the past. He was ordered by a judge to perform 75 hours of community service for resisting arrest after a late night incident last May 8 in Chapel Hill. Smith was understandably less than amused with this news.

Rice will be pushed for his starting position this year by freshman Derrick Phelps and sophomore Kenny Harris. Smith will not be afraid to use Phelps as a starter if Rice does not show improvement in his outside shooting. Rice will begin the season as a starter, and it is felt that he will use the competition to push him to finish his career on a positive note.

With a returning senior starter at point guard and two talented youngsters on the depth chart, North Carolina should be in good shape at the position this year.

HENRIK RODL (6-7, 195 lbs., JR, G/F, #5, 2.3 ppg, 0.7 rpg, 21 assists, 4 blocked shots, 13 steals, Heusenstamm, West Germany & Chapel Hill HS/Chapel Hill, N.C.) Rodl played in all 34 games last year in his first year as a Tar Heel. Rodl graduated from high school in 1988, but went back to West Germany for one year before enrolling at North Carolina. As a result of NCAA guidelines governing foreign athletes, Rodl has only two years of eligibility remaining even though he's only a sophomore academically. As a senior he led Chapel Hill HS to a North Carolina state title before he went back to West Germany.

Rodl gives North Carolina versatility as he can play either at the wing guard or the small forward spot. Last year Rodl showed that he could shoot the ball on the major college level as he connected on 27-of-55 shots (49 percent). He also attempted 30 three-pointers, nailing 13 of them for a 43 percent accuracy rate. He has a quick release and is not uncomfortable creating his own shot off the dribble. At 6-7, Rodl can also make strong, aggressive moves to the basket, and he has excellent court vision which allows him to spot open teammates when he penetrates. Rodl has the making of an excellent, well-rounded offensive player.

He will be competing for more playing time this season and he will get a chance to play almost exclusively at the off-guard spot during the pre-season. If his offense continues to impress, and he can prove that he has quick enough feet and effective positioning to be a good defender, then Rodl may get the starting nod at second guard. Even if he does not start, though, Rodl will be called upon to contribute at least 20 minutes per game in Smith's revolving door system.

MATT WENSTROM (7-0, 250 lbs., SO, C, #55, 0.9 ppg, 0.6 rpg, 2 assists, 5 blocked shots 1 steal, Mayde Creek HS/Katy, Tex.) Wenstrom saw action in 32 games last season as a freshman. He become a solid center in the ACC as he has a soft touch and good passing ability from his position in the low post.

Wenstrom is beginning to add muscle to his huge frame and this will allow him to establish and maintain his position more effectively down low after he goes after rebounds. Coming out of high school he had a soft upper body and even though he could occasionally overcome his lack of strength with his long arms and height, Wenstrom will be more consistently effective with his increased bulk.

He looked to be North Carolina's center of the future last year but this is no longer the case as a result of Dean Smith's most recent recruiting class. Smith landed 7-0 high school All-America Eric Montross from Indianapolis, a player who is a better athlete and much more highly regarded coming out of high school than Wenstrom was. Wenstrom will have to have a terrific pre-season to take playing time away from Montross.

He does have some offensive skills. With Wenstrom and Montross, North Carolina is set in the pivot for the next four years.

★ NEWCOMERS ★

ERIC MONTROSS (7-0, 245 lbs., FR, C, #00, 20.5 ppg, 16.0 rpg, Lawrence North HS/Indianapolis, Ind.) There is one thing for certain about Eric Montross. He is not afraid to take an unpopular stance. When you are the best high school pivot in the country and live in Indiana, it is virtually assumed you will sign with Bob Knight and head to Bloomington. Last spring, Montross considered Indiana and Michigan, but came to the conclusion that the place for him was Chapel Hill. His decision, as expected, was not exactly popular in the Hoosier state. Montross received some nasty letters and was booed at the Kentucky-Indiana All-Star series.

While Shawn Bradley, of Castle Dale, Utah, who is a freshman at Brigham Young, has more long range potential, Montross was definitely the best pure, strong low post pivot in the high school ranks last year. He has a well developed upper body, good overall strength, mobility and coordination. Montross shed his baby fat early. It's unusual for a center this good to arrive on the collegiate scene who does not have to mature, at least somewhat physically.

''. . . plays a hard-nosed inside game that brims with sturdy virtues,'' wrote Austin Murphy in *Sports Illustrated*.

''And this year 'year of the big men' Montross gets our vote as the premier prep center. He proved his mettle and ability at the Nike All-America camp, outplaying all the nation's other top big men, and simply overpowering superbly talented 7-5 Shawn Bradley. Montross already has the body of an NBA pivotman, and is extremely strong, rugged and physical. We rate him as the top rebounder in his class, as well as the most offensively advanced low-post performer. He is presently much better prepared for the collegiate game than any of the other centers . . . Montross is an ominous presence inside and a defensive 'stopper'. He's an excellent outlet passer, and has a soft, accurate medium range jumper,'' wrote Bob Gibbons in *All Star Sports*.

As a junior, Montross powered Lawrence North HS to a 25-4 record and the Indiana state championship.

''Many people see Eric as strictly an offensive player,'' said his high school coach Jack Keefer. ''But he's also a good defensive player. He's not going to be some Bill Russell-type shot-blocker. . .''

When inspired, Montross can be mean in the middle. He is aggressive, strong and very difficult to deal with once he gets the ball inside. He has an effective mix of brawn, talent and brains.

There is no doubt that Montross is the best center at North Carolina since Brad Daugherty graduated in 1986. Smith likes to gradually work his freshmen in, but it won't be long before Montross is a starter.

DERRICK PHELPS (6-3, 180 lbs., FR, G, #14, 15.0 ppg, 9.0 rpg, 5.0 apg, Christ the King HS/Middle Village, N.Y.) Despite Smith's penchant to bend over backwards to accommodate his seniors, it seems hard to imagine Phelps, if he can take his game to the next level, not overtaking King Rice at point guard before too long. In terms of ballhandling, passing, defending and seeing the floor, Phelps can do, at least, what Rice does. Plus he can score —via the perimeter jumper or off penetration. He is quick and can create.

The once-in-a-generation exploits of Kenny Anderson at Archbishop Molloy HS of Queens, the same borough of New York City that Phelps played in, tended to obscure the fact that Phelps was considered one of the most complete and accomplished point guards to come out of New York City in a decade. Comparisons with some of the other great high school point guards out of New York in the '80s such as Kenny Smith and Pearl Washington were commonplace.

He was a second-team *Parade Magazine* All-America selection last year and helped guide Christ the King HS to New York City and state titles.

''A smooth point, he can run the show with the best,'' claimed the *ACC Handbook*. ''He is always in control and has really matured as a floor leader. Range to 18 feet.''

''He plays the point the way it's supposed to be played,'' said Christ the King coach Bob Oliva.

Bob Gibbons of *All-Star Sports* called Phelps ''the best classical point guard in the country.''

He is also a top defensive guard and does not have one glaring weakness. Phelps is definitely the best point guard North Carolina has signed since Kenny Smith.

BRIAN REESE (6-6, 205 lbs., FR, F, #31, 25.0 ppg, 10.0 rpg, Tolentine HS/Bronx, N.Y.) A true star since the beginning of his sophomore year, Reese is unquestionably one of the finest forwards to ever come out of New York City. He was a four-year starter at Tolentine HS. As a sophomore, he was a key player on a Tolentine HS team that won the New York City and state titles and was ranked No. 1 nationally. He was ranked all throughout his senior year as one of the Top

10 high school players in the country.

He has pro range, extension and accuracy on his jumper since the age of 15. Reese can also run the floor like a gazelle, defend and block shots. When Malik Sealy of St. John's graduated two years ahead of him at Tolentine, Reese moved to the pivot and continued to be a two-way force with his long, rangy body. He has a knack for finding open spaces in which to release his twisting jumpers with outstanding body control and hang time. Other times he simply rises over defenders.

"Reese is UNC's best pure athlete since Michael Jordan. He has that hang time, the 42-inch vertical leap, and he can shoot the three-pointer," said Bob Gibbons of *All Star Sports*.

"He has a real, real strong body," said Tolentine coach Bob Mackey. "He's 6-7 and he can handle the ball."

Reese, fellow North Carolina freshman Derrick Phelps and a cast of others made New York City's senior class last year the best in the Big Apple in well over a decade. Smith likes to bring freshmen along slowly, but he's going to have a hard time keeping the lid on Reese. He is potentially an immediate starter, double figure scorer and strong rebounder as a freshman. If Brian Reese doesn't make an immediate impact for the Tar Heels, we'll be surprised.

CLIFFORD ROZIER (6-10, 220 lbs., FR, F, #45, 34.5 ppg, Southeast HS/Bradenton, Fla.) In Rozier, Montross and Reese, North Carolina landed three of the consensus Top 10 high school players in the country last year. Rozier first achieved widespread notoriety at the Nike/ABCD Camp at Princeton University in July of 1989. He led that talent packed camp in rebounding and went on to have a dominant senior year. Last summer Rozier was the co-MVP of the National AAU junior men's tournament in Jacksonville, Fla.

"A real animal on the boards," claimed the *ACC Handbook*, "who believes every rebound is his. He can outlet, fill a lane and dunk on the other end. Runs like a deer."

Clark Francis, publisher of the *Hoop Scoop*, believes Rozier may be the best of the North Carolina freshmen. "He's got those long arms and legs. He's a heck of a talent."

In *Eastern Basketball Magazine*, Bob Gibbons wrote "Rozier is an agile, quick, long-arm 'Sam Perkins-clone'."

Rozier was superb in post-season all-star games scoring 45 points at the Kentucky Derby Festival Classic in Louisville and the McDonald's East-West All-Star Game in Indianapolis.

He is definitely the top rebounding freshman entering college basketball this year. Rozier is also just beginning to blossom as a player. He should be a more athletic, more powerful rebounding power forward than North Carolina has had recently.

KEVIN SALVADORI (6-11, 210 lbs., FR, C, #33, 17.0 ppg, 13.0 rpg, 8.0 blpg, Seton-LaSalle HS/Pittsburgh, Pa.) Salvadori's father, Al, played for legendary North Carolina coach Frank McGuire when McGuire moved to South Carolina. South Carolina, indeed, was the younger Salvadori's primary option before he came out of obscurity to have a big senior year at Seton-LaSalle HS in Pittsburgh. He redshirted last year in order to add some weight to a lamp post-thin frame.

He sees the game well from the pivot and is an outstanding passer. If he continues to add strength, Salvadori could prove something of a sleeper. But probably not for another year.

He had 17 points, 16 rebounds and six blocked shots in the WPIAL Class AA championship game as a senior. He weighed only 195 pounds when he signed.

With Matt Wenstrom already a year ahead of Salvadori and heralded Eric Montross arriving, this probably won't be the year that Salvadori pays big dividends for the Tar Heels.

PAT SULLIVAN (6-7, 225 lbs., FR, F, #3, 26.5 ppg, Bogota HS/Bogota, N.J.) The North Carolina recruiting class is so heralded that Sullivan, ranked as the No. 43 player in the country last spring by *All Star Sports*, is sort of the forgotten man. He was one of the better forwards in the East last year and had an outstanding high school career at Bogota HS.

"Good offensive skills, good hands and timing and a very good offensive rebounder," said Jersey City St. Anthony HS coach Bob Hurley.

Sullivan has a scorer's knack around the basket and has built himself up from 205 pounds to 225 without it affecting his jumping ability, which is very underrated. He also was an excellent stroke out to 18-foot range and good work habits.

"He's somewhere between a small and power forward," said Hurley, "but makes up for the lack of requisite physical stature at power forward with desire and command of basketball skills. He loves to play and will focus on exactly the areas coach Smith will want him to in order to get playing time. He could wind up an overachiever down there in the vein of Matt Doherty."

Sullivan, who played mostly post defense in high school, will find his biggest challenge in trying to match up with quick forwards defensively.

With his five freshmen, Smith practically recruited an entire starting five. North Carolina's recruiting class was not only ranked No. 1 nationally but some think its the best ever in the modern era.

"What North Carolina did, I haven't seen in a long, long time," said South Carolina coach George Felton. "He's (Dean Smith) recruited an entire team."

★ QUESTIONS ★

Chemistry? Smith will be attempting to blend four established players (Rice,

Fox, Chilcutt and Lynch), three of them seniors, with freshmen talent considered so outstanding, it is said to represent one of the finest recruiting classes in history. This is a situation that often leads to initial friction. But Smith is precisely the coach to prevent that type of bad blood.

★ STRENGTHS ★

Dean Smith! No other coach in college basketball has built a program that has made 10 Final 16 appearances in a row but Smith. He is criticized for not getting North Carolina into the Final Four since 1982, but no other coach so consistently has his team within striking distance either.

The star studded freshman class! Simply one of the finest collections of high school talent, spanning four positions, ever assembled.

Depth! The quality of the freshman class means a lot of talent is going to be pushing a lot of high-level experience at nearly every position. North Carolina should have some great practices this year and the competition should mean many players will improve considerably individually.

Frontcourt height! North Carolina is big and powerful up front.

★ BLUE RIBBON ANALYSIS ★

Freshmen or no freshmen, the likes of Eric Montross, Derrick Phelps, Brian Reese and Clifford Rozier should not take long to provide the Tar Heels with more offensive weapons than any other team in the country. Moreover, senior Rick Fox is a proven force who can rebound and score both inside and outside and could be a first round NBA draft choice.

Last season North Carolina was disappointing during the regular season, at least by the program's high standards, and the Tar Heels had to knock out no less than Oklahoma, the top seed in the whole NCAA tournament, to keep alive its string of Final 16 appearances. In the Oklahoma upset, Fox rose to the occasion, including a major league move on the right baseline to receive and hit a short jumper at the finish which gave the Tar Heels the victory.

Senior Pete Chilcutt remains in the picture as an important inside contributor and senior point guard King Rice ought to be able to concentrate on the positive parts of his game —passing, handling and defense —now that the displeasure he absorbs for inability to handle a scoring role will be rendered inconsequential.

Reese will score —he'll probably have eight points by the time he walks out of the lockerroom the first game. Phelps will run the show — he'll score and do everything else, too. Both will put serious pressure on the returning starters. And, of course, both Reese and Phelps will have to measure up to the defensive scrutiny Smith directs at freshmen. But neither are alien to that concept and each was more accomplished at the defensive end of the floor than most high scoring prep stars. Rozier will probably put together his share of double figure scoring and rebounding nights. He'll also block some shots. Like Phelps and Reese, he'll need to adjust to the North Carolina system. But that system does accommodate ability. Contrary to popular conception, many freshmen (Michael Jordan, Phil Ford, Kenny Smith, Jeff Lebo, J.R. Reid, etc.) have had major impact in the first year at Chapel Hill. Which leads to sophomore forward George Lynch, who also put forth a pretty strong freshman year for the Tar Heels and will only get stronger as an inside scorer, defender and rebounder.

About the only place North Carolina didn't bring in a big time recruit was at second guard. While counting their blessings up front — Fox, Chilcutt, Lynch, Rozier, Reese, Montross —the Tar Heels are not particularly overloaded in the backcourt. It's not inconceivable that Phelps and Rice could play together, though. And there's also some decent returning experience in juniors Hubert Davis and Henrik Rodl.

Defensively, this North Carolina team has the athleticism and quickness suited to the half court pressure schemes and run-and-jump double teams that Smith enjoyed success with several years ago. The Madden-Fox-Chilcutt-Rice-Williams nucleus was a bit lumbering a year ago by North Carolina standards.

The Tar Heels lost two important players in Kevin Madden and Scott Williams. However, there are many options to replace Madden's inside scoring and rebounding. Williams' lane clogging defenses are a different story. If Montross is ready to be an active defensive presence, there shouldn't be a major drop off. Plus, Rozier could be an additional factor. But until the freshmen prove it, North Carolina could be tested in the middle by teams with quality height. Still, there is enough defensive ability so that Williams' departure can be absorbed.

Overall, this North Carolina team possesses as many weapons, if not quite the same overall experience, to go with them, than any team in the country. This contingent should be a lock for its 11th straight Final 16. Smith has taken teams with equal or less talent (the 1981 team with Al Wood, Mike Pepper and Jimmy Black starting comes to mind) to the Final Four.

North Carolina should win a very competitive ACC this year after being chased hard by Duke and Virginia. Smith has not been to the Final Four since 1982 and is certainly overdue.

LAST SEASON		1990-91 NORTH CAROLINA SCHEDULE		
#James Madison	80-79	Nov.	24	San Diego State
#Villanova	78-68		27	Jacksonville

#Missouri	73-80	@Wake Forest	72-67
@Alabama	93-101	@Virginia	80-81
Central Florida	92-42	Maryland	76-80
Towson State	87-70	@Clemson	61-69
##Georgetown	81-93	Georgia Tech	81-79
@Iowa	74-87	@Duke	87-75
DePaul	70-51	**Virginia	85-92OT
###Kansas State	79-63	***Southwest Missouri State	83-70
####Kentucky	121-110	***Oklahoma	79-77
*Colorado State	67-78	****Arkansas	73-96
*Colorado	106-101		
Old Dominion	90-78	@ Road Games	
Pepperdine	95-69	# Maui Classic, Lahaina, HI	
@Maryland	88-98	## ACC/Big East Challenge, East	
Virginia	92-70	Rutherford, NJ	
Duke	79-60	### Charlotte, NC	
@North Carolina State	91-81	#### Louisville, KY	
Wake Forest	73-61	* Mile High Classic, Denver, CO	
Clemson	83-60	** ACC Tournament, Charlotte, NC	
@Georgia Tech	75-102	*** NCAA Tournament, Austin, TX	
Miami (FL)	87-74	**** NCAA Tournament, Dallas, TX	
North Carolina State	77-88		

NOTES: North Carolina will face South Carolina, for the first time in years, in the opening round of the Tournament of Champions in Charlotte on Nov. 30 . . . the ACC/Big East Challenge game on Dec. 6 with Connecticut is part of a doubleheader in the Dean Dome. Wake Forest plays Villanova in the other game . . . North Carolina is schedule to play DePaul in the

Nov. 30-	#Tournament of	
Dec. 1	Champions	
Dec. 6	##Connecticut	
10	Kentucky	
15	Alabama	
22	@Purdue	
29-30	*Citrus/Red Lobster Classic	
Jan. 3	@Cornell	
5	**Notre Dame	
9	Maryland	
12	@Virginia	
16	North Carolina State	
19	@Duke	
23	@Wake Forest	
27	Georgia Tech	
31	@Clemson	
Feb. 6	@North Carolina State	
9	Virginia	
13	Wake Forest	
16	@Maryland	
18	The Citadel	
23	Clemson	
28	@Georgia Tech	
Mar. 3	Duke	
8-10	***ACC Tournament	

@ Road Games
# Charlotte, NC (Houston, Iowa State & South Carolina)
ACC/Big East Challenge
* Orlando, FL (Central Florida, DePaul & Stanford)
** Meadowlands Arena, East Rutherford, NJ
*** Charlotte, NC

first round of the Citrus/Red Lobster Classic . . . in a September article in *USA Today*, various television announcers rated their favorite college towns. Dick Vitale chose Chapel Hill. "Every time I go to a game there, it's a happening. The area is beautiful, the restaurants are excellent, the clubs are exciting," Vitale said.

UNLV

LAST SEASON: 33-5
CONFERENCE RECORD: 16-2
STARTERS LOST: 1
STARTERS RETURNING: 4
CONFERENCE: BIG WEST
LOCATION: LAS VEGAS, NV
HOME FLOOR: THOMAS & MACK CENTER (18,500)
NICKNAME: RUNNIN' REBELS
COLORS: SCARLET AND GRAY

★ COACH'S PROFILE ★

JERRY TARKANIAN (Record at UNLV, 446-102. Career record 774-145) As far as winning is concerned, Tarkanian has few peers. He is the nation's winningest active college basketball coach by percentage — .826 —and he also probably leads the nation's coaches in off the court controversies. The extreme dichotomy of Tarkanian's situation was evidenced this year by the fact he won the national championship in runaway style last April 2 at McNichols Arena in Denver. His UNLV Runnin' Rebels stomped Duke 103-73 for the largest margin of victory in an NCAA championship game. The victory was considered ironic in light of Tarkanian's 13-year battle with the NCAA. "I don't look on this as sweet revenge, just sweet," said Tarkanian.

Just two days before UNLV took the court in the semifinals of the Final Four, Tarkanian signed papers ending his 13-year battle. Under the agreement, the NCAA was not to pursue enforcement of a two-year suspension it asked UNLV to impose on Tarkanian in 1977. The suspension was a result of an infractions case that was resolved with UNLV being placed on probation for two years. UNLV served the probation, and Tarkanian went to court, obtained an injunction against the NCAA and the university and continued coaching. Tarkanian blocked the suspension in state court and the case was in the courts until December 1988, when the U.S. Supreme Court ruled in the NCAA's favor. Under the agreement, Tarkanian will pay $20,004 in court costs and legal fees incurred by the NCAA. He also is to pay nearly $350,000 in his own legal fees.

Then on January 20, the NCAA banned UNLV from post-season play this season. UNLV officials and Tarkanian were justifiably outraged by the sanction.

"No other American citizen can be punished for the same offense twice. . ." Tarkanian said. "Players on this year's team, as well as most of the students attending UNLV, were six or seven years old when this began. They are paying the price of the NCAA's vindictive decision."

The NCAA sanction does not limit the school's number of available scholarships and will not keep the Runnin' Rebels off television. It does unjustly keep what could be one of the best college teams of all-time from defending its national

championship. The post-season ban also cost Tarkanian two landmark recruits. In the past, Tarkanian has hotly pursued some of the biggest high school stars, but generally would end up second or third in the hunt. He had to construct his teams with junior college transfers, transfers from other four-year institutions and players supposedly a notch below the "supers." That changed last spring when he signed Ed O'Bannon, a 6-8 forward from Artesia HS in Lakewood, Calif., and 6-5 guard Shon Tarver from Santa Clara HS in Oxnard, Calif. O'Bannon was widely considered the No. 1 high school player in the country as well as the best in southern California. Tarver ranked second behind O'Bannon in southern California and was a national level recruit himself. Tarkanian advised O'Bannon and Tarver against signing a national letter of intent with UNLV because of the NCAA investigation unrelated to the post-season ban. When the Runnin' Rebels were denied the opportunity to defend their national championship this year, O'Bannon and Tarver went to UCLA. The irony of O'Bannon and Tarver leaving for UCLA was not lost on Tarkanian who had lost many recruiting battles over the years with the Bruins.

UNLV will appeal the NCAA decision but is not expected to win.

Tarkanian's ongoing saga with the NCAA has overshadowed what has been a brilliant career. He is entering his 30th year of college coaching, his 23rd at the Division I level and his 18th at UNLV. His winning percentage is only six-one hundred thousands behind the legendary Clair Bee for the best all-time. Tarkanian will most assuredly pass Bee this season.

He has truly built a "Dynasty in the Desert" at UNLV. Tarkanian has coached UNLV to 11 NCAA tournament appearances, including the last eight consecutive years. Over those last eight seasons, Tarkanian has led UNLV to the nation's best record of 247-39 (.864) and he has averaged a seasonal mark of 31-5. Prior to last season's national championship, Tarkanian guided UNLV into the Final Four in 1977 and 1987. He has an overall post-season record of 37-18 (.673) and 26-10 in NCAA tournament appearances at UNLV, 4-3 in the NIT at UNLV, and 7-5 in the NCAA tournament at Long Beach State, before coming to UNLV.

In his 17 years at UNLV, the Runnin' Rebels have failed to win at least 20 games in a season only once. Also, UNLV has dominated the Big West Conference (formerly the PCAA) under Tarkanian like no other team has in another conference. UNLV has won or tied for the conference championship for eight consecutive years and had an unprecedented undefeated campaign (18-0) in 1986-87. In eight years in the Big West, UNLV is 129-13 in the regular season. He is the first coach in conference history to win 100 or more conference games at the same school.

In addition to his problems with the NCAA, Tarkanian is known for his willingness to take a chance on players with checkered backgrounds and his ability to recruit and get the most out of junior college transfers.

"My reputation started with John Q. Trapp. He'd been dropped from three schools," Tarkanian told Michael Hurd of *USA Today*. "He was a problem to a lot of guys. He was a mean, tough guy and I got a lot of recognition because of him. . .

"The rules were set up 15 years ago for middle-class white kids. The kids from the inner city can't get a quarter from home. Some of the nicest kids are not A students. But I don't look down on (inner city players).

"I did some of the same things when I was in school. I went to every party and did things I'm greatful not many people know about. I tell them you have to be accountable."

"I don't know why a kid who comes out of a junior college is perceived as not being as good a kid as one who went to a four-year school and had a higher SAT score. But they have to live with that, I guess," he said.

Another of his trademarks is the constant chewing of a wet towel throughout the game. UNLV's managers are instructed to fold his towel exactly to the same specifications every time, damp it slightly and put it under the bench for Tarkanian to chew on. With his sad sack face and worrying ways, Tarkanian looks like he has the weight of the world on his shoulders.

He is a native of Euclid, Ohio. While in high school his family moved to Pasedena, Calif. Tarkanian attended Pasedena City College before graduating from Fresno State in 1955. He played basketball at Fresno State. More importantly, he met his wife, Lois, at Fresno State.

His first coaching job was at San Joaquin Memorial HS in Fresno in 1956. He then moved on to Antelope Valley HS in Lancaster, Calif., in 1958 before eventually moving on first to Redlands (Calif.) HS and to Riverside City College. Tarkanian's first season at Riverside City College was 14-13, but after that he built a dominant program. He led Riverside to four straight 30 or more victory seasons and four consecutive California junior college championships. Tarkanian recorded a perfect 35-0 mark in 1963-64. He was 145-22 (.868) overall in five years at Riverside.

From Riverside he went to Pasedena City College for two seasons beginning in 1966, compiling a 67-4 (.944) two-year mark and another California junior college crown. In 1968, he took over at Long Beach State. He spent five years at Long Beach State and compiled a 116-17 record and put four of his teams in the NCAA tournament.

His coaching philosophy is to run, run, run on offense and constant, strong pressure defense. Tarkanian has to be considered one of the leaders of the up-tempo movement that has taken hold in college basketball. And he started to let his teams run before it was fashionable. His 1977 team averaged a then NCAA record 110 points per game. Tarkanian shuttled players in and out on that 1977 team like a hockey coach and since then, multiple substitutions and playing eight to 10 players regularly has become commonplace. Not too many schools have ever changed their nickname, like UNLV has from Rebels to Runnin' Rebels, because a team's style of play becomes so synonymous with its name.

He also works his teams extremely hard in practice and is a stickler for conditioning.

The success of his Runnin' Rebels has put UNLV on the map. The school is only 32 years old and until recently it was both undistinguished and small. In a survey of colleges, the *U.S. News & World Report* ranked UNLV in his list of 32 "up and coming" colleges. School officials acknowledge that the publicity generated by Tarkanian's teams has defined and benefited the university.

Now that he has a national championship, it will be interesting to see how much longer Tarkanian stays in coaching. He is a wealthy man and the protracted battle with the NCAA has certainly taken its toll. He has been pursued by NBA teams several times. The NCAA is expected to hand down penalties on other alleged infractions and it is questionable how much more of this Tarkanian can endure.

★ PLAYERS NOT RETURNING ★

DAVID BUTLER (6-10, C, 15.8 ppg, 7.4 rpg, 64 assists, 29 blocked shots, 33 steals) Butler was the Runnin' Rebels' starting center last year. He was ineligible at the beginning of the season, along with fellow senior forward Moses Scurry, and after they returned UNLV started to come together. Butler was very quick and played a key role in UNLV's defense. He finished third on the team in scoring, second in rebounding and fourth in blocked shots. Butler had a good turnaround jumper in the lane and complemented Runnin' Rebel star Larry Johnson well.

Butler salvaged his college career at UNLV. He was not allowed to play during his senior year in high school at Coolidge in Washington, D.C. He enrolled at San Jacinto (Tex.) JC, became a junior college All-America and came to UNLV.

"David is a super kid who has worked so hard," Tarkanian said.

In years to come, Butler might become known as the originator of "the scream." Every time he grabbed a rebound Butler would let out a primal scream and he even started screaming at the free throw line.

STACEY CVIJANOVICH (6-3, G, 2.6 ppg, 1.1 rpg, 63 assists, 3 blocked shots, 8 steals) Cvijanovich was a reserve guard who played in 33 games for 351 minutes. He was a good three-point shooter who made 15 treys last season. Cvijanovich nailed his free throws —27-of-30 (.900), and was a reliable ballhandler. He was a good, capable reserve.

JAMES JONES (6-8, C, 3.9 ppg, 2.8 rpg, 9 assists, 31 blocked shots, 9 steals) Jones started seven games when Butler was academically ineligible at the beginning of the season. He was a good shotblocker, strong and did anything Tarkanian asked. Jones was a solid player in two years at UNLV after transferring from Mt. San Antonio JC in California.

His shot blocking and defense will be missed but UNLV should be strong in the middle again with the addition of junior college transfers Melvin Love and Elmore

Spencer, plus the return of redshirt senior George Ackles.

MOSES SCURRY (6-7, F, 7.7 ppg, 4.1 rpg, 25 assists, 7 blocked shots, 31 steals) Scurry was the first reserve off the bench for UNLV last year. He was a strong rebounder and an aggressive player who helped set the tone for the Runnin' Rebels. The value of Scurry and Butler to UNLV was evidenced last season when they were ineligible. The Runnin' Rebels lost two games early in the season before Butler and Scurry returned to the team.

He could be missed as the possible replacements for Scurry off the bench this year are players who have never before played at UNLV.

★ RETURNING PLAYERS ★

GEORGE ACKLES (6-10, 208 lbs., SR, C, #44, Manteo HS/Manteo, N.C. & Garden City CC/Garden City, Kan.) While we are listing Ackles as a returning player, he also could go under the "Newcomers" section as well. He started 27 of UNLV's first 29 games two years ago before being redshirted last year. Ackles broke the navicluar bone in his wrist during a summer pickup game prior to last season and Tarkanian had considered redshirting him anyway. Tarkanian wanted to redshirt Ackles because he has little basketball experience. Ackles began playing the game in his junior year in high school and has played only five years of organized basketball. Prior to taking up basketball, he was an outstanding goaltender in soccer.

Ackles grew up in small Manteo, N.C., but his family has since moved to Pittsburgh, Pa. He was a standout for two years at Garden City CC in Kansas before transferring to UNLV. Two years ago he averaged 4.6 points, 5.6 rebounds, handed out 19 assists, recorded 20 steals and blocked a school record 64 shots. He frequently found himself in foul trouble, Ackles fouled out of 10 games, and showed most of his offense close to the hoop.

"George has the potential to be a great player," said Tarkanian. "He is very athletic and the only thing he is lacking is more basketball experience. He's very coachable and a great kid."

He is the leading candidate to replace starting center David Butler.

GREG ANTHONY (6-2, 190 lbs., SR, G, #50, 11.2 ppg, 3.0 rpg, 289 assists, 16 blocked shots, 106 steals, Rancho HS/Las Vegas, Nev.) Anthony is one of returning starters for UNLV. Even more than his actual statistical contributions, Anthony will long be remembered in Las Vegas for his courageous play in UNLV's championship season. On January 15 in a UNLV win at Fresno State, Anthony suffered a broken jaw after a jarring collision while driving to the basket. Team doctors believed Anthony would be out two to three weeks. However, Anthony far exceeded their original expectations. Three days after the accident, Anthony, his jaw wired shut, sparked UNLV to a 109-86 victory over national ranked New Mexico State. He wore a mask to protect his nose, because he might not have been able to breath if he had broken his nose while his jaw was wired shut. The oral surgeon who performed the work on Anthony's jaw, or one of his associates, carried wire cutters to UNLV games in case the jaw, which was wired shut, needed to be opened.

Anthony led UNLV with 289 assists (7.4 apg) and 106 steals. He was fifth on the team in scoring.

The Las Vegas native began his collegiate career at the University of Portland where he was a WCAC Freshman of the Year before transferring back home. He averaged 15.3 points and 4 assists as an off-guard for the Pilots. He has played point guard at UNLV and originally had difficulty making the switch to a new position. He was a second-team All-Big West selection as a junior and an honorable mention All-America last year.

He set a UNLV single season steals record with 85 as a sophomore and broke that last year with 106. Anthony is one of the best defensive guards in the country. He is extremely quick, goes to the basket well and also nailed 45 three-pointers (.375) last year. Anthony made .457 of his field goal attempts and .682 of his free throws.

Anthony is not the stereotypical jock. He is a Political Science major and a member of the Young Republicans of Nevada. Two summers ago he served as an intern in Washington, D.C., for Nevada Congresswoman Barbara Vuconovich. He has stated in the past that he would like to one day represent his home state in Washington and also expressed interest in opening an advertising agency. During last season, Anthony deliberated on whether to get a second degree in economics or work on his MBA.

"Everytime he opens his mouth, Anthony punctures one stereotype or another. Anthony is a young, black, moderate Republican. Anthony may have to switch parties before long because he has one idea that might not sit too well with the GOP. Anthony wants college athletes to form a union that would seek pay for players," wrote Michael Wilbon in *The Washington Post.* " 'UNLV (and the other Final Four teams) are getting $1.5 million,' he said. " 'I'm not trying to diminish scholarships but lots of people on campus have scholarships who don't help bring in $1.5 million.' "

Anthony is very outspoken about the unsavory image of the UNLV program.

"It's unjust and unwarranted," Anthony told Michael Hurd of *USA Today.* "If we were to allow the media and others to mold our own characters and personalities and change what we do, we would have problems.

"I guess there is always going to be a negative side to a situation and ours happens to be the reputation we've carried through the past few years.

"It doesn't bother us."

Anthony and fellow senior Anderson Hunt give UNLV arguably the finest backcourt in the country. There is no doubt that Anthony and Hunt are the premier defensive backcourt in the country.

STACEY AUGMON (6-8, 206 lbs, SR, F, #32, 14.2 ppg, 6.9 rpg, 143 assists, 49 blocked shots, 69 steals, John Muir HS/Pasadena, Calif.) After struggling offensively through the regular season, Augmon came alive and shined in the NCAA tournament. He averaged 18.2 points and eight rebounds over six games and was named the MVP of the West Region. He had 22 points and nine rebounds in the semifinal victory over Georgia Tech in the Final Four and held Yellow Jacket star Dennis Scott to just 3-of-9 shooting for nine points in the second half. Augmon's defensive job on Scott further enhanced his reputation as perhaps the finest individual defender in the collage game.

Offensively, Augmon is not a great outside shooter. He made 16-of-50 three-pointers (.320). He gets most of his points on drives and dunks on the fast break. Augmon has exceptional speed, quickness and jumping ability. His extremely long wingspan also aids his defensive ability. On the boards he is a relentless offensive rebounder. Defensively, he is active both on the perimeter and inside. Augmon is the most versatile defender in the country.

Augmon's defensive prowess earned him a spot on the 1988 U.S. Olympic team. Olympic coach John Thompson stated throughout the trials that he needed a defensive specialist to guard the high scoring international players on the perimeter. He picked Augmon for that role.

Augmon sat out his first year at UNLV. In his first year he was Freshman of the Year in the Big West Conference. He was named an honorable mention All-America after his sophomore year as well.

He came to UNLV as a highly regarded high school All-America and considered himself a big scorer. Soon, though, Augmon learned how important defense is to Tarkanian. "I'm asking why we're running so much. We're out in 105-degree heat on the track running and sweating," Augmon said.

"Then we go inside and practice. Coach says we spend 50 percent of the time on defense, but I think it's more than that."

Last season Augmon was ranked as the No. 4 small forward in college basketball by *Sport* magazine. "Stacey's got the ultimate defensive body," said North Carolina Charlotte coach Jeff Mullins. "Skinny, but strong, with extra-long arms. And no chest, so he can mirrow the ball so well and yet not foul. His quickness and effort are impeccable, but I still have some questions about his offense."

Stacey Augmon had 34 points in a blowout of Utah State and 33 in UNLV's 30-point romp over Loyola Marymount in the finals of the West Region.

"Stacey is the backbone of this team, the glue," said UNLV star Larry Johnson.

Rumors swirled after the Final Four that Augmon would go pro. There was no doubt that he would have been a Top 10 selection in the draft. However, Augmon decided to stay.

"The strength of this team is its togetherness," Augmon said. "I'd never been on a team that's been closer. Maybe all we've had to go through this season has served to make us more tougher."

UNLV will need that special closeness this year as the Runnin' Rebels have to find inner motivation to stay dominant without the opportunity of being able to defend their national championship.

TRAVIS BICE (6-4, 152 lbs., JR, G, #3, 4.3 ppg, 0.6 rpg, 46 assists, 4 blocked shots, 11 steals, Simi Valley HS/Simi Valley, Calif.) Bice missed the 1988-89 season after being injured in an automobile accident. He required over 150 stitches. He may be the skinniest player in major college basketball, but he is also one of the most dangerous three-point shooters. Bice came off the bench to make 36-of-75 three-point shots (.480). He led UNLV in three-point percentage. Bice also made 9-of-11 free throws (.818) and 49-of-102 field goals (.480). Seventy-five of his 102 attempted field goals were three-pointers. The fact that Bice got to the free throw line only 11 times in 367 minutes shows you that he is first and foremost a long range bomber.

His performance is ever more impressive when it is considered that Bice had to overcome chickenpox last year as well. He had 19 points against Iowa.

He is a former walk-on who was a lightly regarded high school teammate of UCLA star Don MacLean at Simi Valley HS in southern California's San Fernando Valley. He had surprising quickness and toughness.

After missing the 1988-89 season and overcoming the injuries he suffered in the car wreck and the chickenpox last year, Tarkanian is understandably excited about what Bice can contribute this year. He should be a dangerous offensive threat off the bench for the Runnin' Rebels again.

BRIAN EMERZIAN (5-11, 165 lbs., JR, G, #15, 0.0 ppg, 0.4 rpg, West HS/Waukegan, Ill.) Emerzian is a walk-on guard who appeared in eight games for a total of 15 minutes last year. He missed all five field goal attempts and his only free throw last year.

ANDERSON HUNT (6-1, 176 lbs., JR, G, #12, 15.9 ppg, 2.2 rpg, 158 assists, 8 blocked shots, 43 steals, Southwestern HS/Detroit, Mich.) Hunt blossomed last year and became UNLV's second leading scorer behind superstar Larry Johnson. He also was second on the team in assists behind Greg Anthony and fourth in steals. Hunt was the MVP of the Final Four. He closed the season with 29 points in the championship game against Duke.

Hunt made 99-of-258 three-point field goals (.384) last year. He connected on 230-of-478 field goals (.481). From the line he was 61-of-92 (.663). He moved into the starting lineup in mid-February of his freshman year and started the last 14 games of the season and UNLV was 12-2 during that period. He was a member of the Big West Conference All-Freshman team. The biggest moment of Hunt's

freshman year came when he nailed a three-pointer, with just two seconds left, that gave UNLV an upset victory over Arizona in the semifinals of the West Region.

Hunt also scored 31 points in UNLV's 107-105 loss at LSU on Super Bowl Sunday last year in late January. He scored 28 points each in back-to-back wins over Arkansas and Fullerton State. Hunt opened the season with 26 points in the first round win in the Dodge NIT over Loyola Marymount. He not only can bomb from long range but is an excellent finisher on the break, penetrates well and is a quality ballhandler who had only 60 turnovers against 158 assists.

Hunt and his starting backcourt partner, Greg Anthony, formed the premier defensive guard tandem in the nation. Throughout the Runnin' Rebels' run to the NCAA title, opposing teams commented on how difficult it was to deal with Hunt and Anthony's defense.

"We couldn't get the ball past the hash marks," said Duke's Christian Laettner about Hunt and Anthony's defensive work. "It was just scary watching them," said Duke center Alaa Abdelnaby. "They engulfed us."

Hunt simply rolled over the Duke guards offensively as well. It was one of the most dominant performances a pair of guards has given in recent memory in the Final Four.

Hunt and Anthony were a very underrated starting backcourt last year. This year that should change as UNLV's dynamic backcourt duo should get deserved recognition. In fact, they could be the best starting backcourt in the nation in 1990-91.

CHRIS JETER (6-8, 216 lbs., SR, F, #53, 1.1 ppg, 0.4 rpg, 3 assists, 3 steals, Morse HS/San Diego, Calif.) Jeter originally signed with Missouri but never played for the Tigers before transferring to UNLV. He has seen limited action since coming to Las Vegas. As a sophomore, he appeared in 15 games and last year Jeter saw action in 18 games for a total of 92 minutes. He is limited offensively —11-of-30 (.367) from the field —but does run the court well. Jeter suffered a dislocated kneecap in February of 1989, but came back to full health last year.

He could be more of a factor this year as UNLV has lost three frontcourt players —starting center David Butler and reserves Moses Scurry and James Jones.

LARRY JOHNSON (6-7, 250 lbs., SR, F, #4, 20.6 ppg, 11.4 rpg, 84 assists, 56 blocked shots, 65 steals, Skyline HS/Dallas, Tex. & Odessa JC/Odessa, Tex.) In Jerry Tarkanian's 17 years at UNLV he has certainly had some great players. The talent level at UNLV is usually considered among the highest in the nation. While he has played only one year at UNLV, there is no doubt that Larry Johnson is the premier player ever to wear a Runnin' Rebel uniform.

He came to UNLV with a tremendous buildup and great expectations. Johnson certainly didn't disappoint as he was the guiding force that turned UNLV from a good, Top 20 team into the most dominant club in the nation. He was named the Big West Conference Player of the Year, the MVP of the conference tournament and was a finalist for the 1990 John Wooden award. He led UNLV in both scoring and rebounding while starting all 40 games. Johnson was a first-team All-America selection by *Associated Press*, *United Press International* and the *U.S. Basketball Writers Association*.

"Larry is such an outstanding player, but even more than that, he's just such an outstanding person," Tarkanian said. "He is such an unselfish, team-oriented player. He has the same kind of effect on the team that Magic Johnson has, because of his positive attitude . . . He's everything I thought he would be, plus more."

Johnson had some dominating games last year: 25 points and 10 rebounds vs. California, 32 points in a win over DePaul in the Dodge NIT, 29 at Oklahoma, 26 points and 12 rebounds at Temple, 30 points and 12 rebounds against talented Long Beach State, 28 points and 14 rebounds vs. NCAA tournament participant California-Santa Barbara, 24 points and 16 rebounds vs. North Carolina State, 22 points and 15 rebounds in a win over Louisville, 31 points at Utah State, 32 points and 14 rebounds in the Big West tournament vs. Fullerton State, 23 points and 16 rebounds in a second round NCAA tournament win over Ohio State, and 18 rebounds in the finals of the West Region vs. Loyola Marymount.

"Let's simplify this," Duke center Alaa Abdelnaby told Michael Wilbon of *The Washington Post*, "when he gets the ball on the block, it's a bucket. Let's say there are 50 possessions. We denied him the ball 35 to 40 times. Those 10 to 12 times he got the ball, it was over. He seems like he's almost too good. I knew he was good, but we had to play against him to really find out how good. TV doesn't do his game justice."

Abdelnaby's inside partner at Duke, Christian Laettner was also very impressed by Johnson. "He does things really slow," Laettner said. "He moves around kind of slow. But you can't get away. You can't move him. Plus, he hits some threes and a couple of J's. And he didn't just get rebounds, *he got rebounds*."

Duke coach Mike Krzyzewski said Johnson's strength is "astonishing. He's got to be the strongest guy in college basketball. Plus, he's got agility and a soft touch. He's a special player now and he will be a special player for 10 years."

Johnson, in the opinion of some experts, was the premier high school player in the country in 1987. He attended Dallas Skyline HS and signed with Southern Methodist. He passed the SAT test with enough points to be eligible under Proposition 48, but the Southern Methodist administration, which was reeling at the time from a football scandal, accepted his application but told him he would have to sit out a year. Johnson decided to go to Odessa JC, instead, and dominated the junior college ranks. He may be the greatest junior college player ever. Johnson played for Kansas coach Larry Brown on a U.S. Junior team that played in a tournament in Italy and became close with Brown. After Brown left Kansas for the San Antonio Spurs, UNLV moved in and became his top choice.

After the Final Four, there were rumors that Johnson would turn pro. After all, he had won a national championship in his junior year and he had a legitimate chance to be the first pick in the NBA draft. However, those that knew Johnson well claimed that he is loyal and there was no way he would leave UNLV even though there was a potential threat the Runnin' Rebels could receive NCAA sanctions. Basically, Johnson is very happy at UNLV and wanted to spend another year with Tarkanian and his teammates.

''You know how you teach youngsters to be loyal?'' Johnson's coach at Skyline, J.D. Mayo, told Jeff Miller of *Inside Sports.* ''I mean, we're talking about millions of dollars here. But he said, 'I made a two-year commitment to UNLV. Didn't you always tell us to hold to our commitments?' ''

Johnson enters this season as a unanimous first team All-America. There is also a strong case that can be made that Johnson is the national player of the year as well. Even though it looks as if UNLV will not be able to defend its national championship, don't think that Johnson will let down. He is too committed and loyal to not follow up last year's sensational season with another.

DAVE RICE (96-4. 205 lbs., SR, G, #30, 1.1 ppg, 0.4 rpg, 3 assists, 3 steals, Claremont HS/Claremont, Calif. & Mt. San Antonio JC/Walnut, Calif.) Rice was a late summer addition to the Runnin' Rebels last year. He saw limited action, playing in 16 games for a total of 50 minutes. Rice made 6-of-21 field goals (.286) and 5-of-13 three-pointers (.385). He is best suited for the second guard position and will add depth to a strong UNLV backcourt.

BARRY YOUNG (6-7, 223 lbs., SR, G/F, #33, 4.2 ppg, 2.0 rpg, 36 assists, 7 blocked shots, 10 steals, Mt. Hebron HS/Ellicott, Md.) Young is an offensive presence off the bench who would be a starter in most programs. He connected on 31 three-pointers last year (.323). Young played in 39 games, starting two, for a total of 449 minutes last year. He is considered one of the best pure shooters on the UNLV team.

He has good skills and should be a more important player this year for the Runnin' Rebels. Young was an outstanding high school player at Mt. Hebron in Ellicott, Md. He was named player of the year by the *Baltimore Evening Sun* after his senior season for the Baltimore Metropolitan area. His older brother, Perry Young, starred at Virginia Tech and later played in the NBA.

★ NEWCOMERS ★

EVRIC GRAY (6-7, 205 lbs., SO, F, #23, Bloomington HS/Bloomington, Calif. & Riverside CC/Riverside, Calif.) UNLV has one of the most elaborate ''farm systems'' in college basketball. Tarkanian usually signs several players each year who are ''farmed out'' to junior college before coming to UNLV. Gray is one such player. He signed with UNLV in 1988 and played a season at Riverside CC in southern California before transferring and sitting out last season at UNLV.

Gray is a tremendous athlete with great running and jumping ability. He was one of the top players in southern California as a senior at Bloomington HS. Gray certainly is tailor-made for the UNLV system. He can also rebound and is a scoring threat. Gray should be able to get some immediate playing time. UNLV has lost three frontcourt players from last year and needs some reenforcements off the bench. Gray could be one of those. His role should increase significantly next year after starting forwards Larry Johnson and Stacey Augmon graduate.

BOBBY JOYCE (6-7, 245 lbs., JR, F, #42, Santa Ana HS/Santa Ana, Calif. & Riverside CC/Riverside, Calif.) Like Gray, Joyce was signed by UNLV out of high school, spent a year at Riverside CC, and then transferred in and sat out last season. He was one of the premier players in southern California as a senior at Santa Ana HS. Joyce is extremely strong and effective under the boards. He should be a capable backup for Larry Johnson at power forward this season and may step into a starting role next year.

Tarkanian used to coach at Riverside and has great ties to the junior college system. Joyce should be able to adequately replace Moses Scurry as UNLV's top inside reserve.

MELVIN LOVE (6-10, 240 lbs., JR, C, #40, Cajon HS/San Bernadino, Calif. & Salt Lake CC/Salt Lake City, Utah) Love is another outstanding junior college player who transferred in and sat out last season at UNLV. He is strong, can get up and down the floor with the Runnin' Rebels and block shots. Love was considered one of the best junior college center prospects two years ago.

The San Bernadino, Calif., native should provide strong depth in the pivot for UNLV. With Love and Elmore Spencer, another highly regarded junior college transfer, plus redshirt senior George Ackles, UNLV has excellent depth in the pivot.

ELMORE SPENCER (7-0, 265 lbs., JR, C, #24, 20.3 ppg, Booker T. Washington HS/Atlanta, Ga. & Connors State JC/Warner, Okla.) Spencer is the most highly regarded big man Tarkanian has landed at UNLV. Spencer was considered the top junior college center in the nation last year and was ranked as the No. 3 JC transfer overall by *All Star Sports.*

Spencer was a highly regarded high school All-America, Top 25 in the country, at Booker T. Washington HS in Atlanta. He averaged 27 points, 17 rebounds and eight blocked shots as a senior while leading Washington HS to the Georgia AAAA championship. In the summer following his senior year in high school, Spencer led an Atlanta team to the championship of the prestigious Boston Shootout. He scored 27 points and 11 rebounds in the championship game against New York.

''He looks like a little Bob Lanier,'' said Dick Vitale after watching Spencer in high school.

''This mountain masquerading as a young man is in 'the truth' an Atlanta

prep basketball . . . Spencer is so strong, and so massive, that it is scarry to think of him playing against mere schoolboys. He might accidentally step on them. He is an awesome rebounder and rejector and has an accurate shooting touch. According to his coach, Robert Bell, 'we just get the ball to him on the block, and Elmore stuffs it','' wrote Bob Gibbons in *All Star Sports.*

Spencer signed with Georgia. He spent 36 days in the psychiatric ward of Atlanta's Grady Memorial Hospital during the summer before enrolling at Georgia. He apparently had symptoms of manic-depression, took medication for the condition and received out-patient treatment.

He redshirted in the 1987-88 season at Georgia because he fell behind in his schoolwork due to his health problems and had to take a medical withdrawal from school. He came back in 1988-89 to average 12 points and 5.3 rebounds with 21 assists, 29 blocked shots, and nine steals in 11 games. Georgia was 9-2 with Spencer in the lineup. However, he then broke his foot and eventually left school. He played all of last season at Connors State JC.

He can definitely score down low, block shots and rebound. The key with Spencer is can he get in shape? Reportedly over the summer he worked harder than ever on his game and physical conditioning in Las Vegas.

Spencer is not as mobile as graduated center David Butler, but he is much bigger. His responsibility will not be too great this year as the Runnin' Rebels have four returning starters including All-America forwards Larry Johnson and Stacey Augmon. However, next season the UNLV inside game should center on Spencer.

H WALDMAN (6-2, 180 lbs., FR, G, #31, 18.0 ppg, 9.0 rpg, 3.0 apg, Clark HS/Las Vegas, Nev.) Yes, H is his true first name. Waldman has more than just a unique first name, he was an outstanding player, the best in Nevada, as a senior at Clark HS. Waldman led Clark to a 29-3 record and a second-place finish in the Nevada AAA state tournament.

''He's a pure point guard and a tremendous passer,'' said Clark HS coach Hal Overholtzer. ''He's a tremendous passer. Jerry Tarkanian made the comment that he may be the best passer he's ever seen in high school. I'm sure he's exaggerating a little, but H is a good one.''

In the prestigious Las Vegas Holiday Prep Classic last year, Waldman was MVP. He also made 16-of-26 three-pointers.

''UNLV may have gotten more than they bargained for in this team leader. He hits the three, is totally unselfish and can handle the ball against pressure,'' wrote Garth Franklin in *Hoop Scoop.*

Waldman played for the West All-Stars in the prestigious Dapper Dan Roundball Classic in Pittsburgh last year. He will be Greg Anthony's backup at point guard this year.

★ QUESTIONS ★

Keeping the Runnin' Rebels focused and motivated without a chance to defend their national championship? Normally when a team goes on probation, it is hard to keep them focused and motivated. However, UNLV has four senior starters who may be able to overcome this potential problem and keep the Runnin' Rebels dominant all year long.

★ STRENGTHS ★

Larry Johnson! He is arguably the finest player in the country and is definitely the best ever at UNLV. Johnson was all he was advertised to be, and even more, last year for the Runnin' Rebels.

Defense! UNLV is an underrated defensive team. If you don't believe us, ask Duke, Loyola Marymount and others the Runnin' Rebels rolled over on the way to the national championship.

The starting backcourt of Greg Anthony and Anderson Hunt! Anthony and Hunt comprise the top defensive backcourt in the country and possibly the best overall backcourt as well.

Depth in the pivot! Even though UNLV has lost starting center David Butler, junior college transfer Elmore Spencer is the best pivot man to ever sign with the Runnin' Rebels. The starting center from two years ago, George Ackles, is returning from a redshirt season and another JC transfer, Melvin Love, is also potentially an outstanding player.

Tark! All he does is win big year after year.

Depth and big time athletic ability!

★ BLUE RIBBON ANALYSIS ★

UNLV dumped Duke by a 30-point margin in the NCAA championship game last year. The margin of defeat was the largest in the history of the NCAA tournament. The championship was vindication for UNLV coach Jerry Tarkanian but in July the NCAA ruled the Runnin' Rebels couldn't defend their title this season. While UNLV will appeal, it isn't likely the decision will be overturned.

UNLV is also under NCAA investigation for other matters. However, the decision to bar UNLV from the NCAA tournament was a travesty of justice. The decision was the final chapter of the NCAA's 13-year battle with Tarkanian in court over a 1977 ruling that UNLV should suspend him for two years. The current UNLV players were in elementary school when the original decision was handed down, so it is not exactly their fight. The post-season ban will prevent UNLV`from being the first team since UCLA in 1973 to successfully defend its national title.

Post-season ban or not, UNLV is the premier team in college basketball. Four starters return including superstar forward Larry Johnson, the best player in UNLV history and the pick of most experts for national pre-season player of the year. He was everything advertised and more last year.

Johnson is not all UNLV has to offer, either. Starting guards Anderson Hunt and Greg Anthony destroyed Duke defensively and were unchecked offensively. Hunt and Anthony have started together for two years and are the top defensive backcourt, and possibly the best overall backcourt in the nation.

Senior forward Stacey Augmon got hot in the NCAA tournament and was devastating. The former Olympian is the best defensive forward in college basket-ball and one of the Top 10 players in the game.

Starting center David Butler is gone but George Ackles, the starting center two years ago, is back from a redshirt season. Also in the pivot are 7-0 Elmore Spencer and 6-10 Melvin Love. Both are JC transfers. Spencer started his career at Georgia and is the most highly regarded big man to ever sign with UNLV.

Johnson and Augmon turned down NBA megabucks to return for their senior years and now they are denied a chance to defend their national title. Most teams in similar circumstances would suffer from motivation problems. However, don't expect that from this senior dominated, mature UNLV team. The Runnin' Rebels are focused and intent on dominating even though they can't play in the NCAAs. Johnson, Augmon, Anthony, Hunt and company will still be the premier team in the country anyway. UNLV cannot defend its crown but the Runnin' Rebels can become one of college basketball's all-time great teams.

LAST SEASON			
#Loyola Marymount	102-91	@California-Irvine	99-77
#California	101-81	Louisville	91-81
##Kansas	77-91	@California-Santa Barbara	70-78
##DePaul	88-53	@Utah State	84-82
@Oklahoma	81-89	@Fullerton State	103-85
@Pacific	79-65	###Fullerton State	115-93
Iowa	97-80	###Pacific	99-72
Long Beach State	78-58	###Long Beach State	92-74
Arkansas	101-93	*Arkansas-Little Rock	102-72
Fullerton State	94-66	*Ohio State	76-65
@San Jose State	100-80	**Ball State	69-67
@New Mexico State	82-83	**Loyola Marymount	131-101
@Temple	82-76	***Georgia Tech	90-81
@Fresno State	84-75	***Duke	103-73
California-Irvine	103-67		
@Long Beach State	86-77	@ Road Games	
California-Santa Barbara	69-67	# Dodge NIT	
@LSU	105-107	## Dodge NIT Final Four, Madison	
Utah State	124-90	Square Garden, New York, NY	
North Carolina State	88-82	### Big West Tournament, Long	
San Jose State	105-69	Beach, CA	
Pacific	116-76	* NCAA Tournament, Salt Lake City,	
Oklahoma State	100-84	UT	
Fresno State	69-64	** NCAA Tournament, Oakland, CA	
New Mexico State	109-86	*** Final Four, Denver, CO	
Arizona	95-87		

1990-91 UNLV SCHEDULE			
Dec.	1	#Alabama-Birmingham	Feb. 21 Pacific
	8	@Nevada	23 California-Irvine
	15	##Michigan State	25 @New Mexico State
	19	Princeton	Mar. 2 @Fullerton State
	22	Florida State	@ Road Games
	30	Old Dominion	# Vancouver, British Columbia
Jan.	4	Fullerton State	##Auburn Hils, MI
	7	San Jose State	
	9	Utah State	
	12	@Fresno	
	14	@Pacific	
	17	@California-Irvine	
	19	Long Beach State	
	21	@California-Santa Barbara	
	26	###Louisville	
	28	@Utah State	
	31	@San Jose State	
Feb.	3	Memphis State	
	7	Fresno State	
	10	@Arkansas	
	14	California-Santa Barbara	
	16	New Mexico State	
	18	@Long Beach State	

NOTES: UNLV will play the Soviet National Team, on NBC, in Las Vegas on Nov. 17 . . . Dexter Boney, a 6-3 guard from Wilmington, Del., via Hagerstown, Md. JC, will set out this year at UNLV. He will be a junior in eligibility next season. Boney was ranked as the No. 22 TC prospect in the country by All Star Sports last spring . . . ESPN is scheduled to broadcast five UNLV games: Princeton, (Decv. 19), California-Santa Bar-bara (Jan. 21), Utah State (Jan. 28), Long Beach State (Feb. 18) and New Mexico State (Feb. 25).

THE NEXT WAVE

Alabama   Oklahoma
Duke   Pitt
Georgia Tech   Syracuse
Indiana   Texas
LSU   UCLA
Ohio State   Virginia

ALABAMA

LAST SEASON: 26-9
CONFERENCE RECORD: 12-6
STARTERS LOST: 2
STARTERS RETURNING: 3
CONFERENCE:
SOUTHEASTERN (SEC)
LOCATION: TUSCALOOSA, AL
HOME FLOOR: COLEMAN
COLISEUM (15,043)
NICKNAME: CRIMSON TIDE
COLORS: CRIMSON AND WHITE

CRIMSON TIDE

★ COACH'S PROFILE ★

WIMP SANDERSON (Record at Alabama, 218-100.) He did it again! Yes, that down home talkin' ugly, plaid sportcoat wearin' worrier supreme pulled off another great season. As usual, the national media basically ignored another strong and successful Alabama team for more so called "colorful" stories.

For the second straight year Alabama posted a 12-6 SEC record en route to a second place regular season finish and then went on to win the SEC tournament title and gained the conference's automatic berth in the NCAA tournament. In the second round of the NCAAs, on a western court in Long Beach, Calif., Alabama simply stopped, or as Sanderson would say "Gave 'em a good lickin'," an Arizona team (by a 77-55 score) that entered the tournament as a hot team many thought would advance at least to the region finals. However, as usual, little attention was paid to Alabama after its big win as the Crimson Tide was overshadowed by Cinderella stories such as Loyola Marymount and Xavier. Alabama bowed out of the tournament in the semifinals of the west region in a close 62-60 loss to Loyola Marymount.

In an era in college basketball where coaches are literally kings in their areas and national media celebrities, Sanderson has gotten little national recognition other than for his carnival barker-like plaid suits and perpetual sideline scowl. If some of the young, glib "mediagenic" coaches who have had a hot team or two had equalled Sanderson's accomplishments over the last decade he already would have been annointed to genius status. In the last 10 years, Sanderson has guided Alabama to eight NCAA tournament appearances including five trips to the Sweet 16. The Crimson Tide has also won four SEC tournament championships. Alabama has also won twenty or more games on seven occasions. In the 1980's, Alabama was second to Kentucky in the SEC in terms of overall winning percentage. Alabama also won more SEC tournament games, 17, in the '80s than any other program. Yet you never hear Sanderson's name mentioned among the premier coaches in the country or even on an all-underrated list. He may be a little country and his wardrobe could use some sprucing up, but there's no getting around the fact that the man can coach!

Few Division I coaches have a longer association with their current school than Sanderson does with Alabama. In June, 1960, he joined the Alabama staff as a graduate assistant while working towards a post-graduate degree in school administration. He graduated in 1961 and was made a full-time assistant, responsible for on-court coaching, recruiting and scouting. He has been a fixture on the Alabama bench both as an assistant and the head coach for the past thirty straight seasons.

He was born in Florence, Ala., and had an outstanding athletic career at Coffee HS in his hometown. He enrolled at Abilene Christian College (Texas) but transferred to the University of North Alabama (Florence State) for his sophomore year. While at North Alabama, he earned three basketball letters and was elected team captain in his junior and senior seasons. After graduating from college in 1959, Sanderson began his career as a high school coach at Carbon Hill HS in Walker County, Ala. He was 25-4 and took his team to a district's championship in his only year there.

Sanderson was named national coach of the year by basketball times after the 1987 season. He has twice been named SEC coach of the year as well. The *Lexington Herald-Leader* selected Sanderson as the "*SEC Coach of The Decade*" for the '80s.

His 1986-87 team won 28 games which set an Alabama record for the most wins in a season. After winning consecutive SEC tournament titles in 1989 and '90, Alabama became the first school in the conference since the 1948 and '49 Kentucky teams' to win back-to-back conference tournament titles.

Sanderson has been around Alabama so long that he has seen 858 basketball games at the University, 47 percent of all the games in which Alabama has participated. After ten seasons he ranks as Alabama's second-leading all-time winning coach behind Hank Crisp who won 264 games in twenty seasons. Sanderson is only 46 wins behind Crisp.

"I came for a year and it turned into thirty," said Sanderson about his career at Alabama. "I really didn't intend to stay more than a year, but before I could look up, I'd been here thirty. It has been an exciting time and hopefully, I've been able to add something to the sport of basketball at Alabama."

Thirteen Alabama players in Sanderson's ten years as Alabama's head coach have been selected in the NBA draft. Five Alabama players have been first round selections. Last season, four former Alabama players were on NBA rosters. He generally does not recruit the true, towering center who is 6-11 on up but instead seems to have teams with many 6-8 greyhounds who can run, jump and rebound. Sanderson's best players have been around that 6-8 size range, give or take an inch, such as Derrick McKey, Buck Johnson, Eddie Phillips and Michael Ansley. Last season, the top four players on the team were 6-6 to 6-9 greyhounds who could go up against players much bigger and more than hold their own. His teams are also always strong defensively. Alabama also seldom has a big scoring star and the Crimson Tide generally have several players who score a mid-double figures and can be counted upon consistently. Don't look for anything to change at Alabama for years to come. Sanderson will still be pacing the sidelines with his ever-present scowl and wearing one of those loud, plaid coats. The Crimson Tide will generally be underrated nationally and usually won't even be picked as the team to beat in the SEC. However, at the end of the year Alabama will be a strong factor in the SEC race and headed for another NCAA tournament appearance. As long as Sanderson is around, Alabama will be underrated but successful.

★ PLAYERS NOT RETURNING ★

KEITH ASKINS (6-6, G/F, 9.9 ppg, 5.1 rpg, 46 assists, 30 steals, 23 blocked shots) Askins was Alabama's sixth man for the past few seasons. He basically was a starter in everything except title as he averaged 27.9 points per game and was the team's fourth leading scorer and rebounder. Askins was one of the most versatile and top defenders in the country. He shut down LSU All-America guard Chris Jackson last January when the Crimson Tide blew out the Tigers and started to come to the forefront in the SEC.

Askins was not a great shooter but he developed into a decent scorer. Even though he was not a big name player with gaudy offensive statistics and a non-starter, many NBA teams pursued Askins hard for their summer rookie/free agent camps. Only 54 players are now selected in the NBA draft and Askins was regarded as one of the top five free agents who were not selected in the draft.

His versatility, leadership and excellent work habits will be missed.

DAVID BENOIT (6-8, C, 10.5 ppg, 6.1 rpg, 29 assists, 20 steals, 19 blocked shots) Benoit was Alabama's No. 3 scorer and rebounder last season. He was a versatile player who could hang tough under the boards, muscle up a power layup against bigger opposition or take his man out on the floor and hit a perimeter jumper. Benoit made 9-of-20 three-pointers (.450).

The departure of Benoit leaves a major void in the Alabama front line. There doesn't appear to be anyone on the roster who can match his combination of inside strength and perimeter shooting ability. Benoit was not selected in the NBA draft but he did try out for the Los Angeles Lakers, and was impressive, but decided to play in Spain this year rather than go to pre-season camp with an NBA team.

JAMES SANDERS (6-2, G, 8.1 ppg, 3.4 rpg, 159 assists, 21 steals, 2 blocked shots) Sanders started 23 games in the Alabama backcourt. He averaged 27.5 minutes per game and was third on the team in made three-point field goals (26). He was a scrappy type who did not back down and was competitive game after game.

Sanders certainly did a credible job for Alabama last year but he will be more easily replaced than Askins or Benoit. Freshman guard James Robinson looked outstanding in practice last year before he was forced to miss the season due to a question concerning his scores on the standardized college admission test. He is considerably more gifted than Sanders and has a chance to become the best guard to ever play at Alabama.

★ RETURNING PLAYERS ★

ERNEST BROWN (6-1, 180 lbs., SR, G, #11, 2.2 ppg, 0.5 rpg, 4 assists, 4 steals, 1 blocked shot, Jackson-Olin HS/Birmingham, Ala.) One of the five seniors on the Alabama team, Brown is nicknamed "Snake" and has become a crowd favorite in Tuscaloosa. He appeared in 15 games last year for a total of 58 minutes (3.9 mpg). Brown is a good shooter who made 11-of-19 field goals (.579) and 3-of-7 three-pointers (.429). His role at Alabama has been limited throughout his career as Brown played in 14 games each as a freshman and sophomore.

The intense and always hustling Brown earned the Tuscaloosa Tip-Off Club's "Hustle Award" following his sophomore season. His role will basically be the same this year as Alabama lost one starting guard and reserve, Keith Askins, but will have the services of two gifted newcomers, James Robinson and Marcus Jones, at guard so Brown is slated for limited action again.

MARCUS CAMPBELL (6-7, 220 lbs., SR, F, #32, 3.0 ppg, 1.8 rpg, 11 assists, 1 steal, 10 blocked shots, Livingston HS/Livingston, Ala.) Campbell came off the bench last season and played in 32 games for an average of 7.9 minutes per game. Offensively, he shot the ball extremely well going 38-of-56 (.679) from the floor.

He has excellent strength and can be a physical rebounder. Campbell is a hustler but he hasn't developed as quickly as expected. He was the MVP in Alabama's Class 4A as a senior at Livingston HS and led his team to the state championship.

Sanderson will need a stronger contribution from Campbell this year. He is one of the likely candidates to receive increased playing time and extra responsibility in order to replace graduated David Benoit.

MELVIN CHEATUM (6-8, 200 lbs., SR, F/C, #44, 15.7 ppg, 6.7 rpg, 28 assists, 25 steals, 22 blocked shots, Winnsboro HS/Winnsboro, La.) One of the more underrated players not only in the SEC but the entire south, Cheatum emerged as a force last year both offensively and on the boards. He led Alabama in scoring and rebounding. Cheatum is a slightly built, highly explosive athlete who gets a great deal done inside despite his lack of bulk. He was the MVP of the SEC tournament.

Cheatum's consistency did not go unnoticed by the SEC coaches as they put him on their second-team all-conference squad. He had a three-game total of 50 points and 27 rebounds in the SEC tournament. Cheatum's best game as a junior came at Georgia where he scored 23 points and pulled down 11 rebounds. The Georgia game was one of five games where Cheatum scored 23 points. He also was named SEC player of the week for Jan. 29 through Feb. 4 when he had 40 points and 11 rebounds against Florida and Vanderbilt.

He averaged 9.5 points and 6.3 rebounds as a freshman starter in 1987-88 but slumped as sophomore to averages of 6.7 points and 3.2 rebounds due to a leg injury. He basically plays small forward but also can fill in a power forward as well. Cheatum steps up and delivers at critical times late in games, plays well with his back to the basket and just has special timing around the goal.

In Cheatum and junior Robert Horry, Alabama should easily have the best pair of starting forwards in the SEC.

ROBERT HORRY (6-9, 200 lbs., JR, F, #25, 13.1 ppg, 6.2 rpg, 67 assists, 24 steals, 51 blocked shots, Andalusia HS/Andalusia, Ala.) Horry was second on the squad behind Melvin Cheatum in scoring and rebounding. After coming off the bench as a freshman, Horry emerged as a productive starter last year. He also showed that he was the most talented player in the Alabama program last season. Horry is a more skilled perimeter player at this point in his career than former Alabama star Derrick McKey, now with the Seattle SuperSonics, was at this stage.

Horry led Alabama in three-point field goal percentage at .427 (50-of-117). He also was third in assists as well. He led Alabama in blocks by a wide margin and also was third on the team in field goal percentage (.760). Horry was ranked as one of the Top 16 6-5 and taller inside/outside threats by *The Sporting News*.

He was the MVP of the San Juan shootout, an early season tournament Alabama won in Puerto Rico last season. In three games in the SEC tournament Horry had 37 points, 22 rebounds and 11 blocked shots, including six blocks against Auburn in the semifinals. In the NCAA tournament, he had 27 points in Alabama's opening win over Colorado State and then 21 against Loyola Marymount. Horry was a third-team All-SEC selection.

He tried out for the U.S. National team over the summer and was impressive before eventually being cut. He is one of the smoothest and most versatile offensive players for his size in the entire nation. In fact, some Alabama observers feel he should be a guard. The main knock on Horry is that he must become tougher inside. If he gets tougher and keeps developing, Horry could eventually become the best NBA player the Alabama program has produced so far.

BRYANT LANCASTER (6-3, 185 lbs., SR, G, #21, 2.1 ppg, 0.8 rpg, 15 assists, Valley HS/Fairfax, Ala.) Lancaster started the first 12 games of the season at the off-guard spot, before Sanderson moved senior James Sanders into the lineup. His best game of his career came during a 101-93 home victory over North Carolina when he scored 15 points. For the season, Lancaster averaged 8.7 minutes per game and saw his role decrease after starting the first 12 games.

Lancaster came to Alabama with high expectations. However, he was a high school inside player who had to learn to play guard at the SEC level and that transition has not come easy. He is the best defensive player on the team this year. Now that super defensive stopper Keith Askins is gone, Lancaster's role could be more important. He is limited offensively and made only 16-of-45 field goals (.356) last year and has yet to shoot over .375 for a season. He also is weak at the foul line and is .500 free throw shooter for his career.

His experience and defensive ability could earn Lancaster a bigger role but he will have to stay ahead of two talented newcomers, James Robinson and Marcus Jones.

ANTHONY LAWRENCE (6-8, 220 lbs., SO, F, #34, 1.4 ppg, 1.1 rpg, 3 assists, 2 blocked shots, 2 steals, Lakewood HS/St. Petersburg, Fla.) Lawrence's role was limited as a freshman. He played in 15 games for a total of 57 minutes. His best outing came against Augusta College as he scored 8 points and pulled down five rebounds. Interestingly, Lawrence was 10-of-17 from the field (.588) but just 1-of-7 (.143) from the line. He redshirted the 1988-89 season.

Lawrence has worked hard on his strength and conditioning since coming to Alabama and has showed improvement in both areas. His role is expected to be limited once again.

KENNETH RICE (6-4, 190 lbs., SO, G, #4, 1.0 ppg, 0.5 rpg, 8 assists, 2 steals, 1 blocked shot, Austin HS/Decatur, Ala.) After being redshirted in 1988-89, Rice came back to play in 21 games for a total of 70 minutes last year. He is known as an outside shooter but made only 3-of-15 field goal attempts (.200) and was 2-of-6 (.333) from three-point range. He tallied a career-high of five points in home wins against Augusta College and Kentucky. An off-guard, Rice is considered one of the five best prospects in Alabama when he came out of Austin HS.

After spending three years in the program, Rice should be ready for more playing time this year but the Alabama backcourt is going to be stronger.

DARBY RICH (6-4, 185 lbs., JR, G, #23, 0.5 ppg, 0.5 rpg, 1 assist, Riverside HS/Greer, S.C.) Rich was a limited contributor last year. He redshirted the 1988-89 season and played in 13 games for a total of 31 minutes last year. He is a dedicated athlete who has gotten stronger while at Alabama but the talent level of the program is so high that it is difficult for him to become a key player.

GARY WAITES (6-2, 180 lbs., SR, G, 4.7 ppg, 1.7 rpg, 168 assists, 34 steals, 4 blocked shots, Towers HS/Decatur, Ga) Waites has led Alabama in assists from his point guard spot the past two years. He is definitely a set up the offense type point guard rather than a scorer. Waites averaged fewer than five shots per game last year and was 56-of-150 from the field (.373) and 22-of-61 (.361) from three-point range. He was a reliable .711 (32-of-45) from the line.

He is a smooth ball handler who can deliver the ball to the right people at the most opportune time. Waites also runs the fast break well. He suffered a severe knee injury prior to enrolling at Alabama and although he has rehabilitated the knee, Waites is not as quick as he was prior to the injury.

His selfless play and skill as a playmaker will work well again with an Alabama team that should have three big scorers in forwards Melvin Cheatum and Robert Horry plus freshman guard James Robinson.

MARCUS WEBB (6-8, 262 lbs., JR, F/C, #54, 4.1 ppg, 2.1 rpg, 16 assists, 6 steals, 11 blocked shots, Sidney Lanier HS/Montgomery, Ala.) Webb started seven games last year. He played a total of 323 minutes (11.1 mpg). He showed glimpses of strong play and gave Sanderson hope for the future. Consistency was a problem for Webb but at times he was impressive such as against LSU when he held his own against massive Stanley Roberts. His role will increase significantly this year as Webb could be the replacement for David Benoit at center.

He started the first seven games last year before Benoit reemerged and afterwards he came off the bench. He scored 13 points against Eastern Michigan, 12 in a home win over North Carolina and 11 at Virginia Tech. After that stretch, his only double figure game came when he had 17 points in a road loss against LSU.

His father, George Pugh, is the head football coach at Alabama A & M and played in the NFL. Pugh was a great football player at Alabama. Webb was also a high school football star and was heavily recruited in that sport. However, he didn't want to deal with the inevitable comparisons to his father and chose to concentrate on basketball in college.

He possesses great strength and has the bulk to play physical defense in rebound with just about anyone he will face. Webb is a crucial player for Alabama this year. He has to be more consistent and able to replace the rebounding of Benoit if Alabama is to take the SEC title again.

DEAN WILSON (6-0, 170 lbs., SO, G, #23, 0.3 ppg, 1 assist, Lawrenceburg HS/Lawrenceburg, Ind.) One of two walk-on candidates who made the Alabama varsity last year, Wilson saw action in four games for a total of five minutes. He missed his only field goal attempt and was 1-of-2 from the line.

★ NEWCOMERS ★

GREG GLASS (6-7, 180 lbs., FR, G/F, #30, 23.1 ppg, 9.8 rpg, Todd Central HS/Elkton, Ky.) Glass is the first Alabama recruit from Kentucky in years. He was ranked as a No. 12 senior in the state of Kentucky by the *Hoop Scoop*. Glass was a finalist for the Kentucky— Indiana all-star series and connected on 50.4 percent of his field goal attempts.

"Very athletic. Will be a wing player on the upper level-doesn't like the inside chores. Has 20' range, is a nice passer, and plays good 'D'," wrote Tom Goins in *Hoop Scoop*.

Glass will probably be brought along slowly at least for his first two years at Alabama.

MARCUS JONES (6-3, 175 lbs., SO, G, #20, 23.3 ppg, 7.0 rpg, 5.1 apg, Westwood HS/Memphis, Tenn.) Jones sat out last year at Alabama and will have three years of eligibility beginning this season. He was regarded as an outstanding second guard prospect at Westwood HS in Memphis and led his team to a 31-6 record as a senior. Jones was not only an All-Tennessee selection in high school but also was considered one of the Top 100 players in the nation.

He is expected to make an immediate impact as a first year player at Alabama. Jones is a proficient scorer, passes well and can defend. He can also play some point guard when the need arises. No program in the SEC has two better backcourt newcomers then Jones and James Robinson.

CEDRIC MOORE (6-9, 185 lbs., FR, C, #51, 25.7 ppg, 17.5 rpg, 7.2 apg, 7.0 blpg, Woodlawn HS/Birmingham, Ala.) Moore was a recipient of Alabama's Mr. Basketball Award last year. Most publications ranked him as the top player in the state. He was also considered one of the Top 75 players in the country and was named to the *Orlando Sentinel* Dixie Dozen Team, comprised of the 12 best players in the south. Moore and DePaul recruit Michael Ravizee led Woodlawn to a 35-3 record and the Alabama 5A state title.

"Moore is a very offensive minded player who goes right up and over most of his competition," said Tom Goins of the *Hoop Scoop*.

He needs more strength but is potentially a big league offensive player.

"His game is somewhat similar to that of Derrick McKey, although Moore is not nearly as accomplished now as the former Bama star. Cedric is actually a small forward in a big forward's body. He has good perimeter skills, including an accurate outside jumper. He runs well and is a quick leaper. Moore has exceptional timing and will develop into a 'swat artist'," wrote Bob Gibbons of *All-Star Sports*.

Moore is the latest in a long line of Birmingham prep phenoms who have come to Alabama. Sanderson is usually tough on the freshman and it takes them awhile to become used to his manner. However, Moore is talented enough to become a significant contributor as a freshman.

PHILLIP PEARSON (6-2, 170 lbs., FR, G, #13, Jeff Davis HS/Montgomery, Ala.) One of two walk-ons who were on the Alabama roster last year, Pearson was held out of competition and redshirted. He was an All-City selection at Montgomery's Jeff Davis HS. His role is expected to be limited this year.

JAMES ROBINSON (6-2, 180 lbs., FR, G, #31, 40.7 ppg, 8.3 rpg, 3.7 apg, 3.6 stpg, Murrah HS/Jackson, Miss.) The most heralded player in recent Alabama basketball history, Robinson is the top newcomer in the SEC this season. He practiced for two weeks with Alabama last year but his standardized tests scores were questioned and Robinson was held out of competition. He never got a ruling until the season was over. He won an arbitration case and as a result has four years of eligibility beginning this season.

Robinson was not able to practice with Alabama after the first two weeks but in that time he was sensational. Many close observers of the Alabama program believed the Crimson Tide would have been able to beat Loyola Marymount and make a run at UNLV in the finals of the West Region if Robinson had been eligible. Offensively, Alabama struggled often last year but the points will not be as hard to come by with James Robinson in uniform.

As a senior at Murrah HS in Jackson, Miss., Robinson was not only the top player in the state of Mississippi but he was a consensus national Top 20 selection as well. Robinson set Murrah records for points in a game (66), season (1,383) and career (3,022).

Robinson first gained attention as a junior when he outscored former LSU All-America Chris Jackson and Georgia's Litterial Green in head-to-head duels. He was a consistent three-point threat throughout high school and is truly an exceptionally gifted athlete. As a junior in high school, Robinson dabbled with track and recorded a Mississippi state record 38.72 seconds time in the 300-meter intermediate hurdles. At the McDonald's East-West Game after his senior season, Robinson won the slam dunk competition.

One recruiter called Robinson a "mixture of Isiah Thomas and Byron Scott." He definitely has a NBA level outside shot.

"He can flat out play. He can shoot the 3 from NBA range and gives you 94' of hardnosed tough aggressive basketball," said Van Coleman of the *National Recruiters Cage Letter*.

Expect big things from James Robinson from Day One at Alabama. He is a special talent who could go on to become the best guard ever in the history of the Alabama basketball program.

LATRELL SPREWELL (6-5, 185 lbs., JR, G/F, #42, 26.6 ppg, 9.2 rpg, Washington HS/Milwaukee, Wisc. & Three Rivers CC/Poplar Bluff, Mo.) Sprewell was regarded as one of the premier junior college players in the nation last year. He was ranked No. 11 among junior college sophomores by *All-Star Sports*. He led Three Rivers to a 32-8 record and a spot in the national junior college Final Four. Sprewell canned an amazing 77 percent of his shots from the floor.

Sprewell will probably come off for the bench for over 20 minutes per game much like Askins did over the last few seasons at Alabama. Sprewell is not the defender Askins was but is a better ballhandler and scorer. He is an explosive scorer who can put points on the board in many ways. The Alabama coaching staff is confident Sprewell can make an immediate impact for the Crimson Tide.

★ QUESTIONS ★

Rebounding? "Our biggest concern for this year is rebounding. We do not have a proven rebounder coming back. Our team does have a couple of people who are big and strong and look like rebounders, but they don't rebound," Sanderson said.

Outside shooting? Sanderson also questions the Crimson Tide's outside shooting, but newcomers James Robinson and Marcus Jones could keep that area from becoming a deficit.

★ STRENGTHS ★

Wimp! Sanderson generally gets a lot out of his teams and we don't expect this season to be any exception. Alabama plays very close to Sanderson's game plan.

Defense! You can count on a Wimp Sanderson coached Alabama team to be strong defensively.

Improved offensive punch! Alabama should be more explosive offensive this year with the additions of new guards James Robinson and Marcus Jones. Often last season it was difficult for Alabama to score but points should be easier for the Crimson Tide to come by this year.

★ BLUE RIBBON ANALYSIS ★

Even though Alabama has lost last two SEC tournament titles and advanced to the semifinals of the West Region last year, coach Wimp Sanderson is not the type to go overboard in his praise of a team in pre-season. Sanderson is concerned that his team will not be as athletic this year. Alabama's outside shooting worries him as does the Crimson Tide's rebounding strength. He also wonders how quickly it will take highly touted guards James Robinson and Marcus Jones to become consistent players after sitting out last year.

While Sanderson's concerns are valid, Alabama's strengths will far outweigh its questions in 1990-91. Alabama should be very strong defensively and an unselfish, team-oriented club. Alabama also has a good contingent of seniors and offensively the Crimson Tide should be much more explosive this year.

At forward, Alabama should have the best starting pair in the SEC. Senior Melvin Cheatum led Alabama in scoring and rebounding last year and junior Robert Horry has a chance to be the best frontcourt player the program has ever produced. Sanderson will need 6-8, 262-pound junior Marcus Webb to come through in the pivot. Senior point guard Gary Waites is limited offensively but runs the club well. Robinson is talented enough to eventually become the best guard to ever play at Alabama and Webb was a big time player during his days at Westwood HS in Memphis. Cedric Moore, a 6-9 freshman, was rated the best player in Alabama last year and has drawn comparisons to former Crimson Tide great Derrick McKey.

We like the looks of this Alabama club. Sanderson is rightfully concerned about replacing David Benoit and Keith Askins, but he'll find a way to get it done. Alabama, LSU and Georgia appear to be the class of the SEC heading into the season. Don't be surprised if Alabama takes a third-straight SEC tournament title this March. The Crimson Tide should be back in the Sweet 16 of NCAA tournament this year.

LAST SEASON		1990-91 ALABAMA SCHEDULE		
#Western Kentucky	79-72	Nov.	24	Delaware
#Eastern Michigan	64-61		27	Wake Forest
#Clemson	57-48		30	#Southern Mississippi
North Carolina	101-93			
@Virginia Tech	75-76	Dec.	4	@Wichita State
##Eastern Kentucky	71-52		15	@North Carolina
Augusta College (GA)	94-67		18	Virginia Military Institute
Baptist College (SC)	63-32			
@Wake Forest	65-67		21	@Tennessee-Chattanooga
###Iona	78-39			
###@Santa Clara	64-48		28-29	##Blue Angels Classic
Vanderbilt	67-68			
@Mississippi	66-48	Jan.	3	@Auburn
Georgia	79-62		5	@Mississippi
@Mississippi State	62-57		9	Florida
@Alabama	82-65		12	@Vanderbilt
LSU	70-50		15	LSU
@Tennessee	70-78		19	Georgia
Auburn	78-59		23	@Mississippi State
Florida	57-44		26	Kentucky
@Vanderbilt	65-56		30	@Tennessee
Mississippi	74-64	Feb.	2	Auburn
@Georgia	64-75		6	Mississippi
Mississippi State	74-86		9	@Florida
Kentucky	83-58		13	Vanderbilt
@LSU	69-75		17	@LSU
Tennessee	87-73		20	@Georgia
@Auburn	80-65		23	Mississippi State
@Florida	63-54		26	@Kentucky
*Mississippi State	59-44	Mar.	2	Tennessee
*Auburn	87-71		7-10	*SEC Tournament
*Mississippi	70-51			
**Colorado State	71-54	@ Road Games		
**Arizona	77-55	# Birmingham, AL		
***Loyola Marymount	60-62	## Pensacola, FL (Navy, North Carolina Charlotte & Towson State)		
@ Road Games		* Nashville, TN		
# San Juan Shootout, San Juan, PR				
## Birmingham, AL				
### Santa Clara, CA				
* SEC Tournament, Orlando, FL				
** NCAA Tournament, Long Beach, CA				
*** NCAA Tournament, Oakland, CA				

NOTES: Alabama will face Towson State in the first round of the Blue Angels Classic . . . Sanderson has three sons and all are in the collegiate coaching profession. Jim is an assistant coach at Western Carolina, Scott serves as an assistant at Colorado and Barry is a graduate assistant at Texas A&M . . . Alabama will play North Carolina, Auburn, LSU and Kentucky on ESPN. CBS will televise the Jan. 19 matchup with Georgia and ABC is set to show the Feb. 17 game at LSU . . . "I don't take much validity in what a person has done, until I can see it for myself. Our team has never been centered around one individual. At Alabama, it is a team effort. Everything we do is in the best interest of our basketball team," Sanderson said.

DUKE

LAST SEASON: 29-9
CONFERENCE RECORD: 9-5
STARTERS LOST: 3
STARTERS RETURNING: 2
CONFERENCE: ATLANTIC
   COAST (ACC)
LOCATION: DURHAM, NC
HOME FLOOR: CAMERON
   INDOOR STADIUM (8,564)
NICKNAME: BLUE DEVILS
COLORS: ROYAL BLUE & WHITE

★ COACH'S PROFILE ★

MIKE KRZYZEWSKI (Record at Duke, 231-101. Career record, 304-160.) Few coaches in the history of the college game have experienced the level of success Krzyzewski has enjoyed over the last five seasons at Duke. Krzyzewski has led the Blue Devils to four NCAA Final Fours during that span, including three times in a row, while averaging slightly more than 29 wins a season. Krzyzewski's teams during the last five years have also had some lofty individual accomplishments as well. Duke has had five All-Americas, two of which, Johnny Dawkins and Danny Ferry, were national players of the year, and nine former Blue Devils have been drafted into the NBA in the past five years.

When Krzyzewski's ten-year career at Duke is looked at as a whole, the numbers are even more staggering: seven 20-win seasons, seven-straight upper division finishes in the ACC, two ACC championships and three ACC coach of the year honors. Coach K, as he is also known, also tops all active college coaches (yes, Bob Knight included) with a .750 career winning percentage (21-7 overall) in NCAA tournament games.

Krzyzewski became Duke's all-time winningest coach last year as he jumped over second place Vic Bubas (213 career wins) early in the season, and with a 35-point Blue Devil thrashing of Richmond in the tournament's first round, he overtook No. 1 Eddie Cameron (226 wins). Quite simply, Krzyzewski has built the Duke program to the point where almost all great high school players with better than average academic credentials at least look at Duke, even if they decide to go elsewhere. His recruiting has reached such heights that even graduation losses of key players will not push Duke into periods of transition and rebuilding.

He grew up in Chicago and attended Army where he was a point guard and floor leader for a young head coach by the name of Bobby Knight. Krzyzewski learned a great deal from Knight during his playing days at Army, particularly with regard to man-to-man defense, a concept which he has used as a foundation of all his teams. Krzyzewski eventually returned to West Point, after the obligatory stint in the Army, and took over the Academy's basketball program. The major character trait Krzyzewski exhibits as a head coach is a subdued and quiet intensity on the sidelines during games. This is quite a difference compared to Knight, who was and always will be prone to volatile blow-ups at both officials and his own players. Krzyzewski cultivated a low key, yet very intense, outlook on the game while at Army and his players always respected his sincerity and even temper. He spent five seasons at West Point where he accumulated a solid 73-59 record and methodically learned his trade.

When the head coaching job at Duke opened up after the 1979-80 season, Bob Knight was there again for Krzyzewski as he pushed him to take the job and highly recommended his former point guard to the Duke administration. The dramatic move from Army to Duke was one which many ACC observers thought Krzyzewski would have difficulty making. Krzyzewski was given the Blue Devils reins and in his first year the team struggled through a 17-13 campaign. Duke made it to the NIT, but it was a disappointing ending to senior forward Gene Banks' sensational career at Duke. The doubts about Krzyzewski's ability to handle the Duke job continued as the Blue Devils endured successive 10-17 and 11-17 campaigns. In the year in which Duke won 11 games, the problems were compounded by the fact that up the road, in Raleigh, N.C., North Carolina State was celebrating a national championship victory.

The 1982-83 season, which at the time seemed to be a nightmare for Krzyzewski and the Blue Devils, was actually the beginning of a glorious stretch which has vaulted Duke into the national spotlight as the most consistently successful program in major college basketball in the late '80s and through the first year of the new decade. Freshman Johnny Dawkins, Mark Alarie, David Henderson and Jay Bilas all gained invaluable experience as they all saw more action than any ACC freshmen could realistically expect. This baptism by fire caused these players to grow up quickly and they proceeded to lead Duke to three straight 20-win seasons and three NCAA tournament berths before their careers ended. Duke's class of '86 accomplishments were highlighted by a record setting 37-3 campaign in 1985-86 which concluded with a three-point loss to Louisville in the NCAA championship game. The '86 team was one of the best of the decade and was better than many teams who have actually won national titles. Krzyzewski had ridden this outstanding class

to unprecedented heights where both he and the Duke program have remained ever since.

Last season, Krzyzewski guided Duke to yet another Final Four and this program's second national championship game in five years. The Blue Devils advanced further than anyone could have expected and even though the season ended with a 103-73 blowout at the hands of UNLV, it may have, all things considered, been Krzyzewski's finest year at Duke. After the season was over, Krzyzewski was reportedly offered his first head coaching job in the NBA. Newly installed Vice President of Basketball Operations for the Boston Celtics, Dave Gavitt, reportedly offered Krzyzewski a multi-year contract which would have guaranteed the 43-year-old coach millionaire status immediately. Krzyzewski considered the offer before coming to the conclusion that Duke was where he should remain.

"I think I learned I should be thankful I'm doing what I'm doing where I'm doing it," Krzyzewski said after turning down the Celtics' offer.

After coaching the Blue Devils to the national championship game and considering the Celtics offer, Krzyzewski presided over the tryouts for the U.S. National team, held in Colorado Springs, Colo., in late May. He coached the U.S. team at the Goodwill Games in Seattle and the World Basketball Championships in Buenos Aires, Argentina. Much like some other big name college coaches whose teams failed to win the Gold Medal in international competition —Louisville's Denny Crum at the '87 Pan-American Games and John Thompson in the '88 Summer Olympics — Krzyzewski found out first hand just how difficult it is for a team of American college age players to win international championships these days. The U.S. team finished with a Silver Medal in the Goodwill Games (losing to the Soviet Union and Yugoslavia along the way) and took the Bronze at the World Basketball Championships in Argentina (again losing to the Yugoslavs).

"As long as it says USA, we'll never be able to say, 'No, we aren't the favorite'," Krzyzewski said.

Despite seeing his American college age team not come away with the Gold Medal in either of the two tournaments over the summer, Krzyzewski still believes that college players should represent the United States instead of an all-NBA team. "It adds to the interest level of international competition," he told Michael Wilbon of *The Washington Post*. "That it's not Michael Jordan and those guys kicking butt. You don't know how it's going to turn out. They're kids. I don't know if that's all bad. It's not all bad for me.

"One of the great joys we have is seeing kids going to the World University Games, to the Jones Cup, and represent the U.S. They come back much better players and it's a great educational experience for them. If we lose, does that make it a bad experience? We have to look at the big picture. . ."

He has shown the ability to adapt his team and strategy to varying situations. Krzyzewski has perfected a system in which individual talents blossom but not at the expense of the team.

"Krzyzewski teams frustrate those who like defined, position basketball. His philosophy involves a motion offense that stresses freedom and a tenacious man-to-man defense that is almost a misnomer because it is played with such togetherness," wrote Sally Jenkins of *The Washington Post*.

"Our lineups are so funny sometimes," Krzyzewski told Jenkins. "People ask me who plays what. I'm like, 'I don't know, do they seem to care?' I don't know who the hell my four man is, or my three or my two. It's like, if you grow a plant in a jar, it will take on the shape of the jar, but if you just let it grow, who knows what can happen?"

His touch is everywhere in the Duke program. Krzyzewski oversees recruiting, knows what his players are doing in the classroom and leaves nothing to chance.

"We see him as someone we'd want the kids to spend as much time around as possible," said Duke President Keith Brodie. "At some programs they want to protect the kids from the coach. Not here."

Although he is criticized by some for taking his teams to four Final Fours so far without winning the national championship, there is no doubt that Krzyzewski deserves to be ranked among the elite coaches in the country. At this time, we can't think of anyone who is any better.

★ PLAYERS NOT RETURNING ★

ALAA ABDELNABY (6-10, C, 15.1 ppg, 6.6 rpg, 27 assists, 48 blocked shots, 26 steals) After three seasons of what could charitably be described as inconsistent play, Abdelnaby finished with a bang his senior year at Duke. As opposed to past years when Abdelnaby had his finest outings early in the season against weaker competition, he got stronger as the season progressed in 1989-90. His best all-around game of the season had to have been in Duke's 79-78 overtime victory over Connecticut in the finals of the East Region of the NCAA tournament. He scored 27 points and pulled down a season-high 14 rebounds. Abdelnaby led the Blue Devils in both categories that day and his play on the offensive and defensive ends vaulted Duke into its third consecutive Final Four and fourth in the last five years.

He was a third-team All-ACC selection last year and his 62 percent field goal shooting placed him second overall in the conference. Abdelnaby finished among the ACC's Top 20 players in scoring (15th), rebounding (12th), blocks (4th) and free throw percentage (8th) in addition to his fine field goal shooting. He may very well may have been the ACC's most improved player in 1989-90. This improvement resulted in Abdelnaby being selected in the first round of the NBA draft by the Portland Trail Blazers, an accomplishment that was unthinkable prior to late in his senior year.

Entering his senior season, Abdelnaby was often overlooked when senior leadership of the 1989-90 Blue Devils was discussed. He was upset and decided to do something to change his status. ''When you come to Duke, there's a progression, so that when you reach your last year, you're supposed to be a player that the younger guys can look up to. But I wasn't in that position,'' Abdelnaby said. ''Then I thought that this was the last year I was going to be able to play here and I wanted to make it worth something.''

His quest to have a major impact in his last college season led Abdelnaby to bulk up during the off-season and become a more serious and responsible individual. The increased strength allowed him to bang inside effectively and his off the court attitude made him a leader to the younger players.

It took awhile but Abdelnaby finally begin to live up to the high expectations he created as a high school star in New Jersey. He was truly a force late last season and Duke will miss Abdelnaby greatly in the upcoming year.

ROBERT BRICKEY (6-5, F, 11.7 ppg, 5.4 rpg, 60 assists, 27 blocked shots, 34 steals) The captain of the 1989-90 Blue Devil squad excited fans in Durham and throughout the rest of the ACC with his athleticism and incredibly quick and destructive dunking style. His leadership last year was outstanding, even though he was relegated to doing some of it from the sidelines rather on the floor. Brickey missed eight games last year due to a knee injury suffered in Duke's first conference game against Virginia. He recovered physically to the point where he was an effective presence on the floor for the second half of Duke's season, but it never seemed like Brickey fully regained his all-out, hell-bent style of play. He looked tentative on the offensive end, at times reluctant to take his explosive first step to the basket. His stamina was never quite the same after his injury, either, as he would need breathers often during games and he found it difficult to spring above the pack for rebounds off of the offensive and defensive boards.

Brickey was the type of player Duke usually does not normally have in its lineup: An incredible athlete whose game is not well-refined but who can change the flow with a dunk or a blocked shot. His big play ability will be missed.

JOE COOK (6-2, G, 1.9 ppg, 0.3 rpg, 11 assists, 1 blocked shots, 4 steals) Cook did not get the chance to play much during his career at Duke. He played only 73 minutes for an average of 4.1 minutes per game last year. He was beset by academic difficulties and decided to drop out of Duke before his senior year. Cook will not be allowed to reapply for admission this fall and his career at Duke now appears to be over.

PHIL HENDERSON (6-4, G, 18.5 ppg, 3.8 rpg, 85 assists, 5 blocked shots, 56 steals) Henderson finished his career at Duke with a steady, often spectacular senior season in which he was the team's leading scorer. He was a second-team All-ACC selection last year and his impressive statistics placed him among the conference's Top 10 in scoring (sixth), free throw percentage (tied for first), and three-point field goal percentage (third). Henderson started all 37 games he played in last year, missing only a mid-season game against East Carolina due to an injury. As the season progressed, Henderson became Duke's best scorer in critical game-deciding situations. He often would take matters into his own hands when Duke needed a big basket to either maintain a lead or launch a comeback. Many of his team-leading 79 three-pointers were important and he was one of the nation's best at canning the high pressure long range jumpshot. He was a second round selection of the Dallas Mavericks.

Henderson was definitely on his game in post-season. He averaged 24 point per game in Duke's two ACC tournament games and assumed more of a leadership role as he took the entire team to task with a scathing commentary on the Blue Devils' lethargic play in a team meeting following the semifinal loss to Georgia Tech. He then went on to average 21.7 ppg during Duke's run to the national championship game.

It would seem that Krzyzewski would have difficulty replacing Henderson, but he has found ways to replace big scorers in the past. Johnny Dawkins, Mark Alarie and Danny Ferry have all come and gone through the Duke program, but the Blue Devils have remained a constant presence among the elite programs in the nation.

★ RETURNING PLAYERS ★

CLAY BUCKLEY (6-10, 235 lbs., SR, F/C, #45, 1.8 ppg, 1.2 rpg, 2 assists, 2 blocked shots, 5 steals, Conestoga HS/Berwyn, Pa.) A co-captain as one of only two seniors on this year's team, Buckley will be looked to for both leadership and, even more importantly, increased responsibility on the floor for the '90-91 Blue Devils. Buckley played in 17 games last year, contributing a total of 113 minutes. With the departure of Abdelnaby up front, Buckley will be called upon often to assist Christian Laettner on the inside. He is an intelligent player who will not make spectacular plays but will certainly be effective for up to 18 minutes per game as an aggressive rebounder and tough interior defender. His father, Jay Buckley, was an All-ACC performer for the Blue Devils' Final Four teams in '63 and '64.

He played important minutes for Duke in last year's NCAA tournament third round game against UCLA. Early in the second half, with Duke struggling and

Laettner and Abdelnaby on the bench in deep foul trouble, Buckley checked in and played several minutes of solid basketball. He was not intimidated and he allowed Krzyzewski the luxury of sitting his two big men without losing ground to the Bruins.

Buckley readily admits that he came to Duke as a freshman ill-prepared for his role as he possessed solid perimeter skills but was not comfortable with the rough and tumble world of the low post. As a result, Buckley had to learn then, and is really still learning now, the true basics of post play, from drop steps to hook shots on offense and from proper positioning to rebounding and fighting through screens on defense.

''For me, I really have to concentrate on the little things,'' said Buckley. He has worked, learned and gained the admiration of Krzyzewski. As a result, with Abdelnaby graduated and Duke lacking a player 6-10 or taller to complement Laettner and share some of the rebounding load, Buckley may very well be Krzyzewski's man for that role.

''That position just really has to rebound and play defense and learn how to screen, and when the ball is there to not just score, but get fouled,'' said Krzyzewski. ''It could be a very simple role, a great role, but a simple role. Clay has knowledge. Clay is one of our smarter players. A big guy can't just be smart, he's got to be tenacious. It's just too tough on the boards in our league. Being smart only gets you so far.''

After three years watching and learning from the bench, Buckley should be able to bring the needed tenacity to his game to allow him quality minutes as a power forward and center for Duke this season.

BRIAN DAVIS (6-6, 195 lbs., JR, G/F, #23, 5.0 ppg, 2.2 rpg, 28 assists, 25 steals, Bladensburg HS/Bladensburg, Md.) As a sophomore last season, Davis developed into a solid reserve for Duke as both his offense and defense improved steadily throughout the year. He played in 37 of the team's 38 games, missing only the second game of the season against Canisius due to an injury. He more than doubled his offensive output from his freshman year and his shooting percentage showed marked improvement (.477 in '89-90 as opposed to .385 in '88-89). Davis had six games during the season in which he scored in double figures, the most impressive of which came in a mid-season win at home against Georgia Tech as he contributed 16 points and made key plays both offensively and defensively in Duke's 88-86 win. Coming off a freshman year in which Davis showed flashes of brilliance but just as many flashes of undisciplined, irresponsible play, last season's performance was a pleasant sight.

Davis came to Duke with a reputation for strong, tough defensive play, so to see that part of his game flourish is really not a major surprise. He moves his feet well on defense and he understands where he should be on the floor as he attempts to shut down big scorers at both the small forward and off-guard positions. His versatility makes him an even more valuable commodity, as he has the quickness to play in the backcourt and the size and strength to handle the inside game. His rebounding is outstanding as he is the type of player who is impossible to keep off the boards and who always seems to outwork others to get in perfect position for a rebound.

Last year Davis' offensive skills came to the forefront which allowed him more minutes as the season progressed. He proved that he could bury the 15-18 foot jumpshot, and he also showed a quick first step on drives to the basket. His athleticism allows him to score against bigger people once he gets into the lane. The only real question mark for Davis offensively is the range on his jumper as he did not attempt a three-point shot all season. That should change this season as Davis will see more playing time in the backcourt and he will shoot the ball with confidence from the perimeter. Krzyzewski no longer has qualms about using Davis in the backcourt as last year he showed much improved ballhandling skills. In his freshman year, Davis was second in the ACC in the negative category of turnovers versus minutes played. He averaged a turnover every 8.45 minutes of playing time. Last year, Davis improved to the point where he was committing a turnover every 14.75 minutes he played. This new found ability to handle the ball responsibly and with poise makes Davis that much more beneficial to the Blue Devils. This year Davis will be a major cog in the Duke machine and Krzyzewski will give him every opportunity to become a starter at either the small forward or wing guard position.

THOMAS HILL (6-4, 195 lbs., SO, G/F, #12, 3.4 ppg, 2.2 rpg, 25 assists, 24 steals, Lancaster HS/Lancaster, Tex.) Hill had an excellent freshman season at Duke. The left-handed shooter showed that he could bury the outside shot as he connected on close to 52 percent of his field goal attempts. He also hit 43 percent from three-point range, but that was based on a limited sample of only seven attempts. Still, he showed that he can score at the major college level and with his incredible physical attributes, he should do nothing but improve this season.

Hill has been described as someone who plays hard all the time and has a complete repertoire of aggressive moves to the basket. Add to this mix the fact that he is also an outstanding shooter with a delicate touch and you have quite an offensive talent. Hill also has a knack for playing especially tough perimeter defense. Hill has often been compared in this regard to Robert Brickey and Billy King, two strong former Blue Devil defenders, but Hill's offensive talents make him a superior player to the one-dimensional King and the somewhat unrefined Brickey.

Hill also has an affinity for rebounding, particularly on the offensive boards. He is intense, quick, smart and blessed with great leaping ability, all of which add up to a strong rebounder. The last of these traits, leaping ability, probably was inherited from his father, Tommy Hill, who won a Bronze Medal in the 110-meter hurdles at the 1972 Summer Olympics in Munich, West Germany. (His father is the academic coordinator for the Oklahoma Athletic Department.) The younger

Hill's vertical leap is close to 40 inches. Hill, who played in 34 games last year for Duke and saw substantial time off the bench throughout the season and in the NCAA tournament, grew up quickly and this year he will be expected to compete along with Brian Davis for minutes at both the wing guard and small forward positions. Krzyzewski has a lot of faith in Hill and loves his on-court discipline and understanding of the game. •

"He's a very versatile defender, and he will do anything to win," said Krzyzewski. "He can handle the ball. He can shoot well. He's a very well-rounded player."

Once again, Duke has tremendous versatility due to players like Hill. With his man-to-man defensive skills, a must in Krzyzewski's system, and his potentially big time offensive skills, the sky is truly the limit for Thomas Hill at Duke.

BOBBY HURLEY (6-0, 160 lbs., SO, G, #11, 8.8 ppg, 1.8 rpg, 288 assists, 1 blocked shot, 67 steals, St. Anthony's HS/Jersey City, N.J.) What more can be said about Hurley as he is coming off one of the best freshmen years any point guard has ever had in ACC history. He came to Duke and was immediately given the ballhandling responsibilities as the Blue Devils' starting point guard. He started every game for Duke last season and his 1,268 minutes played (33.4 per game) led the team by a considerable amount. His 288 assists were by far a Duke single-season record and also a league high, and his average of 7.6 assists per game placed him third in the ACC behind freshman sensation Kenny Anderson of Georgia Tech and steady Chris Corchiani of North Carolina State. Hurley finished second to Anderson for ACC Rookie of the Year honors, and he was the catalyst for Duke both offensively and defensively all year long. He not only handled the intense pressure of playing point guards Anderson, Corchiani, John Crotty of Virginia and the other point guards of the ACC all season long, but he also single-handedly broke the full court pressure that Connecticut and Arkansas threw at Duke last year in the NCAA tournament. Nothing seemed to phase Hurley and even though he looks like he's still in high school, his game is major college all the way. As St. John's assistant coach Brian Mahoney said, "Hurley looks like an altar boy, but he's a tough son of a gun."

Krzyzewski had confidence in Hurley's ability to run the club right from the start of last season, and as the season progressed, Hurley's freshman status really didn't mean much. "I think I've shown Bobby as much confidence as any freshman who has ever played for me," Krzyzewski said. "And it deserves that. He earned that. And he's not a freshman anymore, anyway."

His defensive skills are excellent and Hurley rarely, if ever, gets beaten one-on-one off the dribble by another guard. His ballhandling and decision-making are impeccable and he is completely unselfish.

The only part of Hurley's game which was lacking last year was his outside shooting. While he knocked down important shots during the year in crucial games against Michigan, Georgia Tech, St. John's and UCLA, to name a few, his shooting percentage overall was a poor 35.1 percent. He does have good range on his jumper, but it almost seemed like last year he was so concerned with distributing the basketball that he was hesitant to shoot even when being given the shot by the defense. Hurley needs to develop a more selfish attitude at times and take his shots without concerning himself with whether or not someone else should have the ball. He can be a good shooter who can score 12 to 14 points per game and still make the right decisions and distribute seven to eight assists per game. Barring injury, Hurley will be on the court virtually every minute of every game.

He spent much of the summer practicing with the U.S. National team, coached by Krzyzewski, which played in the Goodwill Games. Hurley was cut from the team before it left for the World Basketball Championship in Buenos Aires, Argentina. However, the experience was beneficial for him as he faced the likes of Kenny Anderson, Arkansas' Lee Mayberry, Connecticut's Chris Smith, and other great players every day in practice.

GREG KOUBEK (6-6, 205 lbs., SR, F, #22, 4.7 ppg, 2.4 rpg, 18 assists, 3 blocked shots, 19 steals, Shenedehowa HS/Clifton Park, N.J.) Last season was one which started out with great promise for Koubek. With Brickey and Henderson already slated in as starters at forward and guard, respectively, Koubek was a key reserve off the bench who could play more than adequately at both positions. He had gained experience over his previous two seasons (playing considerable minutes on two Final Four participants), and it was believed that the shooting woes that had plagued him during his apprenticeship would no longer exist as his offensive role was expanded. Unfortunately for Koubek, the season turned out to be a disappointing one for the hard working junior. His outside shot again was erratic and he looked uncomfortable handling the ball. His expected top reserve role was diminished as sophomore Brian Davis and freshmen Thomas Hill and Bill McCaffrey earned some of Koubek's playing time. As the season wound down, he would often see action only after those three had already made their appearances.

The highlight of Koubek's season came in a win at Georgia Tech when he contributed 16 points and nine rebounds off the bench. He cannot sustain this type of production, however, and his output was minimal in Duke's charge in the NCAA tournament. Koubek's shortcomings, which have hindered his development in his three years at Duke, were painfully evident in the Blue Devils' 103-73 loss to UNLV in the national championship game. He was inserted into the game in the first half as the wheels were beginning to fall off for Duke. Koubek was responsible for inbounding the ball against the full court UNLV pressure as Hurley and Laettner were sitting with early foul trouble. Koubek could not get the ball in bounds and he panicked a couple of times and either threw passes away or directly to UNLV players which led to easy baskets. He looked like a freshman who hadn't played all year and was

unsure of what he was supposed to be doing. Koubek's experience was not in evidence at that point and his role on this year's team is very much uncertain. Koubek is a senior co-captain and should be a starter based on seniority, but he needs to have a big senior surge much like Abdelnaby gave Duke last year.

Koubek, through good times and bad, has always given his all and is an enthusiastic player. He has developed into a good rebounder and physical defender who will continue to be given every chance by Krzyzewski to move into an expanded role on the floor.

CHRISTIAN LAETTNER (6-11, 235 lbs., JR, F/C, #32, 16.3 ppg, 9.6 rpg, 84 assists, 41 blocked shots, 59 steals, The Nichols School/Angola, N.Y.) Laettner was Duke's most valuable player last year as he came out from behind the shadow of Danny Ferry and emerged as one of the premier players in America. Laettner was 10th in the ACC in scoring, third in rebounding, seventh in steals, eighth in blocked shots, tenth in field goal percentage and first in free throw percentage. He was a second-team All-ACC selection and may have had the most complete season of any player in the league. He started all 38 games for Duke and played an average of 30 minutes per contest. With all of the minutes that he played and the physical nature of playing on the inside, one would think that Laettner would have probably been somewhat limited in games due to foul trouble. However, he played strong defense in the paint against opponent's best big people and fouled out of only four games all year long.

After the departure of Ferry, Laettner was called upon to be the main man in the middle for Duke. He certainly fulfilled those expectations as the Blue Devils won 29 games and finished second in the nation with Laettner and Abdelnaby carrying the load inside. Laettner was voted the MVP of the NCAA East Region. He also made one of the biggest shots in the history of the Duke basketball program. With Duke trailing Connecticut by one point in overtime, with 2.6 seconds left on the clock, Laettner inbounded the ball and got it right back for a medium range shot which he nailed and Duke was on the way to Denver for its fourth Final Four appearance in the last five years. He also played a key role in Duke's win over Georgetown in the finals of the East Region the previous year when he dominated the Hoyas' Alonzo Mourning.

Laettner did appear extremely fatigued late in the year. He twisted a knee in a game at Maryland and although he did not miss any action, the injury did seem to slow him down. He had single digit scoring performances against Wake Forest (four points), North Carolina State (six points) and Arizona (eight points). His shooting appeared laborious and his defense was not at its normally intense level. Laettner may have been run down, but he came back strong for post-season play.

He played over the summer for Krzyzewski's U.S. National team which took the Silver Medal in the Goodwill Games in Seattle and a Bronze at the World Basketball Championships in Buenos Aires, Argentina. This season Laettner will be Duke's lone experienced big man and he will be called upon to score more, rebound at least as well and play the strong Duke defense. Even though Laettner had a season worthy of All-America consideration last year, he cannot rest on his laurels and must dominate both ends of the floor game after game for Duke to be in the running for another Final Four appearance.

BILL McCAFFREY (6-3, 175 lbs., SO, G, #5, 6.6 ppg, 0.7 rpg, 34 assists, 1 blocked shot, 25 steals, Central Catholic HS/Allentown, Pa.) McCaffrey played in all 38 games for Duke and averaged 13.9 minutes per game. He played both backcourt spots, although his time at the point was limited due to the fact that Bobby Hurley did not miss much action. McCaffrey came to Duke with the label of a long range bomber with excellent ballhandling ability. His shooting was not as consistent as expected as McCaffrey nailed 45 percent of his field goal attempts and was only 8-of-25 (32 percent) from three-point range. His form is good and he has a quick release, but McCaffrey's confidence wavered.

He can get his shot off over the athletic guards of the ACC and is a good leaper and shoots well off the dribble. Last year he shot the ball with apprehension, a common freshman problem, but that should change. McCaffrey is also a solid defender and will be an even stronger defensive presence as he builds up his lanky frame. He has quick feet and hands and his 25 steals last year came in limited playing time. Krzyzewski is impressed with McCaffrey's defensive instincts.

His brother plays football at Stanford and is an All-America caliber wide receiver. With the departure of Phil Henderson, McCaffrey should be in line for more playing time. He is a more refined perimeter player at this point than Thomas Hill or Brian Davis, although McCaffrey is not as explosive athletically or as versatile as those two.

CRAWFORD PALMER (6-9, 235 lbs., JR, C, #34, 1.5 ppg, 2.2 rpg, 1 assist, 6 blocked shots, 4 steals, Washington & Lee HS/Alexandria, Va.) Palmer's playing time increased from 119 minutes his freshman year to 143 minutes last year. Still, he was a bit performer, appearing in 21 games and generally not in key situations. However, this year Palmer will compete with senior Clay Buckley for minutes at the post position alongside Christian Laettner.

Palmer is a decent athlete whose offensive moves in the paint are fast developing to match his strong defensive play. The summer after his freshman season, Palmer spent six weeks in Russia as part of a foreign study program. He did not play much basketball and as a result was not improved. His lack of development was annoying to Krzyzewski, who would have liked Palmer to have worked harder on his game while on the trip.

His brother, Walter, recently graduated from Dartmouth and was a second round choice of the Utah Jazz. While Crawford was more highly touted coming out of high school than Walter, he is also three inches shorter.

Palmer has been plagued by foul trouble and had almost as many personal fouls (23) as points (31) last season. He plays hard but does not always wisely use his aggressiveness. He is very strong and sturdy and could develop into a tough inside presence. Laettner cannot be Duke's sole, consistent inside presence this year and either Palmer or senior Clay Buckley have to come through if Duke is to retain its recent level of success.

★ NEWCOMERS ★

CHRISTIAN AST (6-8, 205 lbs., FR, F, #54, 25.6 ppg, 12.7 rpg, Heidelberg, Germany & High Point HS/Beltsville, Md.) Ast came to America as a German exchange student and became a highly recruited player who many experts thought might fit well into the Duke system. He was an All-Metro player in the Washington area last year. Ast has a strong knowledge of the game and understands the importance of positioning on both the offensive and defensive boards, plus the defensive end of the court. He has soft hands and could develop into a good scorer at the ACC level.

Ast will be given the opportunity to contribute as a freshman as he is one of Duke's larger frontcourt players. He will probably be called upon to contribute at the power forward on occasion, and he will be looked to for rebounding and tough defense. His offense will begin to develop as he gets the opportunity in the future to play some at the small forward position, but with his size and nose for the boards, he may be more comfortable back at power forward early on.

The talent just keeps rolling into Duke year after year.

KENNY BLAKENEY (6-4, 190 lbs., FR, G, −4, 17.5 ppg, 5.6 rpg, DeMatha HS/Hyattsville, Md.) Blakeney is just the latest in a long line of high school All-Americas to play for legendary coach Morgan Wooten at DeMatha. DeMatha is also the alma mater of former Duke All-America Danny Ferry.

A powerfully built, explosive slashing scorer, Blakeney was used on both the perimeter and inside by Wooten at DeMatha. He could regularly outpower high school guards because of his great strength. He was ranked as the No. 34 player in the nation prior to his senior season by *All-Star Sports* and No. 98 at the conclusion of the season.

Although talented and physically mature enough to play immediately in the ACC, Blakeney will have quite a bit of competition for playing time. Sophomores Bill McCaffrey and Thomas Hill, plus junior Brian Davis all are more experienced than Blakeney and in the running for playing time at second guard. There is a possibility that he could be a redshirt candidate.

MARTY CLARK (6-6, 200 lbs., FR, G, #3, 18.0 ppg, 7.0 rpg, St. Joseph's HS/Westchester, Ill.) Clark moved from Denver to the Chicago area for his senior year and attended St. Joseph's HS, the alma mater of Detroit Piston star Isiah Thomas. Clark will be wearing Phil Henderson's uniform number and could step in and help fill the void left on the perimeter with Henderson's departure.

Clark comes to Duke with the reputation as an excellent outside shooter with outstanding range. However, he is not blessed with outstanding quickness and that could hinder his development in Duke's man-to-man defensive scheme.

As is the case with fellow freshman Kenny Blakeney, Clark will be competing with an outstanding group of players for playing time at the wing position. His size and shooting ability could make him attractive to Krzyzewski but he will have to grasp the defensive responsibilities quickly in order to see significant playing time. Look for Clark to be a limited factor as a freshman.

GRANT HILL (6-7, 205 lbs., FR, F/G, #33, 29.0 ppg, 11.0 rpg, South Lakes HS/Reston, Va.) Hill was signed during the early signing period last November and he is unquestionably the jewel of another outstanding Duke recruiting class. The son of former NFL star running back Calvin Hill, he was definitely one of the Top 10 high school players in the nation last year. He played all over the floor for South Lakes and could be almost as versatile during his career at Duke.

"Grant Hill is a youngster in a man's body. The South Lakes basketball standout has been talked about on television, written about in newspapers and basketball publications . . . with ballhandling skills that defy and disguise a soft and accurate perimeter shot, Hill has become king of the hill in the northern region (of Virginia)," wrote Bobby Kaplow in *The Washington Post*.

Hill's skills are refined enough for him to be effective immediately in the ACC as a freshman. He is also an outstanding competitor and an excellent rebounder. He shoots the ball very well out to 18 feet and his range should expand in college.

"Hill is a remarkably mature young man, a fact that shows in his game as well as his conversation," wrote Michael Gee in *The Boston Herald*.

Hill wouldn't mind seeing time in the backcourt for Duke and he is versatile enough to play there.

"Grant Hill is another player whose best attribute is his versatility. It's hard to stop the 6-7 forward from Reston, Va., South Lakes because he can handle the ball and hit the three-pointers as well as take it to the hoop and dunk," wrote Barry Tempkin in *Basketball Weekly*.

With spots in the starting lineup open at the wing guard and small forward positions, Hill should be able to claim one. He should be the latest in a string of Duke freshmen who have started and played very well as freshmen.

TONY LANG (6-8, 185 lbs., FR, F, #21, 21.5 ppg, 5.5 rpg, 3.0 apg, LeFlore HS/Mobile, Ala.) Lang was Duke's last signee as he committed to the Blue Devils during the spring recruiting period. He was ranked as the 14th best prospect in the country by *All-Star Sports*. He is an excellent perimeter shooter who made 60.9 percent of his field goal attempts last year.

"Tony is a youngster who is at the highest level both academically and athletically," said Krzyzewski. "We feel very fortunate to get a youngster like Tony. He fits in perfectly with our style of play and he definitely fits in well academically."

He was the valedictorian of his high school class with 4.38 grade point average on a 5.0 scale while taking a full course load of honor classes.

Lang began playing organized basketball at the age of five. He had an incredible growth spurt as a youngster as he grew from 5-11 to 6-8 between the seventh and ninth grades. Due to the unnatural growth, Lang suffered from Osgood Schlater's disease, a condition that causes a great deal of pain in the knee. Because of this pain, which still exists for Lang, he continues to wear knee pads. His doctors also believe that Lang will most likely still grow and that he will level off at 6-10 or possibly 6-11. With that kind of size to go along with his uncanny finesse skills he already possesses, Lang could be an All-America candidate down the line.

He led his LeFlore HS team to a 31-1 record in an Alabama Class 6A state title as a junior. LeFlore was 27-6 in his senior year.

"Not a flashy performer, Lang's style is quite excellent . . . he is very accomplished in the fundamentals, and is a prototypical team player. Lang is a dead-eye marksman with three-point range, and a superlative defender," wrote Bob Gibbons of *All-Star Sports*.

Duke's ability to sign Lang demonstrates just how strong the Blue Devils' program has become. Five years ago Duke could not have gone into a deep southern town such as Mobile, Ala., and signed a player the caliber of Lang. Lang and Grant Hill also offer the best combination of basketball skills and athlete ability anyone Duke has signed in the 6-7 to 6-8 range in the Krzyzewski era. Lang should be an immediate factor for Duke even though he could use more strength and there is going to be a great deal of competition for playing time at his position.

★ QUESTIONS ★

Finding a complement for Laettner down low? Duke will sorely miss Alaa Abdelnaby's presence inside this year. If someone from the group consisting of Clay Buckley, Crawford Palmer or even freshman Christian Ast do not emerge, Laettner could be worn out late in the year from the defensive attention given to him and the enormity of his load.

Replacing the clutch perimeter shooting of Phil Henderson?

★ STRENGTHS ★

Coach K! No coach in the nation is better than Krzyzewski.

Laettner and Hurley! Laettner and Hurley give the Blue Devils a solid one-two, inside-outside combination. Those two were outstanding last year and they look to be getting even stronger and more consistent. Laettner is one of the Top 10 players in the country and Hurley is a capable point guard.

The homecourt edge in Cameron Indoor Stadium! Duke has amassed an impressive 68-6 record in the friendly, claustrophobic confines of Cameron over the past five years. The Blue Devils only loss last year was to archrival North Carolina in the last regular season game. Basketball is a game which is almost larger than life on Duke's campus, and the intelligent and innovative student body does not even attempt to be good hosts to opposing teams visiting Cameron.

Another strong freshman class! Five outstanding freshmen will be on the Duke campus this fall. Grant Hill and Tony Lang are two of the most refined, intelligent players to ever sign with Duke. Christian Ast, Marty Clark and Kenny Blakeney are also talented and could have outstanding careers at Duke.

★ BLUE RIBBON ANALYSIS ★

Duke coach Mike Krzyzewski just does not seem to understand what the word "rebuild" means. The Blue Devils do not rebuild, Krzyzewski just digs into his bench or uses a touted freshman, fills in a gap and has another Final Four team.

This year Krzyzewski is excited about the Blue Devils but he also has his usual questions.

"I think we'll have a team that will move up and down the court even quicker than last year," Krzyzewski predicts. "We have a number of perimeter people and will be perimeter strong. But are we so strong that we play four perimeter players with Christian (Laettner) or do we play with Christian and another big guy?"

The lofty accomplishment of Duke teams over the last five years (four of which were Final Four teams) aren't fair to hang on the heads of this year's edition. However, as a result of an outstanding recruiting class and the return of some experienced players, expectations will again be high. Another 25-win season will be a minimum achievement.

"It's probably the least mature team age-wise since I've had since 1983," said Krzyzewski. "We have kids who all can play. It's just a matter of how old they are. We actually start out with a younger team, but we have more anchors than a year ago. Both Bobby Hurley and Christian Laettner come back in their same roles this season, where last year we didn't know where everyone was in the beginning."

Krzyzewski will have to find some players to surround Hurley and Laettner. Krzyzewski has been able to successfully replace key players time and time again, but he might have more trouble replacing Alaa Abdelnaby inside than he had finding replacements for such stars as Johnny Dawkins and Danny Ferry. This is not to suggest that Abdelnaby was better than Dawkins or Ferry, but the players in line to inherit Abdelnaby's position are limited.

Duke's freshman class was outstanding again. Rated by all recruiting experts as one of the top ten in the nation. Freshman swingman Grant Hill was one of the Top 10 high school players in the country last year and freshman Tony Lang has tremendous potential.

Duke is versatile with many players who can play several positions and the Blue Devils should be strong defensively. Duke will easily win 20-plus games for the eighth consecutive year under Krzyzewski. Duke will battle North Carolina and Virginia for the ACC title. If Duke gets suitable perimeter play to replace Phil Henderson, a capable inside presence to offset some of the load on Laettner and if Hill or Lang are as good as advertised, Duke could make a fourth consecutive Final Four appearance.

LAST SEASON			
Harvard	130-54	East Carolina	84-51
Canisius	102-66	Wake Forest	71-56
@Northwestern	103-77	@North Carolina State	71-76
#Syracuse	76-78	Arizona	78-76
@Michigan	108-113 OT	@Clemson	93-97
@Davidson	89-44	North Carolina	75-87
Washington	74-64	*Maryland	104-84
##Drake	101-77	*Georgia Tech	72-83
##Cincinnati	95-83	**Richmond	81-46
##Hawaii	87-75	**St. John's	76-72
The Citadel	108-69	***UCLA	90-81
Virginia	76-68	***Connecticut	79-78 OT
@Georgia Tech	96-91	****Arkansas	97-83
Maryland	91-80	****UNLV	73-103
@North Carolina	60-79		
@Wake Forest	97-69	@ Road Games	
@William & Mary	109-76	# ACC/Big East Challenge, Greensboro, NC	
North Carolina State	85-82 OT	## Rainbow Classic, Honolulu, HI	
Georgia Tech	88-86	### Orlando, FL	
Clemson	94-80	* ACC Tournament, Charlotte, NC	
Notre Dame	88-76	** NCAA Tournament, Atlanta, GA	
@Virginia	69-72	*** NCAA Tournament, East Rutherford, NJ	
@Maryland	114-111 OT	**** Final Four, Denver, CO	
###Stetson	102-67		

NOTES: In a recent article in *USA Today*, NBC's Al McGuire rated Durham as his favorite college town. ''You can go ten miles outside of town and be in a bar that serves pickled eggs and pigs' feet . . . it's hard to avoid talking basketball when in Durham. Everyone in the town is aware of the

1990-91 DUKE SCHEDULE				
Nov.	14	#Marquette	Feb.	16 @Wake Forest
	26	East Carolina		20 North Carolina State
Dec.	1	North Carolina Charlotte		24 @Arizona
				27 Clemson
	5	##@Georgetown	Mar.	3 @North Carolina
	8	Michigan		8-10 *ACC Tournament
	19	@Harvard		
	22	@Oklahoma	@ Road Games	
	29	Lehigh	# Dodge NIT. If Duke defeats Marquette, the Blue Devils will play a second round game on Nov. 16. The semifinals and finals of the tournament will be held on Nov. 21 & 23 at Madison Square Garden, New York, NY.	
Jan.	2	Boston University		
	5	@Virginia		
	9	Georgia Tech		
	12	@Maryland		
	14	Wake Forest		
	16	@The Citadel	## ACC/Big East Challenge	
	19	North Carolina	* Charlotte, NC	
	23	@North Carolina State		
	26	@Clemson		
	30	@Georgia Tech		
Feb.	2	@Notre Dame		
	7	Virginia		
	9	Maryland		
	10	LSU		
	13	Davidson		

game. Everyone is geared up, it's a way of life there,'' said McGuire . . . ''Duke recruit Grant Hill is the best all-around player coming out of high school,'' said Dick Vitale.

GEORGIA TECH

LAST SEASON: 28-7
CONFERENCE RECORD: 8-6
STARTERS LOST: 3
STARTERS RETURNING: 2
CONFERENCE: ATLANTIC COAST (ACC)
LOCATION: ATLANTA, GA
HOME FLOOR: ALEXANDER MEMORIAL COLISEUM (9,800)
NICKNAMES: RAMBLING WRECK & YELLOW JACKETS
COLORS: OLD GOLD AND WHITE

★ COACH'S PROFILE ★

BOBBY CREMINS (Record at Georgia Tech, 181-99. Career record, 281-167.) The simple fact that best sums up Bobby Cremins' impact on the Georgia Tech

basketball program is in the Institute's entire history, only seven of its teams have been invited to the NCAA tournament. Cremins has coached six of them.

In his nine years at Georgia Tech, Cremins has had five All-America players, 11 All-ACC performers and six ACC-Rookie of the Year picks. At least five of Cremins' former Georgia Tech players will play in the NBA this year, including three first round draft choices.

Last season was Cremins most successful and satisfying to date during his tenure at Georgia Tech. Not only was it Cremins' first Final Four team, but it was a team that had succeeded pre-season expectations. Heading into the season, Georgia Tech supposedly had a suspect inside game, star forward Dennis Scott was coming off an average sophomore season in which he became a one-dimensional three-point shooter with a significant weight problem and the Yellow Jackets would have to depend on a freshman point guard named Kenny Anderson to become a major dominating force from Day One. Well, all the possible problems were solved early on —the inside game was creditable, Scott lost 25 pounds in the off-season and became one of the most dynamic offensive players in the nation and Anderson quickly established himself as arguably the finest point guard in the country. Georgia Tech roared off to a 10-0 start and climbed as high as sixth in the national polls. The Yellow Jackets were 13-0 in non-conference play and defeated the champions of the Metro Conference (Louisville), the SEC (Georgia) and the Atlantic 10 (Temple). Georgia Tech finished tied for third in the ACC and had an 8-1 record against Top 20 opponents. Cremins guided the Yellow Jackets to their second ever ACC tournament crown. In the NCAA tournament, Georgia Tech blew out a good East Tennessee State team, came back from a sizable deficit to defeat an inspired LSU and hung tough in victories over Big Ten powers Michigan State and Minnesota to earn a trip to the Final Four in Denver. While Georgia Tech was knocked out in the semifinals of the Final Four by eventual national champion UNLV, the Yellow Jackets lost by only nine points (two days later UNLV defeated Tech's ACC rival Duke, by 30 points in the largest margin of victory in the history of the NCAA championship game). A most telling statistic of the 1989-90 season was the fact that through Georgia Tech's first 34 games, its largest margin defeat was only five points.

The silver-haired 43-year-old Cremins wears his success well. He is popular not only with his players and the Georgia Tech fans but is even well liked by the media. He is an affable New York Irishman who is accessible to all. He also has recently developed a sense of perspective concerning the whirlwind merry-go-round of big time college basketball. A part of the perspective was based on the fact that his 1986 team was expected to contend for a national championship but lost in Atlanta in the region semifinals and he lost some of the luster from his glowing reputation as the hottest of the hot young coaches. Over the next three years, the Georgia Tech program slipped a bit on the national level. The Yellow Jackets lost three years in a row in the first round of the ACC tournament and twice Tech was knocked out in the first round of the NCAA tournament. Then last fall his father died and his obsession with winning the national championship waned.

"I saw a lot of great coaches who'd been to the Final Four, or football coaches who'd won national championships, getting left by the wayside," he said in Denver during the Final Four. "In a few weeks, I'll be having a gin and tonic in some lonely place and all this may feel important to me. Right now, it's not.

"It's scary. You get caught up in this rat race, you're going to get burned."

Cremins grew up as somewhat of a street urchin in a tough section of the Bronx in a poor Irish family. He was a gang member as a kid and a very indifferent student. However, he was an outstanding basketball player at All Hollows and that proved to be a saving grace. He had to prep for a year at Frederick Military Academy in Virginia before taking the underground railroad that legendary coach Frank McGuire had established from New York City to South Carolina. Cremins is still close to McGuire and brought him to the Final Four.

"The first time my father met coach McGuire, he said, 'You're going to South Carolina with that Irishman whether you like it or not.'

"Without Frank McGuire, I'd be nothing. I'd be in New York City somewhere, hopefully working."

He was a three-year starter at point guard at South Carolina. The plucky Cremins helped lead some of South Carolina's most successful teams. Cremins and All-America John Roache teamed to give the Gamecocks a potent backcourt. In Cremins' senior year, South Carolina was 14-0 in regular season ACC play and finished the year 25-3. Unfortunately, this was back when the NCAA tournament was smaller in size and only the conference champions were given bids. The ACC tournament champion was the only team from the conference to advance into the NCAAs. In the ACC tournament championship game that year, Cremins missed a key free throw in the final minute that would have given South Carolina the title. The Gamecocks went on to lose the game and Cremins was so distraught that he went and hid out in a cabin in the mountains of North Carolina for a week. It literally took years for Cremins to come to grips with that defeat.

After graduating from South Carolina, Cremins spent one year playing professional basketball in Ecuador before beginning his collegiate coaching career as an assistant at Point Park College in Pittsburgh in 1971. He returned to his alma mater as an assistant to McGuire in 1972.

In 1975 Cremins was chosen as the head coach at Appalachian State. At the time the 27-year-old Cremins was the youngest Division I head coach in the country. His first team at Appalachian State was 13-14 but after that Cremins posted a five-year record of 87-56, a 60 percent winning mark, while capturing three Southern Conference titles. His 1978-79 team was 23-6 and in his last year at Appalachian State, 1980-81, Cremins put the Mountaineers in the NCAA tournament.

He is the only current ACC coach to have played and coached in an ACC tournament championship game. He definitely can be considered a "players' coach" and few can personalize the recruiting process like Cremins. When he hones in on a prospect, Cremins almost becomes like an older brother to the recruit. His genuine, personal touch is reflected in all aspects of the Tech program.

By all criteria, Cremins has done everything that could have been expected and much more in his first nine years at Georgia Tech. He's made Georgia Tech an attractive place for the best prospects in the country, produced winning teams and has done it with style.

★ PLAYERS NOT RETURNING ★

KARL BROWN (6-2, G, 3.8 ppg, 1.9 rpg, 108 assists, 2 blocked shots, 40 steals) Brown was a key figure off the bench for Georgia Tech's 28-7 team a year ago. He was the third guard in Cremins' backcourt rotation. While Brown was not a flashy player or a big scorer, he passed the ball well, pushed it up the court on the break and was one of the better defensive guards in the country. Brown was able to take some of the pressure off starting guards Kenny Anderson and Brian Oliver. Brown's athletic ability and defensive prowess so impressed Denver Broncos'

coach Dan Reeves that he brought Brown in for a free agent tryout last spring. However, Brown decided to return to his native England and play professional basketball instead of going to the Broncos' training camp.

JOHNNY McNEIL (6-9, C, 5.8 ppg, 5.3 rpg, 25 assists, 15 blocked shots, 20 steals) McNeil was Georgia Tech's starting center last year. While not a great player, McNeil and freshman forward Malcolm Mackey combined to give Tech a capable inside game, certainly one that was much better than Cremins expected at the beginning of the season. Like fellow senior Karl Brown, McNeil was a strong defender. He played good post defense on many big name centers last year. He also chipped in some rebounding, was able to convert the shots that were given to him and rebounded.

He certainly played his role well but Georgia Tech is expected to be better at center this year with the arrival of 7-0 junior Matt Geiger, a transfer from Auburn.

BRIAN OLIVER (6-4, G, 21.3 ppg, 6.0 rpg, 111 assists, 5 blocked shots, 28 steals) A second round choice of the Philadelphia 76ers, Oliver was only the third player in ACC history to score 1,500 points, grab 500 rebounds and pass out 500 assists in a career. He was the MVP of the ACC tournament last year.

Oliver was an integral part of Georgia Tech's Lethal Weapon 3 perimeter attack along with Dennis Scott and Kenny Anderson. That potent triumvirate was the only threesome in the ACC history to each average 20 points a game or better over the course of an entire season.

Oliver was a player who wasn't great in any facet of the game, but was sound in all areas. He played both backcourt spots during his career at Georgia Tech, was a decent outside shooter, could score inside and rebounded well for a guard. He was a consistent, tough player who managed to perform despite a stress fracture in his leg which left him severely hobbled late in the season. Georgia Tech is going to dearly miss Oliver. There is no doubt that whoever replaces Oliver in the lineup, there will be a big drop off at that spot for the Yellow Jackets.

DENNIS SCOTT (6-8, F, 27.7 ppg, 6.6 rpg, 71 assists, 30 blocked shots, 62 steals) What a difference a year and 25 lost pounds made. Before Kenny Anderson arrived, Dennis Scott was the most highly regarded player Cremins had recruited to Georgia Tech. He had a good freshman year, but his sophomore year was disappointing despite a 20.3 average. He weighed close to 250 pounds as a sophomore and seemed obsessed with the three-point line. Scott did little that year other than hoist three-pointers and his overall game suffered greatly. In the off-season, he decided to shed the weight. The result was a terrific season and Scott was propelled back into the national limelight.

He was named national player of the year by *The Sporting News* and made four different first-team All-America squads. He was the ACC player of the year as well. Scott led Georgia Tech in scoring and shattered a 28-year-old ACC single-season scoring record. He made 137 three-point field goals (.414). He scored 42 points against Pitt, 37 in a home blowout of North Carolina, 36 in four different games and 40 in Georgia Tech's win over Minnesota in the finals of the Southeast Region. In all, Scott scored 30 or more points in 17 games.

Scott's junior season was so spectacular that he decided to pass up his final year of eligibility and enter the NBA draft. The Orlando Magic made the Scott the fourth overall pick in the draft and signed him for a five-year contract reportedly worth more than $12 million.

Georgia Tech's sophomore Kenny Anderson may well be the best player in the country, but without Oliver and Scott around, there is no way Georgia Tech can be as explosive and successful this year.

★ RETURNING PLAYERS ★

KENNY ANDERSON (6-2, 166 lbs., FR, G, -12, 20.6 ppg, 5.5 rpg, 285 assists, 3 blocked shots, 79 steals, Archbishop Molloy HS/Rego Park, N.Y.) Since freshman eligibility was reinstated in 1972 most of the highly regarded freshmen in both major college basketball and football haven't lived up to their advance billing. The transition from high school superstar to freshman superstar at the major college level is too tough for all but the truly elite to make. Kenny Anderson's first year was one of the greatest any freshman major college basketball or football player has had since freshman eligibility was reinstated in 1972.

Anderson came out of Archbishop Molloy HS billed as the greatest guard to ever come out of New York City. Anderson lived up to every word of his advance billing. He not only stepped in and became Georgia Tech's starting point guard from Day One, but he was also the sixth Yellow Jacket in the last eight years to be honored as ACC Rookie of the Year. He was named national freshman of the year by *UPI*, *Basketball Times*, the U.S. Basketball Writers Association, and *Scripps-Howard News Service*. Anderson was a first-team All-ACC pick. He was only the second freshman in ACC history to achieve the honor. He also was made second-team All-America by the National Association of Basketball Coaches and the *Sporting News*, and third-team by *Associated Press* and *UPI*.

Anderson led the ACC in assists average (8.1 apg) and ranked fourth in the nation. His 285 assists were an ACC record for a freshman, and the third-best single season mark in conference history. He also ranked fifth in the ACC in scoring and set a conference record for scoring by a freshman, totaling 721 points and bettering Mark Price's mark of 568 in 1982-83. Anderson ranked ninth in the ACC in field goal percentage at .515 and second in steals (2.2 stpg). His 79 steals established a Georgia Tech record. His 32-point, 18-assist, 12-rebound performance, against Pitt in the finals of the Kuppenheimer Classic in Atlanta, was only the triple-double in ACC history.

Cremins called Anderson, "one of the most exciting basketball players I've seen in my lifetime."

"He is fantastic," said former Soviet National coach Alexander Gomelsky. "I don't now, maybe he doesn't sleep all night, practicing his dribbling."

Anderson was so spectacular as a freshman that many experts who have viewed the game for decades believe he is the greatest freshman guard to ever play the game. "Everybody knows I've said Anderson is the best freshman guard to play college basketball in the last 50 years," said Marty Blake, the NBA Director of Scouting.

Anderson was a legend in high school at Archbishop Molloy in Queens, N.Y. He was the MVP of the state Catholic School tournament as a freshman, established a new scoring record in New York state and was the only player to ever to make first-team All-New York City for four years. Cremins saw Anderson play at least 40 times before he was even allowed to talk to him due to NCAA rules. Cremins even gave Molloy student manager Giuseppe Liantonio a full manager's scholarship at Georgia Tech. Anderson became sold on the fact that he could start immediately in Cremins' system. He also felt more comfortable with Cremins than the other head coaches who were recruiting him.

Anderson failed to score in double figures only twice and had 18 games over 20 points. He turned in a 29-point, 12-assist performance in a road win over Louisville, making all four of his three-point attempts. He was honored as the ACC Rookie of the Week a record of 10 times in 13 weeks. He also became the first ACC player ever to win the league's player and rookie of the week honors in the same week.

Anderson is the most spectacular and gifted ballhandler in the college game today. The basketball is literally an extension of his hand and he has supreme confidence leading the fast break or penetrating in traffic. Anderson can shake any defender at any time and get to wherever he wants on the court. Only some of the true greats of the game such as Bob Cousy, Pete Maravich, Magic Johnson and a few, rare others, have been blessed with his ability to see the court, find an opening and deliver the ball. Anderson's rare ballhandling gifts are magnified because he is also a proficient scorer. Defenders have to respect his offense but at the same time worry about Anderson's penetration and ability to deliver the ball. He is truly an indefensible player.

Anderson played during the summer for the U.S. National team which won the Silver Medal in the Goodwill Games in Seattle and the Bronze at the World Basketball Championships in Yugoslavia. While many of his teammates were hampered by the physical nature and different style of the international game, Anderson still excelled.

"Kenny's one of the best in the college game," said Cremins. "Some of the challenges he has is to try to keep going. But he has proved himself as one of the premier guards in the country . . . I think he needs to get stronger and keep working on defense and moving a little better without the ball. I'm real excited to be able to coach a Kenny Anderson-type player."

The rumor mill is running rampant concerning whether Anderson will go pro after his sophomore season. Reportedly, the Georgia Tech coaches are recruiting point guards this year with the pitch that Anderson is leaving and there will be a vacancy at the position for the 1991-92 season. A comment Anderson made to *Sports Illustrated* last February reveals why we think Anderson will be headed to the NBA after this season.

"I didn't come from an estate," he said. "I wasn't born with a gold spoon in my mouth. If they offer me a lot of money, I definitely would jump on it."

DARRYL BARNES (6-8, 202 lbs., SO, F, #15, 1.5 ppg, 1.4 rpg, 1 assist, 19 blocked shots, 1 steal, Franklin K. Lane HS/Brooklyn, N.Y.) Georgia Tech did not have a deep bench last year, particularly up front, but Barnes was not able to contribute as much as expected. He averaged just eight minutes per game and a mere 1.5 points and 1.4 rebounds. Barnes is extremely gifted physically with superb leaping ability and timing as a shotblocker, he had 12 blocks last year, but his offensive ability is limited to dunks, put-backs off the offensive boards, and shots just a few feet from the rim. The fact that Barnes had just one assist last year indicates that he needs to become a more skilled and versatile player and not just a great athlete.

"Darryl Barnes had a rough year," said Cremins. "He's got to come back and improve himself. He has the ability. He's a great kid. He's got to learn the game a little bit. I can't expect him to be a factor right now, but I'd love for him to be a factor.

"I think the key to Darryl is working hard this summer. We definitely need him. He's just really raw. He needs to play a lot this summer. Darryl Barnes is the type of kid I'd like to coach year round, but I can only coach him from October 15 to the end of the season. We've got to get him in good playing situations during the summertime."

Barnes grew up in Hazelhurst, Miss., and moved to Brooklyn, N.Y., for his final two years in high school. He was a second-team *Parade Magazine* All-America pick and once blocked 17 shots in a high school game.

If Barnes would develop a more diversified game and become a bigger factor this year, it would help Georgia Tech immensely.

BRIAN DOMALIK (5-11, 164 lbs., SR, G, #3, 0.9 ppg, 0.3 rpg, 4 assists, 1 steal, Flint Hill HS/Leesburg, Va.) Domalik has lettered in each of his two years at Georgia Tech after transferring from Augusta College (Ga.). He was a close friend and teammate of Dennis Scott at Flint Hill HS in the northern Virginia suburbs of Washington, and his relationship with Scott played a role in Domalik's decision to transfer to Georgia Tech.

He has been a limited contributor, playing just 44 and 55 minutes, respec-

tively, in each of the past two seasons. He has good shooting ability from the perimeter although he has not shot the ball well — .250 from the field and .333 from three-point range last season —in his two years at Georgia Tech.

Domalik can push the ball up the floor but needs to become better defensively in order to see more playing time. Domalik is an extremely hard worker and could be more of a factor this year as a backup point guard in relief of Kenny Anderson.

MALCOLM MACKEY (6-10, 243 lbs., SO, F, #32, 7.2 ppg, 7.5 rpg, 16 assists, 41 blocked shots, 13 steals, Brainerd HS/Chattanooga, Tenn.) While Georgia Tech's Lethal Weapon 3 received all of the media attention last year, the role of freshman Malcolm Mackey in the Yellow Jackets' Final Four season went largely unnoticed. He stepped into the starting lineup and became a solid rebounder, he led Georgia Tech in rebounding and was the fourth leading scorer on the team. He also led Georgia Tech in blocked shots.

"Mackey's got to mature more," said Cremins. "I thought he had an excellent freshman year on the court. He's got to get more serious about his game. He'll have the opportunity. He has a lot of talent. He could be a very, very good basketball player. I expect him to have a good summer and come in and control one of the starting positions. He's got to get a little better offensively with his shooting. He's just got to work harder overall. He could be a very fine player."

Mackey made .559 of his field goal attempts but was only 26-of-59 (.441) from the line. He is strong, runs the court well, and averaged 24 minutes per game last year. Mackey ranked sixth in the ACC in rebounding. He had a season-high of 15 points and 17 rebounds against Marist and tied the school freshman mark for rebounds in that game. He also had 17 rebounds in a home loss to Duke, and reached double figures in rebounding five other times. One of Mackey's most impressive games was a nine-point, 14-rebound outing in Georgia Tech's comeback victory over LSU in the NCAA tournament.

Last year Mackey was successful as a role player. This year he will need to step up and be a double figure scorer and a consistent offensive threat if Georgia Tech is to be able to offset the losses of Brian Oliver and Dennis Scott.

JAMES MUNLYN (6-11, 228 lbs., SR, C, #24, 1.0 ppg, 1.5 rpg, 7 assists, 12 blocked shots, 5 steals, South Aiken HS/Aiken, S.C.) Munlyn started four games last year and played 178 minutes. His role was limited as graduated Johnny McNeil held down the center spot and Malcolm Mackey also saw considerable minutes up front. Munlyn began last year as a starter in the first four games and then came off the bench the rest of the season. He had a season-high of five points against Marist and grabbed a season-best five rebounds against Pitt. He just did not exhibit the aggressiveness and presence inside that Cremins had expected. He has been hampered by a lack of confidence and strength.

"There's an opportunity here for James," said Cremins. "He did not get a lot of playing time last year, but he is a good player. He needs to gain more confidence himself and we've got to have more confidence in him as a staff. He's really a fine person. He's exactly the kind of person we want at Georgia Tech. But he can't get down on himself if he doesn't get playing time right away. He's got to continue to work hard. But he has a chance to play."

Munlyn has some physical tools such as good quickness and agility and he runs well. He can score inside or shoot a jumper from the foul line area. Munlyn has also shown some shotblocking skills. However, he has never been a big factor at Georgia Tech. Munlyn started one game in his first two years in the program and averaged 2.9 points and 2.2 rebounds as a freshman and 2.6 points and 2.9 rebounds as a sophomore. He redshirted the 1988-89 season. Munlyn is one of four frontcourt players 6-9 or taller Cremins can call on.

GREG WHITE (6-2, 168 lbs., JR, G, #31, 0.7 ppg, 0.4 rpg, 1 assist, Norcross HS/Norcross, Ga.) White was a walk-on in 1988 and also made the team last year. He played in 11 games as a freshman and nine as a sophomore. White is a good perimeter shooter who is not afraid to put the ball up. He wore No. 14 his first two years at Georgia Tech, but that number has gone to junior college transfer Jon Barry and White will wear No. 31 this season.

★ NEWCOMERS ★

ROD BALANIS (6-3, 192 lbs., FR, G, #34, 11.3 ppg, 4.4 rpg, 7.6 apg, DeMatha HS/Williamsburg, Va.) Balanis has not played organized basketball for two years. He finished high school in 1988 but did not enroll at Georgia Tech until September of 1989 after suffering injuries in a automobile accident. He then suffered a broken wrist last year and was redshirted. Balanis played his high school basketball at famed DeMatha HS in Hyattsville, Md. He was DeMatha's second leading scorer on a 30-3 team his senior year that was ranked No. 8 nationally by *USA Today*. He connected on 43.7 percent of his three-point field goals during his senior year and posted an 84.7 free throw percentage. His father, George Balanis, was the head basketball coach at William & Mary from 1974-76.

He is an excellent outside shooter who could be a contributor if he has fully recovered from his injuries and the two year layoff.

"Rod's a good player," said Cremins. "He could help us. He's an excellent shooter. He made a terrific comeback from his injuries. I'll be looking forward to seeing him at 100 percent."

JON BARRY (6-4, 175 lbs., JR, G, #14, 17.1 ppg, 3.6 rpg, 3.0 apg, 3.0 stpg, DeLaSalle HS/Oakland, Calif. & Paris JC/Paris, Tex.) Barry is the son of former NBA star and Hall of Famer, Rick Barry. His older brother, Scooter, played on Kansas' 1988 national championship team.

Barry is a shooting guard who played one year at Paris (Tex.) JC. He shot 53 percent from the field, 40 percent from three-point range, and 78 percent from the line while starting all 30 games for an 18-12 Paris team last year. He transferred to Paris from Pacific where he averaged 9.5 points per game with 108 assists and 39 steals as a freshman.

"Jon Barry's a good shooter and he's a tough kind. He knows the game and he has talent," Cremins said.

Barry is also considered a good defensive player. He is expected to compete for the starting off-guard spot with another junior college transfer, sophomore Bryan Hill.

BRIAN BLACK (6-1, 178 lbs., FR, G, #23, 6.5 ppg, 2.0 apg, Marietta HS/Marietta, Ga.) Black was a walk-on last year and redshirted after he hurt an ankle in preseason practice and underwent surgery. He has good range and accuracy on his shot. Black needs to work on his quickness and ballhandling. He was a 45 percent three-point field goal shooter in high school.

MATT GEIGER (7-0, 234 lbs., JR, F/C, #52, Countryside HS/Clearwater, Fla.) With the graduation of Brian Oliver, the early departure of Oliver Scott for the NBA and with Geiger being eligible after sitting out last season following his transfer from Auburn, Georgia Tech is expected to be a more inside-oriented team in 1990-91 after relying on a predominately perimeter attack last year.

Geiger averaged 15.9 points and 6.6 rebounds as a sophomore at Auburn. He started all 27 games as a sophomore. As a freshman, Geiger also earned his way into the starting lineup and averaged 6.4 points and 4.1 rebounds. He is a quality shooter with a hard to block turnaround jumper in the lane. Geiger also is a good passer and runs the court. He has improved defensively, especially as a shotblocker, since coming to college. Since enrolling at Auburn, Geiger has sprouted one inch and gained 35 pounds.

"Geiger has two years of Southeastern Conference ball under his belt," said Cremins. "I expect him to contribute like a very experienced player. I expect him to come in there and take control of one of the starting positions. He's got to do it. He'll be challenged, but with his experience and ability he should be a starter. He knows the game. He's an excellent scorer and rebounder. He could turn out to be a really fine player."

Geiger's career-high at Auburn was 30 points and he had seven 20-point games. He had five double figure rebounding games. Last May, he tried out for the U.S. National team, and was cut after the first round of tryouts in Colorado Spring, Colo. The experience was beneficial for Geiger and he held his own against outstanding competition.

Georgia Tech will need an outstanding year from Geiger. Kenny Anderson may be the best player in college basketball and sophomore Malcolm Mackey showed some potential as an inside scorer last year. However, Georgia Tech will need much more if the Yellow Jackets are to contend for the ACC title and high national honors. Geiger must be able to score enough to take some of the pressure off Anderson and help Mackey on the boards. We don't see how Georgia Tech can have a great season without a strong year from Geiger.

BRYAN HILL (6-4, 210 lbs., SO, G, #11, 10.5 ppg, 3.6 rpg, W.T. Woodson HS/Arlington, Va. & Chowan JC/Murfreesboro, N.C.) Hill will compete with fellow junior college transfer Jon Barry for the starting second guard spot. He committed to Maryland out of high school, but went to junior college instead and played one season at Chowan JC. He is the second player Cremins has recruited out of Chowan, the first being Johnny McNeil.

Hill made the switch from an inside player in high school to the backcourt in junior college very well. He played both guard spots and passed out 131 assists last year. Hill made 51 percent of his three-point field goal attempts. Hill is a physical wing player in the mold of former Georgia Tech standouts Bruce Dalrymple and Brian Oliver. His past experience and success as point guard will also give Cremins a possible substitute at that position for Kenny Anderson.

"Bryan Hill's got some talent. He's a good athlete and a tough kid," Cremins said.

Hill is a key player for Georgia Tech this season. Someone needs to emerge as a suitable complementary player for Anderson in the backcourt and Hill is the most likely candidate.

IVANO NEWBILL (6-9, 224 lbs., FR, F, #33, 13.0 ppg, 9.5 rpg, 2.0 apg, 3.4 stpg, Southwest HS/Macon, Ga.) Newbill was redshirted last year and was impressive in practice. Newbill has improved rapidly after first beginning to seriously play basketball at the age of 16. He has added weight and strength since enrolling at Georgia Tech and is expected to compete for the power forward position.

Newbill played only two years of high school basketball, but as a senior was named the player of the year in the state of Georgia by USA Today and the Atlanta Tip-Off Club, as well as the *Atlanta Journal-Constitution*. All Star Sports rated Newbill the nation's 56th best prospect.

"Newbill is someone I expect a lot from because he really came on after midseason," said Cremins. "He's a talented kid. I really think he could come in and take over a starting position. He's an excellent rebounder and a bright kid. He's tough. It will be interesting to see how he comes along. I really like him."

With the additions of Newbill and Auburn transfer Matt Geiger, Georgia Tech should be much stronger up front than last year's Final Four team.

★ QUESTIONS ★

Compensating for the enormous loss of Dennis Scott and Brian Oliver? Scott and Oliver averaged 27.7 and 21.3 points, respectively, last season.

Finding a guard to complement Kenny Anderson as a scoring threat?

Overall backcourt depth? Kenny Anderson is the only proven guard on the roster.

★ STRENGTHS ★

Kenny Anderson! He is not only the best point guard in the nation by far, but Anderson also is a strong candidate for national player of the year honors. Many experts thought last year that Anderson was the finest freshman point guard they had ever seen.

An improved inside game! Georgia Tech should be much stronger inside this year with the additions of Auburn transfer Matt Geiger and redshirt freshman Ivano Newbill.

Bobby Cremins! Last year was his finest coaching job at Georgia Tech. Cremins has a good feel for dealing with players individually and his teams seem to play hard and respond to him.

★ BLUE RIBBON ANALYSIS ★

Georgia Tech rode the backs of its Lethal Weapon 3 triumvirate of Brian Oliver, Dennis Scott and Kenny Anderson to a school record 28 victories and the program's first-ever Final Four appearance. Oliver, Scott and Anderson became the first threesome in ACC history to each average 20 points or better over the course of an entire season. This year, Georgia Tech coach Bobby Cremins will have to find an alternative to "Lethal Weapon 3" as Oliver and Scott have gone on to the NBA. In all, Georgia Tech has lost players who contributed 65.7 percent of its offense, participated in 63.1 percent of the minutes played, grabbed 59.6 percent of the rebounds, and contributed better than 50 percent of its assists.

"Overall, this will be a different team," Cremins said. "Last year we were a highly visible perimeter team. We lost three of those four perimeter players. The only one we have back is Kenny (Anderson). I really think, overall, we are going to be more of an inside team. We might go from a Lethal Weapon perimeter team to a team with three big guys."

Cremins will have to shuffle his starting lineup, but he won't lose a wink of sleep over his point guard play this year as Anderson heads into his sophomore year ranked as undoubtedly the finest player in the country at that position. He also may be the best player at any position in college basketball this year. Anderson shattered the ACC freshman scoring record (721 points) by more than 130 points last year, recorded the third-highest single season total of assists in conference history while also shooting 51.5 percent from the field and .733 from the line.

Expected to join Anderson in the starting lineup is sophomore power forward Malcolm Mackey who led the Yellow Jackets in rebounding last year and was fourth in scoring. Mackey also gave Tech a quality shotblocker unseen since the days of John Salley and he will share more of an offensive load this year plus get competition from redshirt sophomore Ivano Newbill, who was impressive in practice last season.

At center is expected to be Auburn transfer Matt Geiger, a good shooting big man who had two fine years at Auburn. Georgia Tech will have four players 6-9 or taller up front this year.

While Georgia Tech looks to be much improved on the front line, the Yellow Jackets will be untested on the perimeter except for Anderson. A pair of junior college transfers, 6-4 sophomore Bryan Hill and 6-4 junior Jon Barry, will be seeking Oliver's second guard slot. Hill is more physical and Barry is the younger son of Hall of Famer Rick Barry and an excellent perimeter shooter.

"I think this team is going to go through some tough times," Cremins said. "But we'd like to keep Georgia Tech going. We've got a good name. We had a great year last year. We'd like to keep a very competitive basketball program. We need great years from Newbill and Geiger. We need at least one of the two junior college players to come in and play well.

"We'll stick to our same style. This year will be another challenge. I'm into my tenth year and it's exciting. I'm really proud of the program we have here. I just want to keep it going."

Cremins will be able to keep it going at Georgia Tech. This should be Anderson's last year even though he's just a sophomore as all reports indicate he will head to the pros. Anderson, alone, is enough to keep Georgia Tech in the Top 20. He should be absolutely spectacular and dominant this year. If one of the junior college transfers emerge at point guard and Geiger is a capable center, Georgia Tech should be able to stay in the top four in the ACC. The Yellow Jackets are our pick for fourth in the ACC this year.

Georgia State	108-83	Clemson	85-69	
Richmond	87-74	*North Carolina State	76-67	
#Pitt	93-92	*Duke	83-72	
North Carolina A&T	101-87	*Virginia	70-61	
##Georgia	92-89	**East Tennessee State	99-83	
Coastal Carolina (SC)	109-82	**LSU	94-91	
###Morehead State	98-76	***Michigan State	81-80 OT	
###Pitt	111-92	***Minnesota	93-91	
Marist	86-77	****UNLV	81-90	
@Wake Forest	91-79			
Duke	91-96	@ Road Games		
North Carolina State	92-85	# ACC/Big East Challenge, Hartford, CT		
Temple	59-57			
@Virginia	79-81 OT	## The Omni, Atlanta, GA		
@Clemson	90-91	### Kuppenheimer Classic, Atlanta, GA		
@Duke	86-88			
North Carolina	102-75	#### Madison Square Garden, New York, NY		
@Maryland	90-84			
Wake Forest	79-70	* ACC Tournament, Charlotte, NC		
@Louisville	94-84			
Maryland	80-78	** NCAA Tournament, Knoxville, TN		
####Fordham	83-78			
@North Carolina State	95-92 2 OT	*** NCAA Tournament, New Orleans, LA		
Virginia	71-73			
@Notre Dame	88-80 OT	**** Final Four, Denver, CO		
@North Carolina	79-81			

NOTES: Georgia Tech will open in the Sugar Bowl Tournament with Tulane . . . Tech's game with Arizona in the Meadowlands on Feb. 17 will be the second annual ''Hoops for Help'' benefit game for the homeless. Each team will bring home $50,000 for homeless assistance in its respective areas. The remaining proceeds will be donated to the homeless in New York City and Newark, N.J. . . . . The schedule may be the most difficult

Nov.	24	Augusta College (GA)	Mar. 2	@Clemson
	27	Morgan State (MD)	8-10	**ACC Tournament
Dec.	1	@Richmond		
	5	#St. John's	@ Road Games	
	8	Fordham	# ACC/Big East Challenge, Landover, MD	
	15	@Temple	## The Omni, Atlanta, GA	
	19	##Georgia	### New Orleans, LA (Auburn, Tulane & Villanova)	
	22	##Loyola Marymount	* Meadowlands Arena, East Rutherford, New York, NJ	
	27-28	###Sugar Bowl Tournament	** Charlotte, NC	
Jan.	2	Howard University		
	6	Wake Forest		
	9	@Duke		
	13	@North Carolina State		
	19	Virginia		
	24	Clemson		
	27	@North Carolina		
	30	Duke		
Feb.	1	Maryland		
	3	North Carolina State		
	9	@Wake Forest		
	13	@Maryland		
	17	*Arizona		
	19	@Virginia		
	24	Louisville		
	28	North Carolina		

ever in Tech history. The Yellow Jackets could play as many as 16 of 27 regular season games against teams that appeared in last season's NCAA tournament . . . This year's Tech team is the most inexperienced in the Cremins' era as the returnees accounted for only 36.9 percent of the playing time last year and the vast majority of that came from Anderson and Mackey.

INDIANA

LAST SEASON: 18-11
CONFERENCE RECORD: 8-10
STARTERS LOST: 0
STARTERS RETURNING: 5
CONFERENCE: BIG TEN
LOCATION: BLOOMINGTON, IN
HOME FLOOR: ASSEMBLY HALL (17,357)
NICKNAME: HOOSIERS
COLORS: CREAM AND CRIMSON

★ COACH'S PROFILE ★

BOB KNIGHT (Record at Indiana, 430-148. Career record, 352-198.) When October 15 rolled around last year, one of the best college basketball recruiting classes in recent memory gathered at Assembly Hall in Bloomington, Ind., for the first session of pre-season practice. Five of the seven recruits were rated among the Top 75 high school players in the country. The freshmen believed they were there to lay waste to the Big Ten. Indiana coach Bob Knight immediately broke his squad into two teams, the returning veterans and the would-be world conquering freshman class. The two teams squared off on the court and Knight sat back and watched. As he had hoped, his disciplined veterans ran circles around the talented youngsters. When this sting operation was mercifully ended, the master had proved his point. It was time to stop reading the press clippings and play fundamental, team basketball, the Indiana way.

Knight begins his 20th season at Indiana and in his previous 19 years in Bloomington, there have been some tremendous successes as well as some memorable controversies. His accomplishments are almost too numerous to mention: Three NCAA championships ('76, '81 and '87), and without an injury to star Scott May, there could have been a fourth in '75), an NIT crown ('79), the inaugural Commissioner's Association title in '74, and Gold Medals in the '84 Summer Olympics and the '79 Pan American Games, nine shared or outright Big Ten titles and the all-time victory leader in Indiana and Big Ten history. When compared with other Big Ten coaches over the last 19 years, Knight's record at Indiana stands head and shoulders above all. He has produced more Big Ten championships, more NCAA and NIT appearances, more Big Ten MVPs, more first-team All-Americas, more first-team All-Academic All-Big Ten selections, more first-team academic All-Americas, more Top 10 season-ending rankings, more NBA first round draft choices and more second round choices as well. His Big Ten record of 235-95 is far and away better

than any conference coach. Knight is also among the youngest head coaches to have won 200, 300 and 400 games in his career. In achieving undefeated regular seasons in 1975 and '76, Indiana won an unbelievable 37 straight games overall. From 1973 through '76, Indiana won four consecutive Big Ten titles. The Hoosiers took back-to-back crowns in 1980 and '81, a seventh title in '83, an eighth in '87 and another in '89. Based on these accomplishments, one can make the claim that Knight is not only one of the premier coaches in the game right now, but of all-time.

Another important statistic that will support this claim is that no less than nine former Knight aides are currently head coaches in the collegiate ranks, not to mention countless players who are high school coaches and college assistants throughout the country. Knight has definitely set a phenomenal standard of excellence that never may be matched.

While his coaching reputation is unequalled, his off-the-court controversies are well known on an national and international level. One such international incident occurred in Puerto Rico during the 1979 Pan American games. During a team practice, Knight got into a shoving match with a local police officer trying to run the Americans out of the practice facility. Knight continued to coach the team, eventually to the Gold Medal, but was charged with assault, tried, convicted and sentenced to six months in jail in absentia. Puerto Rico proposed, but did not demand extradition. Indiana Governor Robert Orr was prepared to intervene on Knight's behalf if needed.

The most memorable Knight incident occurred during the first half of the Purdue game at Assembly Hall in February of 1985. Knight, near-volcanic with the inconsistent officiating during the game, tried to grab something on the Indiana bench to throw. Team physician Dr. Brad Bomba recalled, ''I grabbed everything I could . . . water bottles, towels, his clipboard . . . anything. The only thing I didn't grab was coach's seat.'' Knight flung his chair across the court and through the lane before it came to rest next to the photographers on the opposite side of the court. Ironically, it was the first game Knight wore his now-trademark red sweater. He has stated many times he had turned around looking to throw his sportscoat. It all seemed comical — another Knight blowup and the fans had become used to it; they had seen it all before but they had never seen chair throwing. But this incident was different. Knight came close to resigning his post soon after. He immediately recognized his error and was remorseful, but still was forced to serve a one-game suspension imposed by then Big Ten commissioner Wayne Duke. To this day, the seats on the Indiana bench are padlocked together. During the NCAA tournament in 1987, which Indiana eventually won, Indiana was fined $10,000 for Knight destroying a court side phone after receiving a technical foul for coming onto the court during a timeout.

Knight is an imposing public figure. He can be loud, animated and abrasive. Many revere him and his beliefs while an equal amount are outraged by his comments and actions. This past fall, at his annual standing room only address before the Indiana student body, he ridiculed a student for being grossly overweight and out of shape for his age. He further challenged this student to lose the weight and if he didn't have the will power, Knight and Indiana trainer Tim Garl would personally supervise his weight loss program. The student lost the weight and Knight had won over another critic.

A product of the midwest, Knight grew up in Orrville, Ohio. It was in this northeast Ohio community that he started as a high school basketball player. He was recruited by Fred Taylor at Ohio State and was part of one of the greatest recruiting classes ever. John Havlicek, Jerry Lucas and Mel Nowell were other members of that Ohio State class with Knight. Ohio State won Big Ten titles in 1960, '61 and '62 and took the NCAA tournament championship in 1960. Knight was a reserve on those Indiana teams. Ironically, he was a weak defender as a player, which is hard to imagine because he has put such a premium on defense as a coach.

Only Knight and North Carolina's Dean Smith have ever coached and played on NCAA championship teams.

After graduating from Ohio State, Knight was an assistant at Cuyahoga Falls (Ohio) HS for a season before enlisting in the Army. While in the Army he was assigned to assist coach Tates Locke at West Point. Locke moved from West Point to Miami of Ohio in 1965 and Knight succeeded him. The 24-year-old Knight, with no prior head coaching experience, led his first Army squad to an 18-8 record and a fourth-place finish in the NIT. His reputation quickly grew as he posted a 102-50 record in his six seasons at West Point. Ironically, Knight almost took the vacant head coaching position at Wisconsin before he was hired at Indiana. How different the history of Big Ten basketball would have been with Knight in Madison instead of Bloomington. In 1972, he assumed the head coaching duties at Indiana and the rest, as they say, is history.

''I don't think the presidents have ever gotten together and told the chemistry department what the hell to teach or how to lecture. I don't why they are any more qualified to tell the athletics department what the hell to do.

''Now, there are some things the presidents could do that would help kids. The seven o'clock (basketball) starting time would be one,'' Knight told United Press International.

Despite his vast accomplishments and the fact that Knight has run an honest program and seen to it that his players graduate, he was turned down three years ago when he first came up for election to the Basketball Hall of Fame. Since then, he has refused to let the Hall consider him for induction. Unlike its counterparts in other sports, basketball's Hall must ask the candidates permission before putting their names on the ballot.

''When a coach gets voted into the Hall of Fame, the honor really belongs to all those who played for him,'' said Knight. ''I don't like to see all of the great kids we've had throughout the years insulted.''

When Knight came to Indiana in 1972, he brought a brand of basketball not seen in the Big Ten for many years. He reintroduced defense to the Big Ten. The year before Knight arrived, Iowa had won the league scoring title averaging 100 points per game. The Big Ten scoring average was 86 points per contest at that time. The ball-you-man theory of defense had been around a long time, but it was Knight who made it an art form. Contest every pass, each shot with total man-to-man defense. His first Indiana teams were feared defensive units. In Knight's second year, Indiana placed third in the NCAA tournament and it was the only time a Knight-coached team has reached the Final Four and didn't win the national championship. He often tells his players, ''You get me to the Final Four and I'll do the rest.'' And who is to argue?

Probably Knight's greatest attribute is his ability to change and adapt to new strategy and thinking. Although man-to-man defense is his staple, zone defenses have been seen in the Indiana repertoire. Once, Knight opened a game with a 2-3 zone defense against his good friend, Digger Phelps of Notre Dame, causing Phelps to throw up his hands in amazement. Of course, Knight was sitting back with a grin on his face enjoying the confusion Phelps felt.

When Indiana was consistently getting beat by quicker, more athletic teams in the mid '70s, he decided to restructure his roster to include more superior athletes. To reach that goal, he had to tap into the junior college system, something he had never done. Two junior college transfers, Keith Smart and Dean Garrett, played key roles on Indiana's 1987 national championship team.

''Evaluating players is meaningless. This is not an individual game,'' he once said. ''It's what can we put together that can play well together as a team.''

Knight is still going strong and has not lost his zest for the game or strong competitive nature. His son, Pat, is a freshman basketball player at Indiana this year and Knight is expected to coach the Hoosiers at least through his son's career and possibly longer.

''If I live long enough, what happens next is I outlive my enemies. I'll be an elder statesman and everyone will like me. That's my next step,'' Knight said.

★ PLAYERS NOT RETURNING ★

JEFF OLIPHANT (6-5, G, 2.5 ppg, 0.8 rpg, 9 assists) Oliphant showed promise when he came to Bloomington from tiny Lyons & Marco HS in rural Indiana. He had great shooting range, fine court vision and was a good defender. He was the latest in a long line of small town Indiana kids who had come to Bloomington to find success.

Unfortunately, things didn't work out the way Oliphant and Knight had expected. Injuries to his right foot and left knee sidelined him for two years and when healthy, two pretty fair shooting guards, named Steve Alford and Jay Edwards, stood in his way. To his credit, Oliphant never gave up and was an inspiration to his younger teammates. His play will not be missed by this young team, but his leadership will.

MARK ROBINSON (6-5, F, 3.2 ppg, 2.1 rpg, 6 assists, 1 blocked shot, 17 steals) Rarely has an Indiana team not been adversely affected by the loss of its seniors. Robinson played in 21 games last season, starting five, but contributed little overall. He was a great athlete but never seemed to catch on to Knight's disciplined schemes. He was just average defensively and it is hard to be a key player at Indiana and not a strong part of the Hoosiers' defensive scheme. He followed former junior college teammate and ex-Hoosier Dean Garrett to Indiana. Robinson averaged 25.4 points and 11.4 rebounds during his last season at San Francisco City College and much was expected of him at Indiana, but his potential was not realized.

The loss of Robinson is not a strong barrier to success for this Indiana team.

★ RETURNING PLAYERS ★

ERIC ANDERSON (6-9, 223 lbs., JR, F, #32, 16.3 ppg, 7.0 rpg, 24 assists, 16 blocked shots, 10 steals, St. Francis DeSales HS/Chicago, Ill.) Anderson truly came into his own last year as a second-team All-Big Ten performer. He finished seventh in the Big Ten in rebounding, 12th in scoring and eighth field goal percentage (182-of-339, .537). He scored in double figures in 27 of 29 games last year and recorded seven double-doubles in scoring and rebounding. He was Indiana's only consistent inside threat as he shifted in between the forward and center positions in Knight's lineup. Anderson was relied upon to defend the opposition's low post threat, usually without much help, and more often than not beat his man. Against Purdue's Steve Scheffler, the Big Ten player of the year, he poured in a career-high 30 points and grabbed nine rebounds in an overtime loss. Also, Anderson had a career-high 16 rebounds against Iowa State's Victor Alexander in a Hoosier rout of the Cyclones. Although Anderson hasn't received the national recognition of his fellow classmates such as Georgetown's Alonzo Mourning, Duke's Christian Laettner and Syracuse's Billy Owens but Anderson has quietly developed into one of the better junior frontcourt players in the country.

Anderson is the top returning big man in the Big Ten now that Scheffler graduated. Michigan's Terry Mills and Loy Vaught have moved on and Michigan State's Ken Redfield and Richard Coffey of Minnesota are gone. Anderson will emerge as a dominant frontcourt player in the Big Ten. With expected improvement, he could also be an All-America candidate as well.

Anderson played on a severely bruised ankle towards the end of last season and was still a force. If anything, the loss of mobility caused by the ankle injury allowed him to showcase his fine outside shooting touch. Against California in the East Region of the NCAA tournament, Anderson was everywhere on the court. While the young Indiana guards were tentative and had trouble shooting over California's zone, Anderson took it upon himself to hit the long jumpers coming off screens, evoking memories of Hoosier great Steve Alford. He scored 20 points and grabbed eight rebounds with virtually no help. That same problem may continue to plague Anderson this year as well as there are no new additions to the Indiana frontcourt and he will be the player opponents key on game after game.

Anderson needs only 123 points to become the 27th player in Indiana's long and storied history to score 1,000 career points. When he's through, Anderson will go down as one of the great Hoosier forwards of all-time.

CALBERT CHEANEY (6-6, 200 lbs., SO, F/G, #40, 17.1 ppg, 4.6 rpg, 48 assists, 16 blocked shots, 24 steals, Harrison HS/Evansville, Ind.) Of the seven outstanding freshmen entering the Indiana program last year, the least was known about a skinny kid from Evansville named Calbert Cheaney. When last season was over, it was clear that Cheaney, a third-team All-Big Ten performer, was the standout of the class and is the most gifted player in the entire program. He started the first game of the year against Miami of Ohio and promptly led the Hoosiers in scoring with 20 points in the season-opening win. He never relinquished that starting role and was the only Hoosier to start all 29 games. Cheaney led Indiana in scoring 12 times and finished second to Ohio State's Jimmy Jackson as the Big Ten freshman of the year. Cheaney finished ninth in scoring in the Big Ten, fifth in field goal percentage (199-of-348, .572) and led Indiana in three-point field goals made (25) and shared team high honors in steals (24) and blocked shots (16). He nailed a season-high 32 points against eventual Big Ten champion Michigan State, on the road, which was the fourth highest output by an Indiana freshman in school history.

Cheaney, who is the only left-handed shooter ever to play for Knight at Indiana, is a smooth, athletic performer who can jump and run with the best. He is at his best shooting on the run and his size presents problems for smaller guards and forwards in the Big Ten. He would seem to have a starting role for the next three years. Simply, Knight needs Cheaney's scoring ability, confidence and leadership on the floor. Many times last season, the young Hoosiers, with the exception of Cheaney, were reluctant to take the open shot in favor of looking inside or continuing to work for an even better shot. What they often found, in many cases, was a bottled up Eric Anderson and no better shot from the perimeter. Cheaney has the confidence and ability to work for the open jumper and to create his own offense.

He tried out for the U.S. National team that participated in the Goodwill Games and World Basketball Championships over the summer but was cut early in the selection process. He started for the U.S. team that traveled to Uruguay over the summer and won the Junior Men's Championship of the Americas. The international experience should help Cheaney.

Cheaney has to continue to grow as a player and have a solid season if Indiana is to challenge for the Big Ten title.

GREG GRAHAM (6-4, 167 lbs., SO, G, #20, 9.7 ppg, 2.6 rpg, 59 assists, 13 blocked shots, 23 steals, Warren Central HS/Indianapolis, Ind.) Graham endured a rollercoaster ride of a freshman year. He began the year as a starter and played spectacularly in a win at home over Kent State. Against Kent, Graham hit on a season-high 24 points and led Indiana with six rebounds. This was only the second game of his college career. He also had 16 points in an early season win over Notre Dame. As December and January rolled on, however, Graham's shooting tailed off and his overall game slipped from its previous level. Thankfully, for Graham and the Hoosiers, his defensive intensity never waivered and that alone was enough to keep him in Knight's rotation. Through February, Graham regained his scoring touch and began to see increased playing time. He played in all 29 games for Indiana last season and started 16, the majority of his starts coming during the Big Ten stretch in late February and early March. He scored in double figures in 13 games last season and was second on the Indiana assist list with 59. Graham also finished sixth in the Big Ten in free throw percentage (91-of-117, .778).

Graham has unquestioned big time athlete ability. Whether he has the consistent outside jumper and the necessary intangibles to stay a starter in the talent rich Indiana backcourt remains to be seen. To his credit, Graham is an excellent defensive player who uses his superior athletic talent to his advantage. Knight has said that Cheaney and Greg Graham were the two best fundamental defensive players he has ever recruited to Indiana and that speaks volumes for their defensive prowess. It should then come as no surprise that of the seven incoming freshmen last year, Cheaney and Greg Graham saw the most playing time and had the most starts.

Graham attended Warren Central HS in Indianapolis, which has had a few other big name alumni, namely Jane Pauley, the noted television personality, and Jeff George, the former Illinois quarterback who was made the top choice in the 1990 NFL draft by the Indianapolis Colts.

The Indiana backcourt only gets deeper with the addition of phenom Damon Bailey and available playing time becomes more scarce. Graham's exceptional defense will get him playing time, but his scoring will have to improve if he is to retain his starting spot.

PAT GRAHAM (6-5, 200 lbs., SO, G, #33, 7.7 ppg, 1.6 rpg, 44 assists, 1 blocked shot, 14 steals, Floyd Central HS/Floyds Knobs, Ind.) While phenomenal long range shooting was his trademark in high school, inconsistency marked Pat Graham's freshman year at Indiana. The high points of his freshman season ranged from a season-high 23 points and five assists in a win over Iowa, a three-pointer with 18 seconds left, in the Hoosiers' second conquest of the Hawkeyes, and 21 points, including 9-of-9 free throw shooting in a loss to Minnesota. The low points were being used sparingly at several junctures throughout the season.

Defensively, Graham seemed a step slow at times and he also looked hesitant to pull the trigger on his shot. Whatever his inconsistency may stem from, several questions arise concerning Graham, the obvious being which Pat Graham will show up on October 15 —the aggressive, intelligent shooting guard or the deliberate, tentative player most saw last season?

Graham led Indiana in free throw shooting last season, hitting 67-of-80 for a .838 mark. He enters the year with a streak of 28 straight free throws (the Indiana record being 37 set by Keith Smart). From the floor, Graham shot at a .504 clip (67-of-133) and scored in double figures nine times last season.

During the summer, Graham played in the U.S. Olympic Festival in Minneapolis where he helped lead the South to the Gold Medal. Hopefully for Graham and the Hoosiers, this additional playing time will benefit him. No less than seven guards will be battling for playing time and Graham will need to develop consistency if he is to stay in the top playing rotation. One scenario may have Graham as the first player off the Indiana bench as an instant offense type. This may relieve any undue pressure from him and would allow him to flourish as a super sub like former Indiana sixth man John Laskowski, who was one of the best ever at Indiana coming off the bench.

LYNDON JONES (6-2, 195 lbs., SR, G, #4, 6.1 ppg, 1.7 rpg, 55 assists, 1 blocked shot, 10 steals, Marion HS/Marion, Ind.) There wasn't a bigger disappointment in the Big Ten last season than Lyndon Jones. After coming off a good sophomore season, Knight was counting on Jones to be the leader in the young Indiana backcourt. However, what Knight got was an unmotivated player who showed the freshmen guards how easy it was to get into Knight's doghouse. Two years ago on Indiana's Big Ten title team, Jones started 29 of 34 games, including 17 of 18 Big Ten games. He averaged 8.4 points and was third on the team in assists with 115. Last year, Jones only played in 22 of Indiana's 29 games, starting 12, and slumped to a 6.1 scoring average. Furthermore, his assists took a nosedive to 55. Jones did match his career-high of 21 points in a victory against Wisconsin and he tallied 20 points in a rousing come from behind win over Michigan before a national television audience, but his contributions were few and far between.

Jones is an enigma. With all the talent in the Indiana backcourt, it is easy to overlook him, but if his attitude and motivation return, Jones could easily be an All-Big Ten performer. It is hard to say how much he was affected by the loss of close friend and runningmate Jay Edwards as last season was the first time in eight years that Edwards wasn't at Jones' side. Jones is the lone senior on the

Indiana team and it still can be *his* team. The talent is there and he has shown it in the past, but whether it comes to the forefront remains to be seen. Knight may look to employ the three-guard offense once again this season and Jones could be a very important factor. Hopefully for Knight and the Hoosiers, now that Jones is completely out of Edwards' shadow, he will exhibit his own court savvy and leadership.

CHRIS LAWSON (6-9, 242 lbs., SO, C, #54, 3.6 ppg, 3.1 rpg, 15 assists, 7 blocked shots, 5 steals, Bloomington South HS/Bloomington, Ind.) Although a bulky center in the Kent Benson mode (complete with red hair), sophomore Chris Lawson made a large transition last season. In high school, Lawson was more of a perimeter player who excelled with an excellent outside shooting touch. He rarely camped out down low and played power basketball in high school. Last season, however, Lawson showed flashes of becoming an excellent low post player. He scored a season-high 20 points in a loss at Michigan on 7-of-9 shooting and 6-of-6 from the line. He had his best game of the year in an Indiana rout of Iowa State when he came off the bench to score 13 points and grab a season-high of 16 rebounds. Lawson also recorded 10 rebounds against Illinois and another eight against Minnesota. He came into his own late in the Big Ten season when he averaged 11 points per game during a stretch of four consecutive starts.

Lawson will be a very important player in Knight's frontcourt rotation and looks to possibly start in the pivot. By all accounts, Lawson had a solid rookie campaign, but much more will be needed to take the heat off Eric Anderson. Lawson must continue to develop his low post game in order to create a secondary low post offensive threat to Anderson. Also, Knight expects superior defensive play and rebounding from the pivot and Lawson will start if he can approach Knight's lofty expectations. The pivot position is not strong in the Big Ten this year and Lawson could mature into one of the better players at that spot in the conference.

TODD LEARY (6-5, 175 lbs., SO, G, #30, 2.3 ppg, 0.6 rpg, 24 assists, 5 steals, Lawrence North HS/Indianapolis, Ind.) Leary typifies the typical Indiana high school player: excellent shooter, with good court vision and basketball intelligence plus a strong will to compete. It didn't matter that he was the last recruit in Indiana's heralded incoming class, or that it was speculated he was only given a scholarship to help lure high school teammate Eric Montross to Bloomington (he went to North Carolina instead). Leary's scholarship only came open when Jay Edwards decided to turn pro early. That didn't matter to Leary as he was an Indiana Hoosier, proud of it and came to school ready to prove that he belonged.

Leary is an excellent shooter who saw action in 22 games last season, starting two, both of which were Indiana victories. He came off the bench to pour in a career-high 14 points in a comeback win at Iowa and he also had personal bests of three rebounds and 3 three-pointers in that game. Leary also scored six points and dished out a season-high five assists in his first collegiate start against Texas A&M. For the year, he made 17-of-49 field goals (.347) and 8-of-27 three-pointers (.296). From the line, Leary was 9-of-13 (.692).

He will be a role player again for Indiana and can provide some instant offense off the bench or defensive help from the backcourt.

JAMAL MEEKS (6-0, 192 lbs., JR, G, #23, 4.0 ppg, 2.3 rpg, 106 assists, 1 blocked shot, 11 steals, Freeport HS/Freeport, Ill.) Jamal Meeks has become a Knight favorite. The two-year letterman is an excellent ballhandler who possesses exceptional quickness and leaping ability. He is a solid defensive player who rarely makes mistakes. Meeks became a starter towards the end of last season and led Indiana with 106 assists. He scored a career-high of 16 points in a crucial late season win over Ohio State, hitting 4-of-5 from the field and 8-of-8 from the line. That win helped to lock up an NCAA tournament bid for Indiana. Meeks averaged 13.3 points in his last three regular season starts and handed out 47 assists while committing just 13 turnovers in his last eight regular season games. With the descent of Lyndon Jones on the Indiana depth chart, Meeks has capitalized and is the starting point guard heading into fall practice.

He is not a consistent scorer, but on any Indiana team the point guard doesn't have to be. That's where the Grahams, Jones, Leary or freshman Damon Bailey will have to step forward. Knight is looking for continued solid play and leadership from the point guard slot and Meeks should fill that bill. The Indiana backcourt was the source of many of the Hoosiers' problems last year and if Meeks can offer solid play and leadership from the beginning of the year, Indiana should be much stronger overall.

MATT NOVER (6-8, 226 lbs., SO, F, #24, 5.3 ppg, 3.4 rpg, 13 assists, 12 blocked shots, 6 steals, Chesterton HS/Chesterton, Ind.) Nover has added over 15 pounds of muscle since he came to Bloomington and is becoming a true factor in the low post for Indiana. He is an excellent rebounder with great leaping ability. Nover led Indiana in rebounding five times last year. Unfortunately, Nover was a step slow at times and often got into foul trouble. He fouled out of four games last year and was used in many situations to save fouls on Anderson and Lawson. He did start 14 games, including the final six games of the season. Nover is a good shooter as is evidenced by his .527 percent (48-of-91) field goal mark. He tossed in a season-high of 16 points in Indiana's NCAA tournament clinching win over Ohio State. He also had seven rebounds and three steals in that game.

Nover will be an important figure in Knight's frontcourt rotation. He is one of only three experienced frontcourt players (Anderson and Lawson being the others) on the Indiana roster. Freshman forward Pat Knight is the only other true frontcourt player on the team. The Hoosier frontcourt is slim which makes it imperative that Nover play up to his ability without getting into foul problems. He is a complementary player with a good future at Indiana.

CHRIS REYNOLDS (6-1, 179 lbs., SO, G, #21, 3.2 ppg, 1.7 rpg, 54 assists, 2 blocked shots, 24 steals, Peoria Central HS/Peoria, Ill.) Reynolds was one of the more highly regarded members of Indiana's freshman class last year. He ended up starting 12 games as a freshman. He has excellent quickness and is generally considered Indiana's best defensive guard. Knight often compares Reynolds to former Hoosier great Quinn Buckner. That's very high praise considering Buckner is one of Knight's all-time favorite players.

Reynolds shared the team lead with 24 steals while only averaging 15 minutes per game. He led Indiana to a win over Notre Dame with season-highs of 14 points, seven assists and five steals while playing all 40 minutes.

Knight will have a hard time keeping his best defensive guard on the bench. However, Reynolds is not as capable a shooter as either Pat or Greg Graham and rates behind Jamal Meeks as a floor general. Reynolds is very important, though, due to his quickness and defensive tenacity. In Indiana's comeback win over Michigan at Assembly Hall last January, it was Reynolds who keyed the Hoosier charge with his stifling defense on Michigan's All-America Rumeal Robinson. He was so intense and played so hard that Reynolds practically collapsed in Knight's arms as he came to the sidelines for instruction during a break in the action.

Even though none of the three are great scorers, Indiana could be strong at point guard this year with Reynolds, Meeks and Jones. All three have shown the ability to be prime time Big Ten guards.

★ NEWCOMERS ★

DAMON BAILEY (6-3, 193 lbs., FR, G, #22, 31.4 ppg, 9.4 rpg, 6.8 apg, Bedford-North Lawrence HS/Heltonville, Ind.) You never know how a newcomer will adjust to the rigors of college basketball. The Big Ten can be an especially difficult proving ground for new players. However, nothing that happens in the future can detract from the storybook career Damon Bailey enjoyed in high school. He is already one of the most recognized players in the history of Indiana basketball. His high school accomplishments rank him right up there with the likes of Oscar Robertson, George McGinnis, Rick Mount, Steve Alford, Larry Bird and the many greats who have proceeded through the ranks of Indiana high school basketball.

Bailey was selected as the high school player of the year by *USA Today*, the Naismith Foundation and Gatorade. He was named the Indiana high school player of the decade, Indiana's 1990 Mr. Basketball, and is the only four-time, first-team all-state selection in the illustrious history of Indiana high school basketball. He topped off his Chip Hilton-like career by taking Bedford-North Lawrence HS to the Indiana state title in front of a crowd of over 42,000 in the Hoosier Dome in Indianapolis last March.

Bailey has been in the national spotlight since John Feinstein mentioned him in his best seller *The Season on the Brink*. In that book, Knight was quoted as saying that Bailey was better as a freshman high school guard than any guard on his 1986 team. The following year *Sports Illustrated* brought him to New York for a photo session and honored Bailey as the best ninth grader in the country. It is no wonder that Bailey was a must recruit for Knight. He verbally committed to Indiana over two years ago and basically never seriously considered another school.

"What Bailey lacks in athletic ability, he makes up for with brains," said recruiting expert Rick Bolus. "The best part of his game is his passing. He makes other players around him better . . . he's a fundamentally sound player who does the little things it takes to beat you."

Bailey finished his career as Indiana's all-time leading high school scorer with 3,134 career points. As a senior, he shot .626 from the field and .789 from the free throw stripe. Over his career, Bedford-North Lawrence HS was 99-11. He played for the Silver Medal North team at the U.S. Olympic Festival in Minneapolis last July. Bailey led the North team with 25 points in the championship game. He also led the Indiana All-Stars to two wins over the Kentucky All-Stars in the annual summer showdown between the two border states. Despite his vast accomplishments, some experts outside of Indiana doubted his ability. However, Bailey's showing at the U.S. Olympic Festival silenced his critics.

"He's better than what I expected," said Dick Vitale after watching Bailey at the festival. "He's not overrated like I've been hearing. Bailey has a great understanding of what the game is about."

The often repeated compliment that experts make about Bailey's game concerns his intelligence. "From the neck up, he is the best player in the America," said Tom Konchalski of the *HSBI Report*.

Yes, Damon Bailey is for real. While he played at every position at some point during his high school career, the backcourt spots will be his home in Bloomington for the next four years. If there ever was a prototypical Bob Knight Indiana Hoosier, it surely would be Bailey. Although he lacks experience, Bailey is already a better player than anyone in the Indiana backcourt. He will be a key contributor as a freshman, probably in a starting spot before long, and go on to become one of Knight's all-time favorite players.

PAT KNIGHT (6-6, 190 lbs., FR, G, #25, 14.0 ppg, 6.0 apg, Bloomington North HS/Bloomington, Ind. & New Hampton School/New Hampton, N.H.) How could any incoming player compare to Bailey in Knight's eyes? You might say he would have to be the coach's son. Knight's younger son, Pat Knight, returns home to Bloomington after prepping for a year at the New Hampton School in New Hampton, N.H. A "cutter" as local Bloomington kids are known, you might have seen that designation in the movie *Breaking Away*, Knight graduated from Bloomington

North HS where he averaged 16.8 points as a senior and earned all-conference, all-sectional and all-regional honors.

Illinois coach Lou Henson was very interested in Knight but shied away from recruiting him. "I didn't want to make the home visit," said Henson.

Pat Knight has good court vision and is a good leaper who is projected as a small forward. He has grown up around his father's program, certainly knows the system, and what the expectations are. He is expected to sit out this year as a redshirt.

"I'll probably be about 35 by the time I graduate," Pat quipped.

★ QUESTIONS ★

Leadership? Lyndon Jones is the only senior on the squad and if it weren't for the bad examples he set last year, he wouldn't have set any at all. For now, this is Eric Anderson's team. The youngsters will follow his lead and he is only a junior.

Frontcourt depth? When talented but enigmatic Lawrence Funderburke left after the sixth game last year, Indiana was left with a limited number of frontcourt players. Freshman Pat Knight, Bob Knight's son and a player who is expected to redshirt, is the only frontcourt addition to the team.

Establishing a regular playing rotation? Knight used 22 different starting lineups last year and a regular playing rotation was never established. Throwing freshman Damon Bailey into the mix may further cloud the picture.

★ STRENGTHS ★

Bob Knight! The General is one of the all-time greats and he seems to be moded to make another run at a national championship in the near future.

Backcourt depth! As slim as the depth is up front, the opposite is the case in Indiana's well stocked backcourt. Good shooters abound, quality point guards are in place and then there is Mr. Damon Bailey.

The scoring ability of Calbert Cheaney and the all-around play of Eric Anderson! Cheaney and Anderson have shown that they are two of the top talents not only in the Big Ten but in the college game.

★ BLUE RIBBON ANALYSIS ★

As Indiana coach Bob Knight ends his second decade on the Hoosier bench, he goes after his tenth Big Ten title with one of his youngest squads ever. Only one senior and two juniors make up a limited Indiana upperclass. The rest of the roster consists of seven sophomores and two freshmen. While Big Ten title talk might sound premature, all sophomores started at some point during the past season and one of the freshmen, Damon Bailey, was voted the Indiana player of the decade. He is already a living legend, a virtual Paul Bunyan in sneakers.

This edition of the Hoosiers is young, but talented and could figure prominently on the national scene. As all Indiana teams have done under Knight, the 1990-91 Hoosiers will play from their strengths, those being backcourt depth, Calbert Cheaney and Eric Anderson. Look for the nation to take notice of the consistency and leadership of Anderson this season. Cheaney led Indiana in scoring last year and started all 29 games for the Hoosiers as a freshman. He is also one of the top young talents in the college game. However, the rest of the Indiana lineup remains a mystery.

The incumbent point guard is junior Jamal Meeks, but that doesn't guarantee he will start on opening day. If senior Lyndon Jones returns to form, he could start due to his ability to score as well as distribute the ball. Jones has the ability to be an All-Big Ten performer, but whether he can provide consistent leadership is unknown. Don't be surprised if Bailey starts at the point. He has excellent court vision, is a great passer and can shoot in the Steve Alford-Indiana tradition. The final guard spot looks to be a battle between Pat and Greg Graham. Pat is the shooter while Greg is the better defender. Neither was very consistent as a freshman. Sophomore point guard Chris Reynolds should also see quality time.

In the pivot, sophomores Chris Lawson and Pat Nover will probably split time. Lawson has more weight to throw around, is taller and the better shooter.

The Big Ten appears to be weaker from top to bottom than usual, but the top three teams (Indiana, Michigan State and Ohio State) will be highly ranked national factors. Without much depth in the frontcourt, Indiana will be hard pressed to overtake Michigan State, the pre-season favorite in the Big Ten, but we have learned to never count out a Knight-coached team. The last time Knight went to the three-guard offense, it produced a Big Ten championship. He may not get the same results this time if he goes to that alignment, but Indiana will finish no lower than third in the Big Ten after coming in at a surprisingly low seventh place with an 8-10 conference mark last year.

Miami (OH)	77-66	Iowa	118-71
Kent State	79-68	@Purdue	49-72
#Kentucky	71-69	@Michigan State	66-72
Notre Dame	81-72	Minnesota	70-75
##South Alabama	96-67	@Wisconsin	70-68
##Long Beach State	92-75	Ohio State	77-66
@UTEP	69-66	Illinois	63-69
Iowa State	115-66	*California	63-65
###Wichita State	75-54		
###Texas A&M	94-66	@ Road Games	
@Ohio State	67-69	# Bank One/Big Four Classic, In-	
Michigan	69-67	dianapolis, IN	
@Northwestern	77-63	## Indiana Classic, Bloomington,	
Purdue	79-81 OT	IN	
@Iowa	83-79	### Hoosier Classic, Indianapolis,	
Michigan State	57-75	IN	
@Minnesota	89-108	* NCAA Tournament, Hartford, CT	
Wisconsin	85-61		
@Illinois	65-70		
@Michigan	71-79		
Northwestern	98-75		

NOTES: Indiana will open up with Northeastern in a nationally televised game on ESPN in the Maui Classic . . . the Big Four Classic game at Louisville will be played in the Hoosier Dome in Indianapolis while the Hoosier Classic will be held in Market Square Arena in Indianapolis . . . Lawrence Funderburke, the most highly regarded member of Indiana's freshman

Nov.	22-25	#Maui Classic		21	Iowa
	28	@Notre Dame		24	Michigan
Dec.	1	##Louisville		28	@Michigan State
	4	@Vanderbilt	Mar.	2	@Wisconsin
	7-8	###Indiana Classic		7	Minnesota
	15	Western Michigan		10	@Illinois
	18	Kentucky			
	22	@Iowa State	@ Road Games		
	27-28	*Hoosier Classic	# Lahaina, HI (Chaminade, Iowa State,		
Jan.	2	Illinois	Loyola Marymount, Northeastern, Santa		
	5	Northwestern	Clara, Syracuse & Toledo)		
	14	@Purdue	## Big Four Classic, Indianapolis, IN		
	19	@Iowa	### Bloomington, IN (Niagara, North		
	21	Ohio State	Carolina Wilmington & University of San		
	24	@Michigan	Diego)		
	26	Michigan State	* Indianapolis, IN (Marshall, North Texas		
	30	Wisconsin	& Ohio University)		
Feb.	3	@Minnesota			
	7	@Northwestern			
	10	Purdue			
	17	@Iowa State			

class last year, is back in Bloomington. He registered for classes at the beginning of the fall semester and is expected to attend Indiana through the first semester before transferring to another school. He is not expected to play for Indiana this year, but stranger things have happened.

LSU

LAST SEASON: 23-9
CONFERENCE RECORD: 12-6
STARTERS LOST: 1
STARTERS RETURNING: 4
CONFERENCE: SOUTHEASTERN (SEC)
LOCATION: BATON ROUGE, LA
HOME FLOOR: PETE MARAVICH
  ASSEMBLY CENTER (14,164)
NICKNAME: TIGERS
COLORS: PURPLE AND GOLD

★ COACH'S PROFILE ★

DALE BROWN (Record at LSU, 342-182) Dale Brown may be mellowing into middle age . . . but only a little.

These updates:

• He's not mad at the NCAA any more. The same coach who once compared the ruling body of college sports to the Gestapo is now ready to work within the system, mainly because Dick Schultz has replaced his old nemesis Walter Byers, as the NCAA's Executive Director. "Dick Schultz is like a breath of fresh air leaking into the Kremlin," Brown said.

• The Bobby Knight Feud, entertaining as it was, is now over with no blood spilled. Recall that Brown once offered to "wrestle Knight naked in a locked room and see who comes out." He added that Knight "dehumanized" the game. Knight later fired back some strong volleys of his own. The feud began at the 1981 Final Four, when, the night after Indiana beat LSU in the semifinals, Knight allegedly stuffed a Tiger fan into a restaurant garbage can. It ended, Brown said, when he realized how insignificant it all was. That day came when Brown watched a television interview with the parents of a young Baton Rouge woman who was killed when teenagers threw a large boulder through her car's windshield from a highway overpass.

When the parents said they could forgive their daughter's killers, Brown said a chill went through his body as he thought about how long he had carried his grudge for Knight.

Within days, he said he called Knight and the two called a truce.

• The SEC may be big enough for Brown and Kentucky's Rick Pitino after all. They made quite a splash in their first meeting in Baton Rouge. After a minor scuffle between two players at the start of a time out, the two charged each other at midcourt, with Pitino having to be restrained and Brown shaking his fist at Pitino. "We straightened it out," Brown said. "It was blown way out of proportion."

Of course, any or all of the above could change at any minute. That's part of the Dale Brown charm.

He still thinks Propositions 48 and 42 stink, that freshmen should not play, and he was beating the drums to put more NCAA-generated riches into players pockets long before it was fashionable.

"The athlete is a whipping boy for all of the problems in our schools. It's true our educational system stinks, but just don't single out the athlete," Brown claimed. "What about the teacher? What about the parents? Shouldn't they have responsibility?"

Mellowing? Perhaps. But never dull. There is no way Brown can ever be considered dull. He has been a colorful, outspoken figure since the day he arrived on the national scene.

It was just a little blip on the sportswire, hardly worthy of notice, 19 years ago when unknown Dale Brown was named head basketball coach at LSU. Another fast-talking, positive-thinking basketball coach blindly believing he could sell basketball in a football market. Louisiana hasn't been the same since. Brown didn't invent LSU basketball any more than Henry Ford invented the automobile. Bob Pettit played at LSU in the 1950s, Pete Maravich in the 1960s.

But like Ford in the auto industry, it was Brown who made it feasible, made it fashionable and, yes, made it profitable. Dale Brown is LSU basketball.

If Brown had any doubts that he had arrived, that he had carved his own special niche at a football school and a football state, he got the proof he needed before last season began. The LSU football team was off to its second worst start in school history. Around LSU, two straight football losses usually attracts a lynch mob with a rope looking for the head coach. But nobody cared —or at the least they were distracted enough by the anticipation of basketball season to leave football coach Mike Archer in relative peace. That's a far cry from when Brown first came to LSU. At that time, the other athletes had to get out of the way at the athletic training table when the football players came through.

While demanding fans have long been the bane of LSU football coaches, Brown was estatic the first time he tuned in the radio and heard Tiger fans calling for his scalp. "When I got here, nobody cared if we won or lost," he remembers with a laugh. "I thought it was great. People cared!"

His LSU team was one of only nine schools to have been in the last seven NCAA tournaments; one of only seven schools to have participated in 12 straight post-season tournaments. Brown has led LSU to two Final Fours, 1981 and 1986, and made the Region Finals on two other occasions. He was named National Coach of the Year in 1981 with a team that went 31-5.

He has outlasted five football coaches and five athletic directors at LSU and he may outlast five more of both. Basketball tickets at LSU are now as treasured as their football counterparts, a far cry from the early days when Brown toured the state a stranger, passing out purple and gold nets for barren, long neglected rims around Louisiana. He had long since "arrived" in Louisiana by the time he rented the Superdome in New Orleans on January 20, 1989, for a date with powerful Georgetown. But he put an exclamation point on it when the most people ever to witness a regular season NCAA basketball game —54,321 actual turnstill count —showed up to watch the game. LSU was unranked and the then No. 2 Hoyas could have claimed the No. 1 spot with a victory. In typical Brown fashion, however, LSU pulled off a monumental 82-80 upset on Ricky Blanton's put-back at the buzzer.

Brown is an Underdog's Underdog. In 1986 he took a lightly-regarded LSU team, a No. 9 regional seed in the NCAA tournament, and showed up unexpectedly at the Final Four in Dallas. It was no easy road. But when the Tigers in succession defied the experts and upset No. 8 seed (Purdue), No. 2 (Memphis State), No. 3 (Georgia Tech) and No. 1 (Kentucky), Brown was just retracing the steps of his life.

Born in Minot, N.D., Brown grew up without a father (he left three days after Brown's birth). Brown and a sister were raised by their mother in a one-bedroom apartment atop a bar, subsisting on a welfare check of $42.50 per month. Stigmatized by the poverty of his youth — he often tells his teams about the tribulations he faced growing up — Brown has run in fear of failure ever since. He admits if he hadn't been a fine high school athlete, it's doubtful his life would have turned out so successfully. "I was a potential loser," he said, before he was pointed in the right direction. Brown was the leading scorer in both football and basketball at Minot HS, leading the state in the latter, as well as winning the state 40-yard dash in track. From there he went to tiny Minot State (now North Dakota-Minot), where he is still the only athlete in school history to earn 12 letters (basketball, football and track).

He coached at two high schools in North Dakota, leaving both due to minor disputes —"it was the principle of the thing," over his salary. With no job and a new infant daughter, he and his wife, Vonnie, packed all of their belongings and headed to California, where he finally landed a junior high school job in Berkeley, then a high school position in Palm Springs. Brown got his big break when Ladell Anderson hired him as an assistant at Utah State, where he quickly gained a reputation as a great recruiter.

He left Utah State in a huff, too, however, when he was passed over for the head job after Anderson left. The next stop was Washington State, also as an assistant and also brief. A year later LSU athletic director Carl Maddox changed the face of Louisiana forever when he hired Brown.

The rest, as they say, is history, but it was hardly easy.

Brown, perhaps, remembering his wrong-side-of-the-tracks childhood, refused to accept second-class treatment for himself, his program, or his players. Soon enough, predictably, there were run-ins with football coach Charlie McLendon as Brown openly took on the LSU football machine.

He also basically built the program from nothing. His first team at LSU, 1972-73, might have been his favorite. That team was a rag-tag collection with little talent that he nicknamed "The Hustlers." They went 14-10, including a 94-81 upset of national runner-up Memphis State. A picture of that team occupies a prominent spot on his office wall today. However, Brown faced a long road to establish LSU basketball. His next three seasons were all losing years. The football fans yawned, but Maddox liked what he saw and stuck by Brown. Before the 1976-77 season, Brown landed his first big time recruit, forward Durand "Rudy" Macklin from Louisville, and LSU finished with a 15-12 record. But the following year was the breakthrough season for Brown.

If you can split the Brown Era into The Struggle and The Reward, the 1977-78 season is the divider, specifically a night in February when national champion-to-be Kentucky visited LSU. The young but blossoming Tigers took the Wildcats into overtime, and, even though all five LSU starters fouled out, hung on for a 95-94 victory. Brown won his first of three SEC championships the following season and began the string of 12 straight post-season trips.

Once considered only a motivator and recruiter by many, Brown began to get his due as a floor coach in the mid-1980s when he took a mildly talented team to the Final Four in 1986 and was within one point of returning the following season. The key to those teams was Brown's "freak defense," the confusing array of consistently switching man-to-man, zone and matchup alignments. He had used it 25 years earlier, he said, while a high school coach because it allowed teams to neutralize superior talent.

Along the way Brown has accumulated an interesting variety of devoted friends, from Dr. Norman Vincent Peale, to UCLA coaching legend John Wooden, to comedian/activist Dick Gregory, Jesse Jackson and a host of others. He even invited Mother Theresa to last year's Superdome charity game —Hoops for the Homeless—against Notre Dame (she declined). Brown is also a voracious reader of philosophy and history, a world traveler who has visited over 50 countries, climbed mountains, gone down the Amazon in a canoe, tried to break the speedboat record down the Mississippi River and searched for Noah's Ark. He often stays up for days at a time without sleep and occasionally fasts ("just to prove I can do it").

Last summer while coaching his South team to the championship of the U.S. Olympic Festival in Minneapolis, Brown visited imprisoned televangelist Jim Bakker, invited American Indians to his locker room and met with a man recently released from a Minnesota prison who credited Brown with being a positive influence on his life. "Dale's got a heart this big," said South assistant coach Pete Herrmann of Navy, holding his hands wide apart.

He recently announced plans to donate some of the money he receives from sneaker endorsement contracts to help athletes finish their academic requirements after their eligibility expires and to deal with sudden emergencies during their playing days.

"He let's it be known how he feels players should be treated," former LSU standout Ricky Blanton told Thomas O'Toole of Scripps Howard News Service. "He's definitely a player's coach. And he's no different in a press conference or the locker room. He's in this to see his players grow."

"I was told when you leave the program, you'll respect and appreciate him even more, and that's what I'm finding out. He's taught me about life, not just basketball."

Last season was a difficult one for Brown. He has always been more comfortable in a role of David, but found himself playing Goliath to the slings and arrows of upstarts. LSU came into last season with the most impressive array of talent any Tiger basketball program has ever had. Guard Chris Jackson was the second leading scorer in the country as a freshman and big men Shaquille O'Neal and Stanley Roberts were both first-team high school All-America picks. The Tigers were considered prohibitive favorites in the SEC and a probable Final Four team. However, LSU never developed a team personality, was extremely inconsistent and finished a disappointing 23-9.

"I didn't handle it very well," Brown said of last year. "I'd never been in that situation before. But I always learn from my experiences."

This year with Jackson gone to the NBA and Roberts in Spain, the expectations are diminished and Brown can literally lay in the grass and do some ambushing of his own. LSU should be a much happier team and more successful this year.

★ PLAYERS NOT RETURNING ★

RANDY DEVALL (6-4, G, 4.7 ppg, 3.7 rpg, 106 assists, 4 blocked shots, 28 steals) It's hard to figure how much the Tigers will miss Devall, who was lost to the team due to academics. He started 16 games, but saw less and less playing time as Maurice Williamson developed at the other guard spot alongside Chris Jackson. He did a lot of things decently, but nothing spectacular. A Baton Rouge native, Devall had played only one year at LSU after transferring from Garden City (Kan.) JC. He has another year of eligibility, and Brown expects he will remain in school and regain his eligibility next year.

CHRIS JACKSON (6-0, G, 27.8 ppg, 2.5 rpg, 102 assists, 1 blocked shot, 52 steals) Jackson, a sophomore last season, announced immediately after LSU's final game that he would enter the NBA draft two years early, with Dale Brown's blessing. It proved to be wise decision as the Denver Nuggets made Brown the third overall choice in the draft.

In his only two years of college play, he was a two-time first-team All-America and two-time SEC player of the year. He set NCAA freshman scoring records for a season (965), season scoring average (30.2 ppg), and single game (55 against Mississippi, breaking his own record of 53 set earlier in the year against Florida). His freshman scoring record gave LSU possession of all scoring records in each class (the late Pete Maravich, before freshman eligibility was reinstated, holds the sophomore, junior and senior records in college basketball).

In 64 games at LSU, Jackson had 11 games of 40 points or more, and four of 50 or more. He was unquestionably one of the greatest scoring guards ever in college basketball and although his stay at LSU was brief, Jackson is definitely one of the three best players ever produced by the school along with Bob Pettit and Maravich.

The LSU basketball team might replace Jackson easier than will the state of Louisiana. One of the most charismatic and nationally publicized players the last few years, Jackson would draw crowds at home and away like no SEC player since Maravich. It is fair to say he was so popular that Jackson became almost like a rock star. Within Louisiana, he was a treasure, and 50 or so youths congregated outside the LSU dressing room after every home game. He was on the cover of virtually every pre-season magazine last fall and even made the cover of Sports Illustrated as a freshman.

But at times, it was a bittersweet season on the court last year for Jackson. As a freshman, the shy youngster sometimes looked ill at ease under the media spotlight that dogged his every step, but forgot it all when he took the court. As a sophomore, often the opposite appeared true. Relaxed and much more talkative and open off the court, at times he struggled (relatively speaking) with the massive influx of talent that joined him on the court last season.

LSU never really blended the talents of Jackson with its seven-foot twin towers, Shaquille O'Neal and Stanley Roberts. Jackson could be dominant from outside or the Tigers could pound it inside, but rarely did they mix the two strategies smoothly on the same night. He took some heat for his assists to turnover ratio of 102-117, but in fairness a lot of Jackson's more creative would-be assists became turnovers off the hands of mere mortal teammates.

The influx of talent also failed to relieve Jackson of the constant array of double- and triple-teams, particularly within the SEC where he was often double-teamed even when he didn't have the ball. He wasn't entirely comfortable with the leadership role under which he was thrust on a team with no seniors; it was much easier as a freshman. Ricky Blanton handled those chores and he worried only about his shots falling.

Despite somewhat difficult times, he was an easy choice as the SEC player of the year. He had a season-high 51 points against Texas (in Houston). One of Jackson's more remarkable games came at Mississippi, where he was held scoreless in the first half, but responded with 28 points in the second half as LSU rallied for a 79-77 victory.

Yes, Chris Jackson will certainly be missed. However, Tennessee-Martin transfer Mike Hansen is more of a pure point guard than Jackson and Brown will be able to emphasize the talents of Shaquille O'Neal.

STANLEY ROBERTS (7-0, C/F, 14.1 ppg, 9.8 rpg, 40 assists, 60 blocked shots,

20 steals) Roberts struggled academically during his entire two years at LSU and finally became ineligible in August. He signed a lucrative contract with one of the premier teams in Europe, Spain's Real Madrid, and should be a high first round choice in next June's NBA draft.

Roberts was LSU's second leading scorer, rebounder and shotblocker. While he certainly did not have a bad first year, considering he had sat out the preceding season, Brown was never pleased with Roberts' work habits. Brown also felt that Roberts slowed down the LSU defense. This year, Brown had vowed to dismantle the Tigers' Twin Tower look.

Roberts did show some finely developed all-around offensive skills last year. He used the glass well, could post up for a turnaround jumper from 10 to 12 feet on in, and powered his way inside as well. Roberts scored in double figures 23 times last year and was in double figures rebounding in 16 games. He tied a SEC record against Loyola Marymount when he made a perfect 10-of-10 field goal attempts. His season highs were 26 points and 16 rebounds, both coming against Texas.

On the down side, he fouled out of eight games, even with the experimental six-foul rule for SEC play, and he was a terrible free throw shooter (.460). Roberts was a third-team All-SEC choice last year and probably would have made first team if he had played for any other conference program except LSU, where the shadow of O'Neal hurt his playing time.

LSU will not be as dominant inside without Roberts. However, it has been proven recently in college basketball that two great big men are not necessarily more effective than one. Kentucky reached the Final Four in 1984 with a Twin Tower tandem of Sam Bowie and Melvin Turpin, but the Wildcats were blown out in the semifinals by Georgetown. So far, in two years together, Georgetown's Twin Towers of Alonzo Mourning and Dikembe Mutombo have not been enough to take the Hoyas to the Final Four. Last year, Georgetown was knocked out in the second round of the NCAA tournament and didn't win either the regular season or conference tournament crown in the Big East.

We have always been impressed with Roberts' offensive skills. He definitely has more potential than any of the centers chosen in last year's NBA draft. However, without him, Brown will be able to emphasize the best center in the country, O'Neal, and put a smaller, quicker, better defensive unit on the floor. It will also reduce the possible combinations he can use and LSU should have a more consistent lineup.

DENNIS TRACEY (6-1, G, 0.7 ppg, 0.5 rpg, 4 assists, 1 steal) Tracey was one of college basketball's most heartwarming rags-to-riches story in 1988-89, but a serious knee injury in pre-season last year downgraded him to only 24 minutes of playing time and led to his decision not to try to play this year. Thus, he really cannot be counted as a loss for this year's team. Tracey, however, has etched his spot in LSU basketball lore. Overlooked out of high school, he enrolled at Brevard JC in Coco Beach, Fla., but stayed only six weeks before leaving to enroll at New Orleans in his hometown. He wasn't wanted at New Orleans, so he transferred to LSU and spent the 1987-88 season playing on an intramural team. Dale Brown announced he would not hold walk-on trials before the 1988-89 season, but changed his mind when Tracey wrote him a letter begging for a chance to play.

The rest followed a Hollywood script as Tracey became a key defensive role player for LSU in 1988-89. His best game came when he shut down Georgetown's Charles Smith in the second half of the Tigers' upset of the Hoyas in the Superdome.

★ RETURNING PLAYERS ★

HAROLD BOUDREAUX (6-9, 242 lbs., JR, F, #32, 2.4 ppg, 2.1 rpg, 8 assists, 8 blocked shots, 10 steals, Cecilia HS/Arnaudville, La.) A Parade Magazine All-America coming out of high school, Boudreaux sat out his freshman year then gradually found his niche late last season for LSU. Although he played in all 32 games last season, he saw limited playing time until late in the season. He started four games, although he played less than 10 minutes in all but his first start and seemed more effective off the bench.

Boudreaux (a common name in Cajun Country in Louisiana, pronounced ''Boo-dro'') should play a much larger role for the Tigers this season even if he doesn't start. He has excellent shooting range, for his 6-9 size and as a starter made 4-of-13 three-point attempts. His best game was the regular season finale, in which he scored 10 points and grabbed eight rebounds at Mississippi. For the season Boudreaux made 32-of-70 field goals (.457) and was 5-of-12 (.417) from three-point range. He connected on 8-of-12 free throws (.667).

Boudreaux is definitely an important player for the Tigers this season. Some forwards have to come through consistently to take some of the load off Shaquille O'Neal. He is a more gifted player than the other key forwards, Wayne Sims and Vernell Singleton.

GEERT HAMMINK (7-0, 263 lbs., SO, C, #43, Didam, Netherlands) Hammink redshirted last season after playing in 25 of 32 games as a freshman in 1988-89. For the season Hammink averaged 2.0 points, 2.2 rebounds, handed out four assists and blocked three shots.

Before coming to LSU, Hammink was a star on the 12-country European Junior National team. He led that team in scoring with a 27.7 average and was the second leading rebounder with 14.4 per game. However, as a freshman he was often overwhelmed by the pace of American major college basketball. He has a decent shooting touch, however, and should benefit from a year practicing against Stanley Roberts and Shaquille O'Neal.

Hammink will back up O'Neal. He attended a big man's camp in Nashville, run by former Tennessee State head coach Ed Martin, who also spent several years as an assistant at Vanderbilt. Martin said at the conclusion of the camp that Hammink was farther along at a similar stage than ex-Vanderbilt star Will Purdue (Chicago Bulls).

RICHARD KRAJEWSKI (6-10, 227 lbs., SR, C, #41, 0.4 ppg, 0.5 rpg, 2 assists, 2 blocked shots, 3 steals, Grafton HS/Grafton, N.D.) Krajewski was an All-State player in Dale Brown's motherland of North Dakota, but has seen limited playing time since coming to LSU. He played in 26 games last year, but logged only 95 minutes for the season. Krajewski made 4-of-13 field goals (.308) and was 2-of-5 (.400) from the line.

Basically, he can give the Tigers a few minutes when O'Neal gets in foul trouble. His role isn't likely to change much this season.

SHAQUILLE O'NEAL (7-1 1/2, 295 lbs., SO, C, #33, 13.9 ppg, 12.0 rpg, 61 assists, 115 blocked shots, 38 steals, Robert G. Cole HS/San Antonio, Tex.) Without a doubt, O'Neal is one of the most awesome physical specimens in all sports, not just college basketball. The scary thing about O'Neal for opposing coaches is that he has likely just scratched the surface of his potential. He did not turn 18 until the SEC tournament last March.

Despite his inexperience, O'Neal played only two years of American high school basketball, in Texas, because his father was stationed overseas in the Army, he would have likely been the No. 1 overall selection in the NBA draft if he had left school last spring. Although still very much of a young talent, O'Neal is in our estimation the premier center in college basketball.

He's built like Adonis, runs like a (very tall) deer, strong as an ox, had the best grade point average on the LSU team last year, and, for those looking at future development, possesses a work ethic of a packmule. This is not just another lumbering seven-footer. This is a 7-1/2 athlete. Patrick Ewing, Akeem Olajuwon, David Robinson . . . NBA scouts see bits and pieces of all of them in O'Neal.

''There's absolutely no limit to how good he can become,'' Brown said. ''I look at Shaquille as a young, wonderful stallion. By the end of (last) season, he was running pretty well. He has a love and a desire for the game that is unseen in other players. He is fearless and he's a great leader. He has great heart. He's not the type who's going to be a prima donna and stop (developing). Shaquille is a warrior.''

''I don't have any trouble working out on my own and pushing myself,'' O'Neal said. ''I'm the kind of player that gets better, not worse. I just say to myself, 'I want to be the best'.''

Although he was overshadowed somewhat nationally as a freshman by the Chris Jackson show, O'Neal shattered the SEC record for blocked shots with 115 last season (3.6 blpg), breaking a record of 95 set the previous year by Florida's Dwayne Schintzius. He destroyed the SEC record for most rejections in a game, first blocking 10 against Texas, then 12 against Loyola Marymount. O'Neal blocked six or more shots in seven games. He also led the SEC in rebounding with a 12.0 average. Nationally, O'Neal ranked sixth in the country in blocked shots and ninth in rebounding.

His season-highs of 26 points came against Lamar and his 24 rebounds against Loyola Marymount. O'Neal recorded 21 double figure points and rebound games.

''He's got a heart bigger than this arena,'' Brown told Dave Hanson of the New York Post. ''He'd step on a land mine, and shrapnel wouldn't keep him off the court. My opinion is, he'll wind up being one of the all-time great players to play this game.''

Navy coach Pete Herrmann assisted Brown with the South team in the U.S. Olympic Festival and made this comparison of O'Neal and David Robinson, his former player, to Hanson: ''Both run the floor very well,'' Herrmann said. ''Both need work on their offense. When David was a freshman, he averaged six points. Shaquille is much ahead at this stage. He's a harder-nosed competitor. Tougher.''

O'Neal was a big hit at the U.S. Olympic Festival. Not only did he lead the Brown coached South team to the Gold Medal, but he basically took a sledgehammer to all of the pertinent festival records. He opened the festival with a triple-double (26 points, 10 rebounds and 10 blocked shots). He scored 89 points in the first three games to break the old record of 77 points for three games and ended the four-game tournament with 98 points, 55 rebounds and 27 blocked shots, all records. He also set the single game record with 39 points.

Still, O'Neal was unimpressed with his performance. ''I think I've been as dominant as I should be,'' he told the New York Times. ''I mean, I'm 7-1, 285 pounds. Seven foot means dominance. When you're seven foot, you're supposed to kill and go for the kill.''

His superb attitude and work ethic come from a strong, spare-the-rod-spoil-the-child father, Phillip Harrison (O'Neal uses his mother's maiden name). Harrison is a career military man, a no-nonsense sergeant straight from Central Casting. In fact, Brown can thank the military for O'Neal being in a LSU uniform. Some years ago, Brown, on one of his regular globetrotting missions, was delivering a speech at a clinic in Wildflecken, West Germany. Afterwards, a 6-8 youth approached Brown for further tips on how to improve his vertical leap. ''How old are you, soldier?'' Brown asked. ''Sir, I'm only 13 years old,'' the young O'Neal replied.

Brown's next question was direct and to the point: ''Son, I'd like to meet your father!''

Brown was so excited he walked into the base sauna fully clothed to seek out Sergeant Harrison, and was quickly in his speech about how O'Neal would grow to be seven, eight or maybe nine feet tall. Harrison stopped him in mid-syllable (no easy chore, if you know Brown).

"He said he wasn't interested in Shaquille playing basketball," Brown remembers. "He was interested in Shaquille getting a degree. He wanted him to develop his intellect. He said that blacks needed to become doctors, lawyers, professors, and that education was the best way to do that.

"I stopped him and said, 'Sarge, we're going to get along just fine'." And evidently they did. Brown stayed in touch and tough O'Neal would return to the states and average 32 points, 22 rebounds and six blocked shots per game for Robert G. Cole HS in San Antonio. He never really considered any school but LSU.

O'Neal did have the normal ration of freshman growing pains last year. Even with the SEC's experiment with six fouls, he fouled out of nine games. He was scoreless in one game and held to only two points in another. He doesn't block out very well on rebounds, grabbing most with sheer physical ability. O'Neal needs to develop a better jump shot, a drop step, and he didn't even toy with a hook shot until arriving at LSU. And, he was a terrible free throw shooter, once missing seven straight (five on the front end of one-and-ones) that sparked an LSU collapse against Georgia. For the season he shot only .556 from the line.

With his work ethic, though, no one seems to doubt that consistent greatness will come. It's worth noting, for instance, that after the Georgia debacle, he shot an improved 61 percent from the line for the rest of the season. Shortly after LSU's season ended, O'Neal returned home to San Antonio, where he met NBA rookie of the year David Robinson.

"I saw him play all year," Robinson said. "The thing I really noticed about him was the aggressiveness that he had all the time. He takes the ball strong to the hole and he is a tremendous rebounder. I'm real impressed with the impact he's made in such a short period. He has a tremendous future. I've got to get ready for him in a couple of years."

There is no doubt that O'Neal will be the first pick of the NBA draft whether he lasts through a full four years of college or opts for early entry. However, O'Neal and his family are adamant at this point about him staying in school for the full four years.

Sergeant Harrison told David Flories of the *San Antonio Express-News*: "Sure, everyone needs money. But you also need peace of mind. We said it from the beginning: Shaquille is going to college for four years. People always ask us if Shaquille is jumping to the pros early, and the answer is always the same: 'No.' He's going to get his degree. We're going for the education. Money is not a big factor."

"I want to stay at LSU because college is supposed to be the best four years of your life," O'Neal told Steve Woodward of *USA Today*.

By March, O'Neal could be the most dominant force in the college game.

WAYNE SIMS (6-7, 245 lbs, SR, F, #44, 7.8 ppg, 4.8 rpg, 58 assists, 11 blocked shots, 22 steals, DeRidder HS/DeRidder, La.) Sims was easily the biggest mystery on the LSU team last year, not to mention the biggest disappointment. He had started 45 of 48 games in his freshman and sophomore years and the first 28 last year before finally losing his spot for the post-season. A player with less history of productivity probably would have lost a starting job much sooner.

Sims, who made the All-SEC freshman team in his first year at LSU, scored in double figures in nine of LSU's first 11 games, but then went into a slump from which he never recovered. True, his role changed greatly with the addition of Shaquille O'Neal and Stanley Roberts to the LSU lineup, but those who watched the Tigers had expected him to be perhaps the biggest beneficiary of the Twin Towers.

In his first two years, Sims was called upon to bang the boards and provide muscle inside, but he also displayed a deadly accurate medium range jumper. Who would guard against that with Roberts and O'Neal demanding so much attention? Yet Sims scoring average dropped from 13.3 to 7.8 ppg and by the second half of the season his confidence was shot.

Sims scored a season-high of 19 points in LSU's wild 148-141 victory over Loyola Marymount, but he turned the game into an adventure when, entrusted to inbound the ball against the Lions' relentless full court pressure, he turned the ball over so much one sportswriter wondered in print if he hadn't led the Lions in assists.

He probably needs to lose some weight to play effectively in LSU's new uptempo system; it wasn't so much of a factor when he played power forward his first two years, but he was always a step or two behind as a small forward last year.

There is no doubt that Sims is a proven SEC-caliber performer. A return to his past form would be a big lift for the Tigers, but in the current system, he figures to struggle for playing time this season.

VERNEL SINGLETON (6-7, 212 lbs., JR, F, #24, 8.4 ppg, 4.8 rpg, 27 assists, 19 blocked shots, 26 steals, South Natchez HS/Natchez, Miss.) Before the Twin Towers arrived at LSU, Singleton was forced to play (out of position) at center his freshman year and made the All-SEC freshman team and third-team freshman All-America squad. Last year, he struggled early not only adjusting to his new small forward role, but to have that role clearly defined. He also spent some time in Dale Brown's doghouse for trying to do too much early in the season. But he's one of the more valuable players on the team and finished strong once he started playing within himself, scoring in double figures in nine of the last 13 games.

Singleton is an agile athlete with a big wing span, capable of buzzing around the lane like a helicopter. His scoring dipped to 8.4 ppg from 10.8 his freshman season, but that was largely due to his new role as a defensive stopper, usually drawing the opponent's top scorer. Singleton shot 59 percent from the floor last year, mainly driving inside; he has only an average jump shot with very limited range.

One of the most versatile players on the team, he could even play off-guard in a pinch. Singleton is an oddity on a team full of blue chip recruits. He signed

with LSU late and was lightly regarded coming out of high school.

MAURICE WILLIAMSON (6-0, 174 lbs., JR, G, #10, 12.2 ppg, 2.3 rpg, 118 assists, 5 blocked shots, 55 steals, Wilbur Cross HS/New Haven, Conn.) Williamson is academically ineligible until at least mid-December. However, he is expected to be eligible at that point unless something unforeseen happens in the fall. Williamson is well suited to play either backcourt spot, although Brown's plan going into the season is to leave him at off-guard and let newcomer Mike Hansen replace Chris Jackson at the point. Williamson is a complete guard, a good ballhandler who can either drive to the basket or shoot from long range.

He sat out his first year at LSU and experienced the normal ups and downs of a first-year player last season. Williamson was a bit turnover prone at times like against Villanova in the NCAA tournament when he had 13 turnovers. However, he can be a dynamic scorer who could emerge as one of the SEC's best guards now that the long shadow of Jackson is gone. In fact, he was named third-team All-SEC last season by *UPI*.

Williamson emerged in the second half of the season. He averaged only 4.8 points per game in his first nine games, while shooting only 33 percent from the field. He was also suspended for one game, according to Brown, for "not paying proper attention to academics."

He came on strong in the second half of the season, topping the 20-point mark four times, including a season-high 31 against Vanderbilt. From three-point range, he shot only .381 for the season, but hit 43 percent over the second half of the year. He had 26 points in a LSU victory over eventual national champion UNLV, including 4-of-7 three-pointers that caused Runnin' Rebel coach Jerry Tarkanian to remark: "We knew about Jackson, where did he (Williamson) come from?"

Against Vanderbilt, Williamson had his best game as he scored 31 points —4-of-7 from three-point range —and handed out 10 assists.

"Maurice gives us an entirely new dimension," Brown said. "He's been able to put his dynamic ways on the court. He played a little out of control early. When he got under control, he really helped us."

His father, John Williamson, was an All-America guard at New Mexico State and averaged 17.8 points per game in eight NBA seasons with three different teams.

LSU needs a big year from Williamson to offset the scoring loss of Chris Jackson. Also LSU enters the season as a questionable outside shooting team and Williamson could help rectify that potential problem.

★ **NEWCOMERS** ★

LENEAR BURNS (6-7, 215 lbs., FR, F, #21, 23.2 ppg, 14.0 rpg, Varnado HS/Angie, La.) Burns sat out last year as a true redshirt, not a Proposition 48 player. Thus, he was able to practice with the team and showed some promise, particularly on defense. Burns runs and jumps well, has good skills and gained 20 pounds since coming to LSU. Over the summer, he toured Argentina with the Score International team.

At Varnado HS, Burns led his team to the Louisiana AA state championship. He also played in the prestigious Dapper Dan Roundball Classic in Pittsburgh. Burns played football at Varnado HS.

The LSU coaching staff is high on Burns and believes he will play a key role this year.

SHAWN GRIGGS (6-6, 205 lbs., SO, F/G, #22, 28.3 ppg, 14.3 rpg, Ferriday HS/Ferriday, La.) Griggs is from the same Louisiana small town, adjacent to the Mississippi state line, as Rock and Roll legend Jerry Lee Lewis, and evangelist Jimmy Swaggart. While Griggs will probably never match those two in terms of fame, he is a crucial player to this year's edition of the LSU Tigers.

Griggs sat out last year at LSU and was not allowed to practice with the team. He was the Louisiana player of the year in high school and led Ferriday to two Louisiana Class 3A championships.

Over the summer in pickup games in Baton Rouge, Griggs was very impressive. He may be the best athlete on the LSU team. Griggs is blessed with tremendous strength and quickness and is already being compared favorably to former LSU standout Leonard Mitchell. There is even some talk that he could be a starting off-guard, but outside shooting is not his forte. He can defend, rebound and basically do everything but consistently nail the outside shot.

There is no doubt that Griggs should be a major factor for LSU at both small forward and big guard this year. The former high school All-America selection could be one of the better players in the SEC in a few years.

MIKE HANSEN (6-1, 175 lbs., SO, G, #11, Madrid, Spain & University Heights Academy/Hopkinsville, Ky.) Hansen is easily the most important player among LSU's newcomers as he will be given the first chance to replace Chris Jackson at point guard. Hansen has already made a major impact at LSU even though he is yet to play a game for the Tigers. After last season, he was named a team co-captain along with Shaquille O'Neal.

"He's a born leader," Brown said.

Hansen sat out last season after transferring from Tennessee-Martin and has three years of eligibility remaining. At Tennessee-Martin he averaged 20.0 points per game and was named freshman of the year in the Gulf South Conference. He hit 82.3 percent of his free throws and 77-of-179 three-pointers (.430). Hansen also averaged 2.9 rebounds and three assists per game as a freshman at Tennessee-Martin. He was the third leading scorer in the Gulf South Conference.

He first attracted attention at LSU when he bombed in 40 points against the

Tigers in a December, 1989, game at the Pete Maravich Assembly Center. Until the late Hank Gathers scored 48 points last January, it was the highest scoring output by an LSU opponent in the history of the building.

He grew up in Madrid, Spain, and has dual citizenship as his father is a native American, who ran track for the University of Maine, and his mother is a Spanish national. He was named to the Junior All-Europe team in 1987 and tabbed as Spain's most valuable player the same year. His team was the champion of the city of Madrid three times and European champion in 1985.

He moved to the United States for his senior year and averaged 22 points and 7.2 assists per game at University Heights Academy in Hopkinsville, Ky. He also played quarterback and safety on the University Heights football team.

He practiced with the Tigers last year and was impressive. Hansen proved that he is a legitimate three-point threat, ran the offense well, displayed his leadership qualities and did not get embarrassed guarding Chris Jackson. Some LSU insiders have compared him to former Georgia Tech star Mark Price (now with the Cleveland Cavaliers). He also has good strength and quickness.

In many respects, Hansen is more of a pure point guard than Jackson. He should be able to run the show for LSU and be a scoring threat so defenses cannot collapse on O'Neal. If Hansen plays as well as the LSU coaching staff expects, the Tigers will be a Top 10 team and have legitimate Final Four possibilities.

DANNYEL "DANNY" MOSCOVITZ (6-1, 160 lbs., FR, G, #25, Blitch HS/Ramatgan, Israel) With the additions of Hansen and Moscovitz, Brown has had players from seven countries in his program. Moscovitz was signed late in the summer as Brown scrambled for backcourt depth after Randy Devall was ruled academically ineligible. Former LSU Tiger Willie Sims, who plays in Israel, alerted Brown to Moscovitz.

A 21-year-old freshman, Moscovitz has already served as a sergeant in the Israeli Air Force. He was born in Vilnus, Lithuania, and his parents —both doctors of engineering —moved to Israel when he was a young child.

A point guard prospect, Moscovitz played for Israel's National Youth team and the Maccabi Ramatgun Club team, where he averaged 25 points and 15 assists. He was an honor student in high school.

He arrived in Baton Rouge late in the summer and almost didn't make it out of Israel. With the crisis in the Persian Gulf heating up, if Moscovitz had stayed much longer he would have been called up by the Israeli Air Force.

JOHN PICOU (6-2, 175 lbs., FR, #12, 16.0 ppg, 6.0 rpg, 7.0 apg, St. McGill-Toolen HS/Mobile, Ala.) Picou will likely redshirt this season. He was signed late last spring after LSU missed on two of the nation's top recruits, Antonio Lang of Mobile, Ala., and California's Ed O'Bannon. He was originally expected to be a walk-on, but the late recruiting developments enabled him to get a scholarship.

Picou can play either backcourt spot. His high school team made it to the state finals for the first time in school history in 1989 and returned to the state tournament in 1990. He shot 58 percent from the field and 90 percent from the free throw line. His father was the basketball MVP of Louisiana's Class AA at Baker HS, located outside of Baton Rouge, in 1963. His father is a professor of Anthropology at South Alabama.

Picou will see limited action this year.

T.J. PUGH (6-1, 175 lbs., JR, #20, 16.1 ppg, 8.4 apg, 6.0 stpg, Broadmoor HS/Baton Rouge, La. & Garden City CC, Garden City, Kan.) Pugh has come home to LSU and should be a backup point guard for the Tigers this year. As a freshman at Garden City CC, he was a teammate of Randy Devall, an LSU guard who is academically ineligible. Pugh is a good outside shooter who led the Kansas Jayhawks Conference, arguably the toughest junior college conference in the country, in assists and steals. He was named to the U.S. Junior College All-Star team that played the Texas JC All-Stars. Pugh was also a junior college academic All-America selection.

He also has outstanding quickness and should provide needed depth to the LSU backcourt.

★ QUESTIONS ★

Dealing with the loss of Chris Jackson? For two years, there was no doubt that Jackson was LSU basketball.

Defense? Dale Brown made his reputation with pesky defense — remember the freak defense that carried the underdog Tigers to the 1986 Final Four? But over the last two years, LSU has not been strong defensively.

Free throw shooting? Last year LSU let at least four games slip away with shoddy free throw shooting. As a team the Tigers shot only 67 percent —and that's with Jackson, shooting the ball for them, at 91 percent. Take away Jackson and the rest of the Tigers shot only 58 percent.

Forcing the tempo? LSU can be awesome when running, but quite average when the pace slows to a crawl. Last year the Tigers were seldom able to dictate which should be played.

Keeping Shaquille O'Neal out of foul trouble? Even with the six-four experimental rule in the SEC last season, O'Neal fouled out of nine games.

★ STRENGTHS ★

Shaquille O'Neal! Although he played only two years of high school basketball and his experience is limited by today's standards, O'Neal is the premier center

in the country. He also has only scratched his potential and could be the most dominant player in the college game by March.

Rebounding! Even with the loss of Stanley Roberts, who averaged 9.8 rebounds per game last year, LSU should be dominant on the boards.

Offensive potential! Even without Jackson, the Tigers should be very hard to defend and able to put points on the boards easily.

Transition game! The Tigers were awesome in high gear last year. Ask Loyola Marymount and defending NCAA champion UNLV, the No. 1 and No. 8 respectively, scoring teams in the country last year, as LSU ran with both and defeated them last year.

A rejuvenated Dale Brown! Still the master motivator, Brown learned from last year and cannot wait to get going this season.

Depth! LSU should go at least nine deep this year.

Improved leadership! Last year LSU was a leaderless team but Brown believes that both O'Neal and newcomer Mike Hansen can solve that problem.

★ BLUE RIBBON ANALYSIS ★

LSU's publicity office worked overtime last year putting a happy face on the season. A 23-9 record, the fewest losses since LSU's 1981 Final Four team, would be a sparkling success by most standards. However, realistically or not, more was expected of a team that possessed more talent than Dale Brown had ever assembled under the Assembly Center roof. Compounding the disappointment was the fact that the Tigers were eliminated in the first round of the SEC tournament and won only one game in the NCAA tournament. The Tigers were all but conceded the SEC title by league coaches in pre-season, yet finished tied for second with Alabama.

Ups and downs? LSU twice overcome double-digit deficits to beat national champion UNLV and won a 148-141 overtime thriller with Loyola Marymount. But the Tigers also lost to a Florida team that was considered by many to be the least talented group in the SEC in 10 years.

Brown, of course, did not exactly disavow knowledge of the lofty expectations, and in fact, fanned the flames with strong pre-season predictions. However, the expectations were unreasonable, despite the Tigers' talent level, as LSU started new three players last year, all of them playing college basketball for the first time.

"I thought it would be fun," Brown said. "It never was. I didn't like my own team, I didn't like the job I did. I lost a little of my own work ethic."

This year expectations are not nearly as high in Baton Rouge. Gone is celebrated guard Chris Jackson and his 1,854 career points. Although Jackson was one of the greatest guards ever in college basketball, as well as one of the top three players so far in LSU history, the Tigers can still be strong, and maybe even better come March, without him. Brown cannot replace Jackson's 27.8 points per game, but Tennessee-Martin transfer Mike Hansen is more of a pure playmaker. Sophomore center Shaquille O'Neal established a new SEC single season blocked shot record last year with 115 and is poised to become one of the best big men of all-time. He will be the No. 1 pick in whatever NBA draft he enters. The Tigers' other Twin Tower from a year ago, Stanley Roberts, flunked out of school and is now playing with the Real Madrid team in Spain. Roberts was a great offensive player and a big league rebounder when motivated, but O'Neal will now have the middle to himself and should blossom even quicker.

The key to this LSU team will be defense and the related ability to force the game in an up-tempo mode. Basically, last year O'Neal's and Roberts' ability to block shots in volume was the only defense LSU had —the defense of last resort as it were. It prevented a lot of points, but did little to force the fast pace the Tigers craved. Particularly within the SEC, stall tactics to neutralize the LSU talent became the norm and were often quite effective. LSU was quite average when forced to play half court.

"The teams that went out and ran at them were crazy," said an SEC coach. "Even Las Vegas couldn't beat them like that. But if you were deliberate and forced them to be patient, they weren't nearly as good."

The lessons weren't lost on Brown and he is ready to use a quicker lineup that will be able to force the issue both offensively and defensively. LSU must also improve another problem area —foul shooting —and that could be tougher to correct. Mainly due to brick-laying at the line, the Tigers were glued to double-digit leads last year. In five of their seven SEC losses, LSU had double-digit leads at one point. A truly amazing stat is that LSU lost three games a year ago in which the Tigers trailed for a grand total of 11 seconds in regulation.

With more depth on the wings and at forward, Brown will have more options as to how he lines his team up this season. The most likely scenario will have Hansen, who was impressive in practice last year, at the point and Maurice Williamson, when he becomes eligible in December, at off-guard. However, both can play either backcourt spot and some even believe sophomore Shawn Griggs will play in the backcourt. Junior Vernell Singleton, a talented athlete who drives to the basket well and is the best one-on-one defensive player on the team, will be at small forward. Harold Boudreaux, a 6-9 power forward with three-point range, will get the first look there, with the Warrior, O'Neal, swatting flies in the middle. Senior Wayne Sims, a proven SEC caliber player, is the utility forward.

The loss of Jackson alone should take a lot of the spotlight off of LSU, allowing a looser team to play without the burden of sky high expectations. "This is going to be well-disciplined team, well-oiled," Brown said. "It's going to be a talented team that is going to have fun playing."

If the Tigers adopt that approach, they have the talent to win the SEC and much, much more. Brown is laying low this season but is privately relishing the thought of what this Tiger team can achieve if the pieces come together. There is no doubt LSU should be much stronger and more a factor in the NCAA tournament than last season.

<table>
<tr><td colspan="6">**LAST SEASON**</td><td colspan="3">**1990-91 LSU SCHEDULE**</td></tr>
<tr><td colspan="3">#Southern Mississippi</td><td>91-80</td><td>Mississippi State</td><td>86-68</td><td>Nov.</td><td>24</td><td>#Villanova</td></tr>
</table>

LAST SEASON					1990-91 LSU SCHEDULE		
#Southern Mississippi	91-80	Mississippi State	86-68	Nov.	24	#Villanova	Feb. 8 @Georgia
#Kansas	83-89	Auburn	82-71		26	Southeastern Louisiana	10 @Duke
McNeese State	85-49	@Tennessee	119-113		30	Texas	13 Auburn
Lamar	116-76	@Kentucky	95-100	Dec.	7	Chapman College (CA)	17 Alabama
Cal State Los Angeles	82-57	@Vanderbilt	121-108		8	Arizona	20 @Mississippi
Northwestern State	73-63	Alabama	75-69		18	Arkansas State	23 Tennessee
Hardin-Simmons (TX)	100-66	@Georgia	85-86		20	Loyola Marymount	27 @Florida
##Texas	124-113	@Florida	63-76		22	@Illinois	Mar. 2 @Mississippi State
@Mississippi State	80-87OT	Mississippi	103-94		29	Nicholls State (LA)	7-10 ##SEC Tournament
@Auburn	77-70	*Auburn	76-78	Jan.	2	Vanderbilt	
Tennessee	111-94	**Villanova	70-63		5	@Kentucky	@ Road Games
Kentucky	94-81	**Georgia Tech	91-94		7	Georgia	# Tip-Off Classic, Springfield, MA
Vanderbilt	101-72				12	@Auburn	## Nashville, TN
###Notre Dame	87-64	@ Road Games			15	@Alabama	
@Alabama	55-70	# Dodge NIT			19	Mississippi	
Georgia	92-94OT	## Houston, TX			22	@Tennessee	
Florida	70-52	### New Orleans, LA			26	Florida	
UNLV	107-105	* SEC Tournament, Orlando, FL			30	Mississippi State	
@Mississippi	79-77	** NCAA Tournament, Knoxville,		Feb.	2	@Vanderbilt	
Loyola Marymount	148-141OT	TN			5	Kentucky	

NOTES: LSU has two guards sitting out this year who should be eligible next season. The best is 6-3 Jamie Brandon. One of the most highly publicized players to ever attend LSU, Brandon was arguably the top off-guard in the high school ranks last year. From Martin Luther King HS in Chicago, Ill., Brandon originally signed with Illinois but was academically ineligible, got out of his commitment and transferred over the summer to LSU. 6-5 Justin Anderson is a transfer from California-Irvine. A North Dakota native, Anderson's father has known Brown for a long time . . . in a

recent article in *USA Today*, several network announcers listed their favorite college towns. James Brown, of CBS, listed Baton Rouge as his favorite. "Southern down-home friendliness," is how Brown described Baton Rouge. "There's a genuine feeling of warmth. They (the people) make you feel like you are at a second home . . . ten minutes from the (LSU) campus you've got a slew of eateries —Mom-and-Pop down-home cooking places. I find a different place each time I go."

OHIO STATE

LAST SEASON: 17-13
CONFERENCE RECORD: 10-8
STARTERS LOST: 0
STARTERS RETURNING: 5
CONFERENCE: BIG TEN
LOCATION: COLUMBUS, OH
HOME FLOOR:
    ST. JOHN ARENA (13,276)
NICKNAME: BUCKEYES
COLORS: SCARLET AND GREY

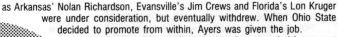

★ COACH'S PROFILE ★

RANDY AYERS (Record at Ohio State, 17-13) If Randy Ayers' career at Ohio State is as successful as his first year at the Buckeye helm, his stay in Columbus should be very long. Although the Buckeye's 17-13 record may not sound like very much, Ohio State won 10 games in the Big Ten, the most conference wins by the Buckeyes since the 1985 season. Ayers also led Ohio State to wins over six teams ranked in the Top 20 and a first round NCAA tournament win over Providence. In the second round of the West Region, Ohio State acquitted itself well before losing 65-76 to eventual national champion UNLV.

The way Ohio State came together is even more impressive considering the Buckeyes lost three of their first five games. Ohio State came together brilliantly at the end of the year to win nine of its last 14. In that stretch drive, Ohio State recorded wins over Louisville and Michigan on national television before downing Providence in the first round of the NCAA tournament. With all 12 lettermen returning from last year, the future in Columbus certainly looks bright for Ayers and the Buckeyes.

The 35-year-old Ayers is the youngest head coach in the Big Ten and one of the youngest in college basketball. He was appointed Ohio State head coach on July 30, 1989, after six years as a Buckeye assistant. The Ohio State coaching position became vacant when Gary Williams left Columbus following the 1988-89 season to accept the head job at Maryland. Many prominent head coaches such

as Arkansas' Nolan Richardson, Evansville's Jim Crews and Florida's Lon Kruger were under consideration, but eventually withdrew. When Ohio State decided to promote from within, Ayers was given the job.

"It's everything and more than I expected. It's a great opportunity for me and also a great challenge," Ayers told Todd Jones of the *Scripps Howard News Service*.

Ayers was the choice of the Ohio State players for the job. "We said we would love to have him as our coach," said Buckeye Jamaal Brown. And that sentiment held up through Ayers' first season as head coach.

"He relates to the players real well," said Buckeye guard Alex Davis. "When a coach relates to his players well, the players play harder for him."

A native Ohioan, Ayers was an All-State basketball player at Springfield North HS and became an All-Mid-American Conference player at Miami (Ohio). He was a four-year starter for the Redskins and helped last Miami to back-to-back MAC titles and successive visits to the NCAA tournament his last two years. He recorded the school's first-ever triple-double as a junior and was selected team captain as a senior. Ayers graduated from Miami in 1978 and was picked in the third round of the NBA draft by the Chicago Bulls. He lasted until the final pre-season cut and played a year of minor league basketball in the defunct Western League before returning to Miami to work on his Masters Degree and serve as a graduate assistant. After receiving his Master's in 1981, Ayers joined the staff as a full-time assistant.

In 1983, Ayers joined the Ohio State staff as a part-time assistant under Eldon Miller. When Gary Williams took over in 1986, he retained Ayers, elevating him to full-time status the following year.

"I learned about recruiting from Rick Barnes (former Ohio State assistant who is now the head coach of Providence)," Ayers told the *Washington Post*," and . . . he was always very aggressive in going after people, trying to build up a rapport with players. That's what I try to do and stay actively involved with recruiting. . .

"We started recruiting kids in their freshman year in high school," he said. "You don't like to say that 'cause I think the kid should be able to concentrate on his academics and his basketball, but you have to do it because everybody else is doing it, and you want to try to compete with everybody else. . ."

In his first year at Ohio State, Ayers proved that he is also a hard worker in addition to a coach with a good rapport with his players. He also showed that he is his own man and modified the full court pressure defense, multiple substitution system his predecessor, Gary Williams, employed.

Not only do all 12 lettermen return from last year, but Ohio State will also only lose two seniors off this year's team. Ayers will not have to have a big recruiting year immediately. Ohio State has a long and illustrious basketball history and there is no reason why Ayers shouldn't be able to continue it. This is a great program, belongs to one of the three best leagues in the country and is located in one of the rapidly emerging cities in the nation. Ohio and the bordering midwest have a strong talent pool that Ayers and his staff should regularly be able to tap. Ayers couldn't have stepped into a better situation.

★ PLAYERS NOT RETURNING ★

None.

★ RETURNING PLAYERS ★

MIKE BAKER (6-1, 180 lbs., JR, G, #30, 9.1 ppg, 2.4 rpg, 109 assists, 4 blocked shots, 38 steals, Dunbar HS/Dayton Ohio) After sitting out the 1988-89 season at Ohio State, Baker started 15 games last season and averaged 29 minutes per game. He started the final 14 games and played a key role in the Buckeyes' 9-5 finish at the end of the year. Baker improved dramatically as the season went on and he gained more experience.

Baker was third on the team in scoring and second in both assists and steals, finishing just one shy of team leader Jim Jackson in both categories. He finished seventh in the Big Ten in assists with a 4.1 average. Baker's .530 field goal percentage (96-of-181) was the second best mark on the squad. From three-point range his percentage dipped to .250 (3-of-12). Baker made 78-of-127 field goals (.614).

He had 19 points in a home loss to Michigan State which was his high scoring game. Baker is a spectacular athlete who is very difficult to defend one-on-one. He routinely drives into the lane, splits defenders and scores over taller players. He is an excellent creator who can get the ball to the open man and makes great decisions on the break. The explosive Baker can stand directly under the basket and dunk the ball two handed without taking a step.

He scored in double figures 12 times, 10 of those performances coming in the last 14 games of the season. He recorded a season-high of 10 assists against Iowa. Baker played well in the NCAA tournament, particularly against Providence, netting 17 points and handing out eight assists. He also was one of Ohio State's better free throw shooters in the final two minutes of games.

Some Big Ten observers believed that Baker was the best point guard in the conference from January on last season. With the year experience, Baker could become the best point guard in the conference all season long this year.

TOM BRANDEWIE (6-8, 215 lbs., SO, F, #31, 1.5 ppg, 0.7 rpg, 1 blocked shot, 2 steals, Fort Loramie HS/Fort Loramie, Ohio) In his first year in the program, Brandewie was used sparingly, in 11 games for a total of 45 minutes. He was 7-of-14 from the field (.500), missed his only free throw attempt and was 2-of-3 (.667) from the free throw line. Brandewie's longest playing stint last year was 12 minutes in the season opener at DePaul.

He saw most of his action early on, playing in four of the first six games while starting forward Perry Carter was recovering from a bruised kidney. Brandewie scored a total of 16 points for the year with half of that total coming against Northwestern, where he hit 3-of-4 shots and both free throw attempts.

He lacked stamina last year, but has increased his upper body strength in the off-season. Brandewie is an intelligent player who has a variety of shots close to the basket and he could be a three-point threat, especially from out front. The Ohio State coaching staff feels Brandewie has a promising future in the program, but he may not be a key player for the Buckeyes until next season when power forwards Perry Carter and Treg Lee graduate.

JAMAAL BROWN (6-4, 188 lbs., JR, G, #30, 7.8 ppg, 3.4 rpg, 54 assists, 5 blocked shots, 32 steals, Sam Houston HS/Arlington, Tex.) Brown has started all 64 games the past two years and is Ohio State's most experienced backcourt player. He divided his time between point and second guard last year, with 15 starts coming at each position. He is probably better suited to the second guard because of his size and junior Mark Baker, who played well last season, should be a fixture at the point.

Brown played well during Ohio State's stretch drive, averaging 9.8 points in his last 13 regular season games. He reached double figures 10 times with a high of 15 in the home upset of Michigan. Brown had a career-high nine rebounds against North Carolina State. Last season he made 80-of-191 field goals (.419) and was a mediocre 12-of-52 (.231) from three-point range. Brown made 62-of-83 free throws (.747).

He is not a big scorer, but does look for his offense when the game is on the line. Brown is an excellent defender whom almost always draws the opposition's top backcourt threat. An explosive leaper, he makes big plays at both ends of the court because of his great athletic ability. Brown is a team leader and a winner.

With the return of Brown, Mark Baker, Alex Davis, standout swingman Jim Jackson and Chris Jent to the backcourt plus the addition of highly regarded freshman, Jamie Skelton, Ohio State may now have the top backcourt in the Big Ten.

PERRY CARTER (6-8, 225 lbs., SR, C/F, #32, 15.2 ppg, 7.8 rpg, 31 assists, 25 blocked shots, 23 steals, Gonzaga HS/Washington D.C. & Maine Central Institute/Pittsfield, Me.) Carter is in his fourth year as a starter at Ohio State and he second as a team captain. He is undoubtedly one of the top centers in the Big Ten and he can also spend some time at power forward if Bill Robinson continues to develop.

The leading returning rebounder in the Big Ten (7.8 rpg) Carter has led Ohio State in both rebounding and field goal percentage the past two seasons. Last year he made 172-of-318 (.541) of his field goal attempts and 96-of-149 (.644) of his free throw attempts. Carter was Ohio State's top shot blocker two of the past three years. Carter was Ohio State's co- MVP last year.

He was an honorable mention All-Big Ten choice as a junior. Carter missed nearly three weeks of practice and the season opener with a bruised kidney last year. He played in the final 29 games, starting the last 26, and scored in double figures 20 times and had eight 20-point games. Carter led Ohio State in scoring 10 times and in rebounding 17 times. He had double- double games (double figures in both scoring and rebounding). His career-high 29 points came at Michigan and he had 16 rebounds at Illinois. Carter was fourth in the Big Ten in rebounding and third in blocked shots.

Ever since he began playing the game in his native Washington D.C., Carter has become known for his great strength. He is one of the most powerful players in the college game and is almost impossible to stop when he gets the ball in the lane. He does not have great range on his shot and is a limited ball handler (31 assists against 90 turnovers last year). He is a big time power player who works hard game after game and gets results.

Carter participated in the World Championship/Goodwill Games tryout last May in Colorado Springs, Colo. He was cut after the first round of the tryouts.

The presence of Carter is one major reason why Ohio State can make a legitimate run at the Big Ten title this year.

ALEX DAVIS (6-1, 170 lbs., SO, G, #20, 10.7 ppg, 2.1 rpg, 41 assists, 25 steals, Forest Park HS/Cincinnati, Ohio) Davis enjoyed an excellent freshman year. He started 15 games, averaging 24 minutes per game and was Ohio State's third leading scorer. Davis was named to the Big Ten all-freshman team.

In the second game of the year, Davis started at second guard and stayed in the starting lineup through the 16th game of the season. He had 23 points in Ohio State's home opener against Mt. St. Mary's. He also had 19 points against North Carolina State in the first round of the Diet Pepsi Tournament of Champions in Charlotte, N.C. Davis reached double figures in scoring in 16 games and came off the bench and scored 20 points at Northwestern. He led Ohio State in free throw shooting with a .909 clip.

After his freshman year, there is no doubt that Davis is considered one of the better offensive talents in the Big Ten. He can score points quickly when he gets on one of his patented hot streaks. Davis was the hero of last year's overtime win against Providence in the NCAA tournament, coming off the bench to score a season-high 24 points, including a three-pointer at the buzzer that sent the game into overtime. He has a picture- perfect jumper and great work ethic.

Davis would have stayed in the starting lineup last year, but he seemed to tire easily and Ayers decided to use him off the bench instead of a starter. Ayers is hopeful that a rigorous off-season conditioning program will increase Davis' strength. He can play either backcourt spot, but is more effective at second guard because of his outside shooting ability.

STEVE HALL (6-8, 218 lbs., JR, F, #42, 0.8 ppg, 0.5 rpg, 4 assists, 3 blocked shots, 3 steals, Wayne Trace HS/Payne, Ohio) Hall is a solid reserve who has spent most of his career at power forward. However, he can play any of the three frontcourt spots. He played in 17 games last year for a total of 70 minutes.

While Hall scored just 13 points, but took only 11 shots for the year. He made 4-of-11 field goals and was a perfect 1-for-1 from three-point range. Hall connected on 4-of-5 free throws. Although not an offensive-minded player, Hall does have a good jumper and can get points around the basket because of his ability as an offensive rebounder. He has good hands, runs the floor well and is a better than average athlete.

His high point game was four against Northwestern. Hall played nine minutes in the season opener at DePaul and had an impressive six-minute stint at Indiana. He was named to the Big Ten All-Academic team last year and is a two-time Ohio State scholar-athlete. He also received the Fred R. Taylor Award for combined excellence in athletics and academics.

He comes from a rural high school and has had to make a big adjustment to play at this level. He seemed to gain more confidence last year and could see increased playing time. Hall is a good defender and can come in and play without hurting the Buckeyes.

NICK HODAK (6-6, 185 lbs., SR, F, #23, 1.5 ppg, 0.5 rpg, 1 assist, St. John's HS/Toledo, Ohio) Hodak is a walk-on who played in two games last year for a total of four minutes. He was 1-for-5 from the field and 1-of-2 from three-point range. Both of the games he played in came in the Big Ten portion of the schedule.

JIM JACKSON (6-6, 210 lbs., SO, F/G, #22, 16.1 ppg, 5.5 rpg, 110 assists, 14 blocked shots, 39 steals, Macomber HS/Toledo, Ohio) Ohio State has had its share of great players over the years, such as Jerry Lucas, John Havlicek, Jim Clemons, Herb Williams, Clark Kellogg, Dennis Hopson and many others. The latest in the long line of Ohio State greats is 6-6 sophomore swingman Jim Jackson.

Jackson was Ohio State's co-MVP last year along with Perry Carter, a second-team All-Big Ten selection and the Big Ten freshman of the year. He started all 30 games at small forward and led the Buckeyes in scoring (16.1 ppg), assists (110) and minutes played (1,035). He also tied for the team lead in steals (39) and was second in offensive rebounds (83). Jackson set an Ohio State freshman record for points with 482, breaking the old mark of 452 set by Herb Williams in 1978. He was twice named Big Ten player of the week and scored in double figures 28 times including the last 21 games. His season-high was 28 points at Iowa, and against Illinois. Jackson led Ohio State in scoring 14 times and in rebounding seven times. In all, he topped the 20- point plateau five times.

For the season, Jackson made 194-of-389 field goals (.499) and was 21-of-59 (.356) from three-point range. He nailed 73-of- 93 free throws (.785).

Jackson was ranked as one of the Top 16, 6-5 and taller inside/outside threats by *The Sporting News*. He not only has outstanding physical gifts such as great strength, but his intangibles are as impressive. Jackson has remarkable poise for a young player, is very intelligent, team-oriented and has a proven ability to take over a game and key junctures. Last season, he seemed to score, or have a hand in, every critical basket when the game is on the line.*

His last second baskets against Louisville and Michigan iced wins for Ohio State. This year Ayers would like to play Jackson some in the backcourt.

He was one of the few freshman invited to the World Championship/Goodwill Games trials in Colorado Springs last May. Jackson made the first cut from 66 down to 25. Later in the summer he starred for the runner-up North team at the U.S. Olympic Festival in Minneapolis.

During his career at Macomber HS in Toledo, Jackson earned a national reputation. He used to sign countless autographs at away games in high school and became known as one of the all-time greats in the Buckeye state. So far, Jackson has certainly lived up to his advance billing.

It will be interesting to see where he spends most of his time this year. As previously mentioned, Ayers wants him to play in the backcourt and the word is that Jackson has been promised that. He has always seen himself as a guard, however, Ohio State had considerable success last year in a lineup with Jackson at power forward. He gets most of his points offensively going to the basket rather than shooting from the perimeter.

CHRIS JENT (6-7, 220 lbs., JR, F/G, #21, 6.8 ppg, 4.3 rpg, 53 assists, 6 blocked shots, 39 steals, Sparta HS/Sparta, N.J.) Jent is an up and down player who started all 30 games last year. He played mainly at power forward after seeing most of his action at small forward and second guard as a freshman. Depending on how quickly the younger inside players develop for the Buckeyes, Jent may play more on the perimeter this year.

Jent came to Ohio State billed as a long distance shooting threat. While he was second on the team in made three-point baskets last year (30), Jent has been an erratic outside shooter. He was 30-of-85 (.353) from three-point range last year and 76- of-223 (.341) from the field. He had five double figure scoring games with a career-high 18 at Minnesota. Jent's career-best 11 rebounds came against South Carolina. He shot .824 from the line in Big Ten play, but made just 17 trips to the line, a figure that Ayers wants to see increased.

The emotional Jent is a battler who is rarely outhustled. His play often provides a lift for the Buckeyes and gets the fans in Ohio State's St. John arena excited. He is also a good offensive rebounder.

While playing power forward last year, Jent sacrificed some of his offensive skills and helped the team in other areas. He is a good ballhandler as well.

Jent is one of five returning starter of Ohio State. He was selected by his teammates as the Buckeyes' Most Inspirational Player last season.

TREG LEE (6-8, 220 lbs., SR, F, #34, 5.4 ppg, 3.4 rpg, 51 assist, 12 blocked shots, 8 steals, St. Joseph's HS/Cleveland, Ohio) Lee came to Ohio State with a major buildup. He was a big time High School All-America at the alma mater of former Buckeye star Clark Kellogg. However, he was not always a dominating presence in high school. This probably was the first sign that maybe Lee would have some trouble in college.

He had to sit out his first year at Ohio State and averaged 4.4 points and 2.3 rebounds as a sophomore. Lee was hampered by an ankle injury as a sophomore. Last season he did not start a game and averaged 19 minutes per game off the bench.

He is a streaky player who runs the floor well, is a big time dunker and has the quickness and ballhandling skills to be a more productive player than he is. However, Lee is not ideally suited for the Ohio State system. He is not mentally tough and is not a post player. He perceives himself as a small forward rather than a power forward. Lee also is not a consistent outside shooter. Last season he made 67-of-144 field goals (.465), missed his only three-point attempt and was 22-of-37 (.595) from the line.

He scored in double figures five times with a high of 14 against Iowa. Lee helped Ohio State to a win over Louisville with his play off the bench, scoring 10 key points for the Buckeyes. He had nine rebounds against La Salle and turned in a fine defensive effort against the Explorers All-America Lionel Simmons in that game. Lee also had 10 points in the season finale against UNLV.

Lee should be in the hunt for a starting spot at power forward.

SCOTT REEVES (6-0, 170 lbs., SR, G, #24, 1.0 ppg, 0.3 rpg, 1 assist, Eastmoor HS/Columbus, Ohio) Reeves was one of two walk-ons on the Ohio State team last year. He appeared in four games for a total of 15 minutes. Reeves made 2-of-9 field goals and missed his only three-point attempt.

BILL ROBINSON (7-0, 240 lbs., JR, C, #54, 3.9 ppg, 3.1 rpg, 7 assists, 12 blocked shots, 11 steals, McKinley HS/Canton, Ohio) Robinson could challenge for the starting center job this year, allowing Perry Carter to move to power forward. Even if he doesn't start, the tallest Buckeye will be a key backup on Randy Ayers' second Ohio State team. Last year he was much improved over his freshman year. Robinson started four games, played in all 30, and averaged 12 minutes per game. He made 46-of-91 field goals (.505) and was 24-of-46 (.522) from the line. Robinson reached double figures three times with a career high 14 against Mt. St. Mary's.

He also pulled down a career-high nine rebounds against Providence in the first round of the NCAA tournament.

Robinson was considered one of the more improved players in the Big Ten last year. The Ohio State coaching staff selected him as the Buckeyes' most improved player. During the last half of the Big Ten season, Robinson began to get more confident and aggressive. He had big games against Michigan (five points, seven rebounds and a key block) and Minnesota (13 points and five rebounds), both important Ohio State wins.

If Ayers starts Robinson he has a possible dilemma as it would slow down the Buckeyes. Ohio State presses and Robinson is not well suited for that style. Also, the more Robinson plays, the less playing time some other Buckeyes such as Treg Lee and Chris Jent will receive.

★ NEWCOMERS ★

JIMMY RATLIFF (6-8, 195 lbs., FR, F, #44, 23.2 ppg, Middletown HS/Middletown, Ohio) Ratliff was generally considered the second best senior in the state last year behind fellow Buckeye freshman Jamie Skelton. *Hoop Scoop* ranked the three Ohio State freshman - Ratliff, Skelton and Joe Reid - as the top three players in the state.

Ratliff was ranked as the No. 109 senior in the country last spring by *All Star Sports*. He is considered an outstanding perimeter shooter with good speed and jumping ability. However, Ratliff is a bit on the soft side to tackle the Big Ten on a full-time basis as a freshman. He also has to move up through an extremely deep Ohio State depth chart. Ayers is expected to use Ratliff at least initially at small forward.

JOE REID (6-7, 215 lbs., FR, F, #50, 18.0 ppg, University HS/Chagrin Falls, Ohio) Prior to his senior year, Reid was considered the top player in the state of Ohio. He slipped some as a senior, but was still ranked among the state's top three. Reid is truly an exceptional athlete. He also is a big time rebounder but a poor shooter.

"Reid is one of those guys who starts to go after the offensive rebound before the shot leaves his hand because he knows it won't go in," said an Ohio source.

"I expect all (three) freshmen to compete for playing time this year," said Ayers of his first recruiting class.

JAMIE SKELTON (6-2, 180 lbs., FR, G, #15, 27.6 ppg, Meadowdale HS/Dayton, Ohio) Skelton was ranked as the top senior in Ohio last year. He also carried his marginally talented Dayton Meadowdale HS to the Ohio state tournament.

"Jamie Skelton, who is one of the nation's top guards has carried this team on his back into sweet 16. Skelton . . . is a combo guard who can do it all - whether it be shooting or passing, the whole package is there," wrote Jerry "JL" Watson in *Hoop Scoop*.

Skelton is considered a truly electrifying leaper. He is a big time scorer with deep three-point shooting range. However, he is not a true point guard at this time and will have to learn that position. Ayers recruited Skelton as a point guard, but with his tremendous athletic ability and scoring potential he will pay dividends even if he doesn't totally master the position.

There's no question that Skelton is a big time prospect. The question is how Ayers will get him some playing time this year. The entire backcourt returns and sophomore Jim Jackson is expected to see more time in the backcourt this year. It will be interesting to see if Ayers decides to use Skelton this year, when there are some possible dilemmas concerning playing time. Will he be redshirted?

★ QUESTIONS ★

Consistent perimeter shooting? Ohio State is not a prolific perimeter shooting team. The Buckeyes made only .324 of their three-point attempts last year. Outside of Alex Davis, the other top returnees are not consistent outside shooters.

★ STRENGTHS ★

A strong returning cast! All 12 lettermen returned from last year. Ohio State coach Randy Ayers is one of the few coaches in the country who does not have to worry about replacing a key player.

Buckeye backcourt! Junior Mark Baker may be the best point guard in the Big Ten, sophomore Alex Davis is a proven scorer, junior Jamaal Brown is an excellent defender and a two-year starter, sophomore sensation Jim Jackson will see more time in the backcourt and freshman guard Jamie Skelton was one of the better high school guards in the country last year. Combined they should give Ohio State possibly the strongest backcourt in the Big Ten.

Versatility! Ohio State has a number of players who can play more than one position.

Impressive Depth!

★ BLUE RIBBON ANALYSIS ★

Randy Ayers first year at Ohio State was unquestionably a success. The Buckeyes won 17 games, knocked off six teams ranked in the Top 20, posted the most

Big Ten wins (10) of any Buckeye team since 1985 and won an opening round game in the NCAA tournament. With all 12 letterman returning, Ohio State appears ready to make a major leap in the national standings in his second year as the head coach of this proud program.

The list of holdovers include sophomore swingman Jim Jackson, a second-team All-Big Ten selection and the freshman of the year in the Big Ten, and senior center Perry Carter, who paced Ohio State in scoring and rebounding. Jackson has potential to go on to be an All-America and one of the best ever from this tradition rich program.

Junior Mark Baker could be the best point guard in the Big Ten as he was excellent down the stretch for the Buckeyes. Junior guard Jamaal Brown is a two-year starter and is in a true defensive stopper. Junior forward Chris Jent is an emotional player who ignited the Buckeyes frequently last year and started at power forward. Sophomore guard Alex Davis led Ohio State in three-point field goal percentage last year and was third on the team in scoring. He is one of the premier young guards in the Big Ten. Junior center Bill Robinson was Ohio State's most improved player last year and should see more action than the 12 minutes per game he averaged last year. If senior forward Treg Lee could shake the inconsistency which has plagued him so far in his career, Ohio State would have even more offensive potential. Lee was one of the most highly regarded high school players ever in Ohio.

Junior Steve Hall and sophomore Tom Brandewie, both forwards, are also capable players. Ayers first freshman class consists of the top three seniors in the state last year. Keep an eye on freshman guard Jamie Skelton as he is an electrifying leaper who could be one of the premier guards in the Big Ten in a few years.

"A year ago we were a young team learning a new system," said Ayers. "We go into this season as a much more experienced team. Hopefully, we can take up in October where we left off in March.

"In addition to more experience, we have better depth than we had a year ago," Ayers pointed out. "And, like last year, we have a number of players who could play more than one position. I like the versatility that gives us."

Ohio State is also aided by the fact that this appears to be the weakest Big Ten in recent memory. Traditional Big Ten powers Michigan and Illinois are down, Iowa is not going to have a vintage club, and two teams that enjoyed great success last year - Minnesota and Purdue - have to decline at least somewhat this year. Road victories should come easier this year in the Big Ten than usual.

Ohio State is capable of pushing pre-season favorite Michigan State for the Big Ten title. The Buckeyes should finish no lower than third in the conference, easily win over 20 games and stay in the Top 20 all year. Ohio State hasn't advanced to the Final 16 of the NCAA tournament since 1983. This should be the best Ohio State team in a decade.

LAST SEASON			
#@DePaul	53-71	Michigan State	75-84
Mt. St. Mary's (MD)	102-63	@Wisconsin	68-58
##North Carolina State	54-68	Michigan	64-61
##Oklahoma State	59-81	@Purdue	70-75
American University	74-64	Illinois	86-80
Robert Morris	78-51	@Northwestern	95-86
South Carolina	59-46	@Indiana	66-77
###LaSalle	62-74	Minnesota	93-83
###New Orleans	74-66	*Providence	84-83OT
Indiana	69-67	*UNLV	65-76
@Iowa	79-73		
@Michigan State	68-78	@ Road Games	
Wisconsin	68-53	# Dodge NIT	
@Michigan	88-90	## Diet Pepsi Tournament of Champions, Charlotte, NC	
@Minnesota	78-83		
Purdue	66-78	### USF&G Sugar Bowl Classic, New Orleans, LA	
@Illinois	81-92		
Northwestern	101-77	* NCAA Tournament, Salt Lake City, UT	
Louisville	91-88OT		
Iowa	98-80		

1990-91 OHIO STATE SCHEDULE

Nov.	25	Bethune-Cookman (FL)	Feb.	11	Michigan
	28	Delaware State		14	@Wisconsin
Dec.	1	Youngstown State		17	Indiana
	8	Chicago State		20	@Illinois
	12	Wright State (OH)		23	Minnesota
	15	@American University	Mar.	3	Michigan State
	17	Tennessee State		6	@Purdue
	22	#Georgetown		9 or 10	@Iowa
	27-28	##West Palm Beach Classic			
Jan.	3	Iowa	@ Road Games		
	5	@Michigan	# Las Vegas, NV		
	10	@Northwestern	## West Palm Beach, FL (Miami of Florida, Miami of Ohio & Mississippi State)		
	12	Wisconsin			
	19	Illinois			
	21	@Indiana			
	24	@Minnesota			
	31	@Michigan State			
Feb.	3	@Purdue			
	9	Northwestern			

NOTES: Ohio State will open up with another *Blue Ribbon* Top 40 team, Mississippi State, in the first round of the West Palm Beach Classic . . . the actual date of the season ending game at Iowa will be determined, by television requirements, after the beginning of the season . . . over the years, Ohio State has appeared in 16 NCAA tournaments, including the first one in 1939 when the Buckeyes finished as runners-up. Ohio State has made it to the Final Four eight times and appeared in four championship games. In the NCAA tournament, Ohio State has an overall record of 26-15 in its 16 appearances.

OKLAHOMA

LAST SEASON: 27-5
CONFERENCE RECORD: 11-3
STARTERS LOST: 5
STARTERS RETURNING: 0
CONFERENCE: BIG EIGHT
LOCATION: NORMAN, OK
HOME FLOOR: LLOYD NOBLE CENTER (10,871)
NICKNAME: SOONERS
COLORS: CRIMSON AND CREAM

★ **COACH'S PROFILE** ★

BILLY TUBBS (Record at Oklahoma, 257-83. Career record, 363-151) The colorful, brash and outspoken Tubbs will get one of his sternest tests this year. For the first time in Oklahoma basketball history, the Sooners return no starters from the previous year's team. From last season's 27-5 team, Oklahoma has lost 82 percent of its scoring and 80.7 percent of the rebounding. Despite those negative statistics, Tubbs believes he will have another championship contending team at Oklahoma. After what he has done so far with the Sooner basketball program, you shouldn't doubt him.

The controversial Tubbs has never backed down from a challenge since his youth when he grew in Tulsa, Okla., fatherless and somewhat of a street urchin. Tubbs also knew he had a challenge ahead of him when he took over at Oklahoma

in 1980. The Sooners' basketball program did have some success before him. John MacLeod, who coached Phoenix and Dallas in the NBA, and Dave Bliss, who is now at New Mexico, were successful at Oklahoma. Alvin Adams, who went on to a long career in the NBA with Phoenix, was an All-America player at Oklahoma. However, the basketball program was definitely a poor stepchild of the school's fabulously successfully football program. There was no comparison between the excitement level at Lloyd Noble Center, the Sooners' basketball home, and the frenzy Barry Switzer's football program generated. While the football program has experienced a resurgence this fall after the Sooners were hit with NCAA probation and Switzer resigned, Tubbs has created an unprecedented level of excitement and interest for basketball at Oklahoma. He realized early that Oklahoma fans needed a good show in addition to a winning team. So, he became determined to put a product on the floor that was exciting enough for Oklahoma fans weaned on football blowouts and dazzling, Heisman Trophy caliber running backs. Tubbs' system has achieved things not even the cocky coach would have dreamed in his wildest imagination. Oklahoma spent most of the last decade in a scoring frenzy. The Sooners have set more than 100 Big Eight Conference records in the past decade, and ranked nationally in the Top 10 in scoring every year in the '80s. In the process, the Sooners helped send college basketball on an up-tempo trend. Many coaches believe college basketball is headed in the '90s to an extremely up-tempo game with full court pressure defense the norm.

"There's nothing wrong with a game in the '50s or '60s if it's for a conference championship or national championship," Tubbs told B.G. Brooks of the *Rocky Mountain News*. "But in helping some people get jobs, I'm asked all the time about the kinds of game they coach. Up-tempo? Or hold the ball? I think you know what the fans want to see.''

After a 9-18 initial season at Oklahoma, Tubbs has never won fewer than 22 games in any of the last nine seasons. Three times his Sooners have won 30 or more games in a season. In 1983-84 Oklahoma won 29 games and last year the Sooners won 27. He put Oklahoma in the Final Four in 1988 and the Sooners have become fixtures in the national Top 10.

"For the last two or three years, really, I've seen our program change direction," Tubbs told Jim Thomas of the *St. Louis Post-Dispatch*. "I have seen a lot of respect coming on our team. I actually think it started about three years ago, the year we were beaten by Iowa (in the Sweet 16 of the NCAA tournament) . . .

"We've always played tough defense, but we kind of joked our defense off. We really wouldn't talk about it. We took a redirection in our defense two years ago. That was when we fully committed to the fullcourt pressure defense.''

Tubbs is not reluctant to admit that he will kick, stomp and mutilate any team that gets in his way. He is not exactly the favorite of many coaches and definitely will pour it on when he gets a chance. Last season Oklahoma opened up with a 72-point blowout of U.S. International, then 146-51 and 130-62 bashings of Northeastern Illinois and Angelo State, respectively.

"We play hard," Tubbs said. "We give no quarter, and we ask for none.''

He was born in St. Louis in the height of The Depression. His father died when Tubbs was a child and his mother took him and an older son to her parents' small farm in Oklahoma. She later moved to Tulsa when Tubbs was in the fourth grade. His mother died of a heart attack when he was 14. Her death devastated Billy and he moved in with his older brother who had a family of his own. He spent his share of time on the streets and was a combative youngster who would fight it out if needed. That combativeness is still present in Tubbs today.

He was a good high school player and went on to Lon Morris JC in Jacksonville, Texas, and played in the national junior college tournament. Maybe that is why Tubbs is one of the top recruiters and coaches of junior college players along with Jerry Tarkanian of UNLV. Both Tubbs and Tarkanian are two of the few big time coaches who actually played junior college basketball. He transferred to Lamar Tech (now Lamar University) where he played and obtained a B.S. Degree in Physical Education. Tubbs served as an assistant at Lamar and North Texas for many years before starting his head coaching career in 1971 at Southwestern University in Georgetown, Texas. He spent two years at Southwestern, compiling a 31-22 record, before going back to his alma· mater. Tubbs spent four years at Lamar. After a losing 12-17 record in his first year, the Cardinals were 18-9, 23-9 and 22-11 in subsequent years under Tubbs. He led Lamar to upsets over highly ranked Oregon State and Missouri in the NCAA tournament before accepting the Oklahoma job in the spring of 1980.

Tubbs is one of the most quotable and wittiest coaches in college basketball. Last year after Oklahoma won at Seton Hall, Tubbs took a jab at the Big East Conference. "It's like going to a slow dance," Tubbs said of the Big East. "We like to rock'n'roll. This is like slow waltzing. Playing this kind of tempo is like a vacation.

"I wouldn't say it's boring, but in Oklahoma now, you need a prescription to watch a Big East game. They prescribe it instead of sleeping pills.''

"I think the game should be fun. It should be enjoyable for players and for fans. We take ourselves a little too seriously. It's becoming too much of a business,'' he told Jim O'Brien of *Basketball Weekly*.

"You're in deep trouble when you can't laugh or take a joke. I grew up in places where you had to joke your way through just to stay sane. People resent you having a good time. When we step on the floor, nobody plays harder than we do, or cares as much as we do. But you have to laugh once in awhile, too. Remember, when it's all said and done, basketball is still a game . . .''

He has one goal that has never been fulfilled —seeing his team score 100 points in a half and 200 points in a game. And who knows, one of these days his "Billy Ball" style of play might achieve those goals.

"I don't ever see pressure out there," Tubbs told O'Brien. "The pressure of what? Expectations? That's the whole fun of it. Nobody has higher expectations than we have for our own program. No one's expectations can exceed mine . . .

"As I was growing up, the most enjoyable years were the years when I was in college. Well, I'm still in college. One of these days I'm going to grow up. When I grow up I'm going to leave school and get my degree.

"I love the college atmosphere. They can be the four or five greatest years of your life. The people you meet . . . the people you associate with. Many people meet their future mate in college. I've been in college for thirty years, and I've enjoyed the college atmosphere.

"When I graduated from college, I knew I wanted to return to college to coach. High school was a place I never wanted to go back to. But the college atmosphere is fantastic.''

Tubbs also expanded on some other matters in his interview with O'Brien in *Basketball Weekly*. "There's been a lot of people who've come through college and it's helped them," he told O'Brien. "Nobody ever programmed me to go to college. I was the first one in our family to graduate from high school. Athletics is not just a big business. You can mold some people. You can get some things in athletics you can't get elsewhere.

"Competition is just like real life. The classroom is not like real life. Maybe some of these high academic qualifiers don't need athletics, but the ones that are involved do need it. We're working with players to get them an education, but you can't force-feed them education.

"There's a pressure in coaching now," he continued. "It's frustrating. You have no rights. Where's any legislation to provide tenure for coaches? If you don't win, you don't have a job. Even winning isn't always enough. You have to be on TV and make lots of money and get to the NCAA Tournament, or you can be tossed out into the street to look for a job.

"Coaches are asked to be many things these days. I understand cheating; I know what cheating is. But we have so many rules. It's tough to keep up with them. It's easy to remember what's out-in-out cheating, but not with some of this Mickey Mouse stuff.''

We concur with the opinion of one of Tubbs' Big Eight rivals, Kansas coach Roy Williams. "There are two things that Oklahoma doesn't get credit for. I don't think they get credit for playing the defense that they really play. And I don't think Billy Tubbs gets credit for doing the job that he does over on the bench.''

Tubbs has not only turned Oklahoma into a national basketball power, but he has done it on his terms with his style of play. In the process, he has played a major role in the up-tempo trend that is now dominating college basketball.

★ PLAYERS NOT RETURNING ★

WILLIAM DAVIS (6-6, C, 16.6 ppg, 8.5 rpg, 38 assists, 18 blocked shots, 39 steals) Davis was only 6-6, yet he started at center for Oklahoma. After struggling to stay healthy as a junior, Davis finished second on the team in scoring and led the Sooners in rebounding last year.

"You got small forward, power forward and stuff. One of our guys, we call him a small center," Tubbs said of Davis.

Davis is one of five lettermen who are not returning for the Sooners this season. He had a successful senior year but Tubbs will probably replace Davis with either 6-9 Martin Keane or 6-8 Bryan Sallier, two highly regarded junior college transfers.

SKEETER HENRY (6-7, G, 17.3 ppg, 5.0 rpg, 141 assists, 11 blocked shots, 59 steals) Henry's emergence was a major reason why Oklahoma did not slow down last year and won 27 games. After averaging 7.0 points per game as a junior, he became a full-time starter as a senior and upped that average to 17.3. He also tied for the team lead in assists. He was a greenlight shooter who had the freedom to pop whenever he wished. He also was a theatrical player who was known to form an imaginary gun with his hand, pull it out of an imaginary holster and fire the phantom gun and blow out the smoking pistol, just like a gunslinger in a western movie, and put it back into the holster. Needless to say he was not a favorite of opposing crowds.

"I like Skeeter as a player, but I don't admire what he does shooting those guns," said Kansas coach Roy Williams. "I think it shows up opponents.''

The fun loving Henry was a prototypical Oklahoma player who loved to run-and-gun and put points on the board. Even though he should be very hard to replace, Tubbs thinks Oklahoma can average 112 to 114 points per game this year.

JACKIE JONES (6-8, F, 15.0 ppg, 7.0 rpg, 51 assists, 64 blocked shots, 44 steals) Jones started 20 games last year and was Oklahoma's third leading scorer and No. 2 rebounder. Instead of returning for his senior year, Jones flunked out and is playing professionally in Spain this year.

If Oklahoma had Jones, the Sooners would be the prohibitive favorite in the Big Eight this year and a probable pre-season Top 10 pick.

TONY MARTIN (6-8, F, 11.1 ppg, 4.6 rpg, 28 assists, 11 blocked shots, 28 steals) Martin was a part-time starter. He started 16 games last year and averaged 18.9 minutes per game. He was Oklahoma's fifth leading scorer. He was a strong physical presence inside. Martin had some big scoring games during his Oklahoma career, he had a 30-point outing against North Texas last year, and was a key player for the Sooners.

He is one of five double figure scorers Oklahoma is missing from last year. Few programs could lose that much scoring and come back strong the next year the way Tubbs believes the Sooners will in 1990-91.

SMOKEY McCOVERY (6-2, G, 10.8 ppg, 2.9 rpg, 132 assists, 2 blocked shots, 68 steals) McCovery started 19 games last year. He was expected to be a senior for the Sooners this year but is academically ineligible. He started 19 games last year and was sixth on the team in scoring. He made 33-of-102 three-pointers (32.3 percent) which ranked McCovery third on the team in three-pointers made. He led the team in steals and second in assists.

McCovery's loss could hurt Oklahoma's pressure defense. Tubbs is concerned that the Sooners will not be as tough defensively without McCovery to pressure the ball on the press.

★ RETURNING PLAYERS ★

TERRY EVANS (6-1, 170 lbs., SO, G, #14, 8.9 ppg, 2.7 rpg, 141 assists, 3 blocked shots, 42 steals, Millwood HS/Oklahoma City, Okla.) Evans started 13 games at the beginning of last season before coming off the bench. He was 95-of-230 from the field (.413) and 58-of-137 (.423) from three-point range. From the line Evans made 40-of-56 attempts (71.4 percent). His 58 three-pointers led Oklahoma in that category.

"He gets the ball down the floor relatively quick," Tubbs told Wendell Barnhouse of *The Sporting News*. "He's got good vision, and he's a good three-point he's a very smart young man. When you talk to him, you know the gears are turning.''

His high scoring game last year was 26 points against North Texas and Evans also had 22 points against Kansas. He averaged 23 minutes per game last year.

Evans' father was a two-time All-Big Eight basketball player at Oklahoma and later served as an assistant coach for the Sooners under head coach John MacLeod. This year, Evans will either start alongside South Carolina transfer Brent Price or be the first guard off the bench for the Sooners. Either way, he's going to be a very important player and will have to be able to help generate the Sooners defensive pressure in the full court press.

KERMIT HOLMES (6-7, 210 lbs., SR, F, #25, 5.0 ppg, 4.1 rpg, 15 assists, 9 blocked shots, 14 steals, Okmulgee HS/Okmulgee, Okla.) If Oklahoma is to win the Big Eight and be a national factor this year, some Sooners, such as Holmes, who have been waiting in the wings for their opportunity, have to emerge. Last year Holmes played in 26 of Oklahoma's 32 games and averaged 11.1 minutes per game. He did not start a game. From the field he was 53-of-99 (53.5 percent) and 25-of-54 (46.3 percent) from the line. His high scoring game was 16 against North Texas and Holmes had 11 against rival Oklahoma State.

Holmes sat out the 1987-88 season and played in only 10 games in 1988-89. He was one of the premier high school players in Oklahoma during his career at Okmulgee HS. He was also highly recruited by the likes of Louisville, DePaul, Houston, Arizona and Oklahoma State. He is tough and athletic, however Holmes has had trouble scoring except off the offensive boards. Tubbs has always liked Holmes but the Oklahoma depth chart was too deep for him to be a significant contributor.

Holmes will compete for the starting power forward job that Damon Patterson should claim once he is eligible.

TERRENCE MULLINS (6-3, 198 lbs., SR, G/F, #24, 5.2 ppg, 1.8 rpg, 15 assists, 3 blocked shots, 18 steals, Riordon HS/San Francisco, Calif.) Mullins is the only Sooner left in the program from the 1988 Final Four team. His role decreased last year. He started 20 games in his first year as a Sooner in 1987-88. As a sophomore he started 29 games and averaged 28 minutes per game. In that season, Mullins played six complete games and was on the court the full 50 minutes against Colorado in a double overtime victory in the Big Eight Conference tournament. He finished second on the team behind All-America guard Mookie Blaylock in assists with 159.

Last season, Mullins' role decreased significantly. He played in 22 games, starting one, and averaged 10.7 minutes per game. He was 23-of-49 (46.9 percent) from three-point range and 42-of-86 (48.8 percent) from the field. Mullins shot a poor 7-of-17 (46.7 percent) from the line.

He can play either backcourt spot, is a talented offensive player but has been inconsistent. Late in his sophomore year when Oklahoma was slumping, Tubbs removed Mullins from the lineup and his role has not increased since then.

This year look for Mullins to be a dangerous three-point shooter and a much more important member of the Oklahoma team. He is the best leaper among Oklahoma's guards and should start the season at small forward.

DAMON PATTERSON (6-7, 205 lbs., SR, F, #31, 11.6 ppg, 6.2 rpg, 49 assists, 31 blocked shots, 41 steals, Central HS/Kalamazoo, Mich.) Patterson is academically ineligible at least through the first semester. He is expected back for Oklahoma's Dec. 22 game with Duke. He was fourth on the team in scoring last year and started 30 games.

For the statistics, Patterson was 154-of-306 from the field (.503 percent) and 14-of-42 (33.3 percent) from three-point range. From the line Patterson made 50-of-73 free throws (68.5 percent). He scored 29 points in a nationally televised game at Loyola Marymount and came through with 24 against Missouri. He averaged 26.4 minutes per game and his playing time rose to an average of 30.7 minutes in Big Eight play.

Patterson is the most gifted Sooner. He can put the ball on the floor to create his shot, hit from the perimeter and go inside to score or rebound. Patterson is a true multi-dimensional force who could star this year as Tubbs plans on accelerating the Sooner offense. He will start at power forward once eligible.

JEFF ROBERTS (6-2, 175 lbs., SO, G, #22, Dale HS/Shawnee, Okla.) Roberts is a walk-on who redshirted last year and practiced with the team. He is a good shooter who is expected to provide some depth for the Sooners in the backcourt.

JASON SKURCENSKI (6-2, 173 lbs., SR, G, #11, 0.6 ppg, 0.3 rpg, 4 assists, Bartlesville HS/Bartlesville, Okla.) Skurcenski is one of four seniors returning for their final season at Oklahoma. He appeared in only eight games last year for a total of 13 minutes. In limited action last year, Skurcenski was 2-of-12 from the field (16.7 percent) and 1-of-5 (20 percent) from three-point range. His season scoring high was three points against Nebraska.

He has not been able to crack the deep Oklahoma depth chart in his first three years with the Sooners. Skurcenski is probably going to be a limited contributor again.

ROLAND WARE (6-6, 225 lbs., SO, F, #42, 3.0 ppg, 2.2 rpg, 2 assists, 2 blocked shots, 4 steals, Central HS/Memphis, Tenn.) In his first season at Oklahoma, Ware appeared in only nine games for a total of 46 minutes. Ware's season high in scoring was six points against Nebraska. Ware made 11-of-25 field goals (44 percent) and was 5-of-12 (41.7 percent) from the line.

He redshirted his first year at Oklahoma before playing last year. Ware was considered one of the better players in Memphis during his days at Central HS. He has excellent strength and can score around the basket. This year his playing time could rise. Tubbs is going to need some players who were not key contributors in the past to come through this year. Ware could be a bigger factor this year.

TOMMY FRENCH (6-5, 177 lbs., SR, F, #34, Albuquerque HS/Albuquerque, N.M.) French finally found a home at Oklahoma after looking for a new place to play for much of the summer. His dilemma was caused when his previous school, Hardin-Simmons University of Abilene, Tex., dropped its basketball program. At first, French seemed headed for Washington State, but over the summer he decided to attend Hawaii instead. Then, in August when the Oklahoma roster was reduced, French decided to come to Norman for his last year of college basketball.

Last season as a junior at Hardin-Simmons, French tied for the spot as the No. 41st scorer in the Division I ranks with Patrick Jones of Niagara. He was 212-of-338 from the field (.627) and 10-of-18 (55.6 percent) from three-point range. French made 164-of-224 free throws (.732). He averaged 21.4 points per game and 4.9 rebounds in 28 games.

French was a second-team All-Trans America Athletic Conference pick. He obviously can score and gets to the basket well.

MAURICE ''KEKE'' HICKS (6-1, 160 lbs., FR, G, #21, 30.5 ppg, Frederick Douglas HS/Atlanta, Ga.) Other than Loyola Marymount under former coach Paul Westhead, no program in the country gives a freer rein to its shooters than Oklahoma. Hicks is definitely a long range shooter in the Oklahoma mold. He was a unanimous All-Georgia selection as a senior. Hicks also made the All-Tournament team at the Boston Shootout and played in the Georgia-Tennessee All-Star game. He connected on 53.3 percent of his three-point field goals last year and hit 51 percent as a junior. Hicks made 52 percent of his field goal attempts overall and 91 percent of his free throws. He was ranked as the 15th best high school shooting guard in the nation by the *National Recruiters Cage Letter*.

''He doesn't even look for other players,'' said Bob Gibbons of *All-Star Sports* in a *Sports Illustrated* article. ''I wouldn't give you a plug nickel for him if not for his ability as a three-point shooter. He's amazing.''

Hicks had a career high 44 points against eventual Georgia state champion Atlanta Southside last year. He selected Oklahoma over Western Kentucky and Clemson.

No coach in the country appreciates a shooter more than Tubbs. Hicks should be able to get some playing time as a freshman and be in the Sooners' top four guard rotation.

MARTIN KEANE (6-8, 225 lbs., JR, C/F, #44, 25.0 ppg, 13.7 rpg, Toronto, Canada & Northeast Nebraska CC/Norfolk, Neb.) Keane was ranked as the sixth best junior college forward/center by the *National Recruiters Cage Letter*. ''Keane is a strong athlete who gets on the boards and is tough to stop. He is a potential force,'' said Van Coleman of the *National Recruiters Cage Letter*.

The Toronto, Canada, native had a strong career at Northeast Nebraska JC. He recorded a career-high of 37 points and 22 rebounds in one game in last year and was a two-time All-Region and All-Conference selection. Keane connected on 56 percent of his field goals and 68 percent of his free throws last year.

''230 pound Canadian will put bulk in the lane, can score around bucket,'' said Rick Ball in *Basketball Times*.

Keane picked Oklahoma over Southern Methodist, Texas Tech, Texas Christian, Wake Forest, Washington, Washington State and St. John's. He is considered an immediate impact player by Oklahoma insiders. There is little doubt that Keane will be in the starting lineup for Oklahoma at the beginning of the season.

BRENT PRICE (6-1, 175 lbs., JR, G, #20, Enid HS/Enid, Okla.) After two years as a starter at South Carolina, Price decided to come back home to Oklahoma and play for the Sooners. He is expected to be an immediate starter at point guard.

As a sophomore on a 19-11 South Carolina team which lost in the first round of the NCAA tournament to North Carolina State, Price averaged 14.4 points, 2.5 rebounds, handed out 128 assists and recorded 52 steals.

Price is the younger brother of Mark Price, former Georgia Tech star and the starting point guard for the Cleveland Cavaliers. He tried out for the U.S. National team last May in Colorado Springs, Colo., and appeared quicker than he was at South Carolina. Price was able to effectively penetrate in the trials and was impressive considering he had been away from organized competition for a year. He missed a month of practice in late August and September due to surgery for a right elbow injury. He is expected to be ready for the opening of pre-season drills on October 15.

Price is one of the premier transfers in the country this year. He was a two-year starter at South Carolina and is a heady playmaker in addition to a three-point threat. He established himself as a solid major college point guard in two years at South Carolina.

The Enid, Okla., native was a High School All-America player and ranked as one of the Top 100 in the country as a senior. Now that he is back home in the most wide open offensive system in the country, Price should put big numbers on the board. Price is one of the main reasons why Tubbs believes this will be his best perimeter shooting team ever at Oklahoma.

DON RICHHART (6-10, 220 lbs., FR, C, #50, 19.0 ppg, 10.0 rgp, Tahlequah HS/Tahlequah, Okla.) Richhart was the top big man in Oklahoma last year. He was an All-State performer and was considered one of the top high school centers in the midwest. ''Richhart is a strong insider with nice offensive skills. Consistent from inside 15-feet and is very capable of running the floor,'' said Van Coleman of the *National Recruiters Cage Letter*.

As a freshman, Richhart will back up junior college transfers Martin Keane and Bryan Sallier in the pivot.

55

BRYAN SALLIER (6-8, 257 lbs., SO, F/C, #40, 9.9 ppg, 9.1 rpg, 68 blocked shots, Port Arthur HS/Port Arthur, Tex. & San Jacinto JC/Pasadena, Tex.) Sallier is making his second appearance at Oklahoma. He originally signed with the Sooners two years ago and came to Oklahoma but left soon after arriving. He transferred to San Jacinto JC, probably the premier junior college program in the country, and played one season there before transferring back to Oklahoma. In his only season at San Jacinto, Sallier was a spot starter who played in all 38 games for a 34-4 team that finished seventh in the national junior college tournament. He averaged 21 minutes per game. Sallier was ranked as the third best junior college center in the country by many scouting services after last season. He led San Jacinto in blocked shots and connected on 53 percent of his field goal attempts and 67.2 percent of his free throws. His best performance was a 17-point, 14-rebound night against Tyler CC (Tex.) in the Region 14 playoff.

Sallier came out of Port Arthur HS ranked as the seventh best center in the nation by *The Sporting News*. He was a two-time 4A player of the year by the Texas Association of Basketball Coaches. He averaged 19.5 points and 15 rebounds a game as a senior on a 29-4 state championship team. He was just as highly recruited in football as he was in basketball. Sallier was a *Parade Magazine* All-America football selection as a tight end. Barry Switzer, who was Oklahoma's football coach at that time, dearly wanted Sallier as a tight end. Switzer thought Sallier could be as good as former Oklahoma All-America tight end Keith Jackson, now with the Philadelphia Eagles, except he thought Jackson was faster. Sallier also seriously considered signing with the Pitt football program, but resisted all gridiron offers to continue his basketball career in college.

He has good range on his shot and is an outstanding shotblocker. Former Oklahoma All-America Stacey King, now with the Chicago Bulls, came back to Norman late in the summer and scrimmaged against the current Sooners. He told several Oklahoma officials that Sallier and Martin Keane were as talented as any players he played with during his collegiate career.

Oklahoma suffered some severe graduation loses, but the Sooners should be stronger in the middle this year with Sallier and Keane. Heading into pre-season drills, Sallier is expected to be the second string center behind Keane. There is no question that he can score, rebound and block shots well enough to help the Sooners, but there is concern about his physical condition. He needs to shed some weight and get in better shape to play at the Oklahoma pace.

JEFF WEBSTER (6-8, 210 lbs., SO, F, #32, Carl Albert HS/Midwest City, Okla.) Although Webster is listed among the returning players by the Oklahoma Sports Information Department, we consider him a newcomer because he redshirted after three games last year. Webster played in three games for a total of 27 minutes, then was afflicted by bone spurs which turned into a stress fracture of his leg. Webster retains his eligibility and is considered a freshman this season.

In his limited action, Webster averaged 5.7 points and 2.7 rebounds. He made 8-of-14 field goals (64.3 percent) and was 1-of-3 from the line (33.3 percent). He scored seven points in an early season game against Northeastern Illinois before being injured.

Webster is one of the most highly regarded high school players ever in Oklahoma. Other than former All-America Wayman Tisdale, Webster is the most highly touted high school player Tubbs has signed at Oklahoma. He averaged 26.0 points and 12.1 rebounds as a senior at Carl Albert HS. Webster was named the Oklahoma player of the year as a senior. He was also a second-team *Parade Magazine* All-America selection and one of eight finalists for the Gatorade National Player of the Year Award. Webster set school records at Carl Albert HS for points in a season (728), career points (1,802), and points in a game (51), in addition to owning every rebound record at the school.

"Top prospect in Oklahoma, Webster is also one of the most-prized combination forwards in the land. He has the athletic ability and physical tools to play both inside or on the perimeter. He will likely be a wing forward in college. Last summer Jeff led his Tulsa AAU team to the championship of the highly competitive 48-team BCI tournament in Tempe, Az. He outperformed many highly-rated individuals to earn the event's MVP award. Veteran mentor Dub Raper praised Jeff's shooting skills, and 'great desire to play the game'," wrote Bob Gibbons of *All-Star Sports* two years ago.

His sister, Sharon, plays on the Oklahoma Women's team. Webster did not easily adapt to the increased intensity of the Oklahoma system in pre-season last year. The coaches felt he needed to learn how to play hard all the time, but he should be further along this year.

Webster and Kermit Holmes are expected to compete for the starting power forward spot. However, Damon Patterson is expected back in time for the December 22 game with Duke and Webster will probably be second-team after that. He should be able to provide some scoring and should be a standout after a full year in the program.

★ QUESTIONS ★

How quickly can Tubbs put together an almost entirely new team? The Sooners were hit hard by graduation and academic problems. Until Damon Patterson regains his eligibility, Oklahoma will be without its top six scorers from a year ago. At least five new players will have key roles this year at Oklahoma.

Defensive pressure from the backcourt? The academic ineligibility of Smokey McCovery leaves the Sooners without a real strong defensive guard to key the press.

Defense? Oklahoma has improved significantly defensively in the last two years but its press may not be as effective with so many new faces.

★ STRENGTH ★

Billy Tubbs! Because Tubbs is such a joker who not only pokes fun at himself but some of the sacred cows of college basketball, he has not been given due credit for the amazing job he has done at Oklahoma. A team does not win 35, 30 and 27 games, respectively, in three straight years without a strong coach and Tubbs is one of the best in the nation.

Perimeter shooting! No coach in the country appreciates shooters more than Tubbs and he has 'em this year. Tubbs feels that this should be the best shooting club he has had at Oklahoma.

A stronger inside presence with 6-9 Martin Keane and 6-8 Bryan Sallier Overall athletic ability and talent!

Homecourt edge! Oklahoma enters the season with a 45-game home winning streak.

★ BLUE RIBBON ANALYSIS ★

At first glance it would appear that Billy Tubbs, the Jack Nicholson sound-alike coach of the Oklahoma Sooners, will finally get his wings clipped after spending the last three years in the headlines due to No. 1 ranked teams and his own wise crackin' humor. Tubbs will never win any Mr. Congeniality Award for his brutal honesty and penchant for running up scores on undermanned opponents.

Oklahoma was hit hard by graduation and academic problems. Four of the top five scorers are gone this year and last year's fourth-leading scorer, senior Damon Patterson, will miss at least eight and maybe more games in November and December due to academic problems. The Sooners will start the season without a returning starter for the first time in Oklahoma basketball history. At least five newcomers will play key roles, but Tubbs is not looking back.

He feels that Oklahoma has a number of players who have been waiting in the wings behind talented teammates in the past and are now ready for an opportunity to keep the Sooners' recent tradition of high scores and national rankings intact. Tubbs firmly believes this is his best shooting team ever at Oklahoma. He feels the Sooners can take around 95 shots a game and average between 112 and 114 points per game.

"If we come close to hitting 50 percent of our shots, no one can beat us," Tubbs said. "We are now faced with the biggest challenge we have faced in quite some time due to lack of experience. Those people, however, who think we'll be tucking in our tail and hiding have another think coming. This team will play hard, play aggressive and score more points than ever."

The Sooners are still extremely talented and lethal offensively. Patterson is the top returnee and he could have a great senior year if he quickly overcomes missing a significant part of the non-conference schedule. Senior swingman Terrence Mullins has been inconsistent but has had big games in the past. South Carolina transfer Brent Price, the younger brother of Cleveland Cavaliers' point guard Mark Price, is expected to come out smoking in Oklahoma's up-tempo system. Hardin-Simmons transfer Tommy French has one year of eligibility remaining. He averaged 21.4 points per game last year at Hardin-Simmons.

Redshirt freshman Jeff Webster was considered one of the Top 20 high school players in the country two years ago and is one of the most highly touted players ever to sign with Oklahoma. Freshman guard Marquis "KeKe" Hicks is one of the best three-point shooters to ever sign with Oklahoma and junior college transfers Martin Keane (6-9) and Bryan Sallier (6-8) will give Oklahoma more size in the middle than the Sooners had last year.

Oklahoma will be underrated in pre-season due to the large personnel losses. The Sooners are still a talented, high-flying bunch, capable of leading the nation in scoring. The only thing lacking in name recognition as this Oklahoma team does not have an established star.

Tubbs knows talent and we are going to take his word that this team could be much better than the experts predict. Oklahoma hasn't won fewer than 24 games since the 1982-83 season and that trend should continue. The Sooners will lead the nation in scoring and win the Big Eight title. This should be another rip-roarin' basketball season at Oklahoma.

LAST SEASON		1990-91 OKLAHOMA SCHEDULE		
U.S. International (CA)	173-101	Nov.	14	#New Orleans
Northeastern Illinois	146-51		26	St. Joseph's
Angelo State (TX)	130-62		28	@Texas A&M
UNLV	89-81	Dec.	1	Angelo State (TX)
@Loyola Marymount	136-121		4	@Texas
James Madison	142-109		8	Virginia Common-
#North Texas	147-94			wealth
#Tulsa	99-78		10	Coppin State
Alaska-Anchorage	101-81		15	Loyola Marymount
@Colorado	66-61		22	Duke
Arkansas-Little Rock	134-81			

56

Texas	103-84	@Oklahoma State	107-94
@Kansas State	51-66	##Nebraska	78-65
@Arizona	74-78	##Kansas	95-77
Iowa State	107-96	##Colorado	92-80
Oklahoma State	109-92	*Towson State	77-68
Nebraska	105-64	*North Carolina	77-79
@Kansas	74-85		
@Iowa State	86-81	@ Road Games	
@Seton Hall	89-84	# All-College Tournament, Oklahoma	
Kansas State	85-69	City, OK	
Colorado	86-64	## Big Eight Tournament, Kansas City,	
@Missouri	90-92	MO	
@Nebraska	88-66	* NCAA Tournament, Austin, TX	
Missouri	107-90		
Kansas	100-78		

NOTES: Oklahoma will play the winner of the Arkansas vs. Vanderbilt game on Nov. 16. Neither Oklahoma or Arkansas, the Sooners probable opponent, wants to play a road game so it will be interesting to see where the game is played . . . Oklahoma will face Illinois State in the opening round of

1990-91 OKLAHOMA SCHEDULE Cont.

Nov.	28-29	##All-College Tournament	Feb.	20	Iowa State
Jan.	5	@James Madison		23	@Kansas
	8	Kansas		27	@Colorado
	12	Colorado	Mar.	2	Kansas State
	15	@Missouri		8-10	*Big Eight Tournament
	19	Oklahoma State	@ Road Games		
	22	Southwestern Louisiana	# Dodge NIT (If Oklahoma defeats New		
	26	Nebraska	Orleans, the Sooners will play a second		
	30	@Iowa State	round game on Nov. 16. The semifinals		
Feb.	2	Missouri	and finals of the tournament will be held		
	5	@Kansas State	on Nov. 21 & 23 at Madison Square		
	9	Seton Hall	Garden, New York, N.Y.)		
	13	@Oklahoma State	## Oklahoma City, OK (Alabama-		
	16	@Nebraska	Birmingham, Illinois State & Tulsa)		
			*Kansas City, MO		

the All-College tournament . . . CBS will telecast two Oklahoma games —Dec. 22, Duke and Feb. 9, Seton Hall. NBC will telecast Oklahoma's Feb. 23 game at Kansas.

PITT

LAST SEASON: 12-17
CONFERENCE RECORD: 5-11
STARTERS LOST: 1
STARTERS RETURNING: 4
CONFERENCE: BIG EAST
LOCATION: PITTSBURGH, PA
HOME FLOORS: FITZGERALD
    FIELD HOUSE (6,798) &
    CIVIC ARENA (16,798)
NICKNAME: PANTHERS
COLORS: BLUE AND GOLD

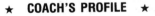

★ COACH'S PROFILE ★

PAUL EVANS (Record at Pitt, 78-45. Career record, 323-155) Paul Evans, who labored diligently but obscurely for eight years at St. Lawrence, was thrust upon the public consciousness through the rise of David Robinson at Navy. On the memorable March afternoon back in 1986 when Navy handed Syracuse its lunch in the Carrier Dome and sent the Orangemen packing from the NCAA tournament, the nation, through the exploits of Robinson, discovered his coach. Many appreciated that even with Robinson, a team needs some direction to dominate an upper level Big East team such as Syracuse on its home court. Also, it was apparent that service academies do not enjoy 30-win seasons without some strong coaching.

Actually, Evans had made his presence known around Navy several years before that—at least to his players. In a story apocryphal to his —let's say rather than intense-style, Evans took a gun out at halftime after a notably lackluster opening 20 minutes by his charges, and starting firing shots in the locker room. That's one way to get a future serviceman's attention, even if they were blanks. Evans also captured Pitt's attention, following six seasons at Navy, and took over the Panther program in 1986.

Those that doubted the success of his hard driving style would meet at the higher Big East level were partially silenced with records of 25-8, 24-7 and 24-7 prior to last season's 12-17 disaster. Yet, despite coaching Pitt to regular season Big East titles in his first two years, Evans became embroiled in several controversies with the Pittsburgh media. First, there was Pitt's 2-3 NCAA tournament record, lowlighted by Barry Goheen's buzzer-beating three-point shot that allowed Vanderbilt to upset the Panthers in the second round of the Midwest Region in 1988. His critics felt there should have been a plan to stop the three-pointer.

When Evans' entire 1989 recruiting class went south academically, he came in for more criticism around Pittsburgh. He angrily noted that several barely missed the 700 score deadline on the SAT test and at least were worth taking a chance on. Then he paid the price for not having enough depth with last year's 12-17 record. This season, with two of the five ready to play after sitting out and several more freshmen coming in that did qualify academically, Evans looks forward to having enough bodies as well as talent to contend for the Big East title.

He was a three-sport athlete in high school at Arcade, N.Y. At Ithica College (N.Y.) Evans was a Dean's List student and ran track plus played football and basketball. He spent two years as a basketball and track coach and teacher in the Kenmore (N.Y.) public school system, where he produced two undefeated track teams and two conference champions in basketball. From there he left to join the coaching

staff at Genesceo State (N.Y.) in 1969 where he stayed for four years. Evans served as the head track coach and assistant varsity basketball coach, as well as an instructor in physical education. In 1973, he became head basketball coach at St. Lawrence University (N.Y.). Evans was also assistant football coach and a professor of physical education at St. Lawrence.

He stayed at St. Lawrence for seven years, compiling a 126-50 record, and his teams advanced to the NCAA Division III tournament five times. His winning percentage of 72 percent was the best in Division III during his tenure. He left St. Lawrence for the Naval Academy in 1980.

For 20 years before Evans arrived at Navy, the Midshipmen had never won more than 14 games in a season. He was 119-60 in six years at Navy and his last three teams averaged 26 wins a season and were 80-19 (.808) overall. The three straight 20-win seasons in Evans' last three years at Navy was the first time that any service academy had achieved three consecutive 20-win seasons in basketball.

The 46-year-old Evans has won more games in his first four years than any other basketball coach in Pitt history. His four Pitt teams and his last three Navy squads have won nearly 74 percent of their games (165-of-223) over the last seven seasons. His teams have won four regular season conference championships in the last seven years and prior to last season had made five consecutive NCAA tournament appearances. He has a Big East Conference mark of 38-26 (.594) in regular season play and an overall 42-30 (.583) conference mark, which includes Big East tournament games.

Evans, unlike some of his rival Big East coaches, has not shied away from competition. Pitt's schedule was rated the toughest in America each of the last two seasons. Through all he has weathered, Evans has maintained a competitive, entertaining team in one of the nation's toughest conferences. He has a team that will enter the 1990-91 season as the favorite in the Big East. There is no doubt that Pitt could win the regular season Big East title for the third time in five tries under Evans.

★ PLAYERS NOT RETURNING ★

ROD BROOKIN (6-5, F, 13.0 ppg, 3.9 rpg, 42 assists, 4 blocked shots, 21 steals) Brookin looked like an unstoppable four-year scoring machine when he arrived at Pitt. Unfortunately, weight problems and academic difficulties grounded him much of his sophomore season and he never totally rebounded as a dominant offensive force. That's not to say he didn't contribute as Brookin had a few blockbuster games and was an integral part of some important Pitt victories. For example, on a Sunday afternoon national television game against Oklahoma his junior year, Brookin simply lit up Fitzgerald Field House with 24 points (on spectacular perimeter shooting), eight rebounds and four steals as he came off the bench to team with Brian Shorter in forging one of Pitt's biggest victories in recent years.

After serving as sixth man most of his junior year, Brookin was back in the starting lineup 16 times last year and was fourth on the team in scoring. He hit 40-of-96 three-pointers and wound up a reliable scorer on a struggling team.

His explosive offensive talent would normally be missed but Pitt is much deeper this year and Evans can compensate for Brookin's departure.

PAT CAVANAUGH (6-3, G, 3.1 ppg, 0.5 rpg, 40 assists, 13 steals) He began as a walk-on and wound up the Panthers' team captain by his junior year. Cavanaugh was also a walk-on quarterback in football. He was not much of a shooter or scorer, but was a scrapper who could handle the ball well enough to play as a competent backup point guard in the Big East. He also sometimes came up with defensive plays.

Because of the absence of starting point guard Sean Miller last year, Cavanaugh averaged 12.6 minutes per game.

Like Brookin, he can be replaced.

GILBERT JOHNSON (6-8, F, 0.7 ppg, 0.6 rpg, 1 assist) Johnson was a reserve who appeared in 15 games for a total of 59 minutes last year. He was 5-of-17 (.294) from the field and a limited contributor.

★ RETURNING PLAYERS ★

BRIAN BRUSH (6-5, 223 lbs., SO, F, #15, 0.9 ppg, 0.5 rpg, 1 assist, 1 steal, Sharpsville HS/Sharpsville, Pa.) Brush is an aggressive inside player who walked-on and had a few solid moments last year. In 20 minutes against Seton Hall, he had five points, a steal and an assist.

He played in 11 games for a total of 49 minutes last year. Brush was 4-of-11 (.364) from the field and 2-of-6 (.333) from the line.

BROCK GENERALOVICH (6-1, 190 lbs., SO, G, #14, 0.0 ppg, 0.5 rpg, Hickory HS/Hermitage, Pa.) The son of former Pitt star Brian Generalovich, Brock walked-on and saw a few minutes time as a backup point guard last year. He played in two games for a total of five minutes last season. He missed his only field goal and free throw attempt.

Despite those meager statistics, Generalovich is an excellent athlete who spent a great deal of time on his game last year and could see playing time as a reserve point guard this year. He earned 10 varsity letters at Hickory HS in football, basketball and baseball. In football he was a versatile player who performed as quarterback, tight end and linebacker, plus was a punter and placekicker. He won the Northwestern Pennsylvania Chapter National Football Foundation and the Hall of Fame Scholar-Athlete Award.

BOBBY MARTIN (6-9, 235 lbs., SR, C, #55, 14.4 ppg, 8.4 rpg, 28 assists, 34 blocked shots, 23 steals, Atlantic City HS/Atlantic City, N.J.) Martin came up big for the Panthers last season as both a power forward and center. Statistically he blossomed. His 8.4 rebounding average was sixth in the Big East. His seven blocked shots against Seton Hall tied a Pitt school record. In a loss at Georgetown, Martin put forth a tremendous 27-point, 20-rebound performance against Georgetown's Twin Towers of Dikembo Mutombo and Alonzo Mourning. This was the type of impact that Martin was expected to have when he arrived at Pitt. He's the consummate power forward, combining strength and mobility to score, rebound and defend inside with the quickness and touch to score from the outside, get up and down the floor and block shots from anywhere.

Despite his vast physical gifts and potential, a lack of consistency almost got him benched early in the season. Evans threatened to ground Martin (and Rod Brookin) after a stunning 74-68 loss to Toledo in which he extended a string of subpar performances. "He stunk against Robert Morris, Duquesne and Toledo," Evans would say later. "And those are games he should have dominated . . . could have career highs."

After hearing his coach's threat, Martin approached Evans and said, "This isn't necessary. Let me go out there and do what I have to do."

Evans let Martin go out there and do what he had to do. Martin went out and got 26 points and 14 rebounds against Oklahoma State, then he posted a 21-point, 14-rebound night vs. Georgia Tech in Atlanta. He followed that with 18 points and nine rebounds vs. Syracuse, 15 points and 12 rebounds against Connecticut, 13 points and 13 rebounds to go with seven blocks vs. Seton Hall.

"When he concentrates and tries to think about what he's going to do, he's pretty good," Evans told the *Pittsburgh Post-Gazette*. "Because he has the athletic ability."

Martin begins the season only 10 points short of 1,000 career points. He was third in the Big East in field goal percentage (.537) and tied for eighth in blocked shots last season. He also sang the National Anthem before Pitt games with Toledo and Georgetown in the 1988-89 season. Martin should project as an All-Big East player this year. Pitt's newfound depth may free him from the ironman-like 34.5 minutes per game he averaged last year. It also may allow him to focus more on defense.

JASON MATTHEWS (6-3, 180 lbs., SR, G, #22, 19.1 ppg, 3.0 rpg, 69 assists, 4 blocked shots, 30 steals, St. Monica HS/Los Angeles, Calif.) Once described as Satin Elegance, Matthews continued to quietly burgeon into one of the Big East's premier perimeter forces. Matthews already has knocked down 93 three-pointers in conference play, second all-time to former Boston College star Dana Barros' 145. He led all Big East players in long bomb percentage (80-of-175 for .457). The rest of Matthews' game is not chopped liver.

Said Connecticut coach Jim Calhoun: "With some of the high-profile guys leaving, Dana Barros and Sherman Douglas and Charles Smith, I thought Matthews and Eric Murdock (Providence) were the two best all-around guards in the league. He (Matthews) shoots well, rebounds well and defends well, and he does it with a whole lot of class. There's no baloney about his game. I'm a fan of his."

As a sophomore Matthews also led the Big East in three-point percentage (.482) as well as free throw percentage (.899). He did that again last season, making 141-of-158 free throws (.892). During the summer prior to last season, Matthews worked to erase the "one-dimensional" tag from his offensive game. After he shot only 1-of-7 from three-point range in a pre-season exhibition against Athletes

In Action, but wound up with 29 points, Evans said in *Basketball Times*: "When his shot was off he was able to take it inside and get his points that way. He has done it very well and couldn't do it at all last year." The trend continued during a 28-point outing vs. Oklahoma State. Half of Matthews' points came on quick drives and from filling the lanes on the break. "He's looking to score every time he gets the ball now," said teammate Brian Shorter. "Even if his shot's not there at first. He has a lot more confidence in himself."

After never playing an entire game as a sophomore, Matthews went the full 40 minutes nine times last year and even played a complete 50 minutes in a double overtime game with West Virginia. Yet, he never fouled out of a game. He threw in 32 against Boston College in the Big East tournament, 29 in a victory over Arizona, and 25 in another win over Providence. In all he was over 20 points 11 times. Matthews made 7-of-11 three-pointers (a school record) on his way to 28 points against Providence in the regular season finale. Matthews (14.4 ppg for his career) already has 1,296 career points.

Growing up, he worked on his shot the old-fashioned way, endless hours of shooting in his backyard. Trouble is, the neighbors were unhappy with his late night 10:00 p.m. to 2:00 a.m. shooting schedule. "They had every right to complain," Matthews said in a *Basketball Times* article. "But I'd be too tired to go right out there after practice. Plus, if I shot at night, it improved my concentration . . . you can't see the rim as well, so you have to concentrate better."

The fruits of Matthews' old late night shooting regimen should be even more apparent this year for the Panthers.

SEAN MILLER (6-1, 185 lbs., JR, G, #3, Blackhawk HS/Beaver Falls, Pa.) Surgery to repair a congenital problem in his left foot cost Miller all of last season. Two tarsal bones were partially fused together causing an arthritic condition. Miller began to rehabilitate the injury in December and ran the Pitt stadium steps. He began full court pickup play in July. Pitt trainer Tony Salesi is very optimistic but says there are no guarantees. If Miller recovers fully, it would provide an immeasurable boost to Pitt's national aspirations. To say the Panthers missed his shooting, passing and skilled ballhandling, not to mention his leadership, is to say a car misses an engine. There's no doubt with a healthy Sean Miller, Pitt would not have been a 12-17, non-post-season tournament team last year.

Miller was on the verge of becoming one of the top point guards in the Big East prior to last season. He averaged 9.5 points and 35 minutes per game over his first two seasons and his 361 assists (180 as a freshman, then 181 as a sophomore) already have him only 89 away from eclipsing teammate Darelle Porter's school record of 449.

Miller, whose father was his high school coach, became the quintessential all-around intelligent floor leader one would expect from that upbringing. His ballhandling reached the point where he was invited to summer camps to give ballhandling exhibitions and he even appeared on the Johnny Carson show as a youngster.

As a free throw shooter, his career mark is over 88 percent, including .914 (74-of-81) as a sophomore. He also combines with Matthews to give Pitt perhaps the best one-two three-point punch in the country. Miller is 114-of-276 (.413) from behind the bonus stripe.

In 1989, Miller led Pitt through the labyrinth of Georgetown's pressure defense with 11 assists and zero turnovers on the way to a Panther win. He dished out 13 assists against Seton Hall's Final Four team, then rose to the occasion with a career-high 22 points in an 82-76 victory over Syracuse. Miller nailed 5 three-pointers on two different occasions —against Connecticut and Villanova. The season before he was Big East freshman of the year. If Miller is fully recovered, he may be the missing piece of a Top 10 team. There are potentially few better all-around point guards in the nation.

DARREN MORNINGSTAR (6-10, 225 lbs., JR, C, #33, 3.8 ppg, 2.8 rpg, 12 assists, 3 blocked shots, 13 steals, Stevenson HS/Stevenson, Wash.) Morningstar transferred from Navy where Evans coached previously and knew of him. He alternated between starting and being the first big man off the bench last year. In all, Morningstar started 11 games. He has a good touch for a big man and knows how to pass. He has dropped his weight from 245 to 225, which should foster a major improvement this season. The increased quickness should help his rebounding.

Morningstar's best game last season was a 10-point (on 5-of-5 shooting), four-rebound effort in 19 minutes against Villanova. He also made an important 10-point contribution against Boston College in the Big East tournament. In 1987-88 at Navy, he averaged 12 points and 6.2 rebounds in five games before transferring. He had a 20-point, 11-rebound game against Iowa. That's the type of ability Evans would like to see redeemed more often.

"If Darren could start and give us quality minutes, we would be that much better," Evans said. "We could do more both offensively and defensively."

If Morningstar can provide a little more scoring, inside rebounding and use his reduced weight to improve his defense, his role could increase.

DARELLE PORTER (6-4, 200 lbs., SR, G/F, #20, 9.8 ppg, 3.9 rpg, 229 assists, 8 blocked shots, 54 steals, Perry HS/Pittsburgh, Pa.) Talk about rising to the occasion. Porter, a small forward by preference, was forced to play point guard because of Sean Miller's absence and responded with a full commitment to the role. All he did was set a school single-season record with 229 assists, while leading the Big East with a 7.9 assist per game average. If Miller can complete his recovery, Porter will go back to the front line. But at least the Panthers know they have some uncommon depth at the point.

The best pure athlete on the team, Porter gives Pitt a welcome local flavor. He grew up on Dunseith Street, virtually across the street from Fitzgerald Field House.

He was an All-City wide receiver in football and an excellent first baseman in baseball at Pittsburgh's Perry HS.

Miller, his roommate, enjoyed watching Porter play his spot last season. "He loves getting the assist," Miller said. "He loves to make the spectacular pass. . ."

Porter enjoyed the point guard experience. "Point guard's nice," he said. "One thing that happens when you're playing point guard, when you have the ball in your hands you're never tired."

It didn't appear that way last season. Porter hit double-digit assists nine times, including a career-high 14 at Syracuse. He surpassed Dwayne Wallace as the all-time Pitt assist leader. Porter also found some time to score: 18 points, to go along with 13 assists against Oklahoma State, a career-high 25 against no less than Georgia Tech in the ACC/Big East Challenge, 21 in a victory over Villanova. Porter, an excellent defender, can get hot from outside and also gets some of his points on exciting breakaway dunks off of his steals. He is considered the team's best defender and strongest penetrator. If he improves his outside shooting, he could rise to All-Big East caliber.

Porter and Sean Miller coached a National AAU 15 and Under team from Pittsburgh over the summer. Porter also benefitted from his experience on a Big East All-Star team that played in Finland and Russia under Connecticut coach Jim Calhoun over the summer. He averaged 10.2 points, 4.7 rebounds and led the squad in steals and assists.

BRIAN SHORTER (6-6, 230 lbs., SR, F, #00, 20.6 ppg, 9.4 rpg, 40 assists, 14 blocked shots, 28 steals, Philadelphia, Pa. & Oak Hill Academy/Mouth of Wilson, Va.) Possibly the strongest 6-6 inside presence since Wes Unseld, Shorter, All-Big East both seasons he's played, is a monster offensive presence in the post. Few are better at receiving the ball near the basket and using their body to find a way to score. Shorter is fifth all-time in the Big East scoring average chart at 20.4 (former Seton Hall star Dan Calandrillo is the leader at 21.7). Shorter led the league in scoring last year and was third in rebounding.

Evans hopes Pitt's influx of talented newcomers will help him improve Shorter's game even more by taking last year's 37-minute per game burden off of him. "I think Brian can now play more aggressively on both boards," Evans said. "In the past I think he's held back a little because he knew we needed him out there all the time."

"This is the strongest player in the country by far," said Massachusetts coach John Calipari, who recruited Shorter when he was an assistant at Pitt in *Sports Magazine*. "He's got rip-your-face off strength. One day in the weight room we set the pin too low on the Nautilaus and I'm telling you, Brian just picked the whole darn machine off the floor . . . his great feel for the position of his defender and smooth yet forceful moves make him almost automatic from eight feet on in. And now he's adding a face-up dimension. I've seen him do it. He's going to be not just a good, but a great shooter."

Shorter's tremendous quickness makes up for his lack of height. He epitomized his power game in a 23-point, 11-rebound outing that carved out a win over Arizona and its king-sized front line. The Wildcats started out putting 6-11 Sean Rooks and 6-11 Brian Williams around him and then came with 6-11 Ed Stokes off the bench. "Those three combined for 56 minutes. Williams got no rebounds, Rooks had two. Stokes added six," wrote Gene Collier in the *Pittsburgh Press*. "Shorter got eight on the offensive board alone."

"I don't think our kids did that bad a job keeping the ball from him," Arizona coach Lute Olson told Collier. "Where he killed us was with the second and third efforts. I can't imagine anybody his size being any tougher than he is."

"He's really strong and he knows how to seal well," said Rooks. "When he gets the ball in the paint, you're in trouble." After the performance, there was some discussion as to Shorter's pro prospects. Olson was certain of one thing: "Our two starting (NBA-sized) big men got pushed all over the floor."

Shorter's .532 field percentage was fourth in the Big East last year. He has 1,185 career points. He had six 20-point or over games in a row and 12-of-15 in one stretch. He collected 29 points and 11 rebounds against Georgia Tech. Against Providence, he was simply overwhelming with a season-high 34 points on 11-of-11 shooting. If he can improve last season's 66 percent average from the foul line, Shorter, who got to the line 308 times, will be even more dominant. He could challenge Syracuse's Billy Owens, Chris Smith of Connecticut and Georgetown's Alonzo Mourning and Dikembe Mutombo for Big East player of the year honors. With Sean Miller back, he should be even more effective.

TRAVIS ZIEGLER (6-5, 195 lbs., SO, F, #23, 0.7 ppg, 0.3 rpg, 1 assist, 1 steal, Jeffersontown HS/Louisville, Ky.) Ziegler played in only three games for a total of six minutes last season. He came to Pitt billed as a long range shooter and missed his only field goal attempt of the season, a three-pointer, and was 2-for-2 from the line.

When he signed with Pitt, Ziegler was considered a marginal Big East prospect. Now that the Panthers are much deeper than a year ago, his role should not change significantly for the better.

★ NEWCOMERS ★

DOMINIC DUMANCIC (6-10, 225 lbs., SO, F, #31, 18.0 ppg, 9.0 rpg, Zagreb, Yugoslavia & Meadville HS/Erie, Pa.) An exchange student from Yugoslavia, Dumancic played well enough at Meadville HS in Erie, Pa., to attract the attention of several Division I programs. He was not eligible last year because of academic requirements

and is finally expected to be eligible in January.

He has great shooting range for a player his size. Dumancic nailed 70 three-pointers as a senior at Meadville HS. He scored 31 points against Fox Chapel HS in the first round of the PIAA state playoffs. Dumancic played for the West Penn All-Stars in the preliminary game of the Dapper Dan Roundball Classic, scoring 14 points and grabbing nine rebounds.

"Dominic is a typical European player in that at 6-10, he isn't a post-up style player," said Meadville coach Norm Price. "He likes to handle the ball and shoot from the perimeter, and he does both very well."

Despite his attractive perimeter skills, if Dumancic is to see consistent playing time in his first year at Pitt, however, he'll have to take his height inside where the Panthers could use some rebounding help for Brian Shorter and added defensive presence.

TIM GLOVER (6-1, 180 lbs., FR, G, #12, 18.0 ppg, Clear Lake HS/ Houston, Tex.) Named the Greater Houston player of the year by the *Houston Chronicle*, Glover was the best player for a team that appeared in two consecutive state championship games. He averaged 12 points and five assists per game as a junior on a state championship team. Glover sees the court extremely well and has three-point range. He scored 9 three-point field goals in one game, setting a Clear Lake HS record. He also set a school scoring record with a 39-point outburst. Glover shot the ball especially well as a senior. He was not highly recruited by national level programs and is probably at least a year away from contributing.

ANTOINE JONES (6-7, 195 lbs., JR, F, #21, 18.8 ppg, 10.4 rpg, 106 assists, 38 blocked shots, Southwestern HS/Baltimore, Md. & Allegany CC/Cumberland, Md.) Jones was a force on a 30-6 Allegany team ranked No. 13 in the nation. His 106 assists and 38 blocks last season attest to Jones' versatility. He shot 55.3 percent from the floor and 65 percent from the free throw line during his final season at Allegany.

Jones moved from the inside to the perimeter last season with little difficulty. In the view of Evans, Jones looks to be the most immediate contributor among the Pitt newcomers. Evans likes Jones' maturity as well as his rebounding, passing and defensive skills.

"He's much more athletic, than you'd expect for a power-type player," Evans told the *Associated Press*. "He doesn't shoot it real well. He's a good passer. A smart player, and a good rebounder. He will help our press."

He was a three-year MVP and led his team in scoring and rebounding all three seasons at Southwestern HS in Baltimore. Jones averaged 24 points, 12 rebounds and four blocked shots per game as a senior and was named an honorable mention All-America selection by *USA Today*.

He is exactly the type of quality player Pitt needed so dearly last year during the disastrous 12-17 season when depth was extremely short.

GANDHI JORDAN (6-6, 195 lbs., FR, G, #4, 11.4 ppg, 5.5 rpg, Anstead, W.Va. & Oak Hill Academy/Mouth of Wilson, Va.) Jordan's seemingly marginal statistics are misleading as he played on an exceptionally talented 29-0 team that finished ranked No. 3 nationally by *USA Today* and No. 2 by ESPN Scholastic Sports America. Jordan averaged just eight shots in 21 minutes a game on a deep Oak Hill team that sent three starters to Division I schools. He was named to the Virginia Top 15 team at the end of his senior year.

Jordan averaged 20 points per game as a sophomore at Midland Trail HS in West Virginia, before transferring to Oak Hill Academy. As a junior he averaged 13.1 points and three assists per game, teaming with current Panther Chris McNeal, on an Oak Hill team that ranked in the Top 10 nationally.

"He's the type of guy you're watching and people say he may not be able to play at Pitt," Oak Hill coach Steve Smith told the *Associated Press*. "But I think he'll earn some minutes."

Jordan is a versatile, second guard prospect who sees the court well and is solid in all facets of the game.

Evans is impressed with Jordan: "Gandhi has been a complete surprise," he said. "We thought he wasn't quite ready, but if I had to start a freshman it would be tough keeping him out of the lineup."

CHRIS McNEAL (6-8, 235 lbs., SO, F, #24, 15.2 ppg, 8.0 rpg, 2.1 blpg, Richmond, Va. & Oak Hill Academy/Mouth of Wilson, Va.) McNeal, who sat out last season, was an outstanding power forward prospect two seasons ago at Oak Hill Academy. An earthshaking power forward, his style has been compared to Brian Shorter.

"He is similar to Brian Shorter," said Oak Hill coach Steve Smith, "though not quite as strong or athletic. He can rebound with almost anyone and shoots the ball from the perimeter better than Brian does."

"Chris is very aggressive off the boards. He should help us with our break. It will be tough keeping him out of the starting lineup," Evans said.

McNeal played on a 22-2 team as a senior at Oak Hill Academy. That Oak Hill team was ranked 11th in the nation by *USA Today*. As a junior he averaged 25 points and 13 rebounds at Hermitage HS in Richmond, Va.

Although some recruiting experts have said that Pitt does not have a great player of the Brian Shorter caliber in its newcomers, the Panthers do have some sorely needed depth. McNeal should see considerable action this year.

JERMAINE MORGAN (6-6, 190 lbs., FR, F, #42, 25.0 ppg, 12.0 rpg, Jeannette HS/Jeannette, Pa.) The WPIAL AA player of the year, Morgan was an all-state receiver and defensive back in football as well as the best senior basketball player in western Pennsylvania. He is the first local recruit for Pitt since Sean Miller in 1987. According to the *Big East Briefs*, Morgan is, "an athletic, versatile player who will help bolster Panthers bench.''

''I think he fits into our style,'' said Pitt assistant John Sarandrea. ''He can run, he's a great athlete, and a very good defender.''

''He (Evans) told me he wouldn't recruit a local kid that wouldn't play. . .,'' Morgan told Mike DeCourcy of the *Pittsburgh Press*.

''Playing in the Big East is just about every kid's dream and it's what I always wanted to do.''

Like teammate Darelle Porter, Morgan turned down football scholarship offers. He felt he got a little more publicity in basketball and had a greater desire to play that sport in college.

He played for the U.S. East team in the Dapper Dan Roundball Classic in Pittsburgh and had an impressive, nine-point performance. His high school coach, Rick Cipullo, believes Morgan needs to improve on his ballhandling, shooting and strength.

OMO MOSES (6-1, 190 lbs., FR, G, #44, 15.0 ppg, 10.2 rpg, 8.7 apg, Rindge & Latin HS/Cambridge, Mass.) From the alma mater of Patrick Ewing and Rumeal Robinson, Moses is one of the best players in Metropolitan Boston. He will figure as a reserve point guard this season and maybe a quality player for the Panthers in a few years.

''Omo's further ahead than I expected at this time,'' Evans told the *Associated Press*. ''He's much more physical than he was a year ago, a good penetrator and makes good decisions.''

He led his team to the Massachusetts state title as a senior and was named Division I player of the year by the *Boston Globe*. He was also selected as the Massachusetts state coaches association player of the year. Like fellow Rindge & Latin alumnus, Rumeal Robinson, Moses is very strong. He bench presses around 245 pounds, which is 50 pounds over his weight.

Despite the fact that Pitt signed a bundle of recruits, some recruiting experts believe the Panthers will need to pick up some impact players in the near future.

''One need that Pitt had was depth,'' Tom Konchalski of the *HSBI Report* told Chuck Finder of the *Pittsburgh Post-Gazette*. ''They got people that appear to fit that need. But as far as getting guys to replace the Bobby Martins, the Brian Shorters, they haven't done that. Eventually, they are going to have to get some piano players. These are piano carriers.''

AHMAD SHAREEF (6-3, 175 lbs., FR, G, #13, 12.0 ppg, 7.0 rpg, 4.0 stpg, Martin Luther King HS/Chicago, Ill.) Shareef was overshadowed at Martin Luther King HS by teammate Jamie Brandon, a big time high school All-America guard who signed with Illinois but is sitting out this year at LSU. Shareef was a starter on a 32-0 Martin Luther King HS team that won the Chicago city and Illinois state titles. King was ranked No. 1 nationally by *USA Today*.

A three-year starter, Shareef averaged 17.8 points per game as a junior. He has three-point range and is a good defender.

''Ahmad is very athletic and can play three positions,'' said Evans. ''He's a good passer and can create his own offense. If he adjusts to the college game quickly, he could play a lot.''

''If he was on any other team, he'd be a star,'' said Martin Luther King coach Landon Cox.

Shareef was considered the top high school prospect signed by Pitt last year. He could use more strength and is expected to back up Jason Matthews.

★ QUESTIONS ★

How quickly and well will the Pitt newcomers fit in? None of Pitt's eight newcomers is a certified blue chipper, but Antoine Jones, Gandhi Jordan, Chris McNeal and Ahmad Shareef are all capable of lending depth and support in important roles. Evans will have to see who is ready to step up and provide the much needed depth to supplement his star studded senior class.

The health of Sean Miller? Miller's leadership and playmaking will be a crucial factor in lifting Pitt to the Final 16 or above, of the NCAA tournament.

Rebounding? Bobby Martin, at 6-9, and Brian Shorter, at 6-6, are the tallest established forces in the lineup that started three forwards and two guards last year. They need help off the defensive boards. It will be up to Darren Morningstar in particular with support from Chris McNeal and maybe Antoine Jones to provide that support. If Sean Miller returns to full strength, the starting lineup will get even smaller, with in effect three guards and two forwards.

Interior defense? Bobby Martin is a shotblocker but not a lane clogger. Darren Morningstar is not quick enough. Brian Shorter has too much responsibility already. Somehow, Pitt must get better interior defense.

★ STRENGTHS ★

Quality experience! Because of last year's thin roster, Bobby Martin, Brian Shorter, Jason Matthews and Darelle Porter all played over 35 minutes a game. And if Sean Miller is back to full health, that adds another two-year starter. All these players know each other and have confidence (rightly so) in their games.

Brian Shorter! Shorter is one of the best, most consistent and reliable low post scorers and rebounders in college basketball.

Depth! Last year's sore point should become this year's blessing. Several of the newcomers are capable of helping in various ways and could push the starters. Chris McNeal will help on the boards, Antoine Jones will help with inside defense

and on the press, and Gandhi Jordan and Ahmad Shareef should also help this year. Evans should have the luxury of being able to pick many more spots in which to rest his starters.

Perimeter shooting! Jason Matthews and Sean Miller (if healthy) form a tremendous one-two zone breaking punch and will force opponents to truly extend their defense. Otherwise, they will just keep raining threes.

★ BLUE RIBBON ANALYSIS ★

Even though they were forced to get used to playing minus Sean Miller without much warning, it's hard to imagine a team with four starters as talented as the Panthers' Brian Shorter, Bobby Martin, Jason Matthews and Darelle Porter going 12-17. Granted seven of the losses (six to quality Big East opposition) were by six points or less and Miller may have turned some of those into victories. Still, there were some times a stronger commitment might have helped. Pitt did, however, play what was rated the nation's toughest schedule for the second year in a row. And that's enough to wear down even teams that have the luxury of depending on more than a 5 1/2 (the half being Darren Morningstar) or a six-man nucleus. Plus, with Bobby Martin the only proven quality player over 6-6, there simply wasn't the necessary defensive presence or rebounding to deal consistently with the total of nine games Pitt played last year against the likes of Syracuse, Georgetown, Georgia Tech and Connecticut.

This season should seem to last year's returning ironmen —Martin, Matthew, Shorter and Porter —less like an NBA marathon season and more like a college campaign. That's because eight newcomers are in Pitt uniforms this year and at least four of them should be able to put in some useful time.

''I feel a lot better going into this year than I have the past two seasons,'' said Pitt coach Paul Evans. ''It's going to be more fun because of the bench and having different options.

''My first year here, we had a walk-on —Pat Cavanaugh —as our sixth man. The next year when we won the league outright, we had a little depth with our freshman class, but two of them (Miller and Matthews) had to start. Other than that, we've really never had any depth. So I think we'll do some things we worked on a little bit last year and had good success with, but couldn't continue for any length of time.''

Offensively, Pitt has as many weapons and as strong and experienced a nucleus as any team in the country with the exception of perhaps UNLV. Moreover, the devastating low post scoring of Shorter and the inside mid-range offense of Martin is balanced beautifully by the three-point shooting of Matthews and Miller. Defensively is where the lack of height may allow quality opposition to score almost as fast, if not faster, than Pitt. The arrival of 6-8 Chris McNeal should go a long way in dealing with the rebounding problem. The defensive depth provided by newcomers Antoine Jones and Gandhi Jordan and perhaps, Ahmad Shareef, will give Evans an opportunity to translate Pitt's athletic ability into more pressure defenses without worrying so much about foul trouble or wearing down his starters. Also, the season Porter was forced to spend at point guard will not only enhance his appreciation of the game but offer quality backup to Miller, who will probably need some breaks as he gradually works his way back after a full year of inactivity and rehabilitation for his broken foot.

Assuming Miller can return to form, Pitt enters the season as the pre-season favorite in a somewhat depleted Big East. Although the Panthers will have matchup problems with Georgetown head-on, they have a vastly greater offensive arsenal to throw at others. Considering the other contenders —Connecticut and Syracuse —don't really have the type of tall scorers to exploit Pitt's defensive vulnerability in the middle, the Panthers have an excellent shot at winning the Big East. With a diminished schedule —Cornell, Siena, St. Francis, Marshall and Toledo all pop up in November and December —20 wins is a more realistic goal. The lack of a tall inside defense will probably catch up to Pitt against the nation's better teams in the NCAA tournament. However, Pitt has the offense, experience, athletic ability, motivation and depth (if the newcomers contribute to expectations) to roll at least to the Final Sixteen. However, it all comes down to how healthy Sean Miller is.

LAST SEASON		1990-91 PITT SCHEDULE		
Siena	101-89	Nov.	27	@Cornell
#Oklahoma State	102-90		28	@Siena
#North Carolina State	87-100	Dec.	1	@St. Francis (PA)
##Georgia Tech	92-93		3	#Virginia
@West Virginia	93-97 2OT		6	Marshall
Robert Morris	88-71		8	West Virginia
Duquesne	92-87		15	Robert Morris
*Oklahoma State	92-81		19	##Duquesne
*Georgia Tech	92-111		22	Toledo
Syracuse	78-80		27-30	###Rainbow
@Connecticut	61-79			Classic
Georgetown	71-87	Jan.	2	##Villanova
@St. John's	70-71		5	*Connecticut
Seton Hall	65-63		7	##Syracuse
@Syracuse	74-83		12	Providence
Arizona	100-92		19	@St. John's

Boston College	110-80	@ Road Games
Villanova	94-82	# Diet Pepsi Tournament of Champions, Charlotte, NC
@Georgetown	81-97	
Providence	117-102	## ACC/Big East Challenge, Hartford, CT
Connecticut	77-80	
@Villanova	68-71	* Kuppenheimer Classic, Atlanta, GA
@Seton Hall	81-86	** Big East Tournament, Madison Square Garden, New York, NY
@Boston College	81-73	
St. John's	75-76	
@Providence	74-85	
**Boston College	88-70	
**Syracuse	55-58	

Jan.	23	@Providence	Mar. 7-9 *Big East Tournament
	27	##Georgetown	
	30	@Villanova	@ Road Games
Feb.	2	@UCLA	# ACC/Big East Challenge, Richmond, VA
	4	Seton Hall	
	9	Boston College	## Civic Arena, Pittsburgh, PA
	12	@Seton Hall	### Honolulu, HI (Alaska-Anchorage, California, Hawaii, Iona, Stetson, Tennessee & Wichita State)
	16	St. John's	
	20	@Georgetown	
	24	@Syracuse	* Hartford, CT
	26	@Boston College	** Madison Square Garden, New York, NY
Mar.	2	Connecticut	

NOTES: Pitt will play Alaska-Anchorage in the opening round of the Rainbow Classic on Dec. 28 . . . there is a player sitting out at Pitt this year that if eligible might have made the Panthers a pre-season Final Four pick. That player is 6-11 center Eric Mobley, who signed with Pitt two years ago while at Salesian HS in New Rochelle, N.Y. He was considered one of the premier defensive centers in the country. Mobley was ineligible last season at Pitt and played at Allegany CC in Cumberland, Md. He should

have three years of eligibility for the Panthers beginning in 1991-92 . . . Pitt will play UCLA for the first time since the 1972-73 season. In four previous meetings with UCLA, the Panthers are winless . . . at least eight Pitt games will be nationally televised this season. CBS is scheduled to televise at least three of the Panthers' games and ESPN will carry at least five more.

SYRACUSE

LAST SEASON: 26-7
CONFERENCE RECORD: 12-4
STARTERS LOST: 2
STARTERS RETURNING: 3
CONFERENCE: BIG EAST
LOCATION: SYRACUSE, NY
HOME FLOOR:
  CARRIER DOME (33,000)
NICKNAME: ORANGEMEN
COLOR: ORANGE

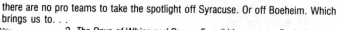

★ COACH'S PROFILE ★

JIM BOEHEIM (Record at Syracuse, 343-108) The numbers are staggering. Fourteen seasons, 14 postseason appearances (12 NCAAs, two NITs). His .761 winning percentage is fourth among all active coaches, trailing only UNLV's Jerry Tarkanian (.825), Temple's John Chaney (.796) and North Carolina's Dean Smith (.788). He reached 100 victories faster than any coach in history (four seasons) and 300 wins faster than all but two. His Orangemen reached the Sweet Sixteen for the second straight season in 1989-90, and only four other schools could say that (Duke, North Carolina, Minnesota and UNLV). It was Boeheim's third Sweet Sixteen appearance in the last four years—he lost in the unforgettable NCAA championship game to Keith Smart and Indiana in 1987—and seventh overall.

It's a portfolio good enough to satisfy the toughest fans and critics—which is exactly what he faces in upstate New York and around the mega-media centers of the Big East.

"We would've had to win every game by 20 if we had Kenny Anderson (the Georgia Tech point guard phenom who almost chose Syracuse), and I'd still be a bad coach," Boeheim said last winter, barely disguising his sarcasm.

He is clearly a victim of several circumstances that make it difficult for this thoroughly likable man to smile.

1. *Great Expectations:* In Syracuse, where roundball has long-since replaced pigskin as the sport of choice, ardent fans don't ask what Boeheim has done for them lately, but rather what hasn't he done. Namely, win a national title or at least return to the Final Four. "I don't think there's any place in the conference like this," Boeheim told *Newsday* last season. "The media people who are here, they have the impression that we're supposed to win every game. Our fans, I think, are like fans everywhere. They want us to win. They're going to get upset when we lose a game, they're going to call the radio shows."

Unlike other Big East cities like New York, Philadelphia, Boston and Pittsburgh,

there are no pro teams to take the spotlight off Syracuse. Or off Boeheim. Which brings us to. . .

2. *The Days of Whine and Roses.* For all his success, Boeheim is no media darling. He is unforgiving of what he perceives as foolish questions by reporters. He isn't glib. No self-deprecating humor, no anecdotes. He is honest, answering questions other coaches duck; he returns phone calls. He just doesn't project the image of a coach who is enjoying his reign among the nation's elite.

Part of that image is formed, no doubt by TV. Syracuse is a regular on ESPN and CBS these days, and what fans see more often than not is an intense Boeheim, gesturing to officials with a pained expression, and believing every call should go his way. He could easily have played the Joe Piscopo character of Saturday Night Live Fame, Mr. Whiner.

3. *Out-Smarted.* To this day, Boeheim says he hasn't watched the tape of Syracuse's last-second loss to Indiana in the 1987 final. Keith Smart's jumper haunts him still. "I dream the whole game out sometimes. I guess I will forever. I really feel that we were the better team."

But until he wins a title, his critics will ignore the numbers.

And that's too bad. Because Boeheim deserves a better rep. His teams are exciting and entertaining year after year, making the Carrier Dome one of the most feared home courts in the nation (the Orangemen are 147-27 at the Dome since it opened). After the NBA failures of players such as Pearl Washington and Rafael Addison, Boeheim should get some of the credit for the success of Sherman Douglas and Rony Seikaly with the Miami Heat. And he was able to keep Derrick Coleman around for four years, watching the Detroit native blossom into a consensus All-America and the first-ever Syracuse player to be the first selection in the NBA draft.

Boeheim grew up in Lyons, N.Y. He came to Syracuse in 1963 as a walk-on guard. He was a three-year starter at Lyons Central HS and an All-Sectional and All-New York State player, but he was not recruited by Syracuse. He made the freshman team, earned three varsity letters and eventually became a starting guard in the same Orange backcourt with Dave Bing, arguably the greatest player in school history and a former NBA great. In 1966, Boeheim and Bing were co-captains of a Syracuse team that advanced to the finals of the East Regional. He averaged 14.6 points per game as a senior and scored 745 career points. After working hard on his jumping ability, Boeheim could dunk the basketball when he was a senior.

"At Army, I coached against Syracuse when Jimmy was a player," said Indiana coach Bob Knight. "I remember him as not having the best talent in the world, but someone who got the most out of what he had."

After graduation, he played in the Eastern League for four years and was twice a member of a league's championship team. He stayed close to the Syracuse program and stayed on and did his graduate work, earning a Master's Degree in Social Science. He also served as a graduate assistant for coach Roy Danforth. Boeheim was 16-2 as the coach of the 1969-70 Syracuse freshman team. Soon after, he became a full-time assistant. He was an assistant on Syracuse's 1975 Final Four team. In 1976, Boeheim succeeded Danforth as Syracuse's head coach.

Last year he had the Orangemen ranked No. 1 in the country for the first time in their history —for six straight weeks. And get this: Syracuse has been ranked in the Top 20 every week since March 5, 1984, the longest run of its kind in the nation. ''If people respect our program, then I hope they have some measure of respect for me,'' he says. They should. Some numbers just can't be ignored.

★ PLAYERS NOT RETURNING ★

DERRICK COLEMAN (6-10, C/F, 17.9 ppg, 12.1 rpg, 95 assists, 67 blocked shots, 51 steals) A stellar career was capped by a spectacular senior year in which he became the school's all-time leading scorer, the NCAA's all-time leading rebounder in the modern era (surpassing Virginia's Ralph Sampson) and Syracuse's first consensus All-America selection since Dave Bing. To say he'll be missed is the understatement of the year. Jayson Williams of St. John's called Coleman ''the best player in the country'' after a 24-point, 17-rebound effort at Madison Square Garden.

Coleman put his stamp on the season with three last-second gems that produced Orange victories. Against upset-minded Seton Hall on Feb. 28, Coleman tipped in a missed shot by Billy Owens at the buzzer for a 71-69 victory. Against Pitt in the Big East tournament, Coleman rejected a dunk attempt by Brian Shorter with eight seconds to play that would've given the Panthers the lead. Instead, Syracuse hung on for a 58-55 win. In the Southeast Region of the NCAA tournament, Coleman duplicated the feat, swatting away a turnaround jumper by Virginia's Bryant Stith in the final seconds preserving a 63-61 triumph.

''He's been good all his life here,'' Boeheim said. ''People don't want to look.'' But fortunately for Coleman, NBA scouts looked closely, and the New Jersey Nets made him the first pick of the June 27 draft.

Said NBA scouting director Marty Blake, ''Obviously, one of the draft's great talents. He can run the court, he can rebound and he's a great passer. He can start right away.''

Adds Utah Jazz director of player personnel Scott Layden, ''Derrick is a young Karl Malone —both have great athletic bodies, both are tireless rebounders and both handle the ball particularly well for their size.''

The A.D. (After Derrick) era is about to begin at Syracuse, and the Dome won't be the same without him.

RICHARD MANNING (6-10, C/F, 3.1 ppg, 2.2 rpg, 9 assists, 15 blocked shots, 8 steals) To transfer or not to transfer, that was the spring-summer dilemma facing Manning after his disappointing sophomore season. Syracuse coaches told him he would start at center or power forward, but his parents thought he should leave. Manning listened to Mom and Dad, even though the transfer to Washington means he'll be sitting out this season. ''It would benefit me in a lot of ways, including having a fifth year. My goal is to make the NBA and the fifth year would make me a better player.''

Off last winter, he needs to make great strides to attract NBA scouts, even if he is 6-10. After a promising freshman season in which he showed some offensive promise, Manning seemed to regress this past year and was a non-factor down the stretch. But, his departure leaves Syracuse thin up front, especially if LeRon Ellis and Conrad McRae do not significantly improve on offense.

ERIK ROGERS (6-11, C, 0.4 ppg, 1.3 rpg, 4 assists, 2 blocked shots, 2 steals) Rogers appeared in only eight games last year for a total of 31 minutes. He only played in one Big East game. His minutes decreased from 82 as a sophomore to 61 as a junior before dropping again to 31 for his senior year. He was never a key contributor for the Orangemen.

TONY SCOTT (6-8, G/F, 5.8 ppg, 1.9 rpg, 9 assists, 4 blocked shots, 1 steal) He became the Syracuse equivalent of Don Baylor late in his career —a one-dimensional designated hitter, or in this case, three-point shooter. His .383 mark on treys (23-for-60) was best on the team, which is both a reflection of Scott's improvement and the sad state of outside shooting at Syracuse. He came up big against Pitt and Connecticut in the Big East tournament, and was a significant substitute when the Orangemen needed instant offense.

Unfortunately, the last shot of his Syracuse career was an ill-advised three-pointer with plenty of time left that assured the Orange of elimination from the NCAA tournament against Minnesota. ''We should've gotten a better shot,'' Boeheim said afterwards. ''But you have to admire the kid's confidence.''

Not much else apparently. One Syracuse insider said the slender Scott refused to lift weights, did not work on his ineffective defense and hardly went to class the second semester. He would have been ineligible academically had he remained, but he opted for a transfer to Texas A&M. Call this one an acceptable loss.

STEPHEN THOMPSON (6-4, G/F, 17.8 ppg, 5.2 rpg, 100 assists, 5 blocked shots, 49 steals) Never mind that he did not get selected in the NBA's two-round draft in June (though fast breaking Denver, where he signed as a free agent, may be just the right spot for his open court skills). Stevie Wonder's legacy is that he was a great college player. If he had to play out of position at point guard, he willingly complied. If he had to go down on the baseline for a slithering move to the hoop, you could count on him. An offensive rebound in traffic? Defend the opponent's top scorer? Thompson was your man. Pro scouts measured him at 6-2 1/2, which made his inside game and dozens of dazzling dunks seem even more remarkable. Has there been a better finisher on the fast break in college basketball. in recent years? And who got from end to end quicker than Thompson? Twice in his

career — against Connecticut and Pitt —he went nearly the length of the court for beat-the-clock dunks that gave Syracuse last second victories.

Even though he never learned to shoot from the field or the foul line, he became Syracuse's all-time leader in field goals (that's right —more than Coleman, Douglas, et al) with 801. He also wound up third on the school's career scoring list (1,940 points, 13.5 average), and that's after averaging only 5.1 ppg as a freshman. During the Coleman-Thompson years, Syracuse was 113-31.

The lefty from L.A. left a huge footprint in the snowbelt, and like fellow co-captain and roommate Coleman, he will be difficult, if not impossible to replace.

★ RETURNING PLAYERS ★

MICHAEL EDWARDS (5-11, 160 lbs, SO, G, #12, 1.1 rpg, 168 assists, 1 blocked shot, 29 steals, Eastern HS/Voorhees, N.J.) Slightly built, but quick and fearless, Edwards led the team in assists with 168, the second highest freshman total in Syracuse history (Pearl Washington had 199). After the Stephen Thompson point guard experiment failed, Edwards sparked a midseason six-game winning streak and did a creditable job at this crucial position. His reward? A probable backup role to freshman Adrian Autry, unless the talented freshman moves to the off-guard, allowing Edwards to continue as a starter.

He had a number of big moments in his rookie season, particularly against Georgetown where he outplayed another freshman point guard named Edwards, David (no relation), both times as Syracuse completed a rare sweep of the Hoyas. But he had more trouble earning respect than he did scoring points.

In the first Georgetown game, the blowout at Capital Centre, Edwards scored eight points, had five assists, and handled the Hoya defense admirably. John Thompson's comment: ''Edwards is quick, and he did an excellent job. But it's more important to see what happens at the end of the year than it is now.''

In the March 4 regular season finale, with first place in the conference at stake, Edwards sank 4 three-pointers in the first half to keep Syracuse in the game, and converted 5-of-7 treys overall en route to a career-high 18 points. He added five assists and just two turnovers in an 89-87 overtime victory. All Thompson would say was, ''We were going to let Edwards beat us with the three-pointer.''

Even Boeheim, who had praised Edwards all year, saying ''Who says we need a point guard, my kid can play,'' lost his patience after Connecticut used a stifling defense to beat Syracuse in the Big East title game. ''Michael Edwards has to at least be able to do something against a zone, he has to bring the ball upcourt against pressure better and not get killed on defense.''

Sounds like the coach was sending Edwards a message for this coming season. But if his rookie year is any indication, Edwards can handle this latest challenge. After all, he showed he's got the right attitude. When thrust into the leadership role last year, he replied, ''I look around me and I see a bunch of guys who are going to be in the NBA. They're all going to be millionaires someday, so I'm thinking I better keep them happy.''

Smart kid.

On the Orangemen's August European tour, in which Syracuse was 1-8 without Billy Owens in games against club teams in France, Italy and West Germany, Edwards made 9-of-21 three-pointers from the longer international distance. He started at point guard for Syracuse; freshman Adrian Autry was not eligible to make the trip.

LeRON ELLIS (6-10, 235 lbs., SR, C/F, #25, 6.0 ppg, 4.0 rpg, 24 assists, 25 blocked shots, 35 steals, Mater Dei HS/Tustin, Calif.) Is this the same guy who averaged a team leading 16.0 ppg at Kentucky in 1988-89? It didn't appear that way most of the time as Ellis was in double figures in scoring only five times all season. ''It's not easy being option No. 5 in the offense,'' Boeheim said, charitably. ''He's never been in that position in his life.''

All well and good, but after losing to Connecticut in the Big East tournament final, Boeheim was less charitable, saying, ''Ellis hasn't fit in at all.''

Things should be different this season. For one thing, Ellis often will be option No. 2, after Owens, and could be the recipient of many passes off penetration by Owens and heralded freshman point guard Adrian Autry. For another, he should be more acclimated to the physical Big East.

Defensively, Ellis was a plus last season, working hard to establish position, blocking out opposing rebounders to free up Coleman, and coming up with his fair share of steals and blocks. With Coleman and Manning gone, Ellis must be solid in the pivot offensively and defensively for Syracuse to harbor any grand post-season plans. Figure on him doubling his scoring and rebounding averages, or beware the wrath of Boeheim.

MIKE HOPKINS (6-5, 190 lbs., SO, G, #33, 2.9 ppg, 1.2 rpg, 26 assists, 4 steals, Mater Dei HS/Laguna Hills, Calif.) Hopkins' biggest assist so far has been his friendship with former high school teammate LeRon Ellis, which played a significant role in recruiting the Kentucky transfer to Syracuse. On the court, Hopkins was a bit of a puzzle in his first season at Syracuse. Reputed to be the team's best outside shooter, he seemed reluctant to take the open jumper in Big East and NCAA tournament games, preferring to pass the ball around the perimeter. He did make .556 of his field goals (20-of-36), but most of them came in non-league games against the likes of C.W. Post and Cornell. He never took more than three shots in a game once the Big East season began.

Boeheim did show more confidence in Hopkins as the season wore on, using him for 12 minutes against Notre Dame and Georgetown and 21 minutes against

Boston College. If he proves to be another Matt Roe (the former Syracuse guard who transferred to Maryland) from the outside, he can be a major contributor this season. If not, he can help by reminding Ellis to take it to the hoop once in awhile.

He gained valuable experience in Syracuse's nine-game European tour in August. Hopkins started at second guard, the Orangemen only took eight players on the tour, and averaged 35 minutes a game.

DAVID JOHNSON (6-5, 210 lbs., JR, G/F, –23, 6.5 ppg, 2.4 rpg, 33 assists, 6 blocked shots, 14 steals, Morgan City, La. & Maine Central Institute/Pittsfield, Me.) A less than fulfilling sophomore season included two moments in the spotlight. Ironically for the 61.1 percent free throw shooter, they came at the foul line. In the season opener against Duke in the ACC/Big East Challenge, he calmly sank two foul shots with three seconds remaining to defeat the Blue Devils, 78-76. "I just focused on what I had to do," said Johnson, after Duke had called time to "freeze" the shooter.

"You have to give him a lot of credit," Boeheim said. "He hasn't had to make those kind of shots before."

He got another chance against St. John's on Jan. 29. With Syracuse leading by three, Johnson made both ends of a one-and-one to clinch a 70-65 decision. Other than those two games, however, Johnson failed to establish his credentials as an effective scorer. He started only 15 of 31 games, reached double figures only eight times, and just once against a Big East team.

The potential is there. He is a better leaper than Stephen Thompson and a decent defensive player with good quickness. He can finish the break, but the big question remains: Can he hit the jumper? Off last season's 40 percent field goal mark, the answer is an emphatic no. He'll have to shoot well early to win a starting job opposite freshman Adrain Autry in the backcourt.

He was yet another disgruntled Orangeman who considered transferring, but chose to remain. On his athleticism alone, that's a plus for the team.

Johnson led Syracuse in scoring, averaging 27 points a game, on the Orangemen's European tour in August. Syracuse was 1-8, without Billy Owens, against club teams in France, Italy and West Germany. The Orangemen's margin of defeat was 20 points. Johnson also continued his poor free throw shooting making only 55-of-92 from the line.

CONRAD McRAE (6-10, 220 lbs., SO, F/C, #13, 1.9 ppg, 2.0 rpg, 4 assists, 16 bocked shots, 4 steals, Brooklyn Tech HS/Brooklyn, N.Y.) Raw offensively, aggressive on defense and off the boards, McRae played in 16 games last year (eight in the Big East). With Richard Manning gone to Washington, he's the likely starter at power forward and could be a key man if he rebounds and defends well. He showed occasional flashes in his brief appearances, especially against patsies Cornell (four blocks in 18 minutes) and C.W. Post (three blocks and five points in 17 minutes). McRae had four rebounds in 14 minutes against Florida State and four rebounds in six minutes against Boston College. Young and restless, he, too, considered transferring.

From the field McRae was 8-of-17 (.471) and he made 15-of-24 field goals (.625).

McRae was considered one of the best big men in high school basketball two years ago. He was inconsistent in high school and lacked a well polished game, but he can be a big time rejector. During the summer he played on a U.S. Junior National squad that won the Gold medal at the Junior Men's Championship of the Americas in Montevideo, Uruguay. He was one of four Big East players on the trip along with Seton Hall guard Terry Dehere, Villanova swingman Lance Miller, and Seton Hall's seven-foot recruit, Luther Wright. McRae averaged 3.0 ppg and 3.0 rpg for the U.S. team. On Syracuse's August European tour against club teams in France, Italy and West Germany, McRae was the team's top rebounder (10.2 rpg) and shot blocker (26 blocks).

BILLY OWENS (6-9, 220 lbs., JR, F, #30, 18.2 ppg, 8.4 rpg, 151 assists, 25 blocked shots, 74 steals, Carlisle HS/Carlisle, Pa.) Finally, it should be the Billy O Show this season. As perhaps the highest profile recruit ever signed by Syracuse, he deftly sublimated his skills in his freshman season, as Sherman Douglas ran the show. Last season, as a sophomore, he led the team in scoring, but still picked his spots to dominate, waiting to see if defenses allowed Derrick Coleman to maneuver down low. But this year, he has the chance to do something no player has ever done under Boeheim —average 20 points a game for a season.

They'll be calling his number early and often under the Dome, with only suspect LeRon Ellis and unproven freshman Adrian Autry appearing capable of providing additional offense. That's a far cry from a year ago, when Dick Vitale said it was "unfair" for Syracuse to have that much frontcourt talent.

Owens showed last year he could dominate a game singlehandedly. He scored a career-high 36 points against Georgetown, leading the Orange to an astonishingly easy 95-76 victory over the Hoyas, which ended an eight-year drought in the Capital Centre for Syracuse. "I had been hearing so much about us not being able to win here," said Owens, who took matters in his own hands in the second half. He scored 23 of his points, mixing in drives, tips, dunks, outside shots and 11 straight free throws.

"He had it going, and when somebody of his ability has it going, he's pretty hard to stop," conceded Georgetown coach John Thompson.

In the March rematch, Owens rebounded from a listless first half to score 21 points in the final 27 minutes, as Syracuse triumphed, 89-87, in overtime, to clinch the top seed for the Big East tournament. A highlight was his two free throws in the waning seconds that forced overtime. "I don't get nervous about anything," Owens said afterwards.

Apparently not. When the going got tough last year, Owens, not Coleman or Thompson, had the ball. Partially, it was because of his team-high free throw percentage (.722), and partly because, as Boeheim has said, "He's the best-passing big man I've seen in a long time." Owens had a remarkable 151 assists against only 79 turnovers.

In the season opener, against Duke in the ACC/Big East Challenge, the score was tied and Syracuse had the ball with 15 seconds left. "All we wanted to do was get the ball in Billy's hands," Boeheim said. "I thought he'd shoot, but he's such a good passer that he got it in David's hands." That would be David Johnson, who sank two free throws for a pulsating 78-76 victory.

Long-time St. John's coach Lou Carnesecca was also tremendously impressed with Owens' varied skills after a 22-point, six-assist, three-steal, two-block effort in a 70-65 Orange victory at the Garden. "You've got to go back to Tom Gola, guys like that," Carnesecca told *Newsday's* Joe Gergen, when asked about Owens' versatility.

Looie was particularly dazzled by a leaning, soft-as-a-kiss bank shot by Owens at a crucial moment late in the game. "That's an NBA move," Carnesecca decided.

No wonder. Owens said later his "friend" Michael Jordan helped him with the move at a summer camp. "He tried to teach me how to make contact and still be in position to shoot."

That shot, and others were on display this past summer when Owens starred for the U.S. National team in the Goodwill Games in Seattle and the World Basketball Championship in Buenos Aires, Argentina. Playing with Alonzo Mourning and Kenny Anderson, Owens was the team's top scorer at the Goodwill Games with a 21.4 average. He was the American's second leading rebounder with a 8.0 average. He had a team-high 34 points against Puerto Rico in the Goodwill Games. In the opening game of the World Basketball Championship in Argentina against Greece, Owens had 31 points, nine rebounds and four assists. He averaged 20 points, 10 rebounds and five assists while shooting 58 percent from the field as the United States went 3-0 in the qualifying round. He hurt his back in the medal round and the U.S. team slumped and took a Bronze Medal.

There is no doubt that Owens was the best player for the U.S. National team from the onset of the trials in Colorado Springs last May, through team practices at Duke, the Goodwill Games and World Basketball Championship. He showed off his shooting (even from three-point range), rebounding, defense and passing, and gave a glimpse of what Syracuse fans can expect this winter: Billy, Billy and more Billy.

"Inch for inch, pound for pound, the most versatile player we have here and potentially the college player of the year," said Al McGuire while watching Owens in an exhibition game that the U.S. National team played against the Soviet National team in Atlanta. "He has no flaw in his game, no Achilles' heel."

It could be a double-edged sword for Boeheim and Company, however. If Owens is as dominating as is likely, given the team's lack of firepower, he could well be one of the most desirable picks in the 1991 NBA draft. That would mean three years and out for Owens, who would undoubtedly break Coleman's school career scoring record if he stayed four years. But let's not get ahead of ourselves. Let's let Owens enjoy this season, one in which he could become national player of the year.

DAVE SIOCK (6-10, 240 lbs., SO, C, #24, Vestal HS/Vestal, N.Y.) After averaging 0.6 points, 1.8 rebounds and blocking two shots in limited action as a freshman, Siock redshirted last season. He stands to benefit from the transfer of Richard Manning.

Siock is the kind of upstate New York player Syracuse used to rely on heavily during the 1960s and '70s (i.e. —Bill Smith, Roosevelt Bouie, Jimmy and Mike Lee), before it recruited nationally. He may be the strongest player on the team, but also possesses a soft shooting touch. If Siock gets aggressive inside, he could earn some important playing time on a thin Syracuse front line.

★ NEWCOMERS ★

ADRIAN AUTRY (6-4, 195 lbs., FR, G, 19.0 ppg, 8.0 apg, Tolentine HS/Bronx, N.Y.) The absolute plum of Boeheim's latest recruiting class and a player whose reputation and skills are such that he could start at either guard position as a freshman. Autry was one of the best players from one of the greatest senior classes in New York City prep history. He selected Syracuse during last fall's early signing period, after being wooed heavily by Kentucky, Louisville, Pitt and St. John's. He recognized Syracuse's need at the point and committed early.

"I saw their personnel and saw who they were recruiting," Autry said. "If I signed first, I felt I could play right away. I fit in with the fellas and felt like I fit in at the University."

He earned a reputation as a defensive whiz when he contained fellow New York City backcourt star Kenny Anderson during Autry's junior year. He excelled in several post-season all-star games this past spring and set a record with 11 assists at the McDonald's East-West Classic in Indianapolis. Autry improved his outside shooting enough so that he's confident at either guard spot. He undoubtedly will draw comparisons to recent Syracuse point guard sensation Pearl Washington and Sherman Douglas.

Autry is stronger than Pearl and a much better shooter. He sees the floor as well as Pearl. Few point guards have ever seen the floor as well as Douglas, but Autry is close. Plus he's stronger and at least four inches taller. He was an impact player at nationally prominent Tolentine from the second he stepped on the floor as a freshman, and, of course, he ran the show on Tolentine's national championship team in 1988 as a mere sophomore.

"He's got a very, very strong upper body," said Tolentine coach Bob Mackey. He's a big kid who really sees the floor well. He's a natural point guard, but he can play the No. 2 or the No. 3."

Autry was a three-year starter and a two-year *Parade Magazine* All-America pick. He and North Carolina freshman Brian Reese helped lead Tolentine to a combined 70-13 record the past three seasons.

Over the summer Autry was impressive. He averaged 18.2 points for the West team at the U.S. Olympic Festival in Minneapolis. His scoring average was the third highest at the tournament and Autry also averaged four assists per game. Later in the summer he averaged 10 assists per game for a New York City Riverside Church team that won the Prince Junior Cup in Italy.

There is definitely an opportunity for Autry to have a major freshman year.

SCOTT McCORKLE (6-5, 220 lbs., FR, G/F, 27.0 ppg, 8.1 rpg, 2.4 apg, Capistrano Valley HS/Mission Viejo, Calif.) Another Californian lured to those brutal, upstate New York winters by the magic of the Carrier Dome, ESPN and the fast-paced Syracuse playing style. McCorkle is reputed to have an outstanding perimeter game. He made 54 percent of his field goals, 40 percent of his three-pointers and 75 percent of his free throws in high school. He is a flatout bomber from the wings and around the key. McCorkle has a good release on his jumper and is strong enough to get the shot off in traffic.

He was considered one of the five best seniors in California last year.

★ QUESTIONS ★

Depth? The transfers of Tony Scott and Richard Manning, and the failure of recruit Lawrence Moten to gain eligibility leaves the Orangemen with nine scholarship players.

Outside shooting? A bugaboo since Greg Monroe and Matt Roe departed. Syracuse overcame it last season with a powerful inside game, but will need the three-pointer this year to open up the inside for Billy Owens and hopefully, LeRon Ellis.

Can Californian Scot McCorkle be the consistent perimeter shooter Syracuse needs as a freshman?

LeRon Ellis? Will the real LeRon please stand up?

Adrian Autry? He has a heavy burden for a freshman point guard, but our reports are that he is equal to the task.

Foul shooting? Probably less of a concern than last season (.647 as a team), but always a concern at Syracuse.

★ STRENGTHS ★

Billy Owens! A terrific talent who seems primed to accept the go-to role, Owens could be the premier player in the college game by March.

The Carrier Dome! Syracuse was 13-3 in the Dome last season, and has won 31 of their last 35 there. The building and its atmosphere are truly phenomenal, except to opponents, who can think of other adjectives. Last season Syracuse set its sixth-straight NCAA Division I attendance crowd and had a national record on-campus crowd of 33,015 for the Georgetown game.

Tradition! Fourteen straight post-season tournaments; two straight Sweet Sixteen appearances. Throw in a Final Four trip in 1987, and you see that the beat just goes on in Syracuse.

Jim Boeheim! His teams are enormously successful as well as entertaining, a must for the rabid fans of the Salt City. It's no accident.

★ BLUE RIBBON ANALYSIS ★

For the first time in several years, Syracuse is not a pre-season Big East Conference favorite. In fact, the Orangemen were seeded fourth in the coaches' poll for the ACC/Big East Challenge, behind Connecticut, Georgetown and St. John's. Graduation will do that to the best of them, and Derrick Coleman and Stephen Thompson were too important for too long not to be missed.

Still, the cupboard is hardly bare. It's just not as overstocked as in previous years. Billy Owens can be expected to flourish as the focal point of the offense. He proved he can handle that role occasionally last season and often over the summer for the U.S. National team in the Goodwill Games and World Basketball Championship. His passing, rebounding, defense and overall court savvy make him one of the best players in the country. If his outside shooting continues to improve, Owens could be simply out-of-sight this season.

Question marks abound at the other spots, however, although Adrian Autry should be solid and senior LeRon Ellis appears capable of scoring more. With its up-tempo style of offense and defense (the latter is often overlooked but Syracuse's press and traps are very effective) could be a drain on this thin team. Would Jim Boeheim consider a slower pace? Not a chance. He knows the Carrier Dome faithful would rather begrudgingly accept a few more defeats with the running game than a better won-loss record with a more deliberate style. Besides, Boeheim is already courting several big time recruits for the fall's early signing period, and not one of them spends much time on the Princeton back-door play.

For Syracuse to keep its place in the Top 10 and in the hunt for the Big East championship, Autry has to be as good as advertised, Ellis, Johnson and McRae must improve dramatically on offense, and Owens must be an ironman and stay free of the nagging back injury that flaired up last year. And, freshman Scott McCorkle must pop from outside with consistency.

Syracuse sports information director Larry Kimball reported that when he talked to the coaching staff over the summer, they all mentioned what happened after the 1985-86 season. "We lost Pearl (Washington), (Rafael) Addison and (Wendell) Alexis and most of the experts didn't expect much from us the next season," Kimball said. "What happened? Sherman Douglas replaced Pearl, (Rony) Seikaly emerged and we went to the Final Four."

It's a valid comparison, without Coleman and Thompson, the Orangemen won't be No. 1 for the first six weeks of 1990, as they were last season. But they can duplicate the magic of '87 (ouch, that's still Smarts!). The Big East does not appear as formidable as usual in many respects. Pitt is the preseason favorite in the league, but the Panthers were 12-17 last year and need big contributions from several newcomers. Georgetown has its devastating Twin Towers of Alonzo Mourning and Dikembe Mutombo, but the Hoyas are extremely suspect elsewhere. St. John's has lost starting point guard Boo Harvey who was arguably the finest buzzer beating shooter in the country last year, Connecticut will dearly miss Nadav Henefeld, Providence lost some key seniors off last year's team and the Friars' two best recruits aren't eligible, Seton Hall is not yet all the way back, and Boston College is still far away from making serious inroads in the conference's upper division.

All of that means that even though Syracuse enters the fall with only nine scholarship players, will have a freshman at point guard and needs a big year from enigmatic LeRon Ellis, the Orangemen can still be serious contenders for the conference crown. That's because Billy Owens should be able to take this Syracuse team, pre-season reservations and all, on his shoulders to a successful season. The Orangemen should finish second in the Big East behind Pitt and return to the Sweet Sixteen of the NCAA tournament for the third straight year.

LAST SEASON		1990-91 SYRACUSE SCHEDULE		
Rutgers	95-79	Nov.	23-25	#Maui Classic
Cornell	108-56	Dec.	1	Cornell
#Virginia Commonwealth	100-73		4	##North Carolina State
#Temple	73-56		7-8	###Carrier Classic
##Duke	78-76		12	Canisius
@Canisius	92-72		15	Long Beach State
Towson State	105-75		20	*Towson State
C.W. Post (NY)	129-72		22	Illinois-Chicago
Lafayette	85-64		29	Wagner (NY)
@Pitt	80-78	Jan.	2	St. John's
Villanova	74-93		5	Villanova
St. John's	81-72		7	@Pitt
@Boston College	81-66		12	@Seton Hall
@Connecticut	59-70		16	Connecticut
Providence	86-87		19	Seton Hall
Pitt	83-74		21	@Georgetown
@Georgetown	95-76		26	@Providence
@St. John's	70-65		28	**Connecticut
###Florida State	90-69	Feb.	2	Boston College
Seton Hall	74-65		9	@Notre Dame
Connecticut	90-86		12	Providence
@Villanova	56-60		16	@Boston College
Notre Dame	65-66		18	Florida State
Boston College	105-69		20	***St. John's
@Providence	93-89		24	Pitt
@Seton Hall	71-69		26	****Villanova
Georgetown	89-87OT	Mar.	3	Georgetown
*Pitt	58-55		7-10	***Big East Tournament
*Villanova	73-61			
*Connecticut	75-78			
**Coppin State	70-48	@ Road Games		
**Virginia	63-61	# Lahaina, HI (Chaminade, Indiana, Iowa State, Loyola Marymount, Northeastern, Santa Clara & Toledo)		
***Minnesota	75-82	## ACC/Big East Challenge, Syracuse, NY		
		### Syracuse, NY (Alaska-Anchorage, Florida & North Carolina Charlotte)		
@ Road Games		* Hershey Park, PA		
# Carrier Classic, Syracuse, NY		** Hartford, CT		
## ACC/Big East Challenge, Greensboro, NC		*** Madison Square Garden, New York, NY		
### Orlando, FL		**** Spectrum, Philadelphia, PA		
* Big East Tournament, Madison Square Garden, New York, NY				
** NCAA Tournament, Richmond, VA				
*** NCAA Tournament, New Orleans, LA				

NOTES: The ACC/Big East doubleheader on Dec. 4 in the Carrier Dome also includes Clemson vs. Seton Hall . . . Syracuse will play Alaska-Anchorage in the opening round of the Carrier Classic . . . recruit Lawrence Moten, a 6-5 forward from Archbishop Carroll HS in Washington, D.C., is expected to enroll in prep school this year as he is not academically eligible. Moten was even more highly regarded as a high school football player . . . the hottest topic in college athletics after the Final Four through the fall was the expansion of major conferences to become "super conferences" so that football television packages can be enhanced. Despite its unparalleled success in 11 years of existence, the Big East is under seige because it doesn't have football. Syracuse will largely determine whether the Big East stays intact as it is an Independent in football and needs to find a conference for its football team. "We're not going to sacrifice everything for basketball," Syracuse athletic director Jake Crouthamel told John Bannon of *USA Today*. "But we're also not going to sacrifice basketball, either." Syracuse is willing to maintain its Independent status in football. "But that depends on what the other independents do. If all of them start getting into conferences then we're going to have to do something," Crouthamel said.

TEXAS

LAST SEASON: 24-9
CONFERENCE RECORD: 12-4
STARTERS LOST: 2
STARTERS RETURNING: 3
CONFERENCE: SOUTHWEST (SWC)
LOCATION: AUSTIN, TX
HOME FLOOR: ERWIN SPECIAL
EVENT CENTER (16,231)
NICKNAME: LONGHORNS
COLORS: BURNT ORANGE AND WHITE

The
TEXAS
LONGHORNS

★ COACH'S PROFILE ★

TOM PENDERS (Record at Texas, 49-18. Career record 319-227) After 16 years of excellent, but unrecognized coaching while waiting for a chance to make the NCAA tournament, Penders certainly made the most of it when the chance came along: Three straight NCAA appearances, two of them as legitimate tournament Cinderellas. Last year's unlikely run through Georgia, Purdue and Xavier stopped one game short of the Final Four on a Travis Mays three-pointer that would have tied Arkansas in the final minute in Dallas wouldn't drop. However, it established what many in the coaching profession had known for awhile: That Penders is one of the nation's premier college basketball coaches. After spurning the offers of several suiters of national prominence, Penders' contract was extended by Texas in a long term, big money deal that finally gave him the financial security he had labored so long and hard for. It also elevated him to a new national level of respect.

Consider that only four years ago when leaving Fordham for Rhode Island, Penders was making only $50,000 per year and could not even get $1,000 from the Fordham athletic department for new uniforms.

Penders' late father was a high school coach at Stratford HS in Connecticut. He played for his father in high school and went on to play point guard at Connecticut. Penders was also a standout baseball player and captained both basketball and baseball teams his senior year at Connecticut. During his college days, Connecticut made the NCAA tournament in 1965 and 1967 and the college baseball World Series in 1965. After he graduated from Connecticut, Penders played two seasons in the Cleveland Indians farm system. His career was ended by an injury and he took up coaching. After his baseball career was over, Penders still played softball for many years for the Raybestos team out of Stratford. He played on several national championship teams for Raybestos.

His coaching career began at Bullard Havens Tech HS (Conn.) in 1968. His second job was at nearby Bridgeport Central. Penders was 59-10 as a high school coach.

His first college job came at Tufts, an academically prestigious institution in Boston. He took over a dismal Tufts program, inheriting a 1-25 squad. He was successful at Tufts, going 54-13 from 1971-73. From Tufts Penders went to Columbia. The Lions had struggled before Penders arrived. Under him Columbia was 16-10 and 17-11.

From Columbia, Penders landed at Fordham in the New York borough of the Bronx. He stayed eight years at Fordham and his teams received five NIT bids. Penders was 125-114 at Fordham.

In the fall of 1985 Penders seemed stuck at Fordham. The Rams were coming off a 13-17 record. When Rhode Island coach Brendon Malone took an assistant coaching position with the New York Knicks, Penders was asked to take over the Rhode Island program. Malone left Penders some quality talent, especially in the backcourt with Tom Garrick (now with the Los Angeles Clippers) and Carlton "Silk" Owens. Penders guided Rhode Island to an NIT appearance in his first year, then a year later Rhode Island pulled off two stunning NCAA tournament victories that propelled Penders into the Texas job. Rhode Island stunned nationally ranked Missouri in the opening round of the 1988 NCAA tournament, then pulled a major upset over Syracuse before losing by a single point to Final Four bound Duke.

The Texas program had stalled under Bob Weltlich, but much like at Rhode Island, Penders found some better than advertised talent, especially in the backcourt, and made an immediate impact. His first Texas team was 25-9, set 22 school records, led the Southwest Conference in scoring with a 94.3 average and also set a conference mark for three-point field goals. The Longhorns made their first NCAA tournament appearance in 10 years and beat Georgia Tech in the opening round before losing to Missouri. Texas' average home attendance rose from 4,000 to 10,000 a game.

Last season Texas was 24-9 and had that splendid run to the finals of the Midwest Region.

There is no doubt that Penders has changed the face and style of Texas basketball. In the two years prior to his arrival, Texas failed to score 100 points in a game. In the past two seasons, the Longhorns have went over the century mark 21 times (any time Texas scores over a 100 points Austin area Whataburger restaurants give out a free breakfast Tacquita).

He has also been at the forefront of a movement to upgrade Southwest Con-

ference officiating. Penders was very outspoken following a couple close Texas losses and had several reprimands from the conference office. The Southwest Conference office has decreed that Penders must serve a one-game suspension when the conference season begins this year. He remains, however, undaunted.

"This (the SWC) will never be a big-time conference until the level of officiating comes up to that of the other major conferences," he said last season. Penders is firmly in favor of a full-time supervisor for Southwest Conference officials. "I definitely feel you need a full-time guy," he told Steve Richardson of *The Dallas Morning News*. "It's a full-time job. It's not just supervising and evaluating. Recruiting is involved in that. And it's hard for a person in another job to do that."

After spending 18 years coaching at eastern schools without great support, Penders is in awe with the resources Texas has at its disposal.

"The facilities are unbelievable," he told Bob Ryan of the *Boston Globe*. "There are none better. And our budget . . . I don't even know what our budget is. If you need a private jet, you get a private jet. We play at Arkansas and after the game there are two jets waiting for us."

"Arkansas has a couple of years' jump on us," Penders told Ryan, "but we can compete with them. In terms of budget and facilities, we have the best situation in the league."

He has instilled a freewheeling attitude in the Texas offense. "I tell my three-point shooters, 'you've already proved to me that you're a great shooter. So, until it's late in the game and we're protecting a lead, you can shoot any time you want and I feel comfortable. If you miss four or five in a row, I don't care,' You have to truly believe in the shot for the strategy to work —and you can't jump on a kid just because he misses a shot."

Texas has long been a "sleeping giant" in college basketball. In his first two years at Texas, Penders has shown that the word, "sleeping," should be eliminated. Texas is on the verge of becoming a true "giant" in college basketball.

★ PLAYERS NOT RETURNING ★

LANCE BLANKS (6-4, G, 20.3 ppg, 4.3 rpg, 96 assists, 11 blocked shots, 87 steals) The son of former Houston Oiler running back Sid Blanks, Lance transferred from Virginia and provided palpitating excitement for two seasons. Blanks' arrival coincided appropriately with Penders' arrival. That circumstance allowed him to freely demonstrate the skills that made him a first round pick by the NBA champion Detroit Pistons last June.

"Coach Penders has done such a great job just letting us go out and play," Blanks said. "He's never told me to tone down my act. He says he doesn't care whether I run in the stands or do whatever I have to do —as long as I put the points on the board."

Blanks did that, albeit with a rather adventurous shot selection at times. He averaged 19.7 points per game as a junior, then 20.3 as a senior. He drilled three-pointers in streaks and hit some defensive streaks on the press just as hot. He launched 512 shots last year and hit 206-of-512 (.402) and made 78-of-214 three-pointers (.364). If he was cold, Blanks would keep throwing up shots until he got hot again. Within Texas' run-n-gun style, that worked. His ever present potential for explosiveness will be missed.

Blanks had 32 points against LSU, 30 in an important win at DePaul, 36 against Baylor, 31 in a three-point victory at Texas Christian, and 27 during a Southwest Conference tournament win over Texas A&M.

TRAVIS MAYS (6-2, G, 24.1 ppg, 5.1 rpg, 72 assists, 16 blocked shots, 58 steals) Mays will probably go down as the best Texas player of all-time, to this point, and certainly one of the best in the history of the Southwest Conference. A two-time SWC player of the year and the conference's leading all-time scorer, Mays was a first round choice of the Sacramento Kings (14th overall). He was a fabulous all-around player —quick, a great shooter, an outstanding penetrator, a smart passer, clutch and the rare offensive player who was so good defensively that he could have earned playing time on that alone. A terrific athlete, Mays flourished within Penders' up-tempo style, nailing quick open three-pointers and playing pressure defense. Yet, Mays was, again a rarity, a player who seldom got so caught up in tempo that he let it affect the intelligence of his floor game. He was a leader and steadying influence.

Against Georgia, Texas' first round win in the NCAA tournament, Mays threw in a Hurculean 44 points. His two free throws with six seconds left in the next round vs. Purdue represented the Longhorns' winning margin in their 73-72 victory (after Panama Meyers' block at the end rescued Texas). Mays was a picture of high-level consistency all season. He was Texas' leading scorer in 20 of 33 games. An exceptional rebounder for his height and position, Mays also won or shared team rebounding honors on five occasions. He scored 35 against Florida, 32 vs. Xavier in the NCAA tournament Final Sixteen, and 30 vs. Texas A&M. Mays scored 772 points last season. For the Longhorns' 49-18 record and two NCAA tournament trips over the last two seasons, not to mention last year's great Final Eight run, Mays was the player most responsible.

Penders is certainly well on his way to having a great career at Texas, but he may never have a backcourt like Travis Mays and Lance Blanks again.

GEORGE MULLER (7-2, C, 1.0 ppg, 1.9 rpg, 2 assists, 19 blocked shots, 1 steal) Muller, limited physically, was not suited to Texas' style under Penders and was not a player of influence. He did contribute some defensively as a backup center when the starters got into foul trouble. He played in 24 games for a total of 163 minutes last year.

★ RETURNING PLAYERS ★

LOCKSLEY COLLIE (6-7, 225 lbs., SR, F, #42, 12.6 ppg, 7.2 rpg, 13 assists, 8 blocked shots, 29 steals, A.F. Adderly HS/Nassau, Bahamas & Lon Morris JC/Jacksonville, Tex.) Collie, at 6-7, was forced to carry a great deal of the rebounding burden on a team that played a three-guard offense. In his first year out of Lon Morris JC, Collie was a bit slow in adjusting but started to really pick it up in January and posted a few great games off the boards, against top opponents, too. (16 points vs. Arkansas, 14 vs. Houston, 16 vs. Xavier in the NCAA tournament.)

On offense, Collie was streaky but liable to break out any time. "He has some unorthodox moves he learned on the Bahamas playgrounds that are tough to stop," said Penders. Collie had a year-long tendency to get two points or so in the first half and then explode in the second. He is a tough, hard-nosed competitor who is expected to be a key inside force. Defensively, he's not overly quick and needs to improve. He was fitted with special shoes last season, after suffering a stress fracture in his foot, which helped his mobility.

Collie led or tied as the Longhorns' leading rebounder 14 times and was a team leader on the boards. He had 12 points and 11 rebounds against Oklahoma, 14 and 10 vs. DePaul, and topped the 20-point mark four times, twice against Texas A&M.

While at Lon Morris JC, he scored 30 points in a half against a San Jacinto JC front line that included Moses Scurry and David Butler, both of whom played on UNLV's national championship team. Collie's brother, Talbot, played college ball at St. John's College in Minnesota.

He is not only an important player on the court for Texas but Collie also was the Longhorns' top recruiter last year. He was a high school teammate of prize recruit Dexter Cambridge at Adderly HS in Nassau, Bahamas. It was Collie who convinced Cambridge to attend Lon Morris JC instead of going to a prep school in Maine for a year, which St. John's wanted. Collie also had a great deal to do with luring Cambridge to Austin.

HANK DUDEK (6-8, 220 lbs., SR, F, #41, 2.8 ppg, 2.8 rpg, 6 assists, 2 blocked shots, 8 steals, Jesuit HS/Dallas, Tex.) Dudek transferred in from Richmond billed as a shooter, but at least last season, did not pan out that way. Dudek made 26-of-60 field goals (43.3 percent) and was a poor 13-of-28 (46.4 percent) from the line. Still, he was a valuable sub who had some good games. He is quick and a good offensive rebounder who runs the floor like a wide receiver and plays very good defense. Dudek's problem has been getting in foul trouble and his poor free throw shooting.

He can fill in at all three front line positions. If he can attain some shooting consistency, he'll pick up some extra playing time this year. Dudek finished the season with strong performances in the NCAA tournament against Georgia and Arkansas. He has been legally blind in his left eye since birth, which is why he wears goggles. Dudek picked up a career-high 12 points at Rice, then scored 10 points in the regular season finale at Houston. He averaged eight points and four rebounds per game at Richmond as a sophomore before transferring back to his home state.

ANDREW FOWLER (6-9, 220 lbs., SR, F, #42, 0.4 ppg, 1.0 rpg, Hillsboro HS/Hillsboro, Tex.) Fowler was a limited contributor last year playing in five games for a total of six minutes. He is a good three-point shooter in practice and is on target to get his degree.

Texas should be very strong up front this year and Fowler probably will not see much more time.

GERRALD HOUSTON (6-8, 235 lbs., SO, F, #33, 1.7 ppg, 1.4 rpg, 1 assist, 4 blocked shots, 5 steals, Douglass HS/Atlanta, Ga.) Houston has bulked up from 210 to 235 which should enhance his Rick Mahorn-style play as a rebounding power forward. His best game last year was six points and seven rebounds in only seven minutes against Rice. He appeared in 19 games for a total of 123 minutes last year. Houston was 13-of-33 (39.4 percent) from the field and 6-of-7 (85.7 percent) from the line.

Texas is strong and deep up front this year so there is a possibility Houston may redshirt.

COURTNEY JEANS (6-2, 190 lbs., SR, G, #11, 2.3 ppg, 1.5 rpg, 31 assists, 1 blocked shot, 20 steals, L.D. Bell HS/Hurst, Tex.) A starter his first two seasons, Jeans is now a solid backup point guard who plays 10 to 15 minutes a game. His role diminished last year because starting point guard Joey Wright stayed out of foul trouble. If Jeans shoots, he'll play more this year. It's just that simple. In the past, he has lacked confidence in his shot. Jeans is an excellent ballhandler and keeps turnovers to a minimum.

He is 2-for-20 for his career from three-point range, including 0-for-6 last season. He averaged 10 minutes per game last year for the Longhorns.

Jeans started his first 41 games at Texas before hyperextending a knee during his sophomore year.

GUILLERMO "PANAMA" MYERS (6-8, 235 lbs., SR, F/C, #44, 4.2 ppg, 6.6 rpg, 12 assists, 52 blocked shots, 28 steals, Panama City, Panama — Madison

HS/Brooklyn, N.Y. & Lon Morris JC/Jacksonville, Tex.) Myers' last second block on Tony Jones to save Texas' 73-72 upset over Purdue in Indianapolis and a trip to the Final 16, will forever be part of Texas athletic lore. Myers, a teammate of Locksley Collie at Lon Morris JC, became one of the most improved players in the country after January. He turned into a great defensive player and rebounder. This year he'll look to improve his inside scoring on post moves and put-backs. He shut off Purdue center Steve Scheffler in the NCAA tournament while blocking his shot four times. For the game, Scheffler, who was named the Big Ten MVP in some polls, made only 6-of-17 field goals.

"He was very responsible and a very big part of our late season run," said Penders.

Myers averaged over 10 rebounds during Texas' six post-season games going against the likes of Carl Herrera (Houston), Alec Kessler (Georgia), Scheffler, Oliver Miller (Arkansas), and Tyrone Hill and Derrick Strong (Xavier). His 52 blocks led the team and were six shy of the Texas school record 58 set by LaSalle Thompson. Myers had 15 points and 16 rebounds in the Southwest Conference tournament against Texas A&M, 10 points and 12 rebounds vs. Long Beach State and 10 and 13 against Arkansas.

Myers, a Panama native, was affected by the U.S. invasion of Panama last December. His father lives there and it took a couple of days to reach him and ascertain that friends and relatives were unharmed.

In the NCAA tournament, Myers had 14 rebounds against Georgia, then 13 vs. Purdue. He should be a major presence on the Texas front line this season, particularly as a post defender.

WINN SHEPARD (6-5, 215 lbs., JR, F, #24, 2.5 ppg, 1.7 rpg, 5 assists, 4 blocked shots, 13 steals, Westbury HS/Houston, Tex.) Shepard is very quick, a good defensive player and can take it to the hole with authority. The problem is Shepard is a power forward in a 6-5 body. For that reason plus his very limited perimeter game, Shepard probably won't play a lot. But he does offer quality experience and is excellent on the press and an ideal player to insert when Penders wants to pick up the tempo.

As a freshman, Shepard averaged 6.4 ppg along with 5.1 rpg, blocked 20 shots and had 47 steals. His freshman field goal percentage was .613, then .667 last season (he's 110-of-176 from the floor for his career). His four baskets down the stretch helped set up a big Texas win over Oklahoma State two seasons ago. Shepard also won the slam dunk competition in Texas' first ever Midnight Madness in October, 1988, by taking off in the middle of the key and soaring over a rack of basketballs. He had 12-point, 13-rebound and 14-point, 10-rebound games against Texas A&M as a freshman.

BENFORD WILLIAMS (6-5, 215 lbs., JR, F, #3, 6.7 ppg, 3.6 rpg, 24 assists, 6 blocked shots, 22 steals, Sweeny HS/Sweeny, Tex.) Williams was first off the bench last season and is expected to stay in his classic sixth-man role this season. Williams is an aggressive, strong inside scorer who can also hit from outside (8-of-9 from three-point range in one high school game). Although he made only 5-of-20 treys (25.0 percent) last season, he can score 30 points in no time if he gets rolling. However, Williams sometimes played out of control and Penders hopes he can add some balance to his game this year. On defense, he tended to reach too often and get into foul trouble. Williams will pull off a few steals on the press and had a big steal at the end of that first half in Texas' tournament win over Purdue.

Williams came up with a monster game at Fayetteville where his 25-point, 11-rebound night got Texas back into the game and nearly propelled the Longhorns to a major upset over Arkansas. He also had a huge 18-point, 12-rebound outing against Oklahoma. Williams has established himself as Texas' resident resounding dunker. He also came up big against Purdue in the NCAA tournament with 10 of his 12 points in the last 12 minutes as the Longhorns came back from a nine-point deficit.

Williams averaged 15 minutes per game last year and started two games.

JOEY WRIGHT (6-2, 180 lbs., SR, G, #12, 19.5 ppg, 4.5 rpg, 126 assists, 4 blocked shots, 56 steals, Gavit HS/Hammond, Ind.) "Wright is the glue of the team, the one player we can't play without," said Penders. Texas' most consistent player, Wright is a true point guard who can also score. He can, in fact, do almost everything and may be one of the nation's Top Five point guards this year. He can shoot (209-of-455 for .459 from the field and 66-of-154 for .429 from three-point range), penetrate, score, pass and create offensively. Wright likes to pull up and score off a penetration move. He's also extremely tough on defense.

Wright will run the Texas offense this year. "It's his ball," said Penders. Wright is also a terrific rebounder out of the guard position. He pulled down an incredible 17 boards against Florida. Wright also lit up Stetson for 46 points on the road. That was the second-highest point total in Texas history. Wright, who transferred from Drake, is already over 1,000 points (1,163) in two seasons at Texas.

He keyed a crucial six-point run that broke a 69-all tie at DePaul and led to an important (in terms of an NCAA bid) intersectional victory. He had 29 second half points against Rice, after going 1-of-13 in the first half, and wound up with 32 points. Wright was fifth in the SWC in scoring, third in three-point accuracy and made second-team All-Conference.

As a sophomore, Wright scored 32 (on 11-of-19 shooting) in an 85-84 win over Oklahoma State. His breathtaking tip-in at the buzzer gave Texas an 88-86 win at Houston during the Longhorns' only regular season ESPN appearance that year. Wright scored in double figures in 31 of 33 games last year, 59-of-60 overall at Texas, and has recorded four 30-plus games. In his sophomore year he came up with 36 big points in a 93-91 win over Southern Methodist in the SWC tournament.

He rose to the occasion last season against the best: He had 25, 24 and 20 points in the three Arkansas games. He also had 20 against Purdue in the NCAA tournament.

If he has a big senior year, Wright should follow his backcourtmates from last year —Travis Mays and Lance Blanks —into the NBA.

★ NEWCOMERS ★

ALBERT BURDITT (6-8, 215 lbs., FR, F, #20, 28.0 ppg, 14.0 rpg, Lenier HS/Austin, Tex.) Burditt was considered the best player in Texas last year (he was selected Mr. Basketball by state basketball coaches) and among the Top 25 freshmen in the country. "He plays above the rim," said Penders. "He has great hands, is a great shotblocker and runs the floor like an antelope." Burditt is a major prospect. He has 15-foot range but has done most of his scoring by taking it to the hole. He is strong and simply jumps over people. His huge hands led to some picturesque dunks.

By landing him in the early period last fall, Texas finally flexed its muscles and established the ability to keep some leading in-state talent home. Before Penders that had been a sore spot was climaxed when Shaquille O'Neal left San Antonio for LSU (even though Dale Brown had prior inroads).

Burditt's father, Bubba, has worked as chief chef in the Texas athletics dining hall since 1974, so he'll be used to school cooking. Texas will get used to him pretty quickly, too. Burditt should see quality time in the Texas front line immediately and become part of a working eight-man nucleus (he and Benford Williams will come off the bench up front, Courtney Jeans in the backcourt).

DEXTER CAMBRIDGE (6-8, 230 lbs., JR, F, #30, 33.4 ppg, 11.0 rpg, A.F. Adderly HS/Eleuthera, Bahamas & Lon Morris JC/Jacksonville, Tex.) After losing two first round draft choices in Travis Mays and Lance Blanks, many feel Texas faces some rebuilding before returning to last year's Final 16 level. That's only because they have not yet been introduced to Dexter Cambridge, the man expected to keep Texas in the hunt for the SWC title and a key factor on the national level.

A high school teammate of Locksley Collie in the Bahamas, Cambridge arrives as the nation's leading junior college scorer (33.4 ppg). The *B/C Scouting Service* has described him as a "James Worthy Playalike" and an "Up-tempo dunking machine with big-time outside agility." Penders expands upon that to characterize Cambridge as a potential cross between Worthy and Karl Malone.

"He loves to get into the open court," said Penders, "and finish off the break."

Cambridge was also a 50 percent shooter from three-point range in junior college. Now that's called an inside/outside game. He also has great hands and is strong and physical enough to go into traffic and pull down rebounds.

He grew up in the town of Eleuthera, about 60 miles from Nassau, Bahamas. In grade school he played basketball by shooting a softball through a bicycle tire rim fastened to a telephone pole. Cambridge did not play organized competitive basketball until his sophomore year in high school. A year later, he went to live with his sister in Nassau. Cambridge went to a better school with a stronger basketball program. St. John's heard about his potential and tried to place him in a prep school in Maine, but former high school teammate Locksley Collie convinced Cambridge to attend Lon Morris. When he first came to Lon Morris, Cambridge had difficulty with the more physical American game. However, his coach Vic Trilli, now a Texas assistant, worked on making Cambridge more aggressive. Also, he began to pattern himself after Karl Malone. Cambridge started to eat more meat and starches, he had basically eaten fish in the Bahamas, lifted weights and gained 30 pounds in a year. A year later he was drawing serious comparisons to UNLV star Larry Johnson, a Texas native who played at Odessa JC.

"He has as much or more talent than a kid like Travis Mays," said Trilli. "Dexter has something Travis doesn't have. Travis is 6-2; Dexter is 6-7. The thing we don't know is if he will work as hard as Travis."

"I saw him maim three guys getting a rebound," said Baylor coach Gene Iba. "Then on the other end of the floor, I saw him hit nothing but net from 20 feet."

"He could dominate in our league," said Texas assistant coach Jamie Ciampaglio.

Longhorn guard Courtney Jeans is also impressed with Cambridge. "I watched him on film, and he can do everything," Jeans told Mark Rosner of the Austin *American-Statesman*.

Like most junior college transfers, Cambridge's offense is ahead of his defense. He figures not only to step into the starting lineup immediately, but also to be one of two focal points in the Texas offense along with Joey Wright. Along with seniors Panama Myers and Locksley Collie, Cambridge will form one of the most imposing, powerful offensive front lines in the country. By the time his two-year career at Texas is up, Cambridge could be a great player.

COREY LOCKRIDGE (6-9, 195 lbs., SO, C, #34, 16.4 ppg, 15.7 rpg, Abilene HS/Abilene, Tex.) Lockridge sat out last year at Texas. He is a good shotblocker, runs the floor and has a nice shooting touch. However, he's reed-thin and needs to bulk up. Lockridge's contributions will likely not start until next season.

TEYON McCOY (6-1, 175 lbs., SR, G, #13, Bishop Noll HS/Hammond, Ind.) Because of Maryland's NCAA probation, McCoy is eligible right away without the usual lay out year. He eagerly anticipates his reunion with Joey Wright, a friend throughout his childhood in Hammond, Ind. McCoy is extremely quick, a good outside shooter (42 percent career from three-point range) and will take some of the ballhandling burden off Wright. He scored 699 points and dished off 294 assists

during his three years at Maryland. Last year McCoy averaged 10.7 points, 2.4 rebounds and 3.6 assists per game on Maryland's NIT team.

He will give Texas, in effect, twin point guard capability in the starting backcourt. "It will be a little like the (Silk) Owens —(Tom) Garrick situation we had at Rhode Island," said Penders, referring to the great Rhode Island backcourt that led the Rams to the Final 16 in 1988. "McCoy should flourish in our system."

At Maryland, McCoy had a 22-point game, including six threes, against North Carolina. His best game as a sophomore came during an Indiana homecoming when McCoy put forth a 10-point, four-assist, zero-turnover game at Notre Dame while holding David Rivers scoreless in the first half of Maryland's 78-77 victory. He also had 15 points in a win over Arkansas.

"I really envied Joey (Wright) last season," McCoy told Mark Rosner of the Austin *American-Statesman*. "I would watch him and Lance Blanks and Travis Mays on television to see how much freedom they had on offense. Our team had so much structure. And Joey used to call all of the time and tell me how much he liked playing for Coach Penders. . .

"I really didn't want to leave Maryland. I liked it there, but I wanted the opportunity to play on television and play for a national championship."

He was recruited to Maryland by Lefty Driesell and arrived on campus after the death of All-America Len Bias from a cocaine overdose at a time when the school's athletic program was in shambles. He never played for Driesell and found himself under another coach, Bob Wade, than the one who recruited him. After his first two years at Maryland, McCoy sat out the 1988-89 season to raise his grades.

When asked to compare his game to childhood friend Joey Wright, McCoy told Rosner: "I'm quicker and a better ball-handler. Joey drives better and is stronger to the basket."

Look for McCoy to have a big year in Penders' up-tempo system in the same backcourt with his childhood friend, Joey Wright.

TONY WATSON (6-3, 180 lbs., FR, G, #22, 28.0 ppg, 10.0 rpg, Pflugerville HS/Pflugerville, Tex.) Watson redshirted last year. He was one of the premier players in Texas during his career at Pflugerville HS and had a 53-point game.

"He's a high wire act," said Penders, "like (Lance) Blanks. But he's less of a shooter, more of a driver and a break finisher."

Watson is a very talented athlete with huge hands and great quickness. He's a streak shooter with a huge vertical leap. His outside shot needs work. Watson won last year's slam dunk contest at the October 15 Midnight Madness practice by soaring over four students, perched on their hands and knees, after taking off just inside the foul line.

Watson will be great on the Texas press and should start to see some quality time this season.

"Tony is as gifted an athlete as I've ever coached," Penders said. "He's a lot like Travis (Mays) was early in his career. Tony is a good defensive player and he goes all out all the time. Our fans won't believe what he can do with the ball on breakaways. He's an exciting player who has a chance to be a big-time player."

★ QUESTIONS ★

Inside defense? Locksley Collie is not that quick or accomplished and Dexter Cambridge is out of junior college which leaves the heavy burden again on Panama Myers. Still, the Longhorns will be bigger and more athletic up front with Cambridge than in last year's three-guard alignment.

Long range shooting? Maryland transfer Teyon McCoy and Joey Wright are perimeter forces but Lance Blanks and Travis Mays (both first round NBA draft choices) represent a lot of lost firepower.

★ STRENGTHS ★

Tom Penders! His teams in the last four years, both at Rhode Island and Texas, have been very successful. His players seem to respond positively to Penders and his system.

A deep frontcourt! With talent like Benford Williams and Albert Burditt coming off the bench, the Longhorns will be five-deep and players who can really get things done offensively up front.

Dexter Cambridge and Joey Wright! Even though Cambridge is a JC transfer from the Bahamas with only two years of American college basketball experience, he could be the best frontcourt player in the SWC and a national factor before long. Wright, with Texas' expanded national television schedule, should be ready to introduce himself to America as one of college basketball's best all-around guards.

★ BLUE RIBBON ANALYSIS ★

In a nutshell, the Longhorns lose a bundle of offense in first rounders, Travis Mays and Lance Blanks, but pickup may be a bigger bundle in Dexter Cambridge, Albert Burditt and Teyon McCoy. Burditt and Cambridge should boost the front line, an Achilles' heel last year because it was undersized. McCoy, a Maryland transfer with one year of eligibility, should complement Joey Wright beautifully given their long standing friendship which will ease what might have been a tricky backcourt transition.

Texas, of course, will go from three guards last season, to three power forwards this year. The Longhorns still lack the classic post-up guys since Alvin Heggs left the season before last. But most of the Longhorns' offense is generated by pressure defense and transition after an opponent misses. And, though Mays and especially Blanks added a great athleticism to the press, the incoming big men, like Burditt and Cambridge, as well as Benford Williams and Panama Myers, have the athletic ability to keep it very effective. So do Joey Wright and Teyon McCoy from the backcourt.

The Longhorns, just like last season, will still give up a lot of points inside and most of their games will be shootouts that require quick-trigger scoreboard operators. Texas will need the three-pointers from Wright, McCoy and maybe Cambridge to make sure it gets more than it gives. The running Longhorns will need to live up to their reputation.

Texas has the experience, depth, coaching and athletes to do that for the most part. If Cambridge is the force he is projected to be, it will not be surprising to see Texas back into the Final 16 or Final Eight again. The Longhorns should present a formidable challenge for Arkansas and the Southwest Conference. Penders has won 25 and 24 games, respectively, his first two years at Texas and should enjoy similar success again.

LAST SEASON			
Texas-Arlington	116-66	Texas Christian	85-77
#Manhattan	108-63	Southern Methodist	79-68
#Texas-San Antonio	89-86	@Texas A&M	79-73
Long Beach State	87-89	@Rice	86-84
Florida	105-94	@DePaul	89-79
VMI	98-74	@Houston	79-84
@Southern Methodist	73-67	*Texas A&M	92-84
@Stetson	102-82	*Houston	86-89
##LSU	113-124	**Georgia	100-88
Texas Tech	109-71	**Purdue	73-72
Baylor	108-89	***Xavier	102-89
@Texas Christian	83-80	***Arkansas	85-88
@Oklahoma	84-103		
Texas A&M	96-94	@ Road Games	
Rhode Island	107-86	# Longhorn Classic, Austin, TX	
@Texas Tech	97-77	## Houston, TX	
@Arkansas	100-109	* SWC Tournament, Dallas, TX	
Rice	86-84	** NCAA Tournament, Indianapolis, IN	
Houston	93-102		
Arkansas	96-103OT	*** NCAA Tournament, Dallas, TX	
@Baylor	96-91		

NOTES: Texas' first round opponent in the Longhorn Classic is Loyola College. The Longhorns open up in the ASU/Tribune Classic with Michigan . . . the Kuppenheimer Classic is a doubleheader at the Omni in Atlanta, Ga. In the other game of the Classic, Georgia Tech faces Loyola Marymount . . . Penders picked up an oral commitment last summer from highly regarded swingman Joel Davis from Angelina (Tex.) JC . . . last season was Texas' first appearance in the Elite Eight of the NCAA tournament

1990-91 TEXAS SCHEDULE			
Nov.	27	@Florida	
	30	@LSU	
Dec.	4	Oklahoma	
	7-8	#Longhorn Classic	
	18	@California-Santa Barbara	
	22	##Georgia	
	28-29	*ASU/Tribune Classic	
Jan.	2	Texas A&M	
	5	Baylor	
	10	@Arkansas	
	12	@Rice	
	17	Houston	
	19	DePaul	
	22	@Texas Tech	
	26	Texas Christian	
	30	Southern Methodist	
Feb.	3	@Texas A&M	
	6	@Baylor	
	9	@Southern Methodist	
	12	Rice	
Feb.	17	@Houston	
	23	Texas Tech	
	25	Stetson	
	27	@Texas Christian	
Mar.	3	Arkansas	
	8-10	**SWC Tournament	

@ Road Games
# Austin, TX (Loyola College, Texas-Pan American & Sam Houston State)
Kuppenheimer Classic, Atlanta, GA
* Tempe, AZ (Arizona State, Michigan & Pennsylvania)
** Dallas, TX

since 1947 . . . Texas' 24-9 season was its second consecutive 20-win campaign. This was only the third time in school history that the Longhorns had won 20 games in consecutive seasons . . . Blanks (651 points), Mays (772) and Wright (644) combined to become the first threesome from the team in the 75-year history of the Southwest Conference to score over 600 each in a season.

UCLA

LAST SEASON: 22-11
CONFERENCE RECORD: 11-4
STARTERS LOST: 1
STARTERS RETURNING: 4
CONFERENCE: PACIFIC-10
LOCATION: LOS ANGELES, CA
HOME FLOOR: PAULEY PAVILION (12,543)
NICKNAME: BRUINS
COLORS: BLUE AND GOLD

★ COACH'S PROFILE ★

JIM HARRICK (Record at UCLA, 43-21. Career record, includes high school, 313-134) Harrick wasn't the first choice of UCLA athletic director Peter Dallis for the Bruins' vacant head basketball coaching position after Walt Hazzard was fired following the 1987-88 season. After all, UCLA once was *the* glamour program in college basketball during the John Wooden dynasty. Dallis wanted a ''high visibility'' coach, not a coach from up the coast at Pepperdine. Dallis went after Duke's Mike Krzyzewski and was turned down. He made a move at Jim Valvano of North Carolina State, and while that looked promising for awhile, Valvano eventually decided to stay in Raleigh. At that time, Kansas coach Larry Brown was a very hot property as he had just taken the Jayhawks through a Cinderella run in the NCAA tournament climaxing with the national championship. Brown had spent two years at UCLA earlier in his career, taking the Bruins to their last appearance in a national championship game, and even though his tenure in Westwood was controversial, he certainly was a ''high visibility'' coach.

The day after winning the national championship, Brown flew to Los Angeles, verbally agreed to become the UCLA coach again, then flew back to Kansas. Shortly after that, Brown decided he couldn't leave Kansas and rejected the UCLA offer. Reeling from the turndowns, Dallis called Harrick in for an interview.

Harrick said he told Dallis, ''You could probably get any coach you want in the United States of America, but, over a long period of time, not one of them would do a better job for you than I will.''

Harrick had a very important supporter in his corner during his quest for the UCLA job, the Bruins' former legendary coach John Wooden. ''I supported Jim all the way through those 13 days,'' Wooden told Tom Kertis of *Sport*. ''He was extremely, and uniquely qualified for this job. His high school coaching experience was invaluable from a teaching point of view. His assistant coach background for recruiting. He was from this area, knew the media, all the high school coaches, the system. He was a highly successful head coach for nine years. And, best of all, he didn't have to be coaxed like those other guys. He wanted the job.''

For Harrick, the UCLA job was the ultimate position in college basketball coaching for him. He headed west in 1960, soon after graduating with a Speech Degree from Morris Harvey College, in Charleston, W. Va., and just married to his college sweetheart. Ever since he started teaching in Crescent City, Calif., a coastal town of about 2,000 near the Oregon-California border, Harrick had dreamed of coaching at UCLA.

''We were just like the Beverly Hillbillies,'' his wife, Sally Harrick said. ''We put everything we had in the trailer and drove across the country and some wilderness we knew nothing about.

''Our families said we were crazy; they were real upset about it. But you know how young couples can be and how they can dream. We wanted to try something new . . . we never looked back.''

Two years after he arrived in Crescent City, Harrick moved south to Hawthorne, Calif., in the greater Los Angeles area. He was hired at a middle school and taught everything but shop. Harrick also worked in a paint factory to supplement his income. He later worked part-time for Mattell, Inc., making toys in one of its southern California factories.

His coaching career began at Inglewood Morningside HS in 1964. He served as an assistant for two years, then became the head coach in 1969. Over the next four years, Harrick compiled a 103-16 record (.866 winning percentage) and his 1973 team was 28-1. *Basketball Weekly* voted Inglewood its No. 1 high school team in 1973.

Shortly after the conclusion of the 1973 season, Harrick was hired by Utah State coach Dutch Belnap as an assistant coach. Harrick had to take an $11,000 salary cut to enter the college ranks. In 1977 he returned to California to work as an assistant at UCLA under Gary Cunningham. He spent two years at UCLA and was named the head coach at Pepperdine in 1979.

In nine years at Pepperdine, Harrick was 167-97. Four of his teams advanced to the NCAA tournament and two more earned NIT bids. Harrick was voted West Coast Athletic Conference Coach of the Year four times. Ironically, he was passed over by Southern California, Oklahoma State and Wyoming for coaching vacancies before getting his dream job at UCLA.

''Everything we do here, every practice, every drill, and even the players' lives *outside* the team, is meticulously planned out,'' Harrick told *Sport*. ''I want our guys to always know exactly what spot to go to. And when a player says, 'Coach, this is so dull,'' well, that's the greatest compliment I could get.''

''Coach Harrick stepped in and broke us down and worked on the fundamentals,'' former UCLA forward Trevor Wilson told Steve Berkowitz of *The Washington Post*. ''Basically, we started fresh, working on fundamental basketball like John Wooden used to teach. And he was very discipline-oriented, which brought the team close together.''

While Harrick has only been at UCLA two years he has put the program close to the point where it can be a national factor every year. He has guided UCLA to its first back-to-back 21-win seasons for the first time since 1982 and '83. Harrick has led UCLA to the NCAA tournament for two straight seasons and last year's appearance in the Sweet 16 was the first by the Bruins since 1980.

''This is 1990 and I think we have different values now,'' Harrick explained to Chuck Landon of the Charleston (W. Va.) *Daily Mail*. ''There are three things that are very important to me.

''No. 1, I want great integrity. I never want there to be a question from the NCAA about our basketball program at UCLA. No. 2, I want high moral values. I want our players to graduate. And I don't want them to have any problems socially. And No. 3, I want to win as big as possible. How big is that? Do we have to go to the Final Four? If we don't, will they find a new coach who can take them there?''

Offensively, Harrick prefers Wooden's high-post offense. However, defensively, he feels his philosophy is more in line with Bob Knight. He is definitely a basketball fundamentalist who believes that if the simple things are taken care, the big things will follow and victory will result. He is definitely a perfectionist.

''I think having been here helped me tremendously,'' Harrick told *The Washington Post*, ''because I know the administration. I know a lot of the boosters, especially the primary ones who really care about UCLA. . . . I know all the high school coaches and junior college coaches, I just think I had a feel.

''I'll say one thing: When you get this job, you'd better darn well be prepared. The magnitude of it is incomprehensible. It's a great situation, but it's ain't easy, pal.''

It may not be ''easy, pal,'' to coach at UCLA, but Harrick certainly looks likes he is going to be in Westwood for a long time. The Bruins survived a five-game losing streak last year and rebounded to advance to the finals of the Pacific-10 tournament before losing to Arizona. UCLA knocked off Alabama-Birmingham and Kansas in the NCAA tournament before losing to Duke in the Sweet 16. Then late this summer he had a major break that can be compared to winning the lottery. Harrick has recruited well in talent rich southern California since taking over at UCLA, a must if the Bruins are to return to consistent national prominence, but he missed out last year on the top two prospects in the state —Ed O'Bannon and Shon Tarver. They committed to UNLV, but did not sign a binding national letter of intent because of the Runnin' Rebels' predicament with the NCAA. In July, UNLV was banned from post-season play this year and O'Bannon and Tarver looked around and decided to come to UCLA. In years to come when Harrick looks back on his career at UCLA, he will consider getting O'Bannon and Tarver on the rebound as one of the biggest breaks he ever received. This August (Christmas) gift puts UCLA in a position to contend with Arizona for the Pacific-10 title.

★ PLAYERS NOT RETURNING ★

DARRIN DAFNEY (6-4, G, 1.2 ppg, 1.0 rpg, 2 assists, 1 steal) Dafney saw limited action in his two years at UCLA and decided over the summer to transfer to Drake. At Drake, Dafney will play for the Bulldogs' new head coach, Rudy Washington. A former assistant at Iowa, Clemson and Southern California, Washington is a Los Angeles native with extensive ties to the area that certainly had something to do with Dafney's decision.

As a freshman, Dafney played in 16 games for a total of 30 minutes. Last season his already limited playing time diminished to a total of 16 minutes in five games. He was diagnosed as having an ulcer after complaining of pain during the Washington State game on March 1 and did play the remainder of the year.

RODNEY ODOM (6-11, C/F) Odom is really not a personnel loss. He redshirted last year and was expected to help shore up the Bruins' weakness in the middle this year, however, the Kingwood, Tex., native transferred back to his home state and is now at San Jacinto (Tex.) JC. *Blue Ribbon's* junior college expert Rick Ball listed Odom in his Honorable Mention Junior College All-America team. It will be interesting to see if Harrick brings Odom back to Westwood.

KEVIN WALKER (6-10, C, 3.7 ppg, 2.1 rpg, 26 assists, 13 blocked shots, 13 steals) Walker started UCLA's first 11 games last year at center and the final regular season home game against Washington. The Bruins were weak in the pivot

last year and Walker was not the answer.

As a junior in 1988-89, he started all 31 games and averaged 9.9 points. Walker was a finesse big man whose main attribute was perimeter shooting. He was not a strong factor on the boards or as a shotblocker. He basically was a forward playing out of position at center because there were few other options left to Harrick.

UCLA is still questionable in the middle this year as the only true centers on the team are 6-9 freshman Rodney Zimmerman, who needs additional seasoning, and 7-6 junior Mike Lanier, a transfer from Hardin-Simmons who need a great deal of work before he can be the answer in the middle.

TREVOR WILSON (6-8, F, 17.2 ppg, 9.1 rpg, 95 assists, 13 blocked shots, 39 steals) Wilson is UCLA's most significant personnel loss. He is the only starting player missing from last year. Although he was not a popular player because he was highly emotional on the court and prone to fiery outbursts until towards the end of his career, Wilson had an outstanding career at UCLA. He was an honorable mention All-America selection last year and a three-year starter for the Bruins. Wilson led UCLA in rebounding for three years. He just missed his third straight Pacific-10 rebounding crown last year, finishing second to Stanford's Adam Keefe.

His value to UCLA was indicated last season after the Bruins got off to a 16-4 start. Wilson injured his wrist in a loss to Southern California and the injury bothered him for the remainder of the season. While he played with the injury, Wilson was not as effective and UCLA lost five straight Pacific-10 games.

In addition to his rebounding prowess, Wilson ran the court well, was the Bruins' second leading scorer and was a major presence defensively. Harrick considered him, ''the heart and soul of our team.''

He was a second round pick of the Atlanta Hawks. Initially, it appeared that UCLA would have a great deal of difficulty overcoming the loss of Wilson. There appeared to be no one on the team at his size who could do the things that Wilson did so well. It looked as if Harrick was faced with the dilemma of trying to replace 17.2 points and 9.1 rebounds per game without anyone who seemed up for the task. However, Harrick's dilemma was solved in August when 6-8 Ed O'Bannon decided not to attend UNLV when the Runnin' Rebels were barred from post-season play this year and hooked up with UCLA. While O'Bannon lacks Wilson's experience and might not defend as well, at last initially, there is no comparison between their ability levels. O'Bannon is considered one of the five best high school players to ever come out of southern California and many experts regarded him as the top prep player in the nation last year. It is never easy to replace a player of Wilson's caliber, but O'Bannon should more than make up for the loss.

★ RETURNING PLAYERS ★

MITCHELL BUTLER (6-5, 200 lbs., SO, G/F, #23, 6.2 ppg, 2.8 rpg, 46 assists, 8 blocked shots, 24 steals, Oakwood School/Inglewood, Calif.) Butler enters the 1990-91 season as a contender for a starting job at either big guard or small forward after establishing himself as one of the top guards off the bench in the Pacific-10. He enjoyed a very productive freshman season as UCLA's third guard. He came off the bench in all 33 games and averaged 18 minutes per game. Butler led UCLA with his .538 field goal percentage. He ranked sixth on the team in scoring, fourth in rebounding and assists. His best game came against Oregon in the opening round of the Pacific-10 tournament, making 6-of-11 shots from the floor and 4-of-5 from the line for a career-high 16 points. He also tied career highs with five assists and three steals in the same game and added five rebounds. He scored in double figures a total of four times, including 13 points against East Tennessee State and 10 vs. the University of San Diego and Arizona.

Butler scored 30 points in the Pacific-10 tournament (10.0 ppg). In the NCAA tournament win over Kansas, he made all six of his free throws en route to eight points and added six points and five rebounds against Duke in the semifinals of the East Region. He grabbed a season-high eight rebounds, including six offensive, against Louisville and had six boards against East Tennessee and American University. Butler was 45-of-72 from the free throw line (.625) and 2-of-11 (.182) from three-point range.

''Butler has outstanding physical abilities and we need to figure out where is the best place on the court for him to play,'' Harrick said.

Harrick is right on that assessment as Butler is a physically superior player. He is an excellent leaper who first dunked in the eighth grade. Butler played center most of his high school career at small Oakwood School in North Holywood. He switched to off-guard during his senior year. Butler also has outstanding quickness, speed and strength. In high school he was an outstanding student who was one of just three Oakwood students to earn the Headmaster Award, the school's highest honor, as a senior.

''He's also one of those guys who's just *got* it,'' Harrick told Tom Kertes of *Sport*. ''This kid is more mature right now than *I* could ever hope to be.''

''Butler is a Michael Jordan-esque tweener who is learning to play guard,'' wrote Kertes.

UCLA has quality depth at second guard with Butler, junior Gerald Madkins and highly touted freshman Shon Tarver. With Butler a possibility at small forward, the Bruins will also be outstanding at that position as Don MacLean and Tracy Murray, both tremendous offensive players, can play this position. Few teams have the quality and quantity at the swing positions —second guard and small forward — of UCLA.

DON MacLEAN (6-10, 220 lbs., JR, F, #42, 19.9 ppg, 8.7 rpg, 35 assists,

16 blocked shots, 18 steals, Simi Valley HS/Simi Valley, Calif.) MacLean is one of the better scoring forwards in the country. He is only the third player in UCLA history to score at least 1,000 points in his first two varsity seasons as Lew Alcindor, now Kareem Abdul-Jabbar, and Bill Walton, are the others. Also, only three UCLA players —Walton (972), Alcindor (927) and Fred Slaughter (549), who is now a well known player agent —had more rebounds after their first two varsity seasons.

Playboy magazine selected MacLean to its pre-season college basketball All-America team. There is no doubt that he is worthy of consideration for such an honor, but despite his considerable accomplishments, MacLean is one of the more unpopular players in college basketball. On the court he is a trash talker supreme who has irritated more than his share of opposing teammates and fans. His irritating ways finally caught up to MacLean at the tryouts for the U.S. National team last May in Colorado Springs, Colo. After a practice session, MacLean and Colorado's Shaun Vandiver got into an altercation. Vandiver popped MacLean in the jaw and was thrown out of camp. MacLean had to return home to Los Angeles and wasn't able to participate in the remainder of the trials. An indication of MacLean's unpopularity is that Vandiver actually received letters of support from fans at other Pacific-10 schools who weren't exactly MacLean supporters. Also, many of the players at the trials openly expressed their support of Vandiver's action.

MacLean is one of the most deadly shooting forwards in the country. Last season he made 238-of-461 field goals (.516) and connected on 179-of-211 free throws (.848). He is especially effective from the baseline area on either side of the basket and can actually accurately pull up on the break for his shot. He led UCLA in scoring (19.9 ppg) and free throw percentage for the second straight year and ranked second in rebounding (8.7 rpg) and field goal percentage. He ranked second in the Pacific-10 in free throw percentage, third in rebounding and fourth in scoring. MacLean was the unanimous first-team All-Pacific-10 selection and an honorable mention All-America pick.

He was at his best in Pacific-10 play, averaging 22.3 points and 10.1 rebounds. He was the only player in the conference to rank in the Top Three in four different categories —scoring, rebounding, free throw percentage and field goal percentage. His 19.9 scoring average was the third-highest ever recorded by a UCLA sophomore behind Lew Alcindor and Bill Walton. MacLean tallied at least 25 points in eight of the 18 league games he played in and scored at least 30 points three times. He led UCLA in scoring 21 times and scored at least 20 points in 17 of 33 games. His season-high 35 points came at home against Southern California. He also added eight rebounds and three assists against the Trojans. MacLean scored 31 points on the road at Oregon, and 32 at Oregon State. He tied a career-high with 16 rebounds against Oregon. MacLean also scored 29 points at Washington State, 27 at California and against Oregon State, 26 against Fullerton State, at Arizona and against Washington State, and 25 at Fresno State and against Oregon in the Pacific-10 tournament. He had a streak of five-straight 20-plus games at one point in the season.

"Obviously, losing a player of Trevor Wilson's caliber is always a blow," said Harrick. "But at the same time, to retain a player like Don MacLean certainly helps to offset the loss of Wilson. Without a doubt, Don enters this year as one of the top returning forwards in the nation. He is a tremendous offensive player who can score with his jumper on the break, off the glass and from the foul line."

"He's a much better rebounder than I expected," Harrick explained. Seeing him in high school, I didn't think he'd be doing so well . . . he's a four-star scorer. He scores in the framework of the offense, on the fast break, on rebounds and on foul shots. There aren't a lot of players who can do it four ways."

MacLean was a big time high school All-America but he had a reputation as a gunner who was a soft player. He has worked to change that image but still needs to continue to get stronger and work on his inside offensive game.

In addition to being an outstanding scorer, MacLean was also an ironman. He played at least 35 minutes, 18 times, including 12 of the final 14 games. He led UCLA in minutes played with 1,111 (33.7 mpg).

There are definitely few forwards in the country who can match MacLean's scoring ability. He made at least half of his shots in 19 of 33 games. All that can hold him back is *himself*.

GERALD MADKINS (6-3, 185 lbs., JR, G, #12, 7.2 ppg, 2.4 rpg, 121 assists, 3 blocked shots, 43 steals, Merced HS, Merced, Calif.) The 1989-90 season was a sweet one for UCLA Bruin Gerald Madkins. As a freshman, he played a key role for UCLA and averaged 5.8 points, served as the team's third guard and earned a spot on the Pacific-10 all-freshman team. The man who recruited him to UCLA, Walt Hazzard, was fired, but Madkins expected to play a big role and knew coach Jim Harrick's system. Unfortunately, on July 25, 1988, his 1988-89 season was ended before it started as Madkins was struck by a car while riding his Moped on the UCLA campus and suffered multiple fractures of his pelvis and torn abdominal muscles. He had surgery twice for the injuries and still has a plate and four pins in his pelvis. The doctors who treated Madkins thought his career was in jeopardy.

However, he worked hard and came back strong last year to start all 33 games at second guard. Madkins became one of UCLA's top three-point shooters making 38-of-90 treys (.422) and also showed that he is still a tenacious defender. The unselfish Madkins was second on the team in assists behind point guard Darrick Martin.

He was also second on the team in steals with 43 last year. Madkins ranked sixth in the Pacific-10 in three-point field goal percentage and tied for 10th in steals. He had a fine all-around game against Duke in the NCAA East Region semifinal, scoring 17 points on 5-of-6 shooting and passing for six assists, one short of his career best. He scored a career-high 20 points in a UCLA victory at California.

He also scored 20 points against Washington State and led the Bruins in scoring with 15 against Louisville and added 14 vs. the University of San Diego. He scored in double figures nine times and averaged 8.5 points in the year's final 12 games. He had a key three-point field goal late in the Kansas game in the second round of the NCAA tournament to pull the Bruins within striking distance. His clutch three-pointer at Washington State also clinched an important early season win.

Madkins had an assist to turnover ratio of almost three to one (121-48). He showed that his stamina had returned by averaging 29.4 minutes per game.

"Madkins is the most unselfish player in America. He's one of the few players I've ever been around who would be happy not to score as long as his teammates performed well and the team wins," Harrick said.

UCLA should have one of the better backcourts in the country with Madkins and junior point guard Darrick Martin. Add reserve Mitchell Butler and highly regarded freshman Shon Tarver and UCLA has a backcourt that can stack up with virtually any in the land.

DARRICK MARTIN (5-11 1/2, 160 lbs., JR, G, #15, 11.3 ppg, 2.2 rpg, 199 assists, 1 blocked shot, 46 steals, St. Anthony HS/Long Beach, Calif.) After starting at the off-guard position opposite All-America Pooh Richardson as a freshman, Martin took over the point guard spot for the Bruins last year. Martin has started 55 consecutive games since moving into the starting lineup as a freshman. He led the Bruins in assists last year and is already sixth on the UCLA's career assist list (289) and should conclude his career second only to Richardson on that list. He also is tied for seventh with 99 career steals.

Martin has great quickness and is an outstanding penetrator. He is developing into a good medium range jump shooter. Last year he made 132-of-283 field goals (.466) and 20-of-63 (.317) from three-point range. From the line, Martin made 90-of-126 free throws (.714).

"We're starting off from strength this year at our guard positions," said Harrick. "Martin's play against Kansas was the key to that victory and we're expecting that type of performance from him all season."

Last year, he not only led the Bruins in assists and steals but was third in minutes played (32.0 mpg) and fourth in scoring (11.3 ppg). He ranked third in the Pacific-10 in assists and tied for eighth in steals. Against Kansas in UCLA's second round NCAA tournament win, Martin tied his season-high with 18 points, making 7-of-12 shots from the floor, tied his career-high with five steals and added six assists. He clearly outplayed Kansas' senior point guard Kevin Pritchard. He also had 18 points in a Pacific-10 tournament semifinal win over Arizona State, making 7-of-10 shots from the floor and 2-of-4 three-pointers. He tied his career-high with six rebounds and passed for seven assists in that UCLA victory. Martin scored 18 points four times, also doing it against Fullerton State and then Oregon. He scored 17 at Arizona State and 19 at Notre Dame. He hit double figures 23 times, including 20 of the last 25 games.

During the summer he started for the U.S. Junior National team that won the Junior Men's Championship of the Americas in Montevideo, Uruguay.

Although Martin signed early with UCLA in his senior year, he tried to find a way out of his letter of intent after Walt Hazzard was fired. Martin didn't know Harrick and was concerned whether the new coach would last through his career. It took Harrick a month to smooth out the situation. Martin's parents were not happy with the situation and Harrick had his work cut out for him. Finally, an accord was reached in a meeting at the home of UCLA Chancellor Dr. Charles E. Young. Both Young and UCLA athletic director Peter Dallis assured Martin that Harrick would be at UCLA for his entire career.

Martin's play was good, not great, last year in his first season as the Bruins' starting point guard. However, this year he could make rather significant improvement. Remember that he was a big time High School All-America. Martin was named to many first and second team high school All-America squads. In fact, he outplayed former LSU All-America Chris Jackson, who was made the third overall pick in the last NBA draft by the Denver Nuggets, at the Nike/ABCD Camp. At that point prior to his senior year in high school, Martin was generally ranked slightly ahead of Jackson. While those rankings are meaningless, it does show where his talent level could be and we expect Martin to have a big year.

ZAN MASON (6-7, 210 lbs., SO, F, #44, 1.5 ppg, 1.5 rpg, 6 assists, 5 blocked shots, 4 steals, Westchester HS/Los Angeles, Calif.) Mason saw limited action as a freshman appearing in 22 of 33 games for 143 minutes without any starting assignments. He is aggressive, can be a good rebounder at this level and takes great pride in his defensive skills. However, Mason showed limited offensive skills away from the basket in his freshman year. He was 13-of-37 from the field (.351) and just 7-of-29 (.368) from the line. Mason had a season-high eight rebounds in a regular season win over Oregon and also had five at Oregon State. He scored six points against East Tennessee State and Oregon. He also scored four points twice.

Mason is a few inches short to be a great player with his type of game. He is just not big enough to be a great power forward on the upper Division I level and not diversified enough to be a big timer from the perimeter.

Mason was a third-team *Parade Magazine* All-America selection as a senior at Westchester HS. He was a three-time All-Los Angeles selection and was considered one of the premier players in California. However, he will have to be fortunate to play a major role this year. Freshman Ed O'Bannon will start at power forward over Mason.

TRACY MURRAY (6-8, 210 lbs., SO, F, #30, 12.3 ppg, 5.5 rpg, 41 assists, 26 blocked shots, 28 steals, Glendora HS/Glendora, Calif.) Murray came to UCLA billed as one of the greatest perimeter shooters to come through the California high school ranks. His 3,053 career points were the highest total ever recorded by a California high school player and Murray was the leading high school scorer in the country in 1988-89 with a 44.3 average. He scored 64 points in a game in the California state tournament and was such a prolific outside shooter that UNLV coach Jerry Tarkanian said that Murray was the best long range shooter he'd ever seen.

While he showed some of that ability last year by leading UCLA in three-point field goals with 46, he made .343 of his treys last year and .442 of his field goals, he also showed impressive toughness and a willingness to help the team by successfully playing out of position at center. Midway through last season, Murray moved into the UCLA starting lineup, replacing senior center Kevin Walker and remained there for 18 of the final 19 games. He finished the year as UCLA's No. 3 scorer and rebounder and earned third-team freshman All-America honors and was a member of the Pacific-10 all-freshman team.

"Tracy has always been a scorer, but what also pleased me with his performance last year was a continued improvement of his rebounding and defensive skills," Harrick said. "Because of his year's experience as a starter, our staff is expecting even more from Tracy this season."

Murray made the two biggest free throws of the year for UCLA with nine seconds remaining against Kansas, converting both ends of a one-and-one to send the Bruins into the Sweet 16 with a 71-70 victory. He led UCLA in blocked shots with 26 and was second only to Don MacLean with his .767 free throw percentage. He averaged 14.9 points and 6.4 rebounds as a starter. Murray became the second-highest scoring freshman in UCLA history with his 407 points and 12.3 average. His 5.5 rebounding average ranks third among all UCLA freshman. He scored a season-high 25 points at California in his first career start, becoming only the third Bruin freshman to score that many points in a game. He was virtually unconscious that afternoon, hitting 9-of-10 field goals against California and making 5-of-6 from three-point range and both free throw tries. He also added a season-high seven assists and six rebounds. He also scored 20 points against both American University and Washington State. Against Washington State, Murray also had a season-high 12 rebounds for his first of two double-doubles on the year. He reached double figures in 24 of the final 29 games and scored at least 15 points on 13 occasions. Murray closed the year by averaging 15.2 points in the final five games of the year (two Pacific-10 tournament games and three NCAA outings). He had 19 points and 10 rebounds in the semifinals of the Pacific-10 against Arizona State.

Murray is an effective offensive rebounder as 80 of his 182 rebounds were on the offensive boards. He ended the season with an impressive 15-point, nine-rebound performance against Duke.

He averaged 26.2 minutes per game. Murray also has the potential to be an accomplished passer in addition to an outstanding scorer. There is no doubt his debut season was one of the best ever by a UCLA freshman. Murray is well on his way to becoming a legitimate big timer. This year, he may have to play out of position again at center as the Bruins still have a gap in the middle.

While the probable starting frontcourt of Murray, freshman Ed O'Bannon and Don MacLean does not have a true center, it should be one of the potentially explosive offensive frontcourts in the country.

KEITH OWENS (6-7 1/2, 200 lbs., SR, C/F, #25, 2.0 ppg, 2.2 rpg, 10 assists, 10 blocked shots, 3 steals, Birmingham HS/Encino, Calif.) A former non-scholarship player who has since earned a scholarship, Owens will see some time again at center. He is not a great scorer and is definitely undersize for a center at this level but he is a hustler who is a good post defender. Owens can make a contribution as a role player for the Bruins.

Just one of two seniors on the team, Owens has developed consistently through his career. He appeared in 26 of 33 games last year and started three times. He was the starting center for UCLA's win over Arizona. In the Bruins' semifinal victory over Oregon in the Pacific-10 tournament, Owens tied his career-high with 10 points, making all five of his field goal attempts and grabbed six rebounds, one shy of his season-high. He also scored 10 points and grabbed five rebounds against East Tennessee State.

He averaged 9.9 minutes in the 26 games he played in. Owens played a season-high 22 minutes at Notre Dame and responded with seven rebounds, one shy of his career best, and four points.

KEVIN WILLIAMS (6-2, 175 lbs., SR, G, #11, 0.4 ppg, 0.3 rpg, 3 assists, Verbum Dei HS/Los Angeles, Calif.) One of just two seniors on the UCLA squad, Williams figures to be a deep reserve again. He started at off-guard for the first nine games of 1988-89, but has not received much playing time since. He appeared in 20 games in 1988-89 for a total of 246 minutes. However, last year his playing time dipped to 19 minutes and he played in a total of nine games.

Williams is known for his defensive skills and he is an intelligent player who can help in spot situations. Last year he made 1-of-8 field goals (.125) and did not attempt a three-pointer. He scored a total of four points, two each against Oregon State and Oregon. He played a season-high five minutes against Louisville. Williams had two assists against Oregon State and three for the year.

The UCLA backcourt is just too deep and experienced for Williams to get significant minutes unless some injuries occur.

★ **NEWCOMERS** ★

MIKE LANIER (7-6, 290 lbs., JR, C, #55, Brother Rice HS/Birmingham, Mich.)

Lanier was the tallest player in the nation last year. This year he will rank as one of the two tallest players in the nation along with Brigham Young freshman Shawn Bradley. When his previous school, Hardin-Simmons University in Abilene, Tex., dropped its program from Division I to Division III, Lanier became eligible immediately at whatever school he decided to transfer to.

He played two seasons at Hardin-Simmons. He appeared in 14 games as a freshman averaging 2.1 points and 1.8 rebounds. As a sophomore, Lanier averaged 6.7 points and 4.2 rebounds while playing 18 minutes per game. He scored 14 points, grabbed eight rebounds and blocked three shots against UTEP in the Miners' strong front line featuring former Bruin Greg Foster. Lanier blocked 28 shots and altered numerous others last year. He made .456 of his field goal attempts and was selected as Hardin-Simmons' most improved player.

He stands 7-7 when he dons his sneakers and can dunk the ball without jumping. Despite his great height, Lanier was only offered one Division I scholarship when he graduated from high school. His rampant growth rate had prevented his body from keeping up in coordination and muscle development. However, his growth has been stopped for over a year and that has allowed Lanier to develop more coordination and improve his game.

"I have to keep adjusting my shot every time I grow," Lanier told the *Associated Press*. "I hope this is it. I don't need to get any taller."

"Watching films, you notice that he alters this man's shot at least eight times a game, forces them to try something they usually don't do," said Hardin-Simmons coach Dennis Harp. "When you do that, you're awesome."

Mike and his twin brother, Jim, who is 7-5 and plays for the University of Denver, are listed in the *Guinness Book of World Records* as the world's tallest twins. They were both 7-4 by their sophomore year in high school. The Laniers' father is 6-3 and their mother is 6-1. They also have a 5-6 sister and a 5-9 brother.

He has never had a car because he cannot fit in them. His parents had to tear the middle seat out of a van so that the twins could fit into the back. Hardin-Simmons had to remodel his dorm room, building a 7 1/2-foot bed, lowering the floor in his shower and raising the ceiling. He could not work out at the Hardin-Simmons' weight room because the angles of adjustment on the equipment were not matched properly for his height. Since the university had no free weights, Lanier was never on a stringent weight training program.

Over 80 schools recruited Lanier after he announced he would leave Hardin-Simmons. After he decided to transfer to UCLA, Lanier said, "I definitely want to play in the NBA, and you can get a whole lot of exposure from going to UCLA."

"To say that Mike Lanier is a big body is certainly an understatement. As a staff, we're looking forward to seeing how quickly he progresses in our system," Harrick said.

Lanier is certainly going to need some time to develop. His height offers some interesting aspects to a UCLA team that has gone without a true center for quite some time. However, Lanier will probably be a spot player for the Bruins at least through this season. It will be interesting to watch his development. Remember that UCLA's last true big man was 7-4 Mark Eaton, who scored only 53 points in his final two seasons with the Bruins, but has since become the starting center of the Utah Jazz and one of the premier defensive centers in the NBA. At this point in his career, Lanier is considered farther along than Eaton. Lanier has more mobility and a better shooting touch.

ED O'BANNON (6-8, 205 lbs., FR, F, #31, 24.6 ppg, 9.7 rpg, 3.4 apg, Artesia HS/Lakewood, Calif.) Jim Harrick has had a string of good fortunes since taking over at UCLA. That good fortune reached new heights early last August when Ed O'Bannon signed with the Bruins. O'Bannon had originally committed to UNLV, but because of the Runnin' Rebels problems with the NCAA, he never signed a binding national letter of intent. When UNLV was barred from post-season play this year, in late August, O'Bannon decided to look elsewhere.

He is not your ordinary, run of the mill highly publicized High School All-America. O'Bannon was named national high school player of the year by *Basketball Times* last year. He was unquestionably the finest player in California and is considered one of the five best talents to ever come out of the state. He is also potentially the best player UCLA has signed since Bill Walton in 1970. O'Bannon is the Newcomer of the Year in this edition of *Blue Ribbon College Basketball Yearbook*.

"I've been around for awhile. He's a great one," Gary McKnight, coach of Mater Dei HS in Santa Ana, Calif., told Mike White of the *Pittsburgh Post-Gazette*. "He's one of the most gifted athletes for a big guy I've seen out here in a long time."

The two-time *Parade Magazine* All-America selection led Artesia to the southern California 4A title and the state Division II championship.

"Ed O'Bannon is the warrior in the class - he can overpower you with his inside game or he can out on the perimeter and beat you with his shooting and finesse. He was our choice last fall (as the top senior in the country), he is our choice today and he'll be our choice tomorrow," said *Hoop Scoop* publisher Clark Francis.

"How good can O'Bannon be? In the same class with Jordan, Bird, Magic and Isiah? Think I'm crazy - well, he has the same work ethic and natural ability to rank alongside of the legends, but one thing (position) may prohibit this from happening. He wants to become a wing forward or even a 2-guard . . . our feeling is that he's best at a 4 (power forward) spot and he's the exception to the rule at 6-8 . . ."

Arizona State coach Bill Frieder, who recruited several eventual NBA players during his tenure at Michigan, has said that O'Bannon was the best player he has ever tried to recruit. UNLV coach Jerry Tarkanian, who gave O'Bannon the option of changing his mind if the Runnin' Rebels were penalized by the NCAA before the start of the fall semester, was equally lavish in his praise.

"O'Bannon will be a three-time All-America no matter where he goes," Tarkanian said.

"This athletic, high-scoring lefthander is ultra skilled, and reminds us somewhat of L.A. Lakers star James Worthy. Like "Jammin' James,' he is an outstanding ballhandler, and has the ability to put it on the floor and take off. O'Bannon possesses an ambidextrous shooting touch around the paint, and with his speed, quickness, and uncanny scoring instincts, he is virtually unstoppable inside. "O'Bannon' has a limitless arsenal of scoring weapons, including a variety of accurate hook shots. We consider him the nation's premier offensive player. He is an effective outside shooter with true three-point range. O'Bannon has the long arms, strength, and competitive spirit to play up front, and the perimeter skills and explosiveness to play in the backcourt," said Bob Gibbons of *All-Star Sports*.

He was the MVP of the West team in the Dapper Dan Roundball Classic in Pittsburgh and scored 19 points in the McDonald's East-West All-Star game. Over the summer he started and averaged 11.5 points for the U.S. Junior National team that won the Junior Men's Championship of the Americas in Montevideo, Uruguay.

"My feelings are the same as when he announced he was going to attend UNLV, except now it gives the Pac-10 two teams this year with Final Four potential," said Southern California coach George Raveling.

SHON TARVER (6-5, 190 lbs., FR, G, #21, 31.6 ppg, 9.2 rpg, 4.0 blpg, 3.5 apg, Santa Clara HS/Oxnard, Calif.) For years UCLA was the program in the west. It took years for the Bruins' challengers to gain ground and eventually equal, and in many seasons surpass UCLA's achievements. UNLV was the first western team, other than UCLA, to win an NCAA title since 1966. After winning the national championship, UNLV signed the two best players in California - Ed O'Bannon and Shon Tarver. UNLV had tried without success to sign the premier player in southern California for over a decade and now the Runnin' Rebels had pulled it off. Then, the NCAA came down hard on UNLV barring the Runnin' Rebels from post-season play this year and O'Bannon and Tarver decided to go elsewhere. Ironically, they both chose UCLA, UNLV's long time nemesis in recruiting.

Tarver was considered the No. 2 player in California behind O'Bannon last year. He was a two-time California Division IV player of the year and led Santa Clara to state titles the last two seasons.

In the finals of the Southern Section 2 AA Division championship, against Los Angeles power Verbum Dei, Tarver not only led his team to the championship, but had a phenomenal 31-point, 12-rebound, 4-block, 3-assist game. At halftime, Tarver had outpointed Verbum Dei, 22-18.

"Has there ever been a more one-sided Southern Sectional final? Has a single player ever dominated so completely?," wrote Steve Henson in the *Los Angeles Times*.

"He's got great size, great instincts and the fact that he's played guard all of his life is a big plus," Harrick said. "He's a good scorer and passes well."

Santa Clara coach Lou Cvijanovich called Tarver the best player he'd coached in his 32 years at the school. Tarver's father, John Tarver, was a standout running back at Colorado. He was a starting running back in the 1973 College All-Star game on a team whose backfield included NFL stars Franco Harris and Robert Newhouse. John Tarver played three years with the New England Patriots and one season with the Philadelphia Eagles. Two of Shon's uncles played football at Southern California and Washington.

Shon Tarver played his first two years of high school basketball at Rim of the World HS in the Lake Arrowhead area of California. His father then moved the family to Oxnard and Tarver had a spectacular two-year career at Santa Clara HS.

After Tarver put up 35 points, seven rebounds and five assists in the state championship game, Cvijanovich said, "He's as good as anybody in the United States. Well, I won't come out and say he's the best, but I would like to see anybody that's better."

"If Shon can shoot the ball like we've been led to believe, he can help us right away," said Harrick.

While Tarver appears to be entering a rather talented and crowed UCLA backcourt, he should still play a key role as a freshman. Tarver is a better pure long range shooter than Bruin guards Darrick Martin, Gerald Madkins and Mitchell Butler.

RODNEY ZIMMERMAN (6-9, 221 lbs., FR, C/F, #14, 25.7 ppg, 13.2 rpg, 10.0 blpg, Air Academy/Colorado Springs, Colo.) Zimmerman was UCLA's lone recruit last November and the only high school player Harrick had lined up before his August sweep netted Ed O'Bannon and Shon Tarver. Zimmerman was a third-team *Parade Magazine* All-America selection. He was selected the *USA Today* Colorado player of the year as well. Most scouting services ranked him as one of the Top 75 players in the country. He helped lead Air Academy to a state title as a sophomore. His father is an Air Force colonel and Zimmerman is a cousin of former St. John's standout Shelton Jones.

While Zimmerman has good mobility and quickness, was an outstanding shot-blocker in high school and scored 44 points on three occasions, he is not the tough, physical center the Bruins need in the pivot. He did have 13 rebounds in a game against LSU All-America center Shaquille O'Neal at the U.S. Olympic Festival, but got pushed around by brawnier centers in the other games.

"I was not mentally or emotionally prepared for that," Zimmerman told Clay Lattimer of the *Rocky Mountain News* about the physical play at the Olympic Festival. "It got to me. Playing down low is impossible for me right now for my size. I'm

not big enough to play down low. . .

"What Harrick is going to find out is that I'm not really a (low-post) man, even though I'm 6-9. I prefer to play small forward but they (UCLA) need post-up guys. That means I have to put on a lot of weight - and I mean a lot. I've got to put on at least 40 pounds between now and the first (UCLA) game. We're talking about sweat and work. . .''

Zimmerman was a little harsh on himself with his critique. Even though he may not be physically ready to handle the banging in the lane in big time college basketball, he is a 6-9 player who can block shots and that's something UCLA didn't have last year. His mere presence will help the Bruins this year and look for Harrick to pull out all stops in trying to make Zimmerman the pivot man UCLA needs so dearly.

★ QUESTIONS ★

The pivot? Harrick was forced to use forward Tracy Murray in the pivot last year. Freshman Rodney Zimmerman (6-9) and gigantic Hardin-Simmons transfer Mike Lanier (7-6) are probably not ready to handle the position on a full-time basis this year. That means UCLA's pivot play will be by committee.

Perimeter shooting from the backcourt? Unless super shooting freshman Shon Tarver comes through, UCLA will be a bit suspect long range shooting club from the backcourt.

Possible lack of senior leadership? UCLA has only two seniors on the team and both could be limited contributors this year.

★ STRENGTHS ★

Overall talent! While UCLA still doesn't have a proven, true center, the Bruins are loaded everywhere else. This is the most talented UCLA team since the Wooden dynasty.

Offensive potential! UCLA already has two bona fide scorers in Don MacLean and Tracy Murray. Freshman Ed O'Bannon and Shon Tarver give the Bruins four legitimate big league scorers. No team in the country has a more lethal group of scoring forwards than UCLA.

Jim Harrick! UCLA is Harrick's dream job and he is producing. He has the experience and skill necessary to keep this extremely talented young team developing at the proper pace.

The backcourt! With the addition of Shon Tarver, UCLA should have one of the strongest backcourts in the country as the top three guards from last year are returning.

★ BLUE RIBBON ANALYSIS ★

The Bruins are back! UCLA rebounded from a five-game losing streak in the midst of the Pacific-10 season last year to upset Kansas in the second round of the NCAA tournament and advance to the Sweet 16 for the first time since 1980. Second-year coach Jim Harrick led the Bruins to back-to-back 20-win seasons for the first time since 1978 and "79. With four starters returning, UCLA appeared to have another 10-win season and possible Top 20 status locked up.

The Bruins' prospects for 1990-91 went from good to possibly out-of-sight in early August when Ed O'Bannon, the *Basketball Times* national high school player of the year last season, and the No. 2 prospect in California, 6-5 guard Shon Tarver, decided to attend UCLA after UNLV was denied a chance to defend its national championship by the NCAA. As soon as O'Bannon's and Tarver's signatures were dry, coaches throughout the west put the burden of high expectations on the Bruins.

". . . they could have the best team in the country. They'll be so talented, it will be unbelievable," said UNLV coach Jerry Tarkanian.

Southern California coach George Raveling said that with the additions of O'Bannon and Tarver, UCLA now gave the Pacific-10 two teams (along with Arizona) with Final Four potential.

The Bruins are without their top scorer and second leading rebounder from last year, forward Trevor Wilson, but the arrival of O'Bannon makes replacing Wilson not nearly as difficult for Harrick. Junior forward Don MacLean is on track to become UCLA's all-time leading scorer during the latter half of his senior year. He led the Bruins in scoring with a 19.9 per game average last year and was one of the most prolific scoring, best shooting forwards in the country.

Sophomore Tracy Murray is the all-time leading high school scorer in California history. He had to play out of position at center last year but responded with averages of 12.3 points and 5.5 rebounds. Murray had one of the best freshman years any Bruin has ever had despite playing out of position. If he ever played full-time at forward, Murray might be even more dangerous offensively than MacLean. Now that O'Bannon has arrived, UCLA should have the most dangerous offensive front line in the country.

The Bruins are still without a proven big time center, but there is more size on the roster than last year. Mike Lanier, a transfer from Hardin-Simmons, is 7-6 and one of the two tallest players in college basketball. He is still developing but some believe he is further along than former UCLA center Mark Eaton. Rodney Zimmerman, a 6-9 freshman from Colorado Springs, Colo., has fine mobility and shotblocking skill but needs to get stronger and tougher before he can handle the pivot on a full-time basis.

In the backcourt, UCLA is lethal and loaded. Starters Darrick Martin and Gerald Madkins return. Martin could develop into one of the premier point guards not only in the west but the country this year and Madkins is an unselfish, strong defender who came back from sitting out the 1988-89 season with a serious pelvis injury. Sophomore Mitchell Butler possesses truly exceptional, explosive athletic ability and looked good as a freshman. Tarver has more offensive ability than any of the returning UCLA guards. He was a sensational offensive player both from the perimeter and driving to the basket in his two years at Santa Clara HS in Oxnard, Calif.

UCLA is still young. There are only two seniors on the roster and both are

slated for limited duty this year. Maturity-wise and as far as experience in big games and playing together as a team, UCLA is still probably a year away from reaching its true potential. However, the Bruins now have the talent necessary to beat anyone in the country on any given day. UCLA will push Arizona for the Pacific-10 crown, win 20 or more games for the third straight year and return to the Sweet 16 of the NCAA tournament. The last time UCLA played in the Final Four was 1980 as Larry Brown's first Bruin team went all the way to the championship game before losing to Louisville. That Final Four was held in Indianapolis. Indianapolis is the site of this year's Final Four. It wouldn't be a major surprise if the Bruins made a return trip to Indianapolis.

LAST SEASON			
Santa Clara	66-62	@Arizona	74-83
@Washington	58-56	California	71-79
@Washington State	68-64	Stanford	69-70
Univ. of San Diego	83-74	@Oregon	99-105
@Notre Dame	84-86	@Oregon State	74-83
American University	89-74	Washington State	96-89
Fullerton State	87-75	Washington	74-61
@Fresno State	74-65	#Oregon	94-76
East Tennessee State	115-66	#@Arizona State	79-78
Southern California	89-72	#Arizona	78-94
@Louisville	80-97	##Alabama-Birmingham	68-56
Arizona State	62-53	##Kansas	71-70
Arizona	73-67	*Duke	81-90
@Stanford	79-87		
@California	106-97	@ Road Games	
Oregon	79-62	# Pacific-10 Tournament, Tempe, AZ	
Oregon State	94-80	## NCAA Tournament, Atlanta, GA	
@Southern California	75-76	* NCAA Tournament, East Rutherford,	
DePaul	87-77	NJ	
@Arizona State	80-72		

1990-91 UCLA SCHEDULE			
Nov.	23-26 #Great Alaska Shootout	Feb.	10 Arizona
Dec.	2 Loyola		14 @California
	5 St. Mary's		16 @Stanford
	8 Notre Dame		21 Oregon
	15 @DePaul		23 Oregon State
	19 Pepperdine		28 @Washington State
	22 @Iowa	Mar.	3 @Washington
	27 Fresno State		7 Washington State
	29 San Diego State		10 Washington
Jan.	2 Southern California		
	5 Louisville	@ Road Games	
	10 @Arizona State	# Anchorage, AK (Alaska-Anchorage,	
	12 @Arizona	California-Irvine, Nevada, Siena, South	
	16 Stanford	Carolina, Texas Tech & Virginia)	
	19 California		
	24 @Oregon State		
	26 @Oregon		
	30 @Southern California		
Feb.	2 Pitt		
	7 Arizona State		

NOTES: The Great Alaska Shootout is one of the few in-season tournaments UCLA has participated in since John Wooden took over the program . . . UCLA retired its first four basketball uniform numbers last February during a ceremony at Pauley Pavilion. The numbers retired were 33 (Kareem Abdul-Jabbar), 32 (Bill Walton), and from the women's program, 15 (Anne Meyers) and 12 (Denise Curry) . . . UCLA recently finalized a deal to televise a package of football and basketball games plus a few other contests in

other sports, in western Europe and Japan. "It's exposure," UCLA associate athletic director Jim Milhorn told Steve Weiberg of *USA Today*. "Some day, it might be worth something. Right now, it's not much." . . . UCLA has participated in 26 NCAA tournaments and won a record 64 games, while losing just 20 for an outstanding .762 winning percentage. Only Kentucky, with 33 appearances, has played in more tournaments, but the Wildcats have won 55 games, nine fewer than the Bruins.

VIRGINIA

LAST SEASON: 20-12
CONFERENCE RECORD: 6-8
STARTERS LOST: 0
STARTERS RETURNING: 5
CONFERENCE: ATLANTIC COAST (ACC)
LOCATION: CHARLOTTESVILLE, VA
HOME FLOOR: UNIVERSITY
** HALL (8,864)**
NICKNAMES: CAVALIERS & WAHOOS
COLORS: ORANGE AND BLUE

★ COACH'S PROFILE ★

JEFF JONES (First year at Virginia) Jones, a member of Virginia's coaching staff for the last eight years and a former standout player for the Cavaliers, was named Virginia's head basketball coach on April 16, 1990. Jones will succeed Terry Holland, who compiled a 326-173 record over the course of his 16 seasons at Virginia. Holland has returned to his alma mater, Davidson, to assume the athletic director's post.

Jones is the eighth head coach in Virginia men's history. He is the third Virginia graduate to coach the Cavaliers and is the youngest head coach in the history of the ACC (30-years-old).

"Any success that we accomplish will be built on the foundation that coach Holland has established," Jones said at a press conference introducing him as the Cavaliers' new head coach. "There'll be some changes, but I promise you that the physical and mental toughness, and the pride with which the players wear the Virginia jerseys will continue.

"There's not another job in the country I'd rather have. This is where I want to be and not all of a sudden because I'm a head coach. This is the place I've wanted to be for a long time."

Jones was a full-time assistant on Holland's Virginia staff the last four years. Prior to that he was a part-time assistant for three years and a graduate assistant for one.

During his playing days at Virginia (1979-82), Jones was a four-year starter at point guard. He was known as a prolific passer and team leader. He played at Virginia in the Ralph Sampson era and Virginia compiled an overall record of 102-28 (.785), competed in two NCAA tournaments and two NITs during his playing career. He was recruited by and played under Terry Holland. The Cavaliers won the NIT in 1980 and advanced to the Final Four in 1981. Jones graduated from Virginia in 1982 with a Bachelor's Degree in Psychology.

He still holds Virginia's career assist record (598) and his 200 assists during the 1979-80 season was Virginia's single-season record until broken by current Cavalier John Crotty each of the last two seasons. Jones was the Cavaliers' team captain as a senior during the 1981-82 season. He averaged 6.6 points and 4.6 assists a game while shooting 52.2 percent from the field and 74.3 percent from the free throw line for his career. Jones was drafted in the fourth round of the 1982 NBA draft by the Indiana Pacers. After being released by the Pacers, he joined the Golden State Warriors until an injury ended his professional aspirations.

He is a native of Owensboro, Ky., and a graduate of Apollo HS. His father, Bob Jones, is the basketball coach at Campbell County HS in Alexandria, Ky. Jones coached Kentucky Wesleyan to the 1973 NCAA Division II title.

Like many coaches who get major college jobs, Jones was not the first choice for his position. The four finalists whom Virginia athletic director Jim Copeland had considered for the job withdrew their names from consideration in a span of two weeks. One of those finalists was rumored to be Xavier coach Pete Gillen. Providence coach Rick Barnes initially accepted Copeland's offer to come to Virginia, but he received some 11th hour pressure from the Big East Commissioner Dave Gavitt, a former Providence coach himself, and decided to remain in his current post. Eventually the list narrowed down to just two candidates: Jones and fellow Virginia assistant Craig Littlepage. Littlepage had previously been a head college coach at Rutgers and Pennsylvania. However, his teams were a combined 63-102 during six seasons at the two schools. Littlepage's record was not lost on Copeland's decision-making process.

"What was unfortunate for Craig was that his head coaching experience did not end up in a very positive way," Copeland said. "Jeff starts out with all the attributes I feel you need in a head coach and a clean slate."

Jones also came highly recommended for this position by a man he will be competing with for years to come: Duke coach Mike Krzyzewski. Copeland contacted Krzyzewski for guidance during the selection process. Krzyzewski emphatically endorsed Jones. He also accumulated support among the players, athletic staff and Virginia boosters.

"This is what everyone wanted," said Virginia All-America forward Bryant Stith.

Holland also was an extremely influential supporter of Jones. "I think we've come out with the best possible result," Holland said. "Jeff is ready for this."

The 30-year-old Jones is only two years older than Niagara's Jack Armstrong, the most junior member of the NCAA Division I head coaching fraternity. Jones' age and lack of head coaching experience, this being his first head coaching position at any level, will raise the typical questions. However, he is more excited than nervous and is confident in his ability to handle this team.

"I'm looking forward to the season," said Jones recently. "It's been a hectic period since being named head coach in April, but it's something that I've always looked forward to and it's a goal that I've had. The thing I enjoy most is being with the team, whether it's in practice, in the locker room or just sitting around talking.

"As far as being on the bench, I hope to have everything covered through practices, team meetings and film sessions because I don't like a lot of surprises. I'm a strong believer that if you're prepared, not only are you ready for virtually any situation, but also you're confident in your ability to handle those situations."

He appears to have his ego firmly in check, is a stickler for details and should benefit from having a talented and experienced team which could go a long way this season. All five starters return from Virginia's 20-12 team last year that advanced to the second round of the NCAA tournament before losing a close game, by a 63-61 score, to Syracuse. Jones will have the services of two All-America players, Crotty and Stith. Freshman Cornell Parker is a potential impact player and makes Virginia even better.

"I know I'm the one making the decisions now and that's a big part of the job. That's why I'm the head coach and I'm certainly looking forward to the challenge," Jones said. "I don't look at it as Jeff Jones going head-to-head with Mike Krzyzewski or Dave Odom or Dean Smith or any of the other coaches in the league. I look at it as the University of Virginia playing whomever our opponent happens to be that night. I certainly respect all the coaches in our league, and all the coaches of the opponents we'll face this season, but I don't intend to be intimidated by anyone."

There is no question that Jones should be extremely successful in his first year at Virginia. He has an excellent relationship with the players and vice versa. He has been around Virginia and the ACC as a player and coach for over a decade. He comes highly endorsed, respects the opposition, but is not in awe. This season should be the start of what should be a long tenure as Virginia's head coach for Jeff Jones.

★ PLAYERS NOT RETURNING ★

MARK COOKE (6-4, F/G, 2.2 ppg, 1.3 rpg, 1 assist, 1 steal) Cooke played in nine games last season for the Cavaliers, six of which were ACC contests. He contributed 64 minutes of playing time as a reserve swingman. Cooke also played on the Virginia football team.

Cooke was a victim of the numbers game last year as he played behind All-America Bryant Stith and starting guard Anthony Oliver, two players who averaged 27-plus minutes per game. Stith played more than 35 minutes per game.

Cooke was a good athlete who could rebound the ball well for a 6-4 player. He was also a solid defender who, when inserted in the games, would not hurt Virginia as he could keep his opposite number in check defensively while playing smart, unselfish basketball on the offensive end of the floor.

JEFF DANIEL (6-9, C/F, 1.0 ppg, 2.1 rpg, 10 assists, 5 blocked shots, 8 steals) Daniel played in 30 of Virginia's 32 games in 1989-90. He was one of the team's top reserves as both a power forward and center last year and he was a tireless worker, both in practice and during games. He was not afraid of the physical contact under the boards and he averaged one rebound every five minutes of playing time. Holland had no reservations about giving Daniel playing time as he displayed a smart, unspectacular brand of basketball which was helpful to the Cavaliers' cause inside.

Daniel's departure will be a real loss for Virginia this year because his interior presence coming off the bench will not be easy to replace. It is tough to find big people who are unselfish and play as hard for as long as Daniel. Even though his talents may have warranted receiving more playing time, he never got frustrated and was always ready.

His role increased in importance in 1989-90 as Virginia lost center Brent Dabbs, prior to the beginning of the season. As a result of Dabbs' transfer to Rutgers, Daniel moved up on the depth chart and averaged 11 minutes per game in the low post. He was a player whose versatility as a forward and center made him a valuable commodity for the Cavaliers. His effectiveness could not be measured solely by statistics as the intangibles which Daniel brought to Virginia were important to the success of the club.

★ RETURNING PLAYERS ★

MATT BLUNDIN (6-7, 226 lbs., SR, F, #30, 3.9 ppg, 5.2 rpg, 30 assists,

3 blocked shots, 13 steals, Ridley HS/Milmount Park, Pa.) Blundin was the Cavaliers' top reserve at the power forward and center positions in 1989-90. He earned his third varsity letter in basketball as he contributed more than 24 minutes of playing time per game last year. His 167 rebounds were the third highest total on the team, and he was the club's most effective offensive rebounder as 47 percent of his boards (a total of 78) came off the offensive glass.

Blundin is an extremely physical player inside, a style which one would not expect from a man who is the second string quarterback on the Virginia football team during the fall. For some reason, we cannot imagine Brigham Young's Ty Detmer and Miami's Craig Erickson avoiding would-be blind side hits on autumn Saturday afternoons and then relishing banging under the boards on the basketball court during the winter.

In football, Blundin is the backup to Virginia's sensational quarterback Shawn Moore. Last fall, he played for Virginia's ACC co-champion football team and did some rigorous double duty during November and December. Blundin not only completed the regular football season and participated in team practices for the Florida Citrus Bowl, which Virginia lost to Illinois, but still managed to play in all 32 basketball games. Virginia football coach George Welsh has made no secret of his displeasure that Blundin did not participate in spring practice. Blundin claimed he was still exhausted and asked out of spring football drills.

"It's going to be tough to do that year after year," Welsh told Pete Williams of The Washington Post. "You see what's happened to Blundin . . . the rigors of the last two years have worn him down."

Even though Blundin was technically a reserve last year, he actually played more total minutes than starting center Ted Jeffries. Blundin's most impressive performance of last season, even though it wasn't statistically his best, came in the semifinals of the ACC tournament against regular season champion Clemson. Blundin spent most of the game battling inside with Clemson's "Duo of Doom," future NBA players Elden Campbell and Dale Davis. Blundin gave away a good four inches to both, but he made his height differential with determination and heart. He scored just two points in 28 minutes, but he had eight rebounds and effectively shut down Campbell all game long. The first-team All-ACC center, Campbell scored just 13 points and he received countless scratches and bruises. Blundin was ecstatic afterwards, saying, "I love going against bigger guys. I love to bang. A physical game lets me take advantage of my strength and let's me do the things I'm capable of doing to help this team."

"More than anything else, he gives us toughness," former Virginia coach Terry Holland said. "He's kind of the heart of this team. When he goes into the game, everyone has to play hard, if just to stay out of his way."

Rookie head coach Jeff Jones knows only too well what Blundin does to help the Cavaliers. "Matt is the heart of our basketball team," said Jones. "He gives us intensity and a strong work ethic that shows in his defensive effort and work on the boards. Matt is the type of player that can be a contributor almost immediately after joining the team (after football is over). He is a very, very important part of our basketball team."

Blundin scored a season-high eight points in Virginia's upset over fourth ranked Duke last February. He had a season-high 13 rebounds and tied his season-high eight points against Clemson. He hauled in 10 offensive rebounds in that game to set a Virginia record. His six assists in the Clemson game last January 9 were the most by any Cavalier except guards John Crotty and Anthony Oliver. He received the Michael McCann Leadership Award at the conclusion of the season and was selected the Cavaliers' best defensive player. Blundin was also a member of Barry Jacobs' All-Overlooked team.

This year Blundin will technically be a reserve again as Virginia returns all five starters. The only question is how soon Jones can get Blundin off the football field and onto the basketball court. The Virginia football team was undefeated and nationally ranked at press-time and seemed destined for a major bowl bid. No matter when he is able to devote all of his energies to basketball, Blundin will average between 26 and 28 minutes a game and will add in valuable experience, leadership, toughness and rebounding to the Cavaliers. He is a co-captain of this year's Virginia team.

JOHN CROTTY (6-1, 179 lbs., SR, G, #22, 16.0 ppg, 2.9 rpg, 214 assists, 4 blocked shots, 34 steals, Christian Brothers Academy/Lincroft, N.J.) Crotty has started the last 71 games for Virginia at point guard and has been one of the ACC's most consistent floor leaders. He enters his senior year 23rd on the school's all-time scoring list and second on the career assists chart. His 514 assists leave him 84 behind all-time leader Jeff Jones, who enters his first year as Virginia's head coach. Jones has been an invaluable help to Crotty as a teacher and role model.

He had a spectacular junior season in every sense. Crotty was a third-team All-ACC selection and an honorable mention All-America pick. He was named ACC player of the week for the week of December 11 and he was the co-recipient of the Bill Gibson Cavalier of the Year award along with Bryant Stith. Crotty was second on the team in scoring and led the Cavaliers in assists. He set a Virginia single-season record for assists with 214 to break the mark he previously set with 208 in 1988-89. He also logged an average of 36.8 minutes per game last year and played the entire game for Virginia five separate times.

He dished out five or more assists in 26 of Virginia's 32 games, including six games, or more. He had a season-high of 12 assists against Virginia Military Institute, Marquette and Syracuse. He topped 20 points eight times and scored a season and career-high 30 points in Virginia's loss at Duke. He made 11-of-15 field goals in that game, with 22 points in the second half as the Cavaliers' furious comeback fell just short. Crotty scored 26 points and handed out 11 assists, with only one turnover in 36 minutes against Samford. He had 25 points and eight assists in 38 minutes in Virginia's victory over Villanova in the ACC/Big East Challenge. He scored eight of Virginia's 14 points in the overtime win over Georgia Tech in Charlottesville, including one four-point play. In Virginia's defeat at North Carolina, Crotty came through with 27 points, dished off eight assists and grabbed a career-high nine rebounds. He also canned 7-of-13 three-point attempts in that game to set team highs for the 1989-90 season. And in Virginia's victory over Notre Dame in the opening round of the NCAA tournament, Crotty scored 28 points.

The only negative side to Crotty's game last year was his outside shooting, which has been a problem for him in the past. While he can get hot and be unconscious from the perimeter at times, he has yet to find a consistent stroke from the outside. Crotty shot only .389 from the field and .340 from three-point distance. He has somewhat of an unorthrodox form as he is a left-handed shooter and often times he shoots the ball more like a slingshot. If he can learn to shoot the ball with the same fluid motion every time and begin to gain more confidence from the perimeter, Crotty will be an unstoppable offensive force. He will be able to knock down the 18-foot jumper and force defenses to extend and play him farther from the basket. If this occurs, he can then use his quickness and superior ballhandling skills to drive to the basket and distribute easy assists to teammates. Crotty is also an excellent leaper.

"John is one of the finest point guards in the nation. In the ACC, he's going up against outstanding competition every night and he doesn't back down from anyone. I think he's improved and matured a lot in his three years at Virginia. Last year I think he really improved the range on his jump shot. He is the man that makes us go and I look for John to have another outstanding season. Hopefully we'll be able to get him a little more rest and a little more help this season so that he doesn't try to shoulder too much of the load. If we can do that, I think his shooting percentage will rise and his turnovers will go down. John really took a physical beating last season in addition to all the minutes he played," Jones said.

Crotty is one of several outstanding point guards in the ACC this season. Georgia Tech's Kenny Anderson is only a sophomore but is already considered the finest point guard in the county. Chris Corchiani, of North Carolina State, is expected to end his career as the all-time assist leader in the ACC. Maryland junior Walt Williams is one of the tallest point guards in the country at 6-8 and he was spectacular at times last season. Duke's Bobby Hurley had a fine freshman year and Crotty is good enough to be one of the best in the country at his position and a first round draft choice next June.

BERNIE FLORIANI (5-10, 156 lbs., SR, G, #5, Dover HS/Dover, Del.) Floriani first made the Virginia team as a walk-on in 1988 and has been a member of the Cavaliers ever since. He played in just two games last season for Virginia and failed to score. He is a scrappy point guard who is a hard working practice player and whose enthusiasm for the game is infectious.

With Virginia returning nine lettermen and adding three new backcourt players, Floriani's role is not likely to increase.

BLAIR FORD (6-2. 170 lbs., SO, G, #23, 0.6 ppg, 0.7 rpg, 2 assists, 1 steal, Marist School/Atlanta, Ga.) A walk-on player, Ford appeared in seven games last year. He saw a total of 23 minutes and missed all five of his field goal attempts. All four of his points came from the free throw line. Ford did have four rebounds against Samford last year and that equalled the Virginia high for the most rebounds by any guard off the bench. He was the only Virginia guard to have more rebounds, five, than points, four, for the season.

Ford was named a first-team Georgia Class AAA all-state selection by both the *Atlanta Constitution* and *Atlanta Journal* as a senior at Marist HS. He was voted Marist's Best Defensive Player during both his junior and senior seasons and scored 17 points in Georgia's 100-98 win over Tennessee in the 1989 Georgia-Tennessee All-Star game. He led his team to a 29-1 record and the Georgia Class AAA state championship as a senior.

His role probably will not be more expanded than last year, but Ford wouldn't hurt the Cavaliers in a key situation.

TED JEFFRIES (6-9, 248 lbs., SO, F/C, #42, 3.5 ppg, 3.9 rpg, 14 assists, 7 blocked shots, 9 steals, DeMatha HS/Bowie, Md. & Fork Union Military Academy/Fork Union, Va.) Jeffries signed with Virginia as a senior at DeMatha HS but decided he needed another year of development and spent a post-graduate season at Fork Union Military Academy in 1988-89. During that year at Fork Union, Jeffries was able to take the low post lessons he learned at famed DeMatha HS and refine them to the point where he made himself a starter as a freshman. Jeffries started 31 of 32 games for Virginia at center last year.

He played with great poise for a freshman considering the fact that he was competing in the always tough ACC. Jeffries averaged one turnover every 22.3 minutes, which was the best turnover ratio on the club. He also grabbed a rebound an average of every 4.8 minutes. All in all, Jeffries did much more than anyone could have expected in his first year in Charlottesville.

"Ted Jeffries far surpassed any expectations that we could have had for him last season, that our fans could have had or that Ted could have realistically had for himself," said Jones. "He improved a great deal during the course of the season."

He was originally expected to be the Cavaliers' third-string center last year behind returning starter Brent Dabbs and backup Curtis Williams. The thought of redshirting Jeffries had even crossed the mind of then coach Terry Holland. But the depth chart was shaken up quite a bit as Dabbs transferred before the season to Rutgers and Williams flunked out after the first semester last year. All of a sudden, Jeffries was the Cavaliers' starting center by default, and he was about to get a baptism of fire in the ACC.

For the year, he averaged 18.8 minutes per game. Jeffries made 42-of-98 field goals (.429) and was 28-of-45 (.622) from the line. He had perhaps his best performance of the year against Virginia Military Institute. In that game he scored 12 points, including 5-of-7 from the field and pulled down seven rebounds. He had eight points and eight rebounds against Georgia Tech. In a win over North Carolina State, Jeffries scored six points and pulled down nine rebounds, had one assist and blocked a shot in 20 minutes of action.

Jeffries is a first cousin of former Maryland standout Adrian Branch. This season he must work on finishing his offensive plays in the lane, especially against bigger players. He has to develop more confidence in taking interior shots. Jeffries appeared nervous about getting his shot blocked last year and once he overcomes his apprehension he should be a more reliable offensive force in the low post. Now that he has a year of starting experience, the expectations are much higher for Jeffries.

"We asked him to spend a good deal of time during the summer working on his low post moves and trying to develop a baby jump hook that he feels comfortable with under any circumstances," Jones said.

These improved offensive moves, along with an emphasis on off-season conditioning which will improve his stamina, have Virginia coaches and fans looking for Ted Jeffries to come into his own and to develop into a quality ACC big man in 1990-91.

DIRK KATSTRA (6-6, 210 lbs., SR, G/F, #24, 1.3 ppg, 0.9 rpg, 3 assists, Blue Valley HS/Stilwell, Kan.) Katstra played in only eight games last year, starting one, for Virginia for a total of 62 minutes. He played in 24 games as a sophomore in 1988-89, but for only 107 minutes. Katstra was also a limited contributor as a freshman playing in only eight games for 23 minutes. His only starting assignment came at North Carolina when he played 17 minutes but did not score. He scored a season-high five points in the season opener against Northeastern.

Forty four of his 66 career field goals have come from three-point range. He is a three-point threat off the bench for Virginia.

He is not expected to be slowed much by arthroscopic knee surgery performed last July. The injury could actually help Katstra in the long run as his rehabilitation strengthened his legs and built up his stamina. He will serve as a Virginia co-captain this year.

TERRY KIRBY (6-3, 212 lbs., SO, G, #4, 3.4 ppg, 1.0 rpg, 10 assists, 1 blocked shot, 10 steals, Tabb HS/Tabb, Va.) We cannot think of another major college basketball team in the country that has two football players on its roster who are as capable roundballers as Terry Kirby and Matt Blundin. Due to Virginia's appearance in the Florida Citrus Bowl last New Year's Day, Kirby did not participate in a basketball game until January 24 against Virginia Tech. He quickly made his presence known by sinking his first shot seven seconds after entering the game. His best performance last year came in a Cavalier loss at North Carolina State. Kirby led Virginia in scoring that day with 18 points in only seven minutes of playing time.

For the season, Kirby played in 17 games for a total of 148 minutes (8.7 mpg). He made 23-of-55 field goals (.418) and was 8-of-29 (.276) from three-point range. Kirby must improve at the free throw line where he made only 3-of-9 attempts (.333).

His strength and overall athletic ability make him an intimidating defender in the backcourt. Last year he combined with Anthony Oliver to shut down Georgia Tech All-America Dennis Scott as the Cavaliers beat the Yellow Jackets in Atlanta at the end of February. Scott was 3-of-16 from the field for 11 points, and Kirby did as fine a job on Scott as anyone did all year. Kirby loves to play a physical style and his quickness allows him to get away with some positional defensive mistakes. Despite the fact he did not shoot the ball particularly well last year, Kirby is confident in his outside shot. He also is a competent ballhandler who should be a more effective scorer off the dribble as his career goes on.

He was one of the most outstanding athletes ever in the Virginia high school ranks. Kirby was a four-year starter in football and basketball at Tabb HS. He was the Virginia Group AA basketball player of the year as a senior and a first-team All-State selection each of his last three years in high school. He scored 2,322 career points at Tabb, averaged 27 points, 4.4 assists and 4.3 steals per game as a senior and led Tabb to the Virginia state semifinals as a senior. He also picked up considerable experience in the summer with the Boo Williams' AAU teams where he was a teammate of former North Carolina star J.R. Reid and Georgetown's Alonzo Mourning. In football, Kirby rushed for a Virginia state record of 7,428 yards and 103 touchdowns during his high school career. He was the *Parade Magazine* National High School Football Player of the Year, *USA Today* National High School Offensive Player of the Year and was voted the Gatorade Circle of Champions High School football player of the year.

In his first season on the Virginia football team, Kirby had to deal with the highest set of expectations any Cavalier athlete has faced since Ralph Sampson arrived a decade earlier. He suffered a rib injury that put him out of three games and then rushed for 311 yards on 63 carries and scored four touchdowns. Kirby closed his freshman football season strong gaining 159 yards on his last 13 carries of the season against Maryland and Illinois in the Florida Citrus Bowl. This fall he is a starting running back and has done well for a nationally ranked Virginia team that has a strong chance to go undefeated in the regular season. The Cavaliers should play again on New Year's Day. Kirby is not expected to be on the court for the Cavaliers' basketball team until mid to late January. Last year he was one of three Cavalier basketball players, along with Matt Blundin and Mark Cooke, to play football.

"Last year, Matt, Mark and I would look at each other and say, "Why are we doing this'?" Kirby told Pete Williams of *The Washington Post*. "And especially when that horn goes off at 7:00 o'clock every morning, I'm like "Why am I here?' but it's that drive, that love - I want to be out there."

Despite his great desire to play both sports in college, Kirby doesn't know if he will be able to combine football and basketball for four years. However, late in the summer Kirby admitted that he wasn't worn out yet and Virginia football coach George Welsh claims that a season of basketball has helped Kirby's quickness.

"We certainly wouldn't have won a couple of games last season if Terry Kirby hadn't been on our roster," said Jones. "It's remarkable how he picked things up so quickly last season after joining the team so late. I think that says a lot for his intelligence and his desire to play and be a contributor."

ANTHONY OLIVER (6-4, 185 lbs., JR, G, #10, 10.1 ppg, 3.2 rpg, 51 assists, 6 blocked shots, 40 steals, North Duplin HS/Faison, N.C.) Oliver started all but one of Virginia's games last year and he was the team's third-leading scorer. He played slightly more than 27 minutes per game, including a 38-minute performance in a win against Duke in February. He also contributed 17 points to the Cavaliers' cause against Duke and he limited high scoring Blue Devil guard Phil Henderson to 4-of-12 shooting from the field. This game displayed Oliver's tremendous versatility and value to Virginia as he scored clutch baskets on the offensive end while playing stiffling man-to-man defense on the other side of the ball.

Oliver usually is given the task of defending the opponent's top scoring guard. As a result of his unselfish dedication to his job, Oliver was voted Virginia's Best Defensive Player last year by his teammates and coaches. Oliver's play on the defensive end in turn gave him added confidence in his overall game. His offense picked up considerably after February and he played so well at both ends of the floor at the ACC tournament that he was named to the second-team all-tournament squad.

"Anthony Oliver was a surprise to a lot of people last season," said Jones. "He started gaining confidence early last season and developed into a very valuable player."

Entering last season, the Virginia coaches didn't know what to expect from Oliver. He played in 32 games and averaged 8.1 minutes per game as a freshman. He was slowed towards the end of the season by two sprained ankles and did not shoot the ball well from the perimeter. Last season his playing time tripled and Oliver was an improved perimeter shooter making 14-of-33 treys (.424) and 135-of-319 field goals (.423).

Oliver is an outstanding complement to point guard John Crotty, and this year he will be called upon to step out of Crotty's shadow somewhat offensively and take some of the scoring and ballhandling burden. Crotty would love to have Oliver share some of those responsibilities.

In Virginia's overtime upset win against Georgia Tech, Oliver made a 16-foot jumper with one second left in regulation to tie the score and send the game into overtime. After the basket, he strained a hip muscle and was forced to watch the overtime period from the bench.

Oliver should continue to develop this year. The Crotty-Oliver starting backcourt should be one of the best in the ACC and possibly the nation this year.

DOUG SMITH (6-1, 170 lbs., SO, G,#11, 0.6 ppg, 0.4 rpg, 19 assists, 3 steals, Lincoln County HS/Fayetteville, Tenn.) Smith was a valuable contributor off the bench for Virginia last year. He was Crotty's caddy at point guard and averaged 5.2 minutes per game.

Smith was the only Cavalier to have more assists (19) than points (18). He made 6-of-22 field goals (.273) and was 2-of-9 (.222) from three-point range. Smith proved to the Virginia coaching staff that he could be a dependable reserve and provide quality minutes whenever Crotty needed a rest. Jones is especially excited about Smith's development and potential.

"I think Doug will come into the season much more confident and more comfortable with the Virginia system, and will be more of a floor general for us," said Jones. "He's a very solid player for us."

He is a reliable ballhandler and knows how to get the ball to the scorers in the half court offense. He has good penetrating ability and is not turnover prone. If he can develop a consistent outside shot, he could put himself in a position to be Virginia's starting point guard when Crotty graduates.

BRYANT STITH (6-5, 202 lbs., JR, F/G, #20, 20.8 ppg, 6.9 rpg, 53 assists, 9 blocked shots, 41 steals, Brunswick HS/Freeman, Va.) As a sophomore, Stith had one of the finest seasons of any player in the nation. His honors earned last year could fill up an entire page by themselves. He was named to the All-ACC first-team as he finished fourth in the league in scoring and rebounding. He was an honorable mention All-America selection by the *Associated Press, United Press International* and *The Sporting News*. Stith was also a member of the first-team All-ACC tournament squad. He was the co-recipient of the Bill Gibson Cavalier of the Year award, along with Crotty, given annually to Virginia's MVP.

"Bryant is a true winner in every sense of the word," said Jones. "He can shoot the three-pointer, he can score inside and this summer he's learning to play on the perimeter, attract the defender and put this ball on the floor for one or two dribbles."

Stith is one of the better offensive rebounders in college basketball. Eighty of his 221 rebounds came off the offensive boards last year. He became only the third Virginia sophomore to score 1,000 career points along with Jeff Lamp (1977-81) and Ralph Sampson (1979-83). It took Stith 57 games to reach the 1,000-point plateau (Lamp did it in 51 games while it took Sampson 61 games). Last season Stith was named the ACC player of the week on three occasions. He led Virginia

in scoring, field goal percentage (.481), free throw percentage (.777), steals (41) and offensive rebounds (80). He was second on the team in assists and rebounding. Stith missed the rebounding lead by three rebounds.

He reached the 30-point mark on five occasions and scored in double figures in 31 of 32 games, including 25 games in a row at one point. He made 34 consecutive free throws in one part of the season. In Virginia's overtime win over Georgia Tech, Stith scored 30 points. In the next game against Virginia Tech, he scored 22 points and took complete control of a close game by scoring 14 of Virginia's 19 points during an 8:25 span midway through the second half. That outburst stretched Virginia's lead from five points to a comfortable 16-point margin. In the Cavaliers' overtime win over Wake Forest, he poured in a career-high 37 points and snatched 10 rebounds. Stith also had 27 points against Louisville, along with seven rebounds, all on the offensive end, and had 27 points, 12 rebounds and no turnovers in 38 minutes to propel Virginia to a victory over North Carolina State. He scored a game-high 32 points and had 11 rebounds at Virginia's upset of North Carolina in the opening round of the ACC tournament.

His defense is continually improving and his quickness and athleticism allow Stith to play man-to-man defense effectively against the best scoring off-guards and small forwards Virginia faces. Despite concentrating heavily on defense, Stith's scoring totals did not drop off.

"If you combine that (his ability) with his willingness to listen and learn, and his competitive spirit, focus and intensity, you've got a player that I would put on the highest level of collegiate competition," Jones remarked.

Over the summer he participated on the U.S. National team, coached by Duke's Mike Krzyzewski that played in the Goodwill Games in Seattle and the World Basketball Championship in Buenos Aires, Argentina. Although Stith did not receive a great deal of playing time, the competition has to be a positive experience for him.

This season, Stith should be one of the most versatile, all-around forces in the college game. He will get a chance to venture outside more and will have much of the Virginia offense geared towards him. He is a legitimate All-America player.

KENNY TURNER (6-6, 227 lbs., SR, F, #12, 12.2 ppg, 7.0 rpg, 50 assists, 16 blocked shots, 33 steals, North Central HS/Indianapolis, Inc.) Turner started all 32 games for Virginia last year and is a three-year letterman. He is one of the Cavaliers' team co-captains for the 1990-91 season. He led Virginia in rebounding and finished ninth in the ACC in that category.

Turner finally made it through a season injury free last year. He had been plagued with knee problems throughout his collegiate career and underwent five knee operations. At 6-6, he became the shortest player to lead Virginia in rebounding since Buddy Reams led the Cavaliers with 223 rebounds in 1966-67 as a 6-5 forward.

Turner was second on the team in free throw percentage (.775) and made 150-of-314 field goals (.478). Turner also made a good contribution as a three-point shooter making 29-of-83 treys (.349). He averaged 32.8 minutes per game. He had an impressive month of January. Turner scored a career-high 21 points, had five assists and three steals against North Carolina and sank 6-of-10 field goals to score 19 points, while also collecting 11 rebounds against Maryland. He also had 13 points and 11 rebounds against Georgia Tech. Against North Carolina last February 14, Turner made a career-best 5-of-9 three-pointers and scored 19 points. He also had nine rebounds, two assists, and no turnovers in 34 minutes of action.

He capped his season with an excellent ACC tournament. Turner scored 17 points and hauled in 10 rebounds in a victory over North Carolina, scored 15 points and grabbed seven rebounds as Virginia upset Clemson and scored 15 points and pulled 11 rebounds in the title game against Georgia Tech. In the opening round of the NCAA tournament, he scored 11 points and had nine rebounds in a Virginia victory over Notre Dame.

He showed a great deal of intensity and heart last season. Turner was one of the smallest power forwards in the ACC last year. Despite having a height disadvantage virtually every game, he used his leaping ability, positioning and work habits to grab countless important rebounds for Virginia. He was a quietly effective offensive player throughout the year and surprised some opponents by making strong moves off the dribble in the lane.

Former Virginia coach Terry Holland loved Turner's grit and determination in first battling back from knee injuries and second, playing so well at the power forward spot. "He gives up 20 or 30 pounds and three or four inches night in and night out," Holland said. "If you look at Kenny and didn't know him, you'd say there was no way he could play power forward in the ACC. Yet, he does it . . . the impressive thing about Kenny is that I don't think his knees are what they were. He can't do all of the things he used to be able to do. He has adjusted to physical limitations."

Over the summer, Turner played with an ACC All-Star team that toured West Germany.

"The big thing that Kenny was able to do last year, was defend and rebound with players that were heavier and taller virtually every night," Jones said admiringly. "He also extended his shooting range well beyond the three-point line. It's a bonus to have a four-man that can go that far away from the basket and be a real threat."

Jones will keep his fingers crossed that Turner has a healthy senior season. If Turner's knees hold up, he gives Virginia a versatile power forward who contributes more than many of the bigger players at his position in the ACC.

★ NEWCOMERS ★

BOBBY GRAVES (6-4, 180 lbs., FR, G, #31, 12.0 ppg, 6.0 rpg, 3.5 apg, Flint Hill HS/Herndon, Va.) Graves joins Virginia as a walk-on. He was the captain of his highly regarded Flint Hill team last year. Flint Hill was ranked in the Top 10 nationally. He is expected to provide capable depth for Virginia at the wing guard position as Graves is a good shooter and dependable ballhandler.

He was an excellent all-around athlete in high school and was the captain of Flint Hill's baseball team last year. The Cavaliers are extremely deep so Graves will probably not be a key player as a freshman.

CHRIS HAVLICEK (6-5, 183 lbs., FR, G, #15, 27.0 ppg, 7.6 rpg, 5.0 apg, Noble and Greenough Prep School/Weston, Mass.) Yes, he is the son of former Boston Celtic star and basketball Hall of Fame member John Havlicek. Havlicek was redshirted last year at Virginia. He is a quality long range shooter who was a four-year starter at Noble and Greenough Prep School.

He is also a good passer, sees the floor well and is a late bloomer. Havlicek will be gradually worked into the Virginia system this year. His biggest need is additional strength.

DERRICK JOHNSON (6-2, 170 lbs., FR, G, #21, 23.5 ppg, 4.0 rpg, 5.0 apg, 6.0 stpg, Plainfield HS/Plainfield, N.J.) Johnson was a second-team All-New Jersey selection as a senior at Plainfield HS. A four-year starter in high school, he holds the Plainfield career scoring record with 1,649 points. He also holds the Plainfield HS record for most games played (98), most games started (98), most three-point shots made in a season (65) and most three-point shots made in a career (91).

He is known as an outstanding defensive player who has good quickness.

"Derrick Johnson can be an outstanding backcourt player for us in the future. I think he can provide quickness that we need in the backcourt and he has the ability to play both guard positions. Derrick has good range on his shot and should enable us to extend our defense and get out after people."

Johnson will compete immediately for playing time with sophomore Doug Smith as John Crotty's backup at point guard. Johnson is probably a more consistent outside shooter than Smith and they should have a real battle. Keep in mind that Crotty graduates after this year and Johnson and Smith will probably be the main competitors for the starting point guard job next year.

CORNELL PARKER (6-7, 200 lbs., FR, G/F, #33, 16.0 ppg, 10.0 rpg, 5.0 apg, Maury HS/Norfolk, Va. & Fork Union Military Academy/Fork Union, Va.) Parker certainly should be one of the more mature freshmen in the country. He spent a post-graduate year at Fork Union Military Academy last year and he signed with Virginia in the spring of 1989. Parker will turn 21 in early April.

He was named team MVP at Fork Union Military Academy last year. As a senior at Maury HS in Norfolk, Parker led his team to a 24-2 record as a senior and was named the Virginia Group AAA co-player of the year. He is extremely versatile and can play either second guard or small forward, can even see some duty at times at power forward, and may even be a part-time point guard before his career is over.

"Cornell Parker is one of the most versatile players coming into college basketball this season. He can play any of four different positions, although I think his best position is around the perimeter. Cornell has shown the ability to play inside and he's an outstanding rebounder. He also has the ability, with added experience and strength, to be a stopper defensively."

Jones should be able to give Parker quality minutes as a valuable utility man. His ability to play in several positions, and rebound and defend should be valuable for Virginia. He is being overshadowed by some of the great freshmen who are entering the ACC this year such as Grant Hill and Tony Lang at Duke and Eric Montross, Clifford Rozier and Brian Reese at North Carolina. However, Parker is going to make a big contribution and he brings more diverse skills off the bench than the two players Virginia lost - Mark Cooke and Jeff Daniel - from last year's team.

COREY STEWART (6-7, 210 lbs., FR, F, #44, 18.2 ppg, 8.6 rpg, Bethel HS/Hampton, Va.) Stewart is expected to be in the mix for significant playing time as a freshman. He was a dominating high school center but never had to play away from the basket and his offensive moves are not well refined. Stewart was a first-team All-Peninsula District selection in Virginia's Tidewater area.

Jones had this to say about Stewart: "Will Corey Stewart be ready to play inside against bigger, stronger and more aggressive players?"

He is an extremely hard worker who wants to improve and has a significant amount of natural ability. It will probably take him awhile to get acclimated to major college basketball and change his game to the level of competition. However, Virginia needs additional help up front and Stewart may be able to provide it as a freshman.

SHAWN WILSON (6-11, 225 lbs., FR, F/C, #52, 17.0 ppg, 9.7 rpg, 3.0 blpg, Brentwood Academy/Franklin, Tenn.) Wilson, like Havlicek, was redshirted last year. He is the tallest Cavalier. Wilson threw the discus at Brentwood Academy. He shot 63 percent from the field as a senior at Brentwood and was an All-District and All-Region selection. He played on a U.S. team that participated in the Albert Schweitzer Games in West Germany.

"And perhaps the biggest question is can Shawn Wilson provide some valuable minutes at the center position? I think Shawn improved a great deal towards the end of last season. He's had a recurring foot problem and his foot was in a cast for six weeks this summer. He's close to seven feet tall and he's a very intelligent player. If he can add strength and aggressiveness, and be able to come in and give us four or five minutes at a time, I think that will go a long way to helping

our frontcourt situation," Jones said.

If Wilson can see some minutes up front as a reserve to Ted Jeffries, Virginia will be in good shape in the pivot.

★ QUESTIONS ★

Outside shooting? Virginia must improve on last year's field goal shooting as the Cavaliers connected on only .434 of their field goal attempts and .343 from three-point range. With Bryant Stith and John Crotty taking most of the Cavaliers' shots from the perimeter, an improved Anthony Oliver and Doug Smith combining with some good shooting newcomers, Virginia should be able to improve in this area.

Lack of great size up front?

Rebounding? The Cavaliers at first glance seem to have a solid overall rebounding season. After all, they outrebounded their opposition over the course of the season by more than 40. However, a closer look will reveal that Virginia was beaten on the boards significantly in ACC games, to the tune of five rebounds per game.

★ STRENGTHS ★

John Crotty and Bryant Stith! They are one of the ACC's best one-two combinations and are both uBlue Ribbonu All-America selections. They will keep Virginia close in virtually any game.

Depth! Virginia has more talent and experience depth this season than in the past few years. Also, with the solid nucleus of five returning starters, some of the newcomers will be able to ease into the ACC without having heavy pressure to perform immediately.

A smooth transition from Terry Holland to Jeff Jones as the Cavaliers' head coach! Jones has been around Virginia basketball as a player and assistant coach for more than a decade and there shouldn't be any significant adjustment with him taking over the program as there could have been with an outsider coming in. The players wanted Jones and he certainly knows the ACC well.

★ BLUE RIBBON ANALYSIS ★

Virginia comes off a successful 20-12 season in 1989-90. The Cavaliers tied for fifth in the ACC but finished strong advancing to the finals of the conference tournament before losing to Georgia Tech. In the NCAA tournament, at nearby Richmond, Virginia easily handled Notre Dame in the opening round before losing in a close, two-point game to Syracuse. Even though long-time head coach Terry Holland has left to become the athletic director at his alma mater, Davidson, Virginia has an excellent chance at being even better in 1990-91.

All five starters return. Forward Bryant Stith and point guard John Crotty are two of the premier players at their respective positions not only in the ACC but nationally as well. Stith is well on his way to be being going down as one of the all-time greats at Virginia and he spent the summer playing with the U.S. National team at the Goodwell Games and the World Basketball Championship. Crotty will break Jones' Virginia career assist record and he also averaged 16 points per game last year.

The returning starter at power forward, senior Kenny Turner, finally overcame chronic knee problems to start every game last year and he led the Cavaliers in rebounding. Turner also is a three-point threat opposing defenses have to take seriously. Junior second guard Anthony Oliver emerged last year into a reliable player at both ends of the floor. Sophomore center Ted Jeffries exceeded all expectations last year and seems set to improve on last year's averages of 3.5 points and 3.9 rebounds. Virginia football players Matt Blundin and Terry Kirby are proven players who should have considerable action off the bench when the Virginia football season is over.

Jones expects immediate help from 6-7 freshman Cornell Parker, who is best suited for the perimeter but can also play up front. Parker is one of the most versatile players coming into college basketball this year and can play any of four different positions. If 6-11 redshirt freshman Shawn Wilson or 6-7 freshman Corey Stewart can provide some quality relief help up front, Virginia's lack of great frontcourt size could be alleviated. And so could a potential rebounding problem.

"I think having five starters and several key reserves back is definitely a benefit," Jones said. "The experience we gained from last year and the success we had whetted our appetites to work harder to be even more successful this year. I think everyone is comfortable with one another. When you're comfortable and feel good about things, confidence stems from that.

"Our guys know how to win. I think they'll come back with the feeling we're going to be a good basketball team and with a willingness to work toward that goal. There's a good nucleus of players with experience and leadership.

"I'm concerned that we're going to be a very small basketball team," Jones continued. "Our three incoming scholarship freshmen should contribute a great deal, but none of them appear to be the kind of player that can step in and fill the needs we have on the front line.

"With five starters returning, we're optimistic, but there are some concerns. One of the things we tried to emphasize to our players as a staff at the end of this academic year, was that while we were successful last year, the margin of error was fairly small. The fact that everyone worked so well together and had a role they were comfortable with was perhaps the bigger factor in our success than any one player or any one area of the game. That's something we're definitely going to stress and hope to continue.''

Jones has a chance to be one of the most successful first year coaches in recent years. Although Virginia is a bit small up front and the Cavaliers had a small margin of error last year, Virginia can legitimately compete for the ACC title this year. Virginia, North Carolina and Duke appear to be the premier teams in the ACC. Virginia is the type of team that could be playing very well together come March and make a big run in the Big Show.

LAST SEASON

#Northeastern	82-60	Louisville	56-72
#Marshall	83-63	@Georgia Tech	73-71
Samford (AL)	87-61	North Carolina State	77-71
@Davidson	71-57	Wake Forest	50-51
@Vanderbilt	64-68	@Maryland	74-89
##Villanova	73-65	**North Carolina	92-85
Houston	72-54	**Clemson	69-66
###Virginia Commonwealth	63-46	**Georgia Tech	61-70
###Richmond	69-57	***Notre Dame	75-67
@Duke	68-76	***Syracuse	61-63
@Clemson	70-76		
@North Carolina	70-92	@ Road Games	
VMI	89-78	# Investors Classic, Charlottesville, VA	
Maryland	72-74		
Georgia Tech	81-79	## ACC/Big East Challenge, East Rutherford, NJ	
*Virginia Tech	77-59		
@Wake Forest	71-70OT	### Richmond Times-Dispatch Tournament, Richmond, VA	
@North Carolina State	58-84		
@Marquette	96-91OT	* Roanoke, VA	
Duke	72-69	** ACC Tournament, Charlotte, NC	
@Clemson	63-74	*** NCAA Tournament, Richmond, VA	
North Carolina	81-80		

NOTES: Virginia has appeared in the NCAA tournament eight of the past 10 years . . . Jones hired two new full-time assistant coaches, Brian Ellerby and Dennis Wolff. Ellerby comes to Virginia from South Carolina. He also served as an assistant at Bowling Green and George Mason. He was a four-year basketball letterman at Rutgers. Wolff comes to Virginia from Southern Methodist. He also was an assistant at Wake Forest, St. Bona-

1990-91 VIRGINIA SCHEDULE

Nov.	23-26	#Great Alaska Shootout	Feb.	13	Fairfield
	30	New Orleans		16	Clemson
Dec.	1	Winthrop College (SC)		19	Georgia Tech
	3	##Pitt		23	@North Carolina State
	8	Vanderbilt		25	Towson State
	20	@Marshall	Mar.	2	Maryland
	29	@Minnesota		8-10	*ACC Tournament
Jan.	2	@Marquette			
	5	Duke			
	8	@Clemson	@ Road Games		
	12	North Carolina	# Anchorage, AK (Alaska-Anchorage, California-Irvine, Nevada, Siena, South Carolina, Texas Tech & UCLA)		
	16	@Maryland			
	19	@Georgia Tech			
	21	Davidson	-- ACC/Big East Challenge, Richmond, VA		
	23	###Virginia Tech			
	26	@Notre Dame	### Richmond, VA		
	29	North Carolina State	* Charlotte, NC		
Feb.	2	Wake Forest			
	4	Radford (VA)			
	7	@Duke			
	9	@North Carolina			
	10	@Wake Forest			

venture and Trinity College in Hartford, Conn. Wolff has head coaching experience as he was the head coach at Connecticut College for two years . . . former Virginia coach Terry Holland will work as a color commentator on television broadcasts of college games this year. Raycom Sports, the network that televises much of the ACC schedule, will audition Holland for a position on its conference broadcasts for next season.

ROUGH CUSTOMERS

California-Santa Barbara
Cincinnati
Clemson
Connecticut
East Tennessee State
DePaul
Georgetown
Georgia

Kansas
Kentucky
Long Beach State
Louisville
Mississippi State
New Mexico
New Mexico State

Notre Dame
Oklahoma State
Princeton
St. John's
Southern Mississippi
Stanford
Temple
Wyoming

CALIFORNIA SANTA BARBARA

LAST SEASON: 21-9
CONFERENCE RECORD: 13-5
STARTERS LOST: 2
STARTERS RETURNING: 3
CONFERENCE: BIG WEST
LOCATION:
SANTA BARBARA, CA
HOME FLOOR: CAMPUS
EVENTS CENTER (6,000)
NICKNAME: GAUCHOS
COLORS: BLUE AND GOLD

★ COACH'S PROFILE ★

JERRY PIMM (Record at California-Santa Barbara, 114-84. Career Record, 266-164.) Entering his eighth year at California-Santa Barbara, Pimm has the Gauchos on sold footing. Pimm has guided the Gauchos to three consecutive 20-win seasons and three straight post-season berths. He came to California-Santa Barbara in 1983 after nine successful years at Utah. He was not an immediate success at California-Santa Barbara going 10-17, 12-16 and 12-15 in his first three years before recording a 16-13 mark in 1986-87, his fourth year at this previously downtrodden program. California-Santa Barbara was in the midst of 10 straight losing seasons and it had tied Georgia State for the longest ongoing losing streak in college basketball plus the Gauchos were coming off a two-year probation for NCAA recruiting violations when Pimm took over. The program had no secretary and the assistant coaches were expected to teach physical education courses. Since then, Pimm has put basketball on the map at California-Santa Barbara. Sellouts are now the norm for key games at the Campus Event Center.

Pimm grew up in East Los Angeles and graduated from Southern California in 1960. He was a three-year starter for the Trojans and was named All-West in his junior and senior seasons. Pimm played one year at Fullerton (Calif.) College, averaging 30 points per game and was a Junior College All-America before coming to Southern California. He was the leading high school scorer in the country in 1956 at Mountebello HS where he averaged 29.6 points per game.

Pimm's coaching career began in 1960 as an assistant at Southern California. A year later he moved on to Utah where he was an assistant coach for 13 seasons before taking over the Utes' program in 1974. In all, he coached at Utah for 22 seasons, nine as a head coach. Pimm recorded a 173-86 overall record and was 95-51 in the WAC while at Utah. The Utes won three WAC titles and made five NCAA tournament appearances. His 1982-83 squad made it to the Final 16 before losing to eventual national champion North Carolina State. His 1980-81 Utah team finished 10th in the country, posted a 25-5 record and won the WAC title. He came to California-Santa Barbara in 1983 to get back closer to his Southern California roots so that he could finish his coaching career near home.

"There were enough good things when I came here, I could see it happening here. We just had to get better student-athletes, and get them working in the off-season," Pimm said.

"Yes, you can have the beaches the bikini bathing suits," he said. "But you also must apply yourself academically and get in the weight room and play in the summer leagues to play here. You can become a better player and person and still have some fun.

"They used to hang their shoes up until October 1 around here. They don't any more."

Like most big time college basketball coaches, Pimm has been obsessed with the game and his own career, but while he was at Utah he learned to slow down and appreciate other aspects of life.

"My children were about 10 when I realized I'd better relax and get to know them. I'd been missing out," he said. "And I also went on a little camping trip with Al McGuire.

"He started his bubbles and balloons and seashells speech and I said, 'What the hell are you talking about, Al? Come back to reality.' And he said, 'No, you're just too concentrated. Basketball is just a little speck in the world. Smell the roses.' And it's true. We're only going to be here so long. Enjoy the days.'"

The 51-year-old Pimm has received considerable attention for his lifestyle. He lives in Santa Barbara Harbor on a 50-foot motor yacht, *My Sweet Love*. Pimm's motor yacht is luxurious with all the trimmings. He had the outer shell and the teak interior made to his specifications in Taiwan and the electrical system, engine

and steering mechanism installed in the United States.

"I like the quieter, easier living so I can get into my own thing. I spend quality time here. It's very private and comfortable. I do have a VCR and a phone. This way I can take care of business and still have my privacy.

"And," he said, "it's not camping out."

Pimm prefers a controlled running game and the Gauchos play a brutal man-to-man defense. California-Santa Barbara was in the Top 10 in the country last year in defensive field goal percentage —allowing opponents just .413 shooting from the field and just .393 in Big West play, while giving up a mere .314 from three-point territory and allowing a stingy 67.5 points per game average. He has coached five players —Tom Chambers, Danny Vranes and Pace Mannion at Utah and Brian Shaw and Conner Henry at California-Santa Barbara —who have gone on to make the NBA. He was an assistant coach on the U.S. team that won the Gold Medal at the World Championships in Spain in 1986. Pimm's winning percentage of .624 in his 16 years as a collegiate head coach is one of the best in the country. He was recently awarded with a new five-year contract by the California-Santa Barbara administration.

"When he's angry, he lets you know," said former Gaucho forward Eric McArthur. "He'll look you dead square in the eye and call you a SOB. But we respect that. We understand what he wants."

After 16 years as a head coach and 34 straight years involved in college basketball as a player, assistant and head coach, Pimm definitely seems to be in the "Golden Era" of his career and truly at peace with himself with his career in order.

"I honestly can say I feel only pressure from myself. And it's such a good thing not to care about what everybody else thinks. I like myself a lot better than 20 years ago when I was a young whippersnapper."

"I don't want to be the winningest coach alive. I don't want to get to the Final Four every year," Pimm said. "You play the game as best you can, but then you get on with life. I get on that boat and just head for Avalon Bay."

★ PLAYERS NOT RETURNING ★

ULYSSES AKINS (6-6, F, 3.8 ppg, 2.6 rpg) Akins was a reserve who averaged just over 10 minutes per game. He was not asked to score much but he rebounded very well. More importantly, Akins was the Gauchos' most physical player and towards the end of the season he was usually on the court in key situations late in the game. His physical play, effectiveness and quiet leadership will be missed.

CARRICK DeHART (6-4, G, 15.9 ppg, 3.6 rpg, 118 assists, 38 steals, 9 blocked shots) One of two starters not returning for the Gauchos and a player who had a big impact on the program's success over the last three years. DeHart was the freshman of the year in the PCAA, now the Big West, in 1986-87. He was a four-year starter and a second-team all-conference selection as both a junior and senior. DeHart left California-Santa Barbara with school record for points in a career (1,687), field goals made in a career (636), field goals attempted (1,409), games played (119), games started (117), consecutive games played (119), consecutive starts (110), three-pointers (196), three-pointers attempted (499) and steals (133).

The impact DeHart made last season cannot be minimized. He moved from the wing to the point guard spot and was guilty of an average of just 2 1/2 turnovers per game. DeHart was not a creative, speed burning type, but he got the Gauchos into their offense and was a scoring threat himself. His leadership will be missed, but sophomore Ray Kelly, a transfer from Texas Christian, should be the quickest point guard to play for Pimm at California-Santa Barbara.

MIKE ELLIOTT (6-3, G, 1.4 ppg, 1.0 rpg, 15 assists) Elliott played in seven games last year for a total of 91 minutes. He had another year of eligibility remaining but decided not to play this year.

ERIC McARTHUR (6-7, F, 15.6 ppg, 13.0 rpg, 43 assists, 51 steals, 91 blocked shots) Like teammate Carrick DeHart, McArthur will go down in California-Santa Barbara history as one of the best basketball players to ever wear a Gaucho uniform. McArthur was the second leading rebounder in the nation last year and a first team All-Big West selection. He led the Big West in rebounding and shotblocking the past two years. McArthur set school records for total rebounds in a career (904), career offensive rebounds (342), free throws attempted in a career (486) and career blocked shots (249). In addition, McArthur set records for rebounds in a season (377) and blocked shots (91).

Replacing McArthur and DeHart will not be easy, but Pimm has done it before. He replaced the best player in the modern history of the school, Boston Celtic guard Brian Shaw, and will find a way to make the Gauchos a power without DeHart and McArthur.

★ RETURNING PLAYERS ★

LUCIUS DAVIS (6-7, 215 lbs., JR, F, #34, 6.5 ppg, 3.5 rpg, 57 assists, 18 steals, 6 blocked shots, Piedmont HS/San Jose, Calif.) After a sluggish start, Davis became one of the team's most valued players by the end of the season. Over the final 13 games of the season, Davis upped his season average of 6.5 points per game to 9.4 points and his 3.5 rebounds to 5.1. He also handed out three assists a game, up from a season averaged of two, over the final 13 games. He was the Gauchos' sixth man. Davis didn't start for most of the season, but did start seven games.

His slow start was due partly to having missed much of pre-season practice with knee problems. While growing an inch and adding nearly 20 pounds of muscle between his freshman and sophomore years. Davis developed tendinitis in both knees.

Davis is a strong defensive player. He has excellent physical strength and leaps well. With McArthur and DeHart in foul trouble at Long Beach State, Davis stepped in with his best performance ever, scoring 19 points and grabbing 10 rebounds, both career highs. Overall, Davis scored 10 or more points seven times, all in the last 20 games, and he grabbed five or more rebounds eight times. He also had at least three assists nine times, including a season-high of five twice.

Davis averaged 20.1 minutes per game overall, but averaged 26.1 per game over the final 13 games he played. He logged 25 minutes or more in 10 games, including the last four of the season. In a poll of the Big West coaches taken by the *Long Beach Press Telegram*, Davis was voted the conference's best sixth man. For the season, he shot .444 from the field and .683 from the line. His field goal percentage rose to .556 over the last 13 games.

This smooth offensive player whose defense and rebounding picked up last year will be a major contributor to either a wing position or inside. He will move into the starting lineup from the sixth man role. It will be difficult to replace McArthur but if Davis builds on his second half of the season performance, the Gauchos can be back in the NCAA tournament.

BOB ERBST (6-9, 235 lbs., SR, F, #44, 1.8 ppg, 2.0 rpg, 5 assists, 8 steals, 7 blocked shots, Katella HS/Anaheim, Calif.) Much was expected of Erbst after transferring from Southern California. He was a highly regarded high school player and a member of the Pacific-10 all-freshman team. He averaged 6.6 points and 5.5 rebounds as a freshman at Southern California and 4.3 points with 3.3 rebounds as as sophomore. However, Erbst was a limited factor for the Gauchos last year.

In 26 games he played a total of 277 minutes. Erbst suffered through shooting woes last year making just .436 of his field goal attempts and connecting on .448 from the line. He had moments of solid play but never showed consistency. Erbst scored a season-high of seven points at UNLV and grabbed a season-high best of eight boards against San Jose State.

Look for Erbst to be a more important contributor for California-Santa Barbara this year. This is his second straight year in uniform for the Gauchos after sitting out a year following a transfer from Southern California. He will not be an all-conference caliber player but a consistent year from Erbst coming off the bench would do wonders for the Gauchos.

GARY GRAY (6-9, 248 lbs., SR, F, #35, 12.9 ppg, 7.7 rpg, 21 assists, 14 steals, Granada Hills HS/Granada Hills, Calif.) The Gauchos' top returning player, Gray's play as a senior will determine if California-Santa Barbara can make a run at the Big West title. Last year his 12.9 points per game average ranked third on the team behind DeHart and McArthur. He was also second on the team in rebounding behind McArthur. Gray was one of the five best rebounders in the Big West last year.

Gray is not a high flying, flamboyant player. He did not block a shot last year and has only three blocks in his 90 game career. At the end of the regular season he had one slam dunk to his credit. He is a position rebounder who worked well with McArthur under the boards. Gray excels at taking charges and post defense.

When Gray arrived at California-Santa Barbara in 1986, he was fat with bad eating habits. Since then he has gotten his weight under control, changed his eating habits and spent a great deal of time in the weight room. He started as a freshman, averaging 6.3 points and 3.8 rebounds but lost his starting job and came off the bench as a sophomore.

"I'm giving the punishment this year rather than taking it," Gray said last season. "I don't feel anything —the shoves or anything. They don't phase me at all. When I set to take the pick at half court, it doesn't phase me or hurt me in the least. I feel I can go in there as tough as nails."

Overall, Gray scored in double figures in 21 of 30 games. He had 24 points and eight rebounds in the season opener against Pepperdine. Gray also had a strong game at Loyola Marymount —21 points and 10 rebounds —and came up big in a key home victory over Long Beach State with 20 points and 13 rebounds. On the season he grabbed 10 or more rebounds nine times. His defensive effort against UNLV's Larry Johnson, Gray held the All-America to five shots and just 10 points, was instrumental in California-Santa Barbara's win over the eventual national champions. He has developed an outstanding jump hook, which keeps big leaping defenders at bay.

Last year he led California-Santa Barbara in field goal percentage with a .536 mark. Look for Gray to be one of the better inside scorers and interior defenders on the West Coast this year.

CHARLIE HILL (6-0, 170 lbs., JR, G, #4, 0.0 ppg, Crenshaw HS/Los Angeles, Calif.) Hill saw little action last year playing in four games for a total of seven minutes. This is his third year in the program and the point guard has played in only 11 games. Hill was an off-guard in high school who has moved to the point guard spot in college. He played on a Los Angeles city championship team at Crenshaw HS in 1987-88.

KASON JACKSON (6-2, 180 lbs., JR, G, #22, 0.3 ppg, Bishop O'Dowd HS/Oakland, Calif.) Jackson is in a similar situation as Charlie Hill. He enters his

third year at California-Santa Barbara as a point guard candidate. He has played in 18 games over the past two seasons and six last year. Last season Jackson played a total of 15 minutes. He is a decent passer who prepped at one of the premier programs in California, Bishop O'Dowd.

PAUL JOHNSON (6-6, 196 lbs., JR, G, #13, 10.e ppg, 3.6 rpg, 83 assists, 32 steals, 12 blocked shots, Santa Barbara HS/Santa Barbara, Calif.) If Johnson can make the same progress from his sophomore to junior season as he did from his freshman to sophomore, he will be a legitimate candidate for All-Big West Conference honors. Johnson played some point guard last year but is expected to be used exclusively at off-guard this year. He was fourth on the team in scoring last year and has played in all 60 games so far in his college career, starting the last 59 in a row. His shooting improved from .441 as a freshman to .471 as a sophomore. His three-point shooting improved dramatically —Johnson made 1-of-7 (.143) as a freshman and was 26-of-57 (.456) as a sophomore. He led the Gauchos in three-point shooting percentage last year. Johnson has a consistent game, an all-around game that is reminiscent in some ways of former Gaucho star Brian Shaw.

"I see him getting stronger —not only physically, but mentally," said former California-Santa Barbara star Eric McArthur. "And he's just a good person. He's not selfish, and he wants to do whatever it takes to win. He'll be there for 41 minutes, if it takes that.

"Paul has been coming along as a leader, also. Brian had that inner strength that only a couple of people could see.

"Brian said whatever he felt. Paul says whatever he feels. Brian pushed the ball and could do it all. Paul is pushing the ball and he's doing it all —whatever it takes to win, you know."

Johnson had arguably his best college game against Boston University last year when he scored 20 points on near perfect shooting (6-for-6 from the field, 7-for-8 from the line), plus he grabbed five rebounds and dished out a game-high six assists.

"He wants to be a complete player," Pimm said, "and so because of that desire he sometimes gets impatient with himself and with me.

"But if he has patience with himself, patience with me, he's going to grow into a very good, complete player, who can do everything."

The lone Santa Barbara native on the squad, Johnson should team with Texas Christian transfer Ray Kelly to give the Gauchos one of the premier backcourts in the west.

IDRIS JONES (6-3, 180 lbs., SO, G, #3, 7.6 ppg, 2.5 rpg, 76 assists, 25 steals, 2 blocked shots, Pasadena HS/Pasadena, Calif.) Whether as a starter, he was in the starting lineup 23 times last year, or off the bench Idris Jones will be a key player for the Gauchos this year. He played both backcourt spots last year and will still get some playing time at the point, but his main spot will be the off-guard spot, a position he seems much more comfortable with. Jones was shooting .479 over the season's first 14 games. After that he was 30-of-129 (.233) from the field. Jones had endurance problems last year, his legs just weren't strong enough and his shot suffered. Jones made only .338 of his field goal attempts last year. He did can 43 three-pointers, but his percentage —.305 —was not good.

Jones put in a great deal of time in the off-season working on his leg strength. He played well in the U.S. Olympic Sports Festival. Jones had five or more rebounds five times. He scored a season-high 25 points, on 7-of-10 from three-point range, in a win at Utah State. Jones was a Big West Conference all-freshman team selection.

If consistent, Jones can be a major factor for California-Santa Barbara.

MIKE MEYER (6-5, 195 lbs., SO, G, #25, 1.8 ppg, 1.3 rpg, 32 assists, 5 steals, 4 blocked shots, Joliet Catholic HS/Joliet, Ill.) Meyer was tentative as a freshman, but he still played in 27 of 30 games for an average of over 11 minutes per game. He can play either wing position. Meyer is an excellent leaper and his court intelligence is also an asset.

His season-high best scoring game was nine points against Bradley. Meyer showed excellent potential as a three-point shooter making 5-of-9 (.556) for the year. As the season went on, his playing time decreased. He played 15 minutes or more 10 times during the season but nine of those appearances came in the first 14 games of the year.

A former All-Illinois and honorable mention High School All-American selection, Meyer has the ability to be a more important factor this year. With the graduation of Carrick DeHart, look for Meyer to be a more important player for the Gauchos.

JOHN SAYERS (6-7, 218 lbs., SR, F, #42, 1.6 ppg, 0.8 rpg, 3 assists, 2 steals, Belarmine Prep/Pleasanton, Calif. & Diablo Valley JC/Pleasant Hill, Calif.) Sayers came to California-Santa Barbara billed as a good shooter. He averaged 18.4 points and eight rebounds per game at Diablo Valley JC during his sophomore season after beginning his college career at the University of San Diego. As a freshman at USD, Sayers was named the West Coach Athletic Conference's freshman of the year and averaged 6.8 points and 4.1 rebounds. However, last year he was a limited contributor playing in just 14 games for a total of 55 minutes.

Sayers did make 7-of-14 field goal attempts (.500) and was 8-of-10 from the line (.800) in his limited playing time. He could see more playing time this year.

★ NEWCOMERS ★

DUANE CARTER (6-8, 195 lbs., FR, F, #30, 12.7 ppg, 6.5 rpg, North Shore HS/Houston, Tex.) A first team All-District performer as a junior and a senior, Carter comes to California-Santa Barbara billed as a hard worker with excellent athletic ability. Carter is blessed with extremely long arms and tremendous leaping ability.

He set a North Shore HS record by hitting .630 of his shots from the field as a senior. Carter led his team to a 30-6 overall record — and district and area championships. He could help the Gauchos in limited playing time as a freshman.

MARK GREENE (6-4, 174 lbs, FR, G, #14, 13.2 ppg, 5.4 rpg, Ganesha HS/Pomona, Calif.) Greene was redshirted last year. He is a walk-on who was an All-Hacienda League choice as a senior at Ganesha HS. He set his school record for triple-doubles and can shoot the ball. Greene does not figure to be high on the Gauchos' backcourt depth chart.

RAY KELLY (5-11, 175 lbs, SO, G, #12, Riordan HS/San Francisco, Calif.) A transfer from Texas Christian who becomes eligible after the first semester, Kelly should be the Gauchos' starting point guard for the next three seasons. He will be the quickest guard to play at California-Santa Barbara in the Pimm era.

Kelly averaged 8.4 points, 3.7 assists, and 2.3 rebounds per game in eight contests for Texas Christian last year before transferring to California-Santa Barbara. He shot .528 from the floor (28-of-53) and hit 2-of-3 from beyond the three-point strip. Kelly was the Southwest Conference's pre-season freshman of the year by a coaches' vote last year. He was named one of the Top 50 incoming freshmen prior to last season by *All Star Sports*. California-Santa Barbara played without a true, quick point guard last year and Kelly's arrival will make the Gauchos more upbeat offensively.

"Kelly especially changes the makeup of the team," Pimm said. "He's a great penetrator, and he could make us more of an up-tempo and pressing team. He can push the ball with anybody. Getting it from free throw line to free throw line, he can, as they say in baseball, bring it in a hurry.

"We could have more of a running game if we can get some people to run with him."

California-Santa Barbara observers believe Paul Johnson, who has great speed, will blossom after Kelly becomes eligible. Lucius Davis, Idris Jones and Mike Meyer could also be much more effective in a running situation.

"He's an excellent ball handler and a great point guard," said Kelly's high school coach, Ron Isola. "He's like a coach on the floor out there and he really made a lot of kids really good."

Kelly considered transferring back to his hometown and the University of San Francisco, but decided California-Santa Barbara lacked a legitimate point guard. The arrival of Kelly is one of the reasons why we think Pimm will be able to compensate for the loss of DeHart and McArthur.

BILL MARTINEAU (6-10, 210 lbs., FR, F, #55, 14.0 ppg, 7.5 rpg, 3.6 apg, Edison HS/Huntington Beach, Calif.) A two-time All-Sunset League selection at Edison HS, Martineau is a good shooter. He set an Edison single season field goal percentage by hitting .640 percent of his shots as a junior. He can also pass the ball well and should give the Gauchos some frontcourt depth. However, his role will probably be limited this year.

SAM ROBSON (6-11, 220 lbs., JR, C, #33, Durham, England & Milford HS/Milford, Ohio) A transfer from North Carolina Charlotte, Robson sat out the 1989-90 campaign. In 1988-89, his sophomore year at North Carolina-Charlotte, Robson started all 29 games and averaged 6.3 points, 5.0 rebounds and 2.7 blocks per game. He was ranked among the nation's leaders in blocked shots.

"I think he has the potential to be a very good big man. He runs the court extremely well for his size and is very active. I think he has a chance, if he works hard, to go on and play in the NBA," said Pimm.

Robson was a limited factor offensively for North Carolina Charlotte but Pimm believes he can become an offensive force at California-Santa Barbara. He had a career-high 24 points against Alabama-Birmingham's 7-2 Alan Ogg.

He came to the United States as an exchange student midway through his junior year of high school. Robson earned All-Ohio and All-Cincinnati area honors as a senior at Milford HS, even though he had started playing basketball only four years earlier. He was recruited heavily by Syracuse and Dayton before settling on North Carolina Charlotte. He first became attracted to California while playing for North Carolina Charlotte in the Cable Car Classic. Robson decided to make a return visit to the Bay Area with several friends at the end of his sophomore year. One of his friends wanted to visit his sister at California-Santa Barbara and Robson became sold on the school.

"I was impressed with Santa-Barbara —the whole environment and the campus atmosphere. The students here don't disappear on the weekends —they stay here. At Charlotte, it's more of a suitcase college."

Robson's redshirt year was not extremely productive. He missed a significant amount of practice time because of an injured hamstring. Despite the missed practice time, the injury and his relative inexperience as a basketball player, Robson can make a big difference for the Gauchos. He could be the best shotblocking big man in the Big West Conference this year. George Ackles, of UNLV, is the only other player in the Big West as big and talented as Robson.

RAY STEWART (6-3, 180 lbs., JR, G, #15, 16.0 ppg, 2.4 rpg, 3.3 apg, Perth Amboy HS/Perth Amboy, N.J. & Utah Valley CC/Orem, Utah) An athletic and smooth playing guard with outstanding leaping ability, Stewart could step in and get significant playing time at either guard spot. He shot .470 from the floor and .410 from the three-point line in his lone season at Utah Valley CC. Stewart was an All-Region and All-Conference player at Utah Valley and his team's MVP. He originally attended Brigham Young-Hawaii out of high school.

At Perth Amboy HS in New Jersey, Stewart averaged 18.3 points, 7.6 rebounds and 7.8 assists per game as a senior. He was an All-New Jersey selection

as well as team MVP. His versatility and athletic ability give Pimm another valuable option in the Gaucho backcourt.

★ QUESTION ★

Replacing Carrick DeHart and Eric McArthur? The Gauchos cupboard is not bare; however, these were two of the greatest players in school history and replacing both in a single season could be difficult.

★ STRENGTHS ★

Jerry Pimm! One of the best coaches not only in the West but the country, Pimm has built a powerhouse at California-Santa Barbara. He is a winner, his teams play consistent ball and Pimm being on the bench is worth several points a game and countless victories per year for the Gauchos.

Defense! The Gauchos are strong defensively and last year ranked in the Top 10 in the nation in field goal percentage defense. Pimm is a stickler for strong defense.

Rebounding! Even without the school's all-time leading rebounder, Eric McArthur, California-Santa Barbara will be a strong rebounding team.

A deep and good shooting backcourt!

★ BLUE RIBBON ANALYSIS ★

Quick, who was the last team to defeat national champion UNLV? The Runnin' Rebels' last loss came on February 26, 1990, at California-Santa Barbara. The win by the Gauchos was no fluke as the Gauchos have won 64 games over the last three years and have made two trips to the NCAA tournament in that span. Gaucho coach Jerry Pimm was a winner at Utah and has turned the California-Santa Barbara program into a West Coach powerhouse.

Under Pimm, the Gauchos play relentless defense. They cover the floor like a tarpaulin and force their opponents into very poor shot selections. The quickness and leaping ability of this team will allow Pimm to keep the defensive pressure on. The Gauchos are also a strong rebounding team. They won the rebounding crown in the Big West Conference last year and even though Eric McArthur, the school's all-time leading rebounder and second in the nation in that department last year, is gone, the Gauchos will still be strong under the boards.

Look for senior Gary Gray to emerge as an inside force in the Big West this year. Most of the teams in the Big West simply cannot keep pace with a strong man like Gray game after game. Former sixth man Lucius Davis will move into the starting lineup and 6-11 Sam Robson, a junior transfer from North Carolina Charlotte, could become the best shotblocker in the Big West. There is depth up front as well.

In the backcourt, the Gauchos should be tough. Junior Paul Johnson is one of the best all-around players in the Big West and could be ready to explode this season due to the arrival of sophomore point guard Ray Kelly. A transfer from Texas Christian, Kelly is the quickest player to ever lace up a pair of Nikes since Pimm arrived at California-Santa Barbara. JC transfer Ray Stewart and sophomores Idris Jones and Mike Meyer are also quality guards.

Losing two quality players such as McArthur and guard Carrick DeHart in one season will make things difficult on Pimm. However, last year he replaced a superb player (Mike Doyle) and didn't miss a beat. California-Santa Barbara has not finished any worse than second in the Big West in the last four years and should be a contender again in the conference.

At worst, the Gauchos should be the No. 3 team in the Big West behind UNLV and New Mexico State. A fourth straight 20-win season and a second consecutive trip to the NCAA tournament is definitely within reach.

LAST SEASON		1990-91 CALIFORNIA-SANTA BARBARA SCHEDULE		
Pepperdine	67-46	Nov.	27	@Pepperdine
@University of San Diego	79-62	Dec.	10	University of San Diego
#Bradley	86-60		15	@St. Mary's
@Iowa	79-85		18	Texas
@Loyola Marymount	101-104		20	Augusta College (GA)
Eastern Washington	72-67		22	@Kansas State
Oregon	70-54		28-29	#Cable Car Classic
Boston University	89-68	Jan.	2	@San Jose State
San Jose State	82-61		4	@Utah State
Utah State	91-66		7	Fresno State
@Pacific	53-75		9	Pacific
New Mexico State	61-74		12	@New Mexico State
Long Beach State	82-67		19	California-Irvine
@Utah State	91-82		21	UNLV
@California-Irvine	73-66		24	Fullerton State
@UNLV	67-69		31	@Pacific
Fullerton State	72-64	Feb.	2	@Fresno State
Pacific	57-45			
Fresno State	78-57			

NOTES: California-Santa Barbara will play another *Blue Ribbon* Top 40 Team, Princeton, in the opening round of the Cable Car Classic . . . the Gauchos will appear five times on ESPN this year, the most appearances by any Big West Conference school other than UNLV . . . the California-Santa Barbara campus is one of the most picturesque in the country. It is bordered on three sides by the Pacific Ocean, and to the east it faces the Goleta

Valley and the Santa Ynez mountains. The main campus buildings are surrounded by trees, lawns and walkways . . . Pimm did not use up his full allotment of 15 scholarships and has set aside some in case a talented transfer decides he wouldn't mind finishing his career in beautiful Santa Barbara.

CINCINNATI

LAST SEASON: 20-13
CONFERENCE RECORD: 9-5
STARTERS LOST: 2
STARTERS RETURNING: 3
CONFERENCE: METRO
LOCATION: CINCINNATI, OH
HOME FLOOR: MYRL
**   SHOEMAKER CENTER (13,200)**
NICKNAME: BEARCATS
COLORS: RED AND BLACK

★ COACH'S PROFILE ★

BOB HUGGINS (Record at Cincinnati, 20-14. Career record, 188-86.) *The Sporting News* gave Huggins its "Most Underrated" award following last season. "A relatively obscure coach who deserves more national recognition is Cincinnati's Bob Huggins," wrote Mike Douchant in *The Sporting News* end of the season awards article. We agree wholeheartedly as what Huggins has pulled off last year at Cincinnati was remarkable. Despite inheriting a team which had only six players returning -and two of those returnees had extremely limited experience —Huggins fashioned Cincinnati's best record in 13 seasons, most Metro Conference victories and highest finish in the standings ever. In the first game of the season, when Cincinnati pulled off an upset over a Minnesota team that would eventually reach the Final Eight, he gave notice that the Huggins Era is going to be an exciting and successful one at Cincinnati.

"I don't think I've had a team that's responded better to coaching than this team has," Huggins said. "There was always somebody who has taken the lead. Peer pressure is a strong determinant of guys being ready to play."

Even though he has had unexpected early success at Cincinnati, Huggins plans a long career there and is not looking ahead to the next plum job like so many successful young coaches. He is in his second year of a five year contract.

"It takes so much energy to build," Huggins said. "I'd like to be able to build things to where you are established. At some point, I'd like to be able to go home at 6:00 o'clock and have dinner with my kids and my wife and not have to do so many other things.

"I like Ohio," Huggins said. "I like the people in Ohio. I think I'm fairly well accepted in Ohio. I know everyone here and everyone knows me. My family can come down and watch us. My kids can be around their grandparents."

His roots run deep in Ohio. Huggins' father was one of the best high school coaches ever in the state of Ohio. He won 87 percent of his games, four state titles and took his Gnadenhutten (Ohio) Indian Valley South HS to an unprecedented five straight state tournaments. Huggins played for his father at Indian Valley South HS. He was a three-year All-Ohio selection and an 1972 Ohio Class A player of the year. His younger brothers, Harry and Larry, followed Bob's lead and earned Ohio player of the year plaudits before launching college careers at Rice and Ohio State, respectively.

Huggins first attended Ohio University but transferred to West Virginia after his freshman year. He had an outstanding three-year career at West Virginia, twice earning academic All-America honors and he was the Mountaineers' MVP as a senior. Huggins was known as a "tough guy" during his college days. In a heated game against rival Duquesne, Huggins knocked the Dukes' star B. B. Flenory out cold. Flenory was hospitalized for over a week.

After graduating from West Virginia, he served as a graduate assistant coach

at his alma mater in 1977-78. He then spent two years as a assistant coach on Eldon Miller's staff at Ohio State before taking the head coaching position at Walsh College in Canton, Ohio. In three years at Walsh, his teams compiled a 71-26 record. His final team at Walsh was 34-1 and the No. 2 seed in the 32-team NAIA National Tournament in Kansas City, Mo. He left Walsh to serve as an assistant at Central Florida for one year before becoming the head coach at Akron in 1984.

The situation Huggins inherited at Akron was similar to the one at Cincinnati. He inherited an Akron program serving an NCAA probation and by his second year had the Zips in the NCAA tournament. Huggins was 97-46 in six seasons at Akron. He put together five straight 20-win seasons and two NIT appearances in addition to his NCAA appearance.

Huggins was a fiery player and he is a fiery coach. He was the unofficial leader among Division I head coaches last year in technical fouls. Huggins was assessed with 15 technical fouls. He also is a tremendous worker who installs a no-frills, strong work ethic among his players.

"(We) work very hard," Huggins said. "And, since it makes no sense to work hard and lose, you keep working until you find how much work it takes to win."

"I don't think winning and losing can get overemphasized," Huggins told the *Cincinnati Post.* "What happens is people take shortcuts and try to do things the wrong way. When they do, bad things happen.

"Everybody says, 'College athletics . . . this is happening and that's happening', but go to your newspaper; there are bad things happening there. There are people taking shortcuts everywhere, and they end up getting in trouble. . ."

Cincinnati basketball has struggled since Gale Catlett left for West Virginia in the late '70s. However, the Cincinnati program has great tradition, Oscar Robertson was a Bearcat and the school won two national championships in the early '60s. Cincinnati has a great facility in the new Meryl Shoemaker Center, and is located in a vibrant, urban area close to a strong talent pool. Huggins signed a strong group of recruits last spring after coming up empty handed last fall and believes that Cincinnati can become a national power again.

"If you're going to recruit national-caliber people, you have to be on national television," Huggins said. "And you have to have a season ticket base that will guarantee you close to a sellout for every game.

"Everyone would like more money, but that's relative. The more successful you are, that's going to happen. You don't have top make an issue out of it."

"I really want to win a national championship and I'd like to do it in a place that's close enough that my family can share in the jubilation. This is as close as any place to be able to do that."

Look for much success this year and in the future for 37-year-old Bob Huggins. He was only 27 years old when he first became a college head coach and he already ranks in the Top 20 among all active major college coaches in winning percentage.

★ PLAYERS NOT RETURNING ★

BRADY HUGHS (6-4, F, 2.0 ppg, 1.3 rpg) A reserve who averaged 8.9 minutes per game last year. He did a decent job in a reserve role but will not be missed as Cincinnati is more talented and deeper this year than last season.

LINDSEY NELSON (6-6, F, 0.4 ppg, 0.4 rpg) Nelson saw action in five games as a freshman. He made the team as a walk-on last fall and will sit out this year as a medical redshirt. Nelson is expected to return to the Bearcats for the 1991-92 season.

STEVE SANDERS (6-2, G, 7.0 ppg, 2.5 rpg, 48 assists, 37 steals) One of five walk-ons who helped fill out the Bearcat roster last year, Sanders was a former football star who eventually cracked the starting lineup. He hit a three-point goal at the buzzer that gave Cincinnati an upset of Top 20 ranked Minnesota in the opening game last year. It was also the opening game in the new 13,200-seat Myrl Shoemaker Center and got Cincinnati's 20-win season off to a good start. Sanders was the leading three-point shooter in the Metro Conference. He certainly was a capable, hustling player who answered the call, but Huggins hopes he will have more manpower in the future and doesn't have to resort into dipping into the football program.

ANDRE TATE (6-5, G, 17.1 ppg, 3.8 rpg, 114 assists, 55 steals) The toughest personnel loss Huggins will have to deal with. Tate was the Bearcats' second leading scorer last year. Tate not only scored consistently but he took care of the ball and was an excellent perimeter defender. Tate was a major part of the Cincinnati press and the overall defensive scheme. He was a second-team All-Metro Conference selection.

Huggins will probably replace Tate in the backcourt by switching senior Louis Banks from his forward spot.

★ RETURNING PLAYERS ★

LOUIS BANKS (6-5, 205 lbs., SR, F, #25, 17.9 ppg, 6.9 rpg, 81 assists, 61 steals, Camden HS/Camden, N.J.) A major reason behind Cincinnati's surge last year was the improvement in Louis Banks. Banks came to Cincinnati in 1986 after averaging 35.6 points and 12 rebounds while leading Camden (N.J.) to the New Jersey state title. Banks' scoring average rose from 13 points as a sophomore to 17.9 points last year. His overall play and consistency also was greatly improved. As a result, Banks was voted to the Metro Conference first-team all-star squad. He was the only player in the Metro Conference to earn conference player of the week honors back-to-back and ranked among the league's top four in four different statistical categories.

"Lou is as good at taking the ball at people as there is in college basketball today," said Cincinnati coach Bob Huggins. "He always was good at penetrating to the basket with the ball, but he has become even more effective as he learned to dish it off. He has gotten so much better at making other people better."

Banks' performance was even more remarkable when it was considered that he fractured a bone in his left (non-shooting) hand in early December after scoring 13, 12 and 12 points in the first three games. In his next outing a week later, playing with the injured hand heavily bandaged, Banks scored a then career-high 31 points against Dayton. His final basket came at the buzzer to break an 89-all tie and led Cincinnati to a victory. He later replayed those last second heroics a week later when he sank a similar game-winning shot against Creighton in the first round of the Rainbow Classic. In the Rainbow Classic, Banks scored 27 points against Duke and 25 at the expense of Rutgers, earning all-tournament honors. He bettered his career scoring high with 32 points against Memphis State and a week later sank his third game-winning basket for a victory over Florida State. He topped the 30 point mark three times and exceeded 20 points in eight other games.

This season Banks will move to the second guard spot vacated by the loss of Andre Tate. His role will expand to include more perimeter shooting and ball handling out on the floor. If he plays well at his new position, Banks could be a sleeper in the upcoming NBA draft. Many Metro Conference observers believe he is a better player and a bigger winner than Louisville's LaBradford Smith.

TARRANCE GIBSON (6-1, 161 lbs., SO, G, #10, 1.2 ppg, 0.9 rpg, 34 assists, 23 steals, Northview HS/Dothan, Ala.) Gibson was used as a key defensive force off the bench by Huggins. He is an outstanding athlete with great quickness and darts through the passing lanes to make deflections and steals. His long arms and jumping ability enable him to be better than expected on the boards and to block a few shots. Gibson has good court vision and awareness and can deliver the ball. He excels in the transition game.

Gibson helps slow down high scoring Metro Conference guards Elliot Perry (Memphis State) and Bimbo Coles (Virginia Tech). His defensive prowess earned him the nickname of "Rat" as a youngster. Gibson is a reluctant shooter who probably won't be asked to provide much more offensive production this year.

"He's got great athletic ability. That's why we signed him," Huggins said.

MICHAEL JOINER (6-3, 175 lbs., SO, G, #4, 3.2 ppg, 0.8 rpg, 10 assists, 8 steals, South Broward HS/Hollywood, Fla.) As a freshman, Joiner averaged 7.6 minutes per game. He made 32-of-76 (.421) of his field goal attempts and 17-of-45 (.378) from three-point range. Joiner found the transition from high school to major college to be a large leap last season but is expected to be used as a designated zone buster this year. He set a Florida state record by making 157 consecutive free throws in high school.

Joiner scored a season-high 14 points against Southern Mississippi in the Metro Conference tournament. He also picked off five steals and had a pair of assists in that game in what was his finest outing of the year. He played an increasingly greater role as he made an adjustment to the tempo of the college games. Joiner should be a bigger factor for the Bearcats this year.

LEVERTIS ROBINSON (6-5, 209 lbs., SR, F, #20, 13.4 ppg, 7.8 rpg, 51 assists, 39 steals, Martin Luther King HS/Chicago, Ill.) Like the other Cincinnati starters, Robinson had his best collegiate season in 1989-90. He is truly one of the outstanding athletes in the college ranks. Also known as "Mr. Levitation" because of his excellent jumping ability, Robinson has outstanding quickness and timing around the basket. He was Cincinnati's top defensive player last year and keyed

the Bear-cats trapping, match-up defense with his ability to cover the entire floor.

"Vert does so many important things for us that do not reflect in the stat sheets," said Huggins.

Last season Robinson underwent an emergency appendectomy on December 6, yet 16 days later saw 20 minutes of playing time. He played despite a pair of ankle sprains and refused to allow a badly sprained right wrist to take him out of the lineup.

The Sporting News named Robinson the "Most Hardnosed" player in the country after last season. "Cincinnati's Levertis Robinson played with injuries, yet showed a blue-collar worker's passion for being in the right position to retrieve missed shots or track loose balls," wrote Mike Douchant of *The Sporting News*.

Robinson had 21 points and eight rebounds against Duke in the Rainbow Classic and keyed Cincinnati's victory over Louisville with 15 points and 11 rebounds. He equalled a career-high with 14 rebounds against South Carolina and matched that effort against Tulane 10 days later. He scored a season high 22 points against Louisville in the regular season finale.

Robinson was a star at Martin Luther King HS in Chicago. He helped his team to a 32-1 record, the Illinois Class AA championship and the nation's No. 3 ranking in 1986. He did not play his first year at Cincinnati and was a part-time starter averaging 8.7 points and 3.9 rebounds in 1987-88. He was also a part-time starter in 1988-89 averaging 10.6 points and 6.6 rebounds.

This year Huggins plans to use Robinson mainly at small forward. He is hopeful that Robinson can score better on the perimeter while still retaining his role as the team's defensive "stopper."

KEITH STARKS (6-7, 206 lbs., SR, C, #42, 11.0 ppg, 5.9 rpg, 39 assists, 55 steals, 24 blocks, Taylor HS/Cincinnati, Ohio) No key returning player had a bad season for the Bearcats. Keith Starks was like the other veterans as he had his best year in 1989-90. In fact, Starks fulfilled the expectations that the coaching staff had for him as well as any Bearcat. At 6-7, he was the team's tallest player and provided defensive size under the boards. He was competitive with pivots five inches and/or 40 pounds heavier, while his excellent quickness enabled him to make steals, knock passes away and keyed the Bearcats' gambling style of play.

"We were a much different team if Keith is not in the lineup," Huggins said.

Starks played through injuries last season. A pair of ankle sprains limited his effectiveness, but not his playing time, in late January. He is a good offensive player with excellent range. Starks establishes his rebounding position well and can score in a crowd. Many of his contributions were not always evident in the box-score. No other Bearcat came up with as many key rebounds when the game was on the line, or was better at forcing a turnover than Starks.

This year the Bearcats have more size and Huggins plans on using Starks at forward.

B. J. WARD (6-5, 180 lbs., JR, F, #40, 1.6 ppg, 1.7 rpg, 9 assists, 13 steals, 7 blocks, Messmer HS/Milwaukee, Wisc. & Laramie County CC/Laramie, Wyo.) Ward played his high school basketball in Milwaukee but his family moved to Cincinnati a few years ago. He made the team as a walk-on last year but injured his right wrist in an auto accident which caused him to miss two valuable weeks of practice. A junior college transfer who attended Ellsworth (Iowa) JC and Laramie County (Wyo.) CC, Ward managed to play only one season in the past two years due to injury. He also suffered an abrasion of his cornea in December and bruised his back in a fall in practice in mid-January. If that wasn't enough, Ward sustained a bruised kidney and some cracked ribs in early February in a game at Memphis State which sidelined him for three weeks. When healthy, Ward was a major contributor, serving as the first frontcourt reserve. He is a solid athlete and helps in the Bearcats' press, plus can crash the boards.

Ward started four games when Robinson was laid up with an appendectomy in early December. He seldom shoots but made 16-of-26 field goal attempts (.615), but with just 9-for-21 (.429) from the line. Ward averaged 10.2 minutes per game last year. If healthy, Ward's role will be similar.

ORLANDO WILLIAMS (6-2, 186 lbs., SR, G, #23, 0.3 ppg, 0.7 rpg, 3 assists, 4 steals, Princeton HS/Cincinnati, Ohio & Cincinnati Technical College) A reserve guard who began the season as one of the Bearcats' top reserves off the bench. However, Williams was struck with aseptic meningitis in late January and did not play until the final game of the season.

Williams has excellent quickness and can be a defensive specialist. He also has good strength, changes directions quickly and can penetrate opposing defenses. He plays hard and is an effective practice player.

★ NEWCOMERS ★

CURTIS BOSTIC (6-5, 205 lbs., FR, F, #32, 22.3 ppg, 15.0 rpg, 2.0 apg, 4.0 blpg, Brockton HS/Brockton, Mass.) A very intriguing newcomer who is one of the most remarkable athletes in all of college basketball. Bostic has a black belt in karate and is a former Massachusetts state kick-box champion. He was an outstanding triple jumper in high school. Bostic is so flexible he can kick his feet way above his head, or sit on the floor, stretch his legs out in a V-shape and touch his forehead to the floor with ease.

"I have never seen anybody who can jump like that and I played five years in the pros," said former Providence All-American Ernie DiGregio who coached Bostic in the Boston Shootout. "That's at the David Thompson level."

"I looked up and saw someone come over the horizon, about three or four feet above the rim,'' said Providence freshman Troy Brown who was also on the Boston team in the Shootout, about one of Bostic's spectacular slams.

A two-time Boston area all-scholastic first-team choice, Bostic's older brother Troy plays at James Madison. Like most young, spectacular leapers Bostic needs to work on his perimeter skills. Still, he is expected to contribute this year and could become a crowd favorite of Bearcat fans at the Meryl Shoemaker Arena.

ALLEN JACKSON (6-3, 175 lbs., SO, G, #52, 15.3 ppg, 4.9 rpg, 3.1 apg, La Salle HS/South Bend, Ind. & Rend Lake JC/Ina, Ill.) As Allen Jackson goes, so will the Cincinnati Bearcats in 1990-91. He is team MVP and best defensive player at Rend Lake (Ill.) JC last year and is projected as a point guard at Cincinnati.

"Allen has all the tools to get the job done at point guard,'' said Huggins.

Jackson is a quality shooter, handles the ball well and has excellent quickness. He needs to get stronger and tougher. He was named freshman of the year in his junior college conference.

HERBERT JONES (6-4, 205 lbs., JR, F, -34, 27.0 ppg, 12.0 rpg, Brown HS/Atlanta, Ga. & Butler County CC/El Dorado, Kan.) Huggins struck out in the early signing period last year and some questioned his recruiting ability. However, he came back strong in the spring and particularly redeemed himself by signing Herbert Jones. Ranked by all scouting services as one of the Top Five junior college players in the country, Jones was listed as the No. 1 JC player in the country by *All Star Sports* and *Tim Timko's Basketball Report*. He finished his career as the all-time leading scorer in the Kansas JC ranks which is quite an accomplishment considering the quality and quantity of players that have come through the state over the years.

"Herbert is really a diverse player,'' Huggins said. "He is great on the block, I mean he can really score on the block no matter how big the opposition is.''

Jones can also get out on the floor and score. He led his team to a 29-6 record last year and the Region VI championship. Jones was twice a first-team all-conference selection.

Herbert Jones is truly an impact newcomer. He is capable of becoming the most influential newcomer in the Metro Conference as well as one of the premier newcomers in the country. Jones is quite a coup for Huggins' first full recruiting class at Cincinnati.

MIKE REICHENEKER (7-0, 240 lbs., JR, C, #41, 8.6 ppg, 9.0 rpg, Choctawhatchee HS/Ft. Walton Beach, Fla. & Panola JC/Panola, Tex.) With the arrival of Reicheneker and 6-10 Jeff Scott, Cincinnati is much stronger and bigger inside than a year ago. Last season, the Bearcats had only one player above 6-6, Keith Starks, and still won 20 games.

Reicheneker originally signed with Middle Tennessee State but never played for the Blue Raiders and transferred to Panola (Tex.) JC. He was Panola's reserve center as a freshman before becoming a strong inside presence last year. Reicheneker is a strong and physical player. He will not back down to anyone. Cincinnati did not have that strong, enforcer in the middle last year and Reicheneker should fill that role.

JEFF SCOTT (6-10, 235 lbs., JR, C, #50, Mount Healthy HS/Cincinnati, Ohio) The fourth transfer in Cincinnati's five-man recruiting class, Scott is a local product who originally enrolled at Miami of Ohio. He was a regular contributor as a backup for two seasons at Miami. Scott averaged 3.2 points and 1.6 rebounds as a freshman and upped those averages to 6.7 points and 4.8 rebounds as a sophomore in 1987-88. He left Miami for California-Santa Barbara but never played for the Gauchos before transferring home to Cincinnati.

While Reicheneker is stronger, taller and more physical, Scott possesses better basketball skills. Former Bearcat Pat Cummings, who was an NBA veteran, played against Scott in the summer and was very impressed.

Expect Reicheneker and Scott to give Cincinnati a great deal of strength and flexibility in the pivot this year.

★ QUESTIONS ★

Will JC transfer Allen Jackson make the grade at point guard? Jackson is a highly regarded player but if he does not get the job done at point guard Cincinnati will suffer dearly.
Perimeter Shooting?

★ STRENGTHS ★

Bob Huggins! Although he does not have a high national profile, Huggins is one of the up and coming young coaches in the game. He worked a near miracle with Cincinnati last year and now has more talent and size at his disposal.
Defense! The Bearcats held opponents to under 70 points per game and just 40.3 percent shooting. This should be another strong defensive team.
Rebounding!
Improved athleticism and depth!

★ BLUE RIBBON ANALYSIS ★

Cincinnati is coming off its finest season in 14 years. In Bob Huggins' initial season, he led the Bearcats to a 20-14 record, a tie for second place in the Metro Conference and a berth in the NIT. All that was accomplished despite the fact

that Huggins had to bring in five walk-ons to fill out the roster last year. There was only one player on the roster taller than 6-6, yet the Bearcats managed to defeat Minnesota and knocked off Louisville on the road. Huggins was selected coach of the year in the Metro Conference and rightfully so.

"A major reason for our success last season was our work ethic. The players dedicated themselves to the goal of getting to a post-season tournament and worked hard day-in, day-out to accomplish that goal. It is important that we have this type of attitude and approach this season. I think our senior leadership will quickly indoctrinate our newcomers to what we have to do to get the job done,'' Huggins said.

The Bearcats will miss second-team All-Metro selection Andre Tate, the team's second-leading scorer, playmaker and a key defender. However, the frontcourt trio of Louis Banks, Levertis Robinson and Keith Starks return. Banks is one of the premier players in the Metro Conference and one of the most explosive offensive players in the country. He is expected to move to the backcourt this year. Robinson, whose leaping ability enables him to play much taller than his 6-5 height, was among the Metro's Top 10 leading rebounders and is an outstanding defender. Starks also was strong defensively.

Huggins' first true recruiting class at Cincinnati was a good one. He added much needed height in 7-0 Mike Reicheneker and 6-10 Jeff Scott. Junior college transfer Allen Jackson is expected to handle the point guard duties and how well he performs is the key to the season. The premier newcomer is 6-5 forward Herbert Jones, considered by some to be the top junior college player in the country last year. He is a terrific scorer, especially down low, and could be the No. 1 newcomer in the entire Metro Conference.

"There is no question that we have the potential to be a much stronger team,'' stated Huggins. "Lou, Vert (Robinson) and Keith will give us good leadership. Their experience, along with that of our other returning players, gives them an understanding of what it takes to win at this level.

"We significantly increased our level of athleticism with our recruiting class,'' Huggins continued. "All of our newcomers have the skills to play pressure defense and crash the boards the way we like to. We'll be bigger and stronger inside and I think we will do a better job of pushing the ball up court in transition.''

Cincinnati will exhibit an aggressive, pressure defense, strong rebounding, plus a deeper bench and a taller front line. The Bearcats set an all-time Cincinnati home attendance record last year and regenerated some of the spirit that existed in the late '50s and early '60s when Cincinnati made five straight Final Four appearances and claimed two NCAA titles.

This season, Huggins will take Cincinnati one step closer to national prominence. The Bearcats will easily register 20 or more victories, should finish second in the Metro Conference, and advance to the NCAA tournament for the first time since the '70s. The Bearcats are definitely on their way back!

LAST SEASON		1990-91 CINCINNATI SCHEDULE		
Minnesota	66-64	Nov.	23-24	#Bearcat Classic
@North Carolina Wilm.	66-55		28	Kentucky
Miami (OH)	59-63	Dec.	1	@Miami (OH)
Dayton	90-88		8	North Carolina
Southern University	83-72			Asheville
#Southwestern Louisiana	88-89		13	Michigan State
#University of Portland	75-53		15	@Evansville
##Creighton	60-58		17	St. Francis (PA)
##Duke	83-95		20	@Minnesota
##Rutgers	79-71		22	East Tennessee
@Louisville	71-66			State
Coastal Carolina (SC)	72-73		29	@Dayton
@Toledo	72-84	Jan.	3	Louisville
Florida State	82-62		10	@Florida State
@South Carolina	53-59		12	@South Carolina
Morehead State	68-61		19	Virginia Tech
@Virginia Tech	62-59		24	@Tulane
@Arkansas State	65-66		26	@Southern Mis-
Tulane	73-64			sissippi
Southern Mississippi	76-83		30	Xavier
@Xavier	88-90	Feb.	2	Memphis State
@Memphis State	64-82		7	Florida State
Alcorn State	89-52		9	South Carolina
@Florida State	72-69		14	@Memphis State
South Carolina	76-51		16	@Virginia Tech
Memphis State	82-76		21	Southern Mississippi
Virginia Tech	94-80		23	Tulane
@Southern Mississippi	63-70		25	Valparaiso (IN)
@Tulane	66-58		28	@Louisville
Louisville	71-86	Mar.	7-9	##Metro Conference
*Florida State	65-64			Tournament
*Southern Mississippi	63-75			
**Bowling Green	75-60	@ Road Games		
**@DePaul	59-61	# Cincinnati, OH (Kent State, Sam		
		Houston State & Texas A&M)		
@ Road Games		## Roanoke, VA		
# U.K.I.T., Lexington, KY				
## Rainbow Classic, Honolulu, HI				
* Metro Conference Tournament,				
Biloxi, MS				
** NIT				

NOTES: Cincinnati will open up with Sam Houston State in the opening round of the Bearcat Classic . . . the NCAA probation restrictions which had limited Cincinnati to 11 scholarships have been lifted and Huggins now has the full complement of 15 scholarships to give out . . . Cincinnati has a commitment from one of the Top Five players in Ohio, 6-7, 250-pound John Jacobs of Cincinnati Withrow HS . . . Cincinnati's Meryl Shoemaker Center was recently ranked among the Top 20 athletic facilities in the country. The arena was opened last year and its stadium club is one of the most ornate dining and banquet facilities housed in any sports arena in the country. Two million dollars was spent on the stadium club and much of its furniture and paneling is made of the highest grade cherry wood. There are even onyx sinks and gold faucets in the bathrooms. No wonder Cincinnati showed the highest percentage of attendance of any college in the country last year.

CLEMSON

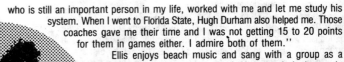

LAST SEASON: 26-9
CONFERENCE RECORD: 10-4
STARTERS LOST: 3
STARTERS RETURNING: 2
CONFERENCE: ATLANTIC COAST (ACC)
LOCATION: CLEMSON, SC
HOME FLOOR: LITTLEJOHN
    COLISEUM (11,020)
NICKNAME: TIGERS
COLORS: ORANGE AND PURPLE

★ COACH'S PROFILE ★

CLIFF ELLIS (Record at Clemson, 119-69. Career record, includes high school, 366-165.) Cliff Ellis' sixth season at Clemson was his most successful one to date. A school record 26 wins, a first-ever ACC regular season title and advancement to the NCAA tournament's Final 16 were all landmark accomplishments for the Tigers and their legion of orange clad fans. Ellis does not receive the media attention his other ACC counterparts such as Dean Smith, Mike Krzyzewski and Bobby Cremins, but he has been successful in his own right since coming to Clemson from South Alabama. Ellis is the first ACC head coach to lead a team to post-season play in each of his first six seasons on the job. Ellis works at the only ACC school which is a national football power with the emphasis clearly on the gridiron rather than the hardwood. Yet, Ellis has managed to create a niche for basketball. Now, the only post-game celebrations at Clemson athletic contests are not just the traditional tearing down of the goalposts as Ellis' basketball Tigers have had a few net cutting ceremonies in Littlejohn Coliseum following major victories. Make no mistake about it, football is still king in Clemson country, but basketball season is not just a rest period between fall and spring football any more. Ellis has been supportive of the Clemson football program and uses its vast support to his advantage. He even spoke to the Clemson football team before the 1988 Florida State game and took the traditional run down a steep hill into Clemson's famed Death Valley Stadium prior to the game with the football team.

Ellis grew up in the Florida panhandle town of Chipley. He graduated from Florida State in 1968. He began his coaching career at Niceville HS in the Florida panhandle and posted a 54-7 record between 1968-71. In 1971-72, Ellis guided another Florida high school, Vanguard of Ocala to a 20-5 mark, the best record in the school's history at the time. The following season he began his college coaching career at Cumberland College in Lebannon, Tenn. In three years at Cumberland, Ellis was 78-12. His 1973-74 team won 27 games in a row and was ranked fourth in the NAIA. Cumberland College averaged 105.1 points per game that season, leading the nation in scoring.

Ellis became the head coach at South Alabama in 1975. The South Alabama program was almost totally unknown at the time. Soon after his arrival, South Alabama joined the Sun Belt Conference. Ellis was very successful at South Alabama (171-84 in nine years). His teams won 20, 23 and 25 straight games between 1978-81. Two of his Alabama teams received NCAA tournament bids; two more were invited to the NIT.

Ellis developed a reputation as a top flight recruiter at South Alabama. Four of his players from the 1980-81 South Alabama team were drafted by the NBA, more than any school in the country. In 1985, South Alabama had three more players drafted and once again no program in the country had more players drafted in that year. One of his South Alabama players — Terry Catledge — was a first round draft choice and two players he has coached at Clemson — Horace Grant and Elden Campbell — have been first round NBA draft choices.

Ellis is one of the few coaches in college basketball to be named coach of the year in three different leagues.

"I wanted to coach from the time I was in the seventh or eighth grade," Ellis said. "I played high school basketball, but I was not quick enough to get a scholarship — to a big school. I broke my ankle my freshman year at Chipola Junior College (Florida) so I took up golf.

"I still studied the game, however. The coach at Chipola, Milton Johnson, who is still an important person in my life, worked with me and let me study his system. When I went to Florida State, Hugh Durham also helped me. Those coaches gave me their time and I was not getting 15 to 20 points for them in games either. I admire both of them."

Ellis enjoys beach music and sang with a group as a youngster and even cut a record. He started singing again publicly when he came to Clemson because beach music is popular in South Carolina.

On his offensive philosophy, Ellis said: "I love the exciting game. My offensive philosophy is one where I love the fast break. I like the excitement of it, and the players like it. And I like the percentages on offense where we are running a set play to try to get the best percentage shots. I detest poor shots, turnovers, and the things that can negate a good offense."

Clemson basketball has made great strides under Ellis, but he knows that consistency will be the ultimate test of his program. "We have made strides in recent years by advancing to the NCAA tournament three of the last four years, winning over 25 games each of the last four years, and, of course, winning the league race last year," said Ellis. "But we must continue to gain consistency. It takes 15-20 years to build a tradition. We enjoyed last year and it was a year of great significance, but we can't look back for we've got to keep going."

While Clemson won't win the conference title every year in the ultra-competitive ACC, the Tigers will continue to get closer to developing a consistent, high profile program under Ellis. He is more successful than expected in his first six years at Clemson and don't look for anything less in the future.

★ PLAYERS NOT RETURNING ★

ELDEN CAMPBELL (6-11, C, 16.4 ppg, 8.0 rpg, 44 assists, 54 steals, 97 blocked shots) Campbell seemed to be a player that pro scouts and media members loved to hate. The California native displayed a laid back, detached demeanor on the court and it often overshadowed what he was accomplishing. The fact that Campbell slipped to the 27th and last pick in the first round (Los Angeles Lakers) is evidence that his game was not given great respect. However, Campbell was a key reserve as a freshman, then became a three-year starter and concluded his career as Clemson's all-time leading scorer and third-best career rebounder. He also concluded his career as Clemson's No. 2 career shotblocker behind Tree Rollins. Bad body language and all, that is a superb college career, especially in the ACC.

"Elden Campbell was a first round draft pick and someone who had outstanding post moves. He was, quite simply, one of Clemson's top players ever," Ellis said.

Clemson still has All-America power forward Dale Davis, but Campbell's departure for the NBA leaves a substantial void in the middle.

MARION CASH (6-3, G, 8.4 ppg, 2.9 rpg, 174 assists, 56 steals, 5 blocked shots) Cash started 34 games at point guard for Clemson last year. He was not a great player and chipped in limited offense. Cash made only .429 of his field goal attempts and was a mere .226 from three-point territory. He was not a big time guard but was adequate. That is the key, *adequate*. Cash was able to get the ball inside to Campbell and Davis and keep the Tiger attack going. Clemson has not had great guard play for quite some time but one of the reasons the Tigers finally won the ACC title last year was that the backcourt play was not a negative.

The Tigers will not be as athletic or experienced at point guard without Cash.

DERRICK FORREST (6-3, G/F, 8.2 ppg, 3.1 rpg, 88 assists, 57 steals, 31 blocked shots) Forest was a starter who played a supporting role in Clemson's march to the regular season ACC title and the Final 16 of the NCAA tournament. He was a shut down defender and made a big difference in many key games for Clemson in the two years he played for the Tigers after transferring in from Chipola (Fla.) JC.

Not a headline grabbing player, but someone who made a substantial contribution to Clemson's success.

KIRKLAND HOWLING (6-4, G/F, 7.4 ppg, 2.9 rpg, 29 assists, 9 steals, 1 blocked shot) A reserve who averaged 16 minutes of playing time per game last year. Howling was one of three junior college transfers who all played perimeter positions and came to Clemson two years ago. He was at full strength last year from the beginning of the season to the end, after undergoing knee surgery in his junior year, and the difference was obvious. Howling was one of Clemson's top two three-point threats and will be missed.

Without Cash, Forrest and Howling, Clemson loses a great deal of experience, athletic ability, versatility, defensive prowess and experience on the perimeter. How well this trio of former junior college transfers is replaced is probably the key to Clemson's season.

★ RETURNING PLAYERS ★

COLBY BROWN (6-8, 200 lbs., SR, F, #44, 1.6 ppg, 1.4 rpg, 9 assists, 6 blocked shots, 3 steals, Westwood HS/Camilla, Ga.) Brown is a reserve forward who saw action in 21 games last season for a total of 84 minutes (an average of four minutes per game). His playing time dipped slightly last year from 123 minutes in 1988-89 to the 89 minutes he saw last year. Brown came to Clemson with a reputation as an excellent shooter, but he has had limited offensive opportunities and has never shot above .391 (last year) from the field for a season. He did knock down 3-of-6 three-pointers and was a near perfect 13-of-15 from the line. He can play both forward spots and may be more of a contributor this year. Brown was used more at small forward last year and possibly a year's experience at the position will pay off for him.

DONNELL BRUCE (6-5, 180 lbs., SR, G, #14, 2.1 ppg, 0.6 rpg, 5 assists, 2 steals, Branchville HS/Branchville, S.C.) Bruce appeared in only ten games for a total of 38 minutes last year. He is a quality athlete with outstanding quickness and can also shoot the ball. However, his opportunities have been limited the last two years. Bruce was an academic All-ACC selection as a freshman, started six games and saw an average of 20.2 minutes per game. However, he broke his wrist on February 1, 1988, at Duke, after going 7-of-11 from the floor, and shot just 7-of-25 the rest of the year.

Bruce came back to play in just nine games for a total of 37 minutes as a sophomore before seeing a rather limited role again last year.

It is hard to project Bruce's role after two years with rather limited playing time. However, he proved early in his career before breaking the wrist that he had the potential to be a decent ACC player, maybe that ability will be exposed in his senior year.

WAYNE BUCKINGHAM (6-9, 235 lbs., SO, F/C, #42, 2.3 ppg, 2.0 rpg, 4 assists, 5 steals, 6 blocked shots, Southside HS/Atlanta, Ga.) Buckingham could be the next in a long line of Clemson frontcourt players who become national level performers. Clemson has had its share of big timers up front in the last 20 years like Tree Rollins, Larry Nance, Horace Grant, Elden Campbell and current senior Dale Davis. Buckingham has the size, strength and potential to one day be rated in that group.

As a freshman, Buckingham was brought along slowly by Ellis. He appeared in 28 games for a total of 162 minutes. He had nine rebounds in a loss at North Carolina but basically was a support player behind Campbell and Davis. He did manage to pace the Tigers in offensive rebounds per minute as he garnered one every six minutes and he was second only to Davis in terms of overall rebounds per minute.

"Buck will see much more playing time this year," said Ellis. "He gained a lot of experience late in the year and improved his baseline post-up moves. He gives us added bulk and strength inside."

Buckingham grew up in a rural area of Tennessee around Shelbyville. He was sent to live in Atlanta for his junior year and quickly gained recognition. By the end of his senior year, Buckingham was rated the best prospect in Georgia by the *Atlanta Constitution*. He had 19 points and seven rebounds in just 24 minutes against the Soviet Junior National team. When Buckingham signed with Clemson, Ellis said he felt that he was as talented a freshman as had been brought into Clemson. Ellis also felt that Buckingham could one day even play small forward.

The physical tools are there and if Buckingham gains consistency he and Davis can be one of the premier inside duos in all of college basketball.

DALE DAVIS (6-10, 225 lbs., SR, F, #34, 15.3 ppg, 11.3 rpg, 21 assists, 36 steals, 58 blocked shots, Stephens County HS/Toccoa, Ga.) Clemson has had its share of front line players who have gone off to the NBA such as Tree Rollins, Larry Nance, Horace Grant and now Elden Campbell. It might not be long before Dale Davis is recognized as the best player to ever put on a Clemson basketball uniform. Last season Davis, along with Campbell, was a first-team All-ACC selection. He led the ACC in both rebounding and field goal percentage (.625). He seemed to get stronger as the season unfolded, and he finished the year with two of his most dominating performances in the NCAA tournament against La Salle (26 points and 11 rebounds) and Connecticut (15 points and 17 rebounds).

"There are not many players around who play the game as hard as Dale Davis," said Duke coach Mike Krzyzewski. "He is a relentless rebounder."

Said Jeff Roulston, the starting center for South Carolina last year, "He (Davis) is one of the best rebounders I've ever played against. I've never been in a game where someone jumped over me so much."

Davis has improved considerably since starting to play basketball in the ninth grade. He averaged 7.7 rebounds per game as a freshman, along with 7.8 points, and upped those totals to 8.9 rebounds and an average of 13.3 points per game as a sophomore. In the summer of 1989 he led an ACC all-star team in scoring with a 25.6 average and rebounding (12.4 rpg) in a five game tournament in Greece. He was the only member of the ACC team to make the all-tournament squad.

Last season Davis ranked 13th in the nation in rebounding and 10th in field goal percentage. He either led or tied for the team lead in rebounding in 24 games last year. One of his better games was a 19-point, 20-rebound outing in a road

loss to Georgia Tech. He had 22 points and 17 rebounds in a win over South Carolina, 25 points and 11 rebounds in a home victory against Georgia Tech, 19 points and 11 rebounds in a victory at Virginia and 21 points and 11 rebounds in a loss in the ACC tournament to Virginia.

"Dale Davis personifies everything you want in a player," said Ellis. "He has a great attitude, is a fine person, and has the work ethic to make it in the NBA. He is right there with Horace Grant and Terry Catledge (who Ellis coached at South Alabama and is now with the Orlando Magic). He strives to meet the challenge, is very coachable, a natural leader. He should be a lottery pick next year."

We concur with Ellis' sentiment. All that stands in the way of Davis' potential stardom in the NBA is a more refined offensive game. Entering the season he ranks as one of the top three senior power forwards along with UNLV's Larry Johnson and Doug Smith of Missouri. In our estimation he is one of the top eight players in all of college basketball who can be classified as power forwards or centers. Even though Clemson suffered strong graduation losses, the Tigers have a shot at finishing in the upper half of the ACC and returning to the NCAA tournament again because of the presence of Dale Davis.

RICKY JONES (6-7, 195 lbs., SR, F, #25, 3.8 ppg, 1.5 rpg, 23 assists, 11 steals, 15 blocked shots, Pendleton HS/Pendleton, S.C.) Those of us directly involved in basketball tend to get a little carried away about high school All-America rankings and recruiting lists. A case in point is Ricky Jones. Coming out of high school, Jones was the most highly regarded player, other than possibly Wayne Buckingham, Ellis has signed at Clemson. Jones was Mr. Basketball in South Carolina for 1985-86 and a consensus national Top 25 pick. However, his career began on a bad note when he had to redshirt the 1986-87 season after playing in just two games due to severe shoulder problems. Jones had surgery on both of his shoulders and did not play any competitive basketball from December of 1986 to the following July. He came back to play in 27 games, starting six, in 1987-88. Jones averaged 5.4 points and 15.9 minutes of action per game. As a sophomore he started 16 games but averaged a mere 4.3 points per game. Last season, on the best Clemson team in ten years, Jones started six games and averaged nine minutes per game. His scoring average dipped again, to 3.8 points per game and he was limited on the boards pulling down an average of 1.5 per game.

Jones is an excellent athlete with great leaping ability. He was also counted on to be an outside shooting threat last year but made only 3-of-15 three-pointers (.200). This year because of the graduation of Derrick Forrest, Jones will get an opportunity to be the full-time starter at small forward.

"We're looking for consistency from Ricky Jones," said Ellis. "He is one of the guys we are counting on from the outside."

SHAWN LASTINGER (6-1, 155 lbs., SO, G, #15, 2.1 ppg, 0.5 rpg, 19 assists, 8 steals, Lakeside HS/Atlanta, Ga.) Starting point guard Marion Cash, who led Clemson in minutes played with 1,105, has departed and Ellis needs a point guard. Cash's heir apparent could be Lastinger. As a freshman Lastinger played in 26 games, starting one, for a total of 204 minutes. He averaged eight minutes per game and may be the player best suited to inherit the ballhandling responsibilities.

The highlight of Lastinger's freshman season came in Clemson's ACC regular season title clinching win against Duke. He was presented with the game ball by his teammates for his ability to hold his own against the Blue Devils' vaunted pressure defense when Cash got into foul trouble. Lastinger guided Clemson's offense to 35 points in his 13 minutes of action, an impressive 2.7 points per minute clip.

He is a member of an athletic Georgia family. Lastinger's brother, John, was the starting quarterback for Georgia in the mid-'80s.

"Shawn Lastinger reminds me of Ohio State's Jay Burson. He can really shoot it from the outside and at the foul line . . . he has all the basketball smarts you need to be a point guard," Ellis said last year.

In his limited action last year, Lastinger made only 14-of-45 field goal attempts (.311) and 10-of-33 three-pointers (.303). He had 19 assists against 26 turnovers on the year. Those statistics are misleading as most freshmen who see limited action in big time conferences do not shoot the ball well. We will get a chance to see just how good Lastinger is with extended playing time. His role will expand greatly this year and there is a strong possibility that as Shawn Lastinger goes, so will the Clemson Tigers.

SEAN TYSON (6-7, 215 lbs., SR, F, #22, 8.5 ppg, 4.1 rpg, 37 assists, 45 steals, 3 blocked shots, Dunbar HS/Baltimore, Md.) The 1989-90 season was a year redemption for Sean Tyson. In the three previous years he had been at Clemson, Tyson had played just one year (1988-89) as he was shelved as a freshman because of academic problems, played 18 games in 1987-88 before being suspended late in the year and then missing the entire 1988-89 season due to gall bladder surgery. Tyson lost 30 pounds during the two months he was out because of the surgery. Last season he developed into a key player for the Tigers.

Tyson was Clemson's No. 3 scorer behind Elden Campbell and Dale Davis. He was also the third-best rebounder on the team behind Campbell and Davis.

"Tyson is a guy who goes at it 100 miles per hour," Ellis said. "Sometimes his style gets us into trouble, but sometimes he gets us out of trouble."

Tyson had one of his best games in Clemson's win over La Salle in the second round of the NCAA tournament as he scored 17 points and grabbed 11 rebounds as the Tigers came back from a major, double figure deficit.

Tyson has good offensive ability, can play both forward spots and is a defensive ballhawk. Tyson will start and be a major player for the Tigers in his senior year.

"He (Tyson) is a player who is ready to be a consistent leader," Ellis claimed. "He has the skill to play professionally. His time has come to step to the forefront."

JOEY WATTS (6-3, 180 lbs., SO, G, #24, 1.3 ppg, 0.7 rpg, 1 steal, Aiken HS/Aiken, S.C.) A walk-on guard who was not even listed in the pre-season media guide last year. Watts appeared in six games for a total of 15 minutes. He was 3-for-6 from the field in his limited action.

DAVID YOUNG (6-4, 175 lbs., JR, G, #11, 6.1 ppg, 1.7 rpg, 142 assists, 42 steals, 13 blocks, Greenville HS/Greenville, S.C.) With four of Clemson's top six scorers gone, and three were guards, it is obvious that the play of 6-4 junior David Young, Clemson's top returnee in the backcourt, is crucial in 1990-91. Young appeared in every game last year and started 27. He was an inconsistent outside shooter making 74-of-204 field goal attempts (.363) and 39-of-132 three-pointers (.295) for the year. However, he seemed to save his best shooting for the big games. Young has 16 points on 6-of-8 field goal shooting in a win against Duke which clinched the ACC regular season title. He also hit an 18-foot jumper to put Clemson ahead of Connecticut 70-61 with one second left in the NCAA tournament. If not for Tate George's desperation shot at the buzzer which beat the Tigers, Young would have been the man responsible for putting Clemson into the Final Eight, and who knows what would have happened from there.

Ellis realizes full well the importance of Young's expanded role. "David will have to be a leader in our backcourt as a 2-3 position player. He did obtain some experience as a point guard last year, but we do not expect to use him at the point this year. However, he will handle the ball more than most two-guards that we have had. With freshman seeing a lot of time in the backcourt, it will be important that working the ball up the court will be a team effort this year."

So far in his two years at Clemson, Young has been a teaser. He appeared in 29 games, averaging 16.4 minutes per game as a freshman, and averaged 6.0 points, 1.5 rebounds and had 58 assists. He hit 5 three-pointers against St. Mary's in the NCAA tournament and led all ACC freshmen in three-point field goals with 36 in 1988-89. At times he showed brilliant floor vision and offensive potential. However, Young has just not been focused and serious so far. There is no denying that Young has the ability to be one of the premier guards in the ACC, he was the second-team *Parade Magazine* All-America selection in high school, and this could be the year he gets it done. After all, Young has to play well all year long for Clemson not to drop off dramatically in 1990-91.

★ NEWCOMERS ★

ANDRE BOVAIN (6-2, 180 lbs., FR, G, #31, 20.0 ppg, 7.0 rpg, Keenan HS/Columbia, S.C.) An all-state selection in South Carolina last season, Bovain will push Shawn Lastinger for playing time at point guard. With Ellis' system this year of having a team effort in the backcourt responsible for ballhandling duties, Bovain could prove to be a very valuable commodity for the Tigers. He was known as an exceptional athlete and can push the ball on the break. It will be interesting to see how Bovain works out. He is the first Clemson recruit in recent memory sneaked out from under the South Carolina campus in Columbia.

ERIC BURKS (6-3, 185 lbs., FR, G, 23.0 ppg, 6.0 apg, McNair HS/Atlanta, Ga.) You can't fault Cliff Ellis for being too selective. He lost three perimeter players so he brought in a six-man freshman class consisting of nothing but perimeter players. If there truly is safety in numbers, Ellis will be able to find some talented guards out of his six-man class. Burks could be a keeper for Ellis.

"He has both the size and body to come into our program and make an immediate impact," said Ellis.

Burks was a consistent long range shooter in high school. He connected on 45 percent of his three-point shots and was also an outstanding free throw shooter, an area in which the Tigers could use some help as Clemson made only .609 of its free throw attempts as a team last year. With Clemson shooting a meager .295 from three-point range last year, Burks' shooting skills couldn't have arrived a moment too soon.

STEVE HARRIS (6-5, 190 lbs., FR, G/F, -13, 23.0 ppg, 9.5 rpg, Hillcrest HS/Simpsonville, S.C.) The most highly regarded of Clemson's six-man freshman class. Harris was a first-team All-South Carolina selection and was a national Top 100 player in many scouting services. His primary area of concentration will be as a small forward, but Harris is versatile and athletic enough so that he could play wing guard and a more inside-oriented role as well. He should immediately bring high quality athleticism and good basketball skills to the Clemson program.

Harris was a high school teammate of Louisville's Everick Sullivan at Hillcrest HS in Simpsonville, S.C. He was a Mr. Basketball award winner in South Carolina last year. The future for Harris looks bright at Clemson, not only because he is talented and the Tigers are in need of perimeter players, but after this year small forward candidates Sean Tyson, Ricky Jones, Donnell Bruce and Colby Brown will leave the program freeing up a great deal of playing time for Harris.

BRUCE MARTIN (6-3, 175 lbs., FR, G, #3, 34.0 ppg, 6.0 rpg, 12.0 apg, Shady Springs HS/Shady Springs, W.Va.) Martin signed with Clemson last fall before suffering a serious knee injury in the middle of the season that ended his high school career. How well he will adjust to ACC level competition and come back off the knee injury remains to be seen. However, one thing is known for certain and that is Martin can put the basketball in the hole from long range. He is a skilled perimeter shooter who was a true dead-eye Dick as a high school player in West Virginia. How well he can get that shot off in major college basketball and play the rest of the game has yet to be determined.

JIMMY MASON (6-1, 190 lbs., FR, G, #10, 17.0 ppg, 4.0 rpg, Pinecrest HS/Southern Pines, N.C.) Mason signed with Clemson last fall. He did not play against the large high schools in North Carolina and will need time to raise his game to the level of competition he will face both in the ACC and in Clemson practices. He is considered physically strong and a good penetrator. Prior to last season, Mason was rated as the No. 18 senior in North Carolina by the *Hoop Scoop*.

Look for possibly Mason and some of the other freshmen to be redshirt candidates. There is no way that all six freshmen will be able to contribute this season.

TYRONE PAUL (6-5, 175 lbs., FR, G/F, #32, 20.5 ppg, 6.0 rpg, Morningside HS/Inglewood, Calif.) Early in Ellis' tenure at Clemson he signed a player from coach Carl Franklin's Morningside HS program. That player was Elden Campbell and the rest is history. Maybe lightning will strike twice for Ellis with the latest Morningside product to head to Tiger country, 6-5 swingman Tyrone Paul.

"Tyrone has a lot of ability and is a gifted basketball player," said Franklin. "Byron Scott (Los Angeles Lakers) played here back in the '70s and Tyrone is the closest player to Scott that I have coached since then. You don't get many players like Tyrone too often."

Paul was the Los Angeles 3-A player of the year last year. He can play both wing guard and small forward, a definite luxury for Ellis. Paul would have an opportunity to see more playing time at wing guard early on as there are many seniors in line for the playing time at small forward.

"Overall, we have signed some players with good basketball sense," said Ellis. "Experience in the NCAA tournament and the attention that comes with your advancement in that tournament was a contributing factor in our successful recruiting last year. Some of these first-year freshmen will have to step in and contribute immediately."

★ QUESTIONS ★

An inexperienced backcourt? Clemson will need a big season from junior David Young, the most experienced returnee to the backcourt. The point guard position will be manned by either sophomore Shawn Lastinger, a limited contributor last season, or a freshman. The Tigers inexperience in the backcourt could be a serious problem all year long.

Consistent outside shooting? Last year Clemson did not take advantage of the three-point shot as the Tigers attempted only 397 treys compared to 519 by their opponents. Consistent outside shooting is even more of a possible problem as Clemson made only .295 of its three-point attempts. Outside shooting will be more crucial this year without Campbell's automatic inside scoring.

★ STRENGTHS ★

Recent tradition! Ellis harps on the fact that Clemson does not have the same tradition as the powers in the ACC. He is correct, but Clemson has made the NCAA tournament two of the last three years and won the conference regular season title outright last year. Clemson is becoming accustomed to winning in basketball.

Dale Davis! When God created power forwards, Davis must have been close to the front of the line. He is a ferocious rebounder both offensively and defensively and has developed an effective arsenal of inside power moves which have made him a legitimate threat to average 20 points per game this year. Davis should be a cinch lottery pick in the upcoming NBA draft.

Homecourt edge! Clemson just does not lose many games in the friendly confines of Littlejohn Coliseum. The Tigers have won 24 straight games at home and the students are so close to the court that they can literally reach out and touch the opposition along the baseline. Clemson is a nightmare for opposing teams.

★ BLUE RIBBON ANALYSIS ★

"We set the same goals each year," said Clemson coach Cliff Ellis when previewing his seventh Tiger team. "We want to go to the NCAA tournament and finish in the top half of the ACC race. But, most importantly, we want to play to our potential; and continue to build a tradition."

Clemson's basketball tradition was enhanced last year as the Tigers won the regular season crown in the ACC, maintained a 24-game winning streak at Littlejohn Coliseum and came a length of the court pass and a heroic turnaround jumper by Connecticut's Tate George with one second left away from a meeting with conference rival Duke in the finals of the East Regional of the NCAA tournament. It was unquestionably the finest season at Clemson since the 1979-80 Tigers advanced to the finals of the West Region before losing to UCLA.

Ellis will be hard pressed to duplicate last year's success as the leading scorer in school history, center Elden Campbell, and three quality perimeter players are gone. Still, All-America power forward Dale Davis is back and there is no reason to feel sorry for Ellis.

If Clemson can come close to matching its overall team defensive play of last year when not one opponent shot over 50 percent from the field against the Tigers, then the inexperience in the backcourt may not be a big problem. Ellis is worried about the prospect of playing an untested freshman or sophomore Shawn Lastinger, who was a spot player last year, at point guard. His concern with the perimeter game is evidenced by the fact he brought in six players who all can play guard.

Sophomore Wayne Buckingham must develop into a solid post player both offensively and defensively and Ellis will need a big year from senior forward Sean Tyson, who was excellent in spurts last year. The play of junior guard David Young is another key to the season for Clemson. Young has the ability to be one of the premier guards in the ACC but has not been a consistent outside shooter. Another inconsistent outside shooter has been senior forward Ricky Jones. His college career has been mediocre.

We will be surprised if Clemson duplicates last season's first place finish in the ACC. The Tigers will probably slip to fifth, but it will be a respectable showing. Clemson's recent tradition will continue as the Tigers should win at least 20 games and advance to the NCAA tournament for the third time in the last four years.

LAST SEASON

#@American Univ. of		North Carolina State	89-81
Puerto Rico	87-73	Furman	85-74
#Stetson	74-61	@Wake Forest	89-75
#Alabama	48-57	North Carolina	69-61
@The Citadel	71-54	Duke	97-93
##Providence	72-71	@Georgia Tech	69-85
Radford (VA)	114-76	@South Carolina	53-54
@North Carolina Charlotte	104-79	*Wake Forest	79-70
###Villanova	71-73	*Virginia	66-69
###Niagara	85-65	**Brigham Young	49-47
@North Carolina State	77-79	**La Salle	79-75
Maryland	82-77	***Connecticut	70-71
@Virginia	76-70		
North Carolina Asheville	78-54	@ Road Games	
@Wake Forest	76-57	# San Juan Shootout, San Juan, PR	
Georgia State	117-59	## ACC/Big East Challenge, Greens-	
Western Carolina	97-61	boro, NC	
Hofstra (NY)	91-58	### Texaco Star Classic, San Diego,	
Georgia Tech	91-90	CA	
@North Carolina	60-83	* ACC Tournament, Charlotte, NC	
@Duke	80-94	** NCAA Tournament, Hartford, CT	
South Carolina	83-65	*** NCAA Tournament, East Ruther-	
@Maryland	75-73	ford, NJ	
Virginia	74-63		

NOTES: 6-2 freshman guard Willie Shears from Marion, Ala., was signed by Clemson last year but is not eligible and will attend a junior college . . . Clemson is a former military school and women were first admitted in 1955. The school gained university status in 1964 . . . Clemson is located a two hour drive northeast of Atlanta and two hours southwest of Charlotte, N.C., nestled along the rim of the Blue Ridge Mountains . . . the actual

1990-91 CLEMSON SCHEDULE

Nov.	24	Maryland-Baltimore Co.		23	@North Carolina
	26	Samford (AL)		24	@Wake Forest
	28	The Citadel		27	@Duke
Dec.	1	Furman	Mar.	2	Georgia Tech
	4	#Seton Hall		8-10	**ACC Tournament
	8	Wisconsin-Green Bay			
	15	North Carolina	@ Road Games		
		Charlotte	# ACC/Big East Challenge, Syracuse, NY		
	17	South Carolina State	* Miami, FL (Coppin State, Florida At-		
	20-21	*Florida International	lantic & Florida International)		
		Invitational	** Charlotte, NC		
Jan.	2	@North Carolina State			
	5	@Maryland			
	8	Virginia			
	12	Wake Forest			
	16	Western Carolina			
	19	Temple			
	24	@Georgia Tech			
	26	Duke			
	31	North Carolina			
Feb.	2	@South Carolina			
	6	Maryland			
	10	North Carolina State			
	16	@Virginia			

population of Clemson, S.C., is one of the smallest among major university towns. The everyday, non-student population at Clemson is about 8,000 . . . Last year the 22,000-plus members of IPTAY, Clemson's athletic fund raising organization, donated $5.3 million setting national record for both revenues and membership in a university sports booster club.

CONNECTICUT

LAST SEASON: 31-6
CONFERENCE RECORD: 12-4
STARTERS LOST: 2
STARTERS RETURNING: 3
CONFERENCE: BIG EAST
LOCATION: STORRS, CT
HOME FLOOR: HARRY A.
   GAMPEL PAVILION (8,302)
NICKNAME: HUSKIES
COLORS: NATIONAL FLAG BLUE AND WHITE

★ **COACH'S PROFILE** ★

JIM CALHOUN (Record at Connecticut, 78-52. Career Record, 328-189.) While taking little known Northeastern to three straight NCAA tournaments during his last three seasons in Boston, Jim Calhoun opened some eyes with records of 27-5, 22-9, and 25-5. Of course, Reggie Lewis (Boston Celtics) helped with some of that. By taking Connecticut to the 1988 NIT championship in his second year at Storrs, Calhoun obtained further recognition. Some attributed the NIT title to a nice run by Cliff Robinson. Last season, however, when the team had no superstar but some of the most unique and pleasing chemistry seen around college basketball in recent years, Calhoun left little doubt of the superb coaching ability most insiders had come to appreciate over his previous 17 years in the game.

"I have all the respect in the world for what Calhoun has done with that team," said Georgetown coach John Thompson. "I think his team, in all the years I've been in the Big East, is the biggest surprise to me. I think Calhoun has done as good a job this year ('89-90) as anyone I've seen in the Big East, consistently at the level he has done it."

What Calhoun had done was help author one of college hoop's all-time Cinderella stories. The Huskies, picked to go nowhere went 31-6 instead, shared their first Big East regular season title and won their first Big East tournament

championship (while knocking off Georgetown, then Syracuse), and were stopped one second short of the Final Four when Duke's Christian Laettner nailed a 14-foot jumper, in overtime. Along the way, Connecticut extended the concept of defense— generated offense to new lengths with furious game-long pressure all over the court.

In the process, Calhoun dismantled the enormous stigma that long hung over a school with one of the most demanding statewide followings in the nation. "I've heard all the criticism," he said. "Nobody in the NBA; well Cliff Robinson (Portland Trail Blazers) may be one of the top five rookies this year. Can't win the big game; we've won the big game. The NBA; can't win post-season games; well we've won (10) in the past (3) years. Can't get the in-state players; Murray Williams, Scott Burrell, Chris Smith. Can't be in the Top 20; were in the Top 20 (actually finished the season, No. 5).

Calhoun, Boston born and bred, lost his father to a heart attack at the age of 15 and he found out what playing center field for a Babe Ruth league baseball team in suburban Braintree, his hometown. At Braintree HS, Calhoun lettered in football, basketball and baseball and made All-League as a senior in both basketball and football. He became an All-America basketball guard in college at American International (Springfield, Mass.) and began his coaching career there as an assistant for two seasons.

At Dedham (Mass.) H.S., his second year as a head coach, Calhoun's team went 21-1. He took a pay cut to take over at Northeastern, then a Division II program, at age 28. Under the Calhoun regime, the Boston commuter school resurfaced from basketball obscurity to win four conference titles and share two more in Division I by getting a NCAA bid in five of Calhoun's last six years. Overall his record at the Huntington Avenue school was 250-137, including a monstrous 74-13 conference slate during the first seven years of the North Atlantic (ECAC North) Conference. During the '80s, Calhoun, a highly regarded rebounding teacher, showed the ability to attract a number of quality out-of-town players, giving the program a new dimension.

Calhoun arrived at Connecticut in 1986, facing a severe challenge with only seven players remaining in the program. The two best then proceeded to flunk out. The Huskies suffered through a 9-19 campaign but came back all the way to 20-14 in the NIT championship in 1988. That set off booming hope for what turned out to be a somewhat disappointing 1988-89 season. Still, Connecticut went 18-13 against a schedule rated of one of the nation's 20 toughest.

Through it all, Calhoun, the father of two sons, has maintained an intense, competitive demeanor while coaching in contrast to a much calmer off-court manner. He can consistently get in his players faces and be a stern disciplinarian.

"You'll either accept him or you'll leave," said former Connecticut guard Tate George, a first round pick of the New Jersey Nets told *Basketball Weekly*. "If I can make it for four years dealing with Calhoun in my face, then I can possibly play in the NBA, or possibly not and go on with my life. He's made me a stronger person."

Calhoun has done that for many, including himself. An avid jogger, he's competed in the Boston and New York Marathons twice each. He is also a long way down the road in what previously was thought to be a Marathon-length endeavor in bringing the Connecticut basketball program to prominence in the Big East. Not only has Calhoun taken the Connecticut program farther, quicker than anyone, including himself expected, he has also taken it farther than it's ever been before.

★ PLAYERS NOT RETURNING ★

TATE GEORGE (6-5, G, 11.5 ppg, 3.5 rpg, 106 assists, 74 steals) George came into his own as a big time collegiate point guard last season. He added consistency and a knack for getting it done in a clutch to his already uncanny ability to see the floor. His season-high 22 points came, appropriately enough, in Connecticut's Big East championship win over Syracuse. Coincidentally, he became the 22nd pick (New Jersey Nets) in the first round of the NBA draft. It was definitely a season in which dreams came true for George. He proceeded over the Huskies resurgence from a disappointing 1988-89 season to a Big East tournament championship and a strong run in the NCAA tournament. Personally, George advanced from an average point guard with some intriguing passing ability and size to a national level player who went in the first round of the draft to the team closest to his Newark, N.J. home. George will also be remembered well into the next century at Connecticut for the most celebrated shot in the school's basketball history. His 15-foot buzzer beater from the right baseline off Scott Burrell's full court pass with one second left, which took Connecticut from a one-point deficit to a victory over Clemson in the semifinals of the East Region in the Meadowlands, is one of the all-time magic moments not only in Connecticut but in NCAA tournament history.

George finished his career in possession of four of the five highest single season assist totals in Connecticut history. The loss of George will be difficult for Connecticut to overcome. He was not only a playmaker but was second on the team in assists and helped key the Huskie's pressure defense. George was not the offensive force that this year's starting guards Chris Smith and John Gwynn are, but without him Connecticut will be nowhere near as pure at the point.

NADAV HENEFELD (6-7, F. 11.6 ppg, 5.6 rpg, 106 assists, 138 steals, 22 blocked shots) The sudden loss of Henefeld in August quickly diminished Connecticut's expectations for the coming season. Even without Tate George, Connecticut had realistic hopes for a Big East title and a possible Final Four trip but those expectations have to be diminished considerably without Henefeld. The Israeli native decided to return home and accept a lucrative contract from Maccabi of Tel Aviv, the dominant team in Israel.

"We will miss him greatly, not just for his athletic skills, but because he is an outstanding young man," said Calhoun. "While I don't agree with the final decision, I feel I can appreciate the great pressures that have been thrust upon him to make this decision. We realize that Nadav would always have to weigh pressure to play in his native country against his desire to remain a part of our basketball program."

Evaluating the loss of Henefeld before the season may be nearly as difficult as trying to replace him once it starts. In his first year in college basketball, Henefeld led Connecticut in rebounding and steals, was second in scoring, three-pointers and free throw percentage and third in assists and blocked shots. Whether Henefeld merely expanded an already outstanding team chemistry from good to unique or actually embodied the definitive, irreplaceable ingredient of that blend is tough to judge.

Enough athletic ability, quality experience, and depth remains to make Connecticut a Top 20 contender. However, when Henefeld unexpectedly popped in on campus, as a 21-year-old freshman and army veteran straight off the Israeli National team, the boost in team spirit and leadership was immeasurable. The Connecticut record setting 138 steals (third in the nation) that won him the nickname, "The Gaza Stripper," can partially be replaced as can his 11.6 points and 5.6 points rebounds per game. What may not be is his court presence. "His understanding of the game is intuitive," said Calhoun. "Not just the defensive anticipation but the passing ability and the sense of where everyone was on the floor."

Henefeld was on his way to becoming one of the major personalities to ever play in the Big East. We're not saying he would ever have been as good as former Big East stars such as Georgetown's Patrick Ewing, St. John's Chris Mullin, Syracuse's Derrick Coleman and others, but his effect on the Huskies and the entire state of Connecticut was literally immeasurable. He was a folk hero in the making. Life will go on at Storrs and the Connecticut basketball program will continue to develop. However, neither may be the same without Henefeld.

SCOTT BURRELL (6-5, 201 lbs., SO, F, #24, 8.2 ppg, 5.5 rpg, 57 assists, 60 steals, 30 blocked shots, Hamden HS/Hamden, Conn.) In all of the excitement that followed Tate George's buzzer-beater against Clemson in the NCAA East Region semifinal, few remember that it was Scott Burrell who had riffled the full court assists which enabled George to make the biggest shot in Connecticut basketball history. Burrell's freshman season was typical of that play —behind the scenes, but always a factor.

There was a question if Burrell would ever play basketball at Connecticut. Prior to his freshman year, Burrell, one of the premier pitchers in high school baseball, was the top draft choice of the Seattle Mariners. He turned down a reported six-figure contract to play basketball at Connecticut. Burrell was drafted again, by the Toronto Blue Jays, in the last spring's major league draft and pitched over the summer in the Blue Jays' minor league system.

"He basically hung up his sneakers and played baseball from April to September. Chris (Smith) was up here playing basketball until 3, 4 in the morning during the summer," said Calhoun. "And here's this guy playing baseball and Nintendo."

Despite the fact that Burrell is one of the few Big East level players who also seriously pursue another sport, he was productive as a freshman and scored a season-high 18 points during a loss at Connecticut and also pulled down 15 rebounds against Clemson in the NCAA tournament. He is a lanky player with outstanding quickness and excellent leaping ability. "He's (Burrell) a very good defensive player and he will be a good passer and ballhandler as he works at it," Calhoun said.

Burrell worked his way into the starting lineup towards the end of the season, he started 20 games and averaged 25.8 minutes per game, and should be in the starting lineup when fall practice begins. With the departure of George and Henefeld, Burrell will be looked to for increased scoring as well as continued solid play on the defensive end of the court. His rebounding will also be important in triggering the Huskies' fast break. His play landed him on the Big East all-rookie team last season and his continued development could land him on the All-Big East team, maybe as soon as this season.

As long as Burrell returns to Storrs each fall after pitching minor league ball, Calhoun won't mind if he plays baseball and Nintendo all summer and stays out of the gym.

DAN CYRULIK (7-1, 251 lbs., JR, C, #55, 3.8 ppg, 3.5 rpg, 9 assists, 13 steals, 8 blocked shots, North HS/Williamsville, N.Y.) Cyrulik started 12 games for the Huskies last season and looks to have a much increased role on this year's squad due to the loss of Henefeld in the frontcourt. Cyrulik continued to develop his low post game last season and was fairly effective for Connecticut when called upon. His bulk was needed to spell Rod Sellers in the middle and to combat Alonzo Mourning, Dikembe Mutombo and the other front line beasts of the Big East. With the departure of Henefeld, Calhoun may opt to move Sellers to the power forward spot in time and insert Cyrulik in the middle. However, Cyrulik may not be ready to assume much responsibility. He was effective for short spurts last season, but he may be too slow and immobile to run with his counterparts in the Big East for more than the 12.7 minutes per game he averaged last year.

Cyrulik scored a season-high 18 points in Connecticut's season opening loss to Texas A&M, at the Great Alaska Shootout. Also, in the inaugural game at the Gampel Pavilion on Connecticut's Storrs campus, Cyrulik scored 13 points and grabbed a season-high 10 rebounds in a 72-58 win over St. John's. They may have helped set a tone as the Huskies were undefeated at Gampel last year. Cyrulik does have solid low post scoring moves and Calhoun will continue to look to him for offense off the bench. However, Cyrulik must improve his quickness and agility if he is to move to the next level.

LYMAN DePRIEST (6-5, 212 lbs., SR, F, #23, 3.2 ppg, 2.6 rpg, 19 assists, 37 steals, 7 blocked shots, Highland Park HS/Highland Park, Mich.) DePriest was a defensive specialist for the Huskies last season and may get a chance to start this fall. He has extreme quickness and outstanding leaping ability which makes him a perfect match for Calhoun's full court pressure defense. Unfortunately, DePriest is not an exceptional shooter or ballhandler and that may end up hurting his chances to move into the starting five. He scored a season-high nine points in Connecticut's 70-59 triumph over Syracuse. More importantly, he came off the bench to contribute five and six-rebound nights on numerous occasions.

As a freshman, DePriest had one of the highlights of his career against high scoring All-America guard Dana Barros of Boston College. In the second half of the NIT semifinals, DePriest chased Barros all over the court and allowed the Eagle star just two points after a 22-point first half.

DePriest's greatest asset is his quickness. He is a superior defensive player and because of that, he will see action. However, with the loss of George and Henefeld, Calhoun will need to get additional scoring from someone. DePriest is not that someone. He will play a great deal and may even start in situations, but look for him to be one of the first Huskies off the bench.

JOHN GWYNN (6-0, 190 lbs., SR, G, #15, 10.6 ppg, 1.7 rpg, 27 assists, 30 steals, DeMatha HS/Hillcrest Heights, Md.) Gwynn was outstanding for Connecticut last season. Nicknamed "Microwave" due to the similarity in style of play with Detroit Piston Vinnie Johnson, Gwynn was one of the best offensive sparkplugs in the nation last season. Despite averaging only 17 minutes of action per contest, Gwynn was still able to manage a 10.6 scoring average. From three-point range, Gwynn shot 34.9 percent on the season but improved to 42.9 percent during Big

East play. With his outstanding quickness and strength, he was also a capable defensive replacement. For his play in the Big East tournament championship game against Syracuse, in which he scored 16 points in 12 minutes, Gwynn was named to the Big East all-tournament team. Gwynn's season-high came in an 89-67 win over Boston College when he knocked home 18 points. In Connecticut's season ending game in the NCAA tournament against Duke, Gwynn came off the bench and pumped in 15 points and grabbed four rebounds in the Huskies' heartbreaking 79-78 overtime loss to the Blue Devils.

As effective as Gwynn was coming off the bench last year, Calhoun will need to start him this year. Gwynn's scoring ability and quickness will be needed to offset the loss of Tate George in the Connecticut backcourt, both offensively and defensively.

OLIVER MACKLIN (6-2, 175 lbs., SO, G, #11, 0.7 ppg, 0.4 rpg, 1 steal, Notre Dame HS/Bridgeport, Conn.) Macklin played very little during his freshman year at Storrs, but that was expected with the glut in the Connecticut backcourt. He was an honorable mention all-state selection in Connecticut two years ago and turned down several Division I offers in order to walk-on at Connecticut. He saw action in only 20 games for the Huskies last season, but his minutes should increase this season. Macklin is a quick, slashing point guard who fits well in the Calhoun's transition game.

STEVE PIKIELL (6-4, 195 lbs., SR, G, #21, 0.9 ppg, 0.5 rpg, 11 assists, 5 steals, St. Paul HS/Bristol, Conn.) Pikiell has had a heartbreaking career at Connecticut. As a freshman he scored 27 points against Boston College in a Big East tournament game, but he has been unable to fulfill that promise over the last three seasons. Finally, it seems that Pikiell has overcome a troublesome shoulder injury and looks to finally make a season-long contribution to the Huskies. Pikiell is an excellent shooter who will see a considerable amount of action if he stays healthy. Although he probably won't start, Pikiell will be a valuable reserve and may assume John Gwynn's role as the first guard off the bench.

Pikiell was a co-captain of the 1989-90 team and will be in graduate school this season while taking advantage of a medical redshirt year. He performed well and injury free during the summer as a member of a Big East Conference all-star team touring Finland and the Soviet Union. A healthy Steve Pikiell will go a long way towards compensating for the losses of George and Henefeld.

TIM PIKIELL (6-4, 180 lbs., JR, G, #31, 0.0 ppg, 0.3 rpg, 2 assist, St. Paul HS/Bristol, Conn.) The younger Pikiell brother saw time in only 12 games for Connecticut last year and doesn't look to improve on that mark considerably this season. He will be a deep reserve in the Huskie backcourt.

ROD SELLERS (6-9, 224 lbs., JR, C/F, #22, 8.2 ppg, 5.3 rpg, 16 assists, 27 steals, 31 blocks, Wilson HS/Florence, S.C.) Sellers returns to start in the middle for Connecticut after an outstanding sophomore season which saw him start 35 games. Sellers saw action in all 37 games despite battling a knee injury during the final few weeks of the season. He has outstanding quickness for his size and is an excellent defensive player who often outplays taller and larger opponents. Sellers is also an aggressive rebounder with great instincts around the hoop once the ball is in the air. He hit for a season-high 22 points in a 95-55 win over Maine and scored in double figures 14 times for the Huskies last year. Sellers also pulled down a season-high nine rebounds on three different occasions. When it was crunch time, Sellers often excelled. Against Boston College in the final game of the regular season, Sellers knocked home 16 points and grabbed eight rebounds in a Connecticut victory. The win enabled Connecticut to tie for the school's first regular season Big East Conference crown. Although still hobbling from his knee injury, Sellers managed to collect seven rebounds against Boston University in the first round of the NCAA East Region.

Sellers was the leading scorer for the Big East all-star squad that toured Finland and the Soviet Union over the summer. He averaged 15 points per game on the tour and was completely recovered from his late season knee problems. Sellers looks to take on an expanded role in the Connecticut offense if focus shifts from the backcourt to the front. With a full season as a starter now behind him, Sellers should continue to blossom. Calhoun will be expecting continued stellar defensive play and he hopes that by season's end Sellers will be recognized for his offensive talents as well.

CHRIS SMITH (6-2, 175 lbs., JR, G, #13, 17.2 ppg, 2.5 rpg, 132 assists, 63 steals, 7 blocked shots, Kolbe Catholic HS/Bridgeport, Conn.) Simply stated, Chris Smith is an All-America caliber guard, one of the very best in the entire nation. After last season's performance, who could argue with that assessment? Smith, with his quick release and often deadly jumper, was an offensive leader for the nation's surprise team. He scored 635 points (the most ever by a Connecticut sophomore and No. 3 on the all-time Connecticut single-season list), earned Big East tournament MVP honors and also received all-tournament recognition in the NCAA East Region.

"I've never seen anybody do the things with a basketball that Smitty can do," said Calhoun. "Plus, straight up on the ball, he's as good a defender as I've ever coached."

Smith has excellent quickness and is a perfect lead player in Calhoun's transition game. He is a decent shooter from the floor (41.7 percent) and better from the line (81.1 percent). Smith poured home a season-high 28 points against Pitt early in the Big East campaign and came up with up with 24 and 20 three-point efforts against California and Clemson in Connecticut's second and third round NCAA tournament East Region games. He also dished out a season high of nine assists against Howard University early in the year.

Make no mistake, with Henefeld and George gone, this is now Chris Smith's team. He is an outstanding leader who is certain to benefit from a season spent with the U.S. National team that competed in the Goodwill Games in Seattle and the World Basketball Championships in Buenos Aires, Argentina.

Smith hails from Bridgeport, Conn., which in the past has produced some pretty fair talent. John Bagley, Wes Matthews, Frank Oleynick, Charles Smith (Pitt) and John Garris were all NBA talents who came from this port city on Connecticut's southern coast. Chris Smith could eventually be better than all the players who have proceeded him from Bridgeport. Calhoun will be expecting increased scoring from Smith and there is no doubt he is up to the task. The Huskies will again employ their patented full court pressure defense with Smith manning the point. He should be in store for a banner year. Expect many post-season honors for Smith, the least being first-team All-Big East.

MARK SUHR (7-1, 242 lbs., JR, C, #30, 0.8 ppg, 0.5 rpg, 1 steal, Cologne, Germany & Lake Tahoe HS/Lake Tahoe, Calif.) Suhr, a native of Germany, saw only 30 minutes of action last year. That came after a total of only four minutes playing time in the 1988-89 season. Needless to say, Suhr does not figure as a major factor for the Huskies.

Suhr sat out the 1987-88 season at Connecticut after being sidelined by Proposition 48. Despite being an excellent student in high school, Suhr was handicapped in taking the standardized tests because he had difficulty translating and answering the questions in English within the allotted time. Despite maintaining a 3.75 grade point average as a freshman at Connecticut, the NCAA turned down his appeal for an additional year of eligibility. He has gained 40 pounds since coming to Connecticut but still lags behind his teammates in terms of basketball ability and experience.

TORAINO WALKER (6-6, 225 lbs., SO, F, #42, 2.7 ppg, 2.8 rpg, 13 assists, 6 blocked shots, 14 steals, Orlando, Fla. & Oak Hill Academy/Mouth of Wilson, Va.) In Connecticut's season of surprises, freshman forward Toraino Walker was one of the most pleasant. He is a solidly built power forward who played a major role for the Huskies in both the Big East and NCAA tournaments at the conclusion of the season. Walker scored 11 points, grabbed six rebounds and had four steals during Connecticut's victory over Syracuse in the Big East championship game. He also contributed excellent defense for the Huskies. Walker helped limit Syracuse's Derrick Coleman, the first player chosen in the NBA draft, to only five total shots and 13 points during the game.

Walker is blessed with excellent quickness and should contribute in a major way. With Sellers and Burrell providing the majority of the frontcourt scoring, Walker could develop into a rebounding machine. He has the natural instincts to go along with solid low post moves.

Don't be surprised if Walker starts for the Huskies at power forward. Although Connecticut would be extremely small across the front line (6-9 Sellers, 6-5 Burrell and 6-6 Walker), this trio would form one of the quickest, most athletic frontcourts in the entire nation. In the overall scheme that Calhoun hopes to develop, Connecticut, like last season, would be a quick, defensive-oriented unit relying on the fast break and full court defensive pressure. Walker makes sense in this alignment.

MURRAY WILLIAMS (6-6, 188 lbs., SR, F, #20, 3.3 ppg, 1.9 rpg, 28 assists, 21 steals, 5 blocked shots, Torrington HS/Torrington, Conn.) It has been a tough two years for Murray Williams. His season two years ago was marred by mononucleosis and strep throat which rendered him ineffective for a good part of the year. Last season, nagging injuries at the beginning of the season kept him from getting on track. Although Williams started seven ball games during the middle of the season, he was eventually replaced by Lyman DePriest in the starting five and saw little action after that. Williams has excellent quickness and is a solid defensive player. In the past Calhoun has said, "Williams has the quickest feet in the Big East." He started 20 games as a freshman on Connecticut's NIT championship team. If healthy, Williams will be a contributor at the small forward spot, but Burrell and DePriest are ahead of him at this point. Williams was one of Calhoun's first recruits when he took over Connecticut and both have experienced the meteoric rise of the Huskies. Williams is a Calhoun favorite and will get quality playing time, but the younger players up front will make it tough on him.

★ NEWCOMERS ★

SHAWN ELLISON (6-7, 211 lbs., FR, F, 20.0 ppg, 14.0 rpg, 6.0 apg, 2.0 stpg, Farmington HS/Hartford, Conn.) A solid forward prospect who decided to stay at home and play for the Huskies. The Hartford native was a first-team All-Connecticut selection and many thought he was the best player in the state last year. He is yet another Husky who has excellent quickness and can score around the basket. He is an up and coming talent who should fit into the Connecticut system well.

Ellison is an important recruit for Calhoun. Signing Ellison showed that Calhoun continues to succeed in his plan to retain the top in-state talent.

GILAD KATZ (6-2, 190 lbs., JR, G, Tel Aviv, Israel) Calhoun cashed in on Israeli import Nadav Henefeld last year and is hoping that point guard Gilad Katz will be another hit. Katz has played with the Israeli National team in the past and comes to Connecticut with two years of eligibility remaining.

"He handles the ball very good. His best point is when he runs the fast break. He is a very strong floor guard who can post up. He is a good perimeter shooter. And a very hard worker," said Henefeld about fellow countryman Katz.

★ QUESTIONS ★

Replacing George and Henefeld? The loss of George to the NBA and Henefeld to the Maccabi of Tel Aviv team in his native Israel strips Connecticut of two of its three best players from a year ago. All-America guard Chris Smith is back, but the leadership, consistency and defensive ability of George and Henefeld will be missed considerably.

Overall team height? This is a relatively small team with the exception of 7-1 Dan Cyrulik, but what it lacks in height it more than makes up for in team speed. The Huskies will try to run and trap their opposition into submission much like they did last year, not rely on inside dominance. That game plan was highly successful last season, but will Connecticut opponents be ready for it this time around?

★ STRENGTHS ★

Jim Calhoun! He wasn't a household name before last year, but he has been around for 18 years as a college coach and has been a consistent winner at every stop. Georgetown's John Thompson said of Calhoun last year, "In 18 years, I've never seen a more exceptional coaching job than the one Jim Calhoun has done this (last) year. I heard some things about that man before I met him. The way he has blended his young people and the way they play so consistently hard, well, the chemistry of his team is really amazing."

Chris Smith! Smith is an all-everything guard. With the exception of Kenny Anderson of Georgia Tech and Michigan State's Steve Smith, Chris Smith may arguably be the best guard in the country. He is a perfect player for Calhoun's defensive system. Smith is also an excellent ballhandler, has fine court vision and plays with intelligence.

Overall team quickness! This is one of the quickest teams in the country, if not the quickest. Smith, Gwynn, Burrell, Sellers, DePriest and Williams are extremely swift players and all are excellent on the defensive end of the court.

★ BLUE RIBBON ANALYSIS ★

"Everyone associated with Connecticut basketball realizes the 1989-90 season was a very special period in our proud basketball history. We're not looking to duplicate or improve on last season," said Connecticut coach Jim Calhoun. "You probably have put those achievements behind us and now we start all over again, trying to make 1990-91 it's own special season. Regardless of the expectations of our fans or the media, we'll set our own goals before the season starts and attempt to reach them."

Calhoun begins his fifth season at Connecticut with a team that has the potential to put together another special season. This Husky story begins with junior guard Chris Smith. He had an excellent sophomore season and was at or near the top in every statistical category for the Huskies last year. Smith will look to take over more of the scoring role and be expected to improve his leadership qualities. Smith will have to come through in a big way as Connecticut is sure to miss starters Tate George and Nadav Henefeld. Both had outstanding seasons and will be remembered for decades to come as two of the finest players in Connecticut history.

John Gwynn, last year's super sub, will move into the backcourt on a starting basis. Fifth-year senior Steve Pikiell is an excellent outside shooter, but he has been ineffective for the past three years due to a shoulder problem.

The small forward spot is well manned for Connecticut. Incumbent Scott Burrell, Lyman DePriest and Murray Williams will all see time in Calhoun's rotation. After an excellent freshman season, Burrell should see the majority of time, but don't count out Williams. Williams, a senior, has battled back from injuries and is a Calhoun favorite. If Burrell falters, look for Williams to start. DePriest flourished in a defensive specialist role for the Huskies last season and will likely fill that role again. In the pivot, Rod Sellers will start after healing his knee over the summer. Sellers started 35 games for the Huskies last year and impressed with his quickness around the basket and defensive tenacity. Junior Dan Cyrulik, the tallest player on the team at 7-1, will also see increased playing time. He has solid post moves and good bulk. However, Cyrulik is still slow and lacks the ability required to start in Calhoun's fast paced transition game.

The power forward position looks to be filled by sophomore Toraino Walker. He came on with solid performances in the Big East and NCAA tournaments and has the ability to be a quality frontcourt player in the Big East.

With the exception of Gwynn, Williams and DePriest, Calhoun's rotation consists of four juniors, three sophomores and one freshman. Almost all are similar athletes. The Huskies are made up of interchangeable parts that never allow the overall machine to break down. Almost all of the Huskies are quick, have exceptional leaping ability and play great defense. All have the characteristics needed to play a nonstop pressure, transition game. As Connecticut showed last season, this style of play can be highly successful. The losses of George and Henefeld are significant, but Connecticut will be able to prosper again this year.

"When we started building our program five years ago, we wanted to be a team that year after year was a consistent winner on the national level. We were 31-6 last season and 69-33 during the past three seasons," Calhoun said. "We hope to sustain our recent success and keep proving that Connecticut basketball is among the top programs on the Division I level."

The Huskies will again be among the top programs on the Division I level this season. With a starting lineup that includes two juniors and two sophomores, Connecticut looks to attain that status for the next couple of seasons as well. The Huskies look to be in a four team race for the top spot in the Big East with perennial favorites Syracuse, Georgetown plus Pitt. Although those teams may have better individual stars such as Alonzo Mourning and Dikembe Mutombo at Georgetown, Billy Owens at Syracuse and Brian Shorter at Pitt, Connecticut may have the better team. At least 20 wins and a tournament berth seem to be a lock for the Huskies and Connecticut will finish no lower than fourth in the Big East. Chris Smith and Jim Calhoun will see to it.

LAST SEASON		1990-91 CONNECTICUT SCHEDULE		
#Texas A&M	81-92	Nov.	24	College of Charleston (SC)
#Auburn	95-81		27	University of Hartford
#Florida State	63-60		29	@Yale
Yale	76-50	Dec.	6	#@North Carolina
Howard University	78-59		9	@Maine
##Maryland	87-65		12	New Hampshire
Univ. of Hartford	79-54		23	##Fairfield
Maine	95-55		28-29	*Connecticut Mutual Classic
Villanova	57-64			
Southern Connecticut	100-37	Jan.	2	@Boston College
###St. Joseph's	83-58		5	Pitt
###Mississippi State	84-68		8	@Villanova
@St. John's	62-93		10	Central Connecticut
Pitt	79-61		12 or 13	St. John's
@Villanova	71-54		16	@Syracuse
@Seton Hall	79-76		19	##Providence
Syracuse	70-59		22	@St. John's
Georgetown	70-65		26	@Seton Hall
Central Connecticut			28	##Syracuse
State	99-77	Feb.	2	Villanova
St. John's	72-58		5	Boston College
@Massachusetts	94-75		11	##Georgetown
@Providence	92-77		16	North Carolina State
Fairfield	74-39		19	@Providence
@Syracuse	86-90		23	@Georgetown
@Pitt	80-77		27	Seton Hall
Boston College	89-67	Mar.	2	@Pitt
Providence	75-72OT		7-10	**Big East Tournament
Seton Hall	79-57			
@Georgetown	64-84			
@Boston College	95-74	@ Road Games		
*Seton Hall	70-58	# ACC/Big East Challenge		
*Georgetown	65-60	## Hartford, CT		
*Syracuse	78-75	* Hartford, CT (Lafayette, Rhode Island		
**Boston University	76-52	& William & Mary)		
**California	74-54	** Madison Square Garden, New York,		
***Clemson	71-70	NY		
***Duke	78-79OT			

@ Road Games
# Great Alaska Shootout, Anchorage, AK
ACC/Big East Challenge, Hartford, CT
Connecticut Mutual Classic, Hartford, CT
* Big East Tournament, Madison Square Garden, New York, NY
** NCAA Tournament, Hartford, CT
*** NCAA Tournament, East Rutherford, NJ

NOTES: Connecticut's top recruit, 6-2 guard Richie Ashmeade from Holy Cross HS in Queens, N.Y., did not pass NCAA academic requirements. Ashmeade will attend St. Thomas More Prep in Oakdale, Conn. He still plans to attend Connecticut next year . . . The Huskies were 5-0 in their new Gampel Pavilion last season . . . CBS will later determine if the St. John's game will be played on Jan. 12 or 13.

DePAUL

LAST SEASON: 20-15
STARTERS LOST: 0
STARTERS RETURNING: 5
CONFERENCE: INDEPENDENT
LOCATION: CHICAGO, IL
HOME FLOOR: ROSEMONT
   HORIZON (17,500)
NICKNAME: BLUE DEMONS
COLORS: ROYAL BLUE
   AND SCARLET

★ COACH'S PROFILE ★

JOEY MEYER (Record at DePaul, 128-61.) After six years on the job, Joey Meyer is clearly out of the shadow of his father, Ray Meyer, who was the Blue Demons' coach for 42 straight years. The younger Meyer ranks second to his father on DePaul's all-time coaching victory list. In each of his six years as DePaul's head coach, Meyer has put the Blue Demons into post-season play. He is only the second NCAA Division I coach to open his career with as many as five straight berths in the NCAA tournament.

The 41-year-old Meyer has been around DePaul since he was an infant. He not only followed his father's teams as a youngster, but graduated from DePaul Academy High School. He then signed with the Blue Demons and scored 1,233 points in his college career and was the team captain as a senior in 1970-71. After graduation, Meyer became the freshman coach for one season. He followed with one year as junior varsity coach and then became a varsity assistant in 1973-74. Meyer was an assistant for 11 years under his father and during that time the Blue Demons went 246-70 (.778) and reached the NCAA tournament seven times.

While working as an assistant under his father, Joey became well known as a recruiter. DePaul's talent pool had been drying up before he aggressively pursued and signed some top notch talent. Meyer is responsible for recruiting Dave Corzine, Mark Aguirre and Terry Cummings, all of whom went on to long careers in the NBA. He also made DePaul a presence in recruiting the talented inner-city areas of Chicago. After the Blue Demons began to get a national profile in the mid to late '70s, Meyer expanded his recruiting efforts nationally.

So far, in his six year tenure at DePaul, Meyer has shown that he is not married to any one style of play. He believes quickness is the most important attribute a successful basketball player can possess. Early last year, Meyer tried to implement an up-tempo, pressing style of play. However, DePaul was just 3-7 after 10 games and Meyer pulled back the press and the Blue Demons were 17-8 during the rest of the season.

"The pot of gold at the end of the rainbow. Look how much the NCAA television package brings in, and how much each school picks up by just being in the tournament," Meyer told *The Associated Press*. "Think of college basketball like a competitive business; think of how many people in big-money business cut corners, and how it's not hard to see where the temptation is coming from."

Meyer has been a part of DePaul basketball for so long that since he became involved in the program as a player in 1967, DePaul is 446-206 (.684). He has been a part of 41 percent of all games ever won by the Blue Demons.

"As a coach, you are very similar to a parent. You want to prepare them for life, like a parent does. You have to know what they are about. Sometimes, I think fans out there see 6-foot-9, 200-pound 'men' and forget they are only 18 or 19 years old. They have girl problems, school problems and being away from home problems just like any other 18 or 19 year old. You can relate back to when you were that age. There's a time to put your arm around their back and a time to kick them in the behind. It's just like being a parent."

There is no coach in the country who has stronger ties to the school he works at than Meyer does to DePaul. He watched the Blue Demons play in practice as a youngster, played in the program (Meyer was once the No. 4 scorer in DePaul history and now ranks 14th) and has never coached anywhere else. It is difficult to imagine Joey Meyer coaching any other team than the DePaul Blue Demons. His job is not in any danger and Meyer should have an outstanding team this year. The biggest concern he and DePaul officials will face in the near future is keeping DePaul a national power in an era where Independents are virtually extinct. Only DePaul and Notre Dame remain as national level programs without conference affiliations. While both schools do not have problems getting into the NCAA tournament, even with as few as 16 wins, regularly make national television appearances and turn a considerable profit from their programs, neither has been dominant nationally in the last five years. Even in this age of parity, teams from the power conferences dominate the college game. No Independent has been to the Final Four since DePaul appeared in 1979. The Blue Demons can be successful but Meyer and school officials will soon have to face the fact that the Independent road is getting increasingly more difficult.

★ PLAYERS NOT RETURNING ★

DERYL CUNNINGHAM (6-7, F, 0.8 ppg, 1.3 rpg, 3 assists, 3 steals, 6 blocked shots) A highly regarded high school All-America from Isiah Thomas' alma mater, St. Joseph's HS in Westchester, Ill., Cunningham came to DePaul billed as one of the Top 20 high school players in the country. However, in his freshman year, he saw only 189 minutes of action (6.8 mpg) for a mediocre 20-15 team. He was unbelievably poor 9-of-53 (.170) from the field and had a grand total of three assists. As expected, Cunningham was not happy with his role and after the season transferred to Kansas State. Despite his big reputation coming out of high school; Cunningham will not be missed.

JAMES HAMBY (7-1, C, 2.1 ppg, 2.3 rpg, 5 assists, 3 steals, 28 blocked shots) Hamby started four games in the pivot for DePaul and averaged 9.5 minutes per game. He provided some important size for the Blue Demons but Meyer can compensate for his departure as two more talented center prospects —6-9 JC transfer Jeff Sterns and 6-8 freshman Michael Ravizee —have joined the team. Hamby is playing professionally in Portugal this year.

CURTIS JACKSON (6-10, C, 1.0 ppg, 0.7 rpg, 1 blocked shot) Jackson was a seldom used reserve who played for a total of 21 minutes last year in 10 games. His loss is not a major blow to the Blue Demons.

Jackson had a bit part in a movie, *Heaven is a Playground*. The movie was filmed over the summer in Chicago and is based on a book published in 1976 and written by a *Sports Illustrator* staff writer Rick Telander. Former Loyola Marymount star Bo Kimble had a major part in the film.

CHARLES SOWELL (6-10, C, 1.5 ppg, 2.6 rpg, 17 assists, 10 steals, 30 blocked shots) Sowell was the most productive of the three big men who have left the DePaul program. He started two games and averaged 10.9 minutes per game. Sowell was second on the team in blocked shots and did lend a physical, defensive presence inside.

Like teammate James Hamby, Sowell is playing professionally in Portugal.

B. J. TYLER (6-1, G, 2.9 ppg, 0.9 rpg, 36 assists, 17 steals, 2 blocked shots) One of the most highly touted guards to ever sign with DePaul, Tyler started four games and played in 17 before being suspended from the team for walking out of a practice. The Port Arthur, Tex., native never returned to the Blue Demons and eventually transferred to Texas where he will have three years of eligibility beginning in the 1991-92 season. Basically, Tyler is not considered a serious loss as the Blue Demons played most of the second half of the season without him.

While Tyler could become a quality player at Texas, it is interesting to note his statistics at DePaul. Tyler shot just .333 from the floor and .167 from three-point range. He had 36 assists but 42 turnovers. Tyler was one of the most highly touted guards in the country two years ago. His trouble showed just how difficult it is for most highly regarded freshmen to come in and make an immediate, major impact. Except for the superstars, and a few fortunate others, it takes most players some time to become accustomed to major college basketball no matter how highly they were regarded in high school.

★ RETURNING PLAYERS ★

DAVID BOOTH (6-7, 192 lbs., JR, F, #30, 16.9 ppg, 6.1 rpg, 68 assists, 48 steals, 45 blocked shots, Manual HS/Peoria, Ill.) The Blue Demons' leading scorer and third-best rebounder last year, Booth is only the third DePaul player to score more than 900 points by the end of his sophomore year. In fact, only Mark Aguirre scored more points as a DePaul sophomore. He was named the *Sports Illustrated* national player of the week (Jan. 22-28) after scoring 37 points, pulling down seven rebounds and making three steals in a victory over Louisville.

Booth scored at least 20 points 10 times as a sophomore. He has been particularly effective against Notre Dame. He scored DePaul's first 14 points, 26 overall, in a win over Notre Dame last year. He had 23 points, seven rebounds and two assists at Notre Dame as a freshman. He had a tendency to get a little out of control in pressure situations last year, hoisting some bad shots, but Booth is one of the most talented small forwards in the country. He has good range on his shot, although he generally is more effective as a wide open three-point shooter when not closely guarded, and is a true slasher who can cut up defenses off the dribble. He also led DePaul in blocked shots last year.

In the off-season, Booth was able to put on much needed weight. He weighed an anemic 178 pounds at the end of last year and is now up to 192 pounds. With two years experience under his belt and added bulk and strength, Booth could be a monster this year. He definitely is DePaul's top gun.

TERRY DAVIS (6-4, 195 lbs., SO, G, #25, 9.8 ppg, 3.4 rpg, 45 assists, 16 steals, 3 blocked shots, Tri-Cities HS/College Park, Ga.) DePaul appeared set in the backcourt for four years last fall with the arrival of two former big time high school All-Americas —B. J. Tyler and Terry Davis. While Tyler struggled, became frustrated and eventually left the program, Davis had one of the best freshmen years ever at DePaul. He started 26 games, averaged 26.7 minutes per game and finished third on the team in scoring. Only seven DePaul freshmen have averaged more points per game (six have gone on to play in the NBA and the seventh is David

Booth). The Blue Demons were 17-9 with Davis in the starting lineup.

"When watching Davis play, it's not easy to tell he's only a freshman. He operates with upperclass cool and rarely strays from where he is supposed to be. In addition, Davis' build belies his age of 18," wrote Scott Gregor of the Arlington, Ill., *Daily Herald*.

Davis is extremely strong and uses his strength to his advantage, posting up smaller guards. He hit a respectable 23-of-61 three-pointers (.377) for a freshman. That percentage is misleading because he was 1-for-10 from three-point range in one early season game. Davis has a great deal of confidence and a past track record of improvement. He has the attitude, the maturity and physical capabilities necessary to become an outstanding guard. If Davis keeps improving he will certainly one day go down as one of the premier guards ever to play at DePaul.

MELVON FOSTER (6-3, 185 lbs., SR, G, #20, 6.2 ppg, 3.2 rpg, 127 assists, 48 steals, 8 blocked shots, Harper HS/Chicago, Ill.) When B. J. Tyler was suspended, Foster took over at point guard. He was respectable, not great, at the position as point guard is not his natural spot. Foster was a frontcourt player in high school who had to adjust to the backcourt in college. He also sat out his first year which affected his development.

Foster is a hard worker who led DePaul in assists and tied for the team lead in steals. However, Foster is a limited outside shooter who made only .364 of his field goal attempts and attempted only 3 three-pointers all year. He also was a .625 shooter from the line.

Foster leads all active players on the team in career starts (52) and started all 35 games last year. DePaul was 17-9 with him as the starting point guard last year. He is also one of the team's top defensive players.

Meyer lured former Loyola Rambler Joe Daughrity back home to Chicago from Oxnard (Calif.) JC and he is a true lead guard. Daughrity will take some of the ball-handling load off of Foster and allow him to play at his natural second guard spot.

BILL HEPPNER (6-9, 225 lbs., JR, S/C, #33, 0.7 ppg, 0.8 rpg, 2 assists, 2 steals, 1 blocked shot, Central HS/Crystal Lake, Ill.) Heppner came to DePaul as one of the most highly rated players in the country. He was ranked third among the nation's post players by *Basketball Weekly* and was a consensus national Top 25 pick. However, his role in college has been rather limited so far. Heppner played in 20 games for a total of 148 minutes as a freshman in 1987-88. He redshirted in the 1988-89 season following knee surgery. Last year, Heppner played in 19 games for a total of 81 minutes. Heppner is regarded as one of the better athletes on the DePaul team. He runs the floor well and is a fine leaper. He also has a decent shooting touch but just has not been able to get much accomplished. The DePaul frontcourt has three starters returning and forward Curtis Price is back after redshirting last year. Newcomers Jeff Stern and Michael Ravizee are highly regarded so it is difficult to see how Heppner's playing time will increase appreciably.

KEVIN HOLLAND (6-8, 215 lbs., SR, F, #15, 8.2 ppg, 7.2 rpg, 45 assists, 45 steals, 20 blocked shots, Cerritos HS/Cerritos, Calif.) Holland has started 43 of the last 44 games he has played in. He leads the current team in career rebounds and minutes played. The team captain of this year's edition of the Blue Demons, Holland was the No. 2 rebounder on the squad behind Stephen Howard. He is a fine leaper, tenacious on the boards and one of DePaul's better jump shooters.

Holland was a limited contributor as a freshman in 1986-87, his role increased dramatically the following season, but he redshirted in 1988-89 campaign due to a back problem. The back injury was not a problem last year as Holland came back strong.

Holland's stability and rebounding will be crucial if DePaul is to get back into the NCAA tournament.

STEPHEN HOWARD (6-9, 225 lbs., JR, C/F, #21, 14.4 ppg, 8.1 rpg, 51 assists, 39 steals, 23 blocked shots, Bishop Lynch HS/Dallas, Tex.) Howard is not only a fine player but is one of the premier student/athletes in big time college basketball. Howard is a pre-law major with a 3.53 grade point average. He was named to the GTE Academic All-America team last year. He was also the winner of the Champion Dodge NIT scholar athlete award. Howard also found time to lead DePaul in rebounding last year.

"So all of these people who don't know me think I'm this nerd with glasses," Howard said about his reputation as a superior student. "People are telling me, 'They're making you out to be this big nerd on TV.' I'm definitely far from that. I just know when to put stuff in perspective. I guess I know when it's time to buckle down and study."

Howard came on strong last year replacing the rebounding void left by the departure of Stanley Brundy. Howard improved his inside, post-up moves. He is also a good passer and an excellent shooter with good range. Howard has the size and strength to work down low against big time opposition.

He scored the winning basket with one second left in DePaul's 61-59 win over Cincinnati in the second round of the NIT last March. He also came through with 28 points at UCLA, 20 points and 11 rebounds against La Salle and 26 points, including the game winning dunk at the buzzer, in DePaul's 63-62 win at Notre Dame. Howard had 28 double figure scoring performances as a sophomore after 16 as a freshman. DePaul was 31-13 when he scores at least 10 points.

With Howard, Holland and Booth all returning up front, Curtis Price coming back after a year on a sidelines and newcomers Jeff Stern and Michael Ravizee arriving, DePaul should have an excellent power game up front.

CHUCK MURPHY (6-1, 165 lbs., JR, G, #12, 5.2 ppg, 1.6 rpg, 94 assists, 22 steals, 4 blocked shots, St. Joseph's HS/Westchester, Ill.) Murphy has been a part-time starter at point guard the past two years for DePaul. He started 12 games as a freshman and five last year, but his playing time rose from 500 minutes as a freshman to 598 as a sophomore. Murphy is a decent shooter who leads all current Blue Demons in three-point field goals made (51).

Murphy had 10 points and nine assists against Creighton last year. He scored at least 10 points in eight of the last 15 games after scoring that many only four times in his first 50 college games. DePaul was 9-3 in his career when Murphy scores at least 10 points. He was a walk-on at the beginning of his freshman year before earning a scholarship.

Murphy will have to hustle to keep his role as junior college transfer Joe Daughrity will make a push for a great deal of playing time at point guard.

BRAD NIEMANN (6-3, 180 lbs., JR, G, #22, Glenbrook South HS/Glenview, Ill.) Until pre-season practice begins this year, it will be impossible to determine if Niemann will be a member of the Blue Demons. He missed last season with a back injury and has not played any basketball since March, 1989. Niemann suffers from a degenerative back condition. He can play golf and is in fact an excellent golfer who won two tournaments last summer. However, he cannot take the pounding that running and jumping on a basketball court give his back.

Niemann played two years for the Blue Demons before redshirting last year. He started 17 games and averaged 8.8 points in 1988-89. Niemann's main attribute is three-point shooting. He made 67-of-154 treys (.435) in 1988-89. During that season, Niemann made 7 three-pointers against Chaminade and six against Dayton. He also knocked down .786 of his free throw attempts.

If Niemann returns, it is difficult to see how he could be at full strength after not playing competitive basketball for over 18 months. However, his perimeter shooting would be a luxury Meyer would love to have.

CURTIS PRICE (6-6, 200 lbs., SO, F, −23, St. Rita HS/Chicago, Ill.) After four games last year, Price suffered a wrist injury, underwent surgery and missed the rest of the year. He averaged 4.1 points and 3.9 rebounds as a part-time starter as a freshman in 1988-89. Price was averaging 4.3 points and 2.3 rebounds last year before being injured. He is considered perhaps the greatest leaper in DePaul history. Price is intense and is also an excellent all-around athlete. He is an improved perimeter shooter.

"The added dimension is Curtis Price who gives us great quickness inside," Meyer said when assessing the Blue Demons.

★ NEWCOMERS ★

JOE DAUGHRITY (6-0, 165 lbs., JR, G, #11, 15.3 ppg, 5.7 rpg, 5.8 apg, Crane HS/Chicago, Ill. & Oxnard CC/Oxnard, Calif.) DePaul did not have a true point after freshman B. J. Tyler was suspended last year. Even when in the lineup, Tyler's inexperience hurt DePaul. This year, the Blue Demons could have a proven floor general if JC transfer Joe Daughrity comes through.

Daughrity was one of the best players in Chicago during his days at Crane HS. He signed with Loyola, but never played for the Ramblers. Daughrity transferred to Oxnard CC in California and played one year there. He has excellent quickness, is a good leaper and handles the ball well. Daughrity is a true point guard who has always played the position.

He is a key player who could make DePaul much improved and an NCAA tournament team in 1990-91.

MICHAEL RAVIZEE (6-9, 250 lbs., FR, C/F, −55, 11.0 ppg, 13.7 rpg, Woodlawn HS/Birmingham, Ala.) DePaul is such a prominent program due to its repeated national television exposure that the Blue Demons can reach into any section of the country and pluck out a key recruit. In addition to Illinois, the DePaul roster features players from California, Texas, Georgia and now Alabama with the addition of Michael Ravizee.

The Birmingham, Ala., native was overshadowed through much of his prep career by a teammate, Cedric Moore, now a freshman at Alabama, but he established himself as a senior as one of the dominant rebounders in high school basketball. Ravizee is a tenacious rebounder who helped lead Woodlawn HS to a 32-3 record and the finals of the Alabama Class 5A tournament. He made .710 of his field goal attempts as a senior.

"Ravizee . . . will be a force in the future at DePaul," wrote Tom Goins in the *Hoop Scoop*.

His role may not be great this year as DePaul already has strong rebounders in Kevin Holland and Stephen Howard up front. However, in the future Ravizee should become one of the most dominate rebounders to ever play at DePaul.

JEFF STERN (6-9, 215 lbs., JR, C, #42, 19.0 ppg, 8.0 rpg, Waxahachie HS/Waxahachie, Tex. & South Plains CC/Levelland, Tex.) Stern is a highly regarded junior college transfer who is expected to help immediately. He was the MVP of the Western Junior College Athletic Conference in 1989-90, one year after UNLV's Larry Johnson earned that honor. Stern led his conference in blocked shots and also led the league in blocks as a freshman. He broke a backboard in a game against Howard (Tex.) JC in 1989-90.

Stern can also run the floor and score inside. He rebounds well and is a leaper. He played with a junior college all-star team that toured Yugoslavia over the summer. Stern is considered more talented than James Hamby and Charles Sowell, DePaul's chief losses up front. Meyer likes to rotate three players into twin post positions and Stern should get plenty of playing time.

Backcourt play? Meyer is concerned about his team's backcourt play. Three-point shooting is a concern due to Brad Niemann's back problem and the Blue Demons were average, at best, at point guard last year.

Low post scoring?

Size in the pivot? DePaul does not have great size in the pivot but there are some athletes who can rebound and run.

★ STRENGTHS ★

Defense! Quietly, DePaul developed into a sound defensive team last year. The Blue Demons were pressing the entire 94 feet early in the year but when Curtis Price went down with an injury, he was the point man on the press, DePaul became more of a half court defensive team and was successful.

Athletic ability up front! DePaul may not be big up front, but the Blue Demons have a strong contingent of athletes who can get off the floor and run the court.

Rebounding! The top three rebounders from last year's team return and newcomers Jeff Stern and Michael Ravizee are strong rebounders.

Returning experience! All five starters return and DePaul will be a team dominated by upperclassmen.

★ BLUE RIBBON ANALYSIS ★

The talent is there and so is the returning experience for Joey Meyer and the DePaul Blue Demons to make a return trip to the NCAA tournament. DePaul was a 20-game winner last year, but also dropped 15 games so the Blue Demons spent March in the NIT, not the NCAAs.

In order for DePaul to reduce those 15 losses, the Blue Demons will have to be a more accurate shooting team. If the team's best outside marksman, Brad Niemann, can return after missing last year with a serious back problem, and that's a huge if, DePaul will be an improved shooting club. If not, Meyer will have to count on improvement from Melvon Foster, Chuck Murphy and Terry Davis. And that may even be a bigger if.

DePaul also had more turnovers than assists (511 turnovers to 496 assists) last year and that figure has to change. Meyer is hoping that junior college transfer Joe Daughrity, a Chicago native who is returning home, can be the answer at point guard.

If the outside shooting improves, and Daughrity is the answer at point guard, DePaul could be dominating up front. There are not too many teams in the country that can boast a frontcourt lineup such as David Booth, Stephen Howard and Kevin Holland up front. Add the return of the team's best athlete, 6-6 sophomore Curtis Price, from a wrist injury, and the addition of two promising 6-9 newcomers —Jeff Stern and Michael Ravizee —and DePaul is a potential frontcourt monster.

Booth is one of the premier offensive small forwards in the country. He should be the next in a long line of DePaul players who have found work in the NBA.

There is depth in the backcourt, even if Niemann is not cleared to play, as Foster and junior Chuck Murphy have experience at point guard and sophomore Terry Davis is coming back after a fine freshman year.

"This is a unique situation for us," Meyer said. "This is having the players back and having to ask them to improve. You know where their potential lies, and you know what it will take for them to reach it. We're more familiar with having the star player gone and having to look at new players to lead in scoring and rebounding. When was the last time we had our leading scorer and leading rebounder coming back?"

The Blue Demons will be strong defensively, tough to beat on the boards and improved offensively. The schedule, as usual, is extremely demanding. However, DePaul has the talent necessary to tackle an ambitious schedule and still come up with 22 to 24 wins. This should be a much improved DePaul team. The Blue Demons are a lock to make it to the NCAA tournament this March.

LAST SEASON			
#Ohio State	71-53	@UCLA	77-87
#North Carolina State	70-63	Fordham	51-38
##St. John's	52-53	@North Carolina State	71-80
##UNLV	53-88	@Miami (FL)	66-49
Univ. of Hartford	64-56	Alabama-Birmingham	68-74
La Salle	62-83	@Notre Dame	63-62
@Houston	49-65	@St. John's	74-77
###Western Illinois	69-72	Bradley	59-48
@North Carolina	51-70	Texas	79-89
Dayton	73-84	Northern Illinois	69-51
Marquette	71-62	Notre Dame	64-59
@Florida International	91-67	*Creighton	89-72
Weber State	55-47	*Cincinnati	61-59
Loyola	71-56	*@St. Louis	47-54
@Duquesne	68-55		
Georgetown	64-74	@ Road Games	
Niagara	73-58	# Dodge NIT	
@Marquette	55-77	## Dodge NIT Final Four, Madison	
@Detroit	87-82	Square Garden, NY	
Louisville	66-62	### First Chicago Christmas Classic	
Miami (FL)	76-48	* NIT	

NOTES: DePaul will play Wisconsin-Green Bay in the first round of the Old Style Classic. The Blue Demons will take on North Carolina in the opening round of the Red Lobster Classic . . . DePaul recruit Brandon Cole, a 6-1 guard from Bloom Township HS in Chicago Heights, Ill., will sit out this season at DePaul. He was ranked as one of the Top 50 high school play-

1990-91 DEPAUL SCHEDULE				
Nov.	24	University of Hartford	20	@Notre Dame
	29	Florida International	23	@Miami (FL)
Dec.	1	@Pepperdine	Mar. 2	St. John's
	8	#Illinois State	6	Miami (FL)
	12	@Louisville	9	Notre Dame
	15	UCLA		
	21-22	##Old Style Classic	@ Road Games	
	29-30	*Red Lobster Classic	# First Chicago Christmas Classic	
Jan.	3	@Dayton	## Rosemont, IL (Oklahoma State,	
	7	Marquette	Southern Illinois & Wisconsin-Green	
	12	Houston	Gay)	
	15	@Northern Illinois	* Orlando, FL (Central Florida, North	
	19	@Texas	Carolina & Stanford)	
	23	Drake		
	26	Duquesne		
	28	@Marquette		
Feb.	3	@Georgetown		
	5	Detroit		
	9	@Bradley		
	13	@Loyola		
	16	@Niagara		

ers in the country last year and would have been a factor at point guard as a freshman . . . DePaul has won more game versus Notre Dame than any other opponent but still trails in the overall series 36-45 . . . In nine seasons at the Rosemont Horizon, the Blue Demons are 143-22 (.867) and have never failed to draw at least 150,000 fans in a season.

EAST TENNESSEE STATE

LAST SEASON: 27-7
CONFERENCE RECORD: 12-2
STARTERS LOST: 0
STARTERS RETURNING: 5
CONFERENCE: SOUTHERN
LOCATION: JOHNSON CITY, TN
HOME FLOOR:
MEMORIAL CENTER (12,000)
NICKNAM: BUCCANEERS
COLORS BLUE AND GOLD

★ COACH'S PROFILE ★

ALAN LeFORCE (First year at East Tennessee State. Career record, including high school, 392-170.) After compiling a 47-19 record at East Tennessee State the last two seasons - 27-7 a year ago - Les Robinson could have run for mayor of Johnson City and won handily. That kind of success was bound to attract attention, though, and when North Carolina State came calling last May, he reluctantly departed for new challenges at his alma mater.

ETSU officials quickly appointed Alan LeForce, formerly associate head coach, to replace Robinson. At 55, LeForce had finally realized a career-long dream of his own.

"You always set goals for yourself," LeForce said. "When I first started coaching high school ball 32 years ago, I wanted to be a Division I head coach. Along the way, I wanted to be a Division I assistant, then head coach at a small college and, finally, a Division I head coach.

"I'd worked hard at every place I went, but as time went on, I began to think my time was running out. When you get a certain age as a basketball coach, people don't seem to want you. You can be President of the United States at age 70, but if you're 55 and a basketball coach, there's something odd about that."

LeForce has no doubts he will be able to maintain the program Robinson left behind. "As far as widsom is concerned, I feel I'm a better basketball coach today than I've ever been," he said. "I feel fortunate for this opportunity. I'm ready."

Just as LeForce said, he prepared for his current job in the conventional way. The Kentucky native started as head coach at Williamsburg (Ky.) High School in 1958. After seven years, he left to become an assistant at Cumberland (Ky.) College. That led to another assistant's job, this time serving under Frank Selvy at Furman.

From Furman, LeForce went to the College of Charleston (S.C), where he served as both head basketball coach and athletic director. LeForce compiled a 138-90 record at Charleston, but missed high school coaching so much he left after nine years to become head coach at Coastal Academy in Myrtle Beach, S.C. He was 125-15 in five seasons there, and 16-9 in one season at East Cooper School in Charleston. In 1985, he left the scholastic ranks again to join Robinson at East Tennessee State.

LeForce's knowledge of the game has earned him the respect of college and high school coaches alike. "I don't think ETSU could have found a better guy to replace Les," said Western Carolina coach Gregg Blatt, who served LeForce as an assistant at the College of Charleston. "He's an outstanding tactician and I've always respected his ability to motivate his players. His teams have always played hard and played together."

The Citadel's Randy Nesbit added: "ETSU might even be better this year. Alan LeForce is an intense coach who stresses defense. With the offense they have, give them a strong defense, and they'll be tough to beat."

Robinson himself has no worries about LeForce. This isn't even the first time LeForce has replaced him. Two years ago, after Robinson had an emergency appendectomy, LeForce coached the team to the championship at a Christmas tournament in Sacremento, Calif.

"Alan LeForce is not new to the program," Robinson said. "He was a big factor in the success at East Tennessee State. He'll do a great job."

LeForce is the fourth former Robinson assistant to become a head coach in the Southern Conference. The others are Blatt, Nesbit and Furman's Butch Estes. Bobby Knight may have more former assistants who became head coaches, but no coach in the country can claim four former assistants who are head coaches in the same league.

Like the more successful former Knight assistants, LeForce will not emulate his old boss in every way. "No two coaches are alike," LeForce said, "but I've got to be very careful. I'm not going to change a lot of things. The train's going

pretty good. I don't want to slow it down or stop it."

On the contrary, LeForce, an intense, defensive-minded coach, may speeds things up with a variety of pressure defenses. "You don't win games with defense, but you can hang in there until your offense comes around," LeForce said. "We're going to be a better defensive team, because we're going to work at it more.

"Les lived and died with the passing game, which was very good to us. I'm on the other end of the spectrum. I stress defense. We're different people. Les was more of a gamesman. He thought we'd win every game, and I'm the type of guy who probably thinks we'll never win a game."

LeForce and Robinson agree the Buccaneers will be good this season, but think a tough schedule may not be reflected in the final record.

"We could be a better basketball team and not win as many games," LeForce said. "We play Brigham Young, North Carolina State, Memphis State, Cincinnati, UNC-Charlotte, George Mason twice and James Madison. That's a pretty rugged lineup when you throw in our conference, which is always tough.

"We've got to go out every day with the blue collar and work hard in practice and then work hard to get better in games. If we take care of those areas, regardless of how many games we win, we'll have been successful in my opinion."

★ PLAYERS NOT RETURNING ★

CHAD KELLER (6-8, F, 8.6 ppg, 6.2 rpg, 40 assists, 13 steals) Keller is the only player not back from a year ago, but he will be missed. A transfer from James Madison, Keller started at ETSU as a sophomore, averaging 14.2 points and 5.4 rebounds. He played in every game that season.

The next two years, Keller was asked to subordinate his skills to allow some of his teammates to score more. Keller moved willingly from a starter into the team's sixth man and averaged eight points and six rebounds in each of his last two seasons.

"Chad did a lot of things for us," LeForce said. "He came off the bench and meant so much to our ballclub with his willingness to sacrifice. He was a good rebounder and was willing to bang inside or do anything we asked him. He will be missed."

★ RETURNING PLAYERS ★

GREG DENNIS (6-11, 205 lbs., SR, C, #11, 19.7 ppg, 6.5 rpg, 53 blocked shots, 50 assists, 12 steals, Charleston HS/Charleston, W.Va.) Like Jennings, Dennis received scant Division I attention as a high school senior. In-state schools Marshall and West Virginia inexplicably showed no interest in Dennis, then a skinny, 6-7 perimeter player.

Former ETSU assistant Dave Hanners recognized potential in Dennis, and when Les Robinson, himself a native of Charleston, W.Va., went to see him play, the deal was done. Much to the dismay of all the coaches who did not recruit him, he grew four inches before he reported to the Buccaneers. Suddenly, the 6-7 perimeter player was a 6-11 center who could hit the three-point field goal as easily as score inside.

Dennis' size and agility have impressed pro scouts and initiated comparisions to the Detroit Pistons' John Salley. The NBA could definitely be in his future.

"If Greg has a good year, if he learns to play the defensive end as well as he does the offensive end, then he cold be a first round NBA draft choice," LeForce said.

Together with Jennings, Dennis gives ETSU an inside-outside combination few teams can match. Dennis runs well for a big man, shoots the jump shot like a small forward and can drive to the basket like a point guard.

Dennis joined Jennings in ETSU's starting lineup as a freshman and hasn't been dislodged since. He led the team in scoring and rebounding and was chosen the Southern Conference freshman of the year in his first season. Dennis also led the Buccaneers in scoring and rebounding as a sophomore and was a first-team All-Conference selection.

Last season, Dennis again led ETSU in scoring and rebounding and received several Player of the Year votes. He was a first-team All-Conference and All-Tournament pick.

"Greg Dennis is a gifted basketball player," Robinson said. "When I was at East Tennessee, we felt fortunate to have signed him. To get a top-notch point guard and a center in one recruiting class, well, that was a big key to our success."

Dennis is not known for his defense, but has developed into a capable shot blocker. His 52 blocks were second in the conference a year ago. "It takes a lot of pressure off me knowing Greg is inside," Jennings said. "If my man drives past me, he has to deal with Greg."

MAJOR GEER (6-1, 160 lbs., SR, G, #12, 10.0 ppg, 1.6 rpg, 65 assists, 21 steals, Chapel Hill HS/Chapel Hill, N.C.) Whether he starts or comes off the bench, Geer's role is clear once he steps on the floor. Geer's a shooter, a long-range shooter.

Last season, he was among the nation's top five three-point shooters until a last-season slump dropped him down a few notches. As it was, Geer still managed to shoot 48 percent from beyond the three-point line, the 18th best percentage in the country.

Thanks in large part to Geer, ETSU was one of the most effective three-point shooting teams in the country. Loyola Marymount and Kentucky received more notoriety for shooting the three, but it was the Bucs who led the nation in three-point attempts (689), far outdistancing runner-up Central Michigan (575). ETSU was also fourth in the country in three-point goals made per game (8.4), and second behind Loyola in three-point goals made (285) overall.

Geer converted six three-pointers in a game against Marshall and four against North Carolina State, helping the Bucs to hot starts in both games, which they eventually won.

"If Major improves his game this year as much as he did last year, he'll be a big factor for us," LeForce said. "He's improved his game on both ends of the floor. He's become stronger and more physical. He's got as nice a three-point stroke as you'll see."

JAMES JACOBS (6-6, 175 lbs, SO, G/F, #20, 0.4 ppg, 0.4 rpg, Pineville HS/Pineville, W.Va.) Jacobs, who redshirted with an injury his first year in the program, did not get much playing time last season. With all the veteran talent returning, he probably won't be much of a factor again this year. He is a good three-point shooter, however.

KEITH JENNINGS (5-7, 160 lbs., SR, G, #22, 14.8 ppg, 3.9 rpg, 297 assists, 84 steals, Culpepper HS/Culpepper, Va.) Small in stature, "Mister" Jennings nevertheless has made giant contributions in ETSU's rise to prominence. Southern Conference coaches thought so much of Jennings last season they chose him the league's most valuable player. He was also the MVP of the conference tournament.

Jennings excels in all facets of the game, though his strength is hitting the open man. He averaged 8.7 assists per game, third in the nation. His total of 297 assists led all Division I players. Jennings was also 27th in the country in steals with an average of 2.5 per game and 18th in total steals with 84. His totals in both categories led the Southern Conference the last three years.

Jennings is also an excellent shooter, making a team-high .574 percent of his field goal attempts last year. He led the team and was seventh in the nation with his three-point field goal percentage of 49.6. Finally, Jennings shot 87.7 percent from the free throw line, 10th in the country.

"Mister's not a giant physically," LeForce said, "but he's a giant at what he does. He plays the offensive end and the defensive end. He's a leader. He's also a tough kid and a very competitive kid. When the game is on the line, he's in control."

Said N.C. State's Robinson: "Mister Jennings is probably the most overlooked and underrated player in the country. I say that based on what opposing players have said about him. Mookie Blaylock, Chris Corchiani, Sherman Douglas, all the point guards he's played against have been impressed with his ability."

Not bad for a player no other Division I school wanted. Most considered him too small.

"That didn't worry us," LeForce said. "We knew he could get it done no matter what his height was. If he was six-foot, we wouldn't have gotten him. If he was 5-10, we wouldn't have gotten him."

Jennings has started since ETSU's first game his freshman season. As a freshman, he set a school record for assists in a season with 183 and was a second-team All-Conference pick. As a sophomore, Jennings improved his assist toal to 202. That year, Jennings nearly led the Bucs to an upset of top-seeded Oklahoma in the first round of the NCAA tournament's Southeast Regional. ETSU led the Sooners most of the game, but lost after Jennings fouled out with less than two minutes to play.

Jennings even has one of the nation's best nicknames. "One day when I was real young, I was playing sandlot football and my dad kept calling me to come home and I wouldn't listen," Jennings said. "Then he said, 'Mister Jennings, come here right now.' I came, and the name stuck."

Jennings is confident of his ability. "I rate myself up there with the best point guards," he said. "My only drawback is my height. Still, I feel confident about playing against anybody."

DARELL JONES (6-10, 205 lbs. SO, C/F, #31, 3.6 ppg, 2.3 rpg, 10 blocked shots, Gaffney HS/Gaffney, S.C.) Jones is similiar in build and ability to Dennis, though he lacks Dennis' touch from outside. Both are tall and thin, yet mobile.

Jones proved he belonged in the Bucs' second game of last season, an 83-70 victory at Tennessee. Subbing for Dennis, who was in foul trouble, Jones scored five points, grabbed five rebounds and blocked a shot in 11 minutes. He scored in double figures in four games and was a key reserve until suffering a bruised retina when a Jennings' pass nearly took his head off in a game at Furman. Jones missed four games.

"If Darell Jones had played anywhere else in the Southern Conference, he'd have been freshman of the year," LeForce said. "With our veteran lineup, he didn't get the minutes last year, but we're expecting a lot from him this year, especially now that Chad Keller's gone."

JERRY PELPHREY (6-6, 185 lbs., SO G/F, #30, 1.8 ppg, 0.8 rpg, Paintsville HS/Paintsville, Ky.) The brother of Kentucky player John Pelphrey, Jerry shows similar traits. He is a rugged competitor who can shoot the ball from three-point range.

"Jerry's one of the candidates who can fill Chad Keller's role for us," LeForce said. "He's got a big body and he's not afraid to bang with people."

ROBERT SPEARS (6-10, 230 lbs. SO C, #50, 1.8 ppg, 1.5 rpg Powell Valley HS/Big Stone Gap, Va.) Spears did not play much last season, but with the loss

of Keller, he should this year. He does not have the mobility of Jones or Dennis, but he is a strong rebounder and has a good shooting touch.

"Robert Spears is going to be a good basketball player," LeForce said. "I'm not saying he'll dominate the league, but he shoots it well and knows how to rebound."

MARTY STORY (6-3, 195 lbs., JR, F, #34, 5.4 ppg, 3.1 rpg, 28 assists, 20 steals, 14 blocked shots, Greeneville HS/Greeneville, Tenn.) Story started most of last season, and though he is not much of an offensive threat, he remains one of the better athletes on the team.

Story originally signed with Clemson to play football. A wide receiver, he decided he missed basketball and transferred to ETSU. He is known as a leaper and outstanding defensive player.

"Marty's got to get us six to eight points and five to seven rebounds a game, play the good defense and be physical," LeForce said. "We have to come up with a sixth man this year. Marty could fill that role."

CALVIN TALFORD (6-4, 175 lbs., JR, G, #24, 16.7 ppg, 4.0 rpg, 44 assists, 42 steals, Castlewood HS/Castlewood, Va.) Talford was another steal for the ETSU coaching staff. Playing as he did in Southwest Virginia, this gifted natural athlete escaped the attention of many Division I schools. His final decision came down to East Tennessee State and Southern Conference rival Appalachian State. Had Talford chosen Appalachian State, the Mountaineers, not the Bucs, could well be two-time defending conference champions.

In basketball, great leapers generally are not great shooters, and great shooters are not great leapers. The exceptions tend to stand out, witness Michael Jordan or David Thompson. Talford is a player in that mold, although he is still unpolished because he was so good in so many other sports. Growing up, Talford simply did not have much time for basketball.

Talford averaged 28 points per game in high school, but he also set Virginia high school records in the long jump and triple jump. He has high jumped seven feet for the ETSU track team. For kicks, Talford went out for football his senior year in high school and scored 22 touchdowns as a wingback. In the summers of 1988 and 1989, he played baseball for the Philadephia Phillies' rookie league team in the Appalachian League.

"Calvin Talford has probably reached 20-25 percent of his potential," LeForce said. "If he wants to be a first-round draft pick or an All-America, he's got to come every day ready to practice. He's got to play both ends of the floor with intensity. So far, he's gotten by on just God-given talent. If we can get him more intense, then the sky's the limit, with his leaping ability, his shooting ability and his speed."

Talford shot 50 percent from the floor, 40 percent from three-point range and 78 percent from the free throw line last season, decent numbers for someone who was not supposed to be a good shooter in high school. He led ETSU in dunks, several coming off well-timed lob passes from Jennings. Talford will be an important part of any success the Bucs have this season.

ALVIN WEST (6-3, 195 lbs., SR., G, #10, 7.7 ppg, 2.9 rpg, 50 assists, 39 steals, Havelock HS/Havelock, N.C.) Another member of the five-man recruiting class that turned around ETSU's program, West has been a part-time starter throughout his career. His shooting touch seems to have no middle ground - it's either on or it's way off.

When West is on, he can literally carry the Bucs. At Drake last season, West scored 25 points, hitting 6-for-10 three-point goals. The next game, West made only one of six three-point attempts against Appalachian State. He shot 41 percent from the floor and 30 percent from three-point range a year ago.

West seems to save his best performances for big games. As a sophomore, he was chosen to the Southern Conference all-tournament team, scoring 56 points in three games. Against Oklahoma in the NCAA tournament, West scored 12 points and grabbed eight rebounds. Last season, despite his shooting slump, West made the conference tournament second-team.

"We've got to get Alvin turned on early," LeForce said. "He's been Mr. February. We've got to get him to where he's Mr. January and Mr. December. He's got to get tougher mentally on both ends. Alvin has to learn he can do other things when his shot isn't falling. He's a great rebounder, a good defensive player, he's a strong kid. He could add 30 to 40 percent more productivity working on other areas."

MICHAEL WOODS (6-5, 180 lbs., SR, G/F, #32, 0.9 ppg, 1.0 rpg, 16 assists, Kings Mountain HS/Kings Mountain, N.C.) Every program needs a player like Woods, an uncomplaining cheerleader who's always ready to fill in when called upon.

Woods was in the same recruiting class as Dennis, Jennings, Geer and West and, for that reason, will go down in school history. No group of players brought in to ETSU ever had such an impact. Woods has not played nearly as much as his four classmates, but peformed admirably as a defensive stopper and backup point guard for Jennings.

"Michael Woods is a role player," LeForce said. "We've asked him to take the other team's leading scorer on defense and to spell Mister at the point. He's a real plus to the program."

★ NEWCOMERS ★

RODNEY ENGLISH (6-5, 185 lbs., JR, G/F, #4, 22.0 ppg, 9.0 rpg, Denmark-Olar HS/Denmark, S.C. & Anderson JC/Anderson, S.C.) Before Robinson left, he told his assistants to find a 6-5 to 6-7 athlete who could rebound. They came back with English, who can score and rebound. He's not as big as Robinson was hoping for, but LeForce will probably insert him into the starting lineup from day one.

English is talented enough to play guard, but will probably play forward for ETSU. Rebounding is his favorite part of the game. "I see the ball, I go after it," English said. "I've just always had the ability to get it."

Neither LeForce, his coaching staff, nor English were worried about whether English will fit in with the group of veterans at ETSU. "I feel as though I've been here all along," English said. "This is a progam on the rise, and it has everything going for it. I wanted to be a part of that, and I think I can help."

ERIC PALMER (5-6, 150 lbs. SO, G, #5, Boiling Springs HS/Boling Springs, N.C.) You read the height correctly. At 5-6, Palmer is one inch shorter than Mister Jennings. Is Palmer "Mister II?"

It would be unfair to compare Palmer, who sat out last season at ETSU, with Jennings, though he has similar skills and some even Jennings doesn't have. Palmer can dunk, and East Tennessee stength coach Lee Morrow says he is the fastest athlete to ever play a sport at ETSU. Palmer ran a 4.2 40-yard dash.

Palmer will earn plenty of minutes subbing for Jennings, who hardly got a rest his first three seasons. At times, LeForce says, he'll use both players in the Bucs' full court press.

TRAZEL SILVERS (6-5, 180 lbs., FR, G/F, #21, 29.0 ppg, 10.0 rpg, 5.0 assists, Ervinton HS/Ervinton, Va.) Silvers represents the ETSU coaching staff's annual recruiting steal. Playing at a high school far removed from media coverage, Silvers did not attract attention from larger schools until it was too late.

Silvers played point guard in high school, but will probably shift to second guard or small forward. He has been compared favorably with Calvin Talford, only more polished as an all-around player at this stage.

"He's a good ball handler for his size, and he's also quick," said Ervinton coach Ed Whitaker. "Because of his size, he'll create matchup problems. He's hard to control in an uptempo game. If he has some room to operate, he can do some damage."

Silvers was MVP of the West team in the Virginia High School Coaches Association all-star game last summer. He came off the bench to score 12 points, grab six rebounds and get four blocked shots. Several Division I coaches who watched the game were impressed.

"Just what they need," said VMI's Joe Cantafio. "Another Calvin Talford."

★ QUESTIONS ★

Defense? Can the Buccaneers play the kind of pressure defense LeForce favors? Will they be able to play solid low-post defense against bigger teams, a weakness underscored in an NCAA tournament loss to Georgia Tech last season?

Rebounding? ETSU was a poor rebounding team last season. Junior college transfer Rodney English may help in that area.

New coach? What effect will changing coaches have on the team? Robinson was immensely popular with the Bucs, but all the players pushed for LeForce to get the job after Robinson departed.

★ STRENGTHS ★

Experience! ETSU's nucleus of players has been together for four years.

Shooting! Few teams in the country shot the ball better than ETSU last year, particularly from three-point range.

Depth! The Bucs can go 12 deep, and with LeForce's pressing defenses, all 12 could get playing time.

Quickness! ETSU doesn't have the biggest team in college basketball, but has been able to counteract size mismatches with superior quickness.

Mister! Keith "Mister" Jennings is one of the top point guards in the country.

★ BLUE RIBBON ANALYSIS ★

Robinson left in May, leaving several holes to fill on ETSU's schedule. LeForce had to fill in as best he could, and the result is a demanding winter that will test even the very experienced Bucs.

ETSU may not win 27 games this season, but will be improved, thanks to another year of maturity for its veteran lineup. The addition of newcomers Rodney English, Trazel Silvers and Eric Palmer will add depth and quickness to the roster.

"We're no longer a surprise and people aren't amazed we can play," LeForce said. "The last couple of years, when we started winning some ball games, we slipped up on people. Now, we won't be able to do that.

"The question now is are we a good basketball team or have the last two years been a fluke? Are we still hungry to get better and go to the next level?

"I think the answer to that is yes, but we'll find out. Our goal, just as it will be every year, is to get in the NCAA tournament and see how many games we can win. It's going to be an interesting season."

And a very happy one. East Tennessee State will win the Southern Conference and could be a real sleeper in the NCAA's.

LAST SEASON			
Univ. of Charleston (WV)	120-83	@Western Carolina	99-88
@Tennessee	83-70	Liberty University	64-49
Carson-Newman (TN)	91-65	@The Citadel	87-86
Newberry (SC)	125-74	@Furman	97-100
#Boston University	73-78	@Appalachian State	98-82
#Monmouth	79-67	Drake	86-71
@North Carolina State	92-82	@Marshall	84-74
##East Carolina	86-80	@Virginia Military	100-81
##Maryland	86-91	*Western Carolina	75-60
##Chaminade	83-89	*Virginia Military	99-94
@UCLA	66-115	*Appalchian State	96-75
Liberty University (VA)	107-91	**Georgia Tech	83-99
@Western Carolina	92-73		
@Tennessee-Chattanooga	75-70	@ Road Games	
Wake Forest	69-73	# Forest Industries Classic, Missoula, MT	
@Furman	94-65	## Chaminade Tournament, Honolulu, HI	
@The Citadel	92-73		
Drake	86-78	* Southern Conference Tournament, Asheville, NC	
@Appalachian State	96-94		
@Virginia Military	77-78	** NCAA Tournament, Knoxville, TN	
@Marshall	99-88		
@Tennessee-Chattanooga	92-73		

1990-91 EAST TENNESSEE STATE SCHEDULE				
Nov.	14	##@Brigham Young	7	Belmont Abbey (NC)
	26	George Mason	9	@The Citadel
Dec.	1	Austin Peay	11	@Furman
	3	Eckerd College (FL)	14	@Liberty University
	5	Wofford College (SC)	16	@North Carolina Charlotte
	8	@James Madison		
	15	@George Mason	18	Western Carolina
	22	@Cincinnati	23	@Marshall
	29	North Carolina State	25	Virginia Military Institute
Jan.	5	Appalachian State		
	10	Liberty University (VA)	Mar.	1-3 ##Southern Conference Tournament
	12	Furman		
	14	The Citadel	@ Road Games	
	19	@Western Carolina	# Dodge NIT. If East Tennessee State defeats Brigham Young, the Buccaneers will play a second round game on Nov. 16. The semifinals and finals of the tournament will be held on Nov. 21 & 23 at Madison Square Garden, New York, NY. ## Asheville, NC	
	21	@Tennessee-Chattanooga		
	26	@Virginia Military Institute		
	28	Marshall		
	30	@Memphis State		
Feb.	2	@Appalachian State		
	4	Tennessee-Chattanooga		

NOTES: The North Carolina Charlotte game on Feb. 16 will be telecast at midnight, live on ESPN . . . former North Carolina guard Jeff Lebo was hired by LeForce as a full-time assistant coach . . . East Tennessee State recruit Melvin Brooks, a 6-7, 235-pound forward/center from Northeast HS in Elizabeth City, N.C., is academically ineligible and will not compete for the Buccaneers this year. At press time, Brooks was trying to find a prep school to enroll in for the upcoming year . . . If East Tennessee State can get by Brigham Young, the Buccaneers will probably face Arizona, in Tucson, in the second round of the Dodge NIT.

GEORGETOWN

LAST SEASON: 24-7
CONFERENCE RECORD: 11-5
STARTERS LOST: 3
STARTERS RETURNING: 2
CONFERENCE: BIG EAST
LOCATION: WASHINGTON, DC
HOME FLOOR: CAPITAL
** CENTER (19,035)**
NICKNAME: HOYAS
COLORS: BLUE AND GRAY

★ COACH'S PROFILE ★

JOHN THOMPSON (Record at Georgetown, 423-142.) As if there was little he could do to elevate his already nearly icon-like status on the hilltop overlooking the Potomac River, John Thompson found a way. By turning down an offer of upwards of $6 million to become general manager and part owner of the Denver Nuggets, Thompson renewed his commitment to Georgetown.

"The timing was not right for me to leave here. I never felt there was nothing left to accomplish at Georgetown," he told Michael Wilbon of The Washington Post. "I've always felt my responsibility was much broader than wins and losses."

Wrote Wilbon: ". . . the NBA is about the business of basketball. Players get in their fancy cars and go home. Players with big cars and $1 million homes don't need John Thompson. A 17-year-old kid whose elementary school is short on textbooks and whose high school has one part-time guidance counselor needs Thompson. That's why college basketball would have missed him."

Said former Hoya Jaren Jackson: "He's such a monument. He's as big as the monument on the Mall. This is his home."

For whatever reason, Thompson turned down the Denver offer after the Nuggets owners twice approached him within a month for their vacant general manager's position. Thompson deliberated for over a week before turning down their last offer. For reasons known only to him, Thompson decided to stay in Georgetown and a collective sigh of relief was heard all over Washington. For John Thompson is not only the embodiment of Georgetown basketball, he is a Washingtonian to the core. Other than his days in college at Providence and a short career with the Boston Celtics, Thompson has always lived in Washington. He is as easily recognizable in the nation's capitol as George Bush.

Thompson unwittingly became embroiled in controversy last winter when Nike advertising was blamed by several writers for fostering an epidemic of robberies for sneakers in the nation's inner-cities. He answered the criticism very appropriately in The Washington Post.

". . . you hear that John Thompson and Michael Jordan and Spike Lee are killing black kids by advertising tennis shoes. That's the most ridiculous, hypocritical thing I've heard in my life, because last year Ballou High School (in Washington), a kid was killed over a boom box. Several kids were killed for their wallets. People of that moral fiber are going to do that without the advertisements."

Since coming to Georgetown in 1972, Thompson has become an almost larger than life figure who is quoted as extensively in the press on topics outside of basketball as he is on the pick and roll. He is a lightning rod for controversy who is viewed with disdain by certain segments of the public and is a hero to others. Thompson has never asked for the role he has been thrust into and neither does he back off and refuse to speak his mind. Virtually all of his players at Georgetown have graduated and most have gone on to successful careers outside of the world of basketball. As a former journeyman NBA player, he knows the inherent risks involved in putting emphasis on a career in professional basketball without a backup plan. Thompson received a strong education and had a backup plan when he decided to end his NBA career after the Celtics left him unprotected and the Chicago Bulls picked him off in the expansion draft.

Thompson thrives on control. He decided to leave the NBA after being picked by Chicago in the expansion draft because he felt he no longer had control over his career. His teams try to control the tempo with constant, stifling defensive pressure. That defensive pressure has been the trademark of Thompson's Hoyas during his 17 years at Georgetown. He controls his players' accessibility to the media and Thompson basically deals with the media on his own terms, not theirs, something that few people in the public eye ever accomplish. He also wants control in the recruiting process. Thompson certainly has had his share of great players at Georgetown, but he has passed up opportunities to get deeply involved in recruitment of many others because he didn't like the situation. Thompson basically outlines the Georgetown program and the responsibilities of being a Hoya on and off the court to a prospective recruit. Thompson is not the type to lavish attention on a prospective recruit and in this day and age when so many of the most highly regarded young players and their coaches and families want constant attention from the coaches courting them, his straight forward, no thrills sales pitch will not always be successful. Sizzle and show biz sell in recruiting these days. You have to respect Thompson for his decision to recruit on his own terms, not on what is in vogue.

When Thompson came to Georgetown in 1972 he inherited a 3-23 team. He was hired by the Georgetown administration after going 122-22 in six seasons at St. Anthony's HS in Washington. The Georgetown program had a very low Division I status, almost intramural, when Thompson took over but he was undaunted. He brought an English teacher from St. Anthony's named Mary Fenlon with him across town to Georgetown to help look out for the academic interests of his players. Fenlon remains at Georgetown today and is one of Thompson's closest advisors.

In his third year at Georgetown, the Hoyas finished the season by winning 11 of their last 12 games and received the school's first invitation to the NCAA tournament in 32 years. In 1975 he landed his first big name recruit, forward Al Dutch from Archbishop Carroll HS in Washington, and a year later he landed two of the premier players in the country, John Duren and Craig Shelton from Washington's Dunbar HS. A few years later he picked up an unheralded guard from Gastonia, N.C., named Eric "Sleepy" Floyd, and the program was off and running, never to look back.

His 1980 team won the first ever Big East championship and advanced to the Final Eight of the NCAA tournament. The Hoyas seemed to have an insurmountable lead in the second half against Iowa but Lute Olson's Hawkeyes played nearly flawless ball down the stretch and defeated Georgetown. That was the year Louisville won the national championship, and many experts thought the Hoyas would have had a real shot at winning the NCAA title if they had been able to get by Iowa. Soon after, Thompson signed Patrick Ewing and the Big East became a dominant presence on the college basketball scene which further enhanced the Georgetown program.

Thompson ranks among the Top 10 active coaches in the nation in winning percentage. Under his guidance, Georgetown has captured six Big East tournament championships, more than any conference member, and has also won four regular season conference titles. Georgetown has had 13 consecutive 20-win seasons and 12 straight NCAA tournament appearances, including five trips to the Final Eight, three appearances in the Final Four and a national championship in 1984. They Hoyas are also the team everyone seems to love to hate and draw tremendous crowds on the road.

Thompson was not a great defensive player himself but he has become one of the strongest defensive coaches in the game. The Hoyas usually rank high nationally in defensive categories such as field goal percentage and points allowed. He looks as much at the defensive potential of a recruit as his offensive game. Thompson believes that defense is a constant that can come through game after game while an offense, no matter how explosive, will have ups and downs throughout a season. While Thompson was criticized heavily for the American's team failure to win the Gold Medal at the 1988 Olympics, and whenever his teams have lost a big game in the NCAA tournament for having a style of play that is too predictable and does not emphasize the half court offensive game enough, his system has proven extremely successful over the long haul.

Thompson is beginning his 18th year at Georgetown. While he does not have any apparent dissatisfaction with Georgetown and still believes there are challenges in the future, he came closer to accepting the Denver Nuggets position than he has with any other offer that has come his way. His son, Ronny, plays for him and is a junior at Georgetown. After Ronny graduates and Alonzo Mourning and Dikembe Mutombo depart for the pros, you have to wonder how much longer the Thompson will stay at Georgetown. He loves the game, but is a complex man with a probing mind who could do many other things. It will be interesting to see if Thompson is at Georgetown long into the '90s.

★ PLAYERS NOT RETURNING ★

ANTHONY ALLEN (6-7, F, 1.9 ppg, 2.2 rpg, 7 assists, 9 steals, 8 blocked shots) Allen came to Georgetown with a big reputation as the best player in Texas, he was from Port Arthur, Tex., and although he never became a major star, Allen was an effective role player during his career. Thompson would quietly start Allen during many games in order to establish an aggressive man-to-man defense. He was very quick and once during his freshman year, Thompson told Allen to guard Syracuse's star Ronny Seikaly. Allen slowed Seikaly down enough to help Georgetown win the game.

He stayed within his role and was a subtly positive force on the team. One of his best games last season was a seven-point, three-rebound effort against Providence. Allen could be missed more than expected as the Hoyas do not have any significant experience up front behind stars Alonzo Mourning and Dikembe Mutombo.

MILTON BELL (6-7, F, 4.2 ppg, 1.9 rpg, 4 assists, 1 steal, 3 blocked shots) Bell played in 10 of the Hoyas' first 17 games, averaging 7.7 minutes per game before transferring to Richmond (in his hometown) midway through his sophomore year. He was a Parade Magazine second-team All-America pick whose arrival at Georgetown was much heralded. However, Bell never seemed to fit into the Hoya system and was a limited contributor as a freshman and early last year. Still, he would have had a role this year as Georgetown's experience up front is almost nonexistent other than Mourning and Mutombo.

DWAYNE BRYANT (6-2, G, 12.3 ppg, 4.3 rpg, 177 assists, 57 steals, 3 blocked shots) Bryant came out of De La Salle HS in New Orleans to forge a solid career at Georgetown. He was a contributor from the outset and his role gradually increased as he became the starting point guard in his final season. One of his best games came his junior year in the NCAA East Regional when Bryant put in 18 points against North Carolina State on a night Charles Smith was sick. Bryant wound up his Georgetown career with a sparkling 527 assists.

A good passer and strong defender, Bryant came in with a solid, intelligent all-around game and on the nights when his outside shot clicked, he was most effective. Bryant's backcourt leadership and steadying influence will be missed. The Hoyas top three guards are all gone and Georgetown has never headed into a season with more uncertainty in the backcourt than this year.

DAVE EDWARDS (5-10, G, 5.4 ppg, 2.3 rpg, 150 assists, 42 steals, 1 blocked shot) After playing in all 31 games last year, averaging 20.3 minutes per game and creating some excitement with his penetration and dazzling ballhandling skills, Edwards transferred to Texas A&M. He will have three years eligibility remaining for the Aggies beginning next year. An exciting, flashy, speed demon, Edwards certainly had his moments of brilliance. But he was a bit too rambunctious —perhaps outrageous at times was a better word —for Thompson to ever feel totally confident with him running the show. He was a different type of point guard than the control minded Thompson has become used to at Georgetown.

Edwards' departure leaves the Hoyas devoid of any experience at point guard. He got his career-high 19 points in the Hoyas' season-ending NCAA tournament loss to Xavier and almost keyed an unlikely comeback. Edwards was a two-edged sword who would create instant offense or instant turnovers. His 150 assists indicate his willingness to give the ball up, even if not quite in the way a coach would always like. The slick, quick and fancy ballhandling Edwards will be heard from at Texas A&M.

SAM JEFFERSON (6-9, F/C, 3.5 ppg, 3.4 rpg, 12 assists, 23 steals, 8 blocked shots) Jefferson was limited offensively and his role was basically on the defensive end and the boards. Once Dikembe Mutombo began to emerge, Jefferson's playing time severely diminished. His career game came as a junior against Duke in the NCAA Final Eight. With Alonzo Mourning on the bench during the waning moments of the game, Jefferson guarded Duke's Danny Ferry while also picking up eight points and seven rebounds.

He averaged 16.2 minutes per game last year and started 12 games. Graduated seniors Anthony Allen and Jefferson may not have been stars, but when Thompson looks down his bench this year he will wish he had them back.

JOHNNY JONES (6-6, G/F, 4.3 ppg, 2.8 rpg, 2 assists, 1 steal, 2 blocked shots) Jones appeared in four games last year for a total of 27 minutes. He completed his eligibility while enrolled in graduate school at Georgetown. Jones was not a key contributor for most of his Georgetown career.

MICHAEL TATE (6-6, F, 3.2 ppg, 2.4 rpg, 22 assists, 5 steals) Only a year ago, Tate arrived at Georgetown from suburban Oxon Hill (Md.) HS as a highly regarded local recruit of high school All-America status. Now he is gone, transferred to James Madison, although the small amount of playing time he got last year would have increased sharply. Tate was player of the year in Maryland as a senior and could have eventually become a big time scorer. He was hindered early on by a knee injury and never found sustained success and playing time.

Tate is strong and a good leaper. For whatever reason, he seldom looked comfortable during his brief stints last season. "Georgetown didn't fit my style," Tate told the Big East Briefs. "Coach Thompson told me to find a place that has more of a running game."

MARK TILLMON (6-2, G, 19.8 ppg, 4.1 rpg, 44 assists, 54 steals, 10 blocked shots) Tillmon, through his career, always displayed great athletic ability and a penchant for strong defense. Last season, he fulfilled a few of his early flashes and became an outside shooter and a true three-point threat. He made 56-of-130 three-pointers (.431) and led Georgetown in scoring with an 19.8 average. In fact, with the graduation of Tillmon and Bryant and the transfer of Edwards, only 24 of the 141 three-pointers made by the Hoyas last year are accounted for by players who are returning this season.

Tillmon emerged as an all-around explosive offensive force. He passed the 1,000-point career scoring mark in the season's first game, then exploded for 27 in the ACC/Big East Challenge win over North Carolina. In a 93-91 win over Providence, Tillmon threw in a career-high 39, the most ever by a Georgetown player in Big East play. He continued the season as a go-to scorer against quality opposition. Tillmon also had 54 steals. His reliable offensive production and perimeter shooting will be sorely missed by Thompson. We cannot emphasize enough how big a void the graduation of Bryant and Tillmon has left in the Georgetown backcourt.

★ RETURNING PLAYERS ★

ALONZO MOURNING (6-10, 240 lbs., JR, C/F, #33, 16.5 ppg, 8.5 rpg, 36 assists, 15 steals, 69 blocked shots, Indian River HS/Chesapeake, Va.) After a fabulous freshman season, Mourning was spoken of as perhaps the best player in the country. Defensively, he was inspiring Patrick Ewing-like comparisons. Offensively, particularly as a low post presence, there was little argument he was far more advanced than Ewing for that stage in his career. Mourning's block —from behind a screen no less —on Princeton's final possession allowed Georgetown to escape a first round NCAA tournament upset that would have been one of the biggest in history.

Last season in an altered role, his statistics went up by three points and one rebound per game. Still, his blocked shots decreased by 100 (169 to 69) and, puzzlingly at times, he did not seem like the totally dominating two-way inside presence he had shown so many signs of being the previous year.

Still, playing with 7-2 Dikembe Mutombo instead of ahead of him, Mourning formed half of the most intimidating twin-tower defensive presence in the college game. Mutombo's equally dominant presence in the paint accounted for much of Mourning's decreased block total. They only give out one block per shot and Mutombo, four inches taller, simply jumped out at some shooters before Mourning could get there. In fact, Mutombo's emergence necessitated several adjustments on Mourning's part. Yet, there were more than a few times he seemed to lack the aggressiveness that helped him set the NCAA all-time single season record for blocks (169 as a freshman).

As a duo, though, Mourning and Mutombo enhanced each other's effectiveness. "I love playing together," Mutombo told Eastern Basketball. "Most of the time we help each other in blocking shots. If we see that a team can cause us foul trouble, he'll step out on his man and I'll jump in from the back and block it."

Mourning's quick on-court temper has been a problem, one that he began to recognize last season. "They are always going to send that hit-man into the game to come in and pester me, try to get my mind out of the game. Hey, I've got to keep my composure, keep myself under control and just play hard and smile things like that off," he said. Mourning managed that with mixed success.

Still, Mourning, second on the team in rebounding and scoring, had his moments. He was the Big East defensive player of the year for the second season in a row and a first-team All-Conference selection. He had 27 points in a win over Virginia Tech and 17 rebounds against Miami. Mourning scored 23 in a 93-91 win over Providence. He threw in 20 more against Connecticut at the Capital Centre. In the Hoyas' NCAA tournament loss to Xavier, Mourning had 15 points and 10 rebounds against the Muskateers' talented senior tandem of Tyrone Hill and Derek Strong.

Mourning came out of high school as one of the five most heralded big men since Lew Alcindor (later to become Kareem Abdul-Jabbar) graduated from New York's Power Memorial HS in the '60s. He barely missed making the U.S. Olympic team right out of high school. That gave him weeks of competition against the best players in the country.

When on his game, Mourning can do it all. He has a soft turnaround jumper from short range, great strength, and unteachable instinct and timing defensively. With the Hoya starting backcourt gone, Mourning will be looked upon to assume more of the offensive burden. He came back strong over the summer while playing for the U.S. National team coached by Duke's Mike Krzyzewski in the Goodwill Games in Seattle and the World Basketball Championships in Buenos Aires, Argentina. He provided the most consistent and dominating inside presence for the U.S. team. In the semifinals of the World Basketball Championship in Argentina, against eventual Gold Medal winning Yugoslavia, Mourning had 28 points and 11 rebounds on 13-of-18 shooting from the floor. He was matched up for most of that game against Vlade Divac, who had a promising rookie year for the Los Angeles Lakers. Mourning used his quickness and intensity to simply embarrass Divac.

We look for Mourning to be ready to redeem himself this year with a strong, productive, All-America type performance.

DIKEMBE MUTOMBO (7-2, 240 lbs., JR, #55, 10.7 ppg, 10.5 rpg, 18 assists, 12 steals, 128 blocked shots, Institute Buboto, Kinshasa, Zaire) As if it was not enough to have the best shotblocker in the country on their team, the Hoyas suddenly discovered they had an even better one on their own bench. Inspired by an off-season dinner suggestion from an old friend (and coach) Red Auerbach, Thompson decided to play Mutombo and Mourning together. The result? Mutombo developed from a 3.9 ppg, 3.3 rpg, limited-time freshman season to emerge as half of perhaps the most frightening defensive presence college basketball has ever seen. He shared Big East defensive player of the year honors with Mourning, led the team in rebounding and added a .709 field goal percentage (129-of-182) to his previous season's mark of .707 (53-of-75). His dunks and shotblocking are already of legendary proportions. Against St. John's, Mutombo established the Big East single game mark with an unbelievable 12 blocks.

"I heard one of our supporters screaming, 'Don't let him catch the ball inside!,'" Texas Southern coach Robert Moreland told Michael Wilbon of The Washington Post. "But how are you going to do that when you're jumping as high as you can, while he's stretching and catching the pass a foot over your head?" Mutombo made 8-of-9 shots and pulled down 16 rebounds in that NCAA opening round win over Texas Southern.

Said David Ramsey in The Sporting News: "Providence center Marty Conlon still shakes his head when he talks about a Mutombo dunk. Mutombo was standing under the basket when he grabbed the ball, leaped and found himself heading straight for the cylinder. So Mutombo curled his back. 'He did a fadeaway dunk,' said Conlon. 'You know those skating contests, the ones where you lean backward under the bar'? That's what Dikembe's dunk looked like. It was the first limbo dunk I'd ever seen.'"

DePaul's 6-9 Stephen Howard drove to the basket against Mutombo. Howard was rising while Mutombo was standing. Howard tried to dunk. Mutombo raised his unbelievably long arms and blocked the dunk attempt —without leaving his feet. "The man doesn't even have to jump," said DePaul coach Joey Meyer.

No player over seven-feet has ever approached Mutombo's quickness, coordination, timing and defensive instincts. This is not to mention his ability to run the floor. His offense is still raw (growing up in Zaire can do that to you) and virtually nonexistent outside the lane. But it's not unfair to say that Mutombo is blessed with the natural ability to become the greatest defensive force ever to play the game. He, of course, still has much to learn about when to go for the block. You can't block shots when you're sitting on the bench in foul trouble. But given how much he has progressed in only two years in college basketball, Mutombo's potential is absolutely frightening.

He did not even begin to play basketball until the age of 16. Mutombo is extremely intelligent and speaks five languages including his native French. At Georgetown he majors in linguistics and political science.

Thompson was reportedly tipped off about Mutombo by Herman Henning, a former Chicago high school coach working for the U.S. Information Agency in Africa. Mutombo attended Institute Buboto, a Jesuit high school in Zaire, and played on the national basketball team.

"I'm still trying to work on my concentration," Mutombo said. "The way you play here is different from what I was accustomed to in Africa. You play here with the crowd, with the coach, with everyone involved. I used to play in front of maybe 700 people. It's very different. The big crowds are intimidating, scary."

Mutombo came on even stronger towards the season's end. He averaged 14.6 points and 12.9 rebounds over the last 10 games prior to the season finale against Xavier. He learned to focus for the whole game and became comfortable with more playing time. Part of the problem had been learning basketball lingo. "His old coach would curse him in French," Thompson told Michael Wilbon of *The Washington Post*. "I curse him in English. He's picking up the game. He's grasping things better."

Mutombo has already had a conversation with Bill Russell, the greatest shotblocker of the all. "He's the guy who has 11 rings and 10 fingers," Mutombo told Steve Berkowitz of *The Washington Post*. "He's asking if God can give him another finger to put this ring on because he's always had to leave one at home."

He spent the summer of 1989 working as an intern for Congressman Robert Matsui (Calif.). "Dikembe is an extremely well balanced person," said Thompson. "He has the whole package . . . He is . . . very intelligent and extremely academically motivated. And he is interested in the world, and not just basketball. He doesn't think basketball is the world."

But within the basketball world, Mutombo should be set to make a giant impact this year. Mutombo's classification is uncertain. He redshirted the 1987-88 season at Georgetown before playing the last two years. The Georgetown Sports Information Department lists Mutombo as a senior, which he is academically, but in terms of eligibility, he's a junior. He could be the No. 1 pick in an upcoming NBA draft.

MIKE SABOL (6-7, 205 lb., SO, F, #44, 1.3 ppg, 1.7 rpg, 6 assists, 1 steal, Gonzaga HS/Washington, D.C.) Sabol passes well and sees the floor. In high school he showed an outside shot but his game was hard to dissect last year as he played only 99 minutes in 17 games for an average of 5.8 minutes per game. Sabol did make 9-of-18 field goals. Sabol's best game was against Florida International when he had eight rebounds in 13 minutes. He was a teammate of incoming Hoya freshman Robert Churchwell and Lamont Morgan at Gonzaga HS in Washington.

The Georgetown bench is slim this year and Sabol, as is everyone else on the team, is a candidate for an increased role and more playing time.

ANTOINE STOUDAMIRE (6-3, 180 lbs., SO, G, #41, 3.1 ppg, 1.1 rpg, 16 assists, 12 steals, 1 block, Jesuit HS/Portland, Ore.) Stoudamire, an excellent long range shooter, should receive ample opportunity to make his mark in Georgetown's depleted backcourt. Against Florida International, he had 24 points, four rebounds and five steals in 22 minutes. He is strong and rebounds well from the guard position.

In high school, Stoudamire led the state of Oregon in both scoring and rebounding, somewhat amazing considering he's 6-3. Heading into the season, the makeup of the Georgetown backcourt is extremely unsettled. Stoudamire has a shot at starting at second guard for the Hoyas this season.

RONNY THOMPSON (6-4, 190 lbs., JR, G, #30, 3.6 ppg, 1.2 rpg, 22 assists, 14 steals, Flint Hill HS/Washington, D.C.) The son of John Thompson, Ronny showed the ability to knock down some important outside shots, including three-pointers, last year. He tied his career high with 11 against North Carolina. For the year, Thompson was 45-of-111 (.405) from the field and 9-of-27 (.333) from three-point range. He played him an average of 12.8 minutes per game.

Thompson is an intelligent, controlled player who can handle the ball and rebound. He plays very hard and defends well. His brother, John III, played at Princeton. Ronny will vie for a great deal of quality time at the off-guard spot this year.

KAYODE VANN (6-1, 175 lbs., JR, G, #11, 0.8 ppg, 0.3 rpg, 2 assists, 2 steals, Berkley-Carroll HS/New York City, N.Y.) Vann saw sparse playing time in some Hoya home games. His hard work the last two years has won him a roster spot. He had five points and two steals against the University of the District of Columbia last year.

★ NEWCOMERS ★

VLADIMIR BOSANAC (6-9, 190 lbs., FR, F, Second Economics HS/Belgrade, Yugoslavia & College of Arts and Sciences/Belgrade, Yugoslavia) The entire Georgetown coaching staff was heavily involved in scouting for the 1980 Olympic Games. Hoya assistants Craig Esheric and Mike Riley made numerous trips abroad to scout the international teams. They developed international contacts and became

impressed the caliber of talent in certain countries such as Yugoslavia.

For those of you who do not keep up on international basketball, Yugoslavia swept the Goodwill Games in Seattle and the World Basketball Championship in Buenos Aires, Argentina over the summer. The Yugoslavian teams knocked off the U.S. National team at both venues. In fact, a United States all-star team has not defeated the Yugoslavians in a top flight international competition in several years. While Bosanac was not a member of the Yugoslavian team which won in Seattle or Argentina, he has to be given respect as his homeland has become the No. 2 talent producer in the world behind the United States. Three Yugoslavians played in the NBA last year and Toni Kukoc, a 6-9 multi-dimensional forward from Split, Yugoslavia, is considered the premier player in the world outside the United States.

The Georgetown coaching staff knows how strong the Yugoslavians have become in recent years. Therefore, after seeing a film of one of Bosanac's workouts, Esherick went to Yugoslavia to watch him play. Esherick liked Bosanac's versatility. He can handle the ball well, and can shoot from the outside, two skills most of the players from his country have mastered.

It is hard to measure how quickly Bosanac will adjust to a new country and the Georgetown program. However, if he can shoot the ball and handle it as well as advertised, he could have a role on this year's Hoya squad.

JOEY BROWN (5-11, 170 lbs., FR, G, 22.0 ppg, 4.0 rpg, 7.0 apg, 5.0 stpg, Morgan City HS/Morgan City, La.) Georgetown has developed a pipeline into Louisiana. Last year's starting point guard, Dwayne Bryant, is from New Orleans. Three other New Orleans natives have played for Georgetown in recent years. Another Crescent City native, Steve Martin, was a standout forward on some of Thompson's early teams at Georgetown.

This was the first time Georgetown went outside of New Orleans to sign a Louisiana player. Thompson reached 85 miles southwest of New Orleans to Morgan City for Brown, an All-Louisiana performer who can play either guard position. In his final two years in high school, Brown led his teams to 35-1 and 32-2 seasons. He was proficient scorer in high school who should get a shot at playing time this year.

ROBERT CHURCHWELL (6-6, 195 lbs., FR, F, 19.0 ppg, 13.0 rpg, Gonzaga HS/Washington, D.C.) Churchwell, who was named to the All-Metro team in the Washington area, is a good defender and rebounder and moves well without the ball. He was also outstanding in track and won the Metro-Washington championship in the high jump, long jump and triple jump.

On virtually every Georgetown team since the beginning of the Big East, a freshman of Churchwell's caliber would have been a candidate for limited playing time. However, this year there is a vacancy at one forward spot and no strong returnee is set to take it. Churchwell could see significant playing time as a freshman.

PASCAL FLEURY (7-2, 220 lbs., FR, C, Dawson Prep/St. Jean-Richelieu, Canada) Few teams in the country will have an international contingent to match the Hoyas this year. Georgetown will have players from Zaire, Yugoslavia and now Canada with Pascal Fleury in the fold.

Fleury is looked upon as a project. He is very thin and only began playing three years ago. "Runs the court and catches the ball well," is the assessment of *Big East Briefs*. "Needs to improve his lateral footwork. Will be redshirted."

Said his coach Olga Hrycak: "You're talking about a guy who's really, really raw. He is still developing his game."

Thompson is hoping that Fleury will benefit from practicing against Mourning and Mutombo. Thompson is a former big man himself and no coach values size more than him. He has been known to take on his share of projects in the past and Fleury is his latest.

CHARLES HARRISON (6-2, 170 lbs., FR, G, 26.3 ppg, 4.0 apg, 3.0 stpg, Archbishop Carroll HS/Washington, D.C.) Harrison was considered not only one of the premier players in the Washington area but one of the best high school guards in the country.

Harrison originally committed to Maryland but signed with the Hoyas just before the early recruiting period ended last November. His game has been offensive-oriented, primarily through outside shooting with some penetration, rather than as a distributing point guard. Harrison does have ballhandling ability and excellent quickness which will allow him to compete for the open point guard spot.

"Probably improved his stock more than any other player in the camp this week. After this camp, we are sure that Harrison will be in everyone's top 30! Possesses one of the best jump shots in America. Rarely out of control with a deadly outside jumpshot that makes Harrison one of the most dangerous guards in camp," was the assessment of the *Hoop Scoop* after Harrison attended the Nike/ABCD Camp.

He is Georgetown's most heralded recruit and a key player for the Hoyas. He should have an immediate impact as a scorer. The Hoyas need an outside threat to balance their strong inside scoring. Harrison could be the starting point guard for Georgetown this year and we don't think the Hoyas can be up to their usual strength without a good year from him.

BRIAN KELLY (6-6, 230 lbs., JR, F, 14.0 ppg, 10.0 rpg, Purcell Marian HS/Cincinnati, Ohio & Cincinnati Tech JC) Kelly was a powerful rebounder in junior college at Cincinnati Tech. He can also play away from the basket. Thompson is hoping that Kelly's junior college experience will be a mature influence on a young team.

"He executes well, does a good job of boxing out, and isn't afraid to take the charge," Cincinnati Tech coach John Hurley told *Big East Briefs*.

Kelly should play a significant role as Mourning's reserve at power forward and maybe even more.

LAMONT MORGAN (6-3, 170 lbs., FR, G, 15.0 ppg, 5.0 rpg, 7.0 apg,

Gonzaga HS/Washington, D.C.) Morgan is one of three Gonzaga graduates on the Georgetown roster. Ronny Thompson went to Gonzaga before transferring to Flint Hill and his brother, John III, who played at Princeton, also graduated from Gonzaga. Morgan is probably the most passing-oriented of the incoming guards and should help at the point. He's an excellent ballhandler and a fine athlete who also lettered in track.

Georgetown signed three possible point guard prospects in the early signing period last November. At that point, the Hoyas still had Dave Edwards and now that he is gone, at least one and probably two of the freshmen guards will have to play immediately.

★ QUESTIONS ★

Point guard? This position is wide open. The Hoyas have no one with significant point guard experience on the Big East level. Either freshman Joey Brown or Charles Harrison will have to adjust their games or another freshman, Lamont Morgan, will have to raise his if the position is to be handled capably.

The backcourt? Overall, the Hoyas will have zero experience at the point coupled with marginal experience at the other guard spot. It will take awhile for the Georgetown backcourt to become familiar with each other, particularly while the Hoya guards are also getting used to prominent roles in a program playing at the highest level in the college game.

Leadership? Mutombo is the only senior on what overall is an extremely young and inexperienced team. Out of the entire roster, only he and Mourning have seen significant playing time. But Mutombo is still adjusting to a new country and the college game. Mourning has not shown significant leadership potential up to this point either. Thompson will be shepherding a very young flock.

★ STRENGTHS ★

John Thompson! His strong father-like influence and guidance will be especially needed and appreciated by this young group.

Mutombo & Mourning! They are two of the very best big men in the college game and certain future NBA Top Three picks. After a year of playing together, they should form the most dominating defensive presence perhaps in the history of the college game. Mourning, if he returns to focusing on it, could be the nation's best low post player. As a combo, Mutombo and Mourning are a terrific inside foundation to build a team around.

Tradition! Over the last decade, this program, under Thompson, has put itself on a level that automatically attracts high-level talent then inspires it to bring out

the best. Several of the newcomers, like Harrison and Brown, as well as returnees like Stoudamire and Thompson, may be motivated to raise their games to fit their surroundings. Georgetown's strong tradition should keep the Hoyas going through some tough moments.

★ BLUE RIBBON ANALYSIS ★

Despite the presence of, potentially, two of the nation's best three or four big men, Thompson faces his biggest challenge since back before the Hoyas entered the Big East and the Patrick Ewing Era began. Beyond Dikembe Mutombo and Alonzo Mourning, this club is virtually devoid of quality experience and even the overall talent of the recruiting class is not up to prior seasons. The transfers of Milton Bell, Dave Edwards and Michael Tate disrupted the entire nucleus planed for the immediate future. What remains —besides Mutombo and Mourning —are two role players (Antoine Stoudamire and Ronny Thompson) who have to prove they can be more, two outstanding freshmen guards who were big scorers in high school (Charles Harrison and Joey Brown), who may be asked to learn the point guard at the Big East level, two international players (Vladimar Bosanac and Pascal Fleury), brand new to the American college game, and three other newcomers (Robert Churchwell, Lamont Morgan and Brian Kelly) who are figured to need some experience before having much impact at this level.

Georgetown has four players —Brown, Harrison, Stoudamire and Thompson —capable of providing perimeter offense. How consistently they can do it will be important to keep what will seem like the entire Big East from sagging on Mourning and Mutombo. How well they can feed the post will also be crucial towards maximizing the effectiveness of the two big men. One positive aspect: It shouldn't take a Magic Johnson to be able to find Mutombo with a decent lob pass.

Defensively, it is questionable if there will be enough overall strength and quickness to implement the pressure Thompson prefers. Georgetown will need that pressure to generate offense and to take advantage of Mutombo and Mourning's terrific ability to run the floor.

The two big men are outstanding enough to project respectability for the Hoyas. But even with a solid, senior backcourt, the Hoyas were vulnerable fairly often and failed to crack the Final 16 of the NCAA tournament. For Georgetown to advance to the Final 16 this year while rising above the tough Big East, freshmen Harrison and Brown must step up quickly and returnees Stoudamire and Thompson must take full advantage of their increased playing time.

It has been a long time since Georgetown entered a season with this much uncertainty. Obviously, any team with a Mutombo and Mourning is a threat to have a big year. However, it might seem like heresy, but Georgetown could fall back into the middle of the pack in the Big East.

LAST SEASON			
#@Hawaii-Loa	109-56	@Providence	90-94
#Hawaii-Pacific	79-57	@Seton Hall	68-60
Florida International	114-67	St. John's	62-63
##North Carolina	93-81	Villanova	83-53
Rice	81-60	Connecticut	84-64
St. Leo (FL)	92-51	@Syracuse	87-89
Univ. of the Dist.		*Providence	78-77
of Columbia	112-39	*Connecticut	60-65
Virginia Tech	97-64	**Texas Southern	70-52
###Northern Iowa	83-49	**Xavier	71-74
@Boston College	83-53		
Providence	93-91	@ Road Games	
@Pitt	87-71	# Hawaii-Loa Classic, Kaneohe, HI	
@DePaul	74-64	## ACC/Big East Challenge, East	
Boston College	68-45	Rutherford, NJ	
@Connecticut	65-70	### Las Vegas, NV	
@Villanova	70-69	* Big East Tournament, Madison	
Syracuse	76-95	Square Garden, New York, NY	
Seton Hall	70-48	** NCAA Tournament, Indianapolis,	
@St. John's	74-67	IN	
Pitt	97-81		
Florida	56-40		

NOTES: Twelve Georgetown games will be telecast on national television . . . for the ninth consecutive year Georgetown will open the season in Hawaii . . . all of the Hoyas' regular season home games will, for the ninth year, be played at the Capital Centre in Landover, Md. . . . When

1990-91 GEORGETOWN SCHEDULE					
Nov.	23	#Hawaii-Loa	Feb.	16	@Seton Hall
	24	#Hawaii-Pacific		20	Pitt
Dec.	1	Southern Indiana		23	Connecticut
	5	##Duke		25	@St. John's
	8	###Rice	Mar.	3	@Syracuse
	12	St. Leo (FL)		7-10	****Big East Tour-
	15	UTEP			nament
	22	*Ohio State			
	29	**Houston	@ Road Games		
Jan.	2	Jackson State (MS)	# Hawaii-Loa Classic, Honolulu, HI		
	5	Seton Hall	## ACC/Big East Challenge		
	8	@Providence	### Summit, Houston, TX		
	12	Boston College	* Las Vegas, NV		
	14	@Villanova	** St. Petersburg, FL		
	19	@Boston College	*** Hartford, CT		
	21	Syracuse	**** Madison Square Garden, New		
	27	@Pitt	York, NY		
	29	St. John's			
Feb.	3	DePaul			
	6	Providence			
	9	Villanova			
	11	***Connecticut			

Georgetown plays Southern Indiana it will be the first collegiate meeting between the Mutombo brothers —Georgetown's All-America Dikembe and Southern Indiana's Ilo. The Mutombos last were on the same court in 1986 when they were members of the Zaire National team.

GEORGIA

LAST SEASON: 20-9
CONFERENCE RECORD: 13-6
STARTERS LOST: 1
STARTERS
   RETURNING: 4
CONFERENCE:
   SOUTHEASTERN (SEC)
LOCATION: ATHENS, GA
HOME FLOOR: GEORGIA
   COLISEUM (10,400)
NICKNAME: BULLDOGS
COLORS: RED AND BLACK

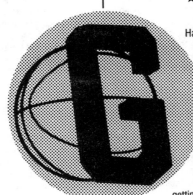

★ COACH'S PROFILE ★

HUGH DURHAM (Record at Georgia, 219-147. Career record, 449-244.) Durham is coming off one of his finest efforts in 1989-90. To begin with, he led Georgia back from a sub-par 15-16 record and a ninth place SEC finish in 1988-89 to respectability and much more in 1989-90. Georgia broke a 57-year drought last year when the Bulldogs captured the SEC regular season crown. It marked the first time in school history that Georgia had won the SEC title. For his efforts, Durham was voted the 1990 SEC coach of the year by *Associated Press* and his fellow league coaches. The coach of the year honor represented the third time in the past six seasons that Durham has picked up that award.

When Durham arrived in Georgia in 1978, the Bulldog program was definitely down. In the 10 seasons before Durham arrived, Georgia had won just 102 games overall and a mere 59 SEC contests. In Durham's first 10 campaigns in Athens, Georgia posted 184 wins overall and captured 89 SEC games. Prior to his tenure, Georgia had never been to a post-season tournament. Georgia has now been to nine post-season events in the past 10 years. Included in that string was a 1983 trip to the NCAA Final Four in Albuquerque, N.M. He is one of only 10 coaches to ever take two different schools to the Final Four as he led Florida State to the 1972 Final Four as well.

Obviously, the talent level at Georgia has risen since Durham took over. In his 12 years at Georgia, the program has produced five All-Americas, two SEC tournament MVPs, two U.S. Olympians and a U.S. Pan American Games team member. In addition, four Bulldogs have been first round NBA draft choices (Dominique Wilkins, Vern Fleming, Willie Anderson and Alec Kessler) in the past eight years.

Durham always seems to appear among the top three in polls ranking the best bench coaches in the SEC. He has always been known as a man-to-man defensive coach and basically prefers an up-tempo offense. However, his teams have not been able to play the way he prefers the last few years because of the depth problems. Durham has shown the ability to adjust to different styles and personnel, plus replace key stars. After Dominique Wilkins left Georgia a year early for the NBA, Durham regrouped the Bulldogs and led them to the Final Four. Last year's team which won the first SEC title in school history was far from perfect. Still, Georgia managed to win the big games when they were most needed.

Durham grew up in Louisville, Ky. He was a star athlete at Eastern HS. Durham earned 14 letters and was an All-Kentucky selection in football and all-region choice in basketball. He went on to become a three-year starter in basketball at Florida State from 1957-59. He scored 1,387 points during his career and averaged 21.9 points per game in 1959. Durham was a high scorer throughout his career, he finished college with an 18.9 career scoring average, and had a single-game high of 43 against Stetson. He received his B.A. degree in Business Administration in 1959 from Florida State and completed work on his Master in Business Administration, also from Florida State, in 1960. He served as an assistant basketball coach for six years at his alma mater after graduation.

Durham took over the Florida State program in 1966. His first team was 11-15, but after that Durham did not have another losing record in his 11 seasons in Tallahassee. Four of his teams at Florida State won over 20 games each. His 1971-72 squad won 27 games which still stands as the most wins in a season at Florida State.

Durham moved into a select group of coaches last year when he notched his 200th victory at Georgia. He is one of three coaches to win 200 or more games at two different NCAA Division I schools.

This will be Durham's 32nd year in college coaching. He is already Georgia's all-time winningest coach. He has accomplished just about everything in 24 years as a college head coach. His three children are out of college and grown up, but Durham is still fiesty, competitive and going strong. Sometimes his teams are better when the expectations were low entering the season.

The talent keeps rolling into Athens and the Georgia program is strong and ready for the future. After 24 years as a college head coach, Durham has had only two losing seasons. Don't look for many more, if any, losing seasons from a Hugh Durham coached team.

★ PLAYERS NOT RETURNING ★

MIKE HARRON (6-2, G, 0.7 ppg, 0.4 rpg, 4 assists, 2 steals) Harron walked-on to the Georgia program as a freshman and was rewarded a scholarship at the conclusion of his freshman year. He received little playing time last year, only 45 minutes, and helped mainly in practice and as a leader. Harron is not a major loss. Georgia has five seniors returning this year and it is Durham's largest senior class, so Georgia is in a better position to handle graduation losses than ever before.

ALEC KESSLER (6-11, F, 21.0 ppg, 10.4 rpg, 37 assists, 19 steals, 15 blocked shots) Kessler enjoyed an almost storybook college career, both on and off the court. His brother, Chad, played at Georgia and that was how Durham found out about Alec. He had no other major Division I offers and redshirted his first year at Georgia. Kessler came to Georgia at 6-8, 180 pounds and left at 6-11, 235. He just kept getting better and better and earned both Academic All-America honors last year while leading Georgia to its first SEC championship. He graduated with over a 3.90 GPA in Microbiology. Kessler was named the SEC Athlete of the Year for the 1989-90 school year. He led Georgia in scoring, rebounding and minutes played last year.

Kessler became the fourth Georgia player in the past eight years to be chosen in the first round of the NBA draft. He was drafted by the Houston Rockets (the No. 12 pick in the first round) and subsequently traded to the Miami Heat.

Durham will not be able to totally replace Kessler, but the Bulldogs' cupboard is certainly not bare. Four starters return and a strong group of newcomers are in the program.

★ RETURNING PLAYERS ★

NEVILLE AUSTIN (6-10, 225 lbs., SR, C, #35, 6.2 ppg, 6.0 rpg, 27 assists, 34 steals, 35 blocked shots, St. Croix, Virgin Islands & Auburn HS/Auburn, Ala.) One of five Bulldogs who stands 6-10 or taller, Austin and Alec Kessler were the only Bulldogs to start all 29 games last year. Austin added nearly 20 pounds to his frame prior to last season and was very effective at times in some big games. He never will be a big time offensive player, but Austin has learned to fill a role as a shotblocker, interior defender and rebounder. The added weight and strength enabled Austin to more than double his scoring and rebounding productivity from his sophomore year.

Austin was able to hold his own against the top front lines in the SEC and he played an underrated role in Georgia's first-ever SEC championship. He would like to get even stronger prior to the opening of the season. Look for Austin to continue to be an effective role player for the Bulldogs.

ARLANDO BENNETT (6-10, 215 lbs., SO, F/C, #32, Madison County HS/Colbert, Ga. & Connors State JC/Warner, Okla.) Bennett played for Georgia as a freshman in 1988-89 and saw action in 20 games. He averaged 2.3 points and 1.7 rebounds in his 20 games as a freshman. He was slated as a possible starter last season but suffered a broken right wrist on the first day of pre-season practice. Bennett left Georgia after the first semester and attended Connors JC for the second semester to work on his academics. He did not play at Connors and retains three years of eligibility.

The Georgia coaching staff has always been high on Bennett. He was ranked as the No. 3 prospect in the state of Georgia coming out of Madison County HS. He led Madison to the Georgia AAA state title as a senior where he averaged 16.5 points and 11.8 rebounds per game. Bennett also blocked 128 shots as a senior. He was highly recruited and chose Georgia over Alabama and Georgia Tech.

Bennett is much more skilled offensively than Neville Austin. However, Austin has had the opportunity to work on his strength and gained weight. Bennett has been unable to lift weights since last fall due to the broken wrist and still is not as strong as he needs to be. Bennett also suffered a broken left wrist shortly after his senior year. He has potential as a shotblocker and swatted away 15 shots during his freshman year. He also suffered a sprained ankle towards the end of his freshman year which limited his effectiveness.

With Bennett back in uniform and some other potentially outstanding shotblockers on the squad, Georgia has more intimidators up front than ever before.

ROD COLE (6-4, 185 lbs., SR, G, #22, 11.0 ppg, 3.5 rpg, 124 assists, 50 steals, 3 blocked shots, Rockdale County HS/Conyers, Ga.) Cole has been the SEC's most underrated player the past couple of years but finally began to earn some recognition last year. He moved to the point guard spot last year and handled the position even though it was his first time performing there on a full-time basis in college. Cole led Georgia in assists with 124 and was guilty of only 63 turnovers for close to a 2-1 assist to turnover ratio. He is not a great shooter but can score and made a respectable .432 (38-of-88) of his three-point attempts.

Cole's performance against LSU in Baton Rouge, in late January, helped set the stage for Georgia's march to the SEC title. He scored 19 points against the Tigers and was fouled with four seconds left while attempting a three-pointer and made all three free throws to send the game into overtime. Georgia won 94-92 in overtime.

"Rod has given us a complete game," said Durham. "He has taken control of our offense, and you see the difference it is making.''

Against Tennessee, Cole had 12 points, nine assists, and three steals and blocked a shot in the final minute to secure the win.

With Cole and talented junior Litterial Green returning to the starting lineup and capable players Jody Patton and Shaun Golden in reserve, the Georgia backcourt is in great shape for the 1990-91 season.

SHAUN GOLDEN (6-3, 180 lbs., SO, G, #10, 3.6 ppg, 1.6 rpg, 43 assists, 32 steals, 3 blocked shots, Riverside HS/Taylors, S.C.) Golden was a key reserve as a freshman averaging over 12 minutes per game. Unlike most highly regarded freshmen, Golden was a strong defender in his first year in college basketball.

''(Golden) was a rarity last year in that he was better defensively as a freshman than he was offensively and that doesn't happen very often,'' Durham said. Durham said Golden was further along defensively as a freshman than any player he has ever coached. Offensively, Golden is not a great shooter and scores more through penetration. He made 36-of-83 field goal attempts (.434) and was 3-of-7 (.429) from three-point range. Golden needs to improve at the free throw line where he made just .546 percent last year. He worked hard over the summer to improve his offensive game.

Golden played for his father at Riverside HS and led his team to an 83-9 record over three years in high school. Riverside won a South Carolina state title and finished second twice during Golden's career.

Georgia's top four guards form one of the best and most complete backcourts in the country. Rod Cole can do a little bit of everything and doesn't make mistakes, Litterial Green is an excellent offensive player, Jody Patton can bomb away from long distance and has three years of experience while Golden is a strong defender who is sure to improve his offense. Lately in college basketball, strong backcourts have become every bit as important as powerful inside games. With a backcourt as good as this one, Georgia cannot help but make a run at the SEC title.

LITTERIAL GREEN (6-1, 185 lbs., JR, G, #11, 17.5 ppg, 2.7 rpg, 120 assists, 37 steals, 4 blocked shots, Moss Point HS/Moss Point, Miss.) According to Durham, Green only needs to improve his consistency to move into the elite category of guards on the national level. Green is the Bulldogs' leading returning scorer and ranks third in the SEC among the conference's returning players.

The streaky shooting Green made 160-of-384 field goals (.417) and 49-of-128 three-point field goals (.383). He had a sensational 30-point game at Auburn that clinched the SEC title for Georgia.

Green played the point guard position almost exclusively as a freshman but moved to a second guard role last year. He also had 28 points in a loss to Georgia Tech, 21 points at Alabama, 24 against Mississippi State and 21 at Tennessee. He possesses excellent strength, explosive quickness and the ability to penetrate defenses and score in traffic against bigger players. Green also is a talented ballhandler. He should be one of the top three guards in the SEC this season along with Allan Houston of Tennessee and Alabama newcomer James Robinson.

LEM HOWARD (6-7, 215 lbs., SR, F, #25, 3.3 ppg, 2.2 rpg, 20 assists, 4 steals, 6 blocked shots, Douglass HS/Atlanta, Ga.) Howard was one of the true super subs in college basketball last year. He was basically the only inside player available off the bench last year and despite a broken hand suffered in mid-January, he played out the season and made a huge contribution to Georgia's championship run. ''We couldn't have won it (the SEC championship) without him,'' Durham said.

A former all-state performer at Atlanta's Douglass HS, Howard began his collegiate career at Miami of Florida. He averaged 7.5 points and 3.6 rebounds per game as a freshman for the Hurricanes before transferring from Miami in January of 1988. He became eligible at the beginning of the second semester during the 1988-89 season and played in a total of 18 games. Georgia was disappointing that year and so was Howard. He suffered from the lack of confidence and averaged only 1.2 points and 0.9 rebounds. Last year he made major strides, gained back his lost confidence and understood his role more clearly. Howard does not need to score in order to be effective. He is strong and can play physical defense, help out under the boards and does a lot of little things that don't show up in the box score.

Now in his fourth year in the Georgia program, including the season he sat out, Howard should be ready to have his most effective year yet. He will bring stability and ability to contribute in many areas to a Georgia front line which should be one of the strongest around.

JODY PATTON (6-4, 190 lbs., SR, G, #12, 7.8 ppg, 2.3 rpg, 28 assists, 8 steals, 1 blocked shot, Tift County HS/Tifton, Ga.) One of the more valuable reserve guards in the SEC, Patton is already Georgia's all-time leader in three-point field goals with 103.

Patton received significant playing time as a freshman and he has been an important player for the Bulldogs ever since. What he lacks in quickness, Patton makes up for in experience and toughness. Patton has had to overcome a knee problem which resulted in surgery and played with a broken nose as a sophomore.

We have mentioned this before, but Georgia's four-man guard rotation is one of the strongest in college basketball.

KENDALL RHINE (6-6, 190 lbs., SO, G/F, #15, 1.1 ppg, 0.9 rpg, 4 assists, 2 steals, Parkview HS/Lilburn, Ga.) As a freshman, Rhine was a limited contributor. He appeared in 18 games for a total of 61 minutes. He did manage to spark the Bulldogs in a few games and Rhine is a capable shooter who made 6-of-12 field goals (.500) in limited action. He is also a quality athlete who was drafted in the 16th round, as a pitcher, by the New York Mets prior to enrolling at Georgia. Rhine turned down the Mets' offer and was a reserve pitcher on Georgia's SEC championship winning baseball team last spring.

It will be interesting to see if Rhine stays with basketball through the next two years. He loves the game, but baseball is the sport in which he has professional potential. With eight lettermen returning and a slew of talented newcomers in the fold, it doesn't appear that Rhine's role will increase this year.

MARSHALL WILSON (6-8, 210 lbs., SR, F, #44, 12.0 ppg, 5.3 rpg, 36 assists, 33 steals, 16 blocked shots, Franklin County HS/Lavonia, Ga. & Connors State JC/Warner, Okla.) Wilson is Georgia's returning starter at small forward. He was the team's No. 3 scorer last year and gained a great deal of confidence and consistency.

''Marshall is getting closer to being the kind of player I want him to be and the kind of player he wants to become,'' Durham said.

He signed early with Georgia during his senior year at Franklin County (Ga.) HS and played one year at Connors State JC before heading back to Georgia. Wilson switched between the small forward and power forward spots as a sophomore, averaged 7.4 points and 4.4 rebounds for the year, and lacked confidence and consistency. He has been held back in the past by a lack of strength but Wilson has gotten stronger over the last year. He scored in double figures in 20 games, including his last seven, after hitting double digits in only six games as a sophomore. Wilson was Georgia's second best rebounder and he hit .521 of his shots from the floor and .790 from the line. He is an excellent athlete who runs the court well and has outstanding leaping ability. Wilson will be asked to help replace the 21 points per game lost with the graduation of Alec Kessler. Both Wilson and Litterial Green have to be consistent scorers for Georgia to be back in the SEC title hunt this season.

★ NEWCOMERS ★

CHARLES CLAXTON (7-1, 225 lbs., FR, C, #33, 22.0 ppg, 14.0 rpg, Carol City HS/Miami, Fla.) The tallest Georgia signee since Troy Hitchcock in 1982, Claxton was one of the top prospects in Florida last year. He is a shotblocker who chose Georgia over UNLV, Louisville, Illinois and Florida State.

Claxton needs to gain more strength and weight, but his shotblocking ability cannot be understated. He will need to learn when to go after shots, Claxton tries to block everything now, but Georgia has never had a big shotblocker before.

Claxton is also a good rebounder and has some offensive tools. He should back up Neville Austin in the pivot and see some time as a freshman.

BERNARD DAVIS (6-0, 170 lbs., FR, G, #23, 22.0 ppg, 5.0 rpg, 5.0 apg, 3.0 stpg, Richmond Hill HS/Richmond Hill, Ga.) A first-team All-Georgia performer, Davis was also voted to the All-Georgia team in all classifications by the Associated Press. He led Richmond Hill to the state Class A Final Four and a 31-1 record as a senior. He also led his team to a 28-4 record and the second-place finish in the Georgia Class A state tournament as a junior. Richmond Hill won the state title his sophomore year and during Davis' four years on the varsity, his teams combined for an 86-6 record. He was regarded as the top senior guard in Georgia last year and is Georgia's only backcourt recruit.

''He gives us some jet-quickness back there,'' said Durham. ''He can be effective both offensively and defensively. I've a good feeling about him.''

Davis enters a rather stacked Georgia backcourt. The Georgia backcourt is talented, versatile and experienced. However, if Davis gets some playing time ahead of the top four guards that are already in the program, the Bulldogs could have unprecedented strength in the backcourt.

ANTONIO HARVEY (6-11, 220 lbs., SO, C, #34, Pascagoula HS/Gautier, Miss. & Connors State JC/Warner, Okla.) After transferring from Southern Illinois and attending Connors State JC, where he did not play last year, Harvey enters Georgia with three years of eligibility. Harvey was the freshman of the year in the Missouri Valley Conference for the 1988-89 season. He started 30-of-34 games for Southern Illinois and averaged 6.9 points, 5.2 rebounds and blocked an impressive 70 shots to lead the MVC in that category.

All who saw Harvey play at Southern Illinois concurred that he had great potential. He needs to get stronger and add some weight.

Harvey's hometown was not far from where teammate Litterial Green (Moss Point, Miss.) grew up. Green and Harvey were two of the top four high school players in Mississippi in 1988 along with former LSU All-America Chris Jackson and Southern Mississippi star Clarence Weatherspoon. The Georgia coaching staff is excited about the potential Harvey brings, especially on the defensive end. With Harvey and Claxton, Georgia has more shotblocking ability than ever.

MARCEL KON (6-10, 200 lbs., FR, F, #51, 13.0 ppg, 8.0 rpg, Boyd Anderson HS/Plantation, Fla.) Georgia is experienced and talented up front so Kon is a probable redshirt candidate. He needs additional weight and strength before becoming a factor in the SEC. He chose Georgia over Penn State, Southern Methodist, Florida State and South Alabama.

Kon's sister, Helene, is member of Georgia's volleyball team. He has a nice shooting touch and good skills. However, he is just not ready for the rigors of the SEC.

REGGIE TINCH (6-5, 210 lbs., JR, F, #24, 14.0 ppg, 6.0 rpg, Westover HS/Albany, Ga. & Connors State JC/Warner, Okla.) We cannot think of another team in the country that has a pipeline with a particular junior college the way Georgia does with Connors State in Warner, Okla. Tinch is one of five Bulldogs who have either played at Connors State or attended that school to get their grades up. Doug Durham, one of Durham's sons, is an assistant coach at Connors. Tinch signed with Georgia coming out of high school but failed to quality for admission and spent the past two years at Connors State. He started for both seasons and played a key role as Connors State finished 36-2 and won the national junior college championship last year. Tinch is known for his terrific strength and athletic ability. He is a "jump out of gym" type and is not afraid to mix it up underneath the basket. He plays bigger than his 6-5 height. Tinch is not a great shooter and scores mainly on the offensive boards and around the basket.

Tinch is another terrific athlete in Durham's arsenal. He makes Georgia deeper and a team with more athletic ability than last year.

★ QUESTIONS ★

Replacing the vast contributions of Alec Kessler? "Alec's record speaks for itself, both on the floor and in the classroom," said Durham. "There's not doubt we're going to miss him. The challenge will be to replace his point production and strong rebounding. But I think it's the intangibles he gave us which will be the most difficult to replace. You don't replace someone with his work ethic, his attitude and his leadership."

Getting consistency from the newcomers? Including Arlando Bennett, who played a year for Georgia before transferring to Connors State JC, Georgia has six new players this year. Durham will need strong years from several of them, including Bennett and Antonio Harvey, who sat out last year at Connors State, for Georgia to successfully defend its SEC title.

★ STRENGTHS ★

Hugh Durham! He is one of the premier bench coaches in the SEC and has made Georgia into a conference power that can compete on a high national level. With few exceptions, Durham has usually found a way to have a successful team at Georgia every year he has been in Athens.

Improved depth!
More overall athletic ability!
Shotblockers! With the arrival of freshman Charles Claxton and transfer Antonio Harvey, Georgia has more shotblocking than it has enjoyed ever before.
An outstanding and deep backcourt!

★ BLUE RIBBON ANALYSIS ★

Georgia surprised the prognosticators by winning the SEC title last year. It was a first SEC title ever for a Georgia basketball team and the accomplishment won't soon be forgotten in Athens.

"Last year was an exciting one and it's one we'll remember for a long time," said Georgia coach Hugh Durham. "Winning a championship is something that coaches and players talk about, but few actually get the opportunity to experience it. We finished second and third before, so we'd knocked on the door. But winning it is a special feeling."

Georgia wasn't particularly deep and the Bulldogs definitely had holes last year, but Georgia came together down the stretch and won the big games when it had to. The Bulldogs will dearly miss their departed leading scorer and rebounder, Alec Kessler, a true All-America, and the fourth Georgia player to become a first round pick in the NBA draft in the Durham Era. Replacing Kessler won't be easy but Durham has the largest senior class (five) he has had since coming to Athens in 1978. He also has a team packed with more depth and athletic ability than last year, possibly the premier backcourt in the SEC and some intriguing shotblockers and a quality small forward in senior Marshall Wilson.

"We have a chance to be a more athletic and deeper team this season," said Durham. "We're counting on many of our new players to contribute early for us. Our new people are going to have an opportunity to help us right away, but we're not going to put any pressure on them to do this. I feel good about our inside with four shotblockers in there. There is some good quickness with our big people. But, we're really only half-big. We have some height, but we don't have the wide-bodies."

Georgia may not have the "wide-bodies" that Durham wants, but the Bulldogs have almost everything else necessary to be strong again in 1990-91. Guards Litterial Green and Rod Cole should be among the elite backcourt players in the SEC. Wilson has All-SEC potential, senior center Neville Austin became a capable, role player last year and the newcomers are impressive.

The SEC is always a difficult league to handicap. At least every few years it seems that the conference champion comes out of the middle of the pack and the predicted favorite fades. However, this year it is difficult to image Georgia not being in the midst of the race for the conference title. LSU and Alabama should be strong and are national level teams. Mississippi State should have its best team in decades, Kentucky gained great respect under Rick Pitino last year, Vanderbilt is coming off an NIT championship, Tennessee has the best returning guard in the league in sophomore Alan Houston, Auburn proved to be no pushover last year, Mississippi is always a difficult trip for all conference teams and Florida has a new coach in Lon Kruger. It will be another competitive year in the SEC, but Georgia still enters the season regarded as one of the upper crust teams in the SEC. Georgia should finish no lower than third in the SEC, win over 20 games again and make the NCAA tournament.

LAST SEASON			
Baptist College (SC)	91-55	Florida	70-65
#Texas Christian	77-72	Alabama	75-64
#@Western Kentucky	76-70	@Vanderbilt	67-66
@Central Florida	92-62	@Mississippi State	82-74
Mercer	85-57	Mississippi	107-83
##Georgia Tech	89-92	LSU	86-85
Jacksonville	91-62	@Tennessee	83-93
###Wisconsin	65-64	@Auburn	94-79
###Arizona State	61-62	*Vanderbilt	74-78 OT
Kentucky	106-91	**Texas	88-100
@Florida	69-97		
@Alabama	62-79	@ Road Games	
Vanderbilt	108-81	# Western Kentucky Invitational, Bowling Green, KY	
Mississippi State	83-69	## The Omni, Atlanta, GA	
@Mississippi	74-84	### Tribune Classic, Tempe, AZ	
@LSU	94-92 OT	* SEC Tournament, Orlando, FL	
Tennessee	85-77	** NCAA Tournament, Indianapolis, IN	
Auburn	88-75		
@Kentucky	77-88		

NOTES: Georgia will play Wichita State in the opening round of the Central Fidelity Holiday Classic . . . the Kuppenheimer Classic is a doubleheader with Georgia facing Texas in the first game with Georgia Tech vs. Loyola Marymount in the second game . . . one of Georgia's early signees from last November, 6-3 guard Justin Thompson of Osceola HS in Kissimmee,

---

1990-91 GEORGIA SCHEDULE			
Nov.	23-24	#Central Fidelity Holiday Classic	8 LSU
	28	Western Kentucky	12 @Florida
Dec.	8	@Mercer	16 Mississippi State
	11	@Vanderbilt	20 Alabama
	14	@Miami (FL)	23 @Auburn
	19	##Georgia Tech	27 Vanderbilt
	22	*Texas	Mar. 2 @Mississippi
	29	Purdue	7-10 **SEC Tournament
Jan.	2	Kentucky	
	5	Tennessee	@ Road Games
	7	@LSU	# Richmond, VA (Dartmouth, Richmond & Wichita State)
	12	Florida	## The Omni, Atlanta, GA
	16	@Mississippi State	* Kuppenheimer Classic, Atlanta, GA
	19	@Alabama	** Nashville, TN
	23	Auburn	
	30	Mississippi	
Feb.	3	@Kentucky	
	6	@Tennessee	

Fla., did not qualify for admission and will attend a junior college this year . . . Georgia was a perfect 12-0 at home last year. The Bulldogs have a streak of 13 regular season victories heading into the season. That is the longest homecourt win streak of any team in the SEC.

KANSAS

LAST SEASON: 30-5
CONFERENCE RECORD: 11-3
STARTERS LOST: 4
STARTERS RETURNING: 1
CONFERENCE: BIG EIGHT
LOCATION: LAWRENCE, KS
HOME FLOOR: ALLEN
FIELDHOUSE (15,800)
NICKNAME: JAYHAWKS
COLORS: CRIMSON AND BLUE

★ COACH'S PROFILE ★

ROY WILLIAMS (Record at Kansas, 49-17.) "I really like watching Kansas play," said one observer. "They're a team. I'd like to see more teams like that."

That compliment of Roy Williams' Kansas team came from none other then the greatest coach ever in college basketball, UCLA's John Wooden. When the Wizard speaks, basketball people listen and his compliment is an indication that Roy Williams hasn't just arrived at Kansas, he is now one of the up and coming young giants in the game after just two years on the job.

Williams' second edition of the Kansas Jayhawks was the surprise of college basketball in 1989-90. At the beginning of the year, the Jayhawks cruised through the Dodge Big Apple NIT, including a win over eventual national champion UNLV, rolled to 19 consecutive wins and a No. 1 ranking. The Jayhawks finished the season with 30 wins —the second most in the school's tradition-rich history —and their five losses were to just three teams (Oklahoma, Missouri and UCLA). Kansas earned an NCAA berth for the sixth time in seven years. Williams was named national coach of the year by the U.S. Basketball Writers Association.

In an era in college basketball when talent rules, the Jayhawks won 30 games the old-fashioned way —through an uncanny spirit of teamwork and an overall team passing ability at a level rarely seen. It is not that the Jayhawks were not talented, but the team did not have any sure-fire superstar or any players that are certain to be big timers in the NBA. For much of the year, the Jayhawks played with the timing and synchronization of a symphony and Williams was the star conductor.

After the Jayhawks romped through the Dodge Big Apple NIT, UNLV coach Jerry Tarkanian said: "The Jayhawks are further along than any team I've ever seen. They're running their offense like it was February."

"They are beautiful to watch," said St. John's coach Lou Carnesecca after Kansas dissected his Redmen in Madison Square Garden. "They reduce the game to simplicity."

"They are like poetry in motion," said former Miami (Fla.) coach Bill Foster after the Jayhawks dismantled his Hurricanes by a 100-73 score. ". . . You look at their athletic talent, and it's not the leaping-and-dunking type talent a lot of teams have. There are probably eight or 10 with more pure talent. But I don't know of anybody else with eight or nine good, smart players. They just kick you with good, basic basketball."

North Carolina coach Dean Smith, a Kansas graduate himself and the man who was responsible for bringing Williams into college basketball said: "They're running our stuff. What bugs me is that they're executing it better. They look better than we do running it."

Williams had never been a head coach at the collegiate level until he left his position as an assistant at North Carolina to take over at Kansas after Larry Brown left for the San Antonio Spurs in the summer of '88. In just two years at Kansas, Williams has succeeded in implementing a system similar to North Carolina's. Like at North Carolina, at Kansas the system always comes first. The Jayhawks hound their opponents on defense, and on offense keep moving and think pass first, shot second. The Kansas system features balanced scoring as five Jayhawks reached double figures last year. The Kansas defense limited opponents to 44 percent shooting from the floor and caused an average of over 19 turnovers per game. Offensively, Kansas averaged 92.1 point per game and their passing ability resulted in a gaudy 53.3 percent shooting from the floor. If Williams keeps it up he may earn a genius tag, like former San Francisco 49ers coach Bill Walsh.

"When people look at basketball players, they focus on athletic ability — running, jumping, shot blocking. That's a huge part of it, but there's a lot more to playing basketball," Williams told Robert Fachet of *The Washington Post.*

"I think your brain and your heart have a lot to do with winning, too. These players have talent, but along with that talent what makes them so good is their work habits, their intelligence, their pride and all those things coaches like to talk about and few of us understand whatever it is."

"Coach Williams' biggest asset is he only recruits a certain type of player," said former Kansas guard Kevin Pritchard, who led the Jayhawks in scoring last year. "He gets people he knows will go to class, knows will be good people. And he gets people he knows will be smart enough to realize his system works."

When Williams took over at Kansas on July 8, 1988, there were Jayhawk supporters who were not only surprised but disappointed. They wanted a big

a proven head coach. However, Kansas athletic director Bob Frederick wanted to take a chance on this relatively obscure assistant coach from Dean Smith's North Carolina program. Being connected with North Carolina certainly didn't hurt Williams' chances for getting the job as Smith certainly has some input at his alma mater. Also, the man Williams succeeded, Larry Brown, was a North Carolina graduate. Those North Carolina ties were important but Frederick also felt strong about Williams both personally and professionally.

"Obviously, there were some risks involved in the decision," Frederick said. "But I became convinced after talking to Roy that he had some qualities this program deserves. He sensed the historical tradition and respected what's happened here in the past with (Dr. James) Naismith and (Phog) Allen and (Adolph) Rupp and (Dean) Smith and (Ralph) Miller. That was significant to him."

Williams took over a Kansas program that was coming off a national championship but also was going on NCAA probation. Kansas was not allowed to participate in post-season play his first year at the school and the coaching staff was restricted from recruiting off campus until last year. Williams managed to keep the Jayhawks' spirits high despite the devastating probation and guided his first Kansas team to a 19-12 record. He was named the 1989 national rookie coach of the year by both *Basketball Times* and Dick Vitale.

Williams is a native of Skyland, N.C., and was an outstanding high school baseball and basketball player. He attended North Carolina and competed as a non-scholarship player on the 1968-69 Tar Heel freshman team. He needed to get a job to pay for his education and was not able to participate in varsity basketball at North Carolina. However, he had known in junior high school that he wanted to be a coach. Williams would often sit in on Dean Smith's North Carolina practice sessions, took notes and furthered his knowledge of the game. He still has those notes and occasionally refers to them. He earned a Bachelor's Degree in Education as well as a Master's Degree in Teaching from North Carolina.

After graduating from North Carolina, he coached for five years at Charles D. Owen HS in Swannanoa, N.C. He also coached freshman football and boys golf, plus served as athletic director. Williams began his collegiate coaching career in 1978 as an assistant at North Carolina. He was the junior varsity head coach, scouted opponents, served as conditioning coordinator, was the assistant director of the Dean Smith Basketball School and even drove 504 miles around the state every Sunday during basketball season delivering copies of the *Dean Smith Show* to television stations. He later assumed the duties of a full-time assistant and recruiter when Eddie Fogler left North Carolina to become head coach at Wichita State. Williams spent 10 years in Chapel Hill before coming to Kansas.

"Tactful and reserved, he seems every bit the Dean's list student. He dresses like a hotel check-in clerk, doesn't smoke or drink, and when he's animated, looks like Huckleberry Hound," wrote Alexander Wolff in *Sports Illustrated.*

With the great job Williams has done in his first two years at Kansas, it is hard to believe that he was just a part-time assistant coach at North Carolina up until four years ago. No one in Kansas questions the decision to hire Williams now. It is obvious that Williams is the latest in a long list of great coaches who have cared and nurtured this great program. His teams have not only been successful beyond the most ardent Kansas fan's dreams, but Williams has also recruited well and has established the philosophy the program will follow. Until Larry Brown spent five years in Lawrence, the least amount of time a Kansas coach stayed at the University was eight years. Williams certainly has an open invitation to stay as long as he wants at Kansas and don't be surprised if his reign goes on into the next century.

★ PLAYERS NOT RETURNING ★

TODD ALEXANDER (6-2, G, 1.1 ppg, 1.0 rpg, 11 assists, 3 steals, 1 blocked shot) A reserve guard who played in 23 games for a total of 90 minutes (3.9 mpg) as a freshman. Alexander saw limited playing time last year but had some ability. He transferred to an NAIA school, Washburn University in Topeka, Kan., after his freshman year was over.

RICK CALLOWAY (6-6, F, 13.1 ppg, 4.3 rpg, 104 assists, 50 steals, 11 blocked shots) Calloway started all 35 games and played well in his only year at Kansas. He spent his first three years at Indiana, played a major role on the Hoosiers' 1987 national championship before becoming dissatisfied with Bob Knight's ways and transferring to Kansas. Calloway thought he would play for Larry Brown at Kansas but that never materialized as Brown left for the NBA and Roy Williams became his coach.

"I wish I could have played here for more than one year. I am a Jayhawk, not a Hoosier. I'm a Jayhawk through and through," Calloway said.

Calloway was Kansas' third-best scorer and rebounder last year. An indication of just how skilled a passing team Kansas was the fact that Calloway ranked fourth on the team in assists even though he had 104. That total would generally be good for first or second on most teams, but not the smooth passing Jayhawks.

He was not drafted in the NBA draft, but tried out for the San Antonio Spurs over the summer. Calloway is one of four starters who are not returning. It seems that it should be difficult for the Jayhawks to be as prominent nationally and strong inside the Big Eight as they were a year ago. However, keep in mind this quote from Williams: "If you looked at what we lost, on paper, compared to what most teams have returning, yes, it would be tempting to leave us out of the polls. But it was tempting last year."

JEFF GUELDNER (6-5, G, 10.7 ppg, 4.6 rpg, 132 assists, 47 steals, 4 blocked shots) One of four starters not returning for the Jayhawks, Gueldner averaged 27.1 minutes per game last year and ranked fifth on the team in scoring. He was one of five Jayhawks who finished the year averaging in double figures. Gueldner was a skilled player who shot the ball well (.527 from the field last year) and was a major three-point threat (69-of-142 for 48.6 percent). He also ranked second on the team in scoring with 132 assists and was guilty of only 59 turnovers, an average of fewer than two per game.

His perimeter shooting and ballhandling abilities will definitely be missed. Gueldner was not a star but he was a skilled, complementary player who made a major contribution in his own way.

It is hard to envision Kansas' passing game being as synchronized this year as it was last year without Gueldner and graduated starters Rick Calloway and Kevin Pritchard.

PEKKA MARKKANEN (6-10, C, 6.9 ppg, 3.9 rpg, 16 assists, 26 steals, 38 blocked shots) A native of Finland, Markkanen played only one year at Kansas but he certainly earned his scholarship. He started 33 games and averaged 19.6 minutes per game. Markkanen was by far the best shotblocker on the team and his 38 blocks more than doubled the total of Kansas' next best shotblocker, Mike Maddox, who had 19. Markkanen was a good defender and had very quick feet for a big man. He fit in well with the Jayhawks and adapted quickly to major college basketball in his first year in the United States.

Markkanen had another year of eligibility but his wife was homesick and he elected to return to Finland. His place in the lineup is expected to be taken by 6-10 David Johanning, a junior college transfer from Hutchinson (Kan.) CC.

KEVIN PRITCHARD (6-3, G, 14.5 ppg, 2.5 rpg, 177 assists, 59 steals, 9 blocked shots) Kansas has a talented sophomore point guard, Adonis Jordan, who can come close to replacing Pritchard statistically. However, Jordan, or anyone else, will have great difficulty replacing the vast intangibles Pritchard contributed to the program. Williams told pro scouts through the year that Pritchard was the toughest competitor he had ever been around.

Pritchard was a starter on the 1988 national championship team. He thrived during his final two years at Kansas under Williams' coaching. Last year Pritchard led Kansas in scoring, assists, steals and minutes played. He was a good perimeter shooter who made .525 of his field goal attempts and was 46-of-108 (42.6 percent) from three-point range. Kansas will undoubtedly miss his competitiveness, leadership, and perimeter shooting.

"I'm asking the NCAA if I can have four more years. But I don't think they're gonna let me," Pritchard said.

He was one of the most underrated guards in the country except in the estimation of the team that drafted him, the Golden State Warriors. Pritchard was a second round choice of the Warriors (the 34th selection overall in the draft) and signed a three-year contract. His contract was considered excellent for a player selected at his position in the draft.

Pritchard will go down as one of the unsung heroes in the history of Kansas basketball.

FREEMAN WEST (6-5, F, 6.0 ppg, 3.7 rpg, 44 assists, 18 steals, 3 blocked shots) West was a solid reserve who averaged 15.8 minutes per game. He was tough defensively and helped on the boards as well. West knew his range and was a solid shooter who made 59.5 percent of his attempts.

In all, Kansas has lost four starters and five of the top eight players last year in terms of scoring and minutes played.

★ RETURNING PLAYERS ★

TERRY BROWN (6-2, 190 lbs., SR, G, –3, 11.0 ppg, 2.5 rpg, 29 assists, 18 steals, 2 blocked shots, Clyde-Savannah HS/Clyde, N.Y. & Northeastern Oklahoma A&M/Miami, Okla.) Few teams in the country could match Kansas' bench strength last year. The Jayhawks' bench contributed 36.7 percent of Kansas' scoring in 1989-90. Terry Brown, who was in his first year in the program after transferring from Northeast Oklahoma A&M, was a big reason why the Kansas bench was so potent. Although he did not start a game, Brown still played in all 35 games and led Kansas in scoring on ten occasions —tying him with Kevin Pritchard for the most on the team.

Brown came to Kansas known as a white-hot, three-point marksman. He lived up to that reputation. Brown's first 11 baskets at Kansas were three-pointers. His 89 three-pointers led Kansas in that category and were just two shy of the Big Eight Conference mark of 91 set by Oklahoma's Mookie Blaylock. He had only 49 two-point field goals for the year. Brown made 42.8 percent of his three-point attempts.

Against Kentucky, he was 7-of-10 from three-point range, setting the Kansas single-game record for three-point shots made. He scored a season-high of 31 points against Kentucky. Seven times last year, Brown knocked in the three-point shot on Kansas' last possession of the first half.

He has an unorthodox shot but it certainly manages to go in. Brown cocks the ball behind his right shoulder before letting it rip. He became such a crowd favorite that Kansas students handed out Xeroxed $3 bills with Brown's photo in

the middle. They read: IN TERRY WE TRUST.

"Terry is a great outside shooter, but he has to improve his defense and ballhandling so he is not just a specialist," Williams said.

Brown was selected to the *UPI* Big Eight All-Bench team along with teammate Mike Maddox. He was also selected to the Big Eight all-newcomer team. He came to Kansas from Northeastern Oklahoma A&M. Brown was selected MVP of the 1989 National Junior College tournament even though he came off the bench for the national championship winners.

With the graduation of Jeff Gueldner, Brown should strongly contend for a starting job at off-guard this season.

ALONZO JAMISON (6-5, 235 lbs., JR, F, #24, 4.9 ppg, 2.0 rpg, 26 assists, 12 steals, Santa Ana HS/Santa Ana, Calif. & Rancho Santiago JC/Santa Ana, Calif.) After becoming eligible, Jamison played the final 17 games of the season. He has extremely quick feet, plays strong defense and can rebound. Jamison averaged 11.1 minutes per game. He made a remarkable 35-of-67 field goals (61.4 percent). He is very effective inside due to superb quickness and a great deal of bulk. However, Jamison needs to do more on the perimeter in order to be a complete player.

He had a season-high of 12 points against Kansas State and recorded five rebounds twice in regular season games. He will be expected to shoulder more of the scoring load this year and could easily become a starter.

"Playing those games (17 after he became eligible) helped Alonzo," Williams said. "He was tight until the very end. This year he has a better chance of getting in game shape. He has quick feet. He may guard players out on the court, yet he's strong, so he'll be asked to play inside. He'll be moved around more than anybody."

ADONIS JORDAN (5-11, 160 lbs., SO, G, #30, 3.0 ppg, 1.2 rpg, 109 assists, 20 blocked shots, Grover Cleveland HS/Reseda, Calif.) As a freshman Jordan averaged 13.3 minutes per game as a backup point guard to Kevin Pritchard. Now this season, Jordan will be the starter and a key player for the Jayhawks. He is a good defender, possesses fine quickness and penetrates well. Jordan was not asked for a big offensive contribution last year and he made 33-of-97 field goals (34.0 percent) and was 14-of-40 (35.0 percent) from three-point range.

Jordan was a member of the Big Eight All-Freshman team last year and played in all 35 games. He was one of four Jayhawks with more than 100 assists and his single-season assist total was the third highest ever for a Kansas freshman. Jordan also had an outstanding assist to turnover ratio as he committed only 47 turnovers with his 109 assists. His season scoring high was 12 points against Iowa State in the opening round of the Big Eight tournament.

Over the summer, Jordan and teammate Mike Maddox toured Spain and the Canary Islands with the Big Eight Select team. Jordan played well against a varying degree of competition. He also got in some sightseeing.

"We went to a bullfight in Madrid. I don't like the way they kill the bulls. They killed six of them," Jordan said. "I don't know if it's sport or entertainment or next week's dinner."

Concerning Jordan, Williams told Gary Bedore of the *Lawrence Journal-World*: "I'd like Adonis to score, it's silly not to ask a guard to score. But he is much different from Kevin (Pritchard). Kevin had a scorer's mentality and could also do the other things. Adonis thinks of running the club, getting in the right offense and defense, getting it inside. Adonis is special to me and I think he'll be a good one."

MIKE MADDOX (6-7, 210 lbs., SR, F, –32, 8.7 ppg, 3.5 rpg, 47 assists, 16 steals, 19 blocked shots, Putnam North HS/Oklahoma City, Okla.) Outside of All-America candidate Mark Randall, Maddox is the only other player on the roster to have ever started a game for Kansas. Behind Maddox, he is the second most experienced frontcourt player on the team. Maddox was a member of the Big Eight All-Bench team last year. He played for the Big Eight Select team over the summer that toured Spain and the Canary Islands. In the summer of '89 he toured Australia with the Big Eight Select team coached by Roy Williams.

Maddox's strength is shooting and last year he made 133-of-233 field goals (.571). He scored a career-high 21 points against Alabama-Birmingham in the first game of the season. Maddox was a double figure scorer in 13 games.

"He's gotta rebound better," Williams told Gary Bedore of the *Lawrence Journal-World*. "Mike's a scorer, yet he has not been the focus of our attack. This year he and Randall may be the focus. If that's the case, defenses will be aimed at them. If that's the case, can they still score?"

Maddox was a reserve on Kansas' 1988 national championship team. He averaged 2.5 points and 1.6 rebounds in limited action as a freshman. In Williams' first year at Kansas, Maddox's sophomore year, he averaged 10.9 points and 3.5 rebounds while starting nine games.

The former player of the year in Oklahoma, Maddox must have his best year yet if Kansas is to stay near the top of the Big Eight Conference. Mark Randall needs some help and Maddox will have to score and rebound consistently to take some of the load off Randall.

MALCOLM NASH (6-7, 195 lbs., JR, F, #43, 1.0 ppg, 1.3 rpg, 2 assists, 3 blocked shots, Vashon HS/St. Louis, Mo.) Nash saw action in 20 games last year and scored a career-high 11 points against Elizabeth City State (N.C.). Last season marked the first time that Nash had been able to practice or play for the Jayhawks because he had to sit out his freshman year at Kansas.

Nash came to Kansas considered as a good rebounder from one of the strongest programs in the midwest. He was the second leading scorer and rebounder for a 30-1 St. Louis Vashon HS team which won the Missouri Class 4A state championship and was ranked fifth nationally by *USA Today*. His brother, Montrell, plays at Memphis State. One of Nash's uncles played at Kansas in the late '60s.

Although the Jayhawks suffered some severe graduation losses, look for Nash's role to be limited.

MARK RANDALL (6-9, 230 lbs., SR, F, #42, 13.3 ppg, 6.2 rpg, 65 assists, 35 steals, 13 blocked shots, Cherry Creek HS/Englewood, Colo.) The lone starter returning from last year's team, Randall turned in a sterling junior season. He was named to the second-team All-Big Eight squad by both the *Associated Press* and *United Press International*. Randall was a third-team All-America selection by the National Association of Basketball Coaches and was a finalist for the prestigious Naismith Award. He finished second on the team in scoring behind Kevin Pritchard and led the Jayhawks in rebounding. Randall also led the Big Eight Conference in field goal percentage (.600). He enters his senior year on course to finish as the top field goal percentage leader in Kansas history ahead of such Jayhawk greats as Wilt Chamberlain and Danny Manning.

"I think he'll have a great year," Williams said of Randall. "He's relaxed, confident after having had two great years. He may be asked to do more than before, carrying more of a scoring load . . . He's one of the best in the conference. Mark can run the court, catches the ball in traffic and is a slashing scorer."

Randall was very highly regarded during his career at Cherry Creek HS in the Denver suburb of Englewood, Colo. He arrived at Kansas weighing 195 pounds and soon found out that he needed more strength and better stamina. Randall played in 31 games and started four as a freshman and averaged 4.5 points and 2.7 rebounds. However, he had trouble adjusting to major college basketball and the expectations of a demanding coach, Larry Brown.

In 1987-88, Randall participated in pre-season drills and played in one exhibition game, but was given a medical redshirt to correct a breathing and jaw alignment problem. He underwent surgery, had his sinus cavities drained and his jaw aligned. The jaw alignment procedure involved breaking the upper jaw in four places and inserting plastic plates to correct an underbite. Randall's jaw was wired for eight weeks following surgery. Even though he missed Kansas' national championship season and was miserable, Randall came back a much better player the following year. Not only was he in better shape, but his confidence soared under Williams.

"When I first got here, Mark was just about the least-confident good player I've ever seen," Williams told Natalie Meisler of the *Denver Post*. "So I took it upon myself to try to build him up. It was easy. I do think he's good. It's not like I was telling him lies. I went overboard at first because I wanted to make sure he understood the positive things. I mean, 'Hey, Mark, you went over there and got a drink of water better than anyone I've ever seen.'"

"By the end of last season he had confidence because he was successful. The experience of the World University Games gave him some confidence he could make that team, and all he's done this year is just improve. He's a better defensive player, a better rebounder, makes better decisions on his passing game. He's just a better player.

"He's getting more defensive attention, which is different from last year, but he has just improved all around, and he's going to continue to improve."

Randall played for the Gold Medalist U.S. team at the World University Games in Duisburg, West Germany, prior to his junior year. His international experience continued over the summer when he made the U.S. National team which competed in the Goodwill Games in Seattle and the World Basketball Championships in Buenos Aires, Argentina. His career certainly has blossomed in the last two years. Randall is not only one of the elite players in the Big Eight but will probably be a first round pick in the upcoming NBA draft.

"Our motto is no one really cares who gets the credit," Randall told Randy Holtz of the *Scripps Howard News Service* about the Jayhawks' espirit de corps. "We're going to pass the ball and hit the open man and whoever gets the best shot is the guy who is going to take it. That all sounds a little hokey, but I truly believe that's the No. 1 key to this team."

Randall also has excelled in the classroom. He was named to the Lee Jeans Big Eight All-Academic team last year.

KIRK WAGNER (6-7, 210 lbs., SR, F, #31, 3.0 ppg, 1.8 rpg, 1 assist, 5 steals, John Muir HS/Pasadena, Calif. & Pasadena City College/Pasadena, Calif.) Last year was Wagner's first season at Kansas and he was a reserve. He played in 21 games for a total of 130 minutes (6.2 mpg). He was out of shape at the beginning of pre-season practice and never caught up with his teammates.

"Kirk a year ago hurt his ankle and reported to school overweight," Williams told Gary Bedore of the *Lawrence Journal-World*. "It took him half the year to get in shape. By the end of the year he was where he should have started. I hope he arrives in condition. He can score."

In limited action last year, Wagner made 28-of-47 field goals (59.6 percent). If he is in shape, Wagner will be a major contributor for Kansas.

★ NEWCOMERS ★

DOUG ELSTUN (6-2, 175 lbs., JR, G, #21, Shawnee Mission West HS/Shawnee Mission, Kan.) Elstun comes back home to Kansas after playing one season at North Carolina, starting for the junior varsity team and serving as a reserve on the Tar Heel varsity. He was an all-state performer in 1986-87 at Shawnee Mission West HS. His father, Gene Elstun, played basketball for Kansas from 1955-57 and captained the Jayhawks as a senior.

Elstun will provide depth to the Jayhawk backcourt.

DAVID JOHANNING (6-10, 220 lbs., JR, C, #54, 10.0 ppg, 8.0 rpg, Bishop Carroll HS/Wichita, Kan. & Hutchinson CC/Hutchinson, Kan.) "He fills a need for us because of our lack of size," Williams said when signing Johanning in April. He comes from one of the premier junior college programs in the country, Hutchinson CC, and is a solid defensive center and a good rebounder. His junior college coach, David Farrar, said Johanning's biggest asset is making his teammates better players. He is expected to replace Pekka Markkanen at center for the Jayhawks.

"I'm not sure David is as good an athlete as Pekka," Williams said. "Pekka had such quick feet. But he faced good competition at Hutch. He's got to step up and give us quality minutes."

Ranked as one of the Top 30 junior college sophomores in the nation by *Basketball Times*, Johanning began his college career at Clemson in 1987-88. He redshirted at Clemson because of a knee injury and transferred to Hutchinson for the 1988-89 season.

PATRICK RICHEY (6-8, 180 lbs., FR, G/F, #12, 18.1 ppg, 7.0 rpg, 5.0 apg, Lee's Summit HS/Kansas City, Mo.) Often when a player signs with a program you wonder how he will fit in that system. That is not the case with Patrick Richey who should easily blend into the Jayhawks' unselfish style of offense. He handles the ball well and is an excellent passer. He needs strength, but Richey's basketball skills are first rate.

He was rated by *All-Star Sports* as the 62nd best prospect in the nation. He was twice named to the All-Missouri team. Richey will find a way to contribute as a freshman and should become an outstanding player in years to come for Kansas.

RICHARD SCOTT (6-6, 215 lbs., FR, F, #34, 21.0 ppg, 12.0 rpg, 6.0 apg, Little Rock Central HS/Little Rock, Ark.) Scott was a heavily recruited swingman in high school and he signed with Kansas last November even though he had not made an official visit to the Lawrence campus. He was ranked as the 68th best player in the country and the top senior in Arkansas by *All-Star Sports*.

"Richard has excellent athletic ability," Williams said. He can score inside and outside and is extremely competitive.

The acquisition of Scott is one of the reasons why Kansas' recruiting class was rated the best in the Big Eight by some recruiting experts. "I'll take any of those kids KU got," said Oklahoma coach Billy Tubbs. "Hey, we were after most of them."

SEAN TUNSTALL (6-2, 175 lbs., JR, G, #22, 18.5 ppg, 7.0 apg, 5.0 stpg, Vashon HS/St. Louis, Mo.) Although Tunstall has been at Kansas for two years he has not been eligible until this season. He signed with Kansas in the 1988 late signing period and was ineligible the following year. He was not eligible for the 1989-90 season after the NCAA ruled there were irregularities in his ACT test scores. He has just two years of college eligibility remaining.

Tunstall was able to practice last year with Kansas. If he can shake the rust off of two years' inactivity, he could be a real factor in the Jayhawk backcourt. Tunstall narrowed his decisions to Kansas and Illinois before signing with the Jayhawks. He was the leading scorer for a 30-1 St. Louis Vashon HS team that won the Missouri Class 4A state championship and was ranked fifth nationally by *USA Today*. He was ranked by one scouting service as one of the Top 65 high school seniors in the nation. Tunstall is a good defender and has some offensive talent.

"He can do some nice things," Williams told Gary Bedore of the *Lawrence Journal-World*. "I now have a better idea of what he can do. He'll be both point guard and second guard. He's probably our best athlete in the backcourt, pretty solid on defense."

STEVE WOODBERRY (6-4, 175 lbs., FR, G, #20, 20.5 ppg, 10.0 rpg, Wichita South HS/Wichita, Kan.) Like fellow freshman Patrick Richey, Woodberry is an excellent ballhandler and shooter. He can play either the point or shooting guard positions.

Woodberry was named the Naismith player of the year in Kansas last season. He led Wichita South HS to two state championships and the Titans only lost three games during his career. He led his high school team in scoring, rebounding and assists last year.

"Woodberry has poise and polish . . . ," Williams said.

Like Richey, all that Woodberry needs is more strength.

★ QUESTIONS ★

Experience? Only two Jayhawks have ever started a game for Kansas.
Rebounding?
Size and depth up front?

★ STRENGTHS ★

Roy Williams! After only two years as a head coach on the collegiate level, Williams is already earning compliments from the likes of John Wooden. He is not just one of the best young coaches in the country but is on his way to becoming one of the best coaches in college basketball regardless of age or experience.

Shooting skill! Kansas made .533 of its field goals attempts last year and led the country in that category. Two years ago the Jayhawks shot .531 percent from the floor. While three of the top six scorers from last year are gone, Kansas should be one of the premier shooting clubs in the country.

Ballhandling ability! The Jayhawks' passing ability virtually brought tears brought tears to the eyes of purists last year. As a team, the Jayhawks passed so well and are so in tune with each other that they almost resemble a high level European team like the Yugoslavians, rather than a typical slam dunking, big time college team.

★ BLUE RIBBON ANALYSIS ★

There was some definite excitement in the air about Kansas basketball in the Sunflower state last year. The Jayhawks were the surprise team of college basketball's regular season as they were ranked No. 1 or 2 in the country most of last season. Kansas won the pre-season Dodge Big Apple NIT and finished with a 30-5 record. While Kansas should be strong again, third-year coach Roy Williams, who earned superlatives from his peers and was voted national coach of the year, has to replace five of the top eight players from last year, including leading scorer Kevin Pritchard. Compounding the difficulty of Williams' task is that three players who were expected to play major roles —center Pekka Markkanen and newcomers Chris Lindley and Cortez Barnes —are not with the Jayhawks this year. Markkanen, a native of Finland, returned to his homeland because his wife was homesick. Lindley, Kansas' top recruit, had his foot amputated in a freak accident last January and Barnes was not eligible under NCAA freshman academic requirements.

"Let's see, if I had to pick now we'd probably go with Adonis Jordan, Terry Brown, Alonzo Jamison, Mike Maddox and Mark Randall," Kansas coach Roy Williams told Gary Bedore of the *Lawrence Journal-World* about his possible starting lineup. "But, if I were a gambler, I would not bet a lot of dollars on it being those five running out there."

Williams believes this is the most inexperienced team he has ever been around, he was an assistant at North Carolina for 10 years before coming to Kansas, and that the Jayhawks are loaded with question marks. Only two Jayhawks have ever started a game for Kansas in the past.

"When camp opens, it'll be very, very difficult for anybody to beat out Mark Randall. But after that, it's survival of the fittest. It'll be a war, because I don't care who starts. These guys are going to earn their spots."

Randall will be the cornerstone of Kansas' attack. He has a chance to finish his career as Kansas' all-time leading percentage shooter as he enters this season at 61 percent for his career. Sophomore point guard Adonis Jordan should be a capable floor leader but not quite the scorer Pritchard was. Seniors Mike Maddox and Kirk Wagner will play major roles up front as will 6-5 junior Alonzo Jamison, who was eligible for the final 17 games of the year and was impressive at times.

Senior guard Terry brown is one of the premier three-point shooters in the country and junior college transfer David Johanning should be capable in the pivot. Williams signed a talented and mature group of newcomers who should be able to provide some help this season.

Heading into the season, the Big Eight race is hard to handicap. Kansas is inexperienced, Missouri is embroiled in controversy concerning an NCAA investigation, Oklahoma's roster was not finalized at the beginning of the school year, and Oklahoma State has a new coach (former Kentucky mentor Eddie Sutton). Iowa State is coming off a disappointing 1989-90 season and Colorado, Kansas State and Nebraska don't appear to be in a position to seriously challenge for the conference title.

The one constant in what could be a wild and unpredictable season in the Big Eight is that Roy Williams should be able to get the Jayhawks to play close to their potential and as a team. Mark Randall is one of the premier players in the conference and the Jayhawks should be hard to handle in Allen Fieldhouse where they were 15-1 last year. We predict a second place finish in the Big Eight for the Jayhawks. Kansas won't hover around the nation's No. 1 mark for many weeks as they did last year, but the Jayhawks will still be Rough Customers.

LAST SEASON			
#Alabama-Birmingham	109-83	@Iowa State	88-83
#@LSU	89-83	Missouri	71-77
##UNLV	91-77	Nebraska	94-67
##St. John's	66-57	@Colorado	103-71
Idaho	87-58	Kansas State	70-58
Maryland-Baltimore Co.	86-67	@Oklahoma	78-100
Tennessee-Martin	103-48	Iowa State	96-63
@Southern Methodist	86-53	*Iowa State	118-75
Kentucky	150-95	*Oklahoma	77-95
Pepperdine	98-73	**Robert Morris	79-71
Arizona State	90-67	**UCLA	70-71
###Texas-Pan American	103-83	@ Road Games	
###Stanford	83-61	# Dodge Big Apple NIT	
@Wichita State	93-66	## Dodge Big Apple NIT Final Four,	
Winthrop (SC)	94-51	Madison Square Garden, New York,	
@Nebraska	98-93	NY	
@Miami (FL)	100-73	### BMA Holiday Classic, Kansas City,	
Oklahoma State	91-77	MO	
Elizabeth City State (NC)	132-65	* Big Eight Tournament, Kansas City,	
@Missouri	87-95	MO	
@Kansas State	85-57	** NCAA Tournament, Atlanta, GA	
Colorado	90-69		
Oklahoma	85-74		
@Oklahoma State	83-76		

1990-91 KANSAS SCHEDULE			
Nov.	23	@Arizona State	
	24	@Northern Arizona	
Dec.	1	Marquette	
	4	Southern Methodist	
	8	@Kentucky	
	15	Rider	
	22	Texas-San Antonio	
	28	@Hawaii-Loa	
Jan.	2	@Pepperdine	
	5	North Carolina State	
	8	@Oklahoma	
	10	Maryland-Baltimore Co.	
	12	@Oklahoma State	
	16	Miami (FL)	
	19	Missouri	
	23	Wichita State	
	26	Colorado	
	29	@Kansas State	
Feb.	2	@Iowa State	
	6	Nebraska	
	9	Oklahoma State	
	12	@Missouri	
	16	Kansas State	
	20	@Colorado	
Feb.	23	Oklahoma	
	26	Iowa State	
Mar.	3	@Nebraska	
	8-10	#Big Eight Tournament	

@ Road Games
# Kansas City, MO

NOTES: As mentioned in the *Blue Ribbon* Analysis, Kansas' top recruit, 6-9 forward Chris Lindley, from Raytown (Mo.) South HS had his right foot amputated after he was run over by a train in the Kansas City stockyards last January. Lindley is still on a basketball scholarship and attending Kansas this year. He will not play this year, but was outfitted with a new, flexible artificial foot in September and is planning on trying to play for the Jayhawks next season. "I'll probably always have to wear a compression bandage on the leg because there was so much damage to the skin and veins in my leg that it's difficult for the blood to flow freely to my feet," Lindley said. "I don't have anything to prove and I know that.

This is just something I have to do for myself. I think if I try —and even if I don't make it —I'll be at rest with myself." . . . Cortez Barnes, a 6-8 forward from Wichita Heights (Kan.) HS was not eligible to play for Kansas this year and is attending Hutchinson (Kan.) CC . . . Sitting out this year is 6-3 guard Rex Walters, who averaged 17.6 points per game as a starter at Northwestern last season. He also dished out 125 assists and shot better than 50 percent from the floor (181-of-360) as a freshman at Northwestern. He was an honorable mention All-Big Ten selection and will have three years of eligibility at Kansas beginning in the 1991-92 season.

KENTUCKY

LAST SEASON: 14-14
CONFERENCE RECORD: 10-8
STARTERS LOST: 1
STARTERS RETURNING: 4
CONFERENCE:
  SOUTHEASTERN (SEC)
LOCATION: LEXINGTON, KY
HOME FLOOR: RUPP
  ARENA (23,000)
NICKNAME: WILDCATS
COLORS: BLUE AND WHITE

★ COACH'S PROFILE ★

RICK PITINO (Record at Kentucky, 14-14. Career college record, 147-88. Career professional record, 90-74.) Midway through last season, posters appeared across the Bluegrass state sporting a smiling Kentucky coach Rick Pitino and the phrase ''What Do You Think So Far?'' Truth be told, the two-year NCAA probation wasn't hurting nearly as much as the doomsayers had predicted or the legions of Wildcat faithful had feared. Maybe a 14-14 record isn't up to Kentucky's legendary basketball standards, and a two-year probation certainly vetoed any post-season plans. But, if anything, last season only added to the already strong legend of Pitino as a miracle worker. And a great time was had by all, something that has not always happened in Kentucky where the program has been on the stuffy and uptight side for years.

Pitino, who previously turned around struggling programs at Boston University, Providence and with the NBA's New York Knicks, inherited two unheard of commodities in Kentucky —a losing team and a honeymoon for the coach. He made the most of both, and looks well on his way to adding the Wildcats to his growing list of turnarounds.

Kentucky will not be back in the NCAA tournament this year, but the Wildcats' television blackout has been lifted. Post-season eligibility returns in 1991-92. Pitino is also coping with other aspects of the probation. Limited to three scholarships last year and this year, the new coach still put together a solid recruiting class that adds talent and depth to a team that last season had little of either.

Fans who tune in the Wildats after a year's absence from television may not recognize what they see. Part of the Pitino charm was his return to the traditional Adolph Rupp style of up-beat, run-and-gun offensive basketball, coupled with full court defensive pressure. It came in marked contrast to the deliberate, often plodding style of Pitino's predecessor, Eddie Sutton.

Not even Rupp, however, had the three-point shot at his disposal. Partly by design, partly by necessity, Pitino's Wildcats unloaded more of them last season than any team in NCAA history. Now in Kentucky custody are the following NCAA records for three-point field goals:

*Most attempts in one game (53 vs. Southwestern Louisiana)
*Most made in one game (21 vs. North Carolina)
*Most attempted in a season (810)
*Most attempts per game (28.9)

Perhaps most amazing of all, on December 19 last year, Kentucky set an NCAA record when eight different Wildcats sank treys against Furman. ''You're trying to score on the other team's made basket before they turn around and match up defensively,'' Pitino said.

His style was entertaining and accepted quickly by Kentucky's fans. Despite a team far below school standards, the 1989-90 Wildcats drew six of the 13 largest home crowds in Kentucky history, including a Rupp Arena-record 24,301 who showed up to see Kentucky upset LSU. Fans hanging around Rupp Arena for Pitino's post-game radio show ballooned from a few hundred to 10,000.

The Kentucky attack was so wide open and up-tempo that some former Kentucky guards said in a *Sports Illustrated* article that they yearned for a chance to play in this style. ''They're allowed so much more creativity than when we played,'' said former Wildcat Dicky Beal, Class of 1984. ''I can see myself really enjoying playing for Coach Pitino,'' claimed former Kentucky All-America guard Louie Dampier, Class of 1967. Lamented Jim Master, Class of 1984: ''If only I were ten years younger. To be able to take those shots from all over the floor and not worry about coming out, that's an incredible feeling.''

''This is the most fun I have ever had in basketball,'' said Kentucky forward Deron Feldhaus. ''This is the way it should be. I've never had this much fun before, and I love it.''

Pitino has written a book titled ''Born to Coach.'' The 37-year-old Pitino grew up on New York's Long Island. He was a standout at St. Dominic's HS in Oyster Bay, Long Island, where he broke several scoring records and captained the basketball team. He was a natural leader as a child and became obsessed with basketball at an early age. Pitino accepted a basketball scholarship from Massachusetts. He served as the Minutemen's captain and graduated in 1974. Pitino had become a favorite of Howard Garfinkel, the colorful boss of the Five-Star Camp, and he con-

vinced Hawaii coach Bruce O'Neil to hire Pitino as a graduate assistant. Pitino was a full-time assistant coach at Hawaii in 1975-76 and served as an interim head coach late in the season when O'Neil resigned. On his wedding night, Pitino met with Syracuse coach Jim Boeheim and took an assistant coaching job at Syracuse. After two years at Syracuse, Pitino was named the head coach at Boston University. He was only 25-years-old when he accepted the Boston University position. Boston University had won only 17 games the previous two years, but went 17-9 in Pitino's first season. He stayed five years and compiled a 91-51 record. He was twice named New England coach of the year and in his final year at Boston University, led the Terriers to their first NCAA appearance in 24 years.

After his five seasons at Boston University, Pitino served as an assistant coach for the New York Knicks under Hubie Brown. Pitino was with the Knicks for two years and in 1985 became the head coach at Providence.

Just like at Boston University, Pitino took over a losing Providence team. The Friars were 11-20 the year before he took over, and using the press and three-point shot as his weapons, the Friars went 17-14 and earned an NIT bid. In his second year at Providence, the Friars had a truly Cinderella-like season. The Friars went 25-9 and upset SEC champion Alabama and Big East titlest Georgetown on the way to the Final Four. Pitino was named the John Wooden national coach of the year and *The Sporting News* coach of the year. In the summer of 1987, Pitino couldn't resist an offer to return to New York and the NBA as the head coach of the Knicks. In his first year at New York, the Knicks were 38-44. In his second year, Pitino orchestrated one of his famed turnarounds as the Knicks moved to a 52-30 mark. He was the youngest head coach in the NBA. He prides himself on being a teacher and Pitino couldn't resist the lure of college basketball and a chance to turnaround the prestigious Kentucky program. So when new Kentucky athletic director C. M. Newton offered the opportunity, Pitino quickly accepted and left New York and the NBA for Lexington and college basketball.

''I think we're changing the attitude of Kentucky basketball,'' Pitino said. ''If a loss occurs, they live with it. If we're doing anything positive, I think we're changing that approach. And I think that's good for Kentucky basketball.''

A major part of Pitino's success is that he is a tremendous teacher who spends a great deal of time working individually with his players. He breaks the offensive fundamentals of the game down into segments and repeatedly works with players individually. His players not only participate in official team practices but are expected to come by during the season almost daily for individual instruction from the coaching staff. In his strategy, Pitino concentrates on what his players can do and gets them to believe in themselves rather than in worrying about their inadequacies. Last season was a perfect example as Kentucky was hardly a perfect team but the Wildcats were competitive and exciting. He definitely has a knack for getting players to overachieve and reach for their potential.

Pitino showed last year that he wasn't afraid of the big names in the college game. At one time or another last year Pitino took on Bob Knight, Denny Crum and Dale Brown and the Kentucky fans loved him for being so combative. His name received the loudest cheer in pre-game introductions and Pitino needed two police escorts to make his way from the arena after games. Even after the probation runs its course and the Kentucky roster is again filled with blue chip players, and the fans' expectations rise dramatically, Pitino will remain successful. There is no doubt that he is one of the premier coaches in the game today. He'll recruit great talent, get those players to reach their potential and find ways to win. Kentucky fans are in for an unprecedented era of exciting basketball.

★ PLAYERS NOT RETURNING ★

DERRICK MILLER (6-5, G, 19.2 ppg, 3.4 rpg, 37 assists, 12 blocked shots, 35 steals) The only departure for Kentucky, Miller was the Wildcats leading scorer last season. He finished an up and down Kentucky career on a high note. Miller was the bombingest of ''Pitino's Bombinos,'' he took 289 of Kentucky's 810 three-point attempts. He finished in the Top Ten nationally in three-pointers made per game, averaging 3.5.

Miller will be hard for Pitino to replace. No Wildcat possesses Miller's combination of outside shooting skill and size.

★ RETURNING PLAYERS ★

NEHEMIAH ''JUNIOR'' BRADDY (6-2, 190 lbs., SO, G, #23, 1.7 ppg, 0.9 rpg, 6 assists, 1 steal, Middleburg HS/Jacksonville, Fla.) Braddy was one of five walk-ons to make the Kentucky team last year. The Wildcats numbers were sorely depleted and Pitino needed the walk-ons to fill out the roster so that full practice scrimmages could be held. Braddy appeared in more games than any of the other walk-ons (20) and earned 102 minutes of playing time last year. He was 13-of-40 from the field (32.5 percent) and made 4-of-18 three-pointers (22.2 percent). Braddy was the only walk-on to attempt a three-pointer for Kentucky last year.

He is extremely strong, especially in the upper body, and is an excellent leaper. Braddy has proven that he can make the open three-point shot. His role and playing time will be similar this year.

JEFF BRASSOW (6-5, 185 lbs., SO, G, #14, 6.8 ppg, 3.5 rpg, 26 assists, 10 blocked shots, 39 steals, Alief Elsik HS/Houston, Tex.) As a freshman, the competitive, hardnosed Brassow showed a great deal of grit and fortitude. He appeared in 28 games, starting two, and averaged 17.3 minutes per game. Brassow was 70-of-170 from the field (41.2 percent) and 32-of-88 (36.4 percent) from three-point range. He is an excellent shooter when open.

Brassow is not blessed with great natural athletic ability. However, he gets the most out of his talent and has honed his skills well.

His best game as a freshman was at LSU as Brassow scored 25 points with seven three-pointers in the second half. He scored in double figures in seven games for Kentucky last year.

Kentucky basketball players have always been extremely popular in the state of Kentucky. The Wildcats are celebrities in their ownright. Brassow's popularity probably soared last year when he was compared in a pictorial spread in the *Lexington-Herald Leader*, called ''Wildcat Look-a-Likes,'' with actor Tom Cruise. Cruise's picture was printed alongside Brassow and there was a strong resemblance.

TONY COOPER (5-9, 150 lbs., SO, G, #20, 0.5 ppg, 0.2 rpg, 2 assists, 2 steals, Windsor Forest HS/Savannah, Ga.) Cooper made the team as a walk-on last year. He appeared in 12 games for a total of 21 minutes (1.8 mpg). Cooper made 3-of-5 of 4 field goal attempts for the season. He is not expected to be a key factor for Kentucky this year.

JOHNATHON DAVIS (6-6, 200 lbs., JR, F, #33, 1.4 ppg, 1.8 rpg, 3 assists, 11 blocked shots, 6 steals, Pine Forest HS/Pensacola, Fla.) Davis' career at Kentucky has never got rolling. He was a limited factor under former Kentucky coach Eddie Sutton. He played in 11 games as a freshman averaging 0.5 points per game. In Sutton's last season at Kentucky, Davis averaged 1.4 points and 1.8 rebounds per game. Last season when Kentucky sorely needed manpower up front, Davis only averaged 7.1 minutes per game. He averaged just 1.4 points and 1.8 rebounds per game.

Davis is an excellent athlete who high jumped 6-9 in high school and also competed in the high hurdles in track. However, he has never developed as a basketball player. His game is strictly around the basket. Davis recorded career highs in points and rebounds when he scored 7 points and pulled down 9 rebounds in 23 minutes last December against Southwestern Louisiana. His most solid effort of the season came against Furman when he scored six points, had six rebounds and blocked three shots. He started his first game ever last year against Indiana in the Big Four Classic in Indianapolis.

His role probably won't expand this year. Pitino signed two big time freshman front court players, 6-8 Jamal Mashburn and 6-9 Gimel Martinez, and both are certain to be a hit of Davis on the depth chart.

RICHIE FARMER (6-0, 180 lbs., JR, G, #32, 7.0 ppg, 1.7 rpg, 73 assists, 2 blocked shots, 32 steals, Clay County HS/Manchester, Ky.) With second-team All-SEC performer Derrick Miller gone, who attempted over one-third of Kentucky's three-pointers, Farmer's role and playing time should increase. He came to Kentucky heralded as one of the all-time great long distance shooters in the storied history of Kentucky high school basketball. Farmer was Kentucky's Mr. Basketball for 1988. He led Clay County to a state championship in 1987 and a 35-2 record and a second place finish in the Kentucky state tournament as a senior. Farmer scored 51 points against Louisville Ballard, whose star was Tennessee's great guard Alan Houston, in the Kentucky state championship game. He finished his career as Clay County's all-time leading scorer with 2,937 points, had his jersey retired, and signed a letter of intent to Kentucky with more than 1,600 people watching him in the school's gymnasium.

Farmer averaged 3.1 points per game as a freshman under Eddie Sutton. His role expanded last year as Farmer averaged 17.4 minutes per game and 7.0 points per game. He had a career-high 21 points and six assists against North Carolina and scored 19 points including 4-of-4 from three-point range, versus Kansas. For the second straight year Farmer was Kentucky's best free throw shooter hitting at an 84.7 percent clip. Farmer saw action in all 28 games, and started one.

There is no doubt he is Kentucky's best pure shooter. However, Farmer does not have outstanding quickness and he is limited by an inability to get his shot off against the bigger, faster, quicker athletes he faces at this level. Also, Miller was 6-5 and Farmer is just 6-0. For those reasons it is not likely he will be able to duplicate Miller's numbers and totally replace Kentucky's top gun from last year's team.

DERON FELDHAUS (6-7, 210 lbs., JR, F, #12, 14.4 ppg, 6.7 rpg, 57 assists, 5 blocked shots, 22 steals, Mason County HS/Maysville, Ky.) Kentucky certainly was not a picture perfect team last year as evidenced by the fact that Feldhaus started 27 of 28 games at power forward. No knock on Feldhaus, as he is an intelligent, hustling player who gets the most out of his ability but he's not the prototypical power forward at the high major college level. Still, Feldhaus was second on the team in rebounding and third in scoring. He managed to pull down a career-high 16 rebounds against Louisville and scored a career-high 27 points against North Carolina. In all, Feldhaus scored 20 points or more in six different games and had 10 plus rebounds five times.

Feldhaus thrived under Pitino's tutelage. He averaged 3.7 points and 3.3 rebounds per game as a freshman under Sutton. (Feldhaus was redshirted in 1987-88 by Sutton). He plays a strong, aggressive brand of ball against all comers, no matter how big. Feldhaus was able to take opposing power forwards away from the basket due to his outside shooting ability.

He benefitted from a rigorous pre-season conditioning program and shed some weight. Feldhaus may not equal his statistics from last year as Pitino brought in two heralded inside players-freshman Jamal Mashburn and Gimel Martinez-but he should be more rested with the additional help. Feldhaus is the epitome of a Pitino coached player. He is also one of the foremost overachievers in college basketball.

REGGIE HANSON (6-7, 200 lbs., SR, F, #35, 16.4 ppg, 7.1 rpg, 44 assists, 40 blocked shots, 61 steals, Pulaski County HS/Somerset, Ky.) After Pitino saw his team in pre-season practice last year he commented that Hanson has professional potential. Some of that potential came out last year as Hanson was Kentucky's MVP even though he played out of position at center. Hanson was the second-team *Associated Press* All-SEC choice and was a *UPI* third-team all-conference. He finished second on the team, behind Derrick Miller, in scoring, and first in rebounding. Hanson finished in the SEC Top 10 in five categories — scoring, rebounding, field goal percentage (49.7), steals (2.7 stpg) and blocks (1.4 blpg). He also led Kentucky in blocked shots with 40.

Even though he gave up several inches and many pounds to most centers he faced, Hanson is effective because of his quickness and ability to take opposing big men away from the hoop due to his threat as an outside shooter. This year he should be able to move back to a natural forward position due to the arrival of more size in the lineup provided by two 6-9 freshman-Jamal Mashburn and Gimel Martinez. Hanson tried out last May in Colorado Springs, Colo., for the U.S. National team. He was cut after the first round of tryouts but was impressive.

MICHAEL PARKS (6-2, 180 lbs., SR, G, #30, 0.2 ppg, 0.2 rpg, 1 steal, Breckenridge County HS/Irvington, Ky.) Pitino needed a contingent of walk-ons to practice with last year so that Kentucky could have full scale scrimmages. Parks was one of five walk-ons who were in the Kentucky program last year. He appeared in 13 games for a total of 29 minutes last year. Parks was 1-of-3 from the field and 1-of-2 from the line. His action is expected to be limited again this season.

JOHN PELPHREY (6-7, 190 lbs., JR, G/F, #34, 13.0 ppg, 5.3 rpg, 76 assists, 21 steals, 61 blocked shots, Paintsville HS/Paintsville, Ky.) Pelphrey became a starter last year and gave a solid performance. He was fourth on the team in scoring, third in rebounding and second in blocks. He tied for the team lead in steals and was second in assists. Pelphrey started 26 of 28 games. At the conclusion of the season he was named to the Academic All-SEC team. He also finished in the Top 5 of the SEC in steals with a 2.2 per game average. He was Kentucky's student-athlete of the year. He was also the Wildcats' best playmaker and Mr. Deflection awards winner.

Pelphrey was Kentucky's Mr. Basketball award winner in 1987. He scored in double figures in all but seven games. He has an excellent feel for scoring around the basket against bigger players, passes well and is described as a true ''coach on the floor'' by Kentucky assistant Herb Sendek.

Last year Kentucky's front line starters had basically no help off the bench other than Jeff Brassow. This year there are some talented newcomers up front so Pelphrey, Hanson and Feldhaus should get some much needed relief.

SEAN WOODS (6-2, 175 lbs., JR, G, #11, 9.1 ppg, 2.3 rpg, 164 assists, 2 blocked shots, 48 steals, Cathedral HS/Indianapolis, Ind.) After sitting out the 1988-89 season at Kentucky, Woods' first full year of eligibility was last year and he started at point guard in all but one game. He led the SEC in assists averaging 5.9 per game and set a Kentucky record for assists by a first-year player with 164. Woods handled the ball with care as he committed only 77 turnovers in 726 minutes (one every 9.4 minutes). His 12 assists against Tennessee Tech fell too short of Kentucky's single-game assists record.

Woods is awfully quick with the ball. He can get in the lane easily and goes by defenders off the dribble. He is fairly strong and has worked hard on the weights to get stronger.

''I'm feeling,'' Woods told John McGill the *Lexington Herald-Leader* last year, ''more fluent. I'm doing it everyday now. I'm getting a lot more seasoned. I've paid my dues as far as being young. I'm trying to force the issue now.''

He is a daring player with a great deal of flair as a ballhandler. Offensively, Woods was 97-of-199 (48.7 percent) from the field and 4-of-14 (28.6 percent) from the three-point range.

In Pitino's frantic, ultra up-tempo system which produced an average of 88.8 points per game last year, Woods is a key player. There is really no one behind him on the Kentucky team with the same ability to push the ball up the court and penetrate defenses. If Kentucky is to continue to improve now that the rest of SEC knows what to expect from Pitino's Wildcats, Woods must continue to raise his game. He made the grade in his first year as a starter and now has to continue to get better.

★ NEWCOMERS ★

TODD BEARUP (6-4, 195 lbs., SO, F/G, #13, Laurel County HS/London, Ky.) A transfer from Utah State, Bearup is the younger brother of former Kentucky Wildcat Bret Bearup. He played 19 of 31 games during the 1986-87 season for Utah State before leaving on a Mormon Church mission. Bearup was expected to play for Utah State last year, but transferred to Kentucky and will be eligible in January. He practiced with the Wildcats last year and the coaching staff feels Bearup can be a factor this year.

He is considered similar in style and strengths to teammates Jeff Brassow and Deron Feldhaus. Like those two, Bearup is fundamentally sound and can shoot the basketball. He is not really a true forward or guard, but can be effective due to his hustle and shooting ability.

Bearup is mature for a player of his eligibility as the class he came into college with has graduated. He will give Pitino more depth and flexibility than Kentucky had last year.

GIMEL MARTINEZ (6-9, 205 lbs., FR, C, #44, 24.2 ppg, 12.1 rpg, 3.0 apg, 4.0 blpg, Miami Senior HS/Miami, Fla.) Martinez is one of two much needed frontcourt players for the Kentucky program. He comes to Kentucky with outstanding prep credentials. Martinez led Miami Senior to a 33-3 record and a second consecutive Florida 4A title last year. He shot 62 percent from the field for the season and was named to the all-tournament at the Florida state tournament. Martinez was runner-up for MVP honors of the Florida state tournament the past two years. More importantly, he was a big winner in high school, playing on teams with a cumulative record of 137-9 and a total of three state championships.

He had 33 points and 16 rebounds in a head-to-head matchup last year with Ed O'Bannon, a UCLA freshman who many considered to be the premier high school senior in the nation last year.

"He's not an athlete with a lot of athleticism," said Wayne Merino, the coach of O'Bannon's Artesia HS of Lakewood, Calif. "But when they got the ball to him, he knew what he wanted to do before he got the ball. He knew where the defensive man was and what move he would make."

He can easily step out to 15-feet and accurately shoot the ball and has a great knowledge of the fundamentals of interior offensive play.

"He knows how to win," said Miami Senior coach Marcos "Shakey" Rodriguez. "Sometimes we get too involved and too caught up in individual statistics and forget that a kid knows how to win."

Martinez should make Kentucky a much stronger team up front. Look for him to thrive under Pitino's program of individual skill development.

JAMAL MASHBURN (6-8, 230 lbs., FR, F, #24, 26.3 ppg, 10.5 rpg, 4.3 apg, Cardinal Hayes HS/Bronx, N.Y.) Mashburn is the most acclaimed prospect in Kentucky's freshman class. He also has more ability than anyone currently in the program. Many experts thought Mashburn was the top senior in New York City last year in a year where the graduating class was better than any in the Big Apple in over a decade.

He led Cardinal Hayes HS to the championship of the New York Catholic League tournament. He also took Cardinal Hayes to the semifinals of the state tournament. Mashburn was voted Mr. Basketball in the state of New York. He was also named player of the year for New York by *Newsday* and was a first-team New York selection by the *New York Daily News* and the *New York Post*.

For his size, Mashburn has excellent agility and deceptive quickness. He is not only proficient offensively around the basket and the baseline, but can drift outside for jumpers and can put the ball on the floor to create his own shot. He played all five positions in every game last year. Some think Mashburn puts the ball on the floor well enough to be a swingman at Kentucky.

After last season, he was ranked as the No. 8 senior in the nation by *All Star Sports*. Mashburn is good enough to be Kentucky's leading scorer and rebounder as a freshman. He will be an immediate starter and should be the freshman of the year in the SEC. He will also have more impact on Kentucky than virtually any other freshman player in the country will on his respective team. If he works and continues to develop, Mashburn is capable of becoming one of the best players to ever come out of this proud program.

HENRY THOMAS (6-4, 170 lbs., FR, G, #21, 21.0 ppg, 7.0 rpg, 3.0 apg, Clarksville HS/Clarksville, Tenn.) Thomas redshirted last year due to knee surgery for a torn anterior cruciate ligament which occurred before he reported to Kentucky. He also fractured an ankle midway through his junior season but rebounded for a strong senior campaign. Thomas was an Academic All-America pick his junior year and an All-Tennessee selection as a senior.

Nicknamed "Blade" in high school for his thin build, Thomas is a good shooter and leaper. The presence of Thomas means Pitino will have more bodies to work with this year and that should make the Kentucky press even stronger.

JODY THOMPSON (6-5, 190 lbs., FR, G, #25, 30.0 ppg, 12.0 rpg, Feds Creek HS/Feds Creek, Ky.) Even though there was no scholarship available and he had other offers, Thompson decided to walk-on at Kentucky. He scored more than 2,000 points in his career at Feds Creek HS. He also had 19 points for the Kentucky AAU team in a game against the Soviet Junior National squad last spring. Thompson was impressive in the Kentucky-Indiana all-star series and scored 21 points in the first game of the series.

Hoop Scoop ranked Thompson the No. 3 player in the state of Kentucky last year. "The best pure shooter in the state —25' range. Excellent ball handler and passer. Smart player. Could qualify for an academic scholarship at Kentucky," said Tom Goins of *Hoop Scoop*.

CARLOS TOOMER (6-4, 190 lbs., FR, G, #42, 13.2 ppg, 6.6 rpg, 3.3 apg, 1.8 stpg, Cornith HS/Cornith, Miss.) When Pitino went to Cornith HS last year to see prep All-America Stephen Davis, who was considered the best senior in the state of Mississippi, he noticed an athletic 6-4 point guard he thought would fit into his defensive system of full court pressure. When Kentucky signed Toomer, it shocked many of the scouting service operators who did not have him high on their lists of top recruits. It also was surprising to many college coaches in Mississippi who did not think Toomer was talented enough to play for Kentucky. Bob Gibbons of *All Star Sports* was surprised that Kentucky signed Toomer, but changed his mind after watching him play in eight games.

"He's an exceptional athlete. He definitely can contribute. He can run, press people and defend," Gibbons said.

While Pitino considers Toomer a point guard prospect, Gibbons believes he is more of a natural wing player. Pitino is high on Toomer and has called him "a big time point guard."

Despite the difference of opinion on Toomer's basketball ability and true position, there is no doubt that his athletic ability and potential effectiveness in Pitino's press should help make him a valuable player early on. The Wildcats pressed successfully last year without what would be considered big time quickness and the addition of Toomer should eventually make the press even stronger.

★ QUESTIONS ★

Replacing designated three-point shooter Derrick Miller? Kentucky set all sorts of national records in three-point field goal categories last year and Miller was a big reason. He attempted over one-third of Kentucky's three-point field goals and made more than twice as many treys as any other Wildcat.

Size and athletic ability up front? Despite the addition of two prize freshmen frontcourt players, Kentucky is still not as big or athletic as a lot of teams at this level up front.

★ STRENGTHS ★

Rick Pitino! Seldom has a coach received as much praise for a 14-14 record as Pitino received last season. He has fully instituted his run and press, hoist the threes system. Many think Pitino is the best coach in basketball and they may not be wrong.

Shooting ability! While Kentucky will have a difficult time replacing Derrick Miller's three-point shooting, most of the Wildcats are proficient outside shooters.

Passing ability!

The addition of Jamal Mashburn to the frontcourt! Mashburn was considered the best senior in New York City last year and he adds a degree of talent up front that Kentucky lacked last year. He could be one of the best players to ever come through the Wildcat program.

★ BLUE RIBBON ANALYSIS ★

Things are looking up for Kentucky. After the Wildcats got nailed by the NCAA and Chris Mills, the top player in the program, transferred to Arizona, it looked as if even the great Rick Pitino would not be able to prevent doom and gloom in Lexington. However, Rupp Arena was a jumpin' joint last year, not a mortuary, as Pitino managed to create a virtual carnival atmosphere with his run-and-gun offensive style coupled with full court defensive pressure. The Wildcats set an NCAA record for most three-point field goals attempted in one game (53) in an early season contest and soon after Rupp Arena was awash in excitement every time Kentucky hit the floor. The Wildcats were undefeated at home in SEC play. "Pitino's Bombinos," as the Wildcats were affectionately known in Lexington, drew six of the 13 largest crowds ever at Rupp Arena. Even playing with a limited team with only eight players on scholarship and five walk-ons, Kentucky was competitive and set a school record with 309 steals.

"His style returned Kentucky basketball to its roots, the Adolph Rupp style," one Kentucky insider said. "A lot of the old-time fans liked that."

This year the numbers will be more in Pitino's favor. Freshmen Jamal Mashburn and Gimel Martinez are impact-caliber recruits who will make Kentucky much stronger up front. Mashburn was the top senior in New York City last year and could develop into one of the best players ever at Kentucky. One of the new walk-ons, freshman Jody Thompson, was ranked as the No. 3 player in the state of Kentucky last year. Throw in a returning redshirt, and Kentucky will have 11 players on scholarship this season.

Pitino claims he needs to use at least 10 men to make his style work. This year Kentucky will be deeper, quicker and stronger up front.

Kentucky averaged 88.8 points per game last year and Pitino has already announced the goal of breaking the 90-point per game barrier. To make that goal, someone will have to pick up the slack of leading scorer Derrick Miller, who set SEC records with 289 three-point attempts and 99 made. A second-team All-SEC selection, Miller launched over one-third of the Wildcats' three-pointers.

This year, although Kentucky will still have matchup problems inside due to a lack of size, they still have enough firepower outside to contend in a SEC not full of dominant centers. One key will be more offensive production from junior guard Richie Farmer to keep the scoring machine running smoothly. Kentucky finished with a surprising 10-8 SEC record, good enough for a tie for forth in the conference. This year SEC foes should be better prepared for Pitino's system. While Kentucky is not allowed to participate in post-season play, the Wildcats can be on television this year and next season all sanctions will be removed. Pitino has a knack for getting the most out of his troops and this season should be no exception. Kentucky has a tough schedule and the Wildcats will have to improve their road record as they won only one away game in the SEC last season. The Wildcats should come close to being unbeatable at home again in the SEC and play better on the road.

The Wildcats should win 18 to 20 games and finish in the SEC's upper division again. Watch out in a few years when Pitino has had a few full recruiting classes and a roster full of blue chip players to implement his style. Happy days are definitely here again at Kentucky.

LAST SEASON

Ohio University	76-73	Mississippi	98-79	
#Indiana	69-71	@Mississippi State	86-87	
Mississippi State	102-97	Georgia	88-77	
Tennessee Tech	111-75	Vanderbilt	100-73	
@Kansas	95-150	@Florida	78-74	
Furman	104-73	LSU	100-95	
##Univ. of Portland	88-71	@Alabama	58-83	
##Southwestern Louisiana	113-116	@Tennessee	100-102	
###North Carolina	110-121	Auburn	98-95	
Louisville	79-86	@Mississippi	74-88	
@Georgia	91-106	@Notre Dame	67-80	
@Vanderbilt	85-92			
Florida	89-81	@ Road Games		
@LSU	81-94	# Bank One Big Four Classic, Indianapolis, IN		
Alabama	82-65	## UKIT, Lexington, KY		
Tennessee	95-83	### Louisville, KY		
@Auburn	70-74			

NOTES: After last year's 14-14 record, Kentucky thought it had relinquished to North Carolina the title of college basketball's winningest all-time program. Then, for a change, came some good news from the NCAA, which ruled that a 1914 Kentucky victory over Louisville had been discovered and added to the overall victory count, giving the Wildcats 1,479 all-time wins. That leaves Kentucky and North Carolina deadlocked . . . Pitino hired a female assistant coach, Bernadette Locke, a former assistant women's coach at Georgia. Her duties will be the same as Pitino's other assistants — on-court coaching and recruiting with a special emphasis on career placement . . . last November 27, Pitino received a verbal commitment from 6-3 guard Chris Harrison, who went on to lead the state of Kentucky in

1990-91 KENTUCKY SCHEDULE

Nov.	24	Pennsylvania	Jan.	26	@Alabama
	28	@Cincinnati		30	@Auburn
Dec.	1	#Notre Dame	Feb.	2	Georgia
	8	Kansas		6	@LSU
	10	@North Carolina		9	@Mississippi State
	15	Tennessee-Chattanooga		13	Tennessee
	18	@Indiana		16	Mississippi
	21	##Western Kentucky		20	@Vanderbilt
	27	Eastern Kentucky		23	@Florida
	29	@Louisville		27	Alabama
Jan.	2	@Georgia	Mar.	2	Auburn
	5	LSU			
	9	Mississippi State	@ Road Games		
	12	@Tennessee	# Bank One Big Four Classic, Indianapolis, IN		
	16	@Mississippi	## Louisville, KY		
	19	Vanderbilt			
	23	Florida			

scoring last season. Harrison is out of Tollesboro HS . . . former Kentucky standout Eric Manuel, who played one season as a freshman in 1987-88 before being implicated in NCAA rule violations that led to sanctions against the Wildcat program, played last season at Hiawassee JC in Madisonville, Tenn. He was ruled ineligible for further competition at NCAA schools and was also ruled ineligible by the NAIA National Eligibility Committee in August. Travis Ford, a 5-11 point guard from Missouri, has transferred back to his home state and will have three years of eligibility for Kentucky beginning next season. Ford was a major high school All-America at North Hopkins HS in Madisonville, Ky.

LONG BEACH STATE

LAST SEASON: 23-9
CONFERENCE RECORD: 12-6
STARTERS LOST: 1
STARTERS RETURNING: 4
CONFERENCE: BIG WEST
LOCATION: LONG BEACH, CA
HOME FLOOR: LONG BEACH
   ARENA (12,000) &
   UNIVERSITY GYMNASIUM (2,200)
NICKNAME: 49ERS
COLORS: BROWN AND GOLD

★ COACH'S PROFILE ★

SETH GREENBERG (First year at Long Beach State) One of the all-time quintessential New York gym rats, Seth Greenberg has long been known around coaching circles not only as one of the hardest workers but also as one of the better talent evaluators. Combine that with his up-beat, streetwise personality, that helps him relate to his players, and you have a man who at 34 is ideally suited for his first head coaching position after serving as an assistant on five Division I staffs.

Greenberg, from the Long Island town of Plainview, graduated from John F. Kennedy HS in 1974, where he was a three-year starter, then went on to Fairleigh Dickinson. He has been associated with the Five Star Basketball Camps, which formed the first large summer gatherings of national high school talent, for over 13 years. Columbia was the first stop on the coaching trail for Greenberg. After two years he went on to Pitt and, under Roy Chipman, was part of consecutive tournament championship teams in 1981 and '82 in the old Eastern Eight Conference. Greenberg then entered the ACC at Virginia and helped mold the 1984 Final Four squad. The rebirth of the Miami (Fla.) program under Bill Foster presented Greenberg's next challenge. He was a major force in recruiting the much touted Tito Horford to that brand new team.

When Joe Harrington arrived on the West Coast to assume control of the

Long Beach State 49ers, Greenberg became his main man in charge of the vast talent-ladened southern California area. Only a UPS delivery man could know his way around metropolitan Los Angeles better than Greenberg, who sifted through the labyrinth of freeways and myriad of high schools from Orange County to the San Fernando Valley in a constant quest to come up with the next sleeper. If you stopped by his office and Greenberg could run down L.A. high school basketball talent like a human computer without looking at any notes or scouting reports. It is that type of care and feel for the game that should mark the foundation for the beginning of a significant coaching career.

Last summer, Greenberg represented the U.S. as an assistant coach at the Maccabiah Games in Israel. He was also a featured speaker at the NABC Convention in Seattle. His brother, Brad Greenberg, was an assistant coach at St. Joseph's and later went on to stints as an assistant with the Los Angeles Clippers and New York Knicks before becoming the player personnel director of the Portland Trail Blazers. His father had a basketball background and played for the legendary Clair Bee at Long Island University.

Under Harrington, who left Long Beach State for Colorado, the 49ers were known as an up-tempo, pressing team with a strong contingent of athletes. Look for Greenberg to continue that style of play and keep the talent pool deep at Long Beach State.

★ PLAYERS NOT RETURNING ★

DARRELL FAULKNER (6-1, G, 4.6 ppg, 0.4 rpg, 15 assists, 8 steals) After averaging 8.4 points per game as a junior, Faulkner's playing time diminished last year when Harrington decided to go with bigger guards. Faulkner appeared in 31 games and made 39-of-87 field goals (.448) and was 16-of-44 (.364) from three-point range. Most importantly, he finished college with a 4.0 GPA.

RUDY HARVEY (6-5, G/F, 6.4 ppg, 2.7 rpg, 16 assists, 9 blocked shots, 17 steals) Harvey was forced to play more on the perimeter last year after being used up front before. He played in 32 games, starting 11, and made .609 of his field goal attempts. Harvey was the 49ers' sixth leading scorer. He contributed some important scoring in spots for the 49ers.

TYRONE MITCHELL (6-4, G, 10.7 ppg, 4.8 rpg, 148 assists, 7 blocked shots, 66 steals) Mitchell, the only starter to depart, could be sorely missed. Unusually physically strong for his position, he was not only a power point guard but the team leader. A great defender, he could shut down opponents anywhere from point guard to power forward. Mitchell was not a shooter (.456 from the field and .290 from three-point range), but he scored and played with great intelligence.

His probable replacement, Bobby Sears, has a big pair of shoes to fill. Mitchell was second on the team in scoring and, incredibly for a point guard, tied for second in rebounding. He was a solid, underrated player.

★ RETURNING PLAYERS ★

KEVIN CUTLER (6-8, 220 lbs., SR, F, #31, 10.5 ppg, 6.6 rpg, 11 assists, 34 blocked shots, 28 steals, Ganesha HS/Pomona, Calif. & Arizona Western JC/Yuma, Calif.) Cutler started at power forward last year and displayed good shooting ability and range for the position. He has 17 to 18 foot range plus runs and jumps well. Cutler averaged over 14 rebounds a game at Arizona Western JC, but has been inconsistent at Long Beach State. He has been prone to foul trouble and tends to get passive when that occurs. He must learn to defend better both in the post and on the perimeter. Cutler needs to focus on running the floor and getting to the glass on every possession. He can be a force if his effort becomes consistent. Cutler is a good athlete and is an important cog in the 49ers team defense.

When on his game, Cutler can be outstanding. He was one of the premier junior college players in the country at Arizona Western. Last year he grabbed 14 rebounds as Long Beach State upset Texas in Austin. He also had a 19-point, 12-rebound outing against Utah State in the Big West Conference tournament. Cutler had double digit rebound games seven times and led the team for the season in rebounding. Greenberg feels Cutler played some of his best ball down the stretch. If he keeps his head in the game, Cutler will play a major role for Greenberg's first Long Beach State team.

FRANKIE EDWARDS (6-8, 225 lbs., JR, F, #20, 5.2 ppg, 4.1 rpg, 20 assists, 17 blocked shots, 16 steals, Millikan HS/Long Beach, Calif.) Edwards is 225 pounds of pure muscle who bench presses 315 pounds and figures as a potentially major force inside. He could start at power forward or center. Edwards posts up well, gets to the glass and is very physical. He also has foul line range on his shot. The question is his consistency but he has worked very hard during the off-season to improve. After sitting out his first year at Long Beach State, Edwards began last season tentatively but started to relax and play better down the stretch. Greenberg felt much of the time he was on a rollercoaster, playing either to extreme highs or lows. The times when he didn't start well early, Edwards would tend to dwell on bad plays instead of mentally returning to the game. He must finish off plays better on the offensive end and go to the boards more consistently. Edwards has worked at that and figures to be much improved this season.

Edwards had 11 rebounds against a tough New Mexico State team and scored 16 points vs Utah State in the Big West Conference tournament. He also missed two games during the season because of a nine-stitch cut in his foot.

Greenberg has always felt that Edwards is physically comparable to former UCLA star Trevor Wilson. Edwards, who is of Samoan descent, could start coming closer to making that comparison reality this year.

LUCIOUS HARRIS (6-5, 190 lbs., SO, G, #30, 14.3 ppg, 4.8 rpg, 52 assists, 49 steals, 5 blocked shots, Grover Cleveland HS/Los Angeles, Calif.) One of the best kept secrets in America, Harris has the potential to become one of the nation's best guards. During a rousing freshman campaign, that featured a 30-point masterpiece in the 49ers win over New Mexico State in the Big West tournament semifinals, he showed the ability to do just about everything. Harris can shoot, run the floor, get over the rim, hit the glass and pull down offensive rebounds. He's a quick jumper with a great first step to the basket and has three-point range on his shot. Extremely talented, Harris is also an excellent defender. He's also clutch. His 22-footer beat Texas at the buzzer late last year in Austin. Harris also had to steal and pass to Kenny Jarvis for the lay-in at the horn that upset Purdue.

Harris has All-America potential and he is being monitored closely by most NBA teams. He scored 22 points against UNLV in the Big West championship game. In three games in the Big West Conference tournament, Harris exploded for 75 points. Long Beach State's leading scorer with a 14.3 average, Harris made 149-of-342 field goals (.430). He was 45-of-136 (.331) from three-point range.

He sees a familiar face every day at Long Beach State as his high school coach, Bob Braswell, is a member of the 49ers coaching staff. He was the Big West Conference freshman of the year and also a second-team all-conference pick last year.

KENNY JARVIS (6-5, 200 lbs., SR, G, #23, 6.3 ppg, 2.9 rpg, 37 assists, 1 blocked shot, 11 steals, Millikan HS/Long Beach, Calif. & College of Southern Idaho/Twin Falls, Idaho) Jarvis is a strong, physical player built somewhat in the mold of former starting point guard Tyrone Mitchell. He'll contest Bobby Sears for the starting point guard job. Jarvis is very unselfish and perhaps needs more ego to command that position but he can help in a lot of ways. An excellent rebounder from the backcourt, he feeds the post well and keeps the ball moving ahead on the break. He also takes the ball well to the basket and can sometimes knock down the three-pointer. Jarvis is not a classic point guard, but he sees the floor.

Last year he started 12 games. Jarvis' top offensive outing was 18 points against UNLV. He also had 16 points and eight rebounds at New Mexico State. He started nine straight games in mid-season and missed the last two games of the year with a sprained ankle. Jarvis made 68-of-183 field goals (.372) and was

15-of-50 (.300) from three-point range.

As with most of the 49ers, Jarvis is more comfortable in transition than the half court game which is why Long Beach State will use heavy defensive pressure to force the tempo.

TROY JOSEPH (6-4, 192 lbs., SR, G, #24, 7.7 ppg, 3.1 rpg, 62 assists, 11 blocked shots, 36 steals, Western HS/Anaheim, Calif. & Fullerton JC/Fullerton, Calif.) Joseph is simply an explosive small forward who is strong, can run and is an extremely quick jumper. He also hits the boards. Joseph needs to bring his game under control, particularly his shot selection.

"We intend to open it up even more this year," said Greenberg. "So we hope Troy realizes he'll get more shots and won't feel the need to force any."

Joseph is a good shooter when open and also the team's defensive stopper. He's extremely strong and great on the press. He had 18 points in as ESPN televised game against North Carolina Charlotte and scored in double figures nine times and had nine points in a game on four occasions. He made 48 percent of his field goal attempts and was accurate 60 percent of the time from the free throw line.

One of Joseph's finest moments last year was when he did a terrific defensive job on Fullerton State's Cedric Ceballos, a first-team All-Big West Conference selection and a second round pick of the Phoenix Suns. Joseph is one of a multitude of great athletes Greenberg can call upon.

MIKE MASUCCI (6-11, 230 lbs., JR, C, #44, 9.3 ppg, 4.4 rpg, 34 assists, 28 steals, 11 blocked shots, Grandview HS/Kansas City, MO) Masucci had to transfer from Kansas after he fell in disfavor with Larry Brown. Masucci was a member of Kansas' 1988 national championship team, but he was basically a member in name only. He was deep in Brown's doghouse and wasn't playing when the Jayhawks reached the Final Four. At press time, his academic status was in question for the upcoming season as, in the opinion of some, is his commitment. When he wants to be, Masucci can be a quality player. He can score in the low post, shoot from the perimeter, is mobile, and an outstanding passer for his size.

He has an excellent all-around understanding of the game as played from the pivot. He showed well against quality opposition last season: 11 points during a victory over New Mexico State, 14 against national champion UNLV, and 16 points and nine rebounds at New Mexico State. However, his most memorable moment last season was shattering a backboard in warmups at San Jose State, causing the game to start 20 minutes late.

For the season, Masucci was 119-of-257 from the floor (.463) and 9-of-24 (.375) from three-point range. He started 32 games.

In high school he was a highly regarded player who was ranked as the tenth best center in the nation by the *National Recruiters Cage Letter*. At Kansas, he averaged 2.1 points and 1.5 rebounds per game in his only season with the Jayhawks.

If eligible, Masucci's playing time could diminish and come when games have already been decided unless he can convince the coaching staff he deserves to be held in the same esteem as teammates that have put in hard work to improve. Still, he has the talent to have an impact for the 49ers. Masucci's skills at center could be a rather valuable commodity for Greenberg.

BOBBY SEARS (6-2, 170 lbs., JR, G, #3, 4.6 ppg, 0.8 rpg, 42 assists, 11 steals, Inglewood HS/Inglewood, Calif.) Sears is the heir apparent to Tyrone Mitchell at the point for the 49ers and as such could be crucial to the team's success.

"Point guard is the position of greatest adjustment on our team," said Greenberg. "We have established starters back and quality depth at the other four positions. We need someone to distribute the ball to them properly."

Sears shoots better than his predecessor, Mitchell, but is not as big or strong. However, he may become the sort of leader Mitchell was for the 49ers.

Sears is a transition-oriented player who has outstanding athletic ability and quickness, plus improved strength. He needs to become a better initiator of the offense in the half court setting and to see the floor while in traffic. He also must work on playing stronger defense on the ball. Mostly, though, his decision making will be of paramount importance.

Last year Sears started one game and played just over 10 minutes per game. He was 34-of-75 from the field (.453) and 7-of-14 from three-point range (.500). His playing time diminished by close to 200 minutes last year even though he played in four more games. He also attempted 45 fewer shots as a sophomore.

His best game last year was a 16-point effort in a win over Southern California for which he was named Prime Ticket's player of the game. He was born in Tokyo, Japan, and professional golfer Calvin Peete is married to his aunt.

KEVIN WILLIAMS (6-8, 200 lbs., SR, F, #34, 2.7 ppg, 1.6 rpg, 1 assist, 4 blocked shots, 5 steals, Martin Luther King HS/Chicago, Ill. & Arizona Western JC/Yuma, Ariz.) Williams has found it difficult to reach his potential ever since he left Brooklyn, N.Y., to spend his senior year at Martin Luther King HS in Chicago. Williams was considered one of the best players in New York during his first two years at Murry Bergtram HS and was highly regarded after his one year in Chicago. Williams played one season at Cincinnati and averaged 3.2 points and 1.7 rebounds before moving on to Arizona Western JC.

Last season was his first in a 49er uniform and Williams played in 23 games for a total of 130 minutes. He did make 26-of-43 field goals (.605). He showed flashes of hope for the future, like when he scored 10 points in the season opener against Stephen F. Austin. Williams has a live body and can shoot from the perimeter. However, he just has never gotten it completely together.

Greenberg was able to recruit Williams because of a strong connection to his family. Williams' older brother, Andre, played at Pitt while Greenberg was an assistant coach there.

RONNIE WINBUSH (6-8, 175 lbs., JR, G/F, #21, 2.9 ppg, 0.9 rpg, 17 assists, 4 blocked shots, 14 steals, Crenshaw HS/Los Angeles, Calif.) Even though Winbush is 6-8, Greenberg talked seriously about using him as a backup point guard. Winbush is also capable of being the purest shooter on the team. Nicknamed "The Long Ranger," Winbush likes to launch three-pointers flatfooted just like former Laker star Michael Cooper. His shot selection is tolerable and Winbush has a good feel for the game. His ballhandling skills are outstanding as is his floor vision. Winbush's problem has been lack of strength as he is extremely, thin for a 6-8 player.

Last season he appeared in 27 games for a total of 233 minutes in his first year in the 49ers' uniform. Winbush was 28-of-75 from the field (.373) and 11-of-36 (.306) from three-point range. He was a perfect 10-of-10 from the line for the season. His quick hands and long reach make him ideal for the 49er press. He contributed significantly down the stretch: 14 points in a win over Utah State, also two big three-point shots from the top of the key against Pacific. He will be a utility contributor this year, backing up Lucious Harris at second guard as well as seeing a little time at lead guard and small forward. Winbush is out of the famed Crenshaw HS program that has produced numerous major college players over the years and some stars such as former UCLA standout and long time pro Marques Johnson, John Williams, who played at LSU and is now with the Washington Bullets, and ex-Syracuse Orangeman Stephen Thompson.

★ NEWCOMERS ★

MIKE ATKINSON (6-7, 220 lbs., FR, F, 22.0 ppg, 10.1 rpg, Bellarmine College Prep/San Jose, Calif.) Atkinson is a physical player who is expected to be a power forward candidate at Long Beach State. He was an All-Bay area honorable mention selection at Bellarmine College Prep and will be redshirted this season.

ROD HANNIBAL (6-5, 185 lbs., FR, G, 14.0 ppg, 9.0 rpg, Long Beach Poly HS/Long Beach, Calif.) Hannibal is a local product who played at Long Beach Poly HS for Ron Palmer, the former coach at Long Beach State. He is an excellent ballhandler who can play either point or shooting guard. The 49ers are deep this season and Greenberg plans to redshirt Hannibal.

ADAM HENDERSON (6-11, 200 lbs., FR, C, -35, Los Angeles HS/Los Angeles, Calif.) Redshirted last season, Henderson has tremendous potential and should step in with immediate impact. He can run, jump, catch and is the second fastest 49er. Remember, he is 6-11 and this is a team full of athletes. Henderson, only 19, is a legit shotblocker and —with Edwards —should give Long Beach State a serious lane-clogging presence. He has a good turnaround with about a 12-foot range and is working on a skyhook. Greenberg is bringing him along gradually, working only on a couple of aspects of his game at a time.

Henderson was also an outstanding track athlete at Los Angeles HS. He finished first in his league and fifth in the city competition in the triple jump.

He is very good around the basket, has great hands and already knows to keep the ball high. Henderson needs to get stronger and if he does he can become a big time college player. Greenberg has told people that he wouldn't be surprised if Henderson emerges quickly in college on the national scene the way David Robinson did at Navy.

TERRANCE O'KELLEY (6-7, 220 lbs., FR, F, 19.8 ppg, 12.0 rpg, Lakewood HS/Lakewood, Calif.) The 49ers are so deep that Greenberg has the same plans to redshirt O'Kelley as he does his two other freshmen — Mike Atkinson and Rod Hannibal. At Lakewood, O'Kelley was known for his inside scoring and rebounding presence. He was a first-team All-More League selection and played for a team that reached the semifinals of the CIF 5AA playoffs.

Few programs in the country are deep enough to redshirt the entire freshman class.

BYRON RUSSELL (6-7, 204 lbs., SO, F, San Bernardino HS/San Bernadino, Calif.) Russell sat out last year at Long Beach State but he still could make an immediate impact on this deep 49er team. At the U.S. Olympic Festival held over the summer in Minneapolis, he broke the single game rebounding record with 20. Dick Vitale was covering the Olympic Festival for ESPN and saw Russell's 20-rebound game. He believes Russell will be a candidate for his All-Windex team comprised of the best rebounders in the country.

"He'll see a lot of time at both forward positions. Russell has great legs and can run all day. He's an excellent defender also, but he needs offensively to work on his shooting range and perimeter skills," Greenberg said.

Russell was ranked as one of the premier small forwards in the country when he was at San Bernadino HS. He was also ranked as one of the Top 10 prospects in southern California.

With his athletic ability and strong rebounding prowess, Russell should be able to create immediate playing time for himself despite the depth of this Long Beach State team.

CHRIS TOWER (6-10, 200 lbs., SO, C, Westminster HS/Huntington Beach, Calif.) Tower is a transfer from New Mexico. He played in 15 games for the Lobos as a freshman and averaged 2.2 points and 1.5 rebounds. He had a high of 10 points and five rebounds, against Prairie View A&M, while at New Mexico.

Tower is most comfortable facing the basket offensively. Defensively, he has good low post fundamental skills. Tower is also a good passer and has gained some strength since transferring to Long Beach State. Greenberg plans to design some offensive plays to utilize Tower's perimeter shooting. He plans to screen for him often to get Tower open.

Tower was also working on a jump hook over the summer. He was ranked

as one of the Top 10 players in southern California's Orange County while at Westminster HS.

Tower could be valuable insurance for Greenberg if Mike Masucci is not eligible. Even if Masucci is eligible, Greenberg has some great flexibility up front with Tower and Adam Henderson.

★ QUESTIONS ★

Point guard? Long Beach State would seem to have most of the right pieces but it is, of course, the job of the man with the ball in his hands to make them fit. The departed Tyrone Mitchell was not only outstanding at his position but also a spiritual leader. Bobby Sears won't have to worry about the leadership —that should fall to others — but his decision making and ability to see the floor and distribute the ball will be crucial to setting free the athletic potential this team has.

Adam Henderson? He arrived highly regarded but has yet to play a game for Long Beach State. If he can begin to fulfill his potential, Long Beach State will have one of college basketball's rarest commodities, an impact center. That would elevate the 49ers to a possible Top 20 status.

Rebounding? This was a major bugaboo last season. But Adam Henderson, Frankie Edwards and Byron Russell ought to be able to remove much of the burden from Kevin Cutler, who was Long Beach State's main man on the boards last season.

★ STRENGTHS ★

Depth! Because most of the 49ers are versatile and can play well at two or three positions, new coach Seth Greenberg will have several quality combinations and options available. There will be talented players pushing each other at most positions.

Experience! With four starters back including potential All-America Lucious Harris, Long Beach State has more than sufficient experience.

Athleticism! The 49ers have strength, quickness and can run all day. There aren't many teams in the country with the athletic ability of the Long Beach State 49ers.

★ BLUE RIBBON ANALYSIS ★

It might sound curious to say the team that returns no one with a scoring average over 14.3 ppg or a rebounding average over 6.6 may be ready to explode on the national scene. However, it could happen to Long Beach State in 1990-91. The 49ers are loaded with the athletic ability to implement ferocious pressure defense, which in turn will generate offense and dictate tempo somewhat in the Loyola Marymount style (although the 49ers will hardly look to be shooting the ball no more than seven seconds in every offensive possession).

Long Beach State has a blossoming star in sophomore guard Lucious Harris, explosive scoring and defense from Troy Joseph, solid inside presence and mid-range shooting from Kevin Cutler and a long range weapon with great flexibility in Ronnie Winbush, and hopefully much improved rebounding presence with the arrival of Byron Russell and Adam Henderson to complement Frankie Edwards under the boards. Henderson also could give the 49ers a strong offensive and defensive threat in the middle.

There is depth, versatility, defensive intensity and offensive balance.

First-year coach Seth Greenberg is concerned about the 49ers consistency, particularly from streaky players like Cutler and Edwards, the speed with which Henderson develops his game, and most of all, whether probable starting point guard Bobby Sears can perform well enough to keep all the talent around him involved and happy. He would appear to be up to the task. However, if the 49ers are forced into a half court, controlled offense, it may be a different story.

Conversely, no matter how much ability there is and how well the 49ers can run the floor, defense is a product of concentration, hard work and defense. Long Beach State lost nine games and narrowly missed an NCAA tournament invitation last season in a controversial decision, now must prove how badly it wants success.

"As a first year coach," said Greenberg, "(the team) not making the tournament last season is a great asset to me. The motivation around here has been tremendous."

Greenberg, noting how much time his players have spent around the weight room, feels every 49er will be dramatically improved. "This is the best group I've ever been around," he said and Greenberg has been a coach at four other Division I schools.

If Long Beach State plays near its potential, UNLV could face a challenge for the Big West crown. And, no matter how that battle turns out, this year the NCAA tournament bid should not escape Long Beach State. Greenberg should have a glorious first year at Long Beach State and the future also looks very bright for him and the program.

LAST SEASON

Stephen F. Austin	105-61	California-Santa Barbara	67-84
Purdue	70-69	North Carolina Charlotte	83-73
@Bradley	94-84	California-Irvine	102-63
#New Hampshire	68-47	@Fullerton State	70-69
#@Indiana	75-92	San Jose State	84-80
@Texas	89-87	Utah State	82-74
North Texas	92-74	@Fresno State	81-75
@UNLV	58-78	Pacific	80-75
Hofstra (NY)	89-69	##Utah State	86-68
Pacific	81-75	##New Mexico State	90-85
Fresno State	66-60	##UNLV	74-92
@California-Irvine	49-48	*@Arizona State	86-71
@California-Santa Barbara	67-82	*@Hawaii	79-84
New Mexico State	72-56		
Fullerton State	79-90	@ Road Games	
UNLV	77-86	# Indiana Classic, Bloomington, IN	
@Utah State	79-78	## Big West Tournament, Long Beach, CA	
@San Jose State	85-83		
@New Mexico State	91-104	* NIT	

1990-91 LONG BEACH STATE SCHEDULE

Nov.	24	@North Texas	Feb.	18	UNLV
	26	Chicago State		21	California-Santa Barbara
Dec.	1	@Arizona		23	@Utah State
	7-8	#Illini Classic		28	Fresno State
	12	Cal State-Northridge	Mar.	2	Pacific
	15	@Syracuse		6-9	##Big West Tournament
	28	Brooklyn College (NY)			
	29	Harvard	@ Road Games		
Jan.	2	@Pacific	# Champaign, IL (Georgia Southern, Illinois & Oregon State)		
	4	@Fresno State	## Long Beach, CA		
	7	@New Mexico State			
	19	@UNLV			
	24	Utah State			
	26	San Jose State			
Feb.	2	New Mexico State			
	6	@California-Irvine			
	9	@California-Santa Barbara			
	11	@San Jose State			
	16	Fullerton State			

NOTES: Long Beach State's first round opponent in the Illini Classic is Oregon State . . . last season's 23 victories were the most wins at Long Beach State in 16 years . . . the 49er athletic program received a considerable amount of national publicity this year with the hiring of former Washington Redskins coach George Allen as the school's football coach.

Allen is 72-years-old and is the oldest head football coach on a Division I level in the country . . . despite having a successful, exciting team, Long Beach State had a tough time drawing fans last year. The 49ers had an average home attendance of just 2,523.

LOUISVILLE

LAST SEASON: 27-8
CONFERENCE RECORD: 12-2
STARTERS LOST: 2
STARTERS RETURNING: 3
CONFERENCE: METRO
LOCATION: LOUISVILLE, KY
HOME FLOOR: FREEDOM HALL (18,865)
NICKNAME: CARDINALS
COLORS: RED, BLACK & WHITE

LOUISVILLE
1989-90 27-8

★ COACH'S PROFILE ★

DENNY CRUM (Record at Louisville, 463-156.) Few coaches ever have matched what Crum has done in 19 years at Louisville. Six times he has guided the Cardinals into the NCAA Final Four, including four times in the last decade. Only former UCLA coach John Wooden and North Carolina's Dean Smith have coached more Final Four teams than Crum. He has directed Louisville to two national championships (1980 and '86), becoming only the eighth coach in NCAA history to win more than two titles.

Louisville has also been to 15 NCAA tournaments under Crum, including 12 of the last 14 years. Three of his squads participated in the NIT as well. The Cardinals have captured or shared 10 Metro Conference regular season titles and eight post-season tournament championships during Crum's tenure. He has engineered Louisville to 20 or more victories in an amazing 17 of 19 seasons. His teams have won an average of nearly 24 games per season while losing just over eight games a year. Amazingly, if Crum were to go winless over the next four years he would still maintain an average of 20 wins per season.

His .748 winning percentage ranks him fifth among active coaches and 13th on the all-time list. His NCAA tournament mark is 32-15 and he has won 22 of his last 28 games in the post-season event. He was the second fastest major college coach to gain his 200th and 300th career coaching victories. At various times in his career, Crum has been named national coach of the year by *The Sporting News*, *Basketball Weekly*, *Playboy* and various other media outlets. He has been Metro Conference coach of the year three times.

While those accomplishments are certainly extraordinary and make Crum one of the all-time greats in the profession, there is reason to believe that his Louisville Cardinals have not been as dominant since winning the national championship in 1986 as they were up until that point. In the September 3 edition of *The Sporting News*, there was an item concerning the records of several prominent coaches since the 45-second shot clock came into existence in the 1985-86 season and the three-point field goal was instituted the following year. Over the last four years, Louisville

has averaged 10 1/2 losses per season. During that span, the Cardinals were 18-24 against opponents from the ACC, Big East, Big Ten, Pac-10, SEC and Independents DePaul and Notre Dame. Louisville's Class of 1990, other than fifth-year senior Tony Kimbro, was the first class at Louisville to never participate in a Final Four since Crum arrived in 1971.

While it certainly is no sin not to make the Final Four in this ultra-competitive age in college basketball, Louisville just hasn't been as dominant a presence on the national scene since 1986. In the past four years, the Cardinals missed out on post-season play in 1987, advanced to the semifinals of the Southeast Region in '88 and '89 Louisville made it to the semifinals of the Midwest Region. Last year the Cardinals were upset in the second round of the West Region by Ball State. In 1987 and '88, the Cardinals were definitely knocked out of the tournament by superior teams —Oklahoma and Illinois, respectively —that went on the Final Four.

Crum was slow, like many coaches, to realize the implications of the three-point field goal both offensively and defensively. That hurt Louisville especially in the 1986-87 season when the Cardinals were coming off the national championship but fell to an 18-14 mark.

When Joe B. Hall was the head coach at Kentucky, Louisville was known as the loose, fun team in the state while Kentucky generally underachieved in the NCAA tournament. Hall was criticized for putting too much pressure on his team and playing his cards too close to his vest. Ironically, the comparison between the two powers in basketball mad state of Kentucky swung 180 degrees as Kentucky under new coach Rick Pitino was a loose, fun group of mad bombers who endeared themselves to their vast legend of fans while Louisville looked more like one of Hall's Kentucky teams in terms of spirit than the Cardinals of old.

"The players look listless, anxious for the season to be done. There is bickering on the floor and boredom on the bench. The coach seems angry and frustrated. The fans are restless, fearful of an NCAA Tournament swoon," wrote Billy Reed in the *Lexington Herald-Leader*.

"Meanwhile, down the road, the state's *other* major college team is having fun. It runs and guns and presses, working its tail off and loving every minute of it. The coach is loose and wise cracking. The fans can't seem to get enough of it.

"Sound familiar? Sure. It does. Except in a rather amazing transferral of roles, the uptight, underachieving team is the Louisville Cardinals of Coach Joe B. Ah, Denny Crum, while the happy campers are the Kentucky Wildcats of Coach Rick Pitino . . .

"Although Crum probably would deny it, his success over the past decade has generated problems very similar to those faced by ex-Wildcat coach Hall in the early 1980s, when the Wildcats were being knocked out of the NCAA tournament by teams like Alabama-Birmingham and Middle Tennessee.

"For one thing, the expectations of the fans are greater. That's what happens when you win two NCAA titles and go to the Final Four more times than any other team in the land. The fans gets spoiled and the atmosphere becomes more intense."

His philosophy has always been to play a rugged schedule to prepare his team for the rigors of the NCAA tournament. Crum is also concerned about burning his players out down the stretch in the long college basketball season and does not have as an intensive pre-season program as most teams of this caliber. He has never pushed his players into the weight room and is a gentle jockey who applies the whip sparingly rather than riding herd on his team from October 15 through the end of the year.

"When people talk of coach Crum and all of his accomplishments, the one thing I think of the most is patience," Jeff Hall, who played for Louisville from 1982 through '86, told Bill Koch of Scripps Howard News Service. "There's going to be days when he's going to get on people to get them to do something, but on a normal day, no. He wants to treat people the way he likes to be treated."

Crum usually seems unruffled on the bench. He was dubbed "Cool Hand Luke," by NBC commentator Al McGuire.

"Coaching is teaching," Crum told Koch. "That's what coach Wooden was. I try to pattern myself after him. He always used to say there's two kinds of mistakes, mistakes of commission and mistakes of omission. He would always say you have to correct all of the mistakes of omission but you don't have to correct all of the mistakes of commission.

"You don't have to tell a kid he threw a bad pass up into the third row. He knows he threw a bad pass. But he said if he doesn't try to make the pass to someone who's open, if you don't correct those kinds of mistakes, you are reinforcing bad habits. So you have to correct all mistakes of omission. And that takes patience."

In his 19 years at Louisville, Crum has never taken a transfer from another four-year program and has signed only three junior college transfers. He also likes to get away from the game and is not obsessed by basketball or his own success. Crum can rarely be found on the summer camp circuit or AAU tournaments in the month of July, when college coaches are allowed to go out and evaluate talent, like most high profile head coaches who are away from home almost the entire month. He likes to spend time with his family on a farm in Jeffersontown, Ky. And he's an avid reader of collector of Louis L'Amour westerns. He also is an outdoorsman.

The 53-year-old native of San Fernando, Calif., Crum attended Pierce (Calif.) JC and went on to play for John Wooden at UCLA. Following his graduation in 1958 from UCLA, Crum stayed with the Bruins as a freshman coach before eventually returning to Pierce JC as its head coach. After four successful seasons at Pierce, Crum returned to UCLA in 1967 where he served as Wooden's top assistant coach and chief recruiter until his move to Louisville in 1971. He became Louisville's 17th head coach.

He will face one of his sternest challenges yet at Louisville in the upcoming season. The Cardinals have lost four players from their regular seven-man rotation of last season and a recruiting class that was ranked as one of the top three in the nation by almost all talent evaluators was decimated by Proposition 42. Louisville's top three recruits are not eligible this season. Other than three returning starters, the Cardinals do not have another player who started a game last year or averaged over 2.8 points per game. This will not be a deep Louisville team and the Cardinals are more limited inside than they have been in years.

★ PLAYERS NOT RETURNING ★

JEROME HARMON (6-4, G, 14.7 ppg, 3.6 rpg, 62 assists, 6 blocked shots, 30 steals) Harmon was Louisville's second leading scorer behind Felton Spencer last year even though he came off the bench and did not start a game. In the off-season he was dismissed from school because of academic problems. Harmon had academic difficulties from the time he enrolled at Louisville. He was academically ineligible his first year and then missed the 1988-89 season due to a back injury. However, Harmon certainly did not show any ill effects from his two-year layoff last year as he was spectacular at times. The high flying Harmon was second on the team with 39 dunks. Outside shooting was not his forte — Harmon was only 2-of-14 from three-point range —but he could cart the ball to the basket as well as practically any player in the nation.

Harmon was expected to become a starter this year. Louisville still should have a quality backcourt without him as LaBradford Smith and Everick Sullivan are talented players. However, the loss of Harmon diminishes Louisville's offensive explosiveness and depth.

CRAIG HAWLEY (6-5, G, 0.7 ppg, 0.6 rpg) Hawley was a reserve guard who saw limited action last year. He played in 21 games, starting one, for a total of 89 minutes. Hawley was just 4-of-23 from the field (.174) and missed all 7 three-point attempts. He provided some experience but is not a key loss.

TONY KIMBRO (6-7, F, 6.2 ppg, 5.0 rpg, 30 assists, 36 blocked shots, 35 steals) Kimbro finished his up and down Louisville career as a part-time starter as a senior. He was seventh on the team in scoring and third in rebounding.

His college career proves that way too much is made of the talent of extremely gifted young players and the result is they often lose their incentive and never develop to the fullest. Kimbro was recognized in ninth grade as a national level player. Many thought he would be the best to ever come out of Louisville. We at Blue Ribbon got sucked up in Kimbro's potential as well and profiled him among the Top 33 Players in the nation in our first ever high school All-America team in the 1982-83 edition.

Kimbro basically improved little, if any at all, from the time he was a sopho-

more in high school until the end of his college career. He did become a contributing factor off the bench for Louisville, but was hardly a big timer. For his career, Kimbro averaged 7.9 points and 4.1 rebounds. He shot .471 from the field, .387 from three-point range, .632 from the line, and handed out 160 assists against 218 turnovers.

Even though he was an underachiever, the loss of Kimbro makes Louisville's bench slimmer this season.

FELTON SPENCER (7-0, 265 lbs., C, 14.9 ppg, 8.5 rpg, 45 assists, 69 blocked shots, 24 steals) Felton Spencer is an old fashioned plugger who kept working on his game and improving bit by bit throughout his career. He is not blessed with the physical ability of a Shaquille O'Neal or Dikembe Mutombo, but Spencer is intelligent and knew what to do with the seven-foot height God gave him. His senior year was the only season Spencer was a full-time starter. He started all 35 games for Louisville as a senior and led the Cardinals in scoring, rebounding and blocked shots.

Spencer was a dependable offensive force who made .681 of his field goal attempts. He scored, rebounded, had his head in the game and plugged away game after game.

His diligence was rewarded in the NBA draft as the Minnesota Timberwolves made him the sixth overall selection in the first round.

Crum is a great coach, but there is no way he can compensate for the loss of Spencer. There is no Cardinal over 6-8 on the roster. Obviously, inside scoring will be harder to come by for Louisville without Felton Spencer.

KEITH WILLIAMS (6-4, G, 9.5 ppg, 3.0 rpg, 162 assists, 13 blocked shots, 41 steals) Williams was one of Louisville's starting point guards. He was basically a full-time starter for his entire career. He started 110 of 126 games at Louisville. Last year Williams was second on the team in assists behind LaBradford Smith. He was a reliable shooter and made .545 of his field goal attempts and was .343 from three-point range. Williams also took care of the ball and averaged slightly over two turnovers per game. He was a capable, steady guard.

LaBradford Smith will be able to handle the point guard position probably as well or better than Williams. However, Louisville's backcourt depth is diminished without Williams.

After it is all totaled up, Louisville has lost 54 percent of its offensive production, 54 percent of its rebounding, 46 percent of last season's assists and 60 percent of all blocks from last year.

★ RETURNING PLAYERS ★

JAMES BREWER (6-3, 190 lbs., SO, G, -11, Bardstown HS/Bardstown, Ky.) Brewer was redshirted last year. He appeared in 26 games for a total of 186 minutes as a freshman in 1988-89. In his freshman year, Brewer played 10 or more minutes in nine games. He made 28-of-53 field goal attempts (53 percent) and was 6-of-12 from three-point range (50 percent). He is truly an exceptional athlete with great leaping ability, speed and quickness.

Brewer was an outstanding football and track athlete at Bardstown HS. He is Bardstown's leading career rusher in football. Penn State and Oklahoma recruited Brewer as a football player. In track, Brewer set school records in the long jump (23'6"), 300-meter low hurdles (37.5 seconds) and 200-meter dash (21.6 seconds).

He's an excellent open court player who is enthusiastic. Brewer has worked hard on his shooting and could be a key player if his ballhandling and decision making are good.

MIKE CASE (6-6, 205 lbs., SO, F, #5, 0.6 ppg, 0.3 rpg, 1 assist, 1 steal, Pendleton Heights HS/Pendleton, Ind.) Case appeared in 18 games last season for a total of 39 minutes. He hit 5-of-14 field goal attempts (.357) and was 1-of-5 from three-point range (.200). His top game was a four-point, two-rebound effort against Austin Peay.

Case redshirted his first year at Louisville. In order to see more playng time, Case must be more aggressive defensively and rebound better. He could be a three-point threat with more playing time.

SHANNON FRALEY (6-0, 175 lbs., SR, G, #10, 1.3 ppg, 0.4 rpg, 1 assist, 3 steals, Pulaski County HS/Somerset, Ky.) Fraley played in nine games for a total of 12 minutes last year. He was 3-for-5 from the field and 1-of-3 from three-point range (.333).

Fraley underwent surgery on his left knee on Jan. 30 to repair a ligament and cartilage damage he suffered in the closing minutes of a game with Southern Mississippi.

Every field goal he attempted as a sophomore (7) was a three-pointer. Fraley walked-on as a freshman. He will long be remembered in Kentucky for hitting the game-winning shot, as a sophomore, to give Pulaski County a 47-45 win over Louisville Pleasure Ridge Park in the state championship game.

CORNELIUS HOLDEN (6-7, 210 lbs., JR, F/C, #30, 10.6 ppg, 5.7 rpg, 16 assists, 57 steals, 14 blocked shots, Crenshaw HS/Los Angeles, Calif.) Last season, in his sophomore year, Holden blossomed into one of the finest frontcourt players in the Metro Conference. He earned a starting role in the 12th game, against UCLA, and never relinquished his potition. Holden finished second behind Felton Spencer in rebounding and blocked shots.

After reaching double figures only once as a freshman, Holden scored in double figures 21 times as a sophomore. His .615 field goal percentage was the third-best single season mark at Louisville.

Holden hit an NCAA record 14-of-14 field goals at Southern Mississippi in the regular season finale. He also hit all four of his free throws, including two for the winning margin with eight seconds remaining, pulled a career-high eight rebounds and made a game-saving steal in the closing seconds.

He improved his free throw shooting from .532 as a freshman to .738 last year. The quick leaping Holden was a force after Crum inserted him in the lineup.

This season Holden's role will expand. He is now the Cardinals' main inside force due to the graduation of Spencer and the academic ineligibility of four frontcourt freshmen. Although he is only 6-7, Holden's quickness, leaping ability and timing will enable him to handle the added responsibility. He also has to stay healthy as there is no one behind Holden who can adequately replace him.

TODD HOWARD (5-10, 165 lbs., SO, G, −15, 0.2 ppg, 0.2 rpg, 1 steal, Ballard HS/Louisville, Ky.) The son of former Cardinal letterman Terry Howard (1972-75), Todd played in 11 games as a freshman. The walk-on hit both of his free throws against Virginia Tech for his only points of the year.

Howard was a high school teammate of Tennessee All-America guard Alan Houston on a state championship team at Ballard HS in Louisville.

LaBRADFORD SMITH (6-3, 200 lbs., SR, G, #23, 13.5 ppg, 3.3 rpg, 226 assists, 4 blocks, 74 steals, Bay City HS/Bay City, Tex.) In 1979-80, a senior guard named Darrell Griffith took charge and led Louisville to its first national title.

If Louisville is to successfully defend its Metro conference title and be a national factor, Smith will have to assume control like Griffith and become a truly dominant player.

He is Louisville's top returning scorer. Smith led Louisville and the Metro conference in assists last year. He also paced the Cardinals in steals (74), free throw percentage (.860) and minutes played (33.3 mpg). He was named the most outstanding player in the Metro Conference tournament with three-game totals of 47 points, 18 assists, 5 steals, and 67 percent shooting from the field. He had 24 points and 9 assists in the championship game against Southern Mississippi, hitting his first nine shots from the field, and earned CBS player of the game honors.

Smith became Louisville's all-time career assist leader (566 career assists) with 11 assists against Tulane on February 27. It was his sixth double figure assist total of the season.

He has become a more team-oriented player since coming to Louisville. Smith admits that as a freshman he was overly concerned about his own scoring. However, he has matured since then and is more team-oriented. He also has learned when to drive the lane and use his prodigious leaping ability. Early in his career, Smith would see a small opening and he'd blast into the lane and knock someone down and get a charge.

Last year he made 158-of-318 field goals (.497) and was 32-of-91 (.352) from three-point range. Louisville was team-oriented last year and Smith attempted an average of just over nine field goals per game. This year look for his offensive output to increase dramatically as we wouldn't be surprised to see Smith average 15 to 20 shots per game.

Smith has started 103 consecutive games at Louisville. He grabbed a career-high of 10 rebounds against UNLV while also totaling 20 points and six assists last year. He handed out a career-high and school record tying 12 assists against both UCLA and Cleveland State. Smith recorded a season-high of four steals on five occasions.

Louisville is a school with a great tradition for high flying slam dunkers. Smith is one of the all-time great dunkers at Louisville and he also has great strength and all-around athletic ability. Smith high jumped over 6-10 in high school and was drafted by the Toronto Blue Jays as a pitcher in 1989. He has a fast ball that was clocked at over 90 mph.

In an argument last year over who was Louisville's best slam dunker, teammate Derwin Webb voted for Smith. ''In my opinion, it's LA, because he does so many things in the air,'' Webb told Russ Brown of the *Louisville Courier-Journal*. ''Any time he dunks, it seems like it's a different variation. When he goes up, you just hold your breath wondering what's going to happen in the air.''

A pre-season second team All-America selection by *Inside Sports*, Smith came to Louisville billed as possibly the greatest high school player ever out of Texas. He has not been a disappointment but neither has Smith dominated like he was expected. Maybe it is because Louisville has so many other options, but Smith has seemed hold back at times. He possesses the basketball skills and physical ability to be one of the premier guards in the country. This year Smith will certainly get a chance to prove he belongs among the elite guards in college basketball. He has to have a big time season if Louisville is to make a serious run at the Metro Conference title and be a solid Top 20 team. In the past Louisville has balanced teams offensively because the Cardinals had many options. This year those options have decreased and the offense will center around Smith, fellow guard Everick Sullivan and Cornelius Holden. Smith is the most experienced and talented of the trio, so this should be his team.

There is no doubt that Louisville will only go as far as the talented and high flying LaBradford Smith can take them. This is his opportunity to end his career ranked among the all-time greats at Louisville.

TROY SMITH (6-8, 205 lbs., SO, F, #24, 2.5 ppg, 1.2 rpg, 5 assists, 4 steals, 6 blocked shots, Ft. Knox HS/Ft. Knox, Ky.) Smith was Louisville's only true freshman scholarship player last year. He appeared in 25 games and generally was used

as the third player off the bench. He saw a total of 154 minutes and was 25-of-50 (.500) from the field. Smith was a poor 12-of-25 (.480) from the line in limited action. He had a season-high of eight points against Florida State. He later equalled his season-high eight points in 15 minutes at Virginia Tech.

Smith originally committed to rival Kentucky, but decided to switch to Louisville when the Wildcats were placed on NCAA probation. He is a good athlete who is making the transition to a more out on the floor role as a forward after a high school career in the pivot.

There is an opportunity for Smith to become a key contributor for Louisville this year. Cornelius Holden is certain to nail down a starting spot up front, but the other two positions are open. Even if he does comes off the bench again, Smith's playing time is certain to rise as this is not a deep Louisville team.

EVERICK SULLIVAN (6-5, 190 lbs., JR, G/F, #34, 12.7 ppg, 4.5 rpg, 102 assists, 11 blocked shots, 44 steals, Hillcrest HS/Simpsonville, S.C.) Crum has always preferred big guards to small ones. He likes the 6-4 and up guards who are tremendous athletes because they can post up inside and offer versatility. Crum will get his wishes this year as he certainly has a big, athletic and versatile backcourt with LaBradford Smith and Everick Sullivan.

Sullivan was the Cardinals' top long range shooter last year, hitting 43-of-114 three-pointers (37.7 percent), just 2 three-point goals short of the school's single-season record set in 1988-89 by Kenny Payne (Philadelphia 76ers). He had a school record 6 three-point field goals (in six attempts) against Virginia and earned NBC/Chevrolet player of the game honors. Sullivan was also second on the squad with 44 steals and was third on the team with 38 dunks and a 2.9 assist average. He scored a career-high of 35 points against Chaminade in the opening game of the Maui Classic, the highest total for a Louisville player in 10 years. Sullivan also had a career-high eight rebounds against both Cincinnati and Virginia Tech.

Sullivan scored in double figures in 25 outings last year.

Like Smith, Sullivan is somewhat turnover prone as he had 103 turnovers to 102 assists while Smith averaged over 3.5 turnovers per game.

He is a competitor and can also score inside. Sullivan is a big time athlete in his own right with excellent leaping ability.

Look for his offensive opportunities to rise considerably. This is a Louisville team that won't have the luxury of balanced scoring and some Cardinals are going to have to step to the forefront offensively, probably Holden, Smith and Sullivan in order for Crum to have another 20-game winner.

DERWIN WEBB (6-4, 190 lbs., SO, G/F, #13, 0.7 ppg, 0.6 rpg, 4 assists, 1 blocked shot, 2 steals, Lawrence North HS/Indianapolis, Ind.) After being redshirted in 1988-89, Webb was used sparingly last year appearing in 25 games for a total of 68 minutes. He was 7-of-17 from the floor (.412) for the season.

Webb is a good defender and rebounder. He was an exceptional football and track performer in high school. He was the top long jumper in Indiana as a senior (23'11 3/4'') and also had the third best high jump (6-10). Webb was a standout wide receiver in high school and could have gone on to major college football.

He plays hard and has worked on his outside shooting. If Webb can provide some offense, his role should become more significant at both second guard and small forward.

Some Cardinals like Webb who have not been key contributors will have to come through if Louisville is to have a season up to its high standards.

★ NEWCOMERS ★

JASON McLENDON (6-8, 210 lbs., JR, F, #33, 19.5 ppg, 9.5 rpg, 3.0 apg, Barron Collier HS/Naples, Fla. & Edison CC/Ft. Meyers, Fla.) McLendon is only the third junior college recruit Crum has signed in his 19-year career at Louisville. He narrowed his choices to Florida State, James Madison and Central Florida before signing with the Cardinals. McLendon was redshirted last year.

He played on a 4-20 team as a sophomore at Edison. In fairness to McLendon, Edison lost two of its guards to injuries and one to dismissal that year. He averaged 15 points and seven rebounds a game as a freshman before suffering a broken finger, which required surgery, forcing him to miss the last 14 games of the season. As a sophomore, he led Edison CC in scoring, rebounding, three-point field goals and steals.

McLendon is known for his leaping ability, shotblocking and rebounding. He was an outstanding track athlete in high school and holds the school record at Barron Collier HS in the long jump at 23 feet and also the triple jump with a 45-foot jump to his credit.

''Jason was the fastest and quickest player on our team,'' said Edison CC coach Hugh Thilmar. ''He can shoot, block shots, run and jump with anyone. He has a wealth of talent.''

He could be a factor for the Cardinals this season. Louisville lost four frontcourt recruits and up front the Cardinals are definitely questionable this year.

KIP STONE (6-4, 180 lbs., FR, G, #20, 22.8 ppg, 5.9 rpg, 4.5 apg, Bolles HS/Jacksonville, Fla.) Stone helped lead Bolles to the Class AA Florida state championship as a sophomore and junior. Last season he paced Bolles to a 26-4 record and the sectional finals. Stone made 60 percent of his field goal attempts, including 40.3 percent from the three-point line. He was first-team All-Florida as a senior and was named the MVP in the Jacksonville area. He was an all-state and all-city selection as a junior and was the MVP of the Florida state tournament as a sophomore.

Stone was also a standout track athlete in high school, competing in the

400-meter dash, long jump and high jump. He also finished third in the state cross country championships as a senior.

"Stone is another great athlete who loves transition, but we question whether he can create well enough to play point guard (which is the position he was recruited for by Louisville). He handles it well in the open court and can knock down the 3-pointer," said Clark Francis of *Hoop Scoop*.

He is the type of guard Crum wants at Louisville —very athletic with good size.

TREMAINE WINGFIELD (6-7, 205 lbs., FR, F, #44, 20.5 ppg, 10.8 rpg, 1.2 apg, Brazaswood HS/Clute, Tex.) Stone and Wingfield are the only two of Louisville's six-man freshman class to predict and earn freshman eligibility. He was a second-team all-state selection at Brazaswood HS in Clute, Tex.

"'67 Tremaine Wingfield (Louisville) is a LaBradford Smith clone. He has a great body, runs the floor well, has excellent speed/quickness, is a strong rebounder, has excellent work habits and plays hard," said Mike Kunstadt of *Hoop Scoop*.

Wingfield appears to be a Louisville type player. He will compete with Troy Smith and Jason McLendon for starting positions up front flanking Cornelius Holden.

★ QUESTIONS ★

Size up front? Louisville had 7-0 Felton Spencer in the middle last year and he was the first center picked in the NBA draft. His replacement will be 6-7 Cornelius Holden, a great leaper in the Louisville mold but a player who lacks great height.

Overall experience up front? Holden is the only experienced frontcourt player for Louisville this season. The rest of the frontcourt playing time will be given to newcomers and returnees who have yet to prove themselves at this level.

Overall depth? There is a definite lack of proven depth both up front and in the backcourt for Louisville this season.

★ STRENGTHS ★

Denny Crum! Even though Louisville has not been as dominant in the last few years, Crum is still one of the elite coaches in the country off his past accomplishments. He has a challenge awaiting him this year and Crum's skill as a bench jockey should come out.

The backcourt of LaBradford Smith and Everick Sullivan! Crum has always liked his guards big and athletic and he certainly has that this year with Smith and Sullivan. This should be an outstanding offensive backcourt as both players can hit from long range or go inside.

Speed, quickness and athletic ability! Louisville will not be tall or deep this year, but the Cardinals do have a good contingent of high level athletes.

★ BLUE RIBBON ANALYSIS ★

Louisville heads into the season with a nation-leading streak of 46 consecutive winning seasons. Some sportswriters have suggested in the off-season that this streak could be in jeopardy as Louisville has more holes and apparent questions than at any time in recent memory. Four of last season's top seven players are gone and a recruiting class that was regarded as one of the top three in the country was ravaged by Proposition 42. Four of Louisville's six freshmen signees are not eligible.

The Cardinals are very questionable, by their standards, up front. the only returnee with significant experience up front is 6-7 junior forward/center Cornelius Holden, an extremely quick shotblocker who will probably have to move into the pivot this year, even though he is not ideally suited for that position. Louisville will have no one over 6-8 up front.

Depth is questionable both up front and in the backcourt. What isn't questionable is that Louisville should have a strong backcourt with 6-3 senior LaBradford Smith and 6-5 junior Everick Sullivan. Smith led the Metro Conference in assists last year and could be ready for a great senior year just like Darrell Griffith had for Louisville's 1980 national championship team. Sullivan is a premier long distance shooter who also can score inside and is an excellent athlete.

The Cardinals do have impressive athletic ability, but this does not appear to be a vintage Louisville team. The Cardinals just don't have the talent and presence up front you would expect at Louisville.

Crum will not have many options and his key players —Smith, Sullivan and Holden —have to come through with big years if Louisville is to defend its Metro Conference title. Louisville should finish third in the Metro Conference behind Cincinnati and Southern Mississippi. There is little margin for error at Louisville this year and the Cardinals could plummet even lower in the Metro Conference standings if the key players do not come through and some other players emerge quickly. This will be an interesting year at Louisville as Crum will have to do some juggling to keep the Cardinals up to their usual high standard.

LAST SEASON

#Chaminade (HI)	89-70
#Missouri	79-82
#Villanova	83-69
##Notre Dame	84-73
Cleveland State	104-77
Vanderbilt	101-75
Western Kentucky	75-61
New Mexico	78-49
Austin Peay	93-59
@Kentucky	86-79
Cincinnati	66-71
UCLA	97-80
@South Carolina	79-66
@Florida State	73-66
@Tulane	109-96
Memphis State	86-69
@DePaul	62-66
Southern Mississippi	105-88
Virginia Tech	96-69
@Ohio State	88-91 OT
Florida State	69-50
South Carolina	95-77
Georgia Tech	84-94
@Virginia Tech	97-78
@Virginia	72-56
@Memphis State	68-82
@UNLV	81-91
Tulane	99-85
@Cincinnati	86-71
@Southern Mississippi	73-71
*Tulane	79-66
*Memphis State	76-73
*Southern Mississippi	83-80
**Idaho	78-59
**Ball State	60-62

@ Road Games
# Maui Classic, Lahaina, HI
Bank One/Big Four Classic, Indianapolis, IN
* Metro Conference Tournament, Biloxi, MS
** NCAA Tournament, Salt Lake City, UT

NOTES: Louisville's recruiting class was rated No. 2 nationally by many experts behind North Carolina. However, four of the Cardinals' six freshmen aren't eligible. Sitting out this year at Louisville and expected to play next season are 6-10 center Brian Hopgood (Millwood HS/Oklahoma City, Okla.), 6-6 Greg Minor (Washington County HS/Sandersville, Ga.) and 6-6 forward Dwayne Morton (Central HS/Louisville, Ky.). Louisville's top recruit,

1990-91 LOUISVILLE SCHEDULE

Dec.	1	#Indiana
	5	Athletes In Action
	12	DePaul
	15	Prairie View A&M (TX)
	17	@Western Kentucky
	19	Cleveland State
	22	@George Mason
	29	Kentucky
Jan.	3	@Cincinnati
	5	@UCLA
	7	South Carolina
	10	Memphis State
	12	@Florida State
	14	@Tulane
	19	South Alabama
	24	Southern Mississippi
	26	UNLV
	30	Virginia Tech
Feb.	2	@Southern Mississippi
	6	@South Carolina
	9	Florida State
	13	@Virginia Tech
	16	@Memphis State
	20	Southwestern Louisiana
	24	@Georgia Tech
	26	Tulane
	28	Cincinnati
Mar.	2	Notre Dame
	7-9	##Metro Conference Tournament

@ Road Games
# Bank One/Big Four Classic, Indianapolis, IN
Roanoke, VA

6-9 forward Anthony Cade (a New York City native who prepped at Oak Hill Academy in Mouth of Wilson, Va.) originally signed with Sullivan College, located in Louisville, but enrolled at Connors State JC in Warner, Okla. . . . The Cardinals will appear seven times on national television this season.

MISSISSIPPI STATE

LAST SEASON: 16-14
CONFERENCE RECORD: 7-11
STARTERS LOST: 0
STARTERS RETURNING: 5
CONFERENCE:
  SOUTHEASTERN (SEC)
LOCATION: STARKVILLE, MS
HOME FLOOR: HUMPHREY
  COLISEUM(10,000)
NICKNAME: BULLDOGS
COLORS: MAROON AND WHITE

★ COACH'S PROFILE ★

RICHARD WILLIAMS (Record at Mississippi State, 50-65.) Richard Williams never played basketball beyond high school, but he has coached at almost every conceivable level since. Williams made an immediate impact as a recruiter when hired four years ago to take over the downtrodden Mississippi State program, and he should finally reap the benefits of that work this season.

Last year, Williams directed the Bulldogs to a 16-14 record, the school's first winning season in seven years. And, if he gets the Bulldogs over the hump and into the SEC's first division this season, he will have accomplished what many believed was impossible.

At the least, the 45-year-old Williams has Mississippi State on firm ground. The Bulldogs spent most of the 1980's as the unquestioned doormat of the Southeastern Conference. Last year's NIT bid was the Bulldogs first post-season action since 1978-79. And, if the Bulldogs' pre-season goal of reaching the NCAA tournament is realized, it would be only the school's second-ever trip and its first in 27 years.

Williams also has made major strides with the age-old problem of selling his program in a rural area with no nearby major population base. Season tickets sales and average home attendance have creeped upward in each of his four years in Starkville.

Born in Oceanside, Calif., while his father was serving in the Marine Corps, Williams grew up in Pearl, Miss., where he lettered in both baseball and basketball in high school. That is also where his playing career ended, but he still managed to learn the game at the foot of a master while an undergraduate at Mississippi State.

As a student worker in the MSU physical education department, Williams was at the school during the final two years of the Babe McCarthyera, the most successful in Mississippi State history. He spent countless hours observing the legendary McCarthy, studying his practice drills and picking his brain on basketball strategy.

After graduating from MSU in 1967, he began the long and varied road back to the head job at his alma mater. Williams' first coaching job was at Montabello Junior High in Natchez, Miss., a post he held for two years before moving to St. Andrew's Episcopal Junior High in Jackson. During his two-year stay there, he found time to earn a Master's degree in School Administration from Mississippi College. From there, it was back to Natchez, as an assistant coach at South Natchez High School, a post he held for two years before being named head coach of the school in 1973.

During his six-year stay, South Natchez averaged 16 victories per season, winning two Big Eight Central Division championships and making the school's first-ever trip to the Mississippi state high school basketball tournament.

Williams joined the hotly competitive Mississippi junior college ranks in 1979 when he was named head coach at Copiah-Lincoln JC (Wesson,Miss.). During five years in that postition, he averaged 18 wins per season and was named National Junior College Athletic Association Region 23 coach of the year in 1983, as well as Mississippi Junior College coach of the year.

Williams used that success to return to Mississippi State as an assistant coach under Bob Boyd in 1984—just in time to see the bottom fall out of his alma mater's program. And it was only when he arrived back in Starkville that he gave up his full-time duties in the classroom, having taught math in junior high, high school and junior college.

When he inherited the headcoaching job two years later, the Bulldogs were coming off an 8-22 season with little prospects for the future. The SEC was no longer Kentucky and nine dwarfs, but Mississippi State had clearly fallen behind the league's basketball boom, which saw one school after another upgrade its program.

Williams was no instant miracle worker—his first team finished 7-21, 3-15 in the conference. But following that season, he put together one of the best recruiting classes in school history, the bulk of which are seniors this year. Williams, with six true freshmen suited up, three starting, and not a senior on the team, doubled

State's victory total in 1989 (14-15 overall, 6-12 in the SEC).

The Bulldogs slipped to 13-15 the following season, but were a slightly better 7-11 in the conference, including a two-game sweep of LSU. The Bulldogs would win five straight over the mighty Tigers in one stretch during Williams' rebuilding period.

Last winter, State was finally a winner (16-14, another 7-11 SEC record). This time around, Williams and his seniors are poised for more.

★ PLAYERS NOT RETURNING ★

MIKE GRANATO (6-5, G, 1.0 ppg, 0.6 rpg) Granato, a freshman last year, left the team in mid-season after playing only 30 minutes in seven games. He transferred to Birmingham Southern.

ROBERT WOODARD (6-4, G, 4.1 ppg, 2.7 rpg, 21 assists, 14 blocked shots) Woodard appeared in all 30 games, but saw the least court time of the eight players who regularly contributed last season, about 12 minutes per game. A gutty player who provided leadership, he should not be missed much on this senior-dominated team.

★ PLAYERS RETURNING ★

CAMERON BURNS (6-7, 200 lbs., SR., F, #21, 18.2 ppg, 7.3 rpg, 26 assists, 18 steals, 18 blocked shots, East Flora HS/Flora, Miss.) Burns sat out his freshman year due to Proposition 48, but has been one of the league's tougher power forwards ever since, starting all 58 games since he became eligible. A blue collar type, Burns will not dazzle you away from the basket, but he plays very physically and takes the ball strong to the hole.

Burns has a long wingspan and a 42-inch vertical jump, plus a good first step toward the basket that help him makeup for the inches he oftens gives away underneath. He rarely strays too far from the paint and does not have much of an outside shot—in three years he has never launched a three-pointer and is only 64 percent from the free throw line—but by concentrating on pounding inside he has led the SEC in field goal percentage the last two years.

The 67.1 percent shooting of his sophomore season set a school record and was second best in the nation that year. Not surprisingly, his favorite shots is the dunk, of which he had a school-record 51 a year ago, including five in an upset victory over Alabama.

"If there's one player on our team that we really, really need in our lineup all the time, he's the guy, "Williams said. Burns took his coach literally. He played all 55 minutes of a triple-overtime victory against Ole Miss.

Nicknamed "Smoke," Burns has been selected to the 10-member All-SEC coaches' team both of his years in the league. He made second-team UPI and Associated Press All-SEC last year, after being a third-team selection on both as a sophomore.

Last year, Burns had season highs of 28 points against Georgia and Baylor and 17 rebounds against Ole Miss.

GREG CARTER (6-6, 215 lbs., SR., F, 13 ppg, 6.8 rpg, 71 assists, 34 steals, 22 blocked shots, Forest HS/Forest, Miss.) Carter has started since he was a freshman at Mississippi State, but spent his first two years primarily as a defensive specialist. Last year, he emerged as a legitimate scorer at small forward after rarely shooting his first two seasons. He more than doubled his points per game, and was second on the team behind Burns in scoring and rebounding. He also led the Bulldogs in blocked shots and was second in assists.

Carter finished the season strong. Six of his team-high seven double-doubles came in the final 13 games of the year, in which he averaged 15 points. He also led MSU in offensive rebounding. That offensive improvement earned him a spot on the both the UPI and Associated Press All-SEC third-team.

Unlike Burns, Carter can score away from the basket, as he has a nice jump shot (41 percent on three-pointers) and was third in the SEC in free throw shooting (83 percent), the best by a Bulldog since 1975-76. His offensive production was one of the pleasant surprises for Mississippi State last season, particularly since it did not seem to harm his defense. Carter normally draws the opponent's top scorer.

DOUG HARTSFIELD (6-1, 190 lbs., SR., G, #20, 11.5 ppg, 3.0 rpg, 158 assists, 39 steals, Utica HS/Utica, Miss.) Hartsfield was second in the SEC in assists last season, but overall the Bulldog backcourt was inconsistent at best, mostly due to erratic outside shooting. If a younger player develops quickly enough, Hartsfield could move to the off-guard—probably his best position—this season. His strong point is outside shooting (43 percent from three-point range), not ballhandling, and he had to worry primarily about the latter last season. A move back to off-guard should increase his scoring output.

Hartsfield was a part-time starter in his first two seasons, averaging 5.0 ppg as a freshman and 6.2 ppg as a sophomore.

KEITH HOOPER (6-5, 185, SR., F, #24, 0.8 ppg, 0.5 rpg, Germantown HS/Germantown, Tenn. & Northeast Mississippi JC/Booneville, Miss.) A junior college walk-on, Hooper played in only seven games, totaling 30 minutes. A good soldier on the roster, his role does not figure to increase much this season.

TODD MERRITT (6-9, 220, SR., C, #30, 8.0 ppg, 6.7 rpg, 38 assists, 14

steals, Dougherty HS/Albany, Ga.) Like many of the SEC centers, Merritt is probably more suited to play forward. And he will play some forward when Carl Nicholls comes in at the pivot.

Still, after two years as a part-time starter, bouncing back and forth from forward to center, Merritt solidified his spot in the middle last season. Merritt took the starting job away from Nicholls midway through the year and started the final 13 games. In the process he was voted the Bulldogs' most improved player by his teammates. After gaining the starting job, he led the team with 11 double figure rebounding efforts.

Merritt is not a flashy player, using muscle more than agility to wedge inside for rebounds. But he has a decent touch from outside, and it is his offense that gives him the edge over Nichols. As a sophomore, his three-pointer at the buzzer beat Kentucky and he hit 20 three-pointers overall last season.

On the down side, aided by the SEC's experimental six-foul rule, Merritt set a school record with 117 personal fouls and, even with the experimental rule, fouled out of six games.

CARL NICHOLS (6-9, 245 lbs., SR., C, #33, 4.4 ppg, 4.7 rpg, Jefferson County HS/Fayette Miss.) Nicholls lost his starting job to Merritt midway through last season, but as a proven player at backup center, it gives Mississippi State some options and flexibility in the frontcourt. An academic All-SEC selection, he is strictly an inside player without much of an outside shot. Opposing teams tended to ignore him on offense last year as he is not much of a scoring threat.

Nichols remains a solid, steady player, but has never lived up to the star potential he displayed as a freshman. That year, he started 27 of 29 games and averaged 9.0 points and 6.6 rebounds. Among freshman in the SEC that year, he was the leader in rebounds and field goal percentage, but his productivity has gone down each season since.

Nichols is also a big liability at the free throw line, hitting only 51 percent last season.

IRA PETERSON (6-2, 180 lbs., SO., G, #32, 0.3 ppg, 0.5 rpg, Broad Street HS/Shelby Miss.) Peterson redshirted as a true freshman, and his progress was slowed by a knee injury which also kept him from practicing. Last year he saw limited playing time, a total of 70 minutes in 13 games.

He averaged 24.5 points per game playing for his father in high school, and has good quickness. But with Mississippi State adding some talented new blood for its backcourt this season, he may struggle for playing time again.

BRAD SMITH (6-6, 175 lbs., SO., F/G, #10, 6.1 ppg, 1.6 rpg, 24 assists, Mendenhall HS/Mendenhall, Miss.) A breakthrough year for Smith would be the biggest lift the Bulldogs could get, and it would not surprise anyone in Mississippi to see it happen. Smith, ranked No. 41 nationally among recruits by Bob Gibbons All-Star Sports two years ago, is the most highly touted prospect Williams has landed. He was slow to make the jump from high school to major college ball last year, but is capable of being a dynamic scorer.

Smith has the potential to be a deadly outside shooter—a Bulldog weakness of a year ago—and can play either off-guard or the wing. Last year he played in all but one game, starting four, and averaged about 13.7 minutes per outing.

Those who saw Smith as one of Mississippi's all-time prep stars know he is capable of much more. At Mendenhall High, he averaged 33.0 points and 8.3 rebounds his senior year. He was named to the Mendenhall Hall of Fame after ending his four-year career with 3,474 points, while the team compiled a composite 123-24 record. Smith once scored 60 points in a high school game against St. Joseph's and, following his senior year, won the slam dunk competition and finished second in the three-point contest at the McDonald's Kentucky Derby Festival in Louisville.

He showed glimpses of all that last year as a freshman at State, scoring in double figures eight times. Williams would like to see more performances like the one he put on at Tennessee—22 points, on a school record six three-pointers. But after scoring 10 points in the rematch with Tennessee, Smith saw his playing time diminish for the remainder of the season. In the final nine games, he made only one more three-pointer, and did not score over five points.

Smith needs to work on his overall game, as he was a bit of one-dimensional player last year. He also needs to get stronger to play in the SEC, having been pushed around as a freshman. It will be interesting to see how he attacks league play after a year to get his bearings straight.

TONY WATTS (6-2, 175 lbs., JR., G, #22, 11.7 ppg, 2.2 rpg, 58 assists, 49 steals, Rolling Fork HS/Rolling Fork, Miss.) After making the All-SEC freshman team two years ago and going on a white-hot streak down the stretch, Watts was plagued by inconsistent shooting and a sophomore slump last season. And his problems mirrored the Bulldogs' woes in the backcourt.

As an example, Watts had eight games of 16 points or more, five of over 20 points. But he was also held to six points or less eight times. Although his scoring was up over his freshman year, his shooting percentage was way down (48 percent to 38 percent).

Watts made a big splash as a freshman, gaining a starting job midway through the season after coming off the bench to hit his first 11 shots in a game against Alabama. The 11 straight field goals broke the school record of 10 set by Jeff Malone, and he finished that game with 24 points. Watts averaged 16.0 ppg over the final 16 games of his freshman year, including a 24-point outburst against Vanderbilt. Interestingly, he was one of four Mississippi natives on the five-man SEC all-freshman team in 1989, but was the only one who stayed in-state to play college

ball (Chris Jackson and Vernel Singleton of LSU, and Litterial Green of Georgia were the others).

His backcourt mate, Doug Hartsfield, had the pressures of the point guard to excuse his shooting woes. Watts was more of a mystery, particularly since he is not much of a defensive player.

Watts is the son of former NBA guard Slick Watts, with whom he spent the summer in Seattle working on his game. Unlike his father, however, Tony has a full head of closely-cropped hair. An expressive, fun player to watch because his three-pointers are often arched high into rafters, he will be even more popular if he regains the shooting touch of his freshman year.

★ NEWCOMERS ★

DERRICK DANIEL (6-6, 225, JR., F, #34, 14.1. ppg, 7.5 rpg, S.R. Butler HS/Huntsville, Ala & Tyler JC/Tyler, Texas) Daniel, a junior college transfer, is a versatile player who should contribute immediately in a backup role. He can play inside, but is a good enough shooter to stay out on the wing as well. He helped lead Tyler JC to the Texas Eastern Conference championship.

DAVID DOMINQUE (6-8, 220, FR., F/C, #42, 14.4 ppg, 9.0 rpg, Notre Dame HS/Crowley, La.) Dominque redshirted last season and reportedly made progress in the weight room, which he will need to play center in the SEC. Before coming to State, he was a teammate of Brad Smith on Team Acadiana, which toured the Canary Islands. He projects as a center, and will probably have to wait until Nichols and Merritt leave to get much playing time.

KEITH DUDLEY (6-8, 240, JR., F/C, #54, 9.1 ppg, 4.4 ppg, Gadsen HS/Gadsen Ala. & Tyler JC/Tyler, Texas) Dudley was a teammate of Daniel's at Tyler JC, where he was a skilled post player with an excellent perimeter touch. He is also considered an top-notch interior defender, who could develop into a strong rebounder for the Bulldogs before the year is out. Brothers Craig (Alabama) and James (Jacksonville State) also played college basketball.

VINCE EMBRY (6-8, 210, FR.,F, #35, 10.6 ppg, 6.2 rpg, Judson HS/Converse, Tex.) Embry may need a year in the weight room, but he possesses good leaping ability. He was slowed his senior year of high school by a severe ankle injury that caused him to miss Judson's first 15 games. Prior to the injury, *Basketball Times* rated him among the nation's ''Best of the Rest'' power forward prospects. Once healthy, he could contribute either down low or on the wing, as he also possesses a fine shooting touch.

NATE MORRIS (6-6, 190, FR., F, #25, 26.0 ppg, 13.0 rpg, 5.0 assists, 3.0 blocked shots, Caldwell HS/Columbus, Miss.) Morris is the most highly touted of Mississippi State's incoming freshmen, a class that Bob Gibbon's All-Star Sports ranked 44th in the country. He was named the Gatorade Circle of Champions Mississippi player of the year last season at Caldwell, where he was an outstanding athlete with explosive leaping ability.

Twice an All-State selection and three times an All-District player, Morris scored over 2,100 career points as a prep performer. He was also chosen the 1989-90 Converse All-America team after leading Caldwell to the championship game of Mississippi's North State tournament.

MSU coaches compare Morris favorably to new teammate Greg Carter—a good inside player who has the shooting range to venture outside. But he also has the strength to spell Burns at power forward.

ORIEN WATSON (5-10, 185, SO., G, #12, 32.7 ppg, Ridgeway HS/Memphis, Tenn.) Watson, who sat out last year after transferring from Memphis State, has three years of eligibility remaining. He can play either guard spot, and MSU coaches believe he could push Hartsfield and Watts for a starting job.

Most likely, Watson will play point guard, which could move Hartsfield to off-guard. Practicing with the team last year, he was the best pointman on the floor. He was also a dynamic scorer in the ultra-competitive Memphis high school ranks.

Watson found several upperclassmen ahead of him his freshman year at Memphis State, but averaged 4.0 ppg before transferring to Mississippi State.

If he can play the point—and Williams has little doubt he can—the Bulldogs will get a lot better immediately. At the least Watson should see considerable action, as he has the potential to be a prolific outside scorer and he also drives the lane well.

★ QUESTIONS ★

Expectations? Arch-rival Ole Miss had the same pre-season giddiness a year ago, and the Rebels were done in by it early.

Home court advantage? The Bulldogs were 2-7 on the road in the SEC last year, about right for their talent level. But they were only 5-4 at home, which is not a first division figure.

Backcourt? On paper it looks like a strength, but on the court it was a liability last season.

Tony Watts? Needs to regain freshman form to solve backcourt woes.

★ STRENGTHS ★

Experience! There are more talented teams in the SEC, but none more experienced.

Depth! All five starters return, and there is a nice blend of newcomers capable of contributing, particularly since they can be brought along slowly.

Frontcourt! Burns and Carter are a fine tandem. Newcomers could give State the luxury of experimenting with different styles.

Cameron Burns! One of the toughest players in the SEC.

★ BLUE RIBBON ANALYSIS ★

It is clearly now or never at Mississippi State. Not only do all five starters return from last year's team, but four are seniors and it is a group that has essentially been playing together for three straight seasons.

If the Bulldogs go with the same starting lineup as last year, it will put four seniors and a junior on the floor. They could end a lot of heartache at a school that had just one winning record in a decade until last year's modest 16-14 mark. And the Bulldogs have still not been above .500 in conference play since the 1978-79 season. That could all change this year, though not without some nagging questions being answered in the positive.

Mississippi State's frontcourt matches up favorably with any team team in the conference, save LSU and Shaquille O'Neill. But the SEC has been a ''guard's league'' in recent years, and certainly inconsistency in outside shooting hampered the Bulldogs progress last season.

However, there is plenty of room for optimism. The backcourt talent is on hand if Tony Watts shakes off his sophomore slump and regains his freshman form. Brad Smith could live up to his advance billing. Newcomer Orien Watson might make enough of an impact at the point to allow Doug Hartsfield to move back to his more natural off-guard.

Mississippi State's biggest hurdle may be mental. This group, experienced as it is, has been content to pull off a few upsets a year, playing spoiler within the conference. One SEC coach said: ''They just play to stay close, and you'll never be a big winner like that.''

Still, you have to like the Bulldogs chances with so many seniors trying to go out with a bang. They got valuable post-season experience last year with two NIT games. This could be the year, finally, that they crack the SEC's first division and make the NCAA tournament for the first time in 27 years.

LAST SEASON			
#Northeast Louisiana	75-68	Tennessee	83-84OT
#@Centenary (LA)	96-80	Auburn	74-77
Centenary	112-74	@Alabama	86-74
@Kentucky	97-102	Georgia	74-82
Christian Brothers (TN)	86-51	@Florida	79-54
@New Orleans	62-55	@Mississippi	67-75
@East Carolina	72-63	Vanderbilt	83-68
##Delaware	66-65	Texas Christian	64-60
##@Connecticut	68-84	*Alabama	44-59
LSU	87-80OT	**Baylor	84-75
@Tennessee	77-82	**@New Orleans	60-65
@Auburn	71-93		
Alabama	57-62	@ Road Games	
@Georgia	69-83	# Centenary Cellunet Classic,	
Florida	98-73	Shreveport, LA	
Mississippi	104-102OT	## Connecticut Mutual Classic,	
@Vanderbilt	68-81	Hartford, CT	
Kentucky	87-86	* SEC Tournament, Orlando, FL	
@LSU	68-86	** NIT	

1990-91 MISSISSIPPI STATE SCHEDULE			
Nov.	26	Tennessee Tech	
	30	@Tennessee-	
		Chattanooga	
Dec.	4	@Jacksonville	
	8	Ball State	
	11	Eastern Kentucky	
	18	Alcorn State	
	22	@Drake	
	27-28	#Eastern Airlines Palm	
		Beach Classic	
Jan.	2	@Tennessee	
	6	Mississippi	
	9	@Kentucky	
	12	Vanderbilt	
	16	Georgia	
	19	@Florida	
	23	Alabama	
	26	@Auburn	
	30	@LSU	
Feb.	2	Tennessee	
	6	@Vanderbilt	
	9	Kentucky	
	13	@Mississippi	
	16	@Georgia	
	20	Florida	
	23	@Alabama	
	27	Auburn	
Mar.	2	LSU	
	7-10	##SEC Tournament	

@ Road Games
# West Palm Beach, FL (Miami of Florida, Miami of Ohio & Ohio State)
Nashville, TN

NOTES: Mississippi State has an intriguing first round matchup in the Eastern Airlines Palm Beach Classic with nationally ranked Ohio State . . . over the past three years, Mississippi State is 5-1 against LSU . . . David Dean, a 6-11 recruit from Carol City HS in the Miami, Fla., area, will sit out this season at Mississippi State. Once in uniform, Dean will be the tallest player ever at Mississippi State . . . the average home attendance in Starkville has risen dramatically since Williams took over the program. The Bulldogs drew 5,740 fans per game last season, up from 2,908 in 1986-87.

NEW MEXICO

LAST SEASON: 20-14
CONFERENCE RECORD: 9-7
STARTERS LOST: 1
STARTERS RETURNING: 4
CONFERENCE: WESTERN
 ATHLETIC (WAC)
LOCATION: ALBUQUERQUE, NM
HOME FLOOR:
 THE PIT (18,100)
NICKNAME: LOBOS
COLORS: CHERRY AND SILVER

★ COACH'S PROFILE ★

DAVE BLISS (Record at New Mexico, 42-25. Career record 261-188.) There are no more loyal fans in the country than those who support the New Mexico Lobos. Last season New Mexico averaged 16,627 fans and the school has been in the Top 10 in the nation in attendance ever since the Pit opened in 1966. In his two years in Albuquerque, Bliss has found out how fervent the New Mexico fans are. The man he replaced, Gary Colson, was openly criticized in both the local media and by the fans for not getting the Lobos into the NCAA tournament. New Mexico was almost an annual participant in the NIT under Colson and that hasn't changed under Bliss. New Mexico has been the post-season NIT in both of Bliss' first two years and last year the Lobos reached the semifinals of the tournament in Madison

Square Garden. He now knows just how much heat Colson took for not getting New Mexico into the NCAA tournament as Bliss has taken some on his own. New Mexico has lacked speed and depth the last two years and Bliss has recruited to give the Lobos those commodities. This should be the year New Mexico is given an NCAA tournament bid after seven straight trips to the NIT.

''They have unrealistic expectations in some regards, but they also have a tremendous loyalty on the other hand,'' Bliss said of the New Mexico fans.

He came to New Mexico after turning the Southern Methodist program around. Bliss was 141-101 (.584) in eight years at Southern Methodist. When he came to Dallas, Southern Methodist was the doormat of the Southwest Conference and his first two teams were just 7-20 and 6-21, finishing last in the Southwest Conference both years. In his final five years at Southern Methodist, Bliss led the Mustangs to post-season play four times, including three trips to the NCAA tournament. In his final year at Southern Methodist, the Mustangs won a school record 28 games and the program's first outright Southwest Conference title in 21 years. He was named Southwest Conference coach of the year in his final season at Southern Methodist. At Southern Methodist his top player was Jon Koncak, now with the Atlanta Hawks.

Before going to Southern Methodist, Bliss coached at Oklahoma. In four years at Oklahoma he was 77-62 (.554) and was twice named Big Eight Conference coach of the year. His 1978-79 Oklahoma team was 21-10 and received an NCAA tournament bid.

Bliss is a native of Binghamton, N.Y. He attended Cornell where he was an All-Ivy League guard in basketball and all-conference outfielder in baseball. Bliss was the Cornell athlete of the year in 1965 and is now a member of the school's Athletic Hall of Fame. He graduated in 1965 with a Bachelor's of Science Degree in Marketing. He attended graduate school and worked for IBM and Proctor and Gamble in Chicago before receiving his MBA from Cornell in 1967.

Bliss was drafted into the Army in 1967. At that point his life's course changed as Bob Knight was able to get Bliss an assistant coaching position at Army. Bliss spent two years at Army with Knight before returning to Cornell for two years as an assistant coach. Prior to joining the Army he had expected to use his Marketing Degree, but basketball became his life's work after he coached with Knight. In 1971, Bliss joined Knight's staff at Indiana and spent four years there before becoming the head coach at Oklahoma.

"The system that I learned under Knight is that you try not to throw the ball away," Bliss said. "Take smart shots and play tough defense and get the maximum out of your players each game."

The WAC Conference is one of the more interesting and underrated in the country. Six of the nine WAC schools have outstanding, on-campus facilities that stack up with virtually any in the country. The home crowds are boisterous and give WAC schools one of the strongest homecourt edges in the country. However, seven of the nine schools operate on Mountain Standard Time and the eastern press rarely gives space to WAC games. Bliss feels the conference needs to aggressively seek publicity. He was disappointed when the conference didn't adopt experimental rules such as the six-foul individual limit.

Bliss told Jeff Miller of *Inside Sports* his recruiting pitch is: "I'm not going to tell 'em we're going to give 'em the best education. What if he says, 'What about Harvard?' What do I say then? I'm going to tell him we have a good school and play in the best supported conference west of the Mississippi."

This is a big year for Bliss' career at New Mexico. He has four starters returning, including the top senior center in the nation in Luc Longley. If he can win either the WAC regular season or tournament title and qualify for the NCAA tournament, it would mean a great deal to his career at New Mexico. If the Lobos receive an NCAA tournament bid next March, Albuquerque will be ecstatic.

★ PLAYERS NOT RETURNING ★

DARRELL McGEE (6-0, G, 8.3 ppg, 2.5 rpg, 205 assists, 41 steals) McGee was New Mexico's starting point guard and a three-year starter. He finished his career as New Mexico's all-time assist leader (684) and games played (137).

Offensively, McGee was 102-of-233 from the field (.438) and 58-of-149 (.389) from three-point range. He was not a great scorer but he could distribute the ball and defend on the perimeter.

Despite the experience lost with McGee, New Mexico should be adequate at the point again. The heir apparent at point guard should be his younger brother, 6-0 sophomore Andre McGee.

OMAR SIERRA (6-8, F, 1.7 ppg, 2.0 rpg, 4 assists, 1 steal) A transfer from Houston Baptist who played only one year at New Mexico, Sierra started five games last year but was shelved after 19 games due to a knee injury which required surgery. New Mexico played 15 games after his injury so Sierra is not a major loss.

DONNIE WALKER (6-1, G, 0.9 ppg, 0.8 rpg, 11 assists, 1 blocked shot, 4 steals) Walker was a reserve point guard who saw limited action during his two years at New Mexico. He appeared in 17 games last year for a total of 84 minutes.

★ RETURNING PLAYERS ★

WILLIE BANKS (6-2, 165 lbs., JR, G, #32, 8.9 ppg, 2.5 rpg, 72 assists, 7 blocked shots, 28 steals, Albuquerque HS/Albuquerque, N.M.) Although he has started only one game in his two years at New Mexico, Banks has had a key role for the Lobos. He has been a true spark plug coming off the bench for New Mexico. Banks averaged 9.3 points and 2.2 rebounds as a freshman. As a sophomore his role decreased and his playing time dipped by 196 minutes. Banks' scoring average also dipped to 8.9.

He has scored in double figures in 34 games and New Mexico was 27-7 in those games. He was the Lobos' fourth leading scorer last year and came on strong averaging 14.2 points per game in the five NIT games. Banks was excellent in New Mexico's NIT win over New Mexico State, scoring 12 of his 14 points in the second half. His play helped spark the Lobo resurgence in mid-February. In the nine games from Jan. 6 to Feb. 10, Banks scored just 32 points, making 11-of-33 field goals. However, in the 12 games thereafter, he notched 147 points, going 49-of-85 from the field and 33-of-46 from the line. In three home wins over Brigham Young, Utah and Hawaii during New Mexico's win streak, Banks scored 15, 16, and 17, respectively, making 17-of-20 shots.

He is extremely quick and an excellent leaper. Banks switched back and forth between point and second guard last year. This year he is expected to be used exclusively at the second guard spot.

With Banks, senior Rob Robbins, senior Marvin McBurrows and talented sophomore point guard Andre McGee plus two promising newcomers, New Mexico should be strong in the backcourt in 1990-91.

J.J. GRIEGO (6-7, 195 lbs., SO, F, #34, 2.5 ppg, 1.3 rpg, 5 assists, 5 steals, Socorro HS/Socorro, N.M.) Griego averaged 7.5 minutes a contest in the 24 games he played as a freshman. He did not play in the first six games of the year before making his collegiate debut against Louisville on ABC-TV. He is considered a good outside shooter —23-of-47 for .489 from the field last year —but needs additional strength and weight. His best scoring game was 10 points in nine minutes against East Carolina. Griego also had a team-high of seven rebounds against Maine.

He was held out of the first six games last year because Bliss was considering redshirting Griego. He was used mainly at power forward last year, but will be switched to small forward this season. New Mexico has a deep roster this year and there is a chance that Bliss might redshirt Griego this season.

LUC LONGLEY (7-2, 265 lbs., SR, C, #13, 18.4 ppg, 9.7 rpg, 108 assists, 117 blocked shots, 31 steals, Scotch College/Perth, Australia) After a great deal of speculation concerning his intentions, Longley finally decided he would stick around for his senior year at New Mexico rather than enter the NBA draft. Longley deliberated a long time about his decision as he probably would have been picked anywhere from fourth to sixth in the draft, and definitely would have been the first center selected. He waited until close to the deadline for underclassmen to declare for the draft before announcing his intentions which made Lobo fans and coach Bliss quite nervous.

Bliss felt Longley felt the need to join his teammates for one more shot at the elusive NCAA tournament bid which New Mexico has not received since 1978. "I really do think that's a large part of his considerations," Bliss told Eric Snouffer of the *Albuquerque Journal* about Longley's desire to help New Mexico gain an NCAA tournament bid. "His commitment runs deep.

"He feels that he has to achieve something . . . That's what drives a guy like Luc."

The two best center prospects in college basketball —LSU's Shaquille O'Neal and Dikembe Mutombo of Georgetown —are not seniors in eligibility, so Longley enters the season as the top senior center prospect in the country. As a junior Longley was first-team All-WAC and an honorable mention All-America pick. He set a WAC record with 117 blocks and his 108 assists are impressive for a center. Longley was triple-teamed on many occasions last year and is expected to be more effective because New Mexico is a more talented team this year. He not only led the Lobos in scoring and rebounding last year, but his 117 blocked shots ranked seventh in the nation. His 108 assists were second on the team, however, he also led New Mexico with 112 turnovers. His best statistical game was 31 points, 11 rebounds and eight blocks in 36 minutes against Towson State. Longley has scored 31 points three times in his New Mexico career and his best rebounding game was 18 against St. Louis in the NIT semifinals in New York. He was the first Lobo to average over nine rebounds a game since Larry Gray led the WAC at 10.4 in 1976.

The biggest rap on Longley is that he does not have great intensity. That has been evidenced in international play. Longley was a seldom reserve who contributed little on Australia's 1988 Olympic team. In the Goodwill Games last July in Seattle, Longley wasn't a starter and had a combined 16 points and 15 rebounds in Australia's first four game. However, he did outplay Georgetown's Alonzo Mourning in Australia's one-point loss to the United States. Against Mourning, Longley had 15 points, 13 rebounds and six blocked shots.

"Luc should play well. He has run out of excuses," Australia coach Adrian Hurley said. "I said, 'if you can't play now, forget it.' He's been promising to play for the last four or five games, and he was running out of games."

"I've always been a role player," Longley told John Bannon of *USA Today*. "My first instinct when I get the ball has been to pass. I have to learn to be more aggressive.

"I guess I'm kind of a laid-back person. I have to work on being intense."

"It's like I told him, 'Luc, you have enough friends.' He's reached a difficult stage where he can never exceed people's expectations," Bliss told Bannon. "If he goes out and gets 30 points and 15 rebounds, you think he could have 40 and 20."

He can be pushed around and handled by much smaller players, but Longley is an exceptional passer for his size. He has good athletic ability but is still learning the game of basketball. Last year, New Mexico depended on Longley too much. "Luc will continue to be the focal point of our offense, but we don't want to rely on him too much," Bliss said.

"We were supposedly going to play a faster style when Luc leaves," Bliss told Eric Snouffer of the *Albuquerque-Journal*. "That's not true. We're going to play a faster style next year . . . we won't be a slow team again. We were a slow team last year. We were a lot slower than I wanted us to be. . .

"He (Longley) has to absolutely take charge —he has to take charge on the floor and take charge in the lockerroom," Bliss said. "He has a lot of understanding (of the team's needs), not just a lot of experience."

Longley enters this season as one of the few players in the country who will have to play themselves out of the NBA draft lottery. There will have to be a virtual tidal wave of significant underclassmen entering the draft and Longley would have to be worse than mediocre, more like atrocious, to play his way out of the big bucks that await a high lottery pick. Even though this should be a much stronger than usual top half of the draft, Longley should go in the first seven.

MARVIN McBURROWS (6-4, 180 lbs., SR, F/G, #20, 6.1 ppg, 3.2 rpg, 34 assists, 8 blocked shots, 8 steals, Andress HS/El Paso, Tex.) After playing just 34 minutes total his freshman year, McBurrows has started in 66 of New Mexico's last 67 games. He will have to work hard to hold his position as some incoming talent will make a run at the starting small forward spot.

McBurrows has been New Mexico's top defensive player over the last two years. He scored in double figures eight times last year and had 14 points twice (against Centenary and Hawaii). He also had a career-high best eight rebounds against Centenary.

Last season McBurrows was 79-of-173 (.457) from the field and 17-of-41 (.415) from three-point range.

He is a good role player type who doesn't make a lot of mistakes, can chip in some offense when needed and excels defensively. He will also be able to play some second guard when needed.

ANDRE McGEE (6-0, 180 lbs., SO, G, #12, 2.0 ppg, 2.8 rpg, 46 assists, 2 blocked shots, 14 steals, King HS/Corpus Christi, Tex.) The McGee family legacy will live on at New Mexico this year. Andre's big brother, Darrell, was a four-year letterman and three-year starter at point guard for New Mexico. He finished his career as the school's record holder in assists (684), game played (137) and games started (104). This year Andre is his brother's replacement at point guard.

McGee is extremely quick going to the basket and New Mexico's best defensive guard. He averaged nearly 11 minutes per game in 28 appearances last year. He made 6-of-7 free throws in the final 3:22 to protect to lead against WAC leading Brigham Young last February. New Mexico was 11-3 when McGee played more than 12 minutes, 7-1 when he was in for 14 or more. His season-highs were seven points and six assists in 18 minutes against Maine.

McGee was a highly regarded high school player at King HS in Corpus Christi, Tex. In fact, he may have more overall ability than his brother. New Mexico should be in good hands at point guard with Andre McGee.

KURT MILLER (6-4, 185 lbs., SR, F, #23, 11.6 ppg, 5.8 rpg, 67 assists, 4 blocked shots, 42 steals, Ben Lomond HS/Ogden, Utah) Miller played the power forward spot all of last year but with the addition of some bigger players, Bliss may move him to the outside. He was put at a disadvantage by being forced to guard the other team's power forward last year and giving up several inches, but Miller is an excellent athlete who compensated. He is acrobatic under the hoop and also uses his quickness well.

Miller played in 32 games last year and started 29. He was New Mexico's leading scorer in the five NIT games averaging 17.6 points plus 7.2 rebounds. He had 19 points and a career-high 11 rebounds against Hawaii in the NIT quarterfinals. Miller scored a career-high of 24 against Oklahoma State in the second round of the NIT. He had a strong night against Oregon in the first round of the NIT with 22 points (tying a career at that time), plus 10 rebounds and a career-high six assists. In the last six games in 1989-90, Miller scored 128 points (16.0 ppg) with 56 rebounds (7.0 rpg) and had 27 assists. He missed the first two games of the year after recovering from two broken bones in his right hand suffered in New Mexico's opening practice last October 15.

He finished second in the WAC in field goal percentage at .573 and converted 61.3 percent of his shots in WAC games, also second in the league. Miller scored double figures in 21 games overall, including 11 of his last 13 and 16 of the last 21.

Even though he will be shifted to more of a perimeter role this year at the small forward spot, look for Miller still to get most of his points inside. He can post up most small forwards and should be fresher offensively because he doesn't have the burden of defending power forwards. Miller improved considerably last year, he averaged 4.6 points per game as a sophomore, and should have a big senior year.

ROB NEWTON (6-9, 215 lbs., SR, F/C, #43, 5.0 ppg, 3.1 rpg, 4 assists, 6 blocked shots, 5 steals, Andress HS/El Paso, Tex. & Eastern Arizona JC/Thatcher, Ariz.) Newton is attempting a comeback after suffering from a broken right leg in the first half of the Air Force game last February 28. He broke both the tibia and fibula near the ankle. Newton is expected to be ready for the beginning of pre-season drills. Bliss is expected to use Newton as a key reserve at power forward and center or possibly as a starter.

At the time of his injury, Newton was providing a boost for the Lobos with his play off the bench. He had developed a quality reserve for Luc Longley at center and Kurt Miller at power forward. His loss affected New Mexico's play down the stretch. Newton had scored 53 points and grabbed 22 rebounds in the seven games before the injury, including a career-high 14 points and 8 rebounds against San Diego State. In the nine games before his injury, Newton was averaging 17 minutes per game.

For the year, Newton was 53-of-83 (.639) from the field. He was shooting .418 percent at the line when injured.

Newton was highly regarded when he came to New Mexico in 1986 from Andress HS in El Paso, Tex. He broke the hearts of UTEP fans in the border city with his decision to play for WAC rival New Mexico. He missed his first year at New Mexico due to academic problems and averaged 1.5 points and 0.9 rebounds in limited action in 1987-88 for former New Mexico coach Gary Colson, who is now at Fresno State. When Bliss took over in 1988, he wasn't happy with Newton and shipped him off to Eastern Arizona JC where he spent a season before coming back to New Mexico.

He was a highly recruited high school player because coaches were intrigued with Newton's athletic ability. He is an excellent runner and jumper for his size but just has never been able to put his entire game together until just prior to breaking his ankle. Newton could be the starter at power forward this year. Miller is expected to be moved to small forward and it could create an opening at power forward which Newton could take if he is healthy.

ROB ROBBINS (6-5, 200 lbs., SR, G, #43, 14.0 ppg, 3.5 rpg, 84 assists, 1 blocked shot, 27 steals, Farmington, HS/Farmington, N.M.) Robbins has started 103 consecutive games in his New Mexico career. Last season, Robbins lead the nation in free throw shooting. He made 101-of-108 free throws (.935). Robbins has always been a great free throw shooter as he converted .829 as a freshman and .917 as a sophomore.

Robbins is on pace to become New Mexico's all time leading scorer. He starts the season seventh on New Mexico's all time scoring list with 1,317 points, 429 shot of the record. He also is already New Mexico's all-time leader in three-point

field goals with 193 in his career.

Robbins came to New Mexico known as a great perimeter shooter but he struggled from the field last year making .421 of his field goal attempts and just .355 from the three-point range. As a sophomore, Robbins shot a sizzling .491 from three-point range.

He played his best game of the season against Oklahoma State in the second round of the NIT, scoring 20 of his 23 points in the first half to rally New Mexico back from a 12-point deficit. Robbins had a season-high 24 points against San Diego State and reached double figures in 29 games. He also converted 52 straight free throws before missing, falling 12 short of the NCAA record. Robbins won his second consecutive Lobo Invitational MVP award last December.

His role in the New Mexico offfense to get open and shoot three-pointers. Robbins was hampered in pre-season practice last year by a knee problem which required arthroscopic knee surgery. He missed over two weeks of pre-season drills.

He enters this season with 71 double figure scoring games to his credit - the New Mexico record is 86 - and starts this season with 23 consecutive free throws made. Look for Robbins to expand his New Mexico and WAC record 52 straight free throws set last season. He also should regain his sophomore shooting form since he does not have to rehabilitate the injured knee.

★ NEWCOMERS ★

BRIAN HAYDEN (6-9, 215 lbs., FR, F, 20.0 ppg, 13.1 rpg, La Cueva HS/Albuquerque, N.M.) Hayden was one of the top players in the state of New Mexico last season and will play power forward for the Lobos. He has been bothered by a nagging foot injury and suffered a stress fracture in his left foot last November that kept him out of action for six weeks. He is a good shooter who is getting bigger and stronger. He will probably need some time to acclimate himself to college basketball. New Mexico is deep up front so Bliss may elect to redshirt Hayden.

TRENT HEFFNER (6-10, 220 lbs., JR, C, 8.4 ppg, 5.9 rpg, McClintock HS/Tempe, Ariz. & Mesa CC/Mesa, Ariz.) Since New Mexico has Longley back for his senior year in the pivot, Bliss might redshirt Heffner and give him two more years of eligibility after Longley departs. Heffner is sound defensively and a good rebounder. He played for a strong Mesa team which finished 32-3 and advanced to the national junior college tournament in Hutchinson, Kan. Mesa was 54-12 and in Heffner's two years.

Heffner has experienced some tough luck in the last year. He had a bout with mononucleosis last season and then was struck by appendicitis. That was followed by the removal of four wisdom teeth and a case of the shingles.

''Every time something happened I wondered what they were thinking over at New Mexico, that maybe they got a lemon.'' Heffner told Richard Stevens of the *Albuquerque Tribune*. ''It was kind of ironic that everything happened after I signed but I don't think I'd even been sick since maybe the eighth grade.''

Heffner admits that he is really not much of an offensive threat, but he enjoys defense and gets more satisfaction out of holding his man down than by scoring a lot of points. If not redshirted, Heffner would like to compete for playing time at power forward.

He is yet another Lobo that was lured to New Mexico by the attraction of The Pit. ''I wanted to be somewhere where I could experience a total basketball environment,'' Heffner told Stevens. ''At MCC (Mesa Community College), we had won thirty games in a row and a thousand people in the stands.''

KHARI JAXON (6-8, 200 lbs., SO, F, 17.0 ppg, 7.0 rpg, Los Angeles HS/Los Angeles, Calif.) Jaxon is eligible this season after sitting out last year at New Mexico. He is expected to have an immediate impact, is probably the Lobos' best leaper and is considered a quality offensive rebounder.

His senior year was marred by a broken wrist that caused Jaxon to miss twelve games. He played in the first ten games of the season and the last five. When he came back from the broken wrist, Jaxon helped lead Los Angeles HS to a spot in the city championship game.

His name is pronounced kuh-HAR-ree. Jaxon's father, Cepheus, played basketball at Wake Forest.

VLADIMIR McCRARY (6-7, 220 lbs., JR, F, 10.4 ppg, 6.0 rpg, Madison HS/San Antonio, Tex. & Hutchinson JC/Hutchinson, Kan.) McCrary is a well traveled young man. He is a 1987 graduate of Madison HS in San Antonio, Tex. and originally signed with Oklahoma. McCrary sat out in 1987-88 season due to Proposition 48 and then transferred to Western Texas JC where he played in 1988-89 before last year's move to Hutchinson JC. In the interim, McCrary's family moved to Dallas.

McCrary played on a strong Hutchinson team that was 29-5 last season. Seven of his teammates are now at Division I programs. The left-handed McCrary is a good defensive player and has leadership potential. He will battle for playing time at power forward with senior Robert Newton and Khari Jaxon. With his toughness and experience, McCrary should be able to carve out a roll this year.

JIMMY TAYLOR (6-2, 170 lbs., SR, G, Campbellsville HS/Campbellsville, Ky. & Cerritos JC/Cerritos, Calif.) Taylor's story is a rare one. He started all 32 games at point guard for a 21-11 New Mexico State team in 1988-89, averaged 8.2 points, 2.4 rebounds and dished out 107 assists. Taylor also had 12 blocks and lead the Aggies in steals with 44. After that one year at New Mexico State, Taylor transferred to rival New Mexico where he will have one year of eligibility.

He was not expected to have a scholarship but after an incoming freshman was lost to Proposition 42, Taylor received his scholarship. He's a good three-point shooter and the son of a basketball coach. Taylor makes good decisions for his point guard spot. At New Mexico State, Taylor scored 23 points in two games against the Lobos.

"Jimmy's in the pool to really compete for a few positions," New Mexico's assistant Doug Ash told David Snyder of the *Albuquerque Tribune*. "He's a very good player. He makes good decisions and he is a good shooter."

Although a natural point guard, Taylor will also be in contingent for playing time at the shooting guard spot. He will probably back up sophomore Andre McGee at the point but still see considerable action.

"I think they'll put somewhere for me to play," Taylor said.

ERIC THOMAS (6-6, 190 lbs., FR, G, 21.0 ppg, 9.8 rpg, 4.0 blpg, Rio Mesa HS/Oxnard, Calif.) An excellent all-round player who made 46 percent of his three-point shots in high school, Thomas is favorably compared to Lobo senior Rob Robbins. Thomas also has good mental toughness and is extremely bright. He won numerous awards in high school for academic achievement and is majoring in Bio-medical Engineering. He would like to become a doctor.

As a senior, Thomas shot 67 percent from the field. He was All-CIF his final two years. Because he is sound and skilled, Thomas may be able to earn some playing time as a freshman.

IKE WILLIAMS (6-5, 200 lbs., SO, G, 18.2 ppg, 9.0 apg, 4.0 rpg, Spruce HS/Dallas, Tex.) Williams sat out last year due to Proposition 48, however, in his first semester at New Mexico, Williams was on the Athletic-Academic Honor Roll. He was ranked as the top guard at Texas and the fifth best player overall in the state in 1989 by the *Dallas Morning News*.

Williams can play either backcourt spot and is expected to even push Rob Robbins for playing time at off-guard. He is tenacious, has excellent strength and can score.

With the additions of Williamson, Taylor and Thomas the New Mexico backcourt is much deeper than last year.

★ QUESTIONS ★

Can Luc Longley shake his laid back attitude, become a little meaner and make the Lobos into a big winner?

Overall team toughness?

Defense? Statistically the Lobos were not bad last year defensively as they allowed only 69.7 points per game and .429 shooting from their opponents. However, Bliss believes New Mexico must become more aggressive defensively if the Lobos are to earn that long awaited NCAA tournament bid.

★ STRENGTHS ★

The presence of Luc Longley! Even though Longley's meanness is questioned, he is the best senior center in the country. He should be a high lottery pick in the upcoming NBA draft.

Improved speed!

More depth!

Offensive potential! Longley is a good scorer, and if Rob Robbins gets his shooting eye back, New Mexico should be potent offensively.

★ BLUE RIBBON ANALYSIS ★

It's now or never time for the New Mexico Lobos. New Mexico may be the only team in the country that has averaged over 20 wins per season for the last seven years but has not received a prize invite from the NCAA Tournament and has had to settle for a NIT bid. New Mexico fans are anxious to see their beloved Lobos in the NCAA tournament and this should be the year.

Four starters are returning including senior center Luc Longley, who toyed with the idea of turning pro last year, but decided to instead return for his senior year. The Australian native needs to become more aggressive and consistent but he is an accomplished passer and scorer. Longley is the top senior center in the country this year.

Senior guard Rob Robbins lead the nation in free throw shooting last year and is on course to become New Mexico's all-time leading scorer. Senior Forward Kurt Miller played well as a power forward last year even though he was short (6-4) for the position and is expected to be used more at small forward this year. Senior forward Marvin McBurrows is a returning starter who can also switch to the backcourt and 6-9 senior Robert Newton is healthy after suffering a broken leg late last season. New Mexico will be stronger up front this year.

Bliss has a quality group of newcomers who should add depth and speed that were lacked last year. Bliss wants the Lobos to press and run more last year and will even sit Longley down if he slows the team down.

"We need to be tougher, more aggressive defensively," Bliss said. "Our increased depth should allow us to use the press more than we have the first two years. Also, our rebounding should improve because of better size."

New Mexico should battle Wyoming and Colorado State (and don't count out UTEP) for the WAC title. There is no reason why the Lobos should not get a NCAA tournament bid this March.

LAST SEASON			
#Hardin-Simmons (TX)	91-57	@Wyoming	82-79
#Monmouth	69-93	Brigham Young	60-51
New Mexico Highlands	106-53	Utah	86-66
@New Mexico State	55-60	Hawaii	82-71
@Tennessee	85-96OT	San Diego State	91-69
New Mexico State	73-74	@Air Force	62-54
@Louisville	49-78	@UTEP	61-78
Centenary (LA)	86-69	**Oregon	89-78
##Maine	94-63	**Oklahoma State	90-88
##Detroit	91-64	**Hawaii	80-58
East Carolina	88-51	***St. Louis	73-80
Towson State	96-68	***Penn State	81-83
Wyoming	87-89OT		
Colorado State	63-61	@ Road games	
@Utah	60-79	# Lobo Classic, Albuquerque, NM	
@Brigham Young	78-79	## Lobo Invitational, Albuquerque,	
@San Diego State	62-78	NM	
@Hawaii	71-74	* WAC Tournament, El Paso, TX	
Air Force	61-44	** NIT	
UTEP	80-82OT	*** NIT Final Four, Madison Square	
@Colorado State	71-75	Garden, New York, NY	

NOTES: New Mexico will open up with Texas-Arlington in the first round of the Lobo Classic. Southwest Texas State is New Mexico's first round opponent in the Lobo Invitational . . . the average attendance in The Pit last year was 16,629 . . . the Lobos are starting a four-game, home and

1990-91 NEW MEXICO SCHEDULE

Nov.	23-24	#Lobo Classic	Feb.	9 @Wyoming
	28	Western New Mexico		14 Brigham Young
Dec.	1	@Texas Tech		23 UTEP
	3	Maryland-Eastern Shore		28 @Air Force
	5	@Arizona State	Mar.	2 @UTEP
	8	New Mexico State	Mar.	6-9 *WAC Tournament
	15	@New Mexico State		
	17	North Texas	@ Road Games	
	20	Tennessee	# Albuquerque, NM (Army, San Francis-	
	28-29	##Lobo Invitational	co & Texas-Arlington)	
Jan.	3	Colorado State	## Albuquerque, NM (Manhattan,	
	5	Wyoming	Southern University & Southwest Texas	
Jan.	10	@Utah	State)	
	12	@Brigham Young	* Laramie, WY	
	17	@San Diego State		
	19	@Hawaii		
	24	Hawaii		
	26	San Diego State		
	31	Air Force		
Feb.	2	Utah		
	7	Colorado State		

home series with Texas Tech and a two-year deal with Arizona State this season . . . Three New Mexico games will be televised nationally, all on ESPN: Tennessee on Dec. 20, Colorado State on Feb. 7 and at home against UTEP on Feb. 23.

NEW MEXICO STATE

LAST SEASON: 26-5
CONFERENCE RECORD: 16-2
STARTERS LOST: 2
STARTERS RETURNING: 3
CONFERENCE: BIG WEST
LOCATION: LAS CRUCES, NM
HOME FLOOR: PAN
   AMERICAN CENTER (13,2222)
NICKNAME: AGGIES
COLORS: CRIMSON AND WHITE

★ COACH'S PROFILE ★

NEIL McCARTHY (Record at New Mexico State, 96-59. Career record, 296-157) After five years at New Mexico State, Neil McCarthy believes he has everything in place necessary to keep the Aggies winning and near the top of the Big West Conference. Last season, McCarthy led New Mexico State to its best record (25-6) since 1970 and the school's first NCAA tournament appearance in eleven seasons.

"I feel like this is my baby now," McCarthy said. "We've got the foundation in place, we just want to keep on building."

Last January McCarthy started negotiations for a new contract. He not only wanted to be rewarded financially and to have security for himself, but he also wanted assurances that additional funding for the program would be made. In June it was announced that McCarthy had signed a new four-year contract. According to New Mexico State athletic director, Al Gonzales, McCarthy will receive a base salary of $115,000 and a total package estimated at $180,000 annually. McCarthy will also get the use of a complimentary car, gas and insurance for the automobile, and will make additional money from radio and television appearances, summer camp and his shoe contract with Nike. His assistant coaches will also receive significant raises. The Aggies' recruiting budget will increase from $35,000 last year to $60,000 next year, and the travel budget will increase from $48,000 to $60,000.

"I am very pleased with the contract," McCarthy said. "I feel it represents a solid commitment by the administration to our basketball program. I signed it, it was time. New Mexico State is where it's at; Las Cruces is where I want to be."

There is no doubt the New Mexico State administration and fans also want McCarthy to stay in Las Cruces. He came to New Mexico State in 1985, from Weber State, and inherited a 7-20 team. He immediately turned the Aggies into winners going 18-12 and reaching the finals of the PCAA tournament in his first year. He became the winningest first-year coach in New Mexico State history. The Aggies' home attendance also increased by approximately 2,000 fans per game in the 1985-86 season.

Last year was McCarthy's best season to date at New Mexico State. The Aggies knocked off national champion UNLV, tied the Runnin' Rebels for the regular season title in the Big West Conference, and were the top seeded team in the conference tournament. McCarthy also led New Mexico State to a berth in the Top 20, reaching as high as 17th in the *UPI* poll. He was named Big West coach of the year for the second straight season. He was also named the Kodak District coach of the year. Maybe his most important achievement, at least in the eyes of the New Mexico State fans, was that the Aggies swept their two games with arch rival New Mexico for the first time in eight years. All this was accomplished even though McCarthy was assimilating five new players into his system.

"I think New Mexico State was a well-kept secret in the last 20 years," McCarthy told John Henderson in an article in *The Sporting News*.

McCarthy has built slowly at New Mexico State. He understands that New Mexico State's remote location makes it tough to recruit high school blue chip players. Instead, he focuses on junior college transfers and players looking for a new start after beginning their career at another four-year school.

"They're different from freshmen," McCarthy told William F. Reed of *Sports Illustrated* about junior college transfers. "The high school player comes with 25 offers, but he thinks college is an extension of high school. A J.C. player says, Hey, I'm fortunate to get this opportunity."

McCarthy feels that he ranks right behind Jerry Tarkanian of UNLV in recruiting junior college players in the west. "I've had good success every year. I understand how to coach J.C. players," McCarthy told Henderson.

Besides his recruiting skill, McCarthy has also been successful because he teaches a matchup zone defense that is one of the best in the country. Last year the Aggies ranked among the Top 10 nationally in field goal percentage defense. The past two years the Aggies also forced opponents into over 20 turnovers per game.

"The matchup zone is a good defense if you want to keep the ball out of the post," McCarthy told *The Sporting News*. "We don't have a lot of tall kids. We need a defense that puts enough pressure on the ball."

As the college game has become more up-tempo due to the 45- second clock, the three-point field goal, and the success of run-n-gun teams like Loyola Marymount, UNLV, and many others, McCarthy has also changed his philosophy in the last few years.

"The first ten years I coached I was more of a half court coach offensively. We didn't run a lot.

"At Weber State we didn't have a lot of kids from the city. My 26-2 team (1980-81) had three starters from Wyoming. We were big, tall, and excellent on offense. We played several defenses but basically we were a big, slow team. At New Mexico State I've made a conscious effort to recruit smaller, quicker players. We press full court and run the break very often. We now do a lot of different things defensively even though we are a wheeling, dealing team on offense. Our matchup zone is the most aggressive type of zone defense you can play.

"Our program is based on defense, not so much containment, but to generate turnovers, and speed the game up. We caused over 30 turnovers in four different games," McCarthy explained.

The 49-year-old McCarthy was born in San Francisco. After graduating from St. Vincent HS. He served in the U.S. Army and during his stint won the heavyweight boxing title at Fort Bliss in El Paso, Tex. Following his stint in the service, McCarthy returned home and enrolled at Vallejo (Calif.) JC. He earned All-League honors on the basketball team and later transferred to Cal State-Sacramento for his final two years where he graduated in 1965 with a Bachelors Degree and later returned to earn a Masters Degree. He later returned to St. Vincent's and served as Dean of Boys in addition to his coaching responsibilities.

Prior to coming to New Mexico, McCarthy coached for ten seasons at Weber State, compiling a 200-98 record that included six regular season or post-season Big Sky Conference titles and five post-season tournament appearances (4 NCAA and 1 NIT). McCarthy received coach of the year honors on four different occasions, which was a Big Sky Conference record. Under McCarthy, Weber State reached the Top 20 four times and was ranked as high as twelfth.

"People who saw my teams play ten years ago have said I have made a philosophical change. Probably I have as I am definitely more of an up-tempo coach now. One of the more interesting things that is happening in college basketball is that there is so much television saturation that if you play half court ball you will lose your fans.

"Part of my recruiting is predicated on the fact that we have to put an exciting product on the floor. We have got to get people to turn off the television set, get out of the house, and plunk down ten dollars per ticket at the Pan American Center.

"Our goal is to be in that class in terms of offensive productivity like an Oklahoma, or a Loyola Marymount," he said.

The Big West Conference is getting stronger each season. However, McCarthy is quite capable of keeping New Mexico State near the top of the Big West. McCarthy has built a firm foundation for the Aggie program.

★ PLAYERS NOT RETURNING ★

MARK ACRE (6-8, C, 1.6 ppg, 1.1 rpg, 1 blocked shot) Acre was a reserve center who appeared in 12 games last year for a total of 28 minutes. He was not a big contributor and can be replaced.

JAMES ANDERSON (6-8, C, 13.6 ppg, 6.4 rpg, 13 assists, 10 blocked shots, 36 steals) Anderson is one of two starters who are not returning. He was New Mexico State's top scorer and rebounder on last year's 26-5 team. Anderson was a co-captain and a major leader.

Junior college transfer James White is Anderson's probable replacement. White is a talented prospect, but whether he can be as productive and replace some of the leadership lost with Anderson is uncertain.

RICK FLUCKEY (6-6, F, 6.0 ppg, 1.3 rpg, 19 assists, 3 blocked shots, 19 steals) Fluckey came off the bench for the Aggies last year and served as the team's top outside shooter. He made 43-of-116 three-pointers (.371) and also led New Mexico State not only in made three-point field goals, but three-point percentage. He averaged 13 minutes per game last year and made some big baskets.

Fluckey was not disenchanted even though he transfered from New Mexico State with a year of eligibility remaining. Fluckey transferred to Quincy College, an NCAA Division II school, in Quincy, Ill. He had lived in Quincy for several years and his transfer to Illinois puts him closer to his family. He also is expected to be a starter at Quincy.

His departure makes the Aggies more questionable from the perimeter this year and could hurt in close games when a big basket is needed.

WARREN HARRELL (6-6, F, 0.7 ppg, 0.0 rpg) Harrell was a freshman on last year's team and saw action in three games for a total of six minutes. The Reseda, Calif. native transferred to Allan Hancock JC back in his home state. McCarthy has said he will let Harrell return to New Mexico State if he desires.

KEITH HILL (6-4, G, 12.9 ppg, 3.8 rpg, 120 assists, 5 blocked shots, 30 steals) Hill is a big loss for the Aggies. He played either backcourt spot and finished his career as New Mexico State's all-time assists leader. He was a first-team All- Big West Conference selection. Hill also hit game winning shots against UNLV and New Mexico.

126

The smart and consistent Hill was a team leader. He will be difficult for McCarthy to replace.

CORY JOHNSON (6-11, C, 0.0 ppg, 0.0 rpg) Like fellow freshman Harrell, Johnson saw limited action, appearing in three games for a total of four minutes. He did not score or get a rebound last season. Johnson transferred to Yavapai JC in Arizona.

"For Cory and Warren (Harrell), they'll get a chance to gain experience at the junior college level. We've left the door open to both of them to return after they have had a chance to play at junior college," McCarthy said.

★ RETURNING PLAYERS ★

WILLIAM BENJAMIN (6-3, 170 lbs., JR, G, #21, 6.4 ppg, 2.4 rpg, 79 assists, 4 blocked shots, 44 Steals, Santa Monica HS/Santa Monica, Calif.) Although he will face some stiff competition, Benjamin is the probable replacement for Keith Hill in the Aggie backcourt. Last season he started one game and played an average of over 19 minutes per game. Benjamin was 65- of-147 (.447) from the field and 9-of-28 (.321) from three-point range. From the free throw line, Benjamin made 58-of-79 (.734).

He has extremely long arms and is blessed with a seven-foot wingspan. Benjamin is a quality ballhandler and passer who can bring the ball up court against tough pressure defense. He is also one of the most aggressive defenders on the team.

Benjamin showed an improved offensive game last year. How much he continues to improve offensively will determine whether Benjamin takes the starting vacancy in the backcourt.

RANDY BROWN (6-3, 190 lbs., SR, G, #3, 13.2 ppg, 3.4 rpg, 109 assists, 14 blocked shots, 91 steals, Collins HS/Chicago, Ill., & Howard County JC/Big Spring, Tex.) Probably the main reason New Mexico State improved last year and earned the co- championship of the regular season of the Big West Conference was the arrival of Randy Brown. Brown was a first-team Big West selection. He was picked as the second best non-freshman newcomer in the league in a poll of Big West coaches, behind UNLV's Larry Johnson.

Brown is a terrific defensive player who has extremely quick hands and feet, and gets his hands on a lot of balls. His 91 steals established a New Mexico State record for the most steals in a season. He was also second on the team in scoring and assists.

He is a catalyst of both the Aggie offense and defense. Brown is a more than adequate shooter who made 131-of-294 field goals (.446) and 16-of-42 (.381) from three-point range. He had a season-high 28 points against Long Beach State in the Big West tournament semifinals despite playing the final 17 minutes of the game with four fouls. Brown's eight-foot jump at the buzzer gave New Mexico State a 71-61 win over Fresno State. He also scored 27 points in the Aggie's 83-82 win over UNLV. Brown's halfcourt shot just before the halftime buzzer against New Mexico was the longest shot of the season for New Mexico State. ESPN, who televised the Aggie-Lobo game, included Brown's shot in its weekly "Plays of the Week."

Brown is not only a great athlete, but he is extremely competitive and has tremendous leadership qualities. He played two years at Houston but became disenchanted with the Cougar's style of play. Houston coach Pat Foster had slowed the Houston attack and Brown felt he wasn't improving. He sat out a year at Howard County JC in Texas and was supposedly headed for UTEP but ended up at New Mexico State when the Miners signed another point guard.

Brown established more respect on the national level with his showing in the tryouts for the U.S. National team. He survived the first tryout camp in Colorado Springs, Colo., and was one of 20 players who advanced to the second phase of the tryouts. Brown was eventually cut before the U.S. team left for the Goodwill Games in Seattle, but the experience benefitted him.

"I think I came in and gave it my best shot and did the things I had to do," Brown said about his experience with the U.S. National team. "I think my biggest question mark was whether I could nail the jump shot. But I think by playing good defense and getting the ball to the right players at the right time really helped me."

Brown's style of play and physical attributes have been favorably compared to former Arkansas star Darrell Walker, a Chicago native who is now with the Washington Bullets. Like Walker, Brown is tough defensively, goes to the basket well, runs the fast break and can go inside on offense. Walker was a first round pick and Brown also has first round potential.

CHRIS HICKMAN (6-9, 255 lbs., JR, C, #35, 3.5 ppg, 2.1 rpg, 2 assists, 2 blocked shots, 4 steals, Clearwater HS/Clearwater Kan.) Hickman was McCarthy's first frontcourt substitute last year. He is a physical rebounder and an above average shooter. Hickman made 29-of-45 field goals (.644) last season. He averaged over seven minutes of action per game.

Hickman's playing time increased over the final two weeks of the season. Over the first 22 games, he was averaging 6.5 minutes, 2.9 points and two rebounds per game. Over the last eight games he became the first big man off the bench and averaged 14 minutes per game while scoring at a 6.2 clip and grabbing 3.3 rebounds per game. Hickman has a GPA of 3.5 in Electrical Engineering, the best grade point average on the team.

He improved significantly over the summer and has lost weight which should make him quicker. Hickman will give McCarthy a three-man pivot rotation along with senior Jason Trask and junior college transfer James White.

REGGIE JORDAN (6-4, 180 lbs., SR, F, #32, 10.6 ppg, 6.0 rpg, 60 assists, 22 blocked shots, 54 steals, Proviso East HS/Maywood, Ill. & Southwestern CC/Chula Vista, Calif.) Jordan is a returning starter at the small forward position. Last season was his first season in the program and McCarthy is impressed with how quickly Jordan became comfortable with the system and made a major contribution. He started 28 games for the Aggies and was the team's fourth leading scorer and No. 3 rebounder. He finished second behind Randy Brown in steals and led the team in blocked shots. He was the top rebounding small forward in the Big West Conference, other than UNLV's Stacey Augmon, last year.

Jordan possesses tremendous leaping ability. He is an acrobatic scorer around the basket who is aided by extremely long arms. Jordan is the Aggie's most spectacular dunker and a great offensive rebounder. He also can drift out to around 18-feet and make his shot which keeps defenses honest.

He scored a season-high 17 points at UTEP and pulled down a season-high of 10 rebounds against Delaware State.

It is hard to believe that Jordan did not play high school basketball in Proviso East HS in Maywood, Ill. He said he "preferred to just be a teenager."

"When we played together (before regular season practices started), I knew we had something," Jordan told Jack Thompson of the *Chicago Tribune* concerning New Mexico State's fast start last season. "We played together well from the start."

Jordan is one of three returning Aggie starters from the Chicago area. The UTEP Miners, one of New Mexico State's two main rivals, have used Chicago as a key recruiting ground over the last five years and it looks like the Aggies are also beginning to benefit from the abundance of talent in the Windy City.

MICHAEL NEW (6-8, 215 lbs., SR, F, #42, 10.4 ppg, 6.8 rpg, 24 assists, 16 blocked shots, 18 steals, Collins HS/Chicago, Ill. & Howard County JC/Big Spring, Tex.) New was one of three first- year starters for the Aggies last year. All three new starters were from Chicago and they meshed much quicker than expected.

"I had no idea it would be this great," McCarthy told Jack Thompson of the *Chicago Tribune*. "These new kids have taken to our system very well, and we've tried to make it fit their abilities."

New was a teammate of Randy Brown at Chicago's Collins HS. Like Brown, he signed with Houston and played with the Cougars before becoming disenchanted. He spent a year at Howard County JC in Texas, along with Brown, before signing with New Mexico State.

New is a consistent scorer who does not attract a great deal of attention. He scored in double figures 17 times last year and finished fifth on the team scoring. He was second in rebounding and blocked shots. New was 112-of-212 from the field (.524) and 99-of-154 (.643) from the line. He had a season-high 17 points against Texas Southern. His season rebounding high was 15 against Fullerton State.

New completes his plays against strong defensive pressure and always works hard. He's an unsung hero type who is not spectacular but does a lot of little things that enable the Aggies to win.

RON PUTZI (6-6, 195 lbs., SO, F, #23, 1.2 ppg, 0.8 rpg, 7 assists, 1 blocked shot, 5 steals, Richmond Senior HS/Richmond, British Columbia, Canada) Putzi played in 19 games for a total of 114 minutes last year. He redshirted his first year at New Mexico State before seeing action last season as a freshman.

He is considered a great shooter but Putzi made only 9-of-29 field goals (.310) and 3-of-16 three-pointers (.188) in his limited action.

He is a member of the Canadian National team and averaged 36 points per game in high school. Putzi is a decent athlete and he could be a more important player this year as designated bomber Rick Flucky has transferred to Quincy College.

JASON TRASK (6-9, 230 lbs., SR, C, 4.4 ppg, 2.6 rpg, 6 assists, 13 blocked shots, 20 steals, Capistrano Valley HS/Capistrano, Calif.) A former transfer from Weber State, Trask was the third big man in the McCarthy's frontcourt rotation last year. He is very physical and active inside. Trask can run the court as well. He loves the bank shot and rarely scores without it. He had a season-high of 13 points against Delaware State and his top rebounding effort was seven against Texas Tech.

His playing time diminished late in the season as Hickman became McCarthy's first frontcourt reserve. For the season Trask was 57-of-114 (.500) from the field and a poor 19-of-40 (.475) from the line.

With the return of Trask and Chris Hickman plus the addition of junior college transfer James White, New Mexico State has depth and strength in the pivot this year.

★ NEWCOMERS ★

TERRY BENNETT (6-0, 180 lbs., JR, G, #5, 22.7 ppg, 7.0 apg, James Madison HS/Milwaukee, Wisc. & Shasta JC/Redding, Calif.) A first-team All-State selection as a freshman in the California junior college system, Bennett was named the MVP in the Golden Valley Conference in 1988-89. He did not play last year due to an injury and enrolled at New Mexico State for the spring semester.

"Terry is quicker than quick. He is right there with Randy Brown in terms of speed and quickness," McCarthy said.

Bennett is also a three-point threat; he made 45 percent of his throws in 1988-89 and he runs the break very well. Bennett also has a good feel for the game.

He has a chance to be a starter for the Aggies. Even if he comes off the bench, Bennett is going to add significant speed, quickness and perimeter shooting to the New Mexico State attack.

TERRY BUTLER (6-5, 200 lbs., JR, F, #4, 25.2 ppg, 12.2 rpg, Thomas Edison HS/Philadelphia, Pa. & Allen Hancock JC/Santa Maria, Calif.) Butler was a first-team-All-State selection among California's junior college players last year. He was the MVP in the Coast Valley Conference and lead the state of California's junior college's in field goal percentage at .726. He also finished fifth in the state in scoring and was fourth in rebounding. Butler earned All-Tournament honors in four different tournaments and was a team captain of a 26-9 Hancock team. Several scouting services rated Butler as the top junior college player in California and the *Sporting News* put him among the Top 30 JC players in the country.

McCarthy plans on using Butler at power forward along with Michael New. Butler was in the military before entering college. He was not a highly regarded player coming out of Edison HS in Philadelphia so he decided to enter the service. In the service, Butler became stronger and improved his game considerably. He also took the GED test and went to California for junior college. He committed to Hawaii but did not play for the Rainbows and came back to junior college. Butler is a great rebounder who has outstanding hands.

"He was rated by all the scouting services as one of the most outstanding front-line players in California," McCarthy said. "He also played in the service so he is a very mature player."

All of New Mexico State's eight junior college transfers are highly regarded. Butler and the rest of the newcomers will make the Aggies deeper, quicker, improved offensively and stronger on the boards.

DAVID LOFTON (6-6, 200 lbs., JR, F/G, #44, 20.7 ppg, 9.2 rpg, Yavapai JC/Prescott, Ariz.) As a high school player, Lofton was MVP of Arizona's small class of schools. After he graduated from high school he went to Yavapai JC in Prescott where he had an outstanding two-year career. Lofton was outstanding in the USA-Texas All-Star game, where he led the USA team in scoring with 21 points. He was named a junior college All-America pick by *Basketball Times*.

"He's one of our best recruits," McCarthy said. "He is very quick, he is very athletic and he shoots the ball well."

Lofton can play either small forward or second guard. He has three-point range on his shot. With so many outstanding recruits, it is difficult to figure out the New Mexico State depth chart.

CHRIS SMALL (6-1, 180 lbs., JR, G, #24, 22.2 ppg, 6.9 apg, Manual Arts HS/Los Angeles, Calif. & Los Angeles City College/Los Angeles, Calif.) McCarthy had a goal of improving New Mexico State's perimeter shooting through his recruiting. The Aggies made only 31.7 percent of their three-pointers last year but that figure should rise appreciably this year as Small, Terry Bennett and David Lofton can all hit the three.

Small shot 49 percent from the field, 42 percent from three-point range and 82 percent from the line as a sophomore at Los Angeles City College. He was a first-team All-Conference selection and second-team All-State pick. As a senior, Small and Fullerton State guard Wayne Williams helped lead Manual Arts to a 27-3 record and the California state title. He scored 30 points in the city championship game against famed Crenshaw HS.

"He's a very tenacious, aggressive player who has good athletic ability," McCarthy said.

Small also knows the game. The New Mexico State backcourt should be strong this year as Randy Brown was a first-team All- Big West selection last year, William Benjamin improved his offense and was impressive last year and newcomers Terry Bennett and Small are talented in their own right.

TRACEY WARE (6-7, 210 lbs., JR, F, #34, 28.5 ppg, 12.8 rpg, Jack Yates HS/Houston, Tex. & Lee JC/Baytown, Tex.) Ware is the most highly regarded member of New Mexico State's impressive recruiting class. He was a third-team Junior College All-America pick. Ware was also a first-team All-Conference selection, first-team All-Region and team MVP at Lee JC. The Houston native has excellent offensive instincts. He also proved himself in one of the toughest new college conferences in the nation.

McCarthy said Ware is "maybe our most athletic big man. He is very springy and has good speed and quickness and is very strong."

Both starting forwards are returning for the Aggies and with Ware, David Lofton and Terry Butler joining the team this year, New Mexico State truly has a big time complement of forwards.

PHILLIP WASHINGTON (6-7, 210 lbs., JR, F, #54, 11.0 ppg, 12.0 rpg, 2.5 apg, 1.0 stpg, Maryvale HS/Phoenix Ariz. & Yavapai JC/Prescott, Ariz.) Washington was a teammate of fellow Aggie newcomer David Lofton at Yavapai JC last year. A scholarship was opened up for Washington when another junior college transfer, 6-7 David Smith, did not qualify academically.

Washington was an All-State honorable mention selection in both basketball and football at Maryvale HS in Phoenix, Ariz. He lead the Arizona junior colleges in rebounding last year. Washington is, like the other junior college transfers, an excellent athlete who can get up and down the floor and leaps well. In informal practices after the beginning of school, Washington looked impressive. In fact, the New Mexico State coaches have said that he is looking much better than they expected after scouting him in junior college.

With the addition of Washington and the other junior college transfers, New Mexico State has more quality athletes than any team in the Big West Conference other than UNLV.

JAMES WHITE (6-9, 220 lbs., JR, C, #10, 12.0 ppg, 10.0 rpg, 4.0 blpg, John Marshall HS/Chicago, Ill. & Westark JC/Fort Smith, Ark.) White is the fourth Aggie from the Chicago area. He is also the probable replacement for James Anderson in the pivot. Last season White helped Westark JC to a 26-8 record and the Arkansas junior college championship.

"He's a tremendous 6-9 athlete that can run, jump and block shots," McCarthy said of White. "He's more of a defensive player than an offensive player, but he's the type of player that can turn the game around with his defensive ability and athletic ability."

"Running center from Chicago should keep this school a winner," wrote junior college expert Rick Ball in *Basketball Times*.

★ QUESTIONS ★

Blending in a large and talented group of newcomers? New Mexico State has eight junior college transfers. How quickly McCarthy can blend them in with the returnees will be the key to New Mexico State's season. However, keep in mind he was successful blending in three new starters last year and is used to dealing with large personnel turnover.

Replacing James Anderson in the Pivot?

★ STRENGTHS ★

Neil McCarthy! He has revitalized the New Mexico State program and has more talent and athletic ability to work with since he came to Las Cruces from Weber State.

Overall team athletic ability! McCarthy believes this is the most athletic group of newcomers he has had at New Mexico State.

The presence of Randy Brown! Brown is one of the premier guards in the country and is especially strong on the defensive end.

Defense! New Mexico State finished in the Top 10 nationally in field goal percentage defense last year and should be strong at that end again.

Senior Leadership!

Competitiveness! "You can't underestimate competitiveness," McCarthy said. This is a team loaded with competitors who come from winning programs.

★ BLUE RIBBON ANALYSIS ★

The 1989-90 season was a memorable one at New Mexico State. In just his fifth year at New Mexico State, coach Neil McCarthy guided the Aggies to their most successful season since the 1970 team reached the Final Four. The Aggies won 25 games, tied UNLV for the co-championship in the Big West Conference and for the first time in 11 years reached the NCAA tournament. Two key starters are gone, but that is not too many for McCarthy to replace as this program generally has to start over again every two years because it relies so heavily on junior college transfers.

Senior guard Randy Brown was outstanding last year. He was one of the final 20 players competing for a spot on the U.S. National team over the summer before being cut. Brown is one of the better defensive guards in the country and is a great leader. Starting forwards Reggie Jordan and Michael New played well in their first years in the program. Jordan is a spectacular leaper and New is a quietly consistent player.

The Aggies should remain strong and close to the top in the Big West because of the addition of eight junior college transfers who form an impressive recruiting class.

"I would say athletically this is the best recruiting class since I've been here-on paper," McCarthy said. "The junior college transfers are not only quality athletes and players but they are competitors and from well coached, winning programs . . . I think the kids we took, we took because we thought they had better character than the others. I think the first step in developing chemistry is getting good people. We think we've (recruited) smart players that will recognize the 'We' concept."

McCarthy believes the Aggies will be faster and quicker than last year and a better shooting and rebounding club. JC transfer forward Tracey Ware was a third-team All-America pick and the rest of the junior college transfers were all highly regarded players.

If JC transfer James White comes through in the pivot and holdovers Jason Trask and Chris Hickman provide capable backup help, New Mexico State should be solid in the pivot. If the newcomers blend quickly with the returnees, something McCarthy is used to doing, New Mexico State could be even better this year.

The Aggies are one of three Big West Conference teams, other than defending national champion UNLV, who are Top 40 teams in *Blue Ribbon*. The Aggies should be strong again in the Big West, finish of this rapidly improving conference, and win more than 20 games. We sincerely hope the NCAA tournament selection committee realizes how tough the Big West is getting and takes California-Santa Barbara, Long Beach State and New Mexico State to the tournament this year.

Eastern New Mexico	85-65	Long Beach State	104-91
@UTEP	72-75	California-Irvine	79-75
New Mexico	60-55	California-Santa Barbara	66-64
Delaware State	104-90	@UNLV	86-109
@New Mexico	74-73	@Fullerton State	65-62
UTEP	62-49	Utah State	103-84
@Texas Tech	74-68	San Jose State	101-70
Sam Houston State	84-66	@Pacific	68-55
Texas Southern	97-76	@Fresno State	82-68
Fresno State	71-69	#Fresno State	72-66
Pacific	81-60	#Long Beach State	85-90
UNLV	83-82	##Loyola Marymount	92-111
@California-Santa Barbara	74-61		
@California-Irvine	88-75	@ Road Games	
@Long Beach State	56-72	# Big West Tournament, Long Beach, CA	
Fullerton State	75-58		
@San Jose State	80-76	## NCAA Tournament, Long Beach, CA	
@Utah State	81-73		

NOTES: Three New Mexico State games will be televised on ESPN: Long Beach State on Jan. 7, at California-Santa Barbara on Feb. 11 and a home game with UNLV on Feb. 25 . . . McCarthy credits assistant coach Gar Forman for improving the Aggies' level of talent. "The last two years with him in charge of my recruiting, our talent level has improved drastically,"

Nov.	23	New Mexico Highlands	Feb.	2	@Long Beach State
	26	Cal State-Northridge		9	@California-Irvine
	29	UTEP		11	@California-Santa Barbara
Dec.	1	Coppin State		14	Fullerton State
	4	@UTEP		16	@UNLV
	8	@New Mexico		21	@Utah State
	15	New Mexico		23	@San Jose State
	22	Texas Tech		25	UNLV
	29	Morgan State (MD)		28	Pacific
Jan.	2	@Fresno State	Mar.	2	Fresno State
	4	@Pacific		8-10	@Big West Tournament
	7	Long Beach State			
	12	California-Santa Barbara			
	14	California-Irvine	@ Road Games		
	19	@Fullerton State	# Long Beach, CA		
	24	San Jose State			
	26	Utah State			

McCarthy said of Forman's efforts. "He's a tireless worker and is very productive." . . . The metropolitan area population of Las Cruces has a population of nearly 100,000. Las Cruces is located 50 miles north of El Paso, Tex.

NOTRE DAME

LAST SEASON: 16-13
STARTERS LOST: 2
STARTERS RETURNING: 3
CONFERENCE: INDEPENDENT
LOCATION: NOTRE DAME, IN
HOME FLOOR: JOYCE ATHLETIC AND CONVOCATION CENTER (11,418)
NICKNAME: FIGHTING IRISH
COLORS: BLUE AND GOLD

★ COACH'S PROFILE ★

RICHARD "DIGGER" PHELPS (Record at Notre Dame, 381-177. Career Record, 407-180). It's hard to believe that Phelps is beginning his 20th year at Notre Dame. It seems like just yesterday he was regenerating the Notre Dame program in the early '70s. He was one of the glamor coaches of college basketball throughout the '70s, but Digger and his program have lost some luster over the past decade as the balance of power in college basketball has shifted towards teams in the super conferences like the Big East, ACC and Big Ten and the independents have shrunk dramatically not only in numbers, but status.

In fact, "Digger Bashing" has become fashionable, not only in South Bend, but across the country among Notre Dame's famed Subway Alumni. His detractors sight the below average NCAA tournament showing by the Fighting Irish (only five wins in Notre Dame's last 13 NCAA tournament games) and the recent surge to national dominance by Lou Holtz's football team has not helped Digger's popularity.

In spite of the outcry from his detractors, Digger continues to weather the storm and run a squeaky clean program. The Fighting Irish continue to qualify for the NCAA tournament, pull of a big upset or two every year, and most importantly, all the players graduate.

Indiana coach Bob Knight challenged the critics: "They can talk all they want about winning the NCAA tournament, but it doesn't happen to a helluva lot of people. It's no criteria to judge a coach on and may be the most invalid. Its the only thing Digger hasn't done. He has consistently good teams, they go to the tournament, they beat so many great teams. I don't think there is anybody that gets kids more ready to play or gets them to play harder than Digger. That's why they win so many big games and they have so many big upsets."

In the 19 years Phelps has been at Notre Dame, the Fighting Irish have recorded upsets of eight No. 1 ranked teams including last season's, 98-67 thrashing of top rated Missouri. The most famous upset occurred on January 19, 1974 in South Bend. The upstart Fighting Irish under their third-year coach upended mighty UCLA 71-70, and ended the Bruins' all-time record 88-game winning streak. That game put Notre Dame solidly in the basketball spotlight.

Phelps is a native of Beacon, N.Y. It was in this small town, an hour drive from New York City, that Phelps received his famous nickname of Digger.

"I got the nickname - Digger - because my father was an undertaker and I worked for him part time," Phelps said. "There were advantages to the job. For instance, when I was dating my wife I sent her flowers every day and she could never quite understand that."

He competed in football, basketball and track at Beacon HS. Phelps attended Rider College in Trenton, N.Y. and played basketball in college. As a senior, he helped lead Rider to the 1963 NAIA national tournament, held each year in Kansas City, Mo. Phelps remained as a graduate assistant at Rider. The Broncos gained national recognition for their stunning 1964 upset of New York University, which ended the Violets' home winning streak which dated back to 1941. Phelps credits that experience more than any as his inspiration to enter the coaching ranks.

"I was a graduate assistant at Rider and I scouted New York University and helped put together the game plan that ended their 23-year homecourt winning streak. It was the first time they had lost on their own campus since 1941. I knew then that I could do it because that's when I got into strategy and how to stop people, how to come up with a game plan."

His first head coaching position came in 1965 at St. Gabriel's HS in Hazleton, Pa. Phelps took St. Gabriel's to a Pennsylvania state title. It was there that he began to lay the foundation of his coaching style. Father Ray Deviney, the former athletic director at St. Gabriel's remembers Phelps well. "He (Phelps) opened his mouth and after he closed it several minutes later after talking about full court pressure, a team that will play hard from one end of the court to another and a code of conduct, I'd hired him. He had a magnetic personality. His players idolized him. In fact, he had a tremendous impact on the whole area. His full court game was revolutionary. He won over the people with his personality and by the way his players conducted themselves on and off the court. Digger made sure they studied and they set the standard for the rest of the student body."

It was also in 1965 that this young coach sent a now-famous letter to Notre Dame head football coach Ara Parseghian. "Eventually, I'd like to coach on the college level," Phelps wrote. "My big dream is to coach at Notre Dame. I love the essence of Notre Dame . . . some day I hope to be a part of that program."

From St. Gabriel's, Phelps moved on to Pennsylvania where he assisted Dick Harter and coached the Quaker freshman team. During his four years as the head coach of the Pennsylvania freshmen, Phelps' squads put together a 65-20 record, including one undefeated 21-0 team. The eastern basketball coaching circle was tight at that time and Phelps was able to move from his assistant coaching position at Pennsylvania to Fordham where he was the head coach of a struggling program. Phelps inherited a 10-15 team and immediately took the Rams to an amazing 26-3 record and a third-place finish in the NCAA East Regional. Notre Dame officials got their first look at this up-and-coming coach when Phelps led his Rams to a 94-88 win over the Johnny Dee-coached Fighting Irish at Madison Square Garden.

The Metropolitan Basketball Writers Association of New York voted Phelps as their coach of the year and he finished fourth nationally in the *UPI* voting. As the luck of the Irish would have it, Johnny Dee retired following the 1970-71 season and Richard "Digger" Phelps became the 14th head basketball coach in Notre Dame history after serving only one year as a head coach on the collegiate level. Tom Sullivan, the center on Phelps' only Fordham team, said, ". . . it was like Digger took a mediocre team, waved a magic wand and turned a local by-line into a national story. I remember the press conference he had when he said he was leaving. Some of the players cried. The way I looked at it, he did a great thing for Fordham and then a great opportunity came up for him and his family. Not any school could have taken him away, he always had a special feeling for Notre Dame.''

Phelps got the Notre Dame job he had dreamed of for years at the young age of 29. With only one returning letterman on his first team, The Fighting Irish finished the season with a disappointing 6-20 mark. His second squad improved to 18-12 and finished second in the NIT. In 1973-74, Phelps led the Fighting Irish to an outstanding 26-3 record and a third-place finish in the Mideast Regional. That season, Notre Dame notched wins over mighty UCLA, Indiana and South Carolina, which was a national power at that time. Phelps was selected as coach of the year by the Metropolitan Basketball Writers of New York, *UPI, The Sporting News* and *Basketball Weekly*. Over the next seven years, Notre Dame averaged 22 wins per season and the Fighting Irish had a Final Four appearance in 1977-78.

The Fighting Irish suffered through a losing season in 1982-83; since then Notre Dame has averaged 21 wins a campaign and has appeared in six straight NCAA tournaments.

His record at Notre Dame has been excellent. Phelps' 381 victories and 100 percent graduation rate speak volumes for this fine program. However, the vast majority of his 17 NCAA tournament victories came in the '70s and last year's disappointing 16-13 campaign has fueled the fires of his critics.

''Of course I get upset when we lose, or in recruiting when I can't convince a kid this place is best for him,'' Phelps said. ''Obviously I want to win the national championship. But I'm not going to make it such a priority in my life that if I don't get it I can't walk away without looking over my shoulder.''

Phelps is one of the most widely quoted coaches in college basketball. He is critical of the rampant commercialism in the sport and of the academic problems which have become so widely documented in the last decade.

''I believe in this place (Notre Dame). We recruit the student-athlete, and I believe you can do both. I never promise anything to an athlete's parents except their son will graduate. I'd emphasize that no matter where I was coaching,'' Phelps said. ''We're coaches, but we can't lose sight that we're supposed to be helping to educate these young people. I hate to say it, but basketball is still a game. After it's over, its time to get back to the real world. No matter whether you win or lose, the sun is going to come up the next day. There is always tomorrow.''

He also has been vocal about the need to develop a cohesive team, put together for a long period of time to compete for the United States in the next Olympics in 1992 in Barcelona, Spain. Phelps has stated that he would like to see a team picked years in advance. Under his plan, the team would stay together for several years before actually competing in the games. He is opposed to the present selection process which produces all-star teams and Phelps does not believe that NBA players should be involved.

Critics have suggested that Phelps is still coaching a game geared for the '60s or '70s instead of one that will play well in the '90s. He does not emphasize the three-point field goal and last year Notre Dame attempted 199 treys for an average of just over six per game. He also has so many plays for various situations that critics believe Phelps' system is too complicated and not free flowing. Defensively, Notre Dame is usually not strong, either.

This may be the most crucial year in Phelps' career at Notre Dame. Many Irish insiders believe he may leave at the end of the season for a career in broadcasting or another endeavor.

★ PLAYERS NOT RETURNING ★

TIM CRAWFORD (6-4, G, 2.4 ppg, 0.2 rpg, 4 steals) Crawford was a walk-on player who saw little action last season (only 10 games for a total of 19 minutes) and is not a key loss.

JOE FREDERICK (6-4, G, 13.0 ppg, 1.6 rpg, 58 assists, 11 steals) Frederick was a solid player in the Notre Dame program over the past three years and his outside scoring will be missed. Frederick, the team co-captain last season, scored over 1,000 points in his Notre Dame career. Although he had a reduced role last year, Frederick still managed to average in double figures in scoring and was a key contributor in Fighting Irish wins over Kentucky, Marquette and Rutgers. He came through with a season-high of 23 points in Notre Dame's 80-67 victory over Kentucky.

Phelps considered Frederick to be his coach on the floor. He was a proven clutch performer who possessed tremendous heart, desire and competitiveness. Notre Dame is not a great three-point shooting club and Frederick led the Fighting Irish in treys with 34. For the season he made 135-of-259 field goals (.521).

His intangibles and perimeter shooting will definitely be missed.

JAMERE JACKSON (6-2, G, 4.4 ppg, 1.2 rpg, 25 assists, 10 steals) Although Jamere Jackson played in all 29 games for Notre Dame last season, his role diminished as the year progressed. He started five games last year, but the majority of those were in the first half of the season. Jackson was one of Notre Dame's most versatile players, but his shooting was not as good as guards Joe Frederick or Elmer Bennett and he was not as quick as point guard Tim Singleton. With the emergence of freshman forward Monty Williams, there was simply no place for Jackson to play. He was often relegated to defensive pressing situations or mopup action. Jackson's season-high came at Southern California when he recorded 15 points in a 86-81 triumph. The high point of his season came when he hit game-winning free throws to beat UCLA last December. However, over the last 15 games

of the season, Jackson only scored 15 points.

Like Frederick, Jackson's leadership will be missed. He was a co-captain of last year's Notre Dame team.

SCOTT PADDOCK (6-9, C, 2.2 ppg, 2.7 rpg, 9 assists, 1 blocked shot, 3 steals) Paddock was a role player and provided depth in the frontcourt. He started four games last year and saw action in a total of 25. He had 13 points and 12 rebounds in an 88-78 win over Wichita State. That was his season-high. He also had 11 points in Notre Dame's 98-67 rout of then No. 1 ranked Missouri on national television.

His strength was rebounding, but with Keith Robinson and LaPhonso Ellis in front of him, Paddock averaged only nine minutes per contest. He adapted well to his role, provided leadership and banged inside. He also will be remembered as one of the worst free throw shooters in Notre Dame history. For his career, Paddock was 49-of-103 from the charity stripe for 48 percent, average.

KEITH ROBINSON (6-9, F, 14.7 ppg, 7.9 rpg, 21 assists, 7 blocked shots, 21 steals) Robinson was an important player for Notre Dame over the last three years and his inside presence will be missed. He was one of only eight Notre Dame players to score over 1,000 points and grab 700 rebounds during a career. He developed into a strong post player and his rebounding ability was an asset that will need to be replaced.

Robinson hit for a career-high 26 points in a win over San Francisco and also during a loss at Dayton. He scored in double figures 25 times last season and recorded 10 double-doubles in scoring and rebounding. He garnered a season-high of 14 rebounds three times (twice against DePaul and once vs. Georgia Tech). All three games were Notre Dame losses.

Although Robinson was a key player, he sometimes hindered the Notre Dame offense when he left the middle to look for his outside jumper. Notre Dame was and is an extremely quick team suited for an up-tempo, fast break offense. When Robinson, Joe Frederick and Scott Paddock were on the court, Notre Dame was reduced to a half court team unable to take advantage of its ultimate strength.

There is no doubt that Keith Robinson will be missed. His points and rebounds will be hard to replace, but with LaPhonso Ellis available for the entire season, the Fighting Irish should have a quicker, more potent lineup that should compensate for Robinson's departure.

★ RETURNING PLAYERS ★

ELMER BENNETT (6-1, 165 lbs., JR, G, –12, 10.9 ppg, 1.6 rpg, 106 assists, 1 blocked shot, 22 steals, Bellaire HS/Houston, Tex.) Elmer Bennett is a lightning-quick guard who will be a starter for the Fighting Irish this season. He is half of the ''Texas Express'' along with Beaumont, Tex., native Daimon Sweet. Bennett played in all 29 games last season and started 17. The majority of his starts came in the second half of the season as Notre Dame made its run towards the NCAA tournament. It was Bennett who nailed a last second shot to upset Syracuse at the Carrier Dome in a game many felt secured a post-season bid for the Fighting Irish. Bennett was the high scorer for Notre Dame four times last season and hit for double figures 18 times. He led the Fighting Irish with 17 points in their first round loss to Virginia in the NCAA tournament.

For the year, Bennett was 112-233 (.481) from the field and 9-of-25 (.360) from three-point range. From the line he was 84-of-114 (.737). With the graduation of Joe Frederick, Bennett enters the season as Notre Dame's top three-point shooter.

He possesses outstanding quickness and is solid defensively. Bennett also has an above average mid-range jump shot and could be a solid scorer. He is an improved playmaker who drives well, has a good work ethic and is most effective in an up and down game.

He can play either backcourt spot and should be a starter all season long. Phelps will need more scoring and solid leadership form Bennett this year. With less depth in the frontcourt, more scoring and leadership will be needed from the Fighting Irish guards in order to relieve pressure on LaPhonso Ellis inside. Bennett showed improvement by cutting down his mistakes and turnovers last season and his continued development will be needed if the Fighting Irish are to improve on last year's 16 wins.

KEVIN ELLERY (6-5, 225 lbs., SR, F, #35, 4.4 ppg, 2.3 rpg, 19 assists, 2 steals, Washington County HS/Springfield, Ky.) If Phelps goes with a big lineup and opts for a halfcourt offense, look for Kevin Ellery to get the call at one forward position. He is a tough competitor who gives the Fighting Irish a rare combination of inside power and outside touch. Ellery will attempt to rebound from a disappointing season in which he saw action in 25 of 29 games for an average of 14 minutes per game.

He was 37-of-77 from the field (.481) and 7-of-16 (.438) from three-point range.

As a sophomore, Ellery played in only eight games before having to sit out the remainder of the season due to academic difficulties. His playing time increased last year but Ellery was inconsistent and often ineffective. He exploded for 17 points and 12 rebounds in a mid-season blowout of Miami (Fla.) and also contributed 11 points against Missouri and 10 in a season-ending loss against Virginia. However, there were also five other games he participated in and didn't register a point or an assist.

Phelps will be looking for increased production and consistency from the only senior on the Notre Dame front line. Ellery is nicknamed ''Pit Bull'' for his tenacity inside against bigger players. That trait may give him some more playing time due to the relative lack of depth up front. Also, the ability to occasionally stick the three-pointer won't hurt Ellery's chances for increased playing time.

LaPHONSO ELLIS (6-9, 238 lbs., JR, F/C, #20, 14.0 ppg, 12.6 rpg, 33 assists, 37 blocked shots, 27 steals, Lincoln HS/St. Louis, Ill.) To put it simply, if Notre Dame is to increase last year's total of 16 victories and crack the Top 20, Ellis must be a franchise player virtually every game. When Notre Dame lost him for the first seven games of last season due to academic difficulties, the Fighting Irish lost three of their first four games. In losses to Louisville and Indiana, Notre Dame had almost no inside presence whatsoever. Ellis is an intimidating force and the Fighting Irish need him academically eligible and out of foul trouble in order to be successful.

He came to Notre Dame regarded as one of the Top 10 high school players in the country in the class of '88. That class also included Alonzo Mourning (Georgetown), Billy Owens (Syracuse) and Shawn Kemp, Chris Jackson and Stanley Roberts who have all left college for the professional ranks. The class of '88 was considered one of the best ever and Ellis was a key member. He is one of the most highly talented players to ever sign with the Fighting Irish. However, Ellis has not been consistent.

He is a good rebounder and led the Fighting Irish by a wide margin in rebounding last year. Even though he missed seven games, Ellis not only had a higher rebounding percentage than the Fighting Irish's second leading rebounder, Keith Robinson, but also pulled down more boards. While he's been tough on the boards, Ellis has not been a strong power player on offense. By this time he should have developed into the go-to player the Fighting Irish rely on when things get tough. However, he's often disappeared for long stretches and just doesn't like to muscle up a power shot. Ellis would rather try to be a finesse player. Offensively, he fancies himself as a small forward in a big man's body.

Ellis was third in the nation in rebounding percentage last year and he recorded 15 double-doubles (double figure in two statistical categories) in scoring and rebounding. Ellis also became Notre Dame's all-time leading shot blocker, as his 37 blocks brought his career total to 90. For the year he was 114-of-223 (.511) from the field and 79-of-111 (.675) from the line.

Ellis needs to keep in mind this Phelps quote: "LaPhonso is definitely the kind of player who can get you to the Final Four," Phelps said. "As he develops and gains game experience, learning the finesse of the game and learning the concepts of the game, he'll be the best we've ever had on the front line.

"We've never had one this good. Probably, (John) Shumate was close as far as being an impact player."

Ellis is extremely quick and unbelievably coordinated for a player his size. He is an opposing figure who has never been in great condition and hasn't worked hard enough in the off-season. When Ellis is on his game he can play with great enthusiasm and that is something the Fighting Irish need more of.

This is Ellis's team and his personality, intelligence and vast ability should allow him to lead the Fighting Irish to significant improvement on last year's disappointing 16-13 season. Now that he will be eligible for the entire year, Ellis may start living up to his vast potential. If he does, watch out for the Fighting Irish.

TIM SINGLETON (6-1, 180 lbs., SR, G, #10, 4.2 ppg, 1.4 rpg, 134 assists, 2 blocked shots, 28 steals, Carver HS/New Orleans, La.) Singleton started 14 games and averaged 21 minutes per game last year as a junior. He was 35-of-61 (.574) from the floor, did not attempt a three-point field goal, and 48-of-74 three-pointers (.649).

Singleton's role decreased last season. As a sophomore he started all but one game and played 30 minutes or more in 15 games. He attempted 44 fewer field goals last year. His assists dropped from 208 as a sophomore to 134 last season.

He is extremely quick, has good strength and is a excellent floor general with outstanding passing skills and floor sense. Phelphs said, "Timmy has been the sparkplug of this team. When we need to get something generated, he is the one we look to. His penetration ability creates things for us."

Singleton has led the Fighting Irish in assists the past two years and enters his final season with 380 career assists, good for fifth place on the all-time Notre Dame assist chart. He also is fifth on the Fighting Irish steals list with 95 career thefts. He had a season high of 12 points in a loss at Duke last February.

"I'm the quarterback. I've got to take charge and be a leader," Singleton said. "It's tough, because I have to get everything started. Everybody looks to you to straighten it out."

If Phelps would let the Fighting Irish go, it would be to Singleton's advantage. He excels in a transition game. Singleton is the elder statesman of this Notre Dame team. He is one of two seniors along with Keven Ellery. If Singleton has a strong year defensively and running the team plus chips in some offense when needed, Notre Dame should be in good shape as juniors Elmer Bennett and Daimon Sweet could blossom offensively. Singleton will either be the first guard off the bench, if Phelps decides to go with Bennett and Sweet, or a starter.

Singleton graduated with a 3.2 average at Carver HS in New Orleans, however, he quickly found out that there was a great deal of difference between high school and college not only on the court but in the classroom.

"I came from a program that was totally different from Notre Dame," Singleton told Fred Robinson of the New Orleans *Times-Picayune*. "Believe me, I had to do some serious adjusting. . .

"It was definitely academics that made adjusting the toughest part of college life. I had to learn to manage my time better.

"I was in the top 10 of my high school class, but when I got here it seemed like everybody had been in the top of their classes, too. It was very competitive," Singleton said.

"There were some times when I was really depressed, but I had some good friends and some upperclassmen to keep me going. It's all helped me be stronger, in life, period. Notre Dame has given me a better perspective on a lot of things.

"Coach (Digger Phelps) is always telling us we've got to make things happen on our own, that you can't sit back and be lazy and expect things to come to you," Singleton said.

DAIMON SWEET (6-5, 200 lbs., JR, G/F, #22, 6.6 ppg, 2.1 rpg, 27 assists, 3 blocked shots, 14 steals, Central HS/Beaumont, Tex.) Sweet is half of Notre Dame's "Texas Express" the other half being Houston native Elmer Bennett, and he has more explosive athletic ability than anyone on the team. Last season Sweet played in 27 games, starting five, and averaged 15 minutes per game. He was 81-of-135 from the field (.600) did not attempt a three-pointer and made 16-of-25 field goals (.640). He hit for double figures in scoring eight times and tied a career-high of 16 points in an early season loss to Indiana.

Sweet truly has NBA level explosiveness as a runner and jumper. His favorite play is the back door alley-oop dunk from his runningmate, Bennett, and Sweet is most effective in the open court. He is an inconsistent perimeter shooter and makes bad decisions in the half court setting.

Sweet should be a valuable player for Notre Dame as either a big guard or a small forward this year. If the Fighting Irish attack is opened up, his quickness and explosive scoring capability in the open court should be important.

A good year with solid double figure scoring from Sweet would definitely make Notre Dame a much improved team.

KEITH TOWER (6-11, 235 lbs., JR, C, #5, 2.1 ppg, 2.7 rpg, 5 assists, 5 blocked shots, 5 steals, Moon Area HS/Pittsburgh Pa.) Tower is the tallest Notre Dame player and will be counted on for a bigger contribution now that Keith Robinson and Scott Paddock have graduated. Tower played in 25 games, starting six, last year for an average of 11 minutes per game. He was 19-of-61 from the field (.311) and 15-of-25 from the line (.600).

Tower played well at the end of his freshman year but tailed off last season and seemed to lose confidence. His shooting percentage dropped dramatically and some Notre Dame insiders thought Tower was way too tight. His season high scoring was six points in a win over Boston College and a loss to La Salle. In an early season win over UCLA, Tower pulled down eight rebounds.

He is strong, intense and looks great in practice. However, Tower has just not been able to get it done in actual games. If he comes through, Phelps would be able to use Ellis at forward and have more flexibility at his disposal.

Either as a starter or reserve, Tower has to play a bigger role this year. There are the 6-9 (Jon) and 6-10 (Joe) Ross twins in the freshman class but they are not ready to be big factors game after game. Tower is going to have to contribute more than ever in his career if Notre Dame is to be successful.

MONTY WILLIAMS (6-7, 205 lbs., SO, F, #32, 7.7 ppg, 3.7 rpg, 31 assists, 16 blocked shots, 15 steals, Potomac HS/Forest Heights, Md.) Monty Williams was a pleasant surprise as a freshman in an otherwise disappointing season at Notre Dame. He saw action in all 29 games as a freshman and started 18. He is a versatile player who is most comfortable with the small forward position, but he can play a number of positions if needed. Williams has excellent leaping ability, runs the floor and is perfectly suited for an up-tempo, style of offense that Phelps should employ this season.

He had a season-high 20 points in a Notre Dame win over Valparaiso (Ind.) and also chipped in 16 in a win over UCLA. In all, Williams hit in double figures ten times and was third on the team in rebounding.

Williams should have a great future at Notre Dame. He is the only sophomore on the team and is the incumbent at the small forward slot. He is a solid outside shooter and his ball handling skills are above average. His perimeter game is well developed. Williams needs to get tougher and more physical, especially on defense, in order to come closer to reaching his potential.

If everything comes together, Notre Dame should have a quality frontcourt. LaPhonso Ellis could be an All-American player, Keith Tower has everything needed to be a competent center, senior Kevin Ellery should be able to generate some offense off the bench and Williams and Daimon Sweet are big time athletes with versatility at small forward.

★ NEWCOMERS ★

BROOKS BOYER (6-3, 185 lbs., FR, G, #15, 21.9 ppg, 7.0 rpg, Lumen Christi HS/Jackson Mich.) Boyer was an All-State quarterback in football who decided to concentrate on basketball in college. He is a combination guard and signed late last spring with the Fighting Irish. Boyer can serve as a floor general type at point guard or shot from the perimeter. He also can penetrate and is an excellent leaper who rebounded well in high school.

He is strong physically and should add depth to the Notre Dame backcourt.

CARL COZEN (6-6, 220 lbs., FR, F, #50, 19.3 ppg, 9.2 rpg, Marist HS/Chicago, Ill.) Cozen is expected to contribute more than any member of Notre Dame's four-man freshman class. He is mainly a power forward but can play some small forward as he had three-point range in high school. Cozen is an excellent rebounder with good low post moves offensively. Many scouts said that if he was just two inches taller, Cozen would be a great player because he has everything a power forward needs but a few inches of height.

131

Look for Cozen to play immediately as a backup power forward.

JOE ROSS (6-10, 215 lbs., FR, F, #53, 14.6 ppg, 10.0 rpg, Northfield HS/Wabash, Ind.) The Ross twins signed with Notre Dame last November. Joe was originally considered to be a lesser prospect than his twin brother Jon. However, since the Ross twins signed Joe has improved more than Jon and they now are comparable.

JON ROSS (6-9, 210 lbs., FR, F, #54, 18.9 ppg, 9.7 rpg, Northfield HS/Wabash, Ind.) This is the tenth edition of *Blue Ribbon College Basketball Yearbook* and we can't remember another set of twins signed by a program of Notre Dame's caliber. The Ross's committed early last fall to Notre Dame and signed in November.

Jon has a better outside shot than his brother Joe and is also more effective in the open court. Originally he was ranked higher but Joe closed the gap last season. Bob Gibbons of *All Star Sports* likens Jon Ross to former Notre Dame player Dave Batton.

"Jon is an excellent outside shooter and he can even play some out in the wing with his touch. He's a pretty good ball-handler," Gibbons told *Blue & Gold Illustrated*. "But I think he'll be kept strictly at power forward because he would have trouble defending quicker people at the wing spot."

Hoop Scoop ranked Joe as the No. 10 senior in Indiana last year and Jon as the state's No. 16 senior.

"In Joe and Jon they'll have two highly-skilled players who are hard workers - no program can oversell that attribute," Gibbons remarked to *Blue & Gold Illustrated*.

★ QUESTIONS ★

Will Digger give up some control and let the Fighting Irish go up and down the court?

Consistency? After coming off a good season in 1988-89 (21- 9), Notre Dame slumped to a 16-12 year even though there were no key personnel losses. The Fighting Irish were the epitome of inconsistency last year.

Frontcourt depth? LaPhonso Ellis is the only proven big time power player Notre Dame has. Keith Tower works hard but has been extremely inconsistent and Kevin Ellery has also had his ups and downs. The other three true inside players are freshmen.

Defense? It remains to be seen if Notre Dame can get after teams consistently and cause havoc on the defensive end of the court.

★ STRENGTHS ★

LaPhonso Ellis! Although Ellis has not lived up to his vast acclaim in his first two years at Notre Dame, this could be the year he explodes on the national scene. He definitely has the talent to rank among the elite players in the country if he produces. Without him Notre Dame would definitely be an also- ran.

A good sized front line which should rebound well!

Versatility! Notre Dame is stocked with quick perimeter players who can run, shoot and handle the ball. If Phelps opens up the attack, Notre Dame can play with virtually any up-tempo team in the country.

★ BLUE RIBBON ANALYSIS ★

This should be a very interesting year at Notre Dame, to say the least. To begin with, some Notre Dame insiders believe that coach Digger Phelps, who is entering his 20th season, could be in his last year. Phelps has been under some heat from Notre Dame's vast Subway Alumni and may be headed for a network announcers job. Look for the Phelps' Watch to go on all year.

Secondly, Notre Dame is coming off a lackluster 16-12 record. The Fighting Irish definitely underachieved last year. However, even though key players Joe Frederick, Keith Robinson and Jamere Jackson are gone, the Fighting Irish are capable of being a much improved team.

The season will come down to how badly LaPhonso Ellis wants to become a great player. If he puts in the strong off-season and gets himself ready, he can become a dominant force on the national level. Ellis has more potential than any inside player at Notre Dame since John Shumate ruled the lane for the Fighting Irish in the early '70s. Remember that even though Ellis was a disappointment last year he still averaged 12.6 rebounds per game.

If Phelps goes with a true up-tempo offense, as the Fighting Irish's talent mandates, sophomore Monty Williams will get the call at small forward. He showed flashes of brilliance last year and just needs to get physically tougher, especially on defense. Guards Tim Singleton, Elmer Bennett, and Daimon Sweet, who will also play small forward are tailor-made for an up and down style of play. Senior forward Kevin Ellery is an aggressive rebounder who should also be an outside threat he will also see considerable playing time.

Another key to Notre Dame's season is the play of senior center Keith Tower. Tower is strong and has looked great in practice but has been erratic in actual games.

The freshman class is expected to provide reserve support as the upperclassmen are going to dominate the playing time.

This is a swift and quick Notre Dame team, in fact, it may be the swiftest group ever in South Bend. "It's like comparing the Edsel with the Corvette," Phelps said. "When you've got the thoroughbreds you let 'em go after it. That's what we've got." Don't be surprised to see an all-out full court game from the Fighting Irish this year. A full court defense and fast break offense should be the game plan no matter the opponent. Instead of slowing the game down, as so many of Phelps' undermanned teams have done in recent years, Notre Dame could run and pressure its opponents into submission. If the Fighting Irish don't dictate the tempo this season something is wrong.

Every coach and program has a down year occasionally and last year certainly was that type of season at Notre Dame. Phelps and his players should be eager to atone for the 16-12 season. If Ellis is ready and Tower can play substantial minutes, this should be an exciting year for the Golden Domers. Notre Dame is capable of winning well over 20 games and making things happen on the national scene.

LAST SEASON

San Francisco	84-64	DePaul	62-63
#Louisville	73-84	Georgia Tech	80-88OT
@Indiana	72-81	@Dayton	79-97
@Marquette	68-80	Missouri	98-67
UCLA	86-84	Kentucky	80-67
Valparaiso (IN)	97-70	@DePaul	59-64
Lafayette	86-71	###Virginia	67-75
Butler	97-65		
@Creighton	75-77OT	@ Road Games	
@Southern California	86-81	# Big Four Classic, Indianapolis, IN	
@Boston College	80-67	## New Orleans, LA	
@LaSalle	78-86	### NCAA Tournament, Richmond, VA	
@Rutgers	74-69		
##LSU	64-87		
Wichita State	88-78		
Miami (FL)	107-60		
Dayton	97-79		
@Duke	76-88		
Southern Methodists	63-49		
@Houston	82-93		
Marquette	79-76		
@Syracuse	66-65		

NOTES: If Notre Dame defeats Fordham in the first round of the Dodge NIT, the Fighting Irish will face the winner of Temple at Iowa . . . Billy Taylor, a 6-6 forward from West Aurora, Ill., HS, gave an oral commitment to Notre Dame last season . . . "This is your chance, Notre Dame. The door is wide open for the only football team in America that doesn't need a conference to spearhead an All-Catholic basketball league (where

1990-91 NOTRE DAME SCHEDULE

Nov.	15	#Fordham	Feb.	16	*Temple	
	28	Indiana		18	Creighton	
Dec.	1	@Kentucky		20	DePaul	
	3	@Butler		23	**St. John's	
	8	@UCLA		26	Dayton	
	12	Southern California	Mar.	2	@Louisville	
	22	Univ. of Portland		4	@Missouri	
Jan.	2	Valparaiso (IN)		9	@DePaul	
	5	##North Carolina				
	6	###USSR	@ Road Games			
	10	@Wichita State	# Dodge NIT. If Notre Dame defeats Fordham, the Fighting Irish will play a second round game on Nov. 17. The semifinals and finals of the tournament will be held on Nov. 21 & 23 at Madison Square Garden, New York, NY.			
	12	@Miami (FL)				
	15	West Virginia				
	17	Marquette				
	22	Rutgers	## Meadowlands Arena, East Rutherford, NJ			
	26	Virginia				
	29	@Dayton	### Springfield, MA			
	31	Boston College	* Hershey, PA			
Feb.	2	Duke	** Madison Square Garden, New York, NY			
	6	La Salle				
	9	Syracuse				
	12	@Marquette				

they could really throw up some prayers). Imagine Notre Dame joined by DePaul, Loyola Marymount, St. John's, Seton Hall, Boston College, Holy Cross, Villanova and Georgetown. With a foot in the New York, Los Angeles, Chicago, Philadelphia, Boston and Washington, D.C., markets, TV would surely see the light," wrote Tom Weir in *USA Today*.

OKLAHOMA STATE

LAST SEASON: 17-14
CONFERENCE RECORD: 6-8
STARTERS LOST: 1
STARTERS RETURNING: 4
CONFERENCE: BIG EIGHT
LOCATION: STILLWATER, OK
HOME FLOOR: GALLAGHER-
   IBA ARENA (6,381)
NICKNAME: COWBOYS
COLORS: ORANGE AND BLACK

★ COACH'S PROFILE ★

EDDIE SUTTON (First year at Oklahoma State. Career record, includes high school and junior college, 632-229) After spending 27 years as a head coach, Sutton spent a year on the sidelines in the 1989-90 season after stepping down as the head coach of the Kentucky Wildcats in March, 1989. His career is beginning again at his alma mater. Sutton played at Oklahoma State under the legendary coach Henry Iba from 1954-58. His first coaching experience came as a graduate assistant under Iba at Oklahoma State in 1958-59.

"I always had a dream I might someday come back to my alma mater . . . I've always thought of Oklahoma as my home," Sutton said.

"We had a horrible experience at the University of Kentucky. Believe me, I learned a lot there. I'm going to supervise staff members a lot more closely than I did there . . . I don't ever want to go through an investigation again, and I know this university doesn't . . . I feel better prepared today to coach Oklahoma State University than at any other time I might have had that opportunity."

Sutton has remained close to Iba. At the news conference announcing Sutton's hiring at Oklahoma State, Iba introduced him, saying, "This is a great day for me and for Oklahoma State. I'm so happy they're here and back where they belong," Iba said of Sutton and his wife, Patsy, who also is an Oklahoma State graduate.

Sutton took over at Kentucky in 1985. His first team (1985-86) was 32-4 and was ranked third nationally by the *Associated Press* and the *United Press International*. Kentucky won the SEC regular season and tournament titles that year. The Wildcats came a game away from winning the Final Four that year, losing to LSU in the finals of the Southeast Region. He was named SEC and National Coach of the Year for his efforts. His second team at Kentucky dipped to an 18-11 mark and lost to Ohio State in the opening round of the NCAA tournament. In Sutton's third year at Kentucky, the Wildcats were 25-5 and ranked sixth nationally by both wire services. Kentucky won the SEC regular season and tournament championship that year. Everything was going fine for him at Kentucky until April, 1988, when a story claiming Kentucky's prize recruit, Chris Mills, had been sent a package containing a video tape and a thousand dollars cash from the Kentucky basketball office. The package allegedly came open at an Emery Air Freight warehouse in Los Angeles. The Kentucky coaching staff, Mills and his father, denied the accusation of the cash payoff. However, the Kentucky program was quickly beset by other problems, such as the alleged cheating on the college entrance examination of Wildcat Eric Manuel and the NCAA investigated and eventually handed down a stiff probation.

Sutton's last year at Kentucky, 1988-89, was a dreadful one. Not only did the Wildcats finish with one of the worst records in the school's illustrious history, 13-19, but controversy swirled all year long. It was basically a season of discontent and misery for Sutton and the Wildcats. He resigned shortly after the season concluded and spent the last year as a consultant for Nike, attending games at his discretion and visiting with college coaches.

"If I had not had this opportunity, it would have been a tough adjustment to be away from this game I have spent my whole life around," Sutton said. "It's been enjoyable, but it's really been a chance to get my batteries recharged . . . It gave me some new insight into the way the game is moving. I think it would be wonderful if a coach could take a sabbatical about this stage in life and get his batteries recharged."

Sutton was not named in any of the violations when the Kentucky basketball program was placed on probation. Therefore, there were no NCAA restrictions against another school hiring him.

He earned praise for admitting to a much speculated drinking problem. Sutton went public with his problem at the news conference announcing his hiring by Oklahoma State.

"There have been many rumors about my drinking in years past. That's been very harmful to my family and to me and I'm here to tell you that some of those rumors were probably true. But many of them were not.

"But I want you to know that I recognized three years ago that there was a problem and I've dealt with it and I think that the fact that I dealt with it better prepares me to be able to help other people and especially to help young people today. I think at this point, I would say that there is a Scripture that has sustained me through all my adversity: 'All things work together for good to them that love the Lord'," Sutton explained.

The 54-year-old Sutton replaces Leonard Hamilton as the head coach at Oklahoma State. Hamilton was the top recruiter at Kentucky and was a member of Sutton's Kentucky staff. Sutton is a native of Bucklin, Kan., and enrolled at Oklahoma State in 1954. After graduating from Oklahoma State and spending a year as a graduate assistant coach, Sutton became the head coach at Tulsa Central HS in 1959. He was 119-51 at Central and in 1967 Sutton took over at Southern Idaho JC. He developed a national junior college power at Southern Idaho and was 83-14 in three years.

Sutton entered the Division I head coaching ranks in 1969 at Creighton. At Creighton, he led the Bluejays to five straight winning seasons including a 23-6 mark in 1974 and an NCAA tournament appearance. In five years at Creighton, Sutton was 82-50.

In 1974 he took over an Arkansas program that had not won a conference title or made an NCAA tournament appearance since 1958. The year before Sutton arrived in Fayetteville, Arkansas posted a 10-16 mark. His first Arkansas team was 17-9 and two years later he led the Razorbacks to a Southwest Conference championship.

At Arkansas, Sutton enjoyed nine straight 10-plus win seasons. He also put Arkansas in the NCAA tournament nine straight times. In 1978, Arkansas was 32-4 and advanced to the Final Four. His Arkansas teams were disciplined, strong defensively and talented. Eight Razorbacks who played at Arkansas under Sutton —the list includes Sidney Moncrief, Alvin Robertson, Darrell Walker and Joe Kleine — went on to significant careers in the NBA.

At Arkansas, Sutton won close to 78 percent of his games, his teams won five Southwest Conference titles and averaged nearly 24 victories a season. He earned National Coach of the Year honors twice and was the Southwest Conference Coach of the Year four times. He also turned Arkansas' Barnhill Arena into one of the most feared homecourts in the country. Arkansas was 128-11 at home during the Sutton Era. He also developed a reputation as one of the best developers of guards in all of coaching.

"Eddie knows offense and defense," said Henry Iba. "And, he knows how to change ends. A lot of coaches know one or the other, but he's one who can coach both and get his players to change ends. He knows the tandem posts like not many do."

When Sutton met with the Oklahoma State team for the first time, he told them the three Ds—Dedication, Discipline and Defense—will be stressed. Discipline will be written on practice jerseys, and defense will be printed on the bottom of the Cowboys' practice shorts.

Hamilton infused the Oklahoma State program with quality big time athletes. The Oklahoma State program is further ahead than it was when Hamilton took over. Now that Sutton is back at his alma mater, look for the Oklahoma State program to continue to improve not only in the Big Eight standings but in the national polls as well. The Big Eight has had unparalleled improvement on the national level over the last decade. With Sutton at Oklahoma State, the conference will be stronger than ever before.

★ PLAYERS NOT RETURNING ★

CHUCK DAVIS (6-0, G, 5.1 ppg, 1.4 rpg, 82 assists, 22 steals) Davis played in 21 of Oklahoma State's 31 games last year. He started one game and was third on the team in assists. A point guard, Davis was more important for his leadership than actual on court performance. He wasn't a great talent, but he did contribute as a playmaker and leader. He is not a major loss.

RICHARD DUMAS (6-7, F, 12.7 ppg, 5.4 rpg, 27 assists, 5 blocked shots, 18 steals) Dumas played in only 12 games last year before being suspended for substance abuse. During his freshman year, it appeared as if Dumas would become a great player. He was a freshman All-America selection and a second-team All-Big Eight pick. He averaged 17.4 points and 6.4 rebounds as a freshman. His scoring average slipped to 15.7 points as a sophomore and he was suspended after the final regular season game, prior to Oklahoma State's game with St. John's in the NIT, to undergo treatment for substance abuse. In the off-season, following his sophomore year, Dumas sprained knee ligaments, underwent arthoscopic surgery on his right knee and suffered a partially torn Achilles' tendon.

Dumas tried to resume his career at Phillips University in Enid, Okla., but was unsuccessful and signed with a professional team in Israel.

CHRIS GAFNEY (6-4, G, 1.6 ppg, 1.3 rpg, 23 assists, 7 blocked shots, 13 steals) Gafney was a reserve guard who started six games last year. He was smart, a leader, but was not a major contributor. Gafney was 16-of-47 (.340) from the field and 8-of-30 (.267) from three-point range.

ROYCE JEFFRIES (6-6, F, 13.9 ppg, 5.7 rpg, 28 assists, 10 blocked shots, 25 steals) Jeffries is by far the toughest player for Sutton to replace. He was second on the team in scoring and rebounding behind Byron Houston last year. Jeffries was a great athlete who played hard every game. He literally left his heart and all he had on the court after every game.

As a junior, Jeffries set an Oklahoma State field goal percentage record (.615) and he made .570 of his field goals last year. He also was third on the team in minutes played last year.

Not only is Jeffries difficult to replace, but there are no front line newcomers on the roster.

★ RETURNING PLAYERS ★

DARWYN ALEXANDER (6-0, 170 lbs., JR, G, #14, 10.2 ppg, 2.3 rpg, 114 assists, 1 blocked shot, 43 steals, Brother Martin HS/New Orleans, La.) Sutton has always been considered one of the premier guard coaches in college basketball. He always had outstanding guards at Arkansas and that trend continued during his four years at Kentucky. In his first year at Oklahoma State, Sutton inherits both starting guards from last year —Darwyn Alexander and Corey Williams. Alexander has led Oklahoma State in assists the past two seasons. He also is a good shooter who led the Big Eight in three-point percentage as a freshman (51.0 percent). He made 103-of-213 field goals (.484) and was 24-of-58 (.414) from three-point range last year. Alexander connected on an excellent 87-of-105 (.829) from the line as a sophomore. He is a point guard but Alexander is such a good shooter that some of his offense is lost when he operates strictly as a playmaker.

His father is the head basketball coach at Xavier University in New Orleans. As befitting a coach's son, Alexander understands the game and is a true playmaker. He possesses excellent quickness. Alexander was second on the team in steals and minutes played last year.

Alexander is the top returning point guard in the Big Eight Conference this year. Oklahoma State's starting backcourt of Alexander and Corey Williams should be the best in the Big Eight and is underrated nationally.

SHAWN DAVIS (6-4, 185 lbs., SO, G, #21, Ferriday HS/Ferriday, La.) Davis redshirted last year. As a freshman in 1988-89, Davis played in 11 games for a total of 34 minutes. He averaged 2.1 points, 0.6 assists and dished out two assists. He made 9-of-15 shots and was 2-of-4 from three-point range. One-third of his made field goals were dunks.

Davis played for a state title team as a senior at Ferriday (La.) HS. Ferriday is also the hometown of rock and roll legend Jerry Lee Lewis and evangelist Jimmy Swaggart.

Davis has improved his strength and skills in the past year. He is a big time leaper with excellent speed. He is the type of athlete Sutton likes in his guards.

BYRON HOUSTON (6-7, 225 lbs., JR, C, #35, 18.5 ppg, 10.0 rpg, 48 assists, 66 blocked shots, 45 steals, Star Spencer HS/Oklahoma City, Okla.) One Cowboy Sutton is certain to become quickly enamored with is Byron Houston. As a sophomore, Houston became the first player in Oklahoma State history to lead the Cowboys in scoring (18.5 ppg), rebounding (10.0 rpg), blocks (66) and steals (45). He finished second in the Big Eight behind Colorado's Shaun Vandiver in rebounding and was a first-team All-Conference selection. He is one of the true warriors in college basketball.

Houston enters his junior year No. 11 on the Oklahoma State all-time scoring chart and ninth on the school's career rebounding list. With another good year, he should finish his junior season ranked among the top four career scorers at Oklahoma State and top three rebounders.

"An animal—when he wants to be," Massachusetts coach John Calipari said in a *Sport Magazine* article. "Gluey hands, superb low-post moves, and so strong, he just swats people out of his way."

Houston made 189-of-358 field goals (.528) and missed all 6 three-pointers he attempted. From the line, he connected on 196-of-268 attempts (.731). He also led Oklahoma State in minutes played with 1,030 minutes in 31 games. He either led or tied for team scoring honors in 16 games and was the Cowboys' leading rebounder, or tied for the lead, in 23 games. He had 15 rebounds at Missouri, 18 rebounds at rival Oklahoma and 15 rebounds against Nebraska. In that win over Nebraska, Houston also scored 35 points. He had 27 points in a loss at national champion UNLV, 25 points in a win over Kansas State and 24 points in an early season victory against Memphis State.

Houston scores almost all of his points from eight feet and in. Houston has great strength, jumps well and has good, but not great, speed. He needs more work on his ballhandling and scoring away from the basket.

All who have been around Houston consider him a quality person. He is soft spoken and has a squeaky, high-pitched voice that reminds some of boxer Mike Tyson. "When I recruited him, I told our staff he talked like Jane and played like Tarzan," said former Oklahoma State coach Leonard Hamilton.

"It hit me real hard (when Hamilton left)," Houston told Mike Baldwin of the *Daily Oklahoman*. "I was in a daze. I thought he would stay here a little longer.

". . . We're getting a real good coach. From what I've heard he's a great coach and he's been a winner everywhere . . . It's like starting over, for him and for us. He told us exactly what he expected. He was straight with us. He said we'll average in the low 80s, which means we'll play a tough, aggressive defense and still run a little."

Expect Byron Houston to not only be one of the premier players in the Big Eight this year, but also the entire country. Some Oklahoma State insiders believe

he will go pro at the end of this year no matter what happens.

EARL JONES (6-2, 155 lbs., SO, G, #3, 1.1 ppg, 0.3 rpg, 2 assists, 6 steals, McLain HS/Tulsa, Okla.) Jones played in 18 games, starting none, for a total of 70 minutes as a freshman. He was 8-of-28 (.286) from the field, 0-of-4 (.000) from three-point range and 3-of-8 (.375) from the line. Jones also had eight turnovers against two assists in his 70 minutes.

He was named the player of the year in the Tulsa area as a senior at McLain HS. He has excellent quickness but is basically an average athlete overall. Jones is heady and is a better perimeter shooter than his statistics indicate, but he needs better stamina and improved ballhandling.

The Oklahoma State backcourt is deep and Jones will probably play about five to seven minutes per game this year.

JOHNNY PITTMAN (7-0, 265 lbs., SR, C, #45, 2.4 ppg, 2.7 rpg, 3 assists, 24 blocked shots, 7 steals, Terry HS/Rosenberg, Tex.) When Sutton took over at Oklahoma State he saw at least one familiar face in Johnny Pittman. He originally signed with Kentucky while Sutton was in Lexington, never played for the Wildcats and transferred to Oklahoma State. Pittman sat out the 1987-88 campaign at Oklahoma State. He averaged 4.0 points and 3.2 rebounds as a sophomore in 1988-89. His role decreased last year as Pittman did not start a game.

Pittman connected on 26-of-58 field goals (.448) and was 19-for-37 (.514) from the line. He was third on the team in blocked shots. He takes up space inside and can bang. His main weakness is an inability to finish a play. Pittman basically cannot score unless it is a dunk shot. He doesn't handle the ball well, either.

Pittman possesses excellent strength. He seems to draw a lot of fouls from opposing teams who concentrate on him more than they should.

He has never lived up to a great high school billing which enabled Pittman to be recruited by the likes of Kentucky.

Oklahoma State should have excellent guard play and get another superb season from Byron Houston. However, if Pittman would contribute more, it could mean the difference in being an NIT team or a participant in the NCAA tournament for the Cowboys.

JOHN POTTER (6-7, 195 lbs., SR, F, #32, 11.0 ppg, 2.7 rpg, 36 assists, 5 blocked shots, 19 steals, Durant HS/Durant, Okla. & Connors State JC/Warner, Okla.) A streaky perimeter shooter, Potter started two games in his first year in the Oklahoma State program. He was fourth on the team in scoring. Potter made 119-of-282 field goals (.422) and was 47-of-127 (.370) from three-point range. He made almost twice as many three-pointers as any other Cowboy. Potter connected on 46-of-61 free throws (.754).

He is a little too emotional for his own good. His lack of emotional control frequently hurt Potter last year. He just tends to lose sight of what he is trying to accomplish on the court.

Potter was a two-time All-Conference selection as well as an All-Region pick at Connors State JC in Warner, Okla. Connors State is one of the premier junior college programs in the country. Potter can jump and run as well as shoot from the perimeter. He had 19 points against Southern Utah State and 23 in a loss to Colorado in the Big Eight tournament last year. With a year's experience in the Big Eight, look for Potter to be an effective and more consistent player as a senior.

MATTIAS SAHLSTROM (6-10, 220 lbs., JR, F, #15, 7.4 ppg, 3.8 rpg, 35 assists, 28 blocked shots, 15 steals, Stockholm, Sweden) A member of the Swedish National team, Sahlstrom started 17 games in his first year at Oklahoma State. He was second on the team in blocked shots and contributed some timely outside shooting. He is not a banger but is more of a perimeter-oriented player. Sahlstrom may be the best passer on the Oklahoma State team. He runs the floor well but needs more strength.

Sahlstrom suffered a knee injury at the end of the last year and wasn't expected to return this season. However, late in the summer he decided to return to Oklahoma State for his second year of college basketball.

Last season, Sahlstrom made 82-of-173 field goals (.474) and nailed 18-of-46 three-pointers (.391). From the line, he was 39-of-56 (.696). He had 20 points in a loss at Missouri and 18 the next game in a win over New Orleans. Sahlstrom came back with 17 points in a close, home loss to Missouri.

"I came away very excited," Sahlstrom told Clay Henry of the *Tulsa World* about his first meeting with Sutton. "He is very direct. He lets you know what he expects, but I think it's great that he's here."

BRIAN WALSH (6-3, 190 lbs., SR, G, #12, Adrian HS/Adrian, Mich.) Walsh was injured last year and did not play for the Cowboys. A transfer from Albion College in Michigan, he averaged 3.6 points and 1.0 rebounds plus handed out 24 assists in 16 games for Oklahoma State in 1988-89. He can play either backcourt position and has a good understanding of the game.

Walsh transferred to Oklahoma State after playing three games as a sophomore at Albion College in 1987. His season was ended by a leg stress fracture. Walsh walked-on to the Oklahoma State program and impressed former Cowboy coach Leonard Hamilton enough to be given a scholarship.

The Oklahoma State backcourt is deep this year, so Walsh probably will not play a key role.

COREY WILLIAMS (6-2, 175 lbs., JR, G, #5, 9.4 ppg, 3.2 rpg, 85 assists, 1 blocked shot, 30 steals, Southwest HS/Macon, Ga.) Williams and fellow junior Darwyn Alexander form the top returning backcourt in the Big Eight Conference. Williams started 30 games last year and was sixth on the team in scoring. His scoring average dipped from 12.4 points per game as a freshman to 10.2 last year, but Williams is still one of the premier guards in the Big Eight.

He is blessed with NBA level speed and quickness. Williams is a great defensive guard, which will endear him quickly to Sutton, and an outstanding all-around athlete. An adequate ballhandler, Williams plays more at the second guard spot. He made 114-of-267 field goals (.427) and connected on 22-of-76 three-pointers (.290). Williams was a consistent free throw shooting going 40-of-53 (.755) from the line.

As a freshman, Williams was a member of the All-Big Eight freshman team and led Oklahoma State in minutes played. Last season he was second on the team in assists and third in steals.

"For Eddie Sutton to coach us is a big-time honor," Williams told Clay Henry of the *Tulsa World*. "I was not sure if he would come here when I heard his name mentioned.

"I felt if we get him it would be kinda like North Texas getting Pat Riley . . . This man knows how to win. There's no doubt in our minds that he will bring joy to our school and team . . . He's fair, honest and concerned about academics, too. He came out and specifically told us we are now part of his family. He told us he would treat us like part of his family."

Williams told Mike Baldwin of the *Daily Oklahoman* this about Sutton: "It's one thing to think offense. It's another to get you to like defense. It sounds like he allows defense to help the offense. He's a veteran. I'm sure he'll capitalize on our strengths and teaching us about our weaknesses . . . I'm sure he will be able to teach us a lot of things because of his experience that coach Hamilton couldn't . . . It's a great opportunity to be taught by a man who has proven he can win ball games."

Look for Williams to blossom this year. Some Big Eight coaches believe that if he can handle the point guard position well, Williams could be an NBA guard.

★ NEWCOMERS ★

MILTON BROWN (6-4, 195 lbs., SO, G/F, #30, 13.8 ppg, 7.8 rpg, Parkview HS/Little Rock, Ark. & Northeastern A&M JC/Miami, Okla.) Brown was signed last spring after Sutton took over at Oklahoma State. He is a native of Little Rock, Ark., an area Sutton certainly knows well, and he could offer an immediate impact. When Sutton was at Arkansas, he preferred big guards who leaped well, could go inside offensively, rebound and disrupt on defense. Brown is at the type of rangy athlete who can do the things out of the backcourt that Sutton wants from his guards. Also, he can possibly play some small forward.

Brown helped Parkview HS to an Arkansas state championship as a junior, while earning All-Conference honors. As a senior, he was named to the All-State team and averaged more than 20 points and 8 rebounds per game.

He is a competitor who will go inside and try to bang with bigger players and is an average shooter. Brown should compete with senior John Potter for a starting small forward spot or swing to the backcourt and backup Corey Williams at second guard.

CORNELL HATCHER (6-4, 195 lbs., JR, G, #24, 9.0 ppg, 6.0 rpg, 4.0 apg, 4.0 stpg, Edison HS/Tulsa, Okla. & Paris JC/Paris Tex.) Hatcher is coming back home to Oklahoma after spending two years at Paris JC in Texas. He was an All-State selection at Tulsa Edison HS and averaged 14.4 points, 7 rebounds and 4 assists per game as a senior.

Like Milton Brown, Hatcher was signed last spring after Leonard Hamilton had left and Eddie Sutton had taken over the Oklahoma State program. He's an athletic rangy guard who offers the inside/outside versatility Sutton wants from his backcourt.

Hatcher is not considered to be as good a prospect as Brown. However, he will add depth to an Oklahoma State backcourt which needed that commodity last year.

SEAN SUTTON (6-1, 185 lbs., JR, G, #20, Henry Clay HS/Lexington, Ky. & Lexington CC/Lexington, Ky.) Sean Sutton played two years for his father at Kentucky, attended classes at Lexington CC but did not play last year and has rejoined his father at Oklahoma State.

As a freshman at Kentucky, Sutton played in 23 games for an average of 6.7 minutes per game. He did not start any games as a freshman and averaged 1.3 points, 0.4 rebounds and had 36 assists against 12 turnovers. Kentucky was 27-6 overall and SEC champions that year. As a sophomore in 1988-89, Sutton was a starting point guard on a 13-19 Kentucky team that was faced with an overwhelming amount of controversy and turmoil. He averaged 5.9 points, 1.6 rebounds, handed out 146 assists and came up with 40 steals.

His game is running the offense and getting the ball to the scorers. Sutton was a good shooter in high school but he did not shoot particularly well in college, but he does have some range with his shot and might become more of a threat since there is less pressure on him this season than there was at Kentucky. He has average physical tools but knows the game and certainly has the confidence of his father.

Sutton was named the sophomore of the year in Arkansas before his family moved to Kentucky. He played in the Dapper Dan Roundball Classic and in the Derby Classic All-Star Games in the spring of 1987. In the Derby Classic, held in Louisville, he scored 19 points and leading the south squad to a 121-91 victory, earning MVP honors in the process. Sutton was an All-State performer as a junior and senior at Henry Clay HS in Lexington, Ky.

He was recruited by Purdue, Michigan and Georgia Tech after leaving Kentucky. Sutton should fit in nicely as a reserve point guard for the Cowboys. He

is experienced against big time competition and that should be beneficial to the Cowboys who lacked backcourt depth last year.

★ QUESTIONS ★

How quickly will the Cowboys adapt to a new coach and system?
Can Oklahoma State win the big conference games, especially on the road? Oklahoma State has hit great potential but the Cowboys were 17-13 and 17-14, respectively, in the past two years. On the road, Oklahoma State is just 3-11 in the big eight over the last two seasons.
Physicalness? Other than warrior Byron Houston, Oklahoma State is a finesse team.

★ STRENGTHS ★

Eddie Sutton! Before the Kentucky program had a disastrous 13-19 season in 1988-89, Sutton was generally ranked by the media as one of the top five colleges coaches in the country. He is a proven winner who is well rested and eager to go after a difficult experience at Kentucky.
Byron Houston! Last season, Houston led Oklahoma State in scoring, rebounding, blocked shots and minutes played. No matter where or who Oklahoma State plays, Houston's performance is a given. He gets it done game after game.
Experience! Most of the core of this team has been through the rugged Big Eight at least twice. The cowboys should have an idea what it takes to win in this strtong and competitive league.
Overall Team Athletic Ability!
The Backcourt of Darwin Alexander and Corey Williams! Entering this season, the Alexander-Williams backcourt of Oklahoma State is the best in the big eight. By the end of the year it could be one of the finest nationally as well.

★ BLUE RIBBON ANALYSIS ★

After an extremely difficult experience toward the end of his career at Kentucky and a year on the sidelines working as a Nike consultant, Eddie Sutton is back in his alma mater and ready to coach again. Sutton played at Oklahoma State in the '50s under legendary coach Henry Iba and his first coaching experience came as a graduate assistant at Oklahoma State.

Sutton inherits a talented team from former Oklahoma State coach Leonard Hamilton who left to take over the Miami (Fla.) program. Ironically, Sutton inherited a Kentucky team, in 1985-86, his first season in Lexington, which Hamilton had recruited and took the Wildcats to a 32-4 record in the final eight of the NCAA Tournament that year. Who is to say that lightning won't strike twice for Sutton and a group of players recruited by Hamilton?

The top talent Hamilton left Sutton is junior forward Byron Houston. As a sophomore Houston became the first player in Oklahoma State history to lead the Cowboys in scoring, rebounding, blocks, steals and minutes played. He is a warrior who literally goes to battle game after game no matter who the opposition is. Houston was the No. 2 rebounder in the Big Eight conference last year and is a true All-America caliber player.

Hamilton also left Sutton a quality backcourt in junior point guard Darwin Alexander and junior guard Corey Williams. The Alexander-Williams backcourt is the best in the Big Eight and could be one of the finest in the country by the end of the season. Alexander is a true point guard with outstanding perimeter shooting ability while Williams is a slashing scorer with great quickness.

Senior small forward John Potter could be another superior outside shooter this year. He made 47 three-pointers last year and was fourth on the squad on scoring. Mattias Sahlstrom, the 6-10 junior from Sweden, started 17 games last year and averaged 7.4 points and 3.8 rebounds in his first season of American college basketball. He is another potentially outstanding perimeter shooter.

Newcomers Milton Brown, Cornell Hatcher, and Sean Sutton (a point guard who played for his father in Kentucky) add depth, ballhandling ability and versatility to the backcourt. If Sutton could get some additional scoring and consistency from the Cowboys' big man, 7-0 senior Johnny Pittman who he signed at Kentucky, Oklahoma State could easily win an excess of 20 games and advance to the NCAA Tournament.

Sutton is a great defensive coach so Oklahoma State should be improved defensively. This is a team that appeared to be on the verge of making a run at the Big Eight title no matter who the coach. Houston, Alexander, Williams and Pittman have been together for two years while Potter and Sahlstrom joined the program last season. If the Cowboys don't get eaten up by power teams, they are basically a finesse outfit, Oklahoma State should do extremely well this year.

We predict a 20-plus victory season in Year One of the Eddie Sutton Era at Oklahoma State. The Cowboys should finish at least third in the Big Eight. Oklahoma State could make some waves in the NCAA tournament this March.

LAST SEASON

North Texas	94-66	Kansas		76-83
#Pitt	90-102	@UNLV		84-100
#Ohio State	81-59	@Nebraska		103-84
Memphis State	93-66	@Kansas State		60-66
Midwestern State (TX)	114-67	Colorado		81-74
Tulsa	80-95	@Iowa State		72-83
Texas Southern	79-77	Oklahoma		94-107
##Pitt	81-92	*Kansas State		82-78
##Morehead State	84-77	*Colorado		72-82
Chicago State	67-59	**Tulsa		83-74
@Missouri	68-78	**@New Mexico		88-90
New Orleans	73-61			
@Kansas	77-91	@ Road Games		
Missouri	71-72	# Tournament of Champions, Charlotte, NC		
Southern Utah State	92-68	## Kuppenheimer Classic, Atlanta, GA		
Nebraska	84-71	* Big East Tournament, Kansas City, MO		
@Colorado	71-68	** NIT		
@Oklahoma	92-109			
Kansas State	89-67			
Iowa State	86-78			

1990-91 OKLAHOMA STATE SCHEDULE

Nov.	24	Colgate	Feb.	13	Oklahoma
	27	@New Orleans		16	Missouri
Dec.	1	Tulsa		19	@Kansas State
	5	Centenary (LA)		24	Colorado
	8	@Wichita State		27	Nebraska
	13	Louisiana Tech	Mar.	2	@Iowa State
	15	Grambling State (LA)		8-10	##Big Eight Tournament
	19	Jacksonville			
	21-22	#Old Style Classic	@ Road Games		
	30	@Marquette	# Rosemont, IL (DePaul, Southern Illinois &		
Jan.	2	@Missouri-Kansas City	Wisconsin-Green Bay)		
	5	@Missouri	## Kansas City, MO		
	12	Kansas			
	19	@Oklahoma			
	23	Southeastern Louisiana			
	26	Kansas State			
	30	@Colorado			
Feb.	2	@Nebraska			
	6	Iowa State			
	9	@Kansas			

NOTES: Oklahoma State will open up with Southern Illinois in the first round of the Old Style Classic . . . the Cowboys would be even stronger this year but their top two recruits are not eligible and didn't enroll in school. Fred Burley, a 6-7 forward from Douglass HS in Oklahoma City, Okla. was the Big School player of the year in Oklahoma last season. He was also considered one of the Top 75 players in the nation. He will play this season at Seminole JC in Seminole, Okla. Randy Rutherford, a 6-3 guard from Broken Bow, Okla., was also signed last fall by Hamilton. He led Oklahoma's Class 4A in scoring last year and was a member of the all-state team along with Burley.

He enrolled at Bacone JC in Muskogee, Okla. . . . as previously mentioned, Sutton is one of the favorite of Oklahoma State's legendary coach Henry Iba. The 85-year-old Iba coached Sutton at Oklahoma State. He gave a fiery introduction at the press conference when Sutton was announced as Oklahoma State's coach. Iba also plans on being visible around Sutton's program. "I'll be at practice," Iba told Clay Henry of the *Tulsa World*. "I want to be around, I want to coach offense, defense — everything." . . . Sutton is only the second Oklahoma State basketball coach to have played collegiately at the school.

PRINCETON

LAST SEASON: 20-7
CONFERENCE RECORD: 11-3
STARTERS LOST: 1
STARTERS RETURNING: 4
CONFERENCE: IVY LEAGUE
LOCATION: PRINCETON, NJ
HOME FLOOR:
JADWIN GYM (7,500)
NICKNAME: TIGERS
COLORS: ORANGE AND BLACK

★ COACH'S PROFILE ★

PETE CARRIL (Record at Princeton, 397-216. Career record, 408-228.) Sure, Princeton is known for its deliberate, lull-'em-to-sleep style, emphasizing sticky defense and patient offensive patterns. And it is known for scaring the big timers in post-season play. But if Tiger teams have one distinctive characteristic, it has to be Pete Carril, their coach of 23 years.

Carril has molded Princeton into the very antithesis of his on-court demeanor. His teams play in control and with composure, while the impish coach stages game-long tantrums on the sidelines. Since coming to Princeton, the former Lafayette hoop star has demanded a cerebral style that mirrors the classroom demands of the Ivy League, frustrating opponents and producing teams that have either won or tied for 10 Ivy titles.

He has done it with future NBA first-round draft choices, and with players who've just done what they've been told. He enters this season with a team favored yet again, this time for its third consecutive league title.

A quick look at Carril courtside might lead one to believe that a chemistry professor had strayed from the laboratory - his unkempt hair and plain black sweater are no match for the sartorial splendor of some NCAA fashion plates. To watch him coach, though, is to believe.

"You do what you can do," Carril said when asked about his teams' style. "You don't do what anyone else does."

What Carril has done is outlasted every other Ivy League coach. He has battled powerful Columbia teams in the 1960's, waged a decade-long war with Penn in the '70's, and taken all comers in the 1980's. The next decade should be equally interesting.

Despite its long-time success, Princeton did not get true national recognition until the 1989 NCAA tournament opening round, when it came within a single blocked shot of upsetting mighty Georgetown. In last year's tourney, the Tigers attacked eventual Final Four qualifier Arkansas before succumbing, 68-64, in another taut first round affair. Those two games changed the nation's perception of Princeton from a boring team in a tiny league to a well-prepared unit capable of scaring anyone. Of course, the hard-driving Carril was not impressed with moral victories after the games, but he understands their significance now.

"Those two games should encourage our guys to work a little harder," Carril said. "It should make them realize they're good players and that the results of their efforts can be satisfying."

As a result of the expanded national attention, the media has discovered Carril. His straightforward style makes him popular with writers, and he's been a target for comment on important NCAA issues, as well as fodder for features in magazines like *Time*. Carril also created some controversy this summer when he expressed his frustration at coaching the East team in the U.S. Olympic Festival.

Bothered by what he perceived to be the team's selfish play, Carril said he did not want to coach an All-Star team next summer. The wire services ran with the item, proclaiming that Carril had ripped his players and was through with coaching in All-Star games.

"Sure I would, some day," Carril told the *Trenton Times* about his desire to direct another group of All-Stars. "It's just that next summer, I'd prefer to stay home, cut the grass and go out with my friends. But another time? Why not?

"It's not that this wasn't an enjoyable experience in a lot of ways. It's just that when it was over, I told the team how I felt about where they came up short of what I'd asked, and then I told the media what I told the team."

On other issues, Carril is equally outspoken. Take recruiting, for instance. "We're the worst recruiters in the league," he told the *Philadelphia Inquirer*. "We don't make many home visits - in fact, only one in the last five years. I don't like it because it's the job of an encyclopedia salesman, or some guy pushing vacuum cleaners. It has the potential for tarnishing a whole relationship between player and coach. That's the reason Bob Cousy quit coaching."

The players who do come, however, get a coach who understands their plight. "Carrill," the *Inquirer* wrote, "knows he's dealing with basketball players with SAT scores that begin in the 1200's, so adjustments must be made."

Said Carril: "I want a kid who goes ahead and does what he knows has to be done, who doesn't give himself an excuse to fail. If a guy misses five shots in a row, will he have the internal fortitude to take the sixth shot? Me, I want a kid who'll take the sixth shot."

Carril began at Princeton in 1967, following one year as head coach at Lehigh. He won 20 games his first season and qualified for the NCAA tournament the next. His 1974-75 team finished 22-6 and won the NIT - back when that meant something. His Ivy League winning percentage of .759 is dominating, and his teams' 20 finishes in the nation's Top 10 in scoring defense is mind-boggling.

"Look," said Carril, "I'd like to have a center who plays like Bill Russell. Forward? Larry Bird. Guard? Maurice Cheeks. But, you see, basketball players are human beings. You'd be surprised how many people forget that."

Carril also worries about other, more important things people forget. "Companies are complaining about not getting people to fill jobs that are only remotely technical," he told the *Inquirer*. "That portends bad things for things for this country. We've got an $8 billion drug problem, and we're giving helicopters to foreign countries when all these kids have to do is stop. I've thought many times about going into politics. Problem is, that may be the biggest compromise of all."

Instead, this little big man continues what he does best. Namely, coach basketball. "The hardest thing in the world to do," he insists, "is to do one thing particularly well for a long period of time at whatever standards you establish." So how does this year-in, year-out practitioner keep exceeding virtually every standard in his profession?

"I draw a general idea about what to do, and little by little, the pieces fall into place," Carril explains. "If they don't, then I'll alter my plans. I don't get a fix on something until I see what I have."

This year, as in those previous, that will be a lot - starting with the coach.

★ PLAYERS NOT RETURNING ★

KYLE HARRINGTON (6-3, G, 2.3 ppg, 0.8 rpg) Harrington played sparingly, seeing time in only six games - all as a reserve. He averaged just 6.2 minutes each time out.

MATT LAPIN (6-7, F, 10.4 ppg, 3.2 rpg, 57 assists, 20 steals, 53.4 percent three-point shooting) Lapin, a second-team All-Ivy selection, will be missed as much for his leadership and court sense as his offensive production and dead-eye shooting.

"What really hurts is that he knew how to play the game," Carril said. "His sense of the game was excellent. He knew when to shoot, when to pass and how to defend. His knowledge of the game is terrific. We don't have anyone coming back who can do that. He's tougher to replace than someone like (1988 grad Bob) Scrabis, and Bob was a much better ballplayer than Matt."

Lapin more than doubled his previous three-year total for three-pointers, draining 71-of-133 shots from beyond the line.

MARVIN WILLIAMS (6-1, G, 1.8 ppg, 0.7 rpg) Williams, who saw time in only nine games last year, decided to forego his junior season to play defensive back for the Tigers' football team this fall. He is already the top high jumper on the Princeton track team, having cleared 7-0.

★ RETURNING PLAYERS ★

JERRY DOYLE (6-3, 165 lbs., SR, G, #5, 4.6 ppg, 1.3 rpg, 43 assists, 42 steals, Bergen Catholic HS/Woodcliff Lake, N.J.) Doyle lost his starting spot last season to Sean Jackson, but still started 10 of the Tigers' games and was first guard off the bench in the others. An excellent shooter and strong ballhandler, he gives Princeton's backcourt depth and will not hurt the first unit when called upon for an emergency start.

As a sophomore, Doyle shot a team-high 45.9 percent from three-point range and nailed 17-of-38 three-pointers (44.7 percent) a year ago.

MATT EASTWICK (6-8, 215 lbs., JR, F, #55, 7.3 ppg, 3.4 rpg, Gilman HS/Baltimore, Md.) Eastwick used his brawn to help anchor the stingy Tiger interior defense. A returning starter, he needs to turn his attention to rebounding with the same fervor he gives to his thunderous, two-handed dunks.

"We were deficient in rebounds by six a game last year," Carril said. "It's tough to believe we won 20 games with that. I have a feeling we'll get more this year."

Eastwick made the all-tournament team at the Met Life Classic early last season and will be called upon for more scoring in Lapin's absence.

"We're hoping Matt can continue where he left off," Carril said, referring to Eastwick's 17 points in the loss to Arkansas. "We're hoping he grows in the knowledge of what he tries to do on the court. He's a good runner and jumps well, but we've got to get him to love to play a little more."

MATT HENSHON (6-5, 180 lbs., SR, F, #35, 6.7 ppg, 2.2 rpg, 1.3 34 assists, 21 steals, Loomis-Chaffee HS/Wilbraham, Mass.) Henshon started the first 20 games of last season, but was sidelined by a groin injury and saw reserve duty thereafter. One of two candidates to replace Lapin, Henshon is an outstanding (80.3 percent) free throw shooter and scored a game-high 20 points in the win against Rutgers a year ago. He was also a member of the District II academic All-America team.

His lack of bulk could limit his minutes up front, since Carril is looking for more rebounding. However, the triple letterwinner will give the Tigers depth in the forecourt.

TROY HOTTENSTEIN (6-2, 170 lbs., SR, G, #12, 4.1 ppg, 0.8 rpg) This senior gunner will give Carril some quick pop off the bench. He started one of the 14 games in which he played last season, and erupted for 12 points in the second half of Princeton's come-from-behind win at Iona.

As a sophomore, Hottenstein tied the Princeton mark for three-pointers in a game with seven, a record Lapin broke last year with eight against Harvard. A highly-regarded high school player, Hottenstein ripped suburban Philadephia defenses for over 1,500 points while at Souderton Area High.

SEAN JACKSON (6-0, 170 lbs., JR, G, #11, 11.1 ppg, 1.3 rpg, 36 assists, 24 steals, Vinson HS/Huntington, W.Va.) Jackson gives the Tigers a lightning-quick two-guard who supplements his fine outside shooting with outstanding defense. A transfer from Ohio University, Jackson started 20 games last year and will team with George Leftwich to give Princeton a solid starting backcourt. His quickness should allow the Tigers to accelerate the pace in their customary bob-and-weave offense.

"I see that we can run some more this year," Carril said. "We have the depth at guard to do it."

Jackson was named honorable mention All-Ivy and made the all-tournament team at the Spartan Cutlass Classic at Michigan State. He shot 44.5 percent from three-point range, second to Lapin among starters.

JIMMY LANE (6-7, 205 lbs., JR, C, #32, 1.2 ppg, 0.9 rpg, Union Catholic HS/Fanwood, N.J.) Lane played in only 10 games last season, averaging just over five minutes an appearance. He gives Carril extra bulk up front for rebounding and possesses a nice shooting touch. He might have to fight off several incoming freshmen for added playing time.

"You never know who's going to make the commitment to try and improve," Carril said. "It doesn't happen by osmosis. It doesn't just come to you. You have to go out and get it."

GEORGE LEFTWICH (6-2, 180 lbs., JR, G, #22, 6.2 ppg, 3.0 rpg, 43 assists, 42 steals, Gonzaga HS/Washington, D.C.) If Carril demands extra effort on defense, he's equally insistent on careful play when the Tigers have the ball. Leftwich meets his coach's requirements. Since the middle of his freshman year, Leftwich has run Princeton's complicated pattern offense with extreme care. He averaged only 1.3 turnovers per contest last

season, a remarkable statistic, considering he played more than 33 minutes each game.

"He hardly ever turns the ball over," Carril said. "I'd like to see him shoot some more, but he"s helped us win some big games."

When he does shoot, Leftwich is deadly. He averaged 62.4 percent from the field last season and should get a chance to take some more shots with Lapin gone. His primary mission in the Tiger offense, however, is to protect the ball and kick-start Princeton's weaves, back-door plays and other annoyances.

Leftwich's father is head coach at the University of the District of Columbia.

CHRIS MARQUARDT (6-8, 190 lbs., JR, F, #30, 2.0 ppg, 1.6 rpg, Clearwater Central Catholic HS/Belleair, Fla.) Lapin's graduation creates an opportunity for the smooth junior. Though he started 13 games as a freshman, Marquardt played considerably less as a sophomore. Still, his good shooting touch (career 40 percent from three-point land) and some increased desire may just put him in the starting lineup this time.

KELLY McDOWELL (6-2, 170 lbs., SR, F, #15, 1.4 ppg, 1.0 rpg, Northeastern HS/Elizabeth City, N.C.) A smaller forward, this lefthander shot 57.4 percent from the field in the seven games in which he played.

KIT MUELLER (6-7, 215 lbs., SR, C, #00, 15.0 ppg, 4.9 rpg, 140 assists, Downers Grove South HS/Downers Grove, Ill.) If it hadn't been for a stray fishbowl, Mueller would be making headlines at some big time Division I school instead of ripping up the Ivies. As a high school senior, Mueller tore up his achilles tendon when he stepped into a fishbowl. The big school scholarships disappeared, and Princeton beckoned.

"I guess we got him by default," Carril said. "It's ironic that he was operated on by a Princeton graduate."

In his three years as a Tiger, Mueller has performed surgery of his own. He has started 80 consecutive games, been named to two straight All-Ivy first-teams and earned last year's Ivy League player of the year. He is eighth on the all-time Princeton scoring list and needs only 11.2 ppg to register 1,452 and soar into second place behind the legendary Bill Bradley (2,503).

Mueller's deft passing and outstanding shooting (55.5 percent) give Carril the solid center needed for Princeton's high-post offense. In addition to his scoring, Mueller is fourth on Princeton's all-time assists list, needing 161 to take over first place.

"Kit has expanded his whole way of playing since coming here," Carril said. "He passes, dribbles and shoots well. He's an all-around player."

Mueller also defends well and gives Princeton a constant presence underneath. Despite averaging over 38 minutes a game last year, he did not foul out. He also was named to the academic All-America team.

CHRIS PAVLIC (6-3, 190 lbs., SO, F, #34, 1.8 ppg, 1.0 rpg, Dover-Sherborn Hs/Sherborn, Mass.) As one of two frosh on last year's Tiger varsity, Pavlic played in only five games. He could provide the Tigers with some instant offense this year, thanks to his outside shooting marksmanship.

MICHAEL SILAS (6-9, 200 lbs., SO, C, #50, 1.4 ppg, 0.8 rpg, Bartlesville HS/Bartlesville, Okla.) The other Tiger frosh last year, Silas played only 12 minutes all season. A project, he could give Princeton some strength underneath in a couple of years.

★ NEWCOMERS ★

MIKE BRENNAN (6-0, 165 lbs., FR, G, Elizabeth HS/Elizabeth, N.J.) Brennan was the point guard on the Elizabeth team that went 23-1 and took the New Jersey state title. He averaged 12.0 ppg and 5.5 assists, and shot 50 percent from three-point range. His teammate, 7-2 giant Luther Wright, will play up the road at Seton Hall.

CHRIS COOK (6-5, 180 lbs., SO, F, Collegiate Schools/Richmond, Va.) A member of Princeton's highly successful junior varsity last year, Cook averaged 12.3 ppg. He is expected to add depth at forward.

BEN GERIG (6-9, 220 lbs., FR, C, Phillips Exeter Academy, N.H./ Athens, Ohio.) An agile big man who averaged 16 points and 12 rebounds at Exeter last year, Gerig will compete for playing time at either center or power forward.

JEFF HICKMAN (6-4, 185 lbs., JR, F, Greenhill HS/Carrolton, Tex.) Another 1989-90 JV veteran, Hickman scored 12.7 ppg and distinguished himself as a strong rebounder.

CHRIS MOONEY (6-6, 190 lbs., FR, F, Archbishop Ryan HS/Philadelphia, Pa.) Mooney earned the MVP in the Northern Division of the Philadelphia Catholic League, and plays the type of cerebral game Carril should love. He is an excellent all-around player who averaged 14.8 ppg in leading Archbishop Ryan to a 21-6 record.

NORBERT VALIS (6-7, 210 lbs., FR, F, Hampton HS/Allison Park, Pa.) Valis came to the United States from Switzerland before his junior year in high school, and started his two years at Hampton High, averaging 20.6 ppg, 12.0 rpg and 5.0 blocks per contest. In Pittsburgh's post-season Roundball Classic, Valis scored seven points and grabbed seven rebounds in 18 minutes.

CHRIS YETMAN (6-4, 205 lbs., FR, F/G, Mater Dei HS/Port Monmouth, N.J.) Yetman averaged 21.0 ppg and 9.5 rpg for Mater Dei, whose 25-2 record included an upset win over highly-regarded St. Anthony's of Jersey City. With Princeton's wealth of guards, Yetman will probably play on the Tiger junior varsity as a freshman.

★ QUESTIONS ★

Size? Eastwick is the tallest Tiger at 6-8. If Carril wants more rebounding, some of the younger, bigger players will have to perform.

Outside shooting? Lapin's three-point gun is gone, and Carril has to find another bomber. Leftwich is a candidate, if he'll just shoot more.

Respect? Will Princeton's last two NCAA tournament performances convince the rest of the country the Tigers are a legitimate threat? Or will they still be considered the best of a weak, albeit smart, bunch?

Coaching! It's tough to find a better coach than Carril. He drums the Princeton style into his players and gets them to execute with intelligence and desire come game time.

Experience! Four returning starters and several tested reserves give Princeton an advantage heading into the always-wacky Ivy League season.

Mueller! The returning Ivy MVP does more than just score, pass and rebound. He exemplifies Carril's cerebral system and keys the team's play with his talent and desire.

★ BLUE RIBBON ANALYSIS ★

Carril seems prepared to lead his Tigers to yet another post-season berth. He will not admit it, but Princeton's four returning starters and strong bench make it the clear favorite for the Ivy League title. Still, Carril doesn't want to hear any of that prognosis stuff.

"Yale has five starters back," he groused. "If you use that as a perspective, then they're the favorites. In my 23 years here, the league has never been settled but once or twice before the final weekend. We're always meeting to decide the best way to break the ties.''

The graduation of forward Matt Lapin, the nation's top three-point shooter (53.4 percent), is the only serious wound the Tigers must heal. Princeton brings back four key backcourt performers, a trio of tested forwards and center Kit Mueller, last season's Ivy player of the year and a good bet for some All-America mention this time.

True, the Ivy League is always crazy, and those Friday-Saturday road trips to bandbox gyms can wear down even the toughest teams, but don't believe Carril's doomsaying. Only a string of major breakdowns will keep the Tigers from the top. And given Carril's track record of preparing his teams, that is not very likely.

Princeton's easy non-league schedule features no big time powers, and could be a catapult toward 22 or 23 wins. It will be an upset if the Tigers do not take the Ivy League title again. But the big question remains: Can Princeton get past the NCAA first round?

As long as the Tigers are matched up against Final Four caliber competition, the smart money says no way. Then again, anyone who bet on Princeton in the last two NCAA tourneys would have looked pretty smart.

LAST SEASON			
Franklin & Marshall (PA)	64-47	@Pennsylvania	50-51
Lehigh	61-50	Harvard	86-73
@Dayton	62-68	Dartmouth	66-28
@Iona	53-41	Brown	74-47
@St. Joseph's	62-47	Yale	62-47
Rutgers	65-60	@Dartmouth	58-49
#Xavier	65-72	@Harvard	63-69
#Canisius	73-59	Cornell	64-41
##Arkansas-Little Rock	59-56	Columbia	73-46
##@Michigan State	49-51	*Arkansas	64-68
Delaware	58-41		
Pennsylvania	56-44	@ Road Games	
@Yale	37-39	# Met Life Classic, San Francisco, CA	
@Brown	64-53	## Spartan Cutlass Classic, East Lansing, MI	
Susquehanna (PA)	75-38		
@Columbia	67-39	* NCAA Tournament, Austin, TX	
@Cornell	60-54		

NOTES: Princeton's first round opponent in the North Coast Tournament is Wright State. The Tigers open up with St. Mary's in the Manufacturer's Hanover Classic. In Princeton's third tournament in the non-conference schedule, the Tigers face another *Blue Ribbon* Top 40 team, California-Santa Barbara, in the first round of the Fujitsu America/Cable Car Classic . . . former Vanderbilt star Jan van Breda Kolff, who played in the NBA, is an assistant coach at Princeton. His father Bill van Breda Kolff coached at Princeton . . . seven of Carrill's teams have led the country in defense,

1990-91 PRINCETON SCHEDULE		
Nov. 24-25	#North Coast Tournament	
27	@Lafayette	
Dec. 3	@Lehigh	
7-8	*Manufacturer's Hanover Classic	
12	St. Joseph's	
15	@Rutgers	
28-29	**Fujitsu America/Cable Car Classic	
Jan. 5	@Pennsylvania	
11	Yale	
12	Brown	
28	Elizabethtown College (PA)	
Feb. 1	Dartmouth	
2	Harvard	
Feb. 5	Pennsylvania	
8	@Cornell	
9	@Columbia	
15	@Brown	
16	@Yale	
22	Columbia	
23	Cornell	
Mar. 1	@Harvard	
2	@Dartmouth	
10	Loyola Marymount	
@ Road Games		
# Cleveland, OH (Cleveland State, Coastal Carolina & Wright State)		
* New Rochelle, NY (Iona, St. Mary's & Wagner)		
** Santa Clara, CA (California-Santa Barbara, Marist & Santa Clara)		

and 20 of his 23 clubs overall at Princeton have been ranked in the Top 10. The Tigers' lowest allowed average points per game was 50.1 in 1983-84 . . . what was the lowest point total by a Division I team last season? Dartmouth's 28, against Princeton, of course . . . in the last three seasons, the Tigers have lost just twice at Jadwin Gym . . . Princeton's loss to Arkansas in first round of the 1990 NCAA tournament was ESPN's highest rated game of the season with a 6.2 share.

ST. JOHN'S

LAST SEASON: 24-10
CONFERENCE RECORD: 10-6
STARTERS LOST: 1
STARTERS RETURNING: 4
CONFERENCE: BIG EAST
LOCATION: JAMAICA, NY
HOME FLOORS: L (6,008) &
 MADISON SQUARE GARDEN
 (18,212)
NICKNAME: REDMEN
COLORS: RED AND WHITE

★ COACH'S PROFILE ★

LOU CARNESECCA, (record at St. John's, 484-180. Professional career record, 114-138). In this changing world, especially in the rapidly changing scene of New York City, it's nice to know there are still a few things you can depend on. After 40 years of coaching basketball; college, high school and the pros and winning over 800 games, Little Looie Carnesecca still paces the St. John's sidelines with the same zest, still eyes referees with the same sense of amazement at questionable calls, lives, loves and talks like a native New Yorker with roots deep into the Big Apple's core. Heading into the '90s, Carnesecca is still a constant if not only on the New York scene but also in a Big East conference with a tradition seemingly far longer than its 11-year run.

Carnesecca now has his own weekly television show on Madison Square Garden Network in a 5-minute pre-game show on 50,000-watt radio giant WCBS. He now

even has his first book out with the release of "Carnesecca, In Season," by Phil Pepp of the *New York Daily News*. Recently, Carnesecca was given the title "Cavallieri," bestowed by the president of Italy on prominent Americans who have distinguished themselves in any field of endeavor.

On the coaching field, Carnesecca has distinguished himself with 16 NCAA Tournament invitations and 6 NIT invites in 22 years at St. John's. That's 22 for 22 in post-season invitations for the Redmen under Carnesecca.

He took his 1985 team to the Final Four. In 11 rugged years in the Big East, Carnesecca has guided St. John's to regular season record of 100-53. St. John's tied for the regular season Big East title and won the conference tournament championship in 1983 and '86. Three times he has been named Big East coach of the year. Five times he has been named metropolitan coach of the year in the New York City area. St. John's has enjoyed 22 consecutive winning seasons in the Carnesecca ERA.

He is entering his 41st year of coaching basketball. At St. John's Carnesecca 20 victory seasons. His winning percentage of .429 ranks him among the nation's winningest active coaches by percentage. St. John's has owned the NIT during Carnesecca's reign as the Redmen have won five NIT titles in his 22 years at St. John's. His in-season tournament titles are also impressive. St. John's has won 15 Lapchick Memorial tournament championships as well as eight ECAC holiday festival crowns.

He was born on January 5, 1925 and raised on Manhattan's east side. His family was a fixture on the east side they owned and operated Carnecessa's Italian Delicatessen. He attended Our Lady Perpetual Help grammar school and graduated from St. Ann's Academy (now Archbishop Molloy HS) in 1943. In 1943-46 he served in the U.S. Coast Guard, pacific Theater of Operations and World War II. He enrolled in St. John's in 1946 and played three games on the 1946-47 junior varsity basketball team. However, his athletic talents were more prominent on the baseball diamond where for four years he hit .300 as a utility infielder. Carnesecca was a member of St. John's first college world series baseball team in 1949. The coach of that team was Frank McGuire the legendary basketball coach who gained fame for opening the "underground railroad" it took New York City talent to North Carolina and South Carolina.

In the fall of 1950, Carnesecca returned to St. Ann's Academy and began his coaching career. He taught health, hygiene and civics and continued to work for a masters degree in educational guidance at St. John's. During his ten years St. Ann's won three national Catholic high school championships in basketball and one in baseball. He returned to St. John's in 1957 as assistant to legendary coach Joe Lapchick. In 1965, when Lapchick retired, he was elevated to position of head basketball coach.

He stayed until 1970 when New York Nets of the now defunct American Basketball Association lured Carnesecca away. In his short ten years in the professional coaching ranks, he posted a 114-138 record and took the Nets to the playoffs each year. Reaching the finals of the league championship in 1972. Carnesecca probably could have hung around the pro ranks for years but he decided that St. John's and college basketball were where he belonged.

His teams are usually good defensively and Carnesecca keeps a reign on the Redmen's tempo. So far, he has not embraced the all-out, up-tempo craze that is sweeping college basketball. Carnesecca likes to keep a degree of control of what's going on.

He has always managed to land his fair share of the vast talented that comes out of the Big Apple. Carnesecca has been very successful at getting disenchanted former New York City high school stars to transfer back home after they find out that the grass is not necessarily greener on the other side of the Hudson. He also has used the junior college ranks well. As the Big East has gained prominence due to its expansive television coverage, Carnesecca has expanded his recruiting horizons. Where before he generally needed only a subway token and a recruit, Carnesecca's staff has needed to consult the travel agent and booked some airline flights recently. In the last five years he has signed players from Walton Beach, Fla., Denver, Colo., Mechanicsburg, Pa., Syracuse, N.Y., Hopkinsville, Ky. and scoured the junior college ranks as well as mined the New York City area talent.

When the Big East decided to experiment with rule giving players six fouls instead of the standard five before disqualification last year, Carnesecca made the following comments of John Bannon of *USA Today*: "We have the only form of entertainment where you make a mistake and you get bounced. Its like going to a play to see a great actor and he doesn't come out for the second act."

There is no doubt St. John's has been extremely successful under Carnesecca's guidance. However, the Redmen have stumbled recently. St. John's is coming off three consecutive seasons of at least ten losses a year and is the only Big East team that hasn't won a game in a conference tournament in the last four years. With eight lettermen returning, including four starters, look for the recent negative trends to be broken by the Redmen this year.

★ PLAYERS NOT RETURNING ★

DARRELL AIKEN (6-0, G, 1.5 ppg, 0.5 rpg, 1 assist, 1 steal) Aiken transferred to St. John's from Division II C.W. Post two seasons back and wound up getting little playing time. He played in 11 games last year for a total of 44 minutes and scored 16 points. Aiken did show some spurts of strong-man backcourt defense but otherwise was not a key contributor.

GREG ''BOO'' HARVEY (5-11, G, 16.5 ppg, 2.2 rpg, 180 assists, 1 blocked shot, 61 steals) After weathering travel, transfers, academic and other troubles, Harvey came back from sitting out the 1988-89 season to put forth his senior year of legend. St. John's was 24-10 last year but would have been 20-14 without Boo. He won or tied four games with three-pointers at the buzzer. The first buzzer beater against DePaul, got the Redmen into the Dodge NIT finals last November. While becoming the most feared clutched shooter in recent seasons in the Big East, Harvey also raised his game from playground scorer to consummate point guard. He led St. John's in assists (180), with second in scoring (16.5 ppg) and first in three-pointers made (46).

Harvey was a unanimous first-team All-Big East pick. He wound up St. John's All-Team leader in three-point field goals (61). He also won two prestigious awards: The Haggerty award for the best college basketball player in metropolitan New York City and the Francis P. Naismith award which is given annually to the nations best player under six feet.

His departure leaves a huge void in the St. John's backcourt and perimeter attack. The talented sophomore David Cain is Harvey's heir apparent at point guard.

BARRY MILHAVEN (6-5, F, 0.3 ppg, 0.3 rpg, 1 assist, 1 blocked shot) Milhaven who once collected 11 points and 8 rebounds in a game his junior year was a hustling, aggressive player who might have been a contributor at a lower level. He began last season with an ankle injury, then came back to find an extremely crowded situation on the Redman front line.

He appeared in 12 games, starting none for a total of 43 minutes last year.

JAYSON WILLIAMS (6-10, FC, 14.6 ppg, 7.8 rpg, 7 assists, 12 blocked shots, 3 steals) Williams, who had risen from a marginal 6-7 high school swingman to a dominating 6-10 Big East power forward, played 21 games last year with broken bones in his foot. He did not play until late December, and after 13 games Williams had to sit out the rest of the year after he re-broke the foot. He was not allowed

to play until well into the summer. Williams averaged 19.5 points and 7.9 rebounds and was a major force on St. John's NIT championship team in 1989. That's why he was a first round choice of the Phoenix Suns even though his senior year was cut short.

If he shows the intensity he played with two years ago, and comes back strong from the injury, Williams could have a long career in the NBA. In actuality, he is not a true personnel loss as St. John's played 21 games without Williams and ended the season with him on the sidelines.

★ RETURNING PLAYERS ★

JASON BUCHANAN (6-2, 155 lbs., JR, G, #12, 6.5 ppg, 2.6 rpg, 126 assists, 3 blocked shots, 39 steals, Nottingham HS/Syracuse N.Y.) After filling in for Boo Harvey at the point as a freshman and vastly exceeding expectations, Buchanan moved to off-guard to accommodate Harvey's return last season. This year, depending on the progress of David Cain he could go back to the point as a starter or backup. Buchanan started all 34 games last season. Even with an accomplished passer like Harvey flanking him at point guard, Buchanan still contributed 126 assists (his 293 total assists ranks him 8th on the St. John's career assists list after only two seasons). He had a 16-point game including 4-of-5 three-pointers to victory over Temple. The season, though, Buchanan was only 28-of-81 from three-point range for 34.6 percent. He was 6th on the team in scoring and averaged 26.3 minutes per game. Buchanan also shot a poor .349 percent (68-of-195) and was 58-of-77 (.753) from the line.

He seems more comfortable as a steady, if unspectacular ballhandler than as a point producing off-guard. Buchanan feeds the post well and usually avoids ill-advised and forced plays. He could use some more strength.

If he stays as the starting second guard, he would leave the Redmen with a probable small backcourt of the 6-2 Buchanan and the 6-0 Cain. St. John's got away with a small backcourt last season because of a big front line but that might not happen this year. If either Chucky Sproling or Carl Beckett can step up at off-guard, Buchanan will be back at the point where he is most effective and comfortable.

DAVID CAIN (6-0, 160 lbs., SO, G, #11, 0.9 ppg, 0.3 rpg, 14 assists, 1 steal, Adlai Stevenson HS/Bronx, N.Y.) After understudying Boo Harvey (a good reason why he saw and average of only 4 minutes a game) Cain will get his chance to take over at the point. The Redmen's fortunes could heavily depend on his progress. There is no question Cain, so-so shooter (41.7 percent from the field and 60 percent from the line as a freshman), will not approach Harvey's outside fire power. Where he can compensate, though, is by running the break and more importantly, by creating some halfcourt offense by feeding Malik Sealy, Billy Singleton and Robert Werdann.

Cain is built as a great passer and the targets will be there for him to hit inside. Carnesecca has called Cain, "a great distributor." He was regarded as a national Top 10 point guard prospect when he signed and was a spectacular player at Adlai Stevenson HS in the Bronx.

During the summer, Cain led the east team in scoring at the US Olympic Fest in Minneapolis. He was coached at the festival by Princeton's Pete Carril. "I liked (Cain) a lot. He's a tough competitor. He plays to win," Carril told *Big East Briefs*. That is high praise considering Carril is not only a tough task master but he basically disliked the games of most of his players on the east team.

If Cain can bring his game under control (he had 14 turnovers to go with 14 assists during his brief action as a freshman) and ran the Redmen at a high major college level, St. John's can contend for a Big East title. This season, Carnesecca will cross his fingers and give Cain an opportunity to make the grade.

TERENCE MULLIN (6-1, 180 lbs., JR, G, #10, 2.0 ppg, 0.1 rpg, 1 assist, 4 steals, Zavierein HS/Brooklyn, N.Y.) Younger brother of St. John's All-Time great Chris Mullin (now and NBA All-Star with the Golden State Warriors), Terence played in 7 games for a total of 41 minutes as a sophomore. He scored 5 points in 17 minutes against Niagara and also had 5 points in 8 minutes in the opening round win in the Joe Lapchick Memorial Tournament over at the University of San Diego.

He hit 2-of-3 from three-point range. As a freshman Mullin, also showed had the confidence to stick and open shot in an eight-point outing against Pitt. He is a spunky player whose strength is definitely hitting the open jumper. Mullin was 5-of-7 from the field (71.4 percent) in his limited playing time.

His playing time will probably be limited this year but don't be surprised if Mullin creates a spark or two somewhere along the way.

SEAN MUTO (6-11, 245 lbs., SR, C, #50, 1.7 ppg, 2.5 rpg, 2 assists, 6 blocked shots, 2 steals, Mechanicsburg HS/Mechanicsburg, Pa.) Muto saved his best game for last, 6-point, 10-rebound effort in only 16 minutes during the Redmen's narrow 76-72 loss to Duke in the second round of the NCAA East Region in Atlanta, Ga. Muto also had a 6-point 7-rebound game vs. Villanova. He served his all season as a confident back up defensive presence in the pivot to starter Robert Werdann, who often wound up in foul trouble.

Muto moves well and has good hands pulling down rebounds in crowds. It was a bit surprising his rebound productivity wasn't a little higher on the year. For the year, Muto was 20-of-47 (42.6 percent) from the field and a poor 5-of-15 (33.3 percent) from the line. He averaged 11 minutes a game and played in 26 of St. John's 34 games. His productivity and role could increase as the St. John's starting front line is not extremely tall. Muto is a plugger whose experience should be an asset.

CHRIS PURSOO (6-1, 165 lbs., JR, G, #24, Long Island Lutheran HS/Westbury, N.Y.) Pursoo made the team as a walk-on but has yet to see action in an actual regular season game during his two years in the program.

MALIK SEALY (6-8, 185 lbs., JR, F, #21, 18.1 ppg, 6.9 rpg, 58 assists, 33 blocked shots, 75 steals, Tolentine HS/Bronx, N.Y.) Sealy blossomed right on schedule into the consistent all- round force that was expected when he came out of Tolentine HS a much celebrated All-New York City player on a national champion high school team.

He has scored in double figures 40 straight times dating back to his freshman year and is already over the 1,000-point career mark (1,015). Sealy has a chance to become only the second St. John's player (Chris Mullin is the other) to reach 2,000 career points. He was the second All-Team selection last year set a school record with his 75 steals and had a season-high of 29 points against Manhattan.

He averaged an incredible 38.4 minutes per game last year and led St. John's in scoring. He was 227-of-432 (.525) from the field and just 2-of-27 (.074) from three-point range. Sealy made .746 (159-of-213) of his free throws. He was third on the team behind Billy Singleton and Robert Werdann in rebounding. And ranked second behind Werdann in blocked shots. Some of his better scoring games against Big East competition were 26 points in a loss at Connecticut, 21 in a win at Georgetown, and 22 in a victory at Pitt. He had 13 rebounds against Pitt at home, 13 in the loss to Connecticut and 12 in a victory against Villanova.

Sealy possesses nearly the complete game for a small forward. He is very quick, a great leaper, conscientious on defense with terrific anticipation and good hands. Because he's a very quick jumper, Sealy plays taller than his size defensively. His biggest project is to work on the mid-range jumper he didn't need as a high school center. He improved on his jumper last season but could get better. Extremely strong for his size, Sealy runs the floor like a gazelle and can score of penetration with good inside moves. He also a consistent rebounding presence.

During the summer he led the New York River Side Church team, that won the Prince Junior Cup in Italy, in scoring (22.0 ppg) in rebounding (8.0 rpg) in the tournament.

This season, Sealy appears ready for an All-Big East major impact season. With the loss of Boo Harvey and Jayson Williams, he'll be asked to become the go-to 20-point per game player on offense. Sealy should become one to the premier forwards in all of college basketball.

BILLY SINGLETON (6-7, 235 lbs., SR, F, #33, 9.9 ppg, 6.9 rpg, 22 assists, 14 blocked shots, 34 steals, Adlai Stevenson HS/Bronx, N.Y.) The under rated Singleton plugged the Dike in exactly the spot needed last year. With Singleton starting 21 games at power forward in place of injured All-America Jayson Williams, the Redmen generally were able to avoid much noticeable dropoff. Singleton, who uses his large body effectively and intensely, made up for his lack of size with bulk and desire. Though not nearly the offense presence of Williams, he held his own on the boards and worked hard defensively. He finished the year second on the team in rebounding.

Singleton was certainly overmatched with some of the elite Big East big men with whom Williams might have coped better. However, he also came up with some big games against quality opposition. He had 19 points against Fordham, 13 rebounds on Houston's imposing front line, 16 points and 12 rebounds against Seaton Hall, and 10 rebounds against Georgetown's twin towers of the Dikemve Mutombo and Alonzo Mourning.

He averaged 30.2 minutes per game last season. Singleton made 116-of-241 field goals (.481). He missed all three of his three-point attempts and was 106-of-147 (.721) from the line. He did have a negative statistic, committing over three times as many turnovers as assists (74 turnovers to 22 assists).

As a sophomore, Singleton showed that he would not be intimidated by the beasts of the Big East. He took the ball right at Derrick Colman and scored a shot in his face that pulled off a big upset at Syracuse at Madison Square Garden. Singleton just cannot be intimidated inside and there are few consistently harder workers.

During the summer he was a member of the Big East team that toured Finland and the Soviet Union and averaged 9.7 points and 4.2 rebounds in 6 games.

In August, he underwent arthroscopic surgery to repair torn cartledge in his left knee. The same knee was operated on two years ago. St. John's trainer Ron Linfonte expects no additional problems from Singleton's knee.

CHUCK SPROLING (6-5, 180 lbs., JR, G, #22, 2.8 ppg, 1.6 rpg, 36 assists, 8 blocked shots, 36 steals, Manuel HS/Denver, Colo.) After sitting out his first year at St. John's Sproling has to be considered a disappointment his first year in uniform. He was looked to for some explosive perimeter offense but because he never seamed to find his outside shot, the rest of his games suffered.

Sproling had been a phenomenal high school player in Denver, averaging 29 points, 11 rebounds and 10 assists as senior at Manuel HS. He played closer to the basket in high school but there seamed little doubt that he had the shot and versatility to play off-guard at a major college level. He did show some strong stretches of defense last year, especially against Georgetown at Madison Square Garden. His season high was 13 points against the University of San Diego and he had 5 rebounds vs. DePaul. Sproling did not have much overall productivity given he got the opportunity to average 15 minutes a game and played in all 34 games. St. John's had an undersized backcourt that Sproling just could not provide the consistent offensive help Carnesecca expected.

For the season he was 35-of-104 (.337) from the field and 10-of-37 (27.0 percent) from three-point range. Sproling also was not impressive from the line as he was 16-of-28 (57.1 percent). He had 33 turnovers to go along with his 36 assists.

Perhaps what Sproling needs is a fresh start this season. Or, perhaps he won't be able to raise his game appropriately to what the Redmen need. Once again St. John's could have an undersized backcourt with a probable starting of 6-0 David Cain at the point and 6-2 Jason Buchanan at off-guard. As Sproling can be more consistent offensively and maintain the level of the rest of his games, the Redmen could use him dearly at off-guard.

He played, as did Robert Werdann, on a NIT sponsored team that compiled a 7-1 record against club teams in West Germany, France, and Switzerland over the summer. Sproling averaged 6.4 points, 4.6 assists and shot 27 percent from three-point range during the tour.

ROBERT WERDANN (6-11, 250 lbs., JR, C, #41, 9.7 ppg, 7.6 rpg, 27 assists, 66 blocked shots, 30 steals, Archbishop Molloy HS/Sunnyside Queens, N.Y.) Suddenly Werdann is a junior and college basketball is still waiting to see if he can concur his vulnerability to foul trouble and achieve enough consistency to fulfill the potential exhibited while playing with Kenny Anderson at Archbishop Molloy HS. Werdann has good mobility and some terrific low post moves but too often he was on the bench early with foul trouble or simply did not assert himself against quality opposition. He averaged over 3 fouls per game and was disqualified in 5 contests.

Werdann did lead St. John's in rebounding and blocked shots. He did have some productive outings (20 points against DePaul) but more often than not his better numbers were weighted against lessor opponents (20 points 16 rebound vs. Wright State for example). Of course, he's still learning. Werdann the son of a Queens fireman only began to seriously play as a high school junior and rapidly emerged as an outstanding big man. He was so impressive late in his high school career, that some veteran New York observers called him ''the next Keven McHale.''

He's an aggressive rebounder but needs to learn better decision making (such as when to go for the block) and improve his defensive footwork. Werdann set a St. John's record with 7 blocked shots against Hofstra this year he has to be looked to as *the man* game after game in the low post for the Redmen. Werdann has the ability to be a consistent scorer and be a big time rebounder. But he must continue to battle his old bugaboo-foul trouble-plus come to grips with his inconsistency. If he doesn't, Werdann could be ready for a 17 ppg, 10 rpg-type season. St. John's dearly needs Werdann to balloon.

Over the summer, Werdann played well for a NIT sponsored team that compiled a 7-1 record against club teams in France, Switzerland and West Germany. He was the team's second leading rebounder (6.8 rpg) before being sidelined by a broken left thumb. He is not expected to be adversely effected by the broken thumb this season.

''He did a great job rebounding and defending the big S,'' NIT coach Jack Powers told *Big East Briefs*. ''He didn't back down from anyone. The competition was very physical and he stayed right in there. He was very aggressive.''

★ NEWCOMERS ★

CARL BECKETT (6-4, 200 lbs., FR, G/F, #30, Christ the King HS/New York, N.Y.) Beckett was a medical register last year. As a senior on a very talented Christ the King HS team that was one of the best high school teams in the country, Beckett averaged 12.0 points, 8.0 rebounds and 4 blocked shots per game. He has a body an athletic ability (particularly for running the floor, leaping and pressure defense) to make an outstanding off-guard. Yet because his entire high school career was spent near the basket, Beckett as of now, doesn't put the ball on the floor or shoot well enough to play in the backcourt full time and he is more of a small forward now. Of course St. John's needs more help at the second guard spot than the small forward where Melik Sealy reigns supreme.

If Beckett applies himself to improving his guard skills, he has the all-round ability to help out in many ways: rebounding, defense, passing and taking the ball to the basket. He played on a great high school team with Khalid Reaves (Arizona), Robert Phelps (North Carolina) and Jamal Faulkner (Arizona State) and help Christ the King to New York State and New York City catholic high school athletic association championships in 1989.

Carnesecca claimed last year that Beckett reminded him of former Kansas State All-America and current golden state warrior Rich Richmond. Although Beckett has a long way to go to fulfilling that praise, and indicates just how outstanding his athletic ability is. In June he played on a Big East team that traveled to Finland and the Soviet Union. Beckett averaged 8.5 points and 3.7 rebounds over the 6-game tour.

SERGIO LUYK (6-8, 200 lbs., FR, F, #3, 23.5 ppg, 14.5 rpg, 5.9 apg, Madrid, Spain & University Heights Academy/Hopkinsville, Ky.) Luyk finished third in the state of Kentucky's Mr. Basketball voting and was a first All-State pick. He was born and raised in Madrid, Spain and arrived in the United States three years ago as an exchange student. His father, Clifford Luyk was an all-sec player at Florida. The elder Luyk played at Florida from 1959-1962 and is one of the Gators all- time leading scorers and rebounders. Originally from Syracuse, N.Y. Clifford Luyk, had a long pro career in Spain and served as an assistant coach for the famed Real Madrid team last year, working for then head coach George Karl, former North Carolina Tar Heal who coached in the NBA at Cleveland and Golden State.

''He can do a lot of things,'' Carnesecca told *Big East Briefs*. ''He can shoot, he can pass, he handles the ball well. He'll give us some flexibility, another weapon.''

Hoop Scoop, a Louisville based publication, ranked Luyk as No. 5 senior in the State of Kentucky last year. "Remember this one-he'll play in the pros some-day. Complete big time wing player with good ball handling skills and 20 range. Jumps well and has improved his quickness. Needs a little strength," said Tom Goings of *Hoop Scoop*

Those who know Luyk well believe he can one day even play at off-guard in college. With his shooting ability and versatility, Luyk can be a contributor as a freshman.

SHAWNELLE SCOTT (6-11, 240 lbs., FR, C, #42, 17.0 ppg, 9.0 rpg, All Hallows HS/Bronx, N.Y.) Scott is coordinated, talented and mobile for his size. Under the careful nurturing of All Hallows coach John Carey, he was just beginning to shed the baby fat and rough edges from his game in high school. How quickly he'll be ready for high level college basketball at the Big East level was uncertain. So was how much of a fire burns inside him. Supported by surrounding cast, Scott had spurts of excellent pivot play but consistent intensity and the dominance that should have been generated by his height and skills escaped him.

Scott was ranked as a No. 72 senior prospect at the completion of last season by *All Star Sports*. Scott should be able to push Werdann in practice and could be an influential player in the future. But he's probably a year away from being a consistent contributor for the Redmen.

★ QUESTIONS ★

Robert Werdann? If Werdann can finally become the major league type inside presence, St. John's will be in for a great year.

Outside Shooting? With Boo Harvey gone, not a proven perimeter shooter of any kind is in the bunch.

Backcourt? Junior Jason Buchanan is the only quality experienced returnee and he has been at the point where he played two seasons ago than second guard where he didn't shoot well enough last year. Sophomore David Cain, who was used sparingly as a freshman, will have to take up over the point or Buchanan may have to play the position again. Junior Chuck Sproling needs to rediscover his game and take over the guard spot. Registered freshman Carl Beckett is a great athlete who has to adjust to the backcourt role after playing close to the basket in high school. And then there is freshman Sergio Luyk who is potentially the best outside shooter on the team. All in all, it is a very unsettled situation in the St. John's backcourt.

★ STRENGTHS ★

Looie! Sixteen NCAA Tournament appearances, and six NIT bids in the 22-year Carnesecca era means the Redmen never have to say their sorry in March. His

record speaks for itself.

Malik Sealy! One of the premier players in the Big East, Sealy is a consummate forward who keeps working on and improving his game. If he can command the mid-range open shot, he'll be and All-America candidate.

Front line depth! Robert Werdann, Malik Sealy, Billy Singleton, Sean Muto, Sergio Luyk, Carl Beckett, maybe even Shawnell Scott . . . that's a lot of players who can be useful near the hoop for St. John's.

★ BLUE RIBBON ANALYSIS ★

Talk about a team with inverted offense! Opponents of St. John's might set and unofficial NCAA record for sagging zone defenses if Lou Carnesecca doesn't find someone who can score reliably outside the lane. St. John's has a lot of players who can do many things, but shooting the basketball from mid to long range does not appear to be foremost in any of their repertoire, save for freshman Sergio Luyk. Chuck Sproling, if he can rediscover his high school touch, might be one remote hope. Luyk could be another.

Junior forward Malik Sealy represents an outstanding offensive foundation to build around. Senior forward Billy Singleton will work hard every night in rebound. Boo Harvey wound up an outstanding point guard and the Redmen with miss his leadership and clutch shooting. He could be replaced by junior Jason Buchanan, who played the point in Harvey's absence two years ago, but what the Redmen really need is for sophomore David Cain to step up and breathe some life into the offense. Whether he's up to the task maturity and control-wise remain to be seen. Sproling is also a huge question mark. So, in a different way, is junior center Robert Werdann. He must turn is up a notch and stay on the floor long enough to provide reliable offense. Werdann has the potential to be a mobile, high scoring pivot man of impact.

Redshirt freshman Carl Beckett has the ability to be a sleeper. And Luyk, a native of Madrid, Spain, could have impact right away. Both will certainly get the chance. Senior center Sean Muto can give quality minutes as a backup pivot man and take some of the pressure of Werdann.

Carnesecca always finds a way to make the Redmen at least respectable, if not better. This year many things will have to come together for St. John's to make a serious serge for the Big East title. However, the Big East is wide open this year as there appears to be no monster team, such as Georgetown in '85 and several other teams that have braced this great conference-so there is hope for the Redmen.

Unless the sky falls in over the St. John's campus in the Jamaica section of Queens, the Redmen, as usual, should attract a NCAA Tournament invitation.

LAST SEASON

#North Carolina A&T	64-57	Rutgers	89-77
#Houston	76-69	Villanova	83-69
##DePaul	53-52	@Seton Hall	90-81OT
##Kansas	66-57	Providence	77-74
###Univ. of San Diego	74-59	@Georgetown	63-62
###Wright State (OH)	76-56	DePaul	77-74
*North Carolina State	58-67	@Pitt	76-75
Hofstra (NY)	58-47	Seton Hall	65-71
@Fordham	68-60	**Villanova	60-70
Manhattan	68-52	***Temple	81-65
Niagara	83-51	***Duke	72-76
Howard University	77-65		
Davidson	83-65	@ Road Games	
Connecticut	93-62	# Dodge NIT	
@Boston College	77-65	## Dodge NIT Final Four, Madison	
@Syracuse	72-81	Square Garden, New York, NY	
Pitt	71-70	### Joe Lapchik Memorial Tourna-	
@Villanova	64-58	ment, Jamaica, NY	
Boston College	65-59	* ACC/Big East Challenge, Greens-	
@Providence	83-75	boro, NC	
@Connecticut	58-72	** Big East Tournament, Madison	
Syracuse	65-70	Square Garden, New York, NY	
Georgetown	67-74	*** NCAA Tournament, Atlanta, GA	

NOTES: St. John's will face Monmouth in the first round of the Joe Lapchick Memorial Tournament. The Redmen's scheduled first round foe in the Cougar Classic is George Mason . . . the actual date of the game at Connecticut (Jan. 12 or 13) will be determined at a later date, probably after the season starts, by CBS . . . St. John's signee Lee Green, a 6-3 New York native who prepped at Chesire Academy in Connecticut, is not academically eligible and will sit out this year. He will have three years of eligibility beginning next season . . . Lamont Middleton, a 6-6 forward

1990-91 ST. JOHN'S SCHEDULE

Nov.	23-24	Joe Lapchik Memorial Tournament
	30	@Niagara
Dec.	5	##Georgia Tech
	7-8	###Cougar Classic
	11	Brooklyn College (NY)
	15	Howard University
	22	Fordham
	27	High Five America (Exhibition)
Jan.	2	@Syracuse
	5	Boston College
	9	@Seton Hall
12 or 13		@Connecticut
	15	Providence
	19	Pitt
	22	*Connecticut
	26	@Villanova
	30	@Georgetown
Feb.	2	*Seton Hall
	5	*Villanova
	9	@Providence
	13	@Boston College
Feb.	16	@Pitt
	20	*Syracuse
	23	*Notre Dame
	25	*Georgetown
Mar.	2	*DePaul
	7-10	*Big East Tournament

@ Road Games
# Jamaica, NY (Central Connecticut, Davidson & Monmouth)
ACC/Big East Challenge, Landover, MD
Provo, UT (Brigham Young, Eastern Kentucky, & George Mason)
* Madison Square Garden, New York, NY

from Walton HS in the Bronx, N.Y. who played two years at the University of Hartford, has transferred to St. John's. He averaged 19 points and eight rebounds per game last year and was a first-team All North Atlantic Conference selection. He will have two years of eligibility beginning next season, however, the St. John's admissions department recommended that Middleton concentrate on his academics while sitting out the season and he isn't permitted to practice with the Redmen this year.

SOUTHERN MISSISSIPPI

LAST SEASON: 20-12
CONFERENCE RECORD: 9-5
STARTERS LOST: 1
STARTERS RETURNING: 4
CONFERENCE: METRO
LOCATION: HATTIESBURG, MS
HOME FLOOR: REED
  GREEN COLISEUM (8,095)
NICKNAME: GOLDEN EAGLES
COLORS: BLACK AND GOLD

★ COACH'S PROFILE ★

M.K. TURK (Record at Southern Mississippi, 212-183. Career record 329-226) Entering his 15th season at Southern Mississippi, Turk is second behind Louisville's Denny Crum in longevity among Metro Conference coaches. In fact, Turk and Crum are far and away the leaders in longevity among Metro Conference coaches. The third spot, behind Turk, in longevity among Metro Conference coaches is held by Pat Kennedy of Florida State and South Carolina's George Felton, who are each entering their fifth season at their respective schools. That figure shows just how volatile the college coaching profession has become when fifth-year coaches are third in a league in longevity. It also shows just how entrenched Turk has become at Southern Mississippi.

There is no doubt that the Southern Mississippi program has improved significantly under Turk's reign. In his four years at Southern Mississippi, Turk has guided the Golden Eagles to three appearances in the NIT and one, last season, in the NCAA tournament. In 1987, Turk led the Golden Eagles to the NIT title and it was the first time ever a Mississippi Division I team had won a national championship in basketball. He was named NIT Coach of the Year in 1987.

The Bradwell, Ky., native is a graduate of Copiah-Lincoln JC in Wesson, Miss., and holds a pair of degrees from Livingston University (Ala.). Following his graduation in 1964 from Livingston, Turk remained on to work for a Master's Degree, left in 1965 to spend two years coaching in the Cobb County (Ga.) school system and then returned to his alma mater to coach the freshman team and to complete work on his Master's in Physical Education. From Livingston, Turk returned to Copiah-Lincoln where he spent six years as athletic director, head basketball coach and chairman of the Department of Health and Physical Education. His 117-43 record at Copiah-Lincoln included a 76-13 record in his final three seasons. Turk's teams won Mississippi JC titles in 1972-73 and '73-74 and finished as runners-up in 1971-72. Copiah-Lincoln also won the Region VII junior college title in 1973-74. He then moved on to Memphis State in 1974-75 where he served as an assistant coach for two seasons before taking the Southern Mississippi post.

"Offensively, we're an up-tempo team. We play the fast break and use a motion offense. Defensively, we play a moderate pressure defense. Basically, our whole league (Metro Conference) is up-tempo," Turk said of his coaching style.

Turk took over a struggling Southern Mississippi program when he came to Hattiesburg in 1976. His first Southern Mississippi team proceeded to go 11-16. However, the Golden Eagles were 13-12 the following year and he has had few losing seasons since. His 1980-81 team was 20-7 and lost in the first round of the NIT to Holy Cross. In 1982 Southern Mississippi joined the Metro Conference and Turk believes that move has played a major role in the success of the program.

"We can never sell short the fact that the most important thing that's happened in the history of our athletic program came when we joined the Metro Conference," Turk said. "It gave us instant credibility. And now, that we've been able to climb, we've added to that credibility."

"As an Independent, we had transfers and juco players. It was so difficult to recruit, but we eventually ended up putting together a good team.

"When you're an Independent, it's so difficult to schedule. If you're decent, no one wants to play you, especially at your place. If you're lousy, good teams would love to play you, but you don't want to get your head beat in. Either way, you can't win," he explained.

"But once we got into the Metro, we could take a totally new approach. We had a new product to sell. We'd be on television in a big-time basketball league, one of the nation's best conferences. We'd be playing in some of the nation's great arenas, and we'd be getting more media attention than ever before."

Probably the most important achievement of Turk's reign at Southern Mississippi has come in recruiting. He has been able to go head-to-head with in-state rivals Mississippi and Mississippi State of the SEC in recruiting wars. Turk has definitely made Southern Mississippi a factor in recruiting the top players in the Magnolia State. Three years ago he successfully recruited Clarence Weatherspoon, a junior on this year's Golden Eagle team, who is the best player in the modern era at Southern Mississippi. Turk feels if he can get just one or two of the best players in Missis-

ippi every year, he can sustain the recent success of the program.

This is a key year at Southern Mississippi. Last season the Golden Eagles advanced to the finals of the Metro Conference tournament for the first time and received an NCAA tournament bid. The tournament bid was a first at Southern Mississippi in decades. This season, usual Metro Conference favorite Louisville is extremely vulnerable. Simply, Southern Mississippi has never had a better chance to win the Metro Conference title. A Metro Conference title would mean a great deal to this program which is rising fast but does not have great tradition.

★ PLAYERS NOT RETURNING ★

MARCUS CROWELL (6-6, G/F, 9.1 ppg, 3.6 rpg, 93 assists, 16 blocked shots, 30 steals) Crowell is the only letterman not returning from last year. He started all 32 games and was fifth on the team in scoring. Crowell was the only Southern Mississippi starter not to average in double figures last year. He was third on the team in assists, steals and blocked shots. Crowell averaged 26 minutes per game. There is no doubt that Crowell was a capable small forward for Southern Mississippi. However, Turk is confident Crowell can be replaced.

★ RETURNING PLAYERS ★

DARRIN CHANCELLOR (6-5, 185 lbs., SR, G, #23, 17.8 ppg, 3.6 rpg, 98 assists, 5 blocked shots, 30 steals, Callaway HS/Jackson, Miss.) Clarence Weatherspoon receives almost all of the ink at Southern Mississippi, so few people realize that Chancellor was actually the Golden Eagles' leading scorer last year. He nudged out Weatherspoon by one point —570 points to 569. He is one of the top guards in the Metro Conference and was the sixth best scorer in the league last year. Chancellor also finished sixth in the Metro Conference in field goal percentage (.533) as well.

For the year, Chancellor also made 23-of-66 three-point field goals (.348) and was 110-of-154 (.714) from the line. Chancellor was second on the team in assists and third in steals. He led the Golden Eagles in minutes played with 1,203 minutes for an average of 38 per game.

He is an excellent scorer who can put the ball on the floor and pull up quickly off the dribble for his shot. Chancellor has improved as a perimeter shooter since coming to Southern Mississippi. He is a solid, key player in the Golden Eagle attack.

Last season Chancellor was remarkably consistent. He scored below his 17.8 average in only nine of 32 games and never two games in a row. He had 24 points against Virginia Tech and 26 vs. Arkansas State. Chancellor also had 11 rebounds against Arkansas State.

Last season, he also led Southern Mississippi in field goals made (218) and three-point field goals made (23). Chancellor's .527 career shooting ranks sixth best all-time at Southern Mississippi. His 204 career assists also ranks tenth at the school, and with another season like he had in 1989-90, Chancellor could become one of the top three scorers in Southern Mississippi history.

There is no doubt that Darrin Chancellor is one of the more underrated guards in the South.

DALLAS DALE (6-2, 175 lbs., JR, G, #3, 1.5 ppg, 0.6 rpg, 29 assists, 3 steals, Denham Springs HS/Denham Springs, La.) Dale played in 25 games last year for a total of 143 minutes, close to an average of six minutes per game. He is a reserve point guard who is an outside shooting threat, is smart and makes few mistakes. Last year Dale was 12-of-28 (.429) from the field and 7-of-17 (.412) from three-point range. Dale made 7-of-11 field goals (.636).

His top scoring game was six points against South Carolina.

Dale's role is expected to be similar this year. Southern Mississippi has a deep team with 11 returning lettermen and two new guards.

DARON JENKINS (6-11, 215 lbs., SR, C, #32, 13.9 ppg, 8.6 rpg, 28 assists, 86 blocked shots, 23 steals, Mendenhall HS/Mendenhall, Miss. & Copiah-Lincoln JC/Wesson, Miss.) In his first year in uniform at Southern Mississippi, Jenkins played well. He wasn't always as consistent as Turk wanted, but Jenkins finished second on the team behind All-America Clarence Weatherspoon in rebounding and led the Golden Eagles in blocked shots. He also was third on the team in scoring.

There is no doubt that Jenkins had a major impact on the Golden Eagles last year. In 1988-89, when he was sitting out at Southern Mississippi, the Golden Eagles were 10-17 and tied for last in the Metro Conference. Last season, Southern Mississippi was one of the most improved teams in the South, and the entire country, finishing 20-12, tied for second in the Metro Conference, advanced to the finals of the conference tournament and earned an NCAA tournament bid. Clarence Weatherspoon had another great year, Darrin Chancellor was one of the finest guards in the Metro Conference, but Jenkins also was extremely influential.

He controlled games with his shot blocking ability. Jenkins blocked 10 shots against Auburn, setting a Metro Conference record and tying the Southern Mississippi record. His total of 86 blocked shots in 1989-90 was the highest single season total ever at Southern Mississippi and places him third all-time on the career ladder. He also led the Metro Conference in blocked shots and finished No. 18 nationally in that category. Jenkins was also the No. 2 rebounder in the Metro Conference behind Weatherspoon.

He scored a season-high of 26 points against Appalachian State and grabbed a career-high 15 rebounds against Northwestern State. Jenkins made .517 (178-of-344) from the field and .690 (87-of-126) from the free throw line.

Jenkins is one of the most mobile and agile big men in the country. He jumps well and has excellent skills. He could use more strength and consistency but no one can question the impact he had last year.

Southern Mississippi is a very talented team. Junior All-America pick Clarence Weatherspoon has to be considered, going into the season, the top player in the Metro Conference. Darrin Chancellor is one of the top guards in the conference and Jenkins has to be considered the best big man in the Metro this year.

RUSSELL JOHNSON (6-2, 215 lbs., SR, G, #22, 12.0 ppg, 3.8 rpg, 180 assists, 3 blocked shots, 34 steals, North Natchez HS/Natchez, Miss. & Copiah-Lincoln JC/Wesson, Miss.) The quality on the Southern Mississippi roster does not end with Darrin Chancellor, Daron Jenkins or All-America selection Clarence Weatherspoon. Senior point guard Russell Johnson also was one of the premier players in the Metro Conference at his position. Last season Johnson finished third in the Metro Conference in assists and finished second in steals. He led Southern Mississippi in assists and started all 32 games. He also averaged 36 minutes per game and started all 32 games.

From the field Johnson was 127-of-241 (.527) and 19-of-51 (.373) from three-point range. He made 112-of-148 free throws (.757). Johnson was guilty of 110 turnovers for an average of over three per game.

Johnson and Daron Jenkins were teammates at Copiah-Lincoln HS and they certainly had a big impact on Southern Mississippi last year. The Golden Eagles won 10 more games in 1989-90 than in the previous year and went from a tie for last to a tie for second in the Metro Conference. Johnson did a great job of getting the ball to Southern Mississippi's scorers. He runs the team very well and possesses good speed and quickness. At 215 pounds, Johnson is also one of the heaviest and strongest point guards around.

He had a season-high of 29 points against Southwestern Louisiana and dished out 11 assists in a win over Auburn and 10 in a victory over Memphis State. His 180 assists were the third highest single season total in Southern Mississippi history. He also was eighth in the Metro Conference in free throw percentage. Johnson rebounds well for a point guard and scores well enough to keep defenses honest. With Johnson and Chancellor on the perimeter, defenses can't pack it in against Southern Mississippi.

JEROME JONES (6-4, 210 lbs., JR, G/F, #20, 5.5 ppg, 2.1 rpg, 31 assists, 3 blocked shots, 15 steals, Stone County HS/Wiggins, Miss.) Jones appeared in 32 games last season. He came off the bench and was Southern Mississippi's top reserve scorer. He made 65-of-172 field goals (.378). Jones was 21-of-76 (.276) from three-point range and 26-of-40 (.650) from the line.

Jones possesses excellent leaping ability and can play either small forward or big guard. He averaged 14 minutes per game and scored a career-high of 12 points against both Tennessee Tech and Marshall. His 21 three-pointers were second best on the team. Jones should be one of Southern Mississippi's top three-point threats.

He is out of the same high school as third-team *Blue Ribbon* High School All-America selection Bubba Wilson. However, unfortunately for Southern Mississippi fans, it looks as though the 6-10 Wilson is not headed for Hattiesburg and probably will go to college elsewhere.

"Jerome has worked hard in the off-season to gain more strength. He is an excellent shooter who should play a lot against zones," Turk said.

RICKY JONES (6-7, 180 lbs., SO, F, #33, Wingfield HS/Jackson, Miss.) Jones was redshirted last year and he appeared in only five games two years ago as a freshman. He averaged 2.0 points and 1.2 rebounds in limited action as a freshman in 1988-89. His season-high of four points came against North Texas and South Carolina.

Despite the fact that Jones saw limited action as a freshman on a 10-17 team, Turk believes this season he will be a much bigger factor. "Ricky is a thin kid with long arms," Turk said. "He is a shot blocker who can shoot and I think he'll help us."

JOHN LACEY (6-7, 195 lbs., SO, F/C, #31, 2.0 ppg, 1.7 rpg, 5 assists, 2 blocked shots, 4 steals, Quitman HS/Shubuta, Miss.) Lacey played in 26 games, starting none, for an average of eight minutes per game. He was basically the Golden Eagles' seventh man last year.

Lacey shot the ball well last year making 21-of-39 field goals (.538), but he was just 11-of-24 (.458) from the line.

He scored a season-high of seven points against Northwestern State and Tulane. Lacey had a season-high five rebounds against both McNeese State and Louisville. He not only shoots the ball well but also possesses good all-around skills. Southern Mississippi coaches feel Lacey just has to continue to get stronger and gain more experience in order to be an outstanding college player.

Lacey's role is expected to expand this year. He will play a great deal as a backup power forward to All-America Clarence Weatherspoon and as the first reserve to starting center Daron Jenkins.

NEWTON MEALER (6-7, 215 lbs., SO, F, #24, 1.2 ppg, 0.8 rpg, 2 assists, Briarcrest HS/Memphis, Tenn.) Mealer is basically the "City Slicker" on the Southern Mississippi team. The Memphis native is from a larger city than any of the Golden Eagles. Southern Mississippi is comprised of basically small town kids.

Mealer was used sparingly last year appearing in just 13 games for a total of 46 minutes. He was 6-of-17 (.353) from the field and 4-of-5 (.800) at the line.

He scored a season-high of six points against Northwestern State and had two rebounds against both South Carolina and Arkansas State.

Mealer is fundamentally sound, works hard and is an effective open shooter. He is considered at least a year away from becoming a more important player in this talent packed program.

RON REMBERT (6-4, 180 lbs., SO, G, #21, 1.7 ppg, 1.3 rpg, 7 assists, 1 steal, Keith HS/Orrville, Ala.) Rembert came off the bench in 26 games last year and averaged six minutes per game. He was 19-of-51 (.373) from the field and just 4-of-17 (.235) from three-point range. Rembert also struggled from the line making 3-of-10 (.300) of his field goals. He also had three times as many turnovers (21) as assists (7).

Southern Mississippi's only left-handed player, Rembert had a season-high of six points and six rebounds against Northwestern State. He also had six points against Metro Conference rival Louisville.

Coming into college, Rembert was billed as an exceptional shooter. He averaged 28 points and 10 rebounds as a senior at Keith HS in Orrville, Ala., where he was also an All-State performer. A younger brother of former Alabama-Birmingham player Larry Rembert, he is considered a skilled player who should get much better in the years to come. Turk is confident that Rembert can generate offense at the Metro Conference level and expects him to be a more important player this year for the Golden Eagles.

CHARLIE SULLIVAN (6-3, 190 lbs., JR, G/F, #12, 0.0 ppg, 0.3 rpg, Seminary HS/Seminary, Miss.) Sullivan saw limited action last year appearing in only eight games for a total of 12 minutes. He did not score during the season. He was hampered by a knee injury that caused him to redshirt the 1988-89 season.

In his freshman year at Southern Mississippi, 1987-88, Sullivan played in seven games and scored two points. He did score 2,332 points in his career at Seminary (Miss.) HS. He is not expected to be a major factor this year.

CLARENCE WEATHERSPOON (6-7, 240 lbs., JR, F, #35, 17.8 ppg, 11.6 rpg, 28 assists, 45 blocked shots, 35 steals, Motley HS/Columbus, Miss.) "You could write a book about what Clarence has accomplished in his first two years here," Turk said about his star player.

The first line of the "Weatherspoon Edition" would have to read that he is unquestionably the finest player in the Metro Conference. He was named player of the year in the Metro Conference in voting by the league media and coaches. The announcement of that award came just prior to the Metro Conference tournament. Weatherspoon followed the announcement with a spectacular performance in the Metro Conference tournament. He had 18 points against Virginia Tech in the opening round, one short of a Metro Conference tournament record of 19. In the semifinals, Weatherspoon grabbed 13 rebounds, scored 14 points and blocked three shots as Southern Mississippi beat Cincinnati for the third time. Finally, against Louisville and the Cardinals' seven-foot center Felton Spencer (the sixth overall pick in the 1990 NBA draft), Weatherspoon grabbed 16 rebounds and scored 19 points. He set a Metro Conference record for the most rebounds in the conference tournament with 47, shattering the old mark of 35 set by Bob Miller of Cincinnati.

Weatherspoon is only the third player in Metro Conference history to win the conference rebounding title two years in a row. Also, his .605 field goal percentage ranked second in the league and 20th in the country. Weatherspoon was also second in the Metro Conference in free throws made with 155, third in free throws attempted with 223, and 10th in scoring. He finished the year ranked 10th in the nation in rebounding.

"Clarence Weatherspoon of Southern Mississippi excited me as much as any player I saw this season. The reason? He does things I've seen from only one other player —Charles Barkley," wrote Keith Drum in *Basketball Times*.

"Weatherspoon is at least 6-6 and extremely strong around the basket. He needs more development of his game, and he doesn't yet have Barkley's arrogance, which might be good. But there are enough similarities to whet the appetite."

Weatherspoon received national attention for his showing in the tryouts for the U.S. National team. He survived the first few cuts and was on the team for the Goodwill Games in Seattle before being cut before the U.S. team traveled to Argentina for the World Basketball Championship.

"He's better than reports indicated," U.S. National team coach Mike Krzyzewski, of Duke, told Steve Wieberg of *USA Today*. "He's a real quick jumper, maybe the quickest jumper in camp. And he's certainly a strong jumper."

"Even though he's not 6-10, Weatherspoon plays very big," Krzyzewski said. "He can play good post defense."

Weatherspoon has started all 59 games since coming to Southern Mississippi. It is also no accident that the Golden Eagles made their first ever NCAA tournament bid last year with him leading the way. He was a second-team All-Metro Conference selection as a freshman and was named Conference freshman of the year. He had 28 points against Northeast Louisiana for his season high. Weatherspoon also had 17 rebounds against Bucknell, 12 rebounds vs. Auburn and twice had 16 rebounds.

"If you look up the word 'physical' in a dictionary, you'll probably find Weatherspoon's picture right beside the definition," said Bucknell coach Charlie Woollum.

Weatherspoon has a great work ethic and is never satisfied with his performance. He not only has great physical strength and is a quick leaper but Weatherspoon also has the most important attribute a rebounder can possess —an unsatiable desire to hit the boards.

Turk calls Weatherspoon "an unusual young man . . . well, you never know he is around except for the good things you hear about him — on the floor and off the floor.

"He never misses a class, he does well in the classroom. He is very quiet, meek and mild-mannered off the floor. But when he walks on to the basketball floor, his personality changes. He becomes the most intense, enthusiastic, competitive young man I've ever coached."

There is no doubt that Weatherspoon's strength is his chief asset. He will rebound against anyone in the country. If he expands his game some on the perimeter, both in ballhandling and shooting, he can be a star one day on the NBA level. There are few around with his combination of strength, agility, quick leaping ability and work habits. It is easy to see why Turk considers him to be the rare player who comes along very seldom in a coach's career.

★ NEWCOMERS ★

JOE COURTNEY (6-8, 240 lbs., JR, F/C, #42, Callaway HS/Jackson, Miss.) Courtney was a teammate of Darrin Chancellor at Callaway HS in Jackson, Miss. He is being reunited with Chancellor after spending two years at Mississippi State. As a sophomore at Mississippi State, Courtney averaged 3.1 points, 3.3 rebounds and handed out two assists, blocked two shots and recorded two steals. His best scoring game at Mississippi State was 19 points against Southeastern Louisiana and 16 against Georgia.

At Mississippi State and in high school, Courtney was a center and power forward. However, Turk believes Courtney has the capability to play small forward and will try him there. He has a soft shooting touch that may be exploited at small forward.

Courtney should get significant playing time in his first season at Southern Mississippi. He will make an already strong Southern Mississippi frontcourt even more powerful.

JOE DUNN (6-5, 190 lbs., FR, G/F, #25, 27.5 ppg, 11.5 rpg, Berry HS/Berry, Ala.) Dunn is one of two freshmen recruits. He was a first team Alabama Class 2A All-State selection and once scored 51 points in a high school game. He holds the Berry HS record for career scoring with 2,233 points.

He is an excellent outside shooter and a smart player. Dunn had a perfect 4.0 GPA in high school.

Southern Mississippi is a very deep, talented and experienced team. Therefore, Dunn is not expected to be a key contributor this year. However, Turk thinks that he can be a quality player at this level a few years from now.

BERNARD HASLETT (6-3, 180 lbs., FR, G, #11, 37.5 ppg, 12.5 rpg, 6.2 apg, Vaiden HS/Vaiden, Miss.) Haslett was the Mississippi player of the year in 1989-90. He can play both point and off-guard and has tremendous three-point range. Haslett scored a career-high of 69 points in one game as a senior. Over his three years at Vaiden HS, he scored 3,074 points.

Turk expects this sizzling outside shooter to help immediately as a freshman. He feels that one of Southern Mississippi's big weaknesses last year was a lack of a consistent long range threat. Darrin Chancellor was the team's top three-point shooter, among the regulars, and he made only .348 and connected on just 23 treys for the season. If Haslett can provide some consistent perimeter shooting, Southern Mississippi should take the Metro Conference crown. If Haslett comes through, opposing teams will find it very difficult to concentrate on Weatherspoon, Chancellor, Jenkins and Johnson who all scored in double figures last year.

★ QUESTIONS ★

Interior defense? Even though Daron Jenkins led the Metro Conference in blocked shots with 86 last year, Turk still questions his team's interior defense.

Consistent perimeter shooting? Southern Mississippi may have a big time long distance shooter in freshman Bernard Haslett, however, none of the returnees exactly shot the lights out from long distance last year.

★ STRENGTHS ★

Clarence Weatherspoon! Not only has he led the Metro Conference in rebounding the last two years, but Weatherspoon is one of the true dominant, impact players on the national level. Last year's Metro Conference's player of the year, Weatherspoon is capable of carrying a team on his back during crunch time against the top teams on the schedule.

Offensive potential! Southern Mississippi should be a big time offensive team this year. Four players return who averaged in double figures last year and freshman Bernard Haslett could be the top three-point threat on the team. Not only does Southern Mississippi have an explosive offensive game, but the Golden Eagles also understand their offense and have good shot selection.

The inside power game with Weatherspoon, Jenkins and others!

Experience! This is a team dominated by upperclassmen. Four starters are returning and three are seniors. Only one freshman is expected to see significant playing time.

★ BLUE RIBBON ANALYSIS ★

Southern Mississippi was one of the most improved teams in the country last year. The Golden Eagles went from 10-17 and a tie for last in the Metro Conference in 1988-89 to 20-12, a tie for second in the conference and an NCAA tournament bid in 1989-90. The NCAA tournament bid was the first in school history. The Golden Eagles also took Louisville to the brink in the finals of the Metro Conference tournament before losing by three points.

Coach M.K. Turk enters his 15th season at Southern Mississippi with a team that should be the best in school history. Junior forward Clarence Weatherspoon has led the Metro Conference in rebounding in each of his first two years at Southern Mississippi and was the conference MVP last year. He gained additional experience with the U.S. National team over the summer and deserves to be recognized as one of the elite players in the country. Weatherspoon can literally dominate a game against any team in the country due to his rebounding prowess, great strength, quick leaping ability and all-out intensity. Some sportswriters have compared him to Charles Barkley.

Senior guard Darrin Chancellor averaged 17.8 points per game and is one of the premier guards in the Metro Conference. Senior center Daron Jenkins could use more consistency, but he still averaged 13.9 points, 8.6 rebounds and blocked 86 shots in his first year in uniform. There is no reason why Jenkins cannot be the best big man in the Metro Conference this year. Senior point guard Russell Johnson also played a key role last year as he handed out 180 assists to go with his 12.0 points per game average.

Only one starter and letterman is gone from last year's 20-game winner. Southern Mississippi has 11 lettermen returning. The returnees are supplemented by 6-8, 240-pound center/forward Joe Courtney, a transfer from Mississippi State, and hot shooting freshman Bernard Haslett, who averaged 37.5 points per game last year and was the Mississippi player of the year.

If Southern Mississippi can play better defense, especially on the interior, the Golden Eagles should win the Metro Conference. Southern Mississippi should be close to unstoppable offensively. Four players return who averaged in double figures last year and if Haslett is as good as advertised, there is no way opposing defenses can key on Weatherspoon or any other individual player.

Southern Mississippi is also an experienced team dominated by upperclassmen as there are three seniors in the starting lineup. The nation is finally beginning to realize how good Weatherspoon is and with the Golden Eagles coming off an NCAA tournament appearance, the program has never been positioned to receive as much national exposure.

There is no reason why this should not be a big year at Southern Mississippi. Not only should Weatherspoon have another great season, but the Golden Eagles are a lock to head back to the NCAA tournament for the second year in a row. Southern Mississippi is our pick to win the Metro Conference.

LAST SEASON		1990-91 SOUTHERN MISSISSIPPI SCHEDULE		
#LSU	80-91	Nov.	30	#Alabama
Tennessee Tech	95-78	Dec.	3	Hawaii-Loa
@Northeast Louisiana	85-81		6	@Tennessee Tech
@Marshall	76-74		15	Northeast Louisiana
@Tennessee-Chattanooga	66-69		28-29	##Cowboy Shootout
##Bucknell	78-71	Jan.	5	Florida State
##Auburn	84-73		10	@South Carolina
Northwestern State	96-67		12	@Virginia Tech
@Florida State	82-113		17	Tulane
@South Alabama	83-91		19	Memphis State
Virginia Tech	87-85		21	Texas-Pan American
@Memphis State	77-93		24	@Louisville
Arkansas State	85-65		26	@Cincinnati
Appalachian State	96-91	Feb.	2	Louisville
Southwestern Louisiana	106-104OT		4	@Appalachian State
@New Orleans	75-77OT		7	Virginia Tech
@Cincinnati	83-76		9	@Memphis State
@Louisville	88-105		11	@McNeese State
Florida State	84-72		14	South Alabama
South Carolina	82-65		16	South Carolina
@Virginia Tech	93-76		18	@Texas-Pan American
Memphis State	86-82		20	@Cincinnati
Tulane	80-71		26	@Florida State
@South Carolina	62-74		28	Southeastern Louisiana
@McNeese State	60-62	Mar.	2	@Tulane
Cincinnati	70-63		7-9	*Metro Conference
@Tulane	92-88			Tournament
Louisville	71-73			
*Virginia Tech	81-67	@ Road Games		
*Cincinnati	75-63	# Birmingham, AL		
*Louisville	80-83	## Casper, WY (Holy Cross, Northern		
**La Salle	63-79	Arizona & Wyoming)		
		* Roanoke, VA		

@ Road Games
# Dodge NIT
Blue Angel Classic, Pensacola, FL
* Metro Conference Tournament, Biloxi, MS
** NCAA Tournament, Hartford, CT

NOTES: Southern Mississippi's first round opponent in the Cowboy Shootout in Casper, Wyo., is Holy Cross . . . the Golden Eagles' opening round game with Alabama, in Birmingham, is one of the better early season matchups in the entire country . . . Southern Mississippi defeated Cincinnati in all three meetings last year. However, the Golden Eagles lost all three games with Louisville and also lost both games with the Cardinals in 1988-89 . . . the Golden Eagles are truly Mississippi's team as 10 of 14 players are in-state products.

STANFORD

LAST SEASON: 18-12
CONFERENCE RECORD: 9-9
STARTERS LOST: 0
STARTERS RETURNING: 5
CONFERENCE: PACIFIC-10
LOCATION: PALO ALTO, CA
HOME FLOOR: MAPLES
   PAVILION (7,500)
NICKNAME: CARDINAL
COLORS: CARDINAL AND WHITE

★ COACH'S PROFILE ★

MIKE MONTGOMERY (Record at Stanford, 80-44. Career record, 234-121) When Mike Montgomery was hired as Stanford's head basketball on April 25, 1986, Stanford acting Director of Athletics Andy Geiger said: "I thought Mike Montgomery's record of achievement at the University of Montana was of very high quality. I feel that his personality and his values as a coach in basketball suit Stanford ideally. . ."

After Montgomery's first four years at Stanford, Geiger's (who is now the Director of Athletics at Maryland) opinion has been proven true. Not only has Stanford enjoyed four consecutive winning seasons under Montgomery, an extremely rare occurrence in the history of this program, the Cardinal has also participated in three post-season tournaments. His first Stanford team was 15-13 and by his second year the Cardinal had risen the victory total to 21 and appeared in the NIT. In 1988-89, his third year at Stanford, the Cardinal was 26-7 and earned the school's first NCAA tournament invitation since 1942. Stanford also finished 12th in the final *United Press International* poll and 13th in the *Associated Press* poll, the highest rankings at the school since the 1962-63 team finished 10th in the *UPI* poll.

During the 1988-89 campaign, Stanford set or tied 26 school, Maples Pavilion, team, individual and Pacific-10 records. Included were a school record 15 conference wins, and a second place finish in the Pacific-10 behind nationally ranked Arizona.

Last season Montgomery had to do some rebuilding as two four-year starters, All-America guard Todd Lichti and forward Howard Wright, graduated, but he managed to put Stanford back in post-season play with an appearance in the NIT.

Under Montgomery's leadership, attendance and enthusiasm has reached a high level. Two seasons ago, Stanford set a single season record by averaging 7,406 fans per game in Maples Pavilion (7,500 capacity), including a record seven sellouts.

The 43-year-old Montgomery came to Stanford from Montana where he spent 10 years. The first two years, he was an assistant coach under Jim Brandenburg, who left Montana for Wyoming and is now the head coach at San Diego State. Montgomery took over at Montana in 1978. He had four 20-game winners at Montana and twice the Grizzlies made it to the NIT. His winning percentage of .667 is the fifth-best of any Big Sky coach in the league's 27-year history. Montgomery never had a losing season in his eight years at Montana.

Four of his players at Montana were drafted into the NBA, including Larry Krystkowiak, a three-time Big Sky Conference MVP who is now with the Milwaukee Bucks.

A native of Long Beach, Calif., Montgomery graduated in 1968 from Long Beach State where he received his Bachelor of Arts degree in Physical Education. He continued his education at Colorado State and received his Master's in Physical Education in 1976. He also served as an assistant coach at the U.S. Coast Guard Academy, Colorado State, the Citadel and Florida before going to Montana.

His teams will fast break when the opportunity is available, but Montgomery emphasizes a well executed, half court offense with a strong power game. In the past two seasons, Stanford has shot nearly 51 percent from the floor. His Stanford teams have also been strong on the boards, outrebounding the opposition in 46 of the last 63 games. Montgomery is also a good defensive coach and last season Stanford allowed 63.7 points per game, first in the Pacific-10.

"Montgomery, a volatile coach by nature, has tailored his approach to this team in a way that has nurtured its development. Nobody plays as if he is fearful of being exiled to the bench, and that, too, is to Montgomery's credit," wrote Chuck Hildebrand in the *Peninsula Times-Tribune*.

Some long time observers of Pacific-10 and Stanford basketball thought that the Cardinal's outstanding 26-7 season two years ago was an aberration. After all, Stanford had not been to the NCAA tournament since 1942 and, Lichti was the type of player Stanford rarely gets. This year 11 lettermen, five starters, and a legitimate All-America candidate in Adam Keefe return. A top three finish in the Pacific-10, a 20-game winner and an NCAA tournament bid would be a strong statement that Stanford can have consistent success.

★ PLAYERS NOT RETURNING ★

DEREK BRUTON (6-10, C, 3.9 ppg, 2.8 rpg, 10 assists, 12 blocked shots, 3 steals) Bruton was a part-time starter in the pivot. He started 13 games last year

for the Cardinal. He is not a major loss as returning in the middle for Stanford is All-America candidate Adam Keefe. Stanford should also have adequate backups in 6-9 junior Lang Meyer and 6-11 redshirt freshman Jim Morgan.

Bruton is the only letterman not returning for Stanford.

★ RETURNING PLAYERS ★

KENNY AMMANN (6-3, 185 lbs., SR, G, #44, 9.3 ppg, 1.6 rpg, 72 assists, 1 blocked shot, 15 steals, Edison HS/Huntington Beach, Calif. & Rancho Santiago College/Santa Ana, Calif.) Ammann earned a 3.4 GPA in Psychology last year. He not only made the Stanford honor roll but was named to the GTE District-8 Academic All-America team and was also named to the Pacific-10 All-Academic team.

Ammann was not just successful in the classroom as he started all 30 games for Stanford at the off-guard spot last year. He hit .463 from three-point range (47-of-102) which ranked second in the Pacific-10. His three-point percentage was the sixth best ever for a single season at Stanford. Ammann scored at least one three-pointer in 24 of 30 games. He also is an outstanding free throw shooter who made 31-of-36 free throws (.861).

He redshirted the 1988-89 campaign after transferring to Stanford from Rancho Santiago College in Santa Ana, Calif. Last year, in his first season in a Stanford uniform, Ammann scored a season-high of 21 points against UCLA, including 5 three-pointers. He also scored 18 points, including 4 three-pointers at California. His .861 free throw percentage was the fifth-best single season record ever at Stanford.

Ammann also hit the winning basket with no time on the clock to beat Oregon and recorded a team-high eight assists against San Francisco and Hawaii. He was on the all-tournament team at the Stanford Apple Invitational.

Montgomery attempted to recruit Ammann to Montana. He wanted Ammann to sign early with Montana but he thought he could get a better offer and didn't. He verbally committed to Northern Arizona but backed off when he found out that program had five recruits and only three scholarships. He spent his freshman year at California State-Bakersfield, a Division II program, but after the season a new coach brought in his own recruits and Ammann's scholarship was cut. He then transferred to Rancho Santiago College for his sophomore year.

Ammann feels he learned a great deal during his redshirt season practicing against Todd Lichti. While he is certainly no Lichti, he proved to be a capable Pacific-10 player last year.

"Things just worked out too well to be a coincidence," Ammann told Chris Crader of the *Stanford Daily* about ending up in Stanford. "If I could pick just one place to go to school and play basketball, it would be here. I just thank God I'm here."

Ammann is one of five returning starters for the Cardinal in 1990-91.

PETER DUKES (6-4, 195 lbs., SO, G, #22, 1.2 ppg, 1.0 rpg, 27 assists, 9 steals, Roosevelt HS/Seattle, Wash.) As a freshman Dukes appeared in 23 games for an average of nine minutes per game. He was 9-of-36 from the field (.250) and just 3-of-20 (.150) from three-point range. Dukes redshirted the 1988-89 season at Stanford before playing last year. His season scoring high was five points.

He can play either backcourt spot and add some height and versatility to the Stanford backcourt.

PAUL GARRETT (6-9, 235 lbs., SO, C/F, #40, 1.9 ppg, 1.8 rpg, 6 assists, 1 blocked shot, 4 steals, Palisades HS/Pacific Palisades, Calif.) Garrett redshirted in 1988-89 and saw action in 20 games for an average of just over five minutes per game as a freshman. He had a career-high of six points and six rebounds at Arizona last year. For the year, Garrett shot .519 (14-for-27) from the floor. From the line he was 10-of-15 (.667).

Garrett is strong and could eventually be a good player at Stanford. However, he is in a very deep Stanford depth chart at forward and may not see much more action this year.

KENNY HICKS (6-4, 175 lbs., SO, G, #21, 2.4 ppg, 0.9 rpg, 11 assists, 3 blocked shots, 6 steals, Notre Dame HS/Sherman Oaks, Calif.) Hicks was one of two true freshmen to see action for Stanford last year. He played in 20 games and impressed Montgomery with his defensive ability. Hicks is a more proficient driver than perimeter shooter. He made 19-of-48 field goals (.396) and was 4-of-15 (.267) out beyond the three-point stripe.

Hicks scored a season-high of 13 points against Washington State, hitting 6-of-8 shots from the floor against the Cougars. He also collected a career-high four rebounds against Arizona. He possesses excellent quickness and should be the No. 4 guard on the Stanford backcourt depth chart.

All guards are returning for Stanford this year so the backcourt depth should be a strength.

ADAM KEEFE (6-9, 230 lbs., JR, C, #31, 20.0 ppg, 9.1 rpg, 41 assists, 18 blocked shots, 23 steals, Woodbridge HS/Irvine, Calif.) In Keefe, Stanford has the best big man in the Pacific-10 Conference. He played both power forward and center last year and is big, strong, physical and plays with great intensity. He currently holds the Stanford school record for career field goal percentage (.629).

"He's a throwback to the old days," Southern California coach George Raveling told Steve Grimley of the *Orange County Register*. "I haven't seen a guy in a long, long time who knows how to play the post like Keefe does. He could have played back in the days of (Bob) Cousy and (Bill) Sharman and those guys.''

Keefe is a hard driving power player. He broke Stanford records for most free throws in a season (179) and free throw attempts (247). He also tied a school and Pacific-10 tournament record for single game free throw percentage (10-for-10) against California at the Pacific-10 tournament. Keefe made and attempted more free throws than any other player in the conference. He also was Stanford's top scorer and ranked third in the Pacific-10. Keefe tied for first in the conference in rebounding. His 20.0 scoring average was the eighth-best single season mark ever at Stanford.

Keefe led the Pacific-10 in field goal percentage at .627 and his mark was the third best single-season performance ever at Stanford. He scored a career-high 32 points against Colgate while adding 12 rebounds. Keefe had 30 points and 10 rebounds against Hawaii, 30 points and 15 rebounds vs. Washington State and hit 11-for-12 shots from the floor against San Francisco. Keefe had 10 or more rebounds in 14 games and recorded 14 double-doubles (double figures in points and rebounds) last season.

''If I come out of a game and I'm not dripping and my shirt's not clinging to my back, I feel like I've let myself down,'' Keefe told Jerry Crowe of the Los Angeles Times.

Stanford beat out North Carolina for Keefe's services. He decided on Stanford because he plans to live in Southern California and felt a Stanford degree means more there than a degree from North Carolina.

He also selected Stanford because the school has a volleyball team and North Carolina doesn't. Keefe was a great high school volleyball player. The day after the basketball season ends, Keefe begins practicing with the Cardinal volleyball team. Stanford volleyball coach Fred Sturm believes Keefe has the potential to become even better than Karch Kiraly, the greatest player in U.S. volleyball history. He has a legitimate chance to be a member of the 1992 U.S. Olympic volleyball team.

''I feel like I should like I should enjoy basketball more because I've been playing it longer, I've put more hours in, I've worked harder for a longer period of time,'' Keefe said. ''I almost feel an obligation to the sport because it's the one paying the bills.

''On the other hand, volleyball allows me to take a step back and maybe have a little more fun; maybe have 200 people in the gym instead of 7,500; be able to smile a little more. It just seems like the pressure's not there, the TV's not there, my parent aren't going to call and say, 'why'd you argue that call. You look like a fool'.''

Montgomery would like to see Keefe spend less time playing volleyball in the off-season and more involved in weight training and basketball. He believes Keefe has an NBA future but must spend more time on the game in the off-season to reach it.

While Keefe is primarily considered an inside banger, Montgomery believes there is more to his game. ''He's not given much of an opportunity to be a finesse player because people are attacking him,'' Montgomery told Jerry Crowe of the Los Angeles Times. ''If he were softer, weak-hearted, he'd be getting dominated . . . He's got good touch. He's a very good shooter. He doesn't miss very often and he can make those shots while being bumped. It's not fair to say finesse is not part of his game. He's not a bully, but he just seems to be around other people a lot.''

Keefe supposedly was impressive in the off-season. Look for him to have another major season as Stanford returns to the NCAA tournament for the second time in three years.

MARCUS LOLLIE (6-0, 170 lbs., SO, G, #20, 3.0 ppg, 1.1 rpg, 39 assists, 6 blocked shots, 12 steals, Chief Sealth HS/Seattle, Wash.) As a freshman Lollie came off the bench and served as Stanford's third guard. He emerged late in the season as a major factor at point guard and saw extensive playing time in the last nine games, averaging 19 minutes per game. At the conclusion of the season, Lollie was voted by his teammate as the winner of the ''Most Inspirational Award.''

He has excellent quickness and played well defensively for a freshman. He made both ends of a one-in-one free throw situation with 43 second remaining to provide what proved to be the winning point in Stanford's 70-69 victory at UCLA —the Cardinal's first ever win at Pauley Pavilion. He scored a season-high of 16 points against California in the Pacific-10 tournament. He also scored 10 points, pulled down five rebounds, had two assists and one steal at California. Lollie was guilty of only eight turnovers in the final eight games.

Lollie grew up with his mother and grandmother in a tough neighborhood in South Seattle. He was a freshman starter on a state championship team at Chief Sealth HS. At the end of the season, Lollie asked his coach why none of the seniors had been offered college scholarships and was told the reason was because they didn't have the grades. At that point he decided to become academically-oriented and went on to compile a 3.8 GPA.

''He had a tough upbringing, but there was something different about Marcus,'' Tim Sowell, who was Lollie's counselor at Chief Sealth HS, told Rick LaPlante of the Peninsula Times-Tribune. ''He would have a Walkman on, but what the kids didn't know what that he was listening to classical music.''

''When you grow up in an environment where there's a lot of negative things, it's easy to get caught up in them . . . I started doing a lot of things I shouldn't have been doing . . . I was scared to break into houses and stuff like that, but I had friends who were doing it. . .

''I remember this one time I was going to go out with some guys and do some stuff and just decided not to at the last minute and they ended up getting

arrested . . . I never went to jail, but I have a lot of friends who wound up,'' Lollie told LaPlante.

This season, Lollie should be Stanford's first guard off the bench and he may even draw some starting assignments.

LANG MEYER (6-9, 240 lbs., JR, C, #50, 1.1 ppg, 1.7 rpg, 1 assist, 2 blocked shot, 1 steal, McCullough HS/The Woodlands, Tex.) Meyer is considered Stanford's strongest player. He loves the weight room and it shows in his physique. Last season, Meyer appeared in 17 games for a total of 118 minutes. He was just 8-of-25 (.320) from the field and 2-of-7 (.286) from the line.

He can play any one of three frontcourt positions. He appeared in nine games as a freshman in 1987-88, redshirted the 1988-89 season before coming back last year. He has only played organized basketball for five years.

Meyer, who's real first name is Langtry, was named after famed British actress Lillie Langtry who often toured the United States. His father was a business administrator for an oil company and the family moved frequently. Meyer has visited 36 countries, including the Soviet Union, China, Taiwan and India. He speaks fluent French. While growing up, Meyer spent four years in London, two in Paris, one in Mexico City, two in Malta and two in Saudi Arabia. He rode elephants in Thailand and mountain ponies in the Himalayas. He developed a desire to play basketball while living in Malta after watching the movie ''One on One'' with Robby Benson.

He played for three years at McCullough HS in Woodlands, Texas., a superb of Houston.

''He does not have a lot of experience, but he's been a willing participant,'' Montgomery told Mark Soltau of the San Francisco Examiner. ''It's just not natural for him yet. I think he'll improve consistently.''

Two summers ago, Lang started for England in the World University Games in Duisburg, West Germany. He holds duel citizenship and would like to play for the English Olympic team.

Meyer will back up Keefe in the pivot this year.

MIKE MORRIS (6-5, 190 lbs., SO, G, #14, 1.5 ppg, 0.7 rpg, 3 assists, 1 steal, Mater Dei HS/Santa Ana, Calif.) Morris appeared in 10 games last year for a total of 24 minutes. He was 5-of-12 (.417) from the field and 1-of-2 (.500) from three-point range. He made 4-of-5 (.800) free throw attempts. He opened his collegiate career with seven points against Cal-Poly San Luis Obispo and scored only eight points the rest of the season. Morris can play either off-guard or small forward.

He will probably see limited action again this year.

JOHN PATRICK (6-4, 180 lbs., SR, G, #11, 7.7 ppg, 2.6 rpg, 115 assists, 30 steals, Sidwell Friends HS/Vienna, Va.) Stanford's starting point guard, Patrick started all 30 games last year. He led the Cardinal in assists and was second in steals. Patrick scored a career-high of 20 points against Oregon and made 6-of-7 three-pointers against Oregon State, setting a school and Maples Pavilion record.

Patrick was a reserve as a freshman and sophomore before making excellent progress and emerging as a starter last year. His progress is remarkable when it is considered Patrick played only 86 minutes as a sophomore before his playing time jumped to 898 minutes last year.

''The thing most pleasing about Patrick is that he has handled the pressure so very well,'' Montgomery told Cindy Somers of the Tucson Citizen. ''A year ago, he backed up three guys and now he's starting. He has played very solidly for us.''

For the season, Patrick made 73-of-196 field goals (.373) and was 37-of-103 (.357) from three-point range. He connected on 49-of-63 free throws (.778).

Stanford does not have any great guards, but Patrick and fellow starter Kenny Ammann have certainly proven to be quite capable. With two seniors in its starting backcourt who have played a year together, Stanford won't have any problems from its guards.

ANDREW VLAHOV (6-7, 225 lbs., SR, F, #30, 9.2 ppg, 6.6 rpg, 76 assists, 12 blocked shots, 50 steals, Kent Street HS/Perth, Australia) Vlahov was Stanford's fourth leading scorer with a 9.2 ppg average last year. He is a very tough, hard-nosed competitor with a great deal of international experience. Over the summer he played with the Australian National team which competed in the World Championships in Buenos Aires, Argentina, and the Goodwill Games in Seattle. He also played in the 1988 Summer Olympics.

Vlahov is one of the toughest players in college basketball and refuses to be intimidated by anyone. He gives no quarter and asks for none as evidenced by the fact he broke the noses of three opponents last year. He played a large part in Stanford's surprising season last year. Vlahov led Stanford in steals.

''Andrew really understands the game,'' Montgomery told Mark Purdy of the San Jose Mercury-News. ''If you tell him something from the scouting report, like what the other team will run when they hold up a fist, he'll always remember. He could be a coach one day.''

Montgomery began using Vlahov at small forward last year but he finally put him back closer to the basket where he belongs. ''It takes advantage of his strength and he's confident inside,'' Montgomery said.

For the season Vlahov made 108-of-263 field goals (.411) and was just 5-of-40 (.125) from three-point range. His three-point percentage may be one of the worst in the country for a player attempting that many attempts. Vlahov was 55-of-105 (.524) from the line.

In Stanford's 70-69 victory at UCLA, he scored a career-high of 20 points, along with eight rebounds. Vlahov also had 15 points against Oregon State and Southern California and grabbed a career-high of 11 rebounds against Oregon State and California. He had 10 rebounds against four other teams. For the second year in a row, Vlahov was voted Stanford's ''Best Defensive Player.''

He did not play basketball at Kent Street because the school did not have a team. He received his experience in basketball in the United States on two different occasions —once as an exchange student when he attended two terms of junior high school, and later as a senior at South Eugene HS in Eugene, Ore.

Vlahov is one of four senior starters for Stanford this year.

DESHON WINGATE (6-7, 205 lbs., SR, F, #34, 10.0 ppg, 5.3 rpg, 34 assists, 23 blocked shots, 16 steals, Lanier HS/Austin, Tex.) Last season, Stanford was the beneficiary of some improved play by several starters. Not only did point guard John Patrick step up and give a better than expected performance, but so did forward Andrew Vlahov and forward Deshon Wingate.

Wingate averaged 2.7 points as a reserve in 1988-89. Last year he averaged 10.0 points and started 18 games. He was Stanford's No. 2 scorer and third-leading rebounder. Wingate scored a career-high 22 points, along with a career-high 14 rebounds, against Washington. He had 19 points against California-Irvine and in that game he was 8-for-9 from the floor. Against UCLA, he tallied 11 points and 9 rebounds in his second career start. Wingate also led Stanford in blocked shots with 23.

Prior to last season Wingate was not a force. He shied away from contact under the basket and never went straight up with his jump shot around the hoop. "It wasn't so much that I wasn't confident as a shooter," he told Chuck Hildebrand of the *Peninsula Times-Tribune.* "It was just lack of confidence, period. Whenever I got the ball, it was, oh gosh, what to do now."

He was a back-to-the-basket player in high school and struggled his first three years at Stanford making the adjustment to playing on the wing and defending the perimeter. He has great speed and leaping ability but was never able to channel it. Then prior to last season, Wingate started working hard on his game and toured Hungary with a collection of Pacific-10 players. He worked with UCLA coach Jim Herrick on his game and came back much improved.

Now that Wingate has a solid year of experience under him as a starter, look for him to be even better in 1990-91. He is just starting to hit his stride.

★ NEWCOMERS ★

JIM MORGAN (6-11, 235 lbs., FR, C, #55, 15.0 ppg, 11.0 rpg, 5.0 blpg, Wheeler HS/Marietta, Ga.) Morgan is Stanford's tallest player at 6-11. He redshirted last season and is one of the three centers listed on the Cardinal roster. Morgan worked extensively in the weight room last year to prepare for this season.

He was a three-year starter at Wheeler HS in Marietta, Ga. He shot 55 percent from the floor as a senior and Montgomery believes Morgan's shooting touch could be important to the Cardinal.

With the return of starting center Adam Keefe, reserves Lang Meyer and Paul Garrett plus the addition of Morgan, Stanford is well stocked in big physical centers. The Cardinal has many fouls to give in the pivot this year.

BOBBY PATTON (6-0, 160 lbs., FR, G, #23, 21.3 ppg, 8.2 rpg, 4.0 apg, Liberty HS/Youngstown, Ohio) Patton is a pure point guard who is expected to make a contribution as a freshman. He was a first-team All-Ohio selection by *Associated Press* and *United Press International* last year. Patton shot 59 percent from the floor and 86 percent from the line during his senior season as Liberty HS chalked up a 27-1 record. He was also Liberty's top three-point threat from three-point territory, shooting 46 percent. The *Associated Press* named Patton Mr. Basketball in Ohio last year. He was coached in high shool by his father.

At the Ohio state tournament, he set two tournament records for most three-pointers (eight in two games) and three-pointers in one game (five). He also passes the ball extremely well and is very heady. According to Montgomery, "Patton has been bred on basketball his entire life."

With Patton, Marcus Lollie and returning starter John Patrick, Stanford is well stocked at point guard for the upcoming season.

NICK RAVN (6-7, 195 lbs., FR, F, #35, 27.9 ppg, 10.5 rpg, Spencer HS/Spencer, Iowa) Ravn was a three-year starter, All-State and All-League during his senior year at Spencer (Iowa) HS. In one game in high school he scored 51 points and grabbed 12 rebounds. Ravn is considered a good perimeter scorer and an exceptional ballhandler. He has good hands, can score facing the basket and is a hard worker. He's expected to be used mainly at small forward in college.

Stanford is very deep this year and Ravn will probably have to wait his turn.

JASON WEAVER (6-7, 240 lbs., FR, F, #43, 19.5 ppg, 12.5 rpg, 6.0 blpg, Pueblo East HS/Pueblo, Colo.) Weaver is a power forward who was redshirted last year along with two other Cardinal freshmen. He is a very strong player particularly under the boards. At Pueblo East HS, Weaver was a four-year starter and an All-Colorado selection. He was also a perfect 4.0 student and a National Merit Scholar semifinalist. Weaver is one of the few individuals who achieved a perfect math score on the ACT exam.

Weaver should be able to hold his own under the boards immediately at the major college level and he gets up and down the court well. He'll probably need time to work his way through the depth chart but should be an important player for Stanford in years to come.

BRENT WILLIAMS (6-6, 195 lbs., FR, F, #33, 20.0 ppg, 10.0 rpg, 2.7 apg, Curtis HS/Tacoma, Wash.) Williams was one of three freshman who redshirted at Stanford last year. He was a first-team All-Washington selection in the *Seattle Post Intelligencer.* He had a 29-point 14-rebound game in the Washington state tournament.

He worked hard in the weightroom in the off-season and is a quality athlete.

Williams is further along as a freshman than starting forward Deshon Wingate, a player he will backup this year.

★ QUESTIONS ★

Offensive Explosiveness? Stanford only averaged 67.7 points per game last year. Against the two best, most talented teams in the Pacific-10-Arizona and UCLA-Stanford will have to be able to put more points on the board.

Long Distance Shooting? Stanford had only two players, Kenny Ammann and John Patrick, who were long ball threats last year. Outside of those two, Stanford made only 19 other three- point field goals.

★ STRENGTHS ★

Experience! Stanford has 11 returning letterman, including five starters, and the Cardinal are a team dominated by upperclassmen.

Adam Keefe and a strong front line! Keefe is the best big man in the Pacific-10. In addition to Keefe, Stanford has a strong contingent of frontcourt players.

Backcourt depth! All guards are returning from last year and freshman Bobby Patton was voted Mr. Basketball in Ohio last season.

A physical, bruising defense! Stanford led the Pacific-10 in scoring defense, allowing only 63.7 points per game last year. Stanford held its opposition under 50 percent shooting in 22 of 30 games and allowed the opposition a shooting percentage of only .441, second in the conference.

★ BLUE RIBBON ANALYSIS ★

After All-America guard Todd Lichti and four-year starter Howard Wright graduated following Stanford's 26-7 season in 1988- 89 skeptics wondered how long it would take the Cardinal to make another run at the Pacific-10 title and play in the NCAA tournament. After all, Stanford had not been to the NCAA tournament since 1942 and players the caliber of Lichti and Wright have rarely been seen in a Stanford uniform. While last season's 18-12 record was monumental, Stanford did beat UCLA twice and earned an NIT bid. With 11 letterman returning, including five starters, Stanford is poised for a strong run in the Pacific-10 and is a likely NCAA tournament invitee.

Stanford coach Mike Montgomery, who is entering his fifth season as the head of the Cardinal program, is an underrated coach who has proven that he was the right choice to lead the Stanford program when the head coaching position became vacant in 1986. He has led Stanford to three post-season appearances in his four years. Montgomery, an excellent defensive coach, seems to have a knack for getting his players to improve and is an excellent bench coach.

The Cardinal has the premier big man in the Pacific-10 in junior center Adam Keefe. He dominated Pacific-10 statistics last year and tied for the conference lead in rebounding. Flanking Keefe up front are senior forwards Andrew Vlahov and Deshon Wingate, both are coming off of strong junior years. There is also plenty of quality depth up front in three redshirt freshmen who are available this season. In the backcourt, Stanford does not have a big star, but the Cardinal is deep in experience. Senior guards John Patrick and Kenny Ammann played well last year, sophomore Marcus Lollie emerged as a top flight point guard in the latter half of the season and freshman Bobby Patton was voted Mr. Basketball in Ohio last year.

Stanford is a strong team defensively. Last season the Cardinal led the Pacific-10 conference in scoring defense, allowing only 63.7 points per game. The Cardinal's rebounding margin of plus 6.1 was the best in the conference.

Stanford does not have the overall talent and athletic ability to beat out Arizona and UCLA for the Pacific-10 conference championship. However, Stanford should finish a strong third to those two potential powerhouses. This March, Stanford will be back in the NCAA tournament for the second time in three years.

LAST SEASON		1990-91 STANFORD SCHEDULE		
Cal Poly San Luis Obispo	88-56	Nov.	23-24	#Stanford Invitational
@California-Irvine	70-57	Nov. 30-		
#Lehigh	82-59		Dec. 1	##Apple Invitational
#Louisiana Tech	62-59	Dec.	15	Santa Clara
San Francisco	74-53		19	California-Irvine
@Santa Clara	66-51		21	Florida
Colgate	77-66		23	@Colorado
##Missouri-Kansas City	70-50		29-30	*Florida Citrus Bowl/
##Kansas	61-83			Red Lobster Classic
Oregon State	76-77	Jan.	3	@Oregon State
Oregon	58-56		6	@Oregon
@Washington	59-71		10	Washington
@Washington State	69-49		12	Washington State
UCLA	87-79		16	@UCLA
Southern California	74-61		19	@Southern California
@Arizona	61-68		24	Arizona
@Arizona State	53-64		27	Arizona State

LAST SEASON Cont.				
@Oregon	61-62	*California		77-61
@Oregon State	70-84	*Arizona		61-85
Washington State	68-54	**@Hawaii		57-69
Washington	59-48			
@Southern California	62-71	@ Road Games		
@UCLA	70-69	# Apple Invitational, Palo Alto, CA		
Arizona	61-80	## BMA Holiday Classic, Kansas City,		
Arizona State	57-44	MO		
California	63-66	* Pacific-10 Tournament, Tempe, AZ		
@California	79-58	** NIT		

1990-91 STANFORD SCHEDULE Cont.			
Jan.	31	Oregon	@ Road Games
Feb.	2	Oregon State	# Palo Alto, CA (Rider, St. Mary's &
	7	@Washington State	Yale)
	10	@Washington	## Palo Alto, CA (George Washington,
	14	Southern California	Hawaii & Vanderbilt)
	16	UCLA	* Orlando, FL (Central Florida, DePaul
	21	@Arizona State	& North Carolina)
	26	@Arizona	
Mar.	2	California	
	7	@California	

NOTES: Stanford will play Central Florida in the first round of the Florida Citrus Bowl/Red Lobster Classic in Orlando . . . the Cardinal has a long break, with two weeks off after the first four games. Stanford is off from December 1-15. Few non-Ivy League Division I teams have such a long break in their schedule . . . the Pacific-10 conference does not have a conference tournament this year . . . *Sports Travel Magazine* named the Stanford athletic program the best in college sports in a survey published last January.

TEMPLE

LAST SEASON: 20-11
CONFERENCE RECORD: 15-3
STARTERS LOST: 0
STARTERS RETURNING: 5
CONFERENCE: ATLANTIC 10
LOCATION: PHILADELPHIA, PA
HOME FLOOR:
  McGONIGLE HALL(3,900)
NICKNAME: OWLS
COLORS: CHERRY AND WHITE

★ COACH'S PROFILE ★

JOHN CHANEY (Record at Temple, 192-61. Career record, 417-120.) The losses were mounting in the bunker that is Temple basketball. The Owls, ranked in virtually everyone's pre-season Top 20, were a sluggish 6-7 after 13 games. Their starting center, 7-0 senior Duane Causwell, was dismissed from school prior to the second semester. And the critics were cornering John Chaney, saying he had lost his touch just two years after being named national Coach of the Year.

So Chaney did what he does best. He dug in deeper, circled the wagons even moretightly around his team, andwent back to the practice floor. And why not? Chaney is most effective as a teacher with a cause. The Causwell dismissal became a rallying point for the young Owls, who promptly won nine of their next 10 games. They stormed to the Atlantic 10 regular season title, then followed with a convincing three-game sweep of the conference tournament.

It was the sixth NCAA bid in seven years for Temple. And it may have been the most rewarding. The Owls, given up for dead after Causwell's departure, simply got better. Another seven-footer, Donald Hodge, picked up where Causwell left off, and Chaney had the floor balance so vital to his legendary ball-control attack. Guard Mark Maconover came a shooting slump to guide the Owls down the stretch, and all the bygones were bygones.

Or were they? Chaney got in highly-publicized shoving match with Massachusetts coach John Calipari during a triple overtime thriller at Amherst. He threatened to punch an abrasive Philadelphia sports radio personality who suggested the Causwell affair had been mishandled. In one regrettable moment, he even called his own players ''brainless'' and ''spineless.'' And that was *after* a 17-point homecourt victory.

''Some things weighed pretty heavily on my mind,'' Chaney told the *Philadelphia Inquirer*. ''I spent a great deal of my time fighting windmills and dealing with issues, as well as preparing my team. It took a little out of me. I'm not proud of the language I used or the threats I made. But I have to go on fighting for the things I believe in. I'm certainly not ready to give up.''

The Owls never did. That is why they were able to recover in time to salvage their season. They did not hit the wall until St. John's blew them away in the NCAA first round. By the time that happened, though, the critics had all piped down. John Chaney was a winner again, and so were his players. With Chaney, they always are.

''I still enjoy going to work, cracking the whip at practice, seeing the growth in kids,'' he said, closing in on age 59. ''So long as the kids I serve are good kids, who want to try, who want to be their best, then I'll be in this for a while. The kids are the most enjoyable aspect of this job. They come to you with a great deal of innocence. As a coach, one of your responsibilities is to help them prepare for the real world.''

No one quarrels with Chaney in that regard. Temple players ride busses and subways. They go to class. They come to school even when Proposition 48 renders them ineligible. On the court, they are molded into a unit that virtually never loses to a team it should beat. The flip side is that the Owls rarely rise up and pull the huge upset that makes the ESPN highlights. With Temple, what you see is what you get.

The same goes for the coach himself. Chaney's perspective is of a man who grew up in poor surroundings and inner city Philadelphia, and whose own post-high school educational and athletic opportunities were restricted by the segregation of the 1950's. Despite being one of the greatest guards ever to come out of Philadelphia, a city that has been a cradle of guards, Chaney was not recruited by ''name'' schools in the East, settling for Bethune-Cookman College in Daytona Beach, Fla. After a standout career there, Chaney was relegated to the old Eastern League rather than the NBA, as the door for blacks in professional sports had not yet opened.

Chaney has not forgotten. The deeply rooted desire to be equal drove him through 10 glowing seasons at Cheyney State, capped by the 1978 Division II national championship, and it continues to drive him at Temple. That is why, even in the midst of magical seasons like 1987-88 -when the Owls went 32-2 and were ranked number one in every national poll - Chaney often comes across as overprotective or unapproachable.

''All this just comes with the turf,'' said Chaney in *Eastern Basketball*. ''But all I can can do is my job. I can't fight all those bladeson the windmill. All I can dois go onto that 50-by-90 foot turf and hope someone looks through the maze and sees the character you're building, and the teaching you're doing.''

It is what John Chaney does best.

★ PLAYERS NOT RETURNING ★

DUANE CAUSWELL (7-0, C, 11.3 ppg, 8.3 rpg, 48 blocked shots) Causwell started 12 games for the Owls before university administrators pulled the plug on his senior season. With him went the twin-towers frontcourt that had lifted Temple into the pre-season spotlight.

Ironically, Causwell was eligible under NCAA standards at the time of his dismissal. He was a probationary student in his department, however, and did not have the required grade point average at the time he became a second semester senior. His former teammates dedicated the remainder of the season to him, and they wore #31 wristbands throughout their march to the Atlantic 10 championship.

''(The dismissal) hurt,'' said Chaney, ''because some people turned against us and criticized us rather than applaud us for giving him a chance. We've had a lot of success stories under similar circumstances. And, to me, if one kid makes it through college because we gave him a chance, then it's well worth it.''

Causwell did not brood over what might have ruined others in a similar position. He worked out regularly with former NBA coach Jack McKinney at the post-season scouting camps, shined at and became a first round draft pick of the Sacramento Kings.

ERNEST POLLARD (6-6, G, 0.9 ppg, 0.8 rpg) Pollard, out of the basketball factory that is Philadelphia's Roman Catholic High, never became an impact player at the college level. Instead, he became an exemplary student, one who succeeded in spite of Proposition 48. Pollard even paid his own way as a freshman (when it was still permitted), but has elected not to use his final year of eligibility. He graduated on-time with his class last May.

''He had so many credits,'' said Chaney, ''I wish I could give them to some other guys.''

STEFAN THOMAS (6-4, F, 2.0 ppg, 1.0 rpg) A little-used walk-on, Thomas appeared in three games as a freshman. He will not return to the team.

148

JOHNNIE CONIC (6-5, 178 lbs., SO, G, #22, 1.3 ppg, 0.7 rpg, Buena Vista HS/Saginaw, Mich.) Conic, who was originally planning to sit out his first year, became eligible at the last minute for the Owls. Temple officials did not realize until a final review of his SAT results that he had in fact scored the required 700. Thus, he became Chaney's third recruit in as many years from Buena Vista High, whose coach, Norwaine Reed, was the man who delivered Mark Macon to North Philadelphia.

Conic was not nearly as polished as a freshman. He got into 22 games, but threw up wild shots in most every appearance. His shooting from floor (.238) was the lowest on the team, and his three-point percentage (.161) was even worse. That he appeared as often as he did was mostly a statement about Temple's shallow backcourt. With two more guards on board this time around, Conic will have to pick it up a notch to see equal time.

MICHAEL HARDEN (6-2, 185 lbs., SR, G, #4, 8.1 ppg, 2.3 rpg, 144 assists, 44 steals, Southern Lab HS/Port Allen, La.) Harden is another guard who could be on the outside looking in. This despite a better-than-expected junior year in which he lived down most of the ghosts of his shaky 1988-89 debut.

The Owls have two new point guards - Vic Carstarphen and Jonathan Haynes - both of whom Chaney seems to rate ahead of his most experienced veteran. Chaney is also inclined toward senior leadership, however, which could work in Harden's favor. "The competition might push him, too," said another Atlantic 10 coach.

Harden hit some big shots for the Owls, and was much less reluctant with the three-pointer (51-for-147). He started the final 23 games and, once Chaney realized that converted forward Mik Kilgore could not cut it at the point, became a solid, if unspectacular floor leader. The problem is that Chaney demands much more from that position, so Harden will have to fish or cut bait with two highly acclaimed newcomers looking over his shoulder.

"To be fair," said Chaney, "he didn't have the advantage of playing behind someone to learn the position. Nate Blackwell had Terence Stansbury to learn from. Howard Evans had Nate. Michael, because he had to sit out (as a freshman), we just had to throw him in there."

DONALD HODGE (7-0, 230 lbs., JR, C/F, #35, 15.1 ppg, 8.2 rpg, 26 steals, 23 blocked shots, 22 assists, Coolidge HS/Washington, D.C.) The best thing to come out of Causwell's academic dismissal was the emergence of this potential first round NBA draft pick. Given room to roam and some time to shakeoff the rust of a redshirt freshman season, Hodge became the dominant big man in the Atlantic 10. By the year's end, he was holding his own and more often than not outplaying experienced league centers like Penn State's Ed Fogell, Rhode Island's Kenny Green and Rutgers' Keith Hughes. His 31-point explosion against Larry Johnson and UNLV pretty much said it all.

"An All-America, plain and simple," said a rival A-10 coach. "By the end of last year, he was the best player in our league. He's a great testament to (Temple's) ability to teach players, especially big men. Nobody does what he did against Vegas. And this year, he's even stronger."

That Hodge was not a first-team All-Conference selection is merely the result of being in Causwell's shadow for eight weeks. That he probably will not be the pre-season A-10 player of the year is a coincidence made possible only by the presence of Mark Macon. Yet it should be made clear that it is Hodge who can make Temple great. Macon, it has been proven, cannot do it flying solo.

"We have great expectations for him," Chaney understated. "He is a strong presence in the pivot. We are hoping he will influence and impact our other forwards in the power game."

Though not as dominant defensively as Causwell or former first round pick Tim Perry (Phoenix Suns), Hodge is considerably more advanced at the offensive end. He can post up, go to the glass (127 offensive rebounds), or drop in the baby jumper with the touch of a much more experienced player.

MIK KILGORE (6-8, 210 lbs., JR, F/G, #24, 10.8 ppg, 5.7 rpg, 101 assists, 37 steals, 11 blocked shots, West Philadelphia HS/Philadelphia, Pa.) Kilgore is Owls' jack-of-all trades, starting (61 straight games) at virtually every position but center. Last year's experiment was to make him a 6-8 point guard, allowing Mark Macon to play off the ball along with a 7-0, 7-0, 6-9 front line. It did not work. The Owls bogged down offensively early in the season, and the plan was scrapped.

Kilgore went back to the wing, where he and Macon combined for 119 three-pointers. Kilgore was 58-for-159 (.365) from the arc. He also logged the second highest number of minutes after Macon (1155), and is the latest in a long line of homegrown Philadelphia Public League players to star at Temple. His only weakness is an occasional lapse in concentration, an unpardonable sin on Chaney's ship. It was a Kilgore miscue that prompted the "brainless, spineless" tirade last January.

This year, Kilgore may be moved again. Should the Owls want use both Carstarphen and Haynes in the backcourt along with Macon, Kilgore could become the power forward, the position where he began his collegiate career. Chaney may have tipped his hand in pre-season when he said "Mik will have to go to the boards for us and give us strong inside play."

An Atlantic 10 assistant coach added: "He could be a very effective baseline player."

CHRIS LOVELACE (6-11, 215 lbs., JR, C/F, #25, 1.1 ppg, 1.6 rpg, Northrop HS/Fort Wayne, Ind.) Lovelace was doubly handicapped in his debut season. First, he had a year's worth of rust thanks to Proposition 48. Second, he had a cumbersome knee brace thanks to reconstructive surgery following his senior year in high

school. It was hard to tell which hampered him more.

This year, Lovelace is healthier and has a more defined role. He will back up Hodge. Should Chaney want a bigger look on occasion, Lovelace could be the center with Hodge at power forward. Lovelace, for mobility reasons, is pretty much limited to the pivot.

MARK MACON (6-5, 185 lbs., SR, G, #12, 21.9 ppg, 6.0 rpg, 71 steals, 68 assists, Buena Vista HS/Saginaw, Mich.) With Mark Macon - part basketball star, part enigma - it is hard to tell the fact from the fiction. One minute, he was the best freshman in America. The next, he was an out of control gunner shooting under 40 percent from the floor. People remember the regrettable 6-for-29 showing in the 1988 East Regional final against Duke, or the 4-for-22 nationally televised disaster last year against UNLV. They also remember his focused gaze, his expressionless court demeanor.

Lost in the middle is the truth, not to mention literally dozens and dozens of games in which Macon is simply the best player on the floor. He is that most nights, in fact, a rare talent who is much, much more than a shooter. Shooting may even be his least developed skill (.417 career field goal percentage). What veteran Macon-watchers have come to know, though, are that there are so many other ways he can control a game.

Defense. "The best we played against all year," said LaSalle coach Speedy Morris. "A great, great defender," added St. Joseph's assistant Phil Martelli. "Hardly anyone ever mentions that." For three years, he has been far and away the best defender on one of the nation's top defensive teams. His quick feet and quick hands were born to play in Temple's sticky matchup zone.

Leadership. "So often," said Chaney, "he just carries us. He's busting his heart out there, and the other guys are running around dumb. That's not fair." Said Macon himself: "It's my duty and obligation to give back what I've learned. It should be everyone's duty."

Desire. In a major *Sports Illustrated* feature, the player behind that on-court stare was revealed. He is a driven individual, one whom arches to a beat only he can hear. "The mental," said Macon in the story, "is four-to-one over the physical. There are people I've won over just with knowledge."

Defense, leadership, desire. Throw in 1,926 points, already the most in Temple history, and the package appears complete. For some, though, it is not enough. The *Philadelphia Inquirer,* during his deep junior year shooting slump, asked "Whatever Happened to Mark Macon?" No one seemed to notice that the answer came down the stretch that very season.

Freed permanently from the point by the adequate play of Michael Harden, Macon was deadly over the season's final six weeks. In one eight-game stretch that cemented Temple's Atlantic 10 crown, he averaged 25.3 points, 6.1 rebounds and 2.9 steals. He had 28 points at Saint Joseph's, 35 to win a triple overtime game at UMass, 29 against Villanova, 31 to break the Owls' scoring record against Rutgers and 32 in an NCAA tournament loss to St. John's. He was 52-for-112 (.464) in those games.

"He's still one of the top half-dozen guards in America," one A-10 coach said. "The NBA draft will bear that out."

NBA superscout Marty Blake agrees. "I'm not concerned that he's shooting this or that," said Blake. "He's had to take shots he ordinarily wouldn't take. He'll be much better as a pro. He has some very good point guard skills. Hell, he has skills people don't even know about."

As a senior, Macon also has the best supporting class since that magical freshman season. They are plenty of point guards, plenty of big men. He can run and shoot and defend and, well, be darned near the best guard in the country.

"He will move into a comfort area now," said Chaney. "Not as much will be demanded of him." In other words, look out.

JAN POST (6-10, 225 lbs., SR, C, #44, 0.3 ppg, 0.5 rpg, Christian Agrarian HS/Bunschoten, Holland) Little was known about Post when he arrived a year ago, and a full season with the Owls did not add much to his resume. Post appeared in just six games, topping out with 12 minutes in a 17-point rout of St. Bonaventure. He does not figure in Temple's regular frontcourt rotation.

SHOUN RANDOLPH (6-5, 205 lbs., SR, G, #21, 1.0 ppg, 0.9 rpg, Buena Vista HS/Saginaw, Mich.) Macon's high school classmate, Randolph got bumped from the frontcourt as a junior by the arrival of Hodge, Lovelace and Mark Strickland. Asked to play guard, his skills simply could not match those of Macon, Kilgore or Harden. That does not figure to change with the presence of Carstarphen and Haynes.

Randolph is a good soldier, however. He never sulked when his playing time was cut from 597 to 311 minutes. Still, it is hard to see him getting back to the 4.8/3.5 numbers he put up as a sophomore.

MARK STRICKLAND (6-9, 210 lbs., JR, F, #30, 5.0 ppg, 5.2 rpg, 32 blocked shots, 19 steals, McNair HS/Atlanta, Ga.) Another beneficiary of Causwell's departure, Strickland really came into his own when it counted. His 10 rebounds, six points and five blocked shots keyed an Atlantic 10 semifinal win over Rutgers. He added a career-high 13 points in the title game against Massachusetts.

Strickland is a spectacular leaper who will be even better once he learns to play under control. He is already a fine defensive player inside, the ideal complement to the wide-ranging offensive skills of Hodge. He could even share time with Kilgore at forward should Chaney go with three true guards. In either role -starter or sixth man - he has the disposition to be very effective.

"He gives us quickness in the open floor," said Chaney," and is one of the most talented forwards that I have seen."

VIC CARSTARPHEN (6-0, 160 lbs., SO, G, #3, 25.6 ppg, Camden HS/Camden, N.J.) Carstarphen is a transfer who averaged 3.8 points and 1.1 rebounds in one season at Cincinnati. He was a dynamic player at Camden, and Chaney thinks he can step right into the point guard job.

"He gives us a true, lead point guard once again," said Chaney. "He gives our program a new future in terms of leadership."

Carstarphen also practiced with the Owls last year, which figures to give him an edge over fellow newcomer Jonathan Haynes. Carstarphen is more the traditional point man to begin with.

"He started some at Cincinnati," an A-10 assistant observed. "He's more experienced. That's a big factor because of the way (Temple) plays. He should already understand the system."

JONATHAN HAYNES (6-3, 177 lbs., FR, G, #31, 33.6 ppg, 5.3 rpg, Germantown Friends HS/Philadelphia, Pa.) A Top 50 recruit, Haynes could be the next great Philadelphia guard. He certainly chose the right school, where the coach was a superb Philly guard in another era.

Haynes scored over 2,000 points at Germantown Friends. He was the Gatorade Pennsylvania player of the year. "Outstanding in the open court" is the way one A-10 recruiter described him, "and also a great defender."

"He's the best young player I ever coached," said Germantown Friends coach Alfred Johnson, "but he goes way beyond basketball talent. He's a very special youngman." As a senior, Haynes was selected young man of the year by the Germantown Boys and Girls Club, and is involved with the Big Brothers program in Philadelphia.

"His nickname here was 'Clutch'," said Johnson. "Whether we needed a defensive play or whether we needed a bucket, he would get it."

Don't be surprised to see Carstarphen and Haynes play together, with Macon on a wing.

JAMES SPEARS (6-6, 220 lbs., FR, F, Glen Mills School/Glen Mills, Pa.) A native of Maryland, Spears originally accepted a football scholarship following the 1988 season from West Virginia, where he was considered a Top 100 recruit as a linebacker and one of the Mountaineers' very best signees. Spears never enrolled at West Virginia, however, opting instead for another year of prep school at Glen Mills.

With his grades improved, Spears was able to accept a basketball scholarship this summer from Temple, where he enrolled in September. Although football was by far his top sport as a prep player, Spears will play only basketball this year for the Owls. He has not played organized ball since the winter of 1989.

"There is no question in my mind he can play at this level," said Chaney. "He's my kind of player. Big, strong, not afraid to play defense and rebound."

★ QUESTIONS ★

Outside shooting? As much talent as Chaney has had over the years, he has never had a pure sniper. One year he dubbed Nate Blackwell, Howard Evans and Ed Coe the "Blank Brothers." Last year, Macon, Kilgore and Harden were more like the "Clank Brothers." They drew a lot of iron.

Player rotation? The Owls are unusually deep. That means more decisions about playing time. The best Temple teams, ironically, have had a set five or six and not much else.

Expectations? Temple has not won an NCAA game since 1988. The pressure will be onto make it happen in Macon's last hurrah.

★ STRENGTHS ★

Balance! Not many teams can boast an inside-outside combo the likes of Hodge and Macon. Both should be high first round draft picks before they're through.

Coaching! Once Chaney got down to business last year, so did the Owls. Their stretch drive to an NCAA bid is proof that he can still teach with the best in the business.

McGonigle Hall! The Owls have won well over 90 percent of their games at home. West Virginia (1987) and Duquesne (1983) are the only Atlantic 10 teams to ever win there. La Salle and Villanova both did it last year, but those things always happen in Philadelphia City Series games.

★ BLUE RIBBON ANALYSIS ★

Even Chaney is calling this a pivotal year at Temple. He knows the potential of Macon and Hodge, and he knows such a combination may not come along again. He also has the necessary foot soldiers in Kilgore, Strickland, Carstarphen and Haynes.

If this were two or three years ago, and if the Atlantic 10 was still a weak sister, the Owls would be looking at another 30-win season. Instead, Rutgers, Penn State and West Virginia are all capable of knocking off the favorites on a given night. Dates with Iowa, Notre Dame, Georgia Tech and South Carolina also loom.

But Temple should be ready. They went 5-1 on an August tour of Japan, and that was without the new guards Carstarphen and Haynes. By the time real

games start, the Owls will have already meshed. And there isn't much meshing to do, not with five returning starters and two new players who could start very soon.

"We now have a full complement of players who, I think, we need to make us successful," Chaney said. "Balance is a major element of strength as I see it in our scheme of things."

Temple is the odds-on choice in the Atlantic 10 again. Beyond that, they have enough balance and senior leadership to think Sweet 16.

LAST SEASON		1990-91 TEMPLE SCHEDULE		
Pennsylvania	55-54	Nov.	15	#@Iowa
#Arkansas State	64-41	Dec.	1	@Villanova
#@Syracuse	56-73		5	@St. Bonaventure
@Penn State	59-61		8	@South Carolina
St. Joseph's	74-54		15	Georgia Tech
@Illinois	61-78		18	Penn State
Duquesne	93-62		27 & 29	##Valley Bank
La Salle	62-63			Fiesta Bowl Classic
##North Carolina State	71-74	Jan.	3	Pennsylvania
@George Washington	60-57		5	@La Salle
West Virginia	73-69		8	Rutgers
*UNLV	76-82		10	@George
@Georgia Tech	57-59			Washington
@Duquesne	67-43		16	@Duquesne
Massachusetts	86-69		19	@Clemson
Rhode Island	81-70		22	St. Joseph's
@St. Bonaventure	59-46		24	Massachusetts
@St. Joseph's	78-63		26	St. Bonaventure
@Rhode Island	70-86		28	@Rhode Island
St. Bonaventure	81-64	Feb.	2	@Rutgers
@Massachusetts	83-82 3OT		4	@St. Joseph's
Penn State	61-53		7	George Washington
@Rutgers	75-69		10	West Virginia
Villanova	69-71		13	@Penn State
George Washington	86-74		16	*Notre Dame
@West Virginia	51-55		19	Rhode Island
Rutgers	75-70 2OT		21	@Massachusetts
**Duquesne	61-50		24	@West Virginia
**Rutgers	65-57		28	Duquesne
**Massachusetts	53-51	Mar.	2-7	**Atlantic 10 Tournament
***St. John's	85-61			

⁹ Road Games
\# Carrier Classic, Syracuse, NY
\## Atlantic City, NJ
* Spectrum, Philadelphia, PA
** Atlantic 10 Tournament, Philadelphia, PA
*** NCAA Tournament, Atlanta, GA

@ Road Games
\# Dodge NIT. If Temple defeats Iowa, the Owls will play a second round game on Nov. 17. The semifinals and finals of the tournament will be held on Nov. 21 & 23 at Madison Square Garden, New York, NY.
\## Tucson, AZ (Arizona, Iowa State & Pepperdine)
* Hershey, PA
** The first three rounds will be held at the Palestera, Philadelphia, PA. The championship game will be held at the site of the highest remaining seed.

NOTES: Temple will play Iowa State in the first round of the Valley Bank Fiesta Bowl Classic . . . two Temple freshman - 6-4 guard Aaron McKie and 6-6 swingman Eddie Jones are not eligible to play this year but have enrolled in school. Each will have three years of eligibility beginning next year. McKie is from Simon Gratz HS in Philadelphia and Jones is out of Ely HS in Pompano Beach, Fla. . . . Chaney has softened somewhat. He once refused to acknowledge the lost year of eligibility of Proposition 48 players in school publications. Temple rosters now list players by the correct class . . . Temple went 6-1 in an August tour of Japan. Donald Hodge led the Owls in scoring with a 14.5 average on the tour. Macon averaged 13.0 points, Strickland 12.3 and Kilgore 11.0 for the Owls. In all, Temple spent 13 days in Japan.

WYOMING

LAST SEASON: 15-14
CONFERENCE RECORD: 7-9
STARTERS LOST: 1
STARTERS RETURNING: 4
CONFERENCE: WESTERN ATHLETIC (WAC)
LOCATION: LARAMIE, WY
HOME FLOOR: ARENA-AUDITORIUM (15,028)
NICKNAMES: COWBOYS & POKES
COLORS: BROWN AND YELLOW

★ COACH'S PROFILE ★

BENNY DEES (Record at Wyoming, 55-37. Career record, 122-73) Unlike his predecessor, Jim Brandenburg, Benny Dees is very happy to be in Wyoming. Dees got a big raise when he left New Orleans in 1987 to come to Wyoming, but he also returned to his alma mater and a life style he enjoys. The native of Mt. Vernon, Ga. lettered as a guard for the Wyoming basketball team in 1958 and as a shortstop on the baseball team in 1957 and '58. He was among the team leaders in hitting for the Cowboys as a senior and graduated from Wyoming in 1958.

"They think I'm one of 'em," Dees told Theresa Smith of the *Denver Post*. "I really like it here. The people have been so good to me. . ."

After attending junior college, Dees, a self described small town guy, signed with Georgia but felt lost at a big school. "I couldn't get registered; the lines were forever," he told Smith.

He returned to junior college for another quarter, then was recruited to Wyoming for baseball by an assistant football coach. He was a draft pick of the Cleveland Indians out of high school but decided to pursue the college route instead.

"It was just the allure of the West and the atmosphere of a small town," Dees said about his decision to sign with Wyoming. "I signed without visiting."

After graduating from Wyoming, Dees returned to Georgia and became boys' and girls' basketball coach at Ware County HS in Waycross. The next year he was named head coach at Manor (Ga.) HS. From there he began a successful five-year stint at Abraham Baldwin JC in Tifton, Ga.

In 1967, Dees moved on to Virginia Commonwealth, which at the time was a Division II school and was 41-33 in three years at the Richmond school. In 1973, he resigned to become a high school administrator and Dees re-entered the coaching ranks when he joined Dwayne Morrison's staff at Georgia Tech in 1977. In 1981, he joined Wimp Sanderson's Alabama staff, and remained there until accepting the New Orleans job in 1985.

He had not been a head coach for 15 years when he accepted the New Orleans job in 1985. The Privateers were 16-12 in Dees' first season. In his second year at New Orleans, 1986-87, the Privateers achieved the best mark in school history, 26-4, and defeated Brigham Young in the opening round of the NCAA tournament before losing to Alabama. After Southwest Missouri State coach Charlie Spoonhour turned down Wyoming, Dees was hired.

"I wanted to come back," Dees said. "I'm a pick-up truck, two bird dogs and a shotgun kind of guy. I like it that we are the only four-year school in the state and that we have season-ticket holders that drive from Sheridan (six hours away)."

While he was happy to be back in Wyoming, Dees walked into a nearly impossible situation in his first year in Laramie. Brandenburg left him a team that was 24-10 in 1987 and advanced to the Final 16 of the NCAA tournament before being eliminated by UNLV. Wyoming was loaded with returning letterman that year and had two All-America caliber players in Fennis Dembo and Eric Leckner. Expectations for that team in Wyoming bordered on the impossible. *Sports Illustrated* featured Wyoming on the cover of its pre-season issue. When Wyoming lost its first two WAC games that year, on the road at UTEP and New Mexico, the pressure intensified. While Wyoming was 26-6 that year, the most victories by a Cowboy team since 1951-52, upstart Loyola Marymount ran the Cowboys out of the NCAA tournament in the opening round. It was a tough way for Dees to break in.

"Country-boy, Benny Dees doesn't know nothin' about no double-talk he just shoots from the hip with a humorous twist.

"In the college-basketball fraternity, Dees' honesty is refreshing, but sometimes it gets the Wyoming coach into trouble," wrote Theresa Smith of the *Denver Post*.

"He says a lot of racial jokes with the team," said Wyoming guard Travis Butler, "But none of it is negative. You hear the jokes and you put yourself in the place of the person the joke is upon, you can't help but laugh."

"We're so open about race, things like that never offend them," Dees told Smith. "I got to be the least racist guy whoever lived in America. I just don't think about it.

"I kid 'em all the time. I walk by my guys and say things like, "Y'all can't swim." Its just a rapport we have and all my black friends - and I bet I got more black friends than anybody in America, coaches and all - we're just that way. There's no closet racism. And I would never use certain words - never, ever, ever."

As far as his coaching style is concerned, Dees is good at getting his teams to play hard. He also is a good defensive coach who makes adjustments well. He is a true people person who likes recruiting. "I'm just honest with 'em," Dees told Smith about his recruiting. "When I go into a black home (to recruit) I'll say really early to them, - If you have any racism in you, you don't need to come to Laramie. It's an all-white community." I hastily add I think the state of Wyoming is the least prejudiced ever. And I really mean that. That's just not for the paper."

"Now I put my foot in my mouth all the time," he elaborated. "I think I got vaccinated with the victrola needle when I was born. I've been talking ever since. Sometimes people don't take it real well. But I can assure you I'm not the kind of person that would hurt anybody."

There is no doubt that the Benny Dees-University of Wyoming marriage is good for both parties. He is in an environment he feels comfortable in and vice-versa. This year that relationship should grow stronger as Dees will have an outstanding team. Wyoming may not equal the 26 wins recorded in 1987-88, but the Cowboys will be more enjoyable for Dees to coach. This is his team, not Brandenburg's, as this group of Cowboys was recruited exclusively by Dees and his staff.

★ PLAYERS NOT RETURNING ★

CLINT BEAN (6-9, F, 2.6 ppg, 1.2 rpg, 5 assists, 1 steal) Bean was a reserve power forward who started 4 games last year and appeared in 17 for a total of 119 minutes. He was not a key factor for Wyoming and can be replaced. Ten letterman are returning from Wyoming this year, so the graduation losses are certainly bearable.

LEE MAYBERY (6-9, F, 2.3 ppg, 2.3 rpg, 2 assists, 6 blocked shots, 11 steals) There were great expectations for Maybery at Wyoming. He was a in-state product and he came highly regarded. However, he was not a key factor during his first year in the program, appearing in only 24 games and starting none. Maybery just needed more time to get adjusted to major college basketball. With the deep depth chart at Wyoming, Maybery was concerned that he might not become a big factor quickly and he transferred to Fresno State.

KENNY SMITH (6-0, G, 11.7 ppg, 2.5 rpg, 107 assists, 3 blocked shots, 39 steals) Smith was Wyoming's starting point guard. He was the team's third leading scorer and top assist man. However, he was a poor perimeter shooter - only .378 from the field and .333 from three-point range, - and not a true point. He should be easily replaced. Junior college transfer Maurice Alexander is a stronger, more talented player than Smith and could be the best point guard in the WAC by the end of the season.

Dees should easily be able to handle the personnel losses from last year.

★ RETURNING PLAYERS ★

TODD BARNETT (6-3, 176 lbs., SR, G, #5, 4.7 ppg, 1.3 rpg, 80 assists, 19 steals, Messmer HS/Milwaukee, Wisc. & Labatte CC/Parsons, Kan.) Barnett was Kenny Smith's backup at point guard. He hit some big baskets for the Cowboys and started one game last year. For the season, Barnett made 47-of-134 field goals (.351) and connected on 26-of-78 (.333) three-pointers. From the line, Barnett made 16-of-26 attempts (.615).

He can also play second guard as well as the point. He is a decent ballhandler and shooter who can make some shots at times but is not consistent.

On Wyoming's trip to New Zealand in early June, the Cowboys were 8-0 and Dees was impressed with Barnett's improvement. "I thought Barnett improved especially near the end of the trip," Dees said. ". . . We did a much better job on cutting down on turnovers while we were in New Zealand. I thought Barnett, especially, did a better job in that regard."

Although Smith has departed, don't look for Barnett to take over the controls as Wyoming's point guard. That job will go to junior college transfer Maurice Alexander and Barnett will basically be in the same role again this year.

TIM BREAUX (6-6, 210 lbs., JR, G/F, #34, 12.8 ppg, 4.0 rpg, 55 assists, 4 blocked shots, 20 steals, Zachary HS/Zachary La.) Breaux started 29 games for Wyoming as a sophomore. He stepped up and played very well in Wyoming's 10-day trip to New Zealand last June. Breaux averaged over 25 points per game as Wyoming went 8-0 in New Zealand. His outstanding play continued a trend Breaux established late last year. In seven of his last eight games he scored in double figures, and in three of those he hit for 20 or more, including a career-high 26 against Hawaii, in the final regular season game. Breaux averaged 18.3 points per game in his last eight games. He also finished second on the team in scoring and was an honorable mention All-WAC selection.

Breaux was an inconsistent shooter last year (.403 from the field and .365 from three-point range) but is expected to be much improved this year. He can rebound, is extremely strong and the Cowboys' top defender. He struggled during the early part of the last season but the Wyoming coaching staff is convinced Breaux can carry an increased offensive load all season long.

Now that he has experienced success, Breaux should be ready for a great year. He has the potential to be an All-WAC performer this year.

MICHAEL BROWN (6-7, 220 lbs., JR, F, #32, 1.3 ppg, 1.0 rpg, 6 assists, 3 blocked shots, 8 steals, Madison HS/Houston, Tex.) Brown was a part-time starter last year. He started 13 games, but played only a total of 184 minutes. His strength is rebounding, however, Brown struggles defensively and tries to do too much offensively. He just is not capable of putting the ball on the floor against good teams as his 21 turnovers vs. six assists attests. As long as Brown rebounds, plays physical ball and stays within that role he'll be fine. However, once he steps outside of that role his effectiveness diminishes and so will his playing time.

TRAVIS BUTLER (6-5, 185 lbs., JR, G/F, HS/Memphis, Tenn.) Butler was one of several Cowboys Dees thought benefitted from the Cowboys New Zealand trip. He played hard throughout the trip. However, that is nothing new as Butler's intensity has served as a spark for Wyoming for the past two years.

He excels defensively and is a rare player who can attack defensively and create consistent havoc. Butler has great quickness, can rebound and is an adequate shooter. He made 52- of-100 field goals (.520) last year and 16-of-32 three-point attempts (.500). From the line, Butler was 31-of-52 (.596). He also blocked 12 shots.

There is no doubt that this defensive igniter is a key player for Wyoming.

STEVE GOSAR (6-0, 185 lbs., FR, G, #12, Pinedale HS/Pinedale Wyo.) Gosar is one of three Wyoming natives on the team. He is a walk-on who did not appear in any games last year for the Cowboys. His brother is an outstanding linebacker on the Wyoming football team.

RICK HENRY (6-4, 195 lbs., JR, G, #3, 2.9 ppg, 1.5 rpg, 24 assists, 6 blocked shots, 9 steals, Waggner HS/Louisville, Ky.) Henry came off the bench last year for Wyoming and played in 26 of 29 games for 297 minutes. Although Henry struggled from the field last year, he should be one of Wyoming's best outside shooters. He made 23-of-60 field goals (.383) and was 12-of-35 (.343) beyond the three-point arc. From the line, Henry made 17- of-26 free throws (.654). He is one of the Cowboy's best defenders and does a lot of the little things coaches look for that don't show up in the box score.

Henry is not a great player but he is solid and Dees has confidence in him. There is no doubt he should see ample playing time this year.

QUEIN HIGGINS (6-9, 220 lbs., SO, F, #30, 8.5 ppg, 4.8 rpg, 12 assists, 43 blocked shots, 14 steals, Fairhope HS/Fairhope, Ala.) Higgins almost has to be considered a newcomer as for most of the summer it was doubtful he would return to Wyoming. In fact, he was not listed as a returning player and was written up as a personnel loss in Wyoming's summer prospectus. Higgins' godfather, Thad Fitzpatrick, recruited him from Fairhope, Ala. to Wyoming. Last spring, Fitzpatrick left Wyoming to take an assistant coaching position at Miami (Fla.) and Higgins announced he was leaving for a junior college. He did not accompany Wyoming on the Cowboys 10-day trip to New Zealand in June.

Higgins' absence from the New Zealand trip turned out to be somewhat of an advantage for the Cowboys. Some other players got more playing time and the Cowboys gained confidence from winning without Higgins. Late in the summer, Higgins had a change of heart and decided to return to Wyoming for his sophomore year. Higgins is the most highly regarded player Wyoming has ever signed. He was the top prospect in Alabama as a senior and recruited by all the prime programs. He is an excellent shot blocker who led Wyoming in blocks and is extremely quick. Higgins is also an outstanding leaper with great timing.

Offensively, he's still developing as most of his game comes around the basket. He also is not much of a passer and averaged only one assist roughly every 2 games. For the season, Higgins made 97-of-171 field goals (.567) and was 52-of-73 (.712) from the line.

With Higgins' return, no other team in the WAC can match Wyoming's front line. New Mexico has All-America center Luc Longley, but Wyoming has more athletes up front. A member of the All-Newcomer team in the WAC, Higgins has the physical potential to one day be the premier player in the conference. It probably won't happen this year but in the future, Higgins could be a star.

KERRY McINTYRE (6-8, 200 lbs., SR, F, #00, 1.3 ppg, 0.7 rpg, 3 assists, 1 blocked shot, 2 steals, Grossmont HS/La Mesa, Calif. & Arizona Western JC/Yuma, Ariz.) Last season was McIntyre's first at Wyoming. He is a banger and plays tough post defense. He appeared in 12 games last year for a total of 61 minutes. McIntyre was 4-of-13 (.308) from the field and 6-of-12 (.500) from the free throw line.

He is expected to be a spot player again this year when some muscle is needed.

REGGIE PAGE (6-10, 245 lbs., JR, C, #33, 2.8 ppg, 3.6 rpg, 11 assists, 22 blocked shots, 2 steals, Washington HS/Fremont, Calif.) Page originally signed with Arizona, but asked out of his letter of intent when the Wildcats picked up Maryland transfer Brian Williams two years ago. He had to sit out the 1988-89 season at Wyoming before playing last year. He started 25 of 28 games, with limited success. Page made 33-of-69 field goals (.478) and a mere 12-of-23 free throws (.522). The left- handed Page is a good back-to-the basket scorer. He plays strong post defense, possesses good hands, but is not a shotblocker. During the trip to New Zealand, Page improved his offensive skills, stamina and mobility. He had off-season shoulder surgery which appeared to help his game.

Wyoming should have good depth in the pivot this year with Page and 6-9 sophomore Brian Rewers. All-WAC player Reginald Slater could also fill in the pivot when needed.

BRIAN REWERS (6-9, 235 lbs., SO, F/C, #23, 2.0 ppg, 1.7 rpg, 4 assists,

4 blocked shots, 3 steals, Hot Springs HS/Thermopolis, Wyo.) Rewers is originally from Calumet City, Ill., and moved to Wyoming while in high school. He was impressive while on the trip to New Zealand. As a freshman, Rewers started two games and played 204 minutes. He was 23-of-42 (.548) from the field and 9-of-18 (.500) from the line.

Rewers has quick feet for his size and is a physical player with a good feel for the game. Rewers and Reggie Page will share the pivot for Wyoming this year. They are both strong, physical, and could provide some offense and give Dees 10 fouls to work with in the middle.

REGINALD SLATER (6-7, 250 lbs., JR, F, #50, 16.7 ppg, 11.3 rpg, 29 assists, 24 blocked shots, 27 steals, Kashmere HS/Houston Tex.) While Wyoming was basically an inconsistent, disappointing team last year, one Cowboy managed to shine. Reginald Slater managed to stand above his teammates in terms of productivity and consistency. He was a first-team All-WAC performer and finished second in balloting for conference player of the year honors. Slater not only led Wyoming in scoring and rebounding, but topped the WAC in rebounding and field goal percentage (.578). He was the first WAC player to lead the conference in both rebounding and field goal percentage since 1980.

Slater had numerous big scoring and rebounding games. He had 22 points and 18 rebounds in a win over San Diego State, 31 points and 11 rebounds in a home win against Utah, 18 points with 17 rebounds in the non-conference win over Fullerton State and he closed the season with 24 points and 14 rebounds in the season- ending loss to Hawaii in the WAC tournament.

He averaged over 30 points per game on Wyoming's June tour of New Zealand. The powerful Slater is a rock under the boards who is going to score and rebound against anyone in the country. With Slater, Higgins, Pages and Rewers, Wyoming should be very strong up front.

★ **NEWCOMERS** ★

MAURICE ALEXANDER (6-1, 190 lbs., JR, G, #11, 16.5 ppg, 7.0 apg, Waxahachie HS/Waxahachie, Tex. & Tyler JC/Tyler, Tex.) While Reggie Slater led the WAC in rebounding and field goal percentage last year and Wyoming should be very strong up front, the key to the program is a player who is yet to suit up for the Cowboys. The Cowboys have gone the last two years without a true point guard. Last year's starting point guard, Kenny Smith, was not really suited for the position, and the Cowboys suffered without a real playmaker. Also, Wyoming lost many games last year because its outside shooting was poor. Alexander should solve both of those problems.

He is built like a running back and is a great perimeter shooter. Alexander passes extremely well, penetrates and just has excellent all-around skills and physical attributes for a point guard. He was recruited heavily by Cincinnati, Arizona State, Syracuse and Tulane in addition to Wyoming.

A third-team junior college All-America pick, Alexander led Tyler JC to a 22-7 record. He shot 53 percent from the floor and 48 percent from three-point range. He had a season-high of 42 points in one game. His brother Todd played at Minnesota and Southern Methodist.

''A lot hinges on how well he can come in, and play. We expect him to be a hard-nosed guy who can play the point, and the wing. He is a complete package . . . he is a good defender, has good feet, he can shoot the ball. We're really looking forward to him coming,'' Dees said.

Alexander could be the best point guard at Wyoming in quite some time. He has potential to be the best point in the WAC by the end of the season.

PARIS BRYANT (6-2, 175 lbs., JR, G, #22, 29.3 ppg, 3.0 rpg, 3.0 apg, Jeffersonville HS/Jeffersonville Ind. & Walker JC/Jasper, Ala.) Last season, opposing teams packed their defenses in so tight on Wyoming that the Cowboys inside offense was often stifled. Lack of consistent shooting was the major problem for Wyoming all year long. After the season Dees said, ''I don't guarantee much, but I guarantee we are going to get some guards in here who can shoot. We have made a promise to our team, to the fans, to ourselves to recruit some shooters. We aren't bringing in anyone who cannot do that . . . guards are what we are after. . .''

Dees has certainly delivered on his promise with the recruitment of junior college transfers Maurice Alexander and Paris Bryant. Bryant was a second-team junior college All-America and the nation's fifth leading JC scorer last year. He shot 89 percent from the free throw line, 50 percent from the floor, as well as 51 percent from three-point range. He was selected as the MVP of his junior college region.

Bryant is a definite big league shooter. He is not as physical as Alexander and is more of a second guard type. He picked Wyoming over Kansas State and Florida.

BRETT STUDDARD (6-2, 170 lbs., SO, G, #14, 20.9 ppg, 7.0 apg, 2.3 stpg, Westover HS/Albany, Ga. & Abraham Baldwin JC/Tifton, Ga.) Studdard is an outstanding shooter who comes to Wyoming after one season at Abraham Baldwin JC. Dees used to coach at Abraham Baldwin and he knows the Studdard family.

Last year Studdard shot 48 percent from three-point range and over 50 percent from the floor.

He provides some insurance in the backcourt and gives Wyoming another outstanding shooter, something the Cowboys certainly need.

BOBBY TRAYLOR (6-7, 190 lbs., FR, F, #44, 19.0 ppg, 13.0 rpg, Cheyenne East HS/Cheyenne Wyo.) Traylor was selected as the *USA Today* player of the year for Wyoming last season. He signed with the Cowboys during the early signing period last fall and is another good shooter. He led Cheyenne East to three consecutive state tournament appearances and one state championship.

He will need some time to get acclimated to this level of competition and could be a redshirt candidate.

★ QUESTIONS ★

Expectations? The University of Wyoming is the only four-year college in the state and its fans are as demanding as any in the country. Expectations are high in Wyoming this year and that sometimes can cause problems for this program.

How quickly will junior college transfers Maurice Alexander and Paris Bryant mesh with the team?

★ STRENGTHS ★

Tremendous depth! Wyoming is very deep at all positions.

Versatility! This team can run or power the ball inside offensively, press or play strong half court defense.

Improved perimeter shooting! Last season, opposing teams packed their defenses so tight against Wyoming that the Cowboys were often stifled inside. Wyoming was definitely the ''Gang That Couldn't Shoot Straight'' but that should change this year with the arrival of junior college transfers Maurice Alexander and Paris Bryant.

A strong front line!

★ BLUE RIBBON ANALYSIS ★

One basketball sage once said ''the only guard who has ever won a championship is Fuzzy Thurston,'' the former Green Bay Packer All-Pro guard who led Vince Lombardi's line during the Green Bay dynasty. That remark is also in line with the old thinking in basketball that big men were the most important players in the game. Anyone who doesn't think that guards are important should have watched Wyoming in the last two years. Despite the presence of a talented front

line and the leading rebounder in the WAC last year, Reginald Slater, Wyoming finished 14-17 and 15-14, respectively, over the past two years. Simply, the Cowboys could not shoot consistently and were very limited at point guard.

Wyoming coach Benny Dees made finding a true point guard and some shooters his recruiting priority last spring. It looks as if Dees found what he is looking for in two junior college All-America performers, point guard Maurice Alexander and shooter Paris Bryant. Alexander is also a big time stroker who could be premier point guard in the WAC by the end of the season. Bryant is a major league shooter who was the fifth leading JC scorer in the country last year.

If Alexander and Bryant come through, the WAC better look out as Wyoming is loaded elsewhere. Up front, the Cowboys are strong with Slater and have depth in the post with Reggie Page and Brian Rewers. Both Pages and Rewers gained valuable experience on Wyoming's June tour of New Zealand.

Swingman Tim Breaux is Wyoming's best defensive player and he blossomed offensively late in the season and during the New Zealand tour. Another swingman, Travis Butler, is a major defensive presence who ignites the Cowboys off the bench. Forward Quein Higgins almost left the program when his godfather, former Wyoming assistant coach Thad Fitzpatrick, left to take a position at Miami (Fla.) but had a change of heart late in the summer and is back. Higgins was one of the Top 30 high school players in the country two years ago and is the most highly regarded player Wyoming has ever signed. He could eventually be the player of the year in the WAC.

The Cowboys are versatile defensively and deep. They also got a major confidence boost during the 8-0 trip to New Zealand. Wyoming went undefeated on the New Zealand trip without Higgins, graduated point guard Kenny Smith or JC transfers Alexander and Byrant. If success begets success, Wyoming is in great shape.

This year's addition of the Wyoming Cowboys could be better than the 1987-88 team led by Fennis Dembo and Eric Leckner. The Cowboys don't have two players with as much publicity as Dembo and Leckner, but all-round this is a better team. Once Alexander and Bryant get used to their new surroundings, Wyoming could roll. Wyoming should win the WAC and could be a Top 20 team by March.

The WAC tournament will be held in Laramie this year and that is another reason why Wyoming should win the WAC title and advance to the NCAA tournament. The Cowboys should also be well rested come tournament time as their last road game is on February 16.

LAST SEASON			
Sam Houston State	69-72OT	Nebraska	95-65
@Memphis State	75-91	@Hawaii	77-81
@Colorado	77-81	@San Diego State	59-68
Montana	78-58	@Colorado State	71-67
Evansville	66-64	Air Force	80-60
McNeese State	76-50	New Mexico	79-82
Northwestern State	80-68	@Air Force	63-69
Lamar	79-71	Brigham Young	64-75
@Southwest Missouri State	51-77	@Utah	80-76
#Northeast Louisiana	75-66	UTEP	59-70
#Fullerton State	69-51	Hawaii	61-60
@New Mexico	89-87OT	##Hawaii	63-66
@UTEP	62-72		
San Diego State	76-60	@ Road Games	
Colorado State	57-65	# Cowboys Shootout, Casper, WY	
Utah	98-87	## WAC Tournament, El Paso, TX	
Brigham Young	60-65		

1990-91 WYOMING SCHEDULE				
Nov.	24	Marshall	Jan.	26 @Brigham Young
	29	Missouri-St. Louis		31 @Hawaii
Dec.	1	Metro State (CO)	Feb.	2 @San Diego State
	5	@Kansas State		5 @Air Force
	9	@Montana		9 New Mexico
	12	Colorado		14 Utah
	14	Northern Iowa		16 @UTEP
	16	Memphis State		21 Air Force
	23	@Sam Houston State		23 San Diego State
	28-29	#Cowboy Shootout		26 Colorado State
Jan.	5	@New Mexico	Mar.	2 UTEP
	8	@Colorado		7-9 ##WAC Tournament
	10	Hawaii		
	12	College of Charleston (SC)	@Road Games	
	17	Utah	# Casper, WY (Holy Cross, Northern Arizona & Southern Mississippi)	
	19	Brigham Young	## Laramie, WY	

NOTES: Wyoming's first round opponent in the Cowboy Shootout is Northern Arizona . . . Dees has been around the WAC for three years and this is his opinion of the conference: ''The basketball is just as good. It's the exposure and the publicity that's bad,'' he said. ''Geographically, we in the WAC are so far away from each other, if you throw out Colorado State and Air Force, then you have Utah, Texas (UTEP), Hawaii, New Mexico, and California (San Diego State). I've been in the ACC and the SEC, and this is the toughest road schedule because of the distance. You can bus from North Carolina State to Duke or North Carolina in 20 minutes.'' . . . ''I can't even get kids to visit from California,'' Dees quipped. ''They all think I'm Andy Griffith.''

THE REST OF THE COUNTRY

AIR FORCE

LAST SEASON: 12-20
CONFERENCE RECORD: 3-13
STARTERS LOST: 3
STARTERS RETURNING: 2
CONFERENCE: WESTERN ATHLETIC (WAC)
LOCATION: COLORADO SPRINGS, CO
HOME FLOOR: CADET FIELD HOUSE (6,007)
NICKNAME: FALCONS
COLORS: BLUE AND SILVER
COACH: REGGIE MINTON, record at Air Force, 67-105.
Career record, 78-120.

Air Force has established a successful and occasionally nationally ranked football program, but like the other service academies, it has struggled in basketball.

Big men don't fit into the cockpit of a jet fighter very well and many of the cadets at the academy want to be pilots. Added to that are the military requirements and high academic standards for the Falcons.

Air Force has a good season when it doesn't finish last in the WAC, and this year the Falcons will be the pre-season choice for last in the nine-team league again.

The best player in Air Force basketball history, guard Raymond Dudley, has graduated. He averaged 21.4 points a game and was the WAC scoring champion for the second year in a row, although he was bothered much of the season with a knee injury. In his four years at Air Force, Dudley set more than 40 school records including career scoring (2,178 points), most WAC points (1,242), best WAC average (22.6 ppg), and most steals (148). The six-foot Dudley also set a WAC record for most points (1,242) in conference games.

The Falcons finished last in the WAC during the 1989-90 season but had two players chosen all-conference. Jeff Bowling was the best point guard in the league. He averaged 7.0 assists and 8.2 points a game. Bowling and Dudley worked well together. Also gone, besides Dudley and Bowling, is the team's second scorer, Dale French, a 6-6 forward who averaged 13.0 points.

Injuries were a major problem for Air Force last year. Eight players missed a total of 23 games with Dudley and French leading the list.

The Falcons finished 3-13 in the WAC and were seeded last in the conference tournament, but they had their day in the sun. Air Force beat San Diego State, 70-64, in overtime in the opening round. Air Force staged an upset by beating top seeded Colorado State, 58-51, in the quarterfinals. The Falcons were 11-for-11 at the foul line in that game. Air Force managed to put a scare into eventual tournament champion UTEP in the semifinals before losing, 57-54.

Air Force has just five lettermen returning with very little experience at guard. The man who will have to replace Dudley in the scoring column will be 6-4 senior **Chris Lowry** (12.2 ppg, 5.9 rpg). He is capable of shooting three-points and was the leading rebounder on the team last year.

The only other starter coming back is 6-8 senior center **Aaron Benson**. He averaged just 5.7 points and 5.7 rebounds, and will have to contribute a lot more this season.

Brent Roberts (3.9 ppg, 2.5 rpg) a 6-8 junior center, **David Quick** (1.3 ppg, 1.8 rpg), a 6-8 senior forward, and **George Irvin** (2.1 ppg, 1.1 rpg), a 6-1 sophomore guard, are the other returnees, but they were not factors last year. Irvin will be expected to replace Bowling at point guard. The remainder of the roster includes 6-2 sophomore guard **George Bulloci**,

6-4 sophomore guard **Steve Haase**, 6-0 junior guard **Robert Hawking**, 6-5 junior forward **Omar Simpson**, and 6-3 junior guard **Charles Smith**. None are projected as more than marginal contributors.

Air Force has never relied heavily on freshmen. First year cadets usually have trouble adjusting to the rigors of life at a service academy and do not have the time to dedicate to a sport. This year, the Falcons need help right away. Air Force does not give athletic scholarships with everyone at the academy on full military scholarship. So technically, the Falcons don't sign players. Twelve newcomers are expected to try out for the team. On that list are two big men who could fit in. **Clayton Davenport** is a 6-9 center from Von Ormy, Texas, and **Jason Deyoe**, a 6-8 forward from Woodland Hills, Calif.

Coach Reggie Minton lists five of his new players as swingmen who can play guard or forward. The list of new swingmen are **Clark James** (6-4 from San Diego), **Jim Locum** (6-4 from Rinard, Ill.), **Thomas Irvine** (6-7 from South Holland, Ill.), **Coleman Mark** (6-5 from Grand Rapid, Mich.) and **Charlie Simmons** (6-5 from Riverside, Calif.).

The guard position is where Air Force will need the most help. Five new names will try to have an impact. **Frederic Stephens** (6-4 from Colorado Spring, Colo.), **Matthew Powell** (6-4 from Barnesville, Ohio), **Travis Gilley** (6-2 from Carlsbad, Calif.), **Crispin Blanchette** (6-6 from Burke, Va.) and **Ben Caton** (6-3 from Alamosa, Colo.) will all have an opportunity in the backcourt.

BLUE RIBBON ANALYSIS

Air Force should be facing a lean year, but that's nothing new for the Falcons. They lack size, depth and experience.

Minton, however, realizes the limitations facing the Falcons and he allows for them. Air Force plays one of the easiest schedules in Division I basketball. Visiting Air Force this year will be NAIA teams Adams State, Regis College, Mesa State and Doane. Samford and Missouri-Kansas City also are scheduled. The Falcons' nonconference schedule is filled out by Kent State, Valparaiso, the University of Portland and the Met Life Classic (which includes Vermont, Utah State and host San Francisco).

Air Force has tried to play more of an up-tempo game the last two seasons but it might have to go back to slowing the ball down to be competitive this year. But with all new guards, even that could be difficult.

1990-91 AIR FORCE SCHEDULE		
Nov.	24	Adams State (CO)
	26	Regis College (CO)
Dec.	3	@Valpariso (IN)
	6	Mesa State (CO)
	10	@Missouri-Kansas City
	21-22	#Met Life Classic
	31	University of Portland
Jan.	3	@UTEP
	10	San Diego State
	12	Hawaii
	14	Doane College (NE)
	19	Utah
	24	@Brigham Young
	26	@Utah
	31	@New Mexico
Feb.	2	@Colorado State
	5	Wyoming
	7	UTEP
	9	Nicholls State (LA)
	13	@Hawaii
	16	@San Diego State
	21	@Wyoming
	23	Brigham Young

1990-91 AIR FORCE SCHEDULE *(Cont.)*		
Feb.	28	New Mexico
Mar.	2	Colorado State
	6-9	##WAC Tournament

@ Road Games
# San Francisco, CA (San Francisco, Utah State & Vermont)
Laramie, WY

AKRON

LAST SEASON: 16-12
CONFERENCE RECORD: INDEPENDENT LAST YEAR
STARTERS LOST: 2
STARTERS RETURNING: 3
CONFERENCE: MID-CONTINENT
LOCATION: AKRON, OH
HOME FLOOR: JAR ARENA (7,000)
NICKNAME: ZIPS
COLORS: BLUE AND GOLD
COACH: COLEMAN CRAWFORD, record at Akron, 16-12.

As the Zips embark on their new adventure in the Mid-Continent Conference, they will begin with at least one rock-solid offensive foundation — 6-1 senior **Mark Alberts** (15.7 ppg, 1.9 rpg), who emerged last season as one of the nation's foremost proponents of the three-pointer, averaging 4.5 per game. Alberts tied for second in that conference in department while knocking down 122-of-258 attempts, easily a school record. He also found time to dish out 84 assists (exactly three per game), which is fortunate since he was also serving as his own brand of point guard. Alberts' game high 30 points (vs. Southern Utah) was achieved in notable fashion: 10 threes. In fact, Alberts only tried 24 of his 282 field goal attempts from inside the 19-foot, 9-inch arc. Suffice it to say Akron might see a few box-and-ones but not too many straight zones.

When the Zips look inside, the ball will usually wind up in the hands of 6-7 senior center **Pete Freeman** (12.0 ppg, 8.2 rpg), who started 11 games while learning a new system after transferring from Duquesne. Despite starting less than half the season, he led the team in rebounding. Freeman's best two offensive performances (24 and 22 points) were saved for archrival Youngstown State. He showed flashes of dominance but needs to focus carefully on his intensity to attain the needed consistency for conference play.

A pair of 6-6 starters, seniors **Kevin McCarthy** (6.3 ppg, 5.6 rpg) and **John Wilczynski** (4.9 ppg, 3.2 rpg) return at forward. McCarthy transferred from Duquesne with Freeman and had some good games (11 rebounds) against decent competition (Middle Tennessee State). He was relatively consistent, but needs to elevate that consistency to a higher level along with providing some leadership during his senior year. A 240-pounder, McCarthy's increased contribution off the glass will be particularly important. Wilczynski will also be looked to for increased production as a senior, although more as a scoring small forward than a power forward like McCarthy. He is also a good passer, as evidenced by his 52 assists last season.

Akron's other three returnees, 6-3 senior guard **Illya McGee** (1.8 ppg, 2.0 rpg), 6-7 sophomore forward **Bill Kress** (0.7 ppg, 0.4 rpg), and 6-9 sophomore center **Jeff Hrjesa** (0.0 ppg, 0.1 rpg) were not major factors last season. Among them, only McGee figures to be more than that this season. McGee did register 55 assists while rebounding well as a backup at both point guard and off guard.

To bolster their depth, size and athleticism, the Zips went the junior college route for five recruits. **James Smith,** a 6-0 junior point guard (Triton, Ill, CC), and 6-8 junior forward **Marcellus Wright** (Alvin, Tex., CC) spent the second half of last season learning the system while practicing with the team. **Roy Coleman,** a 6-4 junior guard was a first team Division II Junior College All-America last year at Owen Technical College in Toledo, Ohio, where he averaged 25 points per game. Another 6-4 junior guard, **Dian Whitfield,** comes from Lakeland (Ohio) CC by way of Admiral King HS in Lorain, Ohio, a long respected high school program. He was an all-conference pick in the Ohio junior college ranks. Much needed size and rebounding strength will be provided by 6-10 junior **Rodney Tetzloff,** who arrives from Polk CC in Florida. The Zips also landed 6-8 freshman power forward **Mario Bell** (13.0 ppg, 5.0 rpg at Central HS in Memphis, Tenn.).

BLUE RIBBON ANALYSIS

In the first season in the Mid-Continent Conference, the Zips appear to be short on quality and experienced height as far as title contention goes. They will also depend on production from Wilczynski and McCarthy at forward on a different level from what they have yet proven. It is essential they both make the most of their senior year as their offense is necessary to balance the reliable perimeter scoring of Alberts. Unless a couple of newcomers emerge quickly, Freeman will not be able to afford much rest in the middle. If the four returning starters can blend their experience into a chemistry that exceeds its separate elements, Akron could force its way into fourth, which would not be a bad debut in the Mid-Continent.

1990-91 AKRON SCHEDULE

Nov.	24	@Kansas State
	28	Bowling Green
Dec.	1	Northeastern Illinois
	4	Kent State
	7-8	#Heritage Cablevision-Drake Classic
	15	Central Michigan
	22	Western Michigan
	29	Indiana (PA)
Jan.	2	@Cleveland State
	5	@Valparaiso (IN)
	7	@Illinois-Chicago
	12	Western Illinois
	14	Northern Iowa
	19	@Eastern Illinois
	23	@Youngstown State
	26	Wisconsin-Green Bay
	28	Northern Illinois
Feb.	2	Valparaiso
	4	Illinois-Chicago
	9	@Western Illinois
	11	@Northern Iowa
	16	Eastern Illinois
	18	Youngstown State
	23	@Wisconsin-Green Bay
	25	Northern Illinois
	28	@Cleveland State
Mar.	2-4	##Mid-Continent Tournament

@ Road Games
# Des Moines, IA (Drake, Eastern Washington & Lamar)
Green Bay, WI

ALABAMA BIRMINGHAM

UAB Blazers

LAST SEASON: 22-9
CONFERENCE RECORD: 12-2
STARTERS LOST: 3
STARTERS RETURNING: 2
CONFERENCE: SUN BELT
LOCATION: BIRMINGHAM, AL
HOME FLOOR: UAB ARENA (8,500)
NICKNAME: BLAZERS
COLORS: GREEN AND GOLD
COACH: GENE BARTOW, record at Alabama-Birmingham, 254-130. Career record, 536-279.

After ruling the Sun Belt Conference last season, Alabama-Birmingham figures to drop a few rungs in 1990-91. But as long as Gene Bartow remains at the controls, don't count the Blazers out. The conference race should be a close one and, even though UAB is minus three starters, the Blazers have enough talent on hand to give the favorites a fit.

The three missing regulars - 7-2 center Alan Ogg, strong forward Larry Rembert and point guard Barry Bearden - helped UAB earn a berth in the NCAA tournament for the eighth time in the school's 12 seasons. The trio also accounted for almost 31 points and 14 rebounds per game, with Bearden's five assists per night thrown in for good measure. Reserve William DeVaughn (4.2 ppg), who made his 6-9 presence felt, is also gone.

Yet Bartow hopes to have one of his quickest and strongest rebounding teams ever, making it difficult for the opposition to handle the Blazers at both ends of the court. As a bonus, the two returning starters - seniors **Andy Kennedy** and **Jack Kramer** can both bury three-pointers and force the defense to play honest.

A 6-8 swingman who transferred from North Carolina State, Kennedy led the Blazers in scoring (16.9 ppg) a year ago. He is UAB's all-time three-point shooting leader with a 64-game total of 211-for-477 (44.2 percent), and is well on the way toward becoming one of the NCAA's all-time bonus shooters. Kennedy, who can strike from anywhere within 30 feet, also led the Sun Belt in free throw percentage (90.2) and was one of the most accurate foul shooters in the country.

Kramer, a 6-3 transfer from Michigan, led UAB in assists for the second straight season, handing out 5.7 per game while averaging 9.9 points. The heady guard did not put up as many threes as Kennedy, but converted a higher percentage (43.8). Though not fast, Kramer can hurt an unsuspecting team with a barrage from the perimeter.

It might be difficult for Kramer to keep his starting job with 6-3 sophomore **Stanley Jackson** (3.8 ppg, 4.3 rpg) on the scene. A Sun Belt all-freshman team selection, Jackson last year established himself as one of the most exciting players ever to wear a UAB uniform. His remarkable athletic ability and tenacity made him an extremely valuable asset and a crowd favorite. With more playing time, Jackson is capable of improving his numbers dramatically.

Another sophomore who figures to crack the starting lineup is 6-3 guard **George Wilkerson,** who joined Jackson on the league's All-Freshman squad. Wilkerson took advantage of his talents to average 2.8 ppg, 2.3 rpg and 2.1 assists in a relief role and developed into an effective defender as the season progressed. He has the potential to be one of the top guards in the conference.

One of the men underneath for UAB will be 6-7 junior **Elbert Rogers,** arguably the best sixth man in the league last season. Rogers was the Blazers' second-leading scorer (12.0 ppg) and third-leading rebounder (4.7 rpg) despite starting only one game. One could make a case for Rogers being the Blazers' MVP a year ago, and the forward should post even higher numbers as a starter.

Expected to join Rogers on the block is junior college transfer **Stan Rose.** The 6-7, 220-pounder should give Bartow some much-needed strength under the boards. A two-time All-District 18 performer at Utah Valley CC, Rose averaged 21.7 ppg and 9.6 rpg last year. He was ranked among the nation's Top 30 JUCO players by *The Sporting News* and received honorable mention All-America honors from *Blue Ribbon.*

Providing depth in the backcourt is **J.J. Smith,** a 5-11 redshirt sophomore with solid ballhandling skills and a good touch from the perimeter. He played in 30 games in 1988-89, averaging 2.6 ppg. Smith also gives the Blazers another three-point threat who can play either guard position.

Giving the big men some rest will be 6-7 **Willie Chapman,** a sophomore who sat out last year and should help under the boards. Chapman averaged 15 points and 12 rebounds as a senior at Jackson (Ala.) High two years ago. Bartow is also hopeful 7-0 sophomore **Doug Turner** can contribute more after playing in 15 games last year and averaging less than a point.

In addition to Rose, the Blazers have six other newcomers, led by 6-4 guard **Carter Long,** 6-4 swingman **Frank Haywood** and 6-6 forward **Reginald Allen.** Long (Winfield, Ala.), who scored 2,128 points during his career at Winfield High, was first-team All-State as a senior, when he averaged 33.7 ppg and 12.1 rpg along with 7.9 assists. Haywood (Birmingham, Ala.) was a first-team All-City performer at Parker HS, where he averaged 25.6 ppg and 14.6 rpg. Allen (Alexander City, Ala.) averaged 25.3 ppg and 11.5 rpg for Benjamin Russell High en route to first-team All-Area and second-team All-State honors.

The other freshmen are 6-6 forward **Ken Ward** (Montgomery, Ala.), who notched 17 points and 14 rebounds for Carver HS, 6-7 forward **Greg Edmonds** (Grant, Ala.), who averaged 26 points and 12 rebounds for D.A.R. High and 6-8 forward **Clarence Thrash** (Atlanta, Ga.), whose numbers at Westlake HS were 19 ppg and 14 rpg.

BLUE RIBBON ANALYSIS

Bartow's troops will have to play better defense, if only because Ogg is not around to swat away shots in the paint. His presence alone was enough to intimidate many Sun Belt teams. The quickness of Wilkerson and Jackson will help compensate for the loss underneath. As usual, Bartow's coaching savvy will be another strong factor in the Blazers' favor. This will be his 13th season at the helm of UAB, and there has been only one losing campaign.

The Blazers are capable of winning another league title, but are more likely a year away from doing it again. Despite the presence of Kennedy and Rogers, who will probably be the two major offensive contributors, there is a bit too much inexperience for this squad to go all the way. Third place looks like the best bet for UAB. While the Blazers will likely miss the NCAA tournament, count on them appearing in the NIT and giving Bartow yet another post-season appearance.

1990-91 ALABAMA-BIRMINGHAM SCHEDULE

Nov.	23-24	#UAB Invitational
	30	Auburn
Dec.	1	##UNLV
	4	@Oregon
	8	Southern University
	14-15	###UAB Classic
	22-23	*Chaminade Classic

Dec.	28-29	**All-College Tournament
Jan.	3	@North Carolina Charlotte
	5	Western Kentucky
	7	@Virginia Commonwealth
	13	St. Louis
	17	South Florida
	19	@Western Kentucky
	23	Virginia Commonwealth
	25	@New Orleans
	30	@Arkansas
Feb.	2	@Jacksonville
	7	@Old Dominion
	9	Jacksonville
	11	Old Dominion
	14	@South Florida
	16	@South Alabama
	23	South Alabama
	25	North Carolina Charlotte
Mar.	2-4	***Sun Belt Tournament

@ Road Games
# Birmingham, AL (Alabama State, Lamar & Sanford)
Vancouver, British Columbia
Birmingham, AL (Florida A & M, Monmouth & Washington State)
* Kauai, HI (Chaminade, Saint Francis & Virginia Commonwealth)
** Oklahoma City, OK (Illinois State, Oklahoma & Tulsa)
*** Mobile, AL

ALCORN STATE

LAST SEASON: 7-22
CONFERENCE
RECORD:6-8
STARTERS LOST: 3
STARTERS
RETURNING: 2
CONFERENCE:
SOUTHWESTERN
ATHLETIC (SWAC)
LOCATION: LORMAN, MS
HOME FLOOR: SCALPIN' GROUNDS ARENA (10,060)
NICKNAME: BRAVES
COLORS: PURPLE and WHITE
COACH: LONNIE WALKER, record at Alcorn State, 7-22.

Alcorn State's Braves hope to be on the basket-ball warpath this season. And if they aren't, they would at least like to improve 100 percent over last year's dismal showing.

In his first season as head coach, Lonnie Walk-er and the Braves won only seven of 29 games. In Southwestern Athletic Conference play, Alcorn was 6-8, good enough for only fifth place. Outside the SWAC, the Braves were 0-13, yet the former Alcorn assis-tant remains optimistic.

"Things are going to be looking up for us this season," Walker insisted. "We're going to play ex-citing basketball and we're going to be competitive. Last year, we played our first 12 games on the road before getting back to Lorman for a home game.

"This year, we have a few more home games at the start of the season, and that's going to help."

What will not help is the loss of three starters - 6-10 center Clarence Cain (8.0 ppg, 6.1 rpg), and guards Arthur Harris (16.6 ppg, 4.6 rpg, 50 steals) and Larry Smith (6.5 ppg, 3.0 rpg, 76 assists). Cain left the team due to academic problems; Harris, the team's best player, and Smith were seniors a year ago. Also gone are role-playing forwards Michael Malone and Deshawn McDonald.

Fortunately for Braves' fans, three players with

significant starting experience do return, and they may help steer Alcorn back toward SWAC respectability. 6-6 sophomore forward **Levi Wyatt** (8.2 ppg, 5.9 rpg, 55 blocked shots), 6-3 sophomore swingman **Reginald Ward** (7.0 ppg, 3.0 rpg), and 6-7 senior forward **Steve Thomas** (6.7 ppg, 5.0 rpg) give Walker at least some stability in the lineup.

6-3 sophomore **Derald Spears** (5.6 ppg, 2.2 rpg,) was an occasional starter, getting the call 16 times. 6-3 soph **Michael Banks** (4.2 ppg, 2.5 rpg) started 10 games. **Terrance Pace** (1.1 ppg, 1.0 rpg), a 6-6, 215-pound sophomore, adds some beef to the smallish frontcourt.

Still, if the Braves are to make any kind of seri-ous leap forward, the debut of three sophomores who sat out last season will be critical. Walker brought in a host of newcomers last year, but lost three of the best - 6-6 forward **Chris Jones** (Northeast HS/Laurel, Miss.), 6-6 forward **Ernie Tubbs** (Cleveland Heights HS/Cleveland, Ohio) and 5-9 point guard to-be **Don-tae Galloway** (Stone County HS/Wiggins, Miss.). Jones and Galloway were Mississippi all-staters in their final prep seasons.

"My outlook is very optimistic," said Walker. "I can't really put my finger on, it but I feel good about it. Our kids have been working hard in summer leagues and on paper they look tremendous. But you don't win games on paper.

"I'm hoping to make this season exciting, rewarding and enjoyable for the team. The first part of the season we'll try to get our system down and get set for conference games. We hope to make a much better showing in SWAC this year than last."

The one true freshman likely to contribute im-mediately is 6-7 center **John Hall** (Velma Jackson HS/Canton, Miss.). Hall also captured All-State honors for his 27.7 ppg and 12.6 rpg. Other signees include 6-1 guard **Brian Lane** (Dillard HS/Fort Lauderdale, Fla.) and 6-4 Dillard High teammate **King Kindred** (14.5 ppg, 15.1 rpg) was the inside monster on a team which went 29-3. Also from Dillard, via countless rec leagues, is 6-6 **Albert Jones**, a 24-year-old "fresh-man" with no collegiate experience.

Over the long haul, Alcorn's top freshman tal-ent could be 6-0 guard **Shedrick McKenzie** of Wilkin-son High in Woodville, Miss. McKenzie hit the hoops for 30.4 points per game in his senior year at Wilkin-son. Another gunner is 6-2 **Michael Johnson**, (Waltrip HS/Houston, Tex.). A three-point specialist, Johnson averaged 22.4 points per game.

"Kindred can definitely help us," said Walker. "Like Wyatt, he can jump out of the gym. He has a 43- or 44-inch vertical jump. McKenzie could be one of the top shooters in the conference, and (Albert) Jones is a 6-6 kid who weighs 240. He stayed out of college the first three or four years after high school and played recreation basketball. Now, at 24, he wants to go to college. He's a man, and he can play."

Walker says defending regular season champ Southern University and tournament champion Texas Southern remain the SWAC's two top teams.

"Ben Jobe has a habit of winning at Southern and he knows his way around the league," Walker said. "Texas Southern lost several key players, but they'll be back near the top. Andy Stoglin at Jackson State could have the surprise team in the league. He's a good recruiter and a good motivator.

"Alabama State could be dangerous if they can find anybody to get points along with Steve Rogers. Rogers is quite a shooter. Mississippi Valley is another team with a good shooter in Al Ford. The SWAC race should be interesting, and we hope to make it even more exciting."

BLUE RIBBON ANALYSIS

Walker inherited a veteran team in his first year, yet still managed to start 10 players five games or more. This season, with only Steve Thomas claiming more than one year of experience, the Braves don't figure to come together any faster.

There are plenty of young bodies at Alcorn, but similar statements were made a year ago. The ques-tion is whether or not Walker can identify the most talented rotation and stick with it. At least his deci-sion to go up-tempo will extend that rotation by three or four more players.

Wyatt, Hall, Kindred, McKenzie and Galloway have the look of a successful nucleus down the road. The best bet might be just to put them on the floor and let them grow together. Why not experiment? The Braves, not yet close to SWAC contention, have noth-ing to lose.

1990-91 ALCORN STATE SCHEDULE

Nov.	24	Miles College
	27	@North Texas
Dec.	1	@Mississippi College
	3	Western Illinois
	5	Arkansas-Pine Bluff
	7-8	#Jowers Jamboree
	10	Northeastern Illinois
	15	Middle Tennessee State
	18	@Mississippi State
	22	@Northeastern Illinois
Jan.	2	@Morehead State
	5	Mississippi Valley State
	7	Grambling State (LA)
	12	@Jackson State
	14	@Alabama State
	21	@Texas Southern
	26	@Southern University
	28	@Western Illinois
Feb.	2	@Mississippi Valley State
	4	@Grambling State
	9	Jackson State
	11	Alabama State
	13	@Tennessee State
	18	Texas Southern
	23	Southern University
Feb. 28-		
Mar.	2	##SWAC Tournament

@ Road Games
# San Marcos, TX
Houston, TX

AMERICAN UNIVERSITY

LAST SEASON: 20-9
CONFERENCE
RECORD: 10-4
STARTERS LOST: 2
STARTERS
RETURNING: 3
CONFERENCE:
COLONIAL
ATHLETIC
ASSOCIATION (CAA)
LOCATION:
WASHINGTON, DC
HOME FLOOR: BENDER
ARENA (5,000)
NICKNAME: EAGLES
COLORS: RED, WHITE AND BLUE
COACH: CHRIS KNOCHE, first year at American University.

With Georgetown and Maryland dominating the headlines and George Washington, George Mason and Howard University all fighting for attention, the Washington, D.C. area is a tough room to work for American University. Yet, under departed couch Ed Tapscott, the Eagles put together some quietly respec-table seasons (relative to talent level), including a December, 1982, upset of Georgetown. Last year's squad was predicted to be "the best American team in a long time" by rival league coach Dick Tarrant of Richmond. The 1989-90 Eagles indeed lived up to expectations and almost made Tarrant live to rue his prophecy before dropping a 91-90 double overtime decision to Richmond in the second round of the CAA tournament. The cornerstone of that squad, 6-9 all-conference center Ron Draper (16.1 ppg, 12.1 rpg) has departed along with solid starter, 6-7 Daryl Holmes (13.6 ppg, 7.9 rpg). New coach Chris Knoche, Tapscott's assistant for eight years, faces a major task in replacing Draper's inside presence and finding some reliable inside offense.

Knoche can probably start from the outside in, as 6-2 senior guard **Brock Wortman** (14.3 ppg, 2.7 rpg) looks to be the most reliable returning scorer. Wortman missed ten games with a broken elbow last season. The Eagles went 7-2 with him, 5-5 without him, then 8-2 after Wortman returned. He was deadly from three-point range (44-of-91, .484 percent) and shot 85.5 percent from the line. Against Wichita State, Wortman threw in a career high 29. He will also be called up to handle the ball some as well as provide the bulk of perimeter offense. Wortman makes good decisions with the ball.

Wortman will be complemented at the point by 6-2 senior guard **Fred Tillman** (4.8 ppg, 2.1 rpg). Nicknamed "the Sheriff" for his defensive tenacity, Tillman started slow, then came on strong to start the last 19 games. His best was a 23-point effort vs. William and Mary. Tillman is a good athlete and will be looked to for senior leadership at the point.

A very important player up front for the Eagles figures to be 6-6 sophomore swingman **Brian Gilgeous** (10.5 ppg, 3.9 rpg, 51 assists, 35 steals). An all-rookie selection in the CAA, Gilgeous could blossom into an impact player this season, which is what American University needs to replace Draper. Knoche looks for him to be a force at both ends as a mid-range scorer and quick-handed defender.

6-9 sophomore forward **Craig Sedmak** (5.3 ppg, 2.7 rpg) will hopefully ease the loss of Draper as an inside presence. Sedmak averaged 8.6 ppg as a starter in 10 of the last 11 games last season. He came up big in a 59-58 thriller over James Madison with 16 points. "Craig has the talent to be one of the top forwards in the league," says Knoche. "His understanding of the game and offense should be a big plus for our frontcourt." It will have to be as there is little other returning quality experience. 6-6 junior forward **Fred Cooper** (1.6 ppg, 0.9 rpg) transferred from New York University. He will get a chance to show his shooting touch and help off the glass. The strongest part of 6-8 senior center **Ron Davenport's** (2.6 ppg, 2.2 rpg) game is passing. 6-11 sophomore center **Sean Stevens** (1.6 ppg, 0.6 rpg) needs to bulk up. He only began to play as a high school junior. Knoche feels with continued hard work, Stevens' shooting touch, hands, and shotblocking ability will eventually make him a surprise force in the league. "He oozes potential," says Knoche. To realize it, Stevens, at 6-11, will have to average better than half a rebound per game.

In the backcourt, 6-3 sophomore guard **John Rooney** (5.7 ppg) could develop into a contributor. Like Wortman, he is a three-point specialist (47.4 from long range last season). With Rooney and Wortman, American University can open the floor without worrying much about zones.

Knock brought in three high school recruits, a transfer, and a junior college transfer. 5-10 freshman guard **Brian Mackey** (Fairmont Heights HS, Capital Heights, Md.) was a three-year starter, fourth team All-Metro Washington, D.C., and leading scorer in Prince Georges County as a senior. At his height, he'll have to prove he can take his shot to the next level. If so, Mackey will push an already relatively deep backcourt. So will 6-0 junior guard **Donald Grant**, who started 23 games for Old Dominion and averaged nearly five assists per game. His 137 assists (4.9 per game to go with 5.4 rpg) placed him fifth in the Sun Belt. Grant has the experience plus a good jumper that could wind up landing him considerable quality time at both guard positions.

Up front, where the Eagles scream for more im-

mediate help, Knoche will look to 6-7 freshman forward **Bryan Palmer** (14.0 rpg at Garfield HS in Woodbridge, Va.). Palmer played on a state champion team as a junior and will be counted on as an immediate contributor. Also coming into the program will be 6-4 junior guard **Bryan Hawkins** (7.9 ppg, 3.6 rpg at San Jacinto JC of Pasadena, Texas), probably the nation's most celebrated junior college program. Hawkins, originally from Coolidge HS, Washington, D.C., also compiled 111 assists and 32 steals. Hawkins is billed as an excellent athlete with three-point range. Also joining the fold is forward **Erick Grace**, a sophomore — eligible from Kathleen HS in Lakeland, Fla.

BLUE RIBBON ANALYSIS

Coach Ed Tapscott and one of the nation's premier rebounders, Ron Draper, are gone from last year's 20-win edition of the American University Eagles. Former Tapscott assistant Chris Knoche is the new head coach.

Even if Gilgeous takes his game to the next (consistent major force) level, the Eagles are going to sorely miss the bedrock pivot play of Ron Draper. Unless Sedmak emerges quickly or Stevens rises from obscurity, American University looks like a team with an overcrowded backcourt and an understocked frontline. Wortman and company will put points on the board. But do the Eagles have the size, athleticism and talent to stop the other guys from putting up more? Knoche is going to need much improvement out of a lot of inexperience to challenge for the CAA's first division. A drop to sixth place looks most likely.

1990-91 AMERICAN UNIVERSITY SCHEDULE		
Nov.	27	Univ. of the District of Columbia
Dec.	1	Lehigh
	3	Old Dominion
	7-8	#Mile High Classic
	11	@Loyola College
	15	Ohio State
	18	Florida Atlantic
	22	@Santa Clara
Jan.	5	North Carolina Wilmington
	7	East Carolina
	12	@Richmond
	16	William & Mary
	19	@James Madison
	23	@George Mason
	26	Navy
	29	@Maryland
Feb.	2	@East Carolina
	4	@North Carolina Wilmington
	6	Towson State
	9	Richmond
	11	@Navy
	13	@William & Mary
	16	James Madison
	20	George Mason
	23	@George Washington
	25	@College of Charleston (SC)
Mar.	2-4	##CAA Tournament

@ Road Games
# Boulder, CO (Central Connecticut, Colorado & Eastern Michigan)
Richmond, VA

APPALACHIAN STATE

LAST SEASON: 19-11
CONFERENCE RECORD: 8-6
STARTERS LOST: 2
STARTERS RETURNING: 3
CONFERENCE: SOUTHERN
LOCATION: BOONE, NC
HOME FLOOR: VARSITY GYM (8,000)
NICKNAME: MOUNTAINEERS
COLORS: BLACK AND GOLD
COACH: TOM APKE, record at Appalachian State, 62-53. Career record, 251-198.

After winning 55 games the past three seasons and advancing to the finals of the Southern Conference tournament a year ago, Appalachian State enters what coach Tom Apke calls a season of transition.

For the first time since Apke took over the program, the Mountaineers will be without All-Southern Conference center Sam Gibson, point guard Kemp Phillips and top reserve Ben Miller. It was that trio which fueled Appalachian's four-year improvement under Apke, and last year led the Mountaineers to within one game of the NCAA tournament. Their careers, and Appalachian's season, did not end until a loss to East Tennessee State in the Southern final.

Clearly, whether the Mountaineers can equal or improve on last year's 19-11 record depends on how quickly Gibson, Phillips and Miller are replaced. The threesome combined for just under 1,000 points and 400 rebounds as seniors.

"Normally," said Apke, "the two key positions are point guard and post man. We've lost both of them. Plus, we're also missing a forward who started most of his career. Replacing quality players is always a problem, but when they play those positions, it's doubly difficult."

Three starters do return for Appalachian State, including 6-4 junior **Broderick Parker** (12.6 ppg, 4.6 rpg) and 6-8 junior **Steve Spurlock** (12.0 ppg, 5.6 rpg, 27 blocked shots), a pair of quick, athletic forwards. Rodney Peel (11.5 ppg, 3.1 rpg, 98 assists) moves to the point after three years at shooting guard.

Apke has depth and size in the frontcourt, where he must identify a third starter. Possibilities include 6-9 junior **Tim Powers** (3.4 ppg, 3.0 rpg), 6-8 senior **Jimmy Stewart** (1.7 ppg, 1.0 rpg) and 6-6 senior **Pat Lyons** (2.1 ppg, 1.0 rpg). Powers appeared in all 30 games a year ago and Lyons in 25, but Stewart returns after missing all but three games with a broken foot. Others forwards who will press for time are 6-9 sophomore **Spencer Click** (2.0 ppg, 1.0 rpg) and 6-7 senior **Bruck Falkner** (0.5 ppg, 0.0 rpg).

The play of Peel, though, may matter most of all. A 6-0 senior with a string of 87 consecutive games, he has the talent to run the show. Two years ago, Peel filled in when Phillips broke a foot midway through the season and, last year, he led the Mountaineers in minutes, steals and three-point field goals. Among the starters, he trailed only Phillips in assists and free throw pecentage.

6-4 senior **Ed Ward** (4.2 ppg, 2.6 rpg, 31 assists) is a three-year letterman and last year was the first guard off the bench. He committed just 21 turnovers in 469 minutes. If Ward does not get the starting nod alongside Peel, that job may go to 6-6 sophomore **Billy Ross**, (4.6 ppg, 1.8 rpg), a Southern Conference all-freshman team selection. 6-1 sophomore **Joe Sabato** (1.0 ppg, 1.0 rpg) played sparingly behind Phillips last season, but could see more action at the point this year as a backup to Peel.

Apke signed four freshman, at least one of whom should contribute immediately. **Ricky Nedd**, a 6-7 forward, averaged 18 points and 12 rebounds last season at Brewster Academy in Wofleboro, N.H. A New York City native, Nedd averaged 16 points and eight rebounds as a junior at La Salle Academy. At least one rival Southern Conference coach believes Nedd is talented enough to start.

Appalachian's other incoming freshmen, all from in-state, are 6-5 **Jason Lutz**, 6-4 **Tony Thompson** and 6-2 **Jeff Williams**. Lutz (Charlotte, N.C.) averaged 15 points and six rebounds for West Charlotte High. Thompson (Dudley, N.C.) averaged 24 points and eight rebounds at Southern Wayne HS. And Williams (Asheboro, N.C.), a forward at Asheboro High, moves to the backcourt as a collegian after averaging 18 points, six assists and five rebounds in his final scholastic season.

BLUE RIBBON ANALYSIS

Gibson, Phillips and Miller will be missed, but Apke has begun to establish a winning tradition at at Appalachian State. If Parker and Spurlock can increase their scoring output and Peel makes a smooth transition to point guard, the Mountaineers are certain to finish in the Southern Conference upper division.

"I truly hope we have established a winner here," Apke said, "but I still think this is a transition year for us. We have enough question marks heading into the season for me to feel that way."

In other words, the Mountaineers are at least a year away from seriously challenging for an NCAA tournament berth.

1990-91 APPALACHIAN STATE SCHEDULE

Nov.	24	@Arkansas State
	28	Belmont Abbey (NC)
Dec.	1	North Carolina Wilmington
	3	Montana State
	5	@North Carolina Charlotte
	8	East Carolina
	12	Southwestern Louisiana
	20-21	#Hawaii Pre-Holiday Classic
	28	@Montana State
Jan.	2	@North Carolina Asheville
	5	@East Tennessee State
	8	@Davidson
	12	The Citadel
	14	Furman
	19	@Tennessee-Chattanooga
	21	@Western Carolina
	26	Marshall
	28	Virginia Military Institute
Feb.	2	East Tennessee State
	4	Southern Mississippi
	9	@Furman
	11	@The Citadel
	16	Western Carolina
	18	Tennessee-Chattanooga
	23	@Virginia Military Institute
	25	@Marshall
Mar.	1-3	##Southern Conference Tournament

@ Road Games
# Honolulu, HI (Hawaii, North Texas & Wagner)
Asheville, NC

ARIZONA STATE

LAST SEASON: 15-16
CONFERENCE
RECORD: 6-12
STARTERS LOST: 23
STARTERS RETURNING: 2
CONFERENCE: PACIFIC-10
LOCATION: TEMPE, AZ
HOME FLOOR: UNIVERSITY ACTIVITY CENTER (14,287)
NICKNAME: SUN DEVILS
COLORS: MAROON AND GOLD
COACH: BILL FRIEDER, record at Arizona State, 15-16.
Career record, 206-103.

When Arizona State managed to lure Bill Frieder away from Michigan just before the start of the 1989 NCAA playoffs, the Sun Devils knew they had recruited one of college basketball's best recruiters. And Arizona State soon became a part of the best story of that '88-89 season: Michigan athletic director Bo Schembechler refused to allow lame-duck coach Frieder to guide the Wolverines in the playoffs, so his replacement, veteran assistant Steve Fisher, takes the school to its first ever NCAA basketball title.

Frieder critics are certain the Wolverines would not have succeeded if he had stayed. But all of this

only seemed to add to the fast growing Frieder lore. Here is a man who left one of the most successful college basketball programs in the country for another football-is-king school in a state where the arch rival's head coach, Arizona's Lute Olson, can do no wrong.

If anything, Frieder brought Arizona State basketball more exposure and "ink" in one year that the school had experienced in a decade. Stories on Frieder's obsession with basketball at the expense of normal living, stories on his remarkable memory that has had him banned from blackjack tables in Las Vegas, etc.

It all translated into renewed interest in Sun Devil basketball, which had been operating in semi-obscurity for almost a decade. Frieder promised he would start filling the spacious University Activity Center in a year or two. He got almost halfway there in his first season, an average of 6,994 per game that was the best since 1981.

In fact, Arizona State has initiated a priority-seating program, its first ever for basketball. In the past, you could sit just about any place you wanted for most games.

The emphasis last year was on Frieder. He was the man the media was writing about and interviewing on camera. And he showed he didn't enjoy all those 20-win seasons at Michigan without understanding some X's and O's. Among the Sun Devil on-court accomplishments was an upset of No. 1 seed Oregon State in the Pac-10 tournament and the school's first postseason tournament appearance (NIT) since 1982-83. Frieder also found time to land one of the nation's top recruiting classes. The group of five freshmen and one junior college transfer is listed anywhere from second to sixth nationally by various respected recruiting services.

That means the emphasis will switch to the players this season, particularly the new talent. The major question is how soon the newcomers will be major contributors.

Leading scorer Alex Austin, single season assist leader Mike Redhair and power forward Mark Becker were the starters who departed. Frieder figures to rebuild his frontline around 6-10 senior **Isaac Austin** (13.7 ppg, 6.2 rpg). Frieder's first and only recruit in his first spring. Isaac, Alex Austin's younger brother, improved as the year progressed and he got in better shape.

On paper, 6-10 senior **Emory Lewis** (3.5 ppg, 2.8 rpg* is a potential starter. But Lewis has been almost a non-factor for his three seasons because of injuries. Last year he played in 30 games, seven more than his first two seasons because of back, hip or leg problems. At the end of his sophomore season, he scored in double figures in five of the last six games, including one 22-point effort. He has never returned to that form, in part because he has logged only 659 minutes in three years.

Frieder will have to complete his frontline with youth, even if Lewis develops into a starter. The only true center he recruited was 6-10 freshman **Robert Conlisk** (18.5 ppg, 10.5 rpg) from Los Alamitos (Calif.) HS. Sophomore forward **Marlon Jones**, 6-7, logged only ten total minutes a year ago and didn't score a point. He figures to be bypassed by 6-7 forward **Jamal Faulkner** (24.0 ppg, 15.0 rpg) from Christ the King HS (Middle Village, N.Y.) who spent last year at Cheshire Academy in Connecticut after originally signing a letter of intent with Pitt. The other potential freshman starter is 6-8 forward **Ian Dale** (28.0 ppg) from South HS in Houston, Texas. Faulkner, a first team all-New York City player, was considered Top 20 in America coming out of high school. He could be a great catch for Arizona State. Faulkner has the strength and ball sense to rebound inside, the range to score from 15 to 18 feet, and some uncanny, slithery moves with which to create penetration. Dale was rated national Top 60 by Bob Gibbons of *All Star Sports*. Says Frieder, "Faulkner can become a dominant scoring force in the Pac-10 and Dale, with an improved work ethic, can be a great player."

The frontline is a bit thin, numerically. That same problem does not exist in the backcourt. 6-6 sophomore swingman **Brian Camper** (5.5 ppg, 2.3 rpg), who started 20 of 31 games last year after 6-4 senior off-guard **Matt Anderson** went down with a knee injury. Camper developed into a strong defender in the second half of the season, but his offense needs to improve. He shot only .417 from the field and made but one of 14 three-pointers. Anderson (10.7 ppg) led the Pac-10 in three-point accuracy (.513 percent) in 1988-89, but fell off to 38.3 percent last year. He definitely was not at full speed for the last nine games after returning from a six-game layoff with the injured knee.

While Anderson has successfully recovered from his knee problem, the major question mark surrounding Arizona State this season is whether or not **Tarence Wheeler** will be a major contributor. The 6-2 senior was easily one of the top guards in the conference two years ago before a freak (right) knee injury sidelined him for more than a year. He was injured while playing defense against California on January 5, 1989. The knee required major reconstructive surgery and rehabilitation that will have reached 21 months when practice starts. In his 11 games as a junior before going down, Wheeler was averaging 15.5 points, 3.1 rebounds and 3.5 assists per game.

Frieder's best recruiting came in the backcourt. He landed 6-1 guard **Lynn Collins** (17.5 ppg, 5.0 rpg, 4.0 apg) from Odessa (Tex.) JC. Collins was listed by the *1989 Blue Ribbon Basketball Yearbook* as the top junior guard prospect in the country. He is a point guard, and the Sun Devils have a hole to fill there with Redhair's departure.

The best of the newcomers, however, may be 6-2 guard **Stevin Smith** (25.0 ppg) from Spruce HS in Dallas, Texas, who ranked high among the major prep All-America listings and was the eighth best point guard in America, according to *The Sporting News*. Another member of Frieder's highly rated recruiting class is 6-4 guard **Dwayne Fontana** (22.0 ppg) from Riordan HS in San Francisco. He averaged 32.0 ppg in leading the Las Vegas Invitational Tournament in scoring summer before last while sharing MVP honors with the famed Ed O'Bannon (29.0 ppg), a junior guard whose minutes fell off from 414 as a freshman to 76 in his first season under Frieder, does not figure prominently. **Ron Waller** (0.2 ppg), a junior guard whose minutes fell off from 414 as a freshman to 76 in his first season under Frieder, does not figure prominently.

BLUE RIBBON ANALYSIS

If Frieder is worried about exposing his talented new faces to the perils of the road, he has taken care of that. Arizona State plays 18 of its 28 regular season games, plus two exhibitions, at home. The Sun Devils leave home but once, a trip to Brigham Young, in preparation for conference play. That's probably a smart move because the future of the Sun Devil program is with the freshman class. There's new excitement about college basketball building in the Valley of the Sun, and the more times Frieder can expose his young talent to the home folks, the better. Arizona State was 6-12 in the Pac-10 a year ago and should improve on that, even with such youth. Frieder needs Tarence Wheeler to return to the same form he was playing two years ago as a junior. That's probably asking too much after almost two years of rehabilitation.

Wheeler's leadership is needed. Otherwise, newcomer Lynn Collins will have to run the show. If Austin has firmed up what appeared to be an overweight frame last year, he can be a force inside.

Sun Devil fans got a good taste of what's ahead with the Sun Devils' fine showing in the Pac-10 tournament. Frieder's first Sun Devil squad played surprisingly good defense, something his Michigan teams were not noted for.

If the young talent has the same work ethic, the Sun Devils could challenge a 20-win season and should receive another postseason invitation. It could be from the NCAA as the Pac-10's fourth place team. More probably, it will come from the NIT after a fifth place finish.

<table>
<tr><th colspan="3">1990-91 ARIZONA STATE SCHEDULE</th></tr>
<tr><td>Nov.</td><td>23</td><td>Kansas</td></tr>
<tr><td></td><td>24</td><td>Southern Methodist</td></tr>
<tr><td></td><td>29</td><td>Northern Arizona</td></tr>
<tr><td>Dec.</td><td>1</td><td>Drake</td></tr>
<tr><td></td><td>5</td><td>New Mexico</td></tr>
<tr><td></td><td>12</td><td>@Brigham Young</td></tr>
<tr><td></td><td>21</td><td>Southern Utah State</td></tr>
<tr><td></td><td>22</td><td>Montana State</td></tr>
<tr><td></td><td>28-29</td><td>#ASU-Tribune Classics</td></tr>
<tr><td>Jan.</td><td>3</td><td>@Washington State</td></tr>
<tr><td></td><td>5</td><td>@Washington</td></tr>
<tr><td></td><td>10</td><td>UCLA</td></tr>
<tr><td></td><td>13</td><td>Southern California</td></tr>
<tr><td></td><td>19</td><td>Arizona</td></tr>
<tr><td></td><td>24</td><td>@California</td></tr>
<tr><td></td><td>27</td><td>@Stanford</td></tr>
<tr><td></td><td>31</td><td>Washington</td></tr>
<tr><td>Feb.</td><td>2</td><td>Washington State</td></tr>
<tr><td></td><td>7</td><td>@UCLA</td></tr>
<tr><td></td><td>9</td><td>@Southern California</td></tr>
<tr><td></td><td>16</td><td>@Arizona</td></tr>
<tr><td></td><td>21</td><td>Stanford</td></tr>
<tr><td></td><td>24</td><td>California</td></tr>
<tr><td></td><td>28</td><td>@Oregon</td></tr>
<tr><td>Mar.</td><td>2</td><td>@Oregon State</td></tr>
<tr><td></td><td>7</td><td>Oregon</td></tr>
<tr><td></td><td>9</td><td>Oregon State</td></tr>
</table>

@ Road Games
# Tempe, AZ (Michigan, Pennsylvania & Texas)

ARKANSAS LITTLE ROCK

LAST SEASON: 20-10
CONFERENCE RECORD: 12-4
STARTERS LOST: 2
STARTERS RETURNING: 3
CONFERENCE: TRANS-AMERICA (TAAC)
LOCATION: LITTLE ROCK, AR
HOME FLOOR: BARTON COLISEUM (8,303)
NICKNAME: TROJANS
COLORS: MAROON AND GOLD
COACH: JIM PLATT, first year at Arkansas-Little Rock.

It may be cliche to talk about a team entering a new era when a new coach arrives but, in this case, the cliche fits. Mike Newell, the golden-haired golden boy who put Arkansas-Little Rock on the basketball map with 133 wins in six seasons, grew tired of threats of cutting back on the program and left for Lamar.

Taking over in Little Rock is former DePaul assistant Jim Platt, not nearly as flashy as Newell but a solid basketball man just the same. In his time at DePaul, the Blue Demons averaged more than 20 wins per season.

As for the Trojans, Platt inherits a team that lost nearly 60 percent of its scoring and rebounding punch, but still returns three starters. He also inherits a team that stumbled through the middle of last season, prompting the school's chancellor to threaten to shut the program down if it did not show a profit. UALR had secured host duties for the TAAC tournament by outbidding the rest of the conference, and the administration feared taking a financial bath.

"It puts a lot of pressure on these kids," Newell understated on the day following the chancellor's announcement. But the Trojans responded. UALR won eight of its last 10 games, swept through the TAAC tournament as the third seed and earned another NCAA berth.

"They were the best team at tournament time," said one rival TAAC coach. "That's when you have to do it."

The downside for Platt is that the two catalysts for the comeback, guard Carl Brown and forward Derrick Owens, are gone. The pair accounted for 34 points per game. Three starters return, however, and there is quality among them.

Leading the way is junior **Rod Wade** (12.7 ppg, 7.3 rpg), a 6-7 jack-of-all-trades who has been everything from point guard to center for the Trojans. Wade will play the small forward spot, after leading the team last season in "double-doubles." Ten times he hit double figures in both scoring and rebounding. Also up front, junior **James Womack** (12.5 ppg, 8.0 rpg) moves from the post to power forward. During UALR's stretch drive, the 6-6 Detroit native increased his numbers to 14.4 points and 8.6 rebounds.

Another "do-everything" type, 6-2 senior **James Scott** (12.7 ppg, 5.8 rpg), returns with point guard, shooting guard and small forward experience from last season. Scott figures to settle in at the second guard spot this year, and he needs just 64 points to become UALR's all-time leading scorer.

"The best thing about the starters we have coming back is that they're as versatile as they are experienced," Platt said. "That gives a coach a lot of different options."

The rest of the pieces for the Trojans fall together nicely. Newcomer **Erskine Caldwell** (Memphis, Tenn.), a 6-9 junior who sat out last year after leading Mississippi County JC to two Arkansas junior college titles, will battle 7-2 junior **Tony Jones** (2.2 ppg, 2.6 rpg) for the starting job at center. Jones finished strong last season, collecting nine rebounds in UALR's loss to UNLV in the first round of the NCAA tournament. Senior **Dwayne Booker** (4.6 ppg, 2.9 rpg), a 6-7 banger, offers more help at the power positions.

Shooting guard is also crowded, where holdover sophomores **Derrick Hall** (6.8 ppg, 2.3 rpg) and **David Hall** (no relation) will be joined by a pair of newcomers, 6-3 **Robert Greene** (Rochester, Mich.) and 6-5 **David Redmon** (Valparaiso, Ind.). David Hall (7.9 ppg, 2.6 rpg) set a Trojan single-game freshman scoring record when he lit up Georgia State for 36 points. Greene averaged 15.3 points for Coffeyville (Kan.) JC. Redmon was the top prep three-point shooter in Indiana last winter, averaging 28.9 points for Valparaiso High.

Point guard is a toss-up among three more newcomers. 6-1 sophomore **Jamar Banks** (Hammond, Ind.), who sat out last season, has the inside track, but two incoming freshmen, 6-2 **Cordell Robinson** (Oak Park, Ill.) and 6-0 **Darren Erickson** (Fort Worth, Texas), will push.

BLUE RIBBON ANALYSIS

The pieces are in place for a smooth transition from Newell to Platt. The new guy in town will debut with a nice mix of experience and versatility. Scott has demonstrated the ability to take up Brown's scoring load and leadership responsibilities.

Womack and Wade are both ready to play more dominant roles.

Even if Jones is not quite ready to start at center, he should contribute more than last year. Neither he nor Caldwell will be expected to provide much scoring, leaving them free to pound the boards and block shots. Point guard is the real question mark, but either Scott and/or Wade can play there if push comes to shove.

The schedule is tough, with a date at Illinois plus a home-and-home with Louisiana Tech. In addition, the TAAC tournament has been awarded to Stetson.

Several of the conference coaches felt UALR bought itself a championship last year by buying the conference tournament site.

This season, the Trojans probably won't need that advantage. UALR will be on the TAAC leader board all year long.

<table>
<tr><th colspan="3">1990-91 ARKANSAS LITTLE ROCK SCHEDULE</th></tr>
<tr><td>Nov.</td><td>26</td><td>Arkansas State</td></tr>
<tr><td></td><td>28</td><td>@Texas Christian</td></tr>
<tr><td>Dec.</td><td>1</td><td>Louisiana Tech</td></tr>
<tr><td></td><td>5</td><td>@Jackson State (MS)</td></tr>
<tr><td></td><td>7-8</td><td>#First Bank Classic</td></tr>
<tr><td></td><td>15</td><td>@Illinois</td></tr>
<tr><td></td><td>17</td><td>@UTEP</td></tr>
<tr><td></td><td>20</td><td>Austin Peay</td></tr>
<tr><td></td><td>27</td><td>Jackson State</td></tr>
<tr><td></td><td>29</td><td>@Arkansas State</td></tr>
<tr><td>Jan.</td><td>2</td><td>@Louisiana Tech</td></tr>
<tr><td></td><td>10</td><td>Georgia State</td></tr>
<tr><td></td><td>12</td><td>Mercer</td></tr>
<tr><td></td><td>14</td><td>Samford (AL)</td></tr>
<tr><td></td><td>17</td><td>@Texas-San Antonio</td></tr>
<tr><td></td><td>19</td><td>@Centenary (LA)</td></tr>
<tr><td></td><td>23</td><td>@Austin Peay</td></tr>
<tr><td></td><td>31</td><td>##Georgia Southern</td></tr>
<tr><td>Feb.</td><td>2</td><td>##Stetson</td></tr>
<tr><td></td><td>7</td><td>#Georgia State</td></tr>
<tr><td></td><td>9</td><td>@Mercer</td></tr>
<tr><td></td><td>14</td><td>Texas-San Antonio</td></tr>
<tr><td></td><td>16</td><td>Centenary</td></tr>
<tr><td></td><td>21</td><td>@Samford</td></tr>
<tr><td></td><td>28</td><td>@Georgia Southern</td></tr>
<tr><td>Mar.</td><td>2</td><td>@Stetson</td></tr>
<tr><td></td><td>5-7</td><td>###TAAC Tournament</td></tr>
</table>

@ Road Games
# Milwaukee, WI (Marquette, Mississippi Valley State & TBA)
Pine Bluff, AR
Deland, FL

ARKANSAS STATE

LAST SEASON: 15-13
CONFERENCE RECORD: 2-8
STARTERS LOST: 3
STARTERS RETURNING: 2
CONFERENCE: AMERICAN SOUTH (ASC)
LOCATION: JONESBORO, AR
HOME FLOOR: CONVOCATION CENTER (10,563)
NICKNAME: INDIANS
COLORS: SCARLET AND BLACK
COACH: NELSON CATALINA, record at Arkansas State, 109-75.

Even though Arkansas State finished with its sixth consecutive .500 or better season, last year's 15-13 campaign is one head coach Nelson Catalina would just as well forget.

For starters, the Indians' three season streak of 20 or more wins was snapped, as was Arkansas State's three-year string of NIT appearances. The Indians finished fifth in the American South with a 2-8 mark, the poorest conference showing by a Catalina-coached squad in his six years at Arkansas State. And the Indians limped home, losing 11 of their last 16 games.

But most telling was a crisis in mid-February when the players boycotted one practice and returned only after the school's administration listened to their grievances.

"In one sense, it was a disappointing season," said Catalina. "We started off the season 7-1, but we didn't come back from the Christmas break with the same intensity and fire. Then we lost a couple of close games in conference when we didn't do the things we needed to do.'' And it went downhill from there.

''Even with the boycott, we still won 15 games,'' Catalina said. ''After losing four starters from a team (in 1988-89) that went to the NIT quarterfinals, I though a realistic goal for last year's team was 17 wins. So we weren't that far off. People thought the boycott would really hurt our recruitment. But our recruiting went well. Hopefully, last year's situation will make me a better coach.''

Catalina will build his 1990-91 squad around two returning starters, seniors **Bobby Gross** and **DeWayne McCray**. The 6-3 Gross (12.1 ppg, 3.3 rpg, 76 assists, 28 steals) was the Indians' second leading scorer and led the Indians in scoring six times last year. A second team All-America South Conference selection at guard last season, Gross made great strides after averaging less than two points per game as a sophomore. McCray, a 6-6 forward (11.4 ppg, 7.8 rpg, 57 assists, 2 blocked shots, 43 steals), led the team in rebounding and was the team's third leading scorer.

The Indians boast plenty of depth at the forward spots in seniors **Philip McKellar** and **Keith Gray** and sophomore **Fred Shepherd**. A 6-6 forward/guard, McKellar (7.9 ppg, 2.8 rpg, 67 assists, 5 blocked shots, 25 steals) started nine games last season. McKellar, an excellent passer, who sat out all but two games of the 1988-89 season because of arthroscopic knee surgery, should be more of an offensive threat this season. Gray (4.5 ppg, 0.9 rpg), a 6-1 senior guard, connected on 47.6 percent of his three-point attempts (10-of-42). Shepherd, a 6-6 sophomore low-post forward (3.2 ppg, 4.2 rpg), showed promise as a freshman. Despite averaging less than 16 minutes per game, Shepherd finished as the Indians' third leading rebounder. 6-1 sophomore **Brian Reaves** (2.0 ppg, 14 assists, 6 steals) provides depth at point guard.

Because the Indians lost nine players from last year's squad, including three starters —6-9 Greg Williams, 6-2 Barry Mayberry and 6-4 Bobby Collins — several things, particularly inside play, cry out to be replaced. Though Williams' 12.2 points per game average wasn't overly impressive, he led the ASC in field goal percentage (60.2 percent) and was the league's fifth leading rebounder (7.6 rpg). Mayberry led the Indians in assists (107) while averaging 10.9 points per game. Also departed was Al Banister, a 7-5, 290-pounder.

''Our first concern is our post play because we lost those two fine players,'' said Catalina. ''Because of this, we may play smaller and try to be quicker. We have two 6-10's and a couple of 6-7's, but we are awfully young.''

Catalina is banking on four junior college transfers to shore up the post and point guard positions. 6-10 **Kelly Rottinghaus** redshirted last season after averaging nine points, five rebounds and two blocked shots per game as a sophomore at Allen County (Kan.) CC. Catalina likes Rottinghaus' offensive potential, but says his defense must improve if he is to nail down the starting center position.

Catalina says **Tyrone Hall** would be a first round NBA draft choice if he were three inches taller. The 6-5 Hall averaged 14.1 points and 10.6 rebounds per game at Seward County (Liberal, Kan.) CC. An outstanding leaper, Hall is a strong candidate for one of the starting post positions. **Corey Cole**, a 6-1 junior, is ticketed for the starting point guard position after averaging 8.3 points and 5.4 assists per game at Barton County CC in Great Bend, Kan. **Gary Wehrum**, a quick, 6-5 junior small forward who averaged 10 points per game at Cincinnati Technical College, could contribute as a defensive stopper.

Mike Philpot, 6-10, 235 pounds, averaged 20 points and 10 rebounds per game for Manual HS in Louisville, Ky. Though Catalina does not rule out Philpot from contending for playing time, Philpot may be a year away from contributing.

However, 6-8 freshman **Paul Turlais**, who averaged 17 points and 12 rebounds a game at

Effingham (Ill.) HS, should figure into the race for a starting post spot. Catalina's fourth freshman recruit, 6-3 **Chris Norris**, will probably have to wait his turn after averaging 15 points, 3.5 rebounds and four assists at Pine Bluff (Ark.) HS.

''We'll have to wait and see how we develop at the five spot,'' said Catalina. ''We could start a 6-10 guy there. But we may also go with a smaller guy and try to use our quickness.''

BLUE RIBBON ANALYSIS

Last season may have shook the foundation, but the solid program that Nelson Catalina has built in his six years at Arkansas State still stands. Because of his system that's based on outstanding defense and efficient offense, the Indians are a solid bet for between 15 and 20 wins per season.

Nothing should change in 1990-91, although Catalina must blend an unusually high number of newcomers in with his veterans. Bobby Gross, DeWayne McCray and Philip McKellar provide a solid core to build around and junior college transfers Kelly Rottinghaus, Tyrone Hall and Corey Cole offer plenty of exciting talent. Cole's ability to make the transition as floor leader from the junior college ranks to Division I will be very important.

''A lot will depend on how we get started,'' said Catalina, ''and how quickly our players develop in the post. If we can blend the new players in with our veterans, we could contend for the league championship.''

That is a possibility, knowing the track record of Catalina's program. But we think Arkansas State is destined for a fourth place finish this season in the underrated American South Conference.

1990-91 ARKANSAS STATE SCHEDULE

Nov.	24	Appalachian State
	26	@Arkansas-Little Rock
	30-Dec.1	#Boston College Classic
Dec.	7-8	##Citizens Bank Classic
	16	###Mississippi
	18	@LSU
	21-22	*Texaco Star Classic
	29	Arkansas-Little Rock
Jan.	2	Morgan State (MD)
	5	Louisiana Tech
	10	@New Orleans
	12	Southwestern Louisiana
	17	@Central Florida
	24	@Texas-Pan American
	26	@Lamar
	28	Mississippi Valley State
Feb.	2	@Louisiana Tech
	6	New Orleans
	9	@Southwestern Louisiana
	11	@Mississippi Valley State
	14	Central Florida
	21	Texas-Pan American
	23	Lamar
	25	@Texas Tech
Mar.	1-3	**ASC Tournament

@ Road Games
# Chestnut Hill, MA (Boston College, Drexel & Wagner)
Jonesboro, AR (Murray State, Oral Roberts & Texas Southern)
Memphis, TN
* San Diego, CA (Drexel, Lamar & San Diego State)
** Site to be announced

ARMY

LAST SEASON: 10-19
CONFERENCE RECORD: 5-11
STARTERS LOST: 2
STARTERS RETURNING: 3
CONFERENCE: PATRIOT
LOCATION: WEST POINT, NY
HOME FLOOR: CRISTL ARENA (5,043)
NICKNAMES: CADETS & BLACK KNIGHTS
COLORS: BLACK, GRAY AND GOLD
COACH: TOM MILLER, first year at Army.
Career record, 106-164.

Going into 1989-90, there was much optimism surrounding the Army basketball program. Seniors Ron Wilson, Todd Mattson and Steve Rothert, along with high scoring junior Derrick Canada, would give Army opponents more than their share of problems. Les Wothke's Cadets could even surpass their 16-13 record of 1984-85. The Black Knights, it seemed, finally had all their guns armed. So what happened? By the time the season ended, Wilson, Rothert and Canada were all lost to either injuries or disciplinary actions and Wothke had resigned following a 10-19 season.

The question now is: What's left for new head coach Tom Miller to work with? The answer very simply is, not a whole lot, at least not on paper. Mattson did a yeoman's job (to steal a phrase from another branch of the service) late last season, and almost singlehandedly led the Cadets to their first round upset of St. Peter's in the MAAC playoffs. But he is lost to graduation.

That leaves Miller, a Bobby Knight disciple, who last coached at Colorado, just two starters from last season, streaky 6-4 senior forward **Kevin Berry** (6.6 ppg, 2.9 rpg) and 6-5 junior long range bomber **James Collins** (10.0 ppg, 3.0 rpg). Other than that, the Cadets will have to go with a large number of greener than fatigue recruits.

In the frontcourt, 7-0, 270 pound junior **David Ewing** (1.7 ppg, 1.4 rpg) appears to be the heir apparent at center, with 6-7 junior **Greg Clark** (1.1 ppg, 1.1 rpg) filling the other forward spot. Ewing is nothing if not imposing, and Cadet followers are hoping the fiery Miller can make him into the player that many expected him to be on his arrival at The Point. Miller has made it clear that the battle for playing time up front could not be more wide open, and four freshmen, 6-8 **Jeff Casucci** (15.2 ppg at Bergen, N.J., Catholic), 6-6 **Derk Schwieger** (19.1 ppg at Hampton-Dumont HS in Dows, Iowa), 6-5 **Dave Ardafiyo** (22.2 ppg at Southfield, Mich., HS), and 6-5 **Michael Etley** (19.5 ppg at Mansfield, Tex., HS), will also throw their hats into the ring.

In the backcourt, Collins will probably be joined by 6-4 senior **Joe Harris** (2.3 ppg, 0.5 rpg) with classmates 6-3 **Chad Michaelsen** (4.8 ppg) and tough-nosed 6-0 **Larry Gnewuch** (2.1 ppg) also challenging. 5-7 freshman **Chris Eddy** (15.8 ppg at Fairview, Pa., HS) and 6-0 freshman **Glenn Duhon** (10.1 ppg at Lake Highlands HS, Dallas, Tex.) could also see some time, along with little used shooter 6-0 junior **Craig Rose** (0.6 ppg).

Army will be a play-by-play typist's nightmare as Miller searches for a winning combination. The four guard setup of Collins, Harris, Michaelsen and Gnewuch with Ewing in the middle may be a familiar sight. Then again, pick any five players and there is a good chance you could see them together. Depth will not be a problem; quality will.

BLUE RIBBON ANALYSIS

Miller is a graduate of the Academy and knows the value of learning through adversity. This season could provide a lifetime of experience for this group of Cadets. They will always play hard and will never quit, but the talent level is not anywhere near what it was last season. Hopefully, Berry will give Cristl Arena some thrills and Collins is a great open jump shooter. Ewing's size is enough to scare any smaller opponent and Harris can shoot from outside as well, but can they play for 40 minutes? The schedule is not an easy one, and even though they host the first Patriot League tournament, the Cadets will do well to get out of the first round. It is a little scary to think of an Army team that can't shoot. This version will hopefully do better on the range than they probably will do on the floor. Double figure wins is a long shot, sixth place in the Patriot League is a better goal to shoot for.

AUBURN

LAST SEASON: 13-18
CONFERENCE RECORD: 8-10
STARTERS LOST: 1
STARTERS RETURNING 4
CONFERENCE: SOUTHEASTERN (SEC)
LOCATION: AUBURN, AL
HOME FLOOR: JOEL EAVES MEMORIAL COLISEUM (12,500)
NICKNAME: TIGERS
COLORS: BURNT ORANGE AND NAVY BLUE
COACH: TOMMY JOE EAGLES, record at Auburn, 13-18.
Career record, 100-58.

Go figure. For most of the 1980's, Auburn put winning, exciting teams on the floor. Teams with marquee names like Charles Barkley, Chuck Person and Chris Morris, all directed in up-tempo style by a flamboyant, wise-cracking coach, the popular Sonny Smith. And Tiger fans avoided Joel Eaves Coliseum in droves.

Auburn may be the toughest basketball sell in the Southeastern Conference, and Smith finally left in frustration for Virginia Commonwealth. Enter little-known Tommy Joe Eagles - bland, spouting cliches and forced by a cupboard left bare into a deliberate,

blue-collar style that would put you to sleep if not for bodies flying regularly into the press table.

And all those football fans bought it. After years of fan neglect for far superior teams, Auburn faithful finally took a liking to a team that could barely dunk.

They did not pack the arena every night, but a team with no one on the floor over 6-foot-6 pulled in 8,750 fans per game, the second highest total in school history and the most in 14 years. Mainly they fell in love with an overachieving, never-say-die outfit that overcame some glaring deficiencies in talent with a hustling, scrambling attitude.

"I've never seen so many players diving for loose balls," said one SEC coach. Another wit remarked that Auburn fans showed up because the Tigers' blue-collar style could easily be mistaken for football.

Picked almost unanimously to finish dead last in the league for the second straight year, the Tigers were a surprising 8-10, tied for sixth in league play. They also found themselves a shocking 7-7 at one point in the race. Along the way, the Tigers broke a 15-game SEC road losing streak at Mississippi State and Eagles picked up his 100th career victory with a stunning upset of LSU in the first round of the conference tournament.

Imagine if the team had had any real talent? Well, Auburn fans might not have to wonder much longer.

Eagles wasted little time in rounding up a stellar class in his first recruiting effort, and one of the new faces has a familiar name - **Wesley Person,** younger brother of Chuck, the school's all-time leading scorer and a current star with the Indiana Pacers. Person should get a shot right away in place of Derrick Dennison, last season's small forward and the only starter not returning.

A 6-5 off-guard at tiny Brantley (Ala.) HS, Person (33.6 ppg, 10.0 rpg, 44 percent on three-pointers), had three 50-point games in high school. "He'll have a quick impact on our team," Eagles predicted. "He's the prototype player of the 90's with his shooting range and versatility."

Person, like his brother Chuck, was overlooked on many of the national blue-chip lists due to the small size of his school and the suspect competition. Instead, Alabama signee Cedrick Moore of Woodlawn High (Birmingham) was voted the state's high school player of the year.

But recruiting guru Bob Gibbons of All-Star Sports disagrees. "Put Wesley in Birmingham or particularly Atlanta," said Gibbons, "and he'd have been one of the Top Five prospects in the country." Eagles added: "Wesley is a tremendous passer with a soft shooting touch, but he also has the size to to take the ball to the basket and score. He has the athletic ability to play all three perimeter positions."

Look for Person on the wing, as the two guard spots appear to be in good hands for the next three years. The sophomore duo of 6-1 **Ronnie Battle** (17.0 ppg, 79 assists) and 5-10 **Reggie Gallon** (9.8 ppg, 119 assists) started every game as redshirt freshmen last season.

Gallon, the point guard, was named to the SEC all-freshman team. After sitting out his first year with a broken foot, Gallon capped a solid freshman season by being named honorable mention freshman All-America by Basketball Times. He was also a first-teamer on UPI's "Small America" team.

Defensively, Gallon was second on the team in steals (58) and one night held former LSU star Chris Jackson to nine points in Baton Rouge. It was the only time in Jackson's two-year career that he failed to reach double figures.

Battle was also a medical redshirt his first year at Auburn after suffering severe facial lacerations and a bruised knee in a head-on automobile collision while returning to campus for the Tigers' first game. Yet he made up for lost time last year, eventually being named Auburn's offensive MVP and becoming only the second freshman ever to lead the Tigers in scor-

ing (Eddie Johnson was the other in 1973-74). The leading three-point shooter on the team, Battle had 11 games of 20 or more points.

Backcourt depth will come from 6-1 junior walk-on **Champ Wrencher** (1.2 ppg), who played sparingly a year ago (1.2 ppg) and 6-5 senior **Larry Patrick** (3.5 ppg).

Inside, Auburn plays by committee. The Tigers have a lot of bodies, but lack the one dominating big man. Instead, 6-6 senior forward **John Caylor** (8.7 ppg, 6.8 rpg) might have best represented Auburn's hustling, team-oriented style up front. He, too, was granted a medical redshirt when a blood clot in his shoulder was found five games into 1988-89. (If you're keeping score, that's Battle, Gallon and Caylor who all missed Sonny Smith's last hurrah).

When Caylor returned under Eagles, he found his role significantly changed - from glamour to blue collar. One of the league's top three-point gunners as a sophomore (40-for-95), he was asked to mix it up inside and launched only seven treys the entire season. Then a series of nagging injuries forced him to miss three games and eventually prompted him into a valuable sixth-man role.

Yet Caylor was stung by the death of Loyola Marymount's Hank Gathers, and said after the LSU upset that he might not play as a senior in fear of the blood clot. However, extensive medical testing in the off-season resulted in blood-thining medication, and Caylor will be back. He did undergo minor arthroscopic knee surgery in August, but was expected to be fully recovered in time for pre-season practice.

Another forward, 6-6 junior **Chris Brandt** (11.7 ppg, 6.5 rpg) is one of the least impressive physical specimens in the SEC, yet somehow manages to get the job done and started all 31 games last season. He was the team's second-leading rebounder and third-leading scorer. 6-6 senior **Richard Smith** (0.6 ppg), who appeared in 21 games, could also have an expanded role.

Robert McKie (11.6 ppg, 6.6 rpg), a 6-5 sophomore, was the starter at center until an injury sidelined him five games into last season. He may have trouble winning his job back, though, particularly if he does not lose some weight. McKie last reported in the 255-pound neighborhood.

In his absence, 6-6 senior **Zane Arnold** (8.2 ppg, 6.5 rpg, 21 blocked shots) emerged as a quality player and one who will be difficult to unseat. Arnold struggled early, but improved considerably with increased playing time. More inside depth could come from 6-6 freshman **Cameron Boozer** (Lanett, Al.), who averaged 26 points and 12 rebounds at Lanett High.

The remainder of a freshman class rated 12th in the country by All-Star Sports includes 6-8 **Robert Shannon** (Jackson HS/Jackson, Ga.) and 6-5 **Aaron Swinson** (Brunswick HS/Brunswick, Ga.). Both were awaiting final eligibility determinations (see Late Breaking News section).

BLUE RIBBON ANALYSIS

Taking a backseat to football is not hot news in the SEC, but Auburn fans sometimes raised it to an art form, particularly considering the Tigers' success. All of which made Eagles even more qualified to take over the Auburn program.

In his previous stop at Louisiana Tech, Eagles had a four-year record of 87-40, four straight post-season appearances and three straight conference championships. Yet, like at Auburn, those teams were overshadowed - and more often than not out-drawn - by the super successful Lady Techsters' program.

But Eagles knows his way around a sudden influx of talent. At Louisiana Tech, he tutored Karl Malone as an assistant and Dallas Maverick 1989 first-round pick Randy White as head coach. And Eagles, a role-player during his college days at Louisiana Tech, can also instill an honest blue collar philosophy.

It played well at Auburn last year, as the Tigers provided some pleasant surprises to a season that had been written off in advance. This year, however, the Tigers will not have the luxury of sneaking up on unsuspecting teams.

Gallon and Battle could provide as good a backcourt as there is in the SEC and Person could live up to his advance billing, but there are still glaring weaknesses. Auburn managed a virtual draw on the boards with opponents last year, compensating for a lack of height by getting most of the rebounds that ended up on the floor. With the dominating big man still at least one recruiting class away, the Tigers will again have to out-hustle teams inside.

In short, Auburn will be more talented, but last year's 13-18 record was an overachievement. Matching it is a reasonable goal for the short term, but keep an eye on the Tigers down the road.

<table>
<tr><td colspan="3">1990-91 AUBURN SCHEDULE</td></tr>
<tr><td>Nov.</td><td>24</td><td>Texas Southern</td></tr>
<tr><td></td><td>26</td><td>Georgia State</td></tr>
<tr><td></td><td>30</td><td>@Alabama-Birmingham</td></tr>
<tr><td>Dec.</td><td>8</td><td>Ohio University</td></tr>
<tr><td></td><td>13</td><td>@Duquesne</td></tr>
<tr><td></td><td>15</td><td>Florida State</td></tr>
<tr><td></td><td>17</td><td>Texas A&M</td></tr>
<tr><td></td><td>27-28</td><td>#USF&G Sugar Bowl Tournament</td></tr>
<tr><td>Jan.</td><td>3</td><td>Alabama</td></tr>
<tr><td></td><td>5</td><td>@Florida</td></tr>
<tr><td></td><td>9</td><td>@Mississippi</td></tr>
<tr><td></td><td>12</td><td>LSU</td></tr>
<tr><td></td><td>16</td><td>Vanderbilt</td></tr>
<tr><td></td><td>19</td><td>@Tennessee</td></tr>
<tr><td></td><td>23</td><td>@Georgia</td></tr>
<tr><td></td><td>26</td><td>Mississippi State</td></tr>
<tr><td></td><td>29</td><td>Kentucky</td></tr>
<tr><td>Feb.</td><td>2</td><td>@Alabama</td></tr>
<tr><td></td><td>6</td><td>Florida</td></tr>
<tr><td></td><td>9</td><td>Mississippi</td></tr>
<tr><td></td><td>13</td><td>@LSU</td></tr>
<tr><td></td><td>16</td><td>@Vanderbilt</td></tr>
<tr><td></td><td>19</td><td>Tennessee</td></tr>
<tr><td></td><td>23</td><td>Georgia</td></tr>
<tr><td></td><td>27</td><td>@Mississippi State</td></tr>
<tr><td>Mar.</td><td>2</td><td>@Kentucky</td></tr>
<tr><td></td><td>7-10</td><td>##SEC Tournament</td></tr>
</table>

@ Road Games
# New Orleans, LA (Georgia Tech, Tulane & Villanova)
Nashville, TN

AUSTIN PEAY

LAST SEASON: 10-19
CONFERENCE RECORD: 2-10
STARTERS LOST: 2
STARTERS RETURNING: 3
CONFERENCE: OHIO VALLEY (OVC)
LOCATION: CLARKSVILLE, TN
HOME FLOOR: DUNN CENTER (9,000)
NICKNAME: GOVERNORS
COLORS: RED AND WHITE
COACH: DAVE LOOS, first year at Austin Peay.

The Governors' biggest off-season chore was not filling a void on the court, but on the sidelines. Lake Kelly, who led Austin Peay to its only three NCAA tournament berths and owned a career record of 189-122 in two tenures with the Governors, resigned in June for a marketing position with a Lexington, Ky. television station.

Ironically, Kelly's final season was fraught with controversy. The pre-season favorites failed to show much of the time and finished in a tie for last in the

OVC. This despite some bright spots which saw the Governors win the Acme Boot Classic over Texas Tech and score a surprising victory over Tennessee Tech in the first round of the conference tournament. The Governors appeared to have plenty of talent, but never became a cohesive unit.

Peay was also without the services of 1988-89 starters **LaMonte Ware** (12.2 ppg, 4.8 rpg) and **Myron DeVoe** (6.2 ppg, 4.5 rpg), each of whom missed the entire season. Ware, a 6-3 junior, was under an athletic department suspension; Devoe, a 6-8 senior, had academic difficulties. Both figure to be back in the fold this season, which is a definite plus for new coach Dave Loos.

Loos was named to the post in mid-July, coming across Tennessee from the high-profile program at Memphis State. A four-year assistant with the Tigers, Loos had previous head coaching experience at Christian Brothers College in Memphis (1982-86). His instate roots are deep.

Still, Loos has mighty big shoes to fill. He also has the horses to lead the Governors toward the promised land which eluded them a year ago. Austin Peay could be a legitimate title contender, but it is a huge if. That is, *if* everything falls into place.

If Loos can get his system of play installed quickly and efficiently; *if* Devoe and Ware are allowed to return; *if* several key returnees play to their potential under the new system; *if* the recruits follow through with their commitments and take the last train to Clarksville. If, if, if. Otherwise, it could be another long year.

On paper, though, Peay seems to have the thoroughbreds to contend in a three- or four-horse race. ''Austin Peay,'' said a rival OVC coach, ''has a lot of talent, a lot more than they're getting credit for.''

Two big-play people are definitely back in seniors **Donald Tivis** (18.3 ppg, 2.7 rpg, 36 percent three-point shooting) and **Tommy Brown** (13.4 ppg, 8.9 rpg). A 5-10 guard, Tivis was the league's fifth-highest scorer and Brown the OVC's third-best rebounder. The cat-quick Tivis has a dynamite three-point shot and, at 6-7, 230, Brown is hard to push around the frontcourt.

Another individual showing promise is golden-haired **Greg Franklin** (9.3 ppg, 2.7 assists). Franklin, a 6-3 sophomore, was a part-time starter last season and displayed inconsistent flashes of brilliance. He will likely start full-time in the backcourt this year alongside Tivis.

Peay has three other sophomores who saw little, if any action and will need to take a more active role this year if Peay is to amount to anything. 6-0 **Terry Boykin** (2.0 ppg) and 6-4 **Tyronne Baynham** (0.7 ppg) can provide much-needed depth at guard, while 6-6 **Doug Johnson** (0.5 ppg) is a swingman who can spell players at both positions.

But perhaps the real key to whether or not Austin Peay can contend is the status of Kelly's recruits. The Governors had an excellent recruiting campaign, but sources suggested that two and possibly three freshmen might go elsewhere because of the coaching change.

The top newcomer, 6-0 **Geoff Herman** of Chattanooga, is expected to give it at least one season. Herman, a guard, was the Class AAA leading scorer his senior year at Tyner HS, averaging 31.8 points. Other signees expected to show are junior **Toine Murphy** of Oakland (Mich.) CC, a 6-5 swingman, along with 6-0 freshman point guard **Jason Otter** (Merrill, Mich.) and 6-7 freshman forward **Jeff Lewis** (O'Fallon, Mo.).

BLUE RIBBON ANALYSIS

It is transition time in Clarksville. The Kelly era ended not with a bang, but a whimper, leaving Loos to pick up the pieces. Those that return are talented, but the question is how long will it take the new man

to make them fit. They certainly did not fit as planned a year ago.

Like the little girl with the curl, Austin Peay is one of those teams that can be as good - or as bad - as it wants to be. A smooth transition could translate into an OVC crown, but it will not be easy. The league is as balanced from top to bottom as it has been in a long, long time. No one team stands out or looks ready to dominate.

Peay looks like a fifth-place finisher in the regular season, with the horses to make a strong push in the OVC tournament.

<table>
<tr><td colspan="3">1990-91 AUSTIN PEAY SCHEDULE</td></tr>
<tr><td>Nov.</td><td>14</td><td>#@Arizona</td></tr>
<tr><td></td><td>24</td><td>Wisconsin-Green Bay</td></tr>
<tr><td></td><td>26</td><td>Belmont College (TN)</td></tr>
<tr><td></td><td>29</td><td>@Southern Illinois</td></tr>
<tr><td>Dec.</td><td>1</td><td>@East Tennessee State</td></tr>
<tr><td></td><td>7-8</td><td>##Acme Boot Showdown</td></tr>
<tr><td></td><td>15</td><td>@Tennessee</td></tr>
<tr><td></td><td>18</td><td>@Mississippi</td></tr>
<tr><td></td><td>20</td><td>@Arkansas-Little Rock</td></tr>
<tr><td></td><td>28-29</td><td>*Music City Invitational</td></tr>
<tr><td>Jan.</td><td>3</td><td>@Wichita State</td></tr>
<tr><td></td><td>5</td><td>@Murray State</td></tr>
<tr><td></td><td>12</td><td>@Middle Tennessee State</td></tr>
<tr><td></td><td>14</td><td>Bradley</td></tr>
<tr><td></td><td>19</td><td>Tennessee Tech</td></tr>
<tr><td></td><td>21</td><td>Tennessee State</td></tr>
<tr><td></td><td>23</td><td>Arkansas-Little Rock</td></tr>
<tr><td></td><td>26</td><td>@Eastern Kentucky</td></tr>
<tr><td></td><td>28</td><td>@Morehead State</td></tr>
<tr><td>Feb.</td><td>2</td><td>Murray State</td></tr>
<tr><td></td><td>9</td><td>Morehead State</td></tr>
<tr><td></td><td>11</td><td>Eastern Kentucky</td></tr>
<tr><td></td><td>16</td><td>@Tennessee State</td></tr>
<tr><td></td><td>18</td><td>@Tennessee Tech</td></tr>
<tr><td></td><td>21</td><td>Milligan College</td></tr>
<tr><td></td><td>25</td><td>Middle Tennessee State</td></tr>
<tr><td>Mar.</td><td>2, 6-7</td><td>**OVC Tournament</td></tr>
</table>

@ Road Games
# Dodge NIT. If Austin Peay defeats Arizona, the Governors will play a second round game on Nov. 16. The semifinals and finals of the tournament will be held on Nov. 21 & 23 at Madison Square Garden, New York, NY.
Clarksville, TN (Army, Indiana State & Western Kentucky)
* Nashville, TN (Fordham, Rice & Vanderbilt)
** Site to be announced

BALL STATE

LAST SEASON: 26-7
CONFERENCE RECORD: 13-3
STARTERS LOST: 4
STARTERS RETURNING: 1
CONFERENCE: MID-AMERICAN (MAC)
LOCATION: MUNCIE, IN
HOME FLOOR: UNIVERSITY GYM (7,000)
NICKNAME: CARDINALS
COLORS: CARDINAL AND WHITE
COACH: DICK HUNSAKER, record at Ball State, 26-7.

Before we start talking about this year's chances for Ball State, let's stop and applaud a job well done two seasons running. The 1989-90 Cardinals became the first team in 27 years to repeat as regular-season Mid-American Conference champions, and the only team to repeat as MAC tourney champions in the 11 years since the tournament was founded.

The Cardinals also reached the Sweet 16 of the NCAA tournament, the first MAC team in 11 years to do so, and it took eventual national champion Nevada-

Las Vegas to stop them. And barely, you may recall. The spirited romp through the NCAAs made Ball State just the only MAC school in league's 44-year history of the league to win first-round games in consecutive seasons.

Enough, you say. That all happened last year, when the Cardinals went 26-7 and averaged a victory by just under 13 points each time they hit the hardwood.

But what about rookie coach Dick Hunsaker? No coach has ever won more games in his first year at the helm, and only Everett Case, Denny Crum, Jim Boeheim, Nolan Richardson, Pete Herrman and Larry Finch have won as many in their inaugural seasons.

The honeymoon, however, is over. Ball State's undeniably fantastic run - 55-10 over two years - will not be forgotten, but the folks in Muncie must realize the current edition of the Cardinals enters a new era of hardwood wars as a badly depleted team. Seventy-one percent of the scoring is gone, as is 79 percent of the rebounding, 62 percent of the assists, 71 percent of the steals and 83 percent of the blocks. Perhaps that is why this season and the ones that follow will be a truer test of Hunsaker's abilities as a head coach.

The only returning starter is 6-3 junior guard **Chandler Thompson** (11.7 ppg, 5.6 rpg, 58 assists, 32 steals), once called by departed coach Rick Majerus "the greatest player I ever recruited, including Butch Lee or anybody else at Marquette." Overshadowed at times last season by departed stars like 6-7 forward Paris McCurdy (11.8 ppg, 8.3 rpg), 6-9 center Curtis Kidd (10.7 ppg, 6.9 rpg, 67 assists) and 6-3 guard Billy Butts (8.8 ppg, 67 assists), Thompson might now become the premier player in the MAC.

Certainly, the Muncie native was outstanding when it counted most, averaging nearly 20 points and nine rebounds in Ball State's three NCAA contests. Thompson also played well enough during the regular season to earn honorable mention All-MAC status.

Along with 6-1 senior running mate **Emanuel Cross** (7.8 ppg, 72 assists, 25 steals), brother of former Purdue All-America Russell Cross, the Cardinals' backcourt may still be the MAC's best. Cross was listed as a reserve a year ago, but started nearly half the time.

The only other returnee who started any games at all is 5-11 junior guard **Mike Spicer** (1.5 ppg, 64 assists). Yet Spicer must improve both his field goal (.311) and the free-throw (.594) shooting to be of great value as the first guard off the bench this season. Otherwise, Spicer is solid and makes few mistakes. In two seasons, his assists-to-turnovers ratio is almost 2-1, and the former All-Michigan prep star could be a key if Hunsaker goes to a three-guard offense with the athletic Thompson at small forward.

In addition to Thompson, Cross and Spicer, two marginal reserves return in 6-2 senior guard **Keith Stalling** (3.0 ppg, 1.0 rpg) and 6-4 junior forward **Mike Guinta** (1.5 ppg, 1.0 rpg). Neither played much last season and it remains to be seen what they can contribute, although Stalling's quickness - if he is over a leg injury that sidelined him for all but five games in '89-90 - should be an asset. Both he and Guinta should get enough playing time to answer any questions.

Newcomers such as 6-7 senior forward **Marcus Johnson,** a transfer from DeLand (Fla.) CC, figure to be the real key to Ball State's eventual success or failure. Also eligible after transferring from Murray State is 6-3 senior guard **Jeff Robbins**, who was a starter early in his career with the Racers. Other newcomers include a trio of sophomores in 6-7 center **Bill Gillis** (North Central HS/Indianapolis, Ind.), 6-9 forward **Steve Turner** (Madison Heights HS/Anderson, Ind.) and highly-regarded 5-11 guard **Rodney Holmes** (St. Joseph's HS/South Bend, Ind.), each a redshirt freshman last winter.

The three incoming freshmen are 6-9 center **David Broz** (Proviso West HS/Westchester, Ill.), 6-6 forward **Jeermal Sylvester** (Riley HS/South Bend, Ind.) and 6-2 guard **Mike Hardwick** (Jay County HS/Dunkirk,

Ind.). Hunsaker has made it clear that playing time is up for grabs. He also has yet to determine which players get the most minutes, so the door is open for all newcomers to make their impression and earn court time.

BLUE RIBBON ANALYSIS

After winning a remarkable 55 of 65 games over the last two seasons, the Cardinals realize a repeat of that kind of success just wouldn't be realistic. Nonetheless, Ball State has the good fortune of playing in a league that this season offers no clear-cut favorite.

The Cardinals' backcourt, with Thompson et. al., should be as good as any in the MAC and better than most. And don't be surprised if Hunsaker opts to employ a three-guard attack, capitilizing on the versatility and excellent leaping ability of Thompson. He and Cross will also be counted on to score a great deal, whereas balance was the buzzword last season, when no player averaged more than McCurdy's 11.8 ppg.

Team defense could also be a problem, given the lack of proven interior defenders. A key to last year's superior effort was holding opponents to 40 percent shooting.

"With only one starter returning and the loss of nine seniors," understated Hunsaker, "we're very inexperienced and untested. We also don't have a frontcourt player that has one minute of major college basketball. Our pre-season practices will be more evaluation to find our strengths and discover our weaknesses. But we hope to blend into a competitive team by the time the Mid-American Conference schedule begins."

In the meantime watch for Johnson, the junior college transfer, to emerge as an inside force in this rebuilding year for the Cards. Ball State figures to be looking up at the MAC first division most of the season.

1990-91 BALL STATE SCHEDULE

Nov.	24	Washington University (MO)
	28	@Xavier
Nov.	30-	
	Dec. 1	#Cardinal Varsity Club Classic
Dec.	4	Indiana State
	8	@Mississippi State
	12	Valparaiso (IN)
	20	Wisconsin-River Falls
	22	@Butler
	29	Chicago State
Jan.	2	Eastern Michigan
	5	@Toledo
	9	Kent State
	12	Slippery Rock (PA)
	16	@Miami (OH)
	19	Western Michigan
	23	@Ohio University
	26	Central Michigan
	30	@Bowling Green
Feb.	2	Toledo
	6	@Kent State
	13	Miami (OH)
	16	@Western Michigan
	20	Ohio University
	23	@Central Michigan
	27	Bowling Green
Mar.	2	@Eastern Michigan
	8-10	##MAC Tournament

@ Road Games
# Muncie, IN (Campbell, Northeast Louisiana & U.S. International)
Detroit, MI

BAYLOR

LAST SEASON: 16-14
CONFERENCE RECORD: 7-9
STARTERS LOST: 2
STARTERS RETURNING: 3
CONFERENCE: SOUTHWEST (SWC)
LOCATION: WACO, TX
HOME FLOOR: FERRELL CENTER (10,084)
NICKNAME: BEARS
COLORS: GREEN AND GOLD
COACH: GENE IBA, record at Baylor, 73-76. Career Record, 201-171.

Baylor made dramatic improvement last season —winning 11 more games than the previous for the sixth-best victory increase in the Division I ranks. Coach Gene Iba was a consensus Southwest Conference coach of the year as the Bears went to a 16-14 record from 5-22 in 1988-89. The 11-victory increase was significant in a year in the Southwest Conference in which Texas and Arkansas advanced to play each other in the NCAA Midwest Region finals.

The Bears return several top players, but lose two key performers in forwards Julius Denton and Ivan Jones. Denton was Baylor's leading scorer (16.4 ppg) and Jones the leading rebounder with a seven per game average.

To match or improve on last year's showing Baylor will have to have 6-0 junior point guard **David Wesley** and 6-8 junior center **Joey Fatta** stay healthy, hope for the continued improvement of forwards **Kelvin Chalmers** and **Ulysses Asprilla** and have 6-7 junior college transfer **Anthony Lewis** step in as well as Denton did two years ago when he came from Kanakee (Ill.) CC. Wesley proved to be an important catalyst for Baylor last season but he was hampered by several nagging injuries and missed 12 games. He is the team's top returning scorer (11.6 ppg) and showed his ability by having more than 20 points six times. He scored 23 points a piece in back-to-back games against Texas and Arkansas. He made a crucial steal in the final minutes as the Bears upset third-rank Arkansas 82-77, last season. Wesley is a good three-point shooter (25-of-56) and excellent at the line (83.6 percent). He is not near as talented as former Baylor guard Michael Williams, who has been with four NBA teams over the past two years, and led Baylor to the 1988 NCAA tournament. However, the gritty Wesley fits in well with Iba's fiesty style.

Iba will rotate four other guards to team with Wesley in the backcourt. He will try to find the right combination against each opponent by alternating a group of average guards —6-3 senior **Melvin Hunt**, 6-3 junior **Dennis Lindsey**, 6-3 senior **Tim Schumacher** and 6-5 senior **Toby Christian**. All have adequate skills except they suffered frequently from sloppy ball-handling.

Lindsey (8.2 ppg) started 19 games last season, probably has the best balanced game of that group and will likely start. Hunt (7.5 ppg) can be the best defender and rebounder and he will usually be the first guard replacement. Schumacher (4.1 ppg, 1.7 rpg) doesn't produce impressive stats, but can be a steady playmaker. Christian (2.3 ppg, 1.0 rpg) can add a change of pace off the bench because of his height.

At forward, Chalmers (a 6-9 junior) has steadily improved since coming to Baylor with a limited basketball background. Chalmers (11.5 ppg, 6.1 rpg) has an athletic exuberance that can help him be a very good rebounder and shot blocker, but can also get him into foul trouble. He set a school record with 114 fouls and fouled out of 11 games last year. He would probably be an ideal sixth man on teams with depth, but Baylor will likely be forced to use him as a starter.

Lewis is hoped to be the second coming of Denton, but Baylor's second Kanakee CC transfer might be slightly behind the first. Lewis ended his two year junior college career with the 10th best career scoring and rebounding mark at Kanakee while Denton was seventh in both categories before coming to Baylor. Lewis, the MVP of his junior college district, needs to step in as a steady starter immediately.

Another candidate for the starting lineup is 6-5 junior forward **Joe Tanksley** (20.5 ppg, 8.7 rpg) from Highland (Kan.) CC. He has been a consistent scorer and rebounder at every level he has played.

Iba is hoping Asprilla (a 6-9 sophomore) quickly develops into a power forward. He is a native of Columbia who had to sit out last year because of a technicality in foreign transfers under the NCAA Proposition 48 requirements. Asprilla averaged 14 points and 10 rebounds at Lee HS in Houston, Tex., and had signed with Houston Baptist, Iba's previous school, before that institution dropped its basketball program. He has good coordination but must pick up a great deal of basketball savvy.

Two incoming freshmen —6-7 forward **David Hamilton** and 6-4 forward **Willie Sublett** —have a good chance to contribute this season. Hamilton signed with Baylor last November and was a second team all-state selection in Kansas while averaging 20.3 points and 10.6 rebounds at Shawnee-Mission HS in Overland Park, Kan. Sublett works hard inside and has a good left handed baseline move that is sometimes a surprise to defenders accustomed to right handers. He is out of Martin HS in Arlington, Texas.

Herb Baker, from Sam Houston HS in Houston, Tex., is Baylor's third freshman forward and may be redshirted.

The Bears should be solid in the post by alternating Fatta and 6-8 sophomore **Alex Holcombe**. The 6-8 Fatta broke his leg and missed the last half of the season after averaging 4.4 points and 4.9 rebounds. He has a good shooting touch but needs to get tougher inside. Fatta apparently has recovered from his broken leg and has been playing well in summer league action. Holcombe finished strong last season as he averaged 4.9 points and 3.6 rebounds and played a great deal down the stretch when Fatta was on the sidelines. Holcombe had 9 rebounds against Arkansas and 16 points and seven boards against Texas. **Brian Zvonecek**, a 6-7 sophomore, is also back as a reserve center.

BLUE RIBBON ANALYSIS

Baylor surprised the Southwest Conference last year in finishing with a 16-14 record. If Baylor is to carry over that success into the 1990-91 season, the Bears will have to overcome a possible problem with consistency. Baylor won't catch as many opponents off guard this year either. The Bears' overall talent is not much better than it was last year.

Wesley is a hardnosed, productive point guard and if Fatta stays healthy, the Bears will be in good shape in the pivot. Lewis will have to step in and play well from the beginning of the season if Baylor is to match last year's success.

Only three players are gone from last year, but Baylor will be doing well to just repeat last season's surprising success. The Bears are not capable of challenging Arkansas, Texas or Houston for the Southwest Conference's top spot, but could compete for the best of the rest. Color the Bears fourth in the SWC in 1990-91.

1990-91 BAYLOR SCHEDULE

Nov.	27	Sam Houston State
Nov.	30-	
Dec. 1		#Dr. Pepper Invitational
Dec.	3	Brooklyn College (NY)
	5	Iowa State
	14-16	##Phenix Basketball Tournament

1990-91 BAYLOR SCHEDULE (Cont.)

Dec.	27	@San Diego State
	29	@U.S. International
Jan.	2	Houston
	5	@Texas
	9	@Texas Tech
	12	Texas Christian
	16	Southern Methodist
	19	@Texas A&M
	26	Arkansas
	30	@Rice
Feb.	2	@Houston
	6	Texas
	9	Texas Tech
	13	@Texas Christian
	16	@Southern Methodist
	20	Texas A&M
	23	Southeastern Louisiana
	27	@Arkansas
Mar.	2	Rice
	8-10	*SWC Tournament

@ Road Games
# Waco, TX (Delaware State, Northwestern State & Penn State)
Tokyo, Japan (Idaho, Japan All-Stars & La Salle)
* Dallas, TX

BOISE STATE

LAST SEASON: 12-15
CONFERENCE RECORD: 7-9
STARTERS LOST: 3
STARTERS RETURNING: 2
CONFERENCE: BIG SKY
LOCATION: BOISE, ID
HOME FLOOR: BSU PAVILION (12,200)
NICKNAME: BRONCOS
COLORS: BLUE AND ORANGE
COACH: BOBBY DYE, record at Boise State, 124-78. Career record, 481-265.

That Boise State managed to win more games (12) than scholarship players lost (nine) during an injury ravaged 1989-90 season is a reflection of a number of factors:

1) Coach Bobby Dye's ingenuity in a season where game night was like an evening at the improv. Dye rounded up four walk-ons, including two Boise State football players, at mid-season;

2) A comparatively "down" year in the Big Sky. The conference was a weak-sister 44-52 vs. non-league Division I foes, despite the Broncos' own soft non-league schedule of Brooklyn, San Jose State, etc.;

3) The enormous potential housed inside the 6-foot-9, 225-pound body of center **Tanoka Beard**. Beard was a runaway choice as Big Sky freshman of the year last season.

The coach, the league and the center are all back this time around, which might be the first good news Boise State has heard since it went 23-7 and earned an NIT berth in the 1989.

The beleaguered Broncos lost two lettermen (personal reasons) before last season even began. Then, starting point guard Michael Pearson quit after limping through the first month of the season with a stress fracture in his left tibia. In late December, shooting guard Rafeal Peterson, then the team's second leading scorer (9.4 ppg) and steals leader, quit for personal reasons on the eve of a crushing loss at Oregon State.

Stress fractures to since departed 6-5 forward Arthur Charles and returning 6-9 senior center **Jon Johnson** (0.8 ppg, 0.7 rpg), plus slow improvement from 6-11 junior college transfer **Darryl Wright** (0.4 ppg, 0.6 rpg), opened up the middle. So it was out

of necessity that Beard (13.6 ppg, 4.6 rpg) got the chance to show his stuff as a 17-year-old freshman.

Initially a redshirt candidate, Beard played in 25 games, finishing second in the league in field-goal percentage (58.1), third in blocked shots (31) and sixth in scoring. He finished with a career high 28 points in the season finale, an overtime loss at Weber State.

"Beard has the chance to become one of the finest players this league ever produced," said Nevada-Reno coach Len Stevens. "He can be so good, it's almost scary."

With teammates going down at an alarming rate, even Beard did not go unscathed. He missed 10 days with chicken pox late last year, and perhaps because of that, the Broncos missed a berth in the Big Sky post-season tournament for the first time in six seasons. Yet Beard made major strides in overcoming the outbursts of temper he showed as a scholastic star in Ogden, Utah.

Said Dye: "He's developed into a fine player. We couldn't be happier with Tanoka."

With Beard, a healthy Johnson, continued improvement from Wright and the addition of 6-11 freshman **John Coker** -17.9 ppg, 12.0 rpg at Bremerton (Wash.) HS - the Broncos' strength is at center. The rest of the frontcourt is not nearly as settled, given the major loss of 6-5 Brian King (11.2 ppg, school record 47.7 percent three-point shooting.)

University of Washington transfer and Boise native **Jeff Sanor** (8.1 ppg, 2.3 rpg for the Huskies) figures to be one new starter. The 6-5 Sanor is a Pac-10 caliber player who grew disenchanted with the Washington program. Boise State will only have him for one year, but big things are expected. Sanor also has the benefit of tremendous practice time a year ago, when bodies were at a premium.

After Sanor, though, the ranks are thin. Gone also are the Broncos' two leading rebounders, departed seniors David Lowery (9.5 ppg, 5.2 rpg) and Rich Blythe (7.2 ppg, 5.5 rpg), a.k.a. this team's heart and soul. 6-9 Pete Eisenrich (5.5 ppg, 3.7 rpg) left the team in April, citing academic reasons. He was a 4.0 GPA as a freshman and sought a transfer to one of five schools: Stanford, Pepperdine, Santa Clara, Northwestern or Columbia. Also, 6-9 sophomore Dan Evans, who played sparsely, transferred to the College of Idaho, a nearby NAIA school.

The only other frontcourt player with game experience at Boise State is junior **Mark Hadden**, a 6-2 small forward with a varied junior college background. Hadden (5.6 ppg, 1.3 rpg), whom Dye discovered at midseason, showed offensive sparks, but had difficulty blending his talents into a program that preaches patience and defense.

Newcomers up front include freshmen **Orentha Jones**, a 6-6 leaper out of Camelback High in Phoenix, and 6-8 **Derek Stone** (Santa Ana, Calif.), a starter for state champion Mater Dei HS. Junior college transfers such as 6-7 **Dan Jones** of Olympic (Wash.) College and 6-6 **Billy Fikes** of Yavipia (Ariz.) JC are more likely to contribute immediately. It is a decent cast, but who will team with Sanor is anyone's guess.

The backcourt was so short-handed a year ago, Dye resorted to Boise State football players Ricky Hill and Frank Robinson to get through the season. In hopes of averting a similar situation, the Broncos have brought in three transfer guards to go with 6-6 sophomore **Archie Wright** (5.0 ppg, 1.5 rpg), who showed steady improvement and three-point shooting skills. Wright should start. The other spot will be contested by the trio of junior-eligibles.

6-4 off guard **Michael Trotter** (24.0 ppg, 4.0 rpg) led the Golden Gate Conference in scoring last year for San Jose (Calif.) City College. 6-0 **Grayle Humphries** (11.0 ppg, 92.0 free throw percentage) and 6-2 **Vince Hizon** (15.0 ppg, 89.0 free throw percentage) were teammates at Cypress (Calif.) College. Their excellent foul shooting can only improve a category in which Boise State set an all-time season low (61.1 percent).

5-10 sophomore walk-on **Lance Vaughn** (0.1 ppg, 0.6 rpg) rounds out the roster.

For three straight seasons, Bobby Dye's Broncos finished no lower than second in the Big Sky Conference, compiling a glossy 69-21 record. Then came last year, in which Boise State was decimated by a staggering array of injuries, ineligibility and players simply jumping ship. Still, Dye and Co. salvaged a dozen victories and built a foundation for the future.

The return of Beard and Wright, plus the additions of Sanor and a deep cast of junior college and high school talent, should go a long way in moving the seventh-place Broncos back to loftier heights in 1990-91. If all of last year's bad luck has finally been spent - and by rights it should be - Boise State should challenge for a top three finish in the Big Sky.

1990-91 BOISE STATE SCHEDULE

Nov.	23-24	#Real Dairy Classic
	27	@Gonzaga (WA)
Dec.	1	@Wisconsin-Green Bay
	8	Utah State
	15	Pepperdine
	18	@San Francisco
	19	@St. Mary's
	28-29	##Albertson's Holiday Classic
Jan.	3	@Montana State
	5	@Montana
	10	@Idaho State
	12	Eastern Washington
	16	Nevada
	19	Northern Arizona
	24	@Idaho
	25	@Eastern Washington
	31	Montana
Feb.	2	Weber State
	8	@Cal State-Northridge
	14	Idaho State
	16	Montana State
	21	@Nevada
	23	@Northern Arizona
	28	Idaho
Mar.	1	@Weber State
	7-10	*Big Sky Tournament

@ Road Games
# Boise, ID (Eastern Washington, Idaho State & Valparaiso)
Boise, ID (Georgia Southern, Monmouth & Northeastern)
* Site to be announced

BOSTON COLLEGE

LAST SEASON: 8-20
CONFERENCE RECORD: 1-15
STARTERS LOST: 2
STARTERS RETURNING: 3
CONFERENCE: BIG EAST
LOCATION: CHESTNUT HILL, MA
HOME FLOOR: SILVIO O. CONTE FORUM (8,604)
NICKNAME: EAGLES
COLORS: MAROON AND GOLD
COACH: JIM O'BRIEN, record at Boston College, 49-70.
Career record, 116-121.

Two seasons back, Boston College was 12-17 but beat Syracuse, St. John's, Villanova, and Notre Dame in (Seattle Supersonics first round draft choice) Dana Barros' final month. These victories, all against teams with significantly more talent and experience, indicate Jim O'Brien, one of the best point guards in Eagle history from 1968-71, can coach. The question,

after the bottom fell out of the Boston College program last season with an 8-20 record and only one conference victory, is how well he can recruit. For years, the Heights was a haven for good New York City-area, New Jersey, southern Connecticut talent. Lately, the school seems to have been missing out. The players obtained from parts south and west generally have proven second level from these areas. Of course, it is hardly the coaching staff's fault that local player, Bryan Edwards, the hope to replace Barros at point guard, never realized his potential. (Edwards, a persistent discipline problem, was suspended indefinitely in April for skipping a weightlifting session without permission, then kicked off the squad.) Still, with a fine new arena, a great college environment, and one of the nation's premier basketball conferences, it's getting to be put up or shut up time in terms of raising the Boston College program back up to a competitive Big East level.

The Eagles did take a huge step forward in that regard by getting 6-9 freshman center **Bill Curley** to stay home. Curley, the best prep player out of Massachusetts since Patrick Ewing, was Top 25 in the country and is one of, if not the, highest rated recruits in school history. He is an improbable story. Curley is from the small fringe upper middle class suburban town of Duxbury, 35 miles south of Boston, near Plymouth and Cape Cod. He did more to put Duxbury on the state map than anybody since Myles Standish in the 1600s. A blue chipper from Duxbury is as unlikely as a soup kitchen in Beverly Hills. If there ever was going to be a notable athlete from Duxbury, it figured to be someone with skates and a stick. The ice is king on Boston's hockey crazy South Shore. But Duxbury sat up and took notice when its team suddenly jumped up and won the Class B state championship. In a Hoosier-like victory against Salem (an industrial city four times bigger) in the Eastern Massachusetts finals, Curley scored 38 of Duxbury's 65 points, grabbed 20 rebounds and blocked 11 shots. That was his junior year.

Now after averaging 28 points and 12.5 rebounds per game, his senior year at Duxbury HS, Curley will be looked to for immediate major impact. But before even thinking about salvation much less making the starting five, Curley must recover from a stress fracture of the right foot suffered in January. Curley was cleared for light running in June. "He seems to be completely healed," Dr. Diane English told *Big East Briefs*. Curley worked himself back into shape by loading and unloading cases of beer on a Budweiser truck. "In terms of a national stature, he's by far the biggest recruit B.C. has ever recruited," O'Brien told *Big East Briefs*. "But people have to understand he's not going to come here and be the savior. He's not Derrick Coleman, he's not Alonzo Mourning. He's not going to be able to do it by himself . . . We think Hinton is very important."

That would be 6-11 sophomore center **David Hinton** (11.3 ppg, 4.5 rpg), who quietly came on strong in February as a silver lining to Boston College's dark cloud. He began the month with 14 points and nine rebounds in the Eagles' only Big East win over Seton Hall. Three days later, Hinton put up 19 points and took down nine rebounds during a one-point loss to Villanova. He also had an 18 point game vs. Pitt, another vs. Syracuse, and a 15-point, 6-rebound outing against Connecticut. Hinton is coordinated and has some pretty decent moves for his size around the basket. He is not very quick but he is strong. Hinton has the potential, assuming continued improvement, to give the Eagles, with Curley, a very solid twin post presence. Filling out what could suddenly emerge as a very respectable frontline, will be 6-5 senior power forward **Doug Able** (12.0 ppg, 7.4 rpg), the team leader in both scoring and rebounding. Times like his 24-point game vs. St. John's or 21-point game in the regular season finale against Connecticut, make you think Able is ready to turn into a consistent scoring force. Though slightly undersized, he compensates with athletic ability. Able does on occasion show the ability to score

away from the basket. His senior year needs to yield more consistency.

At off-guard, there is also hope in the form of 6-3 sophomore **Lior Arditti** (9.3 ppg), an Israeli import. Although not the all-around athlete compatriot Nadav Henefeld proved to be with Connecticut, Arditti displayed an understanding of the game and nice outside shooting (41-of-90 from three-point range). Although the Eagles will have some offensive potential at four positions, even if not a lot of quickness, none of it will win many games if the point guard doesn't distribute the ball properly and throws off the team's chemistry. That was the problem with Edwards last year. Now that he and his 8.9 ppg and 3.3 apg are gone, this is a team crying out for an effective floor leader.

6-2 freshman **Howard Eisley** (15.0 ppg, 3.5 rpg, 10.0 apg at Southwestern HS, Detroit, Mich.) will get a good shot to fill that role. Eisley arrives from a 27-0 state championship team that was ranked No. 2 in the country (behind Martin Luther King HS of Chicago, Ill.) by *USA Today*. "He's very quick, a slashing type of player," says Boston College assistant coach Happy Dobbs. "He handles the ball very well. He has long arms and can really defend people. He should help us tremendously." If he does, Eisley, who was recruited by the likes of Minnesota, Tennessee, and Cincinnati, could be the missing piece of the puzzle. Keep in mind, though, the adjustment to high level Division I basketball from high school is tougher at the point than anywhere else. And Eisley was not a pure point guard at Southwestern, although he certainly has most of the skills. Other important backcourt help could come from 6-3 off-guard **Malcolm Huckaby**, a big time scorer (24.5 ppg, 8.0 rpg, 5.5 apg) in a good program (Bristol Central HS, Bristol, Conn.). If he isn't forced into too many minutes as lead guard, Huckaby has the potential to contribute double figure scoring as a freshman. He can fill it up. The Eagles also took a flyer on another Detroit area backcourt player, 6-2 off-guard **Gerrod Abram** (30.0 ppg, 9.5 rpg, 5.0 apg, 8.0 steals per game). Abram starred in a small program. He is quick, athletic and a good open floor player but somewhat undersized for his position at this level. Abram also needs, in the estimation of River Rouge coach DeWayne Smith, to develop upper body strength.

Boston College's fourth leading scorer, Michael Reese (8.4 ppg, 3.3 rpg), who would have been a 6-8 sophomore forward of promise was, like Bryan Edwards, a disciplinary problem and dismissed by the team. That leaves seven other returning starters who were all marginal contributors to a bad team: In order of points per game averages, they are 6-3 senior guard **Bobby Moran** (4.8 ppg), 6-9 senior forward **Corey Beasley** (4.2 ppg), 6-7 junior forward **Corey Jackson** (4.2 ppg), 6-4 sophomore guard **Mike Herren** (3.6 ppg), 6-2 sophomore guard **Walter Lundy** (3.5 ppg), 6-9 junior forward **Willy Foley** (2.8 ppg) and 7-2 sophomore center **Randy Hagerdon** (2.3 ppg). None of them pulled down more than two rebounds per game. Until last season Beasley was contributing on a level similar to Able and was being counted on as a solid starter. He will try to redeem a disappointing junior year with some of the quality inside minutes of which he is capable. Moran, a spot starter the past two seasons, is also a potential factor but erratic. He has the athletic ability and quickness but his offense has been inconsistent. Jackson will be looked to mainly for rebounds. Herren, the Massachusetts Player of the Year and 30 point per game scorer at perennial power Dufee HS (Fall River) in 1989, still needs to prove he's not over his head in the Big East. Hagerdon and Foley have a way to go.

BLUE RIBBON ANALYSIS

Curley and Hinton are not going to break any quickness records but they are good enough to form an effective twin post presence in the Big East. Able should produce a solid year at the other forward. Arditti, Huckaby, and Moran offer nice offensive depth at the off-guard. That leaves the point. On few teams will the fortunes of so many depend so much on one position. O'Brien must pray that Eisley can step in right away and do an adequate job there. He will have to find out how many of Eisley's 10 assists per game last season came from playing amidst a bunch of high school All-Americas like Jalen Rose and how many came from seeing the floor.

With Curley and Hinton, the Eagles desperately need a backcourt that can feed the post. If Arditti or Moran have to play lead guard, that will be a major question. If Huckaby has to try it, his scoring will probably suffer. But, if Eisley cannot get it done, one of them will have to step up and do an acceptable job as floor leader. If someone does, the Eagles could steal four or five conference games and be far more competitive in the rest. Still, they are depending heavily on three freshmen —Curley, Huckaby and Eisley — and two sophomores — Hinton and Arditti —to backbone a six or seven man nucleus. If their talent can overcome their inexperience, Boston College may sneak ahead of Seton Hall, avoid the cellar, and finish eighth in the Big East.

```
┌─────────────────────────────────────────────┐
│  1990-91 BOSTON COLLEGE SCHEDULE             │
├─────────────────────────────────────────────┤
│ Nov. 00-Dec.10   #Memphis State              │
│          27      @New Hampshire              │
│ Nov. 30-Dec. 1   ##BC Basketball Classic     │
│ Dec.      3      *Maryland                   │
│           8      Harvard                     │
│          11      Providence                  │
│          15      @Holy Cross                 │
│       28-29      **Hall of Fame Tournament   │
│ Jan.      2      Connecticut                 │
│           5      @St. John's                 │
│           9      Maine                       │
│          12      @Georgetown                 │
│          15      Seton Hall                  │
│          17      Maryland-Eastern Shore      │
│          19      Georgetown                  │
│          22      Villanova                   │
│          31      @Notre Dame                 │
│ Feb.      2      @Syracuse                   │
│           5      @Connecticut                │
│           9      @Pitt                       │
│          13      St. John's                  │
│          16      Syracuse                    │
│          18      @Villanova                  │
│          23      @Providence                 │
│          26      Pitt                        │
│ Mar.      2      @Seton Hall                 │
│        7-10      ***Big East Tournament      │
├─────────────────────────────────────────────┤
│ @ Road Games                                 │
│ # Dodge NIT. If the Eagles defeat Memphis    │
│ State, they will play a second round game on │
│ Nov. 16. The semifinals and finals of the    │
│ tournament will be held on Nov. 21 & 23 at   │
│ Madison Square Garden, New York, NY.         │
│ ## Chestnut Hill, MA (Arkansas State, Drexel │
│ & Wagner)                                    │
│ * ACC/Big East Challenge, Richmond, VA       │
│ ** Springfield, MA (Dartmouth, Massachusetts │
│ & Northwestern)                              │
│ *** Madison Square Garden, New York, NY      │
└─────────────────────────────────────────────┘
```

BOSTON UNIVERSITY

LAST SEASON: 18-12
CONFERENCE RECORD: 9-3
STARTERS LOST: 4
STARTERS RETURNING: 1
CONFERENCE: ECAC NORTH ATLANTIC (NAC)
LOCATION: BOSTON, MA
HOME FLOOR: WALTER BROWN ARENA (4,200)
NICKNAME: TERRIERS
COLORS: SCARLET AND WHITE
COACH: BOB BROWN, first year at Boston University. Career record, 102-71.

Former Boston University coach Mike Jarvis established a level of excellence at Boston University that was almost unparallelled in school history. Under his tutelage, the Terriers went to the NCAA tournament two of the past three years, capped off by last season's 18-12 mark and a meeting with Connecticut in the NCAA tournament opening round. Unfortunately for the Beantown faithful, Jarvis, one of the nation's best kept coaching secrets, left to forge a rebuilding program at George Washington. Even more worrisome is the fact that four starters from the Jarvis era are also gone, leaving former assistant Bob Brown precious little to work with. Translation: It could be a long, cold winter in Matthews Arena.

But take heart, Terrier faithful. Brown is used to long, cold winters . . . ones filled with success, that is. The Boston University graduate takes over the reins after guiding Division III powerhouse Southern Maine to a 66-24 record the past three years, including three NCAA appearances. He also had great success on the Division II level, taking St. Anselm College from a 1-25 mark in '83-84 to a 21-9 record and an NCAA appearance in '85-86. So if the record proves true, Boston University could be back in the winner's circle before too long.

It probably won't be this year, though. Gone from last season's squad are the team's top three scorers: do-it-all guard Steven Key (16.6 ppg), and backcourt mate Bill Brigham (10.9 ppg, 7.3 rpg) along with forward Ron Moses (10.4 ppg, 8.6 rpg). The fourth starter to depart was swingman David King (5.5 ppg, 3.6 rpg), leaving Brown with a host of parttime starters looking to fill in with larger roles.

Two backcourt players will key the attack. 6-3 senior **Reggie Stewart** (9.2 ppg, 2.1 rpg) and 6-3 junior **Mark Daly** (8.4 ppg, 1.7 rpg) will provide leadership while competing for time at the shooting guard spot. Both will bring a different scoring dimension on to the floor, with the explosive Stewart looking to drive and create his shots, while Daly brings the long range touch that should make him one of the best in the NAC. A Greek import, 6-2 sophomore **Sotiris Manolopoulos** (4.3 ppg) also has a fine long range touch and will see much more playing time as he adjusts to collegiate ball.

The point guard spot is where Brown will have his biggest challenge. Key not only led the squad in scoring, but in assists (228) and steals (44) as well. 6-0 junior **Mike Jarvis II** (2.2 ppg), son of the former coach, appears to be the leading candidate, while Rhode Island transfer 6-3 junior **Norbert Pickett**, 6-2 sophomore **Adam Olmstead** (0.4 ppg) and 6-3 freshman **Brian Holden** (16.0 ppg, 6.0 apg, Archbishop Williams HS in Braintree, Mass.) will also battle for playing time. Jarvis has shown steady development over his first two seasons despite limited playing time and should be ready. Pickett saw little time at talent laden Rhode Island but has good quickness and can excel at this level, just a step below the Atlantic-10. Both Olmstead and Holden are unproven, but had stellar high school careers running talented offenses.

In the frontcourt, 6-6 senior captain **Fred Davy** (3.4 ppg, 2.7 rpg) returns, along with 6-7 junior **Jason Scott** (3.4 ppg, 3.2 rpg) and 6-9 center **Russell Jarvis**. Davy must develop more of a shooting touch (just 39 percent) and has to pick up some of the board slack lost with the graduation of Moses and Stewart. Scott continued his development coming off the bench and will be Boston University's key returning inside player. Jarvis, nephew of the former coach and cousin of teammate Mike, sat out last season with a knee injury, but should return to the form which made him one of the NAC's best freshman rebounders and best scoring threats two seasons ago. Two other new faces, 6-6 sophomore walkon **Kevin Harris** and 6-10 freshman center **Rick Rosu-Myles** (18.0 ppg, 11.0 rpg at Arkona, Ontario, North Middlesex HS) will provide what little depth the Terriers will have in the frontcourt.

BLUE RIBBON ANALYSIS

The loss of four starters and the late appointment of Brown has created quite a hole in the Terriers' balloon. The loss of over half of its offense, top two rebounders and leading passer will probably be too much for this largely untested group to overcome. Russell Jarvis is a solid frontcourt player and Daly has great range. Stewart can also score, but the point guard spot is very suspect. The real good news for Boston University is the league, other than traditional rival Northeastern and improving Hartford, is quite thin. That will certainly help build morale.

Brown started off at St. Anselm with a team that had won just once the previous season. This won't be anywhere near as bad, especially with a decent frontcourt in a backcourt-oriented league. The Terriers will be hard pressed to get past 10 wins and fourth place in the NAC this season. After years of prosperity, this season could be as hard and cold as the ice under the court at Matthews Arena.

```
┌─────────────────────────────────────────────┐
│  1990-91 BOSTON UNIVERSITY SCHEDULE          │
├─────────────────────────────────────────────┤
│ Nov.   23-34    #Fleet Classic               │
│          28     Fairleigh Dickinson          │
│ Dec.      1     @Massachusetts               │
│           4     @Maryland-Baltimore CC       │
│           7     Delaware                     │
│          10     @Michigan                    │
│          15     @University of Hartford      │
│          22     @Eastern Michigan            │
│       28-29     ##Shootout Spokane           │
│ Jan.      2     @Duke                        │
│           5     George Washington            │
│          12     @Indiana State               │
│          16     @New Hampshire               │
│          19     Vermont                      │
│          22     @Maryland                    │
│          26     Northeastern                 │
│          30     Maine                        │
│ Feb.      2     University of Hartford       │
│           9     @Maine                       │
│          12     North Carolina A&T           │
│          16     New Hampshire                │
│          19     @Army                        │
│          23     @Vermont                     │
│          26     @Delaware                    │
│ Mar.      3     @Northeastern                │
│         5-9     *NAC Tournament              │
├─────────────────────────────────────────────┤
│ @ Road Games                                 │
│ # Providence, RI (Lafayette, Morgan State &  │
│ Providence)                                  │
│ ## Spokane, WA (Gonzaga, Hofstra & Howard    │
│ University)                                  │
│ * Site to be announced                       │
└─────────────────────────────────────────────┘
```

BOWLING GREEN

LAST SEASON: 18-11
CONFERENCE RECORD: 9-7
STARTERS LOST: 0
STARTERS RETURNING: 5
CONFERENCE: MID-AMERICAN (MAC)
LOCATION: BOWLING GREEN, OH
HOME FLOOR: ANDERSON ARENA (5,000)
NICKNAME: FALCONS
COLORS: BURNT ORANGE AND SEAL BROWN
COACH: JIM LARRANAGA, record at Bowling Green, 57-57.

With five starters and 11 lettermen returning from a team that went 18-11 and appeared in the NIT, Bowling Green has to be considered the team to beat in the Mid-American Conference. Head coach Jim Larranaga called last year "Phase I" of a two-year plan to capture the MAC championship, and it was a rousing success. Among the Falcons' victories as they soared to an 8-1 start was an 81-79 upset over eventual Big 10 champ Michigan State, the first-ever loss for the Spartans in their new Breslin Center.

Leading Phase I was the same player who will be counted on to lead Phase II this winter, 5-11 senior **Clinton Venable** (16.8 ppg, 4.6 apg, 3.2 rpg, 133 assists, 46 steals), a first-team All-MAC selection after tranferring from Allegany CC (Cumberland, Md.). Though he shot just 42.4 percent, Venable ranked seventh in the nation in free throw shooting (.884), and was third in the conference in assists and sixth in steals. He is best at using his quickness to penetrate, setting up a three-pointer (32-for-91, .352), which he hits just well enough to keep most defenses honest.

Venable does not operate alone, however. 6-3 senior **Joe Moore** (12.4 ppg, 7.3 rpg) also returns, a second-team All-MAC selection last year who plays much of the time at small forward. Moore led the conference in field-goal percentage (.603), and scored half of Bowling Green's points in the 75-60 loss at Cincinnati in the opening round of the NIT.

The frontcourt is solid with 6-9 senior **Steve Watson** (10.7 ppg, 6.2 rpg, 22 blocked shots) manning the power forward spot. A transfer from Rutgers who sat out 1988-89, Watson proved capable in all phases of the game, save a .321 percentage on three-pointers, which he probably shouldn't be shooting.

Starting at center is veteran **Ed Colbert** (6.9 ppg, 5.3 rpg, 31 blocked shots), a 6-9 senior who is one of four three-year lettermen. Colbert anchors the Falcons' defense in the paint area and is smart about the shots he takes, shooting nearly 55 percent from the floor last season. While still limited offensively, Colbert has improved every year in that regard and is a hard worker around the glass.

As if the frontcourt presence of Moore, Watson and Colbert was not enough, the Falcons will fly at opponents with even more inside firepower. Also returning is 6-5 junior forward **Tom Hall** (7.9 ppg, 4.6 rpg, 26 blocked shots), who was dubbed "Super Sub" as the team's sixth man last year. Hall's speed and quickness, like that of 6-4 senior **Derek Kizer** (2.7 ppg, 1.4 rpg), are assets any coach would love. Kizer will not produce big numbers, but is a hustler who does not hesitate to take a charge or dive for a loose ball. Adding international flavor to the frontcourt is 6-10 freshman **Jason Crump**, hailing from Tilston, England via Mercersburg (Pa.) Academy. Crump dominated his private high school opponents, averaging 23.6 points and 17.9 rebounds.

The backcourt for the Falcons is nearly as deep, and just as formidable. Two players who split time at the shooting guard spot last season - 6-3 senior **Billy Johnson** (11.5 ppg, 4.1 rpg, 53 assists) and 6-0 junior **Kirk Whiteman** (5.6 ppg, 35 assists) - both return. Johnson, a 10-game starter, showed improvement across the board last season, when he shot just under 50 percent from the field and was the high scorer in five games. Whiteman, though not quite as consistent a shooter, emerged when Johnson was hampered late in the year by a back injury.

The other backcourt returnees, who may find it difficult to earn court time, include 6-1 sophomore **Vada Burnett** (0.8 ppg, 0.3 rpg) and 6-0 sophomore **Joe Bair**, a two-sport athlete who appeared in only nine games last season and did not score. They figure to be joined at the end of the bench by 6-0 sophomore Mike Hugar, who was ineligible last season. Also waiting their turn will be 6-7 freshman Jason Hall (Butler HS/Vandalia, Ohio) and 6-5 freshman Matt Otto (Shawnee HS/Lima, Ohio).

BLUE RIBBON ANALYSIS

"This will be the most experienced team we have had in my five years here," said Larranaga. "This group has enjoyed some success and is anxious to take another giant step forward. They have also worked extremely hard to be in position to win the Mid-American Conference title."

With all five starters returning from a team that went 18-11 and knocked off Michigan State last year, Larranaga has every right to believe his club will do exactly that. And the success Bowling Green has already enjoyed is not modest. These Falcons made BG's first post-season appearance since 1983, finished with their finest record since 1984 and posted the best nonconference mark (9-2) in 27 years.

The strengths of this team are clear: outside shooting (.494 overall a year ago); a host of quality frontcourrt plays; Venable's considerable skills; and, it must be said one more time with emphasis, experience. Even though the MAC is as strong and balanced as ever, the Falcons should win the league and reach the 20-win plateau in the process.

1990-91 BOWLING GREEN SCHEDULE		
Nov.	26	Heidelberg College (OH)
	28	@Akron
Dec.	1	Michigan State
	5	@Western Kentucky
	8	Butler
	14-15	#Ameritus Classic
	28	@St. Peter's
	30	@Siena
Jan.	2	@Miami (OH)
	5	Western Michigan
	9	@Ohio University
	12	Central Michigan
	16	Wright State (OH)
	19	@Eastern Michigan
	23	Toledo
	26	@Kent State
	30	Ball State
Feb.	2	@Western Michigan
	6	Ohio University
	9	@Central Michigan
	13	Youngstown State
	16	Eastern Michigan
	20	@Toledo
	23	Kent State
	27	@Ball State
Mar.	2	Miami (OH)
	8-10	##MAC Tournament

@ Road Games
# Lincoln, NE (Alabama State, Nebraska & Tennessee Tech)
Detroit, MI

BRADLEY

LAST SEASON: 11-20
CONFERENCE RECORD: 6-8
STARTERS LOST: 1
STARTERS RETURNING: 4
CONFERENCE: MISSOURI VALLEY (MVC)
LOCATION: PEORIA, IL
HOME FLOOR: CARVER ARENA (10,401)
NICKNAME: BRAVE
COLORS: RED AND WHITE
**COACH: STAN ALBECK, record at Bradley, 67-51.
Career collegiate record, 276-168.
Career professional record, 352-338.**

In 25 seasons as a head coach on the college and professional levels, Stan Albeck has sat on benches from Irvine, Calif. to the New Jersey Meadowlands, from San Juan, Puerto Rico to Adrian, Mich. And though an 11-20 record may not show it, Albeck may have done some of his best coaching last season at Bradley.

"Normally you always (coach harder) in a losing season," said Albeck, whose fifth year at his alma mater figures to be a lot better than his third and fourth years there. "You have to milk everything you can. For the most part, that's basketball suicide. You have to have kids that are overachievers."

And even though the Braves suffered through their first back-to-back losing seasons since World War II and their first 20-loss season in 35 years, Albeck probably got much more than expected out of a team that began the year with just one established starter. Still, it was basketball in three-part disharmony - a 1-9 start, a 10-4 middle of the season and an 0-7 finish.

The only loss is a big one, 6-9 center Luke Jackson. Jackson started every one of the 118 Bradley games he dressed for and wound up 15th on Braves' all-time scoring list, third on the school's all-time rebounding list and No. 19 in rebounding in Missouri Valley Conference history.

But the rest of Albeck's iron-man starting unit is back, led by Missouri Valley scoring champ **Curtis Stuckey** (23.7 ppg, 5.3 rpg, 62 assists, 37 steals). Stuckey, a 6-1 senior, became the fourth straight Bradley player to lead the league in scoring. And he missed the first eight games after transferring back home (Manual HS/Peoria) from Drake. Once he got going, though, Stuckey wound up with four of the 10 highest-scoring games in the MVC last winter.

Sophomore **Charles White** returns alongside Stuckey at point guard. White, a high school forward at 6-1, 160 pounds, averaged 7.8 points, 3.6 rebounds and 3.6 assists and usually drew the toughest defensive assignment in the backcourt. He was also the first player in Bradley history to record 100 points, 100 rebounds and 100 assists as a freshman.

6-7 **Andy Bastock**, who asked to be released from his scholarship during the off-season, then changed his mind and elected to return, is back for his junior year. The Kurt Rambis replica graded out at .510 in the TANDEX rating system last year, fourth-best among MVC returnees, while averaging 9.9 points and 5.7 rebounds. Bastock is the classic garbage man, the kind of guy who always seems to be in the right place at the right time.

The fourth returning starter is 6-9 **Xanthus Houston**, a junior who averaged 10.7 points and 6.4 rebounds after a rough start. With 6-6 junior transfer **James Bailey** (Fresno State) expected to move into the starting lineup at small forward, Houston could move into Jackson's high-post role and use his effective passing skills. Bailey, who lettered during an injury-plagued freshman season at Fresno State, figures to be an instant contributor. "He can score 16-18 points a game," said Albeck.

Only two other lettermen return, and neither saw much action. **Scott Behrends**, a 6-8 sophomore known as "Big Bird" by his teammates, got into just four games during an injury-filled freshman season. He averaged 3.3 points and 2.2 rebounds. 6-0 sophomore **Duane Broussard** (1.3 ppg) hoped to challenge as the starting point guard, but inconsistent play and a bad back limited him to 22 games and an average of 9.7 minutes.

Among the new freshmen, two of the most interesting are 6-7 **James Hamilton** (Grand Blanc HS/Grand Blanc, Mich.) and 6-2 **Maurice Stovall** (Thornton HS/Harvey, Ill.). Hamilton averaged 30.9 points, 17.3 rebounds and 5.1 assists as a high school senior and was runner-up for Michigan's Mr. Basketball. Stovall played against some tough competition in Chicago's south suburbs and wound up averaging 17.8 points and 3.0 rebounds. Albeck calls him "a potential big-time scorer."

Kwame Brown (Jones HS/Houston, Tex.), a 6-7 freshman, is the kind of athlete Albeck loves to plug into his wide-open style. 6-4 junior transfer **Shawn Smith** (Neosho County CC/Chanute, Kan.) averaged 11.8 points and 3.3 rebounds as a sophomore guard following a switch from forward. "He's a high-flyer," Neosho coach Eddie Vaughn said, "and someone who performs best against the better competition."

6-8 sophomore **Tom Wilson,** who sat out last season, is eligible and should provide the Braves with another quality athlete up front. Wilson, a sub-50 sec. quarter-miler as a high school track man, was also a high school teammate of Stuckey.

Bradley's final newcomer has the potential for the most impact, but it may take time. **Mark Bailey,** a 6-11 freshman from Chesterfield, Mo. (Christian Brothers HS), averaged 14.9 points and 7.3 rebounds in his final prep season. He is a project at this level.

Even with the departure of Jackson and sixth-man Jay Schell (transfer to Wisconsin), Albeck does not figure to be as limited as he was last season. There is both size and depth.

''Things look considerably better,'' Albeck said. ''We anticipate number one, a return to a contending position and, secondly, continuing the winning tradition at Bradley. I'm really excited about the future.''

BLUE RIBBON ANALYSIS

With some experience and depth surrounding him, Stuckey could put up Hersey Hawkins-type numbers for the Braves as the main man in Albeck's pro turnout offense. At worst, Stuckey figures to make it five straight seasons of Bradley producing the MVC scoring champ.

However, the Braves need to turn things around in the win column or there will be some disgruntled alumni in the great Midwest. Thirty-four losses over the past two seasons can make for unrest in a city where Bradley basketball is the main dish.

The schedule includes trips to UTEP and Loyola, as well as home games with Missouri, Dayton and DePaul. That's actually an easier grind than the youthful Braves faced last season, when seven of the first nine games were away from home.

If a motivated Houston shows up to play every night, Bradley could find itself in a contending position in the Missouri Valley Conference. Houston needs to become more assertive on the boards and stay out of foul trouble. Broussard and Stovall must also provide some help at the point, if only so White does not wear down as he did at times last season.

The Braves can finish anywhere from third to sixth. The middle of the MVC pack looks very even between Bradley, Tulsa, Wichita State and newcomer Southwest Missouri State.

1990-91 BRADLEY SCHEDULE

Nov.	24	@Georgia Southern
Nov.	30-	
	Dec. 1	@Disneyland Freedom Bowl Classic
Dec.	4	Chicago State
	10	@UTEP
	12	Missouri
	20	@Illinois State
	22	Dayton
	27	Southern Illinois
	29	@Loyola
Jan.	2	St. Louis
	5	@Creighton
	12	@Drake
	14	@Austin Peay
	19	Indiana State
	21	Creighton
	26	Wichita State
	28	Southwest Missouri State
	31	@Southern Illinois
Feb.	4	Drake
	6	@Wichita State
	9	DePaul
	14	@Tulsa
	16	@Southwest Missouri State
	21	Illinois State
	23	Tulsa
	25	@Indiana State

1990-91 BRADLEY SCHEDULE *(Cont.)*

Mar.	1-5	##MVC Tournament

@ Road Games
# Irvine, CA (California-Irvine, Idaho State & Loyola Marymount)
St. Louis, MO

BRIGHAM YOUNG

LAST SEASON: 21-9
CONFERENCE RECORD: 11-5
STARTERS LOST: 4
STARTERS RETURNING: 1
CONFERENCE: WESTERN ATHLETIC (WAC)
LOCATION: PROVO, UT
HOME FLOOR: MARRIOTT CENTER (23,000)
NICKNAME: COUGARS
COLORS: BLUE AND WHITE
COACH: ROGER REID, record at Brigham Young, 21-9.
Career record, including high school, 171-59.

Shawn Bradley is easily the most celebrated high school player in the history of Utah. Given his mobility for his towering height of 7-6, perhaps the tallest ever for an American player —college or pro — he may be one of the most celebrated anywhere. Just not being a freak at Bradley's astounding stature is an accomplishment. But the freshman center, over seven-feet since the age of 14, has had to fight hard to dodge that classification for awhile now. The progress he has made has been nearly as remarkable as his measurements. In Bradley's first (of two) forays into the Nike/ABCD Camp at Princeton, following his freshman year at Emery County HS in Castle Dale, Utah, he played pretty much like you would expect of a skinny, gangly oversized kid who had no idea of his body: soft, scared, awkward, jerky and mechanical.

A summer later, against Nike's same high level national talent, Bradley was blocking shots, rebounding in traffic, posting up, and sticking short jumpers with a confidence and aggressiveness worthy of smaller, stronger, more athletic big men. This is definitely a kid with a heart. Obviously, if Bradley, at 7-6, can extend that type of play (24 points, 16 rebounds, 8 blocks per game as a senior last season) to the college level, he'll be a major force. The guess here is he will be, but that it may take some learning time and increased upper body strength.

He is expected to play one year for the Cougars before embarking on a two-year Mormon Church mission.

Meanwhile, if the Cougars are to approach last year's surprising 21-9 campaign, Bradley will need help from some other highly regarded new faces (along with a couple of returning from mission old ones) as 6-7 senior forward **Steve Schreiner** (10.6 ppg, 5.2 rpg) is the lone returning starter from a squad losing 55.9 of last year's average of 78.3 points per game. Schreiner possesses good inside offense and works hard off the glass against mostly bigger opponents. But coach Roger Reid has a lot of scoring to replace with the departure of last year's excellent backcourt of Andy Toolson (18.3 ppg) and three year starter Marty Haws (18.5 ppg).

However, 5-11 guard **Nathan Call,** who started alongside Haws in 1987-88 during the Cougars' 17-game season opening winning streak, has returned

from a mission for his junior year. Call (4.8 ppg, 2.0 rpg, 3.0 apg) was a lot more important cog on that team than his statistics indicate. He is an intelligent player who should provide backcourt leadership and complement a scorer if Reid can find one to go with him. But he is still healing from burns on his legs and arm. Most likely to fill the backcourt scoring role should be 6-5 junior off-guard **Mark Heslop** (2.7 ppg, 1.0 rpg). Heslop can fill it up from three-point territory (15-of-26 last year) and will get the chance early and often now that Toolson and Haws are gone.

Up front, Reid will look to highly touted freshman power forwards, 6-8 **Kenneth Roberts** (25.9 ppg, 13.3 rpg, 3.9 apg, 3.1 blocks at Brigham, Utah HS) and 6-9 **Jeff Campbell** (16.0 ppg, 8.0 rpg at Athens, Ala. HS) to take some pressure off Bradley. 6-10 sophomore forward **Gary Trus** (1.3 ppg, 1.0 rpg in 1987-88) also returns from a mission and could figure in the frontcourt picture. The only other returnees with experience are 6-9 sophomore center **David Astle** (1.0 ppg, 1.4 rpg) and 6-1 senior guard **Scott Moon** (2.4 ppg, 1.0 rpg), better known as the defending WAC high jump champion. 6-9 sophomore forward/center **Kirk Davidson** and 6-8 sophomore forward **John Lloyd** are the other returning lettermen.

The Cougar backcourt would have been greatly boosted by the arrival of Ryan Cuff, an archrival of Bradley's in Utah prep circles, but Cuff will spend the next two years on a mission in Argentina. Of the remaining Cougar newcomers, the standout is 6-8 sophomore **Jared Miller** (17.6 ppg, 9.5 rpg, 2.1 blocks, 2.1 steals at Ricks JC in Utah). He'll add to an already crowded inside presence in a frontline that could really use a prototype small forward. Schreiner, who will probably wind up there, spent time as an undersized center last year. Other arrivals are 6-9 freshman forward **Shane Knight** (14.0 ppg, 9.0 rpg, 4.0 blocks at Mt. Carmel HS, San Diego, Calif.), 6-6 junior forward **Robert Jones** (10.0 ppg, 7.0 rpg at Lon Morris JC in Texas), 6-1 junior guard **Marc Thompson** (16.3 ppg, 7.7 apg at New Mexico JC) and 6-4 junior guard **Keegan Kane** (18.7 ppg, 5.2 rpg, 4.5 apg at Ricks JC).

BLUE RIBBON ANALYSIS

For those who casually dismiss Mountain West basketball, Brigham Young, with a roster that included 10 players from Utah, one from Idaho and one from Nevada last year and seven from Utah, one from Idaho and one from Nevada this season, is the great redeemer. Which seems appropriate for a religious school. But despite the arrival of a future All-America in Bradley, the WAC road should get a lot rougher for the Cougars and second year coach Roger Reid this season. Reid is recovering from double hip replacement surgery in April.

Watching the progress of Bradley should speed Reid's recovery. And on sheer volume of participants plus the experience of Schreiner, the power forward slot figures to be an asset. However, there is little reason to expect much early production from the other three starting positions. There is little experience beyond Call and he hasn't competed for two years. Nor is there overwhelming talent. Brigham Young might go with a frontline of Bradley and two power forwards. But Bradley will be depending on an inexperienced backcourt to get him the ball, not to mention one that probably won't shoot well enough from outside to prevent the lane around him from getting too crowded. That's not a fun way to begin a college career. Unless Call, Heslop and Moon can gel quickly or newcomers Thompson or Kane can step up (make that quantum leap up), Brigham Young will probably slide into fourth place in the WAC.

1990-91 BRIGHAM YOUNG SCHEDULE

Nov.	14	#East Tennessee State
	24	Utah State

1990-91 BRIGHAM YOUNG SCHEDULE (Cont.)

Nov.	29	@Weber State
Dec.	1	@Utah State
	4	@La Salle
	7-8	##Cougar Classic
	12	Arizona State
	19	James Madison
	21	Stetson
	22	Tulsa
	27 & 29	*Holiday Festival
Jan.	3	@San Diego State
	5	@Hawaii
	10	UTEP
	12	New Mexico State
	17	@Colorado State
	19	@Wyoming
	24	Air Force
	26	Wyoming
	31	Colorado State
Feb.	2	@UTEP
	7	San Diego State
	9	Hawaii
	14	@New Mexico
	16	@Utah
	23	@Air Force
Mar.	2	Utah
	6-9	**WAC Tournament

@ Road Games
# Dod NIT. If Brigham Young defeats East Tennessee, the Cougars will play a second round game on Nov. 16. The semifinals and finals of the tournament will be held on Nov. 21 & 23 at Madison Square Garden, New York, NY.
Provo, UT (Eastern Kentucky, George Mason & St. John's)
* Madison Square Garden, New York, NY (Maryland, Rutgers & South Carolina)
** Laramie, WY

BROWN

LAST SEASON: 10-16
CONFERENCE RECORD: 7-7
STARTERS LOST: 1
STARTERS RETURNING: 4
CONFERENCE: IVY LEAGUE
LOCATION: PROVIDENCE, RI
HOME FLOOR: PIZZITOLA SPORTS CENTER (2,800)
NICKNAME: BEARS
COLORS: SEAL BROWN, CARDINAL RED AND WHITE
COACH: MIKE CINGISER, record at Brown, 82-155.

Just being in contention in last year's wacky Ivy League race was enough for Mike Cingiser. However, his players should not count on such a low threshold of satisfaction this season.

There was plenty to be excited about in Providence in 1989-90, despite the Bears' overall record of 10-16. Brown's 7-7 Ivy mark was good for a spot in the four-way tie for third behind Princeton and Yale. And the emergence of 6-7, 250-pound freshman forward sensation **Carlos Williams** was downright exhilarating.

Williams detonated with a remarkable first season. Though he averaged 11.0 points and 8.0 rebounds for the entire year, the bullish frosh came alive during Ivy time, improving those totals to 15.9 ppg and 10.0 rpg. He was the league's leading rebounder, its top shooter and seventh-leading scorer. It was hardly a surprise that he was named Ivy freshman of the year, particularly since he was its freshman of the week choice six times. An honorable-mention All-Ivy selection capped his remarkable debut.

"We need to find the right person to play next to Carlos and carry over some of the inside scoring and rebounding load this season," Cingiser said.

Candidates for that role include 6-8 soph **Kirk Lowry** (5.2 ppg, 2.9 rpg) and 6-8 senior tri-captain **Mike Gates** (3.4 ppg, 2.4 rpg), both centers. The small forward spot is even more wide open, with 6-6 senior tri-captain **Bill Coffey** (1.4 ppg) heading a group of four candidates.

The backcourt returns intact. Tri-captain **Rick Lloyd**, a 6-2 junior, was an honorable mention All-Ivy selection who led the Bears in scoring with 13.8 ppg and was second in the league with an .847 free throw percentage. He is joined by **Chuck Savage** (8.7 ppg, 3.5 apg, 3.4 rpg), a 6-1 junior, and 6-3 junior **Jon Drezner** (4.2 ppg).

"We're going to build on our backcourt strength and maybe play three guards, especially in the Ivy League," Cingiser added.

Vernon Clayton (3.7 ppg), a 6-1 sophomore, 6-3 junior **Rod Torbert** (3.4 ppg) and 6-1 soph **Ben Batory** (1.3 ppg) add depth to the strong backcourt. **Chris Gosk** (2.6 ppg, 1.9 rpg) is a 6-3 junior swingman; 6-5 junior **Steve Thomas** (1.3 ppg) and 6-7 soph **Daron Mills** are reserve forwards.

Cingiser is depending on four freshmen to add bulk to the Bears' frontcourt. Leading the class is 6-11 center **Chris Klimas** (Pope John XIII/Hackettstown, N.J.). Joining the big guy are 6-8 **Darrin Pisano** (Point Pleasant HS/Point Pleasant, N.J.), 6-6 **Doug Stewart** (Haddonfield Memorial HS/Haddonfield, N.J.) and 6-5 **Malik Nagel** (Germantown Friends School/Philadelphia, Pa.).

"We made a great move last season, but we must solidify our position to get to the next level," Cingiser said. "Everything we need to do can be done. When it comes together, we'll be ready to step to the top level of the Ivy League."

BLUE RIBBON ANALYSIS

If Williams continues the progress he made at the end of last season, he could be a monster. He has a backcourt to get him the ball, but lacks the mates upfront to prevent double- and triple-teaming.

That burden falls on the other starters up front, namely Lowry and Gates. Both could use to take better advantage of the fact that Williams figures to draw even more defensive attention as a sophomore. Consistent shooting from perimeter folks like Lloyd and Savage would also keep the low post clear.

Cingiser is excited about last year's leap to Ivy respectability, but knows the next step is even taller. If support can be found up front, Brown may escape the Ivy logjam and settle into fourth place. If Williams is lonely, a slide to the league's second division is possible.

1990-91 BROWN SCHEDULE

Nov.	23	Lehigh
	28	@ Providence
Dec.	1	Lafayette
	4	@Rhode Island
	7-8	#Pepsi-Marist Classic
	28-29	##Tampa Tribune Holiday Tournament
Jan.	4-5	*Florida Institute of Tech. Tournament
	11	@Pennsylvania
	12	@Princeton
	19	@Yale
	21	Holy Cross
	23	Bryant College (RI)
	26	Yale
Feb.	1	Cornell
	2	Columbia
	8	@Harvard
	9	@Dartmouth
	15	Princeton
	16	Pennsylvania
	22	Dartmouth
	23	Harvard
Mar.	1	@Columbia
	2	@Cornell

@ Road Games
# Poughkeepsie, NY (Canisius, Lehigh & Marist)
Tampa, FL (New Hampshire, Penn State & South Florida)
* Miami, FL (Detroit, Florida Institute of Technology & TBA)

BUCKNELL

LAST SEASON: 15-14
CONFERENCE RECORD: 6-8
STARTERS LOST: 2
STARTERS RETURNING: 4
CONFERENCE: PATRIOT
LOCATION: LEWISBURG, PA
HOME FLOOR: DAVIS GYM (2,000)
NICKNAME: BISON
COLORS: ORANGE AND BLUE
COACH: CHARLIE WOOLLUM, record at Bucknell, 246-176.

Christy Mathewson is perhaps Bucknell's most famous alumnus. The baseball Hall of Famer helped put the Bison on the map in football and basketball in the early part of the century. On the hardwood, head coach Charlie Woollum has not made anyone forget "The Big Six," but he has quietly built the Bison into a very competitive squad over his 15 seasons. Eight straight winning seasons, three 20-win campaigns and two NCAA bids document Woollum's success in Lewisburg. However, the Bison will be hard pressed to continue that success in '89-90.

Almost 50 percent of the Bison offensive attack, leading scorer Greg Leggett (20.2 ppg) and No. 2 man Mike Joseph (18.4 ppg), are gone from a team that went 15-14 last season, but only 12-14 against Division I opponents. Add in a schedule that includes the San Juan Shootout (Illinois, Northern Iowa, Murray State and St. Louis), NIT qualifiers Fordham and Holy Cross, a road trip to Wake Forest and only one non-Division I school, and Woollum's successful string could come to an abrupt end.

However, Bison fans should not turn to thoughts of the diamond and the gridiron just yet. The Bison returnees are young, but not untalented. Two underclassmen, 6-6 sophomore **Mike Bright** (10.8 ppg, 7.1 rpg) and 6-2 junior **Bill Courtney** (10.6 ppg), appear as the likely candidates to replace Leggett and Joseph. Bright's freshman campaign was just that, leading the team in rebounds and making the ECC All-Rookie team. Courtney started 22 games as shooting guard last season but will look to make the transition to the point this year. 6-10 senior center **Steve Leshinski** (4.6 ppg, 3.7 rpg) started 23 games last season, but will have to put up numbers to match his size for Bucknell to be a success. 6-2 senior **Keith Fenton** (6.8 ppg) will likely replace Courtney at the shooting guard spot, while a pair of untested juniors, 6-6 **Pat King** (0.8 ppg) and 6-5 **Mike Walsh** (1.0 ppg) will battle it out at the second forward spot.

Off the bench, Woollum will look to get bigger contributions out of 6-8 senior **Mike Diver** (1.9 ppg, 2.2 rpg) and 6-8 sophomore **Paul Olkowski** (3.4 ppg, 4.2 rpg) in the frontcourt and a pair of seniors, 6-3 **Rob Joy** (1.8 ppg, 1.0 rpg) and 6-1 **Malik Malone** along with 5-11 sophomore **Russell Peyton** in the backcourt. Diver came on strong during the final quarter of last season, capped off by a 14-point, 10-rebound effort vs. Towson State. But the trio of guards played just 35 minutes combined in '89-90 and could more than quadruple their playing time in '90-91. 6-1 freshman **Chris Simpson** (19.0 ppg, 6.0 rpg, 4.0 apg at St. Stephens HS, Alexandria, Va.) may also see some time at the point. Simpson was named the Virginia State Private School Player of the Year in USA Today and second-team All-Metro by The Washington Post. Bucknell's other three newcomers are 6-6 freshman forward **Raymond Brown** from Lafayette HS, Williamsburg, Va., 6-7 freshman **Matt Sloan** (17.5 ppg, 9.0 rpg at Branson School, Novato, Calif.) and **Jason Janego**, a 6-2 guard from Owasso (Mich.) HS. They will be counted on further down the road.

Woollum has worked wonders motivating underdog teams in recent seasons. This may be his biggest test yet. Bright and Courtney have proven that they can score, but can they be the leaders on and off the floor that Leggett and Joseph were? Leggett set Bucknell's single season scoring mark last year while Joseph is the school all-time assist leader. Replacing them by committee may be the best bet, but that would require a number of players to step forward. Right now Woollum would settle for one or two. Fenton and Leshinski also must play more consistently than they have in their careers. Perhaps more importantly, not that these four players have leadership roles, who will fill their spots coming off the bench? The tougher schedule is not exactly coming at the best of times, nor is the appearance of new Patriot League foes Holy Cross and Fordham, both of whom had twenty win season in '89-90 and could again this year.

This will be a rebuilding year in Lewisburg and if Woollum gets more than 12 wins out of this squad he could be asking the great Mathewson to make a little more room in the Bison limelight. A fifth place spot in the new seven team Patriot League is Bucknell's most likely spot.

1990-91 BUCKNELL SCHEDULE

Nov.	23-25	#San Juan Shootout
	28	Delaware
Dec.	1	Yale
	3	@Fairfield
	5	Lycoming (PA)
	8	St. Francis (PA)
	29	@Cornell
Jan.	2	@Maryland-Baltimore Co.
	4	@Towson State
	7	@Delaware
	9	Drexel
	12	Holy Cross
	14	Maryland-Baltimore Co.
	19	@Army
	23	Fordham
	26	Colgate
	28	Towson State
	30	@Lehigh
Feb.	2	Lafayette
	6	@Wake Forest
	9	@Holy Cross
	11	Mt. St. Mary's (MD)
	13	Army
	16	@Fordham
	20	@Colgate
	23	Lehigh
	25	@Lafayette
Feb. 28- Mar. 2		*Patriot League Tournament

@ Road Games
# San Juan, PR (American University of Puerto Rico, Illinois, Murray State, Nebraska, Northern Iowa, Old Dominion & St. Louis)
* Worchester, MA

BUTLER

LAST SEASON: 6-22
CONFERENCE RECORD: 2-12
STARTERS LOST: 2
STARTERS RETURNING: 3
CONFERENCE: MIDWESTERN COLLEGIATE (MCC)
LOCATION: INDIANAPOLIS, IN
HOME FLOOR: HINKLE FIELDHOUSE (10,800)
NICKNAME: BULLDOGS
COLORS: BLUE AND WHITE
COACH: BARRY COLLIER, record at Butler, 6-22.

An image problem exists for Butler, the only NCAA Division I school in the major Indianapolis market. With Indiana to the south and Purdue to the north, not to mention nearby schools such as Ball State and Indiana State, it is difficult for the Bulldogs to attract much attention. "They (the Indy newspapers) send reporters to West Lafayette and Bloomington, but lump us in with the Division II and Division III schools in the area," said Jim McGrath, Butler's sports information director.

Butler is a quaint, private school of 4,000 students. Hinkle Fieldhouse, built in 1928, is a mammoth structure that used to house the Indiana high school basketball tournament, birthplace of Hoosier Hysteria. Hinkle was even in the movie "Hoosiers" for the state tourney scenes.

Last year, the structure underwent a $1.5 million facelift, adding new locker room facilities, offices and improved seating. On the court, Butler hired Barry Collier, a youthful coach, to try and make the program a success. Collier played at Butler in the 1970's, then held five assistant coaching positions before joining his alma mater.

The Bulldogs have not had a winning season since 1985, and worse, they haven't kept pace with the rest of the burgeoning Midwestern Collegiate Conference. Butler ranked last in attendance, averaging only 1,945 spectators in cavernous Hinkle.

But at least Butler has stopped sitting back waiting for things to improve. Collier, though his rookie season was dismal, has been recruiting athletes who can play up-tempo like the rest of the MCC. The building is better and the schedule has improved, with natural in-state rivals Purdue added this year and Indiana next. Notre Dame and Wisconsin are also new opponents this season.

Given those demands, it is fortunate that the Bulldogs return three starters, including talented 6-4 junior swingman **Darin Archbold**. Archbold, who figures to be a full-time guard this season, led Butler in scoring (11.9 ppg) and finished even stronger, averaging 22.8 points over the final six games.

Sophomore **J.P. Brens**, a 6-9 center, showed flashes of brilliance as a freshman and was named to the MCC all-newcomer team. St. Louis University coach Rich Grawer called Brens "the best freshman in the league," and predicted he would "be a force for a long time." Brens (11.0 ppg, 5.7 rpg) has been working on weights in the off-season to build his upper body strength, a major weakness last season. His endurance also lagged at times, and he found it difficult to hold his own with more aggressive players.

"J.P. is a legitimate threat in the low post," said Collier, "and now we want him to extend his scoring. He needs to become more of a physical presence, particularly on defense. Our ability to rebound and defend will start with him."

The other returning starter is 5-8 point guard **Tim Bowen** (5.7 ppg, 1.1 rpg, 80 assists), a sophomore. **Brian Beauford**, a 6-5 junior transfer from Northeastern Oklahoma A&M, will likely join the starting lineup. He is one of the newcomers who likes to play the full-court game, and will fill the small forward spot.

Brett Etherington, a 6-7 senior, gets the first shot at power forward. He has not really lived up to his potential, but did come off the bench last season against Miami of Ohio and scored a career-high 23 points. For the season, though, Etherington's numbers (5.8 ppg, 2.9 rpg) were disappointing.

Butler's top freshman is **Jermaine Guice**, a 6-2 shooting guard from Westerville (Ohio) South High. Guice averaged 19.2 points, 4.1 rebounds, 7.6 assists and 4.1 steals as a high school senior. Collier hopes he can produce immediately. Guice is also a legitimate three-point shooter, and Butler lost to graduation one of the MCC's premier gunners in Jody Littrell. Beauford replaces the other departed starter, Rodney Haywood, who averaged 9.2 points and 6.3 rebounds last season.

Other recruits include 6-8 freshman **Danny Allen** (Appleton East HS/Appleton, Wisc.), 6-9 junior transfer **Harvey Johnson** (Pratt CC/Pratt, Kan.) and 6-4 freshman **John Taylor** (Rich South HS/Matteson, Ill.). A true swingman, Taylor is another of the new-breed athletes for Butler, versatile enough to challenge for playing time in the up-tempo game.

Additional reserves for Collier include 6-3 senior **Chad Fordyce** (0.0 ppg, 0.2 rpg); 6-6 senior **Wade Gault** (1.3 ppg, 1.7 rpg); 6-4 senior **John Karaffa** (2.7 ppg, 1.3 rpg), 6-5 sophomore **Dave Ryser** (0.0 ppg, 0.0 rpg); 6-1 senior **John Shoup** (5.8 ppg, 1.1 rbg) and 6-0 junior **Michael Wilson** (1.9 ppg, 1.4 rpg). Of the bunch, Karaffa, Shoup and Wilson are most likely to play.

BLUE RIBBON ANALYSIS

Butler's rebuilding process is a painstaking one, and it will take some time. The job is even more difficult given the MCC's surge to national prominence. Throw in recent additions Dayton and Marquette, and it has become a conference in which standing still really means falling further behind.

The Bulldogs finally caught on, hired a coach for the 90's, and now must wait while the mix comes to a boil. It is not there yet, although Collier finally has a handful of his own players with which to build. Xavier, St. Louis, Evansville and others, however, remain considerably more advanced, meaning Butler could be a much better team and still not escape the MCC cellar.

1990-91 BUTLER SCHEDULE

Nov.	24	Western Illinois
	26	@Indiana State
	29	@University of Portland
Dec.	1	@Fullerton State
	3	Notre Dame
	6	Valparaiso (IN)
	8	@Bowling Green
	15	Wisconsin
	20	@Purdue
	22	Ball State
Jan.	2	@Georgia State
	5	@Mercer
	9	@St. Louis
	12	@Detroit
	16	@Jacksonville
	19	Detroit
	24	Dayton
	31	Loyola
Feb.	2	@Marquette
	7	St. Louis
	9	Evansville
	12	@Xavier
	16	@Evansville
	21	@Dayton
	23	Xavier
	28	@Loyola
Mar.	2	Marquette
	7-9	#MCC Tournament

@ Road Games
# Dayton, OH

CALIFORNIA

LAST SEASON: 22-10
CONFERENCE RECORD: 12-6
STARTERS LOST: 2
STARTERS RETURNING: 3
CONFERENCE: PACIFIC-10
LOCATION: BERKELEY, CA
HOME FLOOR: HARMON ARENA (6,578)
NICKNAME: GOLDEN BEARS
COLORS: BLUE AND GOLD
COACH: LOU CAMPANELLI, record at California, 90-68.
Career record, 328-186.

Five years ago, new California head coach Lou Campanelli said his major goal was "learning how to win." The Bears hadn't done much of that since the glory years of Pete Newell that ended in 1960. Campanelli has accomplished that. California has not only become respectable, but the Bears are threatening to become a nationally ranked team.

Perhaps it was last year's 22-win season, including the school's first NCAA appearance since Newell's final season, a second place NCAA finish to Ohio State, that has the Berkeley campus excited about the upcoming year. Perhaps it was the stirring NCAA first-round, 65-63, upset of Indiana. Or perhaps it is the fact that three starters and ten lettermen are back from a year ago.

Campanelli proved last season that he is a coach who adjusts his style of play to the personnel. The Bears' squad of a year ago was thin up front but loaded with guards. So Campanelli changed from a half court, inside oriented attack to an up-tempo approach that emphasized the three-pointer. The Bears rewrote the school record book with 196 treys and 507 bonus attempts. California had three of the top 11 three-point shooters in the Pacific-10 Conference.

Campanelli isn't going to change a thing. He'll still use the three-man perimeter attack and transition game. 6-3 junior guard **Ryan Drew** (9.8 ppg, 2.5 rpg) and 6-3 sophomore guard **Bill Elleby** (8.1 ppg) are the two leading candidates for the two off-guard positions. Last year they combined for the 104 three-pointers between them. Drew has been a streak shooter throughout his career, as evidenced by his 21-point performance (7 three-pointers) in only 24 minutes against Washington sandwiched between four games of six points or less. While he scored in double figures 17 times, Drew was blanked three times and held to five or less 12 times. Elleby is the prime contender to fill the starting spot held by graduated Bryant Walton. The team's sixth man last year, he played more minutes than Walton, almost as many as Drew and led the team in shooting percentage in conference games (.566).

California also recruited a marksman that fits into Campanelli's new style of play. 6-5 freshman **Keith Walker** (32.9 ppg) was the fifth leading scorer in California prep circles at Brea-Olinda HS. The younger brother of UCLA senior Kevin Walker, he possesses terrific range combined with strong driving ability. Sophomore **Billy Dreher** 6-4, who averaged 3.4 points as a freshman for Oklahoma State in 1988-89 before transferring, comes in with the reputation as a solid three-point shooter.

The Bears aren't without some potential problems or question marks. Number one, of course, is finding a capable replacement for graduated point guard Keith Smith. Campanelli has not been without a talented point guard in his five seasons in Berkeley. He had the elusive Kevin Johnson his final two seasons. Then Campanelli turned to Smith, who backed up Johnson for one season, before stepping in for what turned into a California career assist record (546). Smith was the trigger man for the last three years, one of the steadiest floor leaders in the country.

5-11 senior **Sean Harrell** (1.7 ppg, 1.3 apg) is the only returning point guard. While he started seven games at off-guard and logged 334 minutes, Harrell showed little offense, particularly from three-point range (1-for-14). He is, however, an excellent defender. The other possibilities are 6-2 sophomore **DeShon Brown** and 6-0 **Akili Jones**. Brown arrived in the fall of 1988 and sat out that season. Last season he underwent surgery to repair a chronic knee problem and received a medical redshirt year. At Modesto (Calif.) HS, he averaged 19 points, 11 rebounds and 7 assists as a senior and came to Berkeley as a heavily recruited prospect. Jones, from Lowell HS in San Francisco, is a redshirt freshman who was the San Francisco AAA prep player of the year as a senior. However, he was primarily an off-guard in high school, but has been learning to play the point at California.

The Bears are not weak inside. In fact, the double post attack could become the Bears' number one strength this season. 6-8 sophomore **Brian Hendrick** (14.9 ppg, 7.6 rpg) was one of the top freshmen in the country last year, finishing second to USC's Harold Miner for such honors in the Pacific-10 balloting. The son of former major league outfielder George Hendrick, Brian set California freshman records for points (478), scoring average (14.9) and field goal percentage (59.3). He was amazingly consistent, scoring in double figures in 29 of California's 32 games.

6-7 senior **Roy Fisher** (14.9 ppg, 6.3 rpg) already has recorded 74 career starts in three years and is one point shy of becoming California's 21st 1,000-point scorer. Fisher is one of the league's flashiest players. That normally does not translate into consistency, but last season Fisher reduced his bad games to only a handful.

California's inside depth comes from 6-5 sophomore **Rich Branham** (2.7 ppg, 2.6 rpg), 6-9 senior **Andre Reyes** (2.5 ppg, 1.9 rpg), 6-9 junior **Eric McDonough** (1.6 ppg, 1.4 rpg) and 6-6 senior **Matt Brigham** (0.6 ppg, 0.8 rpg).

Campanelli also brought in 6-7 junior **Matt Lien** (18.3 ppg, 5.8 rpg) from Rancho Santiago (Calif.) JC, who could help the undersized frontline as a power forward. Among the recruits who could challenge for some backup playing time is 6-11 freshman **Ryan Jamison** (19.5 ppg, 11.5 rpg, 5.0 bpg) from Loyola HS in Los Angeles. 6-7 **LaDay Smith** (21.6 ppg, 9.0 rpg) from Muir High in Pasadena, Calif., could also be a factor. Jamison, ranked among the nation's Top 100 by many, was highly regarded around Los Angeles and could eventually become an important player. He is very agile for his size, runs the floor well, and has a nice touch near the basket.

California opens it season on the road at Houston and also must visit crosstown rival San Francisco. The nonconference slate also includes a nationally televised home game against Purdue and a visit to the Rainbow Classic.

BLUE RIBBON ANALYSIS

California has a lot of good things going for it. Fisher-Hendrick are a talented inside tandem. Drew and Elleby are experienced guards with shooting range. The bench has experience.

But there's no Keith Smith. And anyone who has seen California play the last three years, particularly last season, knows how important the point guard leadership of Smith was. In addition, Smith was the team's top scorer. He made everyone around him a better player. If the new faces cannot handle the position without a major dropoff, California will have problems freeing its three-point shooters. Fisher and Hendrick, at 6-7 and 6-8, respectively, are no match physically for the towering frontline of Arizona, the team the Bears must catch if they are to make the next step in their basketball resurgence.

California's home court edge will keep it in the Pacific-10 race most of the year. Harmon Pavillion is tough on visitors' nerves —and ears.

The Bears are one player away from having a Top 20 team —either another year out of Smith, which isn't possible, or another talented big man to complement Fisher and Hendrick. How rapidly Jamison develops will prove crucial in this regard. More offense and consistency from Harrell or the adjustment to point guard by the more talented Akili Jones, after his redshirt layoff, must answer the Bears' other big question of floor leadership. Drew has to eliminate his off games, which one would expect from a senior.

Campanelli has a new five-year contract. He has taken the Bears to a higher plateau. The next step is the most difficult. For this season, a fight with Arizona State for the fourth (and perhaps final NCAA) spot in the Pacific-10 seems most likely.

1990-91 CALIFORNIA SCHEDULE

Nov.	24	@Houston
Dec.	1	@San Francisco
	3	San Jose State
	6	Purdue
	19	U.S. International (CA)
	22	@California —Irvine
	27-30	#Rainbow Classic
Jan.	3	@Oregon
	5	@Oregon State
	10	Washington State
	12	Washington
	17	@Southern California
	19	@UCLA
	24	Arizona State
	26	Arizona
	31	Oregon State
Feb.	3	Oregon
	7	@Washington
	9	@Washington State
	14	UCLA
	17	Southern California
	21	@Arizona
	24	@Arizona State
Mar.	2	@Stanford
	5	Cal State-Northridge
	7	Stanford

@ Road Games
# Honolulu, HI (Alaska-Anchorage, Hawaii, Iona, Pitt, Stetson, Tennessee & Wichita State)

CALIFORNIA IRVINE

LAST SEASON: 5-23
CONFERENCE RECORD: 3-15
STARTERS LOST: 1
STARTERS RETURNING: 4
CONFERENCE: BIG WEST
LOCATION: IRVINE, CA
HOME FLOOR: BREN EVENT CENTER (5,000)
NICKNAME: ANTEATERS
COLORS: BLUE AND GOLD
COACH: BILL MULLIGAN, record at California-Irvine, 152-157.
Career record, 484-255.

It's safe to say that the coaching staff at California-Irvine would love to wash the 1989-90 hoop campaign away forever. The 5-23 season was a total disaster, the worst in the school's 25-year history. There was a 15-game losing streak. There were eight losses by six points or less.

Veteran head coach Bill Mulligan, who is beginning his eleventh year at California-Irvine, is very eager to put the past behind him, lock it in a closet somewhere, and then conveniently lose the key. After all, the Anteaters were 12-17 two years ago. The spiraling decline is not a good sign.

Still, the administration at California-Irvine has incredible faith in Mulligan, because they have extended his contract for one year, through the 1991-92 campaign. No need for the proverbial vote of confidence. Mulligan got it in writing, but further on?

How eager is Mulligan to get the 1990-91 season going? He started thinking about it this year one day after Fullerton State sent the Anteaters packing after a defeat in the first round of the Big West tournament.

"For the first time since I began coaching, I want a new season to start the next day, normally I looked forward to a little time off in previous years," Mulligan said. "You get to a point where you want to justify your existence and show that you can turn it around."

Turn it around in a conference like the Big West that just keeps getting stronger and better, top to bottom, with each passing year? Nice motto. However, not easily attained. Throw in the fact that the Anteaters nonconference slate is no prize and you'll see that Mulligan's hopes for instant improvement may be nothing more than pipe dreams.

The Anteaters head to the Great Alaska Shootout with UCLA, Virginia and South Carolina, play host to the Disneyland Freedom Bowl Classic with Bradley and high powered Loyola Marymount, then they hit the road to face Maryland, San Diego State and Stanford in one week in December. All before facing the beasts in the Big West, like last year's national champion UNLV.

Turn it around? Finding an Anteater in New York City is easier. Even Mulligan is aware of that.

"It will be one great year to accomplish a turnaround with a schedule like we have," Mulligan said. "The conference will be as good, if not better, than last year and our nonconference schedule is the best ever. Or worst ever, depending on how you look at it."

However, the Anteaters have a good nucleus back from last year's team, returning four starters. Is that good or bad? The optimist will have to say that the experience gained last year was invaluable. The pessimist? What good does it do having four starters and seven letterwinners back from a team that lost 23 times?

Senior center **Ricky Butler** (13.8 ppg, 6.5 rpg) is the top returnee. The 6-7 Butler started 23 of California-Irvine's 28 games last year, scoring in double figures in 20 of them. He shot a very respectable 54 percent from the floor, considering that most centers in the Big West tower over Butler. Butler came on strong at season's end last year, averaging 19.0 points per game and shooting 70 percent from the floor over the final seven games of the season. He has also lost 15 pounds from his 260-pound frame of a year ago and has seemingly put his weight problems of the past behind him. If the Anteaters are to make vast improvements, then Butler will have to come up big.

Senior forward **Jeff Herdman** (11.4 ppg, 5.3 rpg) also returns. The 6-7 Herdman finished second to Butler on the team in scoring and rebounding. Herdman's big contributions started to come when he came off the bench for the final 10 games of the season, averaging 15.0 points in those contests. However, Herdman shot a dreadful 38 percent from the floor, after clicking on 48 percent as a sophomore and 46 percent as a freshman. At one point in his junior year, Herdman was the nation's top three-point percentage shooter. Those days seem ancient history. If Herdman's numbers return to previous form, then he might return to a starter's role. If not, he'll come off the bench as a senior.

Sophomore forward **Jeff Von Lutzlow** (9.4 ppg, 5.2 rpg) was tossed into the fire as a freshman last year and immediately responded. The lanky 6-9 Von Lutzlow was named to the Big West all-freshman team. He started the last 10 games of the season after Herdman was sent to the bench and led the team in field goal percentage at 56 percent. He was a pleasant surprise. Another sophomore who was forced to learn immediately under game pressures last year was guard **Dylan Rigdon** (7.7 ppg, 1.7 rpg, 62 assists). The 6-3 Rigdon was also named to the Big West all-freshman team. He had a fine shooting night in a win against Fullerton State late in the year, converting on all nine field goal attempts, including seven straight from three-point range. Rigdon gives Mulligan hope for the future, because he averaged 17.1 points per game over the final 12 games of the season, all starts.

"When I look back at it now, I should have used the freshmen earlier in the season," Mulligan said. "They all played very well for us."

Craig Marshall (4.7 ppg, 2.6 rpg, 38 assists) has to be considered among that group. The 6-2 sophomore was the most versatile Anteater a year ago, playing three positions and ending the season as the starting small forward. Mulligan considers Marshall as one of the team's top defenders and is the pre-season choice to start again at small forward. However, shooting percentage is not Marshall's forte, evidenced by his poor 34 percent mark.

Junior forward **Elgin Rogers** (5.8 ppg, 2.9 rpg) should see his playing time increase after his strong showing at the end of last season. The 6-6 Rogers started five games and played very well in losses to UNLV and Fresno State. Junior forward **Don May** (1.7 ppg, 2.6 rpg) played in 27 games last year, starting eight. The 6-9 May received his degree in Economics in just three years and will play for the Anteaters this season while attending graduate school.

Mulligan is hopeful of getting strong performances from two redshirt freshmen —6-6 forward **Khari Johnson** (El Toro, Calif., HS) and 6-10 center **Rick Swanwick** (Trabuco Hills HS/El Toro, Calif.). According to the Anteater coaching staff, Johnson is considered a top flight prospect, a player of impact. He averaged 15.7 points and 8.7 rebounds per game in high school, but really came on in a series of postseason All-Star games around Orange County. The coaching staff is working with Johnson in the hopes of developing an outside game, because he played mostly inside in high school. Swanwick was considered to be the leading candidate as the starting center when he was forced to redshirt a year ago. He was the *Los Angeles Times* player of the year his senior year at Trabuco Hills, where he averaged 21.3 points and 13.8 rebounds. Swanwick led Trabuco Hills to the California Division III championship game, where he scored his team's last 25 points in a 62-61 defeat to Central Valley. He is a very strong inside player and an aggressive rebounder who will see considerable action this season.

Mulligan and his staff are confident that their five signees, three junior college transfers and two freshmen, can help immediately. The cream of the California-Irvine newcomer crop is 6-1 junior guard **Gerald McDonald** (18.0 ppg, 7.5 rpg, 9.2 apg), a transfer from Compton (Calif.) College. The versatile McDonald jumped center at Compton, but will probably start in the point guard slot for the Anteaters this season. The other junior college transfers are 6-5 sophomore forward **Cornelius Banks** (15.6 ppg, 7.8 rpg) and 6-2 junior guard **David Hollaway** (14.7 ppg, 5.7 rpg). Banks and Hollaway were teammates at Crenshaw HS in Los Angeles, Calif. Banks is a transfer from Santa Monica College while Hollaway is entering his third school in four years. He started his career at San Jose State, then transferred to West Los Angeles CC where he played last year.

The two recruits out of the high school ranks were 6-6 forward **Gabe Higa** (23.2 ppg, 10.3 rpg) and 6-10 center **Dan Augulis** (10.0 ppg, 6.0 rpg). Higa is from Quartz Hill HS and is a native of Lancaster, Calif. He is a superb athlete who was the California state triple jump champion. Higa has a soft touch from the perimeter and is considered a talented offensive player. Augulis is considered a project and played on an undefeated Shawnee Mission South team that rolled to the Kansas 6A state championship. He is from Leawood, Kan.

BLUE RIBBON ANALYSIS

Are there better times ahead for Bill Mulligan and the California— Irvine Anteaters? Well, it can't get any worse. But, more than likely, it will not get much better either. On paper, Mulligan's team is not very big up front, so that means they will not be able to power the ball down low against much bigger competition in the Big West. Butler is a bulldog, but he is only 6-7. The loss of weight will add quickness, not strength and height. Von Lutzlow, Herdman and May do not instill fear in the hearts of opponents. Playing a 6-2

small forward like Marshall does not help either.

So what the Anteaters lack in size, they need from the outside and going on past performances, they cannot get it done there either. California-Irvine shot 42 percent from the floor, while opponents shot 47 percent. And a team that perennially averages 85 points per game and more under Mulligan scored just 71.7 points per game last year.

There lies the reason for the 5-23 disaster. Plus, the Anteaters turned the ball over to the tune of 19 miscues per game while dishing out only 13 assists. Too huge of a discrepancy there. Getting McDonald to run the show will help.

Sure, the freshmen gained valuable experience getting thrown to the wolves last year, but that can only account for so much. The Anteaters need more than that and don't appear to have it.

Herdman's shooting percentage has to improve and the Anteaters will need immediate help from another newcomer, perhaps Swanwick or Johnson. The schedule, with the Big West going stronger throughout and the competitive nonconference games predominantly on the road, only make the situation that much worse.

Simply, it looks like another trying season for Bill Mulligan's California-Irvine Anteaters.

1990-91 CALIFORNIA-IRVINE SCHEDULE	
Nov. 23-26	#Great Alaska Shootout
30-Dec. 1	##Disneyland Freedom Bowl Classic
Dec. 8	Utah
11	@Maryland
15	@San Diego State
19	@Stanford
22	California
28-29	*Dr. Pepper Classic
Jan. 2	@Utah State
4	@San Jose State
7	Pacific
9	Fresno State
11	@Long Beach State
14	@New Mexico State
17	UNLV
19	@California-Santa Barbara
24	@UNLV
26	Fullerton State
31	@Fresno State
Feb. 2	@Pacific
7	Long Beach State
9	New Mexico State
16	California-Santa Barbara
21	@Fullerton State
28	San Jose State
Mar. 2	Utah State
8-10	**Big West Tournament

@ Road Games
# Anchorage, AK (Alaska-Anchorage, Nevada, Siena, South Carolina, Texas Tech, UCLA & Virginia)
Irvine, CA (Bradley, Idaho State & Loyola Marymount)
* Chattanooga, TN (Alabama State, San Francisco & Tennessee-Chattanooga)
** Long Beach, CA

CANISIUS

LAST SEASON: 11-18
CONFERENCE RECORD: 5-11
STARTERS LOST: 1
STARTERS RETURNING: 4
CONFERENCE: METRO ATLANTIC ATHLETIC (MAAC)
LOCATION: BUFFALO, NY
HOME FLOOR: MEMORIAL AUDITORIUM (16,476) and KOESSLER ATHLETIC CENTER (1,800)
NICKNAME: GOLDEN GRIFFINS
COLORS: BLUE AND GOLD
COACH: MARTY MARBACH, record at Canisius, 31-53.

The big question around Canisius this fall will be: Which Griffs will show up for 1990-91? They will all be there in body, but will it be the 2-12 team from the season's first 14 games or the squad that went 9-6 over the final 15. Only time will tell.

One thing is for sure: Many expect Marty Marbach's crew to make their long-awaited run this season. Canisius returns all but one key player from last year's 11-18 team, and hopes that a healthy squad can make '90-91 Marbach's first winning season.

Healthy is one thing the Griffs were not last season. Players lost 57 combined games to injury, most notably a pair of big men, 6-9 freshman **Sean Sandel** (27 games —stress fracture) and 6-11 junior **Ed Book** (12 games —torn ankle ligaments). Both hope to return to form this year.

Book ended his season prematurely with his ankle injury January 27 vs. Niagara, but still managed to lead the Griffs in scoring (12.3 ppg) and rebounding (6.5 rpg). His aggressive inside play and ever-improving offensive skills will be paramount to the Canisius attack, and could make him one of the MA-AC's best by season's end. Joining Book in the frontcourt will be burly 6-7 junior **Nixon Dyall** (5.6 ppg, 4.8 rpg) and 6-7 classmate **Harry Seymour** (6.3 ppg, 4.2 rpg).

Both showed marked improvement after Book was lost to injury, and should continue to improve on the mental mistakes which plagued Canisius last season. Another frontcourt player who benefitted from Book's injury was 6-9 senior center **Mike O'Sullivan** (3.8 ppg, 2.7 rpg). The little used reserve was forced into a starting role and had some quality performances in the latter stages, including a 9-point, 10-rebound performance in the Griffs' win over Fordham. Sophomore **Dexter Parker** (2.6 ppg, 2.1 rpg) will also increase his minutes and redshirt freshman Sandel could see time in relief of Book in the middle or at power forward.

More good news is that the starting backcourt of 6-1 senior **Gregg Smith** (9.6 ppg, 2.8 rpg) and 6-3 classmate **Chuck Giscombe** (9.9 ppg, 2.4 rpg) will also return. Smith led the team in steals (51) last season while averaging 28 minutes per game, second-most among the returnees. Giscombe, the Griffs most dependable player, led the team in free throw shooting (.833) while showing the maturity that a very young team needs. He could be their go-to guy in late game situations if Book is not available. 5-9 junior three-point ace **"Hot" Rodney Brown** (8.3 ppg) is also back after hitting 42 percent of his treys and leading the team in assists. The depth will come from scrappy 6-3 sophomore **Joe McCarthy** (5.3 ppg) and 6-2 freshman guard **Dana "Binky" Johnson** (22.0 ppg) from Norristown, Pa., HS. Johnson, a third team all-stater as a point guard, will probably see more early minutes as a two-guard but can help at both positions.

BLUE RIBBON ANALYSIS

It appears like the Griffs should be ready to make a run toward the top of the MAAC. Their two biggest problems last season were injuries and untimely turnovers. Hopefully, luck will help one and experience the other. Surprisingly, Canisius played their best ball after star center Book was lost for the year. If he is healthy, they should be worlds better. Playing within themselves is the key. Giscombe and Brown tried to do too much last season, especially on the offensive side. Time and their surrounding cast should dictate that they tone down a little.

A 15 or 16 win season is most definitely within reach —18 or 19 is a possibility —for this team and second or third in the MAAC is definitely within their grasp, if they don't throw it away. It should be Marbach's best yet in Buffalo.

1990-91 CANISIUS SCHEDULE

Nov.	27	Liberty University (VA)
Dec.	1	Xavier
	4	Elmira (NY)
	7-8	#Pepsi-Marist Classic
	12	@Syracuse
	15	St. Bonaventure
	29	@University of San Diego
Jan.	2	@Cal State-Northridge
	5	@Fairfield
	10	@Manhattan
	12	@Iona
	15	@Niagara
	19	Manhattan
	21	Fairfield
	24	La Salle
	26	St. Peter's
	28	Vermont
	31	@Siena
Feb.	2	Iona
	7	@Loyola College
	9	@La Salle
	13	@St. Bonaventure
	16	Loyola College
	18	Siena
	20	@St. Peter's
	23	Niagara
Mar.	1-4	*MAAC Tournament

@ Road Games
# Poughkeepsie, NY (Brown, Lehigh & Marist)
* Albany, NY

CENTRAL MICHIGAN

LAST SEASON: 13-17
CONFERENCE RECORD: 6-10
STARTERS LOST: 1
STARTERS RETURNING: 4
CONFERENCE: MID-AMERICAN (MAC)
LOCATION: MT. PLEASANT, MI
HOME FLOOR: ROSE ARENA (6,000)
NICKNAME: CHIPPEWAS
COLORS: MAROON AND GOLD
COACH: CHARLIE COLES, record at Central Michigan, 77-70.

First off, let it be known that Central Michigan coach Charlie Coles is an optimistic sort, even during the worst of times. So it is hardly unusual for him to be excited about his Chippewas, this despite a record of 13-17 a year ago. That ledger included a second consecutive 6-10 mark in the Mid-American Conference.

Yet Coles is confident that the Chips will contend for this season's MAC championship. "Most definitely," the coach said. "We have more experience, depth and quickness. I think we will be a greatly improved club." Coles has a basis for at least some of his optimism. For the first time in two years, the Chippewas return four starters, not to mention four letter-winning reserves.

Leading the pack of returnees is 6-9 senior **Jeff Majerle** (12.9 ppg, 4.1 rpg), the left-handed brother of former Central star and current Phoenix Sun forward Dan Majerle. The younger Majerle led the team in scoring and was its most prolific three-point shooter, converting 80-of-172 treys. If Jeff could add some muscle to his slender 195-pound frame, he too could become an NBA prospect.

The other starters back are 6-1 sophomore guard **Sander Scott** (11.6 ppg, 2.1 rpg.), 6-3 senior guard **David Carter** (10.2 ppg, 4.3 rpg, 50 assists) and 6-4 senior swingman **Terrance Colbert** (7.7 ppg, 3.3 rpg, 77 assists). Scott has the most long-term value and was an even more dangerous long-distance shooter than Majerle, getting off fewers three-pointers (56-for-115), but connecting on a higher percentage (.487). He needs to improve on a terrible assists-to-turnovers (59-to-65) ratio, but appears to have a great future ahead. It is the second and final year in the program for Carter (Polk CC, Fla.) and Colbert (Miami-Dade South CC), each transferring in a year ago.

Another part-time starter who returns is 6-6 senior **Melvin Kelly.** After transferring from Lansing (Mich.) CC last summer, Coles claimed Kelly was an NBA prospect. Yet he started only 17 games, shooting .433 from the field and .589 from the foul line. In Kelly's favor is the departure of 6-8 forward Carter Briggs.

Also vying for that final forward spot is newcomer **Darian McKinney,** a 6-6 junior transfer from the University of Detroit. McKinney was a freshman All-America at Detroit and the first rookie to ever lead the Titans in rebounding, but a coaching change there led to his move. The powerful forward is a proven Division I talent, athletic enough to have been recruited in football by such powerhouses as Penn State, Notre Dame and Michigan State.

Joining McKinney on the transfer train is 6-3 sophomore **Calvin Winfield,** another highly acclaimed player from the now-recovering Detroit program. Winfield, a less than steady ballhandler for the Titans, will have to cut down on his errors to help the Chippewas.

Three more letter-winning reserves return their varied skills to the mix. The best is probably 6-8 sophomore **Dennis Kann** (7.3 ppg, 3.1 rpg, 30 blocked shots). Also back are 6-2 sophomore **Aundre Kizer** (1.6 ppg, 1.2 rpg) and 6-5 senior **Scottie Thurman** (1.3 ppg, 0.8 rpg). 5-9 junior **Sean Waters** is back as well, having sat out last season with a broken wrist. Waters averaged 8.5 points, 2.3 assists and 2.0 rebounds in 1988-89.

"That gives us a total of 11 talented players who have played significantly at one time or another," said Coles. "We've never been in that position before."

That also makes it difficult for anyone else to see playing time. Still, 6-5 transfer **Willie Jones** - John Logan (Ill.) CC - is a fine athlete and outstanding defender. Coles says Jones play because of those qualities. 6-4 junior **John Baker,** a walk-on, and 6-7 freshman **Corey Henderson** (Eastern HS/Lansing, Mich.) round out the roster.

BLUE RIBBON ANALYSIS

A quick glance at last season's statistics reveal why the Chips were a second-division team. They were outshot badly from the floor (.467 to .449) and the free throw line (.722 to .694), plus they were outrebounded (34.7 to 31.3 per game). They also collected far more turnovers (432) than assists (392). It is a fatal mixture. If you can't win at least half those minibattles, you can't win.

So while this year's Chippewa tribe runs deep on experience and talent, it is also imperative that they take care of fundamentals - and the ball. The Chips need an inside presence, as well, relying too much on a whopping 575 three-point attempts a year ago. It was well over a third of their attack.

Newcomer Winfield might help steady the backcourt, and fellow transfer McKinney could help Central close the gap in rebounding. He also should provide some better interior defense, which the Chips desperately need. They cannot contend for the MAC title surrendering 72.2 points per game.

"We don't have a big man in the middle," Coles admitted, "but this group might play team defense better than any other I've had at Central." But can they do all the other things? Last season the Chips came on strong and reached the MAC tourney final; this one needs to blend quickly to be a force by tournament time.

1990-91 CENTRAL MICHIGAN SCHEDULE

Nov.	25	Oakland University (MI)
	28	@Michigan
Dec.	1	Detroit
	3	Ferris State (MI)
	6	@Chicago State
	8	Wright State
	15	@Akron
	20	@Michigan State
	29	@Wisconsin-Green Bay
Jan.	2	Western Michigan
	5	Ohio University
	9	Wisconsin-Milwaukee
	12	@Bowling Green
	16	Eastern Michigan
	19	@Toledo
	23	Kent State
	26	@Ball State
	30	Miami (OH)
Feb.	2	@Ohio University
	6	@Siena
	9	Bowling Green
	13	@Eastern Michigan
	16	Toledo
	20	@Kent State
	23	Ball State
	27	@Miami (OH)
Mar.	2	@Western Michigan
	8-10	#MAC Tournament

@ Road Games
# Detroit, MI

THE CITADEL

LAST SEASON: 12-16
CONFERENCE RECORD: 5-9
STARTERS LOST: 3
STARTERS RETURNING: 2
CONFERENCE: SOUTHERN
LOCATION: CHARLESTON, SC
HOME FLOOR: MCALISTER FIELD HOUSE (6,200)
NICKNAME: BULLDOGS
COLORS: BLUE AND WHITE
COACH: RANDY NESBIT, record at The Citadel, 59-81.

Over the years, The Citadel's rivals in the Southern Conference have learned not to take the Bulldogs too casually. Usually picked to finish near the bottom of the league standings, The Citadel never looks strong on paper. Yet somehow, the Bulldogs manage every year to pull their share of upsets and hold their own in conference play.

This season may put that track record to the test, as coach Randy Nesbit readily admits. "We have the look of a team," he said, "that could definitely finish last."

Nesbit never gives up hope, though, and a positive attitude goes a long way at The Citadel. "I feel good about our team," he added. "We don't look real strong on paper. But every year, there's always a team or two in every conference that thrives on intangibles and does better than expected. We have a lot of those intangibles."

The Bulldogs will need all the intangibles they can get. Three starters are gone from last year's 12-16 team, including do-everything frontcourt player Patrick Elmore. Elmore led The Citadel in scoring and rebounding and finished as the seventh leading scorer in school history. "Talent-wise," said Nesbit, "Patrick was the most complete player we've had here in the last six years. There's no way we could come up with a player of equal ability to plug in for him."

Worse, Nesbit will have trouble filling two other holes, both in his backcourt. Gone are Ryan Nesbit (9.5 ppg, 70 assists), the coach's brother, and Johnny Smith (8.6 ppg, 2.8 rpg). Both were capable, experienced players who may have to be replaced by freshman. It is a prospect which makes a coach wince.

No wonder Nesbit is counting heavily on his two returning seniors to help lend stability to a team that has five sophomores and five freshmen. 6-6 forward **Ted Mosay** (10.6 ppg, 5.1 rpg) and 6-7 forward **Robert Dalley** (8.5 ppg, 6.5 rpg, 29 blocked shots) must shoulder a huge load.

Dalley, from Surrey, England, emerged as a solid rebounder and defender a year ago. His blocked shot total was just two short of the school's single-season record. Mosay shot only 43.5 percent from the field, but made 38 percent of his three-point field goal attempts. Nesbit could live with that success ratio.

Who will back up the two forwards? Good question. **Scott VanSchaardenburg** (0.5 ppg, 0.8 rpg), a 6-9 sophomore who played in just 12 games last year, has added bulk and strength and should play more. **Boikai Braggs,** a 6-5 sophomore who did not play at a all as a frosh, will get a chance to earn a backup role. So will Nigerian imports **Augustine Olalere** (0.6 ppg, 0.1 rpg) and **Love Ishie**. A 6-6 senior, Olalere played sparingly last year. Ishie is a 6-9 center who dressed for every game but did not play.

Two returning lettermen will battle for one guard spot, unless Nesbit decides to use them at the same time or switch one to forward. 6-3 sophomore **Aaron Nichols** (8.9 ppg, 3.0 rpg), who made the All-Southern Conference freshman team last year, and 6-3 junior **Todd Holstein** (6.3 ppg, 4.4 rpg), have adequate experience. **Andre Harris** (3.1 ppg, 1.3 rpg), a 6-2 sophomore, should play some, as could 5-9 sophomore **Abe Hodges** (0.5 ppg, 0.3 rpg).

Nesbit is pleased with his freshman class, and at least two of the newcomers will have to contribute right away. **Bobby Flowers,** a 5-9 point guard, averaged 17.5 points and 8.5 assists for Ribault High School in Jacksonville, Fla. "Bobby's got more raw talent than we've had at point guard," said Nesbit.

Another freshman, 6-7 **Gus McDowell,** is one of The Citadel's most heralded recruits in years. "As near as we can figure," Nesbit said, "Gus is only the second recruit in the last 18 years that another Southern Conference team wanted to sign." McDowell averaged 17.5 points and 10.3 rebounds for Eastern Wayne High in Goldsboro, N.C.

Other freshmen are 6-4 **Terry Campbell** (Camden HS/Camden, S.C.), 6-9 **Kevin Smith** (Bishop England HS/Charleston, S.C.) and 6-0 **Lamar Wright** (Fort Campbell HS/Fort Campbell, Ky.).

BLUE RIBBON ANALYSIS

As Nesbit noted, The Citadel will not be highly regarded in any pre-season Southern Conference polls. That hardly bothers him, though. The Bulldogs always seem to play better when they sneak up on their opponents.

The real question is whether or not Nesbit has enough talent to sneak up on anyone. If veteran forwards Mosay and Dalley play to their maximum, if impressive sophomore Nichols improves and if Flowers can handle the point as a freshman, The Citadel could once again surprise the unsuspecting.

The Bulldogs clearly have questions marks. But then that's what people said two years ago when they finished 16-12 and Nesbit was voted the league's coach

of the year. Still, a whole lot will have to go right for The Citadel to repeat those performances.

1990-91 THE CITADEL SCHEDULE

Nov.	24	@Georgia State
	26	Savannah State (GA)
	28	@Clemson
Dec.	1	@College of Charleston (SC)
	3	Benedict College
	6	Coastal Carolina (SC)
	30	Nebraska
Jan.	5	Marshall
	7	Virginia Military Institute
	12	@Appalachian State
	14	@East Tennessee State
	16	Duke
	19	@Furman
	21	Liberty University (VA)
	23	Georgia State
	26	Tennessee-Chattanooga
	28	Western Carolina
	31	Youngstown State
Feb.	2	@Virginia Military Institute
	4	@Marshall
	7	Newberry College (SC)
	9	East Tennessee State
	11	Appalachian State
	16	Furman
	18	@North Carolina
	23	@Tennessee-Chattanooga
	25	@Western Carolina
Mar.	1-3	#Southern Conference Tournament

@ Road Games
# Asheville, NC

CLEVELAND STATE

LAST SEASON: 15-13
CONFERENCE RECORD: 0-0
STARTERS LOST: 3
STARTERS RETURNING: 2
CONFERENCE: MID-CONTINENT
LOCATION: CLEVELAND, OH
HOME FLOORS: WOODLING GYM (3,000), PUBLIC HALL (7,400)
NICKNAME: VIKINGS
COLORS: FOREST GREEN AND WHITE
COACH: Mike Boyd, first year at Cleveland State

Cleveland State is back, but coach Kevin Mackey is not. Less than a month after signing a two-year contract extension, and just prior to a season in which the Vikings are to regain eligibility for post-season play, Mackey's seven-year head coaching career came to an abrupt end.

Mackey, 144-67 at Cleveland State, was arrested in July for driving while intoxicated. He was found to have both alcohol and cocaine in his system, and later admitted to a chemical dependency. Entering a rehabilitation center was not enough to save his job. Mackey's contract was terminated in August.

The timing could not have been more ironic. The Vikings are just finishing a two-year NCAA probation, and are to open a 13,000-seat Convocation Center next season. At press time, veteran Michigan assistant Mike Boyd was named the Vikings' head coach, the first good news following a very muddled summer.

Despite a respectable 31-25 record while on probation, the Vikings were set back by the NCAA sanctions. Before the probation, Cleveland State, along with former Mid-Continent Conference member Southwest

177

Missouri State, had become perennial league power-houses. The Vikings won two conference championships and had made three consecutive post-season appearances before the NCAA came to town.

So, as they return to the conference race, the Vikings face two major questions. What effect will the distressing summer and coaching change have on the team? And will Cleveland State's almost entirely new personnel be as good as their high school and junior college statistics suggest?

On the court, at least, the upcoming season will truly be a new beginning. Three top players from last year—Brian Parker (16.5 ppg, 6.4 rpg, 65.7 field goal percentage), William Stanley (14.3 ppg, 5.4 rpg) and Kenny Robertson (12.0 ppg, 149 assists, 79 steals)—are gone. Parker, who was voted second-team All-Conference, became the school's all-time field-goal percentage leader. Robertson is a co-holder of the NCAA all-time steals record, and the three combined to average 48 points and 17 rebounds per game.

To help replace them, the Vikings have nine new players, including seven who had to sit out last season for various reasons. With Cleveland State's typical 10- to 11-man rotation, as many as six or seven of the newcomers could play regularly. While that makes the Vikings' fortunes for this season rather difficult to assess, the new players have some impressive credentials.

Cleveland State's greatest infusion of new talent is at guard. Three newcomers bring with them the credentials of top-notch scorers. Foremost among them is 6-2 guard Marvin McGrew, a transfer from Morton (Ill.) Junior College, who was the leading scorer in JC Division II last season (33.0 ppg). ''I saw him, and he was one of the best junior-college players (last year),'' said one rival Mid-Continent coach.

A second guard, 6-2 sophomore Mike Wawrzyniak, is eligible after transferring from Missouri. Wawrzyniak is originally from Normandy High in Parma, Ohio, where he averaged 39.4 ppg his senior season. An assistant coach in the league who has seen Wawrzyniak play described him as ''more of a scorer than a shooter. He's an excellent athlete and he's very clever with the basketball.''

A third new guard is 6-2 sophomore Anthony Reed, who also sat out last season. USA Today named Reed the high school player of the year in West Virginia in both his junior and senior seasons. He averaged 28.8 ppg and 12.5 rpg at Park High in Wheeling, and is effective enough around the basket to play some at small forward. He also held the state record in the high jump when he graduated.

With Robertston gone, the Vikings will have a new point guard, with 5-7 Gravelle Craig looking like the heir apparent. Craig, a junior, is a transfer from Richmond who insiders say is one of the best pure playmakers the school ever has had. Another point guard possibility is Pat Campbell, a 5-8 sophomore from St. Edward's High in Cleveland. Campbell hit .322 as a centerfielder for the Vikings' baseball team last year, but did not play basketball.

The newcomers in the frontcourt are expected to make their greatest impact at the power positions. Roy Williams, a 6-8, 225-pound transfer from Compton (Calif.) Junior College, possesses great physical talent, though his basketball skills are a bit crude. He is not a scorer, but the coaches who recruited him say he could be a terror defensively and on both backboards.

Lewis Lambert, a 6-6 sophomore, sat out last season but averaged 20.0 ppg as a junior at Dunbar High School (Baltimore, Md.) before transferring to Maine Central Institute. There, he averaged 16.8 ppg for a team that went 30-1. Derek Allen, a 6-7 junior, is a transfer from Trinidad (Colo.) Junior College who was the third leading rebounder (15.0 rpg) in the JC ranks last season. He should help make up for the loss around the basket of the bulky Parker.

Troy Miller, a 6-4 sophomore from Cleveland (John Adams HS), is the final newcomer. He sat out last season.

The strength of the six returning players on scholarship is at forward. Steve Givens (14.8 ppg, 7.9 rpg), a 6-6 senior, improved dramatically last season, going from a bit player as asophomore to the team's second-leading scorer. He is cousin of former Kentucky All-America Jack ''Goose'' Givens. Desmond Porter (8.7ppg, 3.2 rpg), a 6-3 senior forward, is the team's top defensive player. Both Givens and Porter were starters last year.

Center Shawn Fergus (2.1ppg, 2.0 rpg), a 7-1 sophomore, probably has the best chance of the returning backups to gain significant playing time, though that will depend largely on how much his strength improves. He weighed only 212 pounds going into the fall.

One returning guard, 6-3 junior Greg Allen (6.0 ppg), led the team in three-point percentage (44.1) and should play regularly off the bench. Carlos Hubbard (2.8 ppg), a 6-1 senior, and Don Akins (1.8 ppg), a 5-7 junior, got limited minutes last year and will be hard-pressed to beat out the newcomers this time around.

BLUE RIBBON ANALYSIS

The turmoil from Cleveland State's probation continued with Mackey's arrest and dismissal over the summer. The team itself is also in transition, as the bulk of its considerable talent did not play last season.

So where does that leave the Vikings' on court fortunes this year? Probably in the middle of the pack of the Mid-Continent Conference, which lost Southwest Missouri State to the Missouri Valley Conference but gained newcomers Northern Illinois and Akron.

The new players should get plenty of playing time, especially McGrew and Wawrzyniak, who could be legitimate scorers. Still, Cleveland State does not have the stability to challenge Wisconsin-Green Bay, Northern Iowa and Northern Illinois for the Mid-Continent title. The Vikings probably are a year away from being a leading contender, provided Boyd is able to restore order to a program sorely in need of it.

1990-91 CLEVELAND STATE SCHEDULE		
Nov.	24-25	#North Coast Shootout
	27	Allegheny (PA)
Nov. 30-		
Dec. 1		##Mazda Gator Bowl
Dec.	12	@Eastern Michigan
	15	Marshall
	19	@Louisville
	29	Creighton
Jan.	2	Akron
	5	@Kent State
	7	@Valparaiso (IN)
	9	@Youngstown State
	12	Northern Iowa
	14	Western Illinois
	19	Illinois-Chicago
	21	@Eastern Illinois
	26	Northern Illinois
	28	Wisconsin-Green Bay
Feb.	2	@Illinois-Chicago
	4	Valparaiso
	9	@Northern Iowa
	11	@Western Illinois
	18	Eastern Illinois
	23	@Northern Illinois
	25	@Wisconsin-Green Bay
	28	@Akron
Mar.	3-5	*Mid-Continent Tournament

@ Road Games
# Cleveland, OH (Coastal Carolina, Princeton & Wright State)
Jacksonville, FL (Colorado State, Jacksonville & Navy)
* Green Bay, WI

COLGATE

LAST SEASON: 8-21
CONFERENCE RECORD: 3-9
STARTERS LOST: 1
STARTERS RETURNING: 4
CONFERENCE: PATRIOT
LOCATION: HAMILTON, NY
HOME FLOOR: COTTERELL COURT (3,000)
NICKNAME: RED RAIDERS
COLORS: MAROON, GREY AND WHITE
COACH: JACK BRUEN, record at Colgate, 8-21. Career record, 118-93.

After paying his dues for many years as an assistant to Morgan Wootten at fabled DeMatha HS outside Washington, D.C., assistant at his alma mater Catholic University, then head coach there for seven years, Jack Bruen finally got his shot at Division I last year at Colgate. But, after the way the Red Raiders got blown out by Lafayette in his first game (by 26 points), Bruen must have wondered if he'd gone from Division II back to high school instead of up to the big time. It took awhile for things to get better. However, somehow out of this shambles, despite injuries to his two most productive players, Bruen was able to create a competitive team by conference season. Capped by a huge upset of Hartford, on its own floor, in the first round of the NAC tournament, Colgate's eight victories represented the most for this long dormant program in a dozen years.

This season with four starters back plus some newcomers capable of quick impact, Bruen appears to have the Red Raiders in a continued upswing. No longer is the opposition lining up to schedule them as an automatic W. Meanwhile, Colgate's entry into the brand new Patriot League puts it on equal footing, for the first time with its conference colleagues. Unlike the NAC, all Patriot League schools will operate with the same philosophy Colgate's always had: high academic standards and financial aid awarded on the basis of demonstrated need.

Leading the Red Raiders into this new era will be 6-2 senior guard Jay Armstrong (12.2 ppg, 2.1 rpg), who topped the team in scoring last season. A three year starter, Armstrong was hampered by a fractured ankle last season. He is quick and can handle, penetrate, and defend. He came off the ankle injury to finish strong with several high double digit games. Armstrong has limited shooting range and is not a true lead guard. But unless 6-0 freshman guard Hasan Brown (10.0 ppg. 6.0 apg at Cardinal Hayes HS, Bronx, N.Y.), a floor leader of last year's New York City CHSAA champions, can make a rapid adjustment to college, Armstrong will probably be forced to take over at the point. Brown is the only natural point guard in the program —he is quick, a good passer and sees the floor very well. Colgate hopes he will be up to the task of running the show as the season progresses.

Another key man will be 6-4 senior swingman Devin Hughes (9.9 ppg, 3.0 rpg). Hughes, the team's best three-point shooter, started last season strong then was lost to a knee injury. He came back strong with 18 points including the winning three in Colgate's big NAC tournament upset of Hartford. Hughes is strong, penetrates well and, if the knee holds, could be ready to bust out with a big season.

Up front, another player ready to blossom is 6-7 sophomore forward Darren Brown (11.1 ppg, 6.6 rpg), second in scoring and the team's leading rebounder as a freshman. Brown could become Colgate's best player in recent memory. He made the NAC all-rookie team while establishing four school freshman records. Brown is excellent both inside and outside. He can shoot, penetrate, and is a hard-nosed rebounder. Assuming Hughes winds up as mostly a small forward, the starting frontcourt will be completed by 6-6 junior forward **John Stone** (11.2 ppg, 5.9 rpg). As a makeshift pivotman, Stone started every game, showing big heart despite being overmatched height-wise night after night. He's a good shooter for his size and a tough inside rebounder. Stone had a 29-point game vs. a good Boston University team last season. Knowing he desperately needed to add height to his under-sized frontline, Bruen signed 6-8 power forward **Steve Benton** (16.0 ppg, 11.0 rpg at Saratoga Catholic HS, N.Y.). Benton is a good inside scorer with a nice touch from outside. He will be Colgate's tallest immediate contributor and should be the man needed to boost the Stone-Brown-Hughes combination up front.

Until Hasan Brown takes over, Armstrong will run the point, leaving off-guard to 6-2 senior **Dave Goodwin** (10.8 ppg, 2.8 rpg). Colgate's starting quarterback in football and a pre-season 1-AA All-America pick, Goodwin is obviously a gamer. He is exceptionally intense on defense and great on the press. Goodwin will always have a warm spot in Bruen's heart since his 25-footer at the buzzer gave Bruen his first Division I win at U.S. International. Goodwin also had 19 to key a win over Manhattan. Behind him there is experienced depth in the backcourt. 6-5 junior off-guard **Jack Ehretsman** (5.5 ppg, 20-of-48 threes) emerged as a perimeter force last season. 6-2 sophomore **Brennan Luthery** (1.9 ppg) helped spark the U.S. International win and is a quality athlete and good penetrator. He hopes to push Armstrong for a time at the point. Also returning up front are 6-8 senior center **Paul Pawloski** (1.8 ppg, 2.5 rpg), 6-8 junior center **Dave Heller** (0.3 ppg, 0.8 rpg), and 6-9 sophomore center **Andrew Stephens** (0.9 ppg, 0.5 rpg).

In addition to Benton and Brown, Colgate added three other freshmen of potential influence. 6-4 two-guard **Nathan O'Neil** was all-district in both football and basketball at Binghamton (N.Y.) HS (13.3 ppg, 5.0 rpg). He can shoot and defend, but since he's trying to break into a crowded position, O'Neil's influence is probably a year away. Also from Binghamton HS comes 6-10 freshman center **Jason Whatley** (7.6 ppg, 6.0 rpg). Whatley weighs only 190 pounds and needs to bulk up. But he is an excellent shotblocker as evidenced by more than 100 rejections last season. That's a lot in any league. Bruen feels the sleeper in his freshman class may be 6-3 freshman guard **Kart Wickenheiser** (22.1 ppg, 12.5 rpg at Fairfield HS, Pa.) He is a good all-around scorer and could develop into an impact player at off-guard —Wickenheiser's dad is the president of Mt. St. Mary's College. Down the line the combination of Wickenheiser and Hasan Brown could raise the general talent level of the Colgate backcourt. That, however, is a couple of years away.

BLUE RIBBON ANALYSIS

For those used to looking at Colgate as a perennial doormat, that may be coming to an end under Bruen. With four double figure scorers, 11 of 12 lettermen returning, and a newly balanced league, the Red Raiders seem poised to make a run toward .500. The big question mark is point guard. Bruen likes to run a wide open offense, taking advantage of his three-point shooters, and a tough man-to-man defense. To make this work, the burden will fall on the backcourt, particularly Armstrong at the point. If freshman Hasan Brown can help there, it will boost overall team chemistry because Armstrong can play more comfortably if he doesn't have to worry about bringing up the ball.

If Hughes' knee holds up, Brown progresses on schedule, and Benton can provide some quality height, Colgate can make some noise in the Patriot League. The program has already made tremendous progress under Bruen in only one year. That should be redeemed with at least a fifth place finish this season, maybe a little higher. Next season might mean first division, two words unthinkable for Colgate only a little while ago.

1990-91 COLGATE SCHEDULE

Nov.	24	@Oklahoma State
	30-Dec. 1	#Amana-Hawkeye Classic
Dec.	3	@Drake
	22	Harvard
	29	@Mount St. Mary's (MD)
Jan.	2	@Rider
	5	Yale
	8	Pennsylvania
	10	St. Francis (NY)
	12	Fordham
	14	@Manhattan
	17	Vermont
	19	@Lehigh
	21	@Cornell
	23	Lafayette
	26	@Bucknell
	28	Rider
	31	@Holy Cross
Feb.	2	Army
	6	@Fordham
	11	@St. Francis (PA)
	13	Lehigh
	16	@Lafayette
	20	Bucknell
	23	Holy Cross
	25	@Army
Feb. 28-		
Mar.	2	*Patriot League Tournament

@ Road Games
# Iowa City, IA (Creighton, Iowa & Texas-San Antonio)
* Worcester, MA

COLORADO

**LAST SEASON: 12-18
CONFERENCE RECORD: 2-12
STARTERS LOST: 2
STARTERS RETURNING: 4
CONFERENCE: BIG EIGHT
LOCATION: BOULDER, CO
HOME FLOOR: CU EVENTS/ CONFERENCE CENTER (11,199)
NICKNAME: GOLDEN BUFFALOES
COLORS: SILVER, BLACK AND GOLD
COACH: JOE HARRINGTON, first season at Colorado. Career record, 179-135.**

The most embarrassed face at last season's Big Eight tournament belonged to Colorado athletic director Bill Marolt. Less than two weeks earlier, Marolt had fired coach Tom Miller effective at the end of the season. The Buffaloes had just finished dead last in the Big Eight for the fifth year in a row —the last four under Miller.

Yet, here were the Buffaloes making a mockery of the regular season at the conference tournament in Kansas City. First, they knocked off Missouri, which had been ranked No. 1 on two occasions during the regular season and was the league's regular season champ, in the opening round. Then, they ousted NIT-bound Oklahoma State in the second round. Should the charged-up Buffaloes, playing on emotion for their lameduck coach, somehow topple the mighty Oklahoma Sooners in the championship game, they would gain the Big Eight's automatic berth in the NCAAs despite finishing 2-12 in league play. Marolt would have more than egg on his face. It would be more like a three-egg omelette. The Buffaloes gave the Sooners a run for the money, but lost 92-80. Thus ended the disappointing Tom Miller era, four years in which Colorado went 35-79 and won only 10 of 56 league games.

Enter new coach Joe Harrington, most recently of Long Beach State. Harrington, who cut his coaching teeth under Lefty Driesell, inherits a team that returns four starters and five of its top seven players from last season. But which Colorado team that turns out to be remains to be seen. Will it be the one that has served as Big Eight doormat for the last five years? Or the one that looked ready to take on all comers at the Big Eight tournament?

''I do like the fact that we have the leading rebounder and scorer in the league back,'' Harrington said. That would be 6-10 senior center **Shaun Vandiver** (22.3 ppg, 11.2 rpg), who became the first player to lead the league in both categories in the same season since Wayman Tisdale in 1984. Vandiver isn't the most mobile player around, thanks in part to knee problems he brought with him from Hutchinson (Kan.) JC in 1988. But he is a strong inside player, has good moves and a deft touch around the basket, and is as consistent as the sunrise. Vandiver, who came to Boulder as a sophomore, has scored in double figures in all 58 of his games at Colorado and has registered 39 double-doubles.

Besides Vandiver, who made AP's first team All-Big Eight squad, there's one other thing about the Buffaloes that Harrington likes best, ''the fact that we do have a really good scorer on the perimeter,'' Harrington said.

That would be 6-4 senior guard **Stevie Wise** (20.0 ppg), one of the league's biggest surprises last season. Wise was third in the league in three-pointers made (76) and third in free throw percentage (84.2).

Vandiver and Wise form a formidable one-two punch. Trouble is, the Buffaloes don't have much after that. Up front, the likely starters alongside Vandiver are senior forwards **Asad Ali** (6.9 ppg, 4.4 rpg) and **Rodell ''House'' Guest** (6.2 ppg, 5.2 rpg), both of whom started most of last season. Guest prefers to by his nickname, House, rather than his given name Rodell. And who's to argue, because Guest is as big as a house. Built like a tight end at 6-5, 240 pounds, Guest did in fact try out for linebacker on the Colorado football team last spring and is expected to play for coach Bill McCartney's squad full time next season. He can be an intimidating presence inside, but is foul prone and has marginal offensive skills. Ali, who is 6-7, is coming off a quiet year and needs to improve his consistency. Both Guest and Ali need to improve their scoring to help Vandiver inside.

The returning backups inside, 6-5 senior **Cody Walters** and 6-11 junior **Bill Markham**, scored only 126 points between them last season. Walters doesn't have a world of natural talent, but is a scrapper. Markham has a way to go before becoming a factor on the team.

The Buffaloes' major personnel loss other than their head coach was point guard Reggie Morton, the team assists leader (4.9 apg) and third leading scorer (12.9 ppg). 6-3 sophomore **Johnny Terrell**, the only returning guard on the roster other than Wise, is one possibility to replace Morton. So is 6-0 freshman **Cornell Mann**, a fall signee under Miller who averaged 12.0 ppg and seven assists per game last season at Ferndale (Mich.) HS. But the leading candidate at the point just could be 5-10 junior **Billy Law**, a Harrington recruit from Butler County (Kan.) JC, where he averaged 11.5 ppg and 8.5 assists. Law was a second team All-Jayhawk League pick last season for a 29-6 team. ''I feel great that we were able to sign Billy Law —his team won the state championship in junior college,'' Harrington said.

Actually, Harrington should feel great to have signed anybody since he was hired March 29, less than two weeks before the start of the spring signing period. Other than Law, his only other recruit last spring was **Larry Lockley**, a 6-3 off-guard from El Camino (Calif.) JC. Lockley, who like Law will be a junior, already is 23 years old, thanks to a three-year stint in the Army. Oddly enough, since his days at Banning HS in Los Angeles, Lockley has been recruited by three different Colorado head coaches — Tom Apke, Miller, and now, Harrington. The only other member of a four-man recruiting class is another Miller fall signee —6-7 freshman forward **Charles Gentry** of Kimball HS in Dallas, Texas. Gentry (14.0 ppg, 8.5 rpg) will have a chance to play right away simply because the Buffaloes are so thin up front.

BLUE RIBBON ANALYSIS

Harrington likes the up-tempo style. Through conditioning and recruiting, he plans to turn Boulder's mile-high altitude into an advantage. But it won't happen this year. The Buffaloes just do not have the depth.

And where will the points come from other than Vandiver and Wise? No other returning player averaged more than 6.9 points a game last season. Despite Vandiver's solid contributions, he has yet to show the ability to take over a game. Wise, meanwhile, needs to improve upon his 43 percent shooting from the field.

Harrington may very well be the answer at Colorado, which has had only one winning season in its last nine. Again, it won't happen this year. If the Buffaloes finish as high as fifth or sixth in the league, Harrington should merit consideration as Big Eight coach of the year. Seventh or eighth place (again) seems more likely.

1990-91 COLORADO SCHEDULE		
Nov.	23	Cal State-Northridge
	26	@Rice
	28	@Texas-San Antonio
Dec.	1	@Southwest Missouri State
	4	Wisconsin-Green Bay
	7-8	#Mile High Classic
	12	@Wyoming
	23	Stanford
	29	Tennessee State
Jan.	2	@University of San Diego
	5	Iowa State
	9	@Wake Forest
	12	@Kansas State
	19	Southwest Missouri State
	22	Nebraska
	24	Missouri
	26	@Kansas
	30	Oklahoma State
Feb.	2	@Oklahoma
	9	@Nebraska
	13	Kansas State
	16	@Iowa State
	20	Kansas
	23	@Oklahoma State
	27	Oklahoma
Mar.	2	@Missouri
	8-10	##Big Eight Tournament

@ Road Games
# Boulder, CO (American University, Connecticut & Eastern Michigan)
Kansas City, MO

COLORADO STATE

LAST SEASON: 21-9
CONFERENCE RECORD: 11-5
STARTERS LOST: 3
STARTERS RETURNING: 2
CONFERENCE: WESTERN ATHLETIC (WAC)
LOCATION: FORT COLLINS, CO
HOME FLOOR: MOBY ARENA (9,001)
NICKNAME: RAMS
COLORS: GREEN AND GOLD
COACH: BOYD GRANT, record at Colorado State, 66-32.
Career record, 260-106.

Boyd Grant has built a reputation as a coach who does a lot with a little and he's set up to play that role again this season. He seems to enjoy taking newcomers or players who have sat the bench in the past and winning the WAC with them. The last two seasons, Colorado State has been picked to finish near the middle of the WAC and has either won the league title outright or shared it. The reason for that is defense. The Rams are the best defensive team in the league and they make life miserable for other teams in a high scoring conference.

Colorado State basketball fans first started a love affair with Grant when he was a Colorado State player in 1955. In three years with the Rams, he averaged 13.4 per game. Then he was an assistant coach at Colorado State before going out into the world to stake his claim to fame. Grant had a 194-74 record in nine years as head coach at Fresno State before he took a year off and then left Fresno State to return to his alma mater.

Little was expected from Grant's team the first year, but it finished 22-13 and went to the NIT. In 1989, the Rams went to the NCAA tournament for the first time in 20 years. They beat Florida in the first round before losing to Syracuse.

The tune was familiar last season. The Rams had lost three starters and should have been in a rebuilding mode. Instead, Colorado State had a 21-9 season, that included a 78-67 win over North Carolina, and finished in a tie for first place in the WAC. So don't expect anyone to feel sorry for Grant this season. It doesn't impress anyone that the Rams lost WAC MVP Mike Mitchell (19.5 ppg, 6.7 rpg). He led them in scoring and rebounding.

It also won't make much difference that the other two starters on the Rams' frontline are gone. Andy Anderson (11.0 ppg, 3.3 rpg) and defensive specialist Eric Friehauf (3.9 ppg, 3.2 rpg) also have used up their eligibility. Colorado State also lost seven lettermen from its 1989-90 team. Jamie Hines (5.1 ppg, 3.9 rpg) and Matt Sharp (3.4 ppg, 3.6 rpg) were important role players in Grant's system. Also gone are Dwayne Polk (1.5 ppg, 0.2 rpg) and Carren Wilson (1.4 ppg, 0.4 rpg).

So count the Rams out this year, right?

Wrong. Never count Colorado State out while Grant is coach. He simply slides players out and new ones in and very little seems to change. It is the system that wins for the Rams. Grant has both starting guards back. 6-3 senior guard **Mark Meredith** (12.1 ppg, 72 assists) was the only Ram to start all 30 games last year. He hit 84-of-179 shots from three-point range. He scored in double figures 19 times and shot 92.8 percent from the foul line.

6-4 junior **Lynn Tryon** (8.8 ppg, 109 assists) is the returning point guard. Tryon led the team in minutes played. This season, Tryon and Meredith will be the brains and heart of the Rams.

Colorado State has only two other lettermen coming back. **Dwayne Molyneaux** played in just 15 games last season as a sophomore. He is listed as a 6-6 guard. 6-6 senior forward **Tracy Jordan** (2.0 ppg) is the other.

So newcomers are where Grant will find the help he needs, and he's got some good ones. Leading the list is 6-8 senior **Chuckie White**. He had to sit out last year after transferring from Indiana, where he played in 32 games for the Hoosiers during 1988-89. White is originally from Charlotte, N.C., but played for two years at Dodge City (Kan.) JC, averaging 22.3 ppg and 9.8 rpg. He also led his JC conference in scoring and averaged 3.2 blocked shots. White's ability has never been in question. But in Indiana he often found himself in Bobby Knight's doghouse due mainly to lack of defensive effort. White will find Boyd equally demanding in that regard. How he responds will be crucial to Colorado State's fortunes. White has just one year of eligibility left.

Another big man will be 6-8 **Doug Larson**, a sophomore who sat out last year after undergoing surgery on both knees. Larson's numbers were less

than impressive as a freshman as he made only three field goals during the regular season, played in only four WAC games and didn't score against a conference team. But these are the type of players Grant loves.

The Rams have two junior college players who will have to contribute right away. **Elton Byrd** is a 6-7 junior forward who transferred from Fergus Falls (Minn.) CC, where he scored 1,903 points in two seasons. He scored 30 points or more 14 times in 28 games last season, averaging 30.0 points and 14.5 rebounds. The other JC transfer is 6-1 junior **Wayne Gipson** (19.0 ppg, 7.0 apg) from Cerritos (Calif.) JC. He probably will be Tryon's backup at point guard, but might play shooting guard as well.

Colorado State also has six high school signees. The best prep numbers were put up by 6-6 forward **Aaron Atkinson** (33.5 ppg, 17.0 rpg, 12.0 apg) from Lincoln HS in Los Angeles. Atkinson finished second in balloting for the *Los Angeles Times* prep player of the year.

The other freshmen are 6-7 forward **Damon Crawford** (24.0 ppg, 16.7 rpg), 6-6 forward **Tyson Maroney** (26.7 ppg, 6.3 rpg, 4.2 apg), 6-6 forward **Chris Smith** (16.8 ppg, 12.1 rpg), 6-8 center **Malcolm Smith** (17.0 ppg, 6.5 rpg) and 5-8 guard **Ryan Yoder** (27.5 ppg). Crawford is out of Florissant (Mo.) HS, Maroney is out of Friendswood (Tex.) HS, Smith comes to Colorado State from Carbondale (Ill.) HS and Yoder is a native of Topeka, Ind.

BLUE RIBBON ANALYSIS

The Rams have a tough December schedule with a three-game road trip to Texas-Pan American, Northwestern State and Texas Tech. They also play at Fullerton State and in the Gator Bowl Classic. By the time Colorado State gets to the WAC, Grant will have sorted out his personnel. With White in the middle, Colorado State will rebuild its frontline quickly and effectively if he is ready to end his well traveled college career with a serious commitment.

Grant's teams have never won with offense. The Rams are very patient with the ball and work very hard on defense. With that formula, Colorado State will always be good. Everything this season will depend on the development of White and the youngsters on the frontline. They have to be able to produce some points from inside to give some room to Meredith so he can shoot three-pointers.

Colorado State should again be near if not at the top of the WAC. That has become a way of life since Grant returned to his alma mater. Pencil the Rams in for at least second place.

1990-91 COLORADO STATE SCHEDULE		
Nov.	24	Cal State-Northridge
	26	Marshall
	30-Dec. 1	#Gator Bowl Classic
Dec.	8	Southern California
	15	@Texas-Pan American
	17	@Northwestern State
	19	@Texas Tech
	22	Ohio University
	29	@Fullerton State
Jan.	3	@New Mexico
	5	@UTEP
	8	Wyoming
	12	San Diego State
	17	Brigham Young
	21	Eastern Kentucky
	24	@Utah
	28	Oklahoma City
	31	@Brigham Young
Feb.	2	Air Force
	7	New Mexico
	9	UTEP
	14	@San Diego State
	16	@Hawaii
	21	Utah
	23	Hawaii
	26	@Wyoming

1990-91 COLORADO STATE SCHEDULE (Cont.)

| Mar. | 2 | @Air Force |
| | 6-9 | ##WAC Tournament |

@ Road Games
# Jacksonville, FL (Cleveland State, Jacksonville & Navy)
Laramie, WY

COLUMBIA

**LAST SEASON: 4-22
CONFERENCE
RECORD: 2-12
STARTERS LOST: 0
STARTERS
RETURNING: 5
CONFERENCE: IVY
LEAGUE
LOCATION:
NEW YORK, NY
HOME FLOOR: LEVIEN
GYMNASIUM (3,408)
NICKNAMES: LIONS AND LIGHT BLUE
COLORS: COLUMBIA BLUE AND WHITE
COACH: JACK ROHAN, record at Columbia, 154-161.**

There's no consensus about the best way to reverse a dreadful basketball season, but Columbia is certainly going as far from convention as possible. Take one 4-22, last-place Ivy League finisher and add a new coach who's been off the bench for 16 years. What follows is anyone's guess.

Jack Rohan returns to coaching to begin his 14th season leading the Lions. For most programs, that figure would represent continuity. Since Rohan's first 13 seasons at Columbia's helm came from 1961-74, however, his return provokes more than a few questions.

"It's more of a question why I gave it up in the first place," Rohan explained. "In 1974, my wife wasn't healthy, and I had two small children to take care of. Several times Columbia asked me to come back, but I could not. Circumstances have changed and my children are older. I talked it over with my wife, and decided to come back."

But to what does he return? The 1989-90 Lions were a young team that managed only two league wins and were outscored by an average of 11 points per game, aborting coach Wally Halas' rebuilding plan after just three seasons. Sure, Rohan coached the Lions to their last Ivy title (1967-68), and to three consecutive 20-win and Top 20 finishes in the 1960's. But no one on Columbia's Morningside Heights campus remotely resembles the fulcrum of those teams, All-America forward Jim McMillan.

Rohan spent the last 16 years as chairman of Columbia's Physical Education department, moonlighting as the school's golf coach, but he kept active in college basketball. He broadcast games for several national cable networks, assisted high school and college teams with their shooting, and was a guest instructor at summer camps.

"The biggest change for me will be having my own team," Rohan admitted. "Because I was broadcasting so many other teams, I didn't see Columbia play much. No one left me with a bad impression, so we're starting fresh".

Rohan's new start comes with 12 returning lettermen, including six who started throughout the year - an indication that a double figure win total may not be out of the question. And since none of the Lions' top five returnees is a senior, the future looks even better.

Guard **Eric Speaker**, a 6-5 junior, led the Lions in scoring last season (11.9 ppg) and registered a high of 25 against Marist. **Dane Holmes** (11.6 ppg, 6.9 rpg,

61 blocked shots), a 6-8 junior center, was a force in the middle, while 6-5 sophomore swingman **Buck Jenkins** was good for 10.9 ppg.

There's more good news in the backcourt. Sophomore point guard **Mike Jelinsky** led the Ivy League in assists (153 overall) and registered team highs in steals (35) and minutes, while scoring 8.5 ppg. Forward **Russell Steward** (8.2 ppg, 6.7 rpg), a 6-5 junior, gave the Lions more strength up front.

"My goal is to get this team to play as well as it can", Rohan said. "That's very nebulous, but I have no way in the world of knowing who the top players are. I don't even know what kind of style we're going to play. I'll have to wait and see the kind of team we have".

Columbia has plenty of experience on the bench, led by 6-5 senior forward **Steve Livingston** (4.4 ppg). Other frontcourt reserves include 6-5 sophomore forward **Mark Dumolien** (3.5 ppg, 2.1 rpg), 6-6 senior forward **Scott Bennett** (1.3 ppg), 6-8 sophomore center **Tom Casey** (3.3 ppg, 3.0 rpg) and **Darren DeWilde**, a 6-9 junior pivotman. Sophomores **Tom Brady** (2.6 ppg) and **Omar Sanders** (3.7 ppg) add depth to the backcourt.

The coaching switch did not hinder the Lions' recruiting very much, since assistant coach Kirk Saulny remained to continue enlisting new talent. Leading a crop of four newcomers is 6-5 forward **Jamal Adams** (Loyola HS/Los Angeles). Other frosh include 6-3 guard **Ty Buckelew** (Lovett School/Dunwoody, Ga), 6-7 forward **Steve Marusich** (Servite HS/Mission Viejo, Calif.), and **J.J. Waterer** (Blair Academy/Plano, Tex.), a 6-2 guard.

This year's Lions should show better than the '89-'90 edition, simply because they've experienced a year of the Ivy wars together. How Rohan adjusts to his return to the bench could be almost as important as the maturation of his players.

"We're going to start out with the basic fundamentals as our first test," he said. "As the process goes on, I'll find out what players I can depend on, and what kind of style we'll play."

BLUE RIBBON ANALYSIS

You can't blame Rohan if he daydreams about Columbia's 1960's glory years as the Lions struggle through the current state of Ivy League balance. He may not have McMillan burying jumpers from the corner, but he does have a young team with some talent. Unfortunately, other Ivy teams have experience and talent, too.

Yet things shouldn't be quite as miserable at Morningside Heights this season. With Jelinsky dishing to Speaker, Holmes and Jenkins and a bit of depth on the bench, the Lions may inch out of the Ivy cellar. An unthreatening non-league slate may even build some confidence before the January 11 league opener with Dartmouth.

Still, this is not a first division Ivy League club. One does not go from a 2-12 league mark to the penthouse overnight. The Lions will not finish above sixth place.

1990-91 COLUMBIA SCHEDULE

Nov.	24	Haverford (PA)
	27	Manhattan
Nov.	30-	
Dec.	1	#Hawks Unlimited Tournament
Dec.	5	@St. Francis (NY)
	8	@Rider
	11	Fordham
	28	@Southern Methodist
	30	@Tulane
Jan.	2	@New Orleans
	8	Hofstra (NY)
	11	Dartmouth
	12	Harvard

1990-91 COLUMBIA SCHEDULE (Cont.)

Jan.	19	Cornell
	21	@Lehigh
	26	@Cornell
Feb.	1	@Yale
	2	@Brown
	8	Pennsylvania
	9	Princeton
	15	@Harvard
	16	@Dartmouth
	22	@Princeton
	23	@Pennsylvania
Mar.	1	Brown
	2	Yale

@ Road Games
# Hartford, CT (Hartford, Holy Cross & Long Island)

COPPIN STATE

**LAST SEASON: 26-7
CONFERENCE
RECORD: 15-1
STARTERS LOST: 1
STARTERS
RETURNING: 4
CONFERENCE:
MID-EASTERN
ATHLETIC (MEAC)
LOCATION: BALTIMORE, MD
HOME FLOOR: PULLEN GYMNASIUM (3,000)
NICKNAME: EAGLES
COLORS: BLUE AND GOLD
COACH: RON "FANG" MITCHELL, record at Coppin State, 65-49.
Career record, 292-94.**

For years, college basketball aficionados in Baltimore had waited and wondered which of the fledgling Division I programs in town would be first to the NCAA tournament. Would it be Loyola College or Towson State, two schools that seemed forever spinning their wheels? Morgan State, a one-time college division champion locked in reverse? How about the University of Maryland-Baltimore County, whose president wanted the campus to be king of all it surveyed?

Nobody gave little Coppin State much thought. Until Fang Mitchell arrived, that is. At first, it was only the nickname that drew attention. Plus, Mitchell made good copy. Why leave a great junior college job (Gloucester County, N.J.) near your hometown (Philadelphia) for a position at an inner-city commuter school that had little history?

What Mitchell has accomplished at Coppin has been nothing short of amazing. He has taken the Eagles from an 8-19 record to the NCAA tournament in four years, bringing in a steady stream of players from his old stomping grounds, an area that was a gold mine for him in the eight seasons he led Gloucester CC to a 227-45 record and four regional titles.

Mitchell became more than just a nickname and good copy last December, when Coppin became the first Baltimore area team in nearly 30 years to beat the University of Maryland. The Eagles also won at Creighton on the way to becoming the first Baltimore school to make the NCAA tournament (beating Towson State to the claim by three days).

The Eagles fell quickly in the NCAA's, getting bounced by Syracuse, but Coppin State could be ignored no longer, especially in its own hometown. And with four starters returning from last year's MEAC champions, there should be more folks venturing out Baltimore's North Avenue to see what all the excitement is about.

There is plenty of talent to replace the one starter lost to graduation; replacing his leadership is another story. 6-5 swingman Phil Booth (11.6 ppg, 5.5 rpg), a three-year starter, "was our glue," said assistant coach Derek Brown. "He understood everything that was going on and everything the coaches were trying to do." And though you'll always find 6-8 senior forward Larry Stewart (18.7 ppg, 11.2 rpg, 44 blocked shots) and 6-3 senior guard Reggie Isaac (21.2 ppg, 3.3 rpg, 58 steals) in the middle of the action, both are the strong, silent types. "We'll need someone to step forward and be the leader," Brown said.

Isaac and Stewart, both Philadelphian's, averaged only four minutes of bench time between them last year, and one or the other was the leading scorer in all but one game. Stewart, the MEAC player of the year, is a muscular performer who scores well inside and is strong on the boards at both ends of the court. He can also take the jumper (65 percent field goal shooting) from outside the lane.

Whereas Stewart is a consistent player who makes a regular impact, Isaac is the kind of scorer who can take over any game when he gets hot. He shot only 43 percent from the floor, but was 35 percent (73-for-207) from three-point range, along with 85 percent from the foul line. An All-MEAC pick, Isaac moves well without the ball, but is also capable of moving to the point to spell 6-0 junior Larry Yarbray (8.9 ppg, 3.1 rpg, 225 assists).

Yarbray set new school single-season and career (381) assist records last year. A starter since he arrived at Coppin, Yarbray has grown in the position and will be counted on even more this year. 6-6 sophomore Denny Brown, a transfer from Iona, is a possibility to take over Booth's small forward spot and could also see action behind Isaac. He is a good outside shooter. Others who could see action in the backcourt include 6-4 senior Duane Reed (0.9 ppg, 0.7 rpg), a leaper who can also play small forward, and 6-2 sophomore Michael Johnson (0.5 ppg, 0.8 rpg), who saw limited duty in 18 games last year. Reed will spell Isaac on the rare occasions he takes a break. Johnson is strong on defense and can play both guard positions.

Along with Brown, another possibility for Booth's spot is 6-6 freshman James Mazyck (Hillside HS/Hillside, N.J.), who grew another inch during the summer. A good ballhandler capable of playing anywhere but center, Mazyck sank two free throws in the closing seconds to lift Hillside to the New Jersey Group 2 state championship last spring.

Others in the picture at forward are 6-7 senior Joe Hammond (3.0 ppg, 2.8 rpg) and 6-6 junior Darren Woods (1.5 ppg, 1.9 rpg), another Philadelphian. Hammond, the Eagles' strongest player, started three times last year at center and was the first frontcourt reserve. He is tough on the boards and a decent shooter. Woods saw action in 26 games and will be used much the same way again. 6-6 freshman Tariq Saunders (Linden HS/Linden, N.J.) and 6-8 sophomore Rodney Allen will see limited duty. Saunders can play either forward spot and will eventually push for time. Allen is a walk-on who played in only two games, slowed by an achilles tendon injury.

Larry McCollum, a beefy 6-8, 270-pound senior, will plug the middle again unless moved to the power forward spot. A starter since his freshman year, McCollum (4.5 ppg, 4.8 rpg) does the dirty work on the boards and sets a monstrous pick. He has shown gradual improvement on offense each season. If his offense continues to blossom and if 6-9 sophomore Galen Howard adapts quickly, Mitchell may go with a big frontline of Stewart at small forward, McCollum at power forward and Howard in the middle. Howard sat out last year and was a high school teammate (Chester HS/Chester, PA) of Yarbray, will be thrown in early to see how he fares. Ultimately, he will either start or back-up McCollum.

Besides Booth, the Eagles graduated 6-4 reserve guard Derreck Orr (6.6 ppg, 2.2 rpg), the fifth-leading scorer on last year's squad. Orr averaged 20 minutes per game coming off the bench and, besides Isaac, was the only three-point shooting threat (36-for-101).

BLUE RIBBON ANALYSIS

Even with four starters back, there still are some questions Mitchell must answer before settling on a lineup. There is also more depth this year, which should allow Isaac, Stewart and Yarbray time to get a breather and stay fresh. That is important, because Coppin loves to run and push it at both ends of the court. The Eagles were 20-2 when scoring 70 or more points last year, and only 6-5 when scoring fewer. They were 19-1 when they led at the half, and only 7-6 when tied or trailing.

No longer a mystery to non-conference teams on their schedule like Creighton, Toledo, UTEP and Clemson, the Eagles will have to work that much harder to pull off victories like last season's upsets of Creighton and Maryland. In the MEAC, though, Coppin State should repeat. The Eagles also figure to be experienced and strong enough to win a now-required "play-in" game and return to the NCAA field of 64.

1990-91 COPPIN SCHEDULE		
Nov.	24	@Tulsa
	27	Creighton
Dec.	1	@New Mexico State
	2	@UTEP
	8	Maryland-Baltimore Co.
	15	College of Charleston (SC)
	20-21	#Florida International Tournament
	28-29	##MVP Holiday Classic
Jan.	3	@South Carolina State
	6	@New Orleans
	9	North Carolina A&T
	14	Maryland-Eastern Shore
	19	Florida A&M
	21	Bethune-Cookman (FL)
	24	Morgan State (MD)
	26	@Howard University
	29	@Delaware State
Feb.	2	Howard University
	4	@Morgan State
	6	Delaware State
	9	@Florida A&M
	11	@Bethune-Cookman
	14	South Carolina State
	20	@North Carolina A&T
	23	@Maryland-Eastern Shore
Mar.	2-3	*MEAC Tournament
@ Road Games		
# Miami, FL (Clemson, Florida International & TBA)		
## Toledo, OH (Middle Tennessee State, Samford & Toledo)		
* Norfolk, VA		

CORNELL

LAST SEASON: 12-17
CONFERENCE RECORD: 5-9
STARTERS LOST: 1
STARTERS RETURNING: 4
CONFERENCE: IVY LEAGUE
LOCATION: ITHACA, NY
HOME FLOOR: ALBERDING FIELD HOUSE (4,750)
NICKNAME: BIG RED
COLORS: CARNELIAN RED & WHITE
COACH: MIKE DEMENT, record at Cornell, 54-54.

When Cornell coach Mike Dement took a look at this year's schedule, he couldn't help but smile. Sure, non-league games with Syracuse, North Carolina and Pitt tend to lead coaches to grind teeth, rather than show them, but Dement wasn't worried about battles with the Big Guys. All he was looking at was January 11 and 12.

After two years of opening the Ivy League season on the road, Cornell gets a pair of home dates to open this conference campaign. A nice advantage, plus a bit of history. After all, the last time the Big Red opened the league season at home was 1987-88, its most recent Ivy League crown.

"We hope to get off to a better start in Ivy competition," Dement said. "Starting on the road the last couple of years really hurt us. Winning the early league games at home could give us confidence and momentum."

Dement is smart enough to keep his post-season plans at a minimum. The home court may be a plus, but it alone will not overcome Princeton's experience, Yale's depth or any of the other nutty things that characterize the typical Ivy League race.

Talent wins, and Dement may be smiling because of that, too. He's got back four starters, some solid front and backcourt depth among his nine returning lettermen, and a blue-chip recruit who could start right away.

"We will still be deep in all areas and be able to play a lot of people," he said. "We obviously have some very good shooters returning, and if we can get the ball inside to players like Bernard Jackson and Rich Medina, we have the potential to be a very balanced team."

The Big Red slipped to seventh in the Ivy last season, their 5-9 mark two games below the four-team, third-place logjam. How much Jackson, Medina and Shawn Maharaj improve on last season will determine if Cornell moves further away from the basement.

Maharaj, a 6-2 junior guard, was a second-team All-Ivy selection last season. He averaged 12.6 points per game and finished with a .468 percentage from three-point land - a major reason for Cornell's 10th-place national standing in trifectas. His backcourt mate, point guard and co-captain Monte Boykin graduated, so 6-0 senior Steve Johnson (10.5 ppg, 2.1 apg) should step in.

Jackson (12.4 ppg, 8.3 rpg, 2.8 blocked shots), a 6-9, 240-pound senior, anchors the frontline. The honorable mention All-Ivy choice finished second in the league in rebounding and was a force up front all season. Joining him is Medina (7.4 ppg, 4.3 rpg), a 6-7 junior.

"Rich has to continue to improve his rebounding and scoring around the basket," Dement said. 'We have to keep Bernard Jackson healthy and get him the ball in scoring position more often."

Since the Big Red have so many players back from last year, the recruiting harvest was limited to two. However, 6-4, 200-pound swingman Zeke Marshall (St. Paul's HS/Baltimore) was the Baltimore-Metro player of the year and USA Today athlete of the year in Maryland. Justin Treadwell (Farragut HS/Knoxville, Tenn.), a 6-6 forward, is the other newcomer.

"Marshall could see some quality time for us," Dement said. "He's a wing player and an excellent rebounder. He's a great addition to the team."

Reserves on the guard line include four sophomores - 6-3 Frank Abelson (4.2 ppg), 6-2 Jeff Gaca (4.2 ppg), 5-8 speedster Michael Parker (2.3 ppg) and 6-1 Tom Brayshaw - along with 6-2 junior Terrel Dillard. Rob Hill (4.4 ppg, 2.1 rpg), a 6-8 senior, and 6-11 soph Matt Price (2.8 ppg, 2.3 rpg) lead the frontcourt reserves. Steve George, a 6-4 senior, 6-9 senior Nate Grant, 6-8 senior Paul McRae and 6-11 sophomore Marshall Werner all saw limited time last winter.

"The league will be very much the same as last year," Dement said. "To win the close games, we'll have to get better in two areas, free throw shooting and allowing our opponents chances for second shots."

An early Ivy homestead does not guarantee the Big Red an automatic ticket to the first division. Continued maturation and better performance in the waning moments will. Cornell lost six of its Ivy League contests by six or fewer points last year.

If Jackson and Medina continue to improve, and Maharaj continues his long distance gunning, Cornell could surprise. Should Marshall fulfill Dement's expectation, the first division is not out of the question. The tough non-league schedule should help as well.

Still, there's too much depth returning around the league for Cornell to hope for such a drastic improvement. A jump from seventh to fourth or fifth should be very satisfying.

```
1990-91 CORNELL SCHEDULE

Nov.    26    Pitt
        29    @St. Bonaventure
Dec.     1    @Syracuse
         4    @Army
       7-8    #Cornell Tournament
        15    Binghamton (NY)
        29    Bucknell
Jan.     3    North Carolina
         5    @North Carolina Greensboro
         7    @Winthrop (SC)
        11    Harvard
        12    Dartmouth
        19    @Columbia
        21    Colgate
        26    Columbia
Feb.     1    @Brown
         2    @Yale
         8    Princeton
         9    Pennsylvania
        15    @Dartmouth
        16    @Harvard
        22    @Pennsylvania
        23    @Princeton
Mar.     1    Yale
         2    Brown

@ Road Games
# Ithaca, NY (Kent State, Vermont & Virginia Military Institute)
```

CREIGHTON

LAST SEASON: 21-12
CONFERENCE
RECORD: 9-5
STARTERS LOST: 1
STARTERS
RETURNING: 4
CONFERENCE:
MISSOURI
VALLEY (MVC)
LOCATION:
OMAHA, NE
HOME FLOOR: OMAHA
CIVIC AUDITORIUM (9,300)
NICKNAME: BLUEJAYS
COLORS: BLUE AND WHITE
COACH: TONY BARONE, record at Creighton, 78-74.

Back-to-back 20-win seasons usually are heralded with fanfare and much back-slapping. But at Creighton, last year's 21-12 record and berth in the NIT falls into the disappointing category.

The Bluejays, picked to win the Missouri Valley Conference, wound up second instead and missed out on their second straight NCAA tournament bid. With a chance to tie for the regular-season title on the final day, Creighton lost at Illinois State. Then, with a chance to play for the league's post-season tournament title and gain the MVC's automatic NCAA bid, the Bluejays again lost at Illinois State.

But four starters return from that team. Among them, Creighton's "Dynamic Duo" will be making its final appearance, and you can bet MVC coaches will be glad to see the last of **Bob Harstad** and **Chad Gallagher.**

Harstad earned MVC player of the year honors last season when he averaged 22.2 points and 8.8 rebounds per game. The 6-6, rock-solid forward led the Bluejays in scoring 21 times in 33 games. He is also close to becoming only the fourth player in MVC history to record 2,000 points (he needs 460) and 1,000 rebounds (he needs 148). The others in that elite group are Larry Bird, Oscar Robertson and Xavier McDaniel.

Gallagher, 6-10, was an All-MVC selection and also made the league's all-defensive team. He averaged 17.7 points, 8.1 rebounds and 1.9 blocked shots. Gallagher wound up second to Harstad in voting for MVC player of the year.

The trouble spot for the Bluejays last season was point guard, where coach Tony Barone found replacing James Farr tougher than expected. But by the end of the season, 5-10 junior **Duan Cole** had earned the starting spot, ending up as an honorable mention All-MVC selection with averages of 8.5 points, 4.1 assists and 2.1 rebounds. Creighton was 12-6 in games Cole started at the point, and in those dozen wins he averaged 13.6 points, 7.3 assists and only 2.1 turnovers.

6-1 junior **Latrell Wrightsell,** who made 13 starts at point guard, also returns. Wrightsell is a tenacious defender, but he averaged just 2.3 points. The other starter returning is 6-4 senior **Darin Plautz,** the team's top three-point shooter last year at 42.9 percent, second-best in the conference. Plautz averaged 6.6 points and 3.5 rebounds.

The MVC's top three-point shooter two years ago, 6-7 senior **Todd Eisner,** is back after missing all but the first 10 games last year due to left knee surgery. Eisner, says Barone, "is the glue. We can't play without him." In addition to his long-range shooting ability, Eisner is a heady and unselfish player with outstanding passing ability.

The Bluejays return four other part-time players. 6-3 sophomore **Matt Petty** (1.4 points) started one game and made four of five three-pointers. 6-9 sophomore **Todd Geyer** (0.5 ppg, 0.3 rpg) has a nice touch for a big guy. 6-7 junior **Chris Rodgers** (1.2 ppg, 0.7 rpg) started some games as a freshman, but has had knee trouble since. A hard-nosed rebounder, he played in 11 games a year ago.

Backup center **Bill O'Dowd** (0.3 ppg, 0.4 rpg) doesn't even need basketball. The 7-0 senior graduated in just three years with a double major in math and history, not to mention a perfect 4.0 grade-point average. He was named to the USA Today All-Academic first team last year as one of the Top 25 college students in the country. This year, he will be back working on a master's degree in history and on backing up Gallagher at center.

With 10 veterans returning, Barone will be able to ease four newcomers into the lineup. **Derek Bain,** a 5-10 freshman point guard from Austin, Tex., averaged 20.9 points, 6.6 assists and 6.1 rebounds for Hyde Park Baptist High School. He will provide depth behind Cole, Wrightsell and Petty.

Three other freshmen will learn behind Harstad, Gallagher and company up front. 6-5 **Johnnie Williams** averaged 15.6 points and 6.0 rebounds at Marion (Ind.) HS. 6-9 **Jerry Vanderheydt** averaged 15.0 points and 8.3 rebounds at Pekin High, a member of one of Illinois' toughest high school conferences, the Midstate-Nine. And **Greg Everett,** a 6-5 forward with outstanding defensive skills, also brings 12.1 points and 8.3 rebounds from El Toro (Calif.) HS.

BLUE RIBBON ANALYSIS

Creighton returns 86 percent of its scoring and 79 percent of its rebounding from last year. Harstad and Gallagher are as rough a one-two combination as the league as seen in years. Cole is established at the

point, and guys like Eisner, Plautz and Petty can kill you with the three-pointer.

Add to that mix the Bluejays' outstanding depth and Barone, one of the nation's most underrated coaches, and you've got a team that will be difficult to handle, especially at home. While the other MVC kingpins are reeling from major losses, Creighton returns virtually intact.

Make it three straight 20-wins seasons for the Bluejays, and take them to win the Missouri Valley again on their way to an NCAA tournament slot.

```
1990-91 CREIGHTON SCHEDULE

Nov.    30-
Dec.     1    #Amana Hawkeye Classic
Dec.     4    Missouri
         6    @Nebraska
        17    @South Alabama
        20    Tulsa
        22    UTEP
        26    Louisiana Tech
        29    @Cleveland State
Jan.     2    @Southwest Missouri State
         5    Bradley
         8    Iowa State
        10    @Drake
        15    Wichita State
        19    @Illinois State
        21    @Bradley
        26    Indiana State
        28    @Southern Illinois
        31    Illinois State
Feb.     3    @Siena
         7    @Indiana State
        10    Southwest Missouri State
        16    @Tulsa
        18    @Notre Dame
        21    Drake
        23    Southern Illinois
        25    @Wichita State
Mar.   1-5    ##MVC Tournament

@ Road Games
# Iowa City, IA (Colgate, Iowa & Texas-San Antonio)
## St. Louis, MO
```

DARTMOUTH

LAST SEASON: 12-14
CONFERENCE
RECORD: 7-7
STARTERS LOST: 2
STARTERS
RETURNING: 3
CONFERENCE:
IVY LEAGUE
LOCATION:
HANOVER, NH
HOME FLOOR: LEEDE
ARENA (2,100)
NICKNAME: BIG GREEN
COLORS: GREEN AND WHITE
COACH: PAUL CORMIER, record at Dartmouth, 77-78.

The director of intramurals at Dartmouth must have drawn up the Big Green's 1990-91 schedule. That's about the only way to explain the fact that Dartmouth's first nine games and 15 of its first 17 contests are on the road. It seems like the rest of the undergradutes want to play Leede Arena, and the only way to accomodate them was to send the varsity squad packing.

If Dartmouth played in the Big Ten or another conference that relies heavily on air travel for road games, head coach Paul Cormier might be accused of hoarding frequent-flyer miles for a vacation trip to Hawaii. "It's hard to win on the road, especially for an Ivy team," admitted Cormier, whose extra mileage credit should come instead from Greyhound. "If we can improve day-in and day-out, and not worry about being at the top of our game immediately, we should be all right by the Ivy season.''

A year ago, the Big Green's 7-7 league record was worth a spot in the Ivy's four-way, third-place gridlock. This time, Cormier wants some breathing room. "We think we could have a formidable team,'' he said. ''We've got to have patience early on so we'll be ready for the league.''

Three starters return to help Dartmouth move up. However, gone is 7-1 center Walter Palmer (16.5 ppg, 6.4 rpg), a first-team All-Ivy selection, a second-round draft choice of the Utah Jazz and the school's all-time leading shot blocker. Offsetting the loss of Palmer is the healthy return of 6-0 senior **James Blackwell** (13.1 ppg), who missed much of the season with a knee injury.

''James is one of the most talented guards in the league,'' Cormier said of his co-captain. ''He can score, handle the point and run the fastbreak. He's a tough competitor and the heart and soul of our team.''

Joining Blackwell as returning starters are 6-6 senior forward and co-captain **Brendan O'Sullivan** (9.5 ppg, 6.5 rpg) and 6-7 sophomore forward **John Conley** (3.1 ppg, 3.0 rpg).

''Brendan is a fourth-year starter who's an excellent rebounder and a good defensive player,'' Cormier said. ''Conley has had some ankle and back problems, but he's an excellent shooter, a good defender and an excellent rebounder.''

Bill Taylor (5.2 ppg) a 6-1 senior, will assume the point guard responsibilities, and **Mike Lombard** (6.5 ppg, 3.8 rpg) a 6-8 junior who saw action while Palmer struggled with an injured back, should move into the pivot.

Since Cormier favors an up-tempo style, his bench will be very important. Providing depth in the backcourt are four sophomores - 5-9 **Gary Campbell** (1.7 ppg), 5-11 **Jason Rosenberg** (1.5 ppg), 6-4 **Alex Gayer** and 6-1 **Matt Brzica**. **Jon Wilkins**, a 6-4 junior, gives Dartmouth depth upfront.

Cormier will count heavily on his five freshmen. **Michael Crotty** (Christian Brothers Academy/Spring Lake, N.J.), is a 5-9 point guard and the brother of Virginia standout John Crotty. 6-2 guard **Greg Frame** (Phillips Exeter Academy, N.H. and Waterville, Maine), 6-7 power forward **Demetrius Cheeks** (Midwood HS/Brooklyn, N.Y.), 6-7 center **Stan Kowalewski** (West Genesee HS/Camillus, N.Y.) and 6-6 rebounding forward **Reggie Talbert** (Bryan Station HS/Lexington, Ky.) round out the newcomers.

''If we're going to play the up-tempo game, we're going to need to use 11-12 players a game,'' Cormier said, referring to the need for immediate contributions from his freshmen. Dartmouth very likely needs quick results, or it will long for the days of third place.

''The league is very competitive,'' said Cormier. ''Even though we've lost a lot of players, we're not conceding anything. I think we'll be in a position in the last weekend to win it.''

BLUE RIBBON ANALYSIS

Two years ago, with all-time leading scorer Jim Barton, plus Palmer and Blackwell, the Big Green should have won the Ivy League. Last year, with Palmer and Blackwell, Dartmouth could have won it. This year, well, it's time to start over.

Losing Palmer, even though he was hobbled with the bad back, hurts. A lot. Adding a healthy Blackwell helps, but not enough. His supporting cast is unproven.

If Dartmouth's five frosh can show immediate maturity and contribute the necessary depth, things will be all right. However, a more likely scenario is some shellshock from too much life on the road and a second-division Ivy finish.

DAVIDSON

LAST SEASON: 4-24
CONFERENCE RECORD: NONE
STARTERS LOST: 3
STARTERS RETURNING: 2
CONFERENCE: BIG SOUTH
LOCATION: DAVIDSON, NC
HOME FLOOR: BELK ARENA (6,000)
NICKNAME: WILDCATS
COLORS: RED AND BLACK
COACH: BOB McKILLOP, record at Davidson, 4-24.

After two years as an independent produced an 11-48 record, Davidson must have gotten lonely for conference life. The Wildcats, formerly of the Southern Conference, aligned themselves with the Big South in late spring and are immediately eligible for the league championship. Coach Bob McKillop has to be relieved.

The schedule McKillop inherited for his first season at was a killer. The Wildcats played - and lost to - Wake Forest, William and Mary, Virginia, UNC-Charlotte, Duke and St. John's, and that was just in December. Davidson never recovered from that humbling start, finishing 4-24. Clearly, there is considerable room for improvement, and McKillop signed seven recruits to help him achieve it.

''This is a year when our returning players must demonstrate their ability to earn a starting spot immediately,'' McKillop said. ''They must convert their potential into performance.''

That sounds like an ultimatum. One returning player who is up to the task of is 6-11 sophomore **Detlef Musch** (9.9 ppg, 6.7 rpg, 23 blocked shots). A native of West Germany, Musch followed McKillop to Davidson from Long Island Lutheran High School. He also served notice of his emerging talent with a 27-point, 18-rebound peformance against Miami.

Paul Drobnitch (3.0 ppg, 3.2 rpg), a 6-7 junior, and 6-7 sophomore **J.D. Heuer** (2.4 ppg, 3.2 rpg) were key frontcourt reserves last year and should serve in that role again this season.

At guard, 6-3 junior **Paul Denmond** (13.4 ppg, 4.0 rpg, 65 assists, 17 steals) returns after leading the team in scoring. 6-3 senior **Darry Strickland** (4.2 ppg, 2.5 rpg, 47 assists, 20 steals) started seven times and adds experience to the Wildcats' backcourt. **Sterling Freeman,** (2.6 ppg, 2.1 rpg) a 6-4 junior, played in 25 games a year ago.

McKillop was pleased with his recruiting class and, truth be told, many of the newcomers will have to play a lot. ''The strongest class we've seen at Davidson in quite some time,'' recruiting anlayst Bob Gibbons said. ''A well-rounded group that will help in every area. In the Big South Conference, they have easily the best recruiting class.''

The newcomers include 6-9 junior **Jeff Chapin** of Manatee (Fla.) CC, along with a half-dozen freshmen - 6-2 **Jason Zimmerman** from Warsaw (Ind.) High; 6-6 Yugoslavian **Janko Narat,** a freshman from Fork Union (Va.) Military Academy; 6-6 **Ron Horton** from Gonzaga Prep (Washington, D.C.); 6-0 **Pat Holloway** from George Washington High (Denver); 6-6 **Scott Alford** from Maine Central Institute (Pittsfield); and 6-5 West German **James Marsh** from North Hopkins HS/Madisonville, Ky.

Chapin averaged 16.1 points and 10.2 rebounds for a Manatee team that went 20-8. He was a first-team All-Conference choice and played in the Florida all-star game. He also shot 55 percent from the field and 82 percent from the free throw line.

Zimmerman averaged 18 points and eight assists for a Warsaw team that was 21-3 and ranked No. 1 in Indiana much of last season. Narat led Fork Union scorers with a 13.5 average, and he hit on 45 percent of his three-point attempts. Horton averaged 10 points for a Gonzaga quintet that sent two other players to Georgetown and one to Princeton.

''We filled most of our immediate needs, outside shooting and ball handling,'' McKillp said. ''Narat, Zimmerman, Alford and Holloway are all good perimeter shooters and Chapin has the potential to help us inside.''

BLUE RIBBON ANALYSIS

Winners of just 11 games the last two years, Davidson can only improve this season. McKillop, a respected high school coach, seems capable of leading the Wildcats to better things. The move to the Big South Conference is also a plus. Davidson floundered without a conference affiliation.

If Chapin can help inside and Narat, Zimmerman, Alford and Holloway live up to their billing as outside shooters, the Wildcats will be heard from in their new league. ''I think we can be competitive in the Big South,'' McKillop said. ''Except for one game, we were competitive against Big South teams last year. We're excited to be competing for a conference championship. Rivalries will develop. And now we have a chance to be part of the NCAA tournament.''

A remote chance, for this season at least, but Davidson basketball will pull out of its two-year slump and be respectable.

Jan.	17	Baptist
	19	@Radford
	21	@Virginia
	23	South Carolina
	26	Augusta College (GA)
	28	@North Carolina Charlotte
	31	@Augusta College
Feb.	2	@Miami (FL)
	6	Winthrop College (SC)
	11	@Coastal Carolina
	13	@Duke
	16	@Winthrop College
	20	Campbell
	25	@Liberty University (VA)
Feb.	28-	
Mar.	2	##Big South Conference Tournament

@ Road Games
# Jamaica, NY (Central Connecticut, Monmouth & St. John's)
Anderson, SC

DAYTON

LAST SEASON: 22-10
CONFERENCE RECORD: 10-4
STARTERS LOST: 4
STARTERS RETURNING: 1
CONFERENCE: MIDWESTERN COLLEGIATE (MCC)
LOCATION: DAYTON, OH
HOME FLOOR: DAYTON ARENA (13,455)
NICKNAME: FLYERS
COLORS: RED AND BLUE
COACH: JIM O'BRIEN, record at Dayton, 22-10. Career record, 96-79.

When the powers-that-be decided to take the controversial step of firing Don Donoher after his silver anniversary season, it was a big gamble. Donoher, after all, was the winningest coach in Dayton history. He took his first three teams to the NCAA tournament, and guided the 1966-67 squad to the national championship game before losing to perennial UCLA.

Yet in his 25th year, the Flyers were 12-17. It was Donoher's third straight losing season, and he was fired despite an overall record of 437-275 and a winning percentage of .614.

When a school makes such a move, chances are it will take more than a little while to get the program back on track. But the Flyers hired Jim O'Brien, then 37, to take over. Not only had O'Brien worked under Rick Pitino for two years with the New York Knicks, but he is a disciple and son-in-law of the legendary Dr. Jack Ramsay.

O'Brien immediately shook things up at Dayton, utilizing a full court press throughout the game and giving new meaning to run and gun. And it worked. By the end of last season, Dayton was the best team in the Midwestern Collegiate Conference. The Flyers whipped regular season champion Xavier in the final game before the tournament, then stopped Xavier again in the title game of the MCC tourney.

Having earned a spot in the NCAA's, Dayton proceeded to knock off Illinois in the first round before falling to eventual Final Four entry Arkansas in the second. O'Brien's fast-paced game packed U.D. Arena, and hosting the MCC tournament certainly didn't hurt.

The Flyers averaged 89.7 points per game in 1989-90. They took an incredible 666 shots from three-point range, and banged home 261. Even more impressive was the manner in which Donoher's recruits adjusted to, and flourished under, O'Brien.

So what's next? Four of the five starters were lost to graduation, including NBA-bound Negele Knight (second round choice of the Phoenix Suns). Knight, last year's point man, was the premier guard in the MCC, averaging 22.8 points and 6.8 assists per game. The Flyers also lost their second-leading scorer and leading rebounder in 6-8 power forward Anthony Corbitt (16.3 ppg, 8.3 rpg).

The top returnee is actually a non-starter, although 6-3 senior **Norm Grevey** (9.8 ppg, 1.2 rpg) saw extensive action as did almost everyone on the Flyers' bench. Grevey went 72-for-153 from three-point range, a percentage of .471. He shot .519 overall, best on the team.

The only returning starter is 6-11 junior center **Wes Coffee** (3.2 ppg, 2.9 rpg). Coffee was slow to come around last season because of a bout with mononucleosis in the fall, but he was a factor in the late-season success. 6-4 sophomore **Alex Robertson** (5.0 ppg, 1.4 rpg) and 6-3 senior **Ken Branch** (2.2 ppg, 1.2 rpg) were defensive specialists; 6-9 senior **Sam Howard** (3.9 ppg, 3.3 rpg) and 6-6 junior **David Bradds** (3.2 ppg, 5.3 rpg) had major roles off the bench along with Grevey.

"Although we lose a tremendous amount of talent and experience," said O'Brien, "we feel confident that our returning players have a good understanding of what it takes to be successful playing this style. Certainly, when you look at us having seven new players, it will take some time for us to be comfortable with each other. And although we are somewhat inexperienced in playing as a team, we feel that we have the talent to play well in the conference."

Two junior college recruits step in and should deliver immediately. They are 6-9 junior **Makor Shayok**, a center/forward from Khartoum, Sudan who played last season at Alvin (Tex.) JC, and 6-1 point guard **Chip Jones**, a Cincinnati native who played at San Jacinto (Tex.) JC. Shayok (14.8 ppg, 12.2 rpg) and Jones (13.1 ppg, 4.4 rpg, 2.1 assists, 1.3 steals) are the likely heirs to slots left vacant by Corbitt and Knight.

Other positions are even more up for grabs, although 6-4 freshman **Sean Scrutchins** has an interesting background and may have an inside track. Scrutchins came to Dayton on an academic scholarship last year, red-shirted in basketball, and is now on athletic scholarship. His Scott (Toledo) HS team won the Ohio state championship in 1989, and Scrutchins averaged 17.2 points, 5.2 assists and 4.5 rebounds.

Another interesting freshman is **John Richter**, a 6-5 guard. At Badin High in Hamilton, Ohio, Richter's numbers were 22.9 ppg, 11.5 rpg and 5.2 assists. Other frosh include 6-0 guard **Derrick Dukes** (Woodward HS/Cincinnati), 6-8 forward **Andy Gaydosh** (Richmond HS/Richmond, Ind.) and 6-7 **Antoine Smith** (Westerville HS/Columbus).

BLUE RIBBON ANALYSIS

O'Brien was fortunate last year in that so many of the returning players fit his mold. Of them, it will be especially difficult to replace Knight, who was a demon in the clutch. Knight hit big basket after big basket down the stretch and in close games.

The Flyers this season will be very good at times and very bad at others. Inexperience and a new mix will do that. This is also a transition year, one in which O'Brien begins to mold his own cast of characters for another run at the big time.

The ace in the hole is Dayton Arena, where the Flyers were 16-3. And, once again, Dayton will host the MCC post-season tournament, a major sore spot, with some of the league's coaches. Given everything, look for the Flyers to finish in the middle of the pack during the regular season, but come close to the top in their home-grown tourney.

Nov.	24	Towson State
Dec.	1	Morehead State
	6	@Miami (OH)
	8	Alabama State
	15	Southern University
	19	Robert Morris
	22	@Bradley
	27	Texas Southern
	29	Cincinnati
Jan.	5	DePaul
	10	@Marquette
	12	@Loyola
	17	St. Louis
	19	Evansville
	24	@Butler
	26	@Detroit
	29	Notre Dame
Feb.	2	Xavier
	7	Marquette
	9	Loyola
	14	@St. Louis
	16	@Evansville
	21	Butler
	23	Detroit
	26	@Notre Dame
Mar.	2	@Xavier
	7-9	#MCC Tournament

@ Road Games
# Dayton, OH

DETROIT

LAST SEASON: 10-18
CONFERENCE RECORD: 3-11
STARTERS LOST: 1
STARTERS RETURNING: 4
CONFERENCE: MIDWESTERN COLLEGIATE (MCC)
LOCATION: DETROIT, MI
HOME FLOOR: COBO ARENA (11,241)
NICKNAME: TITANS
COLORS: RED AND WHITE
COACH: RICKY BYRDSONG, record at Detroit, 17-39.

Ricky Byrdsong must have a pretty good feeling about the basketball program at Detroit, the school that spawned Dick Vitale. Byrdsong had a chance to move into the six-figure income bracket during the off-season as head coach at Arkansas-Little Rock, his two teams at Detroit hadn't come close to breaking even, yet he turned the offer down.

Byrdsong said he felt an obligation to remain with the players he had recruited, having brought in 10 in 1989. Interviewed by a Detroit television station after deciding to stay, the coach was asked "is it true you turned down a five-year deal worth $5 million?" Byrdsong laughed and said: "If that were true, then the kids would have to understand (him leaving.)"

Actually, Byrdsong may be staying because he can finally see some light in what had been a dark and lonely job. The Titans return four starters and, for the first time in his tenure, have some size and depth.

"You can't underestimate the difference a year's experience makes for freshman players," Byrdsong said. "But the biggest contributor behind us expecting to make progress this year is size. It's something we just did not have last season, and it was a factor that worked against us."

Last year, Detroit was blessed with some great

185

athletes, but 6-6 sophomore **Michael Lovelace** was its tallest player. That will change dramatically this season. **John Beauford,** a 7-1 sophomore, is an eligible transfer from Ohio University. **Greg Grant,** a 6-11 freshman who red-shirted last year with a chronic stomach ailment, is back and reportedly healthy. **John Buszka,** a 6-10 senior, missed most of last season with a knee injury but is also back after arthroscopic surgery. So big guys abound now, and they should fit in nicely with the players who came aboard last season.

Byrdsong's 1989 recruiting class ranked first in the Midwestern Collegiate Conference and 31st nationally by the *National Recruiter's Cage Letter.* The six are now all sophomores, and they worked hard last year in spite of their size handicap. Detroit's 10 victories were the most by the Titans since 1985-86. The Titans also broke a 37-game road losing streak with a double-overtime win at Duquesne in November, and ended a string of 20 successive road losses in the MCC when they beat Butler in January. All told, Detroit defeated seven teams it had lost to the previous season.

The frosh-now-soph heroes were 6-5 forward/center **Michael Aaron** (10.4 ppg, 6.6 rpg), 6-3 guard **Dwayne Kelley** (10.0 ppg, 1.5 rpg) and Lovelace (9.6 ppg, 5.6 rpg). Aaron and Lovelace were starters.

The other returning starters are seniors, 6-3 guard **Huey Smith** (7.4 ppg, 2.2 rpg) and 6-4 forward **Shawn Williams** (12.4 ppg, 4.0 rpg). Williams is considered the top returning player. A junior college transfer last year, he was 15th in the league in scoring (including a 27-point night vs. Xavier) and was an MCC all-newcomer selection. Williams scored 20 or more points on three occasions, and his best rebounding total was 10 (against Dayton).

Overall, Detroit was well-balanced in scoring and probably will be again this year. Other than guard **Bill Wood** (9.3 ppg, 2.9 rpg), the Titans lost little to graduation. In response, Byrdsong signed no freshmen, probably a wise move considering the six returning sophomores, Beauford and Grant. Two JC transfers are on hand, however, in 6-6 forward **Maurice Benson** of Coffeyville (Kan.) CC and 6-2 guard **Andre Johnson** of Highland Park (Mich.) CC.

Other returnees include the rest of the heralded sophs - 6-4 guard **LaJuan Bell** (1.0 ppg, 1.3 rpg), 6-8 forward **Canonchet Neves** (5.1 ppg, 2.4 rpg) and 6-2 guard **Ramsey Nichols** (4.1 ppg,1.6 rpg) - along with 6-5 senior forward **Kelan Ritchie** (2.1 ppg, 1.1 rpg).

BLUE RIBBON ANALYSIS

Many felt Detroit had the best collection of athletes in the MCC a year ago, yet lack of size and experience hurt. This season, Detroit has both. They also have it in a year in which recent MCC powers are rebuilding.

Byrdsong, who spent six seasons as an assistant at Arizona and worked five of those years under Lute Olson, now has to prove he can coach talent as well as recruit it. He has no more excuses. It is time for the Titans to win some games and be competitive with the big boys in the conference.

Look for Detroit to at least threaten the .500 mark, and to finally gain ground on the rest of the Midwestern Collegiate Conference. A fourth or fifth place finish is not out of the question.

1990-91 DETROIT SCHEDULE		
Nov.	28	Duquesne
Dec.	1	@Central Michigan
	5	Toledo
	8	Michigan State
	15	Eastern Michigan
	22	@Northern Iowa
	30	@Xavier
Jan.	2	@Florida International
	4-5	#Florida Tech Tournament

1990-91 DETROIT SCHEDULE (Cont.)		
Jan.	10	@Evansville
	12	Butler
	16	Northern Iowa
	19	@Butler
	24	Xavier
	26	Dayton
	31	@Marquette
Feb.	2	@Dayton
	5	@DePaul
	7	Evansville
	9	St. Louis
	11	Northeastern Illinois
	14	@Valparaiso (IN)
	16	@St. Louis
	25	@Loyola
	28	Marquette
Mar.	2	Loyola
	7-9	##MCC Tournament

@ Road Games
# Melbourne, FL (Brown, Florida Tech & Univ. of the District of Columbia)
Dayton, OH

DRAKE

LAST SEASON: 13-18
CONFERENCE RECORD: 5-9
STARTERS LOST: 4
STARTERS RETURNING: 1
CONFERENCE: MISSOURI VALLEY (MVC)
LOCATION: DES MOINES, IA
HOME FLOOR: VETERANS MEMORIAL AUDITORIUM (11,678)
NICKNAME: BULLDOGS
COLORS: BLUE AND WHITE
COACH: RUDY WASHINGTON, first year at Drake.

We're talking new look as Drake enters the 1990's. There's a new coach - veteran super-recruiter Rudy Washington - and all kinds of new players, seven in all. Things are so different in Des Moines, one wonders if the pit bull will replace the toothy bulldog as Drake's mascot.

Gone is Tom Abatemarco, who could not survive a player insurrection and was dismissed before last season ended. Also gone are four starters, which might be the good news as Washington looks to end a string of three straight non-winning seasons.

Like Abatemarco before him, Washington comes in with a recruiter's reputation. Washington has also been around winning programs. His resume' the past 10 years includes seven NCAA tournament teams in the Pac-10, ACC and Big Ten. And he comes from just up the road in Iowa City, where he served as chief recruiter for Tom Davis and Iowa the past five seasons. In addition, Washington also coached rebounding at Iowa, and the Hawkeyes led the nation in that category two of the past three years.

Yet the new coach is hardly naive. Nor are his glasses colored rose. "Our mission is transition," Washington says of his first major head coaching job. "It will take some work."

The lone returning starter is 5-11 senior **Kaylon Green,** who averaged 8.0 points and 1.3 rebounds last year. The only other returning lettermen are 6-7 senior **Sam Powell** (2.2 ppg, 1.6 rpg) and 6-9 senior **Calvin Tillis** (2.7 ppg, 2.0 rpg), bit players at best. Two others back have even less experience: 6-6 sophomore **Shane Murphy** (five appearances) and 6-3 soph **Eric Bunce** (10).

Finally, one of the players Washington might have counted on, talented 6-7 forward **Kevin Sams** (12.3 ppg, 4.4 rpg), is not available. Sams will sit out 1990-91 to concentrate on academics, eliminating last season's second-leading scorer and third-leading rebounder.

All of which leaves Washington with a major rebuilding job, and a bundle of new faces with which to do it. One who should contribute right away is 6-4 sophomore **Chris Jones,** Mr. Basketball in Wisconsin during 1988-89. Jones, who sat out last year, averaged 25.5 points, 14.0 rebounds and 4.2 assists at Milwaukee's Hamilton High. How he adjusts to the layoff will be crucial.

Junior **Wayne Embry,** another member of Abatemarco's 1989 recruiting class, is also available. A 5-11 shooting guard, Embry played just three games (8.0 pgg) last year before being sidelined by a stress fracture in his foot.

Drake did manage to sign a pair of recruits with outstanding credentials before Washington even arrived on the scene. Junior college transfer **Adrian Thomas,** a 6-7 forward from Angelina (Tex.) JC, scored 15.9 points per game last season and averaged 10.6 rebounds. He earned second-team All-Texas junior college honors. 6-2 freshman **Brian Williams** (Keokuk HS/Keokuk, Iowa) averaged 25 points, five rebounds and four assists in his final prep season and was a first-team, Class 3A all-state selection.

Washington went to work himself during the spring signing period, corraling four more frosh, two from talent-rich Southern California. 6-6 **William Celestine** could be an especially big-time addition. The Los Angeles Class 4A player of the year at Manual Arts High, Celestine averaged 19.9 points, 12.7 rebounds and 4.2 blocks to lead his team to a 27-4 record and the Los Angeles 4-A city title.

The other Californian is 6-1 guard **Mark Raveling,** who spent last season at New Hampton (N.H.) Prep School. The Los Angeles native averaged 15 points per game, and is the son of Southern California coach George Raveling.

Washington went east to Sterling Heights, Mich. to land 6-4 **Mark Prylow,** a guard who averaged 24 points, eight rebounds and four assists for DeLaSalle High School. The final piece in the recruiting puzzle is 6-8 center **Brian Kueter** from Iowa City, the state Class 3-A runner-up. Kueter, already a solid 225 pounds, averaged 17.1 points, 8.1 rebounds and 3.9 blocked shots per game.

"We'll play an exciting style of basketball at Drake," Washington insisted, "and the fans will sense the enthusiasm of our kids on the court."

BLUE RIBBON ANALYSIS

Washington, long one of the most highly respected assistant coaches in the country, paid his dues for a chance to be someone's head man. But he could have picked a better set of circumstances for his first Division I job.

The Bulldogs will find out right away what they've got. They open at home against Iowa, then play at Arizona State. There are also non-conference games with Mississippi State, Iowa State and Texas Christian. It may be too much, too soon for Washington's get-to-know-us cast.

The amount of new faces will probably add up to another losing season at Drake, its fourth straight and seventh sub-.500 campaign in the last 10. A really good year for the Bulldogs would mean escaping the basement in the nine-team MVC.

1990-91 DRAKE SCHEDULE		
Nov.	27	Iowa
Dec.	1	@Arizona State
	3	Colgate
	7-8	#Heritage-Drake Classic
	13	Wichita State
	15	U.S. International (CA)
	22	Mississippi State

DREXEL

LAST SEASON: 13-15
CONFERENCE RECORD: 7-7
STARTERS LOST: 2
STARTERS RETURNING: 3
CONFERENCE: EAST COAST (ECC)
LOCATION: PHILADELPHIA, PA
HOME FLOOR: PHYSICAL EDUCATION ATHLETIC CENTER (2,500)
NICKNAME: DRAGONS
COLORS: NAVY BLUE AND GOLD
COACH: EDDIE BURKE, record at Drexel, 193-173.

As Drexel embarks on its final East Coast Conference campaign before moving with Delaware to the North Atlantic Conference, the Dragons are coming off a second straight enigmatic season. Picked for sixth in the conference last year, the Dragons finished sixth. Getting there was anything but routine, however. On 11 occasions, the Dragons both led and trailed by eight or more points in the same game. Five times, they lost a game in which they had been leading by at least 10 points; four times, they came from 10 or more points behind to win. Eight of their games were decided on a last shot in the final five seconds; they split those games, including a 75-74 loss in the ECC quarterfinals to Lehigh.

Such inconsistency was the benchmark of Drexel last year. But don't blame the bench. The substitutes accounted for 32 percent of the Dragons' scoring, including an 11-6 mark when their bench outscored the opponents. That bench is even deeper this year. Coming up with the right combination of scorers in the starting lineup is coach Eddie Burke's biggest problem.

Drexel will have to replace the scoring of 5-11 point guard Todd Lehmann (16.6 ppg) and 6-5 swingman Chris Arizin (14.1 ppg). Lehmann led the nation in assists per game with 9.3, and Arizin was an occasional starter who was effective coming off the bench. Also graduated is beefy 6-8 center Brian Raabe (3.6 ppg, 4.6 rpg). He may be the easiest to replace, provided one of several candidates steps forward.

A trio of juniors return to the starting lineup. 6-4 **Michael Thompson** (12.8 ppg, 3.3 rpg) will be the

shooting guard and also will draw the opponent's top guard or small forward. He shot nearly 50 percent from the floor, but will need to work on his outside shooting to keep the pressure off his new backcourtmates, 5-11 junior **Clarence Armstrong** (3.8 ppg, 1.3 apg). The left handed Armstrong hit 3 three-point field goals in the final 17 seconds to give the Dragons a one-point win at Bucknell last year, but will need to improve his overall shooting (31 percent) to make his mark at point. Armstrong has played in every game his two seasons at Drexel including one start, but taking over for the steady Lehmann still is a task.

Vying for time off the bench in the backcourt will be a pair of home grown freshman products. 5-11 **Matt Alexander** (15.0 ppg, 8.0 apg) from Father Judge HS, Philadelphia, Pa.) a two-time second-team All-Catholic League pick by the *Philadelphia Daily News*, will push 5-10 sophomore **John Caruso** (0.6 ppg) for the backup point guard position. 6-3 **Andre Daniel**, who honed his skill for a year at Blair Academy (21.3 ppg, 10.0 ppg, 5.0 apg) after leading the city and state with 31.5 ppg and being named second team all-state and city as a senior at Lamberton HS in Philadelphia, will push Thompson for time.

And although Alexander and Daniel should see extensive time, they may not see as much as another freshman, 6-6 **Mike Wisler** (24.5 ppg, 13.4 rpg at Columbia, Pa. HS). Wisler will start out behind a pair of junior forwards, 6-7 **Jonathan Raab** (10.1 ppg, 6.1 rpg) and 6-6 **Dan Leahy** (5.8 ppg, 2.7 rpg), but he may muscle into the lineup this year. A *USA Today* honorable mention All-America, he finished his high school career with 2,837 points to break the county scoring records held by Sam Bowie (New Jersey Nets) and Jack Hurd (LaSalle). Raab is a strong rebounder and inside shooter (58 percent) and Leahy is strong defensively, but Wisler's scoring ability from outside may force Burke to use him. Also expected to see plenty of action is 6-7 senior **Arthur Clark** (9.4 ppg, 5.9 rpg), who emerged as the top substitute last year after playing only 87 minutes the previous two seasons. Clark led the team in scoring three times and rebounding seven times last year without starting a game. Also expected to see playing time is 6-7 sophomore **Matt Attar**, a transfer from Navy with three years of eligibility left. The Somerset, Mass., product averaged 2.4 ppg as a freshman at Navy. 6-6 senior **Jim Hardy** (0.9 ppg, 0.8 rpg) started six games but has never completely recovered from stress fractures in both feet suffered since being the top reserve in the 1987-88 season. 6-5 senior swingman **Tom Murphy**, a starter as a redshirt freshman, has moved near the end of the bench since spraining an ankle early in his sophomore season. He saw limited action in 10 games last year.

Unless 6-10 sophomore **Jim Fenwick** can contribute, either Wisler or Clark could become a starter in a three-forward frontline. Fenwick saw only mapup duty in 10 games last season after redshirting the previous year.

BLUE RIBBON ANALYSIS

With the exception of Delaware, everybody in the ECC has suffered losses. While the Dragons don't figure to approach last season's team record totals for three-point FGs made (152) and attempted (393), they must find someone to shoot from the perimeter for balance. With a quick indoctrination by the freshman, Drexel can battle with anyone in the ECC for second place.

DUQUESNE

LAST SEASON: 7-22
CONFERENCE RECORD: 5-13
STARTERS LOST: 3
STARTERS RETURNING: 2
CONFERENCE: ATLANTIC 10
LOCATION: PITTSBURGH, PA
HOME FLOOR: A.J. PALUMBO CENTER (6,200)
NICKNAME: DUKES
COLORS: RED AND BLUE
COACH: JOHN CARROLL, record at Duquesne, 7-22.

Perhaps Duquesne coach John Carroll was on to something. Speaking during his first Atlantic 10 conference tournament in March, Carroll quipped that "it's a long way from 7-22 to the Final Four." An assistant at Seton Hall when the Pirates reached the 1989 national championship game, Carroll no doubt realized many times last year just how right he was.

The Dukes, despite Mark Stevenson's wondrous one-year whistle stop (27.2 ppg, A-10 single-season record 788 points), won only a half-dozen regular season games, then were eliminated by Temple in the Atlantic 10 quarterfinals. Such are the dues in Division I, where the road to even the conference final four can be blocked by teams that already know the way.

It is a hurdle Carroll must overcome if he is to lead Duquesne out of the wilderness it has faced since Norm Nixon and the glory years of the 1970's. And he is attacking it the only way he knows: recruit, recruit, recruit.

Up to nine newcomers will dot the Dukes' roster. This season, instead of inheriting a team, Carroll is building one. It is a painful process, one in which success is likely to be incremental. Five of the nine are freshmen, and nobody wins an immediate league championship with that type of mix.

At least Carroll's feeling-out period is over. Presumably, so is the bad luck. Last year's team endured season-ending injuries to likely frontcourt contributors **Keith English, James Felix** and **Leroy Mabins,** plus a season-shortening injury to 6-0 point guard **Clayton Adams** (8.1 ppg, 4.1 rpg, 112 assists, 39 steals).

It is no coincidence that, following Adams'

187

return, the Dukes went 5-7. They were 1-8 without him. That put most of the load on Stevenson, who shattered just about every Duquesne single-season record following his transfer from Notre Dame. Neither of the previous record-holders, Nixon or Sihugo Green, even bettered the 700-point mark.

Adams, now a senior and a former teammate of Stevenson at Roman Catholic (Philadelphia) HS, will not make up for all those points. Instead, he and fellow senior **Tony Petrarca** (11.5 ppg, 4.2 rpg, 40 percent three-point shooting), a 6-3 bomber, should think about stabilizing this younger, deeper bunch while Carroll institutes the fashionable 94-foot game. It is a style Carroll wanted a year ago, but had to forego due to the body crunch.

"It's better for them in the long run," said a rival Atlantic 10 coach. "As good as Stevenson was, this league is too strong anymore to rely on one guy and be successful."

English, a 6-6 sophomore, Felix, a 6-5 senior, and Mabins, a 6-8 redshirt freshman, are among a host of hopefuls for three vacant frontcourt spots. English will have to hold off Iona transfer **Mark Gilbert**, a 6-5 soph, for Stevenson's job, while Mabins may be the backup at center to 6-10 junior **Willie Ladson**, another transfer from Champlain (Vermont) JC. A third transfer, 6-3 junior **James Hargrove**, comes from Southeastern (Iowa) CC and will play behind the returning backcourt starters.

Yet it is the four true freshmen who have the Golden Triangle buzzing. Bob Gibbons' scouting service rated the Dukes' signees second-best in the Atlantic 10, with Carroll and Co. combing typically Big East territory to get them.

Leading the way is 6-8 **Derrick Alston**, a polished frontcourt performer from Hoboken (N.J.) High. Alston can shoot (.610 from the floor) and play pressure defense (2.5 steals). Not far behind is 6-5 guard **Effrem Whitehead** (Brooklyn, N.Y.), who led Grady High to a 27-1 record and the New York state championship.

Alston and Whitehead figure to be first-year contributors. 6-1 **Ganon Baker** (Hampton HS/Hampton, Va.) will have to take his turn behind Adams at the point, while 6-7 **Sean Rooney** (Bayonne, N.J.) settles into a support role similar to the one he played at powerhouse St. Anthony's High. Rooney was also awaiting an eligibility determination (see *Late Breaking News* section).

No one knows what to expect from 6-5 sophomore **Alan Watkins**, who sat out last year. Brought in by former coach Jim Satalin, Watkins is another talented Roman Catholic (Philadelphia) HS product. Walk-ons **Donald Codey** (6-2 senior) and **Thomas Keegan** (6-3 soph) round out the roster.

BLUE RIBBON ANALYSIS

Carroll's second effort is younger, deeper and more versatile. And, despite lacking the obvious "go to" guy, it is also his team. He figures to use up to 10 players regularly, and that should keep internal competition and the energy level high.

Even more than setting a rotation, what Carroll has to overcome is Duquesne's stigma for losing. The Dukes haven't won in so long, no one in the program can remember the formula.

"We've had adversity," admitted Petrarca, the one Duke with the longest memory, "but last year we learned from it. We grew up together, and that's something we're taking into the season."

"Most of the time," Carroll echoed, "we played the game the way it should be played. This year, we hope to play the way we want to play."

Wanting and doing, however, are two different things. The Dukes are too new to seriously challenge the Atlantic 10 establishment, but could at least threaten .500 for the first time in five years. A move toward the middle of the conference pack is also not out of the question. Finally, this is a program headed back in the right direction.

EAST CAROLINA

LAST SEASON: 13-18
CONFERENCE RECORD: 6-8
STARTERS LOST: 0
STARTERS RETURNING: 5
CONFERENCE: COLONIAL ATHLETIC ASSOCIATION (CAA)
LOCATION: GREENVILLE, NC
HOME FLOOR: MINGES COLISEUM (6,500)
NICKNAME: PIRATES
COLORS: PURPLE AND GOLD
COACH: MIKE STEELE, record at East Carolina, 36-52. Career record, 160-92.

Obviously, a team like East Carolina is a lot less equipped to lose an NBA first round draft choice, as the Pirates did when Blue Edwards went to Utah in 1989, and not feel it than an ACC neighbor like North Carolina or Duke. So, the growing pains last year's young squad experienced during its 13-18 campaign were not unexpected. Edwards had lifted East Carolina from conference doormat (8-20 in '87-88) to respectability (15-14 in '88-89).

But even without Edwards consistent offensive presence, the Pirates came on last season to upset Richmond and American University while breaking a 10-game losing streak to archrival North Carolina—Wilmington. With all five starters back, coach Mike Steele's group figures to be that much better for the experience, much of which was gained with four first-year players in the starting lineup.

Two of those players, 6-3 sophomore guard **Steve Richardson** and 6-8 center **Ike Copeland**, made the Colonial all-freshman team. Now they will become cornerstones of a team to keep an eye on. Now in his fourth year, since leaving DePauw University

(Greencastle, Ind.), Steele has quietly emerged as a respected coach and leader. In Richardson (8.5 ppg, 1.5 rpg), he will have a reliable outside force. The Terre Haute, Ind., native broke numerous school three-point records, including the single game mark with eight against Navy. Copeland (8.9 ppg, 6.3 rpg) meanwhile, immediately established himself as a force near the basket. He led the Pirates in rebounding 13 times, tied for season lead in that category, and hit a team high 49.9 percent from the field.

The player Copeland tied for the team lead in rebounding was 6-7 senior forward **Tim Brown** (9.7 ppg, 6.3 rpg). Brown, who transferred after two years at Louisburg (N.C.) JC, also led the team in steals with 36. His 13-point, 14-rebound performance vs. conference champ James Madison last year evidenced his potential as an inside force. The frontcourt will be filled out by 6-5 senior forward **Stanley Love** (5.5 ppg, 3.9 rpg). Love serves primarily as a defensive specialist. However, his three-pointer at the buzzer to tie Richmond set up East Carolina's biggest victory last season. Working beside Richardson in the backcourt will be 6-2 senior point guard **Jeffrey Whitaker** (5.1 ppg, 2.1 rpg, 3.9 apg). Whitaker has a nice shooting touch to go with his ball handling ability.

East Carolina should also profit from an uncommonly deep bench that includes five players with experience. Foremost is 6-6 senior center forward **Darrell Overton** (3.8 ppg, 3.9 rpg). Overton proved out as a major contributor under the basket last season while leading the Pirates in blocked shots with 21. **Paul Childress** (2.0 ppg, 1.6 rpg, 3.5 assists), a 5-10 sophomore, will back up Whitaker at the point. Childress started 18 times last year. His ability to see the floor is reflected in his assist average which was compiled during limited minutes. 6-1 junior guard **Robin House** (2.4 ppg), a hometown guy from Greenville, as well as 6-7 junior center **Casey Mote** and 6-2 junior guard **Jeff Perlich**, saw limited time last year. But all are deemed worthy of contributing this year. How much they'll be called on depends on how fast the Pirates' strong recruiting class emerges.

It is highlighted by three promising freshmen. 6-5 forward **Kevin Armstrong** (15.6 ppg, 12.1 rpg) starred at Hunter Huss HS in Gastonia, N.C., the school that Sleepy Floyd made famous. 6-6 forward **Anton Gill** (26.5 ppg, 12.6 rpg) put up large numbers at Millbrook HS in Raleigh, N.C., while making All-AAAA North Carolina East and Wake County AAAA player of the year. **Lester Lyons**, a 6-2 guard (26.3 ppg, 4.0 rpg at Berties HS in Windsor, N.C.), also made All-AAAA East while leading his conference in scoring. East Carolina also reached out to the Bronx, N.Y., by way of Springfield, Mass. Technical CC, for 6-7 sophomore center/forward **Joe Brightwell**. Brightwell was a big fish in a small league last season, averaging 28 points and 16.6 rebounds while shooting 69.2 from the floor. Steele would be ecstatic with about half that product and three-quarters of that shooting percentage on the Division I level.

BLUE RIBBON ANALYSIS

The Pirates bring back a wealth of experience (10 lettermen) but lack the reliable, go-to offensive force in the Blue Edwards mold of two years ago. They are hoping one of the newcomers, Lyons or Blackwell, being the strong possibilities, can step right up as a consistent scorer.

East Carolina will also need some consistency from Richardson, its best three-point shooter. This is a good rebounding team with a patient offense and some quality at the point. The guards just need some people to throw the ball to. The Pirates' aggressive man-to-man and matchup zone defenses usually get the job done. However, they could use some improvement on the perimeter, particularly in stopping the three-pointer.

Look for East Carolina to be around .500, maybe a little above if it can find enough scoring, and to squeeze in, behind James Madison, Richmond and George Mason, to fourth place in the Colonial.

1990-91 EAST CAROLINA SCHEDULE

Nov.	24	North Carolina Wesleyan
	26	@Duke
Nov.	30-	
Dec.	1	#Boilermaker Invitational
Dec.	8	@Appalachian State
	15	Campbell (NC)
	17	College of Charleston (SC)
	22	Radford (VA)
	29	@Old Dominion
Jan.	2	Georgia Southern
	5	@Navy
	7	@American University
	12	James Madison
	14	George Mason
	19	@William & Mary
	23	Richmond
	26	@North Carolina Wilmington
	30	Liberty University (VA)
Feb.	2	American University
	4	Navy
	6	@Georgia Southern
	9	@James Madison
	11	@George Mason
	14	##Campbell
	16	William & Mary
	20	@Richmond
	23	North Carolina Wilmington
Mar.	2-4	*CAA Tournament

@ Road Games
# West Lafayette, IN (Indiana State, Loyola & Purdue)
Fayetteville, NC
* Richmond, VA

EASTERN KENTUCKY

LAST SEASON: 13-17
CONFERENCE RECORD: 7-5
STARTERS LOST: 1
STARTERS RETURNING: 4
CONFERENCE: OHIO VALLEY (OVC)
LOCATION: RICHMOND, KY
HOME FLOOR: ALUMNI COLISEUM (6,500)
NICKNAME: COLONELS
COLORS: MAROON AND WHITE
COACH: MIKE POLLIO, record at Eastern Kentucky, 13-17.
Career record, 195-109.

The Colonels were the OVC's most improved team in the second half of last season, advancing to the league title game and coming within a minute and a half of defeating champion Murray State on its home court. And they did it the old-fashioned way - with the team concept.

"We had the second-best record in the second half of the season," coach Mike Pollio confirmed, "and we did it without a single 'star'. We didn't have a single player make first- or second-team All-OVC, and we didn't put anybody on the All-Rookie team, either. But we came within a couple minutes of going to the NCAA tournament because of our team concept. We try to stay away from the star system, but we had some great role players."

Eastern Kentucky led the conference in scoring defense and rebounding margin, a tribute to their team concept, and those attributes are expected to carry over this season. The Colonels could even be among the OVC's elite, returning four starters and losing only small forward Mike Davis (10.1 ppg, 6.6 rpg).

So Pollio went hot and heavy in recruiting to fill that position. "We feel like that was our biggest priority," said the second-year coach, "and we think we filled the need."

Topping the list of newcomers is 6-6 junior **Tyrone Arrington** (20.2 ppg, 10.2 rpg), the Mississippi JUCO player of the year at East Mississippi JC. Another key recruit is bookend 6-6 junior **Toi Bell** (17.3 ppg, 8.2 rpg) of Belleville (Ill.) JC. They are joined by another transfer, 6-1 sophomore **Adrian Brown** (Arizona State), who becomes eligible following the first semester. If the transfers blend successfully with the returning talent, Eastern Kentucky can be even more formidable.

The top returnee for the Colonels is 6-3 forward **Aric Sinclair**, the lone contributing senior on a relatively young squad. Sinclair will be asked to take on a leadership role, after averaging 11.9 points and 4.9 rebounds as a junior and earning a spot on the OVC all-tournament team.

Returning at center is 6-9 junior **Mike Smith** (4.5 ppg, 7.9 rpg, 60 blocked shots), who came on strong at the end of the season and was an integral part of the Colonel's conference tournament drive. Although Smith's scoring was modest, his rebounding total was fifth in the league and his blocked shots were nearly twice as many as Tennessee Tech seven-footer Milos Babic, the OVC's only NBA draft pick.

Eastern is even stronger at the guard positions, returning both of last year's starters in 6-2 junior **Jamie Ross** (10.1 ppg, 3.2 rpg, 70 assists, 63 steals) and 6-0 junior **Derek Reuben** (8.9 ppg, 98 assists, 31 steals). Reserves at the guard positions are 6-1 junior **Kirk Greathouse** (7.4 ppg, 3.4 rpg), 6-3 sophomore **Chris Brown** (5.7 ppg), a hometown hero, and 6-1 junior **Brandon Baker** (1.4 ppg). Pollio says Baker will challenge Reuben for the starting point guard job. "Derek came on well for us," he said, "but Baker is pretty good, too."

Future help is also on hand, as the Colonels landed a trio of true freshmen in Pollio's first incoming class. 5-11 point guard **Arlando Johnson** (Owensboro HS/Owensboro, Ky.) and 6-7 forward **Ken Riley** (Southwestern HS/Detroit) were inked during the early signing period; 6-7 forward **John Allen** of nearby Cumberland County (Ky.) High came on board in the spring. Riley started for the Michigan Class A champions; Pollio called Johnson "the best point guard available in the state."

Filling out the roster are 6-8 senior **Vernon Evans** (0.5 ppg, 0.1 rpg), 6-8 junior **Ron Peck** and 6-0 walk-on freshman **Shawn Pfaadt**. Yet Pollio knowns that, for this season at least, it will be up to Sinclair and Smith to carry much of the Colonels' load.

"Smith is 6-9 and still developing," the coach said, "and Aric's role is more important than ever. He doesn't shoot well, but he has a gigantic heart. He's not a great scorer, but he will flat get after you."

BLUE RIBBON ANALYSIS

The Colonels were a middle-of-the-pack team last year, but one that saved its best ball for the stretch drive. If they can get any kind of carryover this season, Eastern Kentucky could vie with Murray State in the Ohio Valley Conference.

Eastern's greatest strengths are team defense and rebounding. If Pollio can somehow find just a little more offensive production (67.2 ppg, last in the OVC), the Colonels could conceivably could win it all. But that is probably asking a lot from a team full of new faces, and the lack of any proven explosiveness figures to keep Eastern Kentucky a notch or two below the league's top dogs.

1990-91 EASTERN KENTUCKY SCHEDULE

Nov.	28	North Carolina Greensboro
Dec.	1	Wilberforce (OH)
	3	Miami (OH)
	7-8	#Cougar Classic
	11	@Mississippi State

1990-91 EASTERN KENTUCKY SCHEDULE Cont.

Dec.	15	Bellarmine College (KY)
	21	North Carolina Wilmington
	27	@Kentucky
Jan.	3	Southern Illinois
	8	@Morehead State
	12	@Tennessee Tech
	14	@Tennessee State
	19	Middle Tennessee State
	21	@Colorado State
	23	@Missouri-Kansas City
	26	Austin Peay
	28	Murray State
	30	@Western Kentucky
Feb.	4	Morehead State
	6	@North Carolina Wilmington
	9	@Murray State
	11	@Austin Peay
	16	Missouri-Kansas City
	18	@Middle Tennessee State
	23	Tennessee State
	25	Tennessee Tech
Mar.	2, 6-7	*OVC Tournament

@ Road Games
# Provo, UT (Brigham Young, George Mason & St. John's)
* Site to be announced

EASTERN MICHIGAN

LAST SEASON: 19-13
CONFERENCE RECORD: 8-8
STARTERS LOST: 2
STARTERS RETURNING: 3
CONFERENCE: MID-AMERICAN (MAC)
LOCATION: YPSILANTI, MI
HOME FLOOR: BOWEN FIELD HOUSE (5,600)
NICKNAME: HURONS
COLORS: DARK GREEN AND WHITE
COACH: BEN BRAUN, record at Eastern Michigan, 76-59.

Eastern Michigan coach Ben Braun does not hedge when asked about his team's chances this season in the Mid-American Conference. As he sees it, the Hurons have a shot to be as good as anyone, even challenging consensus pick Bowling Green for the league title. Braun has nine lettermen returning, including three starters, along with a handful of potentially outstanding transfers and recruits.

"I think Bowling Green will be picked to win the league because they have everyone returning from a strong squad last year," said Braun. "But I would like to think we are one of the teams to be reckoned with. We came on so strong at the end of the MAC schedule."

Of course, the Hurons had to win six of their last eight MAC regular season games just to finish a disappointing 8-8 in the conference. They then split a pair in the MAC tournament before calling it a year.

Leading the list of returnees, who presumably learned from last year's roller coaster ride, is 6-0 senior point guard **Lorenzo Neely** (13.4 ppg, 2.8 rpg, 124 assists, 50 steals). A second-team All-MAC selection, Neely has been among the league's top backcourt men in each of his steady three seasons. His speed and quickness are ideal for a designed role as trigger man in the Hurons' effective full-court and half-court presses. Neely is also durable, not missing a game in 91 starts (Eastern is 57-34), and is plagued only by occasionally spotty shot selection (43 percent) and a higher-than-normal 98 turnovers.

Other starters back from last season are 6-8 junior **Kory Hallas** (12.5 ppg, 6.3 rpg, 35 steals) and 6-4 senior **Carl Thomas** (9.9 ppg, 4.1 rpg, 63 assists). Hallas, the last cut from the 1988 Canadian Olympic team, has shown flashes of being among the MAC's top big men and was honorable mention All-Conference a year ago. Thomas, who attended the same Everett (Lansing, Mich.) High School as Los Angeles Lakers' star Magic Johnson, improved his field goal percentage from .405 as a sophomore to .493 last year, also hitting a respectable 45-for-108 from three-point range (41.7 percent).

The key to any dramatic improvement from Eastern, however, could lie in the hands of 6-7 senior center **Marcus Kennedy.** A transfer from Ferris State, Kennedy must make the most of his one season at Eastern after averaging 20.4 points and 9.1 rebounds at Ferris. Braun agrees. "I think Marcus has the chance," he said, "based on his past performance, to be a very powerful inside player for us. He is a good athlete and runs the floor well."

Other frontcourt newcomers will vie for time in place of departed 6-8 bruiser Brian Nolan (11.0 ppg, 4.8 rpg, 49 blocked shots). Candidates include 6-7 sophomore **Fennoris Pearson,** a transfer from Central Michigan (eligible in Dec.) and 6-8 junior **Mike Boykin.** Although he is transferring from Vincennes (Ind.) JC, Boykin signed originally with Bobby Knight at Indiana. Pearson, at 220 pounds, is the smallest of the group. Among he, Kennedy and Boykin, nearly 700 pounds of beef is available up front.

If all the transfers make a major contribution, they will do so ahead of six other returning lettermen, headed by 6-5 sophomore **Chris Pipkin** (6.0 ppg, 2.9 rpg) and 6-3 senior **Charles Thomas** (5.1 ppg, 3.2 rpg). Pipkin was Pittsburgh's player of the year at New Brighton High; Thomas is the brother of starter Carl and, according to Braun, is "one of the more versatile players in the MAC."

Other returnees include 6-5 senior **Roger Lewis** (4.2 ppg, 2.2 rpg), a defensive specialist and part-time starter, 5-11 junior guard **Joe Frasor** (1.5 ppg, 1.0 rpg), 6-8 senior **Pete Pangas** (1.5 ppg, 1.3 rpg) and 6-2 sophomore **Von Nickleberry** (1.5 ppg).

Two in-state freshman recruits round out the Hurons' roster, 5-10 point guard **Kahlil Felder** (Pershing HS/Detroit) and 6-6 swingman **Jeff Wendt** (Okemos HS/Okemos, Mich.). Felder could be the heir apparent to Neely, coming off a final prep season in which he averaged 14 points, eight assists and seven rebounds, good enough for second-team Class A all-state honors. Wendt averaged 23.8 points and 11.2 rebounds, becoming a third-team All-State choice.

BLUE RIBBON ANALYSIS

With three starters and six other lettermen returning, Braun knows leadership will not be a problem. "We have some real quality players returning," he said, "and the seniors will be the key. Lorenzo Neely has been one of the premier guards in the league for three years, and I anticipate that he will have a strong final year. We also expect that Carl Thomas will give us improved play, and Kory Hallas is a proven offensive player."

Braun is also counting on a faster start and a more physical presence up front to boost the Hurons in conference play. The addition of Kennedy, who could be a star, should help Eastern win most rebounding battles.

"Our overall strength will be significantly improved," said Braun. "Our veterans worked very hard in the offseason to get stronger, and Kennedy, Pearson and Boykin are very strong, physical players. We also ended last year as one of the hottest teams in the league."

Amen. But a second-place finish to Bowling Green is the pick here.

EVANSVILLE

LAST SEASON: 17-15
CONFERENCE RECORD: 8-6
STARTERS LOST: 3
STARTERS RETURNING: 2
CONFERENCE: MID WESTERN COLLEGIATE (MCC)
LOCATION: EVANSVILLE, IN
HOME FLOOR: ROBERTS STADIUM (12,300)
NICKNAME: ACES
COLORS: PURPLE AND WHITE
COACH: JIM CREWS, record at Evansville, 87-60.

At times last season, Evansville coach Jim Crews questioned his team's commitment to winning. He said some of his players talked a better game than they played, and gave only lip service to such things as 100 percent effort.

Frustrated? You bet. The Aces were coming off a 25-6 record two seasons ago, a year in which they even won a game in the NCAA tournament, beating Oregon State. Many thus picked Evansville to contend with Xavier for the Midwestern Collegiate Conference championship.

Then, before the season even began, Crews deleted Reed Crafton from his roster for disciplinary reasons. Crafton had averaged 10.8 points and 6.8 assists the year before and was the heir-apparent to sharp-shooting Scott Haffner (24.5 ppg).

Things went downhill quickly after that. Evansville lost its All-MCC center, Dan Godfread, for most of the season with a broken foot, and the Aces finished fifth in the MCC at 8-6. As for Crews, he was nearly happy to see the season end. "It was really a struggle for these kids," he said. "Too many of them were forced to take on roles that they didn't expect to have."

Now comes 1990-91, and rebuilding is the order of the day. The Aces lost their entire front line to graduation - Godfread (19.9 ppg, 8.3 rpg), Brian Hill (14.9 ppg, 5.4 rpg), and Chris Mack (10.1 ppg, 6.4 rpg). The only returning starters are 6-4 sophomore **Chaka Chandler** (9.1 ppg, 2.7 rpg) and 6-1 junior **Scott Schreffler** (13.2 ppg, 5.8 assists).

Schreffler is the team's top returning player. He led the MCC in free throw percentage (.884), was second in three-point shooting (.434), fifth in assists (184), and 13th in scoring. He needs just 85 assists to pass Haffner and become the Evansville career leader. Twice last season, against Michigan State and St. Louis, Schreffler scored a career-high 27 points.

Evansville, of course, has developed a reputation for winning with three guards and bombs-away three-point shooting. Two years ago, the Aces hit 213 three-point field goals, and last season they again led the MCC by dialing long distance 147 times.

Not surprisingly, the three-pointer is once again a staple of the Aces' arsenal. In addition to Schreffler and Chandler, **Billy Reid,** a 6-4 junior transfer from Purdue, is expected to receive considerable playing time. Another outside shooter, Reid started 10 games for the Boilermakers in 1988-89, but his freshman season was hampered by a knee injury.

Adding suspense and competition to the back-court will be three high-scoring freshmen recruits. 5-10 **Mark Hisle** was an All-State guard at Terre Haute (Ind.) North HS, where he averaged 26.6 points per game. One of the few prep players in the state who outscored Hisle was 6-3 **Parrish Casebier** (South Spencer HS/Rockport, Ind.). Casebier also signed with the Aces, bringing a 32.2 scoring average with him. Finally, 6-1 **Todd Cochenour** (Mooresville HS/Mooresville, Ind.) averaged 24.5 points as a prep senior with a single-game high of 62.

"We obviously have a lot of new faces and that creates a lot of questions," Crews said. "I'm sure we'll do a great deal of experimenting early in the season. Our team had very little depth at guard last season. This year, we have a lot of players at that position."

The opposite is true up front. "For the past three years," said Crews, "we've had a talented and experienced center in Dan Godfread. Now that Dan has graduated, we have a big void to fill."

The coach is really high on 7-0 sophomore **Saacha Hupmann** (2.4 ppg, 3.7 rpg), a hard worker who reached double figures in rebounding three times as a freshman despite twice suffering broken bones in his feet. Offensively unpolished, the West German native was a defensive presence and above average on the boards.

Also returning is 6-9 senior **Mark Jewell** (4.2 ppg, 4.1 rpg). He, too, was a starter early in the season, but missed most of January with a broken foot. That's right - Godfread, Jewell and Hupmann all had foot maladies last season. The only frontcourt veteran who got through the year unscathed is 6-6 sophomore **Eldridge Bolin** (0.9 ppg, 0.6 rpg). 5-8 senior **Shane Barrett** (0.3 ppg, 0.4 rpg) was a deep reserve in the backcourt after walking-on, literally, from a spot as starting midfielder on Evansville's nationally-ranked soccer team. Barrett will again hit the hardwood following soccer season.

Joining the high-scoring freshmen as newcomers are a pair of transfers, 6-4 junior **Charles Chambers** (Wabash Valley JC) and 6-6 junior **Lennox Forrester** (Parkland College, Ill.). 6-6 **Scott Fahnestock** (Avon Lake HS/Avon Lake, Ohio) is the final freshman signee.

BLUE RIBBON ANALYSIS

The MCC is much lot tougher than it was when Evansville used to be one of the dominant teams. It is also deeper than it was two seasons back, when the Aces made their loudest mark in the league and the NCAA tournament.

For the Aces to challenge the first division this winter, Hupmann has got to play enough quality minutes to offset the loss of Godfread. An inside presence is also a must on nights when the threes refuse to fall.

Even with a productive Hupmann, however, Evansville still has too many holes - particularly at forward - to crack the top of the conference. They may even slip below .500 and the middle of the standings as the current rebuilding effort continues.

1990-91 EVANSVILLE SCHEDULE

Nov.	24	@Miami (OH)
	26	@Ohio University
Dec.	1	Valparaiso (IN)
	4	@Northern Illinois
	10	Indiana State
	15	Cincinnati
	18	@Michigan State
	20	Bethune-Cookman (FL)
	22	Samford (AL)
	29	Eastern Michigan
Jan.	2	@Siena
	5	Southern Illinois
	10	Detroit
	12	Dayton
	17	@Xavier
	19	@Dayton
	24	Marquette
	26	@Loyola
	31	@St. Louis
Feb.	2	Loyola
	7	@Detroit
	9	@Butler
	14	Xavier
	16	Butler
	21	@Marquette
	25	Northeastern Illinois
Mar.	3	St. Louis
	7-9	#MCC Tournament

@ Road Games
# Dayton, OH

FAIRFIELD

LAST SEASON: 10-18
CONFERENCE RECORD: 6-10
STARTERS LOST: 2
STARTERS RETURNING: 3
CONFERENCE: METRO ATLANTIC ATHLETIC (MAAC)
LOCATION: FAIRFIELD, CT
HOME FLOOR: ALUMNI HALL (3,022)
NICKNAME: STAGS
COLORS: CARDINAL RED
COACH: MITCH BUONAGURO, record at Fairfield, 64-82

Mitch Buonaguro has seen both sides of the proverbial double-edged sword during his stay in Connecticut. The Stag supporters, unquestionably some of the wildest in the east, hysterically chanted ''Mitch is God'' during Fairfield's MAAC championship seasons of '86 and '87. But recent losing campaigns have turned the tide, and catcalls of ''Ditch Mitch'' could be heard reverberating through noisy Alumni Hall the past two seasons. This could be the pivotal season in Buonaguro's reign as head Stag, especially since he is in the final year of a long term contract.

The talent appears to now be in place. Fairfield returns three starters from last season's 10-18 squad and no less than five other players who saw considerable action in '89-90. Couple that with what on paper is the MAAC's best recruiting class, and the Stags could be ready to make another run toward the top of a cloudy MAAC picture.

6-6 senior forward **Harold Brantley** (11.7 ppg, 7.2 rpg) and a pair of sophomores, MAAC all-rookie pick 6-8 forward **Drew Henderson** (5.5 ppg, 7.6 rpg) and 6-1 guard **Kevin George** (6.0 ppg) are the returning starters. Brantley is a fierce leaper and defender who has continually improved his offensive game all three of his seasons while finishing second on the team in rebounding. Henderson stepped right in to lead the Stags on the boards but will have to step up on the offensive side with the graduation of leading scorer Marvin Walters (12.3 ppg). George finished second on the team in assists last season (67) and showed flashes of the steady play that Buonaguro needs in his very young backcourt.

Like the championship Fairfield teams of the mid-80s, the key to this one will be depth. There is not one franchise player on the squad, like an A. J. Wynder or a Troy Bradford. Instead Buonaguro will go with no less than 11 or 12 players to make the Stag system work. In the frontcourt 6-8 sophomore forward **Todd Holland** and 6-9 junior forward **Ed Newman** will increase their court time. Holland averaged 3.5 ppg and 3.1 rpg in his sophomore season while Newman is looking to bounce back off an injury-plagued campaign that saw him appear in only nine contests (1.0 ppg). 6-5 junior swingman **Terry Fitzsimons** (4.6 ppg) is Fairfield's leading returning three-point shooter, but will have to up his 29 percent average from beyond the three-point mark. 6-5 senior **Mike Rodgers** (1.1 ppg) and 6-1 senior **Mike Plansky** (1.6 ppg) will also gain added backcourt time.

If the key to winning close games, as many say, is free throws and defense, then the Stags are halfway to solving the 10-18 riddle that was '89-90. They held opponents to just 41 percent from the floor to lead the MAAC, but shot a woeful 57 percent from the free throw line. The Stags also finished last in the MAAC in scoring offense (57.7 ppg) and must improve if they are to move up.

The relief should come from a combination of the maturing younger players like George and Holland along with the very talented incoming freshman class. Hot-shooting 6-4 guard **Scott Sytulek** should bring the quickest offensive fix. The all-state selection from nearby New Britain, Conn., averaged 23.0 ppg in his senior year while shooting 57 percent from the floor, even more impressive when you consider that no Stag shot over 50 percent last season. Two other backcourt freshmen, 6-3 **Craig Martin** and 6-1 speedster **Johnnie Jones**, will push hard for playing time. Martin averaged 19.4 ppg for Roselle (N.J.) HS, and like classmate Sytulek averaged over 50 percent from the floor. Jones poured in 15.3 ppg and 3.1 assists while helping lead powerhouse Brewster Academy (N.H.) to the New England Prep School title game.

In the frontcourt, Fairfield adds 6-6 **Chris Barry** and 6-7 **Kris Steele**. Barry also connected on over 50 percent of his high school shots (58 percent) while helping St. Rose HS (Belmar, N.J.) to a 20-6 record. Steele completes the picture as the inside player of the five newcomers. He averaged 18.2 ppg and 12.3 rpg for Southington (Conn.) HS and will also push for quality playing time.

BLUE RIBBON ANALYSIS

Buonaguro appears to have the pieces in place. However, winning with freshmen is no easy task, and it is very hard to break the habit of losing close games, which has become the Stag trademark in recent years. George, Henderson and Holland are solid defensive players. Now, they must prove their offensive ability. The presence of five quality freshmen, four of which could be MAAC all-rookie selections at year's end, will take some pressure off the returnees. Keep in mind that the pressure to win is there, especially given the status of their fiery head coach.

If the Stags get off to a good start it will be a big year in Connecticut. If not, the five freshmen could have a new coach come their sophomore campaign.

This team should be at least .500 and no lower than fourth in the MAAC, but only time will tell if even that is enough for Buonaguro to see his young bucks grow into full Stags. That razor can be very sharp.

1990-91 FAIRFIELD SCHEDULE

Nov.	27	@Harvard
	29	@Miami (OH)
Dec.	1	Marist
	3	Bucknell
	5	@Central Connecticut
	9	Richmond
	11	@Gonzaga (WA)
	23	@Connecticut
Jan.	3	Yale
	5	Canisius
	9	Loyola College
	12	Manhattan
	14	@Maine
	19	@Niagara
	21	@Canisius
	26	Siena
	29	Niagara
	31	@La Salle
Feb.	3	@St. Peter's
	6	@Iona
	9	St. Peter's
	11	La Salle
	13	@Virginia
	16	@Manhattan
	19	@Loyola College
	21	Iona
	25	@Siena
Mar.	1-4	#MAAC Tournament

@ Road Games
# Albany, NY

FAIRLEIGH DICKINSON

LAST SEASON: 16-13
CONFERENCE RECORD: 8-8
STARTERS LOST: 1
STARTERS RETURNING: 4
CONFERENCE: NORTHEAST (NEC)
LOCATION: TEANECK, NJ
HOME FLOOR: ROTHMAN CENTER (5,000)
NICKNAME: KNIGHTS
COLORS: COLUMBIA BLUE, MAROON AND WHITE
COACH: TOM GREEN, record at Fairleigh Dickinson, 135-72.

Tom Green has been very successful from the minute he came to Fairleigh Dickinson from Tulane eight years ago. He built the Fairleigh Dickinson program into one of the best in the Northeast Conference, taking the Knights to the NCAA tournament twice in that span.

But last year had to be somewhat of a disappointment for Green and the Knights, especially after the 1988-89 season ended with such promise and vitality. Two seasons ago, in what was thought to be a rebuilding year, the Knights won 13 of their last 18 games before dropping a hard-fought two-point decision to Robert Morris in the Northeast Conference title game. With four starters returning, that winning attitude was supposed to carry over into the 1989-90 season.

However, it didn't. The Knights stumbled through their Northeast Conference slate, losing five conference games in a row at one point, Fairleigh Dickinson lost some games in the final minutes that they should have won. The Knights lost to teams that were inferior in talent. The result was a mediocre 16-13 season, an 8-8 mark in the league, good for only fifth place and a rapid exit in the Northeast Conference tournament.

However, the outlook is not dismal for the Knights this season. Once again, Green returns four starters from a year ago, including the NEC player of the year, **Desi Wilson**. They have plenty of offensive weapons that should be able to shine in the league. And they have a great crop of newcomers to add to the roster. So, the prospects look good for the Knights to be a force in the NEC this season. Then again, the prospects were bright a year ago and look what happened. There is one given concerning the Knights and that is Wilson will come to play every night and eventually, he will hurt you in some capacity. The 6-7 senior forward did it all last season, winning player of the year honors by averaging 22.3 points and 9.1 rebounds per game. Wilson shot a sizzling 57 percent from the floor and was the nation's 29th leading scorer. He can shoot from the outside and take it to the basket with incredible ease in both facets. He is an aggressive rebounder who gets a good portion of his points on second chance baskets. Wilson is also a very consistent player, reaching double figures in each of the Knights' 29 games last year. He is easily the most dominant player in the NEC, one who can control games offensively on his own. Wilson is also a fine defender, evident by his 34 blocked shots (fourth in the NEC) and 58 steals (first in the league). It's easy to see why Wilson was the NEC player of the year and should be even better this season.

But the wealth of returning talent doesn't stop there. Junior swingman **Brad McClain** is back. The 6-5 McClain (10.7 ppg, 4.6 rpg) started 25 of the Knights' 29 games a year ago, moving back and fourth from shooting guard to small forward. McClain is a deadly long range shooter, connecting on more than half of the Knights' total three-point field goals (56 of the team's 107). McClain is also an aggressive defender and a very heady player. With the departure of Eric Odom, the team's No. 2 scorer a year ago behind Wilson, McClain should see his offensive production numbers skyrocket this season. But McClain is a coach's dream, plays hard, does what he is told and shoots the ball very well. He should have a big season.

Senior point guard **Mel Hawkins** is also back for his final go-round. The diminutive Hawkins (10.2 ppg, 3.2 rpg, 151 assists) stands just 5-9 when perched on the Yellow Pages, but he is aggressive going to the basket and remarkably strong. That strength sends Hawkins to the free throw line constantly. His 122 attempts were third best on the team last season. They represented a very high number of tries for a point guard, a 5-9 point guard no less. Hawkins doesn't let his small stature deter him defensively. He has extremely quick hands, coming away with 44 steals a year ago. Hawkins might not scare you at first sight, but he is a talent to be reckoned with.

More than likely, Hawkins' counterpart in the backcourt will be 6-5 senior **Glenn Harding** (6.9 ppg, 3.0 rpg). Harding started 20 games last year and he also played both small forward and off-guard last season. Harding, with a reputation of being a solid outside shooter and one who could get on a roll at times, never really got a streak going last year. He connected on just 41 percent of his attempts after nailing 48 percent as a sophomore. If Harding can return to his sophomore shooting form, then coupled with the sharpshooting of McClain, the Knights may have the best long range team in the NEC.

Junior forward **Wendell Brereton** (5.2 ppg, 4.2 rpg) will get the first crack at trying to replace Odom up front. The 6-6 Brereton started 10 games last year and was the Knights' top man off the bench in other games, averaging 21.9 minutes per game. Brereton

is a very physical player, using his strength to his advantage close to the basket. He also has a fine shooting touch, hitting 48 percent from the floor.

Senior guard **Todd Zimmerman** (4.8 ppg, 2.3 rpg) is another fine perimeter player for the Knights. The 6-5 Zimmerman started four games last season and became very valuable down the stretch, averaging 8.1 points over the final six contests. Zimmerman shot 49 percent from the floor, but he did even better from three-point land, nailing 51 percent. Zimmerman is the perfect role player who should see more time this season. Senior guard **Tony Warren** (3.6 ppg, 1.8 rpg) started at the point to begin the season before relinquishing the reigns to Hawkins. The 6-0 Warren had some moments of brilliance, including 17 against Indiana State, but saw his playing time dwindle by the season's close. Just how much Warren contributes this season depends on how hard he worked in the off-season to improve his poor 37 percent field goal mark. Sophomore guard **Rodney Caldwell** is the last returnee. The 6-5 Chicagoan saw very little action last year, scoring two points in seven games, totalling just 16 minutes.

Two highly touted freshmen of a year ago, both named Robinson, return to finally make their debuts with the Knights after redshirting as freshmen. Guard **Tony Robinson** (Lorain (Ohio) HS) is a 6-3 flash with all the tools. He averaged 17.3 points and grabbed 8.3 rebounds per game as a senior at Lorain. He is an aggressive player who goes strong to the basket and still has the ability to play the perimeter. Center/forward **Brad Robinson** comes to the Knights from the Great White North. The 6-8, 215 pound Robinson played his high school ball at Peterborough HS in Canada and has good physical skills, especially running the floor and finishing fast breaks.

However, both Robinsons are coming off knee injuries which kept them out of action last year. Just how well they recovered from their respective knee problems remains to be seen.

Two academic casualties of a year ago are now eligible: sophomore forwards **Clive Anderson** and **Louis Wilson**. Anderson, a 6-7 leaper from Kingston, Jamaica, is considered more of a project and last year's failure to gain experience didn't help his chances of seeing quality time this year. However, Wilson is a stud. The 6-7 power forward from Amityville (N.Y.) HS averaged 21.0 points, 11.0 rebounds and four blocked shots per game as a senior. He also has a fine shot from close in and on the short perimeter. Wilson is a solid athlete who will compete with Brereton for the inside slot vacated by Odom.

Green also adds two freshmen signees to the Knights' roster in guards, **David Freeman** and **Anthony Hughes**. Freeman, a 6-2 off-guard from Battle Creek (Mich.) Central HS, averaged 16.1 points and 4.5 assists per game, leading Central into the Michigan Final Four. Hughes, a 5-11 point guard from Covington (Ky.) Holmes HS, averaged 14.5 points, 7.8 assists and three steals per game as a senior. Hughes is as quick as a fox and should fit in well with the Knights' fast break offensive attack.

BLUE RIBBON ANALYSIS

There is no question that Tom Green has the horses necessary to take the Knights into the front of the Northeast Conference this season. There is a nice blend of size, strength, athletic ability, quickness and shooting prowess. It is all there.

But so it was a year ago, and the Knights failed miserably. They will have to find it within themselves to perform on a higher level this time and chances are that the experience of last season will be an extreme motivational factor in 1990-91.

Any team that can return a talent like Desi Wilson has to be reckoned with. If Wilson's career continues to skyrocket toward stardom, the professional scouts will just have to take notice. He is that good. But the Knights also can offer some support for Wilson.

McClain, Harding and Hawkins are all players who can pick up the load if Wilson falters a little. And Louis Wilson is a player of impact.

The Knights should return to contending status in the NEC this year. Most definitely, the talent is there. On paper, they could be considered the favorite to win the league, or to duel Marist to the wire. But that's on paper. On the floor is another tale. If past performances don't haunt the Knights, the rest seems to be in line for a shot at another trip to the NCAA tournament. If so, it would be the school's third in seven years.

1990-91 FAIRLEIGH DICKINSON SCHEDULE		
Nov.	24	@Wake Forest
	28	@Boston University
Dec.	1	Maine
	4	Niagara
	8	@San Francisco
	10	@U.S. International (CA)
	15	@St. Peter's
	22	#Central Connecticut
	29	Yale
Jan.	3	Monmouth
	5	Wagner
	8	@St. Francis (PA)
	10	@Robert Morris
	12	@Marist
	17	@Mt. St. Mary's (MD)
	22	St. Francis (NY)
	24	Long Island
	26	@Wagner
	28	@Monmouth
Feb.	2	Marist
	4	@Rider
	7	Robert Morris
	9	St. Francis (PA)
	11	Northeastern
	16	Mt. St. Mary's (MD)
	21	@Long Island
	23	@St. Francis (NY)
Feb. 26 & 28, Mar. 2		*Northeast Conference Tournament

@ Road Games
# Meadowlands Arena, East Rutherford, NJ
* Site to be announced

FLORIDA

LAST SEASON: 7-21
CONFERENCE RECORD: 3-15
STARTERS LOST: 1
STARTERS RETURNING: 4
CONFERENCE: SOUTHEASTERN (SEC)
LOCATION: GAINESVILLE, FL
HOME FLOOR: O'CONNELL CENTER (12,000)
NICKNAME: GATORS
COLORS: ORANGE AND BLUE
COACH: LON KRUGER, first year at Florida.
Career record, 133-105.

In the category for most convincing performance in a first-to-worst collapse, Florida had few challengers in 1990. Champions of the SEC in 1988-89, by midseason a year ago the Gators fielded a team reminiscent in SEC talent of the 1960's, when league head basketball coaches might be "promoted" to assistant football coach.

But unless a severe NCAA penalty rears its head - still a possibility - the worst should be over at Florida. And, at the end of last year's dizzying downward spiral stood an unexpected glimmer of hope, new head coach Lon Kruger.

Kruger's credentials from a four-year run at Kansas State were impeccable, both on the court (81-46 record, four straight trips to the NCAA's, one game shy of the Final Four in 1988) and off (clean-cut roster, never a hint of scandal, five players last year with B averages or better).

Before returning to Kansas State, where he had been Big Eight player of the year in 1973 and 1974, Kruger spent four years as head coach at Pan American, where he went from a 7-21 first season to 20-8 in his final year. The only shock, even among the Florida faithful, was that he could be lured from his alma mater to the long-running Gainesville basketball soap opera.

Don DeVoe, fresh from an ouster at Tennessee, took over the Gators' program on an interim basis just after the start of practice last season when crusty old Norm Sloan was forced out amid the continual allegations of NCAA wrongdoing. DeVoe got on board just in time for the 7-21 nightmare that followed, and announced late in the season that he did not care to be a candidate for full-time employment. What's more, he said in parting, he doubted any other coach of consequence and sound mind would either.

Yet less than a month later, there stood young, vibrant, headed-to-the-top Kruger at a press conference announcing his acceptance of the job. Florida fans, hardened on controversy, would have been excused for wondering: "Yeah, but what's the catch."

"He's not a good choice," said noted philosopher Dick Vitale. "He's a great choice. I was shocked when I heard it. I didn't think Florida would be able to get such a quality coach under the circumstances."

"I'd say he's in the top five young college coaches in the country," added Orlando Magic general manager Pat Williams. "Florida really pulled one off here." Indeed. Two years earlier, Kruger turned down a similar opportunity from a much more stable situation at Texas.

"Lon was always mentioned as someone we would be fortunate to attract," said Florida athletic director Bill Arnsparger. "At the same time, those same people thought we could not interest Lon from leaving his alma mater."

The eventual cheers in Florida were matched only by the groans in Kruger's home state of Kansas. "A big thing was timing," the new coach explained. "When the Texas job came up, I'd only been home two years."

Even when the Gators' offer came, Kruger insisted he was totally satisfied at Kansas State, but that "Florida just has so much potential for the 1990's." In the end, Arnsparger offered the job to no one else, and when Kruger "just said yes" to a reported $300,000-per-year package, Florida had its first good news since the SEC championship.

Even Sloan, who wasted few opportunities to take pot shots at DeVoe, admitted it was a good choice. "He's a good coach," said Sloan, "and he'll do a fine job as long as he has the talent to win in the SEC. That's what it all comes down to - getting players."

Did anyone mention that Kruger is no virgin to Florida's vast talent pool? That five players on his final Kansas State team were Florida natives? So, too, Kansas State alum Mitch Richmond, the 1989 NBA rookie of the year, who has said of his former coach: "When I was playing as well as I thought I could, he was still able to point out little things that helped make me better."

All of which means Kruger will likely spend a lot of time pointing in his first year at Florida. Arriving in Gainesville just 11 days before the national signing date, he could not make much headway in upgrading the depleted talent pool. He did sign three high school prospects, though none are likely to make a quick impact in the SEC.

But the Gators got immediately better when power forward **Livingston Chatman,** the first star to flee DeVoe's sinking ship last year, joined Kruger at his introductory press conference. Chatman brings

averages of 12.6 points, 7.0 rebounds and 3.7 assists into his final collegiate season after consenting to play just 10 games as a junior.

There is other unpleasantness to take care of before happy days and Kruger's own blend of milk and honey return. Florida should learn once and for all its fate with the NCAA just before the season starts. Some sort of probation seems likely - Sloan himself has predicted as much - but Kruger knew that coming in.

"You're always concerned about something like that," Kruger said, "but it was obvious to me that the university had fully cooperated. They've got everything in order and have made all the appropriate changes."

At the least, Kruger will have a honeymoon with Gator fans, which is more than could be said of DeVoe in his fill-in role. And Kruger will not have the Dwayne Schintzius problem, which may have been DeVoe's undoing.

Schintzius, whose imposing 7-2 presence and soft shooting touch was often offset by his even bigger nose for trouble, is the only player from last year's roster not returning. And he played in only 11 games, quitting the team at the business end of a Great Haircut Debate that dominated January headlines in Florida (At least two local newspapers interviewed Schintzius' barber after DeVoe demanded shorter locks).

Many thought Schintzius' departure was fairly predictable when DeVoe's no-nonsense approach took over the loose ship Sloan had run. The surprise was Chatman, more of an overachieving, blue collar type who defected two weeks earlier. Frustrated by the internal bickering, Chatman cited "burn-out" as his reason for leaving and said he "just needed to get away from basketball for a while."

Minus both of them, Florida physically resembled some of the better SEC fraternity league teams and lost 14 straight games. A late-season victory over LSU is now mentioned as one of the great upsets in conference history.

With Chatman back on board, along with 6-7 senior center **Dwayne Davis** and 6-6 sophomore forward **Stacey Poole,** Kruger and the Gators at least have something to build a team around. It is certainly a better foundation than the post-Schintzius/Chatman Gators, who played stall-ball and hoped for the best. They avoided blowouts, but also victories for the most part.

Kruger, never married to any one style at Kansas State, is not tipping his hand on how the Gators will attack. "We want to be able to dictate on both ends of the floor," he said, painting a few broad strokes. "We want to be able to extend our defense and have it create opportunities offensively. On offense, we want to push the ball and get the first good shot that's available. But there's a lot of things you have to be able to do to play that way. For one, you have to be able to rebound."

Even though the Gators will rarely have anyone on the floor over 6-foot-7, rebounding should be the strength of the team. Chatman (16.1 ppg, 7.0 rpg in 1988-89), a 230-pound monster, was named to the pre-season All-SEC team before last year's ill-fated start and was MVP of the 1989 SEC tournament. A return to his past form would be a major plus, considering the solid development of Davis and Poole.

Davis, a second-team All-SEC selection, instituted the 3-D offense at Florida ("Dwayne Davis Dunks") while leading the team in scoring and rebounding (12.3 ppg, 8.5 rpg). Strictly an inside player, Davis shot 65 percent from point-blank range and was third in the SEC with 45 blocked shots.

Yet Poole was probably Florida's best player over the last half of the season (10.0 ppg, 4.3 rpg), emerging as a real force on the wing. A redshirt freshman who sat out his first year after severing an achilles tendon, Poole was on the 25-member *McDonald's* All-America team coming out of Forrest (Jacksonville) High.

Inside depth will come from sophomore **Travis Schintzius,** Dwayne's younger, smaller (6-8, 210

pounds) and presumably less controversial brother, and 6-7 junior **Tim Turner.** Neither saw much action last year.

6-7 freshman **Louis Rowe** (17.0 ppg, 6.0 rpg at Lakewood HS, St. Petersburg) could help at the wing, but is probably more suited to guard. But the Gators are well-stocked with guards, most of whom started at one time or another. Still, only 6-2 senior **Renaldo Garcia** (11.6 ppg, 2.4 rpg, 66 assists, 25 steals) is a proven scoring threat.

Early favorite for the point guard spot is 6-0 sophomore **Scott Stewart** (5.3 ppg, 1.8 rpg, 41 assists, 23 steals), who made a splash while starting the final 11 games last year. He had eight assists in his first start against Georgia, then scored 16 points in the major upset of LSU.

5-7 senior **B.J. Carter** (5.8 ppg, 45 assists) and 6-0 sophomore **Willie Jackson** (2.9 ppg) could challenge, though Jackson also plays football and will not join the basketball team until those duties are completed. 6-1 sophomore **Hosie Grimsley** (5.9 ppg) started at times at both guard spots and could also push for a full-time job this season.

A lift for the Gators would be more consistent play from 6-2 junior **Brian Hogan,** a three-point specialist (27 of his 30 field goals last year were treys), who hit 40 percent from the outer reaches. Other guard candidates include 6-3 freshman **Craig Brown** (Steelton, Pa.) and 6-4 freshman **Carlos McMillan** (Chattahoochee, Fla.)

BLUE RIBBON ANALYSIS

No one seems to doubt that Kruger will eventually get the job done at Florida, either sooner (with mirrors) or later (if stiff NCAA sanctions put a damper on another recruiting class). For the present, however, it looks like another long, if less controversial season for the Gators.

Florida can field a solid inside game, but has little depth for foul trouble. Depth abounds outside, but with no player to light it up night after night. For this year, getting out of the SEC cellar will be an accomplishment. Reaching the SEC first division, given all that has gone done, will be a major miracle.

1990-91 FLORIDA SCHEDULE		
Nov.	24	@South Florida
	27	Texas
	30	@Florida State
Dec.	5	@James Madison
	7-8	#Carrier Classic
	15	Augusta College (GA)
	21	@Stanford
	30	Miami (OH)
Jan.	2	Mississippi
	5	Auburn
	9	@Alabama
	12	@Georgia
	16	Tennessee
	19	Mississippi State
	23	@Kentucky
	26	@LSU
	30	Vanderbilt
Feb.	2	@Mississippi
	6	@Auburn
	9	Alabama
	12	Georgia
	16	@Tennessee
	20	@Mississippi State
	23	Kentucky
	27	Louisiana State
Mar.	2	@Vanderbilt
	7-10	##SEC Tournament

@ Road Games
# Syracuse, NY (Alaska-Anchorage, North Carolina Charlotte & Syracuse)
@@ Nashville, TN

FLORIDA STATE

LAST SEASON: 16-15
CONFERENCE
RECORD: 6-9
STARTERS LOST: 2
STARTERS
RETURNING: 3
CONFERENCE: METRO
LOCATION:
TALLAHASSEE, FL
HOME FLOOR: TALLAHASSEE-LEON
COUNTY CIVIC CENTER (12,500)
NICKNAME: SEMINOLES
COLORS: GARNET AND GOLD
COACH: PAT KENNEDY, record at Florida State,
76-45.
Career record, 200-105.

The best thing that happened to Florida State coach Pat Kennedy in 1989-90 was he was offered the Tennessee coaching job. That happened at the 1989 Final Four in Seattle. He turned the job offer down, which was gratefully accepted by Louisville assistant Wade Houston.

After his decision, it was pretty much all downhill for Kennedy. The best recruit in Florida State history, 6-9 Doug Edwards of Miami (Fla.) Senior HS, failed to qualify academically and sat out last year. Then, after Florida State won 10 of 11 games in late December and early January, star guard Tharon Mayes was suspended for the month of February after getting in a fight with a campus security officer.

Mayes was among Metro scoring leaders at the time of his suspension. By the time he returned, the Seminoles had lost four of seven games, had blown any chance of a post-season tournament and were lucky to break the .500 mark.

Kennedy, who called the season ''my toughest year in coaching,'' refused to use Mayes' absence as a reason for the late season dive. The season started and ended losing games in the last seconds. The Seminoles lost five games in the final minute, four on last second shots.

''Sometimes, the publicity and notoriety created by your program helped other teams get extremely ready to play us,'' Kennedy said. ''People raised their intensity level when they played us. Our kids didn't understand that and didn't raise their level of play.''

Last season was a shocker for Kennedy, a super recruiter who got used to the program is progression. Since taking over at Florida State in 1986-87, the Seminoles had gone from two 19-11 seasons to 22-8 in 1988-89.

Florida State will gulp early and often this season trying to replace seniors Mayes, a 6-3 guard (23.3 ppg), and 6-9 center Irving Thomas (16.7 ppg, 7.6 rpg). Thomas' 15-foot range on his jumper, combined with relentless board work, made him one of the Metro's most improved players last season.

Kennedy has been counting the days until he gets the services of sophomore Edwards (24.9 ppg, 12.0 rpg), rated by many scouting services as the nation's No. 2 best prep recruit (behind Georgia Tech's Kenny Anderson) in 1989. Edwards' athletic ability allows him to play almost every position on the floor. It's too bad Kennedy cannot clone him. Edwards combines an imposing power forward presence with a reliable mid-range shot. He's the rare talent that has the potential to boost a program immediately —like to the tune of perhaps 20 points and 10 rebounds per game.

At the other forward is someone who doesn't play like his last name —6-7 senior Michael Polite. Two years ago, Polite played six games before contracting a nerve disorder called Guillain'-Barre syndrome. The disease caused him to lose 30 pounds and required he have numerous blood transfusions. Polite must have requested to get the Arnold Schwarznegger blood type because he practically tore down backboards last season. He averaged 14.0 points, 8.5 rebounds and was particularly effective during Mayes' absence. Edwards and Polite are at the top of a seemingly endless supply of Seminole forward talent.

There is also 6-6 seniors Aubry Boyd (6.4 ppg, 3.9 rpg) and David White (1.2 ppg, 2.5 rpg), 6-8 junior Byron Wells (1.2 ppg) and 6-6 freshman Jesse Salters. Boyd started 24 games last season because of his ability to play either small forward or shooting guard. Salters, runner-up for Mr. Basketball honors last season at Tampa (Fla.) Chamberlin High (32.6 ppg, 13.5 rpg), may leap-frog past more experienced players for starting time.

The off-season development of 6-9 sophomore Rodney Dobard (3.0 ppg, 2.8 rpg) at center may have earned him a starting job. But Dobard might not be able to hold off 7-0 incoming freshman Andre Reid of Miami (Fla.) Sunset High. Reid (19.4 ppg, 12.4 apg) runs the floor like a small forward. A Dapper Dan participant and Top 50 national recruit, Reid is a shot-blocking presence and potential impact player as a two-way inside presence.

Sophomore Chuck Graham, a 6-3 guard who was the state of Georgia's 3-A player of the year at Richmond Academy in Augusta as a senior two years ago, lived up to his hype last season. He averaged 10.1 points, the best freshman season in Florida State history. He displayed the confidence and the shooting ability that made teams play him honestly instead of doubling on Mayes. Graham's help will be 6-3 junior Ron Miller (2.7 ppg) and 6-3 sophomore Malcolm Nicholas (16.8 ppg), a teammate of Edwards at Miami Senior HS who sat out last year.

Although there are two somewhat experienced returning players at point guard —6-3 junior Lorenzo Hands (1.9 ppg) and 5-11 sophomore Chad Copeland (3.7 ppg) —one of Kennedy's recruiting priorities was finding an experienced point guard.

After a long recruiting search, he went the junior college route and signed 6-1 junior Derrick Myers of Alleghany CC in Pittsburgh, Pa. Myers (19.1 ppg, 5.0 rpg, 8.0 apg) was named the MVP of the National Junior College Athletic Association national tournament. His floor leadership and ability to run an offense is something the Seminoles didn't have last year in clutch situations. They tended to direct everything at Mayes or Kennedy, never quite got key baskets when needed and folded too much against full court defensive pressure.

Kennedy has certainly placed a challenge before his team with a schedule that may be the best in the Metro besides Louisville. Florida State will play at defending national champion UNLV, at regional semifinalist Syracuse and will play host to NCAA Final Four participant Arkansas as well as NCAA tournament entry LaSalle.

BLUE RIBBON ANALYSIS

Kennedy will challenge his team to show more heart this season at crunch time. With the new infusion of talent, the Seminoles should be able to respond.

The rest of the Metro is wondering how much of an impact Edwards will have on the Seminoles after his year long layoff. If Edwards can shake the bugs out of his game early and handle the pressure that goes along with a player of his stature, the Seminoles could finish high in the league.

Edwards, Polite, Dobard and Reid will need help from an unproven backcourt. Kennedy desperately needs JC transfer Myers to step straight in and run the show. How quickly Reid becomes a pivot force will also be telling.

Even with all of this, don't look for Florida State to finish better than fifth in the Metro. This will be a team that gets better as the season progresses, and watch out for the Seminoles in the postseason conference tournament.

1990-91 FLORIDA STATE SCHEDULE		
Nov.	27	Texas Southern
	30	Florida
Dec.	3	Morgan State (MD)
	8	La Salle
	15	@Auburn
	18	South Florida
	22	@UNLV
	29	@Florida International
Jan.	3	@Tulane
	5	@Southern Mississippi
	10	Cincinnati
	12	Louisville
	14	#Stetson
	19	@South Carolina
	21	Arkansas
	24	@Memphis State
	26	@Virginia Tech
Feb.	2	Tulane
	7	@Cincinnati
	9	@Louisville
	13	Alabama State
	16	@Jacksonville
	18	@Syracuse
	21	Memphis State
	23	Virginia Tech
	26	Southern Mississippi
Mar.	2	South Carolina
	7-9	##Metro Conference Tournament

@ Road Games
# Orlando, FL
Roanoke, VA

FORDHAM

LAST SEASON: 20-13
CONFERENCE
RECORD: 9-6
STARTERS LOST: 3
STARTERS
RETURNING: 2
CONFERENCE:
PATRIOT
LOCATION:
BRONX, NY
HOME FLOOR:
ROSE HILL GYMNASIUM (3,200)
NICKNAME: RAMS
COLORS: MAROON AND WHITE
COACH: NICK MACARCHUK, Record at Fordham,
52-43.
Career record, 201-171.

It is said that ''Those who forget the past are damned to repeat it.'' For Fordham basketball supporters, that may not be such a bad thing.

Nick Macarchuk's Rams had a memorable year in 1989-90, posting 20 wins for only the second time in their history while reaching the MAAC title game and the second round of the NIT. The Rams posted some big wins along the way, including upsets of Tennessee, Seton Hall and Boston College, and were the only team in Division I to have five players finish the season scoring in double figures. However, Macarchuk cautions, those accomplishments are old news. ''We had a great year, but with the loss of two, thousand point scorers, we are going to have to work even harder to improve.''

Fordham enters the new season and new league (Patriot League) looking to replace graduated 1,000 point scorers Andre McClendon and Dan O'Sullivan. McClendon averaged 17.0 ppg last season and finished his career as Fordham's all-time leading three-point shooter, while O'Sullivan was the sixth player in Ram history to join the 1,000 point 600-rebound club. Macarchuk won't look to one player to replace either of these standouts. Rather, he will go with the balanced attack that brought Fordham success last season.

Leading the way will be 6-9, 240-pound senior center **Damon Lopez** (11.3 ppg, 10.2 rpg, 91 blocks). The NIT all-star came into his own during the second half of last season, shooting 65 percent from the floor while averaging 16.0 ppg and 13.0 rpg over the final 23 games. He notched eight double-doubles and a triple-double during that stretch, and became the first Ram in 17 years to average in double figures in rebounding. He also broke his own school record for blocked shots (91) while setting the school mark for field goal percentage (.603). Not bad for a player who never played high school basketball.

"He's as good as anyone we faced all year, maybe the best pure rebounder," said Rutgers coach Bob Wenzel.

"If he develops a shooting touch, he will be an NBA player. His defensive skills are top notch now," said New Jersey Nets executive Willis Reed.

Lopez will get help from a pair of ever-improving junior forwards. 6-6 **Sanford Jenkins** (7.8 ppg, 6.4 rpg) averaged over 10.0 rpg during the Rams' stretch run and finished second on the team in blocks, while showing marked improvement on his fundamentals. 6-9 **Fred Herzog** (10.6 ppg, 3.8 rpg) rebounded from some early season injuries to hit double figures 18 times, while hitting over half of his three-point shots. Both must carry over their second half successes from last season to make the Rams a success. The other returning starter is 6-1 junior guard **Jean Prioleau** (11.1 ppg, 2.4 apg). The Teaneck, N.J., native has played both point and shooting guard in his career, but will probably be counted on more as a scorer with the departure of McClendon. Prioleau showed no signs of a sophomore jinx in 1989-90, becoming the first Fordham player to lead the team in steals and assists his first two seasons while shooting .857 from the free throw line, third best in school history.

Taking over Prioleau's spot at point guard should be 6-0 sophomore **Jay Fazande** (1.2 ppg, 71 assists). The New Orleans native showed great poise running Macarchuk's show during the second half of last season, averaging over four assists per game in the final 15. He topped off the season with an 11-assist, one-turnover gem in the Rams win over Southern University in the NIT.

Looking to the bench, the Rams will again have 6-5 senior swingman **Mike Rice** to fill any gaping holes. Rice played both guard and forward spots last season and showed more maturity and discipline than in his first two years. Rice's classmate, 6-9 **Kevin McBride** (0.6 ppg, 0.6 rpg) has been used mainly on defense during his career, but will have to get involved in the offensive scheme to spell the starters. Two other relatively untested players, 6-3 junior **Dewey Stinson** (2.1 ppg, 1.2 rpg) and 6-3 sophomore **Dave Buckner** (0.5 ppg, 0.6 rpg), will also have to increase their productivity. Stinson showed his ability with a 17-point performance early last season at Hofstra, and will have to use his quick moves to give the Ram attack another dimension. Buckner played sparingly during his freshman campaign (73 minutes) but will look to regain the shooting touch that made him Texas Class 5A player of the year in '88-89. Another junior, 6-6 swingman **Joe McGowan** (1.7 ppg, 0.8 rpg) may also help.

Macarchuk added four frontcourt players to the mix, one of whom may pay some early dividends. The best of the group is 6-7 freshman **Sherwin Content**, a fundamentally solid interior player, who averaged 10.0 points and 11.0 rebounds as a starter for New York City powerhouse Christ the King HS. Two other freshmen, 6-9 center **Nick Gianopoulos** and 6-7 forward **Brett Ayers** may see some early playing time. Gianopoulos averaged 23.0 points and 12.0 rebounds in his senior year, while Ayers hit for 20.0 points per game last season, hitting 45 percent from three-point range. The fourth freshman, 6-9 center **Jeff Swider**, is considered a "project" by Macarchuk, and is not expected to make an impact this year.

BLUE RIBBON ANALYSIS

The Rams returning starters, if they stay healthy, should make them the cream of the fledgling Patriot League crop. Lopez is capable of putting up All-America type numbers, while Herzog, Jenkins and Prioleau could all make All-Patriot League. The question here is depth and whether the Rams will believe their pre-season predictions and take their league foes too lightly. Fordham must get scoring from Buckner and consistent play from Fazande, along with a boost from McBride, Stinson or Content up front. If they can, it will be a great year at Rose Hill.

The non-league schedule is tough as usual (Dodge NIT plus Dayton, Xavier, Georgia Tech, Seton Hall and St. John's), while Holy Cross, Lehigh and Lafayette in the league will be no pushovers (Fordham went 1-3 vs. the group last season). However, the returnees are road tough and Macarchuk is one of the country's most underrated coaches. If healthy, Fordham should return to postseason play for the third time in Macarchuk's four years. Only this time it will be NCAA, not NIT.

1990-91 FORDHAM SCHEDULE		
Nov.	15	#@Notre Dame
	24	Navy
	28	Seton Hall
Dec.	1	@Iona
	3	@St. Joseph's
	5	@Hofstra (NY)
	8	@Georgia Tech
	11	@Columbia
	15	Manhattan
	22	@St. John's
	28-29	##Music City Invitational
Jan.	5	Xavier
	8	Army
	12	@Colgate
	16	Lehigh
	19	@Lafayette
	23	@Bucknell
	26	Holy Cross
	29	@Army
	31	@Manhattan
Feb.	2	Adelphi (NY)
	6	Colgate
	9	@Lehigh
	13	Lafayette
	16	Bucknell
	20	@Holy Cross
	23	*Dayton
Mar.	3-5	**Patriot League Tournament

@ Road Games
# Dodge NIT. If Fordham defeats Notre Dame, the Rams will play a second round game on Nov. 17. The semifinals and finals of the tournament will be played on Nov. 19 & 21 at Madison Square Garden, New York, NY.
Nashville, TN (Austin Peay, Rice & Vanderbilt)
* Madison Square Garden, New York, NY
** Worchester, MA

FRESNO STATE

LAST SEASON: 10-19
CONFERENCE RECORD: 4-14
STARTERS LOST: 1
STARTERS RETURNING: 4
CONFERENCE: BIG WEST
LOCATION: FRESNO, CA
HOME FLOOR: SELLAND ARENA (10,132)
NICKNAME: BULLDOGS
COLORS: CARDINAL AND BLUE
COACH: GARY COLSON, first year at Fresno State. Career record, 487-312.

The basketball situation at Fresno State was not a pretty one in 1989-90. Head coach Ron Adams was asked to resign in the middle of the season, told that it would be his last go-round. The pressures built inside of Adams, sitting in the shoes of a lame duck. He got out, left with four games remaining on the Bulldogs' schedule. Two assistant coaches took over and acted as head coaches in Adams' absence.

The result was a dismal 10-19 season filled with turmoil and strife. Not the way you want to compete in the Big West and certainly not the scenario you want at a school with a rich tradition such as Fresno State, a school which probably possesses the most fanatical following of fans in the West.

The famed "Red Wave" pledge their allegiance to the Bulldogs every year, selling out every home game at the Selland Arena in nine of the past 10 years. The Red Wave love their Bulldogs, but would like to see a return to the winning ways after four lackluster seasons with Adams at the helm.

Fresno State athletic director Gary Cunningham, the former coach at UCLA, believes he found the right coach in new Bulldog mentor Gary Colson.

"We had approximately 40 applicants for our basketball position while I talked to approximately another 45 coaches and then interviewed several others," Cunningham said. "When searching for a coach, it is difficult to find a coach that fits all the criteria we had established for this job. We feel fortunate to have found an established coach with a proven track record. As the 12th winningest active coach in the country, Gary Colson's record speaks for itself."

Colson has been a head coach at Valdosta State, Pepperdine and New Mexico in the past and served the last two seasons as the head assistant at California. Not only does Colson carry a reputation as a winner, evident by his .610 winning percentage (487-312, good for the 34th winningest mark in the history of college basketball), but he is also credited around the coaching circles as being an offensive genius and a superb recruiter —both traits that the Fresno State program desperately needed.

It seems like the perfect marriage. The coach with a winning reputation who can handle adversity, instill new offensive life and get some fresh blood into the program. No wonder Fresno is buzzing about the upcoming season. The Red Wave is ready to roll into a port near you.

And what is making the people at Fresno State even more excited is the instant success achieved by Colson and the Bulldogs during the summer months of 1990. Colson took the Bulldogs north to Canada for a five game tour during the first week of July, to get a feel of the talent he was inheriting and to have the Bulldogs face some quality competition before the season. His mission was accomplished. The Bulldogs faced the Canadian National Team five times and averaged 86 points per game in the five contests. Scoring numbers like that are almost totally foreign to Fresno.

Colson is not taking over a team that will take the world over by storm this year. There is some talent, but in the increasingly competitive Big West, some talent is not enough.

If the Bulldogs are to bounce back quickly, then junior guard **Wilbert Hooker** (15.5 ppg, 4.1 rpg) will have to continue to excel. The explosive 6-3 Hooker is extremely versatile, playing inside, outside, running the floor, you name it. But Hooker had moments of uncontrolled frenzy last season and he shot only 39 percent from the floor. There's no doubt that Hooker will be the Bulldogs' big gun once again this year, but he is going to have to show some self restraint if he is to emerge as a leader under Colson. Colson's running style of offense might make Hooker happy enough to play follow the leader. If under control, then watch out. Hooker is that talented and explosive offensively. His numbers should improve under Colson.

Junior forward **Pat Riddlesprigger** (8.4 ppg, 5.2 rpg) also returns and he too should benefit from Colson's arrival. The 6-6 Riddlesprigger (try and fit that on the back of a uniform jersey) was forced to play bigger than he actually was last year and that hurt his game. He is more of a finesse player who is aggressive but not that physical. Riddlesprigger was one of the rare Bulldogs last season. He could actually shoot the ball. His .512 percentage was tops on a team that shot a horrendous 42 percent. Riddlesprigger is also a very aggressive defender, but that aggressiveness on the defensive end was a bit costly last year, as he fouled out nine times. At the end of last season, the hard working Riddlesprigger was one of the most improved players in the Big West. That trend should continue this season.

Senior forward **Chris Henderson** (9.1 ppg, 6.3 rpg) also returns. The 6-6 battler inside had some moments of brilliance last year, saving his best games for the Bulldogs' best opponents like UCLA and UNLV. But the transfer from DePaul suffered badly from inconsistency after taking considerable time getting ready for the season once becoming eligible after the transfer. Henderson is very strong and physical and makes his living in the paint, collecting garbage other teams leave hanging around. He grabbed a team high 71 offensive rebounds last year. Colson will look for a steady effort from Henderson, and, if received, he could be one of the top players in the conference.

Junior swingman **Tod Bernard** (14.3 ppg, 3.8 rpg) is the Bulldogs' other main offensive threat returning along with Hooker. The 6-5 Bernard was shuffled back and forth from off-guard to small forward and back again. He has a reputation of being a solid outside shooter, but he also suffered last year, connecting on only 40 percent of his shots. But Bernard did nail 37 percent of his three-point attempts. Bernard came to Fresno State with a reputation as a superb talent. He was named the Kansas High School player of the year his senior year at Haven HS. This is the year for Bernard to live up to the high billing.

Sophomore center **Dimitri Lambrecht** (pronounced LAM-BRECK) is the Bulldogs' top returning big man. The 6-9 Lambrecht (2.7 ppg, 2.8 rpg) started seven games in the pivot early in the season, but seemed to lose confidence and with that, lost considerable playing time. Colson thought that Lambrecht played well in Canada, so maybe the confidence has returned under the new mentor.

One player that doesn't lack a bit of confidence is senior point guard **Dave Barnett** (8.4 ppg, 2.1 rpg, 46 assists). Barnett, a Fresno native, showed good poise and leadership capabilities in his nine starts a year ago. The 6-0 Barnett has the ability to nail one from long range, like Hooker and Bernard. He is the pre-season favorite to run the show as the starter this season. But overall, Barnett had his problems shooting as well, canning just 38 percent.

Junior forward **Sammie Lindsey** (2.2 ppg, 2.6 rpg) played in 23 games last year, starting five. The 6-8 Lindsey has a nice shooting touch, evident by his 52 percent mark in limited play last year, but lack of stamina still plagues Lindsey and that will keep his playing time down this season. Lindsey is also a decent defender, blocking 13 shots, fourth best on the team. But in an up-tempo offense, it's necessary to be able to run well. Lindsey is not a stallion. He could be in for a long year. Junior guard **Sammy Taylor** is not a player of impact. The 6-2 Taylor saw action in 12 games totalling 88 minutes, but only scored five points. And he also had a tough time from the floor, going 1-of-10. It was an epidemic, the cold shooting flu bug that bit the Bulldogs.

Two players who sat out last year are now eligible: sophomore center **Ray Young** (Rochester, N.Y./St. Thomas More Prep) and sophomore guard **Carl Ray Harris** (Fresno's Washington Union HS). Young, a 6-9 soft-shooting center, needed to add some bulk to his 215-pound frame and some strength to go along with it. The Canadian trip also seemed to help him. Harris is a star in the making. The 6-2 local product has a tremendous vertical leap and is a fine outside shooter which is an obvious Bulldog need. He had a fine Canadian tour, finishing second on the team in

scoring behind Hooker. Colson is hoping for big things from Harris and more than likely, he will get them.

Colson welcomes back three players who were redshirted as freshmen last season in forward **Ron Willis**, guard **Steve Taylor** and forward **Greg Zuffelato**. Willis is a 6-7 forward out of the Chicago suburbs, who had very limited experience playing basketball (only one year in HS) but has great athletic skills, especially in track and field, where he earned all-state honors throwing the discus, shot and javelin. Thus, the reason for his redshirt. Just to get experience. Taylor is a 6-2 guard, also from Fresno (Bullard HS) who should have some impact on the Bulldogs this year. Taylor averaged 17 points per game as a senior at Bullard and he has a fine shooting touch from the perimeter. Zuffelato is a 6-6 lanky small forward out of Pleasanton, Calif./Foothill HS, who will vie for playing time in an already packed frontcourt.

Colson may also has two transfers at his immediate call. Junior guard **Kevin Cooperwood** comes to Fresno State via Poly-DeAnza (Calif.) JC. Cooperwood averaged 10.4 points and 3.4 rebounds last season and is thought to be a Hooker clone with better physical abilities. The 6-1 Cooperwood is the sure-fire addition to the roster. An eligibility question mark surrounds 6-9 sophomore forward **Fabio Ribeiro**, who played last year at Chaffey (Calif.) JC. The question lies with Ribeiro's eligibility with the NCAA. At presstime, the Fresno State athletic department was petitioning the NCAA to allow Ribeiro to play, despite never having taken either the SAT or ACT tests.

If Ribeiro is deemed eligible to play, then he will be a player of impact and possible starter at small forward. Ribeiro comes to Fresno via Rio de Janiero, Brazil, and will be the Bulldogs' second international player. Dimitri Lambrecht hails from Antiwerp, Belgium. Ribeiro has a great outside shot and averaged 14.0 points and 6.4 rebounds per game for Chaffey last season, earning all-conference honors.

Colson has two freshman signees to complete the roster in 6-8 forward **James Bacon** (Los Angeles, Calif./Dorsey HS) and 6-0 guard **Doug Harris** (Tempe, Ariz./Corona HS). Harris is a great leaper and fine penetrator who led Corona to the Arizona state championship, averaging 24.7 points per game while dishing out nine assists per game. He might be a starter at the point. Bacon will probably sit out the season.

BLUE RIBBON ANALYSIS

If there is a school in the Big West that deserves to have a boost of positive vibes, a shot in the arm, some added excitement, then that school is Fresno State. The Bulldogs have exceptionally loyal fans including a group that follows them to all points of the globe.

The school had to do something to keep the attention on the Bulldogs, not the nearby vineyards. That was accomplished by hiring the veteran coach Gary Colson. Presto, instant excitement. Once again, Selland Arena is a complete sellout for the season. But the fortunes of the Bulldogs may not change immediately.

Colson's offensive approach to the game —up-tempo, run-and-gun — will help the Bulldogs immensely. Last season, former coach Ron Adams nearly reduced the Red Wave to a ripple by playing conservative offense and watching a host of characters hoist up long range shots and hear them clank off the iron. Colson wants the Bulldogs to get more transition chances, more layups. With athletes like Hooker, Barnett, Riddlesprigger and Henderson to run the floor, he seems to have the appropriate personnel.

But the rest of the Big West is so greatly improved and the time lost in hiring Colson hurt Fresno State in the recruiting game. The big prize, Brazilian Ribeiro, may be ineligible. The Bulldogs have to count on returning players improving a lot and that's a huge question mark.

Miracles won't happen this year. The rest of the league is just too strong and the Bulldogs are just too

weak. Even if the shooting numbers improve —and they almost have to —the Bulldogs will finish toward the bottom of the heap in the Big West. If they crack the .500 mark this year, then Colson will indeed have pulled off another miracle. Sixth or seventh place looks more probable.

Attention Red Wave: Be patient. Colson will turn the whole ball of wax around, but just not this year.

1990-91 FRESNO STATE SCHEDULE		
Nov.	23-24	#Coors Light Classic
	28	@Oregon State
Dec.	1	Southern Utah State
	8	@Santa Clara
	18	Mississippi Valley State
	20	Northwestern State
	27	@UCLA
	29	Univ. of Portland
Jan.	2	Fullerton State
	4	Long Beach State
	7	@California-Santa Barbara
	9	@California-Irvine
	12	UNLV
	14	New Mexico State
	17	@San Jose State
	19	@Utah State
	26	Pacific
	31	California-Irvine
Feb.	2	California-Santa Barbara
	7	@UNLV
	9	@Fullerton State
	14	Utah State
	16	San Jose State
	23	@Pacific
	28	@Long Beach State
Mar.	2	@New Mexico State
	6-10	##Big West Tournament

@ Road Games
# Fresno, CA (Montana State, Pepperdine & U.S. International)
Long Beach, CA

FULLERTON STATE

LAST SEASON: 13-16
CONFERENCE RECORD: 6-12
STARTERS LOST: 5
STARTERS RETURNING: 0
CONFERENCE: BIG WEST
LOCATION: FULLERTON, CA
HOME FLOOR: TITAN GYM (4,000)
NICKNAME: TITANS
COLORS: BLUE, ORANGE AND WHITE
COACH: JOHN SNEED, record at Fullerton State 29-29.

Two years ago, John Sneed had the tag "interim" head coach hanging around his neck like a noose. Fullerton State then head coach George McQuarn resigned suddenly for personal reasons three weeks into pre-season practice and Sneed was immediately tossed into the head man's slot.

The Titans were a team in turmoil. Prospects did not look good. Sneed was thought to be just a stop-gap, someone to stop the leak in the dam temporarily with a handy nearby thumb. But remarkably, Sneed was an instant success, winning 18 games. The Titans' brand of up-tempo basketball brought some added life and new vigor to Fullerton. Sneed was rewarded in the form of a three-year contract, a sign of relief and security.

Last year, with basically the same roster intact from Sneed's first year, the Titans struggled a bit to a 13-16 mark, dropping the close games they won in the previous campaign. However, this will be a totally different challenge for Sneed, as he heads into his third season, second of stability. The reason is that no starters return from last year's team. Sneed has to crank it all up from the bottom again, much like he did as the "interim" coach two years ago.

Sneed has to build without one of the finest players to ever play at Fullerton State, graduated forward Cedric Ceballos, who was an All-Big West selection last year and led the conference in scoring and rebounding (23.1 ppg, 12.5 rpg) for the second straight year. Ceballos was a second round choice of the Phoenix Suns.

Filling Ceballos' shoes will not be easy, even though he lived in virtual obscurity, that is, outside of the Big West. In his two seasons with the Titans, Ceballos was the consummate go-to guy, the proficient scorer and big league rebounder that makes every coach's job easier.

The huge loss to the Titan roster does not end with Ceballos' departure —in fact, the Titans will be without four of their top five scorers of a year ago. Sneed loses the entire backcourt of Mark Hill (18.2 ppg, graduated) and Wayne Williams (9.8 points, 209 assists, transferred). So that forces some major league scrambling for replacements all around the floor.

The top returnee is junior forward **Agee Ward** (6.4 ppg, 4.8 rpg). Ward, the son of a Detroit Tigers outfielder, Gary Ward, displayed some versatility in playing forward slots for Sneed last year, starting 13 games. This all occurred after getting a late start on everyone else, due to some illness and injuries suffered just prior to the start of the season. The 6-5, 225-pound Ward was the team's second leading rebounder behind Ceballos and showed a fine shooting touch, connecting on 50 percent of his attempts. Ward is a super athlete who uses his strength and quickness to his advantage. With Ceballos gone, Ward's numbers are sure to rise. Sneed is counting heavily upon Ward's constant improvement, hoping maybe Agee is the man to fill Ceballos' huge sneakers.

Senior forward **Ron Caldwell** (4.0 ppg, 2.4 rpg) is back, this time for a full season. Last year, the 6-8 Caldwell was only eligible to play in 12 games after transferring from Washington. By then, Caldwell was so far behind in his progress (he sat out the previous year with a severe knee injury) that his impact was limited. But Caldwell is a strong inside performer and with a full, injury-free pre-season under his belt, he should be able to contribute much better this time around and should be considered a leading contender for a starting berth up front.

Another potential starter is sophomore center **Aaron Wilhite** (3.7 ppg, 3.1 rpg), who saw some quality playing time behind starter David Moody last year. The 6-7 Wilhite saw action in all 29 Titan contests last season. He is an aggressive defender and rebounder, especially off the offensive end, grabbing more offensive boards than defensive last year. And he displayed a fine shooting touch, connecting on 53 percent of his tries, second on the team. Wilhite, who once hauled down an amazing 39 rebounds in one game while playing for Lincoln HS in San Diego, appears to be the frontrunner for the starting nod in the pivot.

Senior guard **Dareck Crane** (2.3 ppg, 0.5 rpg) also played in every game last year, but only averaged 7.6 minutes. However, the 6-2 Crane has a fine outside touch, nailing 50 percent of his three-point attempts, much better than his overall shooting mark of 38 percent. Crane came to Fullerton State with a fine reputation as a junior college scorer at Orange Coast (Calif.) JC, scoring almost 1,000 points in his final season there. If Crane can reclaim that scoring touch with the Titans, then his quality playing time will skyrocket.

Sophomore forward **Bruce Bowen** (1.7 ppg, 1.0 rpg) studied hard last year, watching Ceballos go to work every night. The 6-5 swingman played in 18 games, but really didn't get to see much action with Ceballos around. If Bowen, who also has a fine shooting touch, learned his lessons well monitoring Ceballos, he will also see more time.

Sophomore guards **Jason Hart** and **Tom Parada** walked on to the Titan roster last year and saw very little action. Hart, a 6-8 sophomore, scored five points and grabbed two boards in six games, totalling 11 minutes, while the diminutive Parada, who stands all of 5-6, scored two points and had two assists in five games. Parada is the favorite of the following at the Titan Gym, with the fans constantly calling for his appearance.

To offset all the losses suffered by graduation and transfer, Sneed and his staff had to go to work in the off-season, hitting the recruiting trail to the tune of nine newcomers, one redshirt transfer, four junior college transfers and four high school signees. Sneed is very high on the influx of newcomers. Junior forward **J. D. Green** is now eligible to play for the Titans, after transferring last year from Southern Methodist. The 6-6 Green, a fine athlete who has good leaping ability and is a great defender, averaged 5.7 points and 2.6 rebounds for Southern Methodist two seasons ago. Green is a product of Fairfax HS in Los Angeles, where he played with former Michigan standout Sean Higgins and Arizona's Chris Mills. Sneed is hopeful that Green steps in and immediately becomes a strong scorer for the Titans.

Heading the crop of junior college transfers is junior guard **Joe Small**. The 6-2 shooting guard led all California JC scorers by tossing in 25.3 points per game for the College of the Sequoias. Small set new school records for points in a season (760) and career (1,337), shooting 53 percent from the field and 86 from the line over the two years there. Small, from Bolsa Grande HS in Garden Grove, Calif., will probably become the Titans' starter at the off-guard slot this season. Junior guard **Aaron Sunderland** comes to Fullerton with a strong winning tradition. The 6-2 Sunderland was the starting point guard from the Connors State JC (Okla.) squad that won the national championship last season. Sunderland, an excellent penetrator and playmaker, scored 12 points and averaged seven assists per game for Connors, which finished 36-2 a year ago. Sunderland could very well inherit the starting point guard position. Junior forward **Kevin Ahsmuhs** joins the Titan roster after two seasons at San Diego Mesa JC. The burly 6-8 Ahsmuhs averaged 16.0 points and 10.0 rebounds per game, earing all-state JC honors in California.

Junior forward **Kim Kemp** will add depth up front. The 6-7 product of San Jose City (Calif.) College averaged 16.0 points and 9.0 rebounds per game last year.

Both Ahsmuhs and Kemp are very strong and will try to maintain their fine rebounding figures on the next level. Guard **Greg Vernon** (Los Angeles, Calif., University HS) is the top freshman signee. The 6-5 sharpshooter averaged 23.0 points and 7.0 rebounds and earned all-league and all-city honors in what was a very competitive season in Los Angeles. Vernon will undoubtedly see considerable action, possibly as Small's understudy in the shooting guard slot.

Guard **Marcus Bell** (Alta Loma, Calif., Etiwanda HS) is a 6-1 versatile performer who played three positions in high school, averaging 23.0 points and 5.5 assists per game. 6-4 swingman **Joe Bertrand** (Los Angeles, Calif., Verbum Dei HS) has a nice touch and rebounds as well. He scored 18 points and 9.0 rebounds per contest for a good Verbum Dei squad.

Sneed got another swingman for good measure in 6-6 **Michael Bloodworth** (Los Angeles, Calif., Palisades HS). Bloodworth averaged 14.0 points and 10.0 rebounds per game last year.

BLUE RIBBON ANALYSIS

It was bad enough that John Sneed lost seven letterwinners. But when you lose a major star like Cedric Ceballos and his consistently reliable performances, well, you just cannot make up a loss like that overnight.

In an ever-growing and powerful Big West, the Titans appear to have made the proper moves to remain competitive, getting nine newcomers with fine reputations as being solid players. Joe Small and Aaron Sunderland are players of impact and will make major contributions right away, possibly even start.

But it also appears that Sneed is counting too heavily on virtually unproven returnees Agee Ward, Ron Caldwell and Southern Methodist transfer J. D. Green. Only Ward has shown anything that resembles consistency in the past. Caldwell and Green are huge question marks. Can Ward emerge bigger than he has shown and fill the huge holes up front?

Two years ago, Sneed had all the pressures of the world on his shoulders and just crossed his fingers and hoped that his thrown together team would play better than expected. The Titans did that, going 16-13 when everyone thought doormat status was inevitable. It looks like some of the same, but this time, Sneed has no ace in the hole like Ceballos.

The returnees are going to have to produce more than the past performances dictate and the newcomers are going to have to perform immediately. That seems to be a lot to ask, especially when it seems like everyone else in the Big West has vastly improved. The Titans will finish in the bottom half of the Big West again this season. There doesn't appear to be any way to avoid that, all things considered. No hope for a return engagement of Sneed's first year.

1990-91 FULLERTON STATE SCHEDULE		
Nov.	26	@Lamar
	28	@Tulsa
Dec.	1	Butler
	5	@San Francisco
	8	@Pepperdine
	15	Mississippi Valley State
	20	University of Portland
	22	Chapman College (CA)
	29	Colorado State
Jan.	4	@UNLV
	7	Utah State
	9	San Jose State
	12	@Pacific
	14	@Fresno State
	17	Long Beach State
	19	New Mexico State
	24	@California-Santa Barbara
	26	@California-Irvine
	31	@Utah State
Feb.	3	@San Jose State
	7	Fresno State
	9	Pacific
	14	@New Mexico State
	16	@Long Beach State
	21	California-Irvine
	23	California-Santa Barbara
Mar.	2	UNLV
	7-9	#Big West Tournament

@ Road Games
# Long Beach, CA

FURMAN

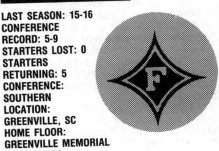

LAST SEASON: 15-16
CONFERENCE RECORD: 5-9
STARTERS LOST: 0
STARTERS RETURNING: 5
CONFERENCE: SOUTHERN
LOCATION: GREENVILLE, SC
HOME FLOOR: GREENVILLE MEMORIAL AUDITORIUM
NICKNAME: PALADINS
COLORS: PURPLE AND WHITE
COACH: BUTCH ESTES, record at Furman, 77-67
Career record, 169-130.

Furman returns five starters from a year ago, a luxury only one other Southern Conference team enjoys this season. Unfortunately for the Paladins, that other team is two-time defending league champion East Tennessee State.

East Tennessee State may be a huge obstacle for Furman to overcome, but coach Butch Estes is nevertheless optimistic. His returning players accounted for 96 percent of the team's scoring and 95 percent of its rebounding last season.

"In the 10 years I've been a head coach, I've never had the pleasure of having all five starters returning," Estes said. "That, plus the experience and talent they have, has us excited about the season."

Estes has put together a solid team, one eager to atone for its erratic play last season. At times impressive, such as in victories over Villanova and East Tennessee State, the Paladins were also disappointing, as their 5-9 Southern Conference record would attest. The latter relegated Furman to a seventh-place finish, dangerously close to cellar-dwelling Western Carolina. Only a two-point victory over the Catamounts in the final game of the regular season kept the Paladins from finishing last.

"I think there were two reasons we didn't have as much success as we'd have liked last year," said Estes. "One, we were not a very good defensive team. Two, I never thought we had the right chemistry. At times, we just didn't play well together."

Some of Estes' counterparts in the Southern Conference believe the Paladins have corrected their weaknesses. "They won't finish in seventh again," said one rival coach. "Furman has enough talent to give East Tennessee a serious run."

That talent begins in the frontcourt, where two former Southern Conference freshmen of the year start side-by-side. The team's best player is 6-7 junior **Bruce Evans** (15.1 ppg, 7.3 rpg), voted the league's top freshman two years ago. Selected to the All-Southern team last season, Evans is a lean 195 pounds, but takes full advantage of his quickness and low-post scoring skills.

Evans will be joined by the league's top freshman of a year ago, 6-7 sophomore **Derek Waugh** (12.3 ppg, 8.3 rpg). Recruited only by Princeton and Furman, Waugh showed he could play when former starter Brent Williams left school in December, earning a full-time starting job.

Waugh's first start came in the Paladins' homecourt victory over Villanova. Playing against 7-3 center Tom Greis, Waugh scored 14 points and grabbed 12 rebounds. The burly Waugh would get even better. He had a 27-point, 12-rebound performance against Marshall, and scored 21 points and grabbed 15 rebounds in the victory over East Tennessee State.

"The challenge this year for Derek is that he'll have a lot more (defensive) attention," Estes said. "Last year, he kind of snuck up on people. This year people know what he can do. I thought Bruce handled the pressure well the year after he was voted freshman of the year. I think Derek can respond the same way."

Completing Furman's front line is 6-5 senior **Tracy Garrick** (11.8 ppg, 4.0 rpg, 20 blocked shots). Garrick started 30 of 31 games after missing most of the 1988-89 season with a knee injury. **Steven Hines,** (4.9 ppg, 2.3 rpg) a 6-5 sophomore, will back him up. 6-7 senior **Tom O'Donnell,** (3.8 ppg, 2.3 rpg), 6-8 senior **Tim Vorel** (3.1 ppg, 1.3 rpg) and 6-10 redshirt freshman **Brian Edwards** should get plenty of minutes in reserve roles.

Furman's backcourt is solid, if not as deep as its front line. The starters are 6-0 junior **Hal Henderson** (9.3 ppg, 2.9 rpg, 136 assists, 53 steals) and 6-3 senior **Chris Bass** (11.5 ppg, 2.1 rpg). They are not sharpshooters, however. Henderson, a fine playmaker and defender, shot just 35 percent from the floor last year, Bass a not-much-better 41 percent. Estes takes some of the blame for those subpar performances.

"We didn't shoot the ball well from the perimeter, which was poor coaching on my part," Estes said. "We didn't put our players in good shot selection situations. This year, we'll try to get them in some better places to shoot."

The only experienced backup guard is 6-3 junior **David Stamey** (3.9 ppg, 1.2 rpg). Stamey did appear in all 31 games.

The Paladins signed just two freshmen, but both should contribute. 6-5 **Adrian Lawson** seems undersized for a forward, but is hardly timid about throwing his weight (230 pounds) around. He averaged 16 points and 10 rebounds at Central Carrollton (Ga.) High. 6-3 guard **Eric Fuller** averaged 17 points last season at Mays High School in Atlanta. He can play either guard position.

"We think we'll get good contributions from both our freshmen," said Estes. "Eric gives us good depth at guard, and Adrian should be a strong player inside for us."

BLUE RIBBON ANALYSIS

Furman's starting lineup, though not as experienced as East Tennessee State's, is one of the best in the Southern Conference. If the Paladins develop the defensive cohesiveness Estes is looking for, they'll be a serious contender in the league.

The continued development of Waugh is also critical. A bruising player, Waugh will draw more defensive pressure this season and his points will not come as easily.

The Paladins guards will also have to shoot better than they did last year. Henderson and Bass are set as the starters, but freshman Fuller figures to earn his share of court time.

"I'm hoping to develop some leaders on this team," Estes said. "I'll look to my seniors first, but I think Hal Henderson and Bruce Evans can be leaders too. The harder those people play, the better we'll be."

Better, maybe, but not quite good enough to knock off East Tennessee State.

1990-91 FURMAN SCHEDULE		
Nov.	23	@Michigan State
	26	Erskine College (SC)
	28	@Mercer
Dec.	2	@Clemson
	4	Lander College (SC)
	12	@South Carolina
	15	@Purdue
	22	@South Carolina State
Jan.	2	Liberty University (VA)
	5	Virginia Military Institute
	7	Marshall
	12	@East Tennessee State
	14	@Appalachian State
	17	@Liberty University
	19	The Citadel
	21	Baptist College (SC)
	24	Wofford College (SC)
	26	Western Carolina
	28	Tennessee-Chattanooga
Feb.	2	@Marshall
	4	@Virginia Military Institute
	6	Maine
	9	Appalachian State
	11	East Tennessee State
	16	@The Citadel
	23	@Western Carolina
	26	@Tennessee-Chattanooga
Mar.	1-3	#Southern Conference Tournament

@ Road Games
# Asheville, NC

GEORGE MASON

LAST SEASON: 20-12
CONFERENCE RECORD: 10-4
STARTERS LOST: 1
STARTERS RETURNING 4
CONFERENCE: COLONIAL (CAA)
LOCATION: FAIRFAX, VA
HOME FLOOR: PATRIOT CENTER (10,000)
NICKNAME: PATRIOTS
COLORS: GREEN AND GOLD
COACH: ERNIE NESTOR, record at George Mason, 40-23.

George Mason's Ernie Nestor has carried on the good work started by former coaches Joe Harrington and Rick Barnes. The Patriots, winners of 20 games in each of the last three seasons and four of the last five, have quietly established themselves as a team to be reckoned with in Division I.

George Mason basketball began 25 years ago as an NAIA program, but has flourished since joining Division I in 1978. The Patriots have a 194-147 Division I record - 95-38 the last five years - with every reason to expect similar success this season.

Nestor has a solid nucleus of three returning starters, all of whom averaged double figures in scoring last season. The most accomplished is 6-7 senior forward **Robert Dykes** (17.1 ppg, 8.5 rpg, 34 steals, 28 blocked shots), who led the Colonial Athletic Association in field goal percentage (61.9, a school record). Dykes put in considerable time in the weight room in the off-season, as a knee injury limited his weight training the previous two years.

"I think you will see more explosion as Robert goes to the basket," Nestor said. "He has been able to work on his leg strength for the first time during the off-season, and we expect improvement in that area."

Center **Byron Tucker** (11.5 ppg, 7.6 rpg), a 6-10 junior, will join Dykes in the frontcourt. The transfer from North Carolina State earned a starting role near the end of last season and was impressive. Against Coppin State, he grabbed a season-high 18 rebounds. Tucker will also benefit from off-season weight training and the playing time he received as a member of the CAA all-star team that toured Yugoslavia in June.

Another ex-transfer returns at forward alongside Dykes. 6-5 junior **Mitch Madden** (6.1 ppg, 2.7 rpg) played for George Mason assistant coach Herb Krusen when the latter was interim head coach at Western Carolina, and is the brother of former North Carolina standout Kevin Madden. Mitch started 18 games last season. 6-6 senior **Danny Dean** (2.4 ppg, 1.6 rpg) , 6-11 senior **Henri Adams** (0.9 ppg, 1.4 rpg) and 6-7 sophomore **Kenny Johnson** (1.0 ppg, 0.8 rpg) will compete for reserve roles up front.

5-10 junior **Mike Harget** (15.3 ppg, 2.6 rpg, 104 assists, 53 steals) solidifies the Patriots' backcourt. Hargett, likely to move to shooting guard in place of graduated Steve Smith (12.9 ppg, 3.6 rpg, 133 assists), led George Mason with 67 three-point goals and his 82.5 percent free throw accuracy. 5-10 sophomore **Jamel Perkins** (3.1 ppg, 1.2 rpg, 53 assists) will probably inherit Harget's point guard responsibilities. Perkins, who played in all 32 games last year, is the team's quickest and fastest player, but needs work on his shooting.

6-4 senior **Steve Moran** (0.8 ppg, 0.4) and 6-4 sophomore **Troy Jackson** (0.3 ppg, 0.1 rpg) return as backcourt reserves.

Two incoming freshmen should at least contribute for the veteran Patriots. **Paul Arthur** is a 6-4 swingman from Brother Rice High School in Birmingham, Mich. A good outside shooter, Arthur averaged 18.6 points and 5.4 rebounds last year. **Ralph Malone**, a 6-0 guard, averaged 22.1 points, 4.5 rebounds and 8.2 assists at Murrah High School in Jackson, Miss. A third recruit is 6-7 **Andrew Fingall**, who averaged 6.9 points, 7.0 rebounds and had 55 blocked shots for Union Catholic High School in Scott Plains, N.J.

BLUE RIBBON ANALYSIS

Two years ago, George Mason won the CAA tournament and advanced to the NCAA's. Last year, the Patriots had a near-identical record but finished second in the Colonial. With its nucleus virtually intact, there is little reason George Mason cannot duplicate its recent success.

"The success of our team in 1990-91 will be in direct relationship to the improvement shown by our veterans and the contributions of the new players," Nestor said. "We have an outstanding nucleus of talented players, but they can't do it by themselves. It is particularly important that some of our veterans step forward to meet the challenge."

1990-91 GEORGE MASON SCHEDULE		
Nov.	24	@Miami (FL)
	26	@East Tennessee State
Dec.	4	@Mt. St. Mary's (MD)
	7-8	#Cougar Classic
	15	East Tennessee State
	17	Coastal Carolina (SC)
	19	Northeastern
	22	Louisville
	28-29	##Oldsmobile Spartan Classic
Jan.	2	@Virginia Commonwealth
	7	@Richmond
	9	William & Mary
	12	@North Carolina Wilmington
	14	@East Carolina
	19	Navy
	23	American University
	26	@James Madison
Feb.	2	Richmond
	6	@William & Mary
	9	North Carolina Wilmington
	11	East Carolina
	14	Old Dominion
	16	@Navy
	20	@American University
	23	James Madison
Mar.	2-4	*CAA Tournament

@ Road Games
# Provo, UT (Brigham Young, Eastern Kentucky & St. John's)
East Lansing, MI (Coastal Carolina, Louisiana Tech & Michigan State)
* Richmond, VA

GEORGE WASHINGTON

LAST SEASON: 14-17
CONFERENCE RECORD: 6-12
STARTERS LOST: 1
STARTERS RETURNING: 4
CONFERENCE: ATLANTIC 10
LOCATION: WASHINGTON, DC
HOME FLOOR: SMITH CENTER (5,000)
NICKNAME: COLONIALS
COLORS: BUFF AND BLUE
COACH: MIKE JARVIS, first year at George Washington.
Career record, 101-51.

This is not a recording. George Washington, after years of perceived underachievement, went north for a new basketball coach. Seeking a reprieve from the college basketball wilderness, the Colonials found their man at Boston University. Repeat, this is not a recording.

Five years ago, George Washington got who they thought was their man. John Kuester, a Dean Smith protege, was a winner in Boston and figured to move easily into a winning situation with the Colonials. Instead, Kuester was the victim of circumstance - mainly injury - and would never capture the imagination of a town saturated by Georgetown and Maryland.

Kuester had one other stigma he could never overcome. In 1988-89, GW was the nation's whipping boy, winning only one game in 28 tries. That was also the year the Colonials saw their virtually entire roster decimated by season-ending injuries. It was also a fact forgotten by the powers that be when it came time to evaluate Kuester at the end of last year.

The Colonials actually improved by 13 games a year ago, a startling turnaround for even the best of programs. But it was not enough to save their coach, who seemed to know as much after a season-ending Atlantic 10 tournament loss to Penn State.

"We played with a tremendous amount of heart all year long," Kuester said. "To go from one to 14 wins really says something. I just don't know it it was enough."

It was not, of course, prompting George Washington to once again look to the north for a savior. The Colonials again believe they have their man. Again he is from Boston University, and again he figures to move easily into a winning situation in Washington.

The track record of Mike Jarvis is impeccable. He has won at every stop, and at every level. After taking the Terriers to two NCAA tournaments the past three years, the former mentor of Patrick Ewing at Cambridge Rindge and Latin (Mass.) High, Jarvis was wooed by any number of Division I programs, most with higher profiles than George Washington. It turns out the new coach, in his decision process, was answering to an even higher authority.

"My wife had refusal rights on any move," Jarvis said. "You only leave Boston for someplace very special. This is the first time we have moved in our entire lives. I just think that Washington will provide us with the laboratory to grow and learn and improve both professionally and personally."

The testimonials also flowed easily. Jarvis, it seems, has never made an enemy.

"Mike Jarvis," said Duke coach Mike Krzyzewski, "is one of the real professionals in college basketball today. Mike is not an isolationist. He understands the big picture. I've been so impressed by his standards both on and off the court. GW got a steal."

"A long-time friend," added former Big East commissioner Dave Gavitt. "I admire him greatly as a person and as a coach. His integrity is impeccable, and he has a great ability to teach and motivate young people."

George Washington athletic director Steve Bilsky was even more succinct. "One of the most impressive things about Mike," Bilsky said, "is that nearly 80 percent of the time he has left the court a winner."

If Jarvis manages that in his first year at GW, he may as well check into the White House. What he inherits is hardly presidential. Plus, in his short time on the job, he was able to add just one recruit. And 5-11 freshman **Alvin Pearsall** (Bartow HS/Bartow, Fla.) is not likely to be an immediate impact player.

For the time being, Jarvis will have to play Kuester's hand. Only one starter - 6-6 forward Mike Jones (10.4 ppg, 8.5 rpg) - is lost from last year's turnaround, but the Colonials remain a team without much size or depth. Jarvis may not even have the horses to push the ball as he did at BU.

What he does have is magnificent 6-3 senior **Ellis McKennie** (16.3 ppg, 3.8 rpg, 179 assists, 82 assists). More than a point guard, McKennie overcame serious

knee surgery to almost single-handedly resurrect the Colonials a year ago. He is a true warrior, taking each loss personally, and was a second-team All-Atlantic 10 selection.

"Ellis," said Kuester, his former coach, "plays with as much heart as any player I've ever seen." He is also the one of the few Colonials athletic enough to respond immediately to Jarvis and the up-tempo approach.

George Washington ended last season by starting McKennie and four almost interchangeable 6-6 players. Three of them are back, led by 6-6 senior **Glen Sitney** (12.9 ppg, 5.9 rpg). A leaper, Sitney is an athletic wing player capable of perhaps one final big season. Also returning are 6-6 sophomore **Sonni Holland** (11.4 ppg, 5.0 rpg), an A-10 all-freshman choice, and 6-6 senior **Matt Nordmann** (8.4 ppg, 2.8 rpg), an unspectacular type. A part-time starter from a year ago, 6-11 center Clint Holtz, transferred to Niagara, robbing the Colonials of their only real size.

6-2 sophomore **Dirkk Surles** (6.3 ppg, 1.8 rpg) is the lone reserve of any significance. 6-9 senior **Byron Hopkins** (1.4 ppg, 2.7 rpg), 6-7 senior **Mark Karver** (2.9 ppg, 1.2 rpg), 6-1 junior **Rodney Patterson** (2.5 ppg) and 6-6 senior **Peter Young** also return. **J.J. Hudock**, a burly 6-8 junior, might help after redshirting the 1989-90 season.

"I'm not going to say we'll win 80 percent of our games right away," said Jarvis. "I won't make any promises like that. I will let you know when that time comes and, when we're the best team in the Atlantic 10, we will go out and prove it."

BLUE RIBBON ANALYSIS

The Colonials are a long way from the top of the Atlantic 10. For now, seventh or eighth place is more likely. It will take some time, probably this year and next, for Jarvis to dig into the D.C. recruiting scene.

"We will be able to recruit our fair share," he insisted, "and I mean our fair share of players from our own backyard. D.C., Virginia and Maryland is a big backyard."

In the meantime, expect the new coach to coax the maximum from his inherited veterans. McKennie alone is proud enough for a handful of wins. A .500 season may be a reasonable goal for George Washington, but the Colonials remain too small and too lean to be a winner just yet.

1990-91 GEORGE WASHINGTON SCHEDULE		
Nov.	24	@Loyola College
	26	St. Joseph's
Nov.	30-	
	Dec. 1	#Apple Invitational
Dec.	4	Univ. of Hartford
	11	Maryland-Baltimore Co.
	22	Virginia Tech
	27	@Duquesne
Jan.	3	@Rhode Island
	5	@Boston University
	10	Temple
	14	@Old Dominion
	17	Rutgers
	19	@St. Joseph's
	24	@West Virginia
	26	Massachusetts
	29	West Virginia
	31	@St. Bonaventure
Feb.	3	Penn State
	7	@Temple
	9	Rhode Island
	12	Duquesne
	16	@Rutgers
	19	@Penn State
	23	American University
	27	St. Bonaventure
Mar.	2-4 & 7	##Atlantic 10 Tournament

@ Road Games
# Palo Alto, CA (Hawaii, Stanford & Vanderbilt)
The first three rounds will be held at the Palestra, Philadelphia, PA. The championship game will be held on the home court of the highest remaining seed.

GEORGIA SOUTHERN

**LAST SEASON: 17-11
CONFERENCE
RECORD: 11-5
STARTERS LOST: 3
STARTERS
RETURNING: 2
CONFERENCE: TRANS
AMERICA ATHLETIC
(TAAC)
LOCATION:
STATESBORO, GA
HOME FLOOR: HANNER
FIELDHOUSE (5,500)
NICKNAME: EAGLES
COLORS: BLUE AND WHITE
COACH: FRANK KERNS, record at Georgia Southern,
171-90.
Career record, 308-168.**

The mark of a solid program is the ability to fill holes neatly and cleanly. Given that, Georgia Southern is a solid program. Coach Frank Kerns, who won his 300th game late last season, loses his top two scorers (Mike Curry and Ben Pierce) and rebounders (Curry and Richard Sherrod) to graduation, but has their replacements already in line.

"I think we filled (the loss of Curry) with recruiting," Kerns said. "You take that with the experienced people we have, and we should have a fine team." That is the kind of program Kerns has put together in Statesboro, consistent if not spectacular. In nine seasons at the school, he was won 171 games - 84 in the last four seasons alone.

"Year in and year out, he's got the kind of team that will pound you at their place and give you fits at home," one TAAC assistant coach said. "He's always got a hole or two to fill, but he always seems to fill it."

The guy who Kerns thinks can replace Curry (16.6 ppg, 7.0 rpg) at small forward is 6-4 junior college transfer **Tony Windless**. In two years at Cowley County (Kan.) CC, Windless scored 1,146 points. Also in the running are sophomore returnees 6-3 **Tommy Williams** (3.6 ppg, 1.4 rpg) and 6-4 **Monty Noblitt** (0.5 ppg, 0.8 rpg), along with 6-7 freshman **Joby Powell** (Jenkins HS/Savannah, Ga.) and 6-8 soph **Chris Scott** (1.0 ppg, 0.7 rpg).

Cal Ferguson (6.0 ppg, 3.7 rpg), a 6-10 senior, leads the hunt for the power forward spot vacated by Sherrod. **Emmitt Smith** (7.2 ppg, 5.1 rpg), a 7-0 senior, will be the full-time starter in the post, but will be pushed by 6-10 senior **Jeff Hagans** (2.2 ppg, 1.9 rpg). Hagans and Ferguson spent the summer on a tightly-controlled weight training program to bulk up for the season.

The backcourt is more of a strength for Kerns. Cat-quick point guard **Charlton Young** (8.8 ppg, 101 assists), a 6-2 sophomore, is back to run the show after earning honorable mention All-TAAC honors as a freshman. 6-1 senior **Derkie Leach** (1.0 ppg, 0.6 rpg) offers relief, along with 6-1 sophomore **Herbert Barlow**, who attended Cowley County CC last year but did not play basketball.

6-4 junior college transfer **Wendell Charles** of Hutchinson (Kan.) CC will open workouts as the starter at the shooting guard, but flashy 6-4 freshman **Dashille King** (Decatur HS/Atlanta), will get an ample chance to win the job. King was a two-time Class AA player of the year in Georgia.

BLUE RIBBON ANALYSIS

An early-season schedule that provides just three home games and a match with Illinois will make it dif-ficult for the new Eagles to get in tune before conference play begins. On top of that, Georgia Southern opens Trans America Conference play against concensus favorite Stetson.

But Kerns has proven again and again he can to re-tool in a hurry, and the pieces are in place. If Windless can continue to score as he did in junior college, if Smith is ready to play a full season like he did the final 10 games last year, and if Young can provide the some old spark, Georgia Southern will make things difficult - or at least interesting - for the rest of the TAAC.

1990-91 GEORGIA SOUTHERN SCHEDULE		
Nov.	24	Bradley
	28	@Murray State
Dec.	1	Middle Tennessee State
	7-8	#Illini Classic
	18	@Augusta College (GA)
	20	@Middle Tennessee State
	28-29	##Albertson's Classic
Jan.	2	@East Carolina
	8	Murray State
	12	Stetson
	17	@Georgia State
	19	@Mercer
	24	Texas-San Antonio
	26	Centenary (LA)
	31	*Arkansas-Little Rock
Feb.	2	@Samford (AL)
	6	East Carolina
	9	@Stetson
	14	Georgia State
	16	Mercer
	21	@Texas-San Antonio
	23	@Centenary
	28	Arkansas-Little Rock
Mar.	2	Samford
	5-7	**TAAC Tournament

@ Road Games
# Champaign, IL (Illinois, Long Beach State & Oregon State)
Boise, ID (Boise State, Monmouth & Northeastern)
* Pine Bluff, AR
** DeLand, FL

GEORGIA STATE

**LAST SEASON: 5-23
CONFERENCE
RECORD: 3-13
STARTERS LOST: 0
STARTERS
RETURNING: 5
CONFERENCE:
TRANS AMERICA
ATHLETIC (TAAC)
LOCATION: ATLANTA, GA
HOME FLOOR: GSU
SPORTS ARENA (4,000)
NICKNAME: PANTHERS
COLORS: ROYAL BLUE AND CRIMSON
COACH: BOB REINHART, record at Georgia State,
49-91.**

This is as close to a sure thing as you will to find in college basketball: the Georgia State Panthers will do better than their 5-23 season in 1989-90. That is not to say they are ready for the NCAA tournament or, for that matter, even the TAAC tournament, but they will definitely have a better year than last.

The reason's are numerous. To begin with, the Panthers' schedule has been toned down. Gone are Georgia Tech and Clemson, replaced by Stephen F. Austin and Texas-Arlington. In addition, there will be no holiday tournaments, giving the Panthers four additional home games.

Secondly, Georgia State will have the most experienced team in the TAAC, returning all five starters. Of course, their most recent experience was losing 23 of 28 games. Head coach Bob Reinhart has 10 lettermen altogether, including his top nine scorers and rebounders.

"They're one team you have to wary of," said a rival TAAC coach. "They struggled, but there were times they showed some ability. A year of experience can only help."

On the floor, senior forward **Chris Collier** (17.2 ppg, 9.9 rpg, 31 blocked shots) will again be Georgia State's main man. The 6-6, 220-pounder led the TAAC in rebounding and was seventh in scoring. His 23 rebounds at Centenary was a single-game conference record.

"He's a big, strong guy who can run the floor," Reinhart said. "What we need more from Chris is leadership."

Frontcourt support for Collier will come from 6-8 senior center **Chuck Armstead** (5.5 ppg, 3.9 rpg), who started seven games last year. 6-9 junior **Bruce Montgomery** (1.3 ppg, 1.8 rpg) and 6-9 sophomore **Arte Cole** (4.3 ppg, 2.6 rpg) will provide support in the low post.

6-8 sophomore **Zavian Smith** (5.7 ppg, 3.9 rpg, 25 blocked shots) is the leading candidate to start alongside Collier at the other forward. 6-6 sophomore **Mike Nalls** (5.0 ppg, 4.9 rpg) was another part-time starter, and he will be challenged by 6-6 junior college signee **Kevin Hines** of Chipola (Fla.) JC.

One backcourt spot is in the very capable hands of 6-2 sophomore **Matt O'Brien** (18.4 ppg, 2.4 rpg, 105 assists, 27 steals). Of course, it may be the wrong kind of statement for a program when a freshman walk-on becomes a team's leading scorer. O'Brien, needless to say, is now on scholarship. His 38 points in the year's biggest win, against Stetson, were just four shy of a school record.

O'Brien's backcourt mate will come from a group that includes 6-1 sophomore **Corey Gauff** (6.4 ppg, 3.4 rpg), 5-11 soph **Sam Wilder** (4.2 ppg, 1.4 rpg) and 6-0 junior **Mark Thompson** (12.4 ppg, 3.4 rpg). Gauff started 20 games last season, Thompson 15 and Wilder seven.

Three junior college transfers - 6-2 **Phil Clark** of Imperial Valley (Calif.) College, 6-1 **Garrett Coley** of Middle Georgia JC and 6-3 **Phillip Luckydo** (Northeast Oklahoma A&M) - along with 5-11 freshman **Courtney Brooks** (Riverwood HS/Atlanta, Ga.) - will also fight for time in the backcourt.

BLUE RIBBON ANALYSIS

Better, yes. Good, maybe not. Collier and O'Brien are both productive players who will help Georgia State make some noise in the Trans America Conference.

But there remain more than a few nagging problems for Reinhart. O'Brien, for instance, hit just 41 percent of his shots from the field. As a team, the Panthers were outscored by an average a 15 points per game, and were beaten by 58 (twice), 45, 31 and 30 points. Not many kept their heads up when things got tough.

The lighter schedule and the more veteran lineup will assure Georgia State of a somewhat better season than last. But if Reinhart doesn't find a leader or two, it will be hard to characterize the year as good. Another season in the TAAC second division is a virtual certainty.

1990-91 GEORGIA STATE SCHEDULE		
Nov.	24	The Citadel
	26	@Auburn
Dec.	3	Florida International
	5	@Florida A&M
	8	@Stephen F. Austin

UNIVERSITY OF HARTFORD

LAST SEASON: 17-11
CONFERENCE RECORD: 8-4
STARTERS LOST: 2
STARTERS RETURNING: 3
CONFERENCE: NORTH ATLANTIC (NAC)
LOCATION: HARTFORD, CT
HOME FLOOR: THE SPORTS CENTER (4,475)
NICKNAME: HAWKS
COLORS: SCARLET AND WHITE
COACH: JACK PHELAN, record at the University of Hartford, 109-144.

The outlook should have been bright for the University of Hartford in the 1990-91 college hoop season. After nine years of trying to make the Hawks soar on the Division I level, things were finally beginning to loop up for coach Jack Phelan. There were certainly plenty of trying times along the way for Phelan and the Hawks —trying to recruit quality players, finding a suitable conference, putting together a competitive schedule, etc. The pieces were all falling into place, evident by the 17-11 mark last year and a third-place finish in the North Atlantic, the school's best season since the shift from Division II. With a spanking new facility in the Sports Center, christened last season, the excitement abounded at Hartford.

No question, the 1990-91 season was going to be the best ever since Hartford moved to Division I. The Hawks were poised to fly into contention in the NAC. With four solid starters returning from a year ago, Phelan had to be chomping at the bit, awaiting the start of the season.

However, the best laid blue prints can sometimes get lost in the shuffle. Those glories of grandeur were diminished severely when it was learned that the team's leading scorer for the past two seasons, 6-6

forward Lamont Middleton, withdrew from the school and announced his intentions to transfer to St. John's.

Middleton was a huge star for the Hawks, a two-time first-team all-NAC selection who averaged 18.9 points and 7.6 rebounds per game last season. He was the first freshman in the history of the NAC to be named to first-team all-league. Middleton was the foundation of the Hawks' high-rise plus was the go-to guy and the team leader. The loss of Middleton hit the Hawks' staff hard and suddenly. There wasn't any hint of Middleton being disappointed or frustrated at Hartford. He just packed his bags and left in search of higher ground.

Any time a program loses its star unexpectedly, it hurts a great deal. There's no question that Phelan recruited around Middleton, knowing that he had a solid scorer to go to for two more seasons. Middleton's decision to transfer will be felt for the next two seasons despite Phelan's efforts to regroup without drastic casualties. Even though the loss of Middleton was a crushing blow, the Hawks still have a plethora of talented players, three starters and 10 letterwinners from Hartford's most successful season ever.

Leading the crop of returnees is senior guard **Ron Moye** (15.1 ppg, 3.0 rpg). The 6-1 off-guard was one of the most improved players in the NAC last year, seeing his point production nearly double over his sophomore season (8.6 ppg to 15.1). Moye is an excellent perimeter shooter, evident by the 46 percent field goal and 42 percent three-point marks he posted as a first-team All-NAC selection last year. His career mark of 40 percent from three-point range is a school record.

Moye will have to pick up some of the slack brought about by Middleton's departure. His consistency was a key last year. As silly as it may sound for someone who reached double figures in 25 of 28 contests last year, Moye might have to be even more consistent this year.

Senior forward **Larry Griffiths** (11.1 ppg, 7.1 rpg) will look to continue the fine play he has displayed for the Hawks over the past two seasons. The 6-8 power forward is a strong player close to the basket, shooting 55 percent from the floor last season and 53 percent for his three-year career. He will get a good shot to improve his scoring totals, now, with Middleton gone, and he can handle it. Griffiths is also a fine defensive player. He is the all-time leader at Hartford in blocked shots with 84. He will be counted upon heavily if the Hawks are to continue their winning ways of late.

Senior guard **Al Jones** (6.9 ppg, 3.4 rpg, 74 assists) shifted from shooting guard to point guard a year ago and handled the move with ease. The diminutive Jones, all of 5-9, is very quick and is a strong ballhandler. His quickness ignited the Hawks' running style of play and just made everyone's level increase as well. However, Jones suffered a knee injury midway through the season last year, forcing him to the sidelines for a month. That knee is still a question mark as is his shooting accuracy. Jones shot 38 percent from the floor and 54 percent from the line. Those are not the numbers coaches like to see coming from their point guard. Jones' assets —like his quickness, ballhandling and leadership —outweigh the negatives.

Sophomore center **Vinnie Baker** (4.7 ppg, 2.9 rpg) will probably get a big chance to start up front for the Hawks this season. The 6-10 Baker set a school record for blocked shots in a season with 47, second in the league. He also shot 62 percent from the floor, tops on the squad. He has a fine shooting touch from short range and is an aggressive scorer and rebounder. Baker came to Hartford with a huge reputation. Now, with Middleton gone and a spot open, Baker will get a solid opportunity to live up to those expectations. His numbers should be vastly improved this year.

Sophomore swingman **David Pritikin** (4.5 ppg, 1.8 rpg) walked onto the Hawks' roster a year ago and by the season's end was one of the team's top reserves. The 6-4 Pritikin has a nich touch from outside, nailing 44 percent from the floor and a remarkable

52 percent from three-point land. He averaged 8.9 points and 3.3 rebounds in the final seven games of the season last year and will more than likely get a shot at starting at small forward this year. Pritikin isn't the best athlete around, but he just plays his heart out and gets the job done with desire and hustle.

Sophomore swingman **Donnail Diggs** (3.1 ppg, 2.6 rpg) was the Hawks' jack-of-all-trades last season, playing off-guard and small forward, switching back and forth to fit Phelan's needs. The 6-2 Diggs is a fine athlete with great leaping ability. He also has a fine shooting touch, connecting on 55 percent of his tries. With some hard work defensively and some ironing out of the rough spots, like ballhandling, Diggs could become a fine player in the NAC. Diggs' health could also be a problem. A knee injury forced Diggs out of action at year's end and deserves watching in pre-season.

Junior forward **Mark Matthews** (1.4 ppg, 1.2 rpg) will try to squeeze his way into the Hawks' lineup up front, possibly at power forward. Even though Matthews is only 6-5, he plays bigger than his size, using quickness, strength and a strong leaping ability to his advantage. His aggressiveness and nice shooting touch (50 percent) might gain him more quality time this season.

Sophomore guard **Paul Spence** (1.3 ppg, 0.5 rpg) saw limited action in 21 games last season, averaging just 7.5 minutes per game. The 5-11 Spence had a reputation of being a solid perimeter player, but he shot just 24 percent from the floor and a miserable 16 percent from three-point range. If Spence wants to see more action, those numbers have to vastly improve. Spence reportedly worked very hard in the off-season on his shooting and ballhandling.

Senior center **Mike Daniel** (1.1 ppg, 1.4 rpg) started 32 games as a freshman and sophomore. He averaged 4.3 points per game in both of those seasons, so Daniel is moving in the wrong direction.

Junior center **Rich Kusmirek** (1.1 ppg, 0.6 rpg) is much like Daniel. Kusmirek is a 6-9 bullmoose, who saw his playing time cut drastically, like Daniel. Kusmirek started 11 games as a freshman, led the team in field goal percentage at 49 percent and averaged 4.7 points per game. Last year, Kusmirek played 21 games, starting none, averaged just four minutes per outing and shot 31 percent from the floor. Not the type of progress a coach likes to see. Kusmirek could be stuck on the pine, deep on the pine, again this year.

The Hawks welcome back three redshirts who are now ready for action this season —one of which may be the comeback story of the year. Senior forward **Vishnue Naraine** was the Rookie of the Year in the then ECAC Metro, now Northeast Conference, way back in 1986-87, at St. Francis (N.Y.). He then transferred to Hartford, but ran into some incredible misfortune, suffering torn anterior cruciate ligaments in both knees, one a year, sitting out both of the last two seasons with the injuries. So Naraine has been out of action for *three* years. Healthy, the 6-5, 220-pound Naraine, will contribute. He averaged 7.1 ppg and 3.4 rpg for St. Francis in 1986-87. But three years away from the game? Has to make Naraine a huge question mark, but certainly one to watch.

Freshman guard **Jack Ayer**, from Coventry (Conn.) HS, was looked upon last season to offer immediate help to the Hawks' backcourt, but knee surgery delayed his debut. The 6-2 Ayer can play either guard position and has good all-around talents, particularly shooting. Ayer had a fine high school career at Coventry, averaging 33 points per game. Ayer won't put up those numbers with the Hawks, but he will be a solid contributor because of his versatility.

The last redshirt from a year ago is freshman forward **Vonsell Johnson**. The 6-5 Johnson was kept on the sidelines to gain some experience. A raw talent, Johnson averaged 11.7 points, 12 rebounds and four blocked shots per game for Danbury (Conn.) HS, leading Danbury to the state title, along with Hawk teammate Diggs. Johnson is a strong athlete who will get better with time.

Phelan's recruiting efforts brought about two quality freshman signees to Hartford in guard **Matt Curtis** and forward **Ricardo Roderick**.

Curtis, a 6-1 guard from Cheshire (Conn.) HS, is Connecticut's third all-time leading high school scorer (2,261 points). He is obviously a prolific scorer, evidenced by his remarkable 35 ppg average last year. Curtis should see a great deal of playing time this season.

Roderick may step in and start right away for the Hawks. He is that talented and was a major recruiting coup for Phelan. The 6-5 small forward from Harwich (Mass.) HS averaged 21 points, 17 rebounds and six assists per game last season for Harwich, leading them to the Eastern Massachusetts state title game. Roderick was named the player of the year by the *Boston Globe* in his classification. His assets include a fine shooting touch, strong athletic skills and the ability to go to the basket with authority. He will be a major factor for the Hawks, if not immediately, then in the near future.

BLUE RIBBON ANALYSIS

Even though Middleton is gone, Phelan is keeping his head up and his hopes up as well. Sure, it would have been nice to have the school's best player ever back for his final two seasons, but life goes on. And Phelan is optimistic.

"I'm very excited about the 1990-91 version of the Hartford Hawks," Phelan said. "I feel we are more balanced as a team and have improved our depth at all positions. This will enable us to press more and sustain a high level of defensive intensity for longer periods of time throughout the game.

"I look forward to the challenge of blending a group of solid veterans with our second-year players and a group of talented freshmen," Phelan said. "This combination gives us a team with tremendous potential. It's the most talent we've had since I've been here."

With one exception. No Lamont Middleton.

Phelan has every right to be optimistic, however, because the Hawks are not about to come plummeting back to earth now that Middleton is gone. The talent is there. Moye and Griffiths are solid Division I players, and will lead the Hawks through the tough times this season. Baker's improvement will be vast and he probably will be the premier post player in the NAC. There is deep depth at small forward. Not many coaches can claim having four swingmen back with experience and the best may be freshman Roderick.

So the Hawks are not going to flounder this season. They will once again be very competitive and in the thick of the hunt for the NAC crown. If Phelan does what he says and turns the Hawks into pressing demons to use their depth and athleticism to the fullest, then the Hawks may even be better off without Middleton. There is no doubt his sudden loss will hurt the Hawks. They might have been a shoo-in for the NAC title. They will more than likely still contend, but may finish second.

1990-91 UNIVERSITY OF HARTFORD SCHEDULE		
Nov.	24	@DePaul
	27	@Connecticut
Nov.	30-	
Dec.	1	#Hawks Unlimited Tournament
Dec.	4	@George Washington
	8	Siena
	11	Dartmouth
	15	Boston University
	22	@Rhode Island
	29	@Jacksonville
Jan.	5	@St. Peter's
	8	@Vermont

1990-91 UNIVERSITY OF HARTFORD SCHEDULE *Cont.*		
	12	@Lamar
	16	@Siena
	20	@Maine
	23	Northeastern
	26	New Hampshire
	30	@Marist
Feb.	2	@Boston University
	4	Delaware
	9	Vermont
	12	Harvard
	16	@Northeastern
	19	Duquesne
	23	Maine
	27	Central Connecticut
Mar.	2	@New Hampshire
	5-9	##NAC Tournament

@ Road Games
# Hartford, CT (Columbia, Holy Cross & Long Island)
Site to be announced

HARVARD

LAST SEASON: 12-14
CONFERENCE RECORD: 7-7
STARTERS LOST: 2
STARTERS RETURNING: 3
CONFERENCE: IVY LEAGUE
LOCATION: CAMBRIDGE, MA
HOME FLOOR: BRIGG ATHLETIC CENTER (3,000)
NICKNAME: CRIMSON
COLORS: CRIMSON, BLACK AND WHITE
COACH: PETER ROBY, record at Harvard, 49-81.

Harvard coach Peter Roby won't have to worry much about people sneaking in to watch the Crimson practice this season. With all the attention he's placing on halfcourt defense, things could get pretty boring. That is not to say his charges won't continue to excite come game-time. It's just that Roby figures his Harvard has the scoring part down. Now he'd like some emphasis on stopping the other guys.

Last year's Crimson specialized in drag-strip basketball, bolting up-and-down the floor and pressuring opponents in the open court on both offense and defense. It wasn't exactly Loyola Marymount, but Harvard did average 77.9 points per game and boasted the Ivy League's first- and third-leading scorers.

Yet all that energy was good for no more than a spot in the league's four-way deadlock for third. And when things slowed down a little, allowing rivals a chance to set up, Harvard really had problems.

"We're a running, pressing team," Roby explained. "We won't change that. We have to force the action, but we have to defend better. We've been sacrificing the half-court defense."

Given the scoring ability of returning stars **Ralph James** and **Ron Mitchell**, the sacrifice may be worth it. When turned loose, those two gave Harvard a potent punch. They could be even more dangerous this year.

James, a first-team All-Ivy selection, is a 6-5 senior swingman who ranked among the league's Top 10 in five different categories, including first in scoring with 22.6 ppg (20.3 ppg, 6.5 rpg overall). He ranks seventh on the all-time Harvard scoring list and set the school single-game record with 41 points against Penn last year.

"Ralph shoots the ball well, and he goes by people and is tremendous in the lane," Roby said. "He has NBA athletic ability and is rugged and strong. He's our marquee player."

Mitchell's name is found among the Crimson

headliners as well. The 6-7, 210-pound senior forward was a second-team All-Ivy choice a year ago and contributed 15.4 ppg and 7.8 rpg to the Harvard cause. "He's a joy to coach," said Roby. "He's a ferocious rebounder, a great defender and he runs like a deer. He gives us tremendous leadership and is the heart of our team."

Returning to distribute the ball to the two stars and kickstart the Crimson running game is 5-10 sophomore **Tarik Campbell** (2.8 ppg, 77 assists). He will be joined in the starting lineup by any combination of 6-6 sophomore forward **Tyler Rullman** (9.4 ppg, 3.1 rpg), 6-8 sophomore center **Peter Condakes** (3.1 ppg, 1.1 rpg) or 6-6 junior forward **Mike Minor** (2.1 ppg, 1.3 rpg).

Matt McClain (1.3 ppg), a 6-2 sophomore, and 6-3 junior **David LaPointe** will provide backcourt depth, while 6-8 junior **Eric Carter** (2.0 ppg, 1.3 rpg) fills up in front.

Roby looked for size on the recruiting trail and came up with some needed frontcourt help. **Jabbar Abdi** (Landon School/Washington, D.C.) and **Anikar Chhabra** (St. Stevens HS/Alexandria, Va.) are 6-7 forwards, and **Chris Wood** (J.A. Faer HS/Little Rock, Ark.) is a 6-8 pivotman. How well those freshmen blend in with the up-tempo Harvard style could determine the Crimson's Ivy performance.

"The league is brutal," Roby said. "It's as even as I've ever seen it, and I've been at Harvard for nine years and graduated from Dartmouth. It creates excitement on everybody's campus and makes for a tight race that comes down to the last weekend."

BLUE RIBBON ANALYSIS

If you get a chance to see Harvard, buy a ticket. James and Mitchell alone are worth scalpers' prices. Both thrive on Roby's wide-open philosophy, and James is a legitimate NBA candidate.

Campbell and Rullman have weathered the Ivy battles, but little else is proven after them. Roby says he should not expect much from his freshmen, but he may need some instant contributions.

On a given night, Harvard can beat anyone in the Ivy League. They proved it last year, knocking off everyone but Brown. Problems for the Crimson will come over the long haul. Figure on a solid third-place finish and lots of scoring.

1990-91 HARVARD SCHEDULE		
Nov.	24	Lehigh
	27	Fairfield
Dec.	1	@Vermont
	3	Brandeis (MA)
	5	Holy Cross
	8	@Boston College
	15	Dartmouth
	19	Duke
	22	@Colgate
	28	#Southern California
	29	@Long Beach State
Jan.	5	Dartmouth
	11	@Cornell
	12	@Columbia
	29	New Hampshire
Feb.	1	@Pennsylvania
	2	@Princeton
	8	Brown
	9	Yale
	12	@Hartford
	15	Columbia
	16	Cornell
	22	@Yale
	23	@Brown
Mar.	1	Princeton
	2	Pennsylvania

@ Road Games
# Long Beach, CA

HAWAII

LAST SEASON: 25-10
CONFERENCE RECORD: 10-6
STARTERS LOST: 4
STARTERS RETURNING: 1
CONFERENCE: WESTERN ATHLETIC (WAC)
LOCATION: HONOLULU, HI
HOME FLOOR: BLAISDELL ARENA (7,575)
NICKNAME: RAINBOWS
COLORS: GREEN AND WHITE
COACH: RILEY WALLACE, record at Hawaii, 46-48. Career record, 129-111.

Every day thousands of visitors board airplanes and leave paradise on their way back to the mainland. But at the end of the spring semester, Hawaii coach Riley Wallace must have been very disappointed to see four people get on one of the many flights that leave Honolulu daily.

The people of Hawaii make a living from those thousands of tourists but those four young men represented a lot more to Wallace. They were 60 percent of his scoring and the nucleus that had turned the Rainbows from a pushover to a contender in the WAC.

While Hawaii is a lovely place to visit, not many good basketball players had wanted to live there until the last few seasons. Wallace is given the credit for making Hawaii basketball respectable, but these four players were the ones who have managed to get Hawaii into the NIT two years in a row. They helped create an interest in basketball in a state that specializes in sandy beaches, sunsets, luas and tropical weather.

A new 10,000-seat arena is being built at Hawaii. It originally was planned as a home for Hawaii's very successful men's and women's volleyball teams. The basketball team threw a wrench into the plans by being so successful that the building was expanded before it was started.

Now that Wallace has created the monster at Hawaii, he has to keep it alive. "We finished the season with the best crowd in Hawaii history and I hope we can continue where we left off."

The Rainbows set a school record with 25 victories last season. They were one game away from going to New York for the semifinals of the NIT. They reached the championship game of the WAC tournament and had a realistic chance of going to the NCAA tournament.

That's all history, however. And it was accomplished with seven lettermen —including the four starters —who now are in the record books and not on the team.

The most painful departure for Wallace was Chris Gaines. Gaines came to Hawaii as the prep player of the year from Iowa and he left as the leading scorer in Rainbow history, something he accomplished in 3 1/2 seasons because he missed a semester during his junior year with academic problems. Last season, Gaines led Hawaii in scoring at 17.6 per game and was the man the Rainbows looked for in the pinch. He was first-team All-WAC.

Also leaving was Terry Houston. He was second on the team in scoring at 15.1 and first in rebounding at 7.0. Gaines was the shooting guard and Houston was the big forward. The starting small forward was 6-4 Vincent Smalls (7.0 ppg, 5.3 rpg). He was an outstanding defensive player, making the WAC's all-defensive team. He might have been the best defensive player in the league.

The other missing starter is 6-8 Chris Beaubrun (8.7 ppg, 5.6 rpg), who normally started at center. When Beaubrun wasn't in the middle, 6-9 Andrew McGuire (5.6 points, 4.1 rebounds), was filling in.

Arlen Bento (1.3 ppg, 0.4 rpg) and Bobby Robinson (1.7 ppg, 0.6 rpg) also left the program.

Troy Bowe, a 5-10 senior, is the only returning starter. He averaged 9.2 points as the starting point guard last year. As the man who runs the team on the floor, Bowe will be carrying a heavy load this year. Bowe has started 51 straight games and has been consistent. He begins the season seventh on the school list in assists and fifth in steals. He had 18 points on 8-of-10 shooting vs. Utah last season.

The backup at point guard is expected to be 6-3 junior **Otis Clay**, who averaged 23.0 points and 4.0 assists last year at Malcolm X JC in Chicago. "We've signed Otis Clay as an insurance policy," said Wallace.

For more insurance, the Rainbows also have 6-4 senior **Joe Hudson** (1.2 ppg, 0.7 rpg), 6-0 junior **Jimmy Lactaoen** (1.6 ppg, 0.4 rpg) and 6-1 junior **Wendell Navalta** (0.2 ppg, 0.3 rpg) returning from last year at point guard.

The starting shooting guard should be **Phil Lott**. The 6-4 junior saw enough time to average 7.1 points last season. He'll have to carry a big part of the scoring load. He has shown flashes of such ability like 25 points on 11-of-14 shooting vs. Air Force last year. Backing up Lott will be 6-2 junior **Andre Stovall**, who averaged 22.2 points last season at Compton (Calif.) CC, and 6-5 junior **Marcus Nash**, who had even better numbers at Los Angeles City College with 22.2 points and 8.7 rebounds per game. Stovall (79 three-pointers last season) is a perimeter force.

Nash might play at small forward, where Wallace has a big hole to fill. **Tim Shepherd** is a returning 6-7 sophomore forward but he averaged just 1.7 points and 1.3 rebounds. **Mike Gilless**, a 6-7 senior forward, also is expected to get some time after averaging 2.2 points and 1.3 rebounds last season. Wallace feels Gilless is capable of being much more productive this year.

Shepherd and two junior college transfers will work at the strong forward position. **Charles McLemore** is a 6-7 junior transfer from Triton (Ill.) CC where he picked up 14.0 rebounds, 9.0 points and a game last season. **Latroy Spann**, 6-7, also went to Triton CC last year where he averaged 9.8 points and 3.0 rebounds.

Wallace really doesn't have any decision or choice at center. **Chip Thompson**, a 6-9 junior transfer from Kansas City (Kan.) CC, will be in the middle. He averaged 17.0 points and 7.0 rebounds last season. Thompson redshirted his freshman year at Wichita State before arriving at Kansas City. He was rated by one scouting service among the Top 20 JC centers in the country.

Backing up Thompson will be 6-10 sophomore center **Phil Addington**, a transfer from Dallas Baptist College by way of Irving, Texas. He was an all-district selection at Irving HS. Last year he averaged 2.0 points and 0.6 rebounds as a reserve center at Dallas Baptist, which dropped basketball after the season.

BLUE RIBBON ANALYSIS

Wallace seems to have found the magical formula at Hawaii by signing junior college players. Most athletes don't get island fever in two years, but a full four or five years is tough. While Wallace was dropping seven players from last year's team off at the airport, he was also picking up six junior college transfers to take their place. "We'll be a better shooting club than last year," said Wallace. "Our overall size is better and our recruits have good athletic ability. I think we'll probably have better quickness."

The key for the Rainbows is how quickly —if ever —the newcomers fit into Wallace's system. He believes in hard work and a team effort, which isn't easy for every player to learn.

So December might be a tough month for Hawaii, which plays in four tournaments (Hawaii Tip-Off, Apple Invitation, Pre-Holiday and Rainbow Classic).

The Rainbows have become hard to beat at home, but have trouble winning on the road. That might seem like a familiar script for many teams, but travel problems are exaggerated for Hawaii, which has to fly over five hours just to reach the mainland.

There is no such thing as a rebuilding year for a team that depends on junior college players to keep the stable full. With two-year players, Wallace always will be replacing, but he won't be rebuilding. If Nash and Stovall can provide the offense they're expected to, Hawaii will remain respectable. But the Rainbows simply lost too much talent and experience not to drop from last year's peak, probably to somewhere around sixth place in the WAC.

1990-91 HAWAII SCHEDULE		
Nov.	23 & 25	#Hawaii Tip-Off Tournament
	Nov. 30-Dec. 1	##Apple Invitational
Dec.	8	Hawaii-Hilo
	14	Illinois-Chicago
	20-21	*Pre-Holiday Tournament
	27-30	**Rainbow Classic
Jan.	3	Utah
	5	Brigham Young
	10	@Wyoming
	12	@Air Force
	17	UTEP
	19	New Mexico
	24	@New Mexico
	26	@UTEP
	31	Wyoming
Feb.	7	@Utah
	9	@Brigham Young
	13	Air Force
	16	Colorado State
	21	@San Diego State
	23	@Colorado State
Mar.	2	San Diego State
	6-9	***WAC Tournament

@ Road Games
# Honolulu, HI (Northeast Louisiana, Southwest Missouri State & Southwestern Louisiana)
Palo Alto, CA (George Washington, Stanford & Vanderbilt)
* Honolulu, HI (Appalachian State, North Texas & Wagner)
** Honolulu, HI (Alaska-Anchorage, California, Iona, Pitt, Stetson, Tennessee & Wichita State)
*** Laramie, WY

HOLY CROSS

LAST SEASON: 24-5
CONFERENCE RECORD: 14-2
STARTERS LOST: 2
STARTERS RETURNING: 3
CONFERENCE: PATRIOT
LOCATION: WORCESTER, MA
HOME FLOOR: HART CENTER (4,000)
NICKNAME: CRUSADERS
COLORS: ROYAL PURPLE AND WHITE
COACH: GEORGE BLANEY, record at Holy Cross, 284-232. Career record, 348-290.

Bob Cousy, Jack "The Shot" Foley, Ron Perry, Tom Heinsohn. All part of the mystique that has comprised the rich history of Holy Cross basketball. A good part of that storied tradition was virtually ancient history to Holy Cross basketball fans of very recent years. Last season, George Blaney's Crusaders did their own version of "Waking Up the Echoes," rolling to a 24-6 record, the MAAC North title, and an NIT berth, the Worcester school's first post-season appearance since 1980-81. Guard Dwight Pernell also etched his name among those mentioned earlier, leading the team in five categories, including scoring (21.6), three-point field goal percentage (.513 —eighth nationally) and free throw percentage (.868 —ninth nationally). His final career point total of 1,891 placed him third on Holy Cross' all-time list. He truly made '89-90 one of the most memorable ever atop Mount St. James, and gave Crusaders faithful memories to last a lifetime.

That, as they say, is history. Pernell and back-courtmate Lorn Davis (10.7 ppg, 3.7 rpg) have both graduated. The question now is, what's next? The answer is, the Patriot League. The former football only group began play in 22 sports this season, including men's basketball. Holy Cross, along with MAAC rivals Fordham and Army, join former ECC members Lehigh, Lafayette, and Bucknell and North Atlantic refugee Colgate for the league's initial season. The road to the NCAA tournament does not include former MAAC rivals LaSalle, St. Peter's and Iona among the league opponents. What does this mean for Blaney's squad? For 1990-91, it should mean more good news.

Holy Cross returns 12 lettermen and three starters from a year ago. Those three starters are all up front, and will again be led by 6-10 senior center **Jim Nairus** (14.3 ppg, 5.9 rpg). The Academic All-American (3.34 GPA in pre-med) had an outstanding junior campaign, emerging to lead the team in rebounding while finishing second in scoring. He also had a very un-bigmanlike outside touch, hitting almost half of his three-point shots (35-of-78). 6-6 senior **Earl Weedon** (9.6 ppg, 5.6 rpg) and junior forward **Leon Dickerson** (8.7 ppg, 4.8 rpg) also return. Weedon excited Holy Cross fans with his strong inside play and great leaping ability in his junior year, while Dickerson showed marked improvement over his sophomore year and could develop into one of the Patriot League's top rebounders. Also seeing more and more time in the frontcourt is 7-0 junior **Scott Martzloff** (3.8 ppg, 4.2 rpg). The Rochester, N.Y., product played in every game last season while beefing up his upper body and making himself into a very capable role player. His development will be a big key to the Holy Cross frontcourt stability.

A pair of 6-7 sophomores, **Rick Mashburn** (3.4 ppg, 2.6 rpg) and **Frank Powell** (5.6 ppg, 3.3 rpg), are coming off solid freshman seasons and will contribute off the bench, along with little used 6-6 junior **Kevin Kerwin** (1.4 ppg). Two 6-9 freshmen, English import **Reece Horton** (13.8 ppg, 11.4 rpg at Nottingham, England Prospect Hall) and **John Young** (24.3 ppg, 12.9 rpg at Staten Island (N.Y.) Academy, may also see some time to spell Martzloff and Nairus.

The key for the Crusader fortunes lies in the backcourt, more specifically in the hands of 6-2 senior scorer **Aaron Jordan** (5.3 ppg, 1.6 rpg). Jordan bounced back from the back injuries that plagued him his first two seasons to have a solid junior year, capped off by his length-of-the-court drive with :06 left to beat Fordham 95-94 in late February. Jordan is not the three-point shooter Pernell was, but he is a good passer and very physical player who can drive to the hoop. He will key the Holy Cross attack. Sharing backcourt duties will be a trio of very inexperienced sophomores, 6-2 **Roger Breslin** (0.6 ppg), 6-2 **Derek Farkas** (0.1 ppg) and 6-3 **Bill Walker** (2.0 ppg). Breslin will likely share time at the point spot with Jordan moves to the shooting spot, with Farkas and Walker playing the off-guard when Jordan runs the show. Of the three, look for the sure handed Breslin to have the biggest input, especially given the scoring load hoisted on Jordan's shoulders. Two others, 5-9 **David Rothstein**, son of Miami Heat coach Ron Rothstein, and 6-5 freshman **David Boyle** (15.9 ppg at Mater Dei HS and a native of Corona Del Mar, Calif.) will also see some time at the point and shooting guard spots, respectively.

BLUE RIBBON ANALYSIS

If this were the highly competitive MAAC, the Crusaders would be a middle of the road team.

However, this is the Patriot League, which is slightly less competitive overall. The frontcourt is formidable. Nairus will be a first team all-league selection, while Weedon, Martzloff and Dickerson are solid contributors. The big question is in the backcourt. As Aaron Jordan goes, so go the Crusaders. No scoring from outside will make it very tough on the inside players to have good seasons. One of the sophomores must also absorb some of the pressure as well. Breslin should emerge from the pack as Holy Cross' point guard of the future.

Still, even with those questions, it should be a good year in Worcester. The only other really talented team in the league is Fordham, and Holy Cross has been able to get by the Rams in recent years (with the exception of last year's MAAC semifinal). Still, the Crusaders will finish in second but come tournament time anything can happen, and Blaney's squad could find themselves in the "bigger" dance for the first time since '79-80.

1990-91 HOLY CROSS SCHEDULE

Nov.	27	Western Michigan
Nov.	30-	
	Dec. 1	#Hawks Unlimited Tournament
Dec.	5	@Harvard
	8	St. Peter's
	15	Boston College
	19	@Mt. St. Mary's (MD)
	28-29	##Cowboy Shootout
Jan.	2	Dartmouth
	5	Providence
	10	Lafayette
	12	@Bucknell
	14	Assumption (MA)
	21	Brown
	23	Army
	26	@Fordham
	28	@Massachusetts
	31	Colgate
Feb.	2	Lehigh
	6	@Lafayette
	9	Bucknell
	11	@New Hampshire
	16	@Army
	20	Fordham
	23	@Colgate
	25	@Lehigh
Feb.	28-	
Mar.	1-2	*Patriot League Tournament

@ Road Games
# Hartford, CT (Columbia, University of Hartford & Long Island)
Casper, WY (Northern Arizona, Southern Mississippi & Wyoming)
* Worcester, MA

HOUSTON

LAST SEASON: 25-8
CONFERENCE RECORD: 13-3
STARTERS LOST: 2
STARTERS RETURNING: 3
CONFERENCE: SOUTHWEST (SWC)
LOCATION: HOUSTON, TX
HOME FLOOR: HOFHEINZ PAVILLION (10,060)
NICKNAME: COUGARS
COLORS: SCARLET AND WHITE
COACH: PAT FOSTER, record at Houston, 78-47.
Career record, includes high school, 427-191.

Houston finally seemed to play up to expectations last season and coach Pat Foster had his best record (25-8) since coming over from Lamar in the spring of 1986. Had the team's top player, 6-8 Carl

Herrera, who led the Cougars last season with averages of 16.6 ppg and 9.2 rpg, not passed up his final year of eligibility, the expectations at Houston might have been as high as they have been since the Akeem Olajuwon-Clyde Drexler led Phi Shamma Jamma era when Guy Lewis coached the Cougars to three straight Final Four appearances.

Herrera was selected by the Miami Heat (the third overall pick in the second round) before being traded to the Houston Rockets. He eventually signed a two-year contract with the Spanish team, Real Madrid.

"Carl's departure is a very big loss," Foster said. "But we have more depth and more experience than last year to make up for it."

Houston still has 6-8 senior forward **Craig Upchurch** (13.1 ppg, 7.0 rpg) at power forward and he will help compensate for the loss of Herrera. Upchurch was a second-team All-SWC selection after being first-team as a sophomore. He led Houston in steals last season and was second on the team in rebounding, assists and field goal percentage plus finished second behind Herrera in scoring. Upchurch, who can be a dominate force because of his quickness, leaping ability and accurate turnaround jumper from the baseline, averaged 18.8 ppg as a sophomore.

Foster is counting on the addition of forwards **Derrick Smith** and **Craig Lillie** to combine with Upchurch and two other starters to keep Houston close to powers Arkansas and Texas in the SWC race. Smith was considered one of Texas' top three high school players two years ago before sitting out last season. The 6-5 Smith was an athletic marvel at Humble HS where he averaged 19.9 points and 12.2 rebounds as a senior. The 6-5 Lillie is a transfer from Angelina (Tex.) JC who averaged 22.6 points and five rebounds per game. He shot 43 percent from three-point range and can also play second guard. Foster believes Smith and Lillie are both good defensive players and their presence will allow the Cougars to press more this season.

Senior forward **Darrell Mickens** was a productive sixth man last season. The 6-5 Mickens averaged 5.2 points and 4.2 rebounds. His 40-inch plus leaping ability often sparked the Cougars with an acrobatic dunk or a big block.

Roger Fernandes, a 6-9 junior from Sao Paulo, Brazil, returns after missing last season with an ankle injury. The soft shooting Fernandes can spell Upchurch at power forward or stand in for 7-1 senior center **Alvara Teheran** (5.4 ppg, 3.4 rpg). Teheran, a Columbian native who transferred from crosstown Houston Baptist, started 10 games but often was used sparingly by Foster. Teheran blocked 30 shots but was also totally lost in many games.

Houston has another seven-footer in junior **Gerry Holmes**. However, Holmes was slow to make the adjustment from junior college and played in only four games.

Transfer **Steve Stevenson**, a 6-10 senior from Prairie View, gives Houston unusual depth in the post. Stevenson was among the NCAA Division I leaders in rebounds (11.7 rpg) and blocks last season. He was expected to have immediate eligibility because Prairie View dropped its program, however, late in the summer the Prairie View program was reinstated so Stevenson's status at Houston could change.

Foster should be able to redshirt 6-9 freshman center **Rafael Carrasco**. A native of Bogota, Colombia, Carrasco is the third international player on the Cougar roster.

Both starting guards return and the backcourt should be deeper, as well, this season. Junior point guard **Derrick Daniels** often played all 40 minutes of a game but still made excellent progress through the season. He appears to be ready to live up to the considerable billing he received as a HS All-America player at Fort Worth Dunbar. The 6-3 Daniels (9.5 ppg) gained confidence in his perimeter shooting and made 41.7 percent of his three-point attempts. He ranked third in the SWC in assists with an average of 5.8 per game.

Shooting guard **Byron Smith** suffered through

a late season slump but should be one of the top scorers in the SWC. Smith, a 6-3 senior, averaged 16.3 points per game and was the SWC's No. 2 three-point shooter (45.6 percent) behind Arkansas' Lee Mayberry. He is a steady player who seemed to thrive on taking and making big shots.

The backcourt depth will come from Lillie and another talented newcomer, 6-2 redshirt freshman **Tyrone Evans**. Two years ago Evans was one of the top players in Louisiana. He averaged 31.6 points, 13.1 rebounds and 5.8 assists as a senior at Atlanta (La.) HS.

Ross Monaco, a 6-2 sophomore, returns after redshirting last year with an ankle injury. He was Daniels' backup two years ago and averaged three points and one assist per game. **Darrell Grayson**, a 6-3 sophomore who averaged 1.1 ppg in seven games, also is back.

BLUE RIBBON ANALYSIS

Everything came together for Houston last year after two mediocre seasons. However, Foster will again have to re-establish his team's chemistry as leading scorer and rebounder Herrera left Houston a year early to play in Spain.

Upchurch, Daniels, Smith and Mickens form a solid nucleus. They provide Houston with a terrific quickness and overall athletic ability that can enable the Cougars to defeat quality opposition and be at least the No. 3 team in the SWC.

The Cougars also have a deeper backcourt, some impressive newcomers and quality depth in the pivot.

Foster should have a 20-game winner and an NCAA tournament team.

HOWARD UNIVERSITY

LAST SEASON: 8-20
CONFERENCE RECORD: 5-11
STARTERS LOST: 0
STARTERS RETURNING: 5
CONFERENCE: MID-EASTERN ATHLETIC (MEAC)
LOCATION: WASHINGTON, DC
HOME FLOOR: BURR GYMNASIUM (2,700)
NICKNAME: BISON
COLORS: NAVY BLUE AND WHITE
COACH: ALFRED "BUTCH" BEARD, first season at Howard University.

For the first time on 15 years, A.B. Williamson will not be pacing the Howard University sidelines. After what happened to the Bison the last two seasons, new head coach Butch Beard better watch where he steps. Williamson wore out the floorboards in Burr Gymnasium.

A fixture who had guided Howard University through some of its best days from the mid-1970's to the mid-1980's, Williamson's fortunes nosedived dramatically. The Bison won only nine and eight games, respectively, the past two seasons. Last year was particularly frustrating, as they were supposed to rebound from a 9-19 record to get back to the .500 mark. Instead, Howard never got untracked, losing its last six games to finish 8-20.

Williamson departed with a 240-182 career record. Hired to rebuild the program was Beard, a nine-year NBA veteran who spent six of the last 11 years as an assistant coach, first with the New York Knicks and then the last two with the New Jersey Nets. A star at Louisville, where he played alongside current Washington Bullets' coach Wes Unseld, Beard also spent three years as a television analyst for the Knicks and the Atlanta Hawks.

"We hope to be competitive and achieve more than we did last year," Beard said. "It will be a year of evaluation and we hope to show improvement from one game to the next."

With all five starters and 13 players returning overall, Beard obviously inherits experienced players. Whether or not the negatives of the last two seasons took an irreparable toll is something he can only find out in time.

The only losses of any consequence are 6-8 forward Guy Owens (2.9 ppg, 1.8 rpg), who shot just 34 percent, and 6-9 center Jack Smith (2.5 ppg, 2.5 rpg). Both drew occasional starts, but fell out of Williamson's top seven.

Even with all the starters back, Beard will look long and hard at everyone at his disposal. There is only one newcomer on the squad but, as with any coaching change, a new system sometimes forces a rearrangement of playing time.

Beard will bring an up-tempo style to the Bison, and that may change past rotations all the more. "The bottom line as to how successful we will be," he said, "will depend on how quickly the team picks up the new system."

6-8 senior **Tyrone Powell** (11.3 ppg. 6.4 rpg) will get the longest look at center. Powell, 106 points shy of becoming the 14th Howard University player to reach the 1,000-point mark, settled into the pivot late last year and played well enough to earn second-team All-MEAC honors. He led the Bison in rebounding and, strangely, three-point shooting percentage (.447), although his place is inside.

The other frontcourt posts will have more com-petition. Power forward has two players who split time there a year ago. 6-7 senior **Tracy King** and 6-8 junior **Charles Chase** return, as well as 6-8 junior **Kelsey Sturdivant**. King averaged 6.3 points, 4.9 rebounds and shot 56 percent from the floor. Chase averaged 5.2 ppg, 3.3 rpg and shot 51 percent. He can also move into the pivot to spell Powell. Sturdivant (1.3 ppg, 1.3 rpg) played 70 minutes in nine games.

6-5 senior **Keith Kirven** (10.7 ppg, 6.7 rpg), who can play any of three positions, is the leading candidate for the small forward spot. He started there 18 times last year. Third in scoring and second in rebounding on the Bison, Kirven will be challenged by 6-6 junior **Julius McNeil**. McNeil transferred from Campbell College and sat out the 1989-90 campaign. The Atlanta, Ga. native is also the only newcomer to the squad. 6-3 junior **Ronnie Gibbs** (1.7 ppg, 1.1 rpg), a swingman, drew one start in 14 appearances last year after transferring from East Carolina.

Although they were the two of Howard's top scorers last season, the inexperience of guards **Milan Brown** and **Martin Huckaby** showed often. Brown, a 6-0 sophomore, averaged 9.0 ppg and had a team-leading 112 assists. He also shot a team-leading 86 percent from the free throw line, but only 35 percent from the floor. Huckaby, a 6-2 junior, led the team in scoring at 11.9 points per game, adding 3.3 rebounds and 85 assists. He was the only player to start all 28 games, and can also play the point.

Like Brown, Huckaby also shot just 35 percent from the floor. Same for 6-2 senior **Milton Bynum** (8.7 ppg, 1.5 rpg), a starter as a sophomore. Bynum drew only four starts last year, but has been a consistent player throughout his career, averaging 9.0 ppg through three seasons.

Others who will vie for attention under the new coaching regime are 6-3 junior **Robert Riddick** (1.3 ppg), 6-1 senior **Ricky Dodson** (0.7 ppg), 5-11 sophomore **Marlon Everett** (0.7 ppg) and 6-0 senior **Sean Mason**. The latter played in two games and did not score.

BLUE RIBBON ANALYSIS

Beard could have picked a better time to debut in college coaching. He will open with a team that returns virtually everyone, but has little history of winning. Next year, six of those players will be gone, and he will have to rebuild with unproven and as yet unidentified newcomers.

Huckaby and Brown are an adequate backcourt, and Powell is a decent performer in the middle. But this is a team that was outscored by nearly double figures a year ago. No coach could turn that around in a hurry without new players.

This looks like a long-term rebuilding job, and another long year for the Bison. Any improvement on last year's record would have to be considered a success.

IDAHO

LAST SEASON: 25-6
CONFERENCE RECORD: 13-3
STARTERS LOST: 3
STARTERS RETURNING: 2
CONFERENCE: BIG SKY
LOCATION: MOSCOW, ID
HOME FLOOR: KIBBIE-ASUI DOME (10,000)
NICKNAME: VANDALS
COLORS: SILVER AND GOLD
COACH: LARRY EUSTACHY, first year at Idaho.

When last seen in March, Idaho was being rudely dispatched by Louisville in the first round of the NCAA tournament. It marked the 12th straight year the Big Sky Conference torch-bearer had its flame snuffed in the opening round.

It was bad news for the league and the 25-6 Vandals, whom Big Sky officials thought - at least privately - had the best talent of any of its post-season representatives in some time. But Louisville, like UNLV the year before and Michigan the year before that, was just too much. So it goes for the two-time defending champion Vandals. For much of the season they are the class of their league, only to be outclassed in the end.

Idaho's storyline isn't likely to deviate much from the recent past in 1990-91, even though its coach, its playmaker and its top scorer are all gone. Kermit Davis took his 50-12 record and back-to-back NCAA appearances to Texas A&M, where it is unlikely he'll match Idaho's regular-season success, but quite possible he will exceed its post-season frustrations.

Former Idaho assistant Larry Eustachy, who worked with Davis when New Orleans coach Tim Floyd was running the Vandals' show, has taken over. Eustachy, who came back via Ball State, wasted no time exacting revenge in the name of Idaho. He was on the Ball State bench when it knocked Louisville out of the NCAA's two days after the Vandals' loss.

Eustachy admits the graduation of guard Otis Livingston, who set assist records for single-game (16) and single-season (262), and center Riley Smith (22.6 ppg, 8.8 rpg.) cut deep. The irrepressible Smith (6-8, 235) scored 28 points and pulled down 12 rebounds against Louisville and 7-0 center Felton Spencer. Both were game-highs and proof of Smith's talent.

Livingston, a cat-quick defender (63 steals), came to Idaho via Kansas. In fact, he started 15 games for the Jayhawks' 1988 NCAA championship team before quitting in early January.

"It will be very difficult to repeat what the Idaho Vandals have done the past two seasons," Eustachy said. "We will be entering the season minus last year's top players - Otis Livingston and Riley Smith. It's very difficult to replace two players of their caliber in such a short period."

6-7 senior center **Sammie Freeman** (6.7 ppg, 3.7 rpg) will be asked to fill the void created by Smith's departure. Freeman, a burly sort with a menacing scowl, has both the disposition and the shooting touch to get the job done.

Clifford Martin, an athletic 6-9 senior, will start at power forward. Martin (10.0 ppg, 4.9 rpg) has the reputation of jumping on the bandwagon during a rout, but seldom driving it when the going is tough. He must shed that tendency if the Vandals are to approach last year's success. Senior **Ricardo Boyd** (13.9 ppg, 4.7 rpg) is a 6-5 small forward with three-point shooting range. Boyd, of Ellisville, Mississippi, rounds out what should be the Big Sky's best front line - again.

"We're very pleased to have Ricardo back for his senior season," Eustachy said. "I may be his third coach (Davis and Floyd the other two), but the style of play hasn't changed all that much. He's accustomed to that style and that should be an added bonus to us besides his obvious athletic ability. We're going to count on Ricardo a lot, especially early."

The supporting cast of frontcourt players is a largely unknown entity. 6-7 freshman **Deon Watson** (T.L. Weston HS/Greenville, Miss.) has been touted as perhaps the most talented, even before he set foot on the Moscow campus. "Deon can do a lot of things very well," said Davis, who recruited him. "It would be a big boost for Idaho is he decides to stay. I hope he does."

Watson, after weighing the coaching change and his options, did indeed stay. If his talent matches his press clippings, the Vandals have themselves a player on which to build.

Junior college transfers **Darryl Mayes** (6-5, 195) of Cleveland State (Tex.) JC, **Terrell Malone** (6-4, 200) of Saddleback (Calif.) JC and **Otis Mixon** (6-5, 195) of Mount San Antonio (Calif.) JC offer athleticism, if not height and bulk. But in the Big Sky, predominantly a small forwards' conference, that should not be a problem.

In the backcourt, 6-3 senior **Leonard Perry** (3.0 ppg, 1.6 rpg) should start at one guard after sharing a spot last season. Perry is a muscular player who likes to mix it up. 6-4 sophomore **Mike Gustavel** played sparingly a year ago (1.5 ppg), but is capable of contributing.

Newcomers at guard include 6-3 junior **Louis Davis**, who averaged 18 points at Copiah-Lincoln (Miss.) JC; 6-2 point guard **Roosevelt Robinson**, a high school teammate of Watson at T.L. Weston HS; and 6-2 freshman **Swede Trenkle**, son of College of Southern Idaho coach Fred Trenkle.

6-1 **Calvin Ward**, yet another junior college transfer - Hiwassee (Tenn.) JC - is cat-quick and should challenge immediately for Livingston's vacated point guard position. Ward, the top assist man at Hiwassee, is one of those "better to give than receive" types who has the tools to do the job.

BLUE RIBBON ANALYSIS

The Vandals have a returning nucleus that is talented enough to defend the Big Sky title. With the league's best front line, and a decent guard in Perry, Idaho is once again the favorite. It is also something Eustachy recognizes.

"My dad once said, 'if it isn't broken, then don't fix it.' And I think it directly relates to the situation that I'm coming into," Eustachy said. "A few years ago, Tim Floyd and Kermit Davis and myself came into town. And we had a formula, or philosophy - call it what you want - and it was not only to improve on winning games, but to bring in players with good character and be the class of the Big Sky."

That much, Floyd and Davis accomplished. What neither was able to do, though, is get over the NCAA tournament hurdle. If Eustachy turns that trick, he'll be revered in Idaho. At least he figures to get the chance. Idaho remains the class of the Big Sky until someone proves otherwise.

IDAHO STATE

LAST SEASON: 6-21
CONFERENCE RECORD: 3-13
STARTERS LOST: 1
STARTERS RETURNING: 4
CONFERENCE: BIG SKY
LOCATION: PPOCATELLO, ID
HOME FLOOR: HOLT ARENA (12,000)
NICKNAME: BENGALS
COLORS: ORANGE AND BLACK
COACH: HERB WILLIAMS, first year at Idaho State.

After his team posted a 6-21 record, the worst in 40 years at Idaho State, Jim Boutin kept his word. He quit. "If I don't get the job done, no one will have to tell me to step down," claimed Boutin, who watched with gritted teeth while the Bengals plummeted from mediocre to morose.

Idaho State endured separate losing streaks of six and seven games. Half of their victories were forged by mid-December. On offense, they shot 42 percent from the field and just 62 percent from the free-throw line. On defense, the porous Bengals yielded more points per game (79.2) than any other team in the Big Sky. On the whole, they were awful.

Boutin, whose strong-willed approach earned him two .500 or better seasons during his five-year stay in Pocatello, finally appeared to succumb to his team's will. When guard **Craig Murray** misfired on an ill-advised three-point shot with Idaho State clinging to a five-point lead over seventh-place Boise State in one late-season game, Boutin winced as if gun shot.

"Why? Why?" he said, to no one in particular. The Bengals went on to a come-from-ahead defeat, and Boutin was never quite the same after that early January disaster.

Now that season, like Boutin, is tucked away in Idaho State's past. Former Michigan State assistant coach Herb Williams is the new man on the job. In doing so, he becomes the first black head coach of a major college sport in Idaho's history. But if the state is catching up with the times, Williams does not want to hear about it.

"I'm not a pioneer, I'm a basketball coach," he shot at a reporter during his inaugural press conference. "I want to be judged by wins and losses, and by how my players perform on the court and in the classroom. Not by the color of my skin."

Clearly, Williams will not be the sort to allow his point guard to take ill-advised shots, no matter what this team's record. "We will play an up-tempo game, but controlled," Williams promised. "It just won't be fire at will."

The new coach inherits four starters, which may or may not be good. Given the results of a year ago, none are guaranteed starting roles. "I only know four guys who'll be there when we tip the ball off for the first time, and they won't be in uniform," Williams said, referring to himself and his staff.

Along the front line, it seems reasonable that **Steven Garrity,** a 6-6 senior and honorable mention All-Big Sky performer, will start at one forward. Garrity (12.0 ppg, 7.2 rpg) is a hard worker who seemed as upset as Boutin by last year's poor play. "I'll accept whatever changes coach Williams makes," Garrity said. "When you're 6-21, you can't assume anything. I hope to play, but I'll understand if he comes in here and cleans house."

Garrity, who was married and put on about 15 pounds prior to last season, neglected his weightlifting routine and his game suffered. "I'm going to put myself full into this because it's my last year," he said.

Marcus Malone (11.2 ppg, 4.6 rpg), an athletic 6-4 forward who has decent post-up skills, could start alongside Garrity. The potentially explosive senior averaged 25 points in one six-game stretch. Yet Malone and Boutin had their differences, among them Boutin's reported belief that Malone did not put out in practice.

How Malone and Williams view each other remains to be seen. "In my directive to each player, I gave them things they must do," said Williams. "It's up to them to make those changes in their attitude, approach, work ethic and attention to their education."

Holdover forwards, such as 6-5 senior **David Fuller** (3.8 ppg, 2.5 rpg), 6-4 junior **Scott Roberts** (4.5 ppg) and 6-5 senior **Byron Young** (5.5 ppg), add depth but not much size.

Meanwhile, incoming freshmen like 6-6 **Kareem Carpenter** (Huron HS/Ann Arbor, Mich.), 6-7 **Jesse Shiel** (Sandy HS/Sandy, Ore.) and 6-7 **Tom Skahill** (Lyons Township HS/LaGrange, Ill.), have come to the land of opportunity. All three were big time prep scorers and could contribute immediately. A pair of junior college transfers - 6-7 **Alexis Kreps** of Golden West (Calif.) CC and 6-7 **Herman Smith** of Lake Michigan CC - are also being counted on.

"For the time of year and the time we had to recruit, we came out with a pretty fair class," Williams said. "We have a lot of work to do to get them acclimated to what we want to do. And we will."

Kirkland Ivory (2.8 ppg, 2.7 rpg), a burly 6-6, 215-pound senior, appears to have the inside track at center. Young should back him up.

In the backcourt, Murray (6.2 ppg, 5.4 assists), a 6-1 senior, should start. Redshirt 6-4 sophomore **Corey Bruce** and 6-2 JC transfer **Tyrone Buckmon** (Coffeeville JC, Kan.) will vie for the other spot.

BLUE RIBBON ANALYSIS

Idaho State fans have not had much to cheer about since the Bengals were a surprise winner in the 1986-87 Big Sky post-season bash. Their reward was a berth in the NCAA tournament, where the Bengals were hammered by UNLV in the first round. Since then, victory has been something of a rare notion.

Williams seems determined to turn things around. His intensity on the court and national recruiting connections off it give hope that Idaho State can return to the Big Sky's upper-echelon. Just don't look for it to happen in 1990-91. Give Williams a year

or two. Until then, and with some luck at that, look for no better than a seventh-place finish.

ILLINOIS

LAST SEASON: 21-8
CONFERENCE RECORD: 11-7
STARTERS LOST: 5
STARTERS RETURNING: 0
CONFERENCE: BIG TEN
LOCATION: CHAMPAIGN, IL
HOME FLOOR: ASSEMBLY HALL (16,153)
NICKNAME: FIGHTING ILLINI
COLORS: ORANGE AND BLUE
HEAD COACH: LOU HENSON, record at Illinois, 270-150.
Career collegiate record, 556-257.

In the summer of Illinois' discontent, the Illini lost more than the nucleus of their 1989 Final Four team. They lost more than five starters and two key reserves from last season's national contenders. Lost more than the services of at least one key recruit.

The Illini lost, period, under the watchful eye of the NCAA, which was expected to conclude its year-long investigation of Illinois basketball in early fall. In the meantime, about all coach Lou Henson could do was hold the fort and try to pick up whatever pieces remained.

"You can't lose five starters off a team and not have it hurt you," Henson understated. And that was before the departure of 6-7 senior-to-be Rodney Jones (7.4 ppg, 4.3 rpg) and the summer suspension of 6-4 sophomore Brooks Taylor (1.5 ppg, 1.0 rpg), two players the Illini were counting on to help replace perhaps the most talented nucleus in Illinois history.

Heading the list of those gone is superlative guard Kendall Gill, the Big Ten scoring champion (20.0 ppg) last year and a first round draft pick of the Charlotte Hornets. Also drafted into the NBA were forward Marcus Liberty (17.8 ppg, 7.1 rpg), who concluded his collegiate career a year early, and point guard Stephen Bardo (9.7 ppg, 6.1 rpg, 139 assists). Both Liberty (Denver Nuggets) and Bardo (Atlanta Hawks) were second round picks. Two more starters — Ervin Small (7.1 pg, 5.4 rpg) and P.J. Bowman (4.2

ppg, 1.2 rpg)—also completed their eligibility.

Henson can celebrate the return of 1989 point guard **Larry Smith,** who sat out last year. Smith, a 6-4 senior, split time at the point during Illinois' Final Four season, averaging 4.9 points, 2.0 rebounds and handing out a team-high 157 assists.

Another returning player with significant experience is 6-6 junior **Andy Kaufmann** (9.8 ppg, 3.2 rpg). Kaufmann played in 12 games as a freshman and started 16 more for the Illini last season. A better-than-average outside shooter (44.6 percent), Kaufmann has excellent range and actually shot better (44.9 percent) from beyond the three-point stripe (22-for-49). A natural small forward with good defensive and passing skills, Kaufmann may be moved by Henson to shooting guard, where, with more consistent scoring, he could recall visions of former Illinois great Doug Altenberger.

Kaufmann's move may be predicated on the eligibility of highly-touted 6-8 redshirt freshman **Deon Thomas** (Simeon HS/Chicago, Ill.), an exceptional talent at forward. Thomas was forced to sit out last year as the NCAA probed Illinois' recruiting of him, and his eligibility this season was expected to be part of the NCAA's fall announcement. Thomas was the state's Mr. Basketball in 1989, averaging 26.2 points, 12.0 rebounds and seven blocked shots as a high school senior. However, he was not even permitted to practice during the NCAA investigation.

6-7 senior **Andy Kpedi** (2.8 ppg, 2.8 rpg) figures to start at center. Kpedi is an excellent leaper and a strong inside player, though not a dominant big man. When not hampered last season by a stress fracture of his right shin, Kpedi showed flashes of solid play. He contributed 12 rebounds in a victory over Indiana State and eight more against Mississippi.

6-5 sophomore **Tim Geers** (1.7 ppg, 1.0 rpg) will make his bid for extended playing time after seeing limited action as a freshman. Geers sees the court very well, is an exceptional passer and possesses a soft shooting touch from medium range. Redshirt freshman **Tom Michael** (Carlyle HS/Carlyle, Ill.) also looks to grab a fair amount of time up front. The 6-8 Michael has great range on his jump shot and, on a team that lost over two-thirds of its scoring, may win himself a job. Michael averaged 25.0 points and 10.0 rebounds in his final scholastic season. 6-8 freshman **Scott Pierce** (Trinity HS/Euless, Tex.) rounds out the frontcourt. Pierce (21.0 ppg, 13.0 rpg) set a school record with 93 blocked shots as a high school senior.

Taylor was expected to compete for a starting position in the backcourt, having played the most of any of last year's freshmen. He is still in school following his suspension, and could return before the year is over. Another potential backcourt starter, 6-4 scoring machine Jamie Brandon (King HS/Chicago, Ill.)—the 1990 Mr. Basketball in Illinois—was ruled academically ineligible and transferred to LSU.

That leaves the rest of the guard line, other than Smith and perhaps Kaufmann, in the untested hands of freshmen **T.J. Wheeler** (Christopher HS/Christopher, Ill.) and **Rennie Clemons** (Calvary HS/Springfield, Ill.). Wheeler, a 6-4 shooting guard, was a two-spot high school star, averaging 32.7 points in basketball and quarterbacking the football team. The 6-0 Clemons, a two-time All-State choice, makes the short trip from Springfield as perhaps the Illinois point guard of the future.

BLUE RIBBON ANALYSIS

It is more than a matter of rebuilding at Illinois. Following the NCAA investigation, it may be a matter of survival. Throw in all the key personnel losses, and it could be a long, long season for the Illini.

The size and strength necessary to compete in the Big Ten are simply not there. Even if the ultra-talented Thomas is eligible, Illinois is looking at a second division finish. And Thomas, once touted as one of the top Illini recruits ever, has not played organized basketball since the winter of 1989.

Call it eighth or ninth place.

ILLINOIS STATE

LAST SEASON: 18-13
CONFERENCE RECORD: 9-5
STARTERS LOST: 3
STARTERS RETURNING: 2
CONFERENCE: MISSOURI VALLEY (MVC)
LOCATION: NORMAL, IL
HOME FLOOR: REDBIRD ARENA (10,500)
NICKNAME: REDBIRDS
COLORS: RED AND WHITE
COACH: BOB BENDER, record at Illinois State, 18-13.

The start of Bob Bender's head coaching career at Illinois State was a page right out of Cinderella. The magic did not end until the Redbirds dropped a narrow decision to defending national champion Michigan in the first round of the NCAA West Regional.

From a 6-9 start, Illinois State put together winning streaks of three, five and four games, and won 12 of its last 15 games altogether. The coup de grace came in the Missouri Valley Conference tournament, hosted and won by the Redbirds.

"I was proud of the way the kids were rewarded for their hard work with success when it counted most," said Bender, a former Duke assistant. "We struggled at times, but they never gave up on the system and eventually turned it around. Our goal was to win the Missouri Valley tournament and get into the NCAA's. We got that."

Repeating the glass slipper act appears to be more difficult this time around. When Bender took over from 11-year coach Bob Donewald, he inherited a team with 12 lettermen and five seniors. The only new face belonged to the 32-year-old head coach.

Now Bender must replace those five graduated seniors, who represented 67.2 percent of the Redbirds' scoring and 63.0 percent of the team's rebounding last year. Gone are the leading scorer, top rebounder, best defender and three widest bodies.

The two returning starters were not even expected to make major contributions when practice began last October. 6-0 sophomore **Richard Thomas** wound up starting at point guard, averaging 8.6 points and 2.0 rebounds (109 assists, 48 steals). Along the way he was named to the MVC's all-newcomer team and wound up second in the voting for the league's Outstanding Freshman award. Thomas was selected over the summer to try out for the USA Junior National Team.

"When Richard started, we couldn't get him out of the lineup," Bender said. "If there's one position you want coming back, it's point guard."

The other returning starter is 6-5 junior forward **Scott Fowler,** who averaged 6.7 points and 3.0 rebounds after moving into the starting lineup just about the time the Redbirds got hot. He averaged 9.7 points over Illinois State's final 16 games.

Said Bender: "We weren't about to push him out of the lineup, either."

Seven other lettermen are back, but none made a major contribution. 6-5 senior **Sam Skarich** averaged 2.2 points, but could help more if he regains his shooting eye (29 percent last year) following major reconstructive knee surgery two years ago. 6-3 junior **Elvin Florez** averaged 2.7 points, but played just 7.6 minutes per game. Junior **Xavier Williams** is a good athlete at 6-6, but must shoot better than the .348 mark he had last year.

Antoine Hicks, a 5-9 junior, backs up Thomas at the point. 5-11 sophomore **Todd Kagel** is a former walk-on who got into 16 games last year. **Rick Bettenhausen** is a 7-0 senior who played in just three games (10 total minutes). A ninth returnee, 6-8 junior and former football tight end **Derek Stokes,** sat out last season after undergoing reconstructive knee surgery. He started 20 games in 1988-89.

All the returnees must shoot better. As a group, the eight who played last season shot just .386 from the field. The best percentage in the group belonged to Florez (.446).

To help fill the many holes, Bender brought in five newcomers, including Illinois State's first junior college recruit in 15 years. **Reggie Wilson,** a 6-6 transfer out of Lincoln (Neb.) College, averaged 12 points and eight rebounds for a team with three Division I signees.

Scott Taylor, who played last season at Bridgton Academy Prep (Newton, Mass.) has the best statistics among four new freshmen. The 6-7 forward averaged 23 points and 13 rebounds per game. Bender also plucked 6-5 **Charles Barnes** (Whitney Young HS) from talent-laden Chicago. Barnes, the nephew of Thomas, averaged 21 points and 10 rebounds last year.

Another former Illinois high school standout, 6-2 **Todd Wemhoener** (Quincy HS), fills the need for a shooter. Womhoener averaged 18.6 points to go with 5.5 assists and 4.5 rebounds on one of the state's top prep teams. The final recruit is 6-7 **Mike VandeGarde** (Jefferson HS/Bloomington, Minn.). VandeGarde averaged 17 points, 10 rebounds, six assists and four block shots per game.

BLUE RIBBON ANALYSIS

As Illinois State tries to become the first Missouri Valley team in 14 years to repeat as post-season tournament champions, the deck is stacked against the Redbirds. Players who had support roles last year will need to come to the forefront and make sizable contributions, offensively and defensively.

Former Redbirds like Rickey Jackson, Jarrod Coleman, Randy Blair and Jon Pemberton were around for a long time and saw a whole lot of playing time. Now it is Fowler, Thomas and Florez who must fill the void from the departure of the graduated seniors.

Bender's biggest task will be getting this group shots it can make. That might take more of a half-court approach, unless two or three of the newcomers make an immediate impact. Pencil the Redbirds for the MVC's second division because of too much youth and inexperience, and too little scoring punch. Seventh place is a possibility.

INDIANA STATE

LAST SEASON: 8-20
CONFERENCE RECORD: 2-12
STARTERS LOST: 1
STARTERS RETURNING: 4
CONFERENCE: MISSOURI VALLEY (MVC)
LOCATION: TERRE HAUTE, IN
HOME FLOOR: HULMAN CENTER (10,200)
NICKNAME: SYCAMORES
COLORS: BLUE AND WHITE
COACH: TATES LOCKE, record at Indiana State, 8-20. Career record, 213-186.

In just about every category that reflected overall athletic ability, Indiana State was at the bottom of the Missouri Valley Conference last season: blocked shots, steals, turnover margin, scoring margin, field goal percentage, rebounding, scoring offense and won-loss record.

But in the departments that reflected "want to," the Sycamores fared much better: first in scoring defense, first in opponents' rebounding, first in three-point shooting, first in free throw shooting.

In his first season at Indiana State, veteran coach Tates Locke tried everything. He used 18 different starting lineups, and no lineup started three straight games. When all was said and done, Locke decided what the Sycamores needed most was a face lift.

Gone are seven lettermen, most with eligibility

remaining. Back are five lettermen - four of them starters - and two redshirts who would have made a difference last year. Add to that 10 newcomers, and you can see that Locke is putting together the kind of team he wants in Terre Haute.

The Indiana State faithful appreciated the efforts of Locke's first team. Attendance was up 30.5 percent last year, and average home attendance was higher than it's been since the 1979-80 season, the year after the Sycamores finished second in the NCAA tournament. Last year's average attendance - 5,459 - was higher than the largest single crowd during the previous season.

Indiana State's top returnee is 6-4 senior forward **Eddie Bird,** who has a chance to end his career as one of the top five scorers in school history. He averaged 14.6 points, ninth-best in the MVC last year, and 3.5 rebounds. In addition, Bird displayed familiar bloodlines in three-point accuracy (46.0 percent) and ranked fifth in the conference in free throw efficiency (80.8).

Dewayne Brown made more starts - 25 - than anybody on the roster, averaging 9.4 points and 3.1 rebounds. Brown is a rugged 6-2 senior, equally comfortable at guard or forward.

Travis Inman, a 6-2 junior guard, averaged 11.5 points and 3.7 rebounds last season and was the third-best three-point shooter in the MVC (.422). He is also one of eight Indiana State players who converted better than 70 percent of their free throws.

The final returning starter is 5-11 sophomore **Greg Thomas** (6.7 points, 2.2 rebounds, 90 assists, 81.6 percent free throw shooting). What it all adds up to is four starters back, but none taller than 6-4. Obviously, Indiana State will look for some size.

That, presumably, will come from among 10 newcomers Locke has assembled. And there is quality as well as quantity in the recruiting class. Leading the way is 6-9 freshman **Marcus Johnson** (Pike HS/Indianapolis), who averaged 14.2 points and 7.1 rebounds while earning some high school All-America mention.

"Marcus is indicative of the type of player we want to come to Indiana State," Locke said. "He comes from an outstanding high school program, where he has already been taught fundamentals and what it means to work hard."

Another high school All-America is 6-8 freshman **Frank Zielinski** (Seaholm HS/Birmingham, Mich.). Zielinski averaged 21.7 points and 11.4 rebounds and, according to Locke, is "a big kid who can score. Frank is the type of player we feel fits our present needs."

The third high school All-America in the class is 6-4 **Juda Parks,** a guard from East Chicago (Ind.) Central who averaged 14.2 points and 7.6 rebounds. Also available is 6-5 freshman **Mike Jovonovich** (Griffith HS/Griffith, Ind.), who finished second in the slam dunk competition prior to the Indiana-Kentucky high school all-star game, and high-scoring **Noah Haynes** (Frontier HS/Chalmers, Ind.). Haynes, a 6-0 freshman, led the state in scoring at 33.8 ppg and finished fourth in the three-point shooting contest at the Indiana-Kenucky all-star series.

The last of seven new freshmen are 6-8 **Dale Springhetti** (Menasha HS/Menasha, Wisc.) and 6-4 **Anthony Ferguson** (Doss HS/Louisville, Ky.). Clearly, Locke has brought in a class capable of filling just about every long-term need. Plus, he has three transfers, two redshirts and one other letterman on hand.

Kenny Rowan, a 6-4 freshman, played just five games a year ago before going down with a knee injury. He averaged 7.8 points and 4.4 rebounds before being sidelined, and at one time attracted interest from a host of Big Ten schools. Another medical redshirt is 6-2 junior **Jeff Lauritzen,** who did not play at all last year because of ankle problems. As a sophomore, Lauritzen averaged 12 points per game and was among the MVC leaders in steals. 6-5 soph **Bubba Burrage** played in 27 games and made nine starts last year, averaging 3.9 points and 3.5 rebounds.

6-9 sophomore **Jim Deister** (Texas-San Anto-

nio), 6-6 senior **Mike Land** (Murray State, Sullivan JC) and 5-10 senior **Quinton Fly** (Hardin-Simmons) add experience as transfers to what remains a very young team.

BLUE RIBBON ANALYSIS

The Sycamores continue on Locke's "Road Back" campaign, and there will be fewer potholes this time around. Indiana State just might be the most improved team in the MVC. The Sycamores will play hard - that includes Bird, or he'll spend a lot of time on the bench - and they will play defense. Locke's teams at Army, Miami of Ohio, Clemson and Jacksonville all played hard-nosed defense, and Indiana State made great strides in that direction last year.

"Of all the jobs I've ever had, when you consider the interest in basketball in this state, who we compete against, our access to players, the facilities, everything, this is the best job I've ever had," Locke says. "The image was just awful, but the potential is endless."

If some of the talented newcomers come on strong, the Sycamores could battle for the MVC first division. The amount of rebuilding, though, does not suggest a finish quite that high. Seventh or eighth place is much more realistic, but don't look for many more 8-20 seasons in Terre Haute. Things have turned around.

1990-91 INDIANA STATE SCHEDULE		
Nov.	26	Butler
Nov. 30-Dec.	1	#Boilermaker Invitational
Dec.	4	@Ball State
	7-8	##Acme Boot Tournament
	10	@Evansville
	13	Northeastern Illinois
	15	Miami (OH)
	18	St. Louis
	22	@Southwest Missouri State
	30	@Southern Illinois
Jan.	5	Illinois State
	12	Boston University
	14	@Illinois State
	19	@Bradley
	24	@Tulsa
	26	@Creighton
	30	Drake
Feb.	2	Tulsa
	4	@Wichita State
	7	Creighton
	9	@Drake
	13	Southern Illinois
	18	Wichita State
	23	Southwest Missouri State
	25	Bradley
Mar.	1-5	*MVC Tournament

@ Road Games
# West Lafayette, IN (East Carolina, Loyola & Purdue)
Clarksville, TN (Army, Austin Peay & Western Kentucky)
* St. Louis, MO

IONA

LAST SEASON: 13-15
CONFERENCE RECORD: 8-8
STARTERS LOST: 1
STARTERS RETURNING: 4
CONFERENCE: METRO ATLANTIC ATHLETIC (MAAC)
LOCATION: NEW ROCHELLE, NY
HOME FLOOR: MULCAHY CAMPUS CENTER (3,200)
NICKNAME: GAELS
COLORS: MAROON AND GOLD
COACH: GARY BROKAW, record at Iona, 55-61.

Television trivia buffs remember New Rochelle, N.Y., as the home of Rob and Laura Petrie of "The Dick Van Dyke Show." Basketball fans remember New Rochelle as the home of the Iona College basketball powerhouses assembled by Jim Valvano and Pat Kennedy. Lately the Gaels have had four mediocre seasons under former Notre Dame All-America, Gary Brokaw, including a 13-15 campaign in '89-90. This year that should change.

All but erratic guard Joey Johnson (10.3 ppg) are back from last year, and the Gaels have the talent to make the run for the MAAC title. Now Brokaw and his staff, which includes new bench coaches Tim O'Toole and standout New York prep coach Steve Post, must motivate the MAAC's most talented group.

The Gaels will again be led by streaky 6-5 senior **Sean Green** (19.8 ppg, 5.0 rpg). His explosive scoring and leaping ability make him one of the most exciting players in the east. But the North Carolina State transfer is also very undisciplined and is not ashamed to shoot from the outer limits of the court (22-of-74 from three-point range last season, only 29 percent). He must become more of an inside player to make the Gaels go. Two classmates will also give Green some frontcourt help, 6-7 senior **Gerald McClease** (3.0 ppg, 3.2 rpg) and monstrous 6-6, 240-pound senior **Jonathan Duck** (7.6 ppg, 5.7 rpg). Both will improve their defensive skills to have the effect needed, while Duck has to overcome the weight problem which has thus far hindered what was projected to be an outstanding college career. 6-6 freshman forward **Danny Golombiewski** (17.0 ppg for Neptune, N.J., HS) could also see some time.

The center spot will once again belong to 6-10 junior and leading rebounder **Kevin Cooper** (5.7 ppg, 6.4 rpg). Cooper, like Duck, was much heralded out of high school but has yet to show the offensive explosiveness that should come with a player of his size and potential. That has not hindered his defensive progress, and he has developed into one of the MAAC's best shot blockers and defensive rebounders. Competing for time behind Cooper will be 6-9 senior **John Savage** (0.6 ppg, 1.5 rpg) and 7-1 freshman **Ian Whyte** (16.0 ppg, 13.0 rpg from Henry Hudson HS in Highlands, N.J.). Savage will be used as a defensive replacement, while Whyte was a real big land for Brokaw; big in that he is Iona's tallest player ever. He will need to put up some numbers to give Cooper some middle help.

The deepest area for the Gaels will be in the backcourt. Senior starter 6-3 **Shawn Worthy** (8.6 ppg, 3.1 apg) and MAAC all-rookie selection 6-3 sophomore **Danny Doyle** (8.5 ppg, 2.3 apg) both return. Worthy came on strong during the season's final weeks, topped off with a career high 21-point effort against Loyola College. The hard-nosed Doyle did all the little things for Iona, playing both guard spots and filling in at small forward. Also back are 5-11 sophomore **Jeremy Green** (1.7 ppg) and 5-11 sophomore **Marvin Goodwine** (0.4 ppg). 6-0 junior guard **Antoine Lewis** and 6-1 freshman **James Brickhouse** (17.0 ppg) from Bishop Ford HS in Brooklyn, N.Y., have also been added. Green, the son of Stanford football coach Dennis Green, should continue to improve on his scoring game while Goodwine will improve upon his minutes and assists. The sleeper of the group and perhaps of the league is Lewis, an all-city performer at Brooklyn's Grady HS and Kansas signee who opted for the junior college route before ending at Iona. He is a big time scorer and playmaker who, with discipline, could turn out to be a real steal.

BLUE RIBBON ANALYSIS

As has been the case in recent seasons, there is a great amount of talent and athletic ability at Iona. Sean Green is a definite NBA prospect, Doyle is very solid and dependable, Worthy is maturing, Cooper will be a major force in the middle and Lewis is an above-MAAC level guard. There is also depth, and with five seniors, the Gaels could finally have a good year.

The question still remains, can Brokaw and his staff make the unpredictable Sean Green play within himself or will it be the wild show of his first two seasons? Furthermore, can Cooper develop into the offensive force that the Gaels need to complement Green? If so, then Brokaw will finally silence his critics.

The prediction here is a bright one. The Gaels have improved, Brokaw has surrounded himself with quality coaches, and Iona should grab second, no lower than third, in the MAAC.

IOWA

LAST SEASON: 12-16
CONFERENCE RECORD: 4-14
STARTERS LOST: 3
STARTERS RETURNING: 2
CONFERENCE: BIG TEN
LOCATION: IOWA CITY, IA
HOME FLOOR: CARVER-HAWKEYE ARENA (15,500)
NICKNAME: HAWKEYES
COLORS: OLD GOLD AND BLACK
COACH: DR. TOM DAVIS, record at Iowa, 93-41. Career record, 363-191.

By Iowa standards, last season's 12-16 overall record and 4-14 mark in the conference was not a good showing for the program. However, it could have been much worse, Hawkeye fans. Forward Ray Thompson, who was averaging 19 points per game was lost after the first semester of last year and has subsequently left school. 6-10 Matt Bullard missed the first half of the season with knee problems and was hampered throughout the rest of the campaign by his bothersome knee. If it wasn't for an inspired effort from Les Jepsen and an outstanding coaching effort by Dr. Tom Davis, 12-16 could have easily been 6-22 or worse.

For the second straight season, Davis will face a major rebuilding task with his Hawkeyes. Iowa returns only eight players from last year's squad, none of

which are seniors, and welcomes seven newcomers to the team. This team is very young and inexperienced, but it is talented.

The starting backcourt of **James Moses** and **Troy Skinner** returns intact to lead the Hawkeyes this year. Moses (18.0 ppg, 2.9 rpg), a 6-4 junior shooting guard, started 24 games last season and returns the highest scoring average for the Hawkeyes. He recorded season high 21-point efforts against North Carolina and Minnesota last year. Moses is an excellent standstill jump shooter and is at his best running off screens and fanning out for the jumper. He will be looked to for increased scoring and leadership which has not yet surfaced on this team. Moses teamed with Skinner (5.0 ppg, 3.8 apg) to form an adequate if not solid backcourt tandem. Skinner, a 6-0 junior point guard, won the job early in fall practice and improved as the season progressed. He had a season high 17-point effort at Illinois late in the season and led the Hawkeyes in free throw percentage at 84 percent. With the loss of over 50 percent of last year's scoring, Skinner must penetrate more this season as well as look for his own shot. Improved scoring and playmaking from Skinner is a must if the Hawkeyes are to improve this year.

Junior College All-America **Val Barnes** arrives from Butler (Kan.) County JC and looks to see considerable time in the Iowa backcourt and may eventually start. Barnes, a 6-2 point guard, averaged 20.0 ppg for Butler and led them to the national junior college tournament. As a senior at Wichita South (Kan.) HS, Barnes averaged 20.9 ppg and was a 63 percent career shooter. His type of talent and scoring ability will be hard to keep on the bench. Davis may employ a three-guard offensive set to complement Barnes and add another element of speed to the Hawkeyes' lineup. Also, with a shooter like Moses already on the court, it may open up Barnes for more opportunities. With the lack of true forwards, the three-guard offense may make even more sense for Iowa.

6-3 junior **Rodell Davis** (4.1 ppg, 2.0 rpg) returns at full strength after two frustrating years missed to knee injuries. Davis, a swingman, returned for the last six games of last year and averaged 11 points in those contests. Included in those performances was a 20-point night at Indiana and a 15-point evening at Illinois. Now healthy, Davis should see plenty of game exposure at the small forward and big guard positions. He would welcome a switch to a guard-oriented offense. Sophomore **Dale Reed** (2.0 ppg, 0.6 rpg) is the only other returning guard with experience. He is not expected to see significant action.

Davis recruited five guards and two swingmen who should help Iowa in the long run. Freshman **Paul Lusk** from Wesclin HS in Trenton, Ill, is a 6-4 shooting guard who was a unanimous first team All-Illinois selection last season when he averaged 28 points, 10 rebounds and six assists for the Illinois Class A champions. Lusk's uncle Gary preceded him at Iowa during the 1970-72 seasons. Lusk is an excellent shooter and rebounder with big play capability. Point guard **Kevin Smith** arrives in Iowa City from Trimble Tech in Ft. Worth, Tex. The 5-11 Smith averaged 19.6 ppg and a hefty 9.8 apg as a senior. He is an excellent penetrater and loves to dish off the the ball. Smith was an All-Texas honorable mention selection in his senior year.

6-6 freshman forward **Jim Bartels** may be a sleeper recruit for the Hawkeyes. An extremely quick, aggressive swingman, Bartels can score and rebound as well. The Freedom (Wisc.) native averaged 16.4 points as a senior plus 9.5 rebounds and 4.5 assists. Bartels scored 31 points in the Wisconsin state championship game and was the state champion in the triple jump as a junior (45'4''). 6-5 freshman swingman **James Winters** is another recruit well suited to the up-tempo style that Iowa employs. Winters, from Joliet (Ill.) Central HS, averaged 19 points and 11 rebounds as a senior and set a school record with a 63 percent field goal shooting mark. Winters is a very physical player who may be a factor in the Big Ten season.

Replacing a frontline of Les Jepsen and Matt

Bullard will be tough for Davis. Bullard, though often injured, was an excellent shooter who opened the middle up for a surging Jepsen. When Jepsen arrived at Iowa he was considered a project at best, but he left Iowa City as the first pick in the second round of the NBA draft by the Golden State Warriors. No doubt that with his outstanding work ethic and his drive to excel he will make a strong impact on a team in search of help in the middle like the Warriors. It also doesn't hurt that his new coach, Don Nelson, is an Iowa Hawkeye legend.

6-10 sophomore **Acie Earl** (6.0 ppg, 3.6 rpg) is the only candidate to replace Jepsen. Earl averaged only 16 minutes per contest his freshman season, but led the entire Big Ten with 50 blocked shots. With outstanding shooters like Barnes and Moses relieving some of the inside pressure, Earl may not have to develop as quickly underneath. By the time the Big Ten season comes, however, the Hawkeyes will need Earl's game to be intelligent and productive. Without Earl's large presence in the lineup, Iowa will be eaten alive in the Big Ten.

One forward spot looks to be filled. Junior **Wade Lookingbill** (6.7 ppg, 3.1 rpg) is a solid role player who doesn't make mistakes. He will complement an up-tempo offense because of his willingness to give up the ball and also set screens. Lookingbill is a smart passer and can knock down the open jumper when left alone. His size (6-7) and his experience will help this young club. Two other returning forwards will provide bench depth, but will probably not see much important playing time. Junior **Brig Tubbs** (1.2 ppg, 1.4 rpg) is a 6-9 small forward who can run the floor and fits well into Davis' offense. 6-8 sophomore **Jay Webb** (2.3 ppg, 2.2 rpg) also will make important contributions before his Hawkeye career is finished. Webb is a 225-pound power forward who specializes in post play and igniting the Hawkeye fast break.

Two freshmen forwards round out the Hawkeye roster. Solid **Chris Street** (6-8), from Indianola HS in Indianola, Iowa, was a three sport star in high school. Street was a three-time all-stater in basketball, passed for 4,271 yards and recorded 34 touchdowns in football and was a first team all-leaguer in baseball. He averaged 20 points and 9.8 rebounds as a senior. Finally, Nigerian born **Phil Chime** will bring more depth to the frontcourt for Iowa. Chime was a dominant 6-7, 215-pound power forward at Madison HS in Houston, Texas. He came to the United States at the age of twelve and has only been playing basketball for four years. As a senior, Chime sparkled, averaging 17 points and 15 rebounds. He was included among the Top 24 power forwards in the nation by *Coach and Player Magazine*.

BLUE RIBBON ANALYSIS

Last season, Iowa was beset by graduation losses, injuries and academic problems and the result was a 12-16 record. Another major rebuilding task faces Davis and the Hawkeyes this season. Gone are Jepsen and Bullard up front and Thompson, the most talented player in the program, has left school.

Only eight lettermen return to the Iowa roster, while seven newcomers arrive in Iowa City. The most promising arrival and the one who looks to start immediately is junior college transfer Barnes at point guard. It is most likely that Davis will have to play with a guard-oriented offense to offset the lack of size down low and to take advantage of his good shooters, Barnes, Moses and Skinner. Davis is potentially a good scorer who will also play a key role.

Earl will be thrust into the starting center role due mainly to the fact that he is the Hawkeyes only legitimate big man. He is still young and needs much seasoning. If Barnes and Moses can start the year well, it will take an enormous amount of pressure off of Earl to develop quickly. Lookingbill will start at the last forward spot. He is an excellent passer and good complementary player. His court intelligence and experience will be a big help to this inexperienced group.

Iowa is very young and a .500 record would be an extremely optimistic outlook for the Hawkeyes. Even with Davis at the helm, it could be a minor miracle. Iowa has a relatively light nonconference schedule with the exception of the pre-season NIT tournament and UCLA at home during the holidays. This may give the Hawkeyes a chance to mature gradually as they head towards the Big Ten schedule. Without a settled frontcourt, however, look for the Hawkeyes to get pounded underneath all year long. Moreover, the rebounding Davis' forward offense is lacking severely in this undersized unit. So might be the overall team pressure defense from which most of his offense is predicated. Although there is a decent amount of athleticism present that may be blended into his system. For Iowa, an eighth or ninth place finish in the Big Ten is likely.

1990-91 IOWA SCHEDULE

Nov.	15	#Temple
	27	@Drake
Nov.	30-	
	Dec. 1	*Amana Hawkeye Classic
Dec.	4	Northern Iowa
	8	Iowa State
	15	Maryland-Baltimore Co.
	18	Chicago State
	22	UCLA
	28	@Hawaii-Hilo
	30	@Chaminade (HI)
Jan.	3	@Ohio State
	5	Michigan State
	10	Michigan
	12	@Minneapolis
	17	@Wisconsin
	19	Indiana
	28	@Illinois
	31	@Purdue
Feb.	2	Northwestern
	7	@Michigan State
	9	@Michigan
	14	Minnesota
	16	Wisconsin
	21	@Indiana
	23	Illinois
Mar.	2	Purdue
	7	@Northwestern
	9 or 10	Ohio State

@ Road Games
# Dodge NIT. If Iowa defeats Temple, the Hawkeyes will play a second round game on Nov. 17. The semifinals and finals will be played on Nov. 21 & 23 at Madison Square Garden, New York, NY.
Iowa City, IA (Colgate, Creighton & Texas-San Antonio)

IOWA STATE

LAST SEASON: 10-18
CONFERENCE
RECORD: 4-10
STARTERS LOST: 1
STARTERS RETURNING: 4
CONFERENCE: BIG EIGHT
LOCATION: AMES, IA
HOME FLOOR: HILTON COLISEUM (14,020)
NICKNAME: CYCLONES
COLORS: CARDINAL AND GOLD
COACH: JOHNNY ORR, record at Iowa State, 151-144.
Career record, 399-290.

A few years ago, Johnny Orr drew up his 1990-91 schedule thinking he would have a Top 20 caliber team at Iowa State. Trouble is, now that he's got a showcase schedule, he no longer has a showcase team.

"When we did this originally, we had (Sam)

Mack and (Mark) Baugh," Orr said. "For the last year and for this year. We thought this year we'd have a great team. All of them would be seniors . . . and then everything hit the fan here."

Boy, did it! The Cyclones lost starters Mack and Baugh before the 1989-90 season. They lost another good one, 6-8 Kirk Baker, to academics during the season. As a result, the undermanned Cyclones were chewed up by one of the nation's tougher schedules. They lost road games to Minnesota, Indiana, Michigan and Houston during non-league play, not to mention seven games to Big Eight powers Kansas, Missouri and Oklahoma. The result was a 10-18 record, Orr's second-worst record in 25 years as a head coach. For only the second time in past six years, the Cyclones failed to earn an NCAA tournament bid. Adding to the frustration was the fact that the Cyclones lost 10 games by five points or less. "That was discouraging, to lose by one point, two points, overtime games," Orr said.

This year, the Cyclones have what could be an even more challenging schedule. Minnesota, Michigan, Indiana and Iowa of the Big Ten are back on the schedule, plus the Cyclones will appear in two prestigious tournaments — the Maui Classic in Hawaii and the Tournament of Champions in Charlotte, N.C. The Cyclones must do it without Mack, Baugh and Baker, none of whom remain on the team. Nonetheless, they have one of the most experienced teams in the Big Eight. Six players return who started eight or more games last year. Back is 70.3 percent of Iowa State's scoring and 77.8 percent of its rebounding from a year ago.

A key once again will be the performance of the Cyclone's man-mountain in the middle, 6-9 senior Victor Alexander. Although he began last season at about 265 pounds, Alexander was closer to 300 pounds by season's end. That limited his effectiveness, his stamina and his defensive play. Oh, his numbers remained good. He ranked among the top five in the league in scoring (19.7 ppg), rebounding (8.7 rpg), and field goal percentage (58.5). But he really didn't show any improvement over his sophomore season. Even with the extra weight, Alexander was an inside force on offense. Once he gets the ball, he's hard to stop. He has soft hands and a deft touch around the basket. If he shows up leaner this season, watch out.

Alexander isn't the only big man on campus in Ames. Former Illinois transfer Phil Kunz (6.3 ppg, 3.9 rpg) got the rust off last season after sitting out the previous year. The 6-9, 230-pound senior figures to see more time, either teaming with or backing up Alexander. The Cyclones have a mid-sized banger in 6-7 senior Paul Doerrfeld (8.0 ppg, 4.6 rpg). The only other holdovers on the frontline are 6-6 junior Norman Brown, who played in only four games in 1989-90 before a shoulder injury ended his season, and 6-7 Mike Bergman, a redshirt freshman who was Iowa's 1989-90 Mr. Basketball at Waverly-Shell Rock HS.

In the backcourt, Orr's biggest concern is finding a replacement for point guard Terry Woods (16.1 ppg, 6.2 apg), who led the league in assists last season and was second on the team in scoring behind Alexander. There are several candidates at the point, including holdovers 6-3 junior Brian Pearson (4.8 ppg), 6-2 sophomore Justus Thigpen (8.9 ppg) and 6-1 senior Doug Collins (12.0 ppg, 4.8 rpg, 4.2 apg). Collins can do a lot of things including play defense. Even if he's not the point guard, he's a big part of the Cyclones' plans and will be out there somewhere. He even played some games at small forward last season, even though he is only 6-1. Thigpen and Pearson are coming off respectable freshman seasons. Thigpen, whose father starred at Weber State, was second on the team in steals (35) and third in assists (86). Pearson made 29 three-pointers, second only to Woods. The only other returning guard, 6-3 sophomore David Washington, arrived in Ames touted as quicker than B. J. Armstrong, who went to the same school: Brother Rice HS of Birmingham, Mich., outside of Detroit. He will need to rediscover his shoot-

ing touch under fire, to redeem that quickness at the Division I level. Washington played just 19 minutes in seven games last season.

Orr brought in six recruits, so even with his solid nucleus of returning talent, he has some new faces to break in. Three of the six newcomers are junior college transfers, which represents a change of strategy for Orr. Until last season, Orr had not signed a single JC transfer since coming to Iowa State from Michigan in 1980. "We've never done that before, but I think you'll see more and more of that everywhere because so many of them now can't pass the (ACT or SAT) test," Orr said. "So everybody will be going to the junior colleges."

The best of the junior college transfers is Mark Chappell, a 6-3 off-guard from Lincoln (Ill.) JC. Here, he was a second-team All-America last season after averaging 22.5 points and 6.5 rebounds. If Orr cannot find the answer at point guard, he may give 5-11 freshman Skip McCoy a look, McCoy averaged 19.0 points and five assists at Bishop Noll HS in Hammond, Ind.

The four other recruits are forwards, including a trio of 6-5 'tweeners in freshmen Saun Jackson and Donnell Bivens and junior college transfer Brad Pippett. Jackson (16.7 ppg, 8.0 rpg) was a first team all-conference pick in the Chicago Public League at Dunbar HS. Bivens was named area player of the year by the *Champaign News-Gazette* after averaging 26.6 ppg and 12.2 rpg for Rantoul (Ill.) HS. The other newcomer up front is 6-8 James Odeh from Vincennes (Ind.) JC. Odeh, who is from Nigeria, averaged 11.0 ppg and 6.2 rpg.

"They're all runners and jumpers," Orr said of his new recruits. "That's a good deal. We'll go back to running a little more."

BLUE RIBBON ANALYSIS

As a senior, Alexander will realize that it's now or never if he wants to impress the NBA scouts. So he figures to come back in shape and go out with a bang. The Cyclones need to find a point guard, and would like a reliable small forward to fill out their lineup. Orr certainly has a lot of candidates in both spots.

Any improvements in defense and free throw shooting might help the Cyclones win some of the close ones they lost last season. As a team, Iowa State was last in the Big Eight in team defense (88.9 ppg) and last in free throw percentage (66.2 percent) last season.

If the Cyclones can keep their wits about them during their rugged non-conference schedule, and even come away with an upset or two, they should bounce back from last year's disaster. Oklahoma, Missouri, Kansas and Oklahoma State appear to be locks for first division finishes, so pencil in Iowa State as the best of the rest in the Big Eight. Another season like the last one and Orr, 63, might begin contemplating retirement.

1990-91 IOWA STATE SCHEDULE

Nov.	23-25	#Maui Classic
	Nov. 30-	
	Dec. 1	##Diet Pepsi Tournament
Dec.	3	Minnesota
	5	@Baylor
	8	@Iowa
	11	@Northern Iowa
	15	Michigan
	22	Indiana
	27 & 29	*Fiesta Bowl Tournament
Jan.	2	Drake
	5	@Colorado
	8	@Creighton
	12	@Nebraska
	15	Illinois-Chicago
	19	Kansas State
	22	Marathon Oil
	26	@Missouri
	30	Oklahoma
Feb.	2	Kansas

1990-91 IOWA STATE SCHEDULE Cont.

Feb.	6	@Oklahoma State
	9	@Kansas State
	13	Nebraska
	16	Colorado
	19	@Oklahoma
	23	Missouri
	26	@Kansas
Mar.	2	Oklahoma State
	8-10	**Big Eight Tournament

@ Road Games
# Lahaina, HI (Chaminade, Indiana, Loyola Marymount, Northeastern, Santa Clara, Syracuse & Toledo)
Charlotte, NC (Houston, North Carolina & South Carolina)
* Tucson, AZ (Arizona, Pepperdine & Temple)
** Kansas City, MO

JACKSONVILLE

LAST SEASON: 13-16
CONFERENCE RECORD: 5-9
STARTERS LOST: 4
STARTERS RETURNING: 1
CONFERENCE: SUN BELT
LOCATION: JACKSONVILLE, FL
HOME FLOOR: JACKSONVILLE COLISEUM (10,000)
NICKNAME: DOLPHINS
COLORS: GREEN AND GOLD
COACH: RICH HADDAD, record at Jacksonville, 35-53.

For the past couple of seasons, the Dolphins have been a hard team to figure. With plenty of talent on hand, Jacksonville has not fared well during the regular season, but has come on strong in the conference tournament. Two years ago, the Dolphins gained the finals of Sun Belt, and last March knocked off Old Dominion to reach the semifinals before losing to eventual champion South Florida.

Coach Rich Haddad is hopeful of carving out a better regular-season mark this time, but unless 6-8 junior **Sean Byrd** (9.4 ppg, 6.2 rpg in '88-89) has completely recovered from knee surgery for the second time - and that appears unlikely - the Dolphins are going to wind up near the bottom of the Sun Belt standings.

That's because Jacksonville lost four starters, including swingman Dee Brown, the All-Sun Belt performer who averaged 19.3 ppg, 6.6 rpg and was the first round selection of the Boston Celtics. The Dolphins will miss his multiple talents, as Brown could take over a game and did so on several occasions over the past two seasons. The other starters who exited the program are guard Curtis Taylor (16.2 ppg, 4.0 rpg), forward Chris Capers (10.7 ppg, 6.8 rpg) and guard Tyrone Boykin (2.9 ppg). They took with them 64 percent of JU's scoring and 51 percent of its rebounding.

The only returning starter is a good one, 6-8 senior forward **Reggie Law,** who laid down the law to the tune of 14.0 ppg and 6.7 rpg last season. Law, with 210 well-constructed pounds on his frame, became just the 20th Dolphin to reach 1,000 career points late last season and now ranks 19th and counting on the school's all-time list. Law is an excellent starting point around which Haddad will again rebuild his squad.

Even without last year's starters, Law has some order, at least underneath, in the presence of 6-8 junior **Tim Burroughs,** 6-9 senior **Steve Gilbert** (5.0 ppg, 4.0 rpg) and 6-8 sophomore **Al Powell** (3.3 ppg, 2.3 rpg).

At point guard, there will be a battle between 6-3 sophomore **Jerome McDuffie** and 5-8 junior **Danny**

Tirado. McDuffie, who averaged less than a point per game a year ago in limited playing time, is a better shooter, but Tirado is a wizard with his passes, accumulating 70 assists a year ago. Also fighting for time will be 6-1 freshman **Nate Burrell** (Nova HS/Fort Lauderdale, Fla.), who hit 61 percent of his three-point attempts in his final prep season while averaging 29 points.

Candidates to start at second guard include 6-4 senior **Tabarris Hamilton** (2.7 ppg), 6-5 freshman **Junior Hanna** (Sarasota HS/Sarasota, Fla.), 6-3 junior **Willie Ivery** (1.2 ppg) and 6-6 junior **Kelly McKinnon,** who averaged 2.2 ppg two years ago at the University of Florida. McKinnon is eligible after the first semester, but give the nod to Hamilton for now. He has been with Haddad for a while and knows the system. 6-5 sophomore **Alonzo Harris** (3.3 ppg) could also see some time at guard, although he is more of a small forward.

As foggy as the starting positions are at guard, they are even more jumbled up front, where a number of combinations could emerge. At small forward, 6-6 redshirt freshman **Kent Shaffer,** who averaged 14.5 points and 6.8 rebounds at Bishop Kenny HS in Jacksonville, will battle Hanna, Harris and Ivery for time. At center, Gilbert looks like the starter because of his experience, although Burroughs, who averaged 20.4 ppg and 13.7 rpg at Delgado, will push him. Burroughs helped Delgado to a 28-6 record and was named a JC All-America. Powell will provide depth. If he recovers fully from two-time surgery, Byrd - at 250 pounds - will also be a huge factor.

BLUE RIBBON ANALYSIS

The Dolphins still have not learned how to win the close ones consistently. Two years ago, 16 of Jacksonville's 30 games were decided by eight points or less, with JU going 7-9 in those contests. Last season, they weren't much better, finishing 7-7 in games determined by 10 points or less.

The Dolphins also lost four games in the last four seconds of regulation or overtime. In all four of those contests, they either missed a free throw (three times) or a field goal (once) with under a half-minute to go and the score tied. Jacksonville did win five games by two points, but will need to find a better way of solving those last-second blues if it wants to challenge for the Sun Belt's first division.

Road woes haunted the Dolphins, as well, as they went 1-9 in enemy gyms, continuing another disturbing trend under Haddad, who may be in trouble if he does not produce a winner soon. JU was also 1-9 on the road two years ago, and things do not figure to get better overnight.

The Dolphins had one of the best recruiting classes in the Sun Belt, and should improve as the season progesses. However, no better than a seventh-place finish looms. Jacksonville is too young and too new, even for its accustomed post-season surge.

1990-91 JACKSONVILLE SCHEDULE

Nov.	24	Flagler College (FL)
	27	@North Carolina
Nov.	30-	
	Dec. 1	#Mazda Gator Bowl
Dec.	4	Mississippi State
	8	Maryland
	15	Bethune-Cookman (FL)
	19	@Oklahoma State
	22	@Pepperdine
	29	Univ. of Hartford
Jan.	7	@South Florida
	10	@Old Dominion
	14	Western Kentucky
	16	Butler

1990-91 JACKSONVILLE SCHEDULE Cont.

Jan.	19	Virginia Commonwealth
	26	@North Carolina Charlotte
	28	@Virginia Commonwealth
	31	Long Island
Feb.	2	Alabama-Birmingham
	4	@Western Kentucky
	7	South Alabama
	9	@Alabama-Birmingham
	11	South Florida
	14	@South Alabama
	16	Florida State
	20	North Carolina Charlotte
	23	Old Dominion
Mar.	2-4	##Sun Belt Tournament

@ Road Games
# Jacksonville, FL (Cleveland State, Colorado State & Navy)
Mobile, AL

JAMES MADISON

LAST SEASON: 20-11
CONFERENCE RECORD: 13-4
STARTERS LOST: 0
STARTERS RETURNING: 5
CONFERENCE: COLONIAL ATHLETIC (CAA)
LOCATION: HARRISONBURG, VA
HOME FLOOR: JMU CONVOCATION CENTER (7,612)
NICKNAME: DUKES
COLORS: PURPLE AND GOLD
COACH: LEFTY DRIESELL, record at James Madison, 36-25.
Career record, 560-249.

Lefty Driesell is building something special at James Madison. Evidence of that came in his first year at the school (1988-89), and it was reinforced last season when the Dukes went 20-11 and won the Colonial Athletic Association regular season championship. By all accounts, there is more in store.

Driesell has all five starters back from a year ago, including the two players most instrumental in last season's success. That success included the first league championship at James Madison in seven years, and a school-record 12-game winning streak. The Dukes also survived a demanding non-conference schedule that included North Carolina, Oklahoma, Florida and West Virginia, then effectively dominated the rugged CAA.

Only a five-point loss to Richmond in the finals of the CAA tournament kept James Madison from its rightful place in the NCAA's. The Dukes settled for the NIT.

"We should be better than last season, but we still have some question marks," Driesell said. "How are we going to come together as a team? Who is going to emerge as our team leader? And how are we going to react to pressure? We won't be able to surprise anyone. People will be ready for us."

The Dukes should be up for the task, thanks in large part to a backcourt that should be of national-level quality. 6-7 senior **Steve Hood** (22.0 ppg, 4.0 rpg, 42 assists, 30 steals), who transferred from Maryland, came into his own at James Madison. Hood went 68-for-141 on three-point shots (48.2 percent), and scored a school-record 682 points. He had 30 or more points in five games, 20 or more in 16 games. Hood's season high of 36 points came against Oklahoma and, after leading the Dukes in scoring in 26 of 31 starts, his selection as CAA player of the year surprised no one.

And Driesell thinks Hood's best days are ahead. "I still think he's got a lot of improving to do," Driesell said. "I want him to rebound better. I want him to handle the ball a little better. But I think he had an excellent year."

Driesell, who has sent 33 players to the NBA, sees pro potential in his star guard. "If he has a good year," said Driesell, "he could go in the first round of the draft."

Hood will be joined in the backcourt by 6-1 senior point guard **Fess Irvin** (11.4 ppg, 2.5 rpg, 117 assists, 35 steals), a transfer from LSU who also enjoyed his best season as a collegian. Irvin shot 53 percent from the floor and 80 percent from the free throw line. **Kenny Brooks** (2.7 ppg, 0.7 rpg), a 6-0 senior, will back him up. Brooks started at the point two years ago.

The James Madison frontcourt also returns intact, led by 6-8 senior **Billy Coles** (11.7 ppg, 7.2 rpg, 44 assists, 38 steals, 13 blocked shots). A transfer from Chowan (N.C.) JC, Coles made an immediate impact for the Dukes. His rebounding average was the highest at James Madison in 10 years, and he shot 57.8 percent from the field.

Barry Brown (5.0 ppg, 4.3 rpg, 66 blocked shots, 13 steals), is a 6-5 senior who plays considerably taller. Brown made the CAA all-defensive team last season and already owns a school-record 166 blocked shots. Brown is not bad offensively, either, converting a JMU-record 66.7 percent of his field goal attempts as a junior. 6-8 senior **John Fedor** (4.1 ppg, 3.1 rpg), a transfer from Palm Beach (Fla.) JC and Florida State, started 14 games last season and also returns.

Yet another transfer will push for playing time on the Dukes' front line. **Chancellor Nichols**, a 6-8 junior from Mississippi State, could start, and will play significant minutes even if he does not. A bruiser at 240 pounds, Nichols averaged 9.2 points and 6.0 rebounds as a freshman and 8.1 points and 5.1 rebounds as a sophomore.

Clayton Ritter, a 6-8 freshman from Fork Union (Va.) Military Academy, is the Dukes' lone freshman recruit. Ritter averaged 22 points and eight rebounds at Kempsville High in Virginia Beach, then prepped for a season at Fork Union and started every game for a team that went 29-1.

James Madison has but 12 players on its roster, so 6-6 junior **Troy Bostic** (2.1 ppg, 1.4 rpg), 6-8 sophomore **Jeff Chambers** (1.8 ppg, 3.1 rpg) and 6-7 senior **Alex Clevinger** (0.5, 0.4 rpg) will get their share of action. In addition, 6-7 senior **Alan Dorsey** is expected to return after sitting out 1989-90. Dorsey averaged 5.0 points per game as a sophomore and 2.0 as a junior.

Two Dukes left the team after last season. Swingman William Davis (8.2 ppg, 2.2 rpg) transferred to New Orleans and senior guard Todd Dunnings (3.3 ppg, 1.0 rpg) will sit out this year for personal reasons. The latter plans to return in 1991. Next season, James Madison will also acquire the services of 6-6 Michael Tate, who transferred from Georgetown after one year there. Tate, a consensus high school All-America, will be groomed for Hood's position. And,

like Hood, he was originally a Maryland signee.

What the Dukes lack in depth this year, they make up for in overall size. Seven players are 6-7 or taller, and six weigh more than 210 pounds.

"We have more size than we had last season," Driesell said. "Physically, we should be stronger and more experienced. Potentially, we can be a good basketball team, but we play a tough schedule and we've got to blend in some new players. We also have players who will have to adjust to new roles."

BLUE RIBBON ANALYSIS

He did it at Davidson, he did it at Maryland and, now, he is doing it at James Madison. Lefty Driesell has had his detractors over the years, but the man wins basketball games. He turned around James Madison's program in one year, and in his second season had the Dukes in a post-season tournament. The "Lefthander" was also the overwhelming choice as CAA coach of the year, giving him that honor in three different conferences.

Look for the Dukes to continue their climb in 1990-91. The only missing ingredient a year ago was depth, and Driesell very likely found it in Nichols and Ridder. If they contribute some, and if the Dukes get past another rugged non-conference schedule, James Madison should once again be the class of the Colonial Athletic Association.

This time around, the Dukes should make it all the way back and into the NCAA tournament. Driesell already knows how to get there.

1990-91 JAMES MADISON SCHEDULE

Nov.	24	Marist
	28	@Virginia Tech
Dec.	1	Maryland-Eastern Shore
	5	Florida
	8	East Tennessee State
	17	@Mt. St. Mary's (MD)
	19	@Brigham Young
	22	@South Alabama
	28-29	#Times-Dispatch Invitational
Jan.	2	Virginia Military Institute
	5	##Oklahoma
	9	Richmond
	12	@East Carolina
	14	@North Carolina Wilmington
	19	American University
	23	@Navy
	26	George Mason
	28	William & Mary
	30	Old Dominion
Feb.	2	@William & Mary
	6	@Richmond
	9	East Carolina
	11	North Carolina Wilmington
	16	@American University
	19	Navy
	23	George Mason
Mar.	2-4	*CAA Tournament

@ Road Games
# Richmond, VA (Richmond, Virginia Commonwealth & Virginia Tech)
Landover, MD
* Richmond, VA

KANSAS STATE

LAST SEASON: 17-15
CONFERENCE RECORD: 7-7
STARTERS LOST: 3
STARTERS RETURNING: 2
CONFERENCE: BIG EIGHT
LOCATION: MANHATTAN, KS
HOME FLOOR: BRAMLAGE COLISEUM (13,500)
NICKNAME: WILDCATS
COLORS: PURPLE AND WHITE
COACH: DANA ALTMAN, first year at Kansas State. Career record, 138-37.

It is a well kept secret outside of the Great Plains, but Kansas State has one of the best basketball traditions around. The Wildcats have made the NCAA tournament 20 times —only Kentucky (33), UCLA (26), North Carolina (24), Notre Dame (24) and Louisville (21) have gone to the Big Dance more often. In addition, since Oklahoma State came aboard to make the Big Seven the Big Eight in 1958, Kansas State has won more conference games (292) than anyone else in the league.

That being said, it looks like tradition will take it on the chin this season in Manhattan, Kan., aka The Little Apple. The Wildcats made a school record fourth straight NCAA appearance last season, but coach Lon Kruger couldn't resist a big money offer from Florida and headed to Gainesville. He didn't leave much behind for Dana Altman, a Kansas State assistant for three years (1986-89) under Kruger. Altman was head coach at Marshall last season.

For starters, there is no more Steve Henson. One of the best players in Kansas State history and one of the better guards in Big Eight history, Henson completed his stellar career last season after setting 43 school and conference records. The league's all-time leader in free throw percentage (90.7) and three-point field goals made (240), Henson led the Wildcats in both scoring and assists in each of the past two seasons. More importantly, he was a master of tempo as the usually outmanned Wildcats routinely managed to stay with or upset some of the league's heavyweights by slowing down the pace. Last season, for instance, every other team in the high scoring Big Eight averaged more than 80 points a game, but the Wildcats averaged a modest 72. Nonetheless, Kansas State finished 7-7 in a conference that featured three teams ranked No. 1 at some time in the season, and upset two of those squads —Oklahoma and Missouri. Henson was a second round choice of the Milwaukee Bucks and signed with a team in Greece.

But what will things be like without Henson?

"We realize that we've got a long way to go," Altman said. And Altman's problems aren't limited to simply replacing Henson. "We realize that we're undermanned on the frontline. We lost four kids that played a lot there, plus Henson, who played 40 minutes. So we realize we've got a lot of minutes to replace. We think **Jean Derouillere** and **'Ski' Jones** are solid players, but we realize we've got a lot of holes to fill other than that."

Derouillere, a 6-5 senior swingman who can shoot the three-pointer some and rebound some, too, was the Wildcats' second leading scorer last season (15.7 ppg) behind Henson (17.4 ppg). Derouillere, who pronounces his name as if it were spelled "Delaware," will have to kick up his scoring if the Wildcats are going to be effective. 6-4 sophomore Askia "Ski" Jones is the only other returning starter. Another swing player, Jones was one of the league's better freshmen last year (8.0 ppg), scoring in double figures in nine of Kansas State's final 11 games. But he is coming off a broken ankle suffered in July in the Olympic Festival. Ironically, he was playing for a North squad that was coached by Kruger.

While Jones and Derouillere are sure starters, the rest of the lineup is one big question mark. 6-0 senior **Jeff Wires** (4.8 ppg) is the heir apparent to replace Henson at the point. He is a penetrator with good quickness. Look for yet another swing player, 6-4 senior **Keith Amerson** (2.1 ppg), to see a lot more playing time than the 10 minutes a game he logged last season. Like Wires, Amerson has the quickness that Altman likes.

There are two other guard candidates among the holdover players, little used 6-4 sophomore **Patrick Sams**, an aggressive defender who should be good in the transition game, and 6-3 sophomore **Marlon Shadd**, who sat out last season. That leaves only two returning players taller than 6-5 on the roster: 6-8 junior **Wylie Howard**, who played only 115 minutes last season, and 6-10 junior **John Rettiger** (5.3 ppg, 3.7 rpg). If Rettiger can match the progress he made last season with similar improvement this time around, he could be a factor inside.

The Wildcats certainly need all the help they can get up front, which explains why Altman made big men his top recruiting priority after being named head coach on April 3. Altman signed three 6-9 players in the spring, junior college transfers **Darryl King** and **Keary Williams** and high school recruit **Hamilton Strickland**. Ready or not, at least two of those three are needed to contribute right away. "They've got to be able to play," Altman said.

King is the brother of former Oklahoma All-America Stacey King, and already has two things in common with his older brother: he's lefthanded and he likes to talk. Darryl King left Midland (Texas) JC midway through his sophomore season after a dispute with his coach. His numbers as a freshman were 10.6 ppg and 6.1 rpg. "Darryl has a lot of things to prove to get where Stacey is," Altman said.

King does have a good shooting touch inside, and should challenge for a starting berth right away. So should Williams, a 235-pounder who averaged 11.0 ppg and 10.0 rpg for a 26-6 Cloud County (Kan.) JC team. Strickland's numbers at Mays HS in Atlanta were 15.0 ppg and 8.0 rpg.

In case Wires isn't the answer at the point, Altman's only other recruit was point guard Marcus Zeigler, who averaged 9.8 ppg and 6.9 apg at Independence (Kan.) JC.

BLUE RIBBON ANALYSIS

New coach Altman is a savvy recruiter. He brought Golden State Warriors star Mitch Richmond to Kansas State in 1986. Many of the holdover players on this year's team were Altman recruits. But, it's clear that he'll need more horses than he has at the moment, particularly up front, to make any kind of run at the Big Eight title.

Altman says he'd like to run, but the Wildcats should consider it a successful season if not too many conference opponents run up the score on them. Quite simply, this shapes up as Kansas State's worst team in awhile. With little height, and no proven scorer other than Derouillere, the Wildcats will do no better than sixth in the Big Eight and could do worse.

1990-91 KANSAS STATE SCHEDULE		
Nov.	24	Akron
	27	Florida A&M
Dec.	1	@Arkansas
	5	Wyoming
	8	Northwest Missouri State
	12	@Tulsa
	15	Lamar
	22	California-Santa Barbara

1990-91 KANSAS STATE SCHEDULE *Cont.*		
Dec.	28 & 29	#BMA Tournament
Jan.	5	Nebraska
	7	@Wichita State
	12	@Missouri
	15	@Missouri-Kansas City
	19	@Iowa State
	21	Missouri-Kansas City
	26	@Oklahoma State
	29	Kansas
Feb.	2	Colorado
	5	Oklahoma
	9	Iowa State
	13	@Colorado
	16	@Kansas
	19	Oklahoma State
	23	@Nebraska
	27	Missouri
Mar.	2	@Oklahoma
	8-10	##Big Eight Tournament

@ Road Games
# Kansas City, MO (Murray State, South Alabama & Texas A&M)
Kansas City, MO

KENT STATE

LAST SEASON: 21-8
CONFERENCE RECORD: 12-4
STARTERS LOST: 3
STARTERS RETURNING: 2
CONFERENCE: MID-AMERICAN (MAC)
LOCATION: KENT, OH
HOME FLOOR: MEMORIAL GYM (6,034)
NICKNAME: GOLDEN FLASHES
COLORS: NAVY BLUE AND GOLD
COACH: JIM McDONALD, record at Kent State, 128-102.

Kent State has appeared in the NIT three times in 74 years. Jim McDonald coached all three of those teams (1985, 1989 and 1990). Only three teams in school history have cracked the 20-win plateau, and McDonald coached two of those clubs.

McDonald, in fact, is the only Kent State coach to ever put together back-to-back 20-win seasons, with the 1988-89 Golden Flashes going 20-11 and last year's group finishing 21-8. Unfortunately for Kent and its wily mentor, the Flashes had the misfortune of posting those records at the same time Ball State was punishing Mid-American Conference competition by winning 27 of 32 league games. That left Kent State as bridesmaids two years in a row, even though McDonald has raked in long-overdue accolades and honors.

It is hard to believe McDonald is entering his ninth season. His 128-102 record makes him the ninth-winningest coach in MAC history, even though he had to wait far too many years to get his shot at a head-coaching opportunity. Presumably, that wait was because of his reserved, polite personality. McDonald is more the grandfatherly type, but he can coach. And forget the grandfatherly analogy, especially during games, as he will administer a tongue-lashing to his players if needed.

Two years ago, when McDonald was voted Ohio college basketball coach of the year by his peers, he finally gained wider recognition for his skills. Last season, even though Ball State ran away with the Mid-American title under rookie coach Dick Hunsaker, McDonald swept MAC coach of the year honors, as voted on by the conference news media association.

But enough about McDonald. He faces quite a challenge this season, because the Flashes have graduated three starters whose combined per game averages last season were 39.4 points, 15.4 rebounds and 6.2 assists. Gone is the entire starting frontline, which included 6-7 forward Ric Blevins (18.2 ppg, 5.1 rpg, 88 assists), 6-3 forward Eric Glenn (13.0 ppg, 5.8 rpg, 50 assists) and 6-9 center David Barnwell (8.2 ppg, 4.5 rpg).

The starting backcourt returns, though, as does the team's top substitute. Leading the way will be 6-1 junior **Harold Walton** (13.4 ppg, 3.8 rpg, 110 assists, 62 steals). The quicksilver point man led the MAC in steals, averaging 2.1 in conference games. He also has three-point range, hittng 38-of-93 attempts last season for a respectable .409 percentage. A fine student - also a Kent State hoops trademark under McDonald - Walton's intelligence carries over to the hardwood. He was named to the academic All-MAC first team, and was honorable mention All-MAC on the court.

Walton's backcourt mate, 6-3 junior **Mike Klinzing** (8.3 ppg, 3.0 rpg, 103 assists) is no slouch, either, be it with the books or running the offense. Klinzing was chosen for the GTE-CoSIDA academic All-District IV team last season, and was honorable mention academic All-MAC. The guy can play, too. Like Walton, Klinzing has three-point range. His percentage (.375) could be better, but he did convert 27of-72.

The top hope for a refurbished frontcourt is 6-5 junior **Tony Banks** (8.0 ppg, 4.8 rpg, 23 blocked shots). Although he started only four games, Banks still ranked among the team leaders in several categories. A fine all-around athlete, Banks' blocked shot total led the Flashes.

A pair of 6-8 freshmen - center **Jason Hunt** and forward **Rod Koch** - should earn playing time right away because of the thinned ranks up front. Hunt averaged 24.0 points and 10.3 rebounds at Watkins High (Petaskala, Ohio), while Koch averaged 19.6 and 10.8, respectively, at Kenton (Ohio) HS.

Trying to hold off the new freshmen will be 6-8 junior **John Wilson** (1.4 ppg, 1.4 rpg), a returning letterwinner, along with 6-9 sophomore **Doug Carr** (only four games last year) and 6-5 sophomore **Gregg Darbyshire** (1.2 ppg, 0.7 rpg). Neither of the latter earned a letter last season.

The only other returning letterwinner is 5-10 junior **Tony Watson** (1.2 ppg), one of several players hoping for backup time behind starters Walton and Klinzing. The others include returning non-lettermen **Mike Albertson**, a 6-2 junior, 6-3 sophomore **Greg Holman** (0.8 ppg, 0.4 rpg) and 6-2 junior **Keith Killian** (1.2 ppg). 6-5 freshman recruit **Jeff Anderson** (Reitz HS/Evansville, Ind.) rounds out the backcourt.

BLUE RIBBON ANALYSIS

All is fine on McDonald's farm, as you can be sure of the following when Kent State takes the court: the Flashes will hound their opponent with good man-to-man defense, they will shoot decent percentages from the field and free throw line, and they will play with a disciplined intelligence that reflects their coach's demeanor.

Last season, for the second consecutive year, Kent State placed three of its players on the academic All-MAC squad, a remarkable accomplishment. As a team last season, the Flashes compiled a cumulative grade-point average of 2.74. This, perhaps more than anything else, is evidence of why McDonald has been able to build such a successful program at a campus previously known as a hoops graveyard.

Hardly the flamboyant type that makes an outstanding recruiter, McDonald relies on enticing intelligent players - true student-athletes who put academics first - to come to Kent State and fit into his scheme of things. Work hard, play smart, and avoid make silly mistakes, and a player of somewhat limited physical skills can flourish in the team setting McDonald emphasizes.

The Flashes also have become quite comfortable and very formidable in Memorial Gym, where crowds of more than 5,000 are becoming habit. Kent went 12-0 at home last season.

As for this year, with the wise veteran backcourt of Walton and Klinzing anchoring an otherwise inexperienced group, anything is possible. But another 20-win season seems unlikely, as it will take McDonald time to sort out his frontcourt. Nevertheless, do not count this team out. They certainly should be competitive (as in middle-of-pack, at worst; top three at best) in a conference that this season offers no overwhelming favorite, other than perhaps Bowling Green.

LAFAYETTE

LAST SEASON: 15-13
CONFERENCE RECORD: 7-7
STARTERS LOST: 3
STARTERS RETURNING: 2
CONFERENCE: PATRIOT LEAGUE
LOCATION: EASTON, PA
HOME FLOOR: KIRBY FIELDHOUSE (3,500)
NICKNAME: LEOPARDS
COLORS: MAROON AND WHITE
COACH: JOHN LEONE, record at Lafayette, 35-23.

Lafayette exited the East Coast Conference after a demoralizing double overtime loss to Delaware in the tournament quarterfinals that epitomized the second half of their season. The Leopards won only six of their last 14 games, but five of their eight losses were by three points or less.

Instead of building as the season went on, Lafayette sputtered and stalled. They had a veteran

team that couldn't get over the hump, despite the rants and raves of coach John Leone, who can stalk the bench area with the best of them. With their entry into the new Patriot League, the Leopards will find it even more difficult getting over the hump. In the new league, they'll be playing all the same teams they faced last year —Army, Fordham, Colgate, Holy Cross and, joining them from the ECC, Bucknell and Lehigh.

Gone are three starters, guard Andy Wescoe, forward Richard Soto and center Matt Roberts, as well as top substitute Greg Bishop. Wescoe (14.9 ppg, 2.7 rpg), a second guard, shot 49 percent from three-point range and was first team All-ECC. The offense revolved around the 6-7 Roberts (10.3 ppg, 4.5 rpg) in the pivot; he led the team with 128 assists and made second-team All-ECC. Those two and 6-7 Soto (10.3 ppg, 5.6 rpg) were the best shooters on the club. The 6-4 Bishop (6.0 ppg, 2.3 rpg) averaged nearly 17 minutes a game, spelling people at three positions.

Steady point guard **Bruce Stankavage** (14.3 ppg, 2.7 rpg, 3.1 apg) will again direct the offense. The 6-2 senior is a standout on defense. He shot a reasonable 47 percent, but hit only 10-of-41 shots from three-point range. 6-0 senior **Tom Kresge** (3.5 ppg, 1.1 rpg), who started four games when Wescoe was injured last year, should move into the starting backcourt. He's a shooter (53 percent from the field, including 44 percent from three-point range) who averaged 15 minutes a game last year. The rest of the backcourt is filled with inexperienced players: 6-3 sophomore **Larry Spigner** (1.0 ppg) played 65 minutes, 6-2 junior **Terry Burke** and 6-0 sophomore **Joe Azzinaro** played 13 and 10 minutes, respectively. Spigner and Azzinaro spent last year learning the system. This year, they'll be expected to contribute. Azzinaro will back up Stankavage. Spigner was a big scorer in high school and his ability to shoot will determine his playing time behind Kresge.

When Stankavage looks to pass, the first person he'll be looking for is 6-5 junior forward **Craig White** (9.8 ppg, 6.0 rpg). White is a leaper who began to come into his own last year, emerging from the shadow of former Leopards' standout Otis Ellis, whom he followed to Lafayette from Philadelphia's Germantown Academy. Comparisons to Ellis may have been too much for him last year, but White will be expected to carry a bigger load this year. He led the team in rebounding last year, and on a team with no height, he'll be looked to for board strength again.

6-6 sophomore **Jeff Antolick** (1.5 ppg, 1.2 rpg) averaged seven minutes in 25 games last year and rates as the most experienced prospect to join White in the frontcourt. He is not a big scorer, but should be able to help on the boards and do a lot of the grunt work (picks and passes) that Roberts handled the last four years. Also returning is 6-6 junior **Keith Van Auken** (1.0 ppg) and 6-6 sophomore **Matt Jens**, both of whom played in only nine games last year. They will have to fend off three frontcourt recruits. With five guards returning Leone went looking for big men to fill his roster. 6-7 **Jamie Panko** (John F. Kennedy HS in Islen, N.Y.), 6-5 **Elliott Fontaine** (Brewster Academy in New Hampshire) and 6-6 **Jon Norton** (Lawrenceville Academy, N.J.).

BLUE RIBBON ANALYSIS

John Leone has his work cut out for him this year. Despite the return of two starters, the Leopards face a major rebuilding effort this year. There is little experience among last year's reserves beyond Kresge. The fact that, outside of White, the recruits of the last two years have not gotten playing time is not a good sign. Leone took the departed Butch van Breda Koiff's team to a 20-10 record his first season but slipped to 15-13 last year with three returning starters and an expectant star in White. How far can they fall this year? A lot. They may be in a new league, but they'll see a lot of familiar faces. It could be a long season.

LAMAR

LAST SEASON: 7-21
CONFERENCE RECORD: 1-9
STARTERS LOST: 1
STARTERS RETURNING: 4
CONFERENCE: AMERICAN SOUTH
LOCATION: BEAUMONT, TX
HOME FLOOR: MONTAGNE CENTER (10,080)
NICKNAME: CARDINALS
COLORS: RED AND WHITE
COACH: MIKE NEWELL, first year at Lamar. Career record, 133-60.

Lamar's once proud basketball program hit rock bottom last season with a 7-21 record, its third losing mark in the past four years. Cardinal second year head coach Tony Branch was dismissed and Lamar turned to Mike Newell, a miracle worker at Arkansas-Little Rock, to restore the winning tradition.

Newell's track record is impeccable. He inherited a program at Arkansas-Little Rock in 1984 that had won 20 or more games only twice in 45 seasons and had drawn less than 96,000 fans total in five previous season. After a 17-13 mark in his rookie season at Arkansas-Little Rock, Newell's next five teams won at least 20 games and made three NCAA appearances and two trips to the NIT. Three times, his teams won conference championships and in 1986, his unknown Trojans stunned No. 10 ranked Notre Dame in the opening round of the NCAA tournament, one of the biggest upsets in the tournament in the '80s.

Newell's .689 winning percentage ranks him among the Top 20 active NCAA Division I coaches. His teams' winning ways and exciting brand of play put people in the stands, as well. By the 1988-89 season, Arkansas-Little Rock sold nearly 5,000 season tickets and the Trojans drew 97,000 customers, more than they had in the five pre-Newell seasons.

Newell is linked with Lamar basketball. He served as an assistant coach four years under Billy Tubbs at

Oklahoma. Tubbs first made a splash on the national college basketball scene at Lamar. Tubbs' 1980 Cardinals upset fifth ranked Oregon State to reach the Sweet Sixteen of the NCAA tournament. And Tubbs' teams began at Lamar an 80-game home winning streak that would be continued under the tenure of Pat Foster.

Basketball was once the kingpin in Lamar's athletic program. Now that the school has disbanded its football program, it will be up to Newell to bring basketball back into national prominence.

"It has been done here before and it will be done again," promised Newell when he accepted the Lamar job. "Lamar will again win 20 games a season; Lamar will again win conference championships; Lamar will again play before packed Montagne Center crowds, and Lamar will again attract postseason attention."

Newell has made an impact already. By midsummer, Lamar had sold 3,000 season basketball tickets, nearly double the amount it had sold for the 1989-90 season.

Four starters return to the Cardinals' nest, including 6-8 senior center **Darryl Reed**, who was named the American South Conference newcomer of the year. Reed (15.8 ppg, 7.5 rpg, 40 assists, 31 blocked shots, 22 steals) scored in double figures in 22 games last year and recorded double figures in points and rebounds in nine games. A former first— team JC All-America at Vincennes University (Ind.) JC, Reed's quickness and soft touch gives Newell a solid pillar in the middle to build the offense around.

Three other starters also return. 6-9 junior forward **Brad Westbrook** (6.8 ppg, 4.4 rpg, 34 assists, 10 steals), 6-6 junior forward **Calvin Rice** (8.9 ppg, 6.0 rpg, 28 assists, 12 steals) and 6-3 sophomore guard **Owen Miller** (7.1 ppg, 2.0 rpg, 36 assists, 14 steals) are the other returning starters. Miller was a high school teammate of former Louisiana State All-America Chris Jackson and his father is Jackson's agent.

The lone missing starter is point guard David Jones, who set a school record by starting in 115 consecutive games in his career. Jones was the Cardinals' second leading scorer with a 14.8 scoring norm and he holds all of the school records for three-point shooting.

Two reserves —6-4 junior guard **Norther Gims** and 6-5 senior forward/post **Keith Harris** —also return. Gims (1.9 ppg, 1.7 rpg) lacks a dependable shooting touch, but can still contribute as a defensive stopper. Harris, a member of the University of Kansas' national championship team in 1988, played in only five games for Lamar after establishing his eligibility late last season. Harris averaged 9.0 ppg and 3.6 rpg and with an advantage of pre-season work, could win a starting position.

A pair of players who sat out last season could provide much needed depth. **Terry Brown**, a 6-9 redshirt freshman post, could become a factor in the middle. Brown averaged 17.5 points and 7.9 rebounds his senior year at Jena (La.) HS. 6-4 junior guard **Mike Hall** sat out last year after transferring from Arkansas State. Hall did not play at Arkansas State, and last saw competitive action at Vincennes (Ind.) JC, where he averaged 11.7 points per game.

Because of the loss of Jones and the fact that no returning guard shot over 40 percent from the field, Newell concentrated heavily on that area, signing four guards among his five recruits.

The newcomers are headed by 6-1 junior **Eric Moore**, who earned third-team National Junior College Athletic Association All-America honors while performing at Pratt (Kan.) CC. Moore, who can play either guard position, averaged 16.1 points, 4.2 rebounds, 5.6 assists and 2.2 steals last season.

Two other junior college guards —6-4 junior **Aaron McFadden** and 6-2 **Terry Bridgeman** —figure prominently in Newell's plans. McFadden played small forward, off-guard and point guard for Ellsworth (Iowa) CC, averaging 18.8 points, 4.7 rebounds and 5.3 assists per game. Bridgeman led Cloud County (Kan.)

in scoring two years in a row, averaging 17.5 points and 3.2 rebounds as a sophomore. He hit 54.3 percent of his shots from the field and 43.8 percent of his three-point attempts.

Another junior college recruit, 6-6 junior **Tommy Smith**, could help up front. Smith averaged 11.5 points and 7.1 rebounds in a 13-game season at Vincennes JC that was cut short by an ankle injury.

Lamar's lone freshman signee, 6-1 **Atiim Browne** is expected to challenge for the starting point guard position. A godson of former NBA star Nate Archibald, Browne averaged 8.7 points and 5.5 assists per game at Maine Central Institute.

BLUE RIBBON ANALYSIS

Mike Newell should give Lamar's basketball program a much needed shot in the arm. As former Lamar head coach and current Oklahoma boss Billy Tubbs said, "Mike will get it done, but he's not going to step in and win 25 games next season, although as an alumnus, I wish he would. You are only as good as your players."

Despite a late start in recruiting, Newell landed enough talented guards to make his running and pressing style work. A .500 season is a reasonable goal for the Cardinals in 1990-91. However, lack of quality depth inside will be a liability in the American South Conference where the Cardinals can expect to finish no higher than fifth.

		1990-91 LAMAR SCHEDULE
Nov.	23-24	#UAB Tournament
	26	Fullerton State
	28	San Jose State
Dec.	4	Sam Houston State
	7-8	*Heritage Cablevision-Drake Classic
	15	@Kansas State
	21-22	**Texaco Star Classic
	31	Southern University
Jan.	5	Texas-Pam American
	8	Tulsa
	10	Central Florida
	12	University of Hartford
	14	@McNeese State
	17	@New Orleans
	19	@Southwestern Louisiana
	24	Louisiana Tech
	26	Arkansas State
	29	McNeese State
Feb.	2	@Texas-Pan American
	9	@Central Florida
	14	New Orleans
	16	Southwestern Louisiana
	21	@Louisiana Tech
	23	@Arkansas State
Mar.	1-3	***ASC Tournament

@ Road Games
# Birmingham, AL (Alabama-Birmingham, Alabama State & Samford)
* Des Moines, IA (Akron, Drake & Eastern Washington)
** San Diego, CA (Arkansas State, Drexel & San Diego State)
*** Held on the home floor of the regular season champion.

LA SALLE

LAST SEASON: 30-2,
CONFERENCE RECORD: 16-0
STARTERS LOST: 1
STARTERS RETURNING: 4
CONFERENCE: METRO-ATLANTIC ATHLETIC (MAAC)
LOCATION: PHILADELPHIA, PA
HOME FLOOR: PHILADELPHIA CIVIC CENTER (10,004)
NICKNAME: EXPLORERS
COLORS: BLUE AND GOLD
COACH: SPEEDY MORRIS, record at La Salle, 100-31. Career record, including high school, 530-144.

Now what? Four years of "Lionelmania" have ended at La Salle, an era that brought this small Catholic college out of the shadow of its larger Philadelphia rivals and into the national spotlight. Lionel Simmons, the Explorers' franchise player, is gone to the financial bounty of the NBA (No. 7 overall pick in the draft by Sacramento). It is time to see what else La Salle has got.

Even if Simmons never donates a nickel of his lucrative pro contract, he has endowed the Explorers with enough good will to warrant statues, speeches and hearty hurrahs all around. The L-Train helped Speedy Morris become only the third Division I coach to win 100 games in his first four years. He was the main reason the Explorers could move their home games to the roomy Philadelphia Civic Center. And he generated an overwhelming amount of national recognition for the program.

Suffice it to say, Simmons established a new standard by which all future Explorers will be measured. He became only the fifth player in NCAA history to top the career 3,000-point mark, finishing with 3,217 - good enough for third on the all-time list. He was a consensus first-team All-America, and the winner of enough Player of the Year awards to fill a cavernous trophy case. And that is only a smattering of the various records and honors accrued during his four years.

"Certainly we have no one to replace Lionel," Morris said. "He made everyone around him better. But life goes on. That's the good thing about college basketball. You get different players every year. The ones we have this year aren't as good as Lionel, but that just means we won't win 30 games again. We'll win 20."

Explorer players, coaches and fans will not have to depend on nostalgia for basketball excitement. Although this year's La Salle team is no threat to the 30-win mark, it should be plenty good enough to reach the stated goal of 20 victories and a fourth consecutive trip to the NCAA tournament.

The main reason for the expected continuity is that Morris was hardly foolish during the Simmons era. Instead of merely surrounding his thoroughbred with complementary types, Morris brought in players whose talent can stand alone.

"I don't think our style will change," Morris said. "We'll still be up tempo, with pressure defense. We just won't have anyone who's a 'go-to' guy like Lionel."

But La Salle will have 6-3 senior **Doug Overton** (17.2 ppg, 6.6 assists, 4.2 rpg, 85 steals), one of the nation's most underrated point guards. Overton already holds the La Salle career assist record and will soar past the 1,500-point mark by mid-season. He kickstarts the La Salle break and can finish things off if needed.

"Like Lionel, he makes everyone better," Morris said. "I don't think that will change. We hope he can score more, but we still need him to distribute the ball. We look for him to do a lot of things."

Overton's backcourt partner will be 6-0 junior **Randy Woods** (13.3 ppg, 3.5 assists, 3.2 rpg), a tenacious defender and a mercurial offensive talent. Woods can harass the finest scoring guards, but tends to play out of control on the offensive end. When on, he can light it up from long distances, as evidenced by his team-high 77 three-pointers. When off, he keeps firing, much to the chagrin of Morris.

"He's a wild player," Morris admitted. "He takes some bad shots, and we have to live with that. We can't restrict him. Toward the end of last year, he fit in well."

Backcourt depth should come courtesy of 6-3 freshman **Lamont Carter** (Hillhouse HS/New Haven, Conn.). Carter averaged 25.5 points, 10.6 rebounds and 6.0 assists to lead Hillhouse to the state big school title. He was named Connecticut player of the year by the *New Haven Register*.

"He may be ready to contribute, but it's a big jump from high school to college," Morris said. Other

Explorer guards include 5-10 junior **Keith Morris** (1.3 ppg), son of the coach, 6-4 sophomore **Mike Bergin** (1.2 ppg) and 6-4 sophomore **Jeff Neubauer** (0.9 ppg).

If the Explorers hope to even approach Simmons' offensive production in the frontcourt, 6-5 junior swingman **Jack Hurd** (8.3 ppg, 3.3 rpg) will have to overcome his disappointing sophomore season. After taking Metro Atlantic Athletic Conference newcomer of the year honors in 1988-89, Hurd's productivity slipped, and his shooting percentage dipped to 38.3 percent.

"If hard work means anything, he'll be back," Morris promised. "He does a lot of things that don't show up in the boxscore. He gets his hands on loose balls to start fastbreaks, and he comes up with a lot of intangibles."

The remaining two frontcourt spots will by filled by any combination of a half-dozen veterans and newcomers. Junior **Milko Lieverst** (4.4 ppg, 4.9 rpg), a 6-9 Dutch import, started at center last season and should be back again this time around. The other frontcourt candidates include burly 6-8 junior **Bron Holland** (4.2 ppg, 2.9 rpg), 6-8 junior **Don Shelton** (1.3 rpg), 6-9 sophomore transfer **Ray Schultz** (Florida Atlantic), 6-6 senior transfer **Broderick President** (Hardin-Simmons), 6-7 freshman **Blitz Wooten** (McCorriston HS/Trenton, N.J.) and 6-5 senior **Mike Stock** (1.4 ppg, 1.2 ppg).

"This could be the deepest team we've had in the four years I've been here," Morris said. "In the past, we've gone with six or seven guys. This year, we'll go eight or nine deep."

That depth will really help during La Salle's challenging non-league slate, which includes Notre Dame, Florida State, Brigham Young, Loyola Marymount, Villanova and Temple. It won't matter as much in the MAAC, a relatively weak conference made weaker by the departure of Holy Cross and Fordham to the Patriot League.

BLUE RIBBON ANALYSIS

Without Simmons, La Salle will no longer be a familiar sight in the national rankings. But it won't be falling into the doldrums, either. Overton and Woods are a quick, slick backcourt, and Carter could be a star in short order. If Hurd emerges from his sophomore slump, La Salle will score plenty of points.

The newcomers give Morris more meat up front than ever. That means rebounds and physical play on defense. Any repeat of last year is out of the question, but the MAAC championship is not. In fact, it is expected. La Salle will be in the NCAA tournament again, you just won't see as much of them the rest of the year.

Losing a legend can do that.

1990-91 LA SALLE SCHEDULE		
Dec.	1	@Pennsylvania
	4	Brigham Young
	9	@Florida State
	14	#Japan All-Stars
	15	#Baylor
	16	#Idaho
	22	@Villanova
	29	Loyola College
	31	@Loyola Marymount
Jan.	5	Temple
	8	@Iona
	12	Niagara
	17	@Loyola College
	21	Siena
	24	@Canisius
	26	@Niagara
	31	Fairfield
Feb.	2	##Manhattan
	6	@Notre Dame
	9	Canisius
	11	@Fairfield
	14	St. Peter's

1990-91 LA SALLE SCHEDULE Cont.		
Feb.	16	St. Joseph's
	18	Manhattan
	20	@Siena
	23	Iona
	26	@St. Peter's
Mar.	1-4	*MAAC Tournament

@ Road Games
# Phenix Bowl, Tokyo, Japan
Madison Square Garden, New York, NY
* Albany, NY

LEHIGH

LAST SEASON: 18-12
CONFERENCE RECORD: 8-6
STARTERS LOST: 2
STARTERS RETURNING: 3
CONFERENCE: PATRIOT LEAGUE
LOCATION: BETHLEHEM, PA
HOME FLOOR: STABLER CENTER (5,800)
NICKNAME: ENGINEERS
COLORS: BROWN AND WHITE
COACH: DAVE DUKE, record at Lehigh, 28-30.

The winds of change continue to blow through Eastern college basketball, and although the newly created Patriot League will barely cause a ripple come Final 64 time, the academic might and old line ties of this conference already has made its presence felt. Instead of having to wait the customary three years before its champion earns an automatic berth into the NCAA tournament, the Patriot League was granted entry into one of the two "play-in" games to fill the field.

For teams like Lehigh, that is great news. For if the Engineers' last two seasons in the East Coast Conference are any indication, they'll be right in the thick of it. Lehigh confounded —or is it astounded? —the experts with their better than expected finish both seasons. A 10-18 record two years ago —when the Engineers had one starter returning —was followed by an 18-12 mark last year. Although four starters returned, Lehigh was picked to finish seventh in the eight team ECC. Instead, they finished in a three way tie for first. They lost two of their last five games, both of them at Towson State, the second defeat coming in the ECC championship game.

The architect of those seasons, David Duke, was honored as ECC Coach of the Year for his work last season. He had five players who started every game and a bench that gave capable support. If the Engineers come up with a point guard to replace Scott Layer, Duke may earn Patriot League coaching laurels this year. The 6-0 Layer (6.4 ppg, 1.5 rpg, 4.3 apg) was not the most prolific scorer, nor was he the flashiest passer. But he was the consummate mid-level Division I point guard and the team's leader. Behind him, and sometimes next to him, was 5-11 guard Neal Fenton (5.3 ppg, 1.2 rpg, 2.2 apg), who also has graduated. Though not as consistent a shooter as Layer (50 percent), Fenton (43 percent) gave the Engineers on-court direction as well. Also departed are starting center Tom Martin (6-7 and 10.9 ppg, 6.3 rpg) and 6-2 reserve guard Peter Rudman (3.2 ppg). Though Martin developed into a solid frontline player and Rudman had his moments off the bench, both can be replaced.

Sophomore **Rich Hudock** and freshman **Mike McKee** will try to take Layer's place at the point. Both are 5-10, Hudock played sparingly behind Layer and

Fenton last year, scoring five points in 25 minutes of action last year (eight games). McKee averaged 8.0 ppg and 8.0 rpg for Roman Catholic HS in Philadelphia, Pa. "Both of them are similar players, good with the ball and smart overall players," Duke said. "Neither one of them turns the ball over, but they both obviously lack collegiate experience. It's going to take some time for them to develop." Duke has no such hesitation about his No. 2 guard position. 6-4 senior **Mike O'Hara** (10.9 ppg, 1.8 rpg) saw the least playing time among the five starters but scored in double figures in 17 of 30 games. He's a good three-point shooter (40 percent on 54-of-133 attempts) and doesn't turn the ball over. **Chuck Penn**, a 6-4 sophomore, returns after sitting out a year and looms as O'Hara's back-up. Penn averaged 5.5 ppg as a freshman.

Solid as a rock are the forward posts, where the team's top two scorers and rebounders return as junior co-captains. 6-5 **Bob Krizansky** blossomed last year, leading Lehigh in scoring (10.0 ppg) and field goal percentage (53 percent) and being named to the All-ECC team and the all-tournament team. He was also second in rebounding (7.5 rpg) and assists (3.5 apg). 6-6 **Dozie Mbonu** was second in scoring (14.7 ppg), first in rebounding (8.1 rpg), was a second team All-ECC pick and an all-tournament selection. He shot 52 percent. "This position no question is the team's strength," Duke said. "We're calling on Dozie and Bob for leadership this season both on and off the court." Two more juniors will back up Krizansky and Mbonu. 6-4 **Jay Hipps** (5.3 ppg, 1.9 rpg) emerged as the top forward reserve last year, averaging 11.4 ppg over the final seven regular season contests, while 6-4 **Steve Yaniga** (2.4 ppg) saw action in 26 games and shot 46 percent. Yaniga can play second guard, too. 6-4 junior **Pat Kilgarriff** (10 points in six games) has had trouble overcoming a couple of knee injuries to accumulate more playing time and 6-5 sophomore **Scott McQuilken** (four points in seven games) will spend another year in waiting.

Center is a jump ball between 6-7 sophomore **John Lynch** (1.4 ppg, 1.1 rpg) and 6-7 freshman **Allan Campbell** (24.0 ppg, 12.5 rpg for Dallastown, Pa., HS). Lynch saw limited action in only 16 games but was the only freshman to letter last year for the Engineers. Both he and Campbell are considered good outside shooters with enough strength to mix it up for rebounds. But as with many little big men at little big schools like Lehigh, center is the toughest position to fill. "It usually takes a couple of years for centers to develop. Lynch and Campbell will get a lot of time early and hopefully they'll develop," Duke said. 6-7 freshman **Jason Kokoszka** (24.0 ppg, 11.0 rpg for the American School in London, England) will also get a look in the pivot.

BLUE RIBBON ANALYSIS

Although there are question marks, Lehigh has the nucleus of a team that's capable of winning the league. The three former East Coast Conference teams (Lehigh, Lafayette and Bucknell) moving over to the Patriot have continually won head-to-head duels with the other new league members (Army, Colgate, Fordham and Holy Cross), and Lehigh remains strong. Dave Duke has quietly built a reputation as motivator and tactician. A new league —one in which they'll play host to the conference tournament in March —and an open shot at the NCAA tournament may be all the motivation the Engineers will need. Solid play from Mbonu and Krizansky should allow the newcomers at point guard and center a chance to settle in.

1990-91 LEHIGH SCHEDULE		
Nov.	23	@Brown
	24	@Harvard
	27	Hofstra (NY)
Dec.	1	@American University
	3	Princeton

1990-91 LEHIGH SCHEDULE *Cont.*

Dec.	7-8	#Marist Tournament
	29	@Duke
Jan.	2	William & Mary
	5	Army
	7	Towson State
	9	@Miami (FL)
	12	@Florida International
	16	@Fordham
	19	Colgate
	21	Columbia
	23	Pennsylvania
	26	@Lafayette
	28	@Drexel
	30	Bucknell
Feb.	2	@Holy Cross
	5	@Army
	9	Fordham
	13	@Colgate
	20	Lafayette
	23	@Bucknell
	25	Holy Cross
Feb. 28- Mar. 2		##Patriot League Tournament

@ Road Games
# Poughkeepsie, NY (Brown, Canisius & Marist)
Worcester, MA

LONG ISLAND

LAST SEASON: 3-23
CONFERENCE RECORD: 1-15
STARTERS LOST: 1
STARTERS RETURNING: 4
CONFERENCE: NORTHEAST CONFERENCE (NEC)
LOCATION: BROOKLYN, NY
HOME FLOOR: ARNOLD AND MARIE SCHWARTZ ATHLETIC CENTER (2,000)
NICKNAME: BLACKBIRDS
COLORS: BLUE AND WHITE
COACH: PAUL LIZZO, record at Long Island, 199-214. Career record, 250-259.

Just how much of a nightmare was the 1989-90 season for the Blackbirds of Long Island? Better yet, do you really need to ask?

The season ended with a 13-game losing streak and there were far too many injuries to count. More players were visiting the trainer's office than the scorer's table. Opponents scorched the Blackbirds to the tunes of 85.7 points per game and a field goal percentage of .515. Head coach Paul Lizzo, the architect of two NCAA tournament teams and one NIT squad, never came close to experiencing anything like last year. Nightmare? Freddy Krueger could have had a nice restful nap watching the Blackbirds.

Eight members of last year's contingent are back again this season, including three or four starters, depending upon how you read it. Lizzo played mix and match for most of the season last year, as 13 of the 15 Blackbirds that saw action last year actually started at least one game.

Senior guard **Brent McCollin** (19.0 ppg, 4.1 rpg) started 15 games of the 22 he played in after returning from a broken jaw suffered early in the season. The 6-1 McCollin exploded down the stretch, scoring 40 or more points in two games and 30 or more five other times, all after January 1. McCollin is an aggressive scorer with a fine shooting touch and the ability to take over games offensively. With a healthy start

this time around, Lizzo can expect some great things from McCollin. At the close of last season, there was no better scorer in the NEC.

Senior swingman **Rich Henry** (17.2 ppg, 5.7 rpg) started 24 games a year ago, which was tops on the club. Henry, who at 6-3 is probably better suited for action at off-guard but plays predominantly at small forward. He is also a strong scorer and good shooter. Henry shot 46 percent from the floor, mostly from long range, but only managed to nail 28 percent of all three-point tries. But he can score in bunches, like McCollin, and was the Blackbirds' leading scorer in nine of the first 13 games of the season, when McCollin was recovering from the jaw injury. Henry is also deadly when in the open floor. His quickness and ability to finish on the break are tremendous assets.

Junior forward **Neil Smith** (13.5 ppg, 5.1 rpg) also returns from a brutal sophomore year. Oh, the numbers were effective and he managed to shoot 55 percent from the floor, among the tops in the NEC, but the 6-4 Smith was forced to play center. Centers that size were out of fashion when the hole was carved out of the bottom of the peach basket, but that's what Lizzo was left with and Smith performed admirably. Smith is a fine player with a soft southpaw touch, but he needs some big help up front.

Senior point guard **Anthony Bogarty** (6.8 ppg, 1.9 rpg, 44 assists) was having a decent season last year at the midway point when he was forced to the sidelines with troubled feet and broken toes. Bogarty is very quick and a good penetrator. But he will not be handed his job back as a starter. That's because sophomore point man **Leroy Wilson** stepped in during Bogarty's absence and did a more than creditable job. Wilson, a 5-10 speedball from Jersey City, N.J. —the land of point guards —transferred to Long Island in mid-season a year ago and played in 10 games, starting eight. Wilson averaged 6.6 ppg and 2.1 rpg and managed to lead the team in assists in just 10 games played with 51. Wilson needs to work on his outside shooting and that's about all, because he does everything else very well, especially defensively.

Sophomore guard **Corbett Smith** (3.1 ppg, 1.8 rpg) also returns. Smith, who came to Long Island after a stint in the Marine Corps, played in 22 games, starting five at off-guard. But Smith can play the point or the small forward slot if needed. Smith is explosive in the open floor and can run like a gazelle. If Smith can play under control, he might be one of the most improved players in the NEC this season.

Senior center **Darwyn Ingram** (0.9 ppg, 1.1 rpg) also returns. At 6-10, Ingram is the lone Blackbird returnee with decent size, but he played very sparingly last season, totalling just 89 minutes in 14 games. How much Lizzo can count on Ingram for quality minutes this year remains to be seen. The final returnee is the coach's son, **Todd Lizzo** (0.5 ppg, 0.7 rpg), a 6-2 sophomore swingman who played in 13 games totalling 28 minutes last year.

Lizzo and his staff welcome six newcomers to the Blackbird roster, four junior college transfers and two freshman signees. In fact, three of the transfers all come from the same school, Manhattan CC in New York. The player of impact among the trio is junior forward **Mark White**. White, a 6-5 power forward, averaged 18.4 points and 12.1 rebounds last season. He is an aggressive rebounder and strong inside player. Junior guard **Fabian Jack**, a 5-11 speedster, will add both quickness and depth to the Blackbirds' lone strength, the backcourt. Jack, who can play either guard role, averaged 15.0 points and 12 assists for Manhattan CC last year.

The last of the Manhattan CC teammates is junior forward **Joe Griffin**. The 6-5 Griffin averaged 15.3 points and eight rebounds per game last season. Griffin is an explosive scorer —but isn't everyone with the Blackbirds, leaving one glaring question: Where's the defense? —who has a nice touch from the outside and goes to the basket very well.

Junior forward **Kevin Taylor** rounds out the Blackbirds' acquisition list from the JC ranks. The 6-6

Taylor, a high school teammate of point guard Wilson at Ferris in Jersey City, averaged 19.0 points and 10.0 rebounds for Mattatuck (Conn.) CC, last season. Taylor is a very versatile performer, with the ability to play inside and grab garbage hoops and lots of rebounds, or head to the far outside, where Taylor has a fine shot from the land of three-pointers. Taylor will contribute in great ways for the Blackbirds.

The top freshman signee —only by need —is 6-9 center **Chris Kozlowski**. Kozlowski hails from Brooklyn, N.Y., and went to St. Francis Prep, a school with a rich hoop tradition and one that has sent many players to Long Island over the years. Kozlowski is a brute, going 230-pounds plus to add to the very welcomed 6-9 frame and good strength. According to some college recruiters, Kozlowski just needs to get tougher and more aggressive and he can be a real find for Lizzo and a possible starter in the pivot.

While Lizzo and his staff were hawking Kozlowski, they spotted a teammate and encouraged him to come along as well. **Vaughn Richmond**, a 6-2 off-guard with a fine shooting touch, joins Kozlowski. The Blackbirds' backcourt is certainly crowded, so Richmond's amount of playing time is unknown. Both are sound fundamentally. Kozlowski averaged 14.0 points and 12.0 rebounds per game. Richmond's numbers were 16.0 ppg and 9.0 rpg.

BLUE RIBBON ANALYSIS

It sounds like a lousy cliche, but really, the Blackbirds can do no worse than last year. Any time a team goes 3-23 and ends the year with 13 losses in a row, you want to quickly think about getting better and forget about that horror show.

Can the Blackbirds improve? Reason says they have to. They have eight players back from last year that have to be hungry for a few W's and anxious to wipe the pain away in a hurry. McCollin and Henry are solid Division I scorers who would end up with 20 points if they were playing in a shoe box. Smith can also put the ball in the basket, but there's no way a team can win on the Division I level with a 6-4 center.

Those three players could play anywhere. They are that talented. After that remains a huge "if." The JC transfers will help. Lizzo has traditionally plucked kids out of the Manhattan CC program —maybe a real Blackbird feeder system, if there is such a thing. The kids from Manhattan CC come to Long Island aggressive and ready to contribute. No need for orientation.

But once again, it appears as if Lizzo is going to ask all of his players to play bigger than what they actually are. And that's not an easy request and certainly even tougher to get those effective results.

The Blackbirds were devastated on the defensive end last year. They gave up 85 points per game and allowed opponents to shoot 51 percent against them. Those numbers are abnormally high and you just don't win games that way. Defense has to be a priority for improvement and it appears as if the huge bodies to make the defense a little more secure are not there.

So will the Blackbirds improve? They just have to. But enough to compete in the NEC? No, they will have another tough year and finish toward the bottom of the conference. But in no way are they headed for another 3-23 disaster.

1990-91 LONG ISLAND SCHEDULE

Nov.	26	Drexel
	28	Central Connecticut State
Nov. 30- Dec. 1		#Hawks Unlimited Tournament
Dec.	5	St. Peter's
	7	Brooklyn College (NY)
	9	@Seton Hall
	15	Old Dominion
	18	Rider

LOUISIANA TECH

LAST SEASON: 20-8
CONFERENCE RECORD: 8-2
STARTERS LOST: 2
STARTERS RETURNING: 3
CONFERENCE: AMERICAN SOUTH
LOCATION: RUSTON, LA
HOME FLOOR: THOMAS ASSEMBLY CENTER (8,000)
NICKNAME: BULLDOGS
COLORS: COLUMBIA BLUE AND RED
COACH: JERRY LOYD, record at Louisiana Tech, 20-8.
Career record, including high school, 122-87.

Louisiana Tech may have changed coaches before the 1989-90 season, but the Bulldogs' successful program went on without skipping a beat. Jerry Loyd took over for Tommy Joe Eagles, who moved on to Auburn, and directed the Bulldogs to a 20-9 record, their seventh consecutive 20-win season.

One would be hard pressed to find a mid-major program that could match Tech's success in the 1980s. The Bulldogs suffered only one losing season in the decade and finished below the 20-win barrier only twice. Louisiana Tech averaged 20.9 wins per season during the '80s and made three trips to the NIT and four to the NCAA tournament during that stretch.

Loyd continued that tradition in his first year. The Bulldogs shared the American South Conference's regular season championship with the University of New Orleans. The Bulldogs also made their seventh consecutive postseason tournament, losing 98-90 in overtime to Vanderbilt in the first round of the NIT.

Another 20-win campaign and postseason appearance appear to be attainable goals for the Bulldogs, who return their entire frontline intact. The Bulldogs' baseline crew is headlined by 6-6, 240-pound junior **Anthony Dade** (18.12 ppg, 7.4 rpg, 37 assists, 6 blocked shots, 18 steals). Following in the footsteps of Tech products Karl Malone and Randy White, Dade became only the fifth sophomore in school history to lead the team in scoring. Dade scored in double figures in all but two of Tech's games last season and went

over 20 points on 11 occasions. A first team all-ASC conference selection, he hit 56.4 percent of his shots from the field. If he improves on his 61.5 percent shooting from the free throw line, the strong lefthander with a soft touch will elevate his scoring average to over 20 points per game.

6-7 senior forward **Eldon Bowman** (9.1 ppg, 6.1 rpg, 25 assists, 22 blocked shots, 18 steals) was a steady performer next to Dade. After redshirting in 1988-89, Bowman moved into the starting lineup eight games into the 1989-90 campaign and could not be moved out. The emergence of Bowman put 6-11 junior P. J. Brown (8.9 ppg, 8.5 rpg, 29 assists, 39 blocked shots, 21 steals) into a reserve role. But Brown still contributed, posting 11 double digit scoring games and 10 double digit rebounding games. A defensive force, Brown blocked four shots in three different contests. He is already the second leading shot blocker in Tech history with 89.

Rounding out the Bulldogs' frontline is 6-5 senior **Roosevelt Powell** (10.7 ppg, 4.5 rpg, 70 assists, 33 steals). Powell was a jack of all trades for the Bulldogs after coming out of Tyler (Texas) JC. Powell led the team in dunks with 29 and was the designated defensive stopper, often guarding the opponent's top scorer. Three other returnees figure prominently in Loyd's plans. **Mark Spradling**, a 6-7, 220-pound sophomore, averaged two points and 1.5 rebounds in back up duty at the post position. A fundamentally sound player who doesn't mind the banging underneath, Spradling offers quality depth. **Reni Mason** saw action in every game last year as a reserve point guard. The 5-11 point guard averaged 1.9 points and 1.3 assists and needs only more seasoning to become a steady point guard. Junior **JoJo Goldsmith**, a 6-3 junior guard, hit 14-of-32 three-point shots (43.7 percent) as a key reserve last year. A streak shooter who averaged 3.5 points per game, Goldsmith will be a contender for the starting shooting guard position. "We've got a good nucleus of returning players," said Loyd. "But we have severe question marks at the guard positions. We lost both of our starters who made (second-team) all-conference. Replacing one all-conference guard is tough, but having to replace two is kind of scary."

The departing point guard Brett Guillory and backcourt mate Reggie Gibbs leaves a void in the backcourt. Guillory averaged 10.4 points per game and led the team in assists with 157 last year. Gibbs was the team's second leading scorer with a 14.6 ppg norm.

While Loyd concentrated on filling the vacancies at guard with his recruiting class, the Bulldogs' top newcomer is a forward, 6-7 junior **Ronald Ellis**. Ellis sat out last year after averaging 19 points and 15 rebounds during his final season at Tyler (Texas) JC. An outstanding athlete, Ellis can play either on the post or at small forward. His versatility has Loyd considering moving Powell to a guard spot to make room for Ellis in the starting lineup. The presence of Ellis gives the Bulldogs' program its best frontline since the Karl Malone-Willie Simmons-Robert Godbolt unit of the mid-1980s.

No less than four new faces will compete for the two openings in the Bulldogs' backcourt. **Antuan Morris**, a 6-4 sophomore, sat out last season. A product of Jefferson Davis HS in Houston, Texas, Martin averaged 23 points and seven rebounds as a senior and was a two-time all-Houston Independent School District selection. Martin may very well be the best athlete in Tech's program.

A pair of junior college signees —6-1 junior **Kenny Rogers** and 6-0 junior **Eric Brown**—could also barge their way into the starting lineup. Rogers, a product of Dodge City (Kan.) CC, will be Mason's chief competition at point guard. Rogers averaged 21 points and four assists while earning All-Jayhawk Conference honors last year. Brown averaged 28.5 points, six rebounds, seven assists and three steals per game last year for Cisco (Texas) JC. The MVP in the North Texas Junior College Conference last season, Brown can play either guard spot.

The Bulldogs also added three quality freshmen —6-1 **Bryan Heaps**, 6-6 **Tron Moller**, and 6-1 **Daniel Magett**. Heaps, an outstanding shooter, averaged 22.0 points, 5.6 rebounds, 4.7 assists and 4.5 steals, while performing for Dallas Christian HS in Mesquite, Texas. Moller is a product of Archbishop Rummel HS in Metairie, La., where he averaged 13.0 points and 13.0 rebounds per game. Magett averaged 18.0 points and 16.0 rebounds per game for Our Savior Lutheran in New York City. As deep as the Tech's frontcourt is, Loyd has not ruled out Magett earning significant minutes during his freshman year.

BLUE RIBBON ANALYSIS

Jerry Loyd carried the torch proudly in his first year as Louisiana Tech's head coach in 1989-90 and there's no reason to anticipate anything less this season.

With Dade, Bowman, Powell and Brown, Louisiana Tech returns the most talented frontline in the American South Conference. If Ellis can overcome a year's layoff and live up to his billing, the Bulldogs could own one of the best and deepest baselines in the south.

The questions arise in the backcourt where last year's starters have departed. But Loyd signed enough quality in Rogers and Brown to stock the cupboard alongside holdovers Mason and Goldsmith.

The competition for starting jobs and quality minutes should be fierce beginning October 15 in Ruston and should only make the Bulldogs better. The Bulldogs have every reason to set their signs on a repeat as American South Conference champions and should at least finish in the money.

If their guards progress and Louisiana Tech can win the league's first automatic berth into the NCAA tournament, Tech has the type of personnel to make noise in the NCAA's Big Show.

219

LOYOLA

LAST SEASON: 7-22
CONFERENCE RECORD: 3-11
STARTERS LOST: 0
STARTERS RETURNING: 5
CONFERENCE: MID-WESTERN COLLEGIATE (MCC)
LOCATION: CHICAGO, IL
HOME FLOOR: ROSEMONT HORIZON (17,500)
NICKNAME: RAMBLERS
COLORS: MAROON AND GOLD
COACH: WILL REY, record at Loyola, 7-22.

For some time now, those in the Midwestern Collegiate Conference have been wondering just how good Loyola could be if coach Will Rey found some players to put around **Keith Gailes** and **Keir Rogers**. They have been the most dynamic scoring duo in the conference the last two years and, as seniors in 1990-91, have the potential to dominate many games.

Rogers, a 6-4 guard, is a complete player. He set the league record for steals last season with 85, and ranked 12th nationally in steals per game (2.9). He also averaged 16.6 points and 8.6 rebounds, and chipped in 2.6 assists per game.

Rogers also is a defensive wizard, and held St. Louis University's Anthony Bonner, headed to the Sacramento Kings as a first round pick in the NBA draft, to just 18 points in the first round of the MCC tournament. The Ramblers upset St. Louis in that game, and then came close to Dayton in the semifinals, with Rogers delivering 25 points in the final game of his junior season. When he finally leaves the Ramblers, Rogers' name will be among the career leaders in scoring, rebounding, steals and assists.

His sidekick is Gailes, a 6-3 guard who is the best pure shooter in the league. He delivers from anywhere on the court, and is a genuine All-America candidate. Last year, Gailes averaged 26.3 ppg, which led the MCC and was 12th nationally. In just two seasons at Loyola, he has scored 1,369 points and averaged 24.4 ppg.

One more important note about this twosome: opponents typically ignored the rest of the Ramblers and concentrated on stopping them, yet they still were successful. The overall picture, though, was never quite good enough. Loyola came close in a lot of games last season, losing in overtime to St. Louis and Marquette, and losing by five or fewer points on seven occasions altogether.

"Our team put forth a monumental effort all of last season," Rey said. "We were ready to play each and every game and we intend to go into each and every game this year with the same philosophy. Last year, this team worked its tail off in practice, during games and especially in their school work. We finished the season with important personal victories. They will work even harder this year. They know what to expect from me, and what I expect from them."

All five starters return from last season's squad. Besides Rogers and Gailes, 6-6 junior **Rob Mizera** (2.6 ppg, 3.0 rpg), 6-7 sophomore **Grant Moehring** (3.7 ppg, 2.7 rpg), and 5-9 junior **Don Sobczak** (2.1 ppg, 2.1 rpg) are back.

Sobczak and Gailes were the only Ramblers to start every game last season, and Sobczak is a feisty player who led the Ramblers in assists (3.9 per game). Also back as Loyola's sixth man in **Brian Wolf**, a 6-4 sophomore who averaged 6.9 ppg. He led the team in three-point shooting percentage (42-for-97, .433). **Spyros Sakellariou**, a 6-9 native of Piraeus, Greece, is a junior who averaged 3.0 ppg and 2.5 rpg last season in a reserve role. The only player of note that the Ramblers lost to graduation was Doug Borders (5.2

ppg, 2.2 rpg).

Loyola has eight newcomers, and it is a good bet Rey will be looking for someone to step forward and help Rogers and Gailes. Among the eight are three transfers, led by 6-3 junior **Hunter Atkins**, eligible after the first semester. Atkins averaged 5.7 ppoints at Mississippi before transfering and, as a high school player in Highland, Ind., scored 26.6 ppg as a senior.

6-3 sophomore **Eric Dolezal** transferred from Nebraska and is eligible immediately. So is 6-4 sophomore **Jason Joseph** (St. Leo College, Fla.), who will challenge for a spot on the front line. The remaining newcomers are true freshmen, including 6-7 **Kerman Ali** (South Shore HS/Chicago), 6-3 **Chris Delaney** (Andrew HS/Tinley Park, Ill.), 6-8 **Craig Meyer** (Black Hawk HS/South Wayne, Wisc.), 6-11 **Bernie Salthe** (Staples HS/Staples, Minn.) and 6-1 **Russell Wilson** (South HS/Minneapolis, Minn.). Salthe and Meyer in particular offer much-needed size, but it remains to be seen if they are ready to contribute at this level.

BLUE RIBBON ANALYSIS

Rey coached under Evansville's Jim Crews, a disciple of Bobby Knight, for five years before getting the Loyola job in his hometown of Chicago. He is a hard worker, and a solid basketball man.

The Ramblers, though, are a long way from the program which won the 1963 NCAA championship. They aren't even the same team which not too long ago dominated the MCC, capturing league titles in 1980, 1983, 1985 and 1987. But four of the last five years have been losing ones.

Make no mistake, Gailes and Rogers are ready for prime time. But it is hard to see that the supporting cast is improved enough to make Loyola an instant winner in their final season together. The Ramblers are a little deeper, a little more experienced. But if that combines for a .500 record, Rey's second effort will have been a success.

1990-91 LOYOLA SCHEDULE

Nov.	24	Western Michigan
Nov. 30-Dec. 1		#Boilermaker Invitational
Dec.	5	Maine
	15	@Northwestern
	19	@Illinois-Chicago
	22	Bethune-Cookman (FL)
	29	Bradley
Jan.	5	Maryland-Baltimore Co.
	7	@Univ. of Portland
	10	Dayton
	12	Xavier
	15	Cal State-Northridge
	19	@Marquette
	21	@Illinois State
	24	St. Louis
	26	Evansville
	31	@Butler
Feb.	2	@Evansville
	7	@Dayton
	9	@Xavier
	13	DePaul
	17	Marquette
	21	@St. Louis
	25	Detroit
	28	Butler
Mar.	2	@Detroit
	7	##MCC Tournament

@ Road Games
# West Lafayette, IN (East Carolina, Indiana State & Purdue)
Dayton, OH

LOYOLA COLLEGE

LAST SEASON: 4-24
CONFERENCE RECORD: 2-14
STARTERS LOST: 1
STARTERS RETURNING: 4
CONFERENCE: METRO ATLANTIC ATHLETIC (MAAC)
LOCATION: BALTIMORE, MD
HOME FLOOR: REITZ ARENA (3,000)
NICKNAME: GREYHOUNDS
COLORS: GREEN AND GREY
COACH: TOM SCHNEIDER, record at Loyola College, 4-24.
Career record, 71-120.

Die Hard.

That's what the Loyola College faithful had done through several mediocre seasons in the Northeast Conference. Then, last year, the Greyhounds trumpeted a move to the Metro Atlantic Athletic Conference and a coaching change. The diehard alumni were pleased to be in the company of the MAAC schools, and with a new coach fresh from the Ivy League. Most knew it would take some time to be respectable in their new conference, but few expected to -

Die Harder.

That's what the folks at Loyola College did, suffering through a 4-24 season. So this year, as a sequel to "Movin' to the MAAC," the Greyhounds will try to "Move Up in the MAAC." It still won't be easy, but some groundwork was laid last year while coach Tom Schneider changed/slowed the team's pace a bit from the endline-to-endline style of his predecessor, Mark Amatucci. Along the way, 11 of 14 players started at least two games, and a capable backcourt began to develop. Now Schneider must focus on sharpening his team's shooting eye —the Greyhounds shot only 41 percent last year— and strengthening the all-around play of the frontcourt. Loyola College was outrebounded by nearly six caroms per game last year, and the frontcourt provided little support in the other phases of the game, either. Part of that may have been the shuttling lineup; 11 players averaged 10 minutes or more per game and only one —shooting guard **Kevin Green** —averaged more than 30 minutes a contest.

For Loyola College to have any chance of improving, they'll have to have another banner season from Green (19.4 ppg, 3.3 rpg, 1.0 apg). The 6-4 junior, a graduate of the famous Dunbar HS program in Baltimore (Reggie Lewis, David Wingate, Reggie Williams, Mugsy Bogues), was the only sophomore named to the All-MAAC team last year. He needs only 27 points to reach the 1,000 mark for his career and is definitely "the man" for Loyola, having taken 28 percent of the team's shots last year and more than twice as many as any other player. Green is both adept at wriggling his way through a crowd to get to the basket and strong enough to power his way in. His shooting (44.5 percent overall; 35.6 percent on three-pointers) could improve with help from his teammates to avoid doubleteaming.

Rejoining Green in the backcourt is expected to be 6-0 sophomore **Tracy Bergan** (9.7 ppg, 2.4 rpg, 3.6 apg), who started 11 of the first 14 games until academic problems forced him to the sidelines. He scored 35 points in an overtime win over Navy. When Bergan had to hit the books, 6-1 sophomore **Mike Malone** (6.0 ppg, 3.6 apg) took over. Although he made all the freshman mistakes, he also showed enough savvy to give the Greyhounds a capable third guard and backup to both Green and Bergan. 5-11 senior point guard **Dave Wojcik** (2.3 ppg), who has seen his playing time decline steadily each year, provides experience, while 6-1 sophomore **Brian Condon** and 6-3 junior **Charles Hatcher** once again will see limited action.

Settling on a frontcourt combination will take Schneider some time. Only one player —6-8 center Stephen Foley (7.5 ppg, 6.6 rpg) — graduated from last year's team, but Foley's dramatic improvement last year means he will be missed more than he would have been though a year ago at this time, especially since the frontcourt was such a weak link. 6-4 junior **Kevin Anderson** (8.3 ppg, 2.3 rpg) emerged as the starting small forward midway through last season. He is perhaps the best athlete on the squad, but his poor shooting (36 percent) and lack of help inside left the door open for others to move into the starting spot this year. They could include 6-6 senior **Marqus Hamwright** (3.7 ppg, 1.9 rpg), who has yet to regain all the moves he showed before a knee injury two years ago, and 6-5 freshman **Jon Haggler** (21.0 ppg, 12.0 rpg for James Madison HS in Vienna, Va.), who is projected as a leaper in the mold of former Greyhound star Mike Morrison (Phoenix Suns). Hamwright started five games a year ago and shot 50 percent from the floor.

There is height at both the power forward and center slots, and a number of players could shuttle between the two positions. A pair of seniors, 6-7 **John Boney** (4.0 ppg, 3.1 rpg) and 6-6 **Derek Campbell** (2.0 ppg, 2.7 rpg), and 6-6 freshman **Brian Pendleton** (Coolidge HS in Washington, D.C.) will battle for time at the power forward spot along with at least one of the losers in the battle for starting center. 6-9 senior **Mark Hauser** (1.8 ppg, 1.6 rpg), 6-7 sophomore **George Sereikas** (4.2 ppg, 2.3 rpg), 6-11 senior **Mike Wagner** (1.6 ppg, 1.3 rpg) and 6-8 freshman **Mark Sparzak** (Calvert Hall HS of Towson, Md.) all will be given a chance at center. Hauser or Sereikas could also end up at power forward, with one the likely winner at center. Hauser is bigger and stronger, and he drew 12 starts last year. But the West German did not shoot (30.5 percent) or rebound well. Sereikas (48 percent shooting) showed improvement as the year progressed. Wagner is slow and has shown little improvement in his first three seasons, so Sparzak may move into the understudy role quickly if he develops some quickness.

BLUE RIBBON ANALYSIS

At season's end, Loyola College was playing much better than a 4-24 team. Four of their last eight losses were by three points or less. Still, the Greyhounds won only one of their last 14 games. The constant shuffling of players to find the right combination didn't work, and coach Tom Schneider will have to settle on a smaller nucleus this year. That may cause some disgruntlement, particularly among the seniors who figure to lose playing time, but it's necessary if this team is to move forward. Kevin Green needs help to turn this team around. Tracy Bergan —if he stays eligible—could provide some, but the frontcourt needs to be settled. We repeat what we said here last year —a 10-18 mark could be judged a success. So would getting out of the MAAC cellar.

1990-91 LOYOLA COLLEGE SCHEDULE

Nov.	30-	
Dec.	1	#Baltimore Beltway Tournament
Dec.	5	@Xavier
	7-8	##Longhorn Classic
	11	American University
	22	@Maryland-Baltimore Co.
	29	@La Salle

1990-91 LOYOLA COLLEGE SCHEDULE *Cont.*

Jan.	7	@William & Mary
	9	@Fairfield
	11	@Siena
	14	@Navy
	17	La Salle
	19	@Iona
	26	Iona
	28	Siena
Feb.	1	@St. Peter's
	4	@Towson State
	7	Canisius
	9	Niagara
	11	Manhattan
	14	@Niagara
	16	@Canisius
	19	Fairfield
	21	@Manhattan
	23	St. Peter's
Mar.	1-4	*MAAC Tournament

@ Road Games
# Towson, MD (Maryland-Baltimore Co., Mt. St. Mary's & Towson State)
Austin, TX (Sam Houston State, Texas & Texas-Pan American)
* Albany, NY

LOYOLA MARYMOUNT

LAST SEASON: 26-6
CONFERENCE RECORD: 13-1
STARTERS LOST: 4
STARTERS RETURNING: 1
CONFERENCE: WEST COAST CONFERENCE (WCC)
LOCATION: LOS ANGELES, CA
HOME FLOOR: GERSTEN PAVILION (4,156)
NICKNAME: LIONS
COLORS: CRIMSON, GRAY AND COLUMBIA BLUE
COACH: JAY HILLOCK, first year at LMU. Career record, 60-50.

Paul Westhead, the man who brought the "four-to-five second" offense to college basketball, is gone. So are the guts of a Loyola Marymount team which won the NCAA team scoring title the past three seasons, establishing NCAA records in that category each of the past two. And, given the September departure of Westhead for the NBA's Denver Nuggets, it is harder than ever to predict where the Lions go from here.

Yet even more than their scoring frenzy, Loyola Marymount last year captured the hearts and minds of college basketball fans everywhere in the wake of the death of senior center and co-captain Hank Gathers. Gathers collapsed and died tragically during a March 4 WCC tournament game against the University of Portland. Feeding off their grief, the Lions blitzed all the way to the NCAA Final Eight before running out of gas against eventual national champion UNLV. Along the way, the Lions punished defending champion Michigan with one of the most dramatic offensive displays in college basketball history.

As a junior in 1988-89, Gathers was only the second player in NCAA history to lead the nation in both scoring(32.7 ppg) and rebounding (13.7 rpg). Wichita State's Xavier McDaniel first accomplished the

feat four years earlier. Gathers was also the first of two Lions to lead the nation in scoring, as former high school teammate Bo Kimble (first round pick of the Los Angeles Clippers) picked up the torch last year to the tune of 35.3 points per game.

As a team, Loyola Marymount averaged a still-incredible 122.4 points per game. Kimble and Gathers (29.0 ppg, 10.8 rpg) led the way, along with guard Jeff Fryer, whose 22.7 average came almost exclusively from long range. All are gone, as is two-year starting forward Per Stumer (8.6 ppg, 7.5 rpg). A former member of the Swedish national team, Stumer elected to play professionally in Europe despite having one more year of college eligibility.

While the Lions showed last year they could play and succeed without marquee players in the lineup for various periods of time, the chemistry at Loyola Marymount is obviously much different now. The new coach will inherit an even newer team and, even should he retain Westhead's explosive attack, there is simply very little experience on the roster.

The Lions' most talented returnee—6'12 junior **Terrell Lowery**—was their top reserve the last two years. He has never started a college game, but is by no means an average reserve. Off the bench last year, he averaged 14.5 points and 6.3 assists (11th and second, respectively, in the WCC). Lowery, in fact, is the leading returning scorer in the conference, and is quite capable of serving as the first string off-guard in almost any lineup.

Lowery will be paired with 6-1 senior point guard **Tony Walker**, the only returning starter. Only a modest scorer by recent LMU standards, Walker (5.6 ppg) is the ignition that makes the Lions' engine rev. He led the conference in assists (227), and was tied for fourth with teammate **Tom Peabody** in steals (1.9 per game). Walker is also a brilliant floor leader and take-charge performer.

The only concern with Walker was off-season surgery to repair a weakened bone is his right wrist. The new coach could choose to redshirt him if not recovered by the start of the season, but that figures to be a last resort. It is hard to imagine Loyola Marymount without its high-octane point man.

The balance of the returnees are mainly role-players, led by Peabody (4.5 ppg, 2.6 rpg). 5-11 sophomore **Greg Walker** (1.3ppg), 6-6 junior **John O'Connell** (2.8 ppg, 2.8 rpg), 6-8 sophomore **Chris Scott** (1.5ppg, 2.3 rpg) and 6-8 junior **Chris Knight** (3.9 ppg, 3.1rpg) also return.

Peabody can play at either backcourt spot and is tough enough even to run at small forward. This year he may have to shoot more, while maintaining a resolve to dive after every loose ball and errant pass. Walker was a walk-on as a freshman, and was capable of playing at the accelerated speed Westhead required.

O'Connell, like Gathers and Kimble, has the toughness learned from playing in their native Philadelphia. He will bang the boards and hit on most of his attempts from short range (66.7 percent from the floor). The stringbean Scott got stronger late in his freshman year, but will have to improve his physical coordination to fill one of the vacant frontcourt positions.

After Gathers' death, the center's job fell into the then unproven hands of Knight. He grew into that great responsibility first mentally, then provided some key rebounds and occasional points in the NCAA's when Kimble was not in position to carry the entire load himself. Even so, it is doubtful Knight can be adominating low-post player. He has neither the muscle nor the bulk.

The new coach will have along list of newcomers for help in the starting lineup and off the bench. He figures to use 6-7 sophomore transfer **Brian McCloskey** (California-Irvine) as the starting small forward. McCloskey's uncle, Jim McCloskey, played for Loyola Marymount in 1980 and 1981, and was a solid mid-range shooter. Brain, although showing signs of also being able to penetrate, looks like he will resemble his uncle in playing style, a good fit for the Lions.

In addition to McCloskey, the Loyola Marymount staff had one of its best-ever recruiting efforts. LMU signed four prep standouts, plus one junior college transfer. **Craig Holt**, a 6-3 guard who averaged 20.0 ppg, 6.5 rpg and 3.0 assists at West Valley (Calif.) JC, will battle for a starting guard position. From the prep ranks, the Lions have stocked up for the future with 6-3 **Rahim Harris** (23.3 ppg, 7.0 apg, Oakland Athletic League player of the year at Skyline HS), 6-4 **Kareem Washington** (24.5 ppg, 12.0 rpg at Sexton HS/Lansing, Mich.) and 6-3 **Greg Evans** (12.9 ppg at Ocean View HS/Huntington Beach, Calif.). 6-7 forward **Ross Richardson** (18.2 ppg for Central HS/Flint, Mich.) was the final signee.

Given the inexperience among the rest of the Lions, most of the newcomers figure to get a long look. While Westhead preferred to bring freshmen along slowly, the new coach may not have that luxury. All may get a turn in the brand new Loyola Marymount rotation.

BLUE RIBBON ANALYSIS

With or without Paul Westhead, Loyola Marymount was inevitably due for a letdown. And, with such a large turnover of players—especially in the starting ranks—it is far too much to expect the Lions to win as many games against one of the toughest non-conference schedules in the country. (The Lions play LSU, Oklahoma, Georgia Tech and UCLA on the road, face Indiana and Syracuse in tournament action, and host LaSalle).

Ultimately, the Loyola Marymount system was only as good as its athletes. Hank Gathers and Bo Kimble fit the mold perfectly. This year, the new coach inherits some talented players and shooters, but none even close to the level of his former stars. Still, the current cast will be in great condition and could confound the bulk of the lightly-regarded West Coast Conference. That does not include pre-season favorite San Diego, or the powerful non-league foes.

It is also impossible to calculate the emotional toll of last season. Gathers' death, Kimble's miracles, the wondrous NCAA run—followed now by Westhead's departure—all exacted a tremendous cost. A lawsuit filed against the school by the Gathers family could also linger throughout the season.

In every way, this is are building year for the Lions. They may still be a winning team, but hardly a juggernaut. Once the early-season rush of media attention fades, it should be a quieter year at Loyola Marymount.

1990-91 LOYOLA MARYMOUNT SCHEDULE		
Nov.	23-25	#Maui Classic
Nov. 30-Dec. 1		*Disneyland Freedom Bowl Classic
Dec.	2	@UCLA
	8	Athletes In Action
	15	@Oklahoma
	20	@LSU
	22	@Georgia Tech
	27	@Pacific
	29	St. Joseph's
	31	La Salle
Jan.	2	Westmont College (CA)
	5	U.S. International (CA)
	11	Santa Clara
	12	Univ. of San Diego
	16	@Pepperdine
	19	Pepperdine
	25	@St. Mary's
	26	@San Francisco
Feb.	1	San Francisco
	2	St. Mary's
	4	@California-Santa Barbara
	7	@Gonzaga
	9	@Univ. of Portland
	15	Univ. of Portland
	16	Gonzaga (WA)
	21	@Univ. of San Diego
	23	@Santa Clara

1990-91 LOYOLA MARYMOUNT SCHEDULE *Cont.*		
Mar.	2-4	**WCC Tournament
	10	@Princeton

@ Road Games
# Lahaina, HI (Chaminade, Indiana, Iowa State, Northeastern, Santa Clara, Syracuse & Toledo)
* Irvine, CA (Bradley, California-Irvine & Idaho State)
** Santa Clara, CA

MAINE

LAST SEASON: 11-17
CONFERENCE RECORD: 6-6
STARTERS LOST: 2
STARTERS RETURNING: 3
CONFERENCE: NORTH ATLANTIC (NAC)
LOCATION: ORONO, ME
HOME FLOOR: BANGOR AUDITORIUM (6,500)
NICKNAME: BLACK BEARS
COLORS: BLUE AND WHITE
COACH: RUDY KEELING, record at Maine, 20-36.

Ah, youth. If you are searching for some lost youth, head to beautiful downtown Orono, because Rudy Keeling has gobbled up as much youth as possible in the constant rebuilding process with the Maine basketball program. Youth? Keeling has plenty of it, quite possibly the youngest team in the Northeast and certainly the diaper bunch of the NAC.

Most coaches would love to have an experienced lineup, filled to the brim with returning veterans. However, Keeling, the long-time assistant at Bradley and Marquette before heading to Maine three seasons ago, doesn't mind the youthful trend at Orono. After all, the Maine program has been struggling for quite some time now. Any change is a breath of fresh air and welcomed with open arms.

Keeling will feature a roster that will have eight freshmen this season. The only five that may be younger than the Black Bears touring the country this year are The New Kids on the Block. Also, throw in one sophomore transfer for good measure.

"I'm more excited about this program than ever before," Keeling said. "I think we have a nice blend of veterans (only five returnees) and newcomers. We've gone out and recruited some kids that will make us very competitive in the conference. We'll make some mistakes because we're young and energetic, but we'll cause a lot of excitement, too."

If Keeling was totally counting on newcomers to run the show, that may be asking a bit much. But since he has a solid bunch of returning veterans, then it could very well be a smooth transition from high school to college ball for the youngsters.

Leading the returnees is 6-3 junior guard **Derrick Hodge** (13.1 ppg, 5.9 rpg). He has the ability to go inside when needed and was the team's leading rebounder last season, quite a feat for a guard. Hodge ranked among the NAC's leaders in four categories (scoring, rebounding, free throw percentage and steals). Where he fits in with the newcomers remains to be seen. With his rebounding skills, he could be moved to small forward. But there is no question, Hodge will be a vital cog in the Black Bears' attack.

Junior point guard **Marty Higgins** (8.3 ppg, 2.0 rpg, 161 assists) is the favorite once again to start at the point for his third straight season. The 5-11 Higgins is a heady leader, a gutsy player with great court sense and awareness. He ranked second in the NAC last season in assists and had a fine summer in his native New Jersey, leading a very competitive summer league in assists. However, Higgins must improve on his 36 percent shooting from the floor. Higgins rare-

ly makes mistakes and plays hard every night.

Junior forward **Shelton Kerry** (6.1 ppg, 2.6 rpg) was one of Keeling's top men off the bench last season. Kerry, a 6-5 small forward, saw action in 27 games last season, starting five. Kerry has a lot of athletic ability and runs very well. But he also suffered greatly from the perimeter, connecting on just 35 percent of his tries. Kerry did connect on 42 percent of his three-point attempts, so he does have a touch, even if it was missing for most of the season last year.

Senior center **Curtis Robertson** (5.8 ppg, 4.8 rpg) will more than likely be the starter in the pivot for the Black Bears again this season. The burly 6-10, 250-pound Robertson had some last minute heroics last season, winning two games with last second rebound baskets. He shot 63 percent from the floor, but only 34 percent from the line. However, Robertson has been a huge puzzle for Keeling and his staff. They cannot understand how anyone so large could score so little. Robertson has worked hard in the off-season with conditioning and adding strength. Maybe the off-season effort will solve the concerns of the past, because he certainly has the body to work with to become a dominant player in the NAC.

Also returning is sophomore forward **Dan Hillman** (1.7 ppg, 1.9 rpg). The 6-8 Hillman sprained his ankle severely in pre-season workouts and never fully recovered, which limited his playing time to just 20 games and 157 minutes. But Hillman is strong, especially close to the basket, and showed much promise before his injury. His numbers could drastically improve this season.

One of the eight freshmen is a redshirt who did see some action last year. Forward **Francois Bouchard** played in four games, starting all four, before suffering a stress fracture of his right tibia in a game against Connecticut in December. The 6-8 Bouchard averaged 5.4 points and 5.0 rebounds in those four games and was being counted upon by Keeling to be a player of impact for the Black Bears. He has the size and the tools to be a good player in the NAC and will more than likely start at power forward this season. Bouchard averaged 28 points and 15 rebounds at Cheverus HS in Portland, Maine, so he came with a solid reputation. Bouchard will get every chance to live up to that reputation this season.

The transfer among the newcomers is sophomore forward **Rossie Kearson**, who came to Maine from Alcorn State and will be eligible to play after the fall semester is completed. The 6-4 Kearson has an excellent shooting touch from the perimeter. Keeling is expecting big things from Kearson and called him "the surprise of the newcomers who should be an instant success." Kearson runs the floor very well and is an excellent defender.

Now, the moment all Black Bear followers have been waiting for, the scroll of incoming freshmen that will more than likely make or break the Maine's chances in the NAC. If they perform up to expectations, then, yes, Maine can actually compete in the NAC this season. The anticipation builds. Drum roll, please.

There are four guards and three forwards among the freshmen. The top freshman gained a great deal of notoriety last year in his native New York. Guard **Donald Taylor** (Brooklyn, N.Y., Prospect Heights HS) is an explosive player with great skills and should be a very good college player. But that's not the entire story. You see, Taylor, a 6-3 guard, was one of New York City's homeless last year. He lived most of the year either on the streets or in a shelter. Yet, he played basketball and played well. His trials and tribulations were chronicled in many national newspapers and his story was told on television features on CBS, ESPN and even the Arsenio Hall Show. For overcoming the huge odds that plagued him, Taylor was recognized by the United States Basketball Writers Association as the Most Courageous Player in the United States. Taylor is not just a player with a tough problem. He's an excellent prospect. Taylor averaged 28 points and nine rebounds per game at Prospect Heights. He can score at will, penetrate very well and has a great leaping ability. Taylor is a player of impact and one to watch in the NAC.

Another of the Black Bears' top recruits is guard **Kevin Terrell**. The 6-0 Terrell (Chicago, Ill./St. Patrick's HS) is a heady player, good passer and solid defender who was named as the Chicago Suburban player of the year, averaging 22.0 points and 5.0 rebounds per game. Terrell can play either guard slot, but more than likely will challenge Higgins for the starting point guard position.

Keeling's time in Peoria at Bradley helped his recruiting game this year, because two other players from Illinois head east to Orono this season. **Deonte Hursey** is a 6-0 point guard from Bloomington (Ill.) HS who averaged 17.6 points, 7.1 rebounds and 4.6 assists per game last season. Hursey is very diversified and a talented ballhandler. Forward **Ed Jones** (Rockford, Ill./Guilford HS) is the other Illinois recruit headed to Maine. Jones is noted as a shot blocking specialist who amassed a remarkable 187 blocks in 28 games last year. Jones, a 6-6 pure physical specimen, averaged 14.2 points and 10.0 rebounds per game for Guilford and was selected as one of the Top 30 players in the state.

Guard **Greg McClaire** (Bronx, N.Y./Leelanau Prep) is also a fine athlete who should see quality time this season. The 6-3 McClaire played power forward in high school, but will play off-guard in college. He averaged 23.0 points and 10.0 rebounds per game at Leelanau. Forward **Tim Dennis** (Pompton Plains, N.J./Pequannock HS) is a 6-7 do-everything who won Morris County player of the year honors last season for Pequannock. Dennis has a nice shooting touch for his size and averaged 18.0 points and 11.0 rebounds per game last year. He is a hardworking athlete who should become a Keeling favorite because of his work ethic.

Meanwhile, don't think that Keeling and his staff traveled the country and forgot about the players in their own backyard. Not at all. Forward **Kenny Barnes** is a highly touted performer from Limestone, Maine, and Maine Central Institute. The 6-6 Barnes is a power forward who averaged 11.7 points and 7.5 rebounds per game for MCI last season.

BLUE RIBBON ANALYSIS

Certainly, Keeling is trying to right the wrongs that have plagued Maine basketball for what now seems like an eternity. He is building the program from the bottom up and certainly seems to be headed in the right direction, as evidenced by the fine recruiting job. On paper, it appears as if Keeling is gambling big by bringing in all these unproven rookies and expecting them to perform like troopers immediately. Most coaches would love to take their time, nurture their freshmen, and work their way into the program slowly and surely. Keeling will not have that luxury.

Freshmen have jitters. That's a given. They work their way into college basketball —and more importantly, college life in general. But this is an impressive group of talented players, ones that can develop quicker than what is expected. Taylor and Terrell is a backcourt to watch for the next four years. They could very well start together this year. Taylor is more than a heart-warming success story. He is pure talent, exciting and a joy to watch.

The returnees will play a huge role in the progress of the youngsters. Higgins is a smart player, a coach on the floor who will only help teammates like Taylor and Terrell develop. If Hodge can find a spot, he will produce. He is one of those players caught in an awkward spot —no real position to play. But Hodge is a player.

The key to the Black Bears' success in 1990-91 is not the progress of the rookies. It's the progress of their inside players, namely Bouchard, Robertson and Hillman. With the size those three have, they should be able to control the backboards and put up solid offensive numbers from close range.

If the Bears' inside game is strong, then so will they. That may be a huge "if." Anyway you look at it, things will get better in Orono. Keeling has done a fine job and the progress will continue. The Black Bears should hover right around the .500 mark and contend in the NAC.

1990-91 MAINE SCHEDULE		
Nov.	23-24	#Central Florida Tournament
	27	Northern Illinois
Dec.	1	@Fairleigh Dickinson
	5	@Loyola
	9	Connecticut
	12	Drexel
	15	##Eastern Illinois
	23	@Delaware
	27	@Furman
	29	@Robert Morris
Jan.	2	Southwest Texas State
	5	New Hampshire
	7	Texas-Pan American
	9	@Boston College
	12	Northeastern
	14	Fairfield
	19	University of Hartford
	22	@St. Bonaventure
	26	@Vermont
	30	@Boston University
Feb.	2	@New Hampshire
	6	@Furman
	9	Boston University
	16	@Rhode Island
	19	@Northeastern
	23	@University of Hartford
Mar.	1	Vermont
	8-10	*NAC Tournament

@ Road Games
# Orlando, FL (Central Michigan, Liberty University & Southeastern Louisiana)
Portland, ME
* Site to be announced

MANHATTAN

LAST SEASON: 11-17
CONFERENCE RECORD: 7-9
STARTERS LOST: 1
STARTERS RETURNING: 4
CONFERENCE: METRO ATLANTIC ATHLETIC (MAAC)
LOCATION: BRONX, NY
HOME FLOOR: DRADDY GYMNASIUM (3,000)
NICKNAME: JASPERS
COLORS: KELLY GREEN AND WHITE
COACH: STEVE LAPPAS, record at Manhattan, 18-38.

Quick, who invented baseball's seventh inning stretch? Many attribute that tradition to former Manhattan College President Brother Jasper, around the turn of the century. Traditions usually die hard. Then again, when you have little tradition, things seem to slip away a little easier. That seems to have been the case with Manhattan College basketball, little tradition, few recent results.

Former Villanova assistant coach Steve Lappas has set out to change all of that, and begin something that would make the former college president proud. The young Jaspers continued their slow but steady rise from the MAAC ashes last season, winning 11 games (most since 1982-83) and posting a 7-9 conference mark, good for second in the MAAC North. Now they have to take the next step.

Manhattan returns four starters from last season's squad, led by impressive MAAC rookie of the year, 6-6 forward **Keith Bullock** (13.6 ppg, 6.6 rpg). The husky sophomore is Manhattan's leading returning scorer, rebounder and free throw shooter and should be the key offensive threat for the Jaspers with the departure of leading scorer Peter Runge (15.4 ppg, 8.4 rpg). Bullock's classmates will also give him a great amount of help.

A pair of Carey's, 6-4 sophomore swingman **Carey Edwards** (4.8 ppg) and 6-3 sophomore guard **Carey Wilson** (4.0 ppg) also had solid freshman campaigns. Edwards emerged during the second half, hitting over 50 percent of his shots from the floor and providing a much needed defensive lift over the final 18 games. Wilson will see action at both guard spots this year after coming off the bench at the shooting guard in his initial campaign, and will have to improve upon the poor shooting (32 percent) which hurt Manhattan last season. Fellow sophomore, 6-4 **Chris Williams** (5.3 ppg), will also see more action in Lappas' rotating guard offense, but must play with more consistency.

Two other impact underclassmen are also returning in the backcourt, 5-9 junior point guard **Charles Dubra** (5.4 ppg, 85 assists) and 6-4 junior shooter **Russ Williams** (9.1 ppg, 2.2 rpg). The smooth handling Dubra will run Lappas' offense again this season as he did in his 24 starts last year, while the older Williams will be looked upon to be the leader of a very young but talented guard corps. Both can score, as evidenced by Dubra's team-best 30 treys in his sophomore season and Williams' .432 field goal percentage, best among the backcourt players. It may be their leadership which will pay Lappas bigger dividends then anything they put in the hoop.

Up front, smooth shooting 6-10 senior **Dave Althaver** (3.6 ppg, 3.2 rpg) will be Manhattan's man in the middle, with help from Bullock, 6-7 junior **David Bernsley** (5.0 ppg, 4.6 rpg), little used 6-10 sophomore **Eric Gottleib** (0.3 ppg, 0.3 rpg) and 6-8 JC transfer **Tom Corrigan** (20.2 ppg, 9.6 rpg at Bergen, N.J., CC). Althaver led the team in blocks (14) and was second to Bullock in field goal percentage (.509) last year, but has lacked the aggressiveness and body strength to be a real force at center. He will have to be much more aggressive to help the attack this season. Bernsley, a transfer from Rhode Island, averaged 5.0 points and 4.0 rebounds in just over 14 minutes per game last season and will be looked to for help on the boards with the graduation of the hard-nosed Runge. Gottleib, a virtual Althaver clone at this stage, should see more time helping the senior in the middle, while Corrigan provides both relief and competition for Bullock and Bernsley. Two freshmen, 6-9 center **Don Elliot** (10.0 ppg, 9.0 rpg at Ashbrook-Gastonia HS in N.C.) and 6-6 **Jake Davalli** (18.0 ppg, 9.0 rpg at Calvert Hall HS in Towson, Md.) will also help out.

BLUE RIBBON ANALYSIS

Lappas is getting it done in the Bronx. Three solid recruiting classes have made Manhattan very dangerous, definitely the sleeper team in the MAAC. The big question is whether the sophomores will continue to develop, and whether the stringbean-thin Althaver can hold his own at center. He will get help from Bernsley and Corrigan, and certainly Bullock can get the job done on both boards.

This team is still a year away from greatness, although the Jaspers up-tempo style will excite and produce 15 to 17 wins and a third place MAAC finish. That will make many stand up and cheer, even ol' brother Jasper himself.

1990-91 MANHATTAN SCHEDULE		
Nov.	24	Hofstra (NY)
	27	@Columbia
Dec.	6	New Hampshire
	8	William & Mary
	15	@Fordham

MARIST

LAST SEASON: 17-11
CONFERENCE RECORD: 10-6
STARTERS LOST: 2
STARTERS RETURNING: 3
CONFERENCE: NORTHEAST (NEC)
LOCATION: POUGHKEEPSIE, NY
HOME FLOOR: McCANN CENTER (3,000)
NICKNAME: RED FOXES
COLORS: RED AND WHITE
COACH: DAVE MAGARITY, record at Marist, 68-45. Career record, 128-121.

Year Two following the departure of Rik Smits, the second pick in the 1988 NBA draft, appeared to portend the continued decline for this program. Instead, the Red Foxes' unlikely recovery made from one of the better little-noticed stories in *Eastern Basketball* last season. Despite lack of a true center, depth, and a go-to force on offense, Dave Magarity's crew somehow rebounded to 17-11 (from the 13-15 of '88-89) and a 10-6, third-place conference finish.

"A lot of what last year's team accomplished had to do with chemistry," said Magarity. "It was a classic case of overachieving."

Boosted by recruiting, Marist would seem to look even better on paper this time around. However, Magarity is concerned with capturing that elusive chemistry. Three returning starters figure strongly in that pursuit. Foremost among them is 6-3 senior guard **Steve Paterno** (14.2 ppg, 4.1 rpg), the Red Foxes' leading scorer, and, even more impressively, third leading rebounder from last year. Paterno comes from a long line of brothers who started lighting it up at Christian Brothers Academy in Lincroft, N.J., down the Jersey shore years ago. Bill Paterno played for the fine Notre Dame teams of the early '70s. Joe Paterno wrapped up a 1,000-point-plus career at Fordham two seasons back. Steve is a shooter in a great family tradition with a career .457 mark from beyond the three-point line. He's deadly from the wings and likes to take the big shot. "He is much improved at creating shots for himself off the dribble," said Magarity.

Improvement was also shown to a considerable degree by 6-4 senior swingman **Reggie Gaut** (11.0 ppg, 4.8 rpg, 2.1 apg) and 6-6 senior forward **George Siegrist** (4.7 ppg, 3.1 rpg). Gaut roared back from a disappointing sophomore season to wind up second on the team in scoring and rebounding. Defense has always been the cornerstone of his game, so now he seems to have acquired the offense to balance it. Gaut made major strides in his outside shooting and ball-handling last year. Siegrist is fulfilling a dream. A freshman walk-on, who worked his way to a scholarship as a sophomore, he started 25 games last year and will captain the team this season. Siegrist is a physical rebounder. He also raised his field goal percentage from 35.3 to 46.1 last season.

Marist got the best of both worlds from 6-3 sophomore guard **Andy Lake** last year: A local hero (from Middletown, N.Y.) and a freshman who could contribute immediately. Lake (8.6 ppg, 2.3 rpg) averaged 19 minutes per game off the bench while playing both guard positions. He scored off penetration and from outside (51.1 percent from three-point range). Lake also converted 23 straight free throws in one 8-game stretch last season. 6-5 senior forward **Rod Henderson** (7.9 ppg, 3.8 rpg) also turned in a solid year off the bench despite being hampered with a back injury. Henderson, a transfer from Pensacola (Fla.) JC, is both quick and strong, a type who can get on a roll and present match-up problems for opponents. 6-3 senior guard **Bobby Reasbeck**, the other returning letterman, had a rough season after a promising sophomore year. Reasbeck (2.0 ppg, 0.9 rpg), a scrappy, intense hustler, missed six games with a leg injury.

Recruiting, however, is what Magarity hopes will raise the Red Foxes back to a dominant level in the NEC. Last year's starting center, Curtis Celestine, was 6-7. This year, Marist has four players 6-7 or taller. 6-7 freshman forward **Jason Turner** (21.4 ppg, 12.5 rpg) at St. Thomas Moore Prep in Connecticut), is a terrific rebounder and transition-oriented player who can really run the floor. **Fred Ingles**, a 6-7 junior forward, was a junior college All-America at Allegheney CC in Pittsburgh. He scored a school record 1,606 points in two seasons while averaging 19.2 points and 8.0 rebounds last year. 6-8 sophomore forward **Sedric Veazey**, who sat out last year at Marist, is a flat-out shotblocker. He rejected six shots per game as a senior at Notre Dame HS in Fairfield, Conn., while averaging 18.0 points and 15.3 rebounds per game. He used his time away from the game last year to build his upper body strength and figures as an immediate contributor. At center, Magarity reached back to the hometown of Rik Smits (Son En Bruegel, Holland) for 7-1, 210-pound sophomore Den Ouden, who sat out last year due to Proposition 48. Smits' father recommended Ouden (12.0 ppg, 11.0 rpg, 4.0 blpg for Eindehoven in the Dutch Junior Club League). Ouden has played only a few years and is a project. He will, however, give Marist a new dimension as a tall presence in the lane.

Magarity also struck newcomer gold in the backcourt. 6-0 freshman **Dexter Dunbar** (6.6 ppg, 6.0 apg at All Hallows HS in the Bronx, N.Y.) may be one of the conference's bigger recruiting coups. Dunbar's ability goes far beyond his numbers. He point guarded one of the best high school teams in the country under an excellent coach, John Carey. Dunbar is very quick with excellent passing ability and court sense. He could have played at a higher level and should excel as a court leader at this one. To complement Dunbar's city game Magarity brought in 6-2 freshman guard **Chad Weikert** (11.3 ppg, 4.2 apg at Memorial HS in Evansville, Ind.), a basic Indiana shooting guard. Weikert shot 45 percent from three-point range and 80 percent from the line while making fourth-team All-Indiana in *Hoosier Magazine*. 6-5 freshman swingman **Izett Buchanan** (33.3 ppg, 13.8 rpg at Goshen, N.Y., HS) needs to solidify his 180-pound frame, but he has the ability to be a factor down the road.

BLUE RIBBON ANALYSIS

Marist started fast and tailed off in February last season. Magarity, himself, best explains why that probably won't happen again.

"I believe the teams in our league have proved you don't necessarily need to have great size as much as solid depth in order to win. We certainly struggled down the stretch. I believe that was caused primarily by a lack of depth at certain positions. The addition of our seven new players should enable us to be much more competitive and fresh late in the season."

While the Red Foxes bring back some quality experience, what they needed most to add was some quality athleticism, particularly with some height attached to it. This they have done. The newcomers, particularly Dunbar, should also give a boost to the backcourt.

"I can't stress enough how important depth is, especially when you have a pressing, uptempo style of play like we do," said Magarity. "I believe we have tremendous depth at the guard position."

This will be even truer, if Dunbar can step into the role of floor leader right away. If so, and Veazey and Turner step up while Lake and Henderson continue to improve, they will combine with the foundation of Paterno-Gaut-Siegrist to give Marist an uncommon number of quality players for this level. Enough to give the Red Foxes the inside track to the Northeast Conference title.

MARQUETTE

LAST SEASON: 15-14
CONFERENCE RECORD: 9-5
STARTERS LOST: 2
STARTERS RETURNING: 3
CONFERENCE: MIDWESTERN COLLEGIATE (MCC)
LOCATION: MILWAUKEE, WI
HOME FLOOR: BRADLEY CENTER (18,000)
NICKNAME: WARRIORS
COLORS: ROYAL BLUE AND GOLD
COACH: KEVIN O'NEILL, record at Marquette, 15-14.

When Kevin O'Neill was named head coach at Marquette in 1989 after three successful seasons as the top assistant to Lute Olson at Arizona, red flags were raised everywhere around the Midwestern Collegiate Conference. Not only was Marquette new to the conference in 1989-90, the Warriors were evidently serious about returning to top-flight basketball.

That was apparent in the selection of O'Neill, regarded as one of the nation's top recruiters and a tireless worker. The new coach did not have to do much recruiting, though, as he brought with him a list of players who quickly decided Marquette was the place to be for the 1990-91. To wit, the Warriors have three returning starters, two valuable reserves and seven new players on this year's roster.

O'Neill's two holes in his second season, though, represent starters who made major contributions. Gone are both 6-3 guard Tony Smith (23.8 ppg, 4.7 rpg), who went to the Los Angeles Lakers in the second round of the NBA draft, and 6-6 forward Tyrone Baldwin (12.4 ppg, 5.3 rpg).

Back is 6-6 senior forward **Trevor Powell** (16.7 ppg, 7.8 rpg). A very consistent performer, Powell has been Marquette's rebounding leader in each of the last three seasons, and needs just 544 points to become the school's all-time career scoring leader. This will be his fourth year as a starter. Also returning are **Mark Anglavar** (8.9 ppg, 3.6 rpg), a 6-3 senior guard, and **Rod Grosse**, a 6-10 senior center who averaged 2.7 points and 5.0 rebounds.

Powell, Anglavar and Grosse were starters last season. Reserve guards **Bruce Hayes** (3.0 ppg, 1.2 rpg), a 5-10 senior, and **Charles Luter** (1.6 ppg), a 6-4 junior, also are back. 6-7 junior **Joe Krysiak** (1.9 ppg) and 6-9 sophomore **Jeff Zavada** add depth up front.

Transfer guard **Keith Stewart**, a 5-10 sophomore from Purdue, will likely take over for Smith at point guard. Stewart originally attended Messmer High in Milwaukee. Baldwin's spot in the lineup could be filled by 6-7 sophomore **Jay Zulauf**, a transfer from Bowling Green, or 6-8 sophomore **Ron Curry**, a transfer from Arizona. Both Zulauf and Curry are versatile players also returning home to the Midwest.

Four freshman recruits add their skills to the mix, and all were rated among the Top 100 recruits in the U.S. They are **Damon Key**, a 6-8 center-forward from Milwaukee's Marquette Prep; **Charles Brakes**, a 6-7 forward from DeLaSalle High in Chicago; 6-3 guard **Robb Logterman** (Craig HS/Janesville, Wisc.); and **Jim McIlvaine**, a 7-1 center from Racine, Wisc (St. Catherine HS). The freshmen all committed in the early signing period; the transfers were already on hand.

"Expectations are going to be too high," O'Neill said. "Eight of our top 12 players will be freshmen or sophomores. We'll struggle early, but hopefully by January, we'll become a pretty good team."

BLUE RIBBON ANALYSIS

It is force-feeding time for O'Neill's young, talented cast. In addition to the now-rugged MCC slate, the Warriors retain home-and-home series with DePaul, Notre Dame and Wisconsin, and could also meet Virginia twice. For good measure, Duke, Kansas and Michigan are also on the schedule. All told, Marquette will face seven NCAA teams from last year and three more from the NIT.

"It is probably the toughest non-conference schedule in the country," said O'Neill. "We will struggle early with all our young players playing tough opponents. We want to play good people and our fans deserve to see us against the top teams in the nation. I ask for their patience early."

Marquette always has a shot at home, though, where it averaged a school-record 13,318 fans at Bradley Center. The 15-14 record was the first winning mark since 1986-87, and the NIT bid was the 22nd post-season apperance in the last 24 years. With much of the MCC rebuilding, the Warriors this year - if they

grow together in a hurry - could be right in line for the conference championship and a berth in that "other" tournament.

1990-91 MARQUETTE SCHEDULE		
Nov.	14	#@Duke
Dec.	1	@Kansas
	4	Wisconsin
	7-8	##First Bank Classic
	19	Prairie View A&M (TX)
	22	@Michigan
	30	Oklahoma State
Jan.	2	Virginia
	5	@Dayton
	7	@DePaul
	10	Xavier
	17	@Notre Dame
	19	Loyola
	21	@North Carolina State
	24	@Evansville
	26	@St. Louis
	28	DePaul
	31	Detroit
Feb.	2	Butler
	7	@Xavier
	9	Dayton
	12	Notre Dame
	16	@Loyola
	21	Evansville
	23	St. Louis
	28	@Detroit
Mar.	2	@Butler
	7-10	##MCC Tournament

@ Road Games
# Dodge NIT. If Marquette defeats Duke, the Warriors will play a second round game on Nov. 16. The semifinals and finals of the tournament will be played on Nov. 21 & 23 at Madison Square Garden, New York, NY.
Dayton, OH

MARSHALL

LAST SEASON: 15-13
CONFERENCE RECORD: 9-5
STARTERS LOST: 3
STARTERS RETURNING: 2
CONFERENCE: SOUTHERN
LOCATION: HUNTINGTON, WV
HOME FLOOR: HENDERSON CENTER (10,250)
NICKNAME: THUNDERING HERD
COLORS: GREEN AND WHITE
COACH: DWIGHT FREEMAN, first season at Marshall.

For the last two years, the fortunes of Marshall's basketball program have risen and fallen like the Dow Jones Industrial Average. The downside began in the spring of 1989, when the school self-reported several NCAA rules violations. The forced resignation of coach Rick Huckabay soon followed.

Huckabay was replaced by Dana Altman, who had a decent first season, coming within an overtime loss to East Tennessee State of winning the Southern Conference regular season championship. But just when things looked on the upswing again, Altman abruptly departed to become head coach at Kansas State.

Altman was replaced by former assistant Dwight Freeman, who has never been a head coach on any level. Freeman was promptly greeted with the news that his program was being placed on NCAA probation. The Thundering Herd cannot participate in post-season play this season, and will be limited to 13 total scholarships next year.

"It's going to be tough the next two years," said Freeman, who turned 31 in June, "but the program has no place to go but up. We've got tremendous support from our administration and fans. With those things in place, we'll just try to go from there. Things have been hectic, but I've got to look at this as an opportunity and something I have to meet head on. With a blessing from the man upstairs, we'll be okay."

Freeman already received one blessing last spring, when 6-2 senior guard **John Taft**, player of the year in the league the last two seasons, decided to remain at Marshall. Because of the probation, Taft could have transferred to any school in the country and been immediately eligible. Prospective schools were lined up for his services, and rumors persisted the Huntsville, Ala. native would bolt for the likes of Auburn, LSU or Wake Forest.

Citing loyalty to Marshall, Taft opted to stay. Freeman, obviously, was elated. "John will be the key to everything we do," the new coach said. "If he has a good season, we'll have a good season. If he struggles, we'll struggle."

Chances are good Taft will not struggle. Last year, he again led the league in scoring, averaging 23.4 points. Taft also grabbed 6.3 rebounds per game, and led the Herd in assists (65) and steals (33). Even more impressive than those accomplishments was Taft's relentless hustle.

"John is the type of player who gives you 200 percent, night in and night out," Freeman said. "The first time I saw him play was in a scrimmage game last year. On one play, he dived over a table after a loose ball - in a scrimmage game. Having somebody who works as hard as John does is a plus. His work ethic rubs off."

Taft attended summer classes at Marshall and put in long hours working on his three-point shooting. That is more bad news for the rest of the Southern Conference. "John has always been able to muscle to the basket with his strength, or go by people with his quickness," said Freeman. "Now, he's an even better three-point shooter. That just adds another dimension to his game."

Marshall's other returning starter is 6-3 senior **Andre Cunningham** (13.2 ppg, 4.8 rpg), the team's best defensive player. "Andre can check anyone from 5-10 to 6-7," Freeman said. "This year, we'll be looking for him to help John in the scoring department."

The Herd lost seven lettermen from last season, so the three remaining starting positions are up for grabs. **Tyrone Phillips**, (2.5 ppg, 1.8 rpg), a 6-6 sophomore, played in 24 games a year ago and is a leading candidate for at least one forward spot.

In the backcourt, 6-2 sophomore **Harold Simmons** (4.5 ppg, 1.6 rpg, 49 assists, 25 steals) showed much promise as a freshman. 6-3 sophomore **Aaron Collie** (2.8 ppg, 0.8 rpg) is also certain to play more than he did a year ago.

Newcomers will have to fill some holes, and quickly. **Torre Baker**, a 6-6, 250-pound forward from Huntington, W.Va., is eligible immediately after transferring from Winthrop (S.C.) College. Baker, who has three years eligibility remaining, never played at Winthrop. As a senior at Huntington's East High School, he averaged 21 points per game.

Two junior college transfers should also play a great deal. **Shawn Clifton** is a 6-4 forward from Allegany CC (Silver Springs, Md.); **Troy Taylor** is a 6-6 forward from Midland (Tex.) JC. Both are juniors in terms of eligibility.

Marshall signed four freshmen, but only two are eligible - 6-5 forward **Chris Patterson** (East HS/Memphis, Tenn.) and 6-8 **Shawn Brailsford** (American HS/Miami, Fla.). Patterson, the top recruit, averaged 18.5 points, 14.0 rebounds and four blocked shots in his final prep season.

BLUE RIBBON ANALYSIS

With all the personnel losses, Marshall, with a demanding schedule, was going to have a tough year anyway. Add the NCAA probation and, well, Freeman would rather not think about it.

"We've still got to go out there and play," he said. "The fact that we're eligible to win the conference regular-season title should be motivation for us."

Freeman, in his first year as a head coach, has at least tried to stay positive. "I know I'll make mistakes," he said, "but a lot of them will be in the learning process. I don't think anyone is prepared for their first head coaching job. We're going to do things the right way here. You have to decide if you want to have a good program, or a good team. Good teams come and go, but if you develop a good program, you'll always have a good team."

Freeman has the right idea, but Marshall fans should not expect too much too soon. The Thundering Herd may not slip as far as the Southern Conference basement, but they will be close.

1990-91 MARSHALL SCHEDULE		
Nov.	24	@Wyoming
	26	@Colorado State
Nov. 30-		
Dec. 1		#Centurion-Marshall Memorial Classic
Dec.	4	West Virginia
	6	@Pitt
	8	@Penn State
	13	Ohio University
	15	@Cleveland State
	20	Virginia
	27-28	##Hoosier Classic
Jan.	3	Virginia Tech
	5	@The Citadel
	7	@Furman
	12	Tennessee-Chattanooga
	14	Western Carolina
	19	@Virginia Military Institute
	21	@Univ. of the District of Columbia
	26	@Appalachian State
	28	@East Tennessee State
Feb.	2	Furman
	4	The Citadel
	9	@Western Carolina
	11	@Tennessee-Chattanooga
	16	Virginia Military Institute
	23	East Tennessee State
	25	Appalachian State
Mar.	1-3	*Southern Conference Tournament

@ Road Games
# Huntington, WV (Mercer, Robert Morris & Texas A&M)
Indianapolis, IN (Indiana, North Texas & Ohio University)
* Asheville, NC

MARYLAND

LAST SEASON: 19-14
CONFERENCE RECORD: 6-8
STARTERS LOST: 3
STARTERS RETURNING: 2
CONFERENCE: ATLANTIC COAST (ACC)
LOCATION: COLLEGE PARK, MD
HOME FLOOR: COLE FIELD HOUSE (14,500)
NICKNAME: TERRAPINS
COLORS: RED, WHITE, BLACK & GOLD
COACH: GARY WILLIAMS, record at Maryland, 17-14. Career record, 226-142.

Going into the 1989-90 college basketball season, not even the most die-hard of Terrapin fans could have felt very good about the state of their beloved program. Still reeling from the many aftershocks of

Len Bias' death in 1986, the Maryland basketball program needed someone to instill immediate stability. This monumental task was tackled by a man who has become known throughout his coaching career as a rebuilder of once-proud programs gone astray. For Gary Williams, the head coaching post at Maryland meant something even more than the opportunity to turn around another program. This was his alma mater, and Williams, a 1968 graduate, was not about to stand by and watch this program, with such great history and alumni (Tom McMillen, John Lucas, Len Elmore, Albert King and Buck Williams to name a few), destroy itself.

Williams put together a 19-win campaign and an NIT caliber club in his first year at Maryland.

This year's challenge could be even greater than last year's, since Maryland, an inside-dominated team last year, lost 67 percent of its scoring and 54 percent of its rebounding from last season, and now must rely on a perimeter-driven offense and a more united defensive effort. To make things even more difficult, Maryland begins a two-year NCAA probation which bans them from any post-season action for the next two seasons. Also, no live television coverage of Terrapin games will be available this year. These sanctions may make it difficult for this young Maryland team, knowing that an NCAA or NIT tournament bid cannot be achieved. It will be a tough task for Williams to keep this team focused on the court with these off-court distractions.

The Terrapins lost two outstanding interior forces —Jerrod Mustaf (18.5 ppg, 7.7 rpg) and Tony Massenburg (18.0 ppg, 10.1 rpg) —who were both selected in the NBA draft. Mustaf went to the Knicks as 17th pick in the first round while Massenburg was chosen by San Antonio in the second round. Mustaf, a 6-10 forward, left Maryland after a sophomore year in which he was a third-team All-ACC selection as he finished seventh in the league in scoring, fifth in rebounding and fifth in field goal percentage (.529). In two seasons at Maryland, Mustaf scored in double figures 50 times, including 30 of the 33 games he played in 1989-90. He was also the Terrapins' ironman last year as he led the club in minutes played with 1,048 (31.8 minutes per contest). Mustaf's consistency on the offensive end and mere presence defensively will be sorely missed. Massenburg, a 6-9 center, may leave a void in the Terrapins' lineup even larger to fill than Mustaf. He was a second-team All-ACC selection in his second year and he and Clemson manchild Dale Davis were the only players in the league to average double figures in both points and rebounds. He was in the league's Top Ten in rebounding (2nd), blocked shots (7th) and scoring (8th). He finished a solid career at Maryland with 1,359 points and 722 rebounds, and in each of his four years he shot better than 50 percent from the field.

The loss of these two dominant players causes some obvious problems for Williams as he enters his second season in College Park. However, Williams will be able to look to a couple of big men who were two of Maryland's top reserves last year to take over some of the lost offense, defense and leadership duties which Mustaf and Massenburg so ably handled. 6-9 senior center **Cedric Lewis**, whose older brother Derrick played at Maryland and finished his career as one of the school's all-time leaders in points, rebounds and blocked shots, played in all 33 games for the Terrapins last year. Lewis is considered one of the best defensive pivotmen in the ACC, having ranked among the conference leaders in blocked shots each of the past two years. Last year Lewis led Maryland with 49 blocks, good enough for third overall in the ACC. Even more amazingly, Lewis, who played a total of 435 minutes last season, averaged one blocked shot every 8.9 minutes of playing time. Lewis also scored 3.1 ppg and collected 3.0 rpg, both averages which should definitely pick up this year with increased playing time and responsibility. He possesses good post-up skills and with his long arms and athletic ability he can score on most opponents inside. A role player

for much of his career at Maryland, Lewis enters this season as the team's most experienced low post player and he will be expected to lead and contribute accordingly.

Evers Burns, a 6-8 sophomore forward, is the Terrapins other experienced inside player. Burns (4.3 ppg, 2.7 rpg as a freshman) showed signs last year of being an outstanding college scorer both on the baseline and in the paint. He will see action this year at both the power forward and center positions, and with his 235-pound frame, he should be able to handle either position when necessary. Burns has a deft touch for a man his size, and he can get his somewhat unorthodox left-handed shot off in heavy traffic. With an increased work ethic, Burns can become an outstanding defensive rebounder and establish himself as an interior presence whom opponents must get through in order to score. **Garfield Smith**, a 6-7 junior forward, will also be called upon to contribute immediately at the power forward position. Smith comes to College Park following two All-America seasons at Coffeyville (Kan.) CC. Smith is a solid 220 pounds and is not averse to mixing it up inside. He is a tenacious rebounder and defender who, it is hoped, will help Lewis and Burns considerably on the inside as they try to effectively deal with the losses of Mustaf and Massenburg. In his two years at Coffeyville, Smith was twice the team's leading scorer, averaging 22.0 ppg as a freshman and 16.1 ppg and 8.0 rpg as a sophomore.

Mark McGlone, a 6-7 freshman from Bladensburg HS in Bladensburg, Md., will also see action at the power forward position. McGlone, Gary Williams' first local signee, will be able to play both forward positions in time, although he thrived at big forward in high school. He has three outstanding attributes: quickness for his size (240 pounds), an effective outside shooting touch and an intensely competitive nature. Last year in high school he averaged 17.0 ppg, 10.0 rpg and three blocks per game, all team highs, and was a second-team All-Metro pick by The Washington Post. Williams is very excited about McGlone and his initial contribution to the Terrapins will be as a workhorse on the boards. Also helping out up front will be 6-7 junior transfer **Eric Kjome**. Kjome comes to Maryland after a three-year stint in the Air Force. He last played collegiately as a sophomore at the Air Force Academy, starting 19 of 27 games and averaging 9.0 ppg and 4.7 rpg in 1986-87. He should help Maryland on the boards and be a competitive offensive force as soon as he gets acclimated following his three-year hiatus.

While Maryland will have to rely on relatively inexperienced players to man the pivot and handle the power forward position, the Terrapins will enjoy the luxury of having the starter and top reserve from last year back in the lineup to handle the small forward responsibilities. **Jesse Martin**, a 6-4 junior who started last year at small forward, returns to College Park looking to improve on his 9.9 ppg and 4.0 rpg average. Martin, who can also effectively play the off-guard when called upon to do so, saw his game take off when the coaching staff last year moved him to the frontcourt virtually full time. Martin proved to be incredibly versatile last year for the Terrapins, as he finished among the team's top five in steals (3rd), assists (3rd), rebounding (4th), and scoring (5th). Martin became the starting small forward in the eighth game last year, and started at the position every game from then on. He showed that he could shoot the ball from the outside effectively as he shot 50 percent or better in 18 games, 60 percent or better 11 times and 70 percent or better five times, finishing the season with a .496 shooting percentage. Martin is also an extremely physical player who has no problems with tight man-to-man defense on an opponent. He also leaps well and, as a result, he will give the Terrapins much needed rebounding help.

Martin's backup last year was 6-3 **Vince Broadnax**, who is back this season for his junior year as well. Broadnax may have been Maryland's most pleasant surprise last year as he started the season as a walk-on and worked his way up to the all-important sixth man role. As a result, Broadnax was granted a scholarship on January 16, 1990. He was probably the team's best defender last year, and Williams grew to love his relentless effort and grasp of the overall defensive scheme. He, like Martin, has the ability to overcome a lack of height to be an effective rebounder by getting great position. Broadnax averaged only 3.5 ppg and 2.1 rpg last year, but as the season progressed and his minutes climbed to the 20-plus mark, his output gradually improved. **Kevin Chamberlain**, a 6-8 sophomore forward, played in only six games all of last year and is an athletic player who, if he does not see much more time at small forward this year than he did last, will still be a contributor in practice and to the team's overall depth.

The frontcourt, excluding the small forward position, is a fairly mysterious commodity as the Terrapins enter this season. Therefore, certainly at the start of the season, look for Maryland to move its game out to the perimeter where they can take full advantage of the skills of the team's best all-around player, 6-8 junior point guard **Walt Williams**. Williams (12.7 ppg, 4.5 apg, 4.2 rpg) was the Terrapins' most versatile, and arguably most valuable, player in 1989-90 even with the presence of Mustaf and Massenburg. His size and ability make him an influential factor in all aspects. He was the only ACC player last year to finish in the league's Top Ten in assists (8th), steals (6th), and blocked shots (10th), while also finishing among the Top 20 scorers (20th). Gary Williams said of his unique point guard: "His size makes him so hard to defend with a typical guard. He sees the whole floor, he gets to the basket in a hurry and gets the ball where it needs to be. He has the ability to be the premier point guard in this league."

Williams is an excellent long-range shooter whose field goal percentage (.483 last year) will definitely improve as the offense becomes more guard-oriented and his main focus is not to push the ball inside every time down the floor. His three-point field goal percentage of .448 would have been among the league's best, but he did not have the minimum number of attempts to qualify. This is Walt Williams' team exclusively this year, and as he goes in all aspects of his game (scoring, rebounding, passing, defending), so too will go the Terrapins.

Williams' backcourt mate this year will be 6-6 **Matt Roe**, a senior transfer who sat out all of 1989-90 after leaving Syracuse following his junior year. Despite his 11.0 ppg average in his junior year, Roe never seemed completely comfortable with his role in his three years at Syracuse. His trademark coming out of high school dead-eye shooting ability, definitely followed him to the major college level, but his game was so one-dimensional that Syracuse coach Jim Boeheim could not afford the luxury of his shooting skills while giving up so much in other aspects of the offensive set and on defense. It will be interesting to see if Roe, who will be thrust into this expansive starting role, will be able to excel as an off-guard at the major college level after a season on the sidelines. He will also be called upon to improve his defensive intensity, since all teams coached by Gary Williams start with defense as the foundation of their overall game plan.

Two more players who will add depth at guard for Maryland are junior newcomer **Matthew "Cougar" Downing** and sophomore **Kevin McLinton**. Downing, a 6-0 true point guard from Dodge City (Kan.) CC, who is expected to back up Williams. "Cougar," the nickname which Downing prefers to go by, averaged 18.0 ppg last year at Dodge City and he possesses an excellent outside shot which could allow him to play some off-guard as well. The son of a high school basketball coach, Downing is as fundamentally sound as anyone on the Terrapins' roster. McLinton, meanwhile, played well at the point for Maryland in their first six games last year before suffering a stress fracture in his leg which caused him to miss the rest of the campaign. His skills will allow him to be a quality backup for the Terrapins at both guard positions.

Maryland's backcourt, while it still should be the most solid part of this year's team, will sorely miss last year's starting off-guard, 6-1 Teyon McCoy, who left Maryland after his junior year and transferred to Texas. McCoy averaged 10.7 ppg, 3.6 apg and 2.4 rpg last year as he established himself as Maryland's most consistent long-range threat. He was a career 42 percent three-point shooter at Maryland, the top percentage on the team, and he finished last season fifth in the ACC in three-point field goal percentage. He started 30 games last year and his experience will be missed as much as his scoring abilities. It is believed that Matt Roe can take over at McCoy's position and be an even stronger offensive threat. The concern, however, is that the absence of McCoy's defensive skills and overall athleticism, both far superior to Roe, may cause serious problems for the Terrapins at this position once they get into the ACC season.

BLUE RIBBON ANALYSIS

This second edition of Gary Williams' Maryland Terps has the potential to be a good, competitive group. "We have an opportunity to be a very good basketball team," said Williams. "We'll be a different team than last year, but we'll be every bit as competitive. We don't have a great deal of depth, but we have players who are committed to working hard and succeeding. We were the underdogs last year, too, and I fully expect to surprise some people this season."

The major difference in this year's team will be more emphasis in the offense on the outside shot, with Williams, Roe and Martin leading the way. With Mustaf and Massenburg gone, the quick development of Lewis, Burns and either Smith, McGlone or Kjome down low is a must for the Terrapins. Coming off last season in which they led the ACC in overall rebounds per game (41.4), Maryland will have to adapt and commit themselves to a five-man unit going to both the offensive and defensive boards rather than relying on just two dominant rebounders to do the dirty work.

Williams will still stress pressure defense, but with a limited bench as far as experience goes, he must make sure that an aggressive defensive posture does not lead to foul trouble, Williams' and Martin's particularly. Maryland will probably start off slowly as they try to mesh their skills together into a cohesive unit. Then, they should come around with Roe's outside shooting and some interior confidence exhibited by Burns and Lewis leading the way. Maryland will be competitive, but that is often times not enough in the always strong ACC. Fifteen wins would be successful, and a last place finish in the ACC seems at this point almost unavoidable.

1990-91 MARYLAND SCHEDULE

Nov.	26	Towson State
	28	Southern California
Dec.	1	@West Virginia
	3	#Boston College
	8	@Jacksonville
	11	California-Irvine
	27 & 29	##ECAC Holiday Festival
Jan.	2	@Wake Forest
	5	Clemson
	7	Maryland-Baltimore Co.
	9	@North Carolina
	12	Duke
	16	Virginia
	19	@South Florida
	22	Boston University
	26	North Carolina State
	29	American University
Feb.	1	@Georgia Tech
	6	@Clemson
	9	@Duke
	13	Georgia Tech
	16	North Carolina
	19	@Virginia Tech

1990-91 MARYLAND SCHEDULE Cont.

Feb.	23	Wake Forest
	27	@North Carolina State
Mar.	2	@Virginia
	8-10	*ACC Tournament

@ Road Games
# ACC/Big East Challenge, Richmond, VA
Madison Square Garden, New York, NY (Brigham Young, Rutgers & South Carolina)
* Charlotte, NC

MASSACHUSETTS

LAST YEAR: 17-14
CONFERENCE RECORD: 10-8
STARTERS LOST: 1
STARTERS RETURNING: 4
CONFERENCE: ATLANTIC 10
LOCATION: AMHERST, MA
HOME FLOORS: CURRY HICKS CAGE (4,024) & SPRINGFIELD CIVIC CENTER (8,200)
NICKNAME: MINUTEMEN
COLORS: MAROON AND WHITE
COACH: JOHN CALIPARI, record at Massachusetts, 27-32.

The 1990 Atlantic 10 championship had just been decided, but it was hard to tell the winners from the losers. Favored Temple had just squeeked into the NCAA tournament, but the other finalist - heavy underdog Massachusetts - seemed to be doing more of the smiling.

There was head coach John Calipari, hugging his young team and reminding them that this was only a beginning. There was **Jim McCoy,** then a sophomore, tugging playfully on his mouthpiece and reflecting on a marvelous A-10 tournament showing. Could this really have been Massachusetts? Lowly UMass? The same Minutemen whose only prior claim to basketball fame was loaning a uniform to a two-year collegian named Julius Erving.

It was indeed UMass, a team that not too long ago seemed forever outclassed by its Atlantic 10 rivals. There have been bad teams in the A-10, of course, but for long stretches Massachusetts seemed like the only hopeless program.

Until Calipari came to town, this is. Promoted from his recruiters' role at Pitt, Calipari did the natural thing. He kept recruiting. The short-term result, in just his second season, was a surprising run to the league final and an NIT berth. The long-term benefit is one of the deepest stockpiles of young talent in the conference.

McCoy, a 6-3 junior, leads the way. Rookie of the year in the A-10 in 1987-88, this sleek shooter just gets better every year. He was magnificent in the postseason, dropping in one clutch bucket after another in consecutive conference tourney victories over West Virginia and Penn State, both higher seeds.

Ostensibly the UMass shooting guard, McCoy (20.7 ppg, 3.3 rpg) pretty much has a free rein from Calipari, who brought him from the Pittsburgh high school ranks along with fellow 6-3 junior **William Herndon** (a transfer from Richmond). A muscular player not outclassed at forward, Herndon (15.7 ppg, 5.7 rpg) really came alive as the Minutemen won five in a row down the stretch.

Joining Herndon up front are a pair of sophomores, 6-6 **Tony Barbee** (11.4 ppg, 4.9 rpg) and 6-7 **Harper Williams** (8.7 ppg, 5.3 rpg). Once he committed to the pair as freshmen starters, Calipari reaped the dividends of their young talent. Though neither is particularly strong, the Atlantic 10 has rarely been a power league down low.

The production of McCoy and Herndon seems a given. Just how high UMass can climb probably depends more on its sophomore forwards. Calipari rides them hard and, as their post-season surge indicates, the young Minutemen responded.

"I was hard on the kids all year," Calipari said, "and I was hard on them in the (A-10) tournament. I had to be hard on them. It's the only way we can win." In doing so, Calipari got a rep around the league as a crybaby. But he can take the heat. Right before the final at Temple, he quipped: "They can say what they want. Look where we are."

Where the Minutemen are now is in contention for a first division finish in the regular season race, this on top of their best year since 1978. They were the league's sixth seed a year ago, despite a 10-8 in-season mark. To improve on that, and to dismiss any notions that last March was just a fluke, UMass needs to discover that ever-elusive ingredient: consistency.

Right before their five-game stretch drive, the Minutemen lost four straight. There was also a five-game losing streak, as well as a six-game winning streak. A lot of that had to do with clustered home and away scheduling in conference play, but even more of it had to do with youth.

McCoy and Herndon should be right in their stride; Barbee and Williams should no longer cower at a Temple, a Rutgers or a West Virginia. They are four talented buliding blocks, with an ample supply of necessary role players right behind.

6-2 senior **Rafer Giles** (7.8 ppg, 1.3 rpg) was beaten out of his point guard job last year by Cary Herer (7.7 assists, 2.4 steals), the only graduated starter. He should return to the first five capably. 6-2 junior **Anton Brown** (1.7 ppg), he of the promising freshman year, backs up McCoy and waits for a break. High-scoring freshmen **Jerome Johnson** (Bassick HS/Bridgeport, Conn.), 6-4, and 6-3 **Mike Williams** (Weaver HS/Hartford, Conn.) continue Calipari's parade of backcourt dynamo's. Johnson averaged 22 points in his final scholastic season, Williams averaged 25.

6-7 senior **John Tate** (5.2 ppg, 5.4 rpg) is the best and most experienced frontcourt reserve. Others returnees there include 6-6 sophomore **Tommy Pace** (2.6 ppg, 3.1 rpg), 6-8 junior **Matt Anderson** and 6-9 junior **Ben Grodski**. Grodski missed all of last season with a hip injury.

The freshmen forwards, unlike Barbee and Williams before them, may have to wait their turn. Signed were 6-9 power players **Ted Cottrell** (Annapolis HS/Annapolis, Md.) and **Kennard Robinson** (Long Island Lutheran HS/Bronx, N.Y.). Calipari also took a chance on 7-2 freshman center **Jeff Meyer** (East HS/Wausau, Wisc.). At worst, the Minutemen finally have some much-needed size to go with their already fine perimeter play.

BLUE RIBBON ANALYSIS

Credit goes to Calipari for taking over at this one-time New England basketball wasteland and turning it around so quickly. He did it the way most young turks do nowadays, recruiting like heck and offering all the available playing time he can.

The first and second wave of talent has now been assembled. As long as the players do not tire of Calipari's iron hand, Massachusetts should continue to get better. They are not ready to win the Atlantic 10 - UMass may not even return to the league championship game - but the Minutemen figure to be more consistent and less prone to long losing streaks.

Ultimately, UMass will need a little more size to seriously threaten the traditional Atlantic 10 powers.

That is probably a year away. In the meantime, the Minutemen are the among the last teams the rest of the conference wants to see. Especially at the pit known as Curry Hicks Cage, which remains one of college basketball's best-kept homecourt secrets.

Massachusetts will be in the A-10 first division all season long.

McNEESE STATE

LAST SEASON: 14-13
CONFERENCE
RECORD: 11-3
STARTERS LOST: 4
STARTERS
RETURNING: 1
CONFERENCE:
SOUTHLAND
LOCATION:
LAKE CHARLES, LA
HOME FLOOR: BURTON COLISEUM (8,000)
NICKNAME: COWBOYS
COLORS: BLUE AND SUNFLOWER GOLD
COACH: STEVE WELCH, record at McNeese State, 37-49.
Career record, includes high school, 53-58.

McNeese State engineered a remarkable rebounding job last year, overcoming an 0-7 start to post a 14-13 record and finish second in the Southland Conference regular season for the second year in a row. After losing four starters off of that team, fourth year head coach Steve Welch is faced with a major retooling job. The Cowboys will be hardpressed to replace 6-10 Anthony Pullard, who was named the Southland Conference's Player of the Year last season. Pullard led the team in scoring (22.5 ppg) and rebounding (9.1 rpg). Pullard led the Cowboys in scoring 16 times last season and scored 27 on nine occasions. Few mid-majors like McNeese State boast a player with the

offensive prowess and versatility as Pullard. Hence, he leaves big shoes to fill.

The other departures include 6-9 center Mark Thompson (9.5 ppg, 6.7 rpg), 6-5 wing Tony Johnson (7.8 ppg, 5.9 rpg) and 6-3 wing Jay Cook (9.5 ppg). Thompson was a two-year starter, Johnson was McNeese's top defensive player and Cook, who started all 27 games as a freshman, was McNeese's top three-point threat (53-of-150). Following the season, Cook transferred to Arkansas State.

"You've got to lean on what you have coming back to keep a consistent basketball program," said Welch, "and that's what we'll do. The keys to us this season is building around those players who have been in the system and adding a couple of players to compliment those players."

The losses will also change, somewhat, the Cowboys' style. A year ago, the Cowboys were the biggest team in the Southland Conference and had the best inside game. But McNeese State was also the slowest team in the league. A major emphasis in the Cowboys' recruiting was to bring more quickness to the lineup.

"On the minus side, we'll be smaller and have less experience than we had a year ago," said Welch. "On the plus side, we should have more quickness and be more athletic."

The lone returning starter, 6-1 sophomore point guard **Danny Servick** (4.4 ppg, 2.3 rpg, 134 assists, 41 steals) performed admirably in his rookie season. Thrust into the starting role after Dewayne Davis, the projected starter, left the squad two weeks before the start of the season, Servick started all 27 games and was the second leading Cowboy in terms of minutes played last season. Servick's assists to turnover ratio was a respectable 134 to 78. He only attempted 80 field goals and made only 36.2 percent of those shots, though. The loss of his four fellow starters will force Servick to become more offensive minded.

Another key returnee is 6-8 senior **Derrick Turner** (10.9 ppg, 7.9 rpg, 17 assists, 23 blocked shots, 14 steals). Filling the sixth man role, Turner earned All-Southland Conference honors despite averaging less than 25 minutes per game. The lone senior on the roster, Turner will be counted on not only to take up some of the slack left by Pullard's departure, but also to become the team's emotional leader.

"To use a baseball term, you always try to be good up the middle and Servick at point guard and Turner at center make us good up the middle," said Welch. Two other returnees, 6-6 sophomore center **Louis Lee** and 6-9 center/forward **Reggie Cogg**, will contend for starting positions. Lee is coming off a redshirt season after undergoing surgery for a leg injury. As a freshman, Lee averaged 2.1 points and 1.7 rebounds on a Cowboy squad that won the Southland Conference's post-season tournament and lost 77-71 to Illinois in the opening round of the NCAA tournament. Cobb averaged 1.3 points and 2.0 rebounds in 12 games last season. A fluid player with good range on his jump shot, Cobb needs to become more hard-nosed in his defensive play.

Two other guards, 6-1 sophomore **Bobby Straface** and 6-3 junior **Terrell Thompson**, should provide depth. Straface averaged 4.3 points and 1.1 rebounds while splitting time between the point and off-guard positions last season. A permanent move to off-guard should help his 30.8 percent field goal accuracy. Thompson (1.2 ppg) saw limited action last year and is best suited to a quick tempo game.

"We try to preach to our players to learn the system and serve their time," said Welch. "Now it's time for players like Lee and Cobb to step up and contribute."

Larone Ford, a 6-2 sophomore guard, who sat out last year because of NCAA academic requirements, will likely start at the off-guard position. An excellent athlete blessed with both quickness and jumping ability, Ford can play either guard position, but will be used primarily at the shooting guard spot in order to take advantage of his scoring. Ford averaged 19.1

points, 5.8 rebounds and 5.2 assists per game during a three-year career at DeRidder (La.) HS.

"Ford gives us more athleticism," said Welch. "He's an explosive, slasher who has outstanding quickness."

Two junior college transfers should also contend for starting berths. **Greg Sims**, a 6-7 junior, averaged 14.3 points and 6.3 rebounds per game last season for Grayson (Texas) CC. An excellent shooter, Grayson can play either the power or small forward position. **Derek Haywood**, a 6-3 junior, averaged 15.1 points and 7.5 rebounds last year for Baytown Lee (Texas) JC.

Martin Yokum, a 6-9 center/forward from St. Louis HS in Lake Charles, headlines the freshman class. Yokum, who was named among the Top 100 prep players in the nation, registered 13.5 points and 10.4 rebounds per game while leading St. Louis to the Class AA state championship last year. A nephew of former McNeese All Americas Edmond and David Lawrence, Yokum has the versatility of a Pullard and can play either on the block or the wing. However, he must adjust to the physical nature of college basketball.

Three other freshman recruits came from a 15-mile radius of Lake Charles. 6-1 **Binky Barrentine** will back up Servick at the point. A more productive offensive player coming of high school than Servick, Barrentine averaged 15.8 points, 5.1 assists per game while spearheading his Sulphur (La.) HS team to a 35-2 record. 6-2 **Carl Klein**, an exceptional shooter, averaged 20.5 points per game as a three-year starter at Barbe (La.) HS last year.

BLUE RIBBON ANALYSIS

The loss of Pullard leaves a major void for Welch to fill, not to mention the departure of three other starters. Turner should become a major factor in the middle with more minutes and Servick is a steadying influence at the point. The bulk of the remaining offense will have to be handled by newcomers Ford, Sims and Hayward. How quickly Yokum adapts to the college game could also be a telling factor in McNeese's season.

Runners-up in the Southland Conference the past two seasons, the Cowboys do not appear to have the experience nor the offensive firepower to make it three second place finishes in a row. In fact, McNeese State will likely be hardpressed to finish higher than fifth in the Southland Conference race.

1990-91 McNEESE SCHEDULE

Nov.	27	Louisiana College
	29	Louisiana Tech
Dec.	1	South Alabama
	3	@Southwestern Louisiana
	5	@Southeastern Louisiana
	8	Chapman College (CA)
	17	@Grambling State (LA)
	29	Mississippi
Jan.	7	Nicholls State (LA)
	10	@Northeast Louisiana
	12	Northwestern State
	14	Lamar
	17	@Southwest Texas State
	19	@Sam Houston State
	21	@Nicholls State
	24	Texas-Arlington
	25	North Texas
	29	@Lamar
Feb.	2	@Stephen F. Austin
	7	Northeast Louisiana
	9	@Northwestern State
	11	Southern Mississippi
	14	Southwest Texas
	16	Sam Houston State
	18	Stephen F. Austin

1990-91 McNEESE SCHEDULE *Cont.*

Feb.	21	@Texas-Arlington
	23	@North Texas
Feb. 28- Mar 3		#Southland Conference Tournament

@ Road Games
# Site to be announced

MEMPHIS STATE

LAST SEASON: 18-12
CONFERENCE RECORD: 8-6
STARTERS LOST: 1
STARTERS RETURNING: 4
CONFERENCE: METRO
LOCATION: MEMPHIS, TN
HOME FLOOR: MID-SOUTH COLISEUM (11,200)
NICKNAME: TIGERS
COLORS: BLUE AND GRAY
COACH: LARRY FINCH, record at Memphis State, 85-43.

What went right for Memphis State in 1989-90? To determine that, let's see what went wrong.

First, **Elliott Perry** and Cheyenne Gibson, the Tigers' veteran guards, suffered through terrible seasons. Perry tried to take too much of the offensive load on himself and Gibson, a senior, was mentally A.W.O.L. most of the year.

Second, the Tigers kept up a three-year streak of having virtually no inside game. Coach Larry Finch was forced to start two freshmen most of the year on the frontline, center **Todd Mundt** and forward **Kelvin Allen**. The lone returning starter on the frontline, **Ernest Smith**, didn't produce until the final 13 games of the year.

Third, Memphis State's inspirational leader, forward **Russell Young**, reinjured a kneecap before preseason work and did not return to full strength until February.

Three strikes and Memphis State went 18-12, was not invited to the NCAA tournament, a rarity for the Tigers. Instead, they got beat on their homecourt by cross-state rival Tennessee in the first round of the NIT. The Tigers had opened the season by beating Tennessee in Memphis.

It was amazing the Tigers won 18 games, considering the team was split with half the players playing team ball and the other half playing for themselves. Subsequently, the Tigers folded too many times in the final minutes of games.

Finch vows he won't tolerate selfishness this season. He is building his nucleus around team-oriented players who look at the scoreboard, not the stat sheet. His building block was supposed to be 6-7 1/2 freshman point guard Anfernee Hardaway of Memphis Treadwell HS. Hardaway (36.3 ppg, 10.1 rpg, 130 assists, 69 steals), who was *Parade Magazine's* 1989-90 high school player of the year, will sit out the season after failing to academically qualify. He was Memphis State's only signee.

Instead, Finch will look to 6-0 senior point guard Perry (16.8 ppg, 150 assists, 82 steals), whose dominance of the ball last season was done with good

intentions. Perry struggled all year with his outside shooting, and defenses began playing him for his drive.

"Most teams played zone defense on us and I basically got my points off the break," Perry said. "It just didn't happen for me."

Coaches such as Florida State's Pat Kennedy said, "We finally figured out how to defend Elliot. You can't attack him and get him cranked up. He loves to shoot off the dribble. He's not a good standstill shooter."

To start this season, Finch may move Perry off the point to the shooting guard spot, and shift 6-1 junior **Tony Madlock** to the point. Madlock (4.0 ppg) showed a nice mix of control and aggressiveness a year ago that impressed Finch.

Memphis State needs production from 6-5 senior guard **John McLaughlin** (3.0 ppg), who wrote the book on injuries last season. McLaughlin, supposedly the team's best three-point shooter, had stitches in his chin and little finger of his right hand, a sinus infection, a stomach virus and torn knee ligaments at the end of the season. If he's breathing in 1990-91, the Tigers will have the outside shooting they lacked a year ago.

Much of the Tigers' success also depends on the off-season improvement of 7-0 sophomore center **Todd Mundt** (7.9 ppg, 3.7 rpg). Mundt, redshirted two seasons ago with a stress fracture, was a fundamentally solid player who lacked strength and intensity last season. He was on the All-Metro freshman team. If Mundt could infuse some of the meanness of 6-7 junior reserve center **Ben Spiva** (6.1 ppg, 3.0 rpg), he'd be unstoppable. Spiva has limited physical ability, but compensates with heady play and a nasty streak that earned him the reputation as one of the Metro's roughest players.

"I'm really a nice guy," said Spiva, who said he hates his play to be compared to Bill Laimbeer of the Detroit Pistons.

Also seeing action at center may be 6-10 sophomore **Montrell Nash** (1.6 ppg, 2.3 rpg), whose specialty as a freshman seemed to be rebounding and defense.

The Tigers' forwards could be offensively productive if 6-5 junior **Russell Young** (5.8 ppg, 3.3 rpg) continues to strengthen his previously injured knee. Before hurting his kneecap early in 1988-89, he was rated as the second best small freshman forward in the country in 1987-88 by *Sport Magazine*. During his comeback late last season, his hustling play was contagious. As Finch said, "Just Russell's attitude makes us a better team." The most pleasant surprise last season was the play of forward **Kelvin Allen**, now a 6-7 sophomore. A lightly recruited high school player from tiny Bolivar, Tenn., he was spotted by Memphis State recruiters in an off-season AAU tournament. By January, Allen (6.0 ppg, 4.4 rpg) was a starter for the Tigers.

Ernest Smith, a 6-5 junior forward (10.6 ppg, 5.7 rpg), who is the best leaper on the team, was a first half disappointment who was the Tigers' best player in the second half of the season. In the final 13 games, he scored in double figures, shot 63.4 percent from the field and said, "I stopped feeling sorry for myself."

Two other forwards who will contribute a little are 6-9 senior **Ronald McClain** (3.6 ppg, 3.2 rpg) and 6-8 junior **Tim Duncan** (1.9 ppg, 1.6 rpg). The reason that Finch vows his team will "have a better talent level this season" is the addition of sophomores **Anthony Douglas** and **Billy Smith**. Both sat out their freshman seasons. Douglas, a 6-7, 258-pound center, and Smith, a 6-5 guard, both starred at Memphis' East High. Douglas, a space eater in the lane, averaged 28.7 points and 18.5 rebounds. Smith, who may instantly become Memphis State's best athlete, averaged 24.3 points and 9.2 rebounds. Douglas was ranked as a national Top 25 player as a high school senior and Smith made most Top 100 lists.

Memphis State seemed to bottom out last season. It wasn't a typical Finch team that played hard down to the final buzzer of every game. There were contests in which the Tigers packed it in a little early, something which infuriated the coaching staff.

There are so many pre-season questions about Memphis State. Can someone relieve the scoring load off Perry? Will Mundt stay intense and play like a seven-footer? Will Young's knee be better than ever Will Douglas and Smith step in and contribute immediately?

While Memphis State fans are moaning over the loss of Hardaway, Finch has always had the attitude of looking forward, not backwards. His optimism has served him well. He won't let the Tigers miss the NCAA tournament two consecutive years. Call it at least a 20-win season for Memphis State, a fourth place finish in the Metro and a trip to the NCAA tournament.

1990-91 MEMPHIS STATE SCHEDULE

Nov.	14	#@Boston College
	27	@Tennessee
Dec.	1	Prairie View A&M (TX)
	4	Murray State
	8	Middle Tennessee State
	13	Mercer
	16	@Wyoming
	19	@Oregon State
	28	Illinois
	30	South Carolina State
Jan.	2	@Missouri
	5	@Virginia Tech
	10	@Louisville
	12	Tulane
	19	@Southern Mississippi
	21	Miami (FL)
	24	Florida State
	26	South Carolina
	30	East Tennessee State
Feb.	2	@Cincinnati
	7	@Tulane
	9	Southern Mississippi
	11	@Miami (FL)
	14	Cincinnati
	16	Louisville
	21	@Florida State
	23	@South Carolina
Mar.	2	Virginia Tech
	7-9	##Metro Conference Tournament

@ Road Games
# Dodge NIT. If Memphis State defeats Boston College, the Tigers will play a second round game on Nov. 16. The semifinals and finals will be held on Nov. 21 & 23 at Madison Square Garden, New York, NY
Roanoke, VA

MERCER

LAST SEASON: 7-20
CONFERENCE RECORD: 2-14
STARTERS LOST: 2
STARTERS RETURNING: 3
CONFERENCE: TRANS AMERICA ATHLETIC (TAAC)
LOCATION: MACON, GA
HOME FLOOR: MACON COLISEUM (9,000)
NICKNAME: BEARS
COLORS: ORANGE AND BLACK
COACH: BRAD SIEGFRIED, record at Mercer, 7-20. Career record, including high school, 96-62.

Mercer enters the 1990-91 season in a good-news, bad-news dilemma. The good news, of course, is that they can only get better after a 7-20 season and a last-place finish in the Trans America Conference.

The bad news is that they will have to do so with a host of unproven players.

Coach Brad Siegfried's three-year rebuilding plan begins its second season with the cupboard all but bare of scoring punch. Scott Bailey (20.0 ppg, 9.6 rpg) and Oscar Moore (15.2 ppg, 4.9 rpg), the two starters lost to graduation, provided more than half the Bears' scoring and almost half their rebounding a year ago. 6-5 junior forward **Scott Waller** is the top returning scorer, but he averaged just 6.4 points per game.

''For us to improve, someone is going to have to step forward as our scorer,'' Siegfried said. ''Fortunately, we have some people who can handle the job.''

A good place to look is in the backcourt, where a battle is shaping up for the shooting guard spot. 6-2 sophomore **Kenny Brown** (South Plantation HS/Fort Lauderdale, Fla.), who sat out last season, has the early inside track. As a high school senior, he averaged 19.2 points and nine rebounds per game.

6-1 senior **Jay Stroman** (0.9 ppg, 0.4 rpg) is also in the running after winning team defensive honors last season. 6-3 freshman **Maurice Parks** (Dalton HS/Dalton, Ga.), who averaged 23 points as a high school senior, and 6-1 junior walk-on **Mark Baynes** (0.4 ppg, 0.2 rpg) are in the fight as well.

6-0 Junior **Flo Davis** (3.2 ppg, 97 assists) is the returning starter at the point. He also led the Bears with 42 steals last season, but will be pushed by 5-11 redshirt sophomore **Yaun Pounds** and 5-10 freshman **Mike Smith** (Pebblebrook HS/Mableton, Ga.).

Waller (6.4 ppg, 3.2 rpg) will move from the backcourt to small forward. He will be tested there, however, by 6-5 sophomore **Chad Boggan** (6.2 ppg, 1.7 rpg) and 6-7 freshman **Donny Woods** (Bradwell Institute/Hinesville, Ga.).

Mike Kennedy (5.3 ppg, 3.5 rpg), a 6-9 sophomore, will move from the post to strong forward, making room for 6-11, 270-pound junior college transfer **Rob Renfroe** (Emmanuel JC/Jacksonville, Fla.). Also on hand is 6-10 freshman **Adam Bowling** (Spencer HS/Columbus, Ga.).

BLUE RIBBON ANALYSIS

Another tough year in Macon, as Siegfried obviously needs a scorer. The rest of the pieces are in place to at least be competitive. Renfroe, Kennedy and Waller form what could eventually be one of the top frontlines in the TAAC. Davis is an experienced point guard who can make things happen between the circles.

Still, the Bears will not be able to win any high-scoring battles. In fact, if Brown and Waller don't develop in a very big hurry, last season's 7-20 season may look pretty good.

1990-91 MERCER SCHEDULE

Nov.	28	Furman
Nov. 30-Dec. 1		#Key Centurion-Marshall Memorial Classic
Dec.	3	@North Carolina Asheville
	6	@Central Florida
	8	Georgia
	10	Ohio University
	13	@Memphis State
	18	@Tennessee-Chattanooga
	22	Davidson
	31	@Augusta College (GA)
Jan.	2	@South Carolina
	5	Butler
	10	@Samford (AL)
	12	@Arkansas-Little Rock
	19	Georgia Southern
	21	Stetson
	26	@Georgia State
	31	@Centenary (LA)
Feb.	2	@Texas-San Antonio
	7	Samford
	9	Arkansas-Little Rock

1990-91 MERCER SCHEDULE Cont.

Feb.	14	@Stetson
	16	@Georgia Southern
	25	Georgia State
	28	Centenary
Mar.	2	Texas-San Antonio
	5-7	##TAAC Tournament

@ Road Games
# Huntington, WV (Marshall, Robert Morris & Texas A&M)
DeLand, FL

MIAMI OF FLORIDA

LAST SEASON: 13-15
STARTERS LOST: 0
STARTERS RETURNING: 5
CONFERENCE: INDEPENDENT
LOCATION: CORAL GABLES, FL
HOME FLOOR: MIAMI ARENA (16,500)
NICKNAME: HURRICANES
COLORS: ORANGE, GREEN AND WHITE
COACH: LEONARD HAMILTON, first year at Miami of Florida.
Career record, 57-63.

Bill Foster was brought to Miami to resurrect a program which simply had not existed since the Rick Barry days of the early '70s. He came in and landed the much-traveled Tito Horford, and the Hurricanes thought they were on their way to basketball prominence. After all, a large recruiting budget, an attractive national schedule, a brand new arena and the beautiful weather of Florida should be all the program needed, right? Well, Miami found out that one talented transfer does not a program make, and Foster left following last season's 13-15 season.

Foster did not leave the cupboard bare for his successor, former Oklahoma State coach Leonard Hamilton, and Miami hoop fans could have the winner they have been hoping for in the very near future. Hamilton has all 12 lettermen from last season's squad back, led by 6-9 senior center **Joe Wylie** (18.4 ppg, 9.5 rpg). Wylie has developed into an aggressive scorer over his first three years and has given Miami more consistent play underneath than Horford did in his short stay. 6-11 senior **Joe Ross** (1.9 ppg, 1.1 rpg) will back up Wylie, and must put up numbers that his size dictates. Athletic 6-8 sophomore center **Hammie Ward** (2.2 ppg, 1.4 rpg) saw some quality time as well in the paint, and will continue to develop. Another still-developing talent up front is 6-7 sophomore forward **Justin Caldwell** (3.3 ppg, 3.0 rpg). The burly Texas native started 16 games last season and spent the summer working on a shooting touch that could make him effective from 15-feet or more. Two juniors, 6-4 **Joseph Randon** (5.3 ppg, 3.3 rpg) and 6-6 **Brandon Adams** (3.4 ppg, 1.9 rpg) back up Caldwell. Randon was second on the team in rebounding last season but must improve his scoring touch to be effective, while Adams provides much needed depth and a quick scoring fix.

A pair of ever improving sophomores will man the opposite forward spot. 6-6 three-point shooter **Samarr Logan** (8.1 ppg, 2.7 rpg) led the team in treys (40-86, .465) last season and will continue to swing between the big guard and small forward spot, with classmate **Doug Elliott** (4.7 ppg, 2.9 rpg), of equal height and range, filling the same role. The two complement each other very well and will split time once again. **Paul Shipe**, a 6-5 redshirt freshman from Osceola HS in Kissimmee, Fla., will back up Logan and Elliott.

The backcourt also returns some talent, although it is painfully short on numbers. Running the Miami show will be 6-2 senior point guard **Thomas Hocker** (7.0 ppg, 139 assists). Hocker has been the steadying force in a very rocky Miami sea the past three seasons and will once again be the one to keep the ball in the hands of a talented frontcourt. Juniors 6-2 **Jake Morton** (11.0 ppg, 2.5 rpg) and 6-3 **Jerome Scott** (8.9 ppg, 2.1 rpg) will likely man the shooting spot, although both must improve on their range (Morton —.311, Scott —.306) from beyond the three-point area to be any kind of offensive help. Scott may be the best of the two this year if he can continue on the 15 points per game pace he had over the season's final 13 games in '89-90. 6-3 sophomore **Trevor Burton** (4.5 ppg) rounds out the backcourt and should see action at the point spot. Hamilton came in late, and given the team's returning experience, brought in no newcomers this season.

BLUE RIBBON ANALYSIS

Hamilton has inherited a team that goes 12 deep and may be ready to make a run at least over .500. The team must improve on the boards (outrebounded by five per game last year) and has to find the intensity level every game that has been lacking in recent years. There were some very bright signs (wins over Dayton, Florida and Florida State) last season, but that lack of consistency also brought losses to the likes of Alabama State and the University of Hartford. The underclassmen should continue to progress, led by the five sophomores, but the backcourt could have problems because of a lack of depth.

One question remains: Will anyone in Miami care? The Hurricanes drew two crowds of less than 1,000 last year and if that keeps up, the administration may again change its commitment. However, no one here thinks that will happen. Hamilton is a winner and once Miami gets into a league they will thrive. For now, a 16-18 win season and an NIT berth for this independent program is definitely in the cards. It has been a somewhat painful building process, but the blocks now appear to be finally falling into place. Not with one star, but with 12 role players.

1990-91 MIAMI OF FLORIDA SCHEDULE		
Nov.	23	George Mason
	27	@Penn State
Dec.	1	@Southern California
	5	@South Florida
	14	Georgia
	17	Dartmouth
	19	@Southern Methodist
	27-28	#Eastern Airlines
		Palm Beach Classic
	30	@Florida
Jan.	3	@St. Joseph's
	5	@West Virginia
	9	Lehigh
	12	Notre Dame
	14	Lafayette
	16	@Kansas
	21	@Memphis State
	25	Penn State
	28	@Wake Forest
Feb.	2	Davidson
	6	St. Joseph's
	9	Virginia Commonwealth
	11	Memphis State
	23	DePaul
	25	South Florida
Mar.	4	Florida International
	6	@DePaul

@ Road Games
# West Palm Beach, FL (Miami of Ohio, Mississippi State & Ohio State)

MIAMI OF OHIO

LAST SEASON: 14-15
CONFERENCE RECORD: 9-7
STARTERS LOST: 1
STARTERS RETURNING: 4
CONFERENCE: MID-AMERICAN (MAC)
LOCATON: OXFORD, OH
HOME FLOOR: MILLETT HALL (9,200)
NICKNAME: REDSKINS
COLORS: RED AND WHITE
COACH: JOBY WRIGHT, first year at Miami (Ohio).

With nine lettermen, including four starters, returning from a team that last year tied for third in the Mid-American Conference, you would think all talk around the Miami basketball program would be positive. It is not. In fact, in the wake of the unexpected dismissal of coach Jerry Peirson, who had compiled a 94-80 record in six seasons as head man for the Redskins, exactly the opposite is true.

The ax fell on Peirson in early August, after considerable debate over his fate. His downfall actually began much earlier, when he elected to give former Miami star Karlton Clayborne an ''A'' for a Basketball Theory course which Carlton never attended and for which he never completed the required work. ''I made a mistake and I'm sorry for it,'' Peirson said. ''I felt I deserved to be disciplined in some manner, but I don't feel the penalty (his firing) fit the violation.''

Miami athletic director R.C. Johnson agreed with Peirson, recommending to university president Paul Pearson that the coach be suspended without pay and banished from teaching. In turn, Pearson said that while he ''has respect for the athletic director's judgment,I have a much broader set of responsibilities. I have to consider the integrity not only of athletics, but of academics, and of the university as a whole.''

So the Peirson by another spelling, after more than 25 years with the school, was sent packing by Pearson the president. His messy and sudden departure has cast an uncertain, dark cloud over the Redskins.

At least new coach Joby Wright, hired in early September, has impeccable credentials. He will also be the ninth Bobby Knight assistant to coach in Division I this year. Wright played on Knight's first team at Indiana, was a three-year starter for the Hoosiers, and had an accomplished professional career with Seattle and San Diego in the NBA, Memphis in the ABA and the Italian League. He has spent the past 10 years on the bench next to his mentor.

Plenty of talent awaits Wright, confused though it maybe. The leading scorer on last year's club was sixth man **David Scott** (14.3 ppg, 2.9 rpg), who returns as a 6-6 junior forward. Scott has outstanding range on his jumpshot, as evidenced by a respectable .402 percentage (37-for-92) from three-point range. He will be joined on a loaded front line by 6-10 senior center **Jim Paul** (13.0ppg, 7.6 rpg) and 6-6 sophomore forward **Craig Michaelis** (12.8 ppg, 4.0 rpg).

Paul has been solid, but occasionally disappointing since getting off to a fast start in his collegiate career. Most MAC observers predicted he would be the league's player of the year by now, as well as its most dominant big man.

Michaelis, meanwhile, earned MAC freshman of the year honors last season, teaming with Scott to correct the shortage of outside shooting that had hampered Miami's recent past.

Part-time starters **Cedric Vanleer** (5.4 ppg, 1.6 rpg), a 6-2 junior, and **Jamie Mercurio** (2.2 ppg, 1.2 rpg), a 6-3 junior, figure to take over full-time in the backcourt, although neither is a true point man in the mold of last season's starter, Derek Walton (6.5 ppg, 120 assists). That job could even fall to 6-0 sophomore **Scott Belyeu** (2.5 ppg, 36 assists), relegating one of the others to a reserve role.

The remaining returning lettermen include 6-6 sophomore forward **Matt Kramer** (2.3 ppg, 1.0 rpg), 6-8 sophomore forward **Braden McCormick** and 6-9 sophomore forward **David Foster** (0.4 ppg, 0.3 rpg). Each saw limited action a year ago and will likely be on the bench again, since 6-7 forward Tim Stewart (13.7 ppg) is the only player missing from the frontcourt, and Scott is available to gobble up most of the extra minutes.

Four freshmen recruits arrive on the scene, only to find the man who recruited them gone. They are 6-5 forward **Maurice Davis**(Case Tech HS/Detroit, Mich.), 6-11 center **John McKenna** (DeSales HS/Columbus, Ohio), 6-3 guard **Jerome Gray** (St. Francis HS/Toledo, Ohio) and 6-6 forward **Vernon Crump** (Woodhaven HS/Flatrock,Mich.). Davis appears the most talented of the bunch, having averaged 22.0 points and 12.5 rebounds as a high school senior. McKenna (18.0 ppg, 11.0 rpg) probably will be groomed as Paul's replacement.

BLUE RIBBON ANALYSIS

Since NCAA investigators informed Miami officials of Peirson's indiscretions in December of 1989, why did it take the university until August to decide the coach's fate? The timing threw everything into turmoil and placed a once-promising season in jeopardy.

This is a team that, despite its considerable returning talent, already faced a number of other questions. Can Paul finally reach the lofty potential for which he so long ago was targeted? Can a suspect backcourt come up with a quality point guard to run the show? And, oh yes, could the Redskins ever win big again without Ron Harper?

It should not be overlooked that Peirson took over as Miami's head coach just when Harper, now a star in the NBA with the Los Angeles Clippers, was only a junior at Miami. After back-to-back 20-win seasons, Harper departed and took his high-wire act to the pros. Peirson's next four editions of the Redskins played mostly mediocre ball, compiling a culmulative 50-62 record.

It will be up to Wright to sort through the recent mess and point Miami back toward respectability. If he is as forceful as his mentor, it may not take long. Under this year's circumstances, however, another .500 season is about the best that can be expected.

1990-91 MIAMI OF OHIO SCHEDULE		
Nov.	24	Evansville
	29	Fairfield
Dec.	1	Cincinnati
	3	@Eastern Kentucky
	6	Dayton
	8	@Xavier
	10	Eastern Washington
	15	@Indiana State
	22	@Nebraska
	27-28	#West Palm Beach Hurricane
		Classic
Jan.	2	Bowling Green
	5	@Eastern Michigan
	9	Toledo
	12	@Kent State
	16	Ball State
	23	@Western Michigan
	26	Ohio University
	30	@Central Michigan
Feb.	2	Eastern Michigan
	6	@Toledo
	9	Kent State
	13	@Ball State
	20	Western Michigan
	23	@Ohio University
	27	Central Michigan
Mar.	2	@Bowling Green
	8-10	##MAC Tournament

@ Road Games
# West Palm Beach, FL (Miami of Florida, Mississippi State & Ohio State)
Detroit, MI

MICHIGAN

**LAST SEASON: 23-8
CONFERENCE
RECORD: 12-6
STARTERS LOST: 5
STARTERS
RETURNING: 0
CONFERENCE:
BIG TEN
LOCATION:
ANN ARBOR, MI
HOME FLOOR: CRISLER
ARENA (13,609)
NICKNAME: WOLVERINES
COLORS: MAIZE AND BLUE
COACH: STEVE FISHER, record at Michigan, 29-8.**

A glorious era of Michigan basketball has finally come to an end. One would be hard pressed to find as talented a group as Rumeal Robinson, Terry Mills, Loy Vaught, Mike Griffin and Sean Higgins at any time in Michigan Wolverine history. As talented and as experienced as this team was, however, the Wolverines often seemed distracted last season. While this glorious era was coming to an unceremonious end under a barrage of Loyola Marymount three-pointers, a new nucleus of players began to bind together with a focus towards the 1990-91 season. Sophomores **Michael Talley** and **Tony Tolbert** looked to form a future backcourt and redshirt sophomore **Eric Riley** showed flashes of brilliance that could make him the dominant big man in the Big Ten for years to come. Michigan will enter the '90s much like they entered the '80s; young and talented, but inexperienced.

Replacing Rumeal Robinson will be a difficult task. Robinson, a first round NBA draft choice of the Atlanta Hawks, will go down as one of the great backcourt players in Michigan history. He ranks in the Top 10 in almost every Michigan career category. As a junior, of course, his two free throws won Michigan's first NCAA championship. As a senior, Robinson averaged 19.2 ppg and 6.1 assists per contest. His leadership and big play capability will be sorely missed in the Wolverines backcourt. The likely candidates to start at the one guard position will be 6-2 senior **Demetrius Calip** (8.5 ppg, 1.9 apg). Calip first came under the Michigan spotlight during the Wolverines run to the national title in 1989. Calip gained head coach Steve Fisher's favor with impressive minutes against North Carolina, Illinois and finally Seton Hall in the championship game. Last season, Calip was a solid starter during the Big Ten campaign alongside Robinson as the Maize and Blue finished 12-6 in the conference. He scored in double figures eight times last year and had a career high of 22 points in Michigan's 127-96 thrashing of Iowa in the season finale. Calip will need to be this year's leader on the floor. He is an excellent ballhandler as evidenced by his 38 turnovers last year in over 600 minutes of playing time. He will be responsible for orchestrating Fisher's attack while still looking to raise his scoring average. Also, look for 5-11 sophomore Michael Talley (3.0 ppg, 1.4 apg) to see a considerable amount of playing time at the point guard slot. Talley led Detroit Cooley HS to three consecutive Michigan state championships while winning the state's coveted Mr. Basketball award his senior season. Talley is an excellent playmaker and may work his way into the starting lineup as the season progresses due to his scoring ability. On a team that lost over 81 percent of its scoring, Fisher may opt for the more potent offensive player in Talley as Big Ten crunch time arrives.

Fellow sophomore Tony Tolbert (6.8 ppg, 1.8 apg) will get the nod at the shooting guard spot. Tolbert, a 6-4 shooter, was instant offense off the bench last season. Fisher needs Tolbert to step forward and become the go-to force on offense. Tolbert definitely has the credentials to take over the role. In his 18 games last year, Tolbert averaged 10 minutes per game and 6.8 ppg with a career high 16 versus Loyola Marymount in the season finale. T and T (Tolbert and Talley) will eventually form a potent backcourt. It will likely be next year, but it may be sooner if Demetrius Calip's jumpers stop falling this season. Another possible factor in the backcourt may be 6-3 junior **Kirk Taylor**. Taylor was an integral part of Michigan's championship team before severely injuring his knee. He averaged 4.5 ppg during that season while sitting out all last year. He could become a factor due to his past experience.

Two sophomores and one newcomer will round out the backcourt, but most likely will not see much action. 6-5 **Rob Pelinka** is a redshirt sophomore who sat out all last year due to tendonitis in his knees. He is a strong outside shooter who may provide some scoring help off the bench. 6-1 sophomore **Sean Dobbins** is a walk-on who will provide depth to an already strong backcourt and should not see any significant playing time. Freshman **Jason Bossard** from Charlotte (Mich.) HS has a chance to be a true impact player at Michigan. He is an excellent perimeter shooter who averaged 30 points as a senior and added five rebounds and five assists. The 6-4 Bossard was a Michigan first-team all-state selection. "He can do a lot of things, but what he does best is shoot the basketball; especially the long range three-point shot. He's an exceptional, hardnosed, gritty competitor and an excellent student," said Fisher.

Replacing Vaught, Mills and Higgins will be a major key to the success of the Maize and Blue this season. These three combined for 47.6 ppg and 22.8 rpg last year. All three were NBA draft choices this past June; Vaught went 15th in the first round to the Los Angeles Clippers; Mills was a first round pick of the Milwaukee Bucks (18th choice), and later traded to Denver before signing with a Greek team, while Higgins, who left Michigan a year early, was selected by the San Antonio Spurs with the last pick in the second round (54th overall). With the exception of 7-0 Eric Riley (2.7 ppg, 3.8 rpg), the frontcourt is extremely unsettled. Riley is a tall, gangly seven-footer who has shown signs of being a decent center. What he needs, more than anything else, is game experience. Riley, a redshirt sophomore, led the Wolverines in field goal percentage last year with a 60.7 mark and tallied a career high 12 points in a late season win against Wisconsin. He will start and it is essential that he provide solid offensive production in the middle.

With the exception of **Chip Armer**, the rest of Michigan's frontcourt is inexperienced to say the least. Armer, a 6-11 junior college transfer from Santa Fe (Fla.) CC is a solid force who can play in the pivot or shift to the power forward spot. A strong rebounder, he set the career blocked shot record at Santa Fe with 120 in one season. The 6-11 Armer and the 7-0 Riley in the lineup at the same time could present a difficult defensive problem for the opposition.

6-9 senior **Chris Seter** (1.1 ppg, 1.6 rpg) may finally get a chance to play this season. Seter has the bulk, but may not have the scoring ability of defensive quickness to challenge for a starting slot. He will be a good complementary role player in Fisher's rotation this season. Sophomore **James Voskuil** (0.9 ppg, 0.8 rpg) is another unproven talent who needs game experience to further develop. Voskuil has a good outside shot and they may get him the call off the bench before his counterpart Seter.

Two excellent freshmen look to vie for the starting forward position. **Rich McIver**, a 6-8 athletic forward from Brazosport HS in Freeport, Tex., may have a legitimate shot at the job. He was the Texas 4A player of the year in 1989-90 when he averaged 20.9 points and pulled down 14.1 rebounds per contest. McIver can shoot the basketball and is a ferocious rebounder. Those characteristics bring to mind Loy Vaught. "He's 6-9, very, very athletic, and pretty much an unknown commodity until last summer when he burst onto the scene with his play in the summer AAU," said Fisher. "He's a young man who's eager to learn and will continue to get better. He's a shot blocker, an inside player, and will be a great addition."

The other freshman player who has a legitimate shot at a starting spot is 6-9 **Sam Mitchell**. A solidly built player, Mitchell was one of the nation's Top 50 players at Loy Norrix HS in Kalamazoo, Mich., two years ago. Last season, Mitchell attended the Brewster Academy in Wolfeboro, N.H. As a senior at Loy Norrix, Mitchell averaged 24.2 points and 15.6 rebounds. Not only can Mitchell play with his back to the basket, but he can also pop out and hit the 10 to 15-foot jumper. "He can play for us as a post player, but the nice thing is that he has a good medium range jump shot. He should be able to fit in nicely with our returning nucleus," Fisher commented.

BLUE RIBBON ANALYSIS

A grand era is now past in Michigan basketball history and Fisher must now begin to mold a team of his own. There is talent on this Michigan club, but most of it is young and inexperienced. Calip looks to have a spot nailed down to start the year. If his scoring doesn't rise, however, sophomore Talley could move into the one guard spot. Talley is an excellent playmaker and is exceptional at working to get his shot. Tolbert looks to also start at the shooting guard spot. He will be counted on to replace the offensive punch Higgins was expected to generate on this team. If Michigan goes with a three-guard offense, Bossard could see some playing time as well as Taylor. Taylor did contribute two years ago on Michigan's national title team but sat out last year with a knee injury. He could be a surprise coming off the bench for Fisher this year. Riley and JC transfer Armer figure to see many minutes in the lineup, whether it is together or on a rotational basis remains to be seen. Most likely, Fisher will let the situation and the opponent dictate which way he goes. The forward spots should be manned by freshmen Mitchell and McIver. Both are powerful rebounders who also have a soft touch around the hoop. They could be future stars.

Michigan has a fairly tough non-conference schedule which is a radical departure from the Frieder days. Michigan will take on Duke on the road, Iowa State and Marquette at home and Texas on the road before they embark on the always tough Big Ten run. With this schedule and the relative inexperience of the Maize and Blue, a .500 record will be a realistic goal for Fisher's crew. Sixth place in the Big Ten should be as far as this team goes. It is a team being rebuilt nearly from scratch that will be heard from again — probably in a year or two.

1990-91 MICHIGAN SCHEDULE		
Nov.	28	Central Michigan
Dec.	1	Utah
	4	Eastern Michigan
	8	@Duke
	10	Boston University
	12	Chicago State
	15	@Iowa State
	22	Marquette
	28-29	#Castus Classic
Jan.	3	@Michigan State
	5	Ohio State
	10	@Iowa
	12	@Purdue
	17	Northwestern
	19	@Wisconsin
	24	Indiana
	26	Illinois
	31	@Minnesota
Feb.	9	Iowa
	11	@Ohio State
	16	@Northwestern
	18	Purdue
	21	Wisconsin

Feb.	24	@Indiana
	28	@Illinois
Mar.	3	Minnesota
	9 or 10	Michigan State

@ Road Games
# Tempe, AZ (Arizona State, Pennsylvania & Texas)

MIDDLE TENNESSEE STATE

**LAST SEASON: 12-16
CONFERENCE RECORD: 5-7
STARTERS LOST: 2
STARTERS RETURNING: 3
CONFERENCE: OHIO VALLEY (OVC)
LOCATION: MURFREESBORO TN
HOME FLOOR: MONTE HALE ARENA (11,520)
NICKNAME: BLUE RAIDERS
COLORS: NAVY BLUE AND WHITE
COACH: BRUCE STEWART, record at Middle Tennesse, 120-67.
Career record, 257-95.**

Last year's record of 12-16 overall and 5-7 in the Ohio Valley Conference was a season of "firsts" for veteran Middle Tennessee State coach Bruce Stewart, but not the kind he would want to claim. Witness the following:

* in 10 years of head coaching at the junior college, NAIA and major college levels, it was Stewart's first losing campaign;

* it was MTSU's first losing record since 1983-84, the year before Stewart took the helm of the Blue Raiders;

* last year's dismal (by MTSU standards) record snapped a string of four straight seasons of 20-plus wins;

* in six seasons at MTSU, it was the first time Stewart's Blue Raiders did not make a national postseason appearance in either the NIT or NCAA tournament; for that matter, it was Stewart's first non-tournament year at any level;

* after a bench-clearing brawl against Tennessee Tech, the Blue Raiders drew the largest suspension in league history, eight players for a total of 22 games.

Stewart was given the option of spreading out the suspensions, but instead chose to get them over with as quickly as possible, resulting in the school's first-ever forfeit and a makeshift lineup for several games. At one point, the roster even included a Dallas Cowboys football player who still had eligibility remaining at his alma mater.

"The suspensions had a great deal to do with the losing record, but it wasn't the only reason," Stewart said. "It just was not the kind of year we are accustomed to, and we have taken steps to make sure it doesn't happen again."

Read that to mean recruiting, and the Blue Raiders had an excellent effort, judged best in the OVC by at least one basketball talent publication. Along with three players who sat out last season, MTSU had a strong enough haul to challenge defending champion Murray State for the 1990-91 crown.

Topping the recruiting effort is 6-7 freshman forward **Jeff Clifton** (Searcy HS/Searcy, Ark.). Listed among the nation's Top 100, Clifton is expected to make an immediate contribution. He averaged 24 points and 11 rebounds his senior season.

The other top newcomers are 6-9, 245-pound sophomore center **Warren Kidd** (Vincent HS/Vincent, Ala.), one of the three Blue Raiders who sat out last season, 6-8, 240-pound junior college transfer **Charles Moore** (Lawson State CC, Ala.) and 6-2 junior guard **Tim Corder** of Murfreesboro, who played at Sullivan (Ky.) JC.

Kidd will give the Blue Raiders some inside muscle they sorely lacked last season, and could battle returning 6-9 junior **Chris Ingram** (10.6 ppg, 5.5 rpg) for the starting center job. Stewart even goes so far as to say that Kidd could become the best player he ever coached.

The two other returning starters are 6-5 sophomore guard **Robert Taylor** (12.8 ppg, 3.2 rpg), and lanky 6-7 junior forward **Quincy Vance** (10.4 ppg, 8.5 rpg). MTSU has no seniors on the team this year, but the six players mentioned give the Raiders a solid nucleus.

Another player who could be a major contributor, if he can learn to control his temper - he touched off the Tech-MTSU fracas - is 6-5 junior guard **Mike Buck** (6.1 ppg, 2.5 rpg). Two years ago, Buck almost single-handedly keyed the Blue Raiders' first-round NCAA tournament upset of Florida State.

Other returnees include steady 6-7 sophomore **David Clark** (5.2 ppg, 3.3 rpg), 6-6 junior **Titus Jackson** (6.1 ppg, 2.5 rpg) and 6-2 junior **Jeff Hunter** (4.3 ppg, 1.4 rpg). Jackson and Hunter may have their playing time cut this year, due to the incoming talent.

MTSU's two other players who sat out last season, in addition to Kidd, are 6-3 sophomore guard **Ramond Davis** (Kingsbury HS/Memphis, Tenn.) and 6-8 sophomore center **John Ruffin** (Butler HS/Augusta, Ga.). Looking for immediate help, Stewart also relied on the junior college route.

One he found has strong family ties to MTSU - 6-3 swingman **Kelvin Hammonds** of Hutchinson (Kan.) JC. His brother, Kerry, starred at Middle several years back and is one of the leading scorers in school history. The younger Hammonds averaged 13 points and four rebounds at Hutchinson after beginning his collegiate career at Minnesota. Another top junior college find was 6-1 guard **Greg Christian** of New Orleans, who averaged 12 points and 11 assists at Howard (Tex.) JC.

Besides the heralded Clifton, MTSU's only other freshman is 6-7 redshirt forward **Jeff Johnson** (McGoavock HS/Nashville, Tenn.), who averaged 10 points and 10 rebounds his senior season.

BLUE RIBBON ANALYSIS

Partially because of the suspensions last year, MTSU was a flop. But the talent level was not up to par, either. The OVC traditionally is a conference won by the team with the best inside talent and muscle, and the Blue Raiders had little. Vance, for instance, had plenty of ability, but was muscled around too easily. With the addition of Kidd, Moore and Clifton, strength should no longer be the question.

The real question is how quickly Stewart can blend the old and new players into a solid fighting (no pun intended) unit. If Stewart can accomplish that task quickly and before the conference race begins, MTSU will challenge Murray State for the OVC crown. A return to at least the league's the upper echelon is a safe forecast.

1990-91 MIDDLE TENNESSEE STATE SCHEDULE

Nov.	23	Mississippi Valley State
	26	Kennesaw College (GA)
	29	@South Carolina State

Dec.	1	@Georgia Southern
	4	Grambling State (LA)
	8	@Memphis State
	13	Belmont College (TN)
	15	@Alcorn State
	20	Georgia Southern
	28-29	#Blade Classic
Jan.	7	Florida International
	9	@Grambling State
	12	Austin Peay
	14	Murray State
	19	@Eastern Kentucky
	21	@Morehead State
	26	Tennessee Tech
	28	Tennessee State
	30	South Carolina State
Feb.	2	@Florida International
	9	@Tennessee State
	11	@Tennessee Tech
	16	Morehead State
	18	Eastern Kentucky
	23	@Murray State
	25	@Austin Peay
Mar.	2, 6-7	##OVC Tournament

@ Road Games
# Toledo, OH (Coppin State, Samford & Toledo)
Site to be announced.

MINNESOTA

**LAST SEASON: 23-9
CONFERENCE RECORD: 11-7
STARTERS LOST: 4
STARTERS RETURNING: 1
CONFERENCE: BIG TEN
LOCATION: MINNEAPOLIS, MN
HOME FLOOR: WILLIAMS ARENA (17,250)
NICKNAME: GOLDEN GOPHERS
COLORS: MAROON AND GOLD
COACH: CLEM HASKINS, record at Minnesota, 61-58.
Career record, 162-131.**

Thaaat Clooose! That close! After thirty-seven and one-half minutes, Minnesota and Georgia Tech were all even in their Southeast Regional final match-up. A trip to the NCAA Final Four and the ultimate comeback for a program once in ruins was that close. Alas, for Gopher fans, this fairytale did not have the desired ending. Georgia Tech went on to Denver while the Maroon and Gold returned to early spring in Minneapolis. In defeat, though, the Minnesota Golden Gophers had reached a new plane, a level the program never before attained. In his fourth year at the helm, Clem Haskins had yielded 23 wins, an impressive run in the NCAA tournament and an NBA lottery selection (Miami Heat) in forward Willie Burton.

While the Gophers have rebounded from the lows of the mid-1980s in a big way, attaining the marks set last season will be a difficult task. Gone are four starters from last year's group who accounted for 64 percent of the Gophers' scoring and 61 percent of their rebounding.

"Defense and rebounding are the areas of our biggest concerns," Haskins said. "Whenever you lose the number of points and rebounds that we lost, it's obvious that some people are going to have to step forward. We have some outstanding basketball players coming back, however, and feel that the level of ability of the freshmen coming in is the best we've ever had."

Replacing Burton, 6-4 guard Melvin Newbern, 6-6 forward Richard Coffey and 6-9 center Jim Shiken

233

janski will be a tall order. Burton was one of the premier players in Gopher history. He finished second on the Minnesota career scoring list with over 1,800 points and ninth in career rebounding with over 700 career caroms. In addition, Newbern finished second on the career assist chart and Coffey placed fourth in total rebounds. These departed seniors scoring and rebounding averages, not to mention their leadership qualities, will be sorely missed. Into this void must step two seniors, **Kevin Lynch** and **Walter Bond**.

Lynch, a 6-5 senior guard, must be the catalyst for this year's team. An honorable mention All-Big Ten selection following last season, Lynch (13.4 ppg, 3.2 assists) returns to the off-guard spot. He is an accurate shooter as evidenced by his 51 percent mark from the field (40 percent from behind the three-point stripe) and 75 percent from the free throw line. Lynch was one of 16 finalists for the USA National Basketball Team that competed at the Goodwill Games in Seattle and the World Championships in Buenos Aires, Argentina. Although Lynch's scoring and rebounding must continue to rise this season, his defensive intensity and his overall court intelligence will be important keys to the success of the young Gophers this season. Lynch showed signs of becoming the leader Clem Haskins was looking for in Minnesota's first round NCAA tournament game last year against UTEP. With the Gophers struggling against the tenacious Miner defense, Lynch stepped up to nail a game high 18 points in the Minnesota 64-61 overtime win. That type of effort will often be needed from Kevin Lynch this year, often.

Bond (10.5 ppg, 4.2 rpg) is a 6-5 slashing forward who looks to be the heir apparent to Burton at the small forward position. Bond started ten games last season, but more frequently was the first man off the bench. For his efforts, Bond's teammates voted him the Minnesota Sixth Man Award at the conclusion of last season. This season Haskins needs Bond to score points. Bond presents a rare inside-outside threat, a soft outside shot as well as the ability to get free underneath for an entry pass.

Replacing the frontcourt trip of Burton, Coffey and Shikenjanski will be a tough task. The threesome combined to start 289 games, score 3,565 points and record over 2,000 rebounds during their careers at Minnesota. While Bond seems a lock to start, the center and power forward positions are as wide open as the entire Big Ten race. 7-0 junior **Bob Martin** looks to get the nod in the pivot, but his commitment and tenacity are still in question. He averaged 2.3 ppg and 2.9 boards per contest off the deep bench. His best effort last season came against Syracuse in the Southeast Regional semifinal. Martin entered the game for the foul-plagued Shikenjanski and scored 10 points, garnered three rebounds and played tough defense against the eventual top NBA draft pick, Derrick Coleman. His offense and defense so frustrated Coleman, the Syracuse strongman actually took a swing at Martin. Martin has shown the ability in spurts, but his play has been often inconsistent. Because of his postseason, Martin should get the job, but whether we see the tough, aggressive Bob Martin or the timid, inconsistent Bob Martin remains to be seen.

If Martin falters, look to Africa-born **Ernest Nzigamasabo** to see playing time in the middle. A transfer student from Burundi, Africa, who played his high school ball at Westonka HS in Mound, Minn., Nzigamasabo was considered by many to be the top recruit in the state during the 1988-89 school year. He is 6-9 and a redshirt freshman who averaged 24.0 ppg and 10.0 rpg as a senior. Nzigamasabo is an exciting player still learning the game who has the potential to evolve into a dominant, powerful center in the next two years. Haskins believes Nzigamasabo has more potential than anyone who has played for him at Minnesota.

Two returning players will get first shot at the vacancy left by Richard Coffey. 6-6 senior **Rob Metcalf** may get a longer look than the rest due to his outstanding shooting touch. Metcalf is an outstanding

athlete who came off the bench to average 1.3 ppg and 1.4 rpg for the Gophers last season. One other possibility at the remaining forward slot is sophomore **Nate Tubbs**. Tubbs, a 6-4 swingman, is known as a supreme defensive specialist. The lightning-quick Tubbs saw limited action last season and averaged 1.0 ppg and 1.3 rpg. In many cases, Tubbs was inserted into a game to apply extra defensive pressure on the opposition's offensive standout. He ballhawked the likes of Steve Smith of Michigan State and Kendall Gill of Illinois. Metcalf and Tubbs present an interesting dilemma: Metcalf is more experienced and can shoot while Tubbs is much quicker and a better defensive player. These two will probably split time early in the year before Haskins decides whether to stick with one player; let the situation dictate who will play or go to one of the youngsters.

One additional sophomore and three freshmen will also view for playing time at a forward position in the Gopher lineup. Sophomore transfer **Dana Jackson** arrives in Minneapolis from San Diego State where he averaged 2.3 points and 3.0 rebounds as a freshman. The 6-8, 220-pound Jackson definitely has the body to bang in the Big Ten and that may rate consideration for playing time alone. If size is a determining factor, 6-8, 225-pound freshman **Randy Carter** may also receive a look from Haskins. Carter, who attended Central High in Memphis, Tenn., averaged 24.4 points with 11.0 rebounds and three blocks per game as a senior.

Freshman **Chad Kolander** arrives in Gold Country with a long list of prep achievements. Minnesota's Mr. Basketball, Minnesota's Naismith Player of the Year and the Gatorade Player of the Year head his impressive list. Kolander led Owatonna (Minn.) HS to a sparkling 66-9 record over his final three seasons. He is a 6-9 leaper who averaged 19.5 ppg, 9.1 rpg and 2.4 blocks per game as a senior. Jackson, Carter and Kolander have outstanding ability. It may be hard for Haskins to keep them on the bench. Finally, redshirt freshman **Robert Roe** will look to add bench support to a talented, young group of forwards. Roe, a 6-7, 200-pound rebounder, attended Haltom HS in Ft. Worth, Tex., where he averaged 19.0 ppg and 11.5 rpg as a senior.

The final open spot in the lineup will be to fill the rather large shoes of point guard Melvin Newbern. Newbern led Minnesota in assists the past three seasons and ended his career 12th on the Gopher career scoring list with 1,224 points. The probable replacement is redshirt freshman **Arriel McDonald**. The 6-2 McDonald came to Minneapolis from Athens Drive HS in Raleigh, N.C., where he averaged 24.0 ppg, six rebounds and nine assists per game as a senior. After sitting out last season, McDonald seems ready to take the reigns from Haskins and direct the Gopher attack. McDonald's playmaking ability and his quickness plus Kevin Lynch's experience, intelligence and shooting range could make for an outstanding backcourt.

Senior point guard **Mario Green** should also see considerable playing time. Green, a steady reserve last season, averaged only 0.7 points, but was looked on more as a defensive replacement. He will again play that role on this Gopher squad.

Two freshmen, **Townsend Orr** and **Jon Laster**, will provide bench depth in the backcourt. Orr, a 6-1 point guard, hails from Thornridge HS in Dalton, Ill. This south suburban Chicago high school is a breeding ground for point guards having spawned Indiana's Quinn Buckner among others. Orr hit on 20.5 ppg as a senior and added 6.5 assists per game while achieving All-Metropolitan Chicago credentials. Shooting guard Laster comes to Minneapolis from Denver's East HS. A three-year starter, the 6-4 Laster scored at a 18.3 ppg clip as a senior and chipped in six boards and six assists per game. Orr and Laster will probably not see much in the way of consistent playing time as the season progresses toward the Big Ten schedule. In time, however, Orr looms as a Big Ten point guard of impact.

BLUE RIBBON ANALYSIS

The Minnesota basketball program, happily, has returned to past glory. In four short years, Haskins has built an impressive program that has the ability to compete in an outstanding conference year after year. The Golden Gophers reached a new high in their long history last season, but lost four starters from that highly successful group.

Only two starting positions seem to be booked. Off-guard Lynch and small forward Bond are solid heady seniors who should and need to have outstanding campaigns for the Gophers to be successful. Junior center Martin remains a major question in the middle. Haskins hopes his fine post-season play last season laid a foundation for consistent improvement. If Martin should falter, Nzigamasabo, the African born transfer, could get a crash course on Big Ten basketball. McDonald will most likely replace Newbern at the point guard spot and should continue to lead an aggressive, up-tempo Gopher attack. At the final forward slot, Metcalf and Tubbs should split time with Tubbs seeing the majority of the time due to his quickness and defensive abilities. Also, look for freshmen Carter and Kolander to see action this season. Both are explosive rebounders with the bodies to withstand the Big Ten wars.

While a third straight NCAA appearance is possible for Minnesota, 17 wins, a sixth place Big Ten finish and an NIT berth seem more realistic. This team has enough quality young talent, however, to again contend for the conference title within two years.

1990-91 MINNESOTA SCHEDULE

Nov.	25	Robert Morris
	27	Augusta College (GA)
Dec.	1	Northern Illinois
	3	@Iowa State
	13	Santa Clara
	15	Oregon State
	20	Cincinnati
	22	@Washington
	29	Virginia
Jan.	5	@Youngstown State
	7	@Wisconsin
	10	@Illinois
	12	Iowa
	17	Purdue
	19	@Michigan State
	24	Ohio State
	26	@Northwestern
	31	Michigan
Feb.	3	Indiana
	10	Illinois
	14	@Iowa
	16	@Purdue
	23	@Ohio State
	25	Michigan State
	28	Northwestern
Mar.	3	@Michigan
	7	@Indiana
	9	Wisconsin

@ Road Games

MISSISSIPPI

LAST SEASON: 13-17
CONFERENCE
RECORD: 8-10
STARTERS LOST: 1
STARTERS
RETURNING 4
CONFERENCE:
SOUTHEASTERN (SEC)
LOCATION:
OXFORD, MS
HOME FLOOR: TAD
SMITH COLISEUM (8,135)
NICKNAME: REBELS
COLORS: CARDINAL RED AND NAVY BLUE
COACH: ED MURPHY, record at Mississippi, 56-62.
Career college record, 200-145.

The University of Mississippi needs to replace only one starter from last year's disappointing 13-17 team.

No problem, you say? Not if the Rebels can find someone who will beg for the ball when every clutch shot is due; who will lead them in scoring, rebounding, assists, steals, three-point goals, field goal percentage, minutes played and free throws; who will rank in the top ten in eight of the nine categories the SEC computes, including first in steals and second (behind only LSU scoring machine Chris Jackson) in scoring.

The replacement would also need to be a consummate team leader, an accomplished Gospel singer and visit orphanages in his spare time. Ole Miss coach Ed Murphy has no illusions. The Rebels do not figure to replace Gerald Glass (24.1 ppg, 7.6 rpg, 121 assists, 70 steals, 30 blocked shots), the 6-5 forward-mostly off guard who became only the 15th player in NCAA history to score 2,000 points and grab 1,000 rebounds. Prior to last season, Glass was named the top college player in America by Dave Heerne's *Basketball Abstract*. He was a first round draft choice of the Minnesota Timberwolves.

"It's just not going to happen," Murphy said. "You don't just hand someone the ball and say 'you're going to get 50 percent better and be Gerald Glass this year.' What you hope for is for everyone to improve 10 percent."

It is not completely out of the question for an Ole Miss team that, even without Glass, will be long on experience with some potential impact players joining the mix. And at least this year's squad will not be carting around the cumbersome baggage of high expectations.

Picked in the pre-season Top 20 in some circles last year, the Glass-led Rebels were assumed to be a lock for their second-ever NCAA tournament appearance. Yet when their star got off to a relatively slow start, the rest of the Rebels followed obediently. Before long, Ole Miss was 0-5 - including losses to Illinois and Arkansas, but also to Division II Metro State - and the season of high promise was shot before it ever got going.

This year, the Rebels will try things without such a clearly defined star system. And Murphy, who admitted last season he may have scheduled too aggressively early on, made sure he did not make the same mistake twice. Mississippi will have a much more user-friendly non-conference slate this time around.

With five seniors back, Murphy has several options on how to begin the post-Glass era. In that group there is some legitimate talent returning, most notably 6-3 senior guard **Tim Jumper** (11.8 ppg, 82 assists, 34 steals), and 6-7 sophomore **Joe Harvell** (13.2 ppg, 5.3 rpg, 45-for-93 on three-pointers). "Jumper," said Murphy, "is probably the key."

The SEC freshman of the year in 1987-88, Jumper is only now fully recovered from a serious knee injury two years ago. He carted around a heavy leg brace for much of his sophomore season, and still was not full speed at the beginning of last year.

Before the injury, Jumper looked to be on his way to becoming one of the league's best players, and may get there yet. Ideally, the Rebels would like to play him at the point, as he did through the final six games last season. In that stretch, Ole Miss went to a bigger lineup and finished 4-2, surprisingly making the finals of the SEC tournament. ("I didn't even bring enough clothes to stay for the finals," Murphy quipped at the time).

"If Jumper hadn't been hurt, my plan all along was to move him to the point," the coach added. "He's smart (pre-law honor student), feisty and tough. But he couldn't play the point dragging that leg brace around."

Jumper averaged 27 points per game in the Jackson (Miss.) summer league and, if he works out as the full-time point man, it could relieve the Rebels of a major headache from last year. A two-man platoon at position brought mixed reviews at best. Both 5-8 senior **John Matthews** (5.6 ppg, 82 assists) and 6-1 senior **David Midlick** (4.6 ppg, 79 assists) had their moments, but Ole Miss was a better team once Jumper took over.

Midlick is a streaky good shooter - he was 33-for-36 from the line - while Matthews is more of a ball handler. 6-4 sophomore **Chuckie Barnes** (1.4 ppg, 1.1 rpg) showed some promise in limited freshman playing time, and 6-5 senior **Greg Jones** (only 12 games) could play a bigger role. Yet Murphy is probably expecting even more help from what easily ranks as his best recruiting class at Mississippi.

"That was one good thing about (last year's) high expectations," said Murhpy. "We parlayed those expectations into a good early recruiting class. I look at who we beat (for players). We've been able to do it on one kid or another, but it's the first time we've been able to get a whole group like this that a lot of people wanted."

Likely to have the earliest and largest impact on the SEC is 6-6 swingman **Stephen Davis** (21.0 ppg, 61 percent from floor, 7.2 rpg, 2.9 assists, 2.1 steals at Corinth HS/Corinth, Miss.). Two-time player of the year in the state, Davis chose the Rebels over Notre Dame, Missouri and Kentucky.
While he could play forward, the best possible scenario would be for Davis to make a home at off guard.

Two other freshmen could also contribute in the backcourt, 6-3 **Dondi Flemister** (Powder Springs HS/Powder Springs, Ga.) and 6-3 **Edmond Fitzgerald** (Newman HS/New Orleans, La.). In the meantime, Harvell, probably Murphy's choicest recruit at Ole Miss (Glass was a transfer from Delta State), will be expected to shoulder much more of a scoring load in his second season.

And if any Rebel can do a plausible Gerald Glass imitation, it might be Harvell, twice Arkansas prep player of the year. He had an up-and-down freshman season, five times scoring over 20 points, three times scoring two or less. But over the last 11 games, he averaged 16.5 points and set an Ole Miss freshman record with 395 points.

Murphy told Harvell before leaving for the summer to concentrate on his offensive game. An all-around athlete, he has the potential to become an All-SEC player at the very least. The Rebels also expect to get more offense from 6-6, 240-pound sophomore **James Bailey** (2.3 ppg, 1.7 rpg), who received increased playing time as last year went on, mainly due to his defense.

More help could also come from another highly-touted freshman, 6-9 **Keith Peel** (16 points, eight rebounds, seven assists at Jessamine County HS/Nicholasville, Ky.). Deeper inside, the development of 6-11 senior **Patrick Eddie** (7.2 ppg, 6.0 rpg, 31 blocked shots) allowed Ole Miss to go to a double-low post with Eddie and the coach's son, 6-11 **Sean Murphy** (5.5 ppg, 6.0 rpg, 47 blocked shots).

Eddie, a transfer from Arkansas State, was not eligible until the seventh game of the season, but emerged as one of the league's better centers over the second half of the year. He can roam outside with a nice, soft touch, and averaged 12.5 points, 11.0 rebounds and 2.5 blocked shots when his role increased. Eddie had his best game (16 points, 13 rebounds) battling LSU's 7-0 twin towers, Shaquille O'Neal and Stanley Roberts.

Murphy, also a senior, has seen his scoring average drop every year and has never really developed into the offensive player many thought he could become. His role diminished somewhat with the development of Eddie, but he remains a hard-nosed, workmanlike player who does not have to apologize for his father putting him in the starting lineup. Murphy even broke the Ole Miss record last year for blocked shots in a season.

6-10 junior **Marc Wilson** (0.8 ppg, 0.9 rpg) also returns, and another possible impact recruit - 7-0 freshman **Wesley Hardin** (Cass HS/Cartersville, Ga.) - will also get a look. Hardin averaged 23 points, nine rebounds and four blocked shots at Cass.

BLUE RIBBON ANALYSIS

Glass was so dominant, the Ole Miss publicity types invented a new statistic for him: "Points Responsible For." It combined scoring with assists, and determined that Glass was "directly responsible for" 42.2 percent of the Rebel's points last season.

Chris Jackson was a distant second in the SEC, responsible for 37.6 percent of LSU's points. No Rebel is likely to approach that figure for this season, which might not be all bad.

A year after Dominique Wilkins left Georgia for the NBA, a group of Bulldog players who had previously caddied for him won the SEC tournament and went to the 1983 Final Four. "The longer we had him, the more we counted on him," Murphy said. Another Mississippi insider said, "the pressure is off now. Last year, everyone was looking at us because of Gerald. That could help us this year."

Thus, the hope in the Rebel camp is that the loss of Glass will be offset by the lack of pre-season expectations. Ole Miss even got a taste of life without him during an 14-day, 10-game August tour of Sweden and Finland, a post-Glass shakedown cruise of which Murphy took full advantage. "I'm going to lie about the scores anyway," he said before leaving. "It really gives us a chance to look at some people and see where we stand."

NCAA rules prohibited the incoming freshmen from making the trip, but at least Murphy got a better understanding of what holes they might fill when pre-season drills began. Basically, Ole Miss needs big years out of Jumper and Harvell, some realistic improvement from the supporting cast, and at least modest input from a promising freshman class.

On paper, the Rebels are part of the logjam in the middle of the SEC pack, any of which, though not likely to challenge Alabama and LSU at the top, could bolt into the first division and be a factor in the race.

1990-91 MISSISSIPPI SCHEDULE		
Nov.	28	Southeastern Louisiana
Nov. 30-		
Dec.	1	#Stetson Hatter Classic
Dec.	3	Northeast Louisiana
	8	Jackson State (MS)
	16	##Arkansas State
	18	Austin Peay
	20	Sam Houston State
	29	@McNeese State
Jan.	3	@Florida
	5	Alabama
	9	Auburn
	12	@Mississippi State
	16	Kentucky
	19	@LSU
	23	@Vanderbilt

MISSISSIPPI VALLEY STATE

LAST SEASON: 11-18
CONFERENCE RECORD: 7-7
STARTERS LOST: 1
STARTERS RETURNING: 4
CONFERENCE: SOUTHWESTERN ATHLETIC (SWAC)
LOCATION: ITTA BENA, MS
HOME FLOOR: HARRISON ATHLETIC COMPLEX (6,500)
NICKNAME: DELTA DEVILS
COLORS: GREEN AND WHITE
COACH: LAFAYETTE STRIBLING, record at Mississippi Valley State, 103-108.

With four starters returning, one of them a true hot-shot, Mississippi Valley State wants to raise its bobbing basketball head to at least the .500 level. And guard **Alphonso Ford** could be just the ticket.

Ford, a 6-1 sophomore, is much more than one of four returning starters. He is an individual force who could make the Delta Devils a team to be reckoned with. Anything would be more palatable than a year ago, when the Devils completed their fourth straight losing season. The only real bright spot, other than the white-hot glow of Ford, was a 7-7 Southwestern Athletic Conference record. But even that modest achievement was good only for a tie for third behind regular season champion Southern University and post-season victor Texas Southern.

The only championship in Itta Bena since the 1986 SWAC title was Ford's narrow victory in the league scoring race. Ford (29.9 ppg, 4.9 rpg, 50 assists, 41 steals) just nipped Alabama State's Steve Rogers (29.7 ppg). He did so mostly by dialing long distance, as witnessed by 104 three-pointers. That alone produced 312 of his Valley freshman record 808 points.

"If (Ford) doesn't come back, I'm not coming back," MVS coach Lafayette Stribling joked. "Seriously, we're so glad he is back with us, but we're hoping we won't have to rely on him quite as much to win games. We want some of the other kids to take up the slack."

At forward, 6-7 sophomore **Derrick Harvey** (13.4 ppg, 4.6 rpg) and 6-5 sophomore **Willie Townsend** (12.5 ppg, 8.2 rpg) both return. They are bolstered by 6-6 senior center **Chequan White** (7.2 ppg, 6.7 rpg).

It is a statistically impressive group, although scoring averages are somewhat misleading in the run-and-gun SWAC.

"These starters," said Stribling, "are probably the best group of four returnees I've had in one season at Valley."

The only starter lost is point guard Reginald Robinson (9.4 ppg, 49 assists). But the point guard is not quite as pivotal in a backcourt featuring the silver bullet of Ford, who creates most of his own opportunities. Still, 6-0 sophomore **James Scott** (eligible after sitting out last year) should be a more than adequate replacement.

Also available at guard are 6-0 sophomore **Mark Clark** (4.2 ppg, 73 assists), along with 6-4 sophomore **Elroy Carey** and 6-4 freshman **Ricky Vance** (Murrah HS/Jackson, Miss.). "We're expecting a lot from James Scott," Stribling said. "Mark Clark could also help us at the point."

Frontcourt reserves include 6-10 sophomore **Phillip Brown** (2.2 ppg, 4.8 rpg), 6-7 sophomore **Keith Bledsoe** (4.2 ppg, 2.2 rpg) and 6-9 junior **Rodney Dillard** (1.8 pg, 1.7 rpg). 6-11 soph **Mark Buford** sat out last year and will watch and try to shake off the rust. 6-6 freshman **Joseph Cooper** (Waynesboro, Miss.) and 6-5 freshman **Thomas Jenkins** (Northwest Rankin HS/Jackson, Miss.) will also compete.

BLUE RIBBON ANALYSIS

Although Stribling has a talented team at Valley, he nominates Southern University and Texas Southern to remain the class of the SWAC. "You've got to," Stribling said. "They've been there before, and they have lots of talent. Our kids are talented, but they haven't played in the NCAA tourney."

They haven't played much defense, either. The Delta Devils were torched for 88.8 points per game a year ago. Improving that stat may be even more important than watching last season's three freshmen starters become sophomores.

Until Ford and friends realize there is more than one end of the court, Valley will not climb much beyond the .500 mark.

MISSOURI

LAST SEASON: 26-6
CONFERENCE RECORD: 12-1
STARTERS LOST: 3
STARTERS RETURNING: 2
CONFERENCE: BIG EIGHT
LOCATION: COLUMBIA, MO
HOME FLOOR: HEARNS CENTER (13,143)
NICKNAME: TIGERS
COLORS: OLD GOLD AND BLACK
COACH: NORM STEWART, record at Missouri, 455-231.
Career record, 552-273.

The 1990-91 Tigers appear destined to go down in college basketball history as one of the most talented teams not to appear in the NCAA tournament. The NCAA was expected to hand down penalties this fall, culminating its 20-month investigation of the Tigers' basketball program. Most observers expect the Tigers to be banned from postseason play this year.

The future of head coach Norm Stewart, the dean of Big Eight Conference coaches, was in doubt because of the 17 allegations of rule violations brought forth by the NCAA. One of those allegations accused Stewart of providing false and misleading information to the NCAA. In addition, Stewart's top assistant coaches —Bob Sundvold and Rich Daly —had their contracts extended only through September, rather than the normal run of April 1 to March 31. Not a good sign for both assistants, who were named in several allegations themselves.

There were transfer rumors involving the Tigers' best players all summer long. 6-4 junior swingman **Anthony Peeler** made some favorable comments concerning Syracuse in the press and it was reported he was even wearing a Syracuse cap around the Missouri campus. At press time Peeler was still in the fold, but 5-11 sophomore point guard Travis Ford (6.4 ppg, 105 assists) finally packed it in in mid-August citing the turmoil surrounding the program as the reason for his departure. He transferred to Kentucky and will have three years of eligibility beginning next season. Ford's exit hurts as he was the only experienced point guard on the Missouri pre-season roster now that Lee Coward (11.2 ppg, 2.6 rpg, 93 assists, 21 steals) has exhausted his eligibility.

The best player on the Missouri roster, 6-10 senior forward/center **Doug Smith**, bypassed the chance to turn pro last May to return for his final season. However, rumors circulated throughout the summer that he may opt for a year in Europe if the Tigers were hit hard by the NCAA. At press time, he was still expected to play for Missouri this season.

The loss of Ford hurts dearly, but Missouri could still be a Top 20 team and is very capable of defending its Big Eight regular season title.

Smith (19.8 ppg, 9.2 rpg, 64 assists, 28 blocks, 44 steals) arguably is the most versatile big man in the college game since Danny Manning. He runs the floor like a guard, cleans the glass like a power forward and posts up like a center. Some combination, right? That array of skills helped make him Big Eight player of the year last season. Although prone to commit silly fouls and occasionally fall into inconsistent play, Smith has refined his game every year at Missouri. If he's not a lottery pick in the next NBA draft, James Naismith didn't invent basketball.

Peeler (16.8 ppg, 5.4 rpg) is a gifted athlete in his own right. The southpaw from Kansas City normally has amazing leaping ability, terrific hang time and great court awareness. Stewart thinks he might be the best passer he's ever had at Missouri —and he's had some good ones over the years such as Larry Drew, Jon Sundvold and last year's point guard, Lee Coward.

Like Smith, Peeler was a first-team all-conference performer last season, when he set a school record for assists (179), tied another record for consecutive free throws made (28), and led the team in steals (63). Trouble is, Missouri fans don't know which Peeler will show up at the start of this season. Will it be the one who averaged 18.8 ppg, and 81.5 percent from the foul line in Missouri's first 26 games? Or the one who averaged 8.5 ppg, 29.5 percent from the field and 47.8 percent from the line in Missouri's final six games?

Smith and Peeler will form the nucleus of the club along with highly touted freshman **Jevon Crudup**, a 6-8 power forward from Raytown South HS (Kansas City, Mo.), who averaged 28.9 points, 14.0 points and four assists as a high school senior. Some Missouri insiders think Crudup was good enough to start last season for the Tigers. He will help keep the pressure off Smith inside and will make it relatively easy for Missouri to get over the loss of 6-9 Nathan Buntin (14.8 ppg, 9.5 rpg), who has completed his eligibility.

Just who will fill out the rest of Missouri's top seven or eight players remains to be seen. Last season, the Tigers went with a three-guard offense that featured Coward, Peeler and John McIntyre (10.4 ppg, 2.8 rpg, 104 assists) on the perimeter (with Ford normally coming off the bench). But with Coward, McIntyre and Ford gone, the Tigers do not have a returning guard on scholarship other than Peeler. So look for Peeler to be more guard than swingman this season.

Teaming with Smith and Crudup up front could be anyone from holdovers **Chris Heller** (2.1 ppg, 1.3 rpg), **Jeff Warren** (2.6 ppg, 2.4 rpg) and **Jamal Coleman** (3.8 ppg, 3.1 rpg) to newcomer **Lamont Frazier**. Heller is a 6-10 sophomore, Warren is a 6-8 sophomore and Coleman a 6-5 junior. Coleman and Warren both averaged 12-13 minutes a game last season and took turns playing the role of the team's seventh man. Heller was highly recruited out of Rockhurst HS in Kansas City, but was held back last season by his lack of strength and aggressiveness, despite having good offensive skills.

Frazier, who is 6-4, could help as a swingman. He led Charleston (Mo.) HS to a 33-0 record and a state title last season, averaged 22.0 points and 12.0 rebounds. Because the Tigers are so thin at guard, freshmen **Melvin Booker** of Moss Point (Miss.) HS and **Reggie Smith** of Socastee HS (Myrtle Beach, S.C.) will get a good look, too. Both were highly recruited for the most part, although the 6-1 Booker posted big numbers at Moss Point (28.4 ppg) and was named Player of the Year in the state by one group. Smith, who is 6-2, averaged 12 assists not to mention 15.9 points at Socastee.

Missouri's only other recruit, 6-7 forward **Derek Dunham** of Jerseyville (Ill.) HS doesn't figure to see much time this year. Ditto for holdovers **Todd Satalowich**, a 6-7 redshirt freshman, **Jim Horton**, a 6-10 junior center, or walk-on **John Burns**, a 6-6 sophomore guard.

BLUE RIBBON ANALYSIS

Because of the NCAA investigation, a cloud of uncertainty remains over the Missouri program. The mid-August defection of sophomore point guard Travis Ford did not add to the stability of the situation. Despite the investigation and the strong possibility of heavy sanctions being levied this fall, and the departure of Ford, Missouri could win the Big Eight title and be a Top 20 team. The Tigers probably have the two best players in the Big Eight in Smith and Peeler. There is no reason to expect that freshman Crudup won't be as good as advertised. If some depth can be developed and one of the freshmen can perform adequately at the point, Missouri will easily be a national factor.

However, the waters were too muddied in Columbia at press time for us to put Missouri in the Top 40. We have never seen a team enter the fall with more uncertainty and controversy hanging overhead. Questions, questions and more questions surround the Missouri Tigers. We will try to provide the latest news in our *Late Breaking News* section.

1990-91 MISSOURI SCHEDULE		
Nov.	27	@Rutgers
	29	Florida A&M
Dec.	1	Oregon
	4	@Creighton
	8	Arkansas
	12	@Bradley
	19	#Illinois
	22	Grambling State (LA)
	27	North Carolina A&T
Jan.	2	Memphis State
	5	Oklahoma State
	9	Prairie View A&M (TX)
	15	Oklahoma
	19	@Kansas
	24	@Colorado
	26	Iowa State
	30	@Nebraska
Feb.	3	Kansas State
	7	@Oklahoma
	12	Kansas
	16	@Oklahoma State
	20	Nebraka
	23	@Iowa State
	27	@Kansas State
Mar.	2	Colorado
	8-10	##Big Eight Tournament

@ Road Games
# St. Louis, MO
Kansas City, MO

MONMOUTH

LAST SEASON: 17-12
CONFERENCE RECORD: 11-5
STARTERS LOST: 1
STARTERS RETURNING: 4
CONFERENCE: NORTHEAST
LOCATION: WEST LONG BRANCH, NJ
HOME FLOOR: ALUMNI MEMORIAL GYM (2,800)
NICKNAME: HAWKS
COLORS: ROYAL BLUE AND WHITE
COACH: WAYNE SZOKE, record at Monmouth, 48-38. Career record, 85-79.

Monmouth County, New Jersey, has always been known as a summer place. For years, thousands of people flock to the beaches for summer relaxation and fun. In the past few seasons, Monmouth College basketball coach Wayne Szoke has made the winter a pretty exciting time down "The Jersey Shore" as well, by turning up the heat on the Hawks basketball opponents.

The Hawks, who finished with a 17-12 record, their best on the Division I level, return four starters from their Northeast Conference finalist team of a year ago. There certainly could be some big doings this year on the beach.

Monmouth's big gun this season will again be 6-7 powerhouse junior **Alex Blackwell** (19.7 ppg, 7.8 rpg). "The Chief" as he is known in the Garden State, was Northeast Conference Newcomer of the Year after sitting out his freshman year, and will certainly continue to improve his dominating game which made him one of the best newcomers in the east last season. Blackwell certainly won't have to get it done alone. 6-5 junior **William "Chill" Lewis** (15.0 ppg, 5.5 rpg) emerged as a nice complement to Blackwell, showing an outside touch (21-of-35 for .600 from three-point range) that freed up the middle for Mr. Blackwell even more. The two also made the most of their offensive efforts, both hitting over 59 percent from the floor. In the middle, 6-9 junior **Alex Sturm** (5.6 ppg, 5.5 rpg) is a defensive force (41 blocks) and will again get help from 6-9 classmate **Jim Keane** (2.0 ppg, 1.3 rpg). **Steve Wriedt**, a 6-11 sophomore transfer from La Salle, could be the sleeper of the group and will certainly contribute as well. 6-6 senior **Harold Mobley** (1.4 ppg) and 6-7 senior **Brian Nymchek** (0.7 ppg) may also see time.

It is in the backcourt where Szoke will have his biggest questions. Their three-point ace, 6-3 senior **Dave Calloway** (14.8 ppg, 97-of-212 treys) is back, as is 6-4 sophomore shooter **Chuck McKay**, who missed all of last season with a knee injury. It is at the distribution end where the Hawks may suffer. Assist leader Brian Kennedy (107) is gone, but so are his team-high 82 turnovers. Still, someone must handle the proverbial rock. If it is not Calloway, sure of hand but slow of foot, it could be unproven 6-1 junior **Andy Partee** (3.7 ppg, 52 assists). Or it could be 6-0 freshman **Steve Ziemian** (6.5 apg at Worcester, Mass., Academy). The most likely candidate is 6-1 freshman **Kevin Rabbitt**, who has the quickness to justify his name. The Overland Park, Kan., import averaged 15 points and seven assists for Shawnee Mission South HS, and led them to the Kansas Class 6A title.

BLUE RIBBON ANALYSIS

If Szoke can get any production from his trio of point guards there will be a lot of winter fun at the beach. If not, it'll be a good year but not a great one. Blackwell is the best in the conference and may draw a look from some All-America committees. Lewis must maintain his pace of last year and Calloway should continue to hit his treys. Wriedt has the body to be a dominating center and complement the bruising Sturm very well, and don't forget about McKay, who has the explosive power to be an All-League performer too. The schedule is tough with trips to tournaments at Alabama-Birmingham and Boise State along with playing St. John's in the Lapchick Tournament opener, but this team is road tough and almost sneaked into the NIT last season. If all goes well, the Hawks should duel Marist for the Northeast title and get 18 to 20 wins in the process.

1990-91 MONMOUTH SCHEDULE		
Nov.	23-24	#Lapchick Tournament
	27	@Army
Dec.	2	@Vermont
	5	Rider
	8	New Hampshire
	11	@Delaware
	14-15	##UAB Tournament
	28-29	*Albertson's Christmas Tournament
Jan.	3	@Fairleigh Dickinson
	8	@Mt. St. Mary's (MD)
	12	St. Francis (PA)
	14	Robert Morris
	17	@St. Francis (NY)
	19	@Long Island
	22	Marist
	28	Fairleigh Dickinson
	31	Wagner (NY)
Feb.	2	@Robert Morris
	4	@St. Francis (PA)
	5	**Marist
	9	Mt. St. Mary's
	14	Long Island
	16	St. Francis (NY)
	23	@Wagner

Feb.	26, 28	
	& Mar. 2	**Northeast Conference
		Tournament

@ Road Games
# Jamaica, NY (Central Connecticut, Davidson & St. John's)
Birmingham, AL (Alabama-Birmingham, Florida A&M & Washington State)
* Boise, ID (Boise State, Georgia Southern & Northeastern)
** Site to be announced.

MONTANA

LAST SEASON: 18-11
CONFERENCE
RECORD: 10-6
STARTERS LOST: 1
STARTERS
RETURNING: 4
CONFERENCE:
BIG SKY
LOCATION:
MISSOULA, MT
HOME FLOOR:
DAHLBERG ARENA
(9,057)
NICKNAME: GRIZZLIES
COLORS: COPPER, SILVER AND GOLD
COACH: STEW MORRILL, record at Montana, 74-44.

Once again, Montana entered the Big Sky Conference post-season tournament as one of the teams to beat. Once again, somebody did. In 1989-90, it was cross-state rival Montana State, this time in the first round.

It has been coach Stew Morrill's four-year legacy of playoff frustration. Morrill buffs and waxes and polishes his team in hopes of an invitation to the big dance, then watches while the Grizzlies turns into pumpkins come playoff time and miss out on the league's automatic NCAA berth.

Last year, it was supposed to be different for the Grizzlies. Going into the playoffs, they had won five straight games by a whopping margin of 18.6 points. Alas, Montana State then ended the Grizzlies' season with the upset that wasn't.

People in these parts have come to expect such collapses from Montana, which has never advanced past the second round of Big Sky post-season play under Morrill. This time around, though, Morrill returns enough talent to put the Grizzlies in position to end all of their post-season madness.

The Grizzlies lose just one starter, 6-6 forward John Reckard (13.0 ppg, 4.8 rpg.), off a very strong team. Back at center **Daren Engellant,** a 6-10, 220-pound junior who averaged 9.9 points on 56-percent field-goal shooting. He was also the Big Sky's leader in blocked shots (50 in 28 games) and fourth in rebounding (7.3 rpg).

Still, he was a disappointment. As a freshman, Engellant raised many eyebrows by averaging 5.9 points and 4.6 rebounds in limited playing time. "Daren Engellent could be one of the premier big men in our conference," Morrill confirmed.

NBA superscout Marty Blake added: "That kid in Montana, Engellant, everybody knows about already. He's got all the tools to be a very fine player, maybe good enough to make 'em forget about (Milwaukee Buck and ex-Grizzlie) Larry Krystkowiak." Suffice it to say Krystkowiak remains legend in Montana. If Engellant reaches his potential, which is tremendous, so will the Griz.

Backing him up is 6-10 senior **Mike Boken** (1.9 ppg, 0.9 rpg), who has a lot of years but little experience under his belt. Also, 6-9 redshirt freshman

Josh Lacheur is available. Like Boken, Lacheur is an unknown quantity.

The forward position is, in a word, loaded. 6-4 senior **Kevin Kearney** (11.8 ppg, 6.1 rpg) was the Grizzlies' MVP and the league's co-newcomer of the year. Kearney shot 54.6 percent from the floor, seventh in the conference. "He should even be improved," said Morrill, "with a year of Division I play under his belt."

A pair of junior college transfers - 6-4 **Devlon Anderson** and 6-4 **Louis Dunbar** (6-4, 180) will battle to start opposite Kearney. A third JUCO, 6-7 **Nate Atchison,** is also in the mix. Anderson was a high scorer (25.0 ppg.) at San Francisco CC, while Dunbar comes by way of Chemeketa (Ore.) CC. Atchison played two years at Carl Sandberg (Ill.) College.

"Devlon and Louis," Morrill said, "will wage an important battle for playing time."

Redshirt 6-6 freshman **Al Brown** (Berkeley, Calif.) and a couple of true freshmen - 6-7 **Matt Kempfert** (Missoula, Mont.) and 6-5 **Anthony Mayfield** (Lafayette, La.) - will likely watch, listen and wait for a chance to contribute this season.

The backcourt features starters 6-4 **Roger Fasting** (9.5 ppg, 2.9 rpg), a junior, and 6-2 junior **Keith Crawford** (3.9 ppg, 2.2 assists), along with part-time starter **Eric Jordan** (4.6 ppg, 4.5 assists), a 6-2 senior. Jordan is the best pure playmaker of the trio, Fasting the purest shooter and Crawford the most versatile and best defender. They form a strong, if unspectacular, threesome. Backing them is 6-2 freshman **Jeremy Lake** (Lambert, Mont.).

If any of the backcourt players should falter - and if the frontcourt turns out to be as well-stocked as it appears on paper - do not be surprised to see either Anderson or Dunbar move to shooting guard.

BLUE RIBBON ANALYSIS

For good reason, Morrill is a well-respected coach in a very good coach's league. He demands discipline from his players, and gets it. He also knows the X's and O's as well as any.

Toss in Engellant, Kearney, Fasting, Anderson and the rest, and Montana has the tools to win the regular-season title. Said Morrill: "I expect this team to be a factor in the Big Sky race, and will be disappointed if we are not a strong team."

With that said, and given Montana's talent in recent years, one wonders why the Grizzlies have not been to the NCAA's. Perhaps Morrill wonders, too, as it remains a touchy subject for him.

Don't be surprised if this is the year Morrill and the Grizzlies win the Big Sky regular-season title, then toss the post-season monkey off their backs by earning a trip to the NCAA's. Of course, no one will be surprised either if the Grizzlies win a regular-season conference championship, then falter again in the first or second round of the playoffs.

1990-91 MONTANA SCHEDULE

Nov.	24	Pacific
	27	@Washington
	Nov. 30-	
	Dec. 1	#Forest Industries Classic XI
Dec.	6	Cal State-Northridge
	9	Wyoming
	12	@U.S. International
	15	Seattle (WA)
	18	@Univ. of Portland
	20	@Oregon
	29	St. Mary's
Jan.	3	Idaho State
	5	Boise State
	10	@Northern Arizona
	12	@Nevada
	17	Idaho
	19	Eastern Washington
	23	Weber State
	26	@Montana State
	31	@Boise State

Feb.	2	@Idaho State
	7	Nevada
	9	Northern Arizona
	14	@Weber State
	23	@Eastern Washington
	25	@Idaho
Mar.	2	Montana State
	7-9	##Big Sky Tournament

@ Road Games
# Missoula, MT (Gonzaga, Southwest Texas State & St. Peter's)
Site to be announced

MONTANA STATE

LAST SEASON: 17-12
CONFERENCE
RECORD: 8-8
STARTERS LOST: 2
STARTERS
RETURNING: 3
CONFERENCE:
BIG SKY
LOCATION: BOZEMAN, MT
HOME FLOOR: WORTHINGTON ARENA (7,848)
NICKNAME: BOBCATS
COLORS: BLUE AND GOLD
COACH: MICK DURHAM, first year at Montana State.

For seven years, Stu Starner toiled and hustled to win 54 percent of his team's Big Sky games (57-48), including a post-season championship in 1985-86 and a regular season title in 1986-87. Ultimately, all the toiling and hustling wore Starner out. Late last season, he asked for and was granted a one-year sabbatical at half-pay.

Saying he was grateful to Montana State, and that he could use to time away from the game to pursue other interests, Starner closed out the season and promptly took the head coaching job at the University of Texas-San Antonio. One wonders if Starner perceives the San Antonio post as the next best thing to a full-blown sabbatical, or if he just had his fill of Bozeman.

In any case, Montana State officials acted swiftly to shed the interim tag from assistant coach Mick Durham's title, and made him the head guy. Durham, a 1979 Montana State grad, was thrilled at the prospect of following in Starner's footsteps.

"I'm excited about the challenges ahead," Durham said. "It's a dream come true to be the head coach at my alma mater." It is difficult to believe Durham is equally excited about the talents of his returning players. None are the dominating type. The Bobcats return three starters - a guard, a forward and a center - with not a star in the bunch.

Up front, undersized 6-6 senior center **Allen Lightfoot** (6.1 ppg, 6.3 rpg) returns to amaze Big Sky fans with an uncanny ability to rebound with little more than good timing and a menacing scowl. **Greg Powell,** a 6-7 senior, has a better shooting touch. Powell (7.9 ppg, 3.6 rpg) should share post duties with Lightfoot, much like they did a year ago.

Statistically, it is a competent center combo. But both so-called big men lack the strength, size and athletic ability to dominate a game. Freshmen **Dwayne Michaels** (Wheaton, Ill.) and **Matt Oyen** (Swink, Colo.), both 6-9, are the future down low.

That leaves **Steve Kunst,** a 6-9 sophomore and occasional starter, as the most talented of the group.

If Kunst (4.2 ppg, 3.2 rpg) develops into the player Durham thinks he can be, Powell and Lightfoot could move to the power forward position, making the Bobcats much more formidable.

Also along the front line, 6-7 **Dave Moritz** is a senior forward who often plays like he wishes he were a shooting guard. Moritz (8.6 ppg, 4.9 rpg) made 34 of 88 three-point goals to finish among the league leaders. Again, if Kunst develops, it would allow Moritz the freedom to roam the perimeter without penalty. Either way, look for Moritz to garner post-season recognition in 1990-91.

Junior college transfers such as 6-6 **Art Menefree** (Southeastern CC/Iowa), 6-5 **Bob Holker** (Ricks JC/Idaho) and 6-7 redshirt freshman **Chris Heriford** (Gardiner, Mont.) all have big numbers on their resume. Along with one true freshman, 6-4 **Robert Belton** (Greeley, Colo.), it should be interesting to see who starts opposite Moritz.

Here at small forward, the loss of graduated Brian Elve (13.2 ppg, 5.2 rpg) is felt most. Elve was a first-team All-Big Sky player and will be difficult to replace.

Guard **Todd Dickson**, a feisty 6-4 junior, was the guy opposing fans loved to hate. His red hair matched a fiery disposition. His statistics (8.1 ppg, 3.6 rpg) were decent. **Johnny Mack,** a gifted 6-2 sophomore, should start opposite Dickson. Mack (5.5 ppg, 1.4 assists) flashed tiny numbers but great promise. He has the shot and the moves to become a high scorer in the Big Sky, given enough minutes.

Junior transfer **Johnny Perkins** (6-0, Iowa Lakes CC), along with freshmen **Kwesi Coleman** (6-3, Detroit, Mich.) and **Ty Elkin** (6-2, Red Lodge, Mont.) will battle for available supporting roles in the backcourt.

BLUE RIBBON ANALYSIS

The Bobcats have several competent players - namely Dickson, Moritz and Mack - but Kunst remains the key. If he can develop as an inside threat, Moritz can look for his outside shot and Lightfoot and Powell can play power forward, where their talents would be better suited.

If not, Montana State will be closer to a .500 team. The Bobcats open with six of their first nine games on the road. Usually, these early-season jaunts bring teams together, almost out of necessity.

Should the Bobcats mesh, and Kunst develop as a low post player, another 17-12 season is not out of the question. In any case, Montana State fans can rest easy knowing Durham will not be seeking a sabbatical to pursue "other interests." His only interest is a berth and subsequent championship in the Big Sky post-season tournament.

1990-91 MONTANA STATE SCHEDULE		
Nov.	23-24	#Sun Met Classic
	28	Rocky Mountain College (MT)
Dec.	1	@Texas Southern
	3	@Appalachian State
	8	Cal State-Northridge
	19	@Southern Utah State
	22	@Arizona State
	28	Appalachian State
	29	Texas Southern
Jan.	3	Boise State
	5	Idaho State
	10	@Nevada
	12	@Northern Arizona
	17	Eastern Washington
	19	Idaho
	25	Weber State
	26	Montana
	31	@Weber State
Feb.	1	@Idaho State
	7	Northern Arizona
	9	Nevada
	16	@Boise State
	21	@Eastern Washington
	24	@Idaho

1990-91 MONTANA STATE SCHEDULE Cont.		
Feb.	27	Southern Utah State
Mar.	2	@Montana
	7-9	##Big Sky Tournament

@ Road Games
# Fresno, CA (Fresno State, Pepperdine & U.S. International)
Site to be announced

MOREHEAD STATE

LAST SEASON: 16-13
CONFERENCE RECORD: 7-5
STARTERS LOST: 3
STARTERS RETURNING: 2
CONFERENCE: OHIO VALLEY (OVC)
LOCATION: MOREHEAD, KY
HOME FLOOR: ELLIS JOHNSON ARENA (6,500)
NICKNAME: EAGLES
COLORS: BLUE AND YELLOW
COACH: TOMMY GAITHER, record at Morehead State, 36-51.
Career record, 106-97.

Just as Morehead State's struggling basketball program was beginning to turn the corner under fourth-year coach Tommy Gaither, the Eagles must now take a step backward. With the graduation of three key players, the team is rebuilding all over again. But there is at least some good news: the front line is mostly intact, and there is definite talent to build upon.

"Just when we got a taste of what winning is like, we're having to start over," Gaither said. "We've slowly built a winning program, and last year was the most wins since 1983-84 (25-6). But I think we've got a good chance for success this season. We're going to have to see how the chemistry fits in, how quickly we can come together as a unit. Then we are going to have to prove it all over again."

Morehead will put its best foot forward with forwards **Brett Roberts** (14.1 ppg, 9.1 rpg), a 6-8 junior, and **Doug Bentz** (9.9 ppg, 6.5 rpg, 21 blocked shots), a 6-9 junior. Both have been starters since they were freshmen.

Three other insiders give Morehead one of the OVC's strongest front lines. They include 7-0 freshman **David Derozier** (Labarth Lede/Toulouse, France), 6-8 returning junior **Vic Gainer** (3.4 ppg, 1.9 rpg) and 6-9 senior **Rod Mitchell**, eligible following a transfer from Clemson, where he also played football.

"We've got five solid post men. We're very strong inside," said Gaither. "Roberts and Bentz give us the experience. Gainer is a dependable role player, and Mitchell is a great athlete. He's really a man." And what about Derozier, a redshirt freshman playing in a league where seven-footers are scarce? "He's the hardest-working seven-footer I've ever been around," Gaither said. "He has worked hard in the off-season to improve himself and he eventually will be a fine, fine player."

It might seem wise to take advantage of all this available inside talent and go with a one-guard offense, but Gaither is quick to dismiss the notion. "In our scheme of play," he said, "we go with two guards, two quick wings and a post player. You can't run the ball when you've got too many big men in there. We will certainly be deep, though."

Morehead has plenty of quick, if unproven guards, led by 6-5 junior **Brian Miller** (9.0 ppg, 3.2 rpg), along with 6-3 sophomore **Greg Wheeler** (0.9 ppg, 0.3 rpg), and 6-7 sophomore **P.J. Nichols** (3.2 ppg, 1.0 rpg). "Nichols," said the coach, "has an NBA-range three-point shot. He's one of the best in the OVC."

Point guard is the big question facing Morehead, since there is not much experience there. 6-0 sophomore **Pat Tubbs** (1.3 ppg, 0.5 rpg, 21 assists) was the backup to playmaker Tracy Armstrong last year and probably will start. Also in the running are 6-1 redshirt freshman **Denny Riffe** (back surgery) and Kent State transfer **Mitch Sowards.** "How these players perform will be the key for us," Gaither said.

If the returnees cannot fill the bill at guard, there are a couple of newcomers who just might do the job. One is 6-0 freshman point man **Mike Helton** (Fairview HS/Ashland, Ky.). Two other freshman signees will provide depth, probably on the wing: 6-5 **Damon Miller** (Eau Claire HS/Columbia, S.C.) and 6-5 **Reese Turner** (Lantana, Fla.).

"With three players gone from last year," said Gaither, "some of these guys will just have to pick up the slack."

BLUE RIBBON ANALYSIS

If it's what's up front that counts, Morehead State will be a contender for one of the top spots in the OVC. Unfortunately for the Eagles, it will take more than frontcourt depth to replace starters Elbert Boyd (19.2 ppg, 6.7 rpg), Tracy Armstrong (12.5 ppg, 125 assists) and Keith Malone (6.4 ppg, 3.0 rpg). Morehead must replace their consistency on the perimeter to really contend.

Overall, the Eagles are likely to sink back below .500 while rebuilding their backcourt and wing positions. There are too many new faces for this group to be a winner right away.

1990-91 MOREHEAD STATE SCHEDULE		
Nov.	24	West Virginia State
	26	Maryland-Eastern Shore
	29	Northeastern Illinois
Dec.	1	@Dayton
	3	Brescia College (KY)
	8	@Maryland-Eastern Shore
	15	@Southern Utah State
	19	@Utah
Jan.	2	Alcorn State
	5	Wisconsin-Milwaukee
	8	Eastern Kentucky
	12	@Tennessee State
	14	@Tennessee Tech
	17	@Northeastern Illinois
	21	Middle Tennessee State
	24	Southern Utah State
	26	Murray State
	28	Austin Peay
	30	@Mississippi Valley State
Feb.	4	@Eastern Kentucky
	6	Liberty University (VA)
	9	@Austin Peay
	11	@Murray State
	16	@Middle Tennessee State
	20	@Youngstown State
	23	Tennessee Tech
	25	Tennessee State
Feb. 28, Mar.	2-3	#OVC Tournament

@ Road Games
# Site to be announced.

239

MURRAY STATE

LAST SEASON: 21-9
CONFERENCE RECORD: 10-2
STARTERS LOST: 1
STARTERS RETURNING: 4
CONFERENCE: OHIO VALLEY (OVC)
LOCATION: MURRAY, KY
HOME FLOOR: RACER ARENA (5,500)
NICKNAME: RACERS
COLORS: NAVY BLUE AND GOLD
COACH: STEVE NEWTON, record at Murray State, 92-56.

Can you say dynasty? Murray State fans can at least dream the impossible. Since Steve Newton took the reins of the Racers' program, Murray has been one of the OVC's strongest and most consistent teams. How consistent? How about three straight league championships, including two outright, and three straight post-season appearances? And they clearly are the pre-season pick for the 1990-91 crown, after last year's ultra-successful - and ultra-surprising - conference championship.

"I sure hate to hear we're the favorite. I'd much rather be picked fifth again, like we were last year," Newton said, laughingly. And he can afford a laugh or two. His team laughed all the way to the NCAA tournament last year, where the 16th-seeded Racers dragged top-seeded Michigan State into overtime before falling in a first-round game.

Murray's outstanding season was a total surprise to OVC observers, as the Racers had lost a combined 56 points per game with the graduation of Jeff Martin and Don Mann the previous year. But no one counted on a young man named Popeye, who indeed proved strong to the finish.

Ron "Popeye" Jones, now a 6-8 junior center, dropped some 60 pounds in between the end of the 1988-89 season and the start of the 1989-90 campaign. And, in doing so, the 225-pound Jones went all the way from a 20-minute reserve to the 1990 OVC player of the year. He led the league in rebounding with an 11.2 average, and his 19.5 scoring average was fourth-best in the conference.

"Ron is a prime example of how we run our system," said Newton. "A lot of the credit goes to our staff, which saw Ron's potential and was able to help him develop into a complete player. Hopefully, his best years are ahead of him. Ron is becoming a very consistent role model for us, but he needs to improve his strength and durability."

Jones did not lead the Racers to the OVC crown single-handedly, and he won't have to go it alone this year, either, as three other starters also return. But the one missing cog - power forward Chris Ogden - may very well be the missing link this season if the Racers do not repeat as anticipated.

"We lost Chris Ogden, who played a very vital role for us," said Newton. "Besides his scoring and rebounding (11.8 ppg, 7.4 rpg), Chris was the team leader and the glue that kept everybody together on the court. We will miss him."

Ogden's replacement likely will be either fifth-year 6-7 senior **Doug Gold,** or 6-4 senior **Donald Overstreet** (1.2 ppg, 0.6 rpg). The other forward spot is manned by capable 6-2 senior **Greg Coble,** who hit the big shot against Michigan State in the NCAA tourney that sent the game into overtime. Coble averaged 9.7 points for the season, but 13.5 in conference play.

The Racers have both starting guards back, a twosome which probably ranks as the steadiest in the OVC. 6-2 sophomore **Frankie Allen** (14.6 ppg, 109 assists, OVC-leading 86.8 percent free throw shooting) is at the point, while 6-4 senior **Paul King** (10.8 ppg) is expected to take Ogden's role as team leader. Between them, King and Allen must continue to draw some of the heat off Jones underneath. "Allen became more of a leader at his position and became very effective for us last year," said Newton, "and Paul will serve as captain, so he is invaluable."

There is no easy way to get to Murray State, except perhaps by helicopter. But that hasn't kept Newton's staff from bringing in top talent year in and year out. His lastest recruiting effort is exceptionally strong, leading one to think the Racers' dominance of OVC is not about to end.

Murray's top prospect is Kentucky all-stater **Cedric Gumm** (25 points, six assists), a 6-1 point guard from Warren Central High in Bowling Green. From Spartanburg (S.C.) High is 6-7 forward **Jerry Wilson** (19 points, eight rebounds), who was the leading scorer in the North Carolina-South Carolina all-star game.

The two freshmen are joined by three junior college standouts, plus 6-2 Western Kentucky transfer **Terry Birdsong** (eligible in December) and 6-3 sophomore guard **Mitch Cothran,** a medical redshirt last year. The JC signees are 6-9 **Scott Adams** from Louisburg (N.C.) JC, 6-6 forward **John Jackson** of John A. Logan (Ill.) JC and 6-4 forward **David Johnson** from Mississippi County (Ark.) CC.

BLUE RIBBON ANALYSIS

The last three seasons (62-29, three league titles, two NCAA trips, one NIT appearance) are a tough act to follow, but the 1990-91 team should be up to the task of keeping the Racers' ball rolling. While not overwhelmingly better than what should be an extremely balanced league, Murray State has just enough to make it four in a row. The biggest question may be what kind of seeding the Racers get from the NCAA tournament committee, chaired by former OVC and current Big Ten commissioner Jim Delany.

Assuming Murray State gets that far, it will again be on the shoulders of Popeye Jones. Even without Ogden beside him, Jones will be the human wrecking ball of the Ohio Valley Conference. Always powerful, Popeye was surprising athletic during his breakthrough season. Along with King, he may also need to assume a leadership role.

A word of caution, though: if the Racers look too far ahead, an Eastern Kentucky, Austin Peay or Middle Tennessee State just might creep up and swipe the Racers' invitation to the big dance.

1990-91 MURRAY STATE SCHEDULE		
Nov.	21-23	#San Juan Shootout
	28	Georgia Southern
Dec.	1	Western Kentucky
	4	@Memphis State
	7-8	##Citizens Bank Classic
	15	@Southern Illinois
	17	Prairie View A&M (TX)
	21-22	###US Air Classic
	28-29	*BMA Holiday Classic
Jan.	2	North Alabama
	5	Austin Peay
	8	@Georgia State
	12	Indiana-Purdue
	14	@Middle Tennessee State
	19	Tennessee State
	21	Tennessee Tech
	26	@Morehead State
	28	@Eastern Kentucky
Feb.	2	@Austin Peay
	4	@Prairie View A&M
	9	Eastern Kentucky
	11	Morehead State
	16	@Tennessee Tech
	18	@Tennessee State

1990-91 MURRAY STATE SCHEDULE Cont.		
Feb.	23	Middle Tennessee State
Feb.	28-	
Mar.	2-3	**OVC Tournament

@ Road Games
# San Juan, PR (American University of Puerto Rico, Bucknell, Illinois, Nebraska, Northern Iowa, Old Dominion & St. Louis)
Jonesboro, AR (Arkansas State, Oral Roberts & Texas Southern)
Dayton, OH (Stephen F. Austin, U.S. International & Wright State)
* Kansas City, MO (Kansas State, Texas A&M & South Florida)
** Site to be announced

NAVY

LAST SEASON: 5-23
CONFERENCE RECORD: 4-10
STARTERS LOST: 0
STARTERS RETURNING: 5
CONFERENCE: COLONIAL ATHLETIC ASSOCIATION (CAA)
LOCATION: ANNAPOLIS, MD
HOME FLOOR: HALSEY FIELDHOUSE (5,000)
NICKNAME: MIDSHIPMEN
COLORS: NAVY BLUE & GOLD
COACH: PETE HERRMANN, record at Navy, 49-67.

Navy basketball. Mention that to the average college basketball fan and visions of David Robinson and coach Paul Evans immediately come to mind. However, all that is past history. Almost as long past in basketball terms as the War of 1812 is in Naval lore. Anyone who wants to study the impact one player can have on a program should look no further than Annapolis. Robinson led the Midshipmen out of the basketball obscurity and into the Final Eight in '86-87. Pete Herrmann's squads have sank slowly and steadily since, finally drifting well below the surface with last season's 5-23 campaign, capped off with the Midshipmen's first loss to the dreaded Black Knights of the Hudson since the late '70s. But things should be getting a little better for Navy in the next few seasons. Herrmann has the most experienced squad at the Academy since '86-87 and they will be leaving the ultra-competitive CAA for the new Patriot League after this season, a move which should bring a few more W's to Halsey Fieldhouse.

That's in the future. Now all the fiesty Herrmann has to do is survive this season, and he has an experienced group to help him make it through. Leading the returnees is 6-6 senior forward **Eddie Reddick** (12.8 ppg, 8.2 rpg). The Midshipmen's captain has done a yeoman's job on the boards against much taller opponents and has the desire and the drive to continue his steady and solid improvement which made him a second-team CAA pick last year. His steady play on both boards will be a big factor in Navy's success. Two other frontcourt players who have benefitted by extended underclass playing time are 6-8 junior forward **Sam Cook** (9.5 ppg, 6.5 rpg) and 6-9 junior center **Nick Marusich** (6.6 ppg, 4.5 rpg). Cook enters the season as Navy's second-leading rebounder and may be Navy's most improved player over his first two seasons, while the burly Marusich should continue to improve on his offensive game after leading the team in field goal percentage (.619) as a sophomore. The two should be a big help on the boards to complement Reddick much more than at any point in his first three seasons. Four sophomores, 6-9 center **Robert Catten** (0.3 ppg, 0.5 rpg), 6-7 **Chris Mang** (0.8 ppg, 0.5 rpg), 6-8 **Larry Parker** (0.3 ppg, 0.0 rpg) and 6-5 **Chuck Robinson** (6.5 ppg, 4.1 rpg) will also see much more playing time. Out of that quartet the key will be Robinson, a smaller version of his older brother, David, who did not disappoint with his great athletic ability during his plebe campaign. More consistent play and a better shooting touch (just 40 percent last year) will be a welcome addition to the attack. Two freshmen, 6-8 **Brad Cougher** (18.0 ppg at Kellogg, Idaho, HS) and 6-7 **Pepper Day** (15.5 ppg at Seattle, Wash., Garfield HS) round out the frontcourt.

Despite the wealth of experience up front, it should be the senior backcourt of 6-2 **Joe Gottschalk** (7.3 ppg, 1.3 rpg) and 6-1 **Erik Harris** (12.9 ppg, 2.0 rpg) that will key Navy's season. Gottschalk has been somewhat of a disappointment since being named to the All-CAA rookie team two seasons ago, and must improve on his 38 percent from the floor in order to free up the inside game. Harris led the team in scoring and assists (140) last year, and will once again be the team floor leader. After those two, Herrmann will look to 6-6 senior swingman **Doug Fee** (5.5 ppg, 2.2 rpg) to increase his scoring range (31-of-72 of his treys last year), and 6-3 sophomore **Michael Burd** (4.3 ppg) to add some much needed depth. 6-3 sophomore **Lance Reinhard** (1.1 ppg) will look to spell Harris at the point, with often injured junior **Corey Bell**, 6-4 sophomore **John Haas** (1.4 ppg) and 6-3 freshman **Victor Mickle** (18.0 ppg at Newport News, Va., Denbigh HS) battling for minutes as well.

BLUE RIBBON ANALYSIS

Herrmann has gone the distance playing his own version of "Raw Recruits" the past three years, and the record has shown it. Now his work should pay some form of dividend. Reddick, Cook and Marusich have come along according to plan and Robinson is developing very nicely. Harris can run the show. The big questions are at shooting guard, where someone must step up if Gottschalk fails again, and at the free throw line, where Navy hit only 47 percent of their shots last year. This team is road tough and will be tested again with eight games away from home to start, but they are a much stronger team than in recent years.

The league schedule will again be a killer and getting out of the basement will be a big step, although it probably won't happen. More likely eight to eleven wins and an upset or two along the way will help Herrmann silence some of his critics. He has plugged some of the holes in what was a very leaky ship, and sailing out of the CAA after this year will make the Midshipmen hoops future quite a bit brighter.

1990-91 NAVY SCHEDULE

Nov.	24	@Fordham
	26	Mt. St. Mary's
Nov. 30-Dec. 1		#Mazda Gator Bowl
Dec.	5	@Towson State
	7	@Pennsylvania
	9	@Hofstra (NY)
	28-29	##Blue Angels Classic
Jan.	2	Lafayette
	5	East Carolina
	7	North Carolina Wilmington
	12	@William & Mary
	14	Loyola College
	16	Richmond
	19	@George Mason
	23	James Madison
	26	@American University
	28	Delaware
Feb.	2	@North Carolina Wilmington
	4	@East Carolina
	9	William & Mary
	11	American University
	13	@Richmond
	16	George Mason
	19	@James Madison
	23	Army
Mar.	2-4	*CAA Tournament

@ Road Games
# Jacksonville, FL (Cleveland State, Colorado State & Jacksonville)
Pensacola, FL (Alabama, North Carolina Charlotte & Towson State)
* Richmond, VA

NEBRASKA

LAST SEASON: 10-18
CONFERENCE RECORD: 3-11
STARTERS LOST: 1
STARTERS RETURNING: 4
CONFERENCE: BIG EIGHT
LOCATION: LINCOLN, NE
HOME FLOOR: BOB DEVANEY SPORTS CENTER (14,478)
NICKNAME: CORNHUSKERS
COLORS: SCARLET AND CREAM
COACH: DANNY NEE, record at Nebraska, 61-64. Career record, 168-131.

Are we imagining things, or does Nebraska seem to hold a talent search every year for a point guard? "Tell me about it," coach Danny Nee said last spring. "That's why I'm biting my lip."

He was biting his lip because between junior college transfer **Jose Ramos** and high school recruit Jamar Johnson, Nee thought he finally had solved the problem. The Cornhuskers haven't had a quality point guard since Brian Carr in 1986-87. Since then, Nee has tried to convert a series of players more suited to the off-guard spot to the point: first Henry T. Buchanan, then Eric Johnson, then **Clifford Scales**. "And they all have done a reasonable job," Nee said. "But getting a kid that's played it his whole life I think would be better. I'd feel better about it."

He felt better about it, that is, until the summer. Jamar Johnson, an all-stater who led Concord HS (Elkhart) to the Indiana state title game, fell short academically. Ramos, a 6-2 junior and a former high school All-America who was considered one of the nation's top junior college prospects at point guard, was ruled ineligible for the first ten games of this season by the NCAA. Coming out of Miami (Fla.) Senior HS, Ramos started 10 games for the Florida Gators as a college freshman. According to the NCAA, he shouldn't have been eligible for those games because of questionable college board exams. Unfortunately for the 'Huskers, they're the ones who must suffer the brunt of the penalty, not Florida. Ramos, by the way, had a falling out with then Gators coach Norm Sloan and left for Central Florida JC where he averaged 16.2 ppg and 6.4 apg last season. When Ramos does return, Nee will need a tight rein to guard against his tendency to, at times, play out of control.

Without Ramos and Johnson, who can play either guard spot, a Nebraska offense that has seemed to lack focus in recent years may be found lacking once again. At least until Ramos regains his eligibility around Christmas. All in all, it was not the kind of off-season news Nee needed. After going 21-12 and finishing third in the NIT in '86-87, his first season at Nebraska, Nee's 'Huskers have fallen upon hard times. In the three years since then, they have had two losing seasons —the schools first since '72-73 —and have won only 11 of 42 conference games. Despite the dip, Nebraska fans and the administration have remained patient with the affable Nee, a Vietnam vet who was a high school teammate of Kareem Abdul-Jabbar, and then became part of Al McGuire's first recruiting class at Marquette.

Will that patience be rewarded this season? Nee does have one of his more experienced Nebraska teams, with four players returning who started 11 or more games and eight players back who are juniors and seniors. One of those veterans is Scales (12..2 ppg, 4.2 apg), who probably will handle the point guard chores until Ramos returns. Scales suffered a broken foot in April, but is expected to be 100 percent this season. He's shown versatility at both off-guard and

small forward where he seems infinitely more comfortable than at point guard on the occasion he's been called to play there. His career game came against LSU two seasons back with 24 points and 13 rebounds. Senior **Keith Moody** (4.7 ppg) is a capable backup at the point. But without Ramos and Johnson, the 'Huskers are short on manpower in the backcourt. Who, for instance, will start at off-guard until Ramos returns? It could be **Chris Cresswell** (4.8 ppg), a 6-4 junior who is the team's top returning three-point shooter. To say Cresswell is a three-point specialist would be an understatement. All but 15 of the 126 points scored last season by the former California-Irvine transfer came on threes.

Another off-guard possibility is **Beau Reid**, a 6-7 senior who has spent most of his college career as a forward. Reid's junior season was a nightmare. Coming off major knee surgery, he tried to play before the knee was ready and at times looked pathetic. He played only eight games. Reid, whose career average entering last season was 10.2 ppg, is said to be healthy. And a healthy Reid could help somewhere on the court. Two other possibilities in the guard equation are 6-4 sophomore **Jamie Cole** and 6-0 freshman **Mario McIntosh**. Cole sat out last season and also underwent major knee surgery in January after suffering an injury in an intramural game. McIntosh is the only other member of Nee's recruiting class besides Ramos and Johnson. As a high school senior, he averaged 14.5 points per game at Benet Academy in Lisle, Ill.

Inside, the 'Huskers will be one of the tallest teams in the nation. At center, there is 7-2 senior **Rich King** (16.1 ppg, 7.4 rpg). King, from nearby Omaha, never has become the franchise player some Nebraskans hoped for, but he has improved steadily since signing with the 'Huskers and is considered an NBA prospect. He led Nebraska in scoring, rebounding, field goal percentage (55.7) and blocked shots (45) last season. King has an adequate backup in 7-0 junior **Kelly Lively**.

The starting forwards probably will be 6-10 junior **Tony Farmer** and 6-8 junior **Carl Hayes** (12.1 ppg, 4.9 rpg), with 6-8 **Dapreis Owens** (8.4 ppg, 4.4 rpg) off the bench. Farmer is a transfer from San Jose State who sat out last season. Hayes was one of the leagues most impressive newcomers last season. He's an athletic type who is well suited to the transition game and could step up to become one of the leagues better players this season. If Nee wants a smaller look up front, he may go to a pair of redshirt freshmen —6-7 **Bruce Chubick** and 6-6 **Eric Platkowski**. Both will bid for playing time. Chubick was Gatorade player of the year for Nebraska coming out of West Holt HS in Atkinson. Platkowski was Mr. Basketball in South Dakota at Stevens HS in Rapid City.

BLUE RIBBON ANALYSIS

This team has been talented in recent years. It is puzzling why the Cornhuskers haven't done better. But the point guard situation has hurt and the Big Eight has never been stronger from top to bottom than it has been in the last five years. This is not the best time in league history to try to move up in the standings.

If King and Hayes have big seasons, and if the team as a whole discovers how to play defense, Nebraska could finish as high as fifth. The Cornhuskers gave up more than 86.1 ppg last season. Scales needs to hold the fort at point guard until Ramos becomes eligible. When that happens, he needs to get in right away without disrupting the team's chemistry. Ramos could be the key to the entire season. Without him until Christmas, and without Jamar Johnson all season, the Cornhuskers may find it tough to avoid finishing seventh for the fourth straight season.

241

1990-91 NEBRASKA SCHEDULE

Nov.	23-25	#San Juan Shootout
	28	Michigan State
Dec.	3	@Eastern Illinois
	6	Creighton
	8	Toledo
	11	@Wisconsin
	14-15	##Ameritas Classic
	22	Miami (OH)
	28	Idaho
	30	@The Citadel
Jan.	2	@Wisconsin-Greenbay
	5	@Kansas State
	9	@Missouri-Kansas City
	12	Iowa State
	22	@Colorado
	26	@Oklahoma
	30	Missouri
Feb.	2	Oklahoma State
	6	@Kansas
	9	Colorado
	13	@Iowa State
	16	Oklahoma
	18	Northern Illinois
	20	@Missouri
	23	Kansas State
	27	@Oklahoma State
Mar.	3	Kansas
	8-10	*Big Eight Tournament

@ Road Games
# San Juan, PR (American University of Puerto Rico, Bucknell, Illinois, Murray State, Northern Iowa, Old Dominion & St. Louis)
Lincoln, NE (Alabama State, Bowling Green & Tennessee Tech)
* Kansas City, MO

NEVADA

LAST SEASON: 15-13
CONFERENCE RECORD: 9-7
STARTERS LOST: 2
STARTERS RETURNING: 3
CONFERENCE: BIG SKY
LOCATION: RENO, NV
HOME FLOOR: LAWLOR SPECIAL EVENTS CENTER (11,200)
NICKNAME: WOLF PACK
COLORS: BLUE AND SILVER
COACH: LEN STEVENS, record at Nevada, is 46-38. Career record, 147-149.

The biggest news out of the University of Nevada this year - aside from the fact that it has officially dropped the ''hyphen-Reno'' from its name - is an increased emphasis on academics. The move was an isolated one, however, and quite costly.

Leading scorer Kevin Franklin, a 6-3 offensive machine from Los Angeles, will sit out his junior season to concentrate on academics. For long stretches last year, Franklin (19.2 ppg, 3.9 rpg) was one of the purest talents in the entire Big Sky, let alone Nevada. He scored 48 points, including eight three-pointers, versus Loyola Marymount in November. He scored 32 points in the second half and overtime to finish with 40 in a two-point victory over Eastern Washington in late January.

Two days later, Franklin left the team when his mother passed away. When he rejoined the Wolf Pack, things never were quite the same. First, his field goal attempts dropped, then his playing time. Ultimately, he was no longer a key cog in coach Len Stevens'

game plan. Franklin's name was also conspicuously absent from the coach's pre-season comments, but forgetting about him will not make the loss disappear.

6-9 forward Jon Baer (11.2 ppg, 8.0 rpg) is also gone, but did manage to make Stevens' pre-season assessment. Baer, who graduated as a first-time All-Big Sky performer, brought a number of positives to the Wolf Pack, not the least of which was his ability to run the floor. Bear was often seen beating daydreaming guards downcourt for easy layups.

Still, even without Franklin and Baer, the Wolf Pack have enough weapons to challenge for the league title. The list begins with honorable mention All-Big Sky players **Matt Williams** (11.8 ppg, 4.2 rpg) and **Ric Herrin** (9.8 ppg, 5.7 rpg.)

Williams, a soft-spoken 6-3 forward, is the quiet leader of this team. Should his senior season exceed last year's fine effort, the Wolf Pack will finish at or near the top. Herrin, amazingly mature as a freshman, played the pivot like he owned it. And, at 6-10, 240, few challenged the issue.

Joining this duo on the front line are forwards **Jarrod Sigsby**, a 6-8 senior, and 6-5 **Gary Scott**, a junior. Sigsby (3.8 ppg, 2.8 rpg) showed a knack for making big plays; Scott (5.6 ppg, 2.6 rpg) displayed more raw talent. 6-8 sophomore **Matt Hankinson**, a redshirt last year, will be hard pressed to start, although Stevens likes him.

''We feel Matt has all the tools to step right in,'' Stevens said. ''He was very impressive last year, watching him work during his redshirt season.''

Battling Herrin for the starting center position will be **Dan Lomas**, a 6-10 junior college transfer from Kishwaukee (Ill.) CC, and **Windell Austin**, a 6-9 redshirt sophomore. ''This is the first time we not only have strength at the post, but we will have backup strength as well,'' Stevens said.

Guards **Kevin Soares** (9.5 ppg, 2.9 rpg, 5.4 assists), a 6-1 junior, and 6-1 senior **Gary Huskey** (6.0 ppg, 2.0 assists) should be tested by **Brian Thomasson**, a 6-2 JC transfer from Skyline (Calif.) CC, where he led the Northern California junior colleges in scoring (25.0 ppg). **Wylie Thomas**, a 6-1 junior transfer from West Valley (Calif.) CC, led all California junior college players in assists.

Rod Brown (3.1 ppg), a 6-2 sophomore who played sparingly a year ago, also returns. 6-5 freshman **Jerry Hogan** (North Kitsap HS/Kitsap, Wash.) is a pure shooter who led Washington state in scoring as a high school senior.

BLUE RIBBON ANALYSIS

The details surrounding Franklin's sudden decision to stop hitting jump shots and start hitting the books remain vague. The obvious explanation is a run-in with Stevens, who at one point last year benched his starters because they were disdaining the pass inside for the jump shot outside. The result was a one-point loss at Weber State, but Stevens said the lesson had to be taught.

Perhaps the coach felt Franklin no longer fit into his plans, despite the guard's high-scoring heroics. The Wolf Pack went 8-4 once he was relegated to a sixth-man role. It seems likely that Franklin, who was unhappy in that capacity, will transfer. His absence leaves the Wolf Pack with a decent backcourt, but a real scoring void pending Thomasson's development.

That loss could ultimately be the difference between Nevada winning the regular- and post-season Big Sky titles, or sliding to another fourth-place finish.

1990-91 NEVADA RENO SCHEDULE

Nov.	23-25	#Great Alaska Shootout
	28	@St. Mary's
Dec.	1	@Northern Iowa
	4	Pacific
	8	UNLV
	11	Washington
	15	Oregon

1990-91 NEVADA SCHEDULE Cont.

Dec.	18	@Santa Clara
	21	Alaska-Anchorage
	27-28	##Capital City Classic
Jan.	3	@Idaho
	5	@Eastern Washington
	10	Montana State
	12	Montana
	17	@Boise State
	18	@Weber State
	24	Idaho State
	29	College of Idaho
Feb.	2	@Northern Arizona
	7	@Montana
	9	@Montana State
	14	Eastern Washington
	16	Idaho
	21	Boise State
	23	Weber State
	28	Northern Arizona
Mar.	2	@Idaho State
	7-9	*Big Sky Tournament

@ Road Games
# Anchorage, AK (Alaska-Anchorage, California-Irvine, Siena, South Carolina, Texas Tech, UCLA & Virginia)
Sacramento, CA (Oklahoma State, Sacramento State & San Jose State)
* Site to be announced

NEW ORLEANS

LAST SEASON: 21-11
CONFERENCE RECORD: 8-2
STARTERS LOST: 3
STARTERS RETURNING: 2
CONFERENCE: AMERICAN SOUTH (ASC)
LOCATION: NEW ORLEANS, LA
HOME FLOOR: LAKEFRONT ARENA (10,000)
NICKNAME: PRIVATEERS
COLORS: ROYAL BLUE & SILVER
COACH: TIM FLOYD, record at New Orleans, 40-22. Career record, 75-47.

Like a magician, Tim Floyd always seems capable of producing another rabbit from his hat. In his first year at New Orleans in 1988-89, he took a team picked late in pre-season polls and with an average height of 6-2-1/2 in the starting lineup and led it to the regular season conference championship and a berth in the NIT.

So how did he top that? With another rabbit. Last year, Floyd guided a team that stumbled out of the gate with a 2-7 record to a 22-11 mark, a regular season co-championship in the American South Conference, the ASC tournament championship and a berth in the quarterfinals of the NIT. That is what makes Floyd one of the brightest, young coaches in the collegiate game.

So what can Floyd do for an encore? Another rabbit? Don't bet against it.

Floyd said, ''it feels like we're starting over,'' because of the departure of 6-3 Tony Harris, the American South player of the year, and Willie Richardson, a two-year second team all-conference choice. Harris averaged 19.9 points per game and was the team's second leading rebounder. Richardson was the team's third-leading scorer (10.4 ppg) and the team's top defensive player.

''Those two were the core of our two conference-championship teams,'' said Floyd. ''But I'm more concerned about replacing their mental and physical toughness than their points.''

But the Privateers' treasure chest is far from empty.

The list of returnees include 6-11 sophomore center **Ervin Johnson**, 6-5 senior forward **Tony Collins**, 6-0 junior guard **Louweegi Dyer** and 5-8 senior guard **Cass Clarke**, who shared the starting point guard duties last year. The newcomers are headlined by 6-8 freshman forward/center **Melvin Simon**, a national Top 25 player. Simon's decision to stay at home represents an enormous catch for a program on this level. He had his pick of schools and is the most publicized recruit to sign with an ASC team in the brief history of the league.

Collins (11.6 ppg, 4.9 rpg, 37 assists, 6 blocked shots, 37 steals) finished second to Harris in scoring last year and averaged 18.3 ppg in New Orlean's three NIT games. "Tank has a lot of talent," said Floyd. "What will benefit him most is that he'll participate in fall practice, which he couldn't do last season because he was a midterm transfer. Tony Harris was in the same situation the year before. If Tank works hard, he could reach the next level of success the way Tony did."

Johnson (6.3 ppg, 6.8 rpg, 29 assists, 62 blocked shots, 29 steals) has been a major surprise ever since he walked into Floyd's office in November, 1988, and said he wanted to play for the Privateers. Floyd said at the time he thought it was a stunt straight out of Candid Camera. After redshirting in '88-89, Johnson led the ASC in blocked shots in his first season of competitive basketball since quitting the team at Block (La.) HS as a 10th grader in 1983. "Ervin is still raw and unproven in many areas," Floyd said, "but we were delighted by his development last season. He exceeded everyone's expectations. In 13 years of coaching, I've never seen a player work harder to improve."

Dyer (8.2 ppg, 2.3 rpg, 106 assists, 24 steals) and Clarke (3.6 ppg, 95 assists, 23 steals) provide experience and solid play at point guard. Dyer tallied 27 points in a triple overtime victory over Louisiana Tech while Clarke had a season high eight assists in the second round of the NIT against Mississippi State.

Two sophomores, 6-3 swingman **Darren Laiche** (0.8 ppg) and 6-5 forward **Fred Hill** (0.7 ppg) also return. Laiche, a walk-on last year, was used occasionally as a defensive stopper and earned a scholarship as a result.

Another front line possibility is 6-10 junior **Sydney Rice**, who played only 46 minutes in five games last year before leaving the team because of mental exhaustion. Floyd said Rice has as much physical talent as any Privateer and could contribute to the team's improved rebounding if healthy.

Simon is an impact recruit of the highest order and he should combine with Johnson and Collins to give New Orleans a formidable frontline. Simon, who was selected to *Blue Ribbon's* Top 44 Prep Players last season, averaged 20.7 points and 10.5 rebounds for Archbishop Shaw HS in Marrero, La. Simon can score from the post and passes well.

"There's no doubt that Melvin can start this season and make an impact on our program," said Floyd. "He's already made an impact just by signing with UNO and desiring to remain part of the community where he grew up. We're excited about what Melvin can be like, both for his good and ours."

Besides Simon, the Privateers' best newcomers may be California junior college players **Reggie Betton**, a 6-5 junior forward who can high jump 7-2, and **Randy Carter**, a 6-4 junior forward, whom Floyd expects to contribute because of defense, not his 23.2 scoring average last season. Betton played only eight games last season for Ventura College because of a stress fracture. He averaged 13.0 points and 3.9 rebounds as a freshman. He has the type of athletic prowess that has become a trademark of Tim Floyd-coached teams. Carter, who played at Oxnard College, earned all-conference honors for the second consecutive year. He could become the Privateers' defensive stopper.

Three other junior college recruits could contribute. **Jacob Edwards**, a 6-3 junior guard averaged

15.2 points, 6.5 rebounds and 2.3 assists for Miami (Fla.) Dade-North CC last season. **Rashone Lewis**, a 6-6 junior forward, boasted 22.8 ppg and 8.6 rpg norms at Fullerton (Calif.) CC last season. And **Dwight Myvett**, a 6-1 guard who enrolled at New Orleans last January and sat out last season, averaged 21.1 ppg as a sophomore at Columbia (Calif.) College. He should challenge Dyer and Clarke for the starting guard position.

A late summer addition, 6-11 junior center **Larry McCloud** from Anderson (S.C.) JC will make New Orleans much stronger. He once signed with Clemson but never enrolled there.

BLUE RIBBON ANALYSIS

In two short years, Tim Floyd has turned New Orleans into a mid-major power, one that can boast post-season play as a realistic goal. ASC player of the year Tony Harris will be difficult to replace, but landing Melvin Simon, the best player in the state of Louisiana last year, was a major coup for Floyd.

"We won't get any breaks in the conference," Floyd said. "Southwestern Louisiana and Louisiana Tech look like the co-favorites. Both are talented and experienced. But the good news is that for the first time ever, our tournament champion will earn an automatic bid to the NCAA tournament. I'm also pleased that the regular-season champion or No. 1 seed will be the host of the conference tournament. We have a shot at both, but I hope the changes aren't a year too late for us."

On paper, Southwestern Louisiana and Louisiana Tech appear to have a slight edge on the Privateers. But don't be surprised if New Orleans finishes higher than third.

NIAGARA

LAST SEASON: 6-22
CONFERENCE RECORD: 4-8
STARTERS LOST: 1
STARTERS RETURNING: 4
CONFERENCE: METRO ATLANTIC
LOCATION: NIAGARA FALLS, NY
HOME FLOOR: GALLAGHER CENTER (3,400) and NIAGARA FALLS CONVENTION AND CIVIC CENTER (6,000)
NICKNAME: PURPLE EAGLES
COLORS: PURPLE, WHITE AND GOLD
COACH: JACK ARMSTRONG, record at Niagara, 6-22.

Not often are 6-22 seasons considered satisfactory. But given the mitigating circumstances facing coach Jack Armstrong when he inherited the team shortly before the season started —seven of the top nine players gone, many unexpectedly, along with a killer early schedule — just staying competitive was cause for celebration. Under America's youngest Division I coach, the Purple Eagles did that and more. They hung tough early and came on to win four conference games. Armstrong was justly rewarded with a four-year contract. He, in turn, rounded up a promising recruiting class. But until the newcomers mature, progress will remain sure but slow.

Niagara only lost one starter. But that was 6-6 forward Patrick Jones, the one and only go-to guy on the squad, with per game averages of 21 points and nine rebounds. Jones' 1,358 points left him ninth on the school career scoring list.

Armstrong will look to replace some of that output at small forward with 6-5 sophomore **Dwayne Daniel** (9.5 ppg, 2.9 rpg), who finished a distant second on the team in scoring. Daniels' season was interrupted by mononucleosis, hampering his late season play severely. He has some fine looking moves but needs to become tougher defensively and be more consistently intense. Daniels' shooting can also stand some improvement. At power forward, Armstrong will have to choose between the passing ability and low post offense of 6-8 sophomore **Brian Clifford** or the athleticism, defense and raw but erratic talent of 6-5 senior **Karl Haire**. Clifford was a highly regarded high school player of Long Island Lutheran of Brookville, N.Y., but has sat out the past two seasons (as an ineligible fifth-year senior in high school, then as a freshman at Niagara). Clifford's defense is a question mark, but he's an outstanding passer and could develop as an offensive force inside if he can shake off the rust. If not, Haire will give a good hard defensive effort every night and maybe steal a few baskets off talent alone. None of these figure to come very far from the basket. Nor can it be predicted when they'll arrive. Haire is as likely to score 10 against Holy Cross as two against Fordham as he did last season in successive games. If he can redeem a bit more of his considerable potential in his final season, the Purple Eagles will get a big boost.

In the pivot, 6-8 senior **Darren Brown** will hold forth once again. Brown (8.8 ppg, 6.2 rpg) started the last 14 games and was Niagara's leading rebounder in six of them. He's strong inside and has shooting range from the foul line in as evidenced by his career high 29 points against no less than Loyola Marymount last season. Armstrong feels Brown has the potential to average double figures in both points and rebounds. The trouble is he needs to stay on the floor long enough to do so. Slow feet defensively have made him consistently prone to foul trouble. When that forces Brown out, 6-11 junior **Sean Schiano** (4.3 ppg, 3.4 rpg) comes in. With numbers like that, at 6-11, you don't

243

need to be John Wooden to figure out Schiano is soft as a pillow inside. Which is a shame, because he's not uncoordinated and can shoot and pass. However, he's not fond of contact and has a knack of picking up quick fouls. If Schiano conditions himself and builds some stamina, he is capable of making some important contributions.

In the backcourt, 6-2 sophomore **Tony Newsom** returns at the point. Newsom (7.6 ppg, 3.0 rpg, 67 assists) is a hardnosed defender and okay floor leader. He can take it to the basket and has 15-foot range. Newsom's season ended with a knee injury after 18 games. He was replaced by 6-0 sophomore **Mike Hartman** (4.1 ppg, 56 assists). Hartman, whose father is the strength coach of the San Diego Chargers, is a solid, heady player who won't hurt you. He'll provide experienced backup at the point. If he can improve his outside shot, he'll see added time. At the off-guard, 5-10 senior **Darrin Bossert** (8.6 ppg, 1.6 rpg, 40 assists) is also back. Obviously small for his position, Bossert compensates with tenacious defense, good penetration and a three-point touch. That touch, in fact, runs in the family. Older brother Gary set a national record several years back by converting 11-of-12 three-pointers for Niagara vs. Siena. On the same night, coincidentally, Darrin hit seven-of-eight bombs for Villa Marie JC in Buffalo. Bossert could be pushed hard at the two position by 6-5 sophomore **E-Lon-E McCracken**, who, if nothing else, should captain this year's all-name team. McCracken, who sat out last year, though, is capable of more. He's a strong, athletic defender and picturesque dunker. McCracken's long arms and 6-5 stature would add seven inches to the Niagara backcourt compared to Bossert. That, of course, is a major factor. But McCracken has two drawbacks: below average ballhandling and no outside shot. He's been taking 200 shots a day to improve. If no improvement is shown, McCracken may have to take his ability to the small forward spot instead. The Purple Eagles could certainly use some depth behind Daniel there.

They might get some from 6-7 freshman **Keith Hocevar** (16.0 ppg, 7.0 rpg at St. Josephs HS, Cleveland, Ohio). Hocevar needs to add strength to his 190-pound frame. But he comes from a winning program and has 15-foot range and solid, if unspectacular, all-around ability. Niagara adds four other freshmen: 6-2 guard **David Bertram** (26.0 ppg, 12.0 rpg at Eldred, N.Y., Central HS); 6-3 guard **Reggie Moore** (24.0 ppg, 8.0 rpg, 7.0 apg at James Monroe HS in the Bronx); 6-4 guard **Scott Ramey** (16.8 ppg, 7.1 rpg, 4.8 apg at Western Boone HS, Thorntown, Ind.); and 6-5 swingman **Kandia Milton** (18.0 ppg, 9.5 rpg, 8.0 apg at University Liggit HS in Detroit). Ramey, a 42 percent three-point shooter, could come on the fastest. Ramey, whose high school coach Ed Shilling was his high school backcourt mate at Miami (Ohio), is your basic Indiana good shooter with a respectable handle. Bertram is a good long range shooter with a quick release. However, he needs to build strength while adjusting from a small town with a single schoolhouse to Division I basketball. He could become a force as a sophomore. Moore also needs to bulk up so as to take advantage of his considerable scoring ability. Milton is a strong small forward, good driver, and good athlete. He'll need some learning time, though.

BLUE RIBBON ANALYSIS

Armstrong has laid a solid foundation for the future toward turning this long dormant program around. But it will take time. The ability of nearly everyone in Niagara's seven or eight man nucleus is tarnished by some kind of flaw: inconsistency, vulnerability to foul trouble, small size, or average tools. In other words, three or four players will have to maximize their talent on the same night to get many victories for with Jones gone there is no remote sign of

an established offensive force.

Several recruits have potential for impact at the MAAC level but cannot be expected to display it right away. Without Jones the starters will need to build entirely new chemistry with the large number of newcomers that have to be blended in. The early schedule is treacherous, not exactly the backdrop you'd want for blending new combinations. If the Purple Eagles survive that, they'll pick up a few wins in the MAAC. Maybe enough to rise above seventh, but probably not. But look out when 6-11 (George Washington transfer) Clint Holtz becomes eligible next season.

1990-91 NIAGARA SCHEDULE		
Nov.	23	@St. Francis (PA)
	26	St. Bonaventure
	30	St. John's
Dec.	4	@Fairleigh Dickinson
	7-8	#Indiana Classic
	11	@St. Bonaventure
	22	##St. Peter's
	27	@Robert Morris
Jan.	5	@Siena
	8	@Northeastern
	10	@Iona
	12	@La Salle
	15	Canisius
	17	Manhattan
	19	Fairfield
	24	St. Peter's
	26	La Salle
	29	@Fairfield
	31	Iona
Feb.	7	@Manhattan
	9	@Loyola College
	12	Siena
	14	Loyola College
	16	DePaul
	19	@Seton Hall
	23	@Canisius
Mar.	1-4	*MAAC Tournament

@Road Games
#Bloomington, IN (Indiana, North Carolina Wilmington & University of San Diego)
##Meadowlands Arena, East Rutherford, NJ
*Albany, NY

NORTH CAROLINA A&T

LAST SEASON: 13-16
CONFERENCE RECORD: 6-10
STARTERS LOST: 0
STARTERS RETURNING: 5
CONFERENCE: MID-EASTERN ATHLETIC (MEAC)
LOCATION: GREENSBORO, NC
HOME FLOOR: CORBETT SPORTS CENTER (6,500)
NICKNAME: AGGIES
COLORS: NAVY BLUE AND GOLD
COACH: DON CORBETT, record at North Carolina A&T, 206-112.
Career record, 365-170.

When perennial Mid-Eastern Athletic Conference power North Carolina A&T slipped to a 9-18 record in 1988-89, the team's fans thought that performance was merely an aberration. Surely the Aggies, who'd won the previous seven MEAC titles and the NCAA tournament bids that accompanied them, could bounce back.

The fans were right, to a certain extent. After a 6-12 start last season, North Carolina A&T won seven of its final 11 games but still finished sixth in the league, just as it did the year before. More encouraging was the team's play in the MEAC tournament., where the Aggies defeated Delaware State in the opening round and Florida A&M in the semifinals before losing to Coppin State in the championship game.

With five starters returning, North Carolina A&T seems set to assume its customary position near the top of the MEAC standings. An NCAA tournament berth is no certainty, however. Even if the Aggies win the conference crown, a new format forces the MEAC and other lesser-light champions to "play-in" to the Big Show.

The conferences involved in the play-in games were selected by the NCAA based on 1990 computer rankings. The four leagues with the lowest non-conference power ratings will compete along with the champions from the Big South and Patriot League, two relatively new conferences, while the MEAC champions' designated opponent will come from the Southland Conference.

Veteran A&T coach Don Corbett probably isn't as worried about the play-in tournament as he is in guiding the Aggies back to their winning ways. If that is accomplished, 6-0 senior point guard **Glenn Taggart** (14.6 ppg, 4.4 rpg, 201 assists) will have played a significant role. Taggart led his team in scoring and the MEAC in assists last season.

"Glenn will be key to our success this year," Corbett said. "He will be our primary ballhandler, and I feel certain he can and will meet the challenge. We'll look to him for leadership on and off the court."

Taggart's backcourt partner is 6-0 junior **Bobby Moore** (13.2 ppg, 2.1 rpg, 55 assists). Moore alternated between shooting and point guard last year. A good outside shooter, he led the team with 48 three-point goals.

Dana Elliott (13.9 ppg, 5.7 rpg, 42 assists, 35 steals), a 6-5 sophomore, is Corbett's top returning player on a young front line. He will be joined by 6-8 sophomore **Colin Spady** (10.3 ppg, 7.5 rpg, 43 steals) and 6-7 sophomore **Wayne Morris** (3.7 ppg, 2.9 rpg). Spady led the team in rebounding and was second in steals. Morris played in 28 games last year, but may have to share time this season with 6-6 senior **Jerry Humphries** (10.3 ppg, 5.8 rpg).

Corbett has no eligible recruits, but had three players sitting out last year who are now ready to contribute. **Chris Johnson**, a 6-9 sophomore from Englewood, N.J., gives Corbett some size. Johnson plays solid defense and rebounds well. He averaged 12 points and 12 rebounds at Dwight Morrow High.

Charles Jackson, a 5-10 guard, will back up Taggart at the point. A good ballhandler, Jackson should play quite a bit. He averaged 19 points and five assists at Pinecrest High (West End, N.C.). The third newcomer is 6-5 sophomore **Thomas Garner**, a transfer from Johnson C. Smith.

BLUE RIBBON ANALYSIS

After dominating the MEAC for seven years, North Carolina A&T fell on hard times the last two seasons. But the Aggies are very nearly back. Corbett has all five starters returning, and adds at least two solid newcomers in Johnson and Jackson.

That experience should put North Carolina A&T back in the MEAC race. Defending champion Coppin State will not go away meekly, however, and the new NCAA "play-in" procedure adds yet another obstacle to a return to the national tournament.

A&T has a shot to leap both hurdles, but is more realistically a year away from gaining its first NCAA bid since 1988.

NORTH CAROLINA CHARLOTTE

LAST SEASON: 16-14
**CONFERENCE
RECORD:** 6-8
STARTERS LOST: 1
**STARTERS
RETURNING:** 4
**CONFERENCE:
SUN BELT
LOCATION:
CHARLOTTE, NC
HOME FLOOR:
CHARLOTTE
COLISEUM (23,338)
NICKNAME: 49ERS
COLORS: GREEN AND WHITE
COACH: JEFF MULLINS, record at North Carolina
Charlotte, 81-69.**

After a spring and summer of rumors involving their coach, Jeff Mullins, and one of their players, **Henry Williams**, competing on the U.S. National team, the 49ers are ready to take on all comers in the Sun Belt race. With a cast that includes youth and experience, UNCC will challenge defending champion South Florida for the conference title.

With five freshmen playing a prominent role, Mullins last year was able to fashion a winning record and direct his team to the championship game of the Sun Belt tournament, where they absorbed a narrow loss to South Florida. The 49ers would like nothing better than another shot at the Bulls, and there is an excellent chance of exactly that happening, especially with Mullins having ignored several pro and college coaching overtures to remain in Charlotte.

UNCC will have to do it without 6-8 forward Cedric Ball, the lone starter absent from 1989-90. Ball averaged 11.6 ppg and a team-high 9.4 rpg, and his enthusiasm will be missed as well as his stranglehold on the power forward position for the past three seasons.

But there is plenty of other talent on hand for Mullins to work with, and the coach has proven in his five years that he knows what to do when he has it. Mullins is just seven victories away from becoming the winningest coach in UNCC history, and it should not take this squad very long to accomplish that.

The main man once again will be Williams, a 6-2 junior, who is rapidly becoming the most recognized UNCC player since Cedric ''Cornbread'' Maxwell led the 49ers to the Final Four in 1977. Even though he was heavily guarded last year, Williams was able to average 21.0 ppg while producing 123 assists and 51 steals. Because of all the attention, however, Williams shot just 41 percent from the floor, which included 40 percent from three-point range.

''I never had a season in my life where I shot so poorly,'' said Williams, the only Charlotte player ever to make the national team. ''My shot felt good, but obviously it wasn't as successful as my first year.''

Williams will continue to draw extra attention from opposing teams, but he has a talented trio of returnees he can pass to when the double- and triple-teaming begins. The other returning starters are 6-7 senior forward **Dan Banister** (8.8 ppg, 5.7 rpg), 6-5 sophomore guard **Cedrick Broadhurst** (7.7 ppg, 3.3 rpg, 96 assists) and 6-10 junior center **Jack Bolly** (4.2 ppg, 4.0 rpg).

Four sophomores who got plenty of court time in Mullins' spread-the-wealth system are 6-9 guard **Benny Moss** (10.8 ppg, 2.8 rpg), 6-10 center **Daryl DeVaull** (4.3 ppg, 3.6 rpg), 6-0 guard **Delano Johnson** (6.3 ppg, 68 assists) and 6-6 forward **Kenneth Wylie** (2.9 ppg, 2.1 rpg). They are expected to be heavier contributors this year. **Chris Baker**, a 6-0 junior guard, and 6-8 sophomore forward **Tim Goodman** will boost UNCC's depth.

Mullins also welcomes what appears to be his finest recruiting class. In addition to four incoming freshmen, UNCC will have the services of 6-6, 230-pound sophomore **Malru Dottin**, who sat out his last year as a Prop 48. Dottin (Saddleback HS/Santa Ana, Calif.) averaged 16.8 points and 9.4 rebounds at Saddleback. The four freshmen - all from North Carolina - are 6-6 forward **Jarvis Lang**, 6-11 center **Jermaine Parker**, 6-0 guard **James Terrell** and 6-3 guard **Bershuan Thompson**.

Lang, the 2-A state player of the year and one of UNCC's highest-ever rated recruits, led Farmville Central High to consecutive state championships, averaging 22.3 ppg and 12.1 rpg last season. Thompson, the 3-A state player of the year, paced D.H. Conley High to the 1990 state title, averaging 19.5 points, 6.9 rebounds and 5.1 assists. Terrell led the state in scoring (32.2 ppg), and helped Louisburg High to the state playoffs for the first time in years. Parker, who grew so much in high school that he did not begin playing basketball until his sophomore year, will not have an impact right away, though he blocked 208 shots last winter at Sanderson High. Doctors project him to a height between 7-1 and 7-3.

The 49ers are especially deep in the backcourt, where a battle for playing time is likely behind last year's tandem of Williams and Broadhurst. Williams will likely become more of a second guard, with Broadhurst assuming traditional point-guard duties. Johnson, a defensive whiz, will get more than 14 minutes per game, and Moss will swing between spelling Williams and playing small forward. Like Williams, Moss is a three-point marksman, having notched 35 treys in his first season. Baker started 12 games last season and will back up the point. Like Moss, Wylie will swing between the two and three spots. He started 13 times a year ago.

In the frontcourt, Banister is expected to replace Ball at power forward. Bolly, who started 14 games

at center last season, and DeVaull (4.3 ppg and 3.6 rpg) will split time in the pivot. DeVaull showed strong rebounding tendencies despite a surgically repaired left thumb. Goodman (2.6 ppg) is back after sitting out the second semester because of an academic suspension.

Expect Dottin and particularly Lang to land considerable playing time in the frontcourt, as well. Both are potentially explosive players and come from excellent prep programs. Terrell and Thompson give the 49ers even more ammunition in a potent backcourt.

BLUE RIBBON ANALYSIS

Despite a schedule as strong as any Mullins has had, the 49ers are definitely on track for their fifth straight winning campaign, something which has not been accomplished at UNCC since 1975-80.

''At this point,'' Mullins said, ''I don't know yet how good we'll be. I do know we'll be a fun team to work with. The cast of characters is made up of a group of young people who will work extremely hard to make themselves and the team better. For example, just since March, you can see a marked improvement in our team's physical strength which, last year, was a weakness for us.''

UNCC could indeed use some strength, particularly after getting outrebounded more often than not a year ago. Playing three games (winning once) against the Canadian National team this summer should also help boost the confidence of the younger 49ers.

Since UNCC returns 86 percent of its scoring, 97 percent of the assists, 77 percent of its rebounding and 100 percent of three-pointers made, the 49ers are a cinch to be in the upper echelon of the Sun Belt. The 49ers should give South Florida quite a battle for the top spot, too, before settling for second place and their third postseason invitation in four years.

NORTH CAROLINA STATE

LAST SEASON: 18-12
CONFERENCE
RECORD: 6-8
STARTERS LOST: 2
STARTERS
RETURNING: 3
CONFERENCE:
ATLANTIC COAST
(ACC)
LOCATION:
RALEIGH, NC
HOME FLOOR:
REYNOLDS COLISEUM
(12,400)
NICKNAME: WOLFPACK
COLORS: RED AND WHITE
COACH: LES ROBINSON, first year at North Carolina State.
Career record, 213-232.

The Jimmy V Era has come to an end at North Carolina State. After ten years at the helm of the Wolfpack, Jim Valvano has left the university this year to pursue a career as a television commentator. During his career in Raleigh, Valvano's teams compiled a 209-114 record, highlighted in 1983 by one of the most unexpected Cinderella runs to the national title in the history of the NCAA tournament Valvano also took the Wolfpack to the tournament's Final Eight twice (in 1985 and '86) and Final 16 once (1989) during his brilliant tenure. But now, following an 18-12 season (6-8 in the ACC) in a year in which the Wolfpack was banned from post-season competition, the program must turn the page and look to reestablish itself as one of the nation's strongest.

The job of bringing basketball glory back to North Carolina State will fall onto the very capable shoulders of Les Robinson. Robinson comes to the Wolfpack after leading East Tennessee State to a berth in last year's NCAA tournament, where they lost to eventual Final Four participant Georgia Tech in the first round. For Robinson, coaching at North Carolina State will be a return to the place where basketball first truly consumed his life. It was in a Wolfpack uniform in 1963-64 that Robinson learned the game under the watchful eye of his coach, the "Old Gray Fox," Everett Case. He then was an assistant coach at his alma mater in 1965-66 under head coach Press Maravich. So now, 24 years later, Robinson is primed to venture back to Raleigh and take over the reins of a program which has had its share of problems over the last couple of seasons.

Robinson is not only lucky to be able to go back to his alma mater to coach, but he will also find that he has some excellent talent to work with when he gets there. The backcourt remains intact as both 6-1 **Chris Corchiani** and 6-3 **Rodney Monroe** enter their senior seasons. This outstanding guard tandem, with Corchiani manning the point and Monroe bombing with dead-eye accuracy from the perimeter, has to be considered the elite backcourt in America. These two outstanding players have been dubbed "Fire and Ice," a description which fits them perfectly. Corchiani, the "Fire" in this backcourt, needs just 23 more assists to give him the all-time Wolfpack mark, 118 to establish a new ACC record and 221 or more to make him the first NCAA Division I player to eclipse the 1,000 assist plateau. He was a third team All-ACC selection in 1989-90, and this year he has an excellent shot at making the first— team while also vying for All-America

honors. As Corchiani goes, so goes the Wolfpack offense. He handles the ball exclusively, distributes it to the right people in the right spots on the floor and he exudes a confidence that borders on bravado. Corchiani is an incredible competitor who has more than his fair share of scrapes and bruises from diving for loose balls over the course of his three years. He already owns the school record for steals (237) and with 39 more he will establish a new ACC career mark. Last year Corchiani (13.1 ppg, 7.9 apg, 95 steals) was an ironman as he played in all 30 of North Carolina State's games and led the team in minutes played with 1,125 (an astonishing 37.5 minutes per game). On top of all this, he also had nine double-doubles (double figures in points and assists) to pace the team.

The only area of Corchiani's game which he has to improve upon would be his outside shooting. Last year Corchiani shot only 42 percent from the field, a figure which included 40 percent (33-82) from three-point range. However, he should be able to knock down the 18-foot jumper with much more consistency this year as he will be given even more freedom to shoot that shot on a regular basis. He has always been an outstanding penetrator who, if he does not get the assist or the easy bucket, will more likely than not get fouled. Once this happens, you can virtually put the two points in the scorebook as Corchiani was third in the conference last year in free throw percentage, connecting on slightly more than 83 percent of his attempts. The only concern that Robinson has about his tremendous floor general is the fact that he spent most of the summer recovering from a stress fracture in his foot. If this injury hampers Corchiani in any way, North Carolina State will be in for a long season. However, it is believed that he will be 100 percent as the season gets underway.

The only way a player of Chris Corchiani's caliber could possibly be overshadowed is if he played in the same backcourt with Rodney Monroe. Monroe, an incredibly smooth 6-3 shooting guard whose nickname "Ice" is well deserved, was a second-team All-ACC selection last year, finishing second in the league in scoring (23.2 ppg), fourth in free throw percentage (.818) and first in three-point field goal accuracy (.483, 84-174). Monroe, like Corchiani, has also had a somewhat difficult summer as he was slowed by mononucleosis. However, this condition should not keep him from playing at full throttle when the season starts. Monroe last season became just the fourth player in Wolfpack history to average better than 20 points in two consecutive seasons as his 23.2 ppg followed a sophomore year average of 21.4. He is already North Carolina State's sixth all-time leading scorer (1,715 points) and with a season average of somewhere in the 20-point range, he will have an excellent chance to break two-time All-America David Thompson's school record of 2,309 points. Monroe is a born scorer who can shoot from long range, create his own shots off the dribble and drive to the basket under control and with a purpose.

As a sophomore, Monroe gave one of the great individual performances in the NCAA tournament history in a second-round game against Iowa. He made an incredible twisting jumper in heavy traffic at the buzzer to tie the game in regulation, then duplicated that feat at the buzzer of the first overtime. In all, he finished with 40 points as the Wolfpack prevailed in double overtime. It has certainly helped Monroe to have an unselfish and intelligent player like Corchiani as a runningmate, and the two seem to feed off of one another. Monroe, who led the Wolfpack in scoring in 25 of 30 games last year, also played in all 30 games and was second to Corchiani in minutes played with 1,095. Even more impressive than the minutes played is the fact that Monroe has yet to foul out of a game at North Carolina State. This is truly incredible because, while not the outwardly tenacious, "bulldog" defender Corchiani is, Monroe still plays outstanding man-to-man defense and is often called upon to guard the opposing team's best all-around player. All in all, the Hagerstown, Md., native enters his senior year with

the opportunity to leave his mark indelibly stamped in both school and conference record books, and with an excellent shot at ACC player of the year and All-America awards. Monroe will almost certainly be a high selection in next summers' NBA draft.

With a healthy and well rested version of this dynamic duo returning in the backcourt, North Carolina State will automatically be competitive under Robinson. The Wolfpack also returns three more players who contributed last year and will be called upon to step into extended roles in 1990-91. Leading this group is 6-9 junior forward **Tom Gugliotta**, who started in 29 of the team's 30 games last year as a sophomore. Gugliotta will be called upon by Robinson to pick up more of the scoring slack at the forward spot as the Wolfpack lost 6-7 Brian Howard (13.0 ppg, 5.1 rpg, started all 30 games) to graduation. In his first season as a starter, Gugliotta averaged 11.1 points and led the team with 7.0 rebounds per contest. While previously considered more of an inside player, Gugliotta showed excellent long range shooting skills as he connected on 48.9 percent of his three-point attempts last year. This number would have led the ACC but for the fact that he did not have the minimum number of attempts. Gugliotta established himself as a solid contributor to the Wolfpack in December of last season as he scored 31 points and grabbed 21 rebounds in two games against Ohio State and Pittsburgh to earn MVP honors, and North Carolina State the team title, at the Diet Pepsi Tournament of Champions. He led the team in rebounding 17 times during the season, seven of which were double digit performances. Gugliotta will be looked to for even more offensive production both on the inside and from the perimeter this season. He also will continue to develop as a rebounder and passer. The latter skill is one which a man his size rarely possesses. Gugliotta knows the game inside and out and his decisions on the floor are often correct and sometimes even spectacular. He is also a workhorse on the defensive end of the court. It is there where increased upper body strength and physical maturity will make him even more of a force for the Wolfpack. Gugliotta will no longer be afforded the luxury of sneaking up on opponents, however, and this year he will have to respond to defenses which will include him prominently in their game plans as they try to throttle the Wolfpack offense.

The other returning lettermen for North Carolina State are 6-6 forward **Bryant Feggins** and 6-9 center **Kevin Thompson**, two sophomores who played high school ball together at Glenn HS in Winston-Salem, N.C. Both players saw playing time off the bench in all 30 games last year, and they contributed a combined 7.5 ppg and 5.3 rpg. Feggins (4.2 ppg, 2.5 rpg) is an aggressive forward who has an enthusiastic "never say die" attitude and is not afraid to put himself in the middle of the action. He showed strong offensive moves when given the opportunity last year and he will most likely start at the other forward spot opposite Gugliotta. Thompson (3.3 ppg, 2.8 rpg) will man the pivot for the Wolfpack and, as his .592 shooting percentage last year showed, he can potentially be very tough from inside 12 feet and will provide a presence down low which cannot be taken lightly by the opposition. Last year North Carolina State got decent production from 6-10 Brian D'Amico (6.8 ppg, 5.5 rpg) on both the offensive and defensive ends of the floor. Thompson has got more refined offensive skills than D'Amico and he should immediately give the Wolfpack a more serious weapon down low.

To this point, things look pretty good for Robinson and the Wolfpack as they will have an outstanding backcourt, one forward with experience and excellent all-around skills and two other front line players who are athletic and received valuable playing time last year as freshmen. However, it is what falls in after these five players which has Wolfpack fans somewhat skeptical and certainly a little bit guarded in their optimism. **Tony Robinson**, a 6-9 forward from Havelock HS in Havelock, N.C., is the only other front line player who has been with the program prior to the

1990-91 season. Robinson gained this distinction when Jamie Knox, a 6-7 junior who averaged 2.4 ppg last year, injured his knee and was lost to the Wolfpack for the active '90-91 campaign. A talented prospect coming out of high school, Robinson spent his first year at State as a redshirt, honing his skills in the team's practices but not dressing for any games during the season. The coaching staff hopes that Robinson can acclimate himself quickly and add to the team's frontcourt depth.

The only other front line reserve will be 6-7 freshman **Marc Lewis**, the MVP of the 1990 North Carolina 4-A state championship game as he led his Greensboro Page team to the state title and perfect 31-0 record. Lewis averaged 23.1 ppg, 10.0 rpg and shot 62.0 percent from the field in his senior year. Lewis should get some minutes off the bench right away, and the fact that he was the star player on an undefeated high school team should say something very positive about his competitive spirit.

Even though the starting backcourt will probably play close to a combined 75 minutes per game this year, there still will be a need for some quality backups over the course of a 30 plus game season. This is an area of great concern as only seldom-used 6-0 junior **Roland Whitley** (0.3 ppg, 0.3 rpg in nine games) returns for the Wolfpack. Two freshmen, **Migjen Bakalli** (25.3 ppg, 10.0 rpg, 6.8 apg, South Points HS, Belmont, N.C.) and **Adam Fletcher** (20.9 ppg, 7.0 apg, Sanderson HS, Raleigh, N.C.) will have to be ready for game action right away if the situation presents itself. Bakalli, 6-6, is the more advanced player of the two as he showed excellent outside shooting skills on his way to first team all-state honors last year. Fletcher, 6-1, is a true point guard who will be Corchiani's backup, a role which in the past has been tantamount to redshirting for a season. However, he will definitely figure into North Carolina State's future so this apprenticeship served under Corchiani will be beneficial for him.

BLUE RIBBON ANALYSIS

The major problem with this first edition of Les Robinson's Wolfpack is the fact that, with only nine active players, intrasquad scrimmages will be tough to organize. Robinson will have some tryouts in the fall to get a player or two as walk-ons from the student body, which will help even things out in North Carolina State's practices. Even though he will be staring at an extremely limited bench, Robinson still stands by a fast-paced, intense style of basketball.

"What I like to see is what I think makes great basketball — uptempo," said Robinson. "We like to shoot the three, and yet we will be able to play a half-court game."

Robinson's East Tennessee State team last year finished with the second-highest number of three-point field goals in the nation, and this year, sporting the likes of Monroe, Corchiani and Gugliotta on the perimeter, Robinson's offensive style should be very similar.

It is on the defensive end where the lack of depth will cause the Wolfpack to make changes. "Defensively my primary preference is man-to-man, but we'll change defenses during the game," explained Robinson. "A team with little depth often has to play more zone defenses in order to stay out of foul trouble."

As a result, State will have to "call off the dogs" and at times not allow its defenders, Corchiani especially, to play with their typical seek and destroy attitude. Still, with Monroe and Corchiani, who both got a well-deserved rest during the summer while nursing ailments and injuries, the Wolfpack will again be competitive in most of the games they play. After all, Monroe and Corchiani have both become accustomed to playing virtually every minute over the course of the past three seasons, so a heavy work load should not bother them at all. Gugliotta must rise to the occasion in his more forceful role on both ends of the floor, and Feggins and Thompson must continue to

develop their all-around games and make sure to avoid stupid fouls which could limit their effectiveness. With contributions from Robinson, Lewis and either Bakalli or Fletcher, more likely Bakalli, North Carolina State will finish in the middle of the conference and win another 16 or 17 games. There is also the outside shot for this State team to get back to the NCAA tournament as they again are eligible for post-season competition this year. These would be great accomplishments for the Wolfpack's first year coach and, as a result, North Carolina State followers will be left excited and in eager anticipation for what lies ahead during this new "Robinson Era."

1990-91 NORTH CAROLINA STATE SCHEDULE

Nov.	23	@Florida International
	28	Baptist College (SC)
Dec.	1	Western Carolina
	4	#@Syracuse
	8	Mt. St. Mary's (MD)
	22	North Carolina-Asheville
	29	@East Tennessee State
Jan.	2	Clemson
	5	@Kansas
	7	Coastal Carolina (SC)
	13	Georgia Tech
	16	@North Carolina
	19	@Wake Forest
	21	Marquette
	23	Duke
	26	@Maryland
	29	@Virginia
Feb.	3	@Georgia Tech
	6	North Carolina
	10	@Clemson
	13	Robert Morris
	16	@Connecticut
	20	@Duke
	23	Virginia
	25	@Tennessee
	27	Maryland
Mar.	2	Wake Forest
	8-10	##ACC Tournament

@Road Games
#ACC/Big East Challenge
##Charlotte, NC

NORTH CAROLINA WILMINGTON

LAST SEASON: 8-20
CONFERENCE RECORD: 3-12
STARTERS LOST: 1
STARTERS RETURNING: 4
CONFERENCE: COLONIAL (CAA)
LOCATION: WILMINGTON, NC
HOME FLOOR: TRASK COLISEUM (6,100)
NICKNAME: SEAHAWKS
COLORS: GREEN AND GOLD
COACH: KEVIN EASTMAN, first year at North Carolina Wilmington.
Career record, 65-22.

North Carolina Wilmington plummeted from 16-14 to its worst season (8-20) in over 20 years. Coach Robert McPherson is out, new coach Kevin Eastman is in and the glory days when Brian Rowsom led the Seahawks must seem a lot further removed than three years, down on the North Carolina coastline. Eastman, successful in his only head coaching stint

at Belmont Abbey (65-22 over three seasons at the school that made Al McGuire famous, or vice versa), followed that with a one-year stay at Tulsa as J. D. Barnett's assistant last season. He will greet four returning starters and ten lettermen from a team that displayed a little talent but a lot of youth a year ago.

"I hope that since we have a large number of players returning that their maturity will be a strength for us," said Eastman, who was hired late and did not have much time to recruit. "We will rely heavily on our returning players."

Foremost among those should be 6-1 senior off-guard **Brannon "Cannon" Lancaster** (11.3 ppg), who led the team in scoring last season, mainly by living up to his nickname by his explosiveness from outside. Lancaster did that largely via the three-pointer, a weapon of which he is one of the league's most accomplished practitioners (79-of-174; 45.4 percent). Lancaster had five trifecta games on five different occasions. Who he'll work with at point guard is a big question. Starter Adam Porter and his 11.2 ppg and 3.1 apg averages are gone. For his job, there are five contenders: 6-3 junior **Joe Cherry** (5.9 ppg, 1.9 rpg), 6-3 junior **Mark Eaton** (3.4 ppg, 3.1 rpg), 6-1 sophomore **Kevin Hayden** (7 minutes total), 6-1 sophomore **Reggie Veney** (0.6 ppg, 0.4 rpg), and 5-10 freshman **Drew Phillips** (21.0 ppg, 10 apg at West Point Prep, Monmouth Co., N.J., via Cardinal Gibbons HS, Baltimore). Cherry would seem to be the leading candidate. But after a strong freshman campaign (7.3 ppg, 2.7 rpg), he never stepped up as a sophomore. He played well as a freshman, before an ankle injury late in the season. Cherry was a 31.0 ppg high school scorer at Riverdale HS in Fort Myers, Fla. Eaton is a hard worker, who showed marked improvement last season. He is, however, 1-of-15 from three-point range in his career so far. Hayden once had a 55-point game in high school, but is low on the depth chart at this point. Veney was a two-year starter for Morgan Wooten at DeMatha's nationally famous prep program in Hyattsville, Md., mainly on the strength of his defense. If Phillips can translate his passing ability to the college level, he'll have a chance at some quality time.

Up front, the Seahawks appear much stronger. 6-6 junior forward **Bryan Withers** (8.4 ppg, 4.5 rpg) and 6-5 sophomore forward **Tim Shaw** (5.0 ppg, 3.0 rpg) form what could be a quality forward combination. Shaw is a talented athlete and a great leaper. He became a starter over the last 11 games and may be on his way to impact status. Shaw had 21 steals on the season and finished strong with 11 points against Richmond in the CAA tournament. Withers is also a leaper with a knack for getting to the foul line. His 92 (of 134) free throws were a sophomore school record last season. Withers' best outing was a 19-point, 10-rebound game vs. East Carolina.

In the middle the Seahawks have depth and experience but not a lot of low post offense. 6-7 senior **Major Wiggins** (7.3 ppg, 5.3 rpg) holds forth as one of the league's premier shotblockers (53 last season). He made the CAA all-defensive team. Wiggins is a good rebounder as well as a strong inside defender. North Carolina Wilmington could use a few more of the type of offensive showings he produced last year against American (30 points, 11 rebounds) or William & Mary (21 points, 9 rebounds). Backing up Wiggins will be 6-10 junior center **Matt Fish** (8.5 ppg, 5.6 rpg), the Seahawks leading rebounder and second leading returning scorer, despite starting only 15 games. Fish shot 56.8 percent from the field by using his 225-pound bulk to good advantage near the basket. He had his biggest night against Duquesne with 27 points and 18 rebounds. Fish could evolve into a go-to man in the paint. Also in the pivot picture is 6-8 junior center **Kenneth Aldrich**, a transfer from Jacksonville. Aldrich was one of the first off the bench for the Dolphins two seasons ago and has a nice touch near the basket. **Scott Tierney**, a 6-7 senior forward (3.6 ppg, 3.2 rpg), will also strengthen the front line. Tierney is 43.8 percent (32-of-73) from three-point range for his career. 6-7 sophomore forward **Jason Moore** lost his entire freshman year to injuries, without seeing any action.

BLUE RIBBON ANALYSIS

It looks like the beginning of a long road back for new coach Kevin Eastman with little returning scoring, no returning rebounder with even six per game, and no newcomers of any projected impact. There is little quality experience at the point either. If Cherry can rally as a floor leader, Lancaster can bomb away and Fish emerges as a consistent scoring force in the post, maybe the Seahawks can surprise a few people. But, that's a lot of ifs. The forward combination of Shaw and Withers, particularly if Shaw can continue to progress, may be enough to keep the offense respectable and competitive. Still, unless there is some major improvement over last season, the CAA cellar beckons.

1990-91
NORTH CAROLINA WILMINGTON SCHEDULE

Nov.	23	North Carolina Greensboro
	26	Campbell (NC)
	29	@North Carolina Charlotte
Dec.	1	@Appalachian State
	4	Stetson
	7-8	#Indiana Classic
	15	North Carolina A&T
	21	@Eastern Kentucky
Jan.	2	College of Charleston (SC)
	5	@American
	7	@Navy
	10	@Campbell
	12	George Mason
	14	James Madison
	19	@Richmond
	21	@William & Mary
	26	East Carolina
	30	@Rutgers
Feb.	2	Navy
	4	American University
	6	Eastern Kentucky
	9	@George Mason
	11	@James Madison
	16	Richmond
	20	William & Mary
	23	@East Carolina
Mar.	2-4	##CAA Tournament

@ Road Games
# Bloomington, IN (Indiana, Niagara & University of San Diego)
Richmond, VA

NORTHEASTERN

LAST SEASON: 16-12
CONFERENCE RECORD: 9-4
STARTERS LOST: 2
STARTERS RETURNING: 3
CONFERENCE: NORTH ATLANTIC (NAC)
LOCATION: BOSTON, MA
HOME FLOOR: MATTHEWS ARENA (6,500)
NICKNAME: HUSKIES
COLORS: RED AND BLACK
COACH: KARL FOGER, record at Northeastern, 75-43. Career record, 108-82.

It appears as if most of the teams in the North Atlantic Conference are facing rebuilding years in 1990-91. A good majority of the teams in the NAC have little experience, quality recruits and hopes for the future. Well, there is one team that is not pointing for good times down the road. And wouldn't you know, that one team thinking the same way as George Allen, that the future is now, would be the Huskies of Northeastern, only the most successful school in recent memory in the NAC.

Northeastern has qualified for the NCAA tournament five times in the last nine years. And for all intents and purposes, diligent head coach Karl Fogel and his staff are making plans for a sixth trip to the Elite 64 in March.

Fogel welcomes back eight seniors and 10 letterwinners from last year's 16-12 team that won the regular season NAC crown only to fall in the league playoffs. And even if the Huskies' leading scorer of a year ago, guard George Yuille, has graduated, Fogel still has a good crop of scorers returning that could fill the shoes of Yuille easily and capably. In fact, the Huskies' scoring attack was so balanced last year, with six players averaging eight points or better and with Yuille leading the way at only 13.9 ppg, Fogel might not feel the sense of urgency usually felt by a coach when a team's leading scorer doesn't return.

Leading the returnees is senior forward **Steve Carney** (13.7 ppg, 10.3 rpg). The 6-7 Carney was a first team All-NAC last year, leading the conference in rebounding. Carney holds most of the NAC rebounding marks. He is an aggressive rebounder and defender and has a fine shot, evident by his 58 percent field goal mark posted last season. Carney's strong inside play is something that Fogel will count on heavily this season. He did count on Carney to improve his game a year ago and he did, doubling the point and rebound totals he put on the board as a sophomore. Carney's hard work down low will be a motivational drive for the Huskies this season.

Sophomore guard **Lamont Hough** will once again run the show from the point. The slender 6-0 Hough started 17 games last season, averaging 11.2 points and 2.5 rebounds. Hough was also the Huskies' chief threat from long range, clicking on 33 percent of three-point attempts. Hough is lightning quick and runs the fast break very well.

Senior forward **Marcellus Anderson** (8.8 ppg, 6.0 rpg) returns for his final season with the Huskies. The 6-5 Anderson is a diligent player, constantly on the move, working hard to get free, a la Bill Bradley. Anderson also works hard to get good shots, evident by his 53 percent shooting mark last year. Anderson's intensity down low complements Carney well off the glass and his defensive skills are a huge asset to the team.

Senior swingman **Dexter Jenkins** (8.8 ppg, 3.0 rpg) will certainly see his share of action this season. There is the only question of where he will play. Last year, Jenkins started 17 games, mostly at small forward. But Jenkins is a quality ballhandler that can play the off-guard slot and he has a fine shot from the perimeter. Jenkins was also the Huskies' top free throw shooter a year ago, clicking on 80 percent of his tries from the charity stripe. Very versatile, Jenkins was second on the team in assists with 72 and was one of a slim few on the Huskies that had more assists than turnovers. Jenkins is also a very clutch performer who comes through in big games.

Another senior swingman on the Huskies' roster is **Ron Lacey** (6.6 ppg, 2.5 rpg). Lacey, at 6-3 and almost a carbon copy of Jenkins, started 13 games last season at both off-guard and small forward and he also has a fine touch from the outside, nailing 49 percent of his tries. Lacey has been plagued by injuries throughout his career. If healthy, he can play a major role in the Huskies' success.

Senior forward **Maurice Brighthaupt** (4.2 ppg, 3.2 rpg) returns. The 6-6 power forward was a key reserve last season, averaging 13 minutes per game over 27 outings. The aggressive Brighthaupt made the most of his opportunities to play, especially rebounding. Brighthaupt also has a knack of being in the right place at the right time and seems to get fouled a lot,

going to the line 45 times in that short time span. His versatility is a great value to the Huskies in the paint.

Another opportunistic Husky is senior forward **Anthony McBride** (4.2 ppg, 2.1 rpg). The 6-6 McBride, who is also a versatile swing player, scored his points in even less playing time than Brighthaupt. McBride, who also has a nice touch from the outside, has the ability to score in bunches and gives Fogel instant offense off the bench.

Senior guard **George Robinson** (1.6 ppg, 0.5 rpg, 28 assists) suffered a knee injury in early December last year and really never recovered enough to be a player of impact for the Huskies. Robinson played in 16 games and started five, but struggled in those outings and his playing time diminished by the season's close. The 5-10 Robinson will be hard pressed to earn quality minutes for the Huskies this season.

Senior forward **Leroy Hodge** (1.5 ppg, 0.3 rpg) will also battle for playing time. Hodge, who is a very good leaper and has been dubbed as the team's dunking specialist, played in only four games last season.

Sophomore forward **Alphonso Barney** (1.5 ppg, 1.8 rpg) played in 18 games a year ago off the bench. The 6-6 Barney came to Northeastern with a reputation as a solid defender and rebounder from Lake Clifton HS in Baltimore, but really didn't develop as well as expected. Fogel feels Barney can become a solid player for the Huskies down the road. Barney did display a nice touch, clicking on 59 percent from the floor.

Fogel headed back down to Baltimore and Lake Clifton to gather in more players to the Husky program. He was very successful, gaining two more players from the very respected Lake Clifton program —forward **Joe Carey** and guard **Ben Harlee**. Carey is a 6-6 superb athlete with a fine shooting touch and the ability to run the floor. Like many of the Huskies, Carey is best suited to play small forward. Harlee is a highly acclaimed 6-3 guard who plays with high intensity and aggressiveness. Both freshmen should see action this season, giving the city of Baltimore reason to actually root for a Boston team.

Fogel didn't limit his recruiting to the city with the fine Inner Harbor. He signed three other quality freshmen that should complement the strong senior contingent very well. The top freshman who should have an immediate impact is 6-8 forward/center **Dan Callahan**, who is the only player listed as a center on the Huskies' pre-season roster. Callahan has great size at 6-8 and 225 pounds and comes to the Huskies from nearby Bedford (Mass.) HS. Callahan is an aggressive scorer and rebounder who may get the starting nod in the pivot provided that Fogel wants to keep Carney happy and healthy at power forward.

The other two new members of the Huskies' roster also come from the state of Maryland, ironically both from the same town of Suitland. Forward **Deo Djossou** is a sharpshooting 6-6 swingman from Suitland HS and **Von Battle** is a 6-0 guard from Forestville HS. Djossou is best slated for the small forward slot while Battle can play either position in the backcourt, but more than likely will see most of his time at the point. Fogel is very high on Battle, saying that Battle "has the ability to be an outstanding ball player for us. He is extremely quick and he is a good outside shooter."

Northeastern is playing one of its toughest schedules in recent memory this year. They are headed to the Maui Classic in Hawaii with Indiana, Syracuse and Loyola Marymount, as well as playing non-conference games with Providence, Rhode Island, Massachusetts, Tulane and Northwestern.

BLUE RIBBON ANALYSIS

With a veteran club like the Huskies have, it would be hard to pick against them in the North Atlantic this season. They have a wealth of talent, a host of good athletes who can shoot the ball and the ability to play solid defense every night. Plus, it is Northeastern, which now has a reputation of excellence in the NAC and that reputation always helps when it comes to gaining instant respect even before the ball is tossed up at center circle.

Carney proved that he is the real thing last year, grabbing every rebound in sight and leading the Huskies through some tough times. You can only expect the same type of improvement this season. With Hartford losing Lamont Middleton, Carney could very well be the top player in the conference.

Hough, Anderson and Jenkins are all proven players, quality athletes with a lot of experience and the ability to come through in the clutch. The bench strength is superb as well. Fogel used that bench to perfection last year and he has received even more help in the form of his five freshman signees, especially Callahan, who may move right into the starting center slot.

So what can stop the Huskies from making yet another journey to the NCAA tournament? Two factors. Stupid fouls and turnovers. The Huskies sent their opponents to the foul line far too many times last year. Sure, every team wants to play aggressive defense, but Husky opponents went to the line on an average of 28 times per game. That's too much.

Turnovers killed the Huskies last year. They had more turnovers (475) than assists (348). No coach wants to see that. Hopefully, the trend will change this year.

If the Huskies continue their individual improvement and then cut down on the fouls and turnovers, the NCAA tournament could be beckoning once again. There is no substitute for experience.

NORTHEAST LOUISIANA

LAST SEASON: 22-8
CONFERENCE RECORD: 13-1
STARTERS LOST: 3
STARTERS RETURNING: 2
CONFERENCE: SOUTHLAND (SLC)
LOCATION: MONROE, LA
HOME FLOOR: EWING COLISEUM (8,000)
NICKNAME: INDIANS
COLORS: MAROON AND GOLD
COACH: MIKE VINING, record at Northeast Louisiana, 150-103.
Career record, includes high school, 335-150.

A year ago, Northeast Louisiana played the role of Secretariat in the Southland Conference. The Indians won the league title by two games over McNeese State and four games ahead of the rest of the field. Along the way, the Indians lost only one league game and their 13 conference wins were the most ever by an SLC team. Northeast Louisiana went on to capture the SLC's post-season tournament and lose 75-63 to Purdue in the opening round of the NCAA tournament.

Northeast Louisiana finished nationally ranked in three categories —No. 9 in three-point accuracy with a school record 43.9 percent, No. 17 in free throw accuracy at 74.6 percent and No. 19 in margin of victory with 10.6 points. The Indians also placed three players —Fred Thompson, **Carlos Funchess** and **Anthony Jones**—on the All-SLC first team, the most from one school ever to make the all-conference first unit.

Thompson, the team's leading scorer, has departed, along with two other starters, post Vincent Lee and point guard Troy Cobb. But with Funchess and Jones, the team's sixth man, returning along with post **Phillip Craig** and a host of top-notch reserves, the Indians should be considered the odds-on favorite to repeat as SLC champions.

"We'll miss a player like Fred Thompson because he was our stroker from outside and he was our hustle man, diving on the floor and getting us going," said Vining. "We lost three starters, but we played 11 people. Starters don't bother me. I like people that contribute. It's finishing that's important."

Jones and Funchess, a pair of 6-3 senior forward/guards who are two marvelous athletes who give the Tribe a one-two punch. Jones (15.1 ppg, 4.0 rpg, 57 assists, 18 blocked shots, 58 steals) led the SLC in steals and hit 45.4 percent of his three-point shots. Jones will likely move into the starting shooting guard role vacated by Thompson.

"I have no reservation about using Anthony in the sixth man role again this year," said Vining. "He did a great job for us coming off the bench and giving us a spark."

Funchess (13.4 ppg, 6.6 rpg, 39 assists, 31 blocked shots, 27 steals) led the SLC in three-point accuracy (46.8 percent).

6-9 senior post **Phillip Craig** (8.7 ppg, 3.2 rpg, 26 assists, 7 blocked shots, 12 steals) was a steady performer last year and is expected to anchor the middle.

Casey Jones, a 5-7 senior, will likely take over the starting point guard position. Jones, originally a walk-on in the Northeast Louisiana program, averaged 3.9 points per game and dished out 84 assists last year.

Other returnees who should factor into the In-

dians' rotation are 6-3 senior forward **Chris Crease** (2.7 ppg, 1.2 rpg) and 6-4 junior forward **Chad Jacobs** (5.2 ppg, 2.6 rpg). 6-3 junior guard **Antoine Martin**, who redshirted last year after averaging 19.5 points per game at Neosho County (Kan.) CC, should also be a prominent member in the rotation.

The Indians added two junior college transfers, one senior college transfer and three high school recruits. The lone weakness in the Indians' camp last year was rebounding where they had an average deficit of 3.6 rebounds per game. Vining and his staff addressed that need by signing 6-7 junior **Scott Byrd** and 6-10 junior **Jeff Murray**. Byrd, whose older brother Jeff was a four year letterman for the Indians, averaged 10.7 points and 7.8 at Walker (Ala.) JC. "Byrd is a board banger," said Vining. "He'll give us the help we need on the boards."

Murray averaged 8.3 points and 6.1 rebounds last year at Hardin-Simmons. Murray transferred to NLU and will be immediately eligible because Hardin-Simmons dropped its basketball program. The other junior college transfer, 6-0 junior **Rodney Redmond**, is expected to challenge Jones at the point guard position. Redmond averaged 16 points and seven assists per outing at Coahoma (Miss.) CC.

Two freshmen will have an opportunity for playing time. 6-8 forward **Anthony Smith** averaged 20 points and 10 rebounds per game at Plaquemine (La.) HS. 6-4 forward/guard **Charles Williams** earned Class AA all-state honors after averaging 23.5 points, 11.0 rebounds, five assists and three steals per game at Jeanerette (La.) HS. Another freshman signee, 6-5 **Herman Myers**, had a 21.0 point and 14.5 rebound norm at Vicksburg (Miss.) HS.

BLUE RIBBON ANALYSIS

While several Southland Conference schools should be improved and capable of closing some of the gap, Northeast Louisiana should repeat as league champions. Funchess and Jones are two of the best athletes in the league and the supporting cast is both talented and well-seasoned.

The only roadblock looming in the Indians' title defense is a wicked schedule. Besides tournaments at Hawaii and Ball State, the Indians will face Arkansas, Ole Miss, Mississippi State and Louisiana Tech on the road in December. If the Indians can maintain their confidence, they should be well prepared to defend their title once conference play opens.

NORTHERN ARIZONA

LAST SEASON: 8-20
CONFERENCE
RECORD: 3-13
STARTERS LOST: 1
STARTERS
RETURNING: 4
CONFERENCE:
BIG SKY
LOCATION:
FLAGSTAFF, AZ
HOME FLOOR:
WALKUP SKYDOME
(9,500)
NICKNAME: LUMBERJACKS
COACH: HAROLD MERRITT, record at Northern Arizona, 0-4 (was named head coach in February after Pat Rafferty resigned).

Harold Merritt said he realized a "dream come true" when named head coach of Northern Arizona on February 22 of last season. That dream might quickly give way to nightmare.

Merritt replaced Pat Rafferty, who resigned in late January, and promptly lost his first four games at the helm. That does not include a 2-8 mark when the former assistant was interim head coach.

Still, Merritt is undaunted. "I was pleased with the way the kids played down the stretch," he said. "We had a four-game swing at the end in which we could have won all four games."

This is optimism at its finest. Lest we forget a 28-point loss to seventh-place Boise State and a 34-point loss to fourth-place Nevada to close out the Lumberjacks' season.

"Some of the things we're going to do will carry over from last year," Merritt said. "So everything won't be brand new to them." Including losing, he could have added, despite the return of four starters and six lettermen off last year's team.

Steve Williams, a 6-1 junior from Tucson, anchors an intact backcourt. Williams (13.0 ppg, 2.3 rpg) has led NAU in scoring each of the past two seasons. He scored over 300 points as a freshman and a sophomore, the first Lumberjack ever to do so. He was also MVP of last year's Hawaii-Hilo Classic, which the Lumberjacks won by defeating the host team. The tournament was notable if only because it snapped NAU's 15-game losing streak, a school and Big Sky record.

The other backcourt starter, **Josh Oppenheimer,** a 6-1 junior from Los Angeles. Oppenheimer (9.4 ppg, 1.4 rpg) sat out the first six games of last season, but soon earned a starting position and led the Lumberjacks in three-point field goals with 42. 6-3 redshirt freshman **Corey Rogers** (La Puente, Calif.) and 6-3 junior **Mickey Walker** (1.0 ppg) provide depth.

At forward, NAU returns starters **Wendell Tull,** a 6-7 senior from Albuquerque, along with **John Akin,** a 6-6 senior from Phoenix. Tull (7.3 ppg, 3.4 rpg) is capable of playing both inside and outside. He led the team in dunks with 24 and also hit 14 three-pointers. Akin, who made the team last year as a walk-on, was second in rebounding with a 5.5 average. He averaged 6.3 points.

Lance Keller, a 6-4 senior, put up small numbers (1.8 ppg, 1.3 rpg) in limited playing time. 6-4 junior **David Truell,** originally from New York City, transferred from Western Arizona JC and will push for a starting role.

The lone starter lost was a key one, 6-9 center Shawn Herman (11.3 ppg, 6.4 rpg). Herman was an honorable mention All-Big Sky performer and easily the most consistent of the Lumberjacks. 6-9 junior

David Wolfe transferred from Brigham Young and will be counted on to fill the void in the middle.

Beyond Wolfe, the Lumberjacks are hurting for size. Freshman **Scott English** (Chaparral HS/Scottsdale, Ariz.) ties as tallest player on the roster at 6-9, followed by fellow newcomer **LeRoy Gaston** (Mesa HS/Mesa, Ariz.) at 6-8. Neither is a muscular type. Little is known about Division I transfers **Mike Herring** (Brigham Young), a 6-5 junior guard, or **Archie Tolliver** (New Orleans), a 6-5 junior forward. They will fight it out with four more new freshmen - 6-8 forward **Ken Bosket** (Clark HS/Las Vegas), 6-3 guard **Jamal Terry** (Buena HS/Sierra Vista, Ariz.), 6-3 guard **Don Leary** (Baning HS/Banning, Calif.) and 6-3 guard **Jeff Plank** (Mohave HS/Bullhead City, Ariz.).

BLUE RIBBON ANALYSIS

The Lumberjacks are 16-48 in Big Sky Conference play over the last four seasons, finishing fifth, sixth and last in successive seasons. Merritt, as optimistic as any first-year coach, believes his team can succeed by playing an up-tempo game.

"We are going to have 10 solid players and we're going to speed the game up a bit," Merritt said. "We're going to be more talented and have more depth. So we're excited already."

It is likely that excitement will wane once the Big Sky season rolls around, maybe sooner. The Lumberjacks were last in the league in rebounding margin and next-to-last in turnover margin. Those kind of numbers make an effective running game highly unlikely.

In the meantime, Merritt points to Montana as the team to beat. "The Big Sky should be competitive again," he said. Maybe too competitive for Northern Arizona. Eighth or ninth place still suits this team.

1990-91 NORTHERN ARIZONA SCHEDULE

Nov.	24	Kansas
	29	@Arizona State
Dec.	1	@Cal State-Northridge
	5	Arizona
	8	Ft. Lewis (CO)
	10	Georgia State
	12	Texas Christian
	22	@Georgia State
	28-29	#Cowboy Shootout
Jan.	3	@Eastern Washington
	5	@Idaho
	10	Montana
	12	Montana State
	17	@Idaho State
	19	@Boise State
	23	Cal State-Northridge
	26	Idaho State
Feb.	2	Nevada
	7	@Montana State
	9	@Montana
	14	Idaho
	16	Eastern Washington
	21	Weber State
	23	Boise State
	28	@Nevada
Mar.	2	@Weber State
	7-9	##Big Sky Conference Tournament

@ Road Games
# Casper, WY (Holy Cross, Southern Mississippi & Wyoming)
Site to be announced.

NORTHERN ILLINOIS

LAST SEASON: 17-11
STARTERS LOST: 0
STARTERS
RETURNING: 5
CONFERENCE:
MID-CONTINENT
LOCATION:
DEKALB, IL
HOME FLOOR: CHICK EVANS FIELD HOUSE (6,044)
NICKNAME: HUSKIES
COLORS: CARDINAL AND BLACK
COACH: JIM MOLINARI, record at Northern Illinois, 17-11.

Last season was an exciting beginning for the Jim Molinari Era at Northern Illinois. "We're really proud of our efforts last year: winning 17 games, finishing fifth nationally in defense (yielding only 61.1 ppg), setting a school record for home victories (at 13-1), and being considered for the NIT. I think all that reflects positively on the attitude we tried to instill in building a solid foundation for our program," Molinari said. Although the Huskies build in relative anonymity to the rest of the college basketball world, people are beginning to take notice. Before last season, *Hoop Scoop* magazine selected Jim Molinari as one of five first-year coaches to watch. He certainly lived up to that billing. Also, *Basketball Times* columnist and scout David Bones tabbed Molinari as one of the year's top 11 "coaching gems."

As the 1990-91 season gets under way, more people will begin to hear about Northern Illinois as the Huskies join the Mid-Continent Conference. While not the Big Ten or the ACC, the Mid-Continent sent two clubs to the NCAA tournament last year and one to the NIT. Northern Iowa recorded a stunning upset of Missouri in the first round and narrowly lost to Minnesota in the second round.

This Northern Illinois squad should more than hold its own in the new conference. All five starters return for the Huskies and the prospects for a successful debut look bright.

5-10 senior point guard **Donald Whiteside** (11.8 ppg, 1.7 rpg), a Francis P. Naismith Award nominee as the nation's best senior under six feet, returns to lead the Cardinal and Black attack. Whiteside is a lightning quick player renowned not only for his stingy defense, but his ability to shoot the basketball. Whiteside shot a team high 59 three-pointers last year and led the Huskies in free throw percentages with a 76 percent mark.

"Donald rates for the Naismith because he plays a sound all-around game," said Molinari. "He can shoot, from the field and from the line, he handles the ball well (only 68 turnovers during a team high 1,019 minutes played), usually defended the opponent's top gunner, and he does the job in the classroom. That's all the factors needed to win the Naismith."

The other star of this year's Northern Illinois squad is 6-4 senior power forward **Donnell Thomas** (17.8 ppg, 8.0 rpg). A strong, athletic player, Thomas specializes in outworking and outhustling his opponents. Thomas can post up as well as step outside and hit the open jump shot. He is currently in eighth place on the all-time Northern Illinois scoring list with 1,325 points. "I know opposing coaches are well aware of Donnell's tremendous work ethic," said Molinari. "I've said it before, nobody works harder. A good example is 15 rebounds against a much taller Nebraska line-up, but his most impressive statistic may have been shooting 48.2 percent from the field.''

In that Husky win versus Nebraska, Thomas garnered 15 boards against a Cornhusker frontline that stands 7-2, 6-9 and 6-7.

Playing alongside Whiteside will be 6-3 junior guard **Stacy Arrington** (8.1 ppg, 3.9 rpg). Arrington led the Huskies with 2.8 assists per contest. He has a soft outside touch and his ability to penetrate makes him doubly dangerous. Molinari commented, ''He (Arrington) made a lot of big plays for us and that award (Assist) indicates his unselfish playing ability.''

6-5 junior **Mike Hidden** (5.7 ppg, 3.1 rpg) will be one of the first Huskies off the bench and the third or fourth guard in Molinari's rotation. Hidden is a quick defender who presents problems for his opponents with his size. He will play an important part in the success of the Huskies this season. 6-3 sophomore guard **David Mitchell** (3.0 ppg, 1.7 rpg) could also see a considerable amount of playing time this year. Mitchell is an outstanding shooter who will be looked to for instant offense off the Huskies bench.

Brian Molis, a 6-8 sophomore transfer from Colorado who sat out last year, should get some action as the season progresses. Molis attended Westchester St. Joseph's HS in suburban Chicago.

Two freshmen, 5-11 **Mark Layton** and 6-3 **Mike Lipnisky**, round out the Husky backcourt. Layton, a stellar point guard, also hails from Westchester St. Joseph's HS. He looks to be the heir apparent to Donald Whiteside at the point guard spot. He can penetrate as well as shoot the basketball. As a senior he averaged 14.0 ppg and 5.0 rpg. Lipnisky is a sharp-shooting all-state guard from Rolling Meadows (Ill.) HS. He signed with Northern Illinois in the early signing period and then exploded for a monster senior season. Lipnisky averaged 30.5 ppg as a senior including a career high 54-point effort against Chicago Weber. He also shot a record 71 consecutive free throws during his senior season. ''The Lip'' has excellent range and should see considerable playing time this season.

In the Husky frontcourt, two seniors, 6-7 center **Andrew Wells** (7.7 ppg, 5.0 rpg) and 6-7 forward **Antwon Harmon** (5.5 ppg, 3.4 rpg) return with starting experience. Wells is a solid pivotman who makes up for his lack of size with quickness and good court intelligence. He is a strong defender who will need to raise his scoring if the Huskies are to ultimately rise. Harmon, the Northern Illinois slam dunk champion, is an athletic forward who likes to run the floor. Harmon had 17 blocked shots to his credit last year, second behind Wells' 23. Molinari will look to Harmon for increased scoring and senior leadership.

6-8 sophomore **Randy Fens** (3.7 ppg, 2.9 rpg) saw a considerable amount of action last season and should see more important minutes this time around. Fens recorded 12 blocked shots last season and will be an important frontcourt defensive replacement this season.

6-6 forward **Brian Banks** (2.9 ppg, 1.0 rpg) and 6-8 forward **Mike Beck** (2.3 ppg, 1.0 rpg) will provide bench depth in the frontcourt. Freshman recruit **Steve Oldendorf** from St. Lawrence HS in Burbank, Ill., should also see action at the center position as the season progresses. Oldendorf, a 7-1 center, hit at a 17.7 ppg mark as a senior and pulled down 6.7 rpg. He is very raw and rates as a project.

BLUE RIBBON ANALYSIS

''We made great progress last year and experience is definitely a strength, but we're still in our second year of development and our first-year in the Mid-Continent race,'' said Molinari.

The most impressive statistic about this Northern Illinois team is that it gave up 25.5 ppg less than the previous year's club. Molinari has transformed this group into a tenacious, scrappy club that has a definite shot at an NCAA tournament berth.

All five starters return for Molinari's club, led by senior point guard Whiteside and senior power forward Thomas. Both must have solid seasons for the Huskies to begin thinking about a post-season tournament. Junior guard Arrington will be an important factor on this Northern Illinois team. He must increase his scoring totals as well as continue to play strong defense. Senior frontcourt starters, Wells and Harmon, will be looked to for solid defensive play and for leadership. Sophomore forward Fens, junior swingman Hidden and freshman Lipnisky will be the first Huskies off the bench.

''One thing we have to stress is the ability to win on the road,'' said Molinari. ''That really tests your mental toughness. I believe the conference schedule will be another positive challenge. It should help create some interest, plus give us a much better chance as post-season play.''

The Northern Illinois non-conference schedule will be taxing, but not impossible. The Huskies will battle Minnesota, Evansville, Rice, DePaul and Nebraska before they enter conference play and their true ability may not be reflected in their record. ''Since we play as tough a non-conference schedule as anyone in the league, I'm sure our record early on may surprise people,'' Molinari admitted. ''But I'm confident we'll finish very strong.'' Look for the Huskies to finish somewhere in the 17 to 19-win range, perhaps as high as second in the conference, with a post-season tournament a strong possibility. To get to the NCAAs, the Huskies will have to win the conference tournament. A strong season and an NIT berth seem to be a more realistic outcome.

1990-91 NORTHERN ILLINOIS SCHEDULE

Nov.	27	@Maine
Dec.	1	@Minnesota
	4	Evansville
	7-8	#Coca-Cola Jowers Jamboree
	17	Idaho State
	20	@Rice
	27	@Chicago State
Jan.	2	Illinois-Chicago
	5	@Northern Iowa
	7	@Western Illinois
	10	Valparaiso (IN)
	15	DePaul
	19	Wisconsin-Green Bay
	21	Illinois Benedictine
	26	@Cleveland State
	28	@Akron
	31	Eastern Illinois
Feb.	2	Northern Iowa
	4	Western Illinois
	7	@Valparaiso
	11	@Eastern Illinois
	16	@Wisconsin-Green Bay
	18	@Nebraska
	23	Cleveland State
	28	@Illinois-Chicago
Mar.	3-5	##Mid-Continent Tournament

@Road Games
#San Marcos, TX (Alcorn State, Southeastern Louisiana & Southwest Texas State)
##Green Bay, WI

NORTHERN IOWA

LAST SEASON: 23-9
CONFERENCE RECORD: 6-6
STARTERS LOST: 2
STARTERS RETURNING: 3
CONFERENCE: MID-CONTINENT
LOCATION: CEDAR FALLS, IA
HOME FLOOR: UNI-DOME (10,000)
NICKNAME: PANTHERS

COLORS: PURPLE AND OLD GOLD
COACH: ELDON MILLER, record at Northern Iowa 65-51.
Career record, 469-292.

Northern Iowa is coming off a breakthrough season. It set a school Division I record for wins (23) and, more importantly, made its first-ever trip to the NCAA tournament, where it became last season's Cinderella by upsetting Missouri in the first round.

The question is, could the Panthers be even better this year? The answer is, it's a possibility. Gone are two key big men - Jason Reese, the school's all-time leading scorer, and Steve Phufe, its leading field goal percentage shooter the last two years - but there are at least five legitimate candidates to take their starting jobs. What the Panthers lose in size and individual production, they could gain in quickness, athletic ability and depth.

''I think they'll become a better defensive team,'' said one Mid-Continent coach. ''And when you're talking defense, you're talking a big reason why a team can be successful.''

Miller, entering his fifth season, turned around Northern Iowa's program in two years, going 23-28 his first two seasons and 52-36 his last three, including 23-9 last year. 1989-90 culminated with a stirring stretch run that saw the Panthers win the Mid-Continent Conference tournament and its automatic NCAA bid, after finishing tied for third in league play. Northern Iowa went on to upset Missouri in the first round of the NCAA's and took Minnesota to the wire before losing in the second round.

''Last year will help us,'' Miller said, ''but we can't dwell on it. We also can't make it any better, but we can do a lot about now.''

The Panthers' biggest difficulty will be replacing Reese's scoring. The 6-10 center led the team each of his four years (19.1 ppg, 7.6 rpg last year), and was the team's high scorer in both NCAA tournament games. ''We do have some critical questions to answer,'' Miller admitted. ''How cohesive will we be offensively and how determined will we be defensively?''

Northern Iowa does not appear to have any one player who can make up for Reese, so the effort will have to be collective. Forward **Troy Muilenburg** (13.8 ppg, 4.8 rpg), a 6-5 senior, is the leading returning scorer. Muilenburg is mainly an outside threat - 37.4 percent shooting on three-pointers, a team-high 131 attempts - who can occasionally take it to the basket. He showed he can score against high-caliber competition, too, managing 16 points against Missouri and 20 against Minnesota.

6-4 forward **Cedrick McCullough** (8.8 ppg, 4.0 rpg), a junior, has been a defensive stopper because of his combination of size and quickness. ''Cedrick is the best defensive player for his age I've ever coached,'' said Miller. McCullough is also a good mid-range shooter, and could be ready to put those tools to better use and become a double figure scorer this year.

6-5 senior **Brad Hill** (5.0 ppg, 2.8 rpg) is a strong forward who also has three-point range. Hill started three games last season and made a crucial three-point shot down the stretch of the Panthers' victory over Iowa last winter in front of 22,797 spectators at the UNI-Dome. He is another player in line for increased playing time after averaging 19 minutes last year.

At least four other Panthers, including three who did not play at all last season, figure to compete for significant playing time at the two power positions. At center, **Terry Merfeld**, a 6-9 redshirt freshman (Hudson HS/Hudson, Iowa), 6-10 junior **Nick Pace** (1.6 ppg, 1.2 rpg) and 6-7 **Troy Vaughn** all have a shot. Merfeld probably has better scoring skills than Pace, but Pace is older and has proven to be a capable defender in limited action. Vaughn, a transfer from Southeastern (Iowa) CC, was ranked by a national recruiting service as one of the top newcomers in the league. He also plays power forward. **David Butler**, a 6-6 transfer from Lincoln Trail (Ill.) JC, was also recruited to help the team immediately.

"They're going to have depth and size," said one Mid-Continent assistant coach. Even 6-5 senior **Ken Pollpeter** (2.0 ppg) and 6-6 sophomore **Steve Deering** (1.2 ppg), two more forwards who played sparingly last year, could help out.

The Panthers will be more immediately skilled on the perimeter, starting a blossoming point guard in 6-2 junior **Dale Turner** (9.9 ppg, 3.2 rpg, 152 assists). Turner developed into a clutch scorer late last season, hitting key baskets down the stretch in conference tournament victories over Southwest Missouri State and Wisconsin-Green Bay. His assist-to-turnover (152 to 64) ratio was nearly three to one. "By the time he's a senior," Miller said, "Dale has a chance to be the best point guard I've ever had."

The Panthers have two solid shooting guards in **Maurice Newby** and **Cam Johnson**. Newby (5.5 ppg), a 6-4 senior, has three-point-plus shooting range. He converted 43.3 percent of his three-point attempts, and it was his 25-footer with two seconds left that stunned Missouri. Newby came off the bench last season, but could be a starter this time around. Johnson (2.9 ppg), a 6-2 sophomore, played in all but one game last season and proved to be a steady player as a freshman.

Northern Iowa also has an intriguing newcomer at guard in 5-10 junior **Louis Armstrong**, a transfer from Lincoln Land (Ill.) JC. Armstrong has a point guard's quickness and ballhandling skills, with a shooting guard's touch (26.0 ppg). He could end up providing backup help at both backcourt positions.

Jon Ellis (Senior HS/Dubuque, Iowa), a 6-7 forward, and **Ed Madlock** (West HS/Waterloo, Iowa), a 6-0 guard, redshirted last season and will be available as freshmen.

BLUE RIBBON ANALYSIS

The Panthers definitely will have a new look. For the past four years they have been mainly a low-post team on offense, dumping the ball to the reliable Reese. This year, their strength will be the outside shooting of Muilenburg, Turner, Newby and Hill, as well as the athleticism of their small forwards and guards.

Matching last year's stretch drive will be difficult, if for no other reason than Northern Iowa is not hosting the conference tournament. But the Panthers' quickness and balance make them a favorite to challenge Wisconsin-Green Bay for the Mid-Continent title.

The Panthers gained big-game experience last year, and also will not have the pressure of being first-time favorites to win the Mid-Continent, a factor which might have contributed to last year's 6-6 showing in the league. With Muilenburg, Turner, McCullough, Newby and the junior college recruits, this will be a good team, good enough to finish in the top three in the conference for sure. The development of some of the young power players could determine whether the Panthers will be even better.

1990-91 NORTHERN IOWA SCHEDULE		
Nov.	23-25	#San Juan Shootout
	29	@Southwest Missouri State
Dec.	1	Nevada
	4	@Iowa
	8	Morningside (IA)
	11	Iowa State
	14	@Wyoming
	22	Detroit
	29	Eastern Illinois
Jan.	2	Wisconsin-Oshkosh
	5	Northern Illinois
	7	Wisconsin-Green Bay
	12	@Cleveland State
	14	@Akron
	16	@Detroit
	21	Valparaiso (IN)
	24	@Illinois-Chicago

1990-91 NORTHERN IOWA SCHEDULE Cont.		
Jan.	26	@Western Illinois
	29	Drake
Feb.	2	@Northern Illinois
	4	@Wisconsin-Green Bay
	9	Cleveland State
	11	Akron
	13	@Eastern Illinois
	16	Illinois-Chicago
	18	@Valparaiso
	23	Western Illinois
	27	@St. Louis
Mar.	4-6	##Mid-Continent Tournament

@ Road Games
# San Juan, PR (American University of Puerto Rico, Bucknell, Illinois, Murray State, Nebraska, Old Dominion & St. Louis)
Green Bay, WI

NORTH TEXAS STATE

LAST SEASON: 5-25
CONFERENCE RECORD: 3-11
STARTERS LOST: 2
STARTERS RETURNING: 3
CONFERENCE: SOUTHLAND (SLC)
LOCATION: DENTON, TX
HOME FLOOR: SUPER PIT (10,000)
NICKNAME: MEAN GREEN EAGLES
COLORS: GREEN AND WHITE
COACH: JIMMY GALES, record at North Texas, 47-70. Career record, includes high school, 240-97.

North Texas began the 1989-90 season with great ambitions, shooting for its third consecutive Southland Conference regular season championship. The Eagles, though, experienced great disappointment and frustration in an enigmatic season, winning only five of 30 contests.

"It was terrible," said Eagles' head coach Jimmy Gales, "especially when I look at the talent that we had. Last year, the team (on paper) was by far the most talent-ladened team that I've had since I've been here. It was sort of like we had a high revving car without a driver, and without a driver you can't go very far."

North Texas lost 17 games in a row at one point in the season, but found new life in the SLC's post-season tournament, upsetting second place finisher McNeese State and Northwestern State to reach the finals, where they lost to regular season champion Northeast Louisiana.

The Eagles lost two starters from last year's team, post Ronnie Morgan and point guard Kevie Gulley. Morgan, who led the team in scoring with a 15.7 points per game and led the SLC in rebounding with 12.6 rebounds per game, will be difficult to replace; Gulley led the team in assists with 131.

The Eagles' climb back to the top will be built around three returning sophomores, who all started as freshmen. 6-3 guard **Ray Schufford** (12.8 ppg, 2.8 rpg, 49 assists, 20 steals) was the team's second leading scorer and set a school record for most made three-pointers in a season (69). 6-7 forward **Jake Short** (4.7 ppg, 4.4 rpg, 32 assists, 19 steals) became a favorite of Gales with his scrappy, hardnosed play on defense and on the glass. 6-7 forward **Ron Griffen** averaged 6.9 points and 2.9 rebounds per game and finished third on the team in made three-pointers with 31.

"I am very encouraged with our three returning starters," said Gales. "Last year, each played with

a great deal of emotion and desire. It is their motivation and want-to that will help to carry us this season."

Four other lettermen return. 6-10 senior center **Doug Schindler** (3.1 ppg, 4.0 rpg) and 6-8 senior forward **Lowell Myrie** (2.8 ppg, 2.1 rpg) offer experience and quality depth. 6-4 sophomore guard **Rusty Walker** (1.7 ppg) and 6-2 senior guard **Kelvene Harris** (1.3 ppg) should figure in the Eagles' bench strength.

The Eagles will boast eight new faces on their roster this season and two transfers from Southwest Conference schools figure prominently in Gales' plans. **Donnell Hayden**, a 6-1 senior, is ticketed for starting duties at point guard. Hayden led Baylor in scoring two years ago with a 13.5 points per game average and scored 25 points when the Bears defeated North Texas 96-95 in four overtimes. "He is the quarterback or car driver that we so sorely missed last year," said Gales. "He's a winner. He wants to win and will take the necessary measures to ensure that he wins."

6-9 junior center **Thomas Gipson** will be counted on to fill the void left by Morgan, who passed up his senior year to play in Europe. Gipson averaged 4.9 points and 4.8 rebounds two years ago at Texas. "Gipson is tough," said Gales. "He has a good work ethic that will help him tremendously. He's not as talented as Ronnie, but that's where his work habits will enhance his overall play."

The Eagles added two junior college players, who should contend for starting positions. 6-2 junior guard **Pat Nash** averaged 17 points per game at Odessa (Tex.) JC. An excellent shooter, Nash will probably find a spot in the Eagles' starting lineup. **Cedric Carson**, a 5-9 junior guard, compiled a 26.9 points per game average at Texas State Technological Institute in Waco, Texas.

Four freshmen could figure in Gales' rotation. 6-7 forward **Jesse Ratliff** (16.0 ppg, 10.5 rpg) and 6-4 guard **Jereld Nunley** (17.4 ppg, 4.2 assists) led Biloxi HS to consecutive Mississippi state championships. "Ratliff and Nunley were a package," said Gales. "They wanted to play together and I'm sure glad they decided to play at North Texas."

Gales called 6-5 **Gavin Diepraam** a steal. Diepraam averaged 15 points per game as a junior at Houston-Dulles HS, but only played in two games as a senior because of a broken hand. 6-6 **Dyalan Beamon** averaged 16 points and 11 rebounds per game at Dallas-Kimball HS.

BLUE RIBBON ANALYSIS

North Texas suffered a great fall last year and faces a substantial climb back to reach the top of the Southland Conference. As usual, the Eagles are well stocked with guards and wings to fuel their run-and-gun attack. But the questions arise in the middle where Morgan, a solid scorer and relentless rebounder, is gone. Gipson may help some but is far from a proven consistent force.

If the Eagles can find a reliable scorer inside, they could return to the upper echelon of the Southland Conference. While North Texas should improve over last year's disastrous showing, the lack of a proven inside scorer probably means they'll finish no higher than fourth in the Southland Conference.

1990-91 NORTH TEXAS SCHEDULE		
Nov.	24	Long Beach State
	27	Alcorn State
	29	Jackson State (MS)
Dec.	1	Weber State
	3	@Texas Southern
	5	Nicholls State (LA)
	8	@Houston
	17	@New Mexico
	20-21	#Pre-Holiday Classic
	27-28	##Hoosier Classic
Jan.	5	@Southeastern Louisiana
	10	@Southwest Texas State
	12	Stephen F. Austin
	17	Northeast Louisiana

NORTHWESTERN

LAST SEASON: 9-19
CONFERENCE RECORD: 2-16
STARTERS LOST: 5
STARTERS RETURNING: 0
CONFERENCE: BIG TEN
LOCATION: EVANSTON, IL
HOME FLOOR: WELSH-RYAN ARENA (8,117)
NICKNAME: WILDCATS
COLORS: PURPLE AND WHITE
COACH: BILL FOSTER, record at Northwestern, 32-80.
Career record, 445-348.

For the second straight season, the Northwestern Wildcats finished with a disappointing 9-19 record and for the sixth straight year, they ended with a 2-16 mark in Big Ten conference play. Unfortunately, things will not get better for head coach Bill Foster and the Wildcats this season. The rebuilding process continues at Northwestern due to the departure of six seniors and the decisions by three underclassmen to transfer to other programs with another to begin a two-year Mormon mission this fall. "Every organization in rebuilding needs patience and careful planning and a touch of luck," the ever optimistic Foster said. "We have not had much of the latter in the last couple of years and are definitely due for a good stretch."

Leading the exodus from Evanston were leading scorer Rex Walters (17.6 ppg, 2.7 rpg), leading rebounder Brian Schwabe (9.4 ppg, 6.5 rpg) and two-time Most Valuable Player Walker Lambiotte (16.8 ppg, 4.9 rpg). Schwabe and Lambiotte were seniors, while Walters decided to transfer to Big Eight power, Kansas. Also gone are senior guard Rob Ross (4.4 ppg, 3.6 apg) and senior reserve forward Don Polite (4.2 ppg, 1.6 rpg). Starting point guard David Holmes (7.2 ppg, 1.9 rpg) and three-time starting forward Kevin Nixon (7.1 ppg 2.7 rpg) also have transferred, further depleting the Wildcat bench. Finally, 6-9 junior forward Evan Pederson, a member of the Mormon Church, has elected to begin his two-year church mission. He will not forfeit any eligibility during his two-year mission. With all these departures, Foster's Wildcats are left with only nine scholarship players. Open tryouts will be held to fill out the squad when fall practice begins on October 15.

The most welcomed piece of news for Foster is the return of often injured 6-8 senior center Larry

Gorman. Gorman has missed the last year and one half following back surgery. As a sophomore, Gorman averaged 9.2 ppg and 4.6 rpg in the nine games he played, but he has yet to play in a Big Ten game. Gorman, a 231-pound player who uses his bulk to his advantage, has won the starting center position in his last two years and will again get the nod this season. His experience will be needed on this extremely young ball club.

Getting the start at power forward will be 6-5 senior **Lucis Reece** (3.3 ppg, 2.3 rpg). Reece is the only returnee with any starting experience, having started three Big Ten contests last winter. He is an explosive leaper who likes to run the floor and Foster hopes he can realize his potential after three disappointing seasons in Evanston.

Looking to get the starting assignment on the other side of the lane will be 6-5 senior **Don Brotz** (2.9 ppg, 0.8 rpg). Brotz missed the last 13 games of last season due to a broken finger suffered at Michigan State. He is a competent role player who hasn't seen much action during his career at Northwestern, but will be pressed into duty this fall. Brotz has a decent outside shot, but will be looked to more for solid defensive play and occasional rebounding.

6-9 sophomore forward/center **Charles Howell** (1.6 ppg, 1.4 rpg) will see plenty of action and may assume a starting frontcourt position if either Brotz, Gorman or Reece don't produce. He played sparingly last season posting highs in points with six against Northeast Illinois and rebounds with five at Iowa. Howell still hasn't added much weight (197 pounds) since his rookie season which may present a problem in Big Ten play, but look for Howell to play nonetheless. Playing time will come soon to 6-11 freshman center **Kevin Rankin**. As a senior at Abbott Pennings HS in DePere, Wisc., Rankin led his team to the Wisconsin private school state championship. He was a Top 150 player in the country last year and averaged 23 points and 12 rebounds per contest during his final season. Foster and the Wildcats are excited about Rankin. They feel he has the size and the ability to be an All-Big Ten performer in the very near future. If Gorman cannot stay healthy, Rankin may learn under fire.

The Northwestern backcourt is unbelievably young. To quote a popular basketball analyst, "these guys are true diaper dandies!" Three freshmen and a sophomore round out this youthful squad. 6-5 sophomore swingman **Todd Leslie** (4.4 ppg, 0.9 rpg) will start at the off-guard spot. Leslie is an excellent outside shooter and led the Wildcats in free throw shooting, making 42-of-49 tries for a solid 86 percent average in his freshman season. He will be looked to for scoring and more scoring. This is a Northwestern team that lost over 86 percent of its scoring from last season. Leslie will be turned loose this season by Foster as will starting point guard, 6-1 freshman **Pat Baldwin**. Baldwin led Leavenworth (Kan.) HS in virtually every statistical category as a senior. He hit on a 21.9 ppg mark with 8.8 rpg and led all Kansas players in large 6-A schools with an average of 5.9 assists per contest. Baldwin also made over 52 percent of his field goals and set a school record with 44 three-point goals in 99 attempts. He will immediately inherit the reins to the Northwestern attack.

6-2 freshman **Eric Simpson** (18.0 ppg, 6.0 rpg, 5.0 apg) will back up Baldwin at the point guard spot. Simpson was the outstanding senior player in the Chicago Catholic League while a senior at St. Ignatius HS. As a three-year starter, Simpson ended his career with over 1,200 points and 150 three-point field goals. Simpson will see a considerable amount of playing time.

The final guard slot will be filled by 6-5 freshman **Kip Kirkpatrick**. He earned first team All-Kentucky honors while hitting on 20 points per game and grabbing nine rebounds a game at Henry Clay HS in Lexington. He is a solid outside shooter who could start if Foster goes to a three-guard set. With all the points that need to be replaced, this may be the game plan for the Wildcats.

BLUE RIBBON ANALYSIS

Graduation, injuries and transfers have hit the Northwestern basketball program hard over the last few years. Gone from this year's squad are four seniors, three transfers and one player (Evan Pederson) who will sit out the next two years due to a Mormon Church mission. Indeed, improving upon a 9-19 record and a 2-16 Big Ten mark will be a tough task. The Wildcats are quick, both defensively and offensively, and they can shoot the basketball. The only drawback seems to be the relative inexperience of the entire roster. Four freshmen and two sophomores make up two-thirds of the scholarship players on the team and the Wildcats may field a starting team that includes three freshmen and a sophomore.

The sure starters look to be sophomore Leslie at shooting guard and freshman Baldwin at point guard. Both are young sharpshooters who will lead an up-tempo, full court attack. Senior Reece will start at power forward and he will be a key to starting the Northwestern fast break. Senior Gorman will start at center if his back has healed sufficiently. He has fine low post moves and he will add experience to this group. If Foster goes with a traditional two guard set, look for senior Brotz to start at forward in the beginning of the season, but freshman Kirkpatrick may take over as the year progresses. Kirkpatrick can shoot and will add speed.

Foster has won at every stop along the way — Rutgers, Duke, Utah and South Carolina. Northwestern, however, has been a much different story for Foster. Northwestern will again finish in tenth place in the Big Ten.

NORTHWESTERN STATE

LAST SEASON: 10-19
CONFERENCE
RECORD: 5-9
STARTERS LOST: 2
STARTERS
RETURNING: 3
CONFERENCE:
SOUTHLAND (SLC)
LOCATION:
NATCHITOCHES, LA
HOME FLOOR: PRATHER COLISEUM (3,900)
NICKNAME: DEMONS
COLORS: PURPLE, WHITE AND ORANGE TRIM
COACH: DAN BELL, record at Northwestern State,
23-35.
Career record, 52-39.

As sometimes happens, Dan Bell suffered through the ''sophomore blues'' in his second year as head coach at Northwestern State. After leading the Demons to a overachieving 13-16 mark in his first year, his second edition slumped to a 10-19 mark.

Northwestern State spent the 1989-90 season restructuring as Bell brought only four players back from his first season. With no seniors and only two second-year players on the team by the time conference play rolled around, the Demons suffered from inconsistency, reflected in the fact that Bell used 13 different lineup combinations and started two true freshmen.

A brutal schedule didn't help matters. Northwestern State, which went 40 days without a home game during one stretch early in the season, lost nine of its first 10 games. Following the season, Bell again separated the wheat from the chaff, retaining only five players from last year's team. But with three starters returning and two quality redshirt transfers ready to step into the lineup, Bell has a positive outlook.

''I feel more confident about the program,'' said Bell. ''The first year, I inherited a group of players I didn't recruit and last year I had only one player who had played Division I basketball.

''I feel now I have the players who will make the commitment to be the kind of players we want in the program, not only on the court but in the classroom.''

A dark cloud remains, though. Northwestern State still faces sanctions for NCAA rules violations that occurred during the tenure of former head coach Don Beasley. Penalties are expected to be handed down in the fall and there's the strong possibility that the Demons will be ruled ineligible for conference championship honors and post-season play by the NCAA.

So much for the bad news. The good news is that while the quantity of returners may be low, the quality isn't.

The most critical starter back is 6-0 senior Roman Banks (14.7 ppg, 4.8 rpg, 157 assists, 50 steals), who earned second team All-Southland Conference honors last year. Banks, the Demons' leading scorer a year ago, finished the season in a rush, scoring 29 and 28 points in two of the last four games. Banks, who is on pace to become the school's all-time career assist leader, will have to provide the leadership in a starting lineup that may include four sophomores.

''Roman came on at the end of last year and has developed into a better player than I ever thought he would be,'' said Bell. ''Making second-team all-conference really helped his confidence. He's our only senior in the program, so he's very important.''

6-7 sophomore post Dexter Grimsley (13.3 ppg,

6.9 rpg, 54 assists, 38 blocked shots, 27 steals) earned freshman of the year honors. Grimsley didn't play like a freshman. During a 10-point loss to LSU, he squared off against Tiger center Shaquille O'Neal. Bell pulled Grimsley aside and said, ''Dex, I don't know if you're stupid enough to bow up on Shaquille O'Neal, but I want you to know, if you are, I'm not stupid enough to go out and try to save you.'' Grimsley, whose ideal position is small forward, should profit from being paired with bigger teammates inside this year.

6-7 sophomore Jethro Owens (10.3 ppg, 6.2 rpg, 43 assists, 15 blocked shots, 35 steals) started 26 games as a freshman last year and led the team with an impressive 55.7 field goal percentage. However, Owens has room for improvement at the free throw line where he shot only 41.9 percent (52-of-124).

The other vets back are 6-6 junior forward Mike Thornton (1.5 ppg, 1.4 rpg) and 6-7 sophomore forward Earl Fleming (0.9 ppg, 0.8 rpg).

Two transfers from East Carolina should move into the starting lineup when they become eligible at the end of the fall semester three games into the season. Jay Sherer, a 6-3 sophomore guard who was named Alabama's player of the year in 1987-88, should give the Demons the consistent shooter they sorely missed last year. Sherer averaged 20.6 ppg while hitting 55 percent of his three-point attempts for Bell's alma mater, Grissom HS in Huntsville, Ala. ''Jay Sherer is the key to our whole team next year,'' said Bell. ''He's a competitor who loves to take the shot in the clutch. He's a winner.''

Sherer will be joined by his former teammate at Grissom HS, 6-9 sophomore center Brooks Bryant. Bryant averaged 19 points and 9.3 rebounds, and shot 58 percent from the field in helping Grissom to the Class 6A Alabama state championship. ''Brooks is a 6-9 guy who is a great shooter,'' said Bell. ''He's going to cause opponents a lot of problems because of his shooting range and because he will take up room on defense. He's not a great athlete, but he's a very good basketball player.''

The Demons signed six freshmen and all should figure in the rotation this season. Bell said 6-3 wing Tarius Brown is capable of being the Demons' second straight SLC freshman of the year. Brown averaged 17.0 points and 10.0 rebounds as a post player for Birmingham (Ala.) West End HS. Bell believes Brown should have no problems converting to the wing.

6-7 forward Eric Kubel, who averaged 18.0 points and 8.7 rebounds per game at Moreno Valley (Calif.) HS, is expected to push Owens for playing time. 6-1 Scott Stapler, another Grissom HS product, will back up Banks at point guard. Stapler, whose father coached Bell at Grissom, averaged 18.3 points and 45 percent from three-point range last year.

Larry Terry, a 6-7 forward from Ponchatoula (La.) HS, and Tony Beaubouef, a 6-5 wing guard/forward from Berwick (La.) HS should also get quality minutes. Terry averaged 23.1 points and 9.2 rebounds per game while Beaubouef had 25.2 ppg and 11.0 rpg norms.

Clem Hopkins, a 6-7 post, averaged 18.0 points and 13.5 rebounds for Gorman HS in Tyler, Texas.

BLUE RIBBON ANALYSIS

After getting mixed results from the junior college route, Bell has decided to forego the quick fixes and build his program with youngsters. Grimsley and Owens were solid producers as freshmen last year. With transfers Sherer and Bryant becoming eligible, the quartet combine to give Bell a promising sophomore class.

The future looks bright for the Demons and they should be a team to be reckoned with down the line. But with only one senior on the squad and only three players who have seen any significant Division I playing time, the Demons have some growing pains left to endure.

Because of the inexperience, Northwestern State will finish sixth in the Southland Conference this year.

1990-91 NORTHWESTERN STATE SCHEDULE		
Nov.	26	Centenary (LA)
Nov.	30-	
	Dec. 1	#Dr. Pepper Invitational
Dec.	8	@Centenary
	10	Ouachita Baptist (AR)
	12	Wiley College (TX)
	17	Colorado State
	20	@Fresno State
Jan.	3	@U.S. International (CA)
	5	@Rice
	10	Sam Houston State
	12	@McNeese State
	14	Northeast Louisiana
	17	@Texas-Arlington
	19	@North Texas
	24	Stephen F. Austin
	26	Southwest Texas State
	31	Southeastern Louisiana
Feb.	2	@Northeast Louisiana
	7	@Stephen F. Austin
	9	McNeese State
	11	@Nicholls State (LA)
	14	Texas-Arlington
	16	North Texas
	18	@Southeastern Louisiana
	21	@Sam Houston State
	23	@Southwest Texas State
	25	Nicholls State
Feb. 28-		
Mar. 2	*SLC Tournament	
@ Road Games		
# Waco, TX (Baylor, Delaware & Penn State)		
* Site to be announced		

OHIO UNIVERSITY

LAST SEASON: 12-16
CONFERENCE
RECORD: 5-11
STARTERS LOST: 3
STARTERS
RETURNING: 2
CONFERENCE: MID-
AMERICAN (MAC)
LOCATION:
ATHENS, OH
HOME FLOOR:
CONVOCATION
CENTER (13,000)
NICKNAME: BOBCATS
COLORS: KELLY GREEN AND WHITE
COACH: LARRY HUNTER, record at Ohio University, 12-16.
Career record, 317-92.

On paper, it looks as if Ohio University doesn't have much to get excited about this season. Their top two scorers are history. Only five lettermen return. But if you know the history of second-year coach Larry Hunter - and are adept enough to read between the lines of a team that needs name tags in practices - you also know that OU might just become a darkhorse contender in the Mid-American Conference.

It helps that, outside of perhaps Bowling Green, the MAC race appears wide open. It also helps that Hunter, operating shorthanded last season, often outmaneuvered opposing coaches and kept the Bobcats in most games they played. Hunter, who won 305 of 381 games in 13 years at Division III Wittenberg University, also had the 'Cats two games above .500 before they fell in their last six outings a year ago.

To avoid a late-season swoon this time around, Hunter's first task will be to replace "Dynamite" Dave Jamerson (31.2 ppg, 6.4 rpg), the 6-5 guard who was a first round selection by Houston in the NBA draft. Jamerson, who was third in the nation in scoring, provided 44 percent of Ohio's offense. Toss in departed point guard Dennis "Dink" Whitaker (10.0 ppg, 5.4 rpg, 104 assists, 35 steals) and the Bobcats not only are missing the best nicknamed backcourt in the MAC, but also nearly 60 percent of their scoring. Also gone is Jerry Lebold (3.0 ppg, 2.9 rpg), a part-time starter at forward.

What still makes OU an interesting team and a possible MAC darkhorse is an exciting combination of returning MAC veterans and capable newcomers. Several players will vie for Jamerson's vacated shooting guard spot, and it is Hunter's hope that, together, they can at least approach Dynamite Dave's explosive offensive output. The top prospect is 6-0 junior **Nate Craig** (7.6 ppg, 4.8 rpg), described by Hunter as "a slashing type of player who likes to take the ball to the basket."

Battling him will be a pair of transfers in 6-3 junior **J. "Don't call me Jay" Barry** from Winthrop (S.C.) College and 6-3 junior **Jim Heffner** (George Mason). Lurking in the wings are 6-4 senior **Tom Jamerson** (2.8 ppg, 1.2 rpg), Dave's younger brother, and 6-2 freshman **Rush Floyd** of Pickerington (Ohio) HS. Jamerson missed the entire MAC season last year after undergoing knee surgery in January, but has good genes and, according to Hunter, is "a very heady player with good passing and shooting skills." Floyd turned down a Division I football scholarship to play hoops for OU, and has three-point range on his jump shot.

"Offensively," said Hunter, "we are trading Dave Jamerson's 30-plus average for three to four players with the ability to score in double figures."

Replacing Jamerson, though, only compensates for half the missing backcourt. Whitaker was OU's point man for four seasons, led the MAC in assists a year ago, and left the program as its all-time assists leader. "Replacing 'Dink' will be as difficult as replacing Dave," Hunter admitted. "The statistics don't begin to reflect the contribution he made to our program with his outstanding ballhandling skills and leadership."

Yet Hunter is confident that Whitaker's shoes can be ably filled by junior college transfer **Dedrick Jenkins,** a native of Waterloo, Iowa who played for Northern Iowa CC last season. Hunter describes Jenkins as "a supreme ballhandler with excellent speed and quickness," while leaving no doubt that he expects the 5-11 junior to step right in and run the offense with minimal difficulty.

The frontcourt is anchored by 6-6 sophomore **Chad Gill** (5.5 ppg, 4.3 rpg), a part-time starter and member of the MAC all-freshman team a year ago, 6-7 sophomore **Steve Barnes** (8.7 ppg, 5.5 rpg in 11 games before being sidelined for academic reasons) and 7-0 senior **Rick Hoffman** (2.6 ppg, 2.6 rpg). The most exciting newcomer is 6-6 junior **Dan Aloi,** a long-range bomber who transferred from St. Bonaventure and sat out last season. He could be the one to replace much of the long-gone offensive firepower.

Also vying for frontcourt time will be 6-9 junior **Robert Stark,** a transfer from Salt Lake City (Utah) CC, and 6-6 freshman **Ryan Greenwood** (Cathedral HS/Indianapolis). Another newcomer, 6-7 freshman **Jeff Boals** (Sandy Valley HS/Magnolia, Ohio), will likely redshirt following a knee injury in Ohio's North-South HS all-star game and subsequent surgery.

BLUE RIBBON ANALYSIS

Of the 15 players on Ohio's current roster, 10 have never logged a single minute in a Bobcat uniform. Yet Hunter, a proven coach who waited a long time for his Division I head coaching shot, is excited about his team's chances. "Our personnel will make us a lot more flexible with the types of defenses and offenses we employ," he said. "We've got more skill

ed players and, overall, better size and quickness. Yet, with the influx of new players, in many ways we will be starting all over again. Our success will depend largely on how well this new group of players comes together as a unit."

Aloi and Barnes could be keys to OU's fortunes, as Hunter projects them to start in the frontcourt along with Gill. Aloi is a long-range gunner with excellent scoring potential, while Barnes proved his worth prior to encountering academic troubles last season. The backcourt, though somewhat untested, appears solid. Jenkins is an exciting prospect at the point, while the shooting-guard-by-committee, led by returnee Craig, should help alleviate the absence of Dave Jamerson and actually make the Bobcats a more balanced team.

Hunter sees Bowling Green, Central Michigan, Miami (Ohio) and Eastern Michigan as the teams to beat in the Mid-American Conference race, but is quick to add that "if we stay healthy, I think we have the ability to be right up there with those teams before it's over. How quickly we mold as a team, as well as team leadership, will be the keys to our season."

So figure on the 'Cats taking a little while to gel, but developing into a force to be reckoned with by MAC tournament time. They should also finish with 16 to 18 wins overall.

1990-91 OHIO UNIVERSITY SCHEDULE

Nov.	26	Evansville
Dec.	1	@Rider
	4	Athletes in Action
	8	@Auburn
	10	@Mercer
	13	@Marshall
	15	Univ. of Charleston (WV)
	17	Youngstown State
	22	@Colorado State
	27-28	#Hoosier Classic
Jan.	2	Wright State
	5	@Central Michigan
	9	Bowling Green
	12	@Eastern Michigan
	16	Toledo
	19	@Kent State
	23	Ball State
	26	@Miami (OH)
	30	Western Michigan
Feb.	2	Central Michigan
	6	@Bowling Green
	9	Eastern Michigan
	13	@Toledo
	16	Kent State
	20	@Ball State
	23	Miami (OH)
	27	@Western Michigan
Mar.	8-10	##MAC Tournament

@ Road Games
# Indianapolis, IN (Indiana, Marshall & North Texas)
Detroit, MI

OLD DOMINION

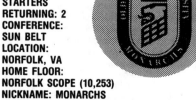

LAST SEASON: 14-14
CONFERENCE
RECORD: 7-7
STARTERS LOST: 3
STARTERS
RETURNING: 2
CONFERENCE:
SUN BELT
LOCATION:
NORFOLK, VA
HOME FLOOR:
NORFOLK SCOPE (10,253)
NICKNAME: MONARCHS
COLORS: SLATE BLUE AND SILVER
COACH: TOM YOUNG, record at Old Dominion, 76-69.
Career record, 510-310.

The 1989-90 Monarchs were a huge disappointment. Picked by many to win the Sun Belt, ODU instead floundered around the .500 mark all season long and finished in a tie for third place. They were beset with injuries for the first month or so, and could never could seem to find the right chemistry thereafter. This despite two of the best players in the conference, **Chris Gatling** and Anthony "AC" Carver.

While that duo averaged almost 42 points between them, the rest of the supporting cast was sporadic. Young couldn't even count on much help from his other starters. For those reasons, ODU struggled to finish as high as it did, and this season promises to bring more of the same.

Carver, the 6-7 forward who led the team and the conference in scoring (21.1 ppg) and also averaged 6.6 rpg, has finally completed his eligibility, as has 6-4 guard Darrin McDonald (14.1 ppg). Chuck Evans, the 5-11 point guard who averaged 5.1 ppg and 6.9 assists, decided to transfer out of the program. Chosen as the top freshman in the Sun Belt, Evans' presence will be missed.

Old Dominion will thus depend even more heavily on Gatling, who averaged 20.5 points and 10.0 rebounds as a junior. The 6-9 center, the returning Sun Belt player of the year, will be the focus of the Monarchs' attack and the onus of opposing defenses. That may curtail his trips to the basket, but experience gained from playing on the U.S. national team over the summer should make Gatling an even smarter player.

"Chris has had two tremendous seasons for us," said Young. "Because of his quickness, he is so versatile. Chris has outstanding moves and great rebounding ability, which make him very tough inside, but his quickness and shooting touch make him just as dangerous outside."

Gatling achieved the double-double (points and rebounds) 14 times last season, and has 26 for his career. The transfer from Pitt scored 20 or more points 16 times, and grabbed 10 or more rebounds on 15 occasions. He is a force to be reckoned with under the basket, but even someone that talented needs at least a little help.

The only other starter returning is 6-7 senior forward **Cyril Cox,** who averaged just 3.0 ppg and 3.5 rpg. The transfer from the University of District of Columbia, hampered by sore knees, did not produce the way Young anticipated and was replaced toward the end of the season by freshman **Keith Jackson,** who started the final six games. Now a 6-5 sophomore, Jackson averaged 9.3 ppg and 4.2 rebounds. As a starter, though, his scoring average increased to 13.2, giving him the inside track to a starting berth this season.

While he suffered through a lackluster season a year ago, 6-7 junior **Ricardo Leonard** (5.8 ppg, 2.8 rpg) should be the starter at power forward. Leonard is capable of using his 225 pounds to good advantage underneath. As a freshman, Leonard averaged 8.1 ppg in seven starts, and Young believes he can produce those kind of numbers again.

The new point guard figures to be 6-0 sophomore **Donald Anderson,** who missed half of last season with an injured spleen. Following his recovery, he averaged 4.1 ppg and 3.9 assists in backing up Evans. Anderson will likely be pushed by 5-11 junior **Barry Smith,** who helped lead Daytona Beach (Fla.) CC to a 25-8 record last season while averaging 9.1 ppg and 7.7 apg. Smith is the younger brother of ODU's Frank Smith (Class of '87), who is the NCAA's fifth all-time assist leader.

Challenging at small forward could very well be 6-7 freshman **Phil Crocker,** who averaged 29.5 ppg and 11.3 rpg for Laurinburg (N.C.) Institute. Another possibility is 6-5 junior **Al Grant,** who helped Champlain (Vt.) CC to a third-place finish (35-2 record) in the JUCO nationals with averages of 15.7 points and 7.3 rebounds.

Adding depth up front will be 7-0 junior **Chris Kerwin** (1.7 pp, 1.8 rpg), Gatling's understudy, and

6-11 redshirt freshman **Allon Wright** (Elizabeth HS/Elizabeth, N.J.), who comes from the same high school as Gatling.

Among the other newcomers that Young hopes will make a contribution are 6-3 junior guard **John Robinson**, who played on the same high school and JC teams as Grant and averaged 18.5 ppg and 3.4 rpg. The pair led Orange (N.J.) High to the AA state championship their senior season (1988).

Other freshmen newcomers include 6-0 **David Bass**, 6-3 **Kevin Larkin** and 6-2 **Joe Leake**. Bass averaged 18.5 points and 4.5 rebounds for Caddo Hills High (Norman, Ark.), which won the Class A state title with a 37-1 record. Leake averaged 21.8 ppg for Princess Anne High in Virginia Beach, and led the Tidewater area by hitting 63 three-pointers, making at least one trey in 32 straight games. Larkin helped Marquette Prep in Milwaukee to a 24-2 record by averaging 9.4 points and 6.2 assists. He also averaged 10.3 ppg for the Milwaukee AAU team.

BLUE RIBBON ANALYSIS

With a young and unproven supporting cast, Gatling is probably going to be frustrated on more than one occasion. Defenses will be collapsing all over him while letting others take the shots. If someone like Jackson or Crocker can hurt the opposition from outside, then Gatling will have an easier time of it. Otherwise, it's going to be a long season for the Monarchs.

While ODU appears destined to finish no higher than fifth in the Sun Belt standings, Young professes confidence. "I feel real good about our team," he said. "We have a lot of depth and balance at each position. We will be even stronger on the boards. And it's especially nice to know you have an outstanding player like Chris in your lineup."

Even with Gatling, though, another .500 season looms for the Monarchs, making it difficult perhaps for ODU fans to understand the two-year contract extension given Young before the end of last season. Although Young continues to get players, as he did for so many years at Rutgers, getting them to stay and play to their ability is another matter.

OREGON

LAST SEASON: 15-14
CONFERENCE RECORD: 10-8
STARTERS LOST: 1
STARTERS RETURNING: 4
CONFERENCE: PACIFIC-10
LOCATION: EUGENE, OR
HOME FLOOR: McARTHUR COURT (10,063)
NICKNAME: DUCKS
COLORS: EMERALD GREEN AND LEMON YELLOW
COACH: DON MONSON, record at Oregon, 97-109. Career record, including high school, 433-282.

Just when it appeared that Don Monson's program at Oregon was in serious trouble, the dean of Pacific-10's coaches came up with what perhaps is his most satisfying season in 31 years of coaching. Monson took the Ducks from a 21-loss season to a winning record (15-14), a first division finish in the Pacific-10 (fifth, 10-8) and a trip to the NIT. And this was a team that everyone had picked to finish last in the conference.

Basketball excitement is back in Eugene because the Ducks return four starters from a year ago, including all-conference guard **Terrell Brandon**. In addition, Oregon brought in Monson's largest recruiting class, including the state's top player for the third straight year. "There's a great deal of optimism with our experienced backcourt in Brandon and **Kevin Mixon**, **Richard Lucas** in the middle for his senior season and **Bob Fife** among the promising youngsters, all returning," Monson admits. "We surprised some people last year, but I don't think we can sneak up on anyone this year. We will have size and quickness and be very versatile. You'd like to have a set lineup, and with four returning starters, we should be able to maintain some consistency. We will have the option of playing a big lineup with two seven-footers in Fife and **(Chuck) Patterson**, and be able to start a three-guard lineup as well."

The player who really brought the Ducks back last year was Brandon (17.9 ppg, 6.0 apg, 1.8 stpg), a 5-11 junior who was forced to miss his freshman season. An all-conference pick, Brandon scored 20 or more points 12 times and was the Ducks' leading scorer 14 times, including 31 against UCLA. Brandon was among the league leaders in three-point percentage (.436). In addition to his impressive numbers, his on-court enthusiasm provided the Ducks with a spark they haven't had in years. Mixon (12.6 ppg, 2.5 rpg) became Oregon's school record-holder in three-pointers in his first year after transferring from El Camino (Calif.) JC. He connected 80 times and shot .414 from bonus land, including two games with seven treys. Mixon also was the team's top backcourt defender.

Lucas (10.9 ppg, 8.5 rpg), a 6-7, 220-pound senior, gives away inches to most opponents, but still ranked fourth in the conference in rebounding and had seven double-doubles (points-rebounds) during the season, while shooting .582 from the floor. He averaged 37 minutes a game and went the distance 14 times. Fife (4.5 ppg, 3.6 rpg), a slender 6-11, 210-pound sophomore, emerged as a starter midway through the season and led the team in blocked shots (38).

Senior guard **Mike Helms** (6-3, 2.3 ppg, 0.3 rpg) had 11 starts as a sophomore and spells Brandon. Senior **David Blair** (6-6, 2.1 ppg, 1.3 rpg) backed up departed small forward Keith Reynolds (15.6 ppg, 4.6 rpg) and will be given a shot at the starting position. He had three starts last year and had 12 points in one of those. **Tony Hargain**, a 6-1 senior, is expected to return after redshirting last year, while competing in

the Independence Bowl with the Oregon football team. Hargain has four career starts.

Among the seven newcomers is Patterson, a 7-0, 225-pound transfer from San Francisco City College (13.0 ppg, 7.0 rpg, in 1988-89) who sat out last year because of academic deficiencies. He is Oregon's first seven-footer since Blair Rasmussen in 1984-85. Patterson is more of a face-the-basket inside player who can knock down jumpers from 15-feet.

The freshman class includes 6-9, 205-pound **Eric Vander Veen** from Amsterdam, The Netherlands. Two years ago he played for Mead High in Spokane, Wash., as a foreign exchange student and averaged 17.0 ppg and 7.0 rpg. Vander Veen is 20 years old and has been a member of his country's National Cadets for two years, averaging 24 points a game. **Orlando Williams**, a 6-2 guard, was Oregon's player of the year while leading Portland's Benson Tech HS to the state title. He averaged 23.4 ppg over his last two prep seasons. Other newcomers include 6-9 forward **Matt O'Neil** (18.0 ppg, 7.0 rpg) from Churchill HS in Eugene; 6-6 forward **Clyde Jordan** (17.0 ppg, 8.0 rpg, 5.0 apg, 4.0 stpg) from West Covina (Calif.) HS; and 6-6 forward **Jordy Lyden** (18.8 ppg, 9.4 rpg) from Beaverton, Ore., HS. O'Neil, son of former Hawaii coach Bruce O'Neil, was a prep player of some national prominence as a center. He has potential to be an impact scorer if he can continue to develop and learn to play facing the basket. Jordan is a good outside shooter and handles well. Lyden may be ready to contribute a bit more quickly than the other freshmen. A very versatile player, he passes well with either hand and shoots well enough to play all three perimeter positions.

Oregon's experience should help early, with a schedule that includes four road games Missouri, Utah, Portland and Nevada —in the first five outings.

BLUE RIBBON ANALYSIS

On paper, Oregon should be even better than last year's surprise season. Even then, the Ducks lost six games by a total of 14 points, including three to archrival Oregon State by a total of six points. With more experience this season, the Ducks figure to turn some of these close decisions around.

If Oregon is to show marked improvement, Fife and Patterson must play like seven-footers. Fife, in particular, must improve his offense. Lucas is solid, if unspectacular, in the middle, but needs rebounding help from the two big men.

Brandon, again, is the player who makes Oregon go. He and Mixon form a solid backcourt. While there's some depth on the bench, it's basically inexperienced, except for Helms. Monson used his reserves sparingly last season, with four starters averaging at least 32 minutes a game.

Monson is a solid coach who received a new lease on his coaching career a year ago when it appeared his job security was in trouble. His recruiting has improved dramatically and has shown up in the won-lost column.

Still, the Ducks will be fortunate to repeat last year's first division finish and NIT invitation. Of the 15 victories, 10 came at home in 12 tries. Venerable McArthur Court still ranks as one of the toughest arenas to visit. If Oregon is to improve, the Ducks will have to win more consistently on the road. Their schedule doesn't favor that.

1990-91 ODO DOMINION SCHEDULE		
Nov.	23-25	#San Juan Shootout
Dec.	3	American University
	5	@William & Mary
	8	Virginia Tech
	15	Long Island
	18	@West Virginia
	22	South Florida
	29	East Carolina
Jan.	3	Richmond
	7	@South Alabama
	10	Jacksonville
	12	Virginia Commonwealth
	14	George Washington
	17	@Western Kentucky
	19	North Carolina Charlotte
	24	South Alabama
	30	@James Madison
Feb.	2	@Virginia Commonwealth
	5	@North Carolina Charlotte
	7	Alabama-Birmingham
	11	@Alabama-Birmingham
	14	@George Mason
	16	Western Kentucky
	21	@South Florida
	23	@Jacksonville
Mar.	2-4	##Sun Belt Tournament

@ Road Games
# San Juan PR (American University of Puerto Rico, Bucknell, Illinois, Murray State, Nebraska, Northern Iowa & St. Louis)
Mobile, AL

1990-91 OREGON SCHEDULE		
Nov.	24	Wisconsin
Dec.	1	@Missouri
	4	Alabama-Birmingham
	6	@Utah
	8	@Univ. of Portland
	15	@Nevada
	20	Montana
	22	Arkansas
	28	Western Michigan

OREGON STATE

LAST SEASON: 22-7
CONFERENCE RECORD: 15-3
STARTERS LOST: 2
STARTERS RETURNING: 3
CONFERENCE: PACIFIC-10
LOCATION: CORVALLIS, OR
HOME FLOOR: GILL COLISEUM (10,400)
NICKNAME: BEAVERS
COLORS: ORANGE AND BLACK
COACH: JIM ANDERSON, record at Oregon State, 22-7.

Last season Oregon State learned that there was life after Ralph Miller.

Now the Beavers are hoping the same is true after Gary Payton.

Oregon State was one of the surprise teams in college basketball last year. Hall of Fame member Miller had retired as one of the game's winningest coaches. Long-time assistant Jim Anderson, who had served as an assistant for almost three decades under Hall of Famer A. T. "Slats" Gill, Paul Valenti and Miller, proved he was capable of making that final step up.

Anderson led the Beavers to the Pacific-10 conference championship, a 22-7 overall record and the NCAA playoffs. However, he could not put a stop to the Beavers' streak of heartbreaking last second setbacks in post-season play. The Beavers lost to Ball State, 54-53, on a three-point play with no time showing on the clock. Oregon State has lost seven straight post-season games, with five of the defeats coming by a total of 13 points. Even the irrepressible Payton couldn't stem this trend.

But it was Payton's overall leadership and talent that took the Beavers to their unexpected heights. He was the *Sports Illustrated* player of the year after averaging 25.7 points, 8.1 assists and 4.7 rebounds per game. He finished with 938 career assists, second only to Syracuse's Sherman Douglas, and accounted for 54 percent of Oregon State's points. In his four years, Payton accounted for 8,728 points, or 46.4 per

cent of the Beavers' total over that span. Included is a school record 2,172 of his own. Payton was rewarded for his stellar career by being the No. 2 overall pick (Seattle) in the NBA draft.

Oregon State always seems to have a cute phrase for its athletic teams. For this year's basketball squad, it's "Post-Payton Place: There's Still Something to Talk About."

Payton isn't the only key player to depart. Forward Earl Martin (11.9 ppg, 5.2 rpg) was a four-year starter. Lamont McIntosh (1.5 ppg, 1.4 rpg) started 23 games in 1988-89 before becoming a key reserve last year. Bob Cavell (1.1 ppg) transferred to an NAIA school to get more playing time in his senior year.

Will Brantley (11.0 ppg, 4.0 rpg) is expected to provide the on-court leadership, although not from the point guard position. The 6-4 senior is an explosive leaper who has had some outstanding games. At Tennessee he scored 24 and teamed with Payton (39 points) for 63 points, the best ever by an Oregon State backcourt duo.

Brantley is a .500 career shooter while starting 65 games, but has made only nine three-pointers. Last year's sixth man, 6-1 senior **Allan Cellestine** (4.1 ppg, 3.0 apg) is expected to move in as point guard. The Beavers obviously will lose considerable firepower and leadership at this position, but Cellestine is a fine defender.

Teo Alibegovic (8.9 ppg, 3.3 rpg), a 6-9 senior forward from Ljubljana, Yugoslavia, has started the last two years. He's a capable, although inconsistent scorer, but a poor rebounder. Rookie coach Anderson moved slender 6-10 sophomore center **Scott Haskin** (8.2 ppg, 4.8 rpg) into the starting lineup at the start of last season. He had one 13-game stretch in which he scored in double figures nine times, but his shooting slumped badly in Pac-10 and NCAA tournament time (4-18). **Karl Anderson** (6-7 junior forward, 4.4 ppg, 3.3 rpg) averaged 20 minutes in the Beavers' last seven games and shot .613 from the field. Also back are **Charles McKinney**, 6-1 sophomore guard (2.6 ppg, 0.9 rpg), **Chris Rueppell**, 6-6 sophomore forward (1.1 ppg, 0.9 rpg), **Kevin Harris**, 6-3 sophomore guard (0.9 ppg, 0.3 rpg) and **Kevin Grant**, 6-3 senior guard (1.4 ppg, 0.8 apg).

The redshirt class of last year could produce two of the best athletes on the squad. **Mario Jackson** (6-4 junior), from Colon, Panama, via North Idaho JC, will compete for one of the starting perimeter spots. He averaged 17.8 ppg in two junior college seasons. **Chad Scott** (6-7 sophomore forward) averaged 32.2 points and 17.3 rebounds per game for Las Plumas HS in Oroville, Calif., in his senior year, 1989. Included were 22 three-pointers in 34 tries.

The Beavers also add 6-7 freshman forward **Travis Stel** from Airdrie, Alberta, Canada, who was invited to the Canadian Junior National team tryouts. He's the third Canadian at Oregon State in the past decade, following guard Alan Tait and center Greg Wiltjer. Freshman **Brent Barry** (6-4 guard, DeSalle HS in Danville, Calif.) is a redshirt possibility. He is the son of former NBA great Rick Barry. Anderson also added 6-9 forward **Henrik Rinsmar**, a sophomore from Upsalla, Sweden, who was recommended by former Beaver Danny Evans, currently playing in Upsalla. And there's a third Anderson, 6-4 **Kereem Anderson**, a freshman swingman from Merced, Calif. (22.5 ppg, 9.1 rpg).

The schedule is the toughest in years, including December visits to New Orleans, Minnesota and the Fighting Illini Classic and non-conference visits by Fresno State, Memphis State and Tennessee.

BLUE RIBBON ANALYSIS

For four years, Payton has carried the Beavers. He made everyone in the supporting cast a bit better, both through his competitiveness and his sharp passes. He cannot be replaced. Brantley, Alibegovic and Haskin are solid returnees. Brantley must show more range,

particularly on the three-pointer, and Alibegovic and Haskin must rebound better if Oregon State is to be competitive. Karl Anderson can rebound but has limited offensive skills.

The Beavers haven't had to change their look much in the last four years. Without Payton, it's a major overhaul, if only in team personality. Payton was a fiery leader but one who could also lead by example. In other areas, the Beavers have been soft, both defensively and on the backboards. These trouble spots could be magnified with Payton gone. This will be a team looking for a new identity. Meanwhile, it will wind up around eighth or ninth in the Pacific-10.

PACIFIC

LAST SEASON: 15-14
CONFERENCE RECORD: 7-11
STARTERS LOST: 1
STARTERS RETURNING: 4
CONFERENCE: BIG WEST
LOCATION: STOCKTON, CA
HOME FLOOR: A. G. SPANOS CENTER (6,000)
NICKNAME: TIGERS
COLORS: ORANGE AND BLACK
COACH: BOB THOMASON, record at Pacific, 22-35. Career record, including high school, 299-182.

When Bob Thomason took the head coaching job at Pacific, his alma mater, two seasons ago, he hoped and dreamed to return the Tigers' program back to its glory days when he played. When Thomason played for the Tigers, he was an integral part of two 20-win seasons and an overall record of 60-21 in three seasons that ended in 1971.

Returning to that era won't be an easy task. After all, the Tigers were 5-24 the season prior to Thomason's hiring. And the new coach suffered through a 7-21 year in his first campaign.

However, Thomason started to see some light last year, when the Tigers were one of the most improved squads in the Big West. Playing an upbeat style that featured the three-point field goal better than it did the power layup, the Tigers bounced back to post a 15-14 mark, the school's first winning season in five years.

That represented major strides toward attaining Thomason's goal of matching yesteryear. This year, the Tigers could come even close toward making Thomason's dreams become reality. Fans around Stockton seem sure it can happen this year.

Thomason welcomes back four starters from last year's bunch of overachieving jump shooters that attained so much success and won seven games in the very tough Big West. Leading the returnees is junior forward **Dell Demps** (15.9 ppg, 4.7 rpg). The 6-4 swingman was the Tiger's leading scorer a year ago, connecting on 49 percent from the floor and 42 percent from three-point range. Demps did it all for the Tigers—passing, ballhandling, rebounding, your basic jack-of-all-trades on the hardwood. He has the ability to be an explosive scorer and a streak shooter. When on a roll, Demps is hard to stop. He finished second on the team in rebounding, assists and steals. His assist to turnover ratio (95 assists to 69 turnovers) was respectable. He is one of the top all-around players in the Big West.

Demps is not Pacific's main gun as senior center **Don Lyttle** is just as important. The 6-10 Lyttle (15.7 ppg, 8.0 rpg) is very versatile as well. Lyttle showed the ability to go inside and outside. While playing power post, he showed a shooting touch from the perimeter, connecting on 48 percent overall and 40 percent from three-point land, a la Bill Laimbeer. Lyttle is also a fine defender as he blocked 22 shots last year. He worked on his strength in the off-season and that should make Lyttle very prepared to make his final season at Pacific a memorable one.

Senior point guard **Anthony Woods** was the third Tiger (Demps and Lyttle being the other two) to start all 29 games last season. The 5-11 Woods is a good penetrator and decent shooter who averaged 8.0 points and 2.6 rebounds to go along with a team-high 131 assists. Woods can also hit the trey (22 made, 33 percent last year), but his biggest asset is his court awareness (an almost 2-1 assist-to-turnover mark), his quickness, plus a strong ability to drive to the basket and then dish off. Woods will once again be the Tigers' catalyst this season.

The final returning starter is senior forward **Rich Ressa** (3.8 ppg, 3.1 rpg). The 6-7 Ressa came to Pacific last year as a transfer from West Valley (Calif.) JC and immediately won a starting role. He is an aggressive rebounder and defender, but Thomason is looking for more offensive punch from Ressa this year to take some of the pressure off of Lyttle and free him to roam outside where he is a big weapon and tough to defend.

Senior forward/center **Scott Hemsath** (3.1 ppg, 1.9 rpg) played in all 29 games last year, starting five. The 6-8, 235-pound Hemsath is a strong, physical player inside and a decent defender. If Ressa doesn't do the job offensively for Thomason this year, then Hemsath may be the answer.

Senior guard **Dan Embick** (1.5 ppg, 1.0 rpg) returns as well. The 6-5 Embick played in four games off the bench last season, scoring six points in 19 minutes. Sophomore guard **Andre Simmons** is another returnee. The 6-2 Simmons saw action in six games, scoring five points.

Sophomore forward **John Hardy** (4.1 ppg, 1.8 rpg) played 18 games last year, starting five. The 6-5 Hardy was expected to battle for a role on the Tigers' roster this year, probably at small forward. But Hardy suffered an injury and his status is questionable now. At press time, it appeared as if Hardy was going to be a medical redshirt.

Thomason welcomes five newcomers to the Tigers' roster this season, three freshmen signees and two junior college transfers. Leading the freshmen class is Stockton's local favorite **Glenn Griffin**. The 6-8 product of St. Mary HS in Stockton led his team to an impressive 33-1 season, averaging 12.8 points and 8.2 rebounds per game. Griffin is a versatile athlete who can play either forward position, but will probably see more time at the power forward slot.

Matt Olin (Carmel, Calif./Robert Louis Stevenson HS) is a 6-8 forward with a lot of potential. Olin averaged 16 points and eight rebounds per game at Stevenson last year. Olin can play center but will also probably break in playing power forward for the Tigers.

Walsh Jordan (Dallas, Tex./Lakehill Prep HS) is a 6-1 point guard who had very impressive numbers in high school —34 points, 15 rebounds, seven assists and six steals per game for the team that won the Texas private school state championship. If Jordan's numbers are for real, then he could be a real find. Thomason is very high on the Tigers' two JC transfers, **Randy Lavender** and **Randy Morphew**. Lavender is a 6-5 forward from Columbia (Calif.) College. He averaged 20 points and eight rebounds per game for Columbia JC last year. Morphew, a 6-7 forward, comes to Pacific from American River (Calif.) JC. Morphew can also play both forward roles, but he is more suited inside, averaging 20 points and 11 rebounds for American River a year ago. Of the newcomers, Morphew is looked upon to be the player of impact.

BLUE RIBBON ANALYSIS

Thomason has worked hard in making his alma mater a formidable foe once again for the teams in the Big West. The Tigers were a laughing stock for too long. Thomason wanted to change that in a hurry and he did. The Tigers won 15 games last year, scared a few good teams and were exciting to watch, especially with all those three-pointers being launched left and right.

Demps and Lyttle are two talented players, keepers in the Big West. Not many coaches have the luxury of sending their 6-10 behemoth of a center out into three-point territory and allow him to hoist away. Lyttle can do that and do it well. Demps can score from all over.

Woods is a solid floor general with a good take-charge attitude. Thomason would like to see him score a little more. He is a good point guard, consistent and dependable.

Where the Tigers need improvement is in rebounding (only 33 per game last year, seven below the national average) and intimidation. Only Lyttle blocked shots last year. That's where the newcomers immediate impact will be felt. Players such as Morphew, Lavender and Griffin will have to help.

Plus, the Tigers lost so many close games last year and their free throw shooting as a team (66 percent) was not good. There were many times that Thomason looked at a box score after a game and said, "If only we made our free throws." The Tigers lost six games by five points or less and better free throw accuracy would have won at least half of those. And with 18 or 19 wins instead of 15, the Tigers would have been off to post-season play for the first time in 20 years.

Thomason is headed in the right direction to make his dream come true. If the Tigers cannot move into the top half of the Big West this year, they will very soon. But this year is not out of the question. The high-flying and long bombing Tigers just might get it done right now. Fifth place or so would be a quantum leap for the program.

		1990-91 PACIFIC SCHEDULE	
Nov.	24	@Montana	
	29	@Santa Clara	
Dec.	1	St. Mary's	
	4	@Nevada	
	7-8	#Pizza Hut Classic	

		1990-91 PACIFIC SCHEDULE *Cont.*	
Dec.	15	San Francisco	
	22	Texas Christian	
	27	Loyola Marymount	
Jan.	2	Long Beach State	
	4	New Mexico State	
	7	@California-Irvine	
	9	@California-Santa Barbara	
	12	Fullerton State	
	14	UNLV	
	17	@Utah State	
	19	@San Jose State	
	26	@Fresno State	
	31	California-Santa Barbara	
Feb.	2	California-Irvine	
	7	@Fullerton State	
	14	San Jose State	
	16	Utah State	
	21	@UNLV	
	23	Fresno State	
	28	@New Mexico State	
Mar.	2	@Long Beach State	
	6-9	##Big West Tournament	

@ Road Games
# Springfield, MO (North Carolina A&M, Prairie View A&M & Southwest Missouri State)
Long Beach, CA

PENN STATE

LAST SEASON: 25-9
CONFERENCE RECORD: 13-5
STARTERS LOST: 1
STARTERS RETURNING: 4
CONFERENCE: ATLANTIC 10
LOCATION: UNIVERSITY PARK, PA
HOME FLOOR: REC HALL (6,846)
NICKNAME: NITTANY LIONS
COLORS: BLUE AND WHITE
COACH: BRUCE PARKHILL, record at Penn State, 98-105.
Career record, 187-180.

A year ago, Penn State coach Bruce Parkhill was guardedly optimistic following a 20-12 season and a berth in the NIT. Now, after a 25-9 record and a trip to the NIT Final Four, the optimism in State College can no longer be guarded.

This is a good team, returning all but one starter. Parkhill is a good coach, good enough to be a finalist for the Virginia job and to be rumored for several other vacancies nationally. It is officially time to toss the jargon and answer the only real question that remains: Can the Nittany Lions get over the hump and into their first NCAA tournament since 1966?

Parkhill, for one, has been around the game too long to just snap his fingers and show up on Selection Sunday. Too many bumps in the road can curtail even the best-laid post-season plans. Smelling the roses was not enough. The Lions must get back to work and finish the job.

"I've asked this group to take a good, hard look at what made us successful last year," Parkhill said. "We won with defense, rebounding and heart. I think last year's team epitomized how much of a factor heart can play in winning."

And the one player who epitomized that concept, 6-9 center Ed Fogell (15.3 ppg, 6.0 rpg, 60.8 percent shooting), is the only loss to graduation. The Lions will have to replace more than his numbers, as Fogell was Penn State's heart and soul. Not a great leaper, hardly the strongest player around, Fogell simply got better every year because he worked at it. With that, it was hard for the rest of the Lions not to do the same.

Said Parkhill: "I don't think there is any way to realistically replace him. Eddie had a fabulous year. He made big plays at both ends of the floor all season long."

Nine of last year's top 12 players do return, though, including the other four starters. The backcourt is particularly strong, and must remain so if Penn State is to pick up where it left off.

A pair of juniors - 6-0 **Freddie Barnes** and 6-3 **Monroe Brown** - will have to add leadership to their already impressive array of skills. Barnes (10.6 ppg, 3.9 rpg, 159 assists, 33 steals) is especially important, setting the table offensively and running the kind of controlled sets which make Penn State difficult to defend. The Lions are a team that, even if well-guarded for 45 seconds, will still run someone off a screen or back cut for a high percentage shot.

Brown (8.2 ppg, 4.3 rpg, 125 assists, 52 steals) is often the trigger man on those sets, although a sophomore shooting slump (.356) slowed his offensive production. A broken finger on his shooting hand didn't help, either, although Brown was not hampered defensively. Of the 17 top opposition scorers he faced, he held 13 below their average.

6-5 sophomore **Michael Jennings** (2.9 ppg, 1.0 rpg) was the first guard off the bench. Erratic at times as a freshman, Jennings showed flashes of athletic ability rarely seen outside the Nittany Lions' football backfield. 6-0 senior **Lem Joyner** (1.1 ppg) usually spells Barnes, and 6-3 senior **Tony Soskich** (0.8 ppg) adds depth.

At small forward, Atlantic 10 freshman of the year **DeRon Hayes** (9.6 ppg, 5.2 rpg) has a job until he graduates. The 6-6 sophomore was among the finest frosh ever at Penn State, recovering superbly from the broken foot which wiped out what was supposed to have been his debut in 1988-89.

"As elated as we were with DeRon," said Parkhill, "the most exciting thing about him is his potential to improve." And if some of that improvement means a bigger nose for the boards, the Lions will not miss Fogell quite so much. Hayes was above average in that department over the summer, when he played for the East squad at the U.S. Olympic Festival.

Behind Hayes are two more sophomores, 6-5 **Eric Carr** (2.2 ppg, 1.0 rpg) and 6-7 **Jim Deitz** (0.8 ppg). Carr is undoubtedly the team's best leaper, and Dietz a radar shooter when given the opportunity.

The power forward, last year's garbage man, is 6-7 senior **James Barnes**. Lost in the hoopla of Penn State's winningest season ever is that Barnes is the Lions' leading returning scorer (11.5 ppg, 6.7 rpg). Once content to play in Fogell's shadow, he emerged as a junior with five double-doubles. He also shot 56.4 percent from the floor and was an NIT all-tournament selection.

"Jimmy was a mainstay for us," said Parkhill. "He had an outstanding year, and I don't see any reason he can't improve statistically in both scoring and rebounding."

There is one reason, actually, namely the level of play at the other low post position. Barnes played off Fogell, and vice versa. In 1990-91, it will be up to 6-9 junior **Dave Degitz** to come up with at least a passable Fogell impersonation. Degitz (4.1 ppg, 2.2 rpg) has appeared in 66 straight games for the Lions and, despite a less than stellar sophomore year, has the brains and the saavy to be the efficient, passing center Penn State requires.

"Dave," said Parkhill, "may have slumped a bit during his sophomore season, but he came on at the end and played well. He is a key player for us, and he should have a good year."

Not far behind is 6-9 sophomore **Rickey Jolley** (1.2 ppg, 1.3 rpg). "He could be a great big kid," said a rival Atlantic 10 assistant. "If he or Degitz can step in and not make (James) Barnes change positions, they won't lose much."

Also in the picture at center are 6-8 senior **C.J. Johnson** (2.7 ppg, 1.9 rpg) and 6-11 freshman **Dan McKenna** (Hunterdon Central HS/Flemington, N.J.). Johnson is already a proven and capable reserve. McKenna is more a long-range project at this stage.

Not a project at all is 6-7 freshman **Elton Carter** (Southwestern HS/Detroit, Mich.). The powerful forward averaged 14.5 points and 10.0 rebounds for the Detroit city and Michigan state champions, and continues Parkhill's recent pattern of excellent out-of-state recruiting. Said Parkhill: "You obviously never know about the transition of a freshman, but Elton looks like he could make an impact."

If he does, the Penn State bench - already the longest in the Atlantic 10 - will be even better. The Lions typically use more players for more quality minutes than any team in the league, and it pays off in defensive intensity over 40 minutes.

BLUE RIBBON ANALYSIS

These are heady times at Penn State. The only problem is, no one seems to know where the Nittany Lions are headed. Next year's ballyhooed move to the Big 10 was clearly a football decision, and it remains undetermined just when the Lions will compete for that league's basketball championship. And, as deep as the Atlantic 10 has become, it also remains to be seen how quickly the Lions can win, if at all, in one of America's original glamour conferences.

In other words, this would be the perfect time for Penn State to grab the brass ring. The A-10 is allowing the Nittany Lions one more season, and State has the experience and talent to make the most of it. Both Freddie and James Barnes are noble, and the wing combination of Hayes and frosh Elton Carter could collectively raise the Lions' overall athleticism.

All it will take for State to be right there again would be modest contribution from someone, most likely Degitz, in the center hole. "You can win in this league with three forwards," said one A-10 coach. "The only team that transcends that is Temple."

The Nittany Lions should have met the Owls in last year's conference championship game, but stumbled against Massachusetts in the A-10 semifinals. And, while the Owls remain a solid favorite, this is Penn State's final shot. It could be that close again.

1990-91 PENN STATE SCHEDULE

Nov.	24	Drexel
	27	Miami (FL)
Nov.	30-	
	Dec. 1	#Dr. Pepper Classic
Dec.	5	Illinois
	8	Marshall
	18	@Temple
	28-29	##Miller Lite Invitational
Jan.	3	Massachusetts
	5	@Rhode Island
	8	@St. Bonaventure
	10	West Virginia
	12	@Duquesne
	17	Rhode Island
	19	Duquesne
	25	@Miami (FL)
	28	Rutgers
	31	@West Virginia
Feb.	3	@George Washington
	7	St. Bonaventure
	9	St. Joseph's
	13	Temple
	16	@Massachusetts
	19	George Washington
	21	@St. Joseph's
	27	@Rutgers
Mar.	2-4 & 7	*Atlantic 10 Tournament

@ Road Games
# Waco, TX (Baylor, Delaware State & Northeast Louisiana)
Tampa, FL (Brown, New Hampshire & South Florida)
* The first three rounds will be held at the Palestra, Philadelphia, PA. The championship game will be held on the home court of the highest remaining seed.

LAST SEASON: 12-14
CONFERENCE RECORD: 7-7
STARTERS LOST: 2
STARTERS RETURNING: 3
CONFERENCE: IVY LEAGUE
LOCATION: PHILADELPHIA, PA
HOME FLOOR: THE PALESTRA (8,700)
NICKNAME: QUAKERS
COLORS: RED AND BLUE
COACH: FRAN DUNPHY, record at Pennsylvania, 12-14.

Fran Dunphy wants Penn basketball fans to look somewhere other than the infirmary for reasons for last year's disappointing Ivy League finish. It would be easy for him to use injuries as a crutch for the Quakers' 7-7 league record and third-place standing. After all, some of his players used them - crutches, that is. But Dunphy isn't willing to write off his first year to Blue Cross.

"I don't want to use injuries as an excuse, and I'm not going to," Dunphy said. "We had enough bodies to do better than we did."

A recitation of the Quaker sick log, though, is evidence that Penn's struggles were not all self-inflicted. Burly forward **Vince Curran,** a 6-7 senior, started the season with 35 rebounds in three games, then missed the rest of the year with a stress fracture. 6-5 senior forward **Scott Schewe** was out of commission for the beginning of the season with two stress fractures, and 6-7 senior **Sean Dineen** played the entire year with a sore back that required post-season surgery. A guard, 6-4 senior **Paul McMahon**, struggled the second half of the year with shin splints.

Still, Dunphy isn't whining. "We just need to be more consistent," he said.

That consistency will start with 6-7, 250-pound senior **Hassan Duncombe**, a first-team All-Ivy selection last year. Duncombe, whose nimble moves belie his bulky frame - a la crosstown NBA star Charles Barkley - averaged 19.1 points and 7.7 rebounds as a junior. He thrilled Palestra regulars with highlights, like his last-second tip-in of a missed foul shot that gave the Quakers a one-point win over arch-rival Princeton, but frazzled Dunphy with constant foul trouble, resulting in nine disqualifications.

"Hassan has to be more consistent," Dunphy said. "He's probably our most talented athlete and a great inside player, but he needs more consistency."

If Duncombe teams up front with the 240-pound Curran (8.3 ppg, 11.7 rpg in three games), and 6-7, 245-pound senior **Ray Marshall** (4.9 ppg, 4.5 rpg), the Quakers may cause an eclipse in the Palestra. A more likely scenario would be two of those three with seniors Schewe (2.2 ppg, 2.4 rpg), 6-5 **Dane Watts** (2.2 ppg, 2.4 rpg) or Dineen. **Bill Helm**, a 6-5 junior, 6-5 sophomore **Jeff Blount** and 6-9 sophomore **Andy Wise** were seldom-used frontcourt reserves. 6-7 junior Mike Milobsky, a transfer from Tufts, is also available.

Dunphy could really use help in the backcourt. Gone are Tyrone Gilliams (10.0 ppg) and second-team All-Ivy performer Jerry Simon (15.1 ppg, 5.4 rpg, 91 assists, 41 steals) - along with their combined 25.1 points and 8.5 rebounds.

Point guard **Paul Chambers** (6.2 ppg, 104 assists, 35 steals), a 5-10 junior, started 23 games last year, and McMahon (8.2 ppg) gave Penn some scoring punch early in the season. Ken Graf (4.0 ppg, 1.4 rpg), a 6-1 junior, and 5-10 soph **Steve Wade** (2.4 ppg) played more than occasionally.

"We have to shoot the ball better from the perimeter than we did last year," Dunphy said.

259

Dunphy brought in seven freshmen, some of whom he hopes can contribute right away. The guards are 6-5 **Will Brown** (Miller Place HS/Miller Place, N.Y.), 6-2 **Gary Langham** (LaSalle-Peru HS/LaSalle, Ill.), 6-2 **Will McAlister** (Highland Regional HS/Blackwood, N.J.) and 6-2 **Dan Purdy** (New Hampton School/New Hampton, N.H.). The forwards include 6-6 **Ken Hans** (Holy Cross HS/Delran, N.J.) 6-3 swingman **Barry Pearce** (Hill School/Pottstown, Pa.) and 6-7 **Joe Warden** (Lawrenceville School/Lawrenceville, N.J.).

"Any one of four freshmen can step in and help at guard," Dunphy said. "At the same time, it's tough for freshmen to come in and play right away. That's asking a lot."

Penn athletic director Paul Rubincam will ask a lot of all the Quakers, putting together an atypical Ivy League non-conference schedule. Along with the usual Philadelphia Big Five rivals (LaSalle, Villanova, Temple and St. Joseph's), there is Kentucky, Southern Methodist and an Arizona State tournament featuring Texas and Michigan.

"I just hope we survive the pre-season," Dunphy said. "In the league, I feel anyone can win at any time. We just have to do the job when we have the chance."

BLUE RIBBON ANALYSIS

With Duncombe, Curran and Marshall, the Quakers have enough bulk to make Penn football coach Gary Steele smile. Dunphy will have the luxury of using these three to bang, or bringing in Watts, Schewe and Dineen to open things up a bit. That could cause matchup problems league-wide.

But Penn's frontcourt versatility could be negated by its backcourt inexperience. Chambers is a hustler who can get the ball to the right guy, but there remains a dearth of outside shooting in what has rapidly become a three-pointers' league.

The Penn-Princeton stranglehold on the Ivy League is long gone, with only the Tigers remaining in the spotlight year-in and year-out. Penn may not have been happy with a third-place finish last year, but a similar spot in this year's deeper Ivy may represent an improvement.

1990-91 PENNSYLVANIA SCHEDULE

Nov.	24	@Kentucky
	28	Southern Methodist
Dec.	1	La Salle
	4	Villanova
	7	Navy
	28-29	#Kactus Klassic
Jan.	3	@Temple
	8	@Colgate
	11	Brown
	12	Yale
	15	@St. Joseph's
	23	@Lehigh
	28	@Lafayette
Feb.	1	Harvard
	2	Dartmouth
	5	Princeton
	8	@Columbia
	9	@Cornell
	15	@Yale
	16	@Brown
	22	Cornell
	23	Columbia
	26	@Princeton
Mar.	1	@Dartmouth
	2	@Harvard

@ Road Games
# Tempe, AZ (Arizona State, Michigan & Texas)

PEPPERDINE

LAST SEASON: 17-11
CONFERENCE RECORD: 10-4
STARTERS LOST: 4
STARTERS RETURNING: 1
CONFERENCE: WEST COAST (WCC)
LOCATION: MALIBU, CA
HOME FLOOR: FIRESTONE FIELDHOUSE (3,104)
NICKNAME: WAVES
COLORS: ORANGE, WHITE AND BLUE
COACH: TOM ASBURY, record at Pepperdine, 37-24.

Third-year Pepperdine coach Tom Asbury believes that once all the pieces - seven returnees and five newcomers - fall into place, the Waves should be a pretty good team. By the end of the season, maybe, and certainly by 1991-92.

Unfortunately for the Waves, there are quite a few games between now and then. A non-league schedule, for one, then another West Coast Conference race. In other words, it is a rebuilding year in Malibu. Time for progress to take priority over wins and losses.

That speaks well for the team's future, but what about now? Losing four of five starters from the past two seasons leaves a void of proven collegiate experience on the roster. The only exceptions are 6-8 junior power forward **Geoff Lear** (13.8 ppg, 8.9 rpg), Pepperdine's power forward, and 6-6 junior **Doug Christie** (8.9 ppg, 4.1 rpg, 4.0 apg, 34 blocked shots), last year's top reserve.

In Lear, the Waves have the only returning All-WCC first-team player. He should be the most complete a player in the league, as he can shoot (57.1 percent from the floor, third best in the WCC), rebound (second in WCC, behind the late Hank Gathers) and intimidate (tied with Christie for the conference lead in blocked shots with 34).

"Lear has the ability to average upwards of 20 points and 12 rebounds a game," said Asbury. "He should rank among the top 15 or 20 rebounders in the country, because he and Christie are going to get all of the minutes they can handle. It's their time to shine."

While Lear and Christie may make for an imposing duo all season, they cannot be the entire Pepperdine team. The bulk of what used to be the Waves - Dexter Howard, Tom Lewis, Craig Davis and Shann Ferch - are gone. It was a foursome which included four double figure scorers, a pair of all-league players, the starting backcourt and a center.

Still, Christie is a very versatile big guard and may prove to be the second best all-around player in the league behind his own teammate. His offensive and defensive skills (44 steals) are quite advanced. "From a purely athletic standpoint, Christie may be the most talented player in the conference," said Asbury. "He has tremendous ability and instinct."

After Lear and Christie, it is anyone's guess as to whom Asbury will turn. The rest of the lineup looks like three questions marks waiting for a period. There were no questions with Howard (17.9 ppg, 6.0 rpg), Lewis (14.8 ppg, 4.8 rpg), Craig Davis (14.0 ppg) and Shann Ferch (10.9 ppg, 3.5 apg). Though there were occasional discipline problems among that foursome, they represented some of the best talent on the West Coast.

Asbury had been counting on the continued development of 6-10 junior center **Mark Georgeson** to ease the team's transition. Georgeson (4.0 ppg, 2.5 rpg) was seriously injured, however, in an off-season automobile accident and is fortunate to be alive. A year ago, he started 17 games and appeared in three others

for the Waves after transferring from Arizona. Much more had been expected for the coming year, but it is not yet known whether his services will be available.

Christie is set in the backcourt. Who will start at the point alongside him? The top contenders are 6-0 junior **Rick Welch** (2.0 ppg, 1.3 apg) and 5-9 freshman **Damin Lopez**, who was a medical redshirt last year after fracturing a bone in his left hand. Lopez was once a top prep recruit out of Apollo High in Glendale, Ariz., where he averaged 27.6 points and 7.6 assists as a senior.

6-4 freshman **Steve Clover** and 6-3 freshman **Rodney Sanders** are the only other guards. Clover averaged 24.0 ppg at Rolling Hills HS (Rancho Palos Verdes, Calif.), while Sanders produced 10 points and seven rebounds per game at Fairfax High in Los Angeles.

Depth and experience will be lacking in the frontcourt as well, after Lear. If Georgeson is not available for the center spot, the Waves may go with three forwards. 6-9 junior **Damon Braly** (0.5 ppg), 6-8 senior **Rex Manu** (2.3 ppg, 2.3 rpg) and 6-8 redshirt freshman **Derek Noether** are center candidates. 6-6 freshman **Dana Jones**, who averaged 19 points and 12 rebounds while leading North Hollywood (Calif.) HS to the Los Angeles City 4A championship, will battle 6-6 sophomore **Steve Guild** (1.2 ppg) for the first-string small forward assignment.

BLUE RIBBON ANALYSIS

Future prospects seem bright for the Waves, after they take their lumps and gain much needed collegiate experience this season. Five of the 12 players on the roster are freshmen, and the lone senior - Manu - played in just 18 games.

If not for the fact that Lear and Christie are two of the top players in the WCC, Pepperdine would be a candidate for last place. Instead, Asbury should be able to maneuver the Waves into fourth - and feel fortunate to be there - by the time players get familiar and comfortable with each other. After two second place finishes in a row, Pepperdine must take a turn in the middle of the pack.

1990-91 PEPPERDINE SCHEDULE

Nov.	23-24	#Sun-Met Classic
	27	California-Santa Barbara
Dec.	1	DePaul
	3	Nebraska-Omaha
	8	Fullerton State
	13	Texas Tech
	15	@Boise State
	19	@UCLA
	22	Jacksonville
	27 & 29	##Fiesta Bowl Classic
Jan.	2	Kansas
	11	University of San Diego
	12	Santa Clara
	16	Loyola Marymount
	19	@Loyola Marymount
	25	@San Francisco
	26	@St. Mary's
Feb.	1	St. Mary's
	2	San Francisco
	7	@University of Portland
	9	@Gonzaga (WA)
	15	Gonzaga
	16	University of Portland
	21	@Santa Clara
	23	@University of San Diego
Mar.	2-4	*WCC Tournament

@ Road Games
# Fresno, CA (Fresno State, Montana State & U.S. International)
Tucson, AZ (Arizona, Iowa State & Temple)
* Santa Clara, CA

UNIVERSITY OF PORTLAND

LAST SEASON: 11-17
CONFERENCE RECORD: 7-7
STARTERS LOST: 3
STARTERS RETURNING: 2
CONFERENCE: WEST COAST (WCC)
LOCATION: PORTLAND, OR
HOME FLOOR: CHILES CENTER (5,000)
NICKNAME: PILOTS
COLORS: PURPLE AND WHITE
COACH: LARRY STEELE, record at the University of Portland, 19-65.

The University of Portland basketball program was once a pitiful sight. With the roster lacking in talent and a head coach with no collegiate experience, the Pilots managed to win just three of 28 West Coast Conference games in their first two years under Larry Steele. A popular player with the NBA's Portland Trail Blazers, Steele was serving in a marketing capacity for that franchise when summoned to take over for long-time Pilots' coach Jack Avina.

Steele has now earned more popularity as a coach, mainly for guiding Portland to 11 wins overall last season and a 7-7 record - good for fourth place in the WCC. Those numbers might not set the world on fire in most places, but it more than doubled the combined conference win total for Steele's first two seasons. Learning on the job, Steele is now adept at subtle game-night strategy and at substitution rotations.

The players also improved with age, though not quite to the championship-contender level. Unlike Steele's NBA experience, however, older players tend to exhaust their eligibility. In all, the Pilots lost six players - including three starters - from their best team in some time. 6-5 guard Josh Lowery (16.7 ppg, All-WCC first-team) and 6-7 center William McDowell (13.3 ppg, 6.6 rpg) are the biggest holes.

Eight returnees - led by 6-5 senior **Ron Deaton** (8.4 ppg, 2.8 rpg, 57 assists), 6-7 sophomore **Matt Houle** (5.8 ppg, 2.4 rpg, WCC freshman of the year) and point guard **Erik Spoelstra** (7.9 ppg, 124 assists) - will help keep Portland competitive in the conference. Deaton is an especially underrated performer who can drive to the basket or shoot from outside, while the self-made Spoelstra is a dangerous passer who will also shoot from three-point range. The 6-1 junior has enough skills to be even more assertive offensively. He still ranked among the league leaders in assists, three-point percentage (.383) and foul shooting (.833).

Deaton figures to start at the off-guard spot alongside Spoelstra. Backing them up at guard will be 6-4 sophomore **Jack Estep** (2.5 ppg), 6-2 freshman **Chris Jones** (20.0 ppg, 7.4 apg, 4.5 steals at Judge Memorial HS/Salt Lake City), and 6-3 junior transfer **Kevin Mason** (11.6 ppg at Hancock JC/Santa Maria, Calif.).

Houle, a starter 19 times as a freshman, should have a first-string frontcourt assignment for the entire season. He will have to rebound effectively, though, as the Pilots need him at power forward. "The battle for playing time in the frontcourt is going to be fierce," said Steele. "We have good size and a tremendous group of competitors, which will make for very intense practices."

What the coach predicts had better come true, as the rest of the frontcourt is either untested or still unproven at the collegiate level. Among the returnees,

Steele hopes that 6-6 **David Roth** (4.6 ppg, 2.3 rpg) and 6-8 **Dan Gray** (1.6 ppg) can muster big senior seasons, or that 6-6 sophomore **Grant Tracy** (1.2 ppg) is ready. The Pilots also have perhaps the tallest player in Division I, 7-5, 250-pound senior **Greg Ritter** (1.2 ppg, 1.3 rpg). Ritter was limited to just six games a year ago after recovering from a stress fracture in his right ankle. Sadly, he is still not mobile enough to help all that much.

Steele's recruits are the best group to sign with the Pilots in a decade, and the coach figures to look to five freshman forward and center candidates for at least one starter. There is size and potential among these newcomers: 6-9 Australian **Leigh Wadeson** (Lebanon HS/Lebanon, Ore.), 6-8 **Curt Ranta** (Cascade HS/Leavenworth, Wash.) and 6-7 **Mike Mueller** (Columbus HS/Columbus, Neb.), who was named "Mr. Basketball" as the top prep performer in his home state. Wadeson was recruited by Indiana and other higher profile schools, enrolling for the second semester last year and practicing with the team.

Another freshman candidate, 6-6 **Erik Payne** (Wilson HS/Washington, D.C.), displayed great all-around ability, averaging 20 points, 17 rebounds and five assists. 6-5 freshman **Nino Samuel** (Clark HS/Las Vegas, Nev.), was All-State as a high school junior, but played in just two games as a senior due to an achilles tendon injury. He looked like a poor man's Charles Barkley in summer league action.

BLUE RIBBON ANALYSIS

Steele, after three years on the scene, has learned to coach and to recruit. He and his team showed enough progress last year to more than justify the continued patience of the university and Pilot fans.

Deaton, Houle and Spoelstra provide a strong base of experience in the starting lineup, but it is questionable whether the many untried and unproven players - on the collegiate level, anyway - will all be able to erase the many Portland question marks. Due to the graduation losses, it is a mini-rebuilding situation for the Pilots.

At least Steele will be stronger, and not just because he now has experience. Toward the end of last season, the coach underwent a medical procedure to correct an irregular heartbeat condition that had been with him all his life.

Overall, despite last year's rapid improvement, the Pilots do not appear ready to contend seriously for a league championship. With all their newcomers, Portland will need another year or two to accomplish that. In the meantime, fourth place is the call here.

1990-91 UNIVERSITY OF PORTLAND SCHEDULE			
Nov.	24	@Washington	
	26	@Eastern Washington	
	29	Butler	
Dec.	6	Chaminade (HI)	
	8	Oregon	
	15	Texas Tech	
	18	Montana	
	20	@Fullerton State	
	22	@Notre Dame	
	29	@Fresno State	
	31	@Air Force	
Jan.	5	@Wisconsin	
	7	Loyola	
	11	@San Francisco	
	12	@St. Mary's	
	16	@Gonzaga	
	19	Gonzaga	
	24	University of San Diego	
	26	Santa Clara	
	31	@Santa Clara	
Feb.	2	@University of San Diego	
	7	Pepperdine	
	9	Loyola Marymount	
	15	@Loyola Marymount	
	16	@Pepperdine	
	21	St. Mary's	
	23	San Francisco	
Mar.	2-4	#WCC Tournament	

@ Road Games
# Santa Clara, CA

PROVIDENCE

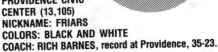

LAST SEASON: 17-12
CONFERENCE RECORD: 8-8
STARTERS LOST: 4
STARTERS RETURNING: 1
CONFERENCE: BIG EAST
LOCATION: PROVIDENCE, RI
HOME FLOOR: PROVIDENCE CIVIC CENTER (13,105)
NICKNAME: FRIARS
COLORS: BLACK AND WHITE
COACH: RICH BARNES, record at Providence, 35-23. Career record, 55-32.

The squad Rick Barnes assembled last season was somewhat of a Big East sleeper and just missed being more. The Friars went down by only one point to Georgetown in the Big East tournament, then blew a nine-point lead with less than three minutes left against Ohio State in the first round of the NCAA tournament. Many felt the Friars could have given UNLV some trouble had they advanced past Ohio State.

This year Providence returns only **Eric Murdock**, albeit a healthy Eric Murdock, from among last year's starters. Given that Providence returns five role players plus Murdock, this is regarded as a rebuilding season by some Providence observers. However, Barnes and his staff are not among them. They believe the Friars can become a factor in the Big East race by February by blending a heavy influx of high quality, if unproven, athletic ability with some solid experience.

The cornerstone of the offense figures to be Murdock, the 6-2 senior guard who has been impressive at both backcourt positions during his first two years. Hampered by a stress fracture that cost him the entire pre-season, Murdock got off to a disappointing start last season but started to pick it up down the stretch as evidenced by his 16.7 ppg average in Big East play, as opposed to 15.4 for the entire season. Murdock also handed out 88 assists. Now fully healed, he should be ready for a big senior year. A good outside shooter as well as a strong and smart penetrator, Murdock has proven he has the guts, court sense and physical requirements necessary to be an impact player. Depending upon the progress of 6-1 sophomore **Trent Forbes** and/or JC transfer **Corey Floyd**, that impact could be at either backcourt spot.

Forbes, a highly touted point guard at Dover-Sherborn HS in Dover, Mass., is explosive and well suited for Barnes' fast-paced offense. However, until he brings his game under control, his playing time won't go much over the seven minutes a game he got last year as an understudy to the now departed Carlton Screen. With Screen gone, though, Forbes (2.6 ppg) will be given every shot to take over the point. He did have 36 assists in 160 minutes last year. If Forbes can tone it down and get in sync with Murdock, Providence would have one of the more talented backcourt duos around. If not, Barnes will look to the 6-3 junior Floyd (16.0 ppg at Hutchinson, Kan. JC). He was the leading scorer on a squad that featured eight players who have gone on to the Division I ranks. Floyd, who excels in the transition game, has seen his own game undergo its considerable transition. In high school he relied on his strength and quickness for penetration. During his two years at junior college, however, he greatly improved his perimeter skills. Floyd was always an intense, athletic defender, ideal for the Friars' pressing man-to-man schemes. Now, the word out of the Jersey Shore League is that he's also sticking three-pointers with regularity. Suffice it to say if he continues that trait and keeps his decision making stable, Floyd will spend a lot of time in the regular backcourt rotation.

Also figuring as a backcourt contributor is 6-3 senior **Chris Watts** (5.4 ppg). Watts, who started the season's first eight games while the healing Murdock came off the bench, is a solid team player. Forty-three of his 48 field goals last season were from three-point range. This fits with a team that emphasizes the three-pointer as an integral of the offense as it did during the Rick Pitino era. Watts, an excellent defender, also shot 85 percent from the line last season. He lost 12 pounds over the summer.

Returning up front are 6-9 sophomore center/forward **Tony Turner** (2.6 ppg, 1.4 rpg), 6-8 junior center/forward **Marques Bragg** (5.9 ppg, 4.0 rpg), and 6-8 sophomore **Marvin Saddler** (2.3 ppg, 2.0 rpg). Of the three, Turner could be a surprise. He arrived in Providence last year from Atlanta at 6-7, 170 pounds. Now he's 6-9 and 200 pounds. Turner's an excellent shooter for a big man and could become a major benefit to the Friars by pulling opposition defenders away from the basket. Bragg is a strong, fearless force who was the team's best defender a year ago. He also made 56 percent of his shots and came up big at times — 15 points, 11 rebounds in 22 minutes at Georgetown, 18 points and six rebounds in 16 minutes at Pitt. Bragg is a garbage man on offense whose numbers could increase significantly if he improves his 44 percent free throw shooting. Saddler was a high school teammate of Watts at St. Joseph's in Trumbull, Conn.

Providence is justifiably excited about its newcomers. In addition to Floyd, Barnes signed two other JC transfers and three freshmen. 6-8 junior forward **Fred Campbell** (14.0 ppg) is a transfer from powerful Midland (Tex.) JC. Campbell has 15-foot range and is a quality athlete. Barnes feels Campbell can contribute immediately. 6-4 junior swingman **Ken McDonald** (25.0 ppg) played on a Loyola Marymount-style, extremely fast-paced team at the Community College of Rhode Island. He made 109-of-218 treys last season.

Among the freshmen, 6-8, 230-pound **Troy Brown** (19.0 ppg, 14.0 rpg at Brewster, N.H., Academy) could have the most immediate impact. Brown is a tremendous athletic talent, compared by some to former Providence star and current Houston Rocket Otis Thorpe. He is a tremendous rebounder who is strong in traffic with good hands.

The other two freshmen may also play major roles, particularly 6-6 forward **Franklin Western**, who did not play his senior year at Manhattan Center in New York City because he began his career as an eighth grader and used up all four years of high school eligibility. Western could be the freshman sleeper of the entire Big East. He's a natural scorer with a nose for the ball and is a great finisher. Western can run, stick mid-range shots and rarely fails to capitalize on a scoring opportunity. He averaged 29 points per game at the National 19 and Under AAU tournament and was co-MVP. 6-10 freshman center **Dickie Simpkins** (27.0 ppg, 13.0 rpg at Friendly HS in Fort Washington, Md.) also is highly regarded. He was a Top 75 selection nationally and an All-Metro pick in the Washington area. Simpkins can shoot, run the floor and is strong and mobile. He needs to improve defensively and get tougher to have an impact this year.

BLUE RIBBON ANALYSIS

Despite the fact Providence lost quality experience and size like Marty Conlon and Abdul Shamsid-Deen (a second round pick of the Seattle SuperSonics) as well as quality point guard Carlton Screen, the incoming talent is probably athletically superior to those departed. Overall, Providence may have more talent. That, however, does not translate into instant success in the Big East. The Friars will need time to find their roles and blend together.

Murdock must be the team leader and Forbes or Floyd have to provide assistance in the backcourt. Up front, Bragg can defend and rebound while Turner

and freshman Brown provide the offense. Newcomers Western and Campbell figure to provide scoring. If freshman Simpkins doesn't come through, rebounding could be a problem.

There is enough talent here to keep the inexperience from dropping Providence to the cellar. Providence's time is coming. Next season when blue chippers Robert Phelps and Michael Smith, who will sit out the 1990-91 campaign, are in uniform, Providence should be a contender for the Big East's upper echelon.

1990-91 PROVIDENCE SCHEDULE

Nov.	23-24	#Fleet Basketball Classic
	28	Brown
Dec.	1	New Hampshire
	5	Northeastern
	8	Rhode Island
	11	@Boston College
	21	Manhattan
	23	@Arizona
	29	Liberty University (VA)
	31	Baptist College (SC)
Jan.	2	@Seton Hall
	5	@Holy Cross
	8	Georgetown
	12	@Pitt
	15	@St. John's
	19	@Connecticut
	23	Pitt
	26	Syracuse
	29	Seton Hall
Feb.	6	@Georgetown
	9	St. John's
	12	@Syracuse
	16	@Villanova
	19	Connecticut
	23	Boston College
Mar.	2	Villanova
	7-10	--Big East Tournament

@Road Games
#Providence, RI (Boston University, Lafayette & Morgan State)
##Madison Square Garden, New York, NY.

PURDUE

**LAST SEASON: 22-8
CONFERENCE RECORD: 13-5
STARTERS LOST: 3
STARTERS RETURNING: 2
CONFERENCE: BIG TEN
LOCATION: WEST LAFAYETTE, IN
HOME FLOOR: MACKEY ARENA (14,123)
NICKNAME: BOILERMAKERS
COLORS: OLD GOLD AND BLACK
COACH: GENE KEADY, record at Purdue, 215-93. Career record, 253-112.**

After a disappointing 15-16 record in 1988-89, Purdue coach Gene Keady, who is a tough, intense type anyway, was even more focused and directed than usual. The result was an impressive turnaround in 1989-90 as Purdue led the Big Ten for most of the season before settling for second place with a 13-5 record. The Boilermakers were ranked in the Top Ten for several weeks and finished 22-8 overall. If Keady had gotten the goal tending call he was looking for, Purdue would have nipped Texas in the second round of the NCAAs and advanced to the Final Sixteen.

Three senior starters, each of whom started all 30 games last year, have graduated. Gone are center Stephen Scheffler (16.8 ppg, 6.1 rpg), point guard Tony Jones (14.6 ppg, 2.9 rpg, 171 assists) and forward Ryan Berning (8.9 ppg, 5.7 rpg, 46 assists). Scheffler was the Big Ten player of the year and finish-

ed his career as the NCAA career field goal leader. He also was a second round pick of the Charlotte Hornets. Jones led the Big Ten in assists and was a second-team All-Conference choice. Berning had a solid senior campaign, ranked second in the Big Ten in free throw percentage and was an honorable mention All-Conference selection.

Keady, the coach of the year in the Big Ten last season, has a challenge awaiting him in trying to replace Scheffler, Jones and Berning. However, Purdue does have nine returning lettermen. Junior guard **Woody Austin** (8.5 ppg, 2.5 rpg, 66 assists) is Purdue's leading returning scorer. The 6-2 Austin was Purdue's Most Improved Player last season. He would have led the Big Ten in three-point accuracy (.565) if he had made one more attempt. He also made 88 percent of his free throws in Big Ten play.

Junior guard **Loren Clyburn** (4.1 ppg, 1.6 rpg, 31 assists) is a talented 6-5 athlete with 12 career starts to his credit. Clyburn was too individually-oriented for Keady's tastes as a freshman and early last season before he joined his mother for a heart-to-heart talk in Keady's office after Purdue's Big Ten opener. Clyburn is now fully acclimated to Keady's system and could be a star this season.

Other returning guards are 6-0 senior **Dave Barrett** (1.2 ppg, 25 assists), 6-6 sophomore point **Matt Painter** (0.8 ppg) and 6-3 **Rich Mount** (0.7 ppg). Barrett has won the team's Mr. Hustle award the past three years and will contend for the starting point guard slot. Painter and Mount saw limited action, 83 and 70 minutes respectively, last year. The Purdue coaching staff believes Painter can be a quality playmaker and Mount was known as a great shooter in high school. He is the son of former Purdue All-America player Rick Mount. Three of Purdue's four freshmen are guards. **Linc Darner** and **Matt Waddell** are shooting guards and **Travis Trice** a quick point. Darner (6-4) averaged 24 points per game as a senior at Anderson (Ind.) HS. He was ranked by most scouting services as a national Top 100 player. Waddell (6-3) pumped in 32.2 points per game for Tipton (Ind.) HS. Trice is 6-1 and averaged 19.3 ppg at Princeton (Ind.) HS.

Up front, Keady will depend heavily on 6-6 senior forward **Chuckie White** (7.8 ppg, 5.5 rpg, 64 assists, 22 blocks) and 6-6 senior forward **Jimmy Oliver** (8.0 ppg, 2.5 rpg, 59 assists). White is a superb leaper who is Purdue's top returning rebounder and inside scorer. He started all 30 games last year. Oliver, who can also swing to guard, started 15 games as a sophomore before coming off the bench last season. He is a quality perimeter shooter and a leader.

Craig Riley, a 6-9 junior, should start in the pivot. He made 56.5 percent of his field goal attempts last year and averaged 1.1 points and 0.8 rebounds. If Riley doesn't get the nod then 6-9 sophomore **Cornelius McNary** will. McNary is a redshirt freshman from Rich South HS in Matteson, Ill. He averaged 14.1 points, 7.3 rebounds and 3.3 blocks as a high school senior. McNary is more talented than Riley and was impressive last season in practice.

Todd Schoettelkotte, a 6-9 sophomore forward, and **Ian Stanback**, a 6-7 freshman forward, are also on the Purdue front line. Schoettelkotte played in only 10 games as a freshman (0.9 ppg), but is an impressive shooter. Stanback averaged 19.7 ppg as a senior at East St. Louis (Ill.) HS. He improved considerably as a senior. Stanback will probably need some time to develop but he has the physical ability to become a quality Big Ten player.

BLUE RIBBON ANALYSIS

"He gets more out of his kids than any other coach in the country," said Michigan State coach Jud Heathcote about Purdue coach Gene Keady. "I have a lot of admiration for him. He takes good players and doesn't necessarily make them into great players, but makes great teams out of them."

Last year, Purdue practiced what Keady preaches

and the result was a second place finish in the Big Ten and a 22-8 record. Duplicating last season's level of success should be difficult as Purdue has lost three key players including Big Ten player of the year Scheffler and outstanding point guard Jones. Still, nine lettermen return. Junior guard Jones, junior guard Clyburn, senior forward White and senior forward Oliver have all done enough in the past to give Keady optimism. If either junior Riley or redshirt freshman McNary come through in the pivot, Purdue can be much better than advertised.

Keady is used to Purdue being picked low in the Big Ten in pre-season. We foresee 18 to 20 wins from the Boilermakers with a fourth place Big Ten finish.

1990-91 PURDUE SCHEDULE		
Nov.	24	Stetson
	26	Massachusetts
Nov. 30-Dec. 1		#Boilermaker Invitational
Dec.	6	@California
	8	@St. Louis
	15	Furman
	20	Butler
	22	North Carolina
	29	@Georgia
Jan.	3	@Northwestern
	5	@Illinois
	12	Michigan
	14	Indiana
	17	@Minnesota
	23	Michigan State
	26	@Wisconsin
	31	Iowa
Feb.	3	@Ohio State
	6	Illinois
	10	@Indiana
	16	Minnesota
	18	@Michigan
	23	@Michigan State
	28	Wisconsin
Mar.	2	@Iowa
	6	Ohio State
	9 or 10	Northwestern

@ Road Games
# West Lafayette, IN (East Carolina, Indiana State & Loyola)

RHODE ISLAND

LAST SEASON: 15-13
CONFERENCE RECORD: 11-7
STARTERS LOST: 1
STARTERS RETURNING: 4
CONFERENCE: ATLANTIC 10
LOCATION: KINGSTON, RI
HOME FLOOR: KEARNEY GYMNASIUM (5,000) PROVIDENCE CIVIC CENTER (12,150)
NICKNAME: RAMS
COLORS: BLUE, WHITE AND GOLD
COACH: AL SKINNER, record at Rhode Island, 28-28.

The most important victory at Rhode Island occurred in the off-season. It came when the NCAA ruled that 6-3 senior guard **Eric Leslie** had a year of eligibility remaining. With one stroke of the pen, the Rams now boast the leading returning scorer in the Atlantic 10.

The decision also means the Rams will be only partially, instead of totally decimated from last season. No eligibility decision will result in the return of A-10 player of the year Kenny Green, whose courage and

persistance while enduring four years of painful knees was at last recognized by media covering the conference.

Green (17.5 ppg, 10.9 rpg, 124 blocked shots) is gone, probably to Italy, and with him the backbone of three winning teams in four years. There is no immediate replacement inside, meaning the Rams will look even more to the perimeter scoring prowess of Leslie (23.0 ppg, 4.6 rpg, 79 assists, 45 steals).

A one-time Villanova signee, Leslie led the Atlantic 10 in 12 statistical categories. "He is a pure scorer," said one A-10 coach, "even more than a shooter. No matter what you did (defensively), the kid got his points."

Of course, most of those defenses were bunched around Green. Rhode Island coach Al Skinner may have to run designed sets to spring his star for the same number of shots this time around.

A key figure there will be 6-2 sophomore **Carlos Easterling,** the returning point guard. Easterling (6.1 ppg, 2.4 rpg, 142 assists) started 27 of 28 games, but needs to shoot a bit more than he did as a freshman. More scoring, and there is a need for plenty, could come from top backcourt reserve **Frenchy Tomlin.** A 6-2 junior, Tomlin (7.0 ppg, 2.2 rpg) had knee surgery a year ago and was limited to 19 games.

Up front, the big returnee - and we mean big - is 6-9, 240-pound junior **Jeff Kent.** To his credit, Skinner stuck with him as a sophomore, and Kent responded with 10.1 ppg and 5.6 rpg. That was alongside Green, however, so the center must now prove he can repeat or increase those numbers as "the man" underneath.

"Jeff played well for us," said Skinner. "I think he can do more." Kent will have to, and he got the chance to learn from the league's best while playing for a touring A-10 all-star team this summer at the Jones Cup in Taiwan.

The final returning starter is Fullerton State transfer **Mike Brown,** a 6-7 junior who started 22 of 24 games after gaining his eligibility. Brown 10.7 ppg, 6.0 rpg) is not the type to set the world on fire, but comes to play most nights and has a shot at becoming an even higher scorer. Brown was second in the Atlantic 10 in three-point accuracy (.456) a year ago.

6-7 senior **Brien Jenkins** (3.7 ppg, 2.8 rpg) will back up Brown and Kent. He could even start if Skinner goes with three forwards, as he got the call twice in a pinch last winter. 6-8 sophomore **Mike Moten** (2.1 ppg, 1.3 rpg) also returns.

Deep backcourt reserves include 6-3 sophomore **Matt Keebler** (1.0 ppg) and 5-11 soph **Art Fitzhugh,** who did not score last year. They will be pushed by 6-2 freshman **Carlos Carfield** (Oak Hill Academy/Mouth of Wilson, Va.), originally from Charlotte, N.C.

Two more freshmen will try to crack the frontcourt, where there is more immediate opportunity. 6-7 **Damont Collins** (Barstow HS/Kansas City, Mo.) and 6-7 **Andre Samuel** (St. John-the-Baptist HS/Massapequa, N.Y.) are the signees there.

BLUE RIBBON ANALYSIS

The Rams, not a great defensive team to begin with, will be even less so without Green's intimidating presence in the middle. Green erased many of the breakdowns, tendinitis and all, by leading the nation in blocked shots. Along the way, he became an honorable mention All-America and the first Ram ever to named Atlantic 10 player of the year.

Rhode Island will miss Green most on defense, as there is probably enough scoring to go around. With Leslie back in the fold and Tomlin healthy again, this could be a fire-when-ready season in Kingston. Skinner may even go with a three-guard offense, Easterling in charge, to offset an average front line. It is hard to imagine Kent, at least this year, becoming a real go-to guy down low.

It is also hard to imagine the Rams remaining in the first division of the Atlantic 10. Somewhere

between sixth and eighth place is the call here. "Without Green," said one A-10 assistant, "they've got to slide at least a little bit."

1990-91 RHODE ISLAND SCHEDULE		
Nov.	24	Keene State (NH)
Dec.	1	@Northeastern
	4	Brown
	8	@Providence
	22	Univ. of Hartford
	28-29	#Connecticut Mutual Classic
Jan.	3	George Washington
	5	Penn State
	9	##St. Peter's
	12	@St. Joseph's
	14	St. Bonaventure
	17	@Penn State
	19	@St. Bonaventure
	21	West Virginia
	24	Duquesne
	26	@Rutgers
	28	Temple
Feb.	1	@Massachusetts
	5	Rutgers
	7	@Duquesne
	9	@George Washington
	14	@West Virginia
	16	Maine
	19	@Temple
	23	St. Joseph's
	27	Massachusetts
Mar.	2-4 & 7	*Atlantic 10 Tournament

@ Road Games
# Hartford, CT (Connecticut, Lafayette & William & Mary)
Meadowlands Arena, East Rutherford, NJ
* The first three rounds will be held at the Palestra, Philadelphia, PA. The championship game will be held on the home court of the highest remaining seed.

RICE

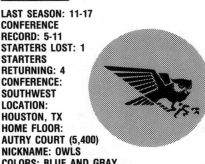

LAST SEASON: 11-17
CONFERENCE RECORD: 5-11
STARTERS LOST: 1
STARTERS RETURNING: 4
CONFERENCE: SOUTHWEST
LOCATION: HOUSTON, TX
HOME FLOOR: AUTRY COURT (5,400)
NICKNAME: OWLS
COLORS: BLUE AND GRAY
COACH: SCOTT THOMPSON, record at Rice, 29-54.

Rice coach Scott Thompson came close to turning the corner with a traditionally poor program but the Owls (11-17) hit a late season slump —ending with seven consecutive losses and 10 losses in their last 11 games.

The Owls return all but one starter and there is every indication that three consecutively strong recruiting classes will pay off. Freshmen accounted for 40.6 percent of Rice's points and sophomores had 43.1 percent.

"We were disappointed that we didn't win more," Thompson said. "But I think we made great strides. When you have a young team, you expect inconsistencies, but we competed in almost every game."

Rice's future hinges on two returning sophomores —**Brent Scott** and **Marvin Moore** —with allconference potential, juniors **Dana Hardy** and **Ken Rourke** and newcomer **Chase Maag** competing with **Scott Tynes** and **David Willie** to make the small forward spot more productive. The Owls also have much better depth than in Thompson's first three years.

The key will be Scott, who was a part-time starter on the U.S. Junior National team which won a gold medal in international competition during the summer. The 6-10 Scott has the body of a banger inside, but the soft-shooting touch of a guard to go along with it. He set an SWC record with 300 points, breaking Rob Williams' mark of 294 set at Houston in 1980. Scott (15.3 ppg, 8.2 rpg) was 10th in SWC scoring and tied for third in rebounding with teammate Rourke. He developed much quicker than some expected, after being recruited out of Everett HS in Lansing, Mich., also the alma mater of Magic Johnson. Scott had eleven 20-point games, including four in a row, which were the most by an Owl since Ricky Pierce scored at least 20 in 11 consecutive games in 1982. ''Brent can be as good as he wants to be,'' Thompson said. ''He has some great tools in his size and strong will. Now, people will be out to stop him. He will have to rise to the next level.''

Rice doesn't have a proven backup for Scott, who proved himself as a workhorse with nearly 30 minutes playing time per game. Redshirt freshman **Dajuan Eubanks** (6-10) still must develop other skills than as a shotblocker. He is out of Kimball HS in Dallas, Tex. It would be a lot to expect incoming freshman **Robert Glaze** to do as well as Scott. The 6-8 Glaze is a banger from Detroit's Cass Tech HS.

The Owls complement Scott well with two good big forwards —who can play simultaneously to spell Scott. Rourke is the starter and the 6-10 lefty has established himself in his first two seasons. He tied with Scott in rebounding at 8.2 per game and was 25th in SWC scoring at 10.6 ppg. When he arrived three years ago, Rourke was pegged as the anchor for the future after a standout high school career in Tulsa, Okla. He has not lived up to that billing, but he certainly has been a quality addition. Rourke's cohort is 6-11 **Greg Price** (9.3 ppg, 6.0 rpg), who can provide a spark off the bench. The slender junior is sometimes timid inside, but he has an excellent outside shot. He had four, three-pointers against Houston in the SWC post-season tournament.

The Owls need to make the most dramatic improvement in the perimeter shooting of their three outside positions. Rice was last in SWC field goal shooting (43.2 percent) and next to last in three-point accuracy (34.6 percent).

Sophomore Scott Tynes (6.0 ppg, 3.1 rpg) did a respectable job at small forward, particularly as a freshman. He will be challenged by Chase Maag, a rare junior college transfer for Rice. Maag is a 6-4 swingman who averaged 22 points and seven rebounds per game at Northeastern JC in Sterling, Colo. He was Rice's only spring signee and was an honorable mention JC All-American.

6-5 junior forward David Willie missed most of last season after undergoing surgery on a broken foot. Willie set a Rice freshman scoring record in 1988, but his scoring fell to 9.3 ppg after 15.3 ppg as a freshman. 6-3 junior **Greg Johnson** (4.0 ppg) could be left with few minutes of playing time and could face competition from incoming freshman **Torrey Andrews** (6-5) of St. Augustine HS, New Orleans, a talented high scoring prospect who was a finalist for the Louisiana Mr. Basketball Award.

The Owls are solid at guard with 6-1 junior Dana Hardy at point and 5-11 sophomore Marvin Moore as the No. 2 slot —although both need to improve shooting consistency. Hardy followed departed senior D'Wayne Tanner as the second Rice player to reach a season triple-triple. He totaled 363 points, 118 rebounds and 113 assists. He had a tendency to run hot and cold, but also showed the knack to make clutch shots late in the game. Hardy's 35 points against SMU two seasons ago was an SWC freshman record.

Moore was the most touted newcomer last season — rated by *Street and Smith's* as the 39th best freshman in the nation. The quick-footed Moore (8.7 ppg) is like a second point guard with his excellent ballhandling, a passing and defense. 6-4 reserve junior **Will Strickland** played sparingly (14 games) and will probably lose minutes to incoming freshmen Andrews and 6-2 **Sam Campbell**, as well as Maag swinging to the off-guard slot. Campbell averaged 21 points, seven rebounds and five assists for Austin (Tex.) Reagan HS. He can play either guard spot and is a capable outside threat.

BLUE RIBBON ANALYSIS

Rice is still trying to break its 19-year drought without a winning season, but the Owls seem to be getting close. Thompson will likely be acknowledged as one of college basketball's bright young coaching stars if he manages to pull it off.

The development of Scott into a national level player is the key for the Owls, who play aggressively under Thompson. Rice is as strong inside as any other SWC team, other than Texas and Arkansas. The need is for better shooting from the outside and developing the ability to make defensive stands. Thompson has an open offense, the Owls set a school record with 98 field goal attempts against Texas A&M last season, but they had a difficult time stopping runs from other teams.

Every SWC coach has commented on the progress made under Thompson, who is praised for teaching skills, recruiting ethics and on-court demeanor. Thompson is quickly improving as a game coach and he has a classy, non-antagonistic style with opponents and referees.

It all helps inspire his players to want to win for him. Home attendance has improved dramatically and the Owls are 17-10 at Autry Court over the last two years. The added experience of the young players should improve on the 3-11 record away from home. If it all comes together, Rice has a shot at fifth place in the SWC.

RICHMOND

LAST SEASON: 22-10
STARTERS LOST: 2
STARTERS RETURNING: 3
CONFERENCE: COLONIAL ATHLETIC ASSOCIATION (CAA)
LOCATION: RICHMOND, VA
HOME FLOOR: ROBBINS CENTER (9,300)
NICKNAME: SPIDERS
COLORS: RED AND BLUE
COACH: DICK TARRANT, record at Richmond, 180-96.
Career record, including high school, 391-157.

The movie ''Arachnophobia'' has nothing on Richmond's basketball program. The Spiders have been putting fear into the hearts of their opponents for years. Nine years, to be precise.

Since 1981, when Dick Tarrant took over as head coach, Richmond has been to the NCAA tournament four times and the NIT three. The CAA's all-time winningest team, the Spiders have averaged 20 victories per season under Tarrant. They have also won the league's regular-season or tournament championship each of the last four years.

One of those NCAA appearances came last year, albeit a forgettable 35-point loss to Duke. If the Spiders want to return to the NCAA's, they will have to replace the talents of point guard Ken Atkinson (18.9 ppg, 2.6 rpg, 99 assists), a first-team All-CAA selection, and forward Scott Stapleton (10.5 ppg, 4.8 rpg), a second-team All-CAA pick.

Tarrant will be operating with a young team. Ten of his 13 players are either freshmen or sophomores. Even the Spiders' lone senior, 6-5 forward **Terry Connolly** (8.2 ppg, 4.8 rpg, 33 assists, 26 steals), has but one previous season in the program after transferring from Shepherd (W.Va.) College two years ago.

Despite that, Connolly is being counted on to provide leadership and was unanimously voted team captain. Connolly started 26 games last year and proved to be a steady performer. He committed just 29 turnovers in 32 games. Generally considered a low-post scorer, Connolly has worked on his jump shot and this season may get more points from the perimeter.

Connolly will be joined at forward by 6-5 sophomore **Kenny Wood** (5.1 ppg, 3.9 rpg). Wood came into his own near the end of last season, providing scoring and rebounding in a reserve role. He averaged 10.1 points and 6.0 rebounds in the Spiders' last six games. Wood was then chosen for the CAA all-tournament team.

Wood, brother of former Tennessee player Howard Wood, could be Richmond's next great player. He gave an indication of his ability with a 21-point game against East Carolina. Nineteen off the points came in the second half. ''Wood doesn't have the quickness or ball-handling skills of most collegiate wings,'' said the *Richmond Times-Dispatch*, ''but he does have the jumper. He also has solid rebounding skills and 230 pounds.''

Richmond's other starting frontcourt position could go to either 6-10 junior **Jim Shields** (5.5 ppg, 3.9 rpg, 22 assists) or 6-8 sophomore **Jim Springer** (3.2 ppg, 2.4 rpg). Shields is considered Richmond's best low-post defender, and he is also capable of putting up some impressive offensive numbers. He scored 28 points and grabbed 11 rebounds against VMI last year. Springer showed his potential in one game a year ago, scoring 13 points and taking 16 rebounds against Army.

Like Wood, Springer impressed Tarrant with his

play as a freshman. ''He's intelligent. He has basketball intellect,'' Tarrant said. ''He's a pretty intense kid. He could be the best big man we've had. When you get a strong body with pretty good skills, a good athlete who understands, you've got something.''

Tim Weathers (2.2 ppg, 1.1 rpg) a 6-6 sophomore and 6-8 sophomore Eric Johnson (0.4 ppg, 0.6 rpg) will probably earn the remaining playing time in the frontcourt.

At guard, 6-3 junior Curtis Blair (12.2 ppg, 4.4 rpg, 93 assists, 39 steals) is Richmond's most experienced player. Blair can score from three-point range or drive to the basket with equal ability. He made 42 of his 110 three-point attempts last year. Blair could be joined in the backcourt by Connecticut transfer Chris Fleming, a 6-6 sophomore. Fleming led New Jersey high school players in scoring in 1988.

Chances are good a freshman will start at point guard, unusual in that Tarrant generally avoids relying on first-year players. The last freshman to have considerable impact on the program was Atkinson. Two 6-0 rookies will battle for the position, Eugene Burroughs of Episcopal Academy (Philadelphia, Pa.) and Gerald Jarmon of Fork Union (Va.) Military Academy and New Bern, N.C. Burroughs was a first-team All-City player last year, averaging 20 points, six assists and steals steals while leading Episcopal to a 21-0 record. Jarmon averaged 12.1 points. 5.2 assists and 3.0 steals for Fork Union, 29-1 a year ago.

Richmond's other two recruits played for the same high school, Beloit Memorial (Beloit, Wisc.). Ty Evans is a 6-4 swingman who averaged 22 points and 10 rebounds. Michael Hodges is a 6-5 forward who averaged 20 points, nine rebounds and three assists for a team that went 23-2 and was ranked second in Wisconsin.

BLUE RIBBON ANALYSIS

Richmond's opponents in the Colonial Athletic Association have come to respect the Spiders during the Dick Tarrant era. In Tarrant's nine seasons, Richmond is 96-38 versus the rest of the CAA, including 17-3 against East Carolina, 12-3 against American University and 15-4 against William and Mary.

The Spiders have also been able to maintain their winning tradition despite an ever-changing lineup. This year will be no exception, though the loss of first-team All-CAA point guard Ken Atkinson and forward Scott Stapleton leaves Tarrant with an unusually inexperienced team.

For Richmond to have a typical Tarrant season, one of two freshman, or both, will have to prove they can replace Atkinson at the point. Both Eugene Burroughs and Jerald Jarmon were winners in high school. If they can make a smooth transition to the college game, Richmond's string of post-season tournament appearances could continue. The Spiders are perhaps a year away from winning the league outright.

RIDER

LAST SEASON: 10-18
CONFERENCE RECORD: 5-9
STARTERS LOST: 0
STARTERS RETURNING: 5
CONFERENCE: EAST COAST (ECC)
LOCATION: LAWRENCEVILLE, NJ
HOME FLOOR: ALUMNI GYMNASIUM (2,200)
NICKNAME: BRONCS AND ROUGHRIDERS
COLORS: CRANBERRY AND WHITE
COACH: KEVIN BANNON, record at Rider, 10-18.
Career record, 155-66.

Kevin Bannon does not like to lose. Having forged a 145-48 career mark and made Trenton State College a Division III powerhouse in his seven years at the helm there, he obviously thought he could do the same for Rider when he moved up the ladder last year. After all, the Broncs hadn't had a winning record since 1983-84, when they won the East Coast Conference championship.

Imagine his frustration at finishing last year with a 10-18 mark. And the way they finished! Oh, there were positives. It's just that they always seemed to be followed with a ''but. . .''

The Broncs won 10 games, double the number of victories of the year before under longtime coach John Carpenter. But it was frustrating because midway through the season, Rider was 9-9 overall and 4-2 and atop the ECC. Rider proceeded to win just one of its last 10 games.

The Broncs broke a 36-game road losing streak that had stretched into its fourth season when they beat Central Connecticut in January. But it was their only away win in 16 contests and they'll take an eight-game road loss streak into this season.

The Broncs are optimistic this year because they return their top eight players. No one yet has followed that with the line, ''but they're the same players who won only 10 games last year.'' That was a learning experience, for the players and Bannon; nine different players started at least two games. Besides, nine of the 15 players on the roster now are Bannon's recruits, including five newcomers this year.

Once again, 6-6 senior forward Jim Cleveland (11.5 ppg, 5.3 rpg) heads the list of returnees. The 1988 ECC Rookie of the Year has never been the star many expected, and in Bannon's scheme of things, he probably won't be this year. But he is solid inside and has a nice shooting touch. With height noticeably lacking on the Broncs, Cleveland's ability to rebound is crucial. He'll get help from 6-6 sophomore William Kinsel (9.9 ppg, 5.9 rpg), who led the team in rebounding last year and made the ECC all-rookie team. A year of experience and strength will help even more.

A holdover and two newcomers may force their way into the frontcourt action, 6-7 junior Jerome Culver (4.2 ppg, 3.6 rpg) started 14 games last year and will try to regain a starting berth. 6-7 Amadi Penn (21.5 ppg, 6.6 rpg for Worcester, Mass., Academy) is a power forward who can score inside. Bannon recruited him out of Xaverian HS in Brookly, N.Y., and now believes he's even better with a year of prep school under his belt. 6-6 freshman Tim Pennix (22.0 ppg, 8.0 rpg for E. C. Glass HS in Lynchburg, Va.) was an early signee who can play inside and outside. Also vying for time with him is 6-6 junior Keith Grim (1.6 ppg), who saw limited action in nine games last year, and 6-7 senior Keith Harvey (1.5 ppg, 1.6 rpg), who played in 17 games (two starts) with mixed results. 6-10 freshman Peter Wasko (14.3 ppg, 9.5 rpg, 6.1 blpg for Whitehall, Pa., HS) may move by all of them. Wasko was a two-year starter at Whitehall. Bannon believes he fits into the Broncs' running style and has the court speed and the hands to dominate the league. His development could alter Bannon's plans to use a three-guard attack.

In the backcourt, 6-0 senior Marcus Pryor (8.6 ppg, 2.2 rpg, 5.7 apg) is back at the point. He came in from the junior college ranks last year and provided the leadership Bannon was looking for. Pryor was the only player who started all 28 games; he needs to cut down on his turnovers to be more effective. 6-1 senior Matt Zaleski (9.8 ppg, 2.5 rpg) was the top outside threat (42-for-112 from three-point range) but needs to improve his overall shooting (only 44 percent from inside the three-point line) to solidify his position. 6-2 sophomore Darrick Suber (13.0 ppg, 2.4 rpg) was the team's leading scorer, shot 50 percent and made the All-Rookie team. He should continue to improve.

None of the starters can rest on their laurels. 6-5 junior Jay Bizyak (6.0 ppg, 1.9 rpg) canned 27-of-50 three-pointers and started seven games. He joins Zaleski as the only true outside scoring threats. Rider recruited two point guards, 6-0 freshman Mark Wilcox and 6-1 junior Norvett Jacques. Wilcox (17.5 ppg, 4.0 apg for St. Peter's HS in New Brunswick, N.J.) a four-year starter at St. Peter's, was the Broncs' top backcourt recruit and is ''our point guard of the future,'' said Bannon. Jacques (16.0 ppg for Barton County, Kan., CC) is from Wichita East HS and gives the Broncs another experienced point guard.

BLUE RIBBON ANALYSIS

Okay, so we were overly optimistic in predicting last year's team would go from five wins to .500. They'll get there this year. Bannon still has some house cleaning to do, but by the time he's done, this could be the East Coast Conference's premier program —if there still is an East Coast Conference.

ROBERT MORRIS

LAST SEASON: 22-8
CONFERENCE
RECORD: 12-4
STARTERS LOST: 1
STARTERS
RETURNING: 4
CONFERENCE:
NORTHEAST
LOCATION:
CORAOPOLIS, PA
HOME FLOOR:
CHARLES L.
SEWALL CENTER (3,056)
NICKNAME: COLONIALS
COLORS: BLUE AND WHITE
COACH: JARRETT DURHAM, record at Robert Morris, 89-82.

You're Jarrett Durham, and you've finally got a winner. After struggling for four years to turn around the Robert Morris basketball program, you've won back-to-back Northeast Conference titles. The first surprised a lot of people. The second proved it wasn't a fluke. Now, with much the same team as last year returning, you're being asked if you can make it three in a row. It's a tough task, but you're not about to duck the question. In fact, you relish it.

"I feel very strongly that this could be the best team in Robert Morris history," Durham said. Not that the Colonials history dates back to the Revolution — this is a one time junior college — but Robert Morris made four trips to the NCAA tournament in the last decade.

"Overall, we should have a quick team with a lot of good athletes who can get up and down the court," Durham said. "We'll miss the inside strength and leadership of Anthony Dickens, and that will be one of the keys — how we're able to compensate for him."

The 6-6 Dickens (12.3 ppg, 9.0 rpg) was the Colonials leading scorer and rebounder a year ago. But on a team that used eight different starters and as many different game high scorers, Dickens' absence won't be felt too much. The only other player not returning is 6-2 guard Moses Moss (9.0 ppg, 2.3 rpg), who started 10 games but was more adept as a spark-plug coming off the bench. Both Dickens and Moss shot 54 percent, but they weren't the only deadeyes; the Colonials shot 50 percent as a team.

As with his last two squads, Durham will be able to go about nine deep. He can play various combinations, but you can be assured that 6-1 senior point guard Andre Boyd and 6-7 junior forward Joe Falletta will be in the lineup somehow. Boyd (12.3 ppg, 2.3 rpg, 3.3 apg) shot 52 percent and was All-Northeast Conference last year. He scored only seven points fewer than Dixon for the team lead and assumed the mantle of team leader down the stretch. Boyd was

also adept from three-point range, shooting 45 percent (32-for-73). His backcourt partner late in the season, 6-3 senior Scott Shepherd (6.6 ppg, 1.7 rpg), also shot 43 percent from three-point range (53-for-118). Shepherd, who hit 8-for-8 against Long Island, made 13 starts last year. Other returning guards who will see action are 5-10 senior Brett Vincent (6.3 ppg, 1.6 rpg) and 5-9 junior Wade Timmerson (5.7 ppg, 2.0 rpg, 2.6 apg). Vincent (18 starts) was used mostly off the bench late in the season because his poor shooting (38 percent) hindered the offense. He can play both backcourt spots. Timmerson drew seven starts, shot 51 percent, and spells Boyd at the point.

Falletta (9.5 ppg, 5.0 rpg, 55 percent shooting) is a solid forward. He started every game last year and made the all-tournament team, mostly off a season high 22-point performance in the semifinals against Fairleigh Dickinson. Along with Falletta, 6-8 junior Ricky Cannon and 6-5 senior Tyrone Steals return. Cannon (10.0 ppg, 3.3 rpg) was the team's third leading scorer despite never starting. He scored 13 points in the 79-71 loss to Kansas in the NCAAs. He'll be looked to for rebounding with Dickens gone. Steals (7.0 ppg, 3.6 rpg) also will be looked to for more rebounding. He started 12 games last year before joining the super-subs that Durham utilized so well. He sparked both conference tournament victories and made the all-tournament team. Robert Jones, a 6-5 sophomore who saw limited action last year, will be in the same spot this year.

Although Durham brought in two freshmen, the biggest newcomer — in size and ability — to hit Coraopolis this year is 6-8 junior center Magdi Bilall, a Sudanese native and transfer from conference rival Long Island. Bilall started for Long Island in the 1988-89 season, averaging 10 points and eight rebounds. He could move into the lineup to give the Colonials extra rebounding strength. The freshmen recruits are 6-5 forward Shelton Carney (17.0 ppg, 8.5 rpg, 2.0 apg for Steubenville, Ohio, HS) and 6-6 guard Craig Conner (17.2 ppg, 9.8 rpg, 3.2 apg for Springfield, Ohio, HS). Carney is a small forward with a good shooting touch and who was honorable mention all-state for a team ranked sixth in Ohio by both wire services. Conner was a late signee who can play either backcourt position.

Also eligible are Zane Vance and Myron Walker, both 6-4 sophomore swingmen. Walker was enrolled at Kent State but did not play there.

BLUE RIBBON ANALYSIS

Seemingly, all the Colonials have to do is keep their heads on straight and they can walk off with their third straight conference title. Bilall could give them a dimension they haven't enjoyed. Durham has been adept at mixing and matching his player combinations and getting everyone involved, and it should be no different this year. A tougher schedule — including eight road games to open the season — may cause the overall record to suffer slightly, but Robert Morris should make up for it by punishing their Northeast Conference foes once January rolls around.

RUTGERS

LAST SEASON: 18-17
CONFERENCE
RECORD: 11-7
STARTERS LOST: 1
STARTERS
RETURNING: 4
CONFERENCE:
ATLANTIC 10
LOCATION:
NEW BRUNSWICK, NJ
HOME FLOOR: LOUIS
BROWN ATHLETIC
CENTER (8,500)
NICKNAME: SCARLET KNIGHTS
COLOR: SCARLET
COACH: BOB WENZEL, record at Rutgers, 36-30. Career record, 124-116.

If Rutgers does not seriously contend this year for the Atlantic 10 championship, it will not be for a lack of players or depth or versatility. It will be a lack of that ever-elusive intangible - chemistry - which dooms the Scarlet Knights.

In back-to-back seasons, perhaps no team in the country has shown just how important chemistry can be. The Scarlet Knights of 1988-89 were the upside, riding the emotional high of Bob Wenzel's first year in New Brunswick to an unexpected conference championship. Everything came together that winter. Players knew their roles. Reserves pulled for starters. And the results were downright magical.

Then, last year, the bottom fell out of a team that seemingly had it all together. Not only had the Knights lost no one from the 1989 A-10 champions, they even added a pair of potentials stars - Keith Hughes and Earl Duncan - as transfers from Syracuse. The results, though, were coyote-ugly. No one knew their role. Players openly pouted for more time. And not even an NIT bid could salvage what was little more than a .500 season.

You've heard of addition by subtraction? For the Scarlet Knights, it was more the other way around. Call it subtraction by addition. "Everyone thought the new blend would take a while," said one rival Atlantic 10 coach. "No one thought it would take the whole year. The talent level was just too high."

The new kids on the block - Hughes and Duncan - were certainly not to blame. At 6-8, Hughes (18.5 ppg, 8.2 rpg, 34 blocked shots) was everything Rutgers expected. He led the Knights in scoring, rebounding, blocked shots and minutes played, and capped the year with second-team A-10 honors that could have been even higher. Now a senior, Hughes will be no less of a monster, and should even draw some NBA attention.

Duncan (13.8 ppg, 2.9 rpg, 122 assists), a 6-3

senior point guard, was also quite productive. But it was the playing time he took from incumbent Rick Dadika that seemed to throw the Rutgers mix out of whack. Dadika (5.9 ppg, 64 assists) was the heart and soul of the '89 champions, and he never got untracked as a backup. Not even Duncan's dramatic game-winning drive against Rhode Island in the Atlantic 10 quarterfinals could rally the Knights.

Dadika is gone, though, so Duncan will no longer need to look over his shoulder. Instead, he can concentrate on blending his considerable talents in the backcourt with 6-4 senior **Craig Carter** and 6-3 sophomore **Mike Jones**. Carter (5.8 ppg, 2.0), like Dadika, also started for most of 1988-89, but got the call just 10 times a year ago. An injured ankle in the A-10 playoffs then cost him the seaon's final four games.

Jones (5.3 ppg, 2.8 rpg, 63 assists) went from invisible at the start of the season to a starter 26 times. He adjusted well to playing off the ball, but figures to take over for Duncan at the point a year from now. As it is, both are capable scorers and neither could be called a traditional lead guard. At one point during last season's backcourt sweepstakes, Wenzel said "it was easier in the old days. Guards were just guards." Backcourt reserves include 6-0 sophomore **Marc Redden** (1.5 ppg) and 6-3 junior **Creighton Drury**.

Up front, Hughes will draw less attention given the presence of 6-9 senior transfer **Brent Dabbs**. Dabbs played his first three years at Virginia, starting at center for the Cavaliers when they advanced to the Final Eight in 1989. He averaged 8.6 points and 7.3 rebounds that season. A pair of junior college transfers - 6-10 **Joe Jarldane** of Fashion Institute of Technology (N.Y.) and 6-9 **Andre Lamoureux** of Cypress (Calif.) CC - join Dabbs in making up for the loss of alternating senior starters **Lee Perry** (5.6 ppg, 4.1 rpg) and **Anthony Duckett** (5.3 ppg, 4.8 rpg).

Small forward is also stacked. 6-7 sophomore **Donnell Lumpkin** (8.5 ppg, 1.9 rpg) was an Atlantic 10 all-freshman selection. He started 19 games, most following the academic suspension of **Tom Savage**, the leading 1988-89 scorer (20.0 ppg) and a previous A-10 first-team choice. Savage, now a 6-5 senior, is also expected back after averaging 12.4 points in last year's shortened season (16 games).

Frontcourt reserves include 6-4 junior **Darryl Smith** (3.8 ppg, 2.4 rpg), along with two new freshmen - 6-7 **Glenn Stokes** (26.3 ppg, 13.0 rpg at Ramapo Regional HS/Ramapo, N.J.) and 6-9 **Charlie Weiler** (17.8 ppg, 11.3 rpg at Haddonfield HS/Haddonfield, N.J.).

BLUE RIBBON ANALYSIS

The horses are there for Rutgers. Again. So are the skeptics. That will happen when a team picked in more than one pre-season Top 20 barely surpasses the .500 mark. "It was a difficult situation over there," said one Atlantic 10 coach. "I'm sure some of the players didn't like playing less."

The issue this year is playing better. Look for Wenzel to establish a rotation early in the season, then turn it loose. The results are likely to be positive, given both the talent level and the extra experience for Hughes, Duncan, Jones and Lumpkin. All were starters a year ago, but few remember it was their first year in the program. The return of Savage provides yet another "go to" guy.

On talent alone, Rutgers is an easy choice for the Atlantic 10 first division. The Scarlet Knights could even challenge Temple for the conference title if someone can locate a chemistry set. A better bet is that the Knights will fight Penn State for second. Either way, this is a team with legitimate post-season aspirations.

		1990-91 RUTGERS SCHEDULE
Nov.	27	Missouri
Dec.	1	St. Bonaventure
	3	Bridgeport (CT)

		1990-91 RUTGERS SCHEDULE Cont.
Dec.	6	@St. Joseph's
	11	@Massachusetts
	15	Princeton
	22	@Seton Hall
	27 & 29	#ECAC Holiday Festival
Jan.	3	Duquesne
	5	Delaware
	8	@Temple
	12	@West Virginia
	17	@George Washington
	19	West Virginia
	22	@Notre Dame
	26	Rhode Island
	28	@Penn State
	30	North Carolina Wilmington
Feb.	2	Temple
	5	@Rhode Island
	9	@St. Bonaventure
	13	St. Joseph's
	16	George Washington
	21	@Duquesne
	24	Massachusetts
	27	Penn State
Mar.	2-4 & 7	*Atlantic 10 Tournament

@ Road Games
# Madison Square Garden, New York NY (Brigham Young, Maryland & South Carolina)
* The first three rounds will be held at the Palestra, Philadelphia, PA. The championship game will be held on the home court of the highest remaining seed.

ST. BONAVENTURE

**LAST SEASON: 8-20
CONFERENCE
RECORD: 3-15
STARTERS LOST: 2
STARTERS
RETURNING: 3
CONFERENCE:
ATLANTIC 10
LOCATION:
OLEAN, NY
HOME FLOOR: REILLY
CENTER (6,000)
NICKNAMES: BONNIES AND BROWN INDIANS
COLORS: BROWN AND WHITE
COACH: TOM CHAPMAN, record at St. Bonaventure, 8-20.
Career record, 266-89.**

Has anybody seen Bob Lanier? Or maybe it just seems that long since St. Bonaventure was a factor on the college basketball scene.

Things got so bad for the Bonnies last season that, by the time the Atlantic 10 tournament rolled around, first-year coach Tom Chapman had only eight players in uniform. The perfunctory first-round defeat was at least merciful, and the Bonnies went back to Olean to continue their perpetual rebuilding job.

Turning St. Bonaventure around after a near decade of decline wasn't supposed to be easy. Chapman, highly successful at Gannon (Division II) College, found that out the hard way. The Bonnies actually took a step backward in his debut, dropping from 13 wins to eight. Worse, they weren't even competitive much of the time.

The Bonnies had very little frontcourt strength, not much depth, and suffered through losing streaks that would have challenged even Chapman's worst nightmares. How else to describe an ordeal that saw St. Bonaventure drop 13 of its final 15 starts? And the Bonnies were within a single digit in only three of those defeats.

"I hope we come back hungrier," Chapman sighed when the death march was over. A quipster

most of the year, not even he could joke about the lost stretch drive. "I hope we learned from the adversity. I hope we took some determination out of it. I know we need more strength."

And more players. Two of the eight St. Bonaventure closed with are gone, both starters. Point guard Rob Lanier (10.7 ppg, 2.5 rpg, 102 assists), Bob's son, never in four years had his father's supporting cast. Small forward Kyle Anglin (7.6 ppg, 3.2 rpg) also graduated. Ironically, neither played much in the season-ending loss to George Washington.

Perhaps Chapman was already looking ahead, trying to boost the confidence of his only go-to guy, 6-4 swingman **Michael Burnett**, who that day had a career-high 27 points. A senior, Burnett (14.6 ppg, 4.9 rpg) is most effective in the open floor, but typically has to challenge bigger players.

"We want to get Michael out on the break earlier," Chapman admitted. "He needs to get the ball ahead of the pack. We need to get him 20 shots a game, and I wouldn't care if they were all 'three's'." Burnett hit just over 40 percent (70-for-174) from beyond the arc as a junior.

Chapman would like open floor action from more than Burnett - offensively and defensively - but simply does not have the personnel. Two other returning starters, 6-8 junior **Kenrick Hamilton** (9.6 ppg, 4.4 rpg) and 6-9 senior **Dan Putney** (5.0 ppg, 4.6 rpg), are more the plodding types. Among the other returnees, only 6-6 sophomore **Jason Brower** (8.2 ppg, 2.9 rpg) is athletic enough to really run. 6-8 senior **Rob Williams** (2.6 ppg, 1.3 rpg) and 6-0 senior **Quinn Smith** (2.3 ppg, 1.2 rpg) are more limited.

"You have to go 10-12 players deep at this level," said Chapman. "Quite simply, we could not. You can't have an 'iron-five'."

The Bonnies may not even have that, unless their three freshmen are ready to play immediately. One who almost certainly is, 6-4 swingman **Garland Mance** (Southwestern HS/Detroit), will be asked for a whole lot. A member of Southwestern's *USA Today* national runner-up, Mance brings a welcome winning attitude in addition to his skills.

"Garland has the whole package," Chapman said, "and the frame of a major college player. He gives us a great attitude and a killer instinct on the floor. He can give us intensity, too." Two Europeans - 6-9 freshman **Tobias Hauff** (Alvik Club/Stockholm, Sweden) and 6-8 freshman **Pieter Hemelaer** (Turnout Club/Breda, Holland) - are not as advanced.

Finally, the point guard job should fall to 6-0 junior transfer **Chris Meadows** (South Mountain CC/Phoenix). It was a long way for SBU to go for a player, but the Bonnies need help that badly. A quick playmaker, Meadows can also shoot the three. Said Chapman: "Chris can push the ball. It gives us a different look at the point position."

BLUE RIBBON ANALYSIS

Has anybody seen Rob Lanier? St. Bonaventure is in such a hole, even the son of its best-ever player would be welcome. Things can only get better for the Bonnies, of course, but that may not even happen right away.

Other than Burnett, Chapman's best pure talent may lie in Mance. And the Atlantic 10 has risen to a level where freshmen - other than a Mark Macon - simply cannot make an immediate difference. The Bonnies will need another recruiting class or two before thinking about a serious dent in the conference race.

In the meantime, it's back to the basement.

		1990-91 ST. BONAVENTURE SCHEDULE
Nov.	24	Concordia (NY)
	26	@Niagara
	29	Cornell
Dec.	1	@Rutgers
	5	Temple
	8	Morgan State (MD)

ST. FRANCIS

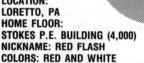

LAST SEASON: 17-11
CONFERENCE
RECORD: 10-6
STARTERS LOST: 0
STARTERS
RETURNING: 5
CONFERENCE:
NORTHEAST
LOCATION:
LORETTO, PA
HOME FLOOR:
STOKES P.E. BUILDING (4,000)
NICKNAME: RED FLASH
COLORS: RED AND WHITE
COACH: JIM BARON, record at St. Francis, 37-47.

You couldn't blame St. Francis coach Jim Baron if he spent the entire off-season force-feeding his players milk and vitamins. He may have even scheduled some time on the rack for certain members of his frontcourt.

Despite returning five starters from last year's 17-11 edition, the Red Flash are not what you would call tall. Though one player is 6-8 and another 6-7, that is hardly intimidating. Hotshot senior guard **Mike Iuzzolino** is all of 5-10. So Baron probably searched for magic beans or miracle fertilizers to give his players a couple extra inches.

Alas, he failed. But the coach is not giving up. There is enough talent on this undersized team to continue the resurgence of the St. Francis program, and maybe enough to win the Northeast Conference title.

"Other teams have some big front line kids," Baron admitted. "Monmouth, Fairleigh-Dickinson and Robert Morris were all able to beat us inside. We're going to look to run, but our key will be how quickly our front line people are able to contribute inside."

Baron's got very little to worry about outside. Iuzzolino is the focus of an experienced backcourt capable of scoring on anyone. The 5-10 senior transfer from Penn State electrified the Northeast Conference last year with his outside marksmanship and impressed his teammates with an uncompromising work ethic.

After averaging only 3.2 ppg as a sophomore

at State College, Iuzzolino erupted for 21.3 ppg (averaging only 12 shots) and 4.8 assists last season. He finished second in the nation in three-point shooting (51.6 percent), and shot 87.1 percent from the free throw line. He also carries a 3.8 grade point average in Secondary Education/Political Science and was first-team COSIDA/GTE academic All-America. *Playboy* named him the winner of its 1990-91 Anson Mount Scholarship for the country's top basketball student-athlete.

"He's one of the hardest-working individuals I've ever been around," Baron said. "He wants to be the very best at whatever he does, on the court and in the classroom."

Joining Iuzzolino in the backcourt is 6-3 senior **John Hilvert** (9.8 ppg, 3.6 rpg), a streak shooter. Though Hilvert's production fell off from his sophomore season (15.6 ppg), he did improve on defense. "We usually put him on the best offensive guard on the other team," Baron said. "He's a physical, hard-nosed type of player."

Completing the solid backcourt triumvirate is 6-3 senior **Harkeem Dixon** (10.2 ppg, 2.6 rpg). Others vying for time at guard include 6-2 junior **Steve Strachan** (0.9 ppg), 6-3 sophomore **Willie Smith** and junior **Rob Pacsi.**

Up front, the Red Flash are small but talented. 6-5 senior **Joe Anderson** (20.7 ppg, 4.9 rpg) is a finesse forward who led St. Francis in scoring as a freshman and a sophomore. **Tom Bennetch** (8.4 ppg, 6.6 rpg), another 6-5 senior, fills the other forward spot. Bennetch missed three games last year with a case of chicken pox and has been troubled by a sore knee.

Baron hopes 6-6 junior **Antoine Patterson** (4.7 ppg, 3.3 rpg) can improve on last season, his first after sitting out 1988-89. **Reggie Lewis** (2.4 ppg, 3.3 rpg), a 6-5 sophomore, is another available forward. **Mike Fink** (3.4 ppg, 3.7 rpg) is the Red Flash center. The 6-7, 200-pound sophomore needs some more upper body strength to bang with bigger opponents, but showed promise last year and started 13 games. **Bill Seaward** (0.7 ppg), a 6-8 sophomore, is St. Francis' backup in the pivot.

The Red Flash welcome three freshmen this season, including 6-1 guard **Steve Cloran** (Cardinal O'Hara HS/Secane, Pa.), 6-4 forward **Jim Horn** (East Palestine HS/New Waterford, Ohio) and 6-5 forward **Leo Nadel** (Kennedy Christian HS/Dominican Republic).

BLUE RIBBON ANALYSIS

Despite its lack of size, St. Francis is a veteran team with proven scoring capabilities. However, Baron needs a big year from Fink and some extra rebounding out of Anderson and Bennetch if the Red Flash are to improve on last season's 17 wins.

"Everyone in the league has good players, but a lot of merit will go to the team that can get over the humps and move through adversity with cohesiveness," Baron said.

Iuzzolino and Hilvert will help with the cohesiveness, not to mention the scoring. But how much the frontcourt can overcome its taller adversaries in the Northeast Conference will determine whether St. Francis remains close to the top or actually scales the peak. The Red Flash are a first division, but not a championship club.

ST. JOSEPH'S

LAST SEASON: 7-21
CONFERENCE
RECORD: 5-13
STARTERS LOST: 1
STARTERS
RETURNING: 4
CONFERENCE:
ATLANTIC 10
LOCATION:
PHILADELPHIA, PA
HOMECOURT:
ALUMNI MEMORIAL
FIELDHOUSE (3,200)
NICKNAME: HAWKS
COLORS: CRIMSON AND GRAY
COACH: JOHN GRIFFIN, first year at St. Joseph's.
Career record, 70-44.

Don't let the pinstripes or the stock quotes or the *Wall Street Journal* fool you. New St. Joseph's coach John Griffin, erstwhile municipal bonds broker, is a basketball guy first and foremost. Make that a Philly basketball guy. Always was, always will be.

Oh, sure, Griffin spent the last four years on Wall Street, trading bonds for Paine Webber. And, sure, it took a lot to lure him out of the financial district and back to his alma mater. But Griffin, who replaces Jim Boyle, was little more than a coach disguised in brokers' clothing. He may have had a head for trading, but his heart was reserved for hoops.

It was that way at Siena College, where Griffin took over in 1982-83 as the youngest head coach in Division I. Four years later, Siena was a two-time 20-game winner and its coach voted the best in the ECAC North Atlantic. Griffin left the program in good enough shape to land an NCAA bid two years later, opting himself for a Paine Webber vice presidency.

For Griffin, a former Rhodes Scholar candidate and the holder of an MBA degree, Wall Street was simply the next logical step. He had accomplished enough in coaching to ensure a return should he ever desire. The call came last spring when Boyle, the third-winningest coach in St. Joseph's history, resigned after nine seasons.

"I had, in my own mind," said Griffin, "an

escape clause at Paine Webber. When Lou Holtz was at Minnesota, the only way he could break his contract was if Notre Dame called. It was the same way for me on Wall Street.

"I had a very good job, with a promising future, but St. Joseph's is a very special place. The opportunity to come back and be a part of this tradition is something I could not pass up."

The coaching tradition, even more than wins and losses, is taken very seriously on Hawk Hill. Jack Ramsay, Jack McKinney, Paul Westhead, Jim Lynam and Matt Goukas all played and coached here. All became head coaches in the NBA, including Lynam (Philadelphia 76ers) and Goukas (Orlando Magic) currently.

Yet it remains wins and losses which Griffin must immediately address. The Hawks slipped badly the past two years, suffering their first losing seasons since the late 1970's. This after four post-season bids in the first six years under Boyle.

In the meantime, the majority of the Atlantic 10 has left St. Joseph's behind. Since their 1986 league title, the Hawks have not been beyond the conference quarterfinals. Still, Boyle - who opted out of coaching voluntarily, and will remain at the school - went out on a high note, leaving Griffin with a recruiting class that could go down as the Hawks' finest ever.

6-3 point guard **Rap Curry** (Penn Wood HS/Lansdowne, Pa.) was the Pennsylvania large school player of the year. He averaged a triple double (19.9 ppg, 12.2 rpg, 10.2 assists) in his final prep season, and finished with the highest assists total (766) in state history. Curry will immediately push incumbent **Chris Gardler** (11.3 ppg, 100 assists), a 5-8 senior.

"It may not happen right off the bat," said Griffin, "but Rap seems like the kind of player who just takes the ball."

Also in the fold is 6-5 sophomore **Jason Warley** (Frankford HS/Philadelphia, Pa.), half of a highly publicized brothers' duo. A slashing, penetrating wing player, Warley sat out last season after leading Frankford to a 49-2 record over two years. Younger brother Carlin Warley, an even higher rated 6-8 low post player, also committed to the Hawks and will be eligible in 1991-92. The two were profiled by *Sports Illustrated* during their final year at Frankford.

Boyle also left behind 6-5 redshirt freshman **Atasho Maloney** (McAteer HS/San Francisco, Calif.) and 6-8 redshirt sophomore **Mike Sell** (Solon HS/Solon, Ohio). Maloney is St. Joseph's first-ever California recruit. Both add depth to a frontcourt that could use plenty.

"I think freshmen can help," said Griffin, "but I'm hesitant to put the pressure of wins and losses on their shoulders."

The new coach then went out and signed one who could be a star. After less than three weeks on the job, Griffin came home with 6-3 freshman scoring machine **Bernard Blunt** (Jamesville-DeWitt HS/Syracuse, N.Y.), the third-leading scorer (2,507 points, 31.3 ppg as a senior) in the history of New York state.

Most assumed Blunt, a Carrier Dome regular, would remain with the hometown Orangemen. By the time Georgia Tech and some other heavyweights got involved, Blunt was Philly-bound instead. After he led all scorers in the Sonny Hill summer league, the *Philadelphia Daily News* ran a headline saying: "To be Blunt, he's very good."

Hawk fans will find out in a hurry. Blunt will start alongside either Curry or Gardler in the backcourt. St. Joseph's best returning player, 6-7 junior **Craig Amos** (16.0 ppg, 6.4 rpg), is the small forward. Amos was an A-10 third-team selection last year. 6-4 senior **Richard Stewart** (11.8 ppg, 2.7 rpg, 54 assists) emerged to start the final 21 games a year ago, but his quick bursts of offense might be better suited to a sixth man's role.

At power forward, 6-8 senior **Marlon Miller** (7.9 ppg, 5.1 rpg) returns for a final shot at realizing his vast potential. 6-11 junior **Ron Vercruyssen** (4.6 ppg, 3.0 rpg) and 6-8 junior **Matt Goukas** (4.0 ppg, 4.1 rpg), son of the Orlando coach, are the likely center candidates. Both could watch, however, if Griffin goes to a small, pressing team with Stewart as a starter.

"That style," said Griffin, "is what fans want to watch, and it's what players like to play. I just don't have an answer yet. I don't know these players well enough."

6-5 junior **Brian Daly** (2.2 ppg, 1.8 rpg), 6-6 sophomore **Eddie Malloy** (2.3 ppg, 1.1 rpg), 5-11 sophomore **Brett McKay** (3.0 ppg) and 6-1 senior **Ray Washington** (2.3 ppg, 44 assists) round out the roster. All have prior experience as starters.

BLUE RIBBON ANALYSIS

Griffin comes with an overachievers' reputation, both as a player and a coach. He is not likely to be outworked, and St. Joseph's fans are sure to welcome his intense game-night demeanor. What they will welcome even more is winning. Back-to-back records of 8-21 and 7-21 have been hard to swallow.

"There are no quick fixes here," Griffin cautioned. "What we're talking about is building a program. To be done right, it has to be done in sequential fashion. You can only take one step at a time."

Step one is being competitive. Many nights last year, the Hawks were simply overmatched. With the talent pool upgraded considerably, that shouldn't happen nearly as often. Griffin - once labeled "one of the best young minds in coaching" by *Eastern Basketball* - simply will not allow it.

Look for the Hawks to threaten, if not quite reach, the .500 mark in his first season back. Give Griffin a year or two, and a return to the glory days is entirely possible.

1990-91 ST. JOSEPH'S SCHEDULE

Nov.	26	@George Washington
	28	@Drexel
Dec.	1	Massachusetts
	3	Fordham
	6	Rutgers
	8	Villanova
	22	@South Carolina
	29	@Loyola Marymount
Jan.	3	Miami (FL)
	5	@Duquesne
	7	@Massachusetts
	10	@St. Bonaventure
	12	Rhode Island
	14	Pennsylvania
	19	George Washington
	22	@Temple
	26	@West Virginia
	28	St. Bonaventure
Feb.	2	Duquesne
	4	Temple
	6	@Miami (FL)
	9	@Penn State
	13	@Rutgers
	16	@La Salle
	21	Penn State
	23	@Rhode Island
	26	West Virginia
Mar.	2-4 & 7	–Atlantic 10 Tournament

@ Road Games
# The first three rounds will be held at the Palestra, Philadelphia, PA. The championship game will be held on the home court of the highest remaining seed.

ST. LOUIS

LAST SEASON: 21-12
CONFERENCE RECORD: 9-5
STARTERS LOST: 2
STARTERS RETURNING: 3
CONFERENCE: MID WESTERN COLLEGIATE (MCC)
LOCATION: ST. LOUIS, MO
HOME FLOOR: KIEL AUDITORIUM (9,300)
NICKNAME: BILLIKENS
COLORS: BLUE AND WHITE
COACH: RICH GRAWER, record at St. Louis, 135-112.

The St. Louis basketball program, which is entering its 75th year, was reborn the last five seasons. Rich Grawer, dean of MCC coaches, has won 105 games and lost only 58 in that span. Three times the Billikens have visited the NIT, and they advanced to the title game in each of the last two years.

When Grawer took over in 1982-83, the St. Louis program was "brain dead." His first team promptly went 5-23. From that less than sizzling start, the Billikens have twice set school records for victories in a season - 25 in 1986-87 and 27 in 1988-89.

All of which is wonderful, but Grawer knows there could be a huge dropoff in 1990-91. For the last five years, the Billikens' success has hinged on the play of three fine athletes turned out by the Public High League in St. Louis. When Roland Gray and Monroe Douglass left after the 1988-89 season, they departed as the first- and second-leading scorers in school history.

When Anthony Bonner, who led the nation in rebounding last season (13.8 rpg), graduated in May, he had become not only the leading rebounder in school history, but also its top scorer. Grawer called him "the greatest player ever to wear a Billikens' uniform." The Sacramento Kings evidently agreed, taking him in the first round of the NBA draft.

Clearly, an era has ended. "It will be strange," said Grawer, "not having the names Douglass, Gray or Bonner in the starting lineup. It's the first time in five years. But I think we have a good blend of returnees, redshirts and newcomers so that we can compete very well."

Two huge question marks face St. Louis in 1990-91. **Melvin Robinson**, a 7-0 sophomore, has the ability to dominate, but has not displayed the desire to do so on a consistent basis. He led the MCC in blocked shots with 51, but averaged only 3.6 rebounds and at times was outplayed by much smaller centers. Robinson's scoring average was 7.4 points, with his best game coming at Eastern Illinois (20 points, 10 rebounds). He also blocked six shots in that one.

The other question mark is **Kevin Footes**, a 6-6 senior who last season had all sorts of growing pains with Grawer as a junior college transfer. Footes (14.0 ppg, 4.3 rpg) finally was suspended from the team after starting 16 of the first 24 games at small forward. Footes has the ability to be a top player in the MCC in 1990-91, but no one at St. Louis is holding their breath. The guy, like Robinson, has been too tough to predict.

Beyond his two problem children, Grawer has back 6-5 senior swingman **Jeff Luechtefeld** (6.9 ppg, 2.9 rpg), who came alive for 13.5 ppg in five NIT games. 6-4 sophomore **Jorge Wallace** (4.5 ppg, 1.8 rbg) was also a solid starter at the end of the season. **John Duff** (5.4 ppg, 2.0 rpg), a gutty 6-3 senior guard, was the team's best outside shooter until he came down with mononucleosis in January. Duff returns as well, and should contend for a starting job at off-guard. The only other returning letterman is 6-2 sophomore

Jeff Gaona (1.3 ppg), a reserve point guard.

In addition to replacing Bonner at power forward, Grawer must find someone to take over for Charlie Newberry (12.8 ppg, 5.8 assists). The point guard, Newberry left as the school's career leader in assists. **Orlando Stewart,** a 5-11 sophomore who transferred from Virginia Commonwealth, will get the first shot. Then comes Gaona, followed by freshman **Kevin Graw er,** the coach's son who was a standout point guard at Christian Brothers High in St. Louis (16.5 points and 5.7 assists per game).

Other returning players are **Carlos Skinner,** a 6-7 freshman who redshirted last season, and **Travis Tadysak,** a 6-10 senior who also redshirted after a recurring back problem put him on the shelf. Newcomers besides Stewart include two JC transfers - **Quit man Dillard,** a 6-5 small forward from Paris (Tex.) CC, and **Lowell Jeffries,** a 6-8 power forward from Belleville (Ill.) Area CC - along with 6-9 freshman **Robert Carr** (Paoli HS/Paoli, Ind.).

BLUE RIBBON ANALYSIS

There are way too many question marks for St. Louis to repeat as a 20-game winner. No program loses its career scoring, rebounding and assist leaders - all at the same time - and recovers overnight.

With Purdue, Houston and Santa Clara on the schedule, as well as continuing regional rivalries with Southwest Missouri State and Southern Illinois - not to mention to MCC grind - the Billikens will do well not to fall below .500 for the first time since 1984-85.

In the first year of the post-Bonner era, do not look for St. Louis to be in post-season play or among the upper division of the Midwestern Collegiate Conference.

1990-91 ST. LOUIS SCHEDULE

Nov.	23-25	#San Juan Shootout
Dec.	1	@Southern Illinois
	4	Houston
	8	Purdue
	11	Santa Clara
	15	Illinois State
	18	@Indiana State
	21-22	##Bud Lite/Billiken Holiday Classic
Jan.	2	@Bradley
	5	@Southwest Texas State
	9	Butler
	11	Southern Illinois
	13	@Alabama-Birmingham
	17	@Dayton
	19	@Xavier
	24	@Loyola
	26	Marquette
	31	Evansville
Feb.	2	Xavier
	7	@Butler
	9	@Detroit
	14	Dayton
	16	Detroit
	21	Loyola
	23	@Marquette
	27	Northern Iowa
Mar.	3	@Evansville
	7-9	*MCC Tournament

@ Road Games
# San Juan, PR (American University of Puerto Rico, Bucknell, Illinois, Murray State, Nebraska, Northern Iowa, Old Dominion & Southern Illinois)
St. Louis, MO (Morgan State, Northwestern & Western Illinois)
* Dayton, OH

ST. MARY'S

LAST SEASON: 7-20
CONFERENCE RECORD: 4-10
STARTERS LOST: 4
STARTERS RETURNING: 1
CONFERENCE: WEST COAST (WCC)
LOCATION: MORAGA, CA
HOME FLOOR: McKEON PAVILION (3,500)
NICKNAME: GAELS
COLORS: BLUE AND RED
COACH: PAUL LANDREAUX, record at St. Mary's, 7-20.
Career record, 324-74.

Having served for 10 years as a head coach on the junior college level, Paul Landreaux is familiar with rebuilding a program every year. However, it is fair to say he was hoping for more stability with the move up to Division I. Instead, the second-year St. Mary's coach will guide an almost completely new Gaels' squad, much as he did in his debut a year ago.

Landreaux has shown he can produce a winner. Each of his 10 junior college teams won 20 games or more, and his nine years at El Camino (Calif.) JC resulted in three state championships and seven conference titles. Noted as an outstanding defensive coach and recruiter, even Landreaux was not ready for what awaited him at tiny St. Mary's in the hills above Oakland.

Last year, there were no returning starters from the team that Lynn Nance guided to a 25-5 record and a West Coast Conference championship in 1988-89. Even worse, only two players - both sophomores - return from Landreaux's first edition of the Gaels.

The most experienced is 6-5 swingman **John Levitt** (8.0 ppg, 3.8 rpg), who led all conference freshmen in scoring. Levitt started 17 games, and was one of only two Gaels to play in all 27. The other returnee is 6-8 forward-center **Danny White** (2.7 ppg, 3.5 rpg in 19 games, five as a starter).

Dissension among the ranks led to five underclassmen electing to transfer after last year, including 6-10 center Eric Bamberger (12.1 ppg, 8.8 rpg), who was the third-leading rebounder and 20th-leading scorer in the league. Others bolting the program were 6-7 forwards Ted Bull (5.4 ppg, 2.4 rpg) and Demetrus Robbins (5.3 ppg, 3.3 rpg), along with 6-2 guards Brian Sitter (5.2 ppg) and Andre Dority (3.7 ppg). Bamberger and Dority were sophomores, the others freshmen. The Gaels also lost 5-10 point guard Mike Vontoure (12.9 ppg, 2.9 rpg, 137 assists) to graduation. Vontoure was the only starter in all 27 games last year.

As a quick fix for 1990-91, Landreaux has turned, by necessity, to the junior college ranks he knows so well. The Gaels have been almost completely rebuilt, with seven of nine newcomers hailing from the JC ranks. "The players we have brought in bring with them a great deal of experience and athletic ability," Landreaux said. "We have signed players at every position, and in doing so, have greatly strengthened our program. We should be much more exciting."

Vying for the starting point guard assignment are 6-1 junior **Allen Caveness** (8.9 ppg, 6.7 apg at El Camino JC) and 6-1 freshman **Darrell Daniel** (23.9 ppg, 6.0 apg at Bishop Montgomery HS/Inglewood, Calif.). Candidates for the starting off-guard spot are on equal footing, with Levitt, 6-1 junior **Kevin Weather by** (17.5 ppg, 4.1 rpg, 4.6 apg, 3.1 steals at Merced JC/Merced, Calif.) and 6-2 **Thurman Watson** (18.8 ppg, 6.4 rpg, 3.1 apg, 2.4 steals at Los Angeles City College) being challenged by 6-6 freshman **Brian Hansen** (Canyon del Oro HS/Tuscon, Ariz.). Hansen

was second-team All-State as a senior, averaging 24.3 points, 6.2 rebounds and 3.3 assists.

In the frontcourt, 6-8 junior **Steve Leary** (12.3 ppg, 9.1 rpg, 64 percent from the field at El Camino JC) should have the upper hand for the starting center spot, while 6-7 junior **Ivan Aralica** (16.0 ppg, 9.2 rpg at Eastern Arizona JC) looks strong at power forward. At small forward, 6-5 junior **Brian Brazier** (18.1 ppg, 8.2 rpg) from the College of the Sequoias (Cal.) will be backed up by Levitt and 6-6 sophomore **Gilbert Myvett** (2.3 ppg at Los Angeles City College).

BLUE RIBBON ANALYSIS

Everyone will need a program, including some of the players, to become familiar with what is essentially a completely new squad at St. Mary's. Last year's Gaels never were able to come together, and this year's squad may have the same difficulty.

Landreaux has been successful at the junior college level in blending new players quickly to form championship teams. But the junior colleges and Division I, even the mid-level West Coast Conference, are different altogether. It will take Landreaux longer than one year to find the right chemistry and win entirely new players. It may take even longer to return the Gaels to the championship level of 1988-89.

For now, it is hard to picture St. Mary's anywhere except the WCC basement.

1990-91 ST. MARY'S SCHEDULE

Nov.	23	#Apple Invitational
	28	Nevada
Dec.	1	@Pacific
	5	@UCLA
	7-8	##Manufacturers Hanover Classic
	12	Cal State Chico
	15	California-Santa Barbara
	19	Boise State
	20	Mississippi Valley State
	22	Weber State
	29	@Montana
Jan.	5	@San Francisco
	11	Gonzaga (WA)
	12	Univ. of Portland
	17	@Santa Clara
	19	@Univ. of San Diego
	25	Loyola Marymount
	26	Pepperdine
Feb.	1	@Pepperdine
	2	@Loyola Marymount
	9	San Francisco
	15	Santa Clara
	16	Univ. of San Diego
	21	@Univ. of Portland
	23	@Gonzaga
Mar.	2-4	*West Coast Conference Tournament

@ Road Games
# Palo Alto, CA (Rider, Stanford & Yale)
New Rochelle, NY (Iona, Princeton & Wagner)
* Santa Clara, CA

ST. PETER'S

LAST SEASON: 14-14
CONFERENCE RECORD: 7-9
STARTERS LOST: 1
STARTERS RETURNING: 4
CONFERENCE: METRO ATLANTIC ATHLETIC (MAAC)
LOCATION: JERSEY CITY, NJ
HOME FLOOR: YANITELLI CENTER (3,500)
NICKNAME: PEACOCKS
COLORS: BLUE AND WHITE
COACH: TED FIORE, record at St. Peter's, 77-40.

Going into last season, hoop fans in Jersey City had two big questions to answer: Who would replace Duke-bound All-America Bobby Hurley for the defending national champion St. Anthony's High School Friars, and who would replace St. Peter's all-time leading scorer Willie Haynes? The talent rich Friars moved on to have yet another highly successful season, while Ted Fiore's Peacocks went bust. This year could be more of the same.

Last season started out well enough for St. Peter's, as they vaulted to a 7-2 pre-Christmas mark. Then the wheels fell off, and they struggled to a 14-14 mark, breaking a run of three straight 20 win seasons. The team shot only 38 percent from the floor and 67 percent from the line while allowing their opponents a touch more offense (66.4 ppg) than they scored themselves (66.3 ppg) for the first time in recent memory. No one player was there to take the big shot that Haynes did for four seasons or provide the steady post defense of Phil Morrison.

But there is some good news amidst this gloom. The Peacocks bring back four starters from last season's .500 squad, including leading scorer 6-6 senior forward **Tony Walker** (16.1 ppg, 6.4 rpg) and his former high school teammate, 6-3 swingman **Marvin Andrews** (8.2 ppg, 4.6 rpg). Walker emerged as a consistent threat last season on both ends, while defensive specialist Andrews had his best games at off-guard, and will see more of the same in '90-91.

Another key returnee in the backcourt is 5-10 senior point guard **Jasper Walker** (8.0 ppg, 3.2 rpg, 6.3 apg). The former St. Anthony's star also showed more offensive punch, hitting on 41 percent of his three-pointers, but had trouble running the offensive show, turning the ball over a team high 96 times. The Peacocks will desperately need more consistent play out of their point guard to have any chance at success. The final returning starter is 6-9 senior center **John Connell** (8.0 ppg, 3.6 rpg). The late blooming center has shown steady improvement in each of his three years, but is at the in-between size that makes it difficult for him to compete with normal size centers. He will have to drastically improve on both ends, but especially on defense, for the Peacocks to succeed.

With veterans Chuck Veterano and Abdul Fox having departed for personal reasons, the rest of the St. Peter's picture resembles the murky Passaic River that flows about a mile west of campus. 6-11 senior center **Ken Mack** (1.1 ppg, 1.0 rpg) will see added time and is expected to help Connell with rebounding, along with little used classmate 6-8 **Matt Anderson** (0.9 ppg, 1.6 rpg). 6-7 sophomore **Oyango Merriman** (0.0 ppg, 0.0 rpg) and 6-7 junior walk-on **Brian O'Sullivan** could also contribute. Merriman missed his freshman season with a back injury while O'Sullivan is considered a still developing project.

In the backcourt, redshirt freshman 6-0 **Antoine Allen** and 5-11 Marquette transfer **Anthony Candelino** will see considerable time. Allen, a lightning quick point guard, will fill in for Walker when he plays the two spot, while Candelino is a veteran point guard and excellent athlete who should help at the point. 6-1 junior walk-on **Corey Taylor** (1.8 ppg) may also see some time.

BLUE RIBBON ANALYSIS

St. Peter's has always had a knack for turning unknown players into a quality unit. This season the athletes do not really appear to be there. Tony Walker and Andrews are solid MAAC players, but if Jasper Walker has another inconsistent season it could be a very long year. Candelino and Allen will help in the backcourt, but the front is painfully weak. St. Peter's lost a good part of its attack prematurely with the departure of the troublesome Veterano (12.8 ppg) and freshman standout Fox (5.0 ppg) and has not replaced it. It will be a rebuilding year in Jersey City, and .500 would be a nice surprise. Thirteen wins and a sixth place MAAC finish is more likely.

SAM HOUSTON STATE

LAST SEASON: 10-18
CONFERENCE RECORD: 8-6
STARTERS LOST: 3
STARTERS RETURNING: 2
CONFERENCE: SOUTHLAND (SLC)
LOCATION: HUNTSVILLE, TX
HOME FLOOR: JOHNSON COLISEUM (6,110)
NICKNAME: BEARKATS
COLORS: ORANGE AND WHITE/BLUE TRIM
COACH: LARRY BROWN, record at Sam Houston State, 10-18.
Career record, including high school, 195-89.

Larry Brown's first year at Sam Houston State wasn't nearly as shaky as the Bearkats' 10-18 record seems to indicate. The Bearkats recovered from a 2-9 record to win five of their first six Southland Conference games and grab a share of the league lead.

However, 6-6 senior Jeff Blice, a key reserve, reinjured his broken foot and was lost for the season. Consequently, the Bearkats won only three of their remaining nine games. Nevertheless, Sam Houston State finished a respectable fourth in the league standings.

The team lived up to its "Run, Gun and Have Fun" motto as it ranked as the highest scoring Sam Houston squad in 17 years, averaging 77.3 points per game.

Entering the 1990-91 season, there are reasons for both concern and optimism in the Bearkats' camp.

Besides Blice, the team lost its two top scorers, Derrick Gilliam and Dennis Green and center Michael Champion. Gilliam, a unanimous first-team All-Southland Conference selection, will be particularly

difficult to replace. He averaged 18.6 points per game and led the Bearkats in scoring and in rebounding 15 times during last season.

Four lettermen return from last year's squad, all of whom saw some starting action. 6-9 senior center **Erik Hammock** (9.2 ppg, 7.6 rpg, 28 assists, 17 blocked shots, 34 steals) started 21 games last year and was the team's second leading rebounder. Hammock ranked third in the SLC in field goal percentage (.579) and fourth in the league in rebounding.

"Erik is one of our main weapons inside," said Brown. "His quickness gives him an advantage over many of the big men in our league. However, he needs to be more consistent."

6-2 junior guard **Gibbiarra Outten** (8.8 ppg, 5.8 ppg, 55 assists, 9 blocked shots, 19 steals) will probably man one of the guard positions for Brown. An impressive 53.3 percent marksman from the field last year, Outten's 41-inch vertical leap and quick hands should help him develop into a complete guard.

Junior guard **Lance Alexander**, 6-0 (7.3 ppg, 1.1 rpg, 67 assists, 19 steals) returns at point guard, but may have a hard time fending off a couple of junior college transfers for the starting duties. Alexander has also been hampered during the off-season by a knee injury. 6-5 junior post **James Sears** (3.8 ppg, 1.9 rpg) will likely contribute off the bench.

Because of the loss of Gilliam and Green, Brown signed five guard —four from the junior college ranks and one from high school.

"We really helped ourselves on the perimeter with our signees," said Brown. "We've got a number of players who can swing between two and three positions. Our quickness on the perimeter should be better."

Juniors **Jim Lewis** and **Ray Johnson** will vie with Alexander for the starting position at the point. The 6-1 Lewis, a former two-time Oklahoma high school state scoring leader, was the starting point guard for Hutchison (Kan.) CC that went 34-4 and finished 1990 ranked seventh nationally. The junior averaged 6.3 points and 4.6 assists per game. Johnson, a 508 junior guard, earned all-conference honors after averaging 8.6 points and 6.1 assists for Western Texas JC.

"Lewis could swing between the two guard positions," said Brown. "He's an excellent scorer."

Joel Donalson and **Kethus Hanks** should both fit into the Bearkats' up-tempo style. Donalson, a 6-3 junior guard, hit 62 percent from the field and averaged 18.1 points per game for Trinity Valley (Tex.) CC. Hanks, a 6-4 junior guard, averaged 16.3 points and made 43 percent of his three-point attempts at Midland (Tex.) JC.

Terry Jefferson and **Milton Hamilton**, a pair of 6-4 juniors, may well man the forward positions. Jefferson is an excellent shooter who averaged 22.1 points and 7.1 rebounds per game for Weatherford (Tex.) JC. Hamilton, more suited for post play, averaged 10.1 points and 7.2 rebounds for Tyler (Tex.) JC.

One freshman signee, **Rico Chilo**, a 6-6 center from Madison HS in Houston, will figure into the Bearkats' rotation. Chilo averaged 15.6 points and 6.7 rebounds. **Roosevelt Moore**, a 5-10 freshman point guard, who averaged 28.0 ppg at A&M Consolidated in College Station, Tex., will compete at the point guard spot.

BLUE RIBBON ANALYSIS

Larry Brown has the Bearkats on the right track and a bevy of guards should help fuel his quick, high scoring attack.

"There are plenty of new faces this year and a lot will depend on how quickly we blend together," said Brown. "I really think this will be a transition year for us. I think we'll be better on the perimeter than we were a year ago."

However, outside of 6-9 Hammock, Sam Houston State is virtually unproven and rather shallow at the post positions. It's hard to imagine Sam Houston

State improving over the 1989-90 season in light of losing two quality players such as Gilliam and Green. And a pre-conference schedule that includes dates with Ole Miss, Southwestern Louisiana, Wyoming, Louisiana Tech and an appearance in the University of Texas Classic is not conducive to a team that has so many new faces.

With only one senior on the roster, Sam Houston State appears to be a team of the future. But in the present, the Bearkats will probably finish seventh in the league race.

UNIVERSITY OF SAN DIEGO

LAST SEASON: 16-12
CONFERENCE RECORD: 9-5
STARTERS LOST: 2
STARTERS RETURNING: 3
CONFERENCE: WEST COAST (WCC)
LOCATION: SAN DIEGO, CA
HOME FLOOR: USD SPORTS CENTER (2,500)
NICKNAME: TOREROS
COLORS: COLUMBIA BLUE, NAVY AND WHITE
COACH: HANK EGAN, record at San Diego, 94-75. Career record, 242-260.

The University of San Diego, for the first time in four years, is the favorite to win the West Coast Conference championship. With all but two players returning from last year's squad that won 16 overall and finished third in the conference race behind decimated Loyola Marymount and Pepperdine, the Toreros have the most returning experience in the league.

Hank Egan, in his seventh season as head coach, should use that experience and a dominant homecourt advantage at the tiny USD Sports Center to enjoy the Toreros' best year since going 24-6 and winning the WCC regular season title in 1986-87. A strong offense that set an all-time school record by averaging 79.1 points per game - third in the WCC - has made USD even more dangerous, as Egan's team also ranked third in defense.

The only two players lost from last season were starters - 6-8 forward and team MVP John Jerome (19.3 ppg, 8.0 rpg) and 6-5 forward Craig Cottrell (9.2 ppg) - but, of the Toreros' 12 returnees, 10 started at least one game last year. It is clearly a strong nucleus for 1990-91.

USD is led in the backcourt by 6-3 senior **Pat Holbert** (12.3 ppg) and 6-2 junior **Wayman Strickland** (8.3 ppg, 169 assists, 60 steals), who figure to be full-time starters for the upcoming campaign. Holbert can put points on the board in a hurry, and is deadly from both three-point range (54-for-117 last year, 46.2 percent, second in the WCC) and the free throw line (83.6 percent, fourth in the conference). Strickland provides strong floor leadership at point guard, having ranked third in the WCC in assists and second in steals.

Backing up the guards will be versatile 6-3 JC transfer **Mike Brown** (13.9 ppg), a transfer from Mesa (Ariz.) CC, who will push hard for a starting spot after playing a key role on Mesa's 32-3 team a year ago, and 6-6 senior **Randy Thompson** (1.7 ppg, 1.4 rpg), who could also see duty at forward. The rest of the backcourt cast is unproven on the Division I level, with 6-6 junior **Carlos Carrillo** (1.3 rpg), 6-3 sophomore **Joe Temple** (1.6 ppg, 1.8 rpg), 5-11 sophomore **Geoff Probst** (9.9 ppg, 7.0 apg at UC-Davis in 1988-89) and 6-3 freshman **Neal Meyer** (Chaparral HS/Scottsdale, Ariz.), who sat out the 1989-90 campaign due to injury.

USD's starting forwards figure to be a pair of 6-5 juniors, **Kelvin Woods** (9.4 ppg, 4.0 rpg) and **Gylan Dottin** (8.6 ppg, 4.2 rpg). Woods has been extremely consistent as a shooter, hitting over 52 percent from the floor last season, and he has the maturity to be a team leader. That is also the case of Dottin, who started 13 of the Toreros' first 15 games last year before suffering a broken nose in a practice mishap. Dottin smacked into the elbow of 6-9 senior center **Dondi Bell** (5.0 ppg, 3.8 rpg).

Bell should be the full-time center this year after starting 11 games toward the end of 1989-90. He suffered a hip injury that caused him to miss USD's final regular season game. Bell still ranked third in the WCC in blocked shots (24) and is capable of returning to the form that earned him All-WCC honorable mention recognition as a sophomore, when he averaged 9.0 points and 5.9 rebounds. He will be pushed by another Mesa CC transfer, 6-8 junior **Reed Watson** (12.4), who can also play forward.

The Toreros have a solid frontcourt bench to complement the starters. 6-4 senior **Anthony Thomas**, when he got regular playing time, averaged 11.4 points over the last seven games (6.9 ppg overall). 6-8 seniors **Keith Colvin** (1.3 ppg) and **Shawn Hamilton** (0.4 ppg), along with 6-8 sophomore **Brooks Barnhard** have height, but must still prove themselves as contributors. That increases the importance of swingmen Thompson, Brown and Watson.

BLUE RIBBON ANALYSIS

There is an old saying: "Two heads are better than one." While Egan, entering his 20th season as a head coach - he served 13 at the Air Force Academy - fits in well with the traditional WCC "coach's league" reputation, it doesn't hurt to add the experience and knowledge of the 10th winningest coach in conference history. That belongs to Jack Avina, formerly of the University of Portland. Avina, now semi-retired, served 17 years as Portland's coach, and has coached a team in Turkey since 1987. Egan will count heavily on Avina's experience in teaching young play-

ers, and will have more time to devote to the many other complexities involved in being a Division I head coach.

The knowledge of Egan and Avina guiding the most experienced roster in the league points to a WCC championship, especially with the skills and intelligence of Holbert, Dottin, Strickland and Woods in the lineup. USD is also overdue for a healthy season.

Except for the Indiana University tournament Dec. 7-8, the Toreros should not be overwhelmed much prior to opening the WCC campaign. Mixed in with home games against Canisius, Hofstra and San Jose State are road games with neighbor San Diego State, Southern Utah State, Cal-Santa Barbara, Eastern Washington and new Division I entry Cal State-Northridge.

It adds up to a championship menu in the West Coast Conference.

SAN DIEGO STATE

LAST SEASON: 13-18
CONFERENCE RECORD: 4-12
STARTERS LOST: 3
STARTERS RETURNING: 2
CONFERENCE: WESTERN ATHLETIC (WAC)
LOCATION: SAN DIEGO, CA
HOME FLOOR: SAN DIEGO SPORTS ARENA (13,471)
NICKNAME: AZTECS
COLORS: SCARLET AND BLACK
COACH: JIM BRANDENBURG, record at San Diego State, 37-53. Career record, 252-165.

Jim Brandenburg left behind the cold winds and bitter winters of Wyoming three years ago for the warm weather and beaches of Southern California. He also left a nationally ranked basketball team at the University of Wyoming to take over a less than successful program at San Diego State. The weather has held up its part of the bargain. It is still cold in Wyoming and warm in San Diego. But Brandenburg has found that creating a winner at San Diego State is a difficult task.

In three seasons, the Aztecs are 37-53 under Brandenburg. They finished eighth in the nine-team WAC last season and lost to Air Force in the qualifying game for the WAC tournament. He has faced drastic changes in his roster every season with players coming and going before they even get their names sewn on their uniforms.

Brandenburg has lost four starters off last year's team. He also has players returning who have starting experience. Out of 12 players on the roster last season, eight started at least six games. Only one player started all 31.

Brandenburg had been searching for that one player he could build his program around, and he feels he might have found him this year. 6-10 **Joe McNaull** from Monte Vista HS in Spring Valley, Calif., is the young man who has Brandenburg looking forward to this season. McNaull averaged 21.1 points, 18 rebounds and six blocked shots during his senior year. And at 6-10, Brandenburg is most impressed with his ability and plans to have him play power forward instead of center.

"He runs like a deer and jumps very well," said Brandenburg. "He is really a '4' (strong forward) prototype." McNaull is expected to start for the Aztecs as a freshman.

The Aztecs will need McNaull and other newcomers right away because the team has lost so much. It seemed that the Aztecs would have a strong nucleus returning until late in the summer when three players left for academic reasons.

Included in the late roster change was Shawn Jamison, a 6-8 strong forward who would have been a senior. Jamison was the biggest loss. He was the only Aztec to start all 31 games. He was the top scorer (16.8 ppg), best rebounder (6.9) and played over 200 more minutes than anyone else on the team. Jamison was a transfer from Pratt (Kan.) CC. Also lost in the late wipeout was Michael Hudson, a 6-5 guard who also would have been a senior. Hudson was fourth in scoring (7.7), fourth in assists (52) and fourth in rebounding for San Diego State last season. He started 10 games.

Also, Michael Best and Rodney Jones are both gone. Best could have been San Diego State's most prolific scorer but he lost a battle to keep off the pounds and was overweight throughout his college career. He should have been the Aztecs' top player but instead started just 20 games and averaged only 11.1 points per game. He was still the man who took charge in close games. Jones started 28 games for San Diego State and averaged 4.1 ppg and 2.3 rpg.

Brandenburg, however, didn't lose everyone. He's more than a little glad to have 7-1 center **Marty Dow** back on the team. Dow started 23 games for the Aztecs but then injured an ankle and his absence hurt San Diego State badly. He averaged 12.3 points and 6.2 rebounds. "Early in the season, he was playing as well or better than any center in the conference," said Brandenburg. "He was a pleasant surprise. But he had torn tendons in his right ankle."

The Aztecs also have 6-11 senior center **Neal Steinly** (1.6 ppg, 1.1 rpg), who started the last six games after Dow went out. And 6-11 center **Mark Pollard** of Orem, Utah, will be back after missing two years on a religious mission for the Mormon Church.

If McNaull starts at strong forward, he'll find plenty of available help behind him. **Keith Balzer** is a 6-8 transfer from Imperial Valley (Calif.) CC. He averaged 19.5 ppg and 12.5 rebounds last season. **Nelson Steward** is a 6-7 redshirt junior from Chicago. At the small forward spot, 6-6 senior **Vern Thompson** (4.5 ppg, 2.5 rpg) will be returning. Also at that position are 6-7 junior **Mike Ferguson** who

averaged 11 points and 6.7 rebounds at McLennan (Tex.) CC last season and 6-7 freshman **Courtie Miller**, a highly regarded redshirt from Torrey Pines (Calif.) HS.

"Thompson started over half of our games there last year and Miller was the player of the year in San Diego the year before," Brandenburg said.

Arthur Massey, who started 16 games last season and played in all 31, should be at point guard. **Chris McKinney**, a 6-2 freshman from East St. Louis, Ill., figures as the backup.

The big guard position was Best's home. 6-1 **Ray Barfield**, who sat out last season, might be moving in. He is a sophomore from Fresno, Calif. Another possibility is **James Lewis**, a 6-2 junior who transferred from Colorado Northwestern CC, where he averaged 26.1 points and broke a school record with 1,499 points in two seasons. Lewis hails from Jefferson, Ind.

The other name on the Aztec roster should be familiar to fans. **Bart Brandenburg**, son of the coach, will be a walk-on freshman who will probably redshirt this season and transfer to an Ivy League school next year.

BLUE RIBBON ANALYSIS

"I like this group for a couple of reasons," said Brandenburg. "I think this is the best recruiting class we've had here because of McNaull, if nothing else. I think he's going to be that good."

The Aztecs will have a blend of the old and the new. With Dow, Massey and Thompson returning and players like McNaull, Steward, Balzer, Lewis, Barfield and Miller mixed in, San Diego State will have more depth and talent than in the last three seasons.

"That's kind of where our program is," explained Brandenburg. "We have more kids back, but we still have a lot of new faces. I think we'll be an improved basketball team, by far. I like my position with this club."

Brandenburg's position isn't real comfortable. San Diego State is building a new arena on campus so the Aztecs don't have to go all the way downtown to play in the Sports Arena. The administration is giving serious thought to pulling out of the WAC, which leaves everything in a state of limbo.

The San Diego State administration wants a winning team out of Brandenburg, feeling he has had the time to produce one. With this group, the Aztecs will be more competitive and will move up in the WAC standings, maybe to sixth. But San Diego State still isn't a true contender for the WAC title.

1990-91 SAN DIEGO STATE SCHEDULE		
Nov.	24	@North Carolina
	27	University of San Diego
Dec.	4	@Southern California
	15	California-Irvine
	21-22	#Texaco Star Classic
	27	Baylor
	29	@UCLA
Jan.	3	Brigham Young
	5	Utah
	10	@Air Force
	12	@Colorado State
	17	New Mexico
	19	UTEP
	24	@New Mexico
	26	@UTEP
Feb.	3	Wyoming
	7	@Brigham Young
	9	@Utah
	14	Colorado State
	16	Air Force
	21	Hawaii
	23	@Wyoming
	27	U.S. International (CA)
Mar.	2	@Hawaii
	6-9	##WAC Tournament

@ Road Games
# San Diego, CA (Arkansas State, Drexel, TBA)
Laramie, WY

SAN FRANCISCO

LAST SEASON: 8-20
CONFERENCE RECORD: 4-10
STARTERS LOST: 4
STARTERS RETURNING: 1
CONFERENCE: WEST COAST (WCC)
LOCATION: SAN FRANCISCO, CA
HOME FLOOR: MEMORIAL GYMNASIUM (5,300)
NICKNAME: DONS
COLORS: GREEN AND GOLD
COACH: JIM BROVELLI, record at San Francisco, 60-80.
Career record, 220-210.

It took five years for Jim Brovelli to build a West Coast Conference champion at the University of San Diego. Brovelli is hoping the timetable for his next championship is the same, now that he is in his fifth season as coach of his alma mater, the University of San Francisco. He seems confident enough, calling this year's edition of the Dons his deepest and most talented team since taking over when USF resurrected its basketball program in 1985-86.

Despite losing four starters off last year's disappointing sixth place squad, Brovelli is confident because of nine returning lettermen and what he calls "the finest recruiting class we have had" in his USF tenure. Heading the list is 6-6 junior forward **Darryl Johnson** (18.9 ppg, 17.0 rpg at Independence CC/Independence, Kan.), the leading rebounder in the national junior college ranks. Johnson was tabbed a JC All-America by *Basketball Weekly*, and was one of 12 players invited to the prestigious Texas-USA national junior college athletic association all-star game in Midland, Texas. Once the prep player of the year in Houston, Johnson was a redshirt freshman at Oklahoma, before transferring to Independence.

Brovelli also signed Johnson's high school teammate, 6-5 junior **Tim Owens** (18.0 ppg, 7.0 rpg for Midland JC, Tex.). Owens played in the Texas-USA national all-star game, as well. Both are "above the rim players who should significantly improve our rebounding capability," Brovelli said. The coach is especially sensitive to that stat, since the Dons ranked seventh on the boards in the WCC a year ago.

Johnson and Owens represent a serious challenge to the first string status of 6-7 senior **James Bell** (7.6 ppg, 4.1 rpg), who is Brovelli's only returning starter. Bell can play either forward spots and made 18 starts last year, his first on the Division I level after transferring from Bellevue (Wash.) CC. He had career highs of 18 points against Virginia Tech and 10 rebounds against Bay Area rival St. Mary's.

After Bell, only 6-7 senior **Scott McWhorter** (7.2 ppg, 2.5 rpg) has any meaningful experience in the frontcourt. In the Dons' final 10 regular season games, McWhorter averaged 10.8 points and shot 54 percent from the floor. Other frontcourt returnees vying for time include 6-9 senior **Jeff Christian** (2.1 ppg) and 6-6 senior **Mike Sestich** (1.3 ppg). 6-10 sophomore **John Glavan** (2.2 ppg, 2.2 rpg) and 6-11 soph **Ben Klash** (1.7 ppg) are reserve centers.

Two freshmen in the frontcourt have glowing, if unproven credentials. Leading the way is 6-5 **Wilson Stephens** (McAteer HS/San Francisco), the San Francisco prep player of the year. Stephens averaged 28.3 points and 11.8 rebounds at McAteer. 6-8 stringbean **Jason Boyd** (Madison HS/San Antonio, Tex.) was also a productive scholastic performer (20.6 ppg, 8.8 rpg).

Newcomers will play an even more significant role in the backcourt, as the Dons have little returning experience there. 6-3 junior guard **Kevin Weeks** averaged 17 points and seven rebounds at the College of the Sequoias (Calif.) before transferring, and a pair of outstanding freshmen - 6-0 **Orlando Smart** (29.2 ppg, 7.0 apg, and 3.2 steals at Crockett HS/Austin, Tex.) and 6-0 **Mike Brovelli** (21.4 ppg, 5.0 apg, and 3.0 steals at San Rafael HS/San Rafael, Calif.) - will get significant minutes right away. Brovelli is the coach's son and was the North Bay Area player of the year.

The only backcourt returnees have minimal experience. They are 6-3 junior **Jeff Perkins** (appeared in just one game), 5-10 sophomore **Leon Clinton** (1.5 ppg) and 6-5 sophomore **Roy Modkins** (0.5 ppg).

BLUE RIBBON ANALYSIS

Brovelli has recruited an outstanding array of players that should bring significant improvement to his team. Johnson alone will fortify the Dons' rebounding strength, where they were terribly weak a year ago. He could even be the same kind of intimidator that the late Hank Gathers was for defending WCC champion Loyola Marymount.

Team chemistry is important, and Bell and McWhorter are the only returnees who made significant contributions. If the freshman are able to fit in right away, USF could return to the front end of the conference standings for the first time in nine years.

Mostly on the strength of the junior college transfers, call it third place for San Francisco, just behind San Diego and Loyola Marymount.

1990-91 SAN FRANCISCO SCHEDULE		
Nov.	23-24	#Lobo Classic
	28	Sonoma State (CA)
Dec.	1	California
	5	Fullerton State
	8	Fairleigh Dickinson
	15	@Pacific
	18	Boise State
	21-22	##Met Life Classic
	28-29	###Red Food Classic
Jan.	2	Marist
	5	St. Mary's
	11	University of Portland
	12	Gonzaga (WA)
	17	@Santa Clara
	19	@University of San Diego
	25	Pepperdine
	26	Loyola Marymount
Feb.	1	@Loyola Marymount
	2	@Pepperdine
	9	@St. Mary's
	15	University of San Diego
	16	Santa Clara
	21	@Gonzaga
	23	@University of Portland
Mar.	2-4	*WCC Tournament

@ Road Games
# Albuquerque, NM (Army, New Mexico & Texas-Arlington)
San Francisco, CA (Air Force, Utah State & Vermont)
Chattanooga, TN (Alabama State, California-Irvine & Tennessee—Chattanooga)
* Santa Clara, CA

SAN JOSE STATE

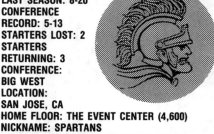

LAST SEASON: 8-20
CONFERENCE RECORD: 5-13
STARTERS LOST: 2
STARTERS RETURNING: 3
CONFERENCE: BIG WEST
LOCATION: SAN JOSE, CA
HOME FLOOR: THE EVENT CENTER (4,600)
NICKNAME: SPARTANS
COLORS: ROYAL BLUE, GOLD AND WHITE
COACH: STAN MORRISON, record at San Jose State, 8-20.
Career record, 211-203.

Some college basketball coaches lose two, maybe three solid players in one year and deem the coming season as a rebuilding year. What Stan Morrison had to do at San Jose State last year was far more than just your ordinary rebuilding. It was more like just plain old building. Morrison basically had to start from scratch last year, after the players rebellion against coach Bill Berry cost the San Jose State program an entire team.

After building from the bottom up, Morrison miraculously found enough players to somehow win eight games with 11 of their 20 loses coming in either overtime or by five points or less. That's quite an accomplishment for the man who had done a fine job at both Pacific and Southern California.

"We made significant progress based on two or three elements," Morrison said. "I sensed a great deal of pride in everyone who was involved with the program. Everyone who was with us at the start of the season was in the team picture five days after the season and they wanted to be in that picture."

The Spartans couldn't brag about that fact the year before. Ten of the Spartans quit the team protesting Berry's coaching techniques. But Morrison, who has had a winner everywhere he has gone, was not pleased with just finishing out a season.

"But my expectations are generally speaking higher than anyone else's," Morrison said. "I was disappointed in terms of the outcome of games where we did not get the job done, 10 losses by five points or less.

"We showed great resiliency throughout the season. No team was emotionally ready as often, which is a key ingredient to any team. We were the underdog every time we stepped on to the floor."

More than likely, the Spartans will have to wear that underdog tag every night this season as well. But at least Morrison has a nucleus of a team, some semblance of continuity to work with this time. Morrison welcomes back 12 players who worked hard for him a year ago. Even though last year's leading scorer and rebounder Kenne Young has graduated, Morrison has a good crop of players to continue the building process at San Jose.

Senior guard **Troy Batiste** (12.4 ppg, 4.2 rpg) is the Spartans' top returning player. The 6-2 Batiste moved into the starting lineup midway through the season last year at off-guard and found instant success there. Batiste had an uncanny way of getting to the free throw line, attempting more free chances than any other Spartan (154), which is remarkable for a guard. He also was the team's third leading rebounder. In addition, Batiste was also the team's leader in steals with 25 and second on the team in assists with 63. However, Morrison has to be concerned with Batiste's shooting numbers, as he connected on only 37 per-

cent from the floor and 30 percent from three-point range. Morrison obviously would like to see those numbers improve greatly. But Batiste is a solid player and more than likely will be the Spartans' go-to guy this season.

Senior guard **Andre Brooks** (9.9 ppg, 1.9 rpg) also returns. The 6-3 Brooks started the first 12 games of the season at off-guard, then became more comfortable in a reserve role. Brooks was the Spartans' main man from three-point land, connecting on 44 percent of his tries, good for second in the Big West. After just one season played, Brooks is fifth on the San Jose career list for three-pointers made. Look for Brooks to play some more while coming off the bench again this year. Brooks is certainly the Spartans' instant offense.

Sophomore forward **Kevin Logan** (7.6 ppg, 6.2 rpg) was a member of the Big West all-freshman team and the only freshman in the Big West to start every one of his team's games a year ago. The 6-7 Logan was a very versatile player, being able to offer inside power as well as outside finesse equally. Logan was the team's leading field goal percentage shooter at 50 percent, second on the team in rebounding and led the team in blocked shots with 26. Logan, who was originally a walk-on two years ago, had so much potential that Berry held him out and redshirted him. He has now become one of the Spartans' top players and will be for the next three seasons.

Sophomore guard **Terry Cannon** (6.8 ppg, 1.9 rpg, 73 assists) played both guard positions as a freshman last year, but ended the season as the team's No. 1 point guard. Cannon, a 6-0 product of Crenshaw HS in Los Angeles, where he was named as the *Los Angeles Times* player of the year as a senior, has all the tools to be a solid guard in the Big West, but Morrison isn't sure if Cannon is totally suited to play the point. That will be one of the things Morrison will look at closely in pre-season. But Cannon is a decent outside shooter (42 percent) and a good penetrator. He led the team in assists with 73, becoming the first freshman ever to turn that trick at San Jose.

Sophomore guard **Charles Terrell** (6.2 ppg, 3.0 rpg) is another guy Morrison pulled out of the intramural league and put into uniform. All the 6-3 Terrell did was start the final 15 games, shot 50 percent from the floor and played aggressive defense. Not bad for a walk-on. Most schools' walk-ons are the guys who sit buried on the bench, wait for any playing time at all and finally get in when the crowd calls their name in the last minutes of a blowout victory. Not for Morrison. He not only used two players off the street, he started two. Terrell's outside touch became better with time and confidence; plus, he is a very good athlete with good strength and leaping abilities. Terrell should be able to contribute this season again and possibly start.

Senior guard **Mike Wasserburger** (4.6 ppg, 0.6 rpg) played in 18 games last year, serving as a role shooter, coming off the bench and hoisting bombs at the basket from long range. More than half of his overall attempts last year were from three-point range (53 threes out of 90 overall). The 6-2 Wasserburger is a solid zone breaker who has no hesitancy in shooting the ball, getting a shot for every minute and a half played last year.

Most of all the top returning players for the Spartans play in the backcourt, with the lone exception being Logan. There is no way that any team can be simply competitive, much less win, in the Big West playing a guard dominated lineup. Size is essential. Enter junior center **Daryl Scott** (3.2 ppg, 2.6 rpg). The 6-8 Scott played in 26 games last year, starting two. Morrison had hopes that Scott would develop into a power in the pivot immediately, but inconsistency plagued him throughout. Scott has all the physical attributes to be a fine player for the Spartans: strength, a decent touch (47 percent last year), ability to crash the offensive glass (39 of his 68 boards were offensive) and good size. And Scott had moments of brilliance last year, but could never keep it up through a solid stretch. If Scott becomes ready to play this October, the center job is his.

Maybe **Robert Dunlap** is the answer if Scott fails. The 6-11, 235-pound sophomore center averaged 2.2 ppg and 2.9 rpg in 18 games last year coming off the bench. But Dunlap, who only played one year of basketball in high school, is still considered a project and may need more time to be a constant contributor. Morrison loves Dunlap's work ethic (he has gained 25 pounds of strength since last year) and he may push Scott out of the starting slot in the pivot.

The final four returning Spartans played very sparingly last season and remarkably, although unfortunately for Morrison, all four are forwards. Senior **Jeff Novitzky** had back surgery in February, which limited his playing time to just two games. The 6-7 Novitzky first attended Arizona on a track scholarship, where he was a high jumper. **Michael Hostetter** played in two games, scoring no points, so the 6-6 forward retained his freshman eligibility. Hostetter is a product of Santa Rosa, Calif., and Cardinal Newman HS. **Andrew Gardiner**, a 6-7 native of New Zealand, played in four games, scored one point and then suffered a groin injury. He also was redshirted, so Gardiner will also be considered a freshman once again. Gardiner, who played on the New Zealand Junior National Team, is also a fine athlete, winning his nation's decathlon championship in 1987. **Matt Romig**, a 6-6 sophomore, was a walk-on of the traditional flavor. He played in one game and much to the chagrin of the fans at the Event Center, Romig didn't score.

Three players that didn't see action last year but were members of the Spartans also return. Leading that group is sophomore guard **Phillip Crump** (Philadelphia, Pa./Ben Franklin HS). The 5-11 Crump was penciled in to start at the point for the Spartans, but then he had to sit out his freshman year. Crump is an excellent penetrator and shooter who averaged 22.7 points and seven assists per game as a senior at Ben Franklin. Very active in the off-season in political affairs in the City of Brotherly Love, Crump hopes to become a Secret Service officer someday. He is also the uncle of the late Hank Gathers' son.

Two players that made the team as walk-ons —a very familiar term in Spartan land —a year ago but were redshirted to gain experience are junior guard **Eddie Fairley**, a 5-9 pepperpot, and junior guard **Ron Hannon**, a 6-2 off-guard.

Morrison and his coaching staff had the benefit of having a full year to recruit for this team. Last year, it was scramble and grab whatever was available. This year, the San Jose State staff were more selective and intent, gaining four frontcourt players, obviously a glaring weakness with the Spartans.

Leading the group of freshman signees (three in all) is center **Rastko Cvetkovic**. The 6-11, 235-pound Cvetkovic is a native of Belgrade, Yugoslavia, where he played for the highly competitive Red Star team that previously sent Drazen Petrovic and Vlade Divac to the United States. The Red Star team toured the United States and played many of the top college teams, especially in the east, last pre-season, and it was then that Morrison spotted Cvetkovic. The burly Cvetkovic averaged 11.2 points and 4.6 rebounds for Red Star in his final season. He could be Morrison's answer in the middle.

Mike Brotherton (Battle Ground, Wash., HS) is a 6-9 forward with a lot of skills. Brotherton averaged 21.9 points and 10.9 rebounds as a senior at Battle Ground, leading his team to the Class AA state title and MVP honors in the state tournament. Brotherton is a strong inside player, aggressive rebounder and solid scorer. With the Spartans' troubles up front, look for Brotherton to contribute immediately.

Jason Allen (Oak Creek, Wisc./Marquette HS) is a 6-5 swingman who averaged 9.0 ppg for the top team in Wisconsin and the 18th ranked team in the nation. Allen has a fine outside touch and is a very solid athlete, evident by his state placing in the shot put and discus. Allen will have to take his time to work his way into the Spartan lineup.

The other Spartan newcomer is JC transfer **Michael St. Julien**. The 6-4 swingman comes to San Jose State from Blinn (Tex.) JC, where he averaged 11.0 points and 12.0 rebounds per game over the two seasons there. St. Julien, who will be a junior for the Spartans, is also a fine athlete who competed in track and field. St. Julien was the national JC champion in the high jump the last two years. With Novitzky and Allen to complement St. Julien, maybe the Spartans should challenge teams to a track meet. Gardiner will handle the decathlon events.

BLUE RIBBON ANALYSIS

There is no question that Morrison deserves a lot of credit for turning the San Jose State program around in a hurry. No one ever imagined the Spartans would finish anywhere but the cellar last year in the competitive Big West. Somehow, they finished eighth. Hardly anyone could have dreamed the Spartans could be competitive after the mass exodus of players during the Bill Berry era. San Jose State won eight games and could have snared a few more with a little luck.

Morrison walked into a troubled position, one that not many people could have handled —and he made things work —immediately. Maybe he was a bit disappointed, but he should have been realistically proud and happy to bounce back after starting with nothing.

Now comes time for Phase Two. Can the Spartans actually leap from an eight-win season to find opportunity and competitiveness in the Big West? It's not very likely.

If the Spartans are to improve and reach at least middle ground — .500 basketball —two things will have to happen:

First and foremost, the Spartans will need some sort of inside help, coming from unknown or yet unproven sources. Someone is going to have to step up and be the leader in the frontcourt. Maybe it's Scott, maybe it's Dunlap, maybe it's one of the two freshmen, Cvetkovic or Brotherton. Someone of that group has to give Morrison double figures in points and at least seven rebounds per game. The Spartans are just too guard-oriented to win consistently in the Big West.

The other factor that needs instant improvement is the Spartans' perimeter shooting. Last year, they shot 42 percent while their opponents clicked on 49 percent.

''We need some people to step forward and play better than what they have shown thus far,'' Morrison said. ''And we have to do a better job of controlling the inside game with rebounding, interior defense and interior scoring. Better shot selection will improve the shooting averages.''

That's where Crump fits in. If he is as talented running the point as anticipated, then Crump will be able to penetrate, get the ball in better shooting position and everything about the Spartans' offense will improve. In reality, the Spartans played all last year without a true point guard to run the show. Crump is a key factor.

However, it appears to be too many ifs for a team that was already in too deep in the Big West. Continued improvement, sure. But radical change in the win column? No. Look for the Spartans to win 10 to 12 games and finish in the bottom half of the Big West, around eighth. However, better times are ahead.

1990-91 SAN JOSE STATE SCHEDULE

Nov.	26	@Texas Christian
	28	@Lamar
Dec.	1	@University of San Diego
	3	@California
	5	Washington State
	20	Santa Clara
	22	@Idaho State
	27-28	#Capital City Classic
Jan.	2	California-Santa Barbara

1990-91 SAN JOSE STATE SCHEDULE Cont.

Jan.	4	California-Irvine
	7	@UNLV
	12	@Utah State
	17	Fresno State
	19	Pacific
	24	@New Mexico State
	26	@Long Beach State
	31	UNLV
Feb.	3	Fullerton State
	9	Utah State
	11	Long Beach State
	14	@Pacific
	16	@Fresno State
	23	New Mexico State
	28	@California-Irvine
Mar.	2	@California-Santa Barbara
	8-10	##Big West Tournament

@ Road Games
# Sacramento, CA (Nevada, Oklahoma State & Sacramento State)
Long Beach, CA

SANTA CLARA

LAST SEASON: 9-19
CONFERENCE RECORD: 6-8
STARTERS LOST: 2
STARTERS RETURNING: 3
CONFERENCE: WEST COAST (WCC)
LOCATION: SANTA CLARA, CA
HOME FLOOR: TOSO PAVILION (5,000)
NICKNAME: BRONCOS
COLORS: BRONCO RED AND WHITE
COACH: CARROLL WILLIAMS, record at Santa Clara, 314-246.

Santa Clara is a basketball program steeped in tradition. Carroll Williams, dean of WCC coaches and in his 21st season at the helm of the Broncos, is by far the winningest ever in conference play with 149 victories. And while it has been traditional for Santa Clara to win close to 20 games year in and year out, when the Broncos do have an off-year, it has been equally traditional for them to bounce right back.

Thus, it is bouncing time by the Bay. The Broncos suffered through the worst record of the Williams era, and the school's worst since 1964, winning just nine games and going 6-8 (fifth place) in conference play. Making it worse was the fact that Santa Clara lost six games by four points or less.

Despite the lack of any senior leadership on this year's roster and the graduation of two of the most talented players in the league - guard Jeffty Connelly (16.2 ppg, 5.0 rpg, 83 assists) and power forward Nils Becker (11.0 ppg, 6.7 rpg) - the Broncos may improve nonetheless. Three prominent junior starters return, led by 7-1 center **Ron Reis** (12.4 ppg, 6.9 rpg, league-leading 62.4 field goal percentage). Also back are 6-0 point guard **Melvin Chinn** (5.3 ppg, 75 assists) and 6-7 forward **Rhea Taylor** (7.2 ppg, 4.1 rpg).

Last year, Reis may have been the most improved player on the West coast, using his height to offset limited mobility in Santa Clara's transition game. Williams knew how to use him, too, and the big guy responded accordingly as a scorer and rebounder. The coach is expecting a still-improved Reis this year, the bulky center having worked 15 pounds off his massive frame to get down to 260. The off-season condition ing program has also helped Reis' jumping and given him the endurance to run up and down the court for 40 minutes. If that is indeed the case, Reis could become one of the most dominant big men in the country.

Santa Clara is also hoping that an added year of maturity will aid Chinn, whose quality of play was inconsistent because of a reported lack of concentration. He was also never 100 percent physically, hampered by nagging groin and ankle injuries. Chinn should be fully recovered this year. As for Taylor, he will continue to improve as he gains confidence in his inside skills and, like Reis and Chinn, should be set in Williams' starting lineup if healthy.

6-0 junior LaCoby Phillips (6.1 ppg), who made 14 starts last year, may have an edge at the off-guard position because of his experience. He and Chinn will be backed up by four other returnees: 6-3 junior James Renfro (3.9 ppg), 6-2 junior Michael Woods (3.0 ppg), 6-1 sophomore Greg Paulson (2.0 ppg) and 6-3 sophomore redshirt Mark Schmitz. Of the backcourt recruits, 6-3 freshman DeWayne Lewis (Hamilton HS/Los Angeles) will probably see the most minutes, although 6-1 freshman John Woolery (Fairfax HS/Los Angeles) will also get a chance to play.

One freshman who will get a chance to start is 6-5 Andy Karich (Mater Dei HS/Surfside, Calif.). Karich figures to get the nod at forward opposite Taylor, although 6-4 junior Jerry Velling (1.6 ppg, 1.9 rpg) merits consideration.

Williams can look to some other young talent thanks to last year's recruiting effort, resulting in three freshmen redshirts this season. They are 6-10 Carl Anderson (Area HS/Sault Ste. Marie, Michigan), who will caddy for Reis, while 6-4 Lyman Casey (Cole HS/Carpinteria, Calif.) and 6-7 Louis Stewart (Kennedy HS/Sacramento) look to contribute elsewhere. The latter is the son of Mike Stewart, Santa Clara's most recent All-America honoree (1972-73).

6-8 sophomore Kevin Fitzwilson, who appeared in just four games last year, also returns.

BLUE RIBBON ANALYSIS

Williams always seems to get the most out of his available talent. Take Reis, for example. Williams has done wonders with his center, serving as the architect of his development in much the same way he did for the late Nick Vanos. After an outstanding career at Santa Clara, Vanos showed promise in his two seasons with the NBA Phoenix Suns before dying in a plane crash.

A coach, however, can only do so much. Even with Reis and Chinn, potentially as quick a guard as there is in the West Coast Conference, Santa Clara has too many question marks. It is doubtful the Broncos will return right away to the form that saw them win 20 games and go to post-season play five times in the 1980's.

Santa Clara has a solid nucleus for the future, but this season should be happy with bettering last year's win total. The Broncos figure to get no higher than sixth in the WCC.

1990-91 SANTA CLARA SCHEDULE

Nov.	23-25	#Maui Classic
	29	Pacific
Dec.	1	San Francisco State
	8	Fresno State
	11	@St. Louis
	13	@Minnesota
	15	@Stanford
	18	Nevada
	20	@San Jose State
	22	American University
	28-29	##Fujitsu America/Cable Car Classic
Jan.	5	University of San Diego
	11	@Loyola Marymount
	12	@Pepperdine

1990-91 SANTA CLARA SCHEDULE Cont.

Jan.	17	San Francisco
	19	St. Mary's
	24	@Gonzaga (WA)
	26	@University of Portland
	31	University of Portland
Feb.	2	Gonzaga
	9	@University of San Diego
	15	@St. Mary's
	16	@San Francisco
	21	Pepperdine
	23	Loyola Marymount
Mar.	2-4	*WCC Tournament

@ Road Games
# Lahaina, HI (Chaminade, Indiana, Iowa State, Loyola Marymount, Northeastern, Syracuse & Toledo)
Santa Clara, CA (California-Santa Barbara, Marist & Princeton)
* Santa Clara, CA

SETON HALL

LAST SEASON: 12-16
CONFERENCE
RECORD: 5-11
STARTERS LOST: 2
STARTERS
RETURNING: 3
CONFERENCE:
BIG EAST
LOCATION:
SOUTH ORANGE, NJ
HOME FLOOR: WALSH GYMNASIUM (3,000) and MEADOWLANDS ARENA (20,149)
NICKNAME: PIRATES
COLORS: BLUE AND WHITE
COACH: P. J. CARLESIMO, record at Seton Hall, 119-128.
Career record, 198-232.

P. J. Carlesimo knew he had to enjoy it all while he could. Enjoy the notoriety, the glamour, the honors, the prestige, the overall attention. The likeable head coach of the Pirates had to know that the Cinderella story that carried the Pirates to the national championship game two seasons ago and just two free throws in overtime away from wearing the national crown would not last forever.

The glory ended in a hurry. The starting five from the national runnersup? All gone. Two key reserves? Gone. After going toe-to-toe with Michigan in Seattle in the NCAA title game, Carlesimo had to start all over again. Carlesimo set out to crank it up again, put the pieces together that would lead the Pirates from perennial doormats in the Big East to national power and almost champion. It would be a long road back.

The end result was a 12-16 season that certainly didn't disappoint. After all, after the years of frustration and tough times, one setback wasn't too hard to handle after two years of huge success. The Pirate fans were patient, mainly because the future looked very bright.

Once again, the Pirates will be a young and spirited team. They will feature just two seniors and only one junior on their roster. Which means that Seton Hall fans may have to be patient for yet another season. Carlesimo is even aware of that.

''Obviously, we're still a very young team,'' Carlesimo said. ''It's difficult to be successful in our league with such a young team. But we believe that we are capable of winning on any night.''

Leading the returnees is sophomore guard Terry Dehere (16.1 ppg, 3.4 rpg). The 6-3 Dehere was the Pirates' leading scorer last year as a freshman, only the fifth freshman in Big East history ever to lead his team in scoring. The sharpshooting Dehere was deadly from long range, especially from three-point land, setting a new freshman conference record with 73 bombs. Dehere, a product of the famed St. Anthony HS in Jersey City, N.J., was a Big East all-rookie team selection, hitting 40 percent from the floor, 39 percent from three and 80 percent from the line. Dehere is also a strong defender, as he led the Pirates in steals with 26. He is a consistent scorer and player who will only get better with experience.

Senior center Anthony Avent (10.5 ppg, 9.4 rpg) had a steady season for the Pirates on paper, but really didn't emerge as expected. Many of the Pirate following expected the 6-9 Avent to step into the shoes vacated by the diligent Ramon Ramos and play even better than Ramos, because Avent was a stronger leaper with a better shooting touch. But Avent was plagued with foul difficulty on most occasions (a team high 117 fouls and seven disqualifications) and lackluster performances on the other nights. Still, with all the troubles, Avent was the Big East's fourth leading rebounder and blocked 53 shots, third highest in school history. And Avent's shooting touch has never disappeared. He can score. However, Avent has hands of stone, turning the ball over 84 times, second on the team. But Avent still has a chance to shine as a senior. The last two centers for the Pirates before Avent, namely, Mark Bryant and Ramos, really didn't become dominant until their final seasons. Avent could do the same. He has the tools, he just needs the confidence and the consistency. Look for Avent to have a solid season all around for the Pirates.

The third returning starter from a year ago is senior point guard Oliver Taylor (8.9 ppg, 1.9 rpg, 91 assists). The 6-0 Taylor also had some bright moments last year in his first year with the Pirates after transferring from Miami Dade North JC, but he also had some tough times as well. Strong teams that used pressure defenses and had big time backcourts ate Taylor up. He still has nightmares of Carlton Screen and Eric Murdock of Providence picking his pocket time and time again and Boo Harvey? Don't mention that name please. The Huskies of Connecticut weren't too kind to Ollie either. Taylor is a good ballhandler and a solid defender. He is a pest on the defensive end, like a gnat at the family picnic that just won't go away. He shot 40 percent from the floor and connected on only 28 percent from three-point range. If Taylor learns to handle pressure a little better this year, then his overall game will improve drastically. Taylor's quickness, ability to penetrate and dish off down low are vital. That's why he will continue to see a lot of playing time this season.

Probably the biggest surprise in college basketball last season was the Pirates' Italian import, sophomore guard Marco Lokar (5.0 ppg, 0.3 rpg, nine assists). When the season began, Lokar wasn't even eligible and when he did become available, he was a total unknown. Carlesimo then started to use the sharpshooting Lokar off the bench in a few games after the first of the year and scored a few points here and there. And then, Lokar gets a start against Pitt late in the season and all the Italian wonder does is score 41 points, only a Big East freshman record. In that game, Lokar canned a school record 7 three-pointers. Then, everyone knew who Marco Lokar was. The 6-1 Lokar is a fine outside shooter in the purest sense. He also made 88 percent of his free throw tries. A favorite with Pirate fans at the Meadowlands, Lokar may be hard pressed to find quality playing time this year with the fine recruits that have entered the program in the off-season.

Junior forward Gordon Winchester (3.7 ppg, 2.6 rpg) played in 26 games off the bench for the Pirates last year, after sitting out his freshman season. When he was recruited out of high school (Mt. St. Michael's Academy in the Bronx, N.Y.), the 6-7 Winchester was thought to be a true blue chipper. He never reached those lofty expectations and it appears as if the year on the sidelines really hurt his game. But Winchester is a solid athlete with very good leaping abilities and who runs the floor very well. His shot needs improvement, as does his ability to play under control. But with a solid pre-season, Winchester may become a player of impact this season.

Sophomore point guard **Daryl Crist** (1.6 ppg, 1.4 rpg, 44 assists) played in every game last year as Taylor's backup and even started four games. The 6-0 Crist is a solid ballhandler, crisp passer and strong defender, but he did get pushed around at times last year by stronger opponents. Crist also didn't shoot that well, connecting on 36 percent of his tries, 25 percent from three-point range and only 46 percent from the free throw line. Those numbers need to improve if Crist is to see more time this year. But he is a very capable reserve.

Sophomore center **Jim Dickinson** (1.5 ppg, 1.4 rpg) also played in every game last year as a freshman. The 7-0, 250-pound bullmoose was a solid clog in the middle, backing up Avent and giving the Pirates a boost off the bench in some key victories notably vs. Wake Forest in the ACC-Big East challenge. He became the first seven-foot player in the history of the Big East to nail a three-pointer and duplicated that later in the season, shooting a perfect 2-for-2 from long range. Dickinson was also a solid defender, going up against some of the best big men in the country. The only knock on Dickinson was his aggressiveness.

Last year's top recruit, 6-7 forward **Jerry Walker**, Dehere's high school teammate at national champion St. Anthony HS in Jersey City, had to sit out last season. He is ready to play this season and will challenge for a starting forward slot. Walker is an aggressive rebounder and scorer, the third highest scorer in St. Anthony history behind former Marquette standout Mandy Johnson and current Duke star Bobby Hurley. Walker is the only four-year starter in St. Anthony's history. His high school career record of 115-5 is a tribute to the heart he showed every night. Walker is certainly a player of impact, but it will be interesting to see how the year's layoff affected him. If Walker is in top shape, he can be a deadly force in the Big East. He is that good.

Carlesimo brought six freshmen into the program, although the top prize, 7-2 center Luther Wright of Elizabeth HS in New Jersey, the nation's No. 2 team a year ago, will sit out the year due to academic difficulties. If Wright were eligible, the Pirates would have moved from a pretender to contender in the blink of an eye. Now, Carlesimo must wait to see big Luther bang in the Big East.

However, the other five freshmen are certainly not to be taken lightly. Once again, Carlesimo has traveled far and wide in search of players that will be immediate impact players for the Pirates, stockpiling the frequent flyer points. In fact, Carlesimo went overseas to lock up two forwards, one sign of glasnost, the other a sign of peace, shalom. Forward **Arturas Karnishovas** comes to New Jersey via Vilnius, Lithuania. The 6-8 Karnishovas is a strong, aggressive power forward who played on the Soviet Junior National Team last year, averaging 17 points per game as the team's leading scorer. Karnishovas will be given every opportunity to replace the graduated Michael Cooper at power forward.

Assaf Barnea joins the Pirates by way of Haifa, Israel. The 6-8 Barnea can play both forward positions and played for the Israeli national team for the last three seasons. Two other Big East schools headed to the Middle East and plucked players from Israel in the past — Boston College got Lior Arditti and Connecticut snatched "The Lonesome Dove," Nadav Henefeld, the Big East rookie of the year last year, who has since headed back to his native land to play professionally. If Barnea can give the Pirates just a tad of the Israeli magic that the Dove gave the Huskies last year, then his acquisition is a fine one.

Carlesimo stayed somewhat local for the Pirates final three additions, two of which come from the Garden State. He got two of the five first-team All-New Jersey selections in guard **Bryan Caver** (Trenton, N.J./McCorristin HS) and forward **John Leahy**

(Cape May, N.J./Middle Township HS). Caver is a 6-3 guard who can do it all — shoot, rebound, handle, defend. He averaged 17.3 points, 9.5 assists, 9.0 rebounds and 4.0 steals per game for the Parochial A state champion. His biggest asset is probably his quickness and because of that, he may get a chance to unseat Taylor as the starting point guard. Leahy, a 6-7 swingman, was originally headed to Maryland, but once the NCAA sanctions were levied upon the Terrapin program, Leahy sought his release and headed north to South Orange. Leahy, who has the reputation as a great pure shooter, averaged 29.9 points and nine rebounds per game as a senior. A good shooter like Leahy (56 percent from the floor, 48 from three) was too good to turn down. Also arriving is forward **Chris Davis** (Chesapeake, Va./Deep Creek HS). The 6-8 Davis averaged 14.4 points and 8.4 rebounds per game as a senior. He is considered a fine athlete with good leaping skills and can run the floor well. Davis was also the Virginia state high jump champion, clearing his own height of 6-8. He will have to fight hard to set quality playing time with all that talent the Pirates have up front.

BLUE RIBBON ANALYSIS

The Cinderella season of two years ago is already ancient history, tucked deep in the archives. True, the excitement may be fresh with Seton Hall faithful, but to the Pirates and to coach P. J. Carlesimo, that's over. So the Pirates trudge on the road back to respectability and they will make major strides in that road this season. With the returnees gaining confidence and experience and some very talented newcomers ready to make a solid impact, the Pirates look to be vastly improved on last year.

Dehere, who had a busy summer playing for the U.S. Junior National Team in South America, will be more of a dominant scorer this time around. He has worked on moving without the ball as well as driving to the basket. Those two improvements will help Dehere's advancement immensely.

Avent will have a better year. History says so. It took Mark Bryant and Ramon Ramos awhile to get settled. With Taylor, Crist and newcomer Caver, along with the Italian flash, Lokar, the Pirates' backcourt is solid and strong, among the best in the league. The questions remain in the frontcourt.

Can Winchester emerge to a higher plateau? What will the year off do to the aggressiveness of Walker? Can the imports from abroad help right away? Those are questions that no one can seem to answer right now, which leaves the status of the Pirates in complete limbo.

If all of those questions can be answered before January 1, then the Pirates might have a surprising season in the Big East. They lost a lot of close conference games last year by just getting worn down and banged up by bigger and stronger opponents down the stretch. If Carlesimo has a deep frontcourt to go to, that will not be a problem. But all four of the names mentioned above —Winchester, Walker, Karnishovas and Barnea have to come through.

The Pirates usually shoot the ball well enough to win, play aggressive defense and rebound. They have to cut down on the turnovers. Seton Hall averaged 18 turnovers to 13 assists as a team last year.

So all the ingredients are there for a solid season for the Pirates. Not enough to crack the Big East elite, but enough to win 16 to 18 games and earn a post-season tournament bid. Carlesimo won't have to spend mid-March in a television studio as an analyst, he will be coaching instead.

1990-91 SETON HALL SCHEDULE		
Nov.	24	Iona
	28	@Fordham
Dec.	1	TBA
	4	#Clemson

1990-91 SETON HALL SCHEDULE *Cont.*		
Dec.	9	Long Island
	12	@Villanova
	22	Rutgers
	27	North Carolina A&T
	29	Winthrop College (SC)
Jan.	2	Providence
	5	@Georgetown
	9	St. John's
	12	Syracuse
	15	@Boston College
	19	@Syracuse
	22	St. Peter's
	26	Connecticut
	29	@Providence
Feb.	2	##St. John's
	4	@Pitt
	9	@Oklahoma
	12	Pitt
	16	Georgetown
	19	Niagara
	23	Villanova
	27	@Connecticut
Mar.	2	Boston College
	7-10	##Big East Tournament

@ Road Games
# ACC/Big East Challenge, Syracuse, NY
Madison Square Garden, New York, NY

SIENA

LAST SEASON: 16-13
CONFERENCE RECORD: 11-5
STARTERS LOST: 1
STARTERS RETURNING: 4
CONFERENCE: METRO ATLANTIC ATHLETIC (MAAC)
LOCATION: LOUDONVILLE, NY
HOME FLOOR: ALUMNI RECREATION CENTER (4,000)
NICKNAME: SAINTS
COLORS: GREEN AND GOLD
COACH: MIKE DEANE, record at Siena, 81-36. Career record, 165-74.

Two years ago Mike Deane's Siena Saints shocked the basketball world, first winning the North Atlantic Conference tournament and then upsetting highly regarded Stanford in the opener of the NCAA tournament. Much of the same was expected last season as the tiny Catholic College in the Albany, N.Y., suburb of Loudonville moved into the MAAC. But sometimes the best laid plans of mice and Saints . . . The team got off to a slow start amidst rumors of dissention among team members. Then the only real big man, 6-11 center **Steve Downey**, went down with a broken foot. The Saints seemed poised to come crashing back to earth, the Cinderella season a distant memory. But instead of going down, Siena kept battling, and posted a somewhat surprising 6-5 mark during the 11 games Downey missed. More importantly, guard **Marc Brown**, who had struggled throughout the early part of the season, turned up his offensive game and scored in double figures the last 17 games of the season, beginning with the first game Downey missed, an 85-62 loss at Fordham. Siena finished a strong 16-13 and second in the MAAC North at 11-5.

This year Saint fans can expect much of the

same. Marc Brown, the 5-11 explosive senior guard returns (16.9 ppg, 196 assists) as does the streaky Downey (10.9 ppg, 5.6 rpg). Brown is a point guard many Big East teams court. It was his do-it-all attitude that led Siena back last season, and he will be looked upon to pick up an even bigger piece of the scoring pie now that all-time leading scorer Jeff Robinson (14.9 ppg) has graduated. Downey, again Siena's only true center, is the key up front. He hit 54 percent of his shots from the floor and finished second in rebounding to MAAC all-rookie selection 6-7 sophomore **Lee Matthews** (6.4 rpg). For the Saints to make a run at the top of the MAAC, Downey must use his size to dominate the other smaller centers in the forward-oriented MAAC.

Joining Downey in the frontcourt is Matthews and 6-4 hardnosed junior **Bruce Schroeder** (11.1 ppg, 4.0 rpg). Matthews had a solid freshman campaign, leading the team in field goal percentage (.597), rebounding and blocks (36). He is a tenacious defender who will be one of the MAAC's best as he matures. Schroeder is the classic overachiever; a tough competitor who plays much bigger than his size. Anyone who watches the Saints will be captivated by his hustle and determination. Other key reserves in the frontcourt include 6-6 junior **Andy Grazulis** (1.3 ppg, 1.7 rpg), 6-6 junior **Dave Foster** (0.9 ppg, 1.0 rpg) and 6-9 redshirt freshman **Andy Shorkey**, who sat out last season with tendonitis. A pair of freshmen, 6-8 **Davor Milardovic** (17.5 ppg, 12.0 rpg of Oakville, Ontario, St. Ignatius HS) and 6-6 **Mike McGee** (18.0 ppg, 10.0 rpg of Texarkana, Tex., Liberty Eylau HS) should also contribute.

Brown will look to a number of players to give him some backcourt help. 6-6 senior swingman **Tom Huerter** (8.1 ppg, 3.6 rpg) will look to up his offensive output a bit when Brown is at the point. He hit on 42-of-106 treys last season despite playing largely at small forward, and will fill a bigger gap in the backcourt this time out. **Mike Brown** (6.0 ppg), a 6-2 junior guard, will also get more time at the second guard spot, but must improve on his 24 percent shooting (14-of-57) from three-point range to be a factor. Flashy 5-11 freshman **Doremus Bennerman** (24.8 ppg, 8.3 apg of St. Joseph's HS, in Trumbull, Conn.) could spell Marc Brown at the point, while 6-4 junior **Joe Middleton** (0.6 ppg, 0.6 rpg) and 6-3 sophomore **Jim Ryder** (2.6 ppg) provide depth.

BLUE RIBBON ANALYSIS

This year's Saints are deeper than last season, especially at the forward spot. However, the key will still be Downey. If he steps up and is able to be a major contributor (15-20 ppg 8-10 rpg), then there will be a lot for the fanatical Saints fans to cheer. If not, it will be a .500 year.

Brown is a great player and can carry games against lesser opponents, but can he score 20 ppg and dish out 10 assists? Maybe, but even that may not be enough. Matthews is developing and will help, especially on the boards, and mighty-mite Schroeder will help with his infectious work ethic. A problem developed last season when Siena did not excel early. That seems to be behind them now, and a shaky start may not mean an awful season. This is not the team of two years ago. However, they will be highly competitive in the wide open MAAC. Expect 16 to 17 wins and a third place finish from Siena. But keep in mind the MAAC tournament is again in Albany. With a distinct home court advantage, the Saints may find themselves back in NCAA heaven again.

1990-91 SIENA SCHEDULE		
Nov.	23-26	#Great Alaska Shootout
	28	Pitt
Dec.	4	@Marist
	8	@University of Hartford
	10	@Western Michigan

1990-91 SIENA SCHEDULE Cont.		
Dec.	22	@Brooklyn College (NY)
	30	Bowling Green
Jan.	2	Evansville
	5	Niagara
	7	St. Peter's
	11	Loyola College
	14	Iona
	16	University of Hartford
	19	@St. Peter's
	21	@La Salle
	24	Manhattan
	26	@Fairfield
	28	@Loyola College
	31	Canisius
Feb.	3	Creighton
	6	Central Michigan
	9	@Iona
	12	@Niagara
	14	LeMoyne College (NY)
	18	@Canisius
	20	La Salle
	23	@Manhattan
	25	Fairfield
Mar.	1-4	##MAAC Tournament

@ Road Games
# Anchorage, AK (Alaska-Anchorage, California-Irvine, Nevada, South Carolina, Texas Tech, UCLA & Virginia)
Albany, NY

SOUTH ALABAMA

LAST SEASON: 11-17
CONFERENCE RECORD: 5-9
STARTERS LOST: 2
STARTERS RETURNING: 3
CONFERENCE: SUN BELT
LOCATION: MOBILE, AL
HOME FLOOR: MOBILE CIVIC CENTER (10,000)
NICKNAME: JAGUARS
COLORS: RED, BLUE AND WHITE
COACH: RONNIE ARROW, record at South Alabama, 49-40.
Career record, 351-83.

With an influx of junior college players, coach Ronnie Arrow was never able to find the right chemistry last season. South Alabama managed to stay around .500 until the season was past the midway mark, but the Jaguars dropped eight of their final 10 games to finish with a losing record for the first time in Arrow's short reign in Mobile.

Arrow may get the Jaguars back on the winning track this time around, but it is not likely they will finish among the top four in the conference. South Alabama will be better, but so will the rest of the league. Unless some of the newcomers prove otherwise, there does not seem to be enough offensive firepower on the squad to allow the Jaguars outscore the opposition consistently.

South Alabama lost two starters, but only the departure of 6-8 forward Alex Stanwood (academics) will really hurt. Stanwood averaged 12.6 points and 7.3 rebounds and was a force underneath. The other starter not returning is 6-5 forward John Jimmerson, who produced 6.1 ppg and 3.3 rpg.

But Arrow is not deterred one bit. He still has seven players who started at least 10 games a year ago, and he figures the experience will make a big difference. "There are two reasons we will be a much improved team," he said. "One, we have experience returning, and two, we have big 'uns this season."

Arrow pointed out that South Alabama has seven seniors on the squad. They are 6-2 guard **Kevin McDaniels**, 6-4 guard **Carl James**, 6-0 guard **Derek Alvin**, 6-5 guard **Marvin Eackles**, 6-6 forward **Neil Smith**, 6-8 forward **Thomas Adams** and 6-9 center **Michael Hurring**.

"For us to have a good season," said Arrow, "we need for them to play like seniors. They have to come back a notch higher than what they were."

Other experienced players are last year's leading scorer, 6-3 junior guard **Derek Turner** (14.3 ppg), and 6-1 sophomore guard **Cedric Yelding** (3.6 ppg). Turner did much of his damage from three-point range, knocking down 42.3 percent of his bonus shots. Yelding started 11 games and handed out 80 assists.

The big 'uns, as Arrow likes to describe his big boys, include four players listed at 6-9. In addition to Hurring (2.5 ppg, 2.2 rpg), there's 240-pound JC transfer **Cesar Portillo**, sophomore redshirt **Alonzo Mitchell** and junior **Brian Hatch**.

Portillo, a highly regarded high school player out of Miami Senior HS (second-team *Parade* All-America), averaged 19.5 ppg and 9.9 rpg for Palm Beach JC last season. Portillo attended Florida for one year (1988-89), where he averaged 2.0 ppg in four games. He also played as a 14-year-old on the Venezuelan national team in the 1983 Pan American Games.

"Cesar is a big, strong inside player," said Arrow. "We expect him to jump right in and get the job done for us.' Arrow would like to believe Portillo can contribute the kind of numbers produced by Gabe Estaba in 1988-89. Estaba averaged 16.6 points and 8.9 rebounds in leading the Jaguars to the Sun Belt tournament championship and a victory over Alabama in the first round of the NCAA's.

Other newcomers include 6-6 junior **Bobby Curtis** (20 points, nine rebounds at Anderson, S.C., JC) and 6-5 junior **Sammie Hines** (12.7 ppg, 5.4 rpg at Chipola, Fla., JC). **Albert Garnett**, a 6-2 freshman guard, led Suncoast High (Riviera, Fla.) to a 36-0 record and the Class 2A state title by averaging 19 points and six rebounds.

"We feel like we recruited well," said Arrow. "Even though we have more than a handful of returnees, these guys will have an opportunity to perform."

Yelding and James (10.8 ppg, 4.9 rpg, 132 assists) will take turns directing the offense from the point-guard position. James started 22 games last year, but his shooting (43.2 percent) left much to be desired. He can also strike from three-point range (36.4 percent).

At the two and three spots, Turner, McDaniels (11.4 ppg, 3.4 rpg) and Eackles (3.7 ppg, 1.7 rpg) will hold forth. "There's not a lot of difference between our number two and three positions," Arrow said. "They're both wing positions in our offense."

Another player who could have a key role on the wing is 6-5 redshirt freshman **Derell Washington**, who is rehabilitating a broken right wrist suffered in mid-June. After breaking his left wrist following his senior prep season (Williamson HS/Mobile), Washington sat out last year.

Portillo, Smith (11.6 ppg, 7.6 rpg), Mitchell and Curtis will fill the power forward and center positions. Curtis, by the way, did not play last year at Anderson because of academics. Hurring, who has never been much of a contributor despite his size, and Hatch give the Jaguars some depth inside.

BLUE RIBBON ANALYSIS

Following his first losing season in 13 years at the junior college and college division levels, Arrow is anxious to get the new season under way. "We have a lot of work to do to return the program to where it was two years ago," he said. "If last season hurt the players as much as it did me, there is no question we'll be back very strong. We have to develop team chemistry early this season, and we have to have leadership from the beginning."

Arrow also needs to instill in his squad the need to play defense. That was perhaps the team's biggest fault a year ago, as the Jaguars allowed the opposition to shoot almost 51 percent from the floor. South Alabama averaged close to 79 points per game, but gave up 80.5. And even with improved defense, the Jags figure to wind up no higher than sixth in the final standings.

Since the Sun Belt tournament is in Mobile, however, the Jaguars will at least have the opportunity to strut their stuff in front of the home folks. Arrow's clubs usually play well at home, too, so watch out for South Alabama in early March.

SOUTH CAROLINA

LAST SEASON: 14-14
CONFERENCE RECORD: 6-8
STARTERS LOST: 1
STARTERS RETURNING: 4
CONFERENCE: METRO
LOCATION: COLUMBIA, SC
HOME FLOOR: CAROLINA COLISEUM (12,401)
NICKNAME: GAMECOCKS
COLORS: GARNET AND BLACK
COACH: GEORGE FELTON, record at South Carolina, 67-49.

The Gamecocks' problems started before last season when star freshman guard Brent Price transferred to Oklahoma. Price, South Carolina's best three-point shooter, had developed an all-around game by the end of 1988-89 when the Gamecocks went 19-11

and earned an NCAA East Regional berth. South Carolina coach George Felton thought he could survive without Price. He probably would have if things had not gone from bad to worse in the first weeks of the 1989-90 season.

6-4 junior guard **Barry Manning** (13.8 ppg) was being called an All-America candidate and "the most unselfish player I've ever coached," by Felton when he went down with a broken bone in his left (non-shooting) hand after four games. Manning received a medical hardship, but that did little to ease Felton's woes.

Then, 6-7 junior swingman **Troy McKoy** (4.8 ppg, 3.5 rpg) whose versatility was a key for South Carolina was ruled academically ineligible after the first semester. Now he'll be a key player shuffling between guard and forward duties.

The frontline was affected in mid-February when 6-8 forward **Joe Rhett** (11.0 ppg, 7.9 rpg) underwent surgery to install a pacemaker for an irregular heartbeat. Rhett, now a junior, has received medical clearance to return to action.

"We didn't have great depth, especially in the backcourt," Felton said of last season. "We tried to buckle up and weather the storm. We tried to play good defense because we weren't talented enough offensively. We made people work for their points."

With the ailing healed, the academically ineligible now eligible and with two possible impact players, South Carolina may be the darkhorse (or is that dark rooster?) of the Metro this season.

"Mark my words —Carolina is going to be good this season," Memphis State coach Larry Finch said. "George has done a nice recruiting job."

The only silver lining from last season was that the squad depletion forced some players to step forward for more playing time than expected. Junior guard **Jo Jo English** was a little-used 6-4 freshman two seasons ago who was pushed into being the Gamecocks' backcourt focal point last season. He played 35 minutes per game, averaged 15.3 points, led the team in three-point shooting (35-of-90, 38.9 percent), was tied for first in assists (2.9), was second in steals (34) and third in rebounding (4.8). And there is one of Felton's international experiments, 6-3 junior guard **Bojan Popovic** of Belgrade, Yugoslavia. Popovic (6.0 ppg, 2.3 rpg) was expected to be brought along slowly last season until he was forced into 31 minutes of action per game.

"We were surprised at his performance," said Felton of Popovic, who had good and bad moments. Popovic shot nearly 50 percent from the three-point line for most of the season, but the hoop Americanization of Popovic wasn't all smooth. He suffered through the embarrassment of giving up a game-winning three-pointer to Memphis State's Elliot Perry after Perry faked Popovic on to his rear end.

Popovic's playing time is likely to shrink this season, especially with the addition of 6-5 freshman swingman signee **Jamie Watson**. He averaged 26.7 points and nine rebounds at Fike HS in Wilson, N.C. Scouting services have rated Watson as South Carolina's most touted signee in more than 15 years. Watson was a member of the gold medal winning South squad in the 1990 Olympic Sports Festival. Watson, who could have gone to Georgetown, North Carolina or Georgia Tech, is a big timer. A great shooter and leaper, he has many around Columbia hearkening back to John Roche, the Gamecocks' great guard of the early '70s, only a taller, more athletic version. Watson, a national Top 25 and *Parade Magazine* third-team All-America, is exceptionally versatile and can take it to the hole from the point or fill it up from long range. He can play the point, second guard or small forward.

The forwards situation will be stabilized if Rhett returns to previous form. **Michael Glover**, a 6-5 senior (6.0 ppg, 4.4 rpg) is a defensive force who usually guards the opposition's best forward. **Chris Leso**, a 6-8 sophomore (3.3 ppg, 2.2 rpg) is a slow footed banger who doesn't have the quickness to be a starter but is an able role player.

South Carolina's biggest surprise this season might be 6-10 sophomore forward **Stefan Eggers** (3.3 ppg, 2.6 rpg) of Osnabruck, West Germany. Eggers showed nice fundamental skills, but little strength last season. If he doesn't get pushed off the block, he can be a force in the Metro as evidenced by 18 points and 12 rebounds in the regular season finale against Clemson last year. The Gamecocks' other foreign front liner, 6-10 Yugoslavian junior forward **Obrad Ignjatovic** (2.1 ppg, 1.5 rpg), was hampered last season with a broken hand.

The Gamecocks may have potentially the two best centers in the Metro. Emphasize that word "potential" because 7-0 junior **Jeff Roulston** hasn't developed an offensive game yet and 6-9 sophomore **Edmond Wilson** sat out last season.

Roulston averaged 8.6 points and 5.7 rebounds last season, getting mainly garbage buckets. He didn't have great post moves and seemed unsure of himself in the pivot once he got the ball. Despite being an offensive liability, he countered on the defensive end by holding opposing centers to about five points below their averages. He blocked 68 shots (including nine in one game).

Wilson, who is 250 pounds, may be one of the Metro's major impact players along with Florida State's Doug Edwards. He averaged 17 points and 10 rebounds at Mt. Pleasant HS in Elliott, S.C., two years ago. He has outside shooting ability, can jump and can run the court.

BLUE RIBBON ANALYSIS

The way Felton has arranged his schedule, it's obvious he wants to find out what his team is made of in November and December. South Carolina is scheduled to play in three killer tournaments —the Great Alaskan Shootout, the Tournament of Champions in Charlotte (where the Gamecocks will play North Carolina for the first time since 1972) and the ECAC Holiday Festival in New York.

Even the Metro schedule is favorable with four of the first five league games at home for the Gamecocks. There's only one three-game Metro road trip in February that could be a problem if South Carolina doesn't mature.

The Gamecocks have recently been erratic and difficult to figure. This season, South Carolina could finish anywhere from second to sixth, depending on the health of Rhett, the contributions of newcomers Watson and Wilson and the improvement of Roulston and Eggers. If he can adjust quickly, Watson has the talent to elevate the program by himself.

But the Gamecocks' talent level hasn't developed yet. It may, but South Carolina will finish in a tie for fifth with Florida State in the Metro. As tight as the Metro will be this season, though, a few wins here and there and South Carolina may even sneak to third.

SOUTH CAROLINA STATE

LAST SEASON: 13-16
CONFERENCE RECORD: 8-8
STARTERS LOST: 1
STARTERS RETURNING: 4
CONFERENCE: MID-EASTERN (MEAC)
LOCATION: ORANGEBURG, SC
HOME FLOOR: SMITH-HAMMOND-MIDDLETON MEMORIAL CENTER (3,200)
NICKNAME: BULLDOGS
COLORS: GARNET AND BLUE
COACH: CYRUS ALEXANDER, record at South Carolina State, 54-37.

After a 25-8 record and the school's first-ever NCAA tournament appearance the year before, South Carolina State took a nosedive last season. For coach Cyrus Alexander, the reasons were obvious.

Graduation stripped the Bulldogs of most of their size and outside shooting ability. South Carolina State won its share of games with speed and quickness last year, but simply did not have the power to match the previous season's success. This time around, Alexander thinks he has corrected the problems.

Anything the Bulldogs accomplish this year will begin with 6-6 senior **Travis Williams** (20.6 ppg, 10.3 rpg, 49 steals, 37 assists, 18 blocked shots), an All-MEAC selection a year ago. As good as Williams was, he could be even better because, this season, there is some inside help.

The first newcomer is 6-10, 240-pound senior **Eric Sanders.** Sanders is eligible after transferring from Virginia Tech, where he started for two seasons. **Jackie Robinson,** a 6-9 sophomore, will also add some size to the front line after sitting out last season. Robinson averaged 23.3 points, 9.0 rebounds, 3.1 assists and 2.9 blocked shots in 1988-89 at Swansea (S.C.) High School.

Two more newcomers, 6-11, 260-pound freshman **Marvin Lucas** and 6-6, 230-pound sophomore **Donald Fogle,** a transfer from Baptist (S.C.) College, are also available in the frontcourt. So is 6-7 junior **Rodney Moore** (5.1 ppg, 4.0 rpg), a starter last season.

The Bulldog backcourt returns intact, with two freshmen competing for playing time as well. **Chris Felix** (13.4 ppg, 4.0 rpg, 29 assists, 24 steals), a 6-6 junior, was the team's best outside shooter last year. 5-7 junior **Curtis Faust** (4.9 ppg, 1.7 rpg, 112 assists,

47 steals) shared time at the point a year ago along with 5-10 junior **Anthony Higginbotham** (7.3 ppg, 2.4 rpg, 143 assists, 52 steals).

Three newcomers will provide depth at guard, including the two freshmen. **Abraham Williams** (Branchville HS/Branchville, S.C.) and **D.D. Hook** (Eau Claire HS/Columbia, S.C.) are bookends. Both are 6-4 and both are good shooters. Hook suffered a stroke last year which limited his effectiveness as a high school senior. **Arnie Lucas,** a 6-4 transfer from Lowndes CC, is the brother of Bulldogs' signee Marvin Lucas.

BLUE RIBBON ANALYSIS

When South Carolina State made its first trip to the NCAA tournament two years ago, the team had size, experience and depth. Last season, the Bulldogs were not as fortunate, and their record reflected as much.

Coach Cyrus Alexander knew he had to recruit some size and shooting talent. Two players who would have made a difference last year, Eric Sanders and Jackie Robinson, were in school but ineligible. They will be in uniform this year, along with 6-11 freshman Marvin Lucas. If those three provide the needed bulk up front, and Abraham Williams and D.D. Hook provide some outside shooting, the Bulldogs will push Coppin State and North Carolina A&T in the MEAC first division.

SOUTHERN CALIFORNIA

LAST SEASON: 12-16
CONFERENCE RECORD: 6-12
STARTERS LOST: 1
STARTERS RETURNING: 4
CONFERENCE: PACIFIC-10
LOCATION: LOS ANGELES, CA
HOME FLOOR: SPORTS ARENA (15,509)
NICKNAME: TROJANS
COLORS: CARDINAL AND GOLD
COACH: GEORGE RAVELING, record at Southern California, 38-78.
Career record, 259-252.

Success has not come quickly for George Raveling at Southern California. In fact, it has yet to arrive. The Trojans have finished no higher than a tie for seventh place in the Pacific-10 Conference in Raveling's four seasons. Southern California has suffered through four consecutive losing seasons and has won less than a third of its games (38-78) under Raveling. In conference play, the percentage drops to .236 with only 17 wins against 55 losses.

Those dismal numbers could change dramatically this season. Raveling finally may have the Trojans headed out of the Pacific-10 second division.

"The pendulum is gaining momentum," Raveling said. "We have the necessary blend of talents to be a winning team. We have veteran-like experience and youthful enthusiasm, a perimeter game and a physical inside game, speed to fast break and size to run a rugged half-court offense."

When Raveling speaks of talent, the first thought is of 6-5 sophomore **Harold Miner** (20.6 ppg, 3.6 rpg). Named to the freshman All-America team last year, Miner was the Pac-10's freshman of the year and is the conference's leading returning scorer. His 20.6 average was second only to NBA first rounder Gary Payton's 25.7 mark. Operating as Southern California's shooting guard, Miner led the Trojans in three-point percentage (60-142, .423) and was the team's top scorer 16 times.

"Harold went through an unusual year where he had to grow up fast because of the frustrations with the box-and-one defense that nearly everyone used against him, the physical beatings he took and the adulation he received off the court," Raveling said. "I don't know if I've ever coached a player in my career who had to make adjustments as quickly as Harold did in a year. And by and large, he handled them pretty well."

Miner's 578 points was the third best total in Southern California's history. He led the team in free throw percentage at 84.1, third best in the conference.

"Most of us live in search of what God put us on earth to do," Raveling said. "I don't think there's any question what Harold Miner is here to do —play basketball"

"It's like one of those underwater explorers. They know the ship is down there. They know there's gold on it. They've just got to find it. That's how we see Harold. He's such a valuable commodity."

Miner is not the only go-to player the Trojans have. Southern California's three-time team MVP, 6-6 senior forward **Ronnie Coleman** (16.6 ppg, 7.1 rpg) is on pace to become Troy's all-time career scoring leader. He has 1,236 points and should have no problems surpassing Wayne Carlander's 1,524 points from 1982-85. Coleman scored 20 or more points in eight games last year, including 27 against UCLA and 26 vs. Notre Dame in back-to-back games. "Ronnie is our force inside," Raveling said. "He's established himself as one of the premier players in the conference."

Joining Miner in the backcourt is 6-2 senior **Robert Pack** (12.1 ppg, 5.9 apg), who was responsible for the Trojans' improved play in the second half of last year. A transfer from Tyler (Texas) JC, Pack's 165 assists was the second best season total in Southern California history. He also scored in double figures in 17 games. When Pack tallied 15 points or more, USC was 8-1.

Calvin Banks (96.2 ppg, 5.1 rpg), a 6-6 senior forward, is the other returning starter. He's a role player who, because of his defensive skills, usually draws the opponent's top offensive threat. If any of the five new frontline players develop quickly, Banks could go back to the sixth man role he had as a sophomore. Sophomores **Keith Greeley** (2.0 ppg, 3.0 rpg), a 6-8 power forward, and **Rodney Chatman** (3.6 ppg, 1.7 rpg), a 6-3 guard, both averaged over 12 minutes a game as freshmen. Chatman played both guard positions and started three games and was the team's second best three-point shooter (.389). Sophomore guards **Phil Glenn** (6-2, 1.0 ppg, 0.3 rpg) and

Cordell Robinson (6-5, 1.6 ppg, 0.6 rpg) round out the returning lettermen. Also back is 6-1 redshirt junior Duane Cooper (4.1 ppg, 2.7 apg, 1988-89), who missed last season because of a broken right foot. His return gives the Trojans six experienced guards, three of whom have started games at point guard in the past two seasons.

The only void in the starting lineup, created by the graduation of 6-9 Chris Munk (8.1 ppg, 8.1 rpg) is center. Raveling is counting on 6-9 junior Yamen Sanders, a transfer from Central Michigan who as a sophomore in 1989 started 27 games and averaged 6.0 points and 4.9 rebounds for the Chippewas. Although he hasn't played a minute for the Trojans, Raveling calls Sanders "a big-time rebounder, perhaps the best I've coached here at USC."

Southern California's recruiting class of four freshmen are all front line performers. Prep All-America Lorenzo Orr (607, 25.0 ppg, 12.0 rpg) from Pershing HS in Detroit has played only three years of organized basketball. His senior year was limited to just 12 games because state regulations stated his eligibility had expired. As a sophomore he had dropped out of school to work and help support his family, but the time out of school counted against his eligibility. At both the McDonald's Western Wildcat Classic and Michigan All-Star game, Orr was crowned dunk champion in pre-game competition. At the McDonald's he performed his "cartwheel" dunk, a slam in which he bounces the ball, does a cartwheel, grabs the ball and stuffs it through in one coordinated move. Kraig Conger (19.8 ppg, 19.1 rpg) is a 6-9, 245-pound all-state center from Wasson HS in Colorado Springs, Colo. He could see time behind Sanders and Greenley. He broke Joe Barry Carroll's 14-year-old state high school playoff record with 25 rebounds in the semifinals.

Raveling also landed two Georgia all-stars in 6-6 Wayne Butts (22.0 ppg, 10.0 rpg) from Baldwin HS in Milledgeville and 6-7, 220-pound Mark Boyd (15.7 ppg, 12.1 rpg) from Redan High in Stone Mountain.

The only other losses besides Munk were reserve guards Tyrone Fuller (2.4 ppg, 0.9 rpg) and Kyle Kazan (1.5 ppg) and substitute forward Turi Carter (1.2 ppg, 0.8 rpg).

"One of the key attributes I really like about this group is its versatility," Raveling said. "We have a lot of guys who can play more than one position. Although I believe we're already a deep team, versatility can double a team's depth."

Raveling has not overmatched his team in December play in recent years. Raveling may want this year's squad to get some real tests because the Trojans are visiting Maryland, Colorado State and Notre Dame prior to conference play. But there are still friendly visits from the likes of Chicago State, Augusta, Harvard and Brooklyn College.

BLUE RIBBON ANALYSIS

The Trojans may have to be taken seriously this season. Probably not as a Pacific-10 title contender, but perhaps the most improved team in the league and a definite first division threat. That's heady stuff for Southern California basketball of late. Miner is easily the top individual talent in the conference. He got frustrated at times last year against the box-and-one defense and forced shots when they finally came his way. Still, he scored in double figures in his last 24 games and was over 20 in seven of his last 10 games, proof that he learned how to beat the gimmick defense. Coleman is a big time player who will give Southern California most of its inside scoring. The trio of Miner, Coleman and Pack combined for 49.4 points per game, which matched UCLA's celebrated trio of Don MacLean, Tracy Murray and Trevor Wilson.

Pack gives Southern California its best court leadership in years. Banks is not a scoring threat and had a miserable time at the foul line (39.3 percent). He probably would be more effective coming off the bench if one of the five new front liners challenge for

a starting position.

Center is the big question mark for Southern California. Departed Chris Munk wasn't flashy but he gave the Trojans some muscle inside. Sanders does have a full season as a starter at Central Michigan to his credit, but was foul prone and blocked only nine shots all season. The Trojans have trouble against the front lines of UCLA and Arizona, one reason they can't be considered title contenders. Still, the firepower and depth is there and it should be Raveling's first winning season.

The question remains whether or not that will bring out the fans to the Sports Arena. Southern California's largest home turnout was 6,455 for crosstown rival UCLA. Arizona and Notre Dame were the only other teams to draw 5,000. The Trojans need more of a homecourt atmosphere to take any giant strides this season. Still, they could climb as high as fifth place.

1990-91 SOUTHERN CALIFORNIA SCHEDULE

Nov.	24	Chicago State
	28	@Maryland
Dec.	1	Miami (FL)
	4	San Diego State
	8	@Colorado State
	12	@Notre Dame
	22	Augusta College (GA)
	28	#Harvard
	29	#Brooklyn College (NY)
Jan.	2	@UCLA
	10	@Arizona
	13	@Arizona State
	17	California
	20	Stanford
	24	@Oregon
	26	@Oregon State
	30	UCLA
Feb.	4	Cal State-Northridge
	7	Arizona
	9	Arizona State
	14	@Stanford
	17	@California
	21	Oregon State
	23	Oregon
	28	@Washington
Mar.	2	@Washington State
	7	Washington
	9	Washington State

@ Road Games
# Long Beach, CA

SOUTHERN ILLINOIS

LAST SEASON: 26-8
CONFERENCE RECORD: 10-4
STARTERS LOST: 2
STARTERS RETURNING: 3
CONFERENCE: MISSOURI VALLEY (MVC)
LOCATION: CARBONDALE, IL
HOME FLOOR: SIU ARENA (10,014)
NICKNAME: SALUKIS
COLORS: MAROON AND WHITE
COACH: RICH HERRIN, record at Southern Illinois, 78-75.
Career record, including high school, 696-284.

Rich Herrin has been a member of the coaching fraternity for 35 years, but not until last March did he make his first real national splash. And it was for all the wrong reasons.

When the NCAA announced the 64 entries in its post-season tournament, Herrin's Southern Illinois team was not among them. A loss at Illinois State in the MVC final wiped out the expected automatic bid. Despite a school-record 26 victories and the regular season Missouri Valley Conference title, SIU was left out of the big party. Herrin was unhappy, and he let everybody know about it. CBS, ESPN, USA Today, you name it. And even though it sounded like sour grapes at the time, one point is indisputable: no team in the country won more games than the Salukis and was left out of the NCAA's.

This year, at least Herrin has regained his optimism. Despite the loss of two main cogs from a team that played in the conference championship game two years in a row, the coach believes the Salukis have a chance to be every bit as good.

"Losing a rebounder like Jerry Jones (14.5 ppg, 10.3 rpg) and an exciting player like Freddie McSwain (17.3 ppg, 103 assists) means we have a couple positions to fill," Herrin says. "But we believe we have the replacements available."

Three starters are back, led by All-MVC selection Sterling Mahan. The 6-0 senior from Isiah Thomas' old high school (St. Joseph/Maywood, Ill.) averaged 15.4 points, 4.2 assists and 2.9 rebounds last year. He also led the conference in steals (57), was a member of the MVC all-defensive team. Mahan also shot a tidy 47 percent from the floor, outstanding for a point guard.

Ashraf Amaya was the league's outstanding freshman, averaging 7.4 points and 6.3 rebounds. The soph-to-be has grown an inch to 6-8, and added 10 pounds to go 220. "Just how good he wants to be," said Herrin, "is how good he's going to be." The third returning starter is 6-8 senior Rick Shipley, an honorable mention All-MVC pick. Shipley averaged 12.0 points, 7.6 rebounds and 3.0 assists last year and was the Salukis' best three-point shooter (.358, 38-for-106) among the starters.

6-4 junior Kelvan Lawrence - "the best sixth man in the MVC," according to Herrin - is back and could move into McSwain's scoring guard spot. Lawrence averaged 6.0 points and 3.0 rebounds in under 18 minutes per game last year. Sophomore Tyrone Bell made tremendous strides during the season and also figures to contest for a starting position. Bell, 6-3, averaged 3.2 points a year ago.

Matt Wynn provided long-range shooting (44.4 percent on three-pointers) off the bench, and the 6-1 junior is back. Also in reserve are 6-3 sophomore Jason Hodges, cousin of NBA three-point bomber Craig Hodges, and 6-4 senior Erik Griffin. Hodges averaged just 1.3 points and shot 33.3 percent; Griffin averaged 1.2 ppg, but can dunk with anybody.

If Southern Illinois is going to repeat as the MVC's top scoring and rebounding team, 6-6 transfer Marvin Kelly will have to step forward right away. Herrin figures he will. "He's a good scorer," the coach said. "We feel very comfortable with him."

And rightly so. Kelly was a first-team junior college All-America last year at Hinds (Miss.) JC, where he averaged 25 points and 10 rebounds. The junior forward figures to be an instant starter and is the early-line choice as MVC newcomer of the year.

Two former Indiana high school standouts hope to give the Salukis some additional scoring help. 5-10 freshman Chris Lowery (Harrison HS/Evansville) shot 52 percent from three-point range as a high school junior and averaged 17 points as a senior. 6-8 freshman Ian Stewart (LaPorte HS/LaPorte, Ind.) averaged 15.1 points and 8.8 rebounds last winter.

After that, the Southern Illinois newcomers take on an international flavor. 6-8 sophomore Emeka Okenwa is a 230-pounder from Owerri, Nigeria who sat out last season. When he last played in his homeland, Okenwa averaged 34.7 points and 16.3 rebounds. 6-7 freshman Mirko Pavlovic is a Yugoslavian (Belgrade) who this summer captained his country's junior national team. 7-0 freshman Marcelo da Silva was a member of three different age-group teams in his native

Rio de Janeiro after graduating from Sao Paulo High School. He becomes one of only three seven-footers in the MVC.

BLUE RIBBON ANALYSIS

After winning its first conference title since 1977, Southern Illinois will find repeating difficult, mostly because of Creighton's strong returning group. But SIU will make a strong bid for the MVC crown and is easily the second-best team in the league.

Getting recognized will not be a problem for Herrin and the Salukis, either. ''I think people know where Southern Illinois is now,'' Herrin said. ''People know we won the league outright. That gives us great visibility. Being Missouri Valley champions is great.''

Nobody in the MVC has as much talent as the SIU, who have improved in each of Herrin's five seasons on the job. But when opponents slow down the pace and play a zone defense, the Salukis have got to be able to respond. Shooting is a problem, and unless a guy like Hodges, Wynn or Lowery steps forward, Southern Illinois just may have a hard time getting unleashed.

1990-91 SOUTHERN ILLINOIS SCHEDULE

Nov.	24	Western Kentucky
	29	Austin Peay
Dec.	2	St. Louis
	8	@South Alabama
	14	Murray State
	21-22	#Chicago Old Style Classic
	27	@Bradley
	30	Indiana State
Jan.	3	@Eastern Kentucky
	5	@Evansville
	8	Southwest Missouri State
	11	@St. Louis
	15	Eastern Illinois
	17	@Tulsa
	19	@Wichita State
	26	Drake
	28	Creighton
	31	Bradley
Feb.	2	@Illinois State
	6	@Southwest Missouri State
	9	Tulsa
	13	@Indiana State
	16	Wichita State
	18	Illinois State
	23	@Creighton
	25	@Drake
Mar.	1-5	##MVC Tournament

@ Road Games
# Rosemont, IL (DePaul, Oklahoma State & Wisconsin-Green Bay)
St. Louis, MO

SOUTHERN METHODIST

LAST SEASON: 10-18
CONFERENCE RECORD: 5-11
STARTERS LOST: 3
STARTERS RETURNING: 2
CONFERENCE: SOUTHWEST (SWC)
LOCATION: DALLAS, TX
HOME FLOOR: MOODY COLISEUM (9,007)
NICKNAME: MUSTANGS
COLORS: RED AND WHITE
COACH: JOHN SHUMATE, record at Southern Methodist, 23-34.
Career record, 81-67.

Dave Bliss left SMU for New Mexico two years ago after the Mustangs had peaked with a Southwest Conference championship. Former Notre Dame star and NBA player John Shumate took over from Bliss and has won just 23 games in two years. With leading scorer and rebounder, John Colborne (18.2 ppg, 7.3 rpg) lost to graduation and only one senior returning, SMU would surpass most expectations with 10 wins.

Shumate seems to have settled on getting more skilled and athletic perimeter players to run the up-tempo style he promised when hired. The Mustangs will run primarily a three-guard offense as four of the seven newcomers are guards.

''I used to think that you built a team from the inside out, but at this level you need to build from the perimeter in,'' Shumate said. ''We're not trying to be Oklahoma, but we want to get the ball up and down.''

The Mustangs' only senior is 6-3 **Rod Hampton** (6.8 ppg, 4.2 rpg, 151 assists), a solid playmaker who was fourth in the SWC in assists. Hampton does not shoot well from outside and that hurt SMU last season. With the exception of Colborne, SMU was a bad shooting team (eighth in the SWC in field goal percentage at .445 percent and last in three-point percentage at .321).

Incoming freshman guard **Chad Allen** may challenge Hampton for a starting job at point guard. The 6-3 Allen was third in Michigan's Mr. Basketball voting last year after averaging 23.5 points, 6.6 rebounds and 4.1 assists for Traverse City HS.

To bolster outside shooting and defense, Shumate added several off-guard candidates to go along with 6-4 sophomore **Gerald Lewis** (7.9 ppg, 3.4 rpg, 92 assists), who was the only Mustang to start all 30 games. Lewis was impressive as a freshman. He had a season high 21 points against Houston, hit a 20-footer with 17 seconds left against Rice to send the game into overtime and nailed two free throws in the closing second to clinch a victory over Tulane. Lewis played with a nagging back injury last year.

Transfer Mike Wilson, a 6-5 sophomore, will likely be the third guard in Shumate's backcourt rotation. Wilson averaged 9.5 ppg as a freshman at Western Kentucky. He had arthroscopic knee surgery in the off-season but is expected to be ready for pre-season drills. In addition to Wilson, two other newcomers should strengthen the Mustangs perimeter game. **Keith Chambers**, a 6-4 1/2 sophomore shooting guard from Temple (Tex.) JC, who averaged 18.5 points per game, was not highly regarded two years ago when he was one of the Dallas area's top scorers with a 31.9 scoring average at Lewisville HS. He improved his stock considerably in one year at Temple. **David Shivers** may be a sleeper who could contribute more than expected as a freshman. Shivers led Boerne (Tex.) HS to the state Class 4A finals. He's an excellent shooter and ballhandler.

Junior **Troy Valentino** (6-2) was considered a skilled outside shooter when recruited by Bliss but has not displayed his touch (6.8 ppg, 38.1 percent from the field and 36.0 percent from three-point territory). With increased confidence and more accurate shooting, Valentino could become a capable role player.

SMU has only one experienced forward —6-6 sophomore **Tim Mason** (3.8 ppg, 3.4 rpg). Mason is not a good shooter but rebounds and defends well. The other candidates at forward are 6-6 junior **John Karl Robertson** (0.5 ppg), a Bliss recruit who hasn't panned out, and three freshmen.

The three freshmen forwards Shumate signed are 6-8 **James Gatewood**, 6-7 **Chris Jessen** and 6-7 **Raymond Van Beveren**. Gatewood is out of Southwest Dekalb HS in Atlanta, Ga., Jessen is from Alief Elsik HS in Houston, Tex., while Van Beveren comes to SMU from Pearce HS in Richardson, Tex. None are ready to make a major impact as first year players.

Greg Kinzer —a 6-10 sophomore who played sparingly last year, 13 games —is SMU's hope in the pivot. Kinzer (2.5 ppg, 3.7 rpg) has strength (245 pounds) and a good attitude. He took Karate during

the summer to improve his agility. Shumate has a knack for developing big men. Both Colborne and Glenn Puddy, SMU's center two years ago, made dramatic strides under Shumate's teaching. And last year SMU had the best rebounding margin in the SWC (plus 3.6).

Junior **Bobby Holkan**, a 6-11 junior who appeared in eight games, is the only other option in the post. He was recruited as a project by Bliss and hasn't developed.

BLUE RIBBON ANALYSIS

Shumate's emphasis on a guard-oriented scheme will take at least a year to develop. He made what many in Dallas consider to be a good decision by hiring Jimmy Tubbs as an assistant. Tubbs, who coached Dallas Kimball HS to a championship in Texas' highest classification last year, should help with local recruiting. His teams were known for their strong defensive and ballhandling fundamentals so he should complement Shumate's ability to develop big men.

Shumate has done a good job instilling his competitive spirit into the Mustangs. SMU could have folded after a seven-game losing streak late last season but rebounded to win three of their last five.

SMU president Kenneth Pye came from Duke and wants the Mustangs program to mirror the national power Mike Krzyzewski has established there. First, SMU has to regain a strong position in the SWC. SMU is a long way away from becoming a SWC power. The Mustangs will have to struggle with a sagging Texas Tech's program to stay out of the SWC cellar.

1990-91 SOUTHERN METHODIST SCHEDULE

Nov.	24	@Arizona State
	28	@Pennsylvania
Dec.	1	Wisconsin
	4	@Kansas
	8	@Tulane
	19	Miami (FL)
	22	@Vanderbilt
	28	Columbia
	30	Texas-Arlington
Jan.	2	Texas Tech
	5	@Texas Christian
	7	Sam Houston State
	9	Texas-San Antonio
	12	Texas A&M
	16	@Baylor
	19	@Arkansas
	23	Rice
	26	Houston
	30	@Texas
Feb.	2	@Texas Tech
	6	Texas Christian
	9	Texas
	13	@Texas A&M
	16	Baylor
	20	Arkansas
	23	@Rice
	27	@Houston
Mar.	7-10	#SWC Tournament

@ Road Games
# Dallas, TX

SOUTHERN UNIVERSITY

LAST SEASON: 25-6
CONFERENCE RECORD: 12-2
STARTERS LOST: 3
STARTERS RETURNING: 2
CONFERENCE: SOUTH-WESTERN ATHLETIC (SWAC)
LOCATION: BATON ROUGE, LA
HOME FLOOR: F.G. CLARK ACTIVITY CENTER (7,500)
NICKNAME: JAGUARS
COLORS: COLUMBIA BLUE AND GOLD
COACH: BEN JOBE, record at Southern Univerity, 88-36.
Career record, 364-162.

Southern University, the class of the South-western Athletic Conference since the middle of the 1980's, hopes to stand tall again. Just as tall as it was in winning 25 of 31 games a year ago, as it was in capturing the 1990 SWAC regular season title and, of course, as it was in making the school's first-ever NIT appearance.

Only in Baton Rouge, and only with highly successful coach Ben Jobe, could those simultaneous accomplishments be a come down. And that is only because the Jaguars, in each of Jobe's first three seasons at Southern, were NCAA bound. They would have been again last year, too, but one of Jobe's most talented teams ever was tripped on the homecourt of Texas Southern in the SWAC tournament final.

One loss should not spoil the Southern record, though. The 1990-91 Jaguars, even without three of last year's starters and four of their top six players overall, will still be a legitimate SWAC contender. Jobe thinks so. Always has, always will. The school evidently agrees. In the off-season, Jobe received a five-year contract extension plus an optional five-year pact that allows either he or the university to discuss his remaining on the bench or working in another capacity until 2003.

In the meantime, this highly underrated coach is searching for new combinations to replace guard Carlos Sample, wingman Joe Faulkner, forward Derrick Stewart and sixth man Derrick Anderson. Sample (17.5 ppg, 214 assists, 85 steals) and Faulkner (21.7 ppg, 9.2 rpg) were the most productive players on a team that has lost just six SWAC games in two seasons. Faulkner, to no one's great surprise, was the SWAC player of the year, with Sample not far behind on the All-Conference squad.

The two starters that return, however, are more than capable of fueling the high-octane Jags. 6-4 senior **Bobby Phills II** was Southern's second-leading scorer last year, and 6-7 junior center **Robert Youngblood** emerged as a true power player in a league featuring few of that breed.

Phills (20.1 ppg, 4.3 rpg, 89 assists, 66 steals) dialed long distance for most of his points, canning 112-for-300 (.373) from three-point range. That kind of perimeter pressure made it even easier for Youngblood (15.2 ppg, 9.1 rpg, 27 blocked shots). It is also the kind of inside-outside game lacking in most other SWAC entries. Call it basic basketball. When all else fails, the Jaguars just keep shooting.

"We always try to keep it simple," Jobe said. "You can do a lot more if you do it that way. Basketball is really a simple game. We lost four top-notch players, but we have some kids returning who understand what we do best."

6-2 junior **Bryan Herbert** (2.2 ppg, 1.2 rpg), 6-0 senior **Mark Guillory** (1.6 ppg) and 6-6 senior **Dwayne Tanks** (3.4 rpg) are the most experienced non-starters returning. They were not in Southern's main rotation, but should be more than adequate with increased roles in Jobe's fire-when-ready offense. Even inexperienced players like to shoot the ball.

The Jaguars also may have gained a potentially productive threesome when fellow SWAC member Prairie View dropped its basketball program. Three seniors - 6-5 forward **Lincoln Browder**, 6-6 forward **Terry Bryant** and 6-7 forward **Lorenzo Tolbert** - originally opted out for one last hurrah in Baton Rouge. With Prairie View since reinstating its program, there was some question over where the trio would play (see *Late Breaking News* section).

"They're good kids," said Jobe. "They'll prove to be valuable additions to the team." Between the transfers and the returnees, a serviceable pair of forwards should be uncovered. That leaves point guard as the only real hole remaining.

Erwin Harper, an athletic 6-4 junior, transferred from Belleview (Wash.) JC and will take over for Sample. 6-0 junior **Dwayne Davis**, a transfer from McNeese State, also has point guard experience. The same goes for Guillory and Hebert.

"We're looking for a floor leader," said Jobe, "and we hope to come up with one by November."

6-5 junior **Derrick Williams** and 6-9 junior **James Wagner** add depth. So do a pair of freshmen, 6-7 **Fred Comanche** (Grambling, La.) and 6-6 **Jervaughn Scales** (Dayton, Ohio). Neither will be rushed.

BLUE RIBBON ANALYSIS

Keep it simple. Remember, that is the Southern Univeristy philosophy. It also works, at least in the Southwestern Athletic Conference, where the Jaguars missed a fourth straight NCAA invitation by an eyelash.

At Southern, simple means shooting the ball at virtually every opportunity. Jobe's idea is that if his team shoots more than yours, it will win more often than not. His record, and his athletes, bear that out. The Jags averaged 99.2 points per game last year, third in the nation and good enough to lead most times a Loyola Marymount is not in the picture.

Said Jobe: "We're going to run a lot, shoot a lot and, hopefully, win a lot of basketball games." Certainly enough to remain in the forefront for another SWAC championship.

1990-91 SOUTHERN UNIVERSITY SCHEDULE		
Nov.	28	Nicholls State (LA)
Dec.	6	Texas College
	8	@Alabama-Birmingham
	15	@Dayton
	18	Xavier (LA)
	28-29	#Lobo Classic
Jan.	2	@Lamar
	5	Grambling State (LA)
	7	Mississippi Valley State
	12	@Alabama State
	14	@Jackson State (MS)
	16	Chicago State
	19	@Texas Southern
	21	@Prairie View A&M (TX)
	23	@Nicholls State
	26	Alcorn State
Feb.	2	@Grambling State
	4	@Mississippi Valley State
	7	@Texas College
	9	Alabama State
	11	Jackson State
	14	Southeastern Louisiana
	16	Texas Southern
	18	Prairie View A&M (TX)
	20	@Southeastern Louisiana
	23	@Alcorn State
Feb. 28-Mar. 2		*SWAC Tournament

@ Road Games
#Albuquerque, NM (Manhattan, New Mexico & Southwest Texas State)
*Houston, TX

SOUTH FLORIDA

LAST SEASON: 20-11
CONFERENCE RECORD: 9-5
STARTERS LOST: 1
STARTERS RETURNING: 4
CONFERENCE: SUN BELT
LOCATION: TAMPA, FL
HOME FLOOR: SUN DOME (10,347)
NICKNAME: BULLS
COLORS: GREEN AND GOLD
COACH: BOBBY PASCHAL, record at South Florida, 41-74.
Career record, 194-159.

While South Florida's successful 1989-90 season, which included winning the Sun Belt tournament for the first time and earning a berth in the NCAA's, may have surprised many, it did not come as a shock to coach Bobby Paschal.

"I'm not surprised with anything this team has done," said Paschal, after the Bulls had beaten North Carolina Charlotte for the Sun Belt championship. "This is the culmination of four years of hard work by everyone associated with the program. The last place progress shows is in wins. And this year, it finally showed there. It's what you work for. If you're going to be surprised by that, I don't think it says much for you."

Indeed, Paschal built the groundwork for a strong program while South Florida was suffering through three straight 20-loss seasons, but everything paid off a year ago, and it should be more of the same in 1990-91. The Bulls will be without 6-7 center Hakim Shahid, who was one of the leading rebounders (12.4) in the country, but virtually everyone else on the squad is back to make another championship run.

With 6-1 guard **Marvin Taylor** returning for his senior year at the point and 6-7 guard **Radenko Dobras** back for his junior year on the wing, the Bulls boast the finest backcourt in the conference and perhaps one of the best in the Southeast.

Taylor joined the Bulls last year after two seasons at Holmes CC and a year of inactivity at Southeastern Louisiana, which dropped basketball. He started 29 games and provided South Florida with its first true point guard in years. An excellent penetrator and passer, Taylor averaged 12.2 ppg and 5.1 assists.

Taylor's emergence allowed Dobras, who started every game at point guard in 1988-89, to move to his more natural position, shooting guard. A native Yugoslavian, Dobras led the Bulls in scoring (16.6 ppg) for the second straight season and enters this year needing only 32 points for 1,000 in his career. A second-team All-Sun Belt selection, Dobras was not able to hit three-pointers (25.4 percent) like he did his freshman year (42.1), but is capable of returning to that form.

Also returning is sixth man **Tony Armstrong,** who averaged 7.6 ppg off the bench and continued to terrorize opponents with his defense. A 6-1 senior, Armstrong is the most experienced player on the roster, having played in 85 games in three years.

A new luxury for the Bulls are swing players. Junior **Bobby Russell** (6.5 ppg, 2.9 rpg), at 6-5, and JC transfer **David Williams**, at 6-6, can play either guard or forward. Both possess good shooting range and can also drive the lane. At 220 pounds, Williams will likely work mostly inside after starring for Pratt (Kan.) CC. Also in the backcourt are 6-1 senior **Maurice**

Webster (1.0 ppg) and 6-1 freshman **Chad Dollar,** a product of national power Douglass High (Atlanta).

South Florida's frontcourt was one of the best in the conference last year, but it lacked depth. So Paschal and his assistants went to work in the off-season, landing three junior college transfers to join 6-7 junior **Gary Alexander,** 6-7 sophomore **Jarvis Jackson** and the returning starters, 6-7 junior **Fred Lewis** and Russell.

Alexander was forced to sit out last season after injuring his knee in a pick-up game and undergoing surgery. His return alone is enough to worry Sun Belt coaches, who watched him average 13.7 points and 8.6 rebounds in his rookie season. Alexander has also added bulk to his upper body, making him even more dangerous.

Lewis leads the returning frontcourt players with his 12.5 ppg average. He added 7.4 rpg and is "the most natural leader I've ever coached," according to Paschal. Lewis was the emotional catalyst for the Bulls a year ago after transferring from the University of Tampa, and should contribute more leadership his second time around.

A 6-7 forward, Jackson played quarterback on his high school football team (Chattahoochee HS/Chattahoochee, Fla.), and is considered the best leaper in several years at South Florida. He figures to lend immediate help as a scorer and rebounder on the inside. Jackson sat out last year.

Scott Roczey, a 6-9 junior forward from Cerritos (Calif.) CC, gives the Bulls both strength and perimeter shooting. Roczey has excellent range, hitting over 40 treys as a sophomore for Cerritos. It remains to be seen who will replace Shahid - can anybody? - but 6-7, 225-pound junior **Landon Edmond** fits the bill physically. Edmond was an excellent rebounder at San Jose (Calif.) CC.

The third transfer is Williams, who originally signed at Auburn and played one season for Sonny Smith (now at Virginia Commonwealth). He was an All-Conference performer at Pratt CC. 6-8 senior Chris Risey (2.1 ppg, 1.8 rpg) and 6-5 senior **Steve Williams** are also back up front.

"Barring injuries," said Paschal, "our frontline should be very physical, talented and deep."

BLUE RIBBON ANALYSIS

The loss of Shahid will be felt by the Bulls, but the return of Alexander helps offset his departure. If this team does not let the tag of favorite bother it, South Florida should beat out North Carolina Charlotte for the regular season Sun Belt title.

The Bulls have plenty of depth, both in the backcourt and along the frontline, and some good shooters. Dobras should have a better year shooting, which will put more pressure on defenses to watch him from the outside. That, in turn, should open up the middle.

Paschal had figured this would be the year the Bulls were capable of challenging for the title. They finished second last season, behind Alabama-Birmingham, before winning the tournament. The confidence gained from those experiences should make the Bulls difficult to beat in 1990-91.

"That group of guys made me very proud," said Paschal of last year's battlers. "They stayed focused on their goals and went after everything they wanted with great intensity."

It's going to take the same kind of effort again, and Paschal's crew appears ready to take on all comers.

1990-91 SOUTH FLORIDA SCHEDULE

Nov.	24	Florida
Dec.	3	Bethune-Cookman (FL)
	5	Miami (FL)
	8	@Florida International
	15	Stetson
	18	@Florida State
	22	@Old Dominion
	28-29	#Tampa Tribune Holiday Invitational

1990-91 SOUTH FLORIDA SCHEDULE *Cont.*

Jan.	2	@Stetson
	7	Jacksonville
	12	Western Kentucky
	17	@Alabama-Birmingham
	19	Maryland
	22	@South Alabama
	26	Xavier
	31	North Carolina Charlotte
Feb.	4	Florida International
	7	@Virginia Commonwealth
	9	South Alabama
	11	@Jacksonville
	14	Alabama-Birmingham
	16	Virginia Commonwealth
	18	@Western Kentucky
	21	Old Dominion
	23	@North Carolina Charlotte
	25	@Miami (FL)
Mar.	2-4	##Sun Belt Tournament

@ Road Games
# Tampa, FL (Brown, New Hampshire & Penn State)
Mobile, AL

SOUTHWESTERN LOUISIANA

**LAST SEASON: 20-9
CONFERENCE RECORD: 4-6
STARTERS LOST: 1
STARTERS RETURNING: 4
CONFERENCE: AMERICAN SOUTH (ASC)
LOCATION: LAFAYETTE, LA
HOME FLOOR: CAJUNDOME (12,000)
NICKNAME: RAGIN' CAJUNS
COLORS: VERMILION AND WHITE
COACH: MARTY FLETCHER, record at Southwestern Louisiana, 60-54.
Career record, 97-129.**

Southwestern Louisiana has produced an impressive graph under Marty Fletcher in the past four years, improving from 11-17 to 12-16 to 17-12 to last year's 20-9 mark. But the 1989-90 was bittersweet for Fletcher and the Ragin' Cajuns. Blessed with what some observers felt was the best talent in the American South Conference last year, the Ragin' Cajuns opened the season by winning 14 of their first 15 games. Included in that blistering start was a 104-96 victory over Kentucky in the championship game of the U.K.I.T., one of only two losses the Wildcats suffered in Rupp Arena last season. That victory over Kentucky was the fourth straight over an SEC team for USL.

The hot start heightened expectations. But a 89-87 overtime loss at home to New Orleans in the opening game of American South Conference play sent USL into a five-game losing skid. The slump caused the Ragin' Cajuns to finish a disappointing fourth in the ASC last year.

Yet, the Ragin' Cajuns were only an eyelash away. Besides the loss to New Orleans, USL lost a two-point overtime decision to Southern Mississippi and a two-point double overtime decision to Texas-Pan American. Turn those three near misses into wins and USL would have had a legitimate shot at an at-large bid to the NCAA tournament.

With four starters and six other lettermen returning from last year's squad the expectations for this season are even greater. The lone loss off of last year's squad was leading scorer Sydney Grider, the nation's 16th leading scorer with a 25.5 ppg average and a three-point expert (40.8 percent).

"When you take somebody who scored 25 points a game and was the second leading three-point shooter in the nation out of your lineup, it will impact your team," said Fletcher, referring to Grider. "But we feel like we can find the 25 points. Hopefully, we can find the leadership and intangible qualities that Sydney gave us."

With 6-8 senior wing **Kevin Brooks** and 6-2 senior point guard **Aaron Mitchell** back, the Ragin' Cajuns' arsenal remains well stocked. Both Brooks and Mitchell could be NBA draft choices next year.

A year ago, USL averaged 90.4 points per game (13th nationally) and broke the century mark nine times. The Ragin' Cajuns excelled on the offensive end. They ranked third nationally in three-pointers made with an average of 8.7 treys per game and ranked seventh nationally, shooting 76.3 percent as a team from the free throw line.

Brooks (20.1 ppg, 7.0 rpg, 61 assists, 18 blocked shots, 14 steals) is the Ragin' Cajuns top gun. A lanky player who is equally adept at shooting the three or creating his shot off the dribble, Brooks ranks as the No. 4 active career scorer in college basketball. With Grider leading the offense, Brooks concentrated on raising his rebound total over 1.5 per game from his sophomore year. He scored in double figures in all but one game last year. Brooks is on track to become the first USL player to collect 2,000 points and 600 rebounds in a career.

Mitchell (13.9 ppg, 5.4 rpg, 264 assists, 48 steals) is one of the best point guards in the south. He ranked second in the nation in assists last year and is ideal for the Ragin' Cajuns game. Mitchell registered double digits in assists in 15 games last year. He is also a tenacious defender, an asset that is sometimes lost in the glare of USL's offensive fireworks.

Two other starters, 6-7 junior **Marcus Stokes** and 6-8 senior **Ken Allen**, return at the post positions. Stokes (11.4 ppg, 9.0 rpg, 48 assists, 47 blocked shots, 31 steals) was a pleasant surprise. He not only led the American South Conference in rebounding — grabbing double figure rebounds in 14 games last year — but was also a steady scorer inside. Allen (3.4 ppg, 1.7 rpg, nine blocked shots) played solid defense, but often gave way to 6-9 sophomore **Todd Hill.** Hill (11.2 ppg, 4.3 rpg, 34 assists, 13 blocked shots, 37 steals) is an even thinner version of Brooks. He averaged 11.2 points in less than 25 minutes per game last season and will probably take Grider's vacant spot in the starting lineup.

The Ragin' Cajuns also should receive a boost from the return of 5-10 junior guard **Eric Mouton,** who sat out the season after injuring his knee in pre-season workouts. A pesky defender, Mouton will not only spell Mitchell but allow Fletcher to move him on occasion to off-guard to take advantage of his scoring.

Other returnees include 6-4 junior forward/guard **Tyrone Jones** (2.1 ppg, 1.3 rpg), 6-8 sophomore forward **Johnny Womack** (1.5 ppg, 1.6 rpg), 7-0 senior center **Mark Considine** (1.5 ppg, 1.7 rpg), 6-2 sophomore guard **Bobby Thigpen** (1.5 ppg, 0.7 rpg) and 6-6 sophomore forward **Russ Harris** (0.2 ppg, 0.6 rpg).

Cedric Mackyeon, a 6-6 sophomore transfer from Oklahoma State, gives the Ragin' Cajuns a strong leaper inside. Mackyeon, who was the top prospect in Louisiana his senior year at East Ascension HS in Gonzales, La., will likely push Allen for a starting berth and will at the least be a solid contributor off the bench.

Two highly touted freshmen, 6-3 guard **Antonio Moore** and 6-5 swingman **Byron Starks**, should be major contributors off the bench. Moore averaged 22.0 points per game last year for Southside HS in Atlanta, Ga. Moore was listed among Georgia's Top 10 players by the *Atlanta Constitution.* "Tony's the best shooter I saw all summer," said Fletcher. "He's a big-time scoring threat and he can also play at both guard positions." Moore led his team to the Georgia state championship and named the MVP of the state tournament.

Starks averaged 24.5 points and 11.3 rebounds while leading Grambling (La.) HS to successive Class A state championships. Starks was listed as the No. 2

prep prospect in Louisiana by the *New Orleans Times Picayune. All-Star Sports* ranked Starks as the 14th best swing player in the country while listing him in its Top 100 prep prospects. ''Byron's the best athlete I saw all year,'' said Fletcher. ''He's capable of being a great, great collegiate player. He's got the size, the quickness and the shooting touch to step in and make a big contribution.''

BLUE RIBBON ANALYSIS

With four starters back from a 20-9 team, the Ragin' Cajuns should be considered the favorites in the American South Conference.

''I think that's where you want to be,'' said Fletcher. ''Those are the things you work for. No matter where you are picked, you want to win the league.''

To win the ASC, USL needs to improve its defense and rebounding from last year. The Ragin' Cajuns allowed 85.2 points per game last year and were outrebounded by 1.4 missed shots per game. If the Ragin' Cajuns can elevate their game in those two areas, they should win the ASC championship and gain the league's first automatic berth into the NCAA tournament.

1990-91 SOUTHWESTERN LOUISIANA SCHEDULE		
Nov.	23 & 25	#Hawaii Tip-Off Tournament
	28	Tennessee Tech
Nov.	30-Dec. 1	##Louisiana Classic Tip-Off
Dec.	3	McNeese State
	12	@Appalachian State
	15	Jackson State (MS)
	20	Tennessee State
	22	Texas Southern
Jan.	2	Prairie View A&M (TX)
	5	New Orleans
	10	@Louisiana Tech
	12	@Arkansas State
	17	Texas-Pan American
	19	Lamar
	22	@Oklahoma
	24	@Prairie View (A&M (TX)
	26	Central Florida
	28	Sam Houston State
	30	Southern Mississippi
Feb.	2	@New Orleans
	7	Louisiana Tech
	9	Arkansas State
	12	@Texas-Pan American
	16	@Lamar
	17	Southern Utah State
	20	@Louisville
	23	@Central Florida
Mar.	1-3	*ASC Tournament

@ Road Games
#Honolulu, HI (Hawaii, Northeast Louisiana & Southwest Missouri State)
##
* Site to be announced

SOUTHWEST MISSOURI STATE

LAST SEASON: 22-7
CONFERENCE RECORD: 11-1 (Mid-Continent)
STARTERS LOST: 3
STARTERS RETURNING: 2
CONFERENCE: MISSOURI VALLEY (MVC)
LOCATION: SPRINGFIELD, MO
HOME FLOOR: HAMMONS STUDENT CENTER (8,858)
NICKNAME: BEARS
COLORS: MAROON AND WHITE
COACH: CHARLIE SPOONHOUR, record at Southwest Missouri State, 152-61.
Career record, including high school, 528-170.

Talent-wise, Southwest Missouri State could have picked a better year to leave the Mid-Continent Conference and join the Missouri Valley. But coach Charlie Spoonhour has been known to pick a rabbit or two out of his hat, so the MVC better be on its toes.

The Bears lose three starters from last season's 22-7 team that won the Mid-Continent regular season title and was ousted in the first round of the NCAA Midwest Regional by North Carolina. Even so, it is a program which has done nothing but win since Spoonhour arrived.

''They bring to the Valley an excellent basketball program and a university with a quality academic background,'' MVC Commissioner Doug Elgin said at the press conference announcing Southwest Missouri State's admission into the conference.

The Bears are eligible for the conference title right away. They have won at least 21 games in each of the past five seasons, and they captured four straight Mid-Continent regular-season titles. When the decade of the 1980s began, Southwest Missouri State was an NCAA Division II school. By the time the it ended, the Bears were regulars in the NCAA tournament, boasting four consecutive appearances.

Along the way, they scored postseason victories over Clemson, Pitts and Marquette. Also in the post-season, Florida, Kansas, UNLV and Seton Hall beat the Bears by a combined total of just 19 points.

With the loss of second-leading scorer and top rebounder Lee Campbell (16.6 ppg, 12.5 rpg) - ''He has a good chance to play in the NBA,'' North Carolina coach Dean Smith said after the Tar Heels' NCAA victory last year - and number three scorer Jeff Ford (11.4 ppg), the Bears will have to rebuild the front line.

The backcourt is in the very competent hands of the Bronx bashers, 6-2 senior **Darryl Reid** and 5-5 senior **Arnold Bernard.** Reid led the Bears in scoring last year at 19.0 ppg and was an easy choice as Mid-Continent newcomer of the year. A real fireplug, Bernard averaged 11.4 points, 6.9 assists, 2.3 rebounds and 1.7 steals. Bernard (Our Saviour Lutheran) and Reid (St. Raymond's HS) were high school rivals, then played in the same backcourt at San Jacinto (Tex.) JC before transferring to Southwest Missouri State.

David Brewer, a 6-9 senior, averaged 5.1 points and 2.6 rebounds off the bench last year. **Lovelace Redmond,** a 6-3 senior, averaged 5.2 and 2.1 in a reserve role. The only other returnees with any experience are 6-5 senior **J.T. Marshall** (1.1 ppg) and 6-1 sophomore **Dale Ribble** (1.3 ppg). **Anthony Jones,** a 5-9 sophomore, appeared in two games and did not score.

That means Spoonhour must turn to newcomers to pick up the slack. To do so, he brought in three junior college transfers, two freshmen guards and one senior transfer.

The best of the recruits is 6-6 junior **Andre Rigsby,** who averaged 28 points and 16 rebounds at Mary Holmes (Miss.) JC. Rigsby probably will take Campbell's place, and those are big shoes to fill. Campbell led the nation in field goal shooting last season (.698) and was the country's fourth-leading rebounder.

6-5 junior **Adbul Muhamad** is on board from Rend Lake (Ill.) CC. He is an outstanding all-around athlete who averaged 15 points and 10 rebounds last year. 6-8 junior **Chris Albright** had modest numbers at Hutchinson (Kan.) JC - eight points, and four rebounds - but is the kind of workmanlike player who fits very well in Spoonhour's system. 6-6 senior **Ryan Thornton** transferred for his final season from Kansas State, and will be eligible after the first semester.

Spoonhour tapped the buddy system again with his freshmen, bringing in former Phoenix Central High (Ariz.) backcourt-mates **Mark Brown** and **Chris Wynn.** Brown, 6-3, was a first-team All-State selection last year, averaging 20.8 points, 11.0 rebounds and 5.0 assists. Wynn, 6-1, averaged 20.4 points, 6.0 assists and 5.0 steals per game and was a second-team All-State selection.

BLUE RIBBON ANALYSIS

The Missouri Valley Conference is very happy to have Southwest Missouri State. The Bears are another true basketball school with a budding national reputation.

League coaches, however, might not be so happy, especially when they travel to Springfield to play in the Hammons Student Center. Southwest Missouri State is 73-10 at home, and the Bears have averaged nearly 8,000 fans per game. Hammons is an old-fashioned pit.

Spoonhour's reputation as an X's and O's man continues to grow. One national publication included him in a list of its ''Top Five Coaches Who Do The Most With The Least.'' Counting his days on the high school level, Spoonhour has won 528 games. In seven years at Southwest Missouri State, he has won 71.6 percent of the time.

And even the losses are contested. Five of the Bears' seven defeatss last season were by four or fewer points. Nothing is ever easy against them, regardless of talent level.

In the MVC, the Bears will need rapid development from their frontcourt players to challenge for the conference title. For the moment, they do not have the horses inside to battle either Creighton or Southern Illinois.

With Reid and Bernard, Spoonhour must go with a guard-oriented attack. Even with that, third place in their first MVC season is a real possibility. The Bears are likely to battle Bradley, Tulsa and Wichita State in the regular season race, a shade behind Creighton and Southern Illinois.

But once the MVC tournament begins in St. Louis, watch out for the Bears. Southwest Missouri State figures to pack the place and create a home-away-from-home atmosphere. If nothing else, the Bears' home record makes it impossible to rule out a fifth straight NCAA bid.

1990-91 SOUTHWEST MISSOURI STATE SCHEDULE		
Nov.	23 & 25	#Hawaii Tip-Off Classic
	29	Northern Iowa
Dec.	1	Colorado
	4	@Tennessee State
	7-8	##Pizza Hut Classic
	12	@Missouri-Kansas City
	15	@Wichita State
	19	Morgan State (MD)
	22	Indiana State
	28-29	*Sun Carnival Tournament
Jan.	2	Creighton
	5	St. Louis
	8	@Southern Illinois
	12	Illinois State
	14	@Drake
	19	@Colorado
	22	Tulsa
	26	@Illinois State
	28	@Bradley
Feb.	2	Wichita State
	6	Southern Illinois
	10	@Creighton
	14	Drake
	16	Bradley
	20	@Tulsa
	23	@Indiana State
Mar.	1-5	**MVC Tournament

@ Road Games
# Honolulu, HI (Hawaii, Northeast Louisiana & Southwestern Louisiana)
Springfield, MO (North Carolina A&T, Pacific & Prairie View)
* El Paso, TX (Texas Tech, UTEP & Washington)
** St. Louis, MO

STEPHEN F. AUSTIN

LAST SEASON: 2-25
CONFERENCE
RECORD: 1-13
STARTERS LOST: 2
STARTERS
RETURNING: 3
CONFERENCE:
SOUTHLAND (SLC)
LOCATION:
NACOGDOCHES, TX
HOME FLOOR: SFA
COLISEUM (7,050)
NICKNAME: LUMBERJACKS
COLORS: PURPLE AND WHITE
COACH: NED FOWLER, first year at Stephen F.
Austin.
Career record, including high school, 432-155.

Stephen F. Austin endured a forgettable season in 1989-90. The Lumberjacks lost 25 of 27 games and finished dead last in the Southland Conference with a 1-13 record.

Second year head coach Mike Martin was dismissed with three games to go in the season and following the campaign, the job of resurrecting the program, which three short years ago reached the NIT tournament, was entrusted to former Tulane head coach Ned Fowler.

Fowler is no stranger to the piney woods of East Texas. From 1978-81, Fowler led Tyler Junior College to a 83-22 mark and a third place finish in the National Junior College tournament. From there, he compiled a 70-45 record in four seasons as head coach at Tulane, guiding the Green Wave to two appearances in the NIT. The trademark of Fowler coached teams has been defense. His first three teams at Tulane allowed less than 60 points per game. In 1983-84, his Green Wave squad was ranked third nationally in scoring defense.

"The coming season will be the most challenging one I've faced in my entire coaching career," said Fowler. "We have two major factors to overcome, youth and a losing syndrome that's developed here during the past three seasons."

Fowler's skills will be tested. Opponents averaged over 86 points per game against the Lumberjacks last year. The average margin of defeat for SFA last year was over 18 points. Foes held the Lumberjacks to 65 or fewer points on 13 occasions. At least, Fowler will have a corp of three returning starters and five other lettermen to work with.

The most promising returnee is 6-7 sophomore post **Tim Holloway** (10.0 ppg, 7.5 rpg, 23 assists, 31 blocked shots, nine steals). Holloway led the SLC in blocked shots and finished sixth in rebounding despite missing four games in the middle of the season because of arthroscopic knee surgery.

"Tim had an endurance problem last year," said Fowler. "He's a good player, one we can build around."

Holloway will likely be teamed on the post by 6-6 senior **Rick Archberger** (8.8 ppg, 4.4 rpg, 20 assists, 9 blocked shots, 9 steals). Archberger finished second in the SLC in field goal percentage with a .561 mark.

6-3 junior guard **Avery Helms** (11.8 ppg, 4.0 rpg, 64 assists, 7 blocked shots, 27 steals) is ticketed to start at the shooting guard position. Helms led the team in scoring last year despite missing eight games with a stress fracture in his foot. "Avery is an excellent player and one of our most experienced guys," said Fowler. 6-1 sophomore **Keithan Ross** (4.0 ppg, 1.8 rpg) will probably move into the starting point guard position.

Depth should be provided by three returnees, 6-7 sophomore **Jeff Williams** (8.2 ppg, 5.7 rpg), 6-3 sophomore guard **Darren Fleming** (5.8 ppg, 2.2 apg), and **Antoine Dooley** (2.1 ppg, 2.5 rpg). Another veteran, 6-7 senior **Daniel Koenigs**, returns after sitting out the past two years. Koenigs averaged 7.3 points and 4.3 rebounds a game as a sophomore. Also available after redshirting last year will be 6-7 freshman forward **Kevin Traylor**.

Fowler landed one junior college signee and four freshman in his first recruiting class for the Lumberjacks. **Jack Little**, a 6-4 junior forward, will be a contender for the starting small forward position after averaging 9.6 points and 2.4 rebounds at Tyler (Tex.) JC last year.

Fowler described 6-6 **Deric Moten** as the best athlete signed by SFA and the one most likely to help because he is the quickest. Moten, out of Huntsville (Tex.) HS, averaged 15.0 points and six rebounds per game as a senior. Another forward, 6-4 **Chris Foreman**, will also likely contribute. Foreman averaged 17.1 points and 9.3 rebounds at Tyler (Tex.) HS.

Trent McClain, another 6-6 freshman, can play either guard position as well as handle small forward duties. McClain averaged 17.2 points and 7.0 rebounds last year at Robert E. Lee HS in Tyler, Tex. Another rookie who will see duty at point guard is 5-10 **Chad Melton**, who averaged 12.0 points and 8.0 rebounds, for Class AAAAA Texas state champion Dallas Kimball HS.

BLUE RIBBON ANALYSIS

Based on Fowler's track record, Stephen F. Austin should make immediate improvements. Fowler's dedication to defense and patient offensive style should pay immediate dividends to a Lumberjack squad that lacks a proven scorer.

"We need to improve in every phase of the game," said Fowler. "The three greatest weaknesses last year were ability, skills and experience. The program hit rock bottom last year. Hopefully, we can build it back up, but it's going to be a slow, gradual process."

Stephen F. Austin will certainly be more competitive in 1990-91, but the Lumberjacks will likely be hard pressed to escape another finish in the Southland Conference cellar.

1990-91 STEPHEN F. AUSTIN SCHEDULE		
Nov.	26	Houston
	29	Texas Southern
Dec.	2	@Nicholls State (LA)
	3	@Southeastern Louisiana
	8	Georgia State
	15	Central Oklahoma State
	17	Southeastern Louisiana
	21-22	#U.S. Air Classic
Jan.	2	@Southern Utah State
	5	@Georgia State
	10	Texas-Arlington
	12	North Texas
	14	Nicholls State
	19	@Southwest Texas State
	24	@Northwestern State
	26	Northeast Louisiana
	29	@Texas Southern
Feb.	2	McNeese State
	7	Northwestern State
	9	@Northeast Louisiana
	14	@Sam Houston State
	16	Southwest Texas State
	18	@McNeese State
	21	@North Texas
	23	Texas-Arlington
Feb. 28-		
Mar. 2		##Southland Conference Tournament

@ Road Games
# Dayton, OH (Murray State, U.S. International & Wright State)
Site to be announced

STETSON

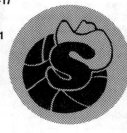

LAST SEASON: 15-17
CONFERENCE
RECORD: 9-9
STARTERS LOST: 1
STARTERS
RETURNING: 4
CONFERENCE:
TRANS AMERICA
ATHLETIC (TAAC)
LOCATION:
DeLAND, FL
HOME FLOOR:
EDMUNDS CENTER (5,000)
NICKNAME: HATTERS
COLORS: GREEN AND WHITE
COACH: GLENN WILKES, record at Stetson, 512-389.

In the Trans America Athletic Conference, two things can get you to the NCAA tournament in a hurry - a dominant player, or host duties in the conference tournament. That being the case, Stetson has to be considered a pretty serious contender for its first TAAC title and a trip to the NCAA's in 1990-91.

The Hatters, who were competent in a 15-17 season last year, return 6-9 senior **Derrall Dumas**, arguably the best player in the TAAC, and will host the conference tourney in early March. "Nobody is conceding anything," said one TAAC assistant, "but you have to look at them first. They've got some horses coming back from a team that wasn't all that bad."

Glenn Wilkes, Stetson's coach for the past 34 years, brings back four starters from a team that won six of its last seven games, including a 25-point blowout of Texas-San Antonio in the first round of the TAAC tournament. In their final game, the Hatters pushed champion Centenary into overtime before losing.

The only loss from that team is, admittedly, a big one. Guard Maurice Cowan led the Hatters in scoring with 18.6 points per game and was one of the top TACC's three-point shooters. Fortunately for Wilkes, there are plenty of scorers returning.

Dumas (15.7 ppg, 8.9 rpg) is the logical starting point. A wide body who controlled the inside, Dumas shot nearly 60 percent from the floor and led the conference in rebounding. He also had 43 blocked shots and, for good measure, 27 steals. **Lorenzo Williams** (7.8 ppg, 8.4 rpg), another 6-9 senior, scored less but was extremely effective inside. The top shot blocker in the conference, he slapped away 121 and pulled down 269 rebounds. Included in that total were 124 offensive boards. 6-9 sophomore **Chris Desiderio** (5.1 ppg, 3.0 rpg) provides the depth in the Hatters' double low post game.

6-5 senior **Jim Horn** (8.2 ppg, 4.0 rpg) is back at forward. Depth comes from 6-7 senior **Donnell Sampson** (7.0 ppg, 4.5 rpg), 6-7 junior **Johnny Walker** and a trio of freshmen - 6-6 **John Kee** (Dillard HS/Fort Lauderdale, Fla.), 6-7 **Marcus Cowart** (Rutherford HS/Panama City, Fla.) and 6-7 hometowner **Karl Bruschayt** (DeLand HS/DeLand, Fla.).

The backcourt is deep and experienced. 6-2 senior point guard **Frank Ireland** is back after averaging 13.3 points and 5.7 assists last year. 6-0 sophomore **Rob Wilkes** (3.8 ppg, 2.5 apg) will back him up.

There is not a shortage of prospects to replace Cowan. 6-2 sophomore **Kenny Daniels** (1.0 ppg) and three more newcomers - 6-4 junior transfer **Mark Brisker** from Polk (Fla.) CC, 6-3 freshman **Mark Southall** (Spruce Creek HS/Daytona Beach, Fla.) and 6-2 freshman **Bryant Conner** (South Plantation HS/Plantation, Fla.) - will all get a chance to take the job.

A schedule that opens with Purdue and includes Pitt and Tennessee should more than adequately prepare the Hatters for conference play.

BLUE RIBBON ANALYSIS

Opportunity knocks. With five of the top six players in their last year of eligibility, the Hatters better answer. It could be now or never for them.

With three 6-9 and four 6-7 frontcourt player, Stetson also has the talent to push any other TAAC team off the court. Ireland is a solid floor leader who can get the ball to Dumas easily enough. Cowan will be missed, but Brisker, the top junior college player in Florida a year ago, should be able to replace a good bit of the lost scoring punch.

With any kind of carry over from the strong 1989-90 finish, Stetson should be able to stay at or near the top in the conference race. Finishing up with two home games will lead nicely into the TAAC tournament on the Hatters' home floor.

Things are looking bright in DeLand. Stetson should win the conference tournament and an NCAA invitation.

1990-91 STETSON SCHEDULE

Nov.	24	@Purdue
	26	@Florida International
Nov. 30- Dec. 1		#Hatter Classic
Dec.	4	@North Carolina Wilmington
	6	Bethune-Cookman (FL)
	15	@South Florida
	21	@Brigham Young
	27-30	##Rainbow Classic
Jan.	5	South Florida
	9	@Bethune-Cookman
	12	@Georgia Southern
	14	###Florida State
	19	@Georgia State
	21	@Mercer
	24	Centenary (LA)
	26	Texas-San Antonio
	31	@Samford (AL)
Feb.	2	*Arkansas-Little Rock
	9	Georgia Southern
	14	Mercer
	16	Georgia State
	18	Florida International
	21	@Centenary
	23	@Texas-San Antonio
	25	@Texas
	28	Samford (AL)
Mar.	2	Arkansas-Little Rock
	5-7	**TAAC Tournament

@ Road Games
# Deland, FL (Bethune Cookman, Hofstra & Mississippi)
Honolulu, HI (Alaska-Anchorage, California, Hawaii, Iona, Pitt, Tennessee & Wichita State)
Orlando, FL
* Pine Bluff, AR
** DeLand, FL

TENNESSEE

LAST SEASON: 16-14
CONFERENCE RECORD: 10-8
STARTERS LOST: 1
STARTERS RETURNING 4
CONFERENCE: SOUTHEASTERN (SEC)
LOCATION: KNOXVILLE, TN
HOME FLOOR: THOMPSON-BOWLING ARENA (24,535)
NICKNAME: VOLUNTEERS
COLORS: ORANGE AND WHITE
COACH: WADE HOUSTON, record at Tennessee, 16-14.

Wade Houston turned down a slew of coaching offers before accepting the top job at Tennessee last season. Cynics might suggest he was just waiting for his son Allan to grow up and join him.

It was good thinking regardless. Wade's rebuilding of a Tennessee team which had lost all five starters from Don DeVoe's final season was made considerably smoother when the Dad threw his first-born male into the equation. Yet the job is far from complete. With all-new starters, the Volunteers had their ups and downs last year, and some obvious holes still demand attention.

But scoring will be no problem for the Vols as long as **Allan Houston** is around. Not since Press Maravich was named head coach at LSU, and brought along his son Pistol Pete, has a father-son duo made such an impact on college basketball as the Houstons did last season.

Wade Houston was the first black head coach in the Southeastern Conference, but little was made of it around the league. Everyone was too busy trying to keep their eyes on his son. If not for the Chris Jackson phenomenon one year earlier, SEC historians would have been searching the archives for evidence of a freshman who made such a strong and immediate impact.

A 6-5 guard, Houston (20.3 ppg, 2.9 rpg, 127 assists, 36 steals) was third in the league in scoring behind only LSU's Jackson and Gerald Glass of Mississippi. Neither of those two will be back this season.

And, while it may be comparing apples and oranges, Houston and 7-1 manchild Shaquille O'Neal of LSU - both true sophomores - will be the only two choices when the SEC argues about who its best player is this season. A unanimous choice for both the *Associated Press* and *United Press International* All-SEC team, Houston was the first Tennessee freshman to win that honor since Bernard King in 1975.

"Allan's a great player," said Glass, who ought to know when he sees one. "He plays the game all over the court. He'll be one of the best players in the country before he leaves Tennessee."

"The sky's the limit for that young man," said Kentucky coach Rick Pitino. "Allan has a great NBA future ahead of him." Added Ole Miss coach Ed Murphy: "This may sound crazy, but I'm glad he's at Tennessee. It's great for this conference."

The latter may be the dissenting view among SEC coaches. After Allan's first tour of the conference, most probably wished he'd gone to Louisville, where his dad was an assistant coach for 13 seasons under Denny Crum. Houston originally chose the Cardinals during the early signing period of his senior year at Ballard (Ky.) High, where he was Kentucky's Mr. Basketball and a first-team *Parade* and *USA Today* All-America. Superscout Bob Gibbons called him the best three-point shooter among the 1989-89 prep stars.

But when Wade Houston landed the Tennessee head job in April of that year, his first order of business was to go home - and recruit. Crum understood the situation and immediately released Allan from his Louisville scholarship, though there was some red tape involved before the Conference Commissioners Association, which administers letters-of-intent, granted him immediate elegibility at Tennessee.

It was more than a package deal for the Vols. It was Christmas morning in Knoxville. Wade Houston, who grew up in Alcoa, Tenn., just 12 miles from Thompson-Boling Arena, finally came home, this time bearing gifts. Allan was the best start he could have had in restoring the winning ways at Tennessee.

Even playing out of position at point guard - he's a true, made-to-NBA-specs off guard - Houston got his freshman inconsistency out of the way in a hurry. You would have expected that, though. He grew up hanging around the Louisville campus, running with ex-Cards who came home from the NBA - Darrell Griffith, Rodney McCray, Milt Wagner, etc.

Houston is an above average ballhandler, has unlimited range on his jumper, possesses good moves toward the basket and is an 80 percent free throw shooter. This year, without the burden of playing point guard, he should sneak in for some rebounds as well.

Last year, Allan was 83-for-192 on three-pointers (43.2 percent) and scored over 30 points on eight occasions, including back-to-back performances of 43 and 37 points against LSU and Kentucky. If all that is not enough, he carried a 3.1 grade point average as a freshman.

Houston spent the summer playing on the USA Junior Men's team that won the Championship of the America's tournament in Uruguay. He was the USA's leading three-point shooter, and was named to the all-tournament team. The Vols would prefer he not play the point this season, as they will go almost exclusively with a three-guard attack. Allan could then function as a small forward against bigger opponents.

The key will be getting someone else to play the point effectively. 6-2 junior **Jay Price** (1.8 ppg, 42 assists in 17 games) will get the first look after starting the final two games of the season there. 6-3 redshirt Norman Marbury (21.5 ppg, 5.2 assists at Lincoln HS/Brooklyn, N.Y.) is probably the point guard of the future, but will sit out this season. 6-4 sophomore **Lang Wiseman** (2.8 ppg, 29 assists) worked on his suspect ballhandling during a summer league in Memphis, and is also a candidate at the point.

Across from Allan Houston, the other shooting guard spot will be in good hands. 6-3 senior **Greg Bell** (16.6 ppg, 3.2 rpg, 65 assists, 36 steals) was probably the biggest beneficiary of the coaching change. The former West Virginia prep player of the year was a productive, but often frustrated sixth man in DeVoe's more deliberate offensive system.

In Wade Houston's up-tempo game, Bell was turned loose and came to life, earning third-team All-SEC honors. His only liability is at the free throw line, where he is barely a 67 percent career shooting. This despite a .431 percentage from three-point range. A backcourt role will also be found for 6-4 sophomore **Steve Rivers** (3.1 ppg, 2.0 rpg), who started 16 games last year as a defensive specialist.

The Vols have far more questions inside, where they must replace 6-8 center Ian Lockhart (13.1 ppg, 10.9 rpg), one of the league's top rebounders despite giving up several inches in most games. 6-8 senior power forward **Ronnie Reese** (9.1 ppg, 5.1 rpg) was a pleasant surpise, voted the team's most improved player last year. He has excellent quickness and good leaping ability.

Reese could be moved to center, since he has an excellent backup at power forward in 6-7 sophomore **Carlus Groves** (6.6 ppg, 4.1 rpg), last year's first man off the bench. Groves also has an adequate outside shooting touch.

Other forwards include 6-9 redshirt freshman **Ronnie Robinson** (1.0 ppg, 1.0 rpg in two games before being lost for the season) and 6-5 senior **Rickey Clark** (1.1 ppg, 1.5 rpg). Robinson has some skills, but needs to add weight. 6-6 freshman recruit **Daryl Milson** (26 points, 12 rebounds at Savannah HS/Savannah, Ga.) will also get a chance

6-9 junior **Michael Curry** (2.1 ppg, 3 rpg) is in the picture to replace Lockhart at center. He needs to be more aggressive, however, and was hampered over the summer after being diagnosed with high blood pressure. He has since been cleared to play, but worked little on his game in the off-season. Another suspect for the post is 6-8 redshirt freshman **Gannon Goodson** (20.2 points, 10.1 rebounds at Shades Valley HS/Birmingham, Ala.). A foot injury shelved him last year after just four collegiate games.

BLUE RIBBON ANALYSIS

Head coach Wade Houston thinks his son Allan could get even better. "He needs to improve defensively," Dad said, "which he has in common with many of his teammates. He could work on being more consistent throughout the season, trying to work on the total package: rebounding, steals, becoming a

287

dominant player.''

As long as Allan is on the floor, though, the Volunteers will always be fun to watch. There is ample outside firepower beside him, too, particularly from Bell.

Still, to improve on last year's record, the Vols will need someone to step in and relieve Houston of the point guard duties, to get some reasonable play at center, to improve their overall defense and to become a better free throw shooting team. Take away Houston's 84 percent accuracy from the line, and the rest of the Vols were a dismal 63 percent.

Tennessee can get away with its three-guard offense in the SEC, where outside of LSU's twin towers, there are few dominating inside games. With a few breaks and a year to work on Wade Houston's aggressive defensive style, the Volunteers might have the best chance to break away from a large pack in the middle of the conference and challenge the Alabama-LSU-Georgia domination at the top.

TENNESSEE CHATTANOOGA

LAST SEASON: 14-14
CONFERENCE RECORD: 7-7
STARTERS LOST: 1
STARTERS RETURNING: 4
CONFERENCE: SOUTHERN
LOCATION: CHATTANOOGA, TN
HOME FLOOR: UTC ARENA (11,218)
NICKNAME: MOCCASINS
COLORS: NAVY BLUE AND OLD GOLD
COACH: MACK McCARTHY, record at Tennessee-Chattanooga, 94-57.

After dominating the Southern Conference in the 1980's, Tennessee-Chattanooga returned to the middle of the pack as the 1990's began. And coach Mack McCarthy was not at all happy with the change of scenery.

In nine previous years, the Moccasins had won five regular season conference championships and averaged 22 victories. That success ended abruptly last season after player defections, academic problems and other off-the-court troubles reduced the Mocs' roster to nine scholarship players.

The shortage of warm bodies made it difficult for McCarthy to conduct a decent practice, much less win games. McCarthy needed help. To get it, he returned to familiar territory, the junior colleges. He signed six junior college transfers, but only three will be eligible. All should contend for starting jobs.

''I think we've got a good nucleus of veterans and some good solid kids coming in,'' McCarthy said. ''We feel good about the coming year. One advantage we've always had was the fact that we knew we were going to win all the time. That's been diminished a little bit, but I don't think to the point where it isn't going to come back and be a factor. I think we still feel like we ought to win the league every year.''

At least one conference rival agrees. ''UTC kind of got off the track a little bit last year,'' Furman coach Butch Estes said. ''They'll be back this year.''

McCarthy might have been able to get by with nine players last season if they were all as talented as 6-6 senior **Derrick Kirce** (20.1 ppg, 7.6 rpg). Kirce, a transfer from Georgia, played all five positions and was the Mocs' primary scoring threat after forward Daren Chandler became academically ineligible in December. Despite double- and sometimes triple-teaming, Kirce managed to get his points.

''Kirce had an amazingly consistent year considering what all went on around him,'' McCarthy said. ''He's such a versatile kid. We've played him everywhere, from point guard to center. He responded really well. This year, he'll be surrounded by better players and I think he'll be even better.''

Two newcomers will probably join Kirce on the Mocs' front line. The first is 6-6 junior **Lavert Threats** (16.2 ppg, 10.1 rpg), a transfer from Indian Hills (Iowa) CC. ''On paper, he's our best recruit,'' said McCarthy. ''He's a big time athlete. Athletically, he could have played in any league in the country. He can run and jump and guard anybody.''

Keith Nelson (14.9 ppg, 9.8 rpg), a 6-7, 230-pound junior from Sullivan (Ky.) Business College, will probably start at center. ''Keith's a big-time rebounder,'' McCarthy said. ''We needed some bulk in the post, and he gives that to us.''

Two returnees will get plenty of minutes as frontcourt reserves. 6-4 senior **Ben Wiley** (6.3 ppg, 3.8 rpg) is on the small side, but can play both forward positions. 6-8 **Maceo Williams** (3.3 ppg, 2.3 rpg) improved throughout last season after being forced into a starting role when the Mocs' roster dwindled.

6-3 junior **Larry Stewart** (4.8 ppg, 3.4 rpg) and 6-3 senior **Tommy Bankston** (9.5 ppg, 4.3 rpg) are capable swingmen. Stewart, the best jumper on the team, started most of the year. Bankston missed the first semester last season and will do so again as he tries to regain academic eligibility. He is one of the few Moccasins capable of hitting the three-point shot with consistency.

Yet another JC signee, 6-3 junior **T.J. Jackson** (18.2 ppg, 7.8 rpg), is being counted on to solidify the shooting guard position. Jackson, a teammate of Threats at Indian Hills, averaged 29 points two years ago, second in the nation among junior college players. ''He's a key player for us,'' said McCarthy, ''because we've had some instability at two guard. We started five different people at that spot last year. T.J.'s a pretty good shooter, but he's more of a scorer.''

Jackson will be joined in the Mocs' backcourt by one of two virtually interchangeable point guards. 5-10 senior **Eric Spivey** (12.2 ppg, 2.9 rpg, 85 assists) is a better shooter, but not as quick as fellow 5-10

---

senior **Tyrone Enoch** (4.6 ppg, 1.9 rpg, 44 assists, 83 steals). ''One of the keys to having a good season will be the play of the point guards,'' McCarthy said. ''Both will be significantly better after a year in our system. They're both talented and quick enough to make up for their size.''

Bart Redden (5.1 ppg, 2.8 rpg), a 6-5 sophomore, and **Pat Shepphard**, a 6-4 junior who redshirted last year, will back up Jackson. Brother of the late Don Redden, a former LSU player, Bart is the team's best outside shooter. Shepphard can fill in at either second guard or the point.

McCarthy has two incoming freshmen. **Brandon Born,** a 6-5 forward, averaged 20 points and five rebounds last year for Ringgold (Ga.) High School. His brother Gerry, playing for Davidson, hit a three-point shot at the buzzer to defeat UTC in the 1985 Southern Conference championship game. That was McCarthy's first season in Chattanooga.

Freshman **Shane Neal,** a 6-2 guard, averaged 20.8 points and 4.1 rebounds at Pope High School (Marietta, Ga). Neal is the brother of former Georgia Tech point guard Craig Neal.

BLUE RIBBON ANALYSIS

Even with all the turmoil of a year ago, UTC's biggest problem was poor shooting. The Mocs shot just 44 percent from the field, and looked worse than that.

''Two things concern me about this year's team,'' McCarthy admitted. ''Shooting is number one. We've got to be able to shoot the ball. The second thing is our schedule. If it doesn't sap our confidence playing all those good people, then I think we're going to be better for it. Playing a tough schedule has helped us in the past, and I think it will again.''

Tennessee-Chattanooga plays Tennessee, Alabama, Kentucky and Mississippi State. If, as McCarthy says, the Moccasins do not get crushed by those Southeastern Conference schools, they might gain from the experience.

Finally, McCarthy is counting on junior college transfers Threats, Nelson and Jackson to start or at least play a great deal. If those three come through to provide scoring and depth, UTC will have a winning season and return to its accustomed spot in the upper division of the Southern Conference.

TENNESSEE TECH

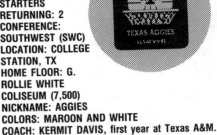

LAST SEASON: 19-9
CONFERENCE RECORD: 9-3
STARTERS LOST: 2
STARTERS RETURNING: 3
CONFERENCE: OHIO VALLEY (OVC)
LOCATION: COOKEVILLE, TN
HOME FLOOR: EBLEN CENTER (10,150)
NICKNAME: GOLDEN EAGLES
COLORS: PURPLE AND GOLD
COACH: FRANK HARRELL, record at Tennessee Tech, 27-26.

The 1990-91 campaign will definitely be a rebuilding year for the Golden Eagles, the only question being just how much needs to be done. Tennessee Tech lost two key performers from last year's squad — forward Earl Wise, the school's all-time leading scorer, and 7-0 Yugoslavian center Milos Babic, taken by the Cleveland Cavaliers in the second round of the NBA draft.

Behind that high-scoring duo, Tech almost made it to the penthouse of the OVC before being upset by area rival Austin Peay in the first round of league's post-season tournament. Even so, losing the services of Wise (19.5 ppg, 7.8 rpg, 85 assists, 56 steals) and Babic (12.4 ppg, 7.2 rpg, 32 blocked shots) does not automatically mean a quick trip to the conference basement. Coach Frank Harrell and staff have accumulated too much talent for that.

Point guard **Van Usher,** an academic question mark over the summer, has been ruled eligible. The 6-0 junior leads a trio of solid returning starters, each of whom scored in double figures a year ago. Usher (11.3 ppg, 4.3 rpg, 189 assists, 80 steals), in particular, has the tools to be one of the OVC's premiere players. 6-2 junior college transfer **P.J. Mays,** from Anderson (S.C.) JC, will back him up. Mays was a big time high school player, who originally signed with Missouri before attending junior college.

Also from Anderson is 6-8 transfer **Charles Edmondson,** who averaged 14 points and eight rebounds in the JUCO ranks. He and Mays are the backbone of what one recruiting service called the second-best talent roundup in the OVC. Three Tech freshmen signees earned state or regional honors last season.

6-3 swingman **Robert West** (Springfield HS/Springfield, Tenn.) was chosen Class AA player of the year by The Tennessean, averaging 26 points and 18 rebounds at Springfield. 6-5 forward **Eric Mitchell** (Pickett County HS/Byrdstown, Tenn.) was Mr. Basketball and the player of the year in Class A for his 22-point, eight-rebound averages. 6-6 forward **Bruce Ogelsby** (Hart County HS/Hartwell, Ga.) was the North Georgia player of the year. The final freshman is 6-8 center **Mike Norris** (Pendleton Heights HS/Pendleton Heights, Ind.).

Senior guard **Bobby McWilliams,** a 5-7 dynamo, is the second returning starter. He averaged 11.5 points and 2.4 rebounds for the Golden Eagles. He also set a school record for three-pointers (63), and was 82.8 percent from the free throw line. McWilliams can also play the point. Fellow senior **Rod Manuel** (2.2 ppg, 1.3 rpg), the 6-5 brother of former Kentucky recruit Eric Manuel, is a defensive standout who would see more time if his offensive game improved.

A pair of sophomores are being primed for the future, but played enough last year to contribute as needed. 6-6 **Mitch Cupples** (6.1 ppg, 2.7 rpg) shot exactly 50 percent (50-for-100) from the field and set a Tech freshman record for free throw accuracy (79.4 percent). 6-8 forward **John Best** (3.1 ppg, 1.7 rpg) saw slightly less action after suffering a broken hand in the now-infamous brawl with Middle Tennessee State.

The top returning forward and the final returning starter is 6-6 senior **Jerome Rodgers** (10.9 ppg, 5.8 rpg, 51.8 field goal percentage). Still, it is the Golden Eagles' weakest position, allowing for the possibility that Edmondson may step right in and start alongside him. That would be Wise's former spot, of course, not an easy position to fill.

6-8 junior **Wade Wester** (5.0 ppg, 4.6 rpg) will have to fill the void left by Babic in the middle. Backing him up is 6-8 sophomore **Derrick Gray** (1.3 ppg, 1.0 rpg), a 280-pounder who is also a defensive lineman for the Tech football team. 6-10 redshirt freshman **Jared Elder** (Henderson HS/Chamblee, Ga.) is in the wings.

6-5 senior **Howard McClain** (0.4 ppg), 5-10 junior **Darrell Stevens** (2.4 ppg) and 5-10 redshirt freshman **Maurice Houston** (Central Catholic HS/Springfield, Ohio) round out the roster.

BLUE RIBBON ANALYSIS

"If everything works out," said Harrell, "we have the makings of a pretty decent team." Maybe so, but the Golden Eagles remain a mystery at this point. It all depends on the development of the freshmen, as well as the contributions of Edmondson in the frontcourt.

Tennessee Tech could conceivably finish anywhere from second to sixth in the OVC. The Golden Eagles could even contend with Murray State, or at least Middle Tennessee, toward the top of the conference standings. On the flip side, the newcomers could be overrated, and Tech could plummet to the second division.

Realistically, call it fourth place for the Golden Eagles.

1990-91 TENNESSEE TECH SCHEDULE

Nov.	23	Bethel College (TN)
	26	@Mississippi State
	28	@Southwestern Louisiana
Dec.	3	Covenant College
	6	Southern Mississippi
	8	@Missouri-Kansas City
	14-15	#Ameritas Classic
	17	@Wisconsin-Milwaukee
	22	Western Carolina
	28	@Western Kentucky
	31	@Wisconsin
Jan.	2	Tennessee-Chattanooga
	5	Tennessee State
	12	Eastern Kentucky
	14	Morehead State
	19	@Austin Peay
	21	@Murray State
	26	@Middle Tennessee State
	30	@Western Carolina
Feb.	4	@Tennessee State
	9	Missouri-Kansas City
	11	Middle Tennessee State
	16	Murray State
	18	Austin Peay
	23	@Morehead State
	25	@Eastern Kentucky
Mar.	2, 6-7	*OVC Tournament

@ Road Games
# Lincoln, NE (Alabama State, Bowling Green & Nebraska)
* Site to be announced

TEXAS A&M

LAST SEASON: 14-17
CONFERENCE RECORD: 7-9
STARTERS LOST: 3
STARTERS RETURNING: 2
CONFERENCE: SOUTHWEST (SWC)
LOCATION: COLLEGE STATION, TX
HOME FLOOR: G. ROLLIE WHITE COLISEUM (7,500)
NICKNAME: AGGIES
COLORS: MAROON AND WHITE
COACH: KERMIT DAVIS, first year at Texas A&M. Career record, 89-32.

Coach Kermit Davis begins his first year at Texas A&M with a completely overhauled program. The 30-year-old Davis led Idaho to consecutive NCAA tournament appearances and is part of A&M's effort to upgrade its program before it falls too far behind the Southwest Conference leaders, Arkansas and Texas. A $16 million, 14,500 seat arena is also being planned for the opening of the 1992-93 season.

Davis is the son of former Mississippi State coach Kermit Davis, Sr. He coached two years at Southwest Mississippi JC before joining Tim Floyd's staff at Idaho. After working under Floyd for two years, Davis took over the Vandal program in 1988.

"My goodness gracious, Kermit Davis just did an outstanding job here," said Idaho athletic director Gary Hunter. "Fifty wins and 12 losses and two Big Sky championships in two years, and for a young man who's only 30 years old, that's extraordinary."

Davis is both having to build for the future and produce a respectable team for this season. The Aggies had gotten used to high turnover in recent years under former, 27-year coach Shelby Metcalf, who usually brought in large numbers of transfers. Davis had little left for him after the Aggies' 14-17 record last season and even less when center David Harris (10.9 ppg, 7.8 rpg, 108 blocks) lost his final year of eligibility because of academic problems. The Aggies also lost All-SWC guard Tony Milton (20.6 ppg, 5.0 rpg, 208 assists), who started two years after transferring from junior college.

Davis signed nine players —with two of the more prominent not being eligible until 1991. Forward Tony Scott, a former Syracuse starter, and guard David Edwards of Georgetown will redshirt this season. Of the seven other newcomers —one is a senior transfer, four are junior college transfers, and two are freshmen. The Aggies' two freshmen recruits —6-4 guard **Artie Griffin** (29.5 ppg, 8.4 rpg at Lee HS, San Antonio) and 6-5 guard **Ed Wheeler** (33.0 ppg. 16.5 rpg at Seagoville, Tex., HS) are promising.

The lone strength that Davis inherits, though, is at guard. Seniors **Freddie Ricks** and **Lynn Suber** are adequate players who have played regularly. The 6-2 Ricks (9.9 ppg) started in 27 games last year and was 10th in the SWC with 114 assists. He had a team high 47.4 percentage on three-pointers. Suber was a part-time starter but seemed to have more of an impact off the bench. He was 12th in the SWC with a 14.0 points per game average. The 6-2 Suber can be exceptional when hot. He had 33 points in A&M's season-opening upset of Connecticut.

Another returning guard is 6-4 sophomore **Brooks Thompson** (8.3 ppg, 2.4 rpg, 69 assists), who started 14 games as a freshman. He's a long range left-handed bomber who's not afraid to shoot but must get more accurate to justify his attempts.

Davis might frequently use a three-guard attack to take advantage of his depth. He might decide to redshirt freshmen Griffin and Wheeler although

Griffin might be hard to keep off the floor. He was considered one of Texas' top prospects last season and was ranked as the No. 83 high school senior in the country by *All-Star Sports*. Davis also signed 6-1 guard **Isaac Brown** (18.0 rpg, 7.8 apg at Gulf Coast, Miss., CC) who could be another redshirt candidate.

At Idaho, Davis did not run a guard-oriented offense but concentrated his team strength on power forward Riley Smith. He won't have that ability at A&M. Two junior college transfers —**Darrin Terry** and **Anthony Ware**—could provide the forward strength Davis is used to. Both are physically strong and athletic. Terry (6-6, 210 pounds) averaged 27.5 points and 12.3 rebounds at Carl Albert (Okla.) JC. The previous year he was an all-conference wide receiver at Tyler (Tex.) JC. Terry was considered one of Texas' top athletes in both sports his senior season at Hughes Springs HS. Ware (6-7, 215 pounds) averaged 18.3 points and 10.4 rebounds at Central Florida JC, the same school that produced Tony Milton. He was a JC honorable mention All-America selection last season by *Blue Ribbon College Basketball Yearbook*. Ware is originally from Crane HS in Chicago.

Shedrick Anderson is a wide-bodied 6-8 junior transfer from Delgado (La.) JC who might be A&M's best possibility in the post. Anderson averaged 19 points and 10 rebounds per game at Delgado.

Another senior transfer, **Maurice Sanders** (8.1 ppg, 6.5 rpg), is a nice 6-5 addition from Marshall but is hardly a player to build around.

Sophomore **Chris Finley** (1.1 ppg, 1.2 rpg) has Mississippi roots like his new coach but the slender 6-10 center is not likely to fit into Davis' plans despite being the tallest Aggie. Finley didn't letter as a freshman and prefers to shoot from outside rather than hang inside.

BLUE RIBBON ANALYSIS

The general consensus is that any Aggie revival will have to wait until at least next year when two Big East transfers —Scott and Edwards—become available. Davis could make some waves behind the SWC's top three —Arkansas, Texas and Houston —but won't be able to nose out any of them for a top spot in the standings.

He did extremely well with a late start in recruiting and will be able to run with any team with a good stable of guards. But Davis will probably have to coach a three-guard, two-forward offense which is a change for him. The Aggies' best hopes to have a winning season rest with the two junior college transfer forwards. If they are athletic and physical at the Division I level, Texas A&M could hurt the generally inside weak SWC. Pencil the Aggies in for fifth.

Davis should win support at tradition-oriented Texas A&M for his decision to start a sixth man at home games that would be a variation of the 12th man tradition of the Aggies' football squad. He plans to have three walk-on players and will let one of them start each home game and play until the opposing team scores its first basket.

TEXAS ARLINGTON

LAST SEASON: 13-16
CONFERENCE RECORD: 6-8
STARTERS LOST: 3
STARTERS RETURNING: 2
CONFERENCE: SOUTHLAND (SWC)
LOCATION: ARLINGTON, TX
HOME FLOOR: TEXAS HALL (4,200)
NICKNAME: MAVERICKS
COLORS: ROYAL BLUE AND WHITE
COACH: MARK NIXON, record at Texas-Arlington, 35-50.

Recent history has not been kind to Texas-Arlington's basketball program. The Mavericks have not enjoyed a winning season since the 1981-82 season, the last time UTA finished in the upper tier of the Southland Conference. But with three starters returning and a host of high scoring junior college transfers coming aboard, a winning season seems to be well within the grasp of the Mavericks in 1990-91.

Heading the list of returning starters is 6-2 senior **Willie Brand**, the most complete guard in the Southland Conference. Brand (18.0 ppg, 4.1 rpg, 61 assists, 5 blocked shots, 30 steals) earned second-team All-Southland Conference honors last season and has already become the school's all-time leading scorer with 1,502 points in three seasons. Brand scored a season high 39 points last year against Prairie View A&M and scored 30 or more points in three other games.

Junior **Bobby Kenyon**, 6-9, responded after being thrust into the starting lineup in the Mavericks' final nine games with a shooting touch around the hole, tallied 19 points and 15 rebounds in the semifinals of the Southland Conference post-season tournament against regular season champion Northeast Louisiana. Kenyon finished the year with 7.4 points and 3.8 rebound averages.

Junior forward **David Allen** (6-6, 9.0 ppg, 6.2 rpg, 34 assists, 8 blocked shots, 23 steals) was a part-time starter last year. Allen was the Mavericks' second leading scorer and rebounder last year. He led Texas-Arlington in rebounding in 11 games in 1989-90. Another letterman returning is 6-6 junior **Ronnie Pruitt** (1.7 ppg).

In past years, as Brand went so went Texas Arlington. Hence, opponents place heavy emphasis on

stopping Brand. Nixon and his staff concentrated on adding firepower to the lineup, signing six junior college players and two high school players, in an effort to take some of the scoring burden off Brand.

"We needed some people to take the pressure off Willie," said Nixon. "With having other people that can score, we feel like it will open things up for Willie."

Headlining the recruiting crop is 5-11 junior point guard **Glover Cody**, a second-team junior college All-America from Mid Plains (Neb.) JC. Cody averaged 19.5 points, 8.5 assists and 4.0 steals per game. Cody had a single game high of 36 points last season. "Glover is an outstanding point guard who could come in and help us right away," said Nixon.

Another impact player is 6-7 junior forward **Eric Gore**. He averaged 27.9 points and 9.2 rebounds per game last year for Western Nebraska JC. Gore had a single game high of 49 points and scored 30 or more points in 16 games last year. Gore hit 54.6 percent from the field, including 44.1 percent from three-point territory in the national junior college tournament. "Eric had a great season last year and he's just what we needed for the power forward position. He can score and rebound," Nixon said.

The other JC signees will contribute. Junior **Robert Mays**, 6-3, will likely back up Brand at guard. Mays averaged 18 points and four rebounds for Mississippi (Ark.) County JC. A member of the Super Team for the state of Arkansas as a prep player, Mays was named the MVP of the Arkansas Junior College League. **Leonard Wilson**, a 6-5 sophomore forward, earned Wyoming All-Conference honors, by averaging 18 points and nine rebounds per game for Casper JC. **Keylian Williams**, a 6-2 sophomore transfer from Seminole (Okla.) JC will understudy Cody at point guard, while 6-4 junior wing **Daniel Baker** from Paris (Tex.) JC will be expected to fill the role of defensive stopper. Another transfer, 6-9 junior **Jerry Neal** who sat out last year after transferring from Texas A&M, will serve as a backup post.

Both freshmen signees earned impressive credentials in Georgia. **Sheldon O'Neal**, a 6-6 forward, was named the Heart of Georgia player of the year, after averaging 21.7 points and 10.3 rebounds per game for East Laurens HS in Dublin, Ga. Like O'Neal, 6-0 point guard **Rodney Hutchinson** earned first-team all-state honors. Hutchinson posted 17.1 ppg, 7.3 apg, 4.1 rpg numbers for Monroe HS in Albany, Ga.

BLUE RIBBON ANALYSIS

The lean years appear to be over at Texas-Arlington. Blessed with a solid nucleus of returnees and, on paper, the best recruiting class in the league, Texas Arlington appears to be poised to move up in the Southland Conference.

Blending the newcomers in with the lies of Brand and Kenyon may take time, but the pre-conference schedule is favorable. If Cody and Gore live up to their billings, Texas-Arlington should finish second to defending champion Northeast Louisiana in the 1990-91 race.

TEXAS CHRISTIAN

LAST SEASON: 16-13
CONFERENCE RECORD: 9-7
STARTERS LOST: 2
STARTERS RETURNING: 3
CONFERENCE: SOUTHWEST (SWC)
LOCATION: FORT WORTH, TX
HOME FLOOR: DANIEL-MEYER COLISEUM (7,166)
NICKNAME: HORNED FROGS
COLORS: PURPLE AND WHITE
COACH: MOE IBA, record at Texas Christian, 42-45. Career record, 186-180.

Coach Moe Iba's 13-year career record is a little better than .500 —186-180. That will probably be the same fate for the Texas Christian Horned Frogs in his fourth season. The Horned Frogs suffered from a high turnover —seven players left since the beginning of the previous season for a variety of reasons —and there were only five scholarship players on campus last spring. But they still will have a competitive team capable of upsetting some of the Southwest Conference's more glamorous favorites because Iba has assembled the type of players to run his defensive-oriented, controlled-tempo, half court style.

''We're not as athletic as we were a year ago,'' Iba said. ''But we have better players. We will be a better shooting ballclub, dribble better and handle the ball better. We have players who are fundamentally better basketball players.''

Junior center Reggie Smith is a reason Iba wants to slow the tempo. The 6-10, 240-pounder has shown flashes of what could be a dominating player. He averaged 10.5 points and 6.2 rebounds last season and had a 1.3 blocks per game average. Smith is strong, he had 25 dunks last season, and could cause big problems for the rest of the SWC which has concentrated on faster guards and forwards. Iba even has an experienced backup in 6-8 senior center Ed Fromayan (2.4 ppg, 1.1 rpg), who has played well sporadically. Incoming freshman Bobby Frain is expected to be able to contribute. The 6-10, 230-pounder (14.0 ppg, 14.0 rpg at Klein Forest HS, Houston) was recruited by several top schools and is not viewed as a project type.

The Horned Frogs lost their most athletic player, forward Craig Sibley (13.9 ppg, 6.6 rpg), who started the last two years after transferring from a junior college. Two junior college newcomers are hoped to be

ready as immediate replacements. Mark Moten is from Santa Monica (Calif.) JC and led his team in both scoring (15.6 ppg) and rebounding (8.0). The 6-7 junior forward is solid defensively, on the boards and as a shooter —the all-around steady, if not spectacular, player that Iba seeks. Jody Bentley (19.0 ppg, 8.0 rpg at Aquinas (Tenn.) JC) fits much the same mold although his strength leans more toward shooting. The 6-6 junior swingman can go to off-guard and give Iba a matchup to exploit. He shot 54 percent from the field last season and 82 percent from the line. He hit 70-of-184 from three-point range for a respectable 38 percent.

Iba's problem is that he has little other options at forward except Moten or Bentley. The Horned Frogs have eight guards and three centers for the rest of their 13-man roster.

Senior Kelvin Crawford will likely start at point and while he's not a great playmaker, he is very good defensively. At 6-2, he can go inside for rebounds (4.3 rpg) which helps slow opponents' fast breaks. Crawford (6.3 ppg) started all 29 of Texas Christian's games last season. Transfer Albert Thomas of Moberly (Mo.) Area JC is hoped to be good enough to challenge Crawford. The 6-2 junior guard had 5.2 assists and 3.1 steals per game last season as well as averaging 17.9 points. He set a school record for career three-pointers (142) at Moberly, which reached the NJCAA Region XVI playoffs.

Dan Dore, from Fajardo, Puerto Rico, showed ballhandling skills the last two years at Central Florida CC in Ocala. The 6-3 junior college transfer (13.5 ppg, 2.7 rpg, 2.0 apg) could work himself into the point guard rotation. Walk-ons Mike Mitchell (6-1) and 5-8 Ernie Morgan are both juniors and saw limited action last year.

Sporadic 6-4 junior swingman Michael Strickland returns at shooting guard. Strickland (13.2 ppg, 3.0 rpg) set a Texas Christian record with 93 three-pointers (93-of-233), which is also the second highest single season SWC total. Strickland and Texas Christian's highlight of last season was his 9 three-pointers in an 81-79 upset of Arkansas. Connecting on 9-of-12, Strickland tied the SWC single game record. He also had 8 three-pointers against Houston, seven against Mississippi Valley State and six vs. Texas Tech. He came from the same school as Dore, Central Florida CC in Ocala. Allen Tolley is a 6-5 sophomore (1.7 ppg), whom Texas Christian coaches still hope can continue to develop into a solid off-guard.

For the future, Iba also added two freshmen guards —6-4 David Preston (19.7 ppg at Macarthur HS in Houston) and 6-2 Ken Fiedler (18.0 ppg, 5.0 rpg, 4.1 apg at Fremd HS, Palatine, Ill.). Preston may redshirt. Fiedler could see some time at the point.

BLUE RIBBON ANALYSIS

Neither of the Ibas, Moe or his cousin Gene at Baylor, are dropping their basketball heritage to join the run-and-shoot styles that Arkansas and Texas have used to gain national prominence. And that may be the best tactic they can employ if not the best way to sell tickets.

Texas Christian cannot recruit the same athletes in a head-to-head battle with Arkansas and Texas so the Horned Frogs wouldn't win many battles that mostly pitted athletic ability. Iba causes those thoroughbreds problems the old fashioned way. Texas Christian beat Arkansas last season and gave Texas fits, losing once by three and another by eight.

Iba will run the same system and may even have better players for doing it this season. The Horned Frogs may be a surprise to the SWC and be the best team to challenge Arkansas, Texas and Houston for the upper division and a probable fourth place finish. The key will be transfer forwards Bentley and Moten stepping in immediately to a high level of play. A strong season by Smith in the post could take Texas Christian into a post-season tournament.

TEXAS-PAN AMERICAN

LAST SEASON: 21-9
CONFERENCE RECORD: 7-3
STARTERS LOST: 4
STARTERS RETURNING: 1
CONFERENCE: AMERICAN SOUTH (ASC)
LOCATION: EDINBURG, TX
HOME FLOOR: PAN AMERICAN FIELDHOUSE (5,500)
NICKNAME: BRONCOS
COLORS: GREEN, WHITE & ORANGE
COACH: KEVIN WALL, record at Texas Pan American, 66-48. Career record, 123-72.

One of the better kept secrets and more interesting programs in college basketball is Texas-Pan American. This institution is located in Edinburg, Tex., some 225 miles south of San Antonio at the mouth of the Rio Grande River. The area is isolated, subtropical, and you'll never see snow in Edinburg in the winter, just palm trees and citrus orchards. Texas-Pan American has one of the largest Hispanic populations of any university —80 percent of the student body.

The Texas-Pan American basketball program has had some well known coaches in the past, such as Abe Lemons and Lon Kruger. While current Bronco mentor Kevin Wall is presently not as well known as Lemons and Kruger, he may be in a few years if he keeps building a reputation as a coach who gets the most out of his material. In fact, Wall and New Orleans coach Tim Floyd are generally regarded as the two best coaches in the up-and-coming American South Conference.

In the first three years the American South Conference has been in existence, Wall has captured two conference coach of the year honors. The Broncos are a team that is annually picked to finish in the lower division of the ASC but generally seems to be more successful. Last year, it was the same story as Texas-Pan American was picked to finish in the lower division of the ASC, but instead posted a 21-9 record, including a strong 12-1 mark at home, and finished third in the regular season race and reached the finals of the post-season tournament, losing 48-44 to New Orleans. The 21 wins were the most by a Pan American team in 12 years and the most ever victories over NCAA Division I competition.

Wall, though, faces a rebuilding job after losing four starters and two top substitutes from last year's team.

"The fact that we will have 10 players on our roster that have never played Division I basketball puts in perspective the job that lies ahead," said Wall. "We're going to be inexperienced, but that doesn't mean we're not going to be good."

Wall will be hard pressed to replace 6-7 Melvin Thomas, the team's leading scorer with a 19-point average last year. Thomas, who also led the Texas-Pan American in rebounding, earned first team All-ASC honors and, in Wall's opinion was the conference MVP. Also gone are starting forward Fred Young (13.1 ppg, 6.1 rpg, 53 assists, 30 steals), starting guards Keith Campbell (10.2 ppg) and Clyde Davis (5.8 ppg) plus key reserves Brett Andrick (9.5 ppg) and Jarrod Harrell (2.8 ppg). Campbell, Davis, Andrick and Harrell all exhausted their eligibility while Young was expected to return for his senior year, but over the summer was accepted into the Houston Police Academy. Young was the Broncos' second leading scorer and rebounder, but his departure is not a major blow to the program. He was inconsistent and the team's worst defensive player.

Only one starter and a total of four lettermen are returning. The lone returning starter is 6-9 sophomore center Chris Jones (5.9 ppg, 4.9 rpg, 10 assists, 22 blocked shots, 13 steals). Jones started 26 games last year and had highs of 20 points and 17 rebounds last year.

6-2 senior off-guard Gabriel Valdez (11.0 ppg, 2.2 rpg, 115 assists, 42 steals) is expected to move into the starting lineup after performing admirably as the Broncos' sixth man last year. He made 27 consecutive free throws which broke a 20-year-old school record.

6-2 senior Arturo Ormond (0.9 ppg, 0.3 rpg) is a strong candidate for the starting point guard position.

"He's made great strides," said Wall of Ormond. "He was a junior college transfer last year and the hardest position for a junior college transfer to handle is point guard. He's probably the best athlete we have."

Randy Henderson, a 6-7 sophomore forward, averaged 0.7 points and 1.0 rebounds in backing up Melvin Thomas. He is the least experienced of the four returning lettermen.

Texas-Pan American has 10 players on the roster who have never played a minute of Division I basketball before. How well Wall can get them ready to handle the rigors of the American South Conference is the key to the season.

Two players —6-7 sophomore forward Henry Thomas and 6-0 sophomore Francisco "Paco" Siller, sat out last year at Texas-Pan American. Thomas averaged 19.3 points and 14 rebounds per game as a high school senior and he has an uncanny knack for scoring inside in traffic. He could move into the position that Melvin Thomas occupied last year. Siller hails from Saitillo, Mexico (which is 200 miles west of Edinburg) and is a former walk-on who improved his English in order to play for the Broncos. He is talented and could end up in the starting backcourt along with Valdez, which would give the Broncos probably the only All-Hispanic starting backcourt in Division I basketball.

Wall picked up three junior college transfers who offer different skills. 6-5 junior forward Jerome Chambers is an inside scorer and rebounder who averaged 16 points and eight rebounds per game at State Fair (Mo.) JC. 6-8 junior Derek Wright is more adept on the wing and shooting the three-pointer. Wright averaged 13 points and seven rebounds per game last year for Northeast Oklahoma JC. The third junior college transfer, David Johnson, is a 6-6 junior small forward. He averaged 13 points and seven rebounds per game last year for Westark (Ark.) JC. Johnson runs the floor well and is an excellent defender.

"We really think Chambers and Wright can come in and have an impact," said Wall. "In fact, if they both come through, we could move them into the forward position."

Wall is banking on his freshman class to add quality depth at the guard positions. 6-3 Travis Harris, 6-1 Oliver Harrison and 6-1 Desi Howard will all contend for playing time at the off-guard position. Harris, an excellent athlete, averaged 13 points and six rebounds per game at Central HS in Beaumont, Tex. Harrison, who can play either guard position, averaged 25 points and seven rebounds per game at St. Ignatius Prep in San Francisco, Calif. Howard, who is deadly from three-point range and beyond, averaged 26 points and 11 rebounds per game at Kountz (Tex.) HS.

Two other freshmen will compete at the small forward position. 6-4 Reuben Fatheree averaged 24 points and 12 rebounds for Nixon (Tex.) Smiley HS. He is a cousin of former Bronco and NBA star Luke Jackson. Fatheree must make the conversion from power forward to small forward. 6-4 Alvin Langley averaged 17.0 ppg and 7.0 rebounds per game at C. E. King HS in Houston, Tex. He is a native American Indian who is a great dunker.

BLUE RIBBON ANALYSIS

Kevin Wall has built a solid program at Texas Pan American. His Broncos have made a habit of finishing higher than expected in the American South Conference race. His school has a small gym and the Broncos have a strong student following, therefore, the Texas-Pan American advantage at home is considerable. Last year the Broncos were 12-1 at home and could be nearly as tough this year.

However, this is not a good year to be in a rebuilding mode in the American South Conference. Southwestern Louisiana, New Orleans and Louisiana Tech are all capable of winning 20 or more games this year and advancing to post-season play. They seem to be a cut above the rest of the conference.

Texas-Pan American looks a second division team on paper, but on the court, it could be another matter. Look for the Broncos to be more than competitive under Wall, despite the loss of four starters, and fight it out with Arkansas State for fourth place in the competitive American South Conference.

1990-91 TEXAS PAN-AMERICAN SCHEDULE

Nov.	24	Grambling State (LA)
	26	Texas-San Antonio
Dec.	1	@Missouri-Kansas City
	3	@Texas Tech
	7-8	#Longhorn Classic
	15	Colorado State
	19	@Texas-San Antonio
	22	Tulane
	30	@Missouri
Jan.	5	@Lamar
	7	@Maine
	12	Central Florida
	17	@Southwestern Louisiana
	19	@New Orleans
	21	@Southern Mississippi
	24	Arkansas State
	26	Louisiana Tech
	28	@Grambling State
Feb.	2	Lamar

1990-91 TEXAS PAN-AMERICAN SCHEDULE Cont.

Feb.	7	@Central Florida
	12	Southwestern Louisiana
	16	New Orleans
	18	Southern Mississippi
	21	@Arkansas State
	23	@Louisiana Tech
	25	Missouri-Kansas City
Mar.	1-3	##American South Conference Tournament

@ Road Games
# Austin, TX (Loyola College, Sam Houston State & Texas)
Site to be announced.

TEXAS SAN ANTONIO

LAST SEASON: 22-7
CONFERENCE RECORD: 14-4
STARTERS LOST: 2
STARTERS RETURNING: 3
CONFERENCE: TRANS AMERICA ATHLETIC (TAAC)
LOCATION: SAN ANTONIO, TX
HOME FLOOR: CONVOCATION CENTER (5,100)
NICKNAME: ROADRUNNERS
COLORS: ORANGE, NAVY BLUE AND WHITE
COACH: STU STARNER, first year at Texas-San Antonio.
Career record, 110-95.

The veteran Roadrunners would like nothing more than to make their swan song in the Trans America Athletic Conference a catchy little tune that lands them in the NCAA tournament. They've got a choir on hand that could give it a shot.

Texas-San Antonio, which next season joins the Southland Conference, returns three starters from a squad that went 22-7 and finished second in the TAAC. The Roadrunners also return four of their six double-figure scorers and three of the top three-point shooters in the league.

About the only thing they don't return is their coach. In one of those little twists of irony that characterizes TAAC life, Ken Burmeister left the Roadrunners to become an assistant at DePaul. That job became open when fellow conference member Arkansas-Little Rock hired Jim Platt away from the Blue Demons as its head coach.

Replacing Burmeister is Stu Starner, who won 110 games in seven seasons at Montana State. Starner is expected to transform the Roadrunners into exactly that - a running, gunning, pressing team.

Of course, that is also the hand he has been dealt. The graduation losses of forward Bruce Wheatley (13.9 ppg, 9.9 rpg) and center Tim Faulkner (11.4 ppg, 5.9 rpg) took most of Texas-San Antonio's inside scoring punch, as well as about a third of its rebounding power.

What's left, though, is not bad. A quintet of shooters - 6-0 senior Darryl Eaton (15.6 ppg, 2.8 rpg, 78 assists, 47 steals, .456 three-point percentage), 5-11 senior Mike Mason (13.9 ppg, 1.7 rpg, 81 assists, 52 steals), 6-4 junior Keith Horne (11.9 ppg, 3.9 rpg, 42 assists, 35 steals, .400 three-point percentage), 6-2 junior Ronnie Ellison (10.5 ppg, 3.2 rpg, 75 assists) and 6-2 senior Preston Ivory (7.8 ppg, 3.3

rpg, .374 three-point percentage) - will be counted on to handle the bulk of the scoring in the Roadrunners' three-guard attack. The five combined for all but one of the team's 199 three-pointers a year ago.

"You wouldn't want to get into an outside scoring duel with them," said one TAAC assistant coach. "They've got guys who were consistent last year and the year before. There's no reason to think they won't be consistent again."

Even more depth in the backcourt will be provided by 6-4 transfer **Thatcher Decker** (Allen County CC/Iola, Kan.) and 6-1 freshman **Troy House** (Ingram, Tex.). House is the all-time Texas schoolboy scoring leader with 4,259 points. Last season, he averaged 40 points per game for state champion Tom Moore High.

The frontcourt for the Roadrunners is as shallow as the backcourt is deep. The absence of Wheatley and Faulkner leave no proven rebounders. Junior **Taju Olajawon** (3.0 ppg, 2.9 rpg), the 6-7 younger brother of Houston Rockets' center Akeem Olajuwon, will be counted on heavily to provide inside muscle. Another junior, 6-8 **Albert Tilman** (1.3 ppg, 1.7 rpg), will battle 6-6 senior **Willie Newson** (1.9 ppg, 1.6 rpg) for the second inside spot.

6-8 transfer **Craig Walker** (Brevard CC/Sandford, Fla.) will also get a chance inside, along with 6-9 freshman **Ken Washington** (Pine Bluff HS/Pine Bluff, Ark.) and 6-6 freshman **Jamell Swader** (Eisenhower HS/Blue Island, Ill.).

BLUE RIBBON ANALYSIS

Because of an unproven frontcourt, Starner will have to put a team on the floor that can create most of its baskets in transition. The key figure may be Horne, a potential swingman who showed flashes of brilliance last year. In a road win over TAAC champion Centenary, he dominated play with a 25-point, 13-rebound effort.

Texas-San Antonio could use a slew of games like that to offset its positional imbalance. The TAAC at least allows teams to dominate from the perimeter, which is what the Roadrunners will have to do.

There is plenty of backcourt scoring to go around. If Olajuwon and the newcomers can at least hold their own up front, Texas-San Antonio should remain in the first division of the Trans America Athletic Conference.

TEXAS SOUTHERN

Robert Moreland liked what happened last season to himself and to his Texas Southern basketball team. This year, however, could be a different matter.

"Last season, we won the Southwestern Athletic Conference tournament and got the automatic bid to the NCAA's," said Moreland, whose Tigers were runner-up to Southern during the SWAC regular season. "It was our first trip to the NCAA tournament, and we're anxious to get back."

Moreland and the Tigers, however, will find the trip a bit rougher this time around. Four starters and the number one sub are gone from a team that finished 10-4 in league play and 19-12 for the season. What's more, the SWAC tourney winner will have to play the Big South Conference champion for a berth in the NCAA's.

"We lost five highly important people from our 1989-90 squad, and they'll be hard to replace," Moreland understated. "The good news is we'll have three kids returning who had considerable playing time last season. In addition, we'll have a couple of redshirts. We also signed a couple of freshmen who could help us."

Gone from last year's team are forwards Charles Price (20.0 ppg, 9.2 rpg) and Fred West (18.0 ppg, 8.4 rpg), along with guards Darrion Applewhite (13.5 ppg, 5.6 rpg, 134 assists) and Michael Brooks (2.5 ppg, 2.6 rpg). Also gone from last season is the Tigers' ace sixth man, guard Tony Gatlin (4.5 ppg, 77 assists). To put it mildly, that's a whole lot of production.

The most experienced returnees are 6-4 senior off guard **Ray Younger** and 6-7 senior center **Charles Parker**. Younger was the only full-time starter, averaging 14.3 points, 4.1 assists and 1.8 steals. Parker (5.5 ppg, 5.6 rpg) started 15 times. Also back with some experience are 6-0 sophomore point guard **Keith Armwood** (2.1 ppg) and 6-7 senior forward **Raoul Collins** (4.5 ppg, 2.8 rpg).

The only other returning lettermen are a pair of junior guards. 6-0 **Sean Gibson** (3.1 ppg) and 6-1 **Chris Tatum** (0.6 ppg) got into 15 games between them.

Moreland may get some help from a pair of reshirts. 6-7 junior **David Arceneaux** could step in and help Parker in the middle. 6-1 freshman guard **Derrick Butler** (Baton Rouge, La.) adds scoring punch to a backcourt that lost plenty of it.

More likely to contribute right away are a trio of JC transfers. 6-7 forward **Scott Davis** (11 points, eight rebounds) comes from South Plains (Okla.) JC; 6-4 swingman **Billy Joe Jefferson** (25 points, nine rebounds) posted high numbers at Lawson State (Ala.) College; and 6-0 guard **Tyrone Sillman** (13 points, nine rebounds) was also a solid performer at Lawson State.

Help from an unlikely source may also be available in the person of 6-2 senior guard **Michael Ervin**. Ervin tallied 14.0 points per game last year at Prairie View before that fellow SWAC member shut down all its varsity sports except track. Prairie View has since reinstated basketball, and there was some question as to where Ervin would play (see *Late Breaking News* section).

"I think it's going to be difficult to replace the players we lost," said Moreland. "This year, we'll need more of a team effort from all our guys. Last year, we counted more on individual performances. We won't be fortunate enough to do that this year.

"Our first four or five players will be okay, but I'm not sure after that. We also won't be as strong off the bench as we were last year. Our first team, though, could play a lot of people tough."

Texas Southern has other talent to look forward to down the road. A pair of freshmen - **Dwayne Price** (Baker HS/Baker, La.) and **Henry Briggs** (Glen Oaks HS/Baton Rouge, La.) - are athletic enough to play the high-octane SWAC game. Price is the younger brother of last year's leading scorer, Charles Price. Both are 6-5 forwards.

"These kids probably won't start, but they can play for us this season," Moreland said. "They'll have to be role players and wait for their chances. They'll play some this year. Later down the line, they'll be able to help us a lot."

BLUE RIBBON ANALYSIS

Give credit where it is due. Texas Southern used a tremendous stretch drive - winning its final six SWAC games - to dethrone Southern University and end the Jaguars' three-year stranglehold on the Southwestern Athletic Conference championship.

It was a home-grown title, however. The Tigers hosted last season's SWAC tournament, and used that fact to full advantage when it counted. It is an advantage that repeats in 1990-91, as the conference again returns to Houston for its post-season bash.

But not even the homecourt can replace four starters. The Tigers are a shell of what they were a year ago. Price and West, in particular, gave Texas Southern the kind of inside consistency rarely seen in the lesser conferences.

Replacing them will be the most difficult assignment for Moreland, as the reshaped backcourt should come together nicely behind Younger. The building process will not be painfully slow, just slow enough to prevent a repeat championship.

The Tigers figure to slip a notch - to third or fourth - in the SWAC this season.

TEXAS TECH

LAST SEASON: 5-22
CONFERENCE
RECORD: 0-16
STARTERS LOST: 2
STARTERS
RETURNING: 3
CONFERENCE:
SOUTHWEST (SWC)
LOCATION:
LUBBOCK, TX
HOME FLOOR:
LUBBOCK MUNICIPAL
COLISEUM (8,174)
NICKNAME: RED RAIDERS
COLORS: SCARLET AND BLACK
COACH: GERALD MYERS, record at Texas Tech,
318-238.
Career record, 350-281.

Texas Tech gave coach Gerald Myers a supreme vote of confidence last year —giving the popular Tech alumnus a four-year contract extension midway through a season that ended with a winless Southwest Conference record (0-16) and an 18-game losing streak. The move was made to quell speculation that Myers would be fired with one year left on his contract and help spur a turnaround of a program that won its last SWC title six years ago under Myers. The Red Raiders have suffered recently after signing several prospects who didn't pan out and by a series of academic casualties. Texas Tech has even lost two returning starters: James Johnson (3.6 ppg, 3.4 rpg) and Cleveland Phelps (6.1 ppg, 1.6 rpg) to grades for this season.

The support for Myers is based in his past success at Tech that has largely come despite not having the benefit of highly regarded players. The Red Raiders do have a talented forward returning in 6-7 sophomore **Will Flemons** and hope to find the right mix among nine newcomers.

Flemons (11.4 ppg) became only the third freshman in league history to lead the SWC in rebounding last season with a 10.0 per game average. His 23 rebounds against Houston were the most by any SWC player since Houston's Akeem Olajuwon had 25 against Texas Tech in 1984. The 225 pound Flemons isn't so much a high leaper as he is a hard worker for position inside. He also seems to have the uncoachable act of timing.

Flemons was remarkably consistent for a freshman —getting 12 double-double in points and rebounds. He was a West Texas hero in high school as he led Class A Paducah to consecutive state titles and a 127-7 record during his tenure, including winning its last 49 games.

Extending Myers' contract was also a way to keep Flemons, who had been rumored to be interested in transferring to Arizona. His decision to remain at Texas Tech in the off-season is the main reason there is hope for the future.

Myers would like to have recruited more inside help for Flemons, but was hurt so much on the perimeter last season that he signed mostly guards.

Senior **Steve Miles** (6.3 ppg, 4.6 rpg) returns as a three-year letterman and has been a part-time starter. The slender 6-8, 210-pounder arrived at Texas Tech with high expectations from Dallas but has not been able to consistently handle the more physical play of college. He'll likely start alongside Flemons since Texas Tech has only three redshirted forwards for depth: 6-6 freshman **Brad Dale**, 6-5 junior **Wes Dawson** and 6-8 sophomore **Kraig Smith**.

The future hope for inside help comes from in coming freshmen 6-7 forward **Mike Brewer** (20.0 ppg, 11.0 rpg at Clovis (N.M.) HS) and 6-9 center **Jeremy Lane** (13.0 ppg, 7.0 rpg at Irondale HS, Minneapolis, Minn.).

Myers thinks he got a steal on Lane but it's hard to determine just how good he could be if he was taken out of Big Ten country by the SWC's last place team. Besides, Myers' record in recruiting "project" big men has been poor lately.

Texas Tech's more immediate need is at guard and Myers will start the season with four newcomers to try to improve on last season's 18.8 turnover average per game. 6-5 senior **Derek Butts** returns as the Red Raiders' leading scorer (11.6 ppg) and he could be a good off-guard, hitting on 42.1 percent of his three-pointers. His weak ballhandling, though, might make him a better small forward. Sophomore **Barron Brown** emerged late in the season to show promise. He ended the season with 21 points against Texas A&M. Tech tried him at point guard but he might be better at the second guard position. The 6-3 Brown was a high school teammate of Duke's promising sophomore Thomas Hill.

Two more shooting guards will help the Red Raiders matchup in the perimeter-oriented SWC. **Stacy Bailey** is a 6-2 junior college transfer from Western Wyoming who averaged 25 points per game and led his team to the regional round of the NJCAA playoffs. Bailey's scoring ability has been consistent throughout his career, going back to his days as a star at Berkeley (Calif.) HS. But he has also had disciplinary problems. Tech's situation apparently made him worth the risk.

Lamont Dale is another key athletic transfer. He is from Hagerstown (Md.) JC where he played all five positions. The versatile 6-3 junior could be a solid role player for the Red Raiders.

Texas Tech hopes its search for a point guard will end with 6-1 **Bryant Moore** from Mesa (Ariz) CC. He averaged 6.0 ppg and five assists per game last season and would be a big help if he could start immediately. He was a good floor leader and defender for Mesa, which ended the regular season atop the national JC poll.

BLUE RIBBON ANALYSIS

The first assignment Texas Tech will have is putting an end to its current 18-game losing streak. It might not come quickly as the Raiders open in the Great Alaska Shootout on Nov. 23, with a field including Virginia and UCLA. The sooner Texas Tech can rid itself of that burden, the faster it can work toward having a better season.

There will still be pressure on Myers to improve, despite his extended contract. The 20-year Texas Tech coach probably never would have been fired outright. He still could be kicked upstairs to another position in the athletic department. Myers added some quality help in the off-season with assistant James Dickey, a long time protege of Eddie Sutton at Arkansas and Kentucky.

Flemons shows every sign of being a consistently good player and Texas Tech must find some help for him. Moore may be the smallest of the Red Raiders, but he probably plays the biggest role in fulfilling a void at point guard. Even if he does, Texas Tech will be a long way from rebuilding a conference contender. The Red Raiders will be lucky to finish above eighth this season.

1990-91 TEXAS TECH SCHEDULE

Nov.	23-26	#Great Alaska Shootout
Dec.	1	New Mexico
	3	Texas-Pan American
	5	Adams State (CO)
	13	Pepperdine
	15	@University of Portland
	19	Colorado State
	22	@New Mexico State
	28-29	##Sun Carnival

1990-91 TEXAS TECH SCHEDULE *Cont.*

Jan.	2	@Southern Methodist
	5	@Texas A&M
	9	Baylor
	12	Arkansas
	16	@Rice
	19	@Houston
	23	Texas
	26	Southern Illinois Edwardsville
	30	@Texas Christian
Feb.	2	Southern Methodist
	6	Texas A&M
	9	@Baylor
	13	@Arkansas
	16	Rice
	20	Houston
	23	@Texas
	25	Arkansas State
Mar.	2	Texas Christian
	7-10	*Southwest Conference Tournament

@ Road Games
# Anchorage, AK (Alaska-Anchorage, California-Irvine, Nevada, Siena, South Carolina, UCLA & Virginia)
El Paso, TX (Southwest Missouri State, UTEP & Washington)
* Dallas, TX

TOLEDO

LAST SEASON: 12-16
CONFERENCE
RECORD: 7-9
STARTERS LOST: 2
STARTERS
RETURNING: 3
CONFERENCE: MID-
AMERICAN (MAC)
LOCATION:
TOLEDO, OH
HOME FLOOR:
JOHN F. SAVAGE HALL (9,000)
NICKNAME: ROCKETS
COLORS: MIDNIGHT BLUE AND GOLD
COACH: JAY ECK, record at Toledo, 43-43.
Career record, 92-56.

Will Toledo fizzle once again in the Mid-American Conference? That question is hanging over the head of fourth-year coach Jay Eck, whose teams have earned a reputation for piling up non-conference victories, only to struggle when the MAC campaign begins.

Last year was no exception. Though the Rockets were only 5-7 in non-conference games, three of those triumphs came over Houston, Pittsburgh and Cincinnati - formidable foes to be sure. Furthermore, Toledo overcame a rocky start to win five of its last eight non-league contests. The run may have given the Rockets false hope, as they promptly dropped four of their first six MAC games to fall quickly from title contention.

"I was pleased with the effort and poise of our players," said Eck, "but we've failed to execute at times, both offensively and defensively. We've played brilliantly in some games and really struggled in others. Those types of things are going to happen when you're dealing with a young team."

This season, the Rockets can no longer be considered young. Three of Eck's top five scorers return, as well as six of his top nine players overall. Leading the pack of returnees, which numbers eight in all, is 6-6 senior forward **Craig Sutters** (13.8 ppg, 8.7 rpg, 39 steals).

Sutters is an inside force in a league where few players are taller than 6-7 or 6-8. He led the MAC in rebounding, ranked eighth in scoring, fourth in field goal percentage (.511), sixth in blocked shots (30) and ninth in steals (39). His value was underscored when a sprained ankle limited him to eight minutes in the

Rockets' MAC tourney opener versus Miami. Toledo lost by 28 points to a team it had beaten twice during the regular season.

Joining Sutters on the return fuselage are fellow starters **Keith Wade** (8.1 ppg, 2.4 rpg, 141 assists, 47 steals), the point guard, and 6-8 junior center **J.C. Harris** (6.7 ppg, 3.0 rpg, 33 blocked shots). Wade was second in the MAC in assists and fourth in steals, but could improve on his assists-to-turnover ratio, which figured to less than the two-to-one average desired by coaches from Toledo to Timbuktu.

Therein lies Wade's problem, and whether or not he can correct it could determine how well the Rockets fare this season. The 6-1 senior has shown flashes of brilliance and is unquestionably an outstanding passer, but he needs to play under better control and learn to steady the team as all good point guards do. Last season, Wade was simply too erratic.

Harris, meanwhile, possesses a nice touch for a big guy, especially from the top of the key. He seemed to come on late last season and should continue to improve as a factor inside, where he and Sutters provide considerable shot blocking ability and defensive intimidation.

Among the other returnees are 6-4 sophomore swingman **Jeff Regez** (5.3 ppg, 1.6 rpg), 6-8 sophomore forward **Tom Best** (3.7 ppg, 3.5 rpg) and 6-2 junior guard **Scott Riley** (2.7 ppg, 0.5 rpg), each of whom saw sporadic action last season because of varied injuries. Regez suffered a pre-season knee injury, came on strong in the middle of the year, then suffered a late-season injury to his elbow and saw his playing time diminish. Best was slowed early by a pulled groin muscle and twisted ankle, while Riley, a three-point specialist, missed 13 games after suffering a broken kneecap in the victory over Pittsburgh.

The remaining letterwinners back for this season are a pair of junior swingmen - 6-4 **Quenton Jordan** (1.2 ppg, 0.8 rpg) and 6-6 **Rick Rightnowar**. Rightnowar logs more minutes, as he is considered a hustling defensive specialist.

Three transfers, all from Kansas junior colleges, and two freshman recruits are on the scene to assist the returning talent. The JUCO transfers include 6-4 swingman **Corey Martin** (Allen County CC/Iola, Kan.), 6-0 guard **Kent Murphree** (Cowley County CC/Arkansas City, Kan.) and 6-8 junior forward **Fernando Righetto**, also from Cowley County CC but by way of Sao Paulo, Brazil.

Murphree, a sharpshooter with three-point range, is the best bet to help immediately. He averaged 23.8 points last season at Cowley County, and two years ago led the nation's junior colleges in free throw percentage (91.0) and was sixth in three-point percentage (54.0). His teammate at Cowley, Righetto (9.5 ppg, 5.5 rpg), can also shoot the trey and possesses an excellent outside touch for a man his size. Martin (8.0 points, 2.0 assists) was a teammate of Harris at Northrop HS (Fort Wayne, Ind.).

The freshmen recruits are 5-10 guard **James Heck** (17.5 points, 8.0 assists at nearby Rossford HS (Rossford, Ohio) and 6-9 center **Andy Schafer**, who played for DeVilbiss HS (Toledo) two years ago and subsequently drew national attention last summer while on a Toledo-based AAU team in Las Vegas. Local heroes both, it remains to be seen if or how much either can help the Rockets this season.

BLUE RIBBON ANALYSIS

Toledo's main problem has been discipline, or rather a lack thereof. The Rockets simply have suffered too many breakdowns offensively and defensively in recent years to be consistent.

Last year, Rocket opponents outshot them from the field (.469 to .464), the free throw line (.715 to .691), outrebounded them (35.0 to 32.7) and passed for far more assists (406 to 353). Though turnovers were virtually even between Toledo and its opponents (398 to 404), the Rockets remained guilty of throwing the ball away far too often. No team can consistently lose those statistical categories and expect to win more than half its games.

''This year,'' said Eck, ''we have more quality depth because of the experience that was gained last season. Our perimeter shooting and rebounding need to improve, and I feel that they will. In addition, we will work to increase our defensive intensity, and to be both physically and mentally tough.

''If we hadn't run into injury problems last year, we would have been able to weather our tough schedule with more consistency. We won some big games early, but then injuries really took their toll and forced us into some tough lineup situations.''

While there is some truth to Eck's complaints about injuries, Toledo's problems with inconsistency run deeper than that. With Sutters and Wade the only seniors on this team, can the Rockets be more disciplined and less mistake-prone on both ends of the court? Can they develop the mental toughness it takes to win on the road, where they were 1-11 last season?

All of that seems doubtful, so a .500 finish at best seems likely in the MAC. Anything less and Eck could be answering even harder questions after the season.

```
            1990-91 TOLEDO SCHEDULE
Nov.    23-25   #Maui Classic
         29     Prairie View A&M (TX)
Dec.     1      St. Mary's (MI)
         5      @Detroit
         8      @Nebraska
         15     Tennessee State
         20     Grambling State (LA)
         22     @Pitt
         28-29  ##MVP Holiday Classic
Jan.     2      @Kent State
         5      Ball State
         9      @Miami (OH)
         12     Western Michigan
         16     @Ohio University
         19     Central Michigan
         23     @Bowling Green
         26     Eastern Michigan
         29     Valparaiso (TN)
Feb.     2      @Ball State
         6      Miami (OH)
         9      @Western Michigan
         13     Ohio University
         16     @Central Michigan
         20     Bowling Green
         23     @Eastern Michigan
Mar.     2      Kent State
         4      Chicago State
         8-10   *MAC Tournament

@ Road Games
# Lahaina, HI (Chaminade, Indiana, Iowa State,
Loyola Marymount, Northeastern, Santa Clara &
Syracuse)
* Detroit, MI
```

TOWSON STATE

LAST SEASON: 18-13
CONFERENCE RECORD: 8-6
STARTERS LOST: 4
STARTERS RETURNING: 1
CONFERENCE: EAST COAST (ECC)
LOCATION: TOWSON, MD
HOME FLOOR: TOWSON CENTER (5,300)
NICKNAME: TIGERS
COLORS: GOLD, BLACK AND WHITE
COACH: TERRY TRUAX, record at Towson State, 90-115.

From the moment the NCAA tournament pairings were announced and Oklahoma forward Jackie Jones said, ''Tulsa, yeah, we played them, they're a physical team,'' you almost knew Towson State wouldn't roll over and play dead. No one, save the Tiger players themselves, dared think they could actually stay with the large and lightning quick Oklahoma Sooners for 40 minutes. Actually, the Tigers fell about two minutes short, which is when Oklahoma stretched a four-point lead to the final 77-68 margin.

That was then; this is now. The Towson State team that extended No. 1-ranked Oklahoma last March will be vastly different from the one that will take the court this season. And it's not just the loss of two-time East Coast Conference player of the year Kurk Lee that the Tigers will be missing. In addition to the 6-3 Lee (26.0 ppg, 4.6 rpg, 2.0 apg, 84 steals), Towson State loses three other senior starters. Kennell Jones (8.7 ppg, 6.8 rpg, 2.9 apg) and Kelly Williamson (10.9 ppg, 5.8 rpg, 2.2 apg) were a pair of 6-5 forwards, both two-year starters and, like Lee, transfers who had returned to their hometown to help put Towson State on the basketball map. Jones set a career field goal percentage record (.582). 6-8 center Mike Morin (4.0 ppg, 2.8 rpg) was the most expendable, but his tenacity in coming back after a two-year layoff was part of the grit that made the Tigers a good story.

The Tigers have replaced nine seniors over the last two seasons, but none had Lee's impact. Above all, it was Lee who led the Tigers to a two-year 37-23 mark and their only winning seasons in 11 years at the Division I level. His dipsy-doodle spinning shots and passes, his put-them-to-sleep-dribble-and-fire three-point shots, his willingness to scrap inside for rebounds and putbacks will be sorely missed.

What the Tigers do have is a couple of experienced guards and a young front line that is potentially exciting. 6-2 junior point guard **Devin Boyd** (11.7 ppg, 3.9 apg, 2.8 rpg) is the lone returning starter, although 5-10 senior **Lewis Waller** (7.1 ppg, 1.7 apg, 1.3 rpg) has had extensive playing time at both backcourt spots for three years, including a couple of starts. Boyd, a starter since the opening game of his freshman year, has been the team's assist leader and second leading scorer both seasons. He made the ECC all-tournament team last year after scoring 40 points and dishing out 19 assists, but he had a shaky game against Oklahoma (0-for-6 shooting). He'll need to erase that memory and give the Tigers more direction this year without Lee as his backcourt partner. Waller will move into Lee's spot. His shot selection (50 percent shooter) has improved each season, and last year he hit 50 percent of his three-pointers.

6-3 junior **Terrance Jacobs** (10.6 ppg, 8.0 apg, 6.6 rpg for Allegany, Md., CC) carries on a tradition of ex-Baltimore high school stars who left and came back, having played a year at Old Dominion before going to Allegany CC. He'll give coach Terry Truax flexibility and Boyd competition at the point. 6-3 junior **Myron Ray**, a former all-state pick from Wheeling (W.Va.) Park HS, becomes eligible after playing one year at St. Bonaventure and missing another with a broken wrist. He'll battle with 6-2 sophomore **Craig Valentine** (1.1 ppg), who saw spot duty in 24 games last year, for time at shooting guard. 6-1 junior **Mike Manns**, another local product (Towson Catholic HS) is eligible in January after transferring from Sheridan (Wyo.) JC.

At small forward, 6-5 junior **Chuck Lightening** (8.5 ppg, 3.5 rpg, 50 percent shooting) is the only returnee, but he could turn out to be all the Tigers need. A transfer from Maryland, Lightening wasn't supposed to play much last year, but his leaping ability and quickness forced Truax to use him and he made the ECC's all-rookie team. His take-no-prisoners dunk over two Oklahoma players in the NCAA Midwest Regionals let the Sooners know Towson State wouldn't go lightly. Behind Lightening are a pair of freshmen, 6-6 **Matt Campbell** and 6-5 **Andrew Mason**. Campbell (26.1 ppg, 16.4 rpg for Broadnack HS in Arnold,

Md) was an All-Metro pick by both Baltimore newspapers and the Anne Arundel County player of the year in the *Arundel Sun*, leading his team to the state regionals. Mason (20.5 ppg, 11.0 rpg, 3.0 blpg for Oxon Hill, Md., HS) is deceptively quick and may eventually move inside. He was an All-Prince George's County pick.

The power forward position is up for grabs between a sophomore and two freshmen. 6-7 **Larry Brown** (1.2 ppg, 1.4 rpg) is the lone holdover. He averaged better than six minutes a game in 24 contests, but needs to improve his shooting and his court presence to solidify the position. **John James**, 6-7, and **Tom Caldwell**, 6-8, figure to get playing time at the position as well. James (21.0 ppg, 18.0 rpg, 8.0 blpg) for St. Elizabeth's HS in Wilmington, Del.) was one of Delaware's Top 15 selections picked by state coaches and a second-team all-state pick by sportswriters. He shot 67 percent from the floor. Caldwell (13.9 ppg, 11.5 rpg for Bishop McCorristin HS in Trenton, N.J.) helped his 27-4 team to the New Jersey Parochial Class A championship after transferring from Petty Prep School.

Sophomores **William Griffin** and **Scott Heidler** return to man the post position. The 6-6 Griffin (1.9 ppg, 2.7 rpg) led the Tigers with 28 blocked shots while playing in all 31 games. He started eight games but at times looked timid. A year of seasoning should have toughened him. Knee problems prior to his freshman season forced Heidler, a stocky 6-8, to redshirt, and he came back last year still somewhat below full strength. He scored 20 points in 18 games with limited playing time. He could be the plug in the middle, but will need to improve his quickness.

BLUE RIBBON ANALYSIS

Truax is not bluffing when he says, ''The expectations should not be so high.'' Replacing Lee and the others and maintaining continuity will be difficult. For the players, trying to win the East Coast Conference will be tough enough. For the coaches, trying to keep the ECC alive will be a bigger challenge. Down to seven teams this year — Bucknell, Lafayette, and Lehigh left; Maryland-Baltimore County and Central Connecticut joined —the league will lose two more members after this season when Delaware and Drexel depart. That could spell the end of the conference, for with only five teams and no chance to make the NCAA tournament as a qualifier, there is little reason for these teams to stay banded together.

Towson State's hopes rely on the added toughness and maturity of Griffin and Lightening's ability to create a spark come conference tournament time. A tougher non-conference schedule (including Dayton, Syracuse, Alabama and Virginia) almost assures a .500 record at best, with a middle of the pack finish in the ECC.

TULANE

LAST SEASON: 4-24
CONFERENCE RECORD: 1-13
STARTERS LOST: 0
STARTERS RETURNING: 5
CONFERENCE: METRO
LOCATION: NEW ORLEANS, LA
HOME FLOOR: FOGELMAN ARENA (5,000)
NICKNAME: GREEN WAVE
COLORS: OLIVE GREEN AND SKY BLUE
COACH: PERRY CLARK, record at Tulane, 4-24.

So what if Tulane has no place to go but up? At least the Green Wave has a direction after Tulane's 4-24 re-entry last season into Division 1 basketball. Tulane basketball was back last season after a four-year absence due to point shaving and allegations that star player John ''Hot Rod'' Williams had been paid to sign at Tulane as well as paid to play there.

There wasn't much to cheer about last season in New Orleans, other than the fact the Green Wave program was breathing again. But there weren't too many times Tulane showed up and died. Tulane coach Perry Clark's team may not have been experienced, but it played hard and pushed opponents to the final buzzer. As Clark said, ''If we played horseshoes instead of basketball, we would have been champions because we were close all year.''

The Wave quickly earned the respect of other Metro Conference teams. Florida State coach Pat Kennedy said of Clark and Tulane, ''He constructed a competitive team. They played people tough. Games went down to the final minutes.''

Tulane had a magical Metro home debut when guard **Michael Christian** tossed in a three-pointer from somewhere in the vicinity of the French Quarter to beat highly-touted Metro foe Memphis State, 81-80.

''I really didn't know what to expect in my first year,'' Clark said. ''It was a mixed bag. I didn't want to pressure my players too much. I wanted everything to be a learning experience, to have a foundation for the program. We were competitive last year, and that was an accomplishment. But I'm not satisfied with being competitive. We have to move up to the next plateau.''

That may take a few years, but Clark's team is still young —there are eight sophomores and three freshmen signees on the 15-man roster.

One of those sophomores didn't play like a freshman last season — 6-9 center-forward **Anthony Reed** (18.4 ppg, 8.4 rpg). Reed was sixth in the Metro in scoring, second in rebounds and sixth in field goal percentage. He was an easy choice for the league's freshman player of the year, was second-team All-Metro and second-team freshman All-America by *Basketball Weekly*.

Reed wasn't a highly regarded high school

player, but Clark began to suspect he got a recruiting steal when Reed won ''Mr. Basketball'' honors at the 1989 Louisiana High School All-Star game. Reed played a fearless game in the middle. It was as if he almost expected to perform as well as he did against the likes of Louisville's Felton Spencer and Southern Mississippi's Clarence Weatherspoon.

Christian, a 6-3 senior, is the other part of Tulane's two-man game. A year ago, he averaged 19.3 points (third in the Metro) and was the Green Wave's designated long bomber. His shot selection was questionable at times, but Clark felt like Christian was the only consistent legitimate three-point threat. Christian and Reed became only the second duo in Tulane history to score more than 500 points each in the same year. Clark went the junior college route to get Christian, who Clark had recruited when he was an assistant at Georgia Tech.

Clark also recruited 6-5 guard-forward **David Whitmore** from Georgia Tech. Whitmore, who sat out last season at Tulane, will be ready to play this year. Whitmore, who averaged 5.2 points in nine games as a starter at Georgia Tech in 1988-89, was a *Parade Magazine* All-America at St. Bernard's HS in Playa del Ray, Calif. He is a sophomore eligible. Whitmore is a great leaper who needs to expand the rest of his game.

The Green Wave has a steady, not flashy group of guards. Junior **Greg Gary**, 6-2, is a true point guard (7.9 ppg) who was second in the Metro in assists (5.7 apg) and first in free throw shooting (87.2 percent). When Clark moved Gary into the starting lineup for the last 12 games, the Green Wave played more consistently.

When defenses began to gang up on Christian last year, **G. J. Hunter** came to the rescue. Hunter, a 6-3 sophomore, averaged 10.8 points, was third in the league in steals (2.2 stpg) and was eighth in the league in assists (3.1 apg). Other Tulane guards are 6-6 sophomore **Carter Nichols** (5.1 ppg), 5-10 sophomore **Bret Just** (0.0 ppg) and 6-4 freshman signee **Kim Lewis**, who averaged 32 points and 14 rebounds as Louisiana's Class AA player of the year at Varnado (La.) HS. Lewis attended the Nike/ABCD camp while in high school.

Tulane opened the season last year as a fast break team because Clark liked its entertainment value for a program trying to rebuild a fan base. Then, he realized he wasn't getting much defense from the fast break style. He backed off, went more to a half court offense and ordered his team to pick their spots to run the break.

Reed leads an inside game that has nice size and that hopefully learned valuable lessons last season. Sophomore **Pete Rasche** and **Matt Popp** started at times last season when Clark was trying to find the right combination. The 6-9 Popp (3.3 ppg, 2.1 rpg) spent much time in foul trouble, but replaced the 6-10 Rasche (3.2 ppg, 1.5 rpg) in the starting lineup late in the season. Senior 7-0 center **Joe Passi** (0.7 ppg) is slow and did little last season.

Clark is hoping he got a recruiting sleeper, like Reed, in 6-9 forward/center **Mekaba Perry** of Clinton (La.) HS, where he averaged 20 points and 18 rebounds as a senior in his only year of varsity basketball. Perry's father, John, played in the NBA for the Lakers and the Knicks.

The rest of the returning forwards are a hodgepodge of minimal talent. **Jerome Conner**, a 6-4 sophomore (4.3 ppg, 3.9 rpg) probably improved more than any Green Wave player last season. **Bernard Parks**, a 6-7 sophomore (1.2 ppg), had few moments of playing time or glory. Joining this group is 6-7 freshman signee **Carlin Hartman** of Grand Island (N.Y.) HS, who averaged 28 points and 14 rebounds as a senior.

BLUE RIBBON ANALYSIS

Clark, who was a super recruiter at Georgia Tech, is slowly building a nice talent base at Tulane.

One of the biggest surprises in the Metro last season was Tulane's competitiveness. The Green Wave rarely quit and had enough talent to hang with most teams through 30 minutes. A lack of depth usually did in Tulane late in tight games.

Reed and Christian provide a nice inside-outside balance. Reed's high-arcing jumpers from the lane will be a familiar site in the Metro for the next three years as he establishes himself as one of the league's best players. Christian provides the Green Wave with a three-point threat that always keeps them within striking distance.

The addition of Whitmore will raise the Tulane talent level, and Perry might be someone who will develop quicker than anticipated. Mired in the Metro cellar last season, Tulane crawls out past Virginia Tech and into seventh place this year. Look for the Green Wave to win at least 10 games as Clark continues to breathe life into a rejuvenated program.

Tulane already has earned back Metro respect. As one Metro Conference assistant said, "If the Hurricanes (potent drinks) at Pat O'Brien's (bar in the New Orleans French Quarter) don't get you, Tulane might."

1990-91 TULANE SCHEDULE

Nov.	23	Rice
	26	Nicholls State (LA)
Dec.	1	Wake Forest
	5	@Texas Christian
	8	Southern Methodist
	22	@Texas-Pan American
	27-28	#USF&G Sugar Bowl Tournament
	30	Columbia
Jan.	3	Florida State
	10	@Virginia Tech
	12	@Memphis State
	14	Louisville
	17	@Southern Mississippi
	20	@Hofstra (NY)
	21	@Northeastern
	24	Cincinnati
	28	New Orleans
	31	@South Carolina
Feb.	2	@Florida State
	7	Memphis State
	9	Virginia Tech
	14	South Carolina
	16	Southeastern Louisiana
	23	@Cincinnati
	26	@Louisville
Mar.	2	Southern Mississippi
	7-9	##Metro Conference Tournament

@ Road Games
# New Orleans, LA (Auburn, Georgia Tech & Villanova)
Roanoke, VA

TULSA

LAST SEASON: 17-13
CONFERENCE
RECORD: 9-5
STARTERS LOST: 1
STARTERS
RETURNING: 4
CONFERENCE:
MISSOURI VALLEY (MVC)
LOCATION: TULSA, OK
HOME FLOOR: MAXWELL CONVENTION CENTER (9,200)
NICKNAME: GOLDEN HURRICANE
COLORS: GOLD, ROYAL BLUE AND CRIMSON
COACH: J.D. BARNETT, record at Tulsa, 88-63. Career record, 271-163.

Piece by piece, J.D. Barnett has been rebuilding the Tulsa basketball program from the 8-20 debacle of two years ago. The finished product will take the court this season.

The Golden Hurricane, for the second year in a row, return four starters and nine letterwinners from a team that tied for second place in the Missouri Valley Conference. Tulsa is neither physically imposing nor extremely gifted in the shooting department, but the sum of its parts far exceeds the individual merits.

Some of the players who seemingly have been around forever are back for their final try at the brass ring. 6-5 senior **Wade Jenkins,** a center/forward, returns after earning honorable mention All-MVC honors last season. He scored 11.0 points per game, and finished among the MVC's top rebounders with a 6.8 average. Perhaps the top pound-for-pound rebounder in the conference, Jenkins missed the entire 1988-89 season due to a knee injury.

Michael Scott was on the MVC's all-defensive team for the second year in a row, although he did not repeat as the league's Defensive player of the year. Scott, a 6-5 senior, can defend inside players as well as guards and also averaged 8.1 points and 4.2 rebounds. This despite missing six games with spinal meningitis.

Marcel Gordon moved into the starting lineup last year after transferring from San Francisco City College. A 6-1 guard, Gordon led the Golden Hurricane with a 12.9 scoring average, 12th-best in the league. He also contributed 4.2 rebounds and was second in the league with 50 steals.

Another player who fit in quickly was 6-0 guard **Reggie Shields,** the MVC's newcomer of the year. Shields, a transfer from Polk (Fla.) CC, led the conference in both assists (147) and steals (51). He also scored 10.7 points per game and was an honorable mention All-MVC pick.

6-3 junior **Jamal West** started two years ago at point guard, averaging 11.1 points, 4.1 assists and 1.7 steals. But he missed all but four games last season due to a knee injury. West, a one-time member of the Tulsa football team, is back, but may find regaining his starting job a difficult task given the presence of Shields and Gordon in the backcourt.

Barnett can also call on four more veterans. 6-5 sophomore **Lou Dawkins** (4.0 ppg, 2.9 rpg) is the most experience of the bunch, starting 12 times as a freshman. Backup center **Alyn Thomsen** (2.5 ppg, 1.9 rpg), a 7-0 senior, is the tallest player on the roster. 6-7 senior **Cornal Henderson** averaged 2.4 points and 1.8 rebounds in a reserve role last season, while 6-6 junior **Jason Ludwig** scored 16 points in 18 appearances.

With six seniors and two juniors among the returnees, Barnett went after just two JC transfers. Both figure to make considerable contributions, however. **Bennie Gibbs,** a 6-4 forward, averaged 20.5 points and 9.5 rebounds at Cloud (Ga.) CC. There is a spot in the frontcourt for either he or 6-6 **Richard Johnson,** who averaged 20.1 points and 6.6 rebounds at Blinn (Tex.) CC.

The other four newcomers all are freshmen, one a question mark because of limited playing time in high school. 6-9 **Tony Jennings** (Cass Tech/Detroit, Mich.) did not play at all as a high school senior due to a knee injury.

A pair of Texans cleaned up in the awards department as prep seniors. 6-4 forward **Gary Collier** (Dunbar HS/Fort Worth, Tex.) was a 5-A first-team All-State selection and the Tarrant county player of the year. He averaged 26 points and 10 rebounds per game at Dunbar. 6-5 guard **Tom Etchison** (Boswell HS/Fort Worth, Tex.) was the Texas 4-A player of the year, averaging 26.1 points and 7.0 rebounds. Some experts have dared to call Etchison a "mini-Larry Bird."

The final freshman also posted some big-time numbers. 6-6 forward **Kelly Wells** (Morehead, Ky.) averaged 25.7 points and 9.0 rebounds for Rowan County High. He is a big-time shooter.

Count on these things at Tulsa: the Golden Hurricane will play as good a brand of defense as there is in the MVC; one player will not be asked to shoulder the offensive burden; and Barnett will be his usual fiery self, taking out his wrath on officials and rival fans alike.

One thing had better change, though, for the Golden Hurricane to contend for the Missouri Valley title. Tulsa has got to find a way to score from outside. The Golden Hurricane shot just .440 from the field last year, and the figure from three-point range was a lowly .329. Take away the .534 mark by Jenkins, the .491 accuracy of Gordon and the .487 mark posted by Scott, and there are some ugly shooting percentages on the roster. The talented Shields, for instance, shot just .357 overall and .336 from three-point range.

Still, with all of its experience, Tulsa will be right in the middle of the chase for the conference title. Creighton's athletes aren't as good, and Southern Illinois does not play defense as well. Tulsa does not have much size, though, and if a team can get the Golden Hurricane into a running game, they have trouble.

Third place and another NIT bid for Tulsa seems like the most realistic prediction.

1990-91 TULSA SCHEDULE

Nov.	24	Coppin State
	28	Fullerton State
Dec.	1	@Oklahoma State
	3	@Louisiana Tech
	12	Kansas State
	20	@Creighton
	22	@Brigham Young
	26	Virginia Commonwealth
	28-29	#All College Tournament
Jan.	2	Mississippi Valley
	5	@Drake
	8	@Lamar
	12	Wichita State
	17	Southern Illinois
	19	Drake
	22	@Southwest Missouri State
	24	Indiana State
	31	@Wichita State
Feb.	2	@Indiana State
	7	Illinois State
	9	@Southern Illinois
	14	Bradley
	16	Creighton
	20	Southwest Missouri State
	23	@Bradley
	25	@Illinois State
Mar.	1-5	##MVC Tournament

@ Road Games
# Oklahoma City, OK (Alabama-Birmingham, Illinois State & Oklahoma)
St. Louis, MO

UTAH

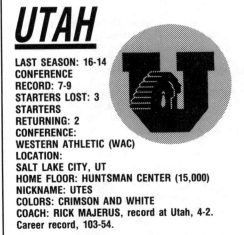

LAST SEASON: 16-14
CONFERENCE
RECORD: 7-9
STARTERS LOST: 3
STARTERS
RETURNING: 2
CONFERENCE:
WESTERN ATHLETIC (WAC)
LOCATION:
SALT LAKE CITY, UT
HOME FLOOR: HUNTSMAN CENTER (15,000)
NICKNAME: UTES
COLORS: CRIMSON AND WHITE
COACH: RICK MAJERUS, record at Utah, 4-2. Career record, 103-54.

Rick Majerus will be starting his first full season as head coach at Utah —again.

At this time last year, Majerus was the new head coach. His Utes had a 4-2 record in December when Majerus was diagnosed as having a heart problem. He underwent heart bypass surgery and assistant coach Joe Cravens took over the team.

Majerus didn't return, making it clear that Cravens was in charge for the season. Majerus switched roles with his assistant with Cravens doing the coaching and Majerus doing the recruiting.

The Utes finished with a 16-14 record and Cravens was credited with doing a good job with a team that wasn't overflowing with talent, size or depth. Utah upset Brigham Young in the first round of the WAC tournament in El Paso, Texas, which ended the season on a positive note.

Utah has lost three starters from a year ago, including both starting guards and the small forward. Most of the ballhandling experience went with them. Four redshirts and three transfers will be giving the Utes new life.

The man Utah probably will miss the most is point guard Tommy Connor (10.1 ppg, 4.4 apg). He was the man who ran the team and was Utah's best three-point shooter. Cravens leaned on him heavily. Jon Hansen (4.2 ppg, 2.6 rpg) and forward Keith Chapman (11.3 ppg, 4.3 rpg) also were intricate parts of the team.

Two reserves also finished at Utah last season as Justin Brooks (1.2 ppg, 1.5 rpg) and Mike Gill (0.3 ppg, 0.5 rpg) are gone.

The good news for Utah is the return of its two big players. **Josh Grant** is big in scoring and rebounding and **Walter Watts** is big in size. Grant averaged 16.5 points and 7.0 rebounds last season. Grant is Utah's best player. The 6-9 junior from Salt Lake City works well under the basket and can shoot from the perimeter, which causes problems for opposing defenses. Grant should move up from second-team to first-team All-WAC this year. He always is the man the Utes look for in the closing minutes of a close game. Majerus has described Watts as a summo wrestler. He is 6-8 and is listed at 280 pounds, but at times Watts has been closer to 300 pounds. Watts can create his own room under the basket. Last year he averaged 10.9 points and 5.4 rebounds from the center position. Watts is a senior.

Two JC players might help Utah right away on the front line. **Paul Afeaki** is a 6-10 center from Nukalosa, Tonga. He averaged 20.0 points and 12.0 rebounds and blocked 89 shots last season at Snow (Idaho) JC. Afeaki and Watts might share the center position. **M'Kay McGrath** is a 6-5 forward who averaged 15.0 points and 9.0 rebounds last season at Mesa (Ariz.) CC.

Larry Cain is a 6-9 sophomore from Ogden, Utah, who saw limited playing time as a freshman, averaging 2.9 points and 1.5 rebounds. The other two returnees might start. **Craig Rydalch** is a 6-4 swingman who was an occasional starter last season. The junior from Oakley, Utah, averaged 5.0 points and 2.3 rebounds. He could be at small forward or the big guard spot for the Utes. **Jimmy Soto** earned a letter, averaging 5.0 points and 2.3 rebounds a game as a freshman last season. He was the backup at point guard and probably will move up to the starting spot. Soto might be the key to Utah's success this season.

Utah has another JC transfer and four redshirts to help in the backcourt. **Anthony Williams** transferred from the College of Southern Idaho, where he scored 17.0 points and averaged 4.0 assists last season. He's a 6-1 junior from Seattle.

Phil Dixon is a 6-5 swingman who will be a redshirt freshman and **Byron Wilson** is a 6-3 redshirt sophomore from Gary, Ind. **Tyrone Tate**, a 6-1 sophomore from Weber HS in Chicago, Ill., sat out last year and **Barry Howard**, a 6-5 guard/forward, will be eligible after sitting out a season after transferring from Washington.

A leaner, healthier Majerus will have to do a lot of coaching in a hurry to mold this team. He has more size and depth than last year, but then again he

coached only six of Utah's games last season. Majerus has a proven track record. He came to Utah from Ball State, where his team had a 29-3 record during the 1988-89 season. He was 43-17 in two years with the Cardinals. He was 56-35 in three seasons as the head coach at Marquette and was an assistant coach for the Milwaukee Bucks for a season. But this is a new Majerus. His heart problems have given him a new prospective on basketball, and life. A seven-way heart bypass has a tendency to do that.

"When you come face-to-face with your mortality, you come face-to-face with what life is all about. It's an interesting experience. Maybe I won't be as driven when it comes to basketball," Majerus said.

"I think it'll be interesting when I yell and get excited the first time and that vein pops up in my neck."

The people of Utah still are getting used to Majerus' quick sense of humor. While he talks seriously about his surgery, he also finds humor in it. When he began his conditioning to get back into shape, he remarked "I went to Santa Monica (Calif.) to run. I wanted to go to a rich city where they have 911 and rich doctors with good equipment. I wasn't going to Watts or Compton (Calif.) where they just let you lay in the street if you have a heart attack."

BLUE RIBBON ANALYSIS

Before Utah started last season, Majerus didn't like what he saw when he looked down the roster. "These are a great bunch of guys if you want to go skiing, but I don't know if they can win basketball games," he joked.

This year, he feels a little better about the team. He has more size and depth, and the Utes needed both.

Grant is a keeper. He's versatile and experienced. He's the type of player you can rebuild a team around, and that's what the Utes are doing. With Watts and Afeaki in the middle, the Utes should be strong under the basket.

The questions are at guard. Soto came a long way, especially defensively, as a freshman. With only junior college transfers and redshirts to back him up, Soto may or may not have help when needed. The Utes will need to find some scoring from the perimeter to take pressure off the inside.

This will actually be Majerus' first team. It's a team he'll have to mold and put together. But he has a proven track record for doing that. He is a good coach and the result should be a good team.

Look for Utah to have a better-than-expected season. The Utes could be the real darkhorse in the WAC. They might struggle some in December when they're still learning their left from their right, but by the first of the year this should be a pretty good basketball team.

UTAH STATE

LAST SEASON: 14-16
CONFERENCE RECORD: 8-10
STARTERS LOST: 1
STARTERS RETURNING: 4
CONFERENCE: BIG WEST
LOCATION: LOGAN, UT
HOME FLOOR: THE SPECTRUM (10,270)
NICKNAME: AGGIES
COLORS: BLUE AND WHITE
COACH: KOHN SMITH, record at Utah State, 26-32.

Many college basketball experts believe that it takes two years for a coach to get settled at a school, to allow time to implement a fresh system with new philosophies. After the two year process is completed, then a program can be ready to take off and flourish.

Kohn Smith has been at Utah State for two years now. There have been many trials and tribulations in those two seasons. Trying to build the Aggies' program into a Big West contender has not been an easy task when considering the incredible growth the conference has experienced in the past three years. This marks Smith's third season with the Aggies. And it appears as if the Aggies are ready to make the move in the Big West to actual contenders.

If that's the case, then Smith's patience and perseverance over the past two seasons is going to pay off with fine dividends this season. There is little doubt that the Aggies will be much improved this season, ready to better the less than .500 campaigns Smith endured in his first two years. They have four returning starters, depth in every position, and enough experience and size to handle the Big West battles.

The only bad news is that while the Aggies have been vastly improving, so have the rest of the teams in the Big West. Which could mean two things: Either the league will be highly competitive top to bottom this year or other schools have been talking and writing a good game in pre-season publications. In any case, the Aggies and Smith should be ready to shine this year.

One of the main reasons for high optimism in Logan these days is the return of junior guard **Kendall Youngblood** (15.4 ppg, 4.9 rpg). The 6-4 Youngblood is extremely versatile and talented. He can do it all. He is a consummate scorer, getting points from all over the floor. He can drive to the basket or nail a long jumper. Youngblood has been predominantly an off-guard and small forward. Youngblood shot very well last season, connecting on 49 percent from the floor and 78 percent from the free throw line. A second-team All-Big West selection last year, he will look to better those numbers this year. He is one of the best returning players in the Big West and the key to the Aggies' hope of making the leap into the role of a contender this season. He has all the tools to make the people in Logan very excited this winter. The one part of Youngblood's game that needs work is ballhandling. Youngblood dished off for 79 assists in 30 games last year, but he turned the ball over 109 times. However, every other facet of Youngblood's game is solid and strong.

Senior forward **Rich Jardine** returns. A 6-8 power forward, Jardine (11.8 ppg, 4.1 rpg) also possesses a fine shooting touch for a big man, hitting exactly 50 percent of his tries from the floor. Jardine was named the Most Improved Player on the Aggies last season, going from an unknown JC transfer to the team's second leading scorer by the end of the season. His outside shooting touch causes havoc for opponents making it difficult to defend him. Look for Jardine to continue his improvement scale this season.

Senior center **Randy Funk** (11.4 ppg, 6.5 rpg) also returns to his spot in the pivot. The 6-7 aggressive inside player was tops on the Aggies in field goal percentage last season at 56 percent and was the team's leading rebounder as well. Known for his constant hard work and dedication, Funk was named as the team's Mr. Hustle last year. He has the knack to get the job done inside against much larger opponents. He's a purist's pleasure, a true blue collar laborer.

Senior point guard **Allen Gordon** (7.2 ppg, 1.7 rpg, 121 assists) will more than likely return to the starting point guard slot, freeing up Youngblood to do a lot more without the ball. Gordon started the final 19 games at the point a year ago and was very effective, shooting 49 percent from the floor and having a plus 40 in assists versus turnovers. Gordon is also a fine defender, as he led the team in steals last year. Smith felt that all Gordon needed was confidence and his performance at the end of the season last year gave the 6-0 Gordon the needed shot in the arm.

Senior forward **Jeff Parris** (6.6 ppg, 5.1 rpg) is a powerful inside player with great strength and agility. The 6-8 Parris is known for his defense (34 blocked shots last year) and rebounding. He was named the Aggies' top defensive player. Parris' only downfall is his inclination to get into foul trouble. He needs to spend more time on the floor and less on the bench this season.

Senior guard **Matt Barnes** (4.3 ppg, 1.3 rpg) started 11 games in the backcourt last season. The 6-0 Barnes is a good role player and has the ability to help immediately off the bench. Barnes' outside shooting suffered last year (only 34 percent) but he is an excellent free throw shooter (82 percent).

Sophomore forward **Gary Patterson** (2.7 ppg, 1.3 rpg) played in 21 games last year coming off the bench. The 6-6 Patterson also has fine shooting numbers, hitting 51 percent from the floor and 76 from the line. Patterson was very effective when opponents threw a zone defense at the Aggies. His long range shooting ability is a big asset.

Sophomore guard **Brent Lofton** (2.4 ppg, 1.4 rpg) has a great athletic ability and is a solid defender. Lofton, a 6-4 ball of energy with long arms, should see considerably more time than the seven minutes per outing he saw last year. Smith is high on Lofton. Maybe he will get a chance to strut his stuff this year. But that might be tough in an already crowded backcourt.

Junior forward **Roger Daley** (1.4 ppg, 1.3 rpg) walked onto the Aggies' roster last year and was a crowd favorite, seeing 72 minutes of action in 13 games. The 6-7 Daley is a good athlete, as evidenced by his Big West championship in discus. When he gets a chance to play, Daley is rugged inside.

Smith and his staff did their recruiting homework in the off-season, acquiring four freshmen signees that will obviously add immediate depth to the Aggies' roster. The top freshman recruit is 6-7 forward **Eric Franson** (American Port, Utah, HS). Franson was one of the best high school players in Utah last season, averaging 27.1 points per game. He showed Smith what he was made of in an all-star game against a touring Soviet Junior National Team last spring, winning Most Valuable Player honors in the game while

scoring 27 points. Center **Charlie Sager** (Grand Prairie, Texas/South Grand Prairie HS) is a 6-10, 220-pound workhorse who may compete for the starting slot in the pivot. Smith is high on Sager, who has great agility and quickness to go along with his sizeable frame.

Byron Ruffner, a 6-6 forward from Orem, Utah (Timpview HS) and **Darren Johnson**, a 6-7 forward from Idaho Falls, Idaho (Bonneville HS) will add depth to an already talented frontcourt.

BLUE RIBBON ANALYSIS

Smith is ready to have his best season since coming to Utah State from Indiana three years ago. He has the personnel, the experience, the shooters and the talent to push the Aggies into the role of actually contending this season. Youngblood should have a fine season as one of the Big West's top players. So should Jardine. Both are excellent all-around players, ones to build a program around. The rest of the returnees are solid and are aware of their roles.

If the Aggies are to improve enough to contend in the Big West, they must do two things. They have to work harder rebounding, as they were outrebounded last year badly, especially within the conference (minus seven in the Big West, 40-33) and they have to work on ballhandling. The Aggies' turnover total was way too high (509 in 30 games). The Aggies have been a team in the past to push the ball up the court, run-and-gun. They should be the same way again this year, which is the predominant style in the Big West. The Aggies shoot the ball very well as a team and the coaching staff is confident that they can do even better shooting the ball this year.

Smith instituted a weight and strength program for the off-season. The Aggies have to be hopeful the program pays immediate dividends. If not, then the Aggies will continue to get pushed around down low by the bigger teams in the Big West.

It's not so much a make-or-break year for Smith, but it is a make year. There will be no excuses this time around. The newness of Smith's regime is over. So is the inexperienced roster. The Aggies just have to be better this year.

Look for Utah State to go around 18-12, and possibly crack the Big West first division.

1990-91 UTAH STATE SCHEDULE

Nov.	24	@Brigham Young
Dec.	1	Brigham Young
	4	@Utah
	8	@Boise State
	13	Weber State
	19	@Weber State
	21-22	#Met Life Classic
	29	Utah
Jan.	2	California-Irvine
	4	California-Santa Barbara
	7	@Fullerton State
	9	@UNLV
	12	San Jose State
	17	Pacific
	19	Fullerton State
	24	@Long Beach State
	26	@New Mexico State
	28	UNLV
	31	Fullerton State
Feb.	9	@San Jose State
	14	@Fullerton State
	16	@Pacific
	21	New Mexico State
	23	Long Beach State
	28	@California-Santa Barbara
Mar.	2	@California-Irvine
	8-10	##Big West Tournament

@ Road Games
# San Francisco, CA (Air Force, Vermont & San Francisco)
Long Beach, CA

UTEP

LAST SEASON: 21-11
CONFERENCE RECORD: 10-6
STARTERS LOST: 2
STARTERS RETURNING: 3
CONFERENCE: WESTERN ATHLETIC (WAC)
LOCATION: EL PASO, TX
HOME FLOOR: SPECIAL EVENT CENTER (12,222)
NICKNAME: MINERS
COLORS: ORANGE, BLUE & WHITE
COACH: DON HASKINS, record at UTEP, 563-243.

There was a rumor going around the west Texas city of El Paso not so long ago that basketball here existed before Don "The Bear" Haskins moved here. But it was wrong.

Oh, there might have been some form of basketball before Haskins was hired, but it certainly did not resemble what the Miners play today. He took the relatively unknown Texas Western program to an NCAA championship in 1966. Since then, the school has changed its name but it hasn't changed its basketball coach. Haskins will be starting his 30th season in El Paso this year. He has gone through two generations and is approaching his third. While there was basketball in Indiana before Bob Knight and the sport will continue to flourish in North Carolina after Dean Smith retires, Haskins is basketball in El Paso. Miner fans cannot imagine what life would be like without Haskins, and they don't want to.

UTEP decided to take a chance on a high school coach from the Texas Panhandle in 1961. At the time, John Kennedy was President and Texas Western was a small mining school that had no name recognition and less money. In the last 29 seasons, there have been seven United States Presidents and Haskins has rolled up an impressive 563 wins and 243 losses.

Haskins is one of the most respected coaches in college basketball. He ranks third in wins among active career coaches. Besides an NCAA title, Haskins has won the WAC six times. He has won four WAC tournaments and has been in the NCAA tournament seven years in a row, for a total of 13 NCAA tournament appearances.

Haskins suffered through the low point of his tenure at UTEP last season. It didn't come in the form of wins or losses, but in a stubborn case of laryngitis. He lost his voice in December and couldn't get it back. Doctors recommended that he stop coaching, so Haskins was not on the bench for the last 24 games of the season. Assistant coach Norm Ellenberger, the former head coach at New Mexico, took over as UTEP's head coach, although everyone still considered it Haskins' team.

The Bear is back this season, and so are the Miners. While UTEP may not be favored to win the WAC, it will be close to the top, and as long as Haskins is coaching, UTEP will be considered the team to watch in the WAC.

Haskins has to replace his two premier big men—6-10 Antonio Davis (10.8 ppg, 7.6 rpg) and 6-11 Greg Foster (10.6 ppg, 6.2 rpg). Davis and Foster entered last season with great expectations but were not as productive as expected nor did they provide the leadership the Miners so desperately needed. Davis was a second round choice of the Indiana Pacers and signed a lucrative contract over the summer with a team in Greece. Foster was a second round choice of the Washington Bullets.

The loss of Davis and Foster would seem to wipe out UTEP's front line, but it actually doesn't. Returning is 6-8 junior forward **Marlon Maxey**, who led the Miners in scoring (12.4 ppg) and rebounding (7.8 rpg). The powerfully built 220-pound Maxey transferred to UTEP from Minnesota and was one of the best forwards in the WAC last season. He has the ability to become the best frontcourt performer to play at UTEP in the last decade. **David Van Dyke** (4.9 ppg, 2.9 rpg) probably will be a starter in the pivot. The 6-9 junior center played in all 32 games last season, starting in just five. He blocked 48 shots in just 535 minutes last year, but was a disappointment. Van Dyke set a UTEP school record for blocked shots in a season with 90 as a freshman and he also averaged 5.6 points and four rebounds per game that year. He needs to get stronger, more assertive and serious about his game if he is to reach his potential.

Another returning letterman on the UTEP front line is 6-8 senior forward **Francis Ezenwa** (0.9 ppg, 1.9 rpg). Ezenwa, a native of Enugu, Nigeria, will never be a prolific scorer but he is a defensive specialist who can rebound.

The UTEP coaching staff expects a strong contribution, and possibly a starting role, from 6-8 sophomore forward **Roy Howard**. A transfer from Tarleton State (Tex.), an NAIA school, Howard was the team MVP two years ago on the best Tarleton State team in school history. He can run the floor and is a strong offensive rebounder. Howard is from Houston, Texas.

UTEP will have 6-4 sophomore forward **Johnny Melvin** back this year. He averaged 5.2 points and 3.1 rebounds as a freshman in 1988-89 before missing last year after being suspended by Haskins. UTEP was a nonemotional, leaderless team last year, and Melvin's intensity, energy and hustle were missed. He had 10 rebounds against New Mexico as a freshman. Melvin is the type of player who does not have a true position on the floor, yet he can play everywhere.

Senior **Mark McCall** (7.3 ppg, 3.3 rpg) was an occasional starter at small forward and big guard. The 6-2 McCall has excellent quickness and big league leaping ability. He is the premier leaper in the WAC and is a decent three-point threat.

Last year's starting point guard, 5-10 senior **Prince Stewart** (8.6 ppg, 180 assists) was declared academically ineligible over the summer. He will not play for at least the first semester and has to pass 18 hours this fall to be eligible. Stewart was moved from the shooting guard spot to the point last year and had trouble adjusting to the position. He also did not provide the leadership the Miners needed. His replacement as the Miners' point guard is expected to be 6-1 junior **Gym Bice**, a transfer from Midland (Tex.) JC. He is a true floor general type who is more suited for the position and probably can provide more consistency than Stewart.

Back at shooting guard is 6-1 sophomore **Henry Hall** (11.7 ppg), who was freshman of the year in the WAC. Hall was UTEP's best three-point shooter. He had 64 treys to lead the team, while no other Miner converted over 18 three-pointers. Hall posted the highest freshman scoring average in UTEP history. He originally signed with Georgetown in high school, but never officially enrolled in school there or played for the Hoyas.

Haskins is expecting contributions from two redshirt freshmen, 6-8 forward **Dallas David** and 6-5 forward/guard **Ralph Davis**. David is from Berkner HS in Richardson, Tex., and was redshirted last fall after missing a good deal of preseason practice due to a broken hand and a back injury. He is an impressive athlete who can shoot the ball, wears a size 16 shoe and may continue to grow. Davis is from St. Benedict's HS in Chicago, Ill. He is also a good ballhandler and shooter who is expected to have an outstanding career at UTEP. Chicago has become a prime hunting ground for the Miners in recent years. Tim Hardaway, the starting point guard for the Golden State Warriors and runner-up in balloting for NBA rookie of the year behind David Robinson, had an outstanding career at UTEP. Several players from Chicago followed his lead

and have played for the Miners in recent years.

UTEP picked up one of the premier junior college players in the country in 6-8 **Von Bennett** (15.0 ppg, 9.0 rpg from Northeastern Oklahoma A&M). Bennett knows the game, can score and rebound and will add stability to the Miners' front line.

The remainder of the UTEP roster consists of 6-2 freshman guard **Chris Walters**, 6-6 freshman forward **Abie Ramerez** and 6-2 freshman guard **David Dick**. Walters, from Antelope Valley HS in Lancaster, Calif., is similar to Mark McCall in that he is a sensational athlete who needs to improve his ballhandling skills and overall guard play. Walters is reportedly a fine defensive player. Ramerez is from Enterprise HS in Redding, Calif. He is an outstanding leaper. Dick is a walk-on from Burgess HS in El Paso.

BLUE RIBBON ANALYSIS

The big news at UTEP is that coach Don Haskins is back for his 30th season after missing most of last year due to an extreme case of laryngitis. While Haskins was away, a highly touted Miner squad never really clicked as senior big man Antonio Davis and Greg Foster didn't play up to their potential, the leadership void caused by the graduation of Tim Hardaway was never filled, and the backcourt play was inconsistent.

Backcourt play will be a concern again as last year's starting point guard Prince Stewart is ineligible for at least the first semester and maybe the entire year, and junior college transfer Gym Bice is the only true point guard on the roster. Still, the Miners could be an improved club not just because Haskins is back on the bench. Even without Davis and Foster the frontcourt will be strong. Junior Marlon Maxey is one of the premier players in the WAC, underachieving junior David Van Dyke can be a premier shotblocker, senior Francis Ezenwa should be a solid role player, and newcomers Roy Howard and Von Bennett both have excellent potential.

The Miners will also benefit from the return of sophomore Johnny Melvin, who will add an emotional lift that was lacking last year. Sophomore guard Henry Hall had his ups and downs as a freshman but still averaged 11.7 ppg and was the freshman of the year in the WAC. Redshirt freshmen Dallas David and Ralph Davis will add outside shooting and ballhandling skills.

Basically, there is a better blend of talent at UTEP this year and the Miners should be a quicker, better shooting team. This is more of a Don Haskins team than last year's highly touted but underachieving edition. The Miners have been to the NCAA tournament the last seven years in a row. With The Bear back on the bench, that streak could continue as the Miners are one of four teams in the WAC, the others being Wyoming, New Mexico and Colorado State, who have legitimate post-season aspirations.

1990-91 UTEP SCHEDULE

Nov.	26	Midwestern State (TX)
	29	@New Mexico State
Dec.	2	Coppin State (MD)
	4	New Mexico State
	6	Maryland-Eastern Shore
	10	Bradley
	15	@Georgetown
	17	Arkansas-Little Rock
	22	@Creighton
	28-29	#Sun Carnival
Jan.	3	Air Force
	5	Colorado State
	10	@Brigham Young
	12	@Utah
	17	@Hawaii
	19	@San Diego State
	24	Hawaii
	26	San Diego State
	31	Utah
Feb.	2	Brigham Young
	7	@Air Force
	9	@Colorado State

1990-91 UTEP SCHEDULE *Cont.*

Feb.	16	Wyoming
	23	@New Mexico
	28	@Wyoming
Mar.	2	New Mexico
	6-9	##WAC Tournament

@ Road Games
# El Paso, TX (Southwest Missouri State, Texas Tech & Washington)
Laramie, WY

VANDERBILT

LAST SEASON: 21-14
CONFERENCE RECORD: 7-11
STARTERS LOST: 2
STARTERS RETURNING 3
CONFERENCE: SOUTH-EASTERN (SEC)
LOCATION: NASHVILLE, TN
HOME FLOOR: MEMORIAL COLISEUM (15,646)
NICKNAME: COMMODORES
COLORS: BLACK AND GOLD
COACH: EDDIE FOGLER, record at Vanderbilt, 21-14. Career record, 82-46.

On his way home from the Southeastern Conference tournament last season, Vanderbilt coach Eddie Fogler stopped off with a few friends at a lounge in the Orlando, Fla., airport. At the lounge, the tournament championship game was on the television, and quickly a player negotiated a reverse dunk between two defenders, bringing oohs and shouts from everyone watching.

"You could use some of that," one of Fogler's friends remarked, pointing at the screen. Fogler did not even look up for the instant replay. "Find it with Vandy SAT's," he replied. "That's the problem."

Instead, Fogler took what he had - the normal Vanderbilt ration of high school valedictorians, college honor students and basketball sharpshooters - and three weeks later wrapped up the NIT title in his first year at the school. It was a nice recovery from a midseason slump that produced seven straight losses (three of them by one point), and wrecked the Commodores in conference play. Vandy, which opened 3-0 in the league, finished a disappointing 7-11, tied for eighth with Mississippi State and ahead of only lowly Florida.

But Fogler overhauled his lineup to break the skid, and the NIT championship victory over St. Louis capped a turnaround that saw the Commodores win nine of their last 11 games. Included was a four-point upset of SEC regular season champion Georgia in the second round of the conference tournament.

A Dean Smith pupil both as an athlete (North Carolina point guard 1967-70) and assistant coach (helping recruit Michael Jordan, James Worthy, Sam Perkins, Brad Daugherty, Phil Ford, J.R. Reid and Kenny Smith among others), Fogler got his first head coaching job at Wichita State. In three years there, he compiled a 61-32 record with two NCAA tournament trips and another to the NIT.

Still, Fogler had a hard act to follow at Vanderbilt, replacing the popular C.M. Newton when the latter left to become athletic director at Kentucky. But the NIT title cemented his own, more aggressive style with Vanderbilt's loyal following.

But two of the key cogs of that late season run will have to be replaced - 5-11 point guard Derrick Wilcox (11.8 ppg, 3.3 rpg, 158 assists) and 6-8 forward Eric Reid (10.5 ppg, 5.8 rpg), the team's best rebounder. On a positive note, the NIT's MVP, 6-2 off guard guard **Scott Draud** (15.6 ppg, 90-for-208 on three-pointers), is back for his senior season. In the game of musical chairs that was the Vandy lineup - eight players started nine or more games - Draud alone started all 35, and he led the Commodores in scoring.

"Winning (the NIT) really highlighted what I think was a good year," Fogler said. "Hopefully, we've built a foundation to have competitive teams and will build on the experience of winning a championship."

There will also have to be some rebuilding, of course, though being a starter is relative with Vanderbilt's user-friendly bench. Last year, nine players averaged 17 or more minutes per game.

"Derrick (Wilcox) was sensational at the end of the year," Fogler said. "He was the catalyst to our stretch run and will be very difficult to replace. Eric (Reid) was a very good defender and our best rebounder."

The Commodores have long relied on outside shooting, and will have to build an offense around Draud, the latest slim, curly-haired, whiz-kid sharpshooter off the Vandy cookie-cutter. Having redshirted in 1988-89 after his sophomore season, Draud has already graduated, with a double major, of course. He will stick around for another year to work on a Master's degree in Psychology with a minor in three-point accuracy.

One of best pure shooters in the SEC (87 percent on free throws), Draud is capable of scoring 30 points on any given night, which he did twice last year. Draud made *United Press International* third team All-SEC last year, and could be one of the league's top guards.

The situation is much less settled at the point. Draud is probably a good enough ballhandler to take over the spot, but Fogler's offensive system puts entirely too much pressure and responsibility on the position to burden his best scorer with it. Sophomore **Kevin Anglin** (4.9 ppg, 2.5 rpg, 88 assists) backed up Wilcox until he earned a starting role in the late-season lineup shuffle, as a 6-4 small forward. Anglin appears to have the court savvy and intelligence to run Vandy's show from the point, but is unproven.

Another sophomore and a pair of promising incoming freshmen could provide backup or move Anglin back to his forward spot. On paper, the prize of the Commodore recruiting class was 6-3 **Matt Maloney** (21.6 ppg, 6.0 rpg, 6.0 assists at Memorial HS/Haddonfield, N.J.). Mentioned on several lists of the nation's Top 100 prospects, the Vanderbilt staff feels he could make an immediate impact in the SEC at either point guard or off guard. He is also the son of Temple assistant and former Niagara head coach Jim Maloney.

More of a pure point guard is a fellow freshman, 5-10 **Aaron Beth** (21.6 ppg, 6.4 assists, valedictorian of his class at Marshall County HS/Calvert City, Ky.). Rounding out the point guard sweepstakes is 6-3 sophomore returnee **Willy Daunic** (1.8 ppg in 12 games).

The backcourt could also get a lift from 6-5 sophomore transfer **Bruce Elder,** who sat out last year as a redshirt after leading Davidson in scoring and rebounding (17.2 ppg, 5.6 rpg) as a freshman in 1988-89. Elder can swing between the similar off guard and small forward spots at Vandy.

At small forward, 6-5 junior **Morgan Wheat** (9.2 ppg, 3.4 rpg) and 6-7 senior **Charles Mayes** (5.3 ppg, 3.2 rpg) both had turns starting before Fogler settled on Anglin for the stretch drive. They will likely split time, perhaps with Elder, this season.

Mayes can also help out deeper inside where Vanderbilt has several solid, interchangeable players, but none who are the dominating types to take over a game. Fogler has already listed better rebounding as one of his major goals for the season.

Mayes' move to power forward could depend on 6-7 sophomore **Dan Hall** (6.0 ppg, 3.7 rpg), who underwent major reconstructive knee surgery after he tore ligaments just before last year's SEC tournament. Hall is credited with the single play that turned around

Vanderbilt's season and sparked them to the NIT title.

Trailing by nine in the regular season finale against Tennessee, Hall came all the way across the court to block an apparent Volunteer dunk, sparking a wild rally that ended in a 24-point Commodore rout of their archrivals. Hall's surgery was successful, but it is extremely doubtful he will play this season given the normal 9-to-12 month rehabilitation period.

Like the off-guard and small forward spots, the center and power forward positions are quite similar in Fogler's system. And just about everyone tried out both last season. The most successful combination had the departed Reid at center, with 6-7 senior **Steve Grant** (7.3 ppg, 4.5 rpg) at forward.

Grant is one of the few Commodores who is not an outside shooting threat, yet he picks his spots well. Though hardly a scorer, he broke the single-season school record for field goal percentage (67.8 percent) by limiting himself to point-blank range. One of the success stories of the late lineup juggle, his averages went up to 9.4 ppg and 5.0 rpg when inserted into the starting lineup for the last 11 games. He was voted Vanderbilt's most improved player.

At center, 6-10 junior **Todd Mulholland** (9.6 ppg, 5.1 rpg) started until the final 11 games. More of a finesse player who can roam away from the basket, he played well early in the year, but mirrored his team's mid-season slump. However, Mulholland probably had his best games after losing his starting job, averaging 12 points off the bench while being named to the NIT all-tourney team. 6-11 junior **Fred Benjamin** is coming off a redshirt season after playing little as a freshman and sophomore. An imposing physical specimen, his role figures to be greatly expanded from his first two years.

Fogler also added two inside players from his freshman class, though both are probably long-range projects at best. The most interesting story is 6-9 **John Amaechi** (12 points, 11 rebounds, 4 blocked shots at St. John's HS/Toledo, Ohio), a Manchester, England native who has only been playing basketball for two years. He grew up playing rugby, but after picking up basketball as a high school junior in England, he decided to spend his senior year in the U.S.

A year on a weight program could benefit 7-1 **Rob Nunnery,** who graduated from high school (Berea HS/Berea, Ky.) one year early and spent last year at Fork Union (Va.) Military Academy.

BLUE RIBBON ANALYSIS

Vanderbilt always seems to have good outside shooters, and this year will be no exception. But Eddie Fogler's system depends heavily on the point guard, and one of the four candidates will have to step forward to make it work. The Commodores also need to take better care of the ball. Last year they had two more turnovers per game than their opponents, and made mental mistakes that belied a team full of honor students.

Part of that was Fogler's almost exclusive use of man-to-man defense with a team bred on C.M. Newton's steady diet of zones. "I think we'll be a better defensive team because of one year of experience with the system," Fogler said.

The coach has the depth to run his up-tempo style, but must get better rebounding, especially since the team is so outside oriented. A nice plus would be a breakthrough season for Fred Benjamin, or a quicker than expected emergence by one of the big freshmen.

Though mostly overmatched athletically in the Southeastern Conference, the Commodores can play with any team on nights when the outside shots are falling. How many nights that happens will largely determine who breaks away from an evenly-matched pack in the second division of the SEC.

VILLANOVA

LAST SEASON: 18-15
CONFERENCE RECORD: 8-8
STARTERS LOST: 2
STARTERS RETURNING: 3
CONFERENCE: BIG EAST
LOCATION: VILLANOVA, PA
HOME FLOOR: DUPONT PAVILION (6,500) and SPECTRUM (18,497)
NICKNAME: WILDCATS
COLORS: BLUE AND WHITE
COACH: ROLLIE MASSIMINO, record at Villanova, 326-211.
Career record, 360-227.

Some say Rollie Massimino did his best coaching job ever with the Wildcats of '89-90. The team was coming off a somewhat lackluster 18-16 season and were still trying to find themselves on the Dupont Pavilion hardwood. An early season schedule that included Louisville, North Carolina and Virginia did not give the Wildcats much time to come together. But come together they did, taking a very sure, steady pace that included a pair of big wins over Syracuse and one each over Connecticut and Clemson. Many of the questions that the critics had, especially the play in the backcourt, were answered positively, and now Massimino appears to be ready to move Villanova back once again toward the Big East heirarchy. They are still a year away, but Villanova is back on the right track.

Leading the way on the Main Line will be the junior backcourt combination of 6-6 **Greg Woodard** (11.9 ppg, 3.4 rpg) and 5-11 **Chris Walker** (11.4 ppg,

128 assists). Walker returns after a sterling sophomore year which saw him emerge as the Wildcats' floor general. He started more games (32) and played more minutes (1022) than anyone else on the squad and showed he can be a threat both distributing and shooting the ball, leading the team in assists (3.9 per game) and three-point field goals (71-183). More importantly the Houston native showed the leadership and consistency of a senior, something which was more important than his scoring ability. If he can improve slightly on his shooting touch (39 percent from the floor and 62 percent from the line) he will continue to establish himself as one of the Big East's best.

Woodard paralleled Walker's development in the backcourt, showing that he can be the inside-outside scorer to complement his smaller partner. He returns as Villanova's leading scorer and third-leading rebounder, but still needs to show a bit more consistency on the offensive end and be more of a take charge offensive leader. His 27-point effort in the 97-74 upset of No. 1 Syracuse last January was no fluke, and he has the capability of putting up the big time numbers that the running Wildcats will need. After those two there is some question, but 6-1 junior point guard **David Miller** (0.9 ppg, 0.6 apg) should provide some help. He averaged almost six minutes per game over the last 24 after recovering from a stress fracture, and is a quality passer. 5-11 redshirt freshman **Lloyd Mumford** (Lexington, Mass.) will also return to the lineup after sitting out last season with a stress fracture of the right tibia, and will help at both spots. Walk-on seniors **Tim Muller** (0.2 ppg) and **Chris Masotti** (0.6 ppg) round out the backcourt.

It is in the frontcourt where the biggest questions have to be answered. Starters **Tom Greis** (13.4 ppg, 6.5 rpg) and **Rodney Taylor** (5.7 ppg, 4.6 rpg) have both graduated, leaving 6-7 junior **Marc Dowdell** (5.9 ppg, 4.3 rpg) as the one returning frontcourt starter. The mobile Christian Brothers Academy (N.J.) product played perhaps his best ball at Villanova during the final 10 games of '89-90, and will be the steadying force in a very young frontcourt. Two years of Big East play have shown that Dowdell is ready to face up to any foe and become the type of aggressive rebounder that Villanova desperately needs. 6-6 sophomore swingman **Lance Miller** (8.4 ppg, 5.5 rpg) will see most of his action up front this year and should continue to improve upon his Big East all-rookie season. His quick moves, clutch shooting and in between size make him very tough to guard. A pair of sophomores, 6-6 **Calvin Byrd** (4.6 ppg, 2.2 rpg) and 6-7 **Arron Bain** (6.8 ppg, 2.4 rpg) also had impressive initial campaigns and will continue to improve. Byrd is an intimidating force on the boards (25 blocks last year) while the soft-shooting Bain is potentially a big time scorer who will be the Wildcats go-to guy in future seasons.

A pair of 6-11 recruits are also expected to make an immediate impact at forward, especially on the defensive boards. One is **Anthony Pelle**, a product of New York powerhouse Adlai Stevenson, the alma mater of former Villanova star Ed Pinckney. Pelle averaged 22 points and 12 rebounds last season while setting a school record with an incredible 17 blocks in one game. He is an aggressive rebounder with good speed for his size. The other newcomer is Raleigh, N.C., native **Ron Wilson** (20.0 ppg, 10.0 rpg at Raleigh-Cardinal Gibbons). Wilson's forte is his shooting touch, and he will become more of a rebounder as his upper body develops. Both Pelle and Wilson should see time in the middle as well, joining Massimino's three returning centers. Mobile 6-10 sophomore **James Bryson** (1.6 ppg, 2.1 rpg) watched and learned a good deal behind Greis last season and appears to be ready to stop in at center. Often injured 6-10 senior **Barry Bekkedam** also returns after suffering a stress fracture in pre-season last year, and will try to silence some of the critics who have called him a huge disappointment in his first three campaigns. 7-2 junior import **Paul Vrind** (1.4 ppg, 1.3 rpg), from Holland, is also back and will see more action this season, although

his inconsistent play could hurt Villanova more this year without a proven center to come right back with.

''We're still a very young team, and this will be another year of putting the pieces together,'' added Massimino. ''Our schedule is very difficult (LSU in the Tip-Off Classic, Wake Forest, Auburn and Arizona along with Big East and Big Five play) and with an unproven center in the middle, it will be a year of adjustment all around.''

BLUE RIBBON ANALYSIS

Villanova took a very big step last year with the quick development of Woodard, Walker, Miller, Bain and Byrd, and it doesn't look like that will stop. Bryson is getting better while Wilson and Pelle should provide a quick fix up front. The big question is depth. Mumford will help in the backcourt but neither Bekkedam nor Vrind will help much up front. Villanova will run and press and steal some games from bigger teams like they always do, but the powerhouse teams will wear them down inside.

Some games were lost last season on inexperience, and that will happen again this year, only it should be one or two instead of five or six games. The rebuilding continues on The Main Line, but that is toward a Big East title, not a winning season. An 18 to 20-win season and sixth place in the Big East is the likely spot.

1990-91 VILLANOVA SCHEDULE

Nov.	24	#LSU
	27	Drexel
Dec.	1	Temple
	4	@Pennsylvania
	6	##Wake Forest
	8	@St. Joseph's
	12	Seton Hall
	22	La Salle
	27-28	*USF&G Sugar Bowl Tournament
Jan.	2	@Pitt
	5	@Syracuse
	8	Connecticut
	10	@Vermont
	14	**Georgetown
	19	Arizona
	22	@Boston College
	26	**St. John's
	29	Pitt
Feb.	2	@Connecticut
	5	@St. John's
	9	@Georgetown
	13	St. Francis (PA)
	16	Providence
	18	Boston College
	23	@Seton Hall
	26	**Syracuse
Mar.	2	@Providence
	7-10	***Big East Tournament

@ Road Games
# Hall of Fame Tip-Off Classic, Springfield, MA
ACC/Big East Challenge, Raleigh, NC
* New Orleans, LA (Auburn, Georgia Tech & Tulane)
** The Spectrum, Philadelphia, PA
*** Madison Square Garden, New York, NY

VIRGINIA COMMONWEALTH

LAST SEASON: 11-17
CONFERENCE RECORD: 5-9
STARTERS LOST: 2
STARTERS RETURNING: 3
CONFERENCE: SUN BELT
LOCATION: RICHMOND, VA
HOME FLOOR: RICHMOND COLISEUM (10,716)
NICKNAME: RAMS
COLORS: BLACK AND GOLD
COACH: SONNY SMITH, record at Virginia Commonwealth, 11-17.
Career record, 214-194.

It was a rough maiden voyage for coach Sonny Smith a year ago. The Rams had a tough time adjusting to his style, and wound up tied for sixth in the Sun Belt standings. A highly touted recruiting class also did not materialize as quickly as forecast, disappointing Virginia Commonwealth fans who hoped Smith would return the Rams to the top of the conference.

VCU had its moments, knocking off Memphis State at home and James Madison on the road, but shooting and rebounding deficiences haunted the Rams all season. It added up to the third losing season in the last five. Will Smith get it turned around? The answer appears to be yes - with highly regarded prep star Kendrick Warren in the fold - but not right away. Warren will sit out this season, and Virginia Commonwealth is not an immediate contender in the Sun Belt race.

The Rams will have to do it without two departed starters, guard Lionel Bacon (10.0 ppg, 3.5 rpg) and center Martin Henlan (7.2 ppg, 7.7 rpg), neither of which performed up to their previous year's standards nor provided the kind of senior leadership Smith expected. Katara Reliford (2.2 ppg, 1.7 rpg), a 6-6 forward who started two games early in the season, transferred out of the program, as did forwards Derek Borden and Horace Scruggs.

Three starters come back, but none are guaranteed their position when practice begins. There could be up to five new faces in the starting lineup. The only sure-bet returnee is 6-3 senior point guard **Carl Weldon,** who can get up and down the floor in a hurry the way Smith likes it. Weldon was not much of a threat to put it up (6.8 ppg), although he handed out 5.4 assists per game.

The other returning starters are 6-4 senior forward **Elander Lewis** and 6-10 senior center **Craig Uhle.** Lewis, a transfer from St. John's, was a big disappointment, despite leading the team in scoring (13.9 ppg) and averaging 5.2 rebounds. Lewis was in Smith's doghouse for several off-the-court activities near the end of the season, and did not play much down the stretch. Uhle was not strong enough to hold his own underneath and never got untracked offensively, averaging 5.6 ppg and 3.7 rpg.

Other returning lettermen include 6-3 sophomore **Chris Brower** (5.3 ppg), 6-2 senior **Dewayne Garner** (6.0 ppg, 1.2 rpg), 6-7 senior **Bobby Reddish** (4.4 ppg, 2.7 rpg), 6-2 senior **Derek Thompkins** (6.1 ppg, 2.6 rpg) and 6-6 senior **Brian Whitley** (1.4 ppg).

Brower and Garner came off the bench on several occasions to spark the Rams, and are capable of getting hot from three-point range. Garner hit 40 percent of his bonus shots, and Brower 36 percent beyond the arc. They are valuable bench players, and Smith will likely continue to use them that way.

Reddish had a wrist operation in the off-season to repair a broken bone, and Smith is hoping it will let him contribute more this year. Thompkins started four games at the end of the season, averaging close to 17 points per game in that stretch.

Off those numbers, Thompkins will have a chance to earn a full-time starting berth at the wing guard spot, along with Lewis, 6-7 freshman **Yann Bonato** and Brower. Bonato, a native of France, led Southern Wayne High (Mt. Olive, N.C.) to a 19-9 record last winter while averaging 24.2 ppg and 6.1 rpg. He is the son of one of the greatest players in French basketball history, Jean-Claude Bonato.

Eric Atkins, a 6-6 transfer from San Jacinto (Tex.) JC, is expected to move in as the small forward in Smith's alignment. Recognized last year as one of the nation's Top 20 JC players, Atkins averaged 15.7 points and 7.7 rebounds for 34-4 San Jacinto. He also shot an amazing 66 percent from the floor, and Smith needs someone like that to improve on last season's 44.4 percent VCU effort.

If nothing else, the Rams will make history in 1990-91, having signed the nation's first Soviet collegiate player. Smith got his first look at 7-2, 21-year-old freshman **Konstantin Pepeliaev** (Leningrad Spartak/U.S.S.R.) while conducting clinic in the Soviet Union last spring. Pepeliaev was permitted by the Leningrad Sports Authority to enroll at a U.S. school because of his academic ability. He is not to be confused with Arvidas Sabonis.

"He is not a great player," Smith admits, "but he has a chance to be very, very good. He has got to gain weight, gain strength and gain confidence. He has to start believing in himself." Pepeliaev must also overcome his inevitable attraction as a curiosity piece.

"The fans' expectations are also too tough," Smith added. "Konstantin may disappoint some people at first. I don't expect him to be a star, but I expect him to play his first year. I expect him to give us some rebounds and some blocked shots. I don't expect him to make a huge impact or be the darling of the fans. But I expect him to help us win, and I think he will."

Other newcomers to the program include 5-10 freshman point guard Rod Ladd, who averaged 23.1 ppg, 6.2 rpg and 11.4 apg for Macon County (Ga.) High, 6-4 freshman guard **Thomas Meredith** (19.6 ppg and 8.3 rpg in Warren's shadow at Thomas Jefferson) and 6-8 forward **Sherron Mills**, a sophomore who becomes eligible in mid-December. Mills, once a star at Snow Hill (Md.) High, transferred from Chowan (N.C.) JC before playing a game there. He was the Maryland high school player of the year in 1988-89.

With all of the firepower, Smith figures he can speed up the Rams this season and surpass last year's 66.5 ppg scoring pace. "I've always liked to run the ball up and down the court," he said, "but we just didn't have the personnel to do it last season. I think now we have the players who can be much more consistent on the offensive end. We should score more points and be stronger inside."

BLUE RIBBON ANALYSIS

With what is regarded as one of the top recruiting classes in the South, the Rams will be better. Even the .500 mark appears attainable, but how much further Virginia Commonwealth can go will depend on how quickly Warren adapts to the college game and whether Smith finds some others to put the ball in the basket consistently.

"We have a lot of talent this year," said Smith, "but until they do it on the court, it doesn't mean too much."

Smith's club is not quite ready to challenge for the Sun Belt title. A fourth-place finish would be regarded as improvement, though VCU fans are starved for another shot at the NCAA's, something that was commonplace during J.D. Barnett's six-year reign.

It took Smith a few years to get the Auburn program on the road to consistent NCAA appearances.

It will be at least next season before the Rams enjoy similar opportunities.

1990-91 VIRGINIA COMMONWEALTH SCHEDULE

Nov.	24	New Hampshire
	28	@Illinois State
Dec.	1	Augusta College (GA)
	5	@Richmond
	8	@Oklahoma
	11	Virginia Tech
	17	@Tennessee
	22-23	#Big Isle Invitational
	26	@Tulsa
	28-29	##Times-Dispatch Invitational
Jan.	2	George Mason
	5	Northeastern
	7	Alabama-Birmingham
	10	South Alabama
	12	@Old Dominion
	15	@South Alabama
	17	North Carolina Charlotte
	19	@Jacksonville
	23	@Alabama-Birmingham
	26	Western Kentucky
	28	Jacksonville
Feb.	2	Old Dominion
	7	South Florida
	9	@Miami (FL)
	16	@South Florida
	18	@North Carolina Charlotte
	23	@Western Kentucky
Mar.	2-4	*Sun Belt Tournament

@ Road Games
# Kauai, HI (Alabama-Birmingham, Chaminade & St. Francis)
Richmond, VA (James Madison, Richmond & Virginia Tech)
* Mobile, AL

VIRGINIA MILITARY INSTITUTE

LAST SEASON: 14-15
CONFERENCE RECORD: 7-7
STARTERS LOST: 4
STARTERS RETURNING: 1
CONFERENCE: SOUTHERN
LOCATION: LEXINGTON, VA
HOME FLOOR: CAMERON HALL (5,029)
NICKNAME: KEYDETS
COLORS: RED, WHITE AND YELLOW
COACH: JOE CANTAFIO, record at VMI, 49-66.

Was that Ramon? Or was it Damon? VMI coach Joe Cantafio never could tell those Williams' twins apart, but it didn't really matter. What was important was that Cantafio could put them on the court, and be certain they'd provide about half the team's scoring, precisely what they did the last three years.

Now the Williams boys - Damon (20.7 ppg, 2.9 rpg, 71 assists, 38 steals) and Ramon (18.6 ppg, 3.0 rpg, 62 assists, 41 steals) - are gone, along with two other starters. Cantafio must rebuild a program that has become, if not the most successful, then at least one of the most competitive in the Southern Conference.

"We've been in this position before," Cantafio said. "Fortunately we're at the level where we had

kids who sat down last year, who didn't have to play. Now those kids are ready to step in."

One of those players ready to step right in was not even eligible a year ago. 6-4 junior **Erek Perry** came to the Keydets in a most improbable manner. He transferred - that's right, transferred - to VMI from Delaware. Perry is the first basketball player ever and the first athlete since 1957 to leave another school for Virginia Military. Football player Sam Woolwine was the last, earning All-America honors after transferring from Georgia Tech.

If Perry's arrival weren't unusual enough, his reason for switching to VMI was an even greater surprise. Two years ago, guard Renard Johnson left the Keydets for Delaware, where his roommate was, oddly enough, Erek Perry. Johnson spoke often of his former school.

"Whatever he told Erek, whether it was good or bad, Erek took it in a positive way," Cantafio said. "He decided VMI was the right place for him to be. You have to have a lot of respect for a kid who comes here, but especially for a kid who was on scholarship somewhere else."

Perry wasn't just on scholarship at Delaware. He started most of the time in his two years there, averaging 9.4 points and 3.4 rebounds. He holds the school record for three-point field goals in a game and made the East Coast Conference all-rookie team in 1988.

"Erek's a very skilled player," Cantafio said, "not a first-team All-America, but very solid. He really plays hard. I like his work ethic."

Perry could play either small forward or shooting guard, where he would team with the Keydets' most experienced player, 6-1 junior **Percy Covington** (9.0 ppg, 2.0 rpg, 152 assists, 62 steals). Covington's emergence and the presence of the Williams' twins the last two years forced Cantafio to a three-guard lineup.

"Percy's really going to be a good one for us," Cantafio said. "He's always had good point guard skills, and now he's improved his shooting." Covington became a legitimate scoring threat near the end of last season, leading the team in field goal accuracy at 51 percent and shooting 43 percent from three-point range.

Kenny Johnson (2.0 ppg, 1.0 rpg), a 6-2 junior, has been a solid reserve guard for two seasons. 6-2 sophomore **Juan Banks** (1.8 ppg, 0.8 rpg) can play point or shooting guard.

Cantafio is counting on 6-7 senior **Greg Fittz** (8.0 ppg, 4.7 rpg) to anchor VMI's front line. Fittz averaged 13 points and eight rebounds in his first four games last season, then was sidelined by a back injury. He was a part-time starter the rest of the year. Fittz will be joined in the frontcourt by 6-7 sophomore **Lewis Preston** (2.7 ppg, 3.6 rpg), who has come a long way since his days as the team's video cameraman.

Preston played just 12 minutes per game last year, but was fifth in the Southern Conference in blocked shots (25). He really displayed his potential in a 14-point victory over Tennessee-Chattanooga in the first round of the Southern Conference tournament, scoring nine points, grabbing six rebounds and blocking five shots.

Cantafio had a good recruiting season, signing five freshmen. They are 6-7 **Jonathan Goodman** (Denmark-Olar HS/Denmark, SC), 6-5 **Larry Jeffries** (George Washington HS/Danville, VA), 6-4 **Jamie Lee** (George Wythe HS/Wytheville, VA), 6-3 **Heath Schroyer** (DeMatha High/Walkersville, MD) and 5-10 **Sean Spriggs** (Maury HS/Norfolk, VA). Goodman averaged 13.5 points, 10.9 rebounds and 3.6 blocked shots for a team that went 30-1. Jeffries, who played center in high school, averaged 14.8 points, 8.5 rebounds and 4.6 assists. Lee was a first-team Virginia all-state selection, averaging 21.5 points, 12.4 rebounds and 5.6 assists. Schroyer was one of three senior starters on DeMatha's Metro-D.C. champions. Spriggs, a pure point guard, averaged 5.7 points, 5.1 assists and 3.5 steals.

VMI will miss Ramon and Damon Williams, who finished their careers as the third- and fourth-leading scorers in school history. The twins accounted for half the Keydets' points the last three seasons. Taking up some of the slack will be an improving Covington, one of the top point guards in the Southern Conference, and transfer Perry, a good shooter and hard worker. Several freshmen will also get a chance to play key roles.

Cohesion could be a problem in the Keydets' revamped lineup. VMI, which was 11-1 at home last season, will always be competitive. But without the Williams twins, things figure to be considerably tougher this time around. "Even though we've got a pretty good nucleus returning, everybody thinks we're not going to be very good," Cantafio said. "One thing we can guarantee is the fact we'll play hard."

Even so, if sounds here like a second division finish.

1990-91 VMI SCHEDULE

Nov.	24	@Virginia Tech
	26	Bluefield College (VA)
	28	Bridgewater College (VA)
	30	Liberty University (VA)
Dec.	3	@Radford (VA)
	7-8	#Cornell Tournament
	18	@Alabama
	20	@Vanderbilt
Jan.	2	##James Madison
	5	@Furman
	7	@The Citadel
	10	@North Carolina Asheville
	12	Western Carolina
	14	Tennessee-Chattanooga
	19	Marshall
	21	Richmond
	23	William & Mary
	26	East Tennessee State
	28	@Appalachian State
Feb.	2	The Citadel
	4	Furman
	9	@Tennessee-Chattanooga
	11	@Western Carolina
	16	@Marshall
	23	Appalachian State
	25	@East Tennessee State
Mar.	1-3	*Southern Conference Tournament

@ Road Games
# Ithaca, NY (Cornell, Kent State & Vermont)
Site to be announced.
* Asheville, NC

VIRGINIA TECH

LAST SEASON: 13-18
CONFERENCE RECORD: 3-9
STARTERS LOST: 1
STARTERS RETURNING: 4
CONFERENCE: METRO
LOCATION: BLACKSBURG, VA
HOME FLOOR: CASSELL COLISEUM (9,971)
NICKNAME: HOKIES
COLORS: CHICAGO MAROON AND BURNT ORANGE
COACH: FRANKIE ALLEN, record at Virginia Tech, 43-45.

The rumblings around the Metro —even from other coaches —is that Virginia Tech coach Frankie Allen has to win or else he'll be seeking another job next season.

It's not a very inviting proposition for Allen, who has to build a team around three seniors. None of the seniors —6-9 center **David Herbster**, 6-8 center **Ibraheem Oladotun** and 6-5 forward **Antony Moses** — are exactly showstoppers.

Virginia Tech made noise in the Metro race in the mid '80s when guard Dell Curry was firing up long range missiles. When Curry took his act to the pros, his green shooting light was passed on to guards Bimbo Coles and Wally Lancaster. After Lancaster played out his eligibility in '88-89, it left Coles all alone to carry a vastly undertalented Tech team in '89-90 that finished seventh in the eight-team Metro. As a result, Coles averaged 25.3 points while shooting horribly (40.4 percent). Coles was a second round pick of the Sacramento Kings and was later traded to Miami. No one else on Virginia Tech's team averaged in double figures. It was Bimbo Coles and the 12 Dwarfs. As a team, the Hokies shot 40.4 percent. They were also blasted on the boards by a deficit of over five a game.

The only consolation of 1989-90 was Virginia Tech ended the regular season with three straight wins, using a lineup of virtually all freshmen.

"I really felt good the last 2 1/2 months of the season," Allen said. "Unless you have an elite group of freshmen, it's tough to step right in and play. Late in the season last year, the freshmen figured out what it took to win."

Allen believes he'll have a wider talent base this season from which to choose a lineup. But it's still a young team with two true freshmen, two redshirt freshmen, four sophomores and a transfer who will be a junior. The best of the returning players is 6-4 sophomore forward **Dirk Williams** (9.8 ppg, 3.6 rpg). Williams, who ran the outside lanes on fast breaks about as well as anyone in the Metro, made the All-Metro freshman team. He scored 32 points at Louisville.

John Rivers, a 6-5 junior forward, was the Hokies leading rebounder (7.3 rpg) last season, but was a disappointment most of the year and lost his starting job for four games. A former high school All-America football player, Rivers will report to the basketball team late this season because he decided to play for Virginia Tech's football team. Perhaps football will toughen him for board battles in the winter. Rivers won't be missed if one of the Hokies other returning forwards —Moses (3.7 ppg, 2.2 rpg), 6-7 sophomore **Thomas Elliott** (2.5 ppg, 2.5 rpg), 6-7 redshirt freshman **Corey Jackson** or 7-0 junior transfer **Eric Wilson** —steps in the front.

Jackson and Wilson are two prime examples why Allen believes he'll have more weapons to play with this season. Jackson may give Virginia Tech the outside shooting boost it has sorely needed. He averaged 18.3 points and 9.7 rebounds at Elsik High in Alief, Texas, two seasons ago and was rated among the nation's Top 10 unsigned college prospects at small forward by Bob Gibbons in April, 1989.

Allen said he expects an immediate contribution from Wilson, who can play both the high and low posts, and can run the floor. Wilson originally signed with Minnesota out of high school where he redshirted before transferring to Hutchinson (Kan.) JC. At Hutchinson, he averaged 5.6 points and four rebounds. He's considered more of a finesse player than a banger, which may not be good news for Allen. One of the Hokies' biggest problems recently has been soft inside play.

Herbster (6.5 ppg, 5.5 rpg) is the returning starting center. But he may be pushed out of the spotlight by Oladotun if the unpredictable Nigerian can play consistently. Oladotun is just starting his fourth year of playing organized basketball, which is why Allen never knew last year what he'd get from Oladotun (3.4 ppg, 3.5 rpg) from game to game. In the regular season finale against Memphis State, Oladotun played more like Akeem Olajuwon. He had career highs of 14 points, eight rebounds and three blocked shots.

"I told Ibraheem to get a tape of the Memphis State game, watch it everyday and play like he played in that game." said Allen.

Center help also may come from 6-10 redshirt freshman **Jimmy Carruth** who averaged 14.2 points, 10.6 rebounds and 7.6 blocked shots as a senior two years ago at Stephen F. Austin HS in Port Arthur, Texas. His 244 blocked shots as a senior broke his own Class AAA record. His shot blocking dimension could add something Virginia Tech has never enjoyed.

The Hokies guards must pick up the scoring slack from the departed Coles. Hopefully, they'll have better shot selection than Bimbo. Returning sophomore guards **J. J. Burton** and **Rod Wheeler** both shot under 36 percent from the field last year. The 6-1 Burton (7.6 ppg, 2.5 rpg) was bothered by ankle injuries most of the season, but managed to start 24 games. The 5-10 Wheeler (8.8 ppg, 1.9 rpg) saw most of his action as a reserve.

"I think a lot of poor shooting by our young kids was a case of nerves," Allen said. "Kids like J. J. shot just horrendously, but it was like being in a batting slump."

Depth at guard is thin with 6-2 junior **Mike Holland** (1.3 ppg), 6-3 freshman **Donald Corker** of Columbia HS in Decatur, Ga. (18.1 ppg, 7.0 rpg) and 6-3 hometown freshman **Jay Purcell** of Blacksburg (Va.) HS (19.0 ppg, 6.0 rpg).

BLUE RIBBON ANALYSIS

Allen is one of the nicest guys in Division I college coaching, but he's in a tough spot.

Even though he played a lot of freshmen last season, his team is still young and his talent base hasn't developed. To make matters worse, the rest of the Metro Conference has improved.

Unless his new players are dynamite and provide Virginia Tech with elements it hasn't had in several years —such as relentless play in the paint —the Hokies are likely to sink to last place in the Metro this season.

1990-91 VIRGINIA TECH SCHEDULE

Nov.	24	Virginia Military Institute
	28	James Madison
Dec.	1	William & Mary
	8	@Old Dominion
	11	@Virginia Commonwealth
	22	@George Washington
	28-29	#Times-Dispatch Invitational
Jan.	3	@Marshall
	5	Memphis State
	10	Tulane
	12	Southern Mississippi
	16	@South Carolina
	19	@Cincinnati
	23	##Virginia
	26	Florida State
	30	@Louisville
Feb.	2	@West Virginia
	4	Richmond
	7	@Southern Mississippi
	9	@Tulane
	13	Louisville
	16	Cincinnati
	19	Maryland
	23	@Florida State
	27	South Carolina
Mar.	2	@Memphis State
	7-9	*Metro Tournament

@ Road Games
# Richmond, VA (James Madison, Richmond & Virginia Commonwealth)
Richmond, VA
* Roanoke, VA

WAKE FOREST

LAST SEASON: 12-16
CONFERENCE
RECORD: 3-11
STARTERS LOST: 1
STARTERS
RETURNING: 4
CONFERENCE:
ATLANTIC COAST
(ACC)
LOCATION: WINSTON-
SALEM, NC
HOME FLOOR:
LAWRENCE JOEL COLISEUM (14,407)
NICKNAME: DEMON DEACONS
COLORS: OLD GOLD & BLACK
COACH: DAVE ODOM, record at Wake Forest, 12-16.
Career record, 50-58.

Dave Odom got off to a rocky start in his first year as the head coach of the Wake Forest Demon Deacons. Wake Forest finished with a 12-16 overall record, low-lighted by a 3-11 mark in the ACC last year. Add to these less than stellar numbers the fact that Wake Forest has not finished with a winning record since 1985 and, even more amazingly, no current Demon Deacon has ever been on a team that has won more than three ACC games in any one season. Optimism would seem to be limited in Winston-Salem, however, despite all those negatives there is reason to believe that the future should be brighter for Wake Forest basketball in the 1990-91 season. A major reason for optimism is that Odom will be able to take a solid returning cast (four of the five starters return from last year) and combine it with one of the finest recruiting classes in the nation. The finished product could be a team that will be able to compete in the upper echelon of the ACC.

Odom will call on a bevy of talented forwards and should rightfully expect quality production from his frontcourt. Highlighting this group will be last year's scoring and rebounding leader, 6-8 junior forward **Chris King**. King (16.1 ppg, 7.4 rpg) also topped Wake Forest in scoring and rebounding his freshman year, thereby making him the first Demon Deacon since All-America Dickie Hemric in 1951 and '52 to capture team scoring and rebounding honors in his first two collegiate seasons. King also led Wake Forest in field goal percentage (54.6 percent, good for fourth in the ACC) and blocked shots (31, the ACC's eighth best mark). His scoring and rebounding totals also placed him in the conference's top dozen, finishing 12th and seventh in the two categories respectively. He likes to do most of his offensive damage on the baseline and his touch from 15-feet on in is outstanding. King almost makes the most of his rebounding prowess on the offensive end. Last year he led Wake Forest with 77 offensive boards and scored a number of baskets on putbacks. King has blossomed into one of the ACC's elite players in his first two years of college basketball.

Another potentially explosive player returning to the Wake Forest frontcourt is 6-8 junior forward **Anthony Tucker** (13.0 ppg, 6.3 rpg, 3.3 apg), second on the team in scoring, rebounding and assists last year while leading the Demon Deacons with 37 steals. Last season was Tucker's first in a Wake Forest uniform after sitting out the 1988-89 campaign after transferring from Georgetown. He was by far Wake Forest's most versatile player as he played substantial minutes at four different positions (every position on the floor but center). Tucker shot an unimpressive 46 percent from the field last year, but this percentage is misleading because he was often called upon to play out of position on the perimeter and found himself shooting 18 to 20-foot jumpers. He has the ability and shooting touch to make these shots on occasions, but he is a more effective player using slashing moves in the lane to free himself up for shots and to distribute the ball to others for easy baskets. For the more experienced and confident backcourt this year, Odom hopes he can use Tucker exclusively in the frontcourt. This would give Wake Forest an athlete who is quicker than most of the opponents he will face up front.

Two other players who return and provide capable backup help in the frontcourt are 6-6 senior forward **Todd Sanders** (2.5 ppg, 1.3 rpg) and 6-9 senior forward/center **Tom Wise** (1.1 ppg, 1.2 rpg). Both players saw action in 16 games last year and they both earned varsity letters in each of their first three years at Wake Forest. Sanders is the more refined, complete player of the two, and with his strong work habits he can be counted on this year to contribute a solid 15 minutes per night. Wise is solid 240-pounder who is not afraid of contact inside and he will be used primarily as a reserve at the power forward position. A third court reserve may be 6-6 sophomore forward **Mike Forester** (0.4 ppg, 0.6 rpg), who saw action in just five games in 1989-90.

The Wake Forest frontcourt will also benefit tremendously from a talent-laden group of newcomers. The premier newcomer at Wake Forest is 6-7 freshman forward **Rodney Rogers** (28.3 ppg, 12.3 rpg). Rogers, from Hillside HS in Durham, N.C., was a *Parade Magazine* All-America pick and the player of the year in North Carolina last year. He should be an immediate impact player. Rogers has the power to battle inside, he is built like the prototype NFL tight end or linebacker, and has the skill to handle himself on the perimeter. He was unquestionably the most physically imposing high school player in the class of '90. "A real bull. A space eater who could not be separated from a rebound with a jackhammer," said Clark Francis, editor and publisher of The Hoop Scoop.

Another North Carolina all-state performer enrolling at Wake Forest this year is 6-8 forward **Trelonnie Owens** (19.5 ppg, 11.1 rpg). Owens led Bladenboro HS to the North Carolina 1A state championship last year and like Rogers, he should be able to come into the program and contribute immediately. He scores well off the baseline and has very reliable hands. Owens is a powerful 240-pounder who will definitely add a strong rebounding presence and offensive potential to the Wake Forest bench and he should see considerable playing time as a freshman.

Two players who will be called upon to handle most of the duties in the post this season are returning lettermen **Phil Medlin** (1.8 ppg, 2.2 rpg in 26 games last year) and 7-0 freshman **Stanley King** (11.6 ppg, 10.1 rpg). Medlin, a 6-9 junior, has been a part-time starter in both of his first two seasons at Wake Forest, but his production both offensively and defensively must improve if he is to become a full-time starter. He showed promise as a freshman starting in 20 games and averaging 4.4 points and 3.3 rebounds while contributing surprisingly solid defensive play as well. However, last year he showed inconsistency as a rebounder and as a result he became a backup to seniors Sam Ivy and Ralph Kitley. King is out of August Martin HS in Jamaica, N.Y. He possesses excellent shotblocking and rebounding potential but he needs refinement on the offensive end. King may not be ready to jump right into the fray in the ACC, but it will not be very long before this freshman with tremendous physical attributes becomes a real factor for the Demon Deacons. Some New York observers see a little Duane Causwell, the former Temple center who entered college with an unrefined offensive game, but with good physical attributes and left a first round NBA draft pick.

The backcourt will be a strength for Wake Forest as last year's starting duo returns. **Derrick McQueen**, a 5-11 junior who started 22 games last year, is the Demon Deacons' point guard. He suffered through a tough season physically as he had a broken nose in December, an ankle sprain in January and capped it off with a concussion in the ACC tournament. As a result of playing banged up, McQueen's statistics (6.1 ppg, 3.1 rpg, 5.2 apg) slacked off last year as compared with some outstanding freshman year numbers. However, his 5.2 assists per game did rank McQueen sixth in the ACC last year, and his floor generalship cannot be overestimated. He also proved as a freshman that he can connect from the perimeter, making 48.3 percent of his field goal attempts. Last year, his percentage fell to 35.5 percent, but again it has to be believed that a healthy McQueen will be able to give a more consistently effective performance. Alongside McQueen in the backcourt again will be 6-3 senior **Robert Siler** (9.9 ppg, 3.0 rpg). A powerful guard, who was an outstanding football player in high school and even toyed with the idea of playing both sports at Wake Forest, Siler has also suffered through injuries his first three years in college. His freshman year was ended after just nine games by ligament damage to his left knee, and he had to undergo a second surgery on the knee immediately following last year. He was not able to play competitive basketball all summer long. It is hoped that the injuries are behind him and that the 1990-91 campaign will be by far his finest. After all, when healthy, Siler can shoot the ball with excellent range, drive aggressively to the basket and rebound the ball as well as any guard in the ACC. Also, when he is healthy, he is one of the best leaping guards in the country. It is absolutely imperative for Siler to be 100 percent effective if Wake Forest is to have a chance to qualify for a post-season tournament for the first time since 1985.

The three top backcourt reserves this year will all be freshmen. 6-3 **Marc Blucas** (20.8 ppg, 10.1 rpg) led his Girard HS team to the Pennsylvania state title last year. Blucas is known as a hardnosed guard who gets after the opposition defensively for a full 94-feet. He has been coined a "Jeff Moe-clone" after the scrappy guard who played at Iowa a couple of years ago. 6-2 **Randolph Childress** (20.8 ppg, 8.1 apg) was an outstanding prep performer at renowned Flint Hill HS in the Northern Virginia suburbs of Washington. The Clinton, Md., native will be a contributor at both the point and second guard positions. He is an outstanding ballhandler. Finally, 6-3 **Robert Doggett** (29.4 ppg, 3.7 rpg) rounds out this talented trio of Wake Forest freshmen guards. He was an all-state performer at Reidsville, N.C., HS, and led the state of North Carolina in three-point shooting.

Steve Ray, a 6-0 senior guard who played in only one game last year after suffering a severe knee injury, will most likely not be ready for the start of the season. He is not expected to play at all for Wake Forest this year and may even be granted a medical redshirt to allow him to finish up his career in 1991-92. Also, **David Hedgecoe**, a 5-11 sophomore, who walked-on in his freshman year and replaced Ray as the backup point guard, will have a difficult time making the team this year. He played in 11 games last year averaging 0.9 points and collecting eight assists.

While the outlook for Wake Forest is indeed bright, there are several players who were lost to graduation whose absence will be felt. First and foremost among these players is 6-7 power forward/center Sam Ivy (10.0 ppg, 5.3 rpg). Ivy's intensity and toughness will be sorely missed. Ivy had a peculiar career at Wake Forest as he achieved second-team All-ACC status as a sophomore, averaging 18.6 points, and 7.6 rebounds, and saw his statistics drop as a junior and really plummet during his senior year. It was almost as if, while Wake Forest was building as strong a program to complement him, Ivy was worn out from carrying the team from the first day he stepped on the floor as a freshman. Teams keyed on Ivy and by the time he was a senior, he had run out of solutions to the doubleteaming down low, that he had faced his entire career. It was also physically draining for Ivy to play quite a bit at center where he consistently gave four and five inches away to his opposite number. David Carlyle (6.0 ppg, 1.9 rpg) and Antonio

Johnson (3.7 ppg, 1.3 apg) will be missed from the Wake Forest backcourt. Carlyle and Johnson were two of the team's better three-point shooters. Finally, 6-10 center Ralph Kitley (1.6 ppg, 3.0 rpg), who started nine games in the middle last season and contributed 14 minutes per contest, has graduated. He was a physical inside presence, who, while unspectacular, would not hurt Wake Forest offensively and defensively and he could be relied on to play an intelligent, unselfish brand of basketball.

BLUE RIBBON ANALYSIS

Wake Forest fans have got to be chomping at the bit to get this season under way. After several years of being ACC doormats, Wake Forest is primed to do some damage of its own. With a frontcourt featuring the talented King and Tucker complemented by guards McQueen and Siler, the Demon Deacons will be close in every game and have a chance to knock anybody in the ACC off. Also, freshmen Rogers is the most highly regarded player to enroll at Wake Forest in quite some time. Owens, another freshman with tremendous strength, should be able to come off the bench and add a positive contribution. Rogers and Owens will immediately let the rest of the ACC know that a game against Wake Forest this year will mean bumps and bruises time.

If the talented newcomers (Odom also signed three quality guards) which Wake Forest has stockpiled, blends as expected with the proven veterans on this team, then there is no doubt that Wake Forest will win between 17 and 20 games and have a real chance at a post-season bid. It is not out of the realm of possibility that Wake Forest can be an upper division team in the ACC this season. Even if the Demon Deacons take longer to develop than expected, Odom knows that his rebuilding days at Wake Forest are now behind him and that there could be an exciting ride back to ACC and national prominence in the future.

1990-91 WAKE FOREST SCHEDULE

Nov.	23	Howard University
	24	Fairleigh Dickinson
	27	@Alabama
Dec.	1	@Tulane
	6	#Villanova
	8	@Davidson
	22	Richmond
Jan.	2	Maryland
	6	@Georgia Tech
	9	Colorado
	12	@Clemson
	14	@Duke
	19	North Carolina State
	23	North Carolina
	28	Miami (FL)
	31	Winthrop College (SC)
Feb.	2	@Virginia
	4	@William & Mary
	6	Bucknell
	9	Georgia Tech
	10	Virginia
	13	@North Carolina
	16	Duke
	23	@Maryland
	24	Clemson
	27	New Hampshire
Mar.	2	@North Carolina State
	8-10	##ACC Tournament

@ Road Games
# ACC/Big East Challenge, Chapel Hill, NC
Charlotte, NC

WASHINGTON

LAST SEASON: 11-17
CONFERENCE RECORD: 5-13
STARTERS LOST: 2
STARTERS RETURNING: 3
CONFERENCE: PACIFIC-10
LOCATION: SEATTLE, WA
HOME FLOOR: HEC EDMUNDSON PAVILION (9,600)
NICKNAME: HUSKIES
COLORS: PURPLE AND GOLD
COACH: LYNN NANCE record at Washington, 11-17. Career record, 230-143.

When the Washington basketball program ran out of West German stars, the Huskies started to experience hard times. Washington enjoyed eight consecutive winning seasons starting in 1980, including two Pacific-10 Conference co-titles. But when NBA first round draftees Chris Welp (1985) and Detlef Schrempf (1987), both West German imports, finished their collegiate careers, the Huskies haven't been able to regroup.

This year's roster doesn't have any foreign players. In fact, 10 of the 13 players are from the state of California, which means either the state of Washington isn't producing the prep talent the Huskies need or that other schools are getting the available in-state players.

Either way, second year coach Lynn Nance, a one-time Washington standout, cannot be expected to produce immediate success. Nance, who came to Seattle off a brilliant 25-5 season at St. Mary's, suffered through a ninth place finish in the Pac-10. Only cross-state rival Washington State was worse.

While the Huskies have three starters and eight lettermen returning, the two graduation losses were severe. The major departure is three time All-Conference guard Eldridge Recasner (16.2 ppg, 3.9 rpg, 3.4 apg). He was the team's leading scorer the past two seasons and was the Huskies' only bona fide three-point threat. Recasner converted 38 treys, twice as many as the rest of the squad. Also gone is 6-7 center Mark West (8.1 ppg, 5.2 rpg), a three-year starter. Sophomore reserve guards Jeff Brown (1.3 ppg, 1.0 rpg) and Ryan Kaps (1.4 ppg, 0.4 rpg) are also gone.

Heading the list of returnees is Dion Brown (11.3 ppg, 6.3 rpg), an athletic 6-5, 203-pound forward. A transfer from Chaminade, Brown is a crowd pleaser who can dazzle fans with his leaping ability (40-inch vertical jump) and power dunks. His problem has been consistency. While Brown scored in double figures in 18 of the 28 games, he has the tendency to disappear at times, both offensively and on the backboards. Foul problems (seven disqualifications) also hampered Brown's effectiveness last year.

If Washington is to show improvement, it will need 6-7 senior Mike Hayward (5.2 ppg, 2.8 rpg) to return to the form that earned him Pac-10 freshman of the year honors. Hayward's career numbers have been on a downward spiral. His scoring has dropped from 14.0 to 9.6 to 5.2. His rebounding has shown the same tendency —from 5.0 to 4.1 to 2.8. Hayward started 25 games last year and broke into double figures in scoring only twice while shooting a meager .434. Hayward has always operated around the perimeter and has never been a productive rebounder, as evidenced by only two double figure rebounding efforts in three seasons. Hayward, like Brown, experienced foul troubles with six disqualifications.

The third returning starter is 6-3 senior guard Brent Merritt (6.7 ppg, 2.6 rpg), a transfer from Contra

Costa (Calif.) College whom the Huskies had hoped to redshirt last season. A standout track performer in junior college, Merritt hit only 42.4 percent from the field and made only two three-pointers. The Huskies did have one of the conference's most productive sixth men in 6-6 junior forward Doug Meekins (10.4 ppg, 6.2 rpg), who sat out his freshman year. Meekins did get ten starts during the year. He was the team's high scorer on four occasions and wound up third in minutes played.

6-10 senior center Todd Lautenbach (3.9 ppg, 2.4 rpg) has always shown offensive promise, but has had his playing time limited because of defensive and rebounding deficiencies. As a sophomore, Lautenbach scored 21 points against conference champion Arizona and 17 against Arizona State, on the road. This after a freshman year in which he totaled 29 points against the same two teams. Injured early last season, Lautenbach never seemed to get going, although two of his three double figure scoring efforts came in the last four games of the year.

Quentin Youngblood (3.4 ppg, 1.6 apg), a 6-4 sophomore, started seven games as a rookie. His shooting (.378) was off all year, although his seven three-pointers were second on the team to Recasner. Steve Hall, a 6-4 junior (2.1 ppg, 1.9 apg), was injured the last part of the season and appeared in only 17 games, although eight were in a starting role. He also had shooting woes (.382). Also back is 6-3 senior guard Anthony Jenkins (2.5 ppg, 0.8 rpg).

The Huskies are getting some sizeable help up front in 6-10 redshirt freshman center Maurice Woods. Just over 200 pounds, Woods averaged 22.0 points, 13.0 rebounds and six blocked shots per game in his senior year at Kennedy HS in Richmond, Calif. Byron Daye (21.8 ppg), a 6-3 transfer from Chabot (Calif.) JC ppg) could challenge for a backcourt starting position. Washington did land one in-state freshman in 6-6 guard Tim Caviezel (17.6 ppg, 7.0 rpg at Mount Vernon HS). He joins 6-4 guard James French (El Cerrito HS of Richmond, Calif.) and 6-7 forward Trent Cornelius (10.5 ppg, 7.8 rpg at Cleveland HS in Reseda, Calif.) on the list of newcomers.

Caviezel was considered a national caliber blue chipper. "He shoots the ball very well from three-point range and is a good ballhandler," said Nance. "In time he'll be one of the top collegiate guards." French was considered one of California's best point guards. Nance feels he'll be an "exceptional player." Cornelius is a solid rebounder.

Nance played a ball-control attack his last year at St. Mary's, a philosophy he said was dictated by the talent available. The Huskies weren't an overly patient club a year ago, nor were they a free wheeling outfit. Surprisingly, Washington was a good rebounding team, averaging more than five rebounds a game advantage, despite the fact the starting front line measured 6-8, 6-7 and 6-5.

A year ago, Nance said his goal for the year was stability, to get to the point where the players knew exactly what to expect from the coaching staff, and vice versa. Now the goal has to be to be more competitive in the Pac-10. Washington has suffered through two 5-13 conference records in the last three seasons. In Seattle, the fans expect more, even if the West German pipeline has dried up.

BLUE RIBBON ANALYSIS

Don't be surprised if Nance slows the Huskies down this year and tries to win on ball control, as he did so successfully at St. Mary's. Washington doesn't have a lot of firepower after the departure of Recasner. The team has no serious three-point threat, and unless Lautenbach emerges, there is no major scorer in the post area. Meekins showed promise of being a big time scorer, while Brown will get his points.

Washington does have some athletes in the backcourt. The problem is that none have shown any consistency as a scorer. Last year the Huskies shot only .460 overall and .326 from three-point range. Washington's best percentage shooter, Mark West (.514), and top three-point threat, Recasner, are gone.

If Nance can mold this roster into a winning team, it will be a solid coaching job. The Huskies don't figure to escape the Pacific-10's second division. It might be a battle to stay out of the basement.

WASHINGTON STATE

LAST SEASON: 22-7
CONFERENCE RECORD: 1-17
STARTERS LOST: 3
STARTERS RETURNING: 2
CONFERENCE: PACIFIC-10
LOCATION: PULLMAN, WA
HOME FLOOR: FRIEL COURT (12,058)
NICKNAME: COUGARS
COLORS: CRIMSON AND GRAY
COACH: KELVIN SAMPSON, record at Washington State, 30-57.

Last season, one that produced only seven victories in all and a miserable 1-17 conference record, magnified the Washington State problems. One was an obvious lack of overall talent. The Cougars tried to cover this by playing a deliberate style, yet one that relied heavily on the three-point shot. However, coach Kelvin Sampson didn't have a consistent shooter from any range. Washington State shot a miserable 42.7 percent for the year and only 35.8 from bonus range while attempting over 17 per game. Lack of depth also was a trouble area. The Cougars lost eight games in which they led at halftime and dropped nine decisions by seven points or less. On the road the Cougars were 0-10.

That was the bad news. The good news is that Sampson brought in four freshmen and four junior college transfers. The emphasis in the recruiting class was finding players who can score. The team's main

threat of a year ago, 6-3 guard Darryl Woods (15.3 ppg, 3.6 rpg) is gone, as are starters David Sanders (6.0 ppg, 2.9 rpg) and 6-8 Neil Evans (6.3 ppg, 4.5 rpg) plus reserves Herb Delaney (4.3 ppg, 2.6 rpg) and Winston Bell (2.1 ppg, 1.5 rpg).

Last year's prize freshmen, 6-0 guard **Bennie Seltzer** (11.7 ppg, 4.2 apg) is back, as is the starting center, 6-10 **Brian Payne** (9.3 ppg, 4.3 rpg). The Cougars again will utilize a three-guard lineup. **Terrence Lewis** (26.5 ppg, 4.0 rpg), a 6-4 transfer from Howard (Tex.) JC, could join Seltzer and 6-3 **Neil Derrick** (27.0 ppg, 4.0 apg), from Trinity Valley (Tex.) JC, in the starting lineup. He is the most highly regarded player to sign with the Cougars in years. Lewis is a native of Birmingham, Ala. He originally signed with Providence, but had to go to Howard JC instead. Lewis was ranked as one of the Top Five JC players in the country.

"Terrence is the best guard in the country," said his junior college coach. "He shoots and hits from everywhere."

Derrick was also one of the premier JC players in the country last year.

Pressing this trip will be 5-10 **Tyrone Maxey** (14.6 ppg, 5.0 apg) from South Plans (Tex.) JC, 6-5 redshirt freshman **Brian Sparrow** and 6-5 senior **Reco Rowe** (4.9 ppg, 1.3 rpg, 1988-89), coming off a medical redshirt season. Another possibility is 6-6 senior letterman **Juan Thomas** (4.5 ppg, 3.0 rpg). Also returning is 5-11 **Sean Tresvant** (1.5 ppg).

Up front the Cougars still have major problems. Payne is 240 pounds but had only one double figure rebounding effort last season. The Cougars were outrebounded by almost six per game a year ago and also committed 701 fouls to 479 for the opposition in trying to battle a height deficit. Senior forward **Jason Thomason** (4.5 ppg, 3.0 rpg), only 6-6, is the other experienced front liner with Payne.

Sampson undoubtedly will have to use new faces at the two inside positions, **Ken Critton** (14.3 ppg, 11.5 rpg), a 6-8, 220-pounder from Snyder JC, figures to play, as does 6-8, 220-pound freshman **Rob Corkrum** (18.5 ppg, 11.5 rpg, 7.0 blpg) from Shady Park HS in Spokane, Wash. He was the top senior in the state a year ago. Freshman **David Vik** (17.5 ppg, 8.4 rpg, 2.4 blpg) from Everett, Wash., is 6-11 but needs to add muscle to his 195-pound frame.

"Up front will be our weakness," Sampson said, "but we're got to find some way to turn our front line's weakness into a strength. I'm really excited about our offensive potential. We'll push the ball up the court and be an exciting team to play. Last year you saw the trend move towards a more up-tempo style of play. That trend is fine. But if you don't have the players to play that way, you're going to get killed.

"However, I think that we've gone out and gotten that type of player, so we can play at a higher tempo offensively."

The massive recruiting class also includes 6-7 freshman **Joey Warmenhoven** (17.2 ppg, 6.9 rpg) from Grandview, Wash., and 6-1 freshman guard **Eddie Hill** (16.3 ppg, 6.7 apg) from Reseda, Calif.

BLUE RIBBON ANALYSIS

Sampson is a realist in looking at the Cougars chances against the likes of Arizona and UCLA, but is not discouraged about his program's situation.

"I guess the rich get richer, but in our situation the poor haven't gotten poorer," he said. "We've gotten better and have managed to steal a little bit from the rich this year. That's going to make it tough on the league when the teams that have been at the bottom, like USC, Arizona State, Washington State and Oregon, make a push. All that does is make the Pac-10 unbelievably strong."

Sampson says he plans to up the tempo this year. The Cougars not only lost often last year, but they weren't much fun to watch with their deliberate attack. The problem will be getting the ball off the

backboards to run with. Washington State doesn't have the height or muscle up front, which may force Sampson to slow it down again midway through the season. The Cougars do have better athletes than they've had in the last several years. However, they're untested in the Pacific-10, and the league is too strong for newcomers to make much of an impact. Last year, with a veteran lineup, Washington State was 0-10 on the road. With so many new faces in the picture, that doesn't figure to improve much. Looks like tenth place again. This definitely is a rebuilding year in the Palouse. Still, it has to be better than last season.

WEBER STATE

LAST SEASON: 14-15
CONFERENCE RECORD: 8-8
STARTERS LOST: 1
STARTERS RETURNING: 4
CONFERENCE: BIG SKY
LOCATION: OGDEN, UT
HOME FLOOR: DEE EVENTS CENTER (12,900)
NICKNAME: WILDCATS
COLORS: ROYAL, PURPLE AND WHITE
COACH: DENNY HUSTON, record at Weber State, 31-26.
Career record, 44-38.

Idaho, Montana and Nevada - all for good reason - are categorized as the Big Sky Conference favorites going into the 1990-91 season. Idaho, after all, is the defending champion and returns three starters. Montana returns four starters off an 18-11 team. And, sooner or later, Nevada is bound to play at a level that matches its considerable talent.

Thus it would be easy to overlook, say, a Weber State. It would also be a major mistake. The Wildcats were the finest sub-.500 team in the league a year ago.

Weber State led the league in rebound margin (plus 6.2). It led in three-point field goal accuracy

(42.1 percent). The Wildcats shot 48.8 percent from the floor and held opponents to 44.0 percent field goal shooting, both figures second in the league. They also defeated every team in the Big Sky at least once except Montana.

Want a darkhorse? Take Weber State. The lone starter gone is first-team All-Big Sky guard Michael Ostlund (11.3 ppg, 3.4 rpg). A heady player with a knack for making the key basket, Ostlund's leadership will be missed. Replacements abound, however.

Tony Nicholas, a rangy 6-4 senior from Oakland, Calif., should start at one guard spot. Nicholas (9.5 ppg, 3.7 rpg) has three-point range and the moves to go to the hole. His offensive prowess showed in a 33-point outburst against Idaho State.

Nicholas should team up with **Jason Joe,** a 6-2 junior from Los Angeles, to form a decent backcourt. Joe (7.3 ppg, 1.8 rpg) assumed a growing role as the season progressed. Quick off the dribble with a nice pull-up jumper, Joe set a Big Sky record by making 12-of-12 free throws versus Nevada in a Big Sky tournament victory.

Backcourt depth, though, is a problem. 6-4 redshirt freshman **Elroy Miller** (Battle Ground, Wash.) and 6-2 true freshman **Robbie Johnson** (Seaside, Calif.) are the lone backups. Neither is experienced.

The front line is considerably stronger, and in every way. Seniors **Aaron Bell** (6-5, 225), **Jerry McIntosh** (6-6, 240) and **Chris Metke** (6-8, 235) are basketball's version of the beef brothers. Bell (11.5 ppg, 5.6 rpg) is surprisingly quick for his size and was third on the team in assists (2.3). He goes to the basket hard, and contesting him is not a pleasant thought.

McIntosh (7.8 ppg, 6.5 rpg) led the Wildcats in rebounding while splitting time between center and power forward. He is burly, naturally, but possesses a soft touch which allows him to catch the ball in traffic. Metke (2.0 ppg, 2.5 rpg) is a player opposing fans love to hate. He plays very physically, and often finds himself in foul trouble because of it.

6-8 junior college transfer **Dave Baldwin** (College of Eastern Utah), 6-6 redshirt sophomore **Al Hamilton** (Dallas, Tex.) and 6-8 redshirt freshman **Kurt Schwan** (Westlake, Calif.) will be hard pressed to unseat the beef brothers. 6-5 freshman Jimmy DeGraffenried (Santaquin, Utah) also joins the ranks at forward.

Anthony McGowan, an honorable mention All-Big Sky performer, is back at center. The 6-8 senior is deceptively strong, with averages last year of 11.1 points and 6.3 rebounds. He also shot 57.7 percent from the field, slightly better than his 56.9 percent from the free throw line.

Mike Pomeroy, a 6-10 senior, backs up McGowan. Pomeroy (2.8 ppg, 2.3 rpg) has a decent touch, but is not naturally aggressive. When he tries to assert himself, he seems to get tagged with fouls. Still, Pomeroy has the kind of size that can pose problems for opponents in the Big Sky. And McGowan rarely needs to be spelled, anyway.

"We were 20th in the nation in rebounding margin," coach Denny Huston said. "And we didn't take a lot of three-point shots, but when we did it well. We were 18th in the nation in three-point accuracy. We need to build upon those positives."

BLUE RIBBON ANALYSIS

Weber State has the talent and a highly respected coach. The Wildcats could contend for a league title. And Huston knows it.

"This year, the hammer is really on us," he said. "We only lose one starter, we have seven experienced players returning, plus now our recruiting effort for two years begins to show itself.

"Hopefully, we can reap the benefits of having experienced players returning to our program. Our competition level on this team is high, which should give us a great deal of flexibility and bench strength. It will allow us to play at many different styles and many different tempos."

It will also allow Weber State to win a decent number of basketball games. The Wildcats could finish as high as second in the Big Sky Conference.

1990-91 WEBER STATE SCHEDULE

Nov.	24	Prairie View A&M (TX)
	26	Southern Utah State
	29	Brigham Young
Dec.	1	@North Texas
	13	@Utah State
	17	@Utah
	19	Utah State
	22	@St. Mary's
	29	Cal State-Northridge
Jan.	3	Western Washington
	5	@Cal State-Northridge
	10	Eastern Washington
	12	Idaho
	18	Nevada
	19	Idaho State
	23	@Montana
	25	@Montana State
	31	Montana State
Feb.	2	@Boise State
	7	@Idaho
	9	@Eastern Washington
	14	Montana
	16	@Idaho State
	21	@Northern Arizona
	23	@Nevada
Mar.	1	Boise State
	2	Northern Arizona
	7-9	#Big Sky Tournament

@ Road Games
# Site to be announced

WESTERN CAROLINA

LAST SEASON: 10-18
CONFERENCE RECORD: 3-11
STARTERS LOST: 3
STARTERS RETURNING: 2
CONFERENCE: SOUTHERN
LOCATION: CULLOWHEE, NC
HOME FLOOR: RAMSEY CENTER (7,826)
NICKNAME: CATAMOUNTS
COLORS: PURPLE AND GOLD
COACH: GREG BLATT, record at Western Carolina, 10-18.

Western Carolina coach Greg Blatt has confused some of his team's fans. "I was talking to someone during the summer about our recruiting class," Blatt said. "He asked me how many people we signed, and I told him nine. He said: 'Are you basketball or football?'"

If it sounds like Blatt is making wholesale changes in the Catamounts' program, well, he is. Before he arrived last season, Western Carolina had been through three coaches in the previous three years. The last one, Dave Possinger, made such a mess of things that Blatt was forced to go through his debut season with only seven scholarship players.

The Catamounts, predictably, finished last in the Southern Conference. Blatt knew he had to go out and find some players. "This year is going to be a completely different situation," he said, "one more conducive to hard work and healthy competition in practice. Last year, you could threaten them with their lives, but with only seven scholarship players, they knew they'd play 30-35 minutes a game no matter what."

Only two returnees, both starters, are likely to figure in Blatt's plans. The first is 6-2 junior guard **David Donerlson** (16.1 ppg, 3.0 rpg, 89 assists, 31 steals). "David was an inconsistent performer last year," Blatt said, "but at times was an excellent shooter." Donerlson shot just 42 percent overall, but made 44 percent (64-for-144) of his three-point attempts.

The other returning starter is 6-6 sophomore **Eric Dailey** (11.2 ppg, 9.6 rpg), who led the Southern Conference in both rebounding and field goal percentage (57.5) last year. He was runner-up for the Southern's freshman of the year award. "We'll see what kind of player Eric is this year," Blatt said. "He played on a team without a lot of depth or talent, and had to put in 35 minutes a game. Still, he was a proven performer as a freshman."

Western Carolina's remaining starting spots will be filled by newcomers. And, though Blatt wants to build his program with freshmen, he knew he needed some immediate help. That meant turning to the junior colleges, where he found two players who will play a great deal.

The first is 6-2 junior **Terry Boyd,** who averaged 24.8 points and 8.3 rebounds at Southern Union (Ala.) State. A third-team All-America selection, Boyd shot 55 percent from the field and made 92 three-point goals last season.

The second JC transfer is 6-7 junior **Cranford Jenkins,** whose numbers were 12.5 ppg and 7.0 rpg at Lees-McRae (N.C.) College. "We don't recruit junior college players unless we expect them to make an instant impact and play a major role," said Blatt. "I believe these two will."

Blatt completed the overhaul with seven new freshmen: 6-4 **Monty Bumper** (Greensboro Day School/Greensboro, N.C.), 6-5 **Bobby Getter** (Northwest Georgia HS/Trenton, Ga.), 6-2 **Ted Portee** (Lake Placid HS/Lake Placid, Fla.), 6-1 **Carey Rich** (C.A. Johnson HS/Columbia, S.C.), 6-6 **Sylvester Smalls** (Cape Coral HS/Cape Coral, Fla.), 6-6 **B.J. Thompson** (The Bolles School/Jacksonville, Fla.) and 6-8 **Lamont Turner** (Bartlett-Yancey HS/Yanceyville, N.C.).

Bumper, the co-player of the year among North Carolina independent schools, averaged 16.6 points and 8.8 rebounds. Getter averaged 29.2 points and 11.1 rebounds, shooting 49 percent from three-point range. Portee, chosen to Florida's 2-A all-state team three seasons running, was good for 28.3 points and 11.0 rebounds.

Rich, who made the South Carolina 3-A all-state team, averaged 23.1 points and 5.6 assists. Smalls, originally of Charleston, S.C., played just one season at Cape Coral but averaged 22.0 points and 12.0 rebounds. Thompson was a second-team 2-A All-State choice, averaging 20.8 points and 8.6 rebounds for Bolles. Turner's numbers were 12.2 points, 12.1 rebounds and three blocked shots per game.

BLUE RIBBON ANALYSIS

Western Carolina's basketball program has struggled the last four years, but better days are ahead under Blatt. Yet with so many new players, those days are likely to be few and far between again this year. The Catamounts will certainly struggle early, but could sneak up on some unsuspecting opponents later in the season.

"We'll be picked to finish at the bottom of the league again," Blatt said, "but I'm very excited and optimistic. We'll be much deeper and more talented than last year, but we've got nine newcomers and seven are freshmen. In the next two years, we'll see some real progress and strides in our program."

In the meantime, the immediate goal for Western Carolina should be to escape the Southern Conference basement.

WESTERN KENTUCKY

LAST SEASON: 13-17
CONFERENCE RECORD: 7-7
STARTERS LOST: 2
STARTERS RETURNING: 3
CONFERENCE: SUN BELT
LOCATION: BOWLING GREEN, KY
HOME FLOOR: E.A. DIDDLE ARENA (12,370)
NICKNAME: HILLTOPPERS
COLORS: RED AND WHITE
COACH: RALPH WILLARD, first year at Western Kentucky.

The Hilltoppers were the surprise team of the Sun Belt a year ago, finishing in a tie for third place after being picked for last. But it was not enough to save Murray Arnold's job. Arnold has been replaced by Ralph Willard, who comes to "The Hill" from the University of Kentucky, where he was an associate coach under Rick Pitino.

Willard has his work cut out for him, and the prospects of finishing out of the Sun Belt cellar appear dim. At least Willard's philosophy, culled from many years as a successful high school school in Long Island (N.Y.), figures to excite the Western Kentucky faithful. Like virtually the rest of the sport these days, Willard preaches an up-tempo, fast-paced game.

"The potential at Western is unlimited," said Willard, mindful of WKU's long and proud history. "I want to put a team on the floor this season that will play an exciting, in-your-face brand of basketball."

Willard will first have to find replacements for departed starters Roland Shelton (18.2 ppg), a second-team All-Sun Belt selection and Western's leading career three-pointer shooter, and Rodney Ross, who blossomed as a senior to become one of the top rebounders (9.5) in the conference. Ross also averaged 8.5 ppg.

At least Willard has some experience with which to build his first team, as three starters and six other lettermen return. Heading the list is 6-8 senior **Jerry Anderson** (12.3 ppg, 5.5 rpg), who showed what he is capable of last winter by exploding for 41 points (the most by a Hilltopper in 19 years) and 14 rebounds against North Carolina Charlotte. Anderson's defensive efforts also resulted in big numbers. His 37 blocked shots and 53 steals both rank as the third highest single-season totals in school history.

Also back are two more senior starters, 6-1 point guard **Anthony Palm** and 6-3 swingman **Joe Lightfoot**. Palm averaged 9.1 ppg while handing out an 159 assists, the fourth-highest single-season number at WKU. Lightfoot, an overachiever with hustle and determination, averaged 5.8 ppg and 3.4 rpg. After suffering through a slump late in the year, Lightfoot broke out in fine fashion in the final four games of the season, averaging 10 points and six rebounds. Willard hopes that late-season scoring trend continues.

Although Anderson, Palm and Lightfoot are not guaranteed starting spots because of the coaching change, the chances are likely they will be in the lineup on opening night. The other two positions, however, are very much up for grabs.

Transfer **Jack Jennings**, a 6-6, 240-pound junior out of Holmes (Ky.) High by way of Sullivan (Ky.) JC, has the inside track at power forward. He posted a team-high 20 ppg last winter to go with eight rebounds. Named MVP of the Kentucky JC Athletic Conference, Jennings led Sullivan to a 31-4 mark and a Top 20 ranking among JC teams.

The other frontcourt spot appears to be a battle between 6-8 junior **Scott Boley** (5.0 ppg, 2.1 rpg) and 6-5 sophomore **Karl Brown** (2.9 ppg, 2.8 rpg). Another player who merits consideration is 6-9 freshman **Jason Eitutis**, who averaged 23.1 points and 10 rebounds for North Hardin High (Radcliff, Ky.). Eitutis led North Hardin to a 25-8 mark and a berth in Kentucky's Sweet Sixteen tournament.

Also returning for the Hilltoppers are 6-3 sophomore **Rich Burns** (6.2 ppg, Sun Belt-leading 52.8 percent three-point shooting), 6-7 sophomore **Bryan Brown** (1.0 ppg), 6-8 sophomore **Will Gregory** (1.1 ppg) and 6-5 senior **Harold Thompkins**. Thompkins suffered a broken foot in pre-season drills a year ago and missed the entire 1989-90 campaign.

Bryan Brown and Gregory were used sparingly last season, but showed signs of marked improvement in the latter stages of the year. Kevin Brown averaged just six minutes per game last season, but figures to put his rugged, 230-pound frame to good use in the future.

Another promising newcomer is 6-1 freshman **Patrick Butts**, who averaged 15 points and seven assists last year for Baldwin County High (Milledgeville, Ga.). Butts was the Baldwin MVP the last two seasons and shot 48 percent from three-point range.

BLUE RIBBON ANALYSIS

Willard will have the Hilltoppers hustling up and down the court and firing up three-pointers, much like his former boss at Kentucky. That will make the players and the fans happy, but whether Western succeeds will depend on how often the shots go in.

Willard needs to get more production out of Lightfoot and Palm, and Anderson will have to be even more of a factor underneath. Two of the newcomers, Jennings and Eitutis, might be the kind of players that could have an impact on the squad right away.

At any rate, the Hilltoppers will not be a serious threat to anyone in the upcoming Sun Belt race, and will be fortunate to escape the league basement. At least Willard seems like the kind of coach who will have the program heading in the right direction before too long.

WESTERN MICHIGAN

LAST SEASON: 9-18
CONFERENCE RECORD: 3-13
STARTERS LOST: 3
STARTERS RETURNING: 2
CONFERENCE: MID-AMERICAN (MAC)
LOCATION: KALAMAZOO, MI
HOME FLOOR: READ FIELDHOUSE (8,250)
NICKNAME: BRONCOS
COLORS: BROWN AND GOLD
COACH: BOB DONEWALD, record at Western Michigan 9-18.
Career record, 217-139.

It has not taken Bob Donewald long to stamp his trademark on Western Michigan basketball, even if it has yet to be reflected in wins and losses. Donewald, you see, likes big players. Real big. The bigger the better, in fact, because he figures about the only thing he cannot teach a reasonably capable Division I ballplayer is height.

So it is that Western Michigan enters this season with a vastly different roster - especially size-wise - than it had a year ago. The 1989-90 club, Donewald's first year in Kalamazoo, frequently started four players who stood 6-2 or under. This season, just one of the 14 players listed on the roster stands below 6-3.

Not coincidentally, this greatly pleases Donewald, who previously posted a 208-121 record in 11 seasons at Illinois State. "Besides being taller," said Donewald, "we hopefully will have a few more good athletes on the floor."

Leading a group of five returning letterwinners, which includes two starters, is the biggest man of the bunch. He is 6-10, 240-pound junior center **Jim Havrilla** (20.8 ppg, 8.6 rpg), who earned first-team All-MAC honors in his first season as a regular. Havrilla should be the best big man in a conference which traditionally lacks players his size who can walk and chew gum at the same time.

Havrilla can do that for sure. He can even run, chew gum and put the ball in the basket. All at the same time. And he should continue to get better as his career progresses.

The only other returning starter is from the other end of the size spectrum. He is 6-0 sophomore **Darrick Brooks** (9.8 ppg, 2.3 rpg), who was forced to play out of position at forward for much of his freshman season. Partly because of that, he shot only 41 percent overall from the field. He should shoot a much higher percentage this season, as evidenced by the .430 mark he fashioned (49-for-114) from three-point range.

Perhaps the most intriguing returnee is 6-5 junior swingman **Jerry Overstreet**, who was redshirted last year after switching academic majors. Overstreet started at forward in 1988-89, averaging 9.3 points and 6.0 rebounds. With better size now available on the front line, he could end up switching to the backcourt and starting at shooting guard opposite Brooks, another ex-forward now slated for point guard.

The remaining returnees are 6-6 junior **Mark Judge** (3.7 ppg, 4.1 rpg) and 6-3 junior **Kelvin Johnson** (3.0 ppg, 2.4 rpg). Judge started a handful of games last year and both saw considerable action, but this year they must beat out three Division I frontcourt transfers.

6-8 sophomore **Mark Frederiksen** (Mercer) is joined by a pair of 6-6 forwards who have more than a little in common. Twin brothers **Shawn** (pronounced Shawn) and **Sean** (pronounced Seen) **Wightman** were freshmen redshirts under Donewald at Illinois State, then followed him to Western, where they had to sit out again and lose one season of eligibility under NCAA rules. Shawn is considered more of an inside player, while Sean is an outstanding outside shooter.

Sometimes that is the only way to tell them apart and, to really complicate things, the twins could spend a great deal of time on the court at the same time. Frederiksen, meanwhile, is an inside banger who should occupy a reserve role and help out considerably on the boards.

Six other newcomers, including yet another Division I transfer - 6-4 sophomore **Michael Pearson** (Hardin-Simmons) - join the Bronco ranks. The others are freshman recruits, including 6-4 swingman **Vinton Bennett** (Rummymede HS/Toronto, Ont.), 6-6 forward **Deon Davenport** (Northwestern HS/Detroit, Mich.), 6-3 guard **Anthony Robinson** (Ladue HS/Ladue, Mo.), 6-3 guard **Toby Whiteman** (Knoxville HS/Knoxville, Ill.) and 7-0 center **Matt VanAbbema** (Berthoud HS/Berthoud, Colo.).

Pearson *averaged* a triple-double in 14 games at Hardin-Simmons (25 ppg, 14 rpg, 10 assists), transferring only after the school shifted to Division III. Among the freshmen, you know VanAbbema, the seven-footer, has to excite Donewald the most. He averaged 15.5 points and 10.0 rebounds while helping Berthoud to a 24-1 record and the Colorado state finals.

BLUE RIBBON ANALYSIS

Could the Broncos possibly be a darkhorse contender in the Mid-American Conference this season? The answer is yes. While seven lettermen are gone from last year, only guard Mark Brown (15.7 ppg, 1.8 rpg, 60 assists) could be considered a highly significant loss.

Havrilla returns, and shows all the signs of becoming the most dominant big man in the conference. Brooks and Overstreet, as well as newcomers

such as Pearson, should help stablize the backcourt and more than compensate for the departure of Brown. That leaves the forward positions to a trio of newcomers in Frederiksen and the Wightman twins, as well as returnees Judge and Johnson.

Out of that fivesome, the Broncos surely can get decent production and are assured outstanding depth. So while it is true that many on this team have never played together, there seems to be just enough experience returning that a coach like Donewald, who specializes in getting the most from his players, can turn this team into a winner.

One area in which the Broncos' improved size should help is interior defense. Last year, the undersized Broncs played little defense at all - surrendering a MAC high of 76.4 points per contest. They should also fare better in and around the paint, as Western was outrebounded a year ago by an average of 35.4 to 32.0.

"I'm primarily concerned about being better defensively," Donewald said. "It's difficult to say which of the new players will help us until we get into the season, but we will need help from some of them."

The Broncos should get it, which in turn would allow Western - a perennial MAC doormat - to finish anywhere from third to fifth place in the conference. And you wouldn't want to play any team with Havrilla, or coached by Donewald, in the post-season.

WEST VIRGINIA

West Virginia coach Gale Catlett, never one to mince words, did not. The Mountaineers had just made a disappointing season even worse, getting blown out by previously unheralded Massachusetts in the quarterfinals of the Atlantic 10 tournament.

Catlett collected his thoughts, then chose his words carefully. "I hate to even play basketball," he said, "when the other team plays harder. When the other team is tougher, more together. I've made my living having it the other way around. Too many times (last) season, the other team just wanted it more. It doesn't get any simpler than that."

Months later, following the first Mountaineer season in 10 without a post-season invitation, Catlett was more reflective, but equally blunt. "I was unhappy with the season we had last year," he said. "We had some breakdowns in different areas, and we're going to make as many changes as we have to."

If that sounds like crack the whip time in Morgantown, beware. The Mountaineers simply have too much talent and coaching acumen to stay down for long. "Down" is also a relative term. A record of 16-12 may be spectacular in some places, but it is flat-out unacceptable to West Virginia loyalists.

Those are the same folks who pack WVU Coliseum, among the most feared arenas in college basketball. They are also the folks who expect, no demand, continuing excellence from Catlett and the Mountaineers. In 1990-91, excellence is what they figure to get.

In addition to four returning starters who already know how to win, Catlett welcomes what even he admits is his best-ever crop of newcomers. The competition they provide, more than any other factor, is likely to be what shoves West Virginia back into the running for post-season play.

Not only were last season's starters too secure, they were often tired, particularly on the road, where the Mountaineers won just two Atlantic 10 games. Even graduated point guard Steve Berger (12.0 ppg, 3.9 rpg, 183 assists, 49 steals) seemed to wear down. Once irrepressible, Berger slumped under the weight of 35-plus minutes each night.

Said Catlett: "We only won two road games in our league last year. And that didn't have so much to do with how poorly we might have played. We played pretty well at Penn State and got beat. We played a pretty good game at St. Bonaventure and got beat. We played a fine game at Rutgers and got beat. We played an excellent game at Temple and got beat."

So the four returning starters - 6-0 junior **Tracy Shelton** (17.8 ppg, 2.6 rpg, 64 assists, 49 steals), 6-7 senior **Charles Becton** (14.1 ppg, 7.6 rpg), 6-6 senior **Chris Brooks** (13.0 ppg, 5.9 rpg) and 6-10 senior **Junior Robinson** (3.6 ppg, 2.4 rpg) - are not the story.

The real news in Morgantown is who else will play, how much, and of course, how soon.

"There been so much talk about this recruiting class," said Catlett, "that it's almost impossible for me not to say something about them. There's probably only three or four teams in the East that had better recruiting years than we did. It's the first time we've had a class that ranks that highly."

Leading the way are a pair of freshman point guards - 6-1 Orange, N.J. native **Mike Boyd** (Maine Central Institute) and 5-8 **Marsalis Basey** (Martinsburg HS/Martinsburg, W.V.) - who will battle to replace Berger. *HSBI* ranked Boyd (23.1 ppg) as the A-10's top newcomer, and Basey (18 points, eight assists) turned down professional baseball to play hoops in Morgantown.

"Michael Boyd," said one rival Atlantic 10 coach, "is not a typical freshman. He's been to two different prep schools (also Oak Hill Academy, Va.), and he has a lot of experience." With Boyd at the controls, Maine Central Institute went 24-0 and won the New England prep school title. Maine Central coach Max Goode said: "There are a lot of kids who want to win. This kid refuses to lose."

As for Basey, he led Martinsburg High to a 23-3 record and the final of the West Virginia high school tournament. Equally outstanding on the diamond, Basey was drafted in June by the Houston Astros and assigned to a rookie team in the Gulf Coast League. He got homesick after just one game, though, then left for a basketball offer from the Mountaineers. The multi-talented Basey was also a Division I recruit in football.

"I think he can play," said former WVU point guard Jay Jacobs, who now works for the Mountaineer Sports Network. "He's the type of kid who can run the break for you, and he's going to play pretty decent defense. He's smart enough not to let himself get caught inside."

Talented 6-5 swingman **Lawrence Pollard** (Boys and Girls HS/Brooklyn, N.Y.) is another freshman signee, as are 6-8 forwards P.G. Green (Fork Union Military Academy, Va.) and **Phil Wilson** (Bowie HS/Bowie, Md.). In June, the Mountaineers added 6-7 freshman **Rickey Robinson** (Canterbury School/New Milford, Conn.).

Originally from Roselle, N.J., Robinson (19.8 ppg, 13.4 rpg) was a Rutgers signee prior to attending prep school. "We thought we had him last year," said Catlett. "He's strong enough to step in and challenge for a position right away." *HSBI* rated him among the Top 100 players in the East.

Wilson led Bowie with 20 points and 13 rebounds per game. "I don't know where he'll play in college," said Bowie coach Tom Hendershot, "but he has good hands, can catch the ball, runs the floor well and can fill the lane on the fast break."

Pollard, one of the best three-point shooters in New York City, comes with a reputation as a zone buster. He averaged 23.1 ppg as a senior. Boys and Girls coach Paul Brown said: "He should make the transition from high school to college very easily. He has a great attitude."

Once a star at Oak Hill (W.Va.) HS, Green (15 points, 10 rebounds) got even better at Fork Union. This after West Virginia player of the year honors and a Class AAA state title at Oak Hill. "I think that by the time Christmas rolls around," said Fork Union coach Fletcher Arritt, "he'll be challenging for a starting berth. I sent Tracy Shelton and Steve Berger to WVU. Green is in the same category talent-wise."

"It says something about your recruiting and the future of your program to get a class this deep," said Catlett. "I think these six guys coming in are really going to have an impact."

"They'll find help in that class, for sure," said an Atlantic 10 assistant coach. "The only thing they really have to deal with is the center position."

Even though Junior Robinson is the returning starter there, West Virginia could use more low post production, especially since Brooks has never exploded with the marquee season many predicted. The Mountaineers' top recruit of the 80's, Brooks has been good as a collegian, but never great. One look at his shooting percentages (54.1 from the field, only 50.0 from the foul line) captures both an ability to play but an occasional inability to concentrate.

Shelton became a very effective scorer as a sophomore, dialing long distance for many of his team-leading 498 points. He went 53-for-122 on three-point shots, a .434 percentage. Becton, the last returning starter, was more of a garbage man. He rarely shot from outside, instead getting most of his points off the glass. He led WVU with a whopping 92 offensive rebounds.

6-10 junior **Tom Kroger** (0.8 ppg, 2.0 rpg) and 6-9 sophomore **Matt Roadcap** (1.3 ppg, 2.0 rpg) will push Junior Robinson, and also try to stay ahead of the freshmen. Roadcap toured with the Atlantic 10 all-stars at the Jones Cup in Taiwan. 6-8 sophomore **Jeremy Bodkin** (2.1 ppg, 2.3 rpg) rounds out the frontcourt.

6-4 junior **Chris Leonard** (9.9 ppg), 6-4 senior **Shaun Jackson** (2.8 ppg), 6-3 junior **Tim McNeely** (1.8 ppg) and 6-6 sophomore **Anthony Williams** (1.7 ppg) are the reserve guards. Leonard, a three-point specialist (.436 percent), will see the most time.

BLUE RIBBON ANALYSIS

Lost in the shuffle of all the new faces is that West Virginia returns four senior starters. Not many teams can say that. Not in the Atlantic 10, not anywhere. It is a versatile group, as well, lacking only the dominant low post player.

The recruits most likely to emerge are Boyd and perhaps Basey. One will have to be the point guard. As in the past, Catlett figures to rotate his forwards more, young and old, maintaining interior defensive pressure and wearing down a few less willing Atlantic 10 opponents.

At the top, the A-10 has become a well above average conference. As deep as the Mountaineers are, they remain a notch below Temple and about even with Penn State, Rutgers and possibly Massachuetts.

West Virginia will be in race, however. They always are. A strong third or fourth place is the call here.

1990-91 WEST VIRGINIA SCHEDULE		
Nov.	27	Robert Morris
Dec.	1	Maryland
	4	@Marshall
	8	@Pitt
	18	Old Dominion
	21	#North Carolina Charlotte
Jan.	3	St. Bonaventure
	5	Miami (FL)
	7	Duquesne
	10	@Penn State
	12	Rutgers
	15	@Notre Dame
	19	@Rutgers
	21	@Rhode Island
	24	George Washington
	26	St. Joseph's
	29	@George Washington
	31	Penn State
Feb.	2	Virginia Tech
	6	@Massachusetts
	10	@Temple
	12	Massachusetts
	14	Rhode Island
	17	@Duquesne
	21	@St. Bonaventure
	23	Temple
	26	@St. Joseph's
Mar.	2-4 & 7	*Atlantic 10 Tournament

@ Road Games
# Rock Hill, SC
* The first three rounds will be held at the Palestra, Philadelphia, PA. The championship game will be held on the home court of the highest remaining seed.

WICHITA STATE

LAST SEASON: 10-19
CONFERENCE RECORD: 6-8
STARTERS LOST: 1
STARTERS RETURNING: 4
CONFERENCE: MISSOURI VALLEY (MVC)
LOCATION: WICHITA, KS
HOME FLOOR: LEVITT ARENA (10,666)
NICKNAME: SHOCKERS
COLORS: YELLOW AND BLACK
COACH: MIKE COHEN, record at Wichita State, 10-19.

Mike Cohen waited a long time to get his chance as a head coach on the college level, but last year was not what he dreamed about during 25 seasons in the wings. The Shockers started miserably and needed to win five of their final 10 games to avoid their first ever 20-loss campaign.

That final five-week stretch —which included victories over Missouri Valley Conference regular season champion Southern Illinois and MVC tournament champ Illinois State —was the result of months of lineup tinkering. In all, 10 different players drew starting assignments for Wichita State, and not until the last month did Cohen settle on a starting unit.

"I think the way we came on at the end of the season should play significantly on our attitude and our players' belief in themselves," Cohen said. "Plus the experience of playing together, the experience of having played one year under me —each of us knows what to expect of the other —will make us a better team."

Classes had barely ended, however, when trouble began anew. Gaylon Nickerson, perhaps the most talented player on the team, was suspended in June for an indefinite period of time and transferred to Butler County (Kan.) JC later in the summer. A junior-to-be, Nickerson was a member of the MVC's all-newcomer team after averaging 10.3 points and 5.0 rebounds. Once moved into the starting lineup, he keyed the revival in the final 10 games and averaged 14.9 points and 6.3 rebounds in that span.

Aaron Davis and Keith Bonds made major contributions off the bench down the stretch, but are no longer in the program. Davis' career was ended by an enlarged heart and Bonds transferred. Davis was the team's third-leading scorer at 10.4 ppg, and also chipped in 47 rebounds. Bonds, a 6-3 guard, averaged 6.1 points, fifth best on the squad, and 2.5 rebounds.

The biggest bright spot for Cohen was the play of 6-6 forward **John Cooper**. Cooper, a senior, averaged 17.0 points, fifth best in the league, and 7.2 rebounds, eight in the conference. He also led the MVC in free throw shooting (820) and was a second team all-conference pick.

"Averages don't really tell what he did for us last year," Cohen said. "When we asked him to score more, he scored. When we asked him to guard the opponent's best offensive player, he played great defense. No one meant more to his team in the league last year than Coop did."

6-3 senior **Paul Guffrovich** is back for his final season. Guffrovich averaged 10.7 points and 3.5 assists last year as the full-time point guard. 6-5 sophomore **Claudius Johnson** moved into the starting lineup late in the year and wound up averaging 3.7 points and 4.4 rebounds. 6-11 junior **Phil Mendelson** also worked his way into the first five and

311

finished with averages of 2.2 ppg and 2.2 rpg. The final returnee is 6-5 sophomore forward **Rick Conn** (0.9 ppg).

Cohen's first recruiting class had some interesting prospects but two key freshmen were ruled ineligible over the summer. The Shocker newcomers are 6-0 junior guard **Robert George** (Southeastern, Iowa, CC), 6-7 freshman forward **Patrice Scott** (Shawnee Mission HS/Overland Park, Kan.), 6-7 freshman forward **Michael Wiggins** (Southwest Dekalb HS/Decatur, Ga.), 6-1 freshman guard **K. C. Hunt** (West Geauga HS/Chesterfield, Ohio), 6-5 sophomore forward **Tony Johnson** (Butler County, Kan., JC) and 6-6 sophomore forward **Calvin Thomas** (John Jay HS/San Antonio, Tex.). George had modest statistics —7.3 points and 4.2 assists per game —but could be the up-tempo point guard to get the Shockers moving. Scott was a third-team All-Kansas selection. Wiggins averaged 17 points and nine rebounds as a senior. Hunt will be a backup point guard. Thomas sat out last year and Johnson was a late summer signee. He is a Wichita native who averaged 9.6 points and 8.3 rebounds at Butler County.

BLUE RIBBON ANALYSIS

Summer was not much fun for Wichita State coach Mike Cohen. Over the summer he lost perhaps the most talented player in the program, Gaylon Nickerson, two other returning veterans, and two recruits.

Shooting is the Shockers' achilles' heel. Wichita State shot just 44 percent from the field last year, and only one regular, Johnson, was over 47 percent. And he took a limited number of shots (65).

Cooper, who wound up as the MVC's No. 3 returnee on the TANDEX rating system (also used to evaluate NBA players), is a quality, do-everything kind of guy. But all the others are strictly role players who must perform night in and night out for the Shockers to thrive.

Due to the unfortunate personnel losses, Wichita State is probably no better than a sixth place team in the MVC.

1990-91 WICHITA STATE SCHEDULE

Nov.	23-24	#Central Fidelity Classic
Dec.	4	Alabama
	6	Delaware State
	8	Oklahoma State
	13	@Drake
	15	Southwest Missouri State
	22	@Utah
	27-30	##Hawaii Rainbow Classic
Jan.	3	Austin Peay
	7	Kansas State
	10	Notre Dame
	12	@Tulsa
	15	@Creighton
	19	Southern Illinois
	23	@Kansas
	28	@Illinois State
	31	Tulsa
Feb.	2	@Southwest Missouri State
	4	Indiana State
	6	Bradley
	9	Illinois State
	12	*St. Peter's
	16	@Southern Illinois
	18	@Indiana State
	23	Drake
	25	Creighton
Mar.	1-5	**MVC Tournament

@ Road Games
# Richmond, VA (Dartmouth, Georgia & Richmond)
Honolulu, HI (Alaska-Anchorage, California, Hawaii, Iona, Oklahoma, Stetson & Tennessee)
* Meadowlands Arena, East Rutherford, NJ
** St. Louis, MO

WILLIAM & MARY

LAST SEASON: 6-22
CONFERENCE RECORD: 2-13
STARTERS LOST: 1
STARTERS RETURNING: 4
CONFERENCE: COLONIAL ATHLETIC ASSOCIATION (CAA)
LOCATION: WILLIAMSBURG, VA
HOME FLOOR: WILLIAM AND MARY HALL (10,000)
NICKNAMES: INDIANS, TRIBE
COLORS: GREEN, GOLD AND SILVER
COACH: CHUCK SWENSON, record at William & Mary, 21-64.

Chuck Swenson was forced to throw a young team into the heat of competition last season, and the results were predictable. Still, the Indians showed signs of improvement, winning two of their last three CAA games, their only two conference victories all season.

If there is one commodity William & Mary still needs, it's experience. There remains only one way to get that, and two of the Indians' top returning veterans had busy summer playing schedules. **Thomas Roberts**, (14.0 ppg, 4.6 rpg, 32 assists, 19 blocked shots) a 6-6 sophomore and CAA rookie of the year last season, played in the U.S. Olympic Festival and with the CAA all-stars, which toured Yugoslavia. Playing for the East team in the Olympic Festival, Roberts averaged 11.3 points and a team-high 23.8 minutes per game. He averaged nine points in six games in Yugoslavia.

Scott Smith (14.6 ppg, 5.6 rpg), a 6-8 junior, joined Roberts on the Yugoslavian tour. "Competition forces player development," said Swenson, who along with Navy's Pete Hermann coached the All-Stars. "Because of that, the Yugoslavian tour will help all of the players involved. We played against some NBA-caliber players, players who were much better than I anticipated. That kind of top-flight competition works to develop a player's confidence."

Roberts served early notice of his ability last year, hitting the game-winning basket with seven seconds to play against Davidson in the Indians' second game of the season. He started 27 of 28 games overall and led William & Mary in scoring 11 times. He scored over 20 points on seven occasions, and his leadership ability earned him tri-captain honors this season.

Joining Roberts on the Indians' front line is the 240-pound Smith, who led the team in scoring and rebounding a year ago. Another of William & Mary's tri-captains, Smith can score inside or drift outside and hit the jump shot. In late February, he was chosen CAA player of the week after a 39-point outburst against George Mason. That was the highest single-game total by a CAA player all year, and it established a new scoring record for George Mason's Patriot Center.

The Indians' third front court starter could be one of three players. **John Leone**, (3.9 ppg, 5.0 rpg) a 6-9 senior, started the last five games a year ago and is a tri-captain this season. He is a strong rebounder who had a season-high 11 against Wake Forest and nine against American. **Ben Blocker** (7.4 ppg, 5.2 rpg), a 6-6 junior, started 18 games last year before being sidelined with a deep thigh bruise.

There was an upside to Blocker's injury, though. His absence allowed 6-7 sophomore **Todd Cauthorn** (6.3 ppg, 3.3 rpg) to get unexpected playing time as a freshman. Cauthorn came off the bench and scored 11 points and grabbed four rebounds against Navy, then started seven of the next nine games. He had a career-high 15 points and grabbed 9 rebounds against

North Carolina-Wilmington, and scored 14 points with 11 rebounds against Richmond.

6-8 senior **Andrew Emory** (1.4 rpg) and 6-5 junior **Eric Wakefield** (0.9 ppg) should get some minutes as frontcourt reserves. Emory, the team's tallest player, is a good shot blocker and rebounder. Wakefield worked hard in the off-season and, as a result should play more than last year, when he averaged just 3.9 minutes a game.

Four returning players will get most of the action at guard. **Jimmy Apple** (10.9 ppg, 1.2 rpg, 36 assists), a 6-2 senior, is a likely starter at shooting guard, though his percentages were not great a year ago. Apple shot 37 percent from the floor and 33 percent from three-point range. **Casey Potts** (2.4 ppg, 1.4 rpg), a 6-5 senior, was a solid reserve a year ago. He scored 14 points in 11 minutes against Duke in his top performance of the season.

At point guard, 6-0 sophomore **Brendan Connor** (3.0 ppg, 1.3 rpg, 89 assists, 23 steals) improved in the final month of last season and will probably start. "Intelligence and leadership from your point guard, whether he scores or not, is an unknown and unappreciated variable on most teams," Swenson said. "Therefore, the development of Brendan is a key to our improvement."

Derrick Peters (2.8 ppg, 1.4 rpg, 36 assists, 12 steals), a 6-2 sophomore, can play either guard position. Nicknamed "Sky Pete" by his teammates, Peters is a creative dunker who was also chosen the team's best defensive player. Peters started five games last season.

Outside shooting has been a weakness at William & Mary in recent years, and Swenson recruited with that in mind. **Chris Ciaccio**, a 6-3 shooting guard from Gloversville (N.Y.) HS, is the all-time leading scorer in Section II of New York state. He scored 2,373 points in four seasons, and averaged 29.8 points, 16.3 rebounds, 4.0 assists and 3.0 steals as a senior. Ciaccio will also play baseball at William & Mary.

Swenson signed another guard, 6-3 **Chris Jensen** of Salt Lake City, Utah. Jensen averaged 19 points and 11 assists at Cottonwood High, where he was chosen to the All-State team. Jensen was once a preseason pick as player of the year in Oregon, where, as a junior, he averaged 28 points at Oregon City HS. A Mormon, Jensen will go on a two-year mission after his freshman year, but will have three years eligibility upon returning.

Two other freshmen will compete for playing time in the Indians' frontcourt. **Charles Payton**, a 6-7 forward from Ettrick, Va., averaged 16.4 points, 11.2 rebounds and 6.0 blocked shots for Matoaca High. **Sean Duff**, a 6-6 forward from Waukesha, Wisc., was William & Mary's only early signee. Another good athlete, Duff averaged 18.5 points and 12.5 rebounds for Waukesha South HS and was chosen second-team All-State. He was first-team All-State in football as a tight end, and was recruited by Big Ten schools Illinois and Wisconsin.

BLUE RIBBON ANALYSIS

William & Mary coach Chuck Swenson is fielding his best team in four seasons at the school. The Indians are young, but have more talent and depth than the last three years.

Guard play will be a big key to any success Williams & Mary has. If Brendan Connor can handle the point and newcomers such as Chris Ciaccio and Chris Jensen provide some much-needed outside shooting, the Indians will show dramatic improvement over last year's 6-22 record.

A winning season may be too much to expect, but the Indians should no longer be a pushover in the Colonial Athletic Association.

WISCONSIN

LAST SEASON: 14-17
CONFERENCE RECORD: 5-13
STARTERS LOST: 1
STARTERS RETURNING: 4
CONFERENCE: BIG TEN
LOCATION: MADISON, WI
HOME FLOOR: WISCONSIN FIELD HOUSE (11,886)
NICKNAME: BADGERS
COLORS: CARDINAL AND WHITE
COACH: STEVE YODER, record at Wisconsin, 100-132.
Career record, 177-194.

Last year was to be a watershed year for Steve Yoder and the University of Wisconsin basketball program. They were coming off an impressive 18-12 year and the school's first trip to a post-season tournament in over 45 years! Those 18 victories were the most by a Badger squad since their NCAA championship team won 20 in 1940. With four starters back, Yoder and the Badgers were primed and ready for a run at 20 wins and a trip to the NCAA tournament. Instead, the inconsistent Badgers achieved only 14 wins and were left only with thoughts of what could have been.

In defense of the scrappy Badgers, they lost nine games by a total of 20 points, including seven Big Ten matchups by a total of 16 points. Included in those near misses were: one-point losses to Georgia and Minnesota on the road, two three-point losses to Big Ten champion Michigan State, a two-point loss to Purdue, a three-point loss to Illinois and two-point losses to Indiana and Northwestern. Typical of the Wisconsin season, the Badgers led Indiana at home on Senior Day by a 68-60 count with less than two minutes remaining only to see the Hoosiers storm back and win 70-68 on a Calbert Cheaney three-pointer at the buzzer. It was a frustrating end to a disappointing season for Steve Yoder and the Badgers.

With four starters back from a team on the verge of doing great things, there is renewed hope in Madison that the Badger program may be back on track. The one starter missing, however, was an important one. Gone is power forward Danny Jones and his 17.7 ppg average. Jones will go down as one of the great forwards in Wisconsin history. He finished in the Top 10 in nearly all Wisconsin basketball statistical categories, but his leadership and experience may be missed more than his points and rebounds.

This year's Wisconsin club will be built around five solid seniors, one junior and three sophomores. The highest returning scorer is 6-5 senior forward **Willie Simms** (13.3 ppg, 4.8 rpg). Simms is an athletic forward who can run as well as shoot from the outside. He scored in double figures 24 times last year and set season high marks of 22 points against Butler and Minnesota. Simms shot 53.9 percent from the field and was tied for the team lead in steals with 33. Yoder needs Simms to raise his scoring and rebounding averages if the Badgers are to be successful this season. Joining Simms on the blocks will be either 6-7 senior **John Ellenson** (1.9 ppg, 1.9 rpg) or 6-5 junior **Bill Douglass** (2.8 ppg, 1.3 rpg). Ellenson may add more size to the lineup, but Douglass can bring increased speed and an ability to score. Ellenson played in thirty games last year and posted his Big Ten highs of six points and five rebounds versus Michigan. Douglass started the final six games of last year and posted a career high 10 points and five assists against Indiana. Douglass plays great defense and should get the nod in a three-guard alignment. He was also a member of the Big Ten All-Academic team.

Starting in the middle again this season will be 6-6 senior **Patrick Tompkins** (6.6 ppg, 6.4 rpg). Tompkins is a muscular pivotman who makes up for his lack of size with quickness and superior leaping ability. Last season, he started 19 games including the final 17. In Big Ten play, he raised his game to 8.1 ppg and 6.8 rpg averages while scoring the game winning field goal at the buzzer against Minnesota before a nationwide television audience on ESPN.

6-8 sophomore **Damon Harrell** (1.1 ppg, 1.0 rpg) should be Tompkins' principal reserve at the center spot. Harrell saw action in 19 games last season including 10 Big Ten games. He is a tough, physical player cut in the same mold as the now departed Danny Jones. As the Big Ten season progresses, look for Harrell to see more action. His physical build will be an asset to this team lacking overall size. Speaking of size, Tompkins and Harrell should receive help from 7-0 redshirt sophomore **Grant Johnson**. Johnson is the heir apparent at the center position.

The backcourt is the strongest and deepest area on this Wisconsin team, but only one player seems assured of starting. 6-4 senior **Tim Locum** (9.8 ppg, 2.3 rpg) will get the call at the off-guard spot. Locum started 19 games last winter and led Wisconsin in three-point shooting with 67-of-143 for an outstanding 46.9 percent average. Locum, the Badgers designated zonebuster, is an excellent standstill jump shooter and has become better at working for his shot. This team needs to replace Danny Jones' scoring and Locum must now shoulder a significantly large scoring role. Two returning players, 6-1 junior **Brian Good** (5.7 ppg, 0.7 rpg) and 6-4 sophomore **Larry Hisle, Jr.** (4.5 ppg, 1.4 rpg) will battle for the final open point guard slot. Good led the Big Ten in free throw shooting with a 90.2 percent mark and collected a season high 15 points in a win at Iowa on February 10. Hisle, the son of former Minnesota Twin and Milwaukee Brewer Larry Hisle, Sr., was one of the top stories of the 1989-90 Badger campaign. He garnered 516 minutes of playing time last year (12 starts) and scored in double figures eight times, including six of the last eight games. He also set a season high against Iowa on February 10 with 19 points. Both Good and Hisle will see plenty of action this season, but look for Hisle to get the starting nod due to his defensive prowess and height.

Also looking to see time in the Badger backcourt is 6-3 redshirt freshman **Jason Johnsen**. Johnsen is an exciting player out of Armstrong HS in Plymouth, Minn. During his senior season he was a finalist for player of the year honors in Minnesota. He was a high school teammate of fellow Badger Grant Johnson. Johnsen is an athletic player who can score as well as distribute the basketball. 6-3 freshman recruit **Kass Weaver** arrives from Rich Central HS in Olympic Fields, Ill. Weaver is an exceptional talent but looks to make his mark sometime in the future. 5-11 **Tracy Webster** is another freshman guard who will add depth to the Wisconsin backcourt. Webster is a playmaker who hails from Thorton Township HS in Harvey, Ill. Finally, 6-1 junior **Jay Peters** rounds out the Badger backcourt. Peters, strictly a reserve, did not see any action last season.

Adding depth in the frontcourt will be a trio of 6-7 forwards. Sophomore **Louis Ely** will see his first playing time this winter after a season of ineligibility. Redshirt freshman **Carlton McGee** is an outstanding athlete who will make an impact on the Wisconsin front line. McGee won the Wisconsin state high jump championship twice and is an excellent three-point shooter as well. Freshman forward **Howard Moore**, from Taft HS in Chicago, could be a sleeper. Moore averaged 14 ppg, nine rpg and three blocked shots per contest as a senior. The Wisconsin staff feels he will blossom with some playing time.

BLUE RIBBON ANALYSIS

By all accounts, last season was a disappointing year for Yoder and the Badgers. Wisconsin came close many times but was unable to knock out its opponent as many as nine different times. However, Yoder accentuates the positive and continues to build the Badger program.

Wisconsin was a tough defensive club last season and will continue to do that this year. The Badgers led the Big Ten in scoring defense for all games, holding their opponents to an average of 64.6 points per game. In Big Ten games only, the Badgers ranked third in scoring defense with a 70.2 points per game mark. Wisconsin's always tenacious style of play limited opponents to a 45.3 field goal percentage as well.

With this small, but quick club, Wisconsin should again be stingy on defense, but will look to do some more running. "But not at the expense of being competitive," remarked Yoder. "We're still going to run a motion offense and we're still going to mix defense. But, I do think we'll have the people to do some running," he added.

Senior forward Simms will be a catalyst on this young squad. Simms returns the highest scoring average and will be looked to for increased rebounding totals as well as continue solid offensive output. His ability to start the Badger fast break will be crucial to the success of the team. Joining Simms in the frontcourt will be senior center Tompkins. He is a quick defender and solid rebounder whose inside presence will be needed especially in the Big Ten. Sophomore Harrell should be the first frontcourt reserve off the bench.

Due to its relative lack of size, Wisconsin will usually run a three-guard set employing Locum, Hisle and most likely, Douglass. Locum will shoot, Hisle will distribute and Douglass will add speed and defense. This set up will see Good as the fourth guard and a possible replacement if one of the first three should falter. Locum has been excellent off the bench providing instant offense and he may continue in that role, although Danny Jones' scoring must be replaced somehow. Look for Locum to start.

This is a small Wisconsin team and as quick as they are, it may not help in the Big Ten. A .500 record is an optimistic outlook for this team and, unfortunately, that may again put Yoder's job in jeopardy. A ninth place finish in the Big Ten should be expected.

WISCONSIN GREEN BAY

LAST SEASON: 24-8
CONFERENCE RECORD: 9-3
STARTERS LOST: 2
STARTERS RETURNING: 3
CONFERENCE: MID-CONTINENT
LOCATION: GREEN BAY, WI
HOME FLOOR: BROWN COUNTY ARENA (5,600)
NICKNAME: PHOENIX
COLORS: KELLY GREEN, CARDINAL AND WHITE
COACH: DICK BENNETT, record at Wisconsin-Green Bay, 76-68.
Career record, 250-147.

The University of Wisconsin-Green Bay's slow, steady climb under coach Dick Bennett is in position to take another significant step. The Phoenix, who last season finished second in the Mid-Continent Conference and played in their first post-season tournament, enter 1990-91 as a favorite for the league title.

The Phoenix have improved dramatically since Bennett took over in 1985-86. That year Wisconsin-Green Bay went 5-23 and tied for last in the league. Since then, it has gone 71-45, culminating last year in a 24-8 record, a second-place finish in the conference, an appearance in the Mid-Continent championship game and a first-round NIT victory. It was the school's best overall record and highest finish in the league since joining Division I in 1981-82.

Lost from that breakthrough team are three important, but not irreplaceable players. With Southwest Missouri State now in the Missouri Valley Conference, the Mid-Continent race is wide open. The Phoenix even rate as a slight favorite over Northern Iowa, the Cinderella team of last year's NCAA tournament.

It is the first time Wisconsin-Green Bay has come into a season with legitimate title expectations, but not the first time Bennett has been a frontrunner. While at Wisconsin-Stevens Point, an NAIA school, his teams won the Wisconsin State University Conference his last four years and went to the NAIA national tournament his last three.

"I don't like it, personally," Bennett said of the favorite's role. "What I don't like is that it affects our players *and* the other players. When they play against you, they're especially ready, and our players feel the heat. If you've won (the title) before, you like it because it puts the pressure on everyone else. If you haven't won, it puts the pressure on you. But it's only a factor at the beginning of the conference season."

The starting point of the Phoenix is the point guard, 6-1 junior **Tony Bennett**. The coach's son, Bennett (16.6 ppg, 155 assists, 38 steals) was first-team All-Conference last season. He shouldered the heaviest burden of any player in the league, controlling the Green Bay passing game on offense as both the primary playmaker and primary scorer. He has range beyond the three-point line (48.2 percent last season) and had enough quickness to get around the best defensive guards in the Mid-Continent.

"Bennett is by far the best player in the league, said one rival assistant coach. "I love Tony Bennett. The first time I saw him as a freshman I said, 'This kid can play'."

About the only uncertainty with Bennett is his health. He has had troublesome injuries in each of his first two seasons, playing the second half of his freshman year with a stress fracture in his shin, and suffering through an arthritic condition in his foot, a pulled muscle in his hip and a badly bruised shin last season.

He has played through the injuries, though, missing only three games in two years. He scored a school Division I-record 44 points against Cleveland State despite the stress fracture and, after bruising his shin in the final regular-season game last year, led the Green Bay to the final of conference tournament and scored 26 points in an upset win at Southern Illinois in the NIT.

"He radiates a confidence and a poise when he's in there," said another Mid-Continent coach. "And he just doesn't make any mistakes."

The player most likely to join Bennett in the starting backcourt is 6-0 sophomore **John Martinez** (2.3 ppg). Martinez was a bit player last year, but is a slick ballhandler and good shooter. For the first time since Bennett has been on the team, he will have a backcourt mate capable of creating offense off the dribble. "There's a special chemistry there," Dick Bennett said of his likely backcourt.

Wisconsin-Green Bay will need the help offensively after losing two top shooters, 6-2 guard Mike Karisny and 6-4 guard-forward Dan Oberbrunner, both of whom graduated. The Phoenix's shooting was crucial in stretching defenses last year, as they finished eighth in the nation in three-point field goal accuracy (43.9 percent). Oberbrunner was third in the country (50.3 percent) and Karisny shot 42.3 percent from three-point range for his career.

The Phoenix are counting on one of two freshmen recruits, 6-2 **Mark Andres** or 6-2 **Tory Smith**, to contribute in the backcourt. Smith, who averaged 23.6 ppg for Buena Vista High (Saginaw, Mich.), was a candidate for Mr. Basketball in Michigan last season and is the more talented of the two. Andres, however, played in a system similar to Wisconsin-Green Bay's in high school and might see more playing time in the short run. He averaged 21.7 ppg for Rhinelander (Wisc.) HS. **Tony Ciaravino**, a 6-2 junior, played sparingly his first two seasons but could provide a three-point threat off the bench.

The foundation on which Dick Bennett has built Wisconsin-Green Bay is its half-court, man-to-man defense, and the keystone for that will again be **Ben Johnson** (4.3 ppg, 2.3 rpg), a 6-3 junior forward. At 200 pounds, Johnson is one of team's most athletic players and is a tireless and physical defender. He has improved each year offensively, going from a liability his freshman season to a decent shooter (36.4 percent on three-pointers) and adequate ballhandler last year. He also is the team's most ferocious rebounder and figures to have his playing time increase (24 minutes per game last season).

The Phoenix lost some depth at small forward when Chris Yates, a 6-5 senior, was redshirted this year for academic reasons. That means that either **Dean Rondorf** (0.2 ppg), a 6-7 sophomore who played only in mop-up roles last season, or the Smith-Andres combo will back up Johnson.

Wisconsin-Green Bay lost its most physical presence in the power positions with 6-8 center Roger Ripley (5.2 ppg, 3.5 rpg) having graduated, but powerful 6-4 senior **Dean Vander Plas** (10.8 ppg, 4.6 rpg, 64 assists, 50 steals) returns. A 230-pound lefty with slippery post moves and excellent court vision, Vander Plas was honorable-mention All-Conference as a junior and was the Phoenix's most reliable scorer around the basket.

Green Bay also returns 6-7 junior **Larry Hill** (7.4 ppg, 3.1 rpg), the quickest and most skilled frontcourt player on the team. Hill made his greatest impact defensively last season, leading the Mid-Continent in blocked shots (44). He might be ready to become a double-figure scorer this year.

This will be Bennett's biggest team at Wisconsin-Green Bay, as he has two reserve post players of 6-8 or taller - 6-9 junior **Scott LeMoine** (1.6 ppg) and 6-8 redshirt freshman **Jeremy Ludvigson. Logan Vander Velden,** a 6-9 redshirt freshman, is also in line for time.

BLUE RIBBON ANALYSIS

Wisconsin-Green Bay returns its most important players from last year's 24-8 team. What it lost in shooting (Oberbrunner and Karisny), it should make up for with the improved athletic ability of its younger players.

"They've got a great player in Tony Bennett, a winner in Vander Plas and they're coming off a good season with their key people coming back," said a rival Mid-Continent coach.

The Phoenix were tested over the summer by a three-week trip to the Republic of the Ukraine in the Soviet Union, a trip on which they went 8-1. The only loss came in the final game to last season's Soviet professional league champions. "That was like playing another whole season," said Bennett of the tour.

Wisconsin-Green Bay's non-conference schedule has improved a notch, as it plays at Clemson, at a tournament at DePaul (Southern Illinois and Alabama are the other two teams), at Colorado and plays host to Nebraska. That should toughen the team even further for the conference season.

The Phoenix also host the Mid-Continent tournament, with the winner getting an automatic NCAA bid. Northern Iowa showed last year what an advantage that was, and Green Bay figures to do the same this time around. Provided Tony Bennett remains healthy, it is Wisconsin-Green Bay's turn for its first conference championship and NCAA berth.

XAVIER

**LAST SEASON: 28-5
CONFERENCE RECORD: 12-2
STARTERS LOST: 2
STARTERS RETURNING: 3
CONFERENCE: MID-WESTERN COLLEGIATE (MCC)
LOCATION: CINCINNATI, OH
HOME FLOOR: CINCINNATI GARDENS (10,400)
NICKNAME: MUSKETEERS
COLORS: BLUE AND WHITE
COACH: PETE GILLEN, record at Xavier, 119-39.**

By any measuring stick, Xavier has been the class of the Midwestern Collegiate Conference. The Musketeers have won four regular season titles, including three in the last five years, under the extraordinary work of coach Pete Gillen.

The Musketeers' post-season record has been even more exemplary. Before losing to Dayton in the final of last spring's MCC tournament, Xavier had never lost a conference tourney game with Gillen at the controls. That is 13-0, good enough for four consecutive NCAA berths. Even the loss at Dayton did not end the real streak. The Musketeers went to the NCAA's as an at-large entry, advancing all the way to the "Sweet Sixteen" before calling it a season.

That is history now, of course, and Gillen these days has new questions to answer. Namely, can Xavier continue to dominate the MCC without Tyrone Hill and Derek Strong. Inquiring minds want to know.

At 6-9 and 6-10, Hill and Strong may have been the best pair of big men in the country last season. At least the NBA thought so. Hill (20.2 ppg, 12.6 rpg) went in the first round of the draft to Golden State, Strong (14.2 ppg, 9.9 rpg) in the second round to Philadelphia. That latter was the best player all summer in the 76ers' rookie camp.

"With the graduation losses," said Gillen, "it would be lunacy to pick us number one. We'd need Mary Poppins at point guard. We could be decent in time, but I think Marquette is the early favorite, based on a great recruiting class and some quality transfers. Detroit may be the team to watch with all of its returnees and some good newcomers."

It should be noted, though, that Gillen was a winner long before Hill and Strong arrived in Cincinnati, so his requisite poor-mouthing should be taken with a grain of salt. He has back two senior guards, both of whom are quick on the break and press and both of whom can shoot. 5-10 **Jamal Walker** (15.1 ppg, 3.5 rpg, 196 assists, 55 steals) is a top player, as is **Michael Davenport** (12.7 ppg, 2.9 rpg, 79 assists). At 6-4, Davenport may move to the front line.

As for Walker, he is often out of control, but few guards in the country possess his baseline to baseline speed or the ability to hang in the air until

he finds an open man. Considering the whole package, he is one of the premier point guards in the country.

6-0 sophomore **Jamie Gladden** (10.2 ppg, 2.3 rpg, 94 assists), though not Mary Poppins, was a more than adequate point guard as a freshman, starting 32 of 33 games. He was also the MCC newcomer of the year. Not too far behind as a rookie was 6-9 sophomore **Aaron Williams** (2.2 ppg, 2.7 rpg, 28 games). With Hill ill for a game with Loyola, Williams took over power forward and contributed eight points, a game-high 10 rebounds and seven blocked shots. He could be a legitimate prospect before too long.

Another player with experience is 6-6 sophomore **Maurice Brantley** (3.6 ppg, 1.9 rpg), who started all three of the Musketeers' NCAA games in place of the injured Davenport. Brantley collected 27 points and 11 rebounds in the three starts. 6-6 senior **Colin Parker** (4.2 ppg, 1.1 rpg) also started once last year and he helps bring stability to an otherwise revamped frontcourt.

Others back for Xavier are 5-9 junior **Eric Knop** (0.6 ppg), 6-6 senior **Dave Minor** (1.7 ppg), 6-8 junior **Mark Poynter** (0.9 ppg) and 6-8 sophomore **Dwayne Wilson** (1.3 ppg, 1.5 rpg). They will be pushed by an impressive group of four freshmen.

6-8 power player **Erik Edwards** (Wilmington HS/Wilmington, Del.) is at the head of the new class, posting averages of 30.2 points and 13.3 rebounds as a high school senior. He was a consensus Top 50 recruit nationally and is the premier freshman in the MCC. Edwards capped his senior year with an impressive showing at the Dapper Dan Roundball Classic in Pittsburgh.

Other freshmen include 6-8 **Brian Grant** (Georgetown HS/Georgetown, Ohio), 6-7 **Dennis Pierre** (Walnut Hills HS/Cincinnati, Ohio), 6-8 **DeWaun Rose** (Leo HS/Chicago) and 6-4 **Tyrice Walker** (Hamilton HS/Hamilton, Ohio). Chris Mack (10.0 ppg, 6.4 rpg), a 6-5 swing player, transferred from arch-rival Evansville. He is not eligible until 1991-92.

BLUE RIBBON ANALYSIS

Davenport, Walker and Gladden are prime time players. Gillen is a prime time coach. Thus, there is no reason to suspect that Xavier will not remain a prime time program. Even the best, though, must rebuild occasionally.

And, for Gillen, it is hardly a complete overhaul. Retooling is perhaps a better description. Without Hill and Strong, he is flexible enough to focus more of the offense on outstanding perimeter players. Xavier's traditionally rugged defensive pressure should also be a strength.

The guess here is that one of the new big men, most likely Edwards, will be at least serviceable in his freshman year. The rest of the roster has enough proven winners so that the predicted MCC slide is not as drastic as many forecast.

Xavier will not win the MCC in 1990-91, but a drop out of the first division is equally unlikely. Other recent glamour teams in the conference have also suffered major losses. The Musketeers should remain in the league's top three.

YALE

**LAST SEASON: 19-7
CONFERENCE RECORD: 10-4
LEAGUE STARTERS LOST: 0
STARTERS RETURNING: 5
CONFERENCE: IVY LEAGUE
LOCATION: NEW HAVEN, CT
HOME FLOOR: PAYNE WHITNEY GYMNASIUM (3,100)
NICKNAMES: BULLDOGS, ELI
COLORS: YALE BLUE AND WHITE
COACH: DICK KUCHEN, record at Yale, 56-50. Career record, 136-162.**

You'll have to pardon the Bulldogs if they appear a little colorblind this season. Even as they fight through Ivy League hues of crimson, red and blue, and brown and green, everything will appear in two colors.

Orange and black. That's the orange and black of Princeton, perennial Ivy League favorite and two-time defending champion. Orange and black as in four starters back from a season where the Tigers scared yet another big-time powerhouse in the NCAA tournament. Imagine that, Halloween every day of the season.

The Bulldogs are not dismissing the rest of the league - you don't get into Yale without some kind of common sense - but since the Eli missed last year's championship by just one game and has everybody back, it will be tough for them not to focus on Princeton.

"Princeton is a tough team, because any game they play, they'll be in," Yale assistant Mike Mucci said. "But the way they play, they always give you a chance to win. You have to take it. You also have to know how to win, and we've shown we know how."

The Bulldogs can apply that knowledge *en masse* this season. They finished last year with their best record since 1947-48. Five starters and 13 letterwinners are back in New Haven to take the next step, but that does not make them the only team hunting Tiger.

"No one in the whole league has lost a lot of guys," Mucci said. "While we're in a great situation, the league is as tough as it's been."

It's people like **Dean Campbell** and **Ed Petersen** who have helped make Yale's condition so favorable. Campbell, a 6-4 senior forward, averaged 14.8 points per game and 5.9 rebounds, en route to a first-team All-Ivy selection. He solidifies the small but tough Yale frontline.

"From the time he came here, he's worked so hard at the game," Mucci said. "He's a very explosive player, and he's got the ability to take over a game."

Where he's matured is that he's doing it more consistently.''

Petersen, a 5-11 junior point guard, was Yale's second-leading scorer (14.2 ppg, 86 assists) and a second-team All-League choice. He shot 40 percent from three-point range and directed the Bulldog offense superbly.

''There may not be a better point guard in the league when the game is on the line,'' said Mucci. ''He's like a coach on the floor, and does some things that we can't believe when we see them on tape.''

The other returning starters are 6-5 senior forward **Travis McCready** (10.4 ppg, 5.9 rpg, 19 blocked shots), 6-7 junior forward **Stuart Davies** (9.6 ppg, 7.4 rpg, 26 blocked shots) and 6-1 sophomore guard **David Brown** (5.5 ppg). All have had the luxury of growing together as a winning unit, perhaps even sooner than Bulldog fans expected.

Depth up front will be provided by 6-7 junior **Casey Cammann** (6.6 ppg, 4.8 rpg) 6-5 senior captain **Steve Keller** (1.0 ppg), 6-8 sophomore **Craig Fairfield** (1.1 ppg, 1.3 rpg), 6-8 junior **Steve Dove** (1.3 ppg, 1.2 rpg) and 6-7 junior **Phil Black** (1.2 ppg, 1.2 rpg).

John Brodsky (1.1 ppg), a 6-0 senior, will spell Petersen at the point, while 6-1 sophomore **Rob Connolly** (3.3 ppg) and 6-4 sophomore **Todd Trimmer** (1.6 ppg, 1.4 rpg) are reserves at the two spot.

Since the Eli were not exactly giants in physical stature last year, head coach Dick Kuchen tried and was successful in luring some height to New Haven.

Five of the six incoming freshman stand 6-4 or taller, the lone exception being 6-1 guard **Damon Franklin** (Chicopee Comp HS/Chicopee, Mass.).

The tall timber, at least by Ivy standards, includes 6-4 swingman **Rodney Burford** (Hunters Lane HS/Nashville, Tenn.), 6-7 **Sean Fitzgerald** (Bishop Moore HS/Orlando, Fla.), 6-8 **Dixon Karmindro** (Liberty HS/Youngstown, Ohio), 6-8 **Robert Fisher** (Julienne-Chaminade HS/Dayton, Ohio) and 6-10 **David Bialski** (John Abbott HS/Quebec, Can.).

''We brought in a lot of size, but with big kids, you just don't know how they're going to develop,'' Mucci said. Yale fans simply hope they develop a healthy appetite for anything wearing orange and black.

BLUE RIBBON ANALYSIS

Is this the Bulldogs' year? Well, maybe. Yale has a lot back and could get some much-needed help up front from the newcomers. Campbell and Petersen solidify a starting five that's as good as any in the league, and Cammann is a solid sixth man.

But there is always the problem of Princeton. If the Tigers had lost a few more players, it would be title time in New Haven. The defending champions, though, may have returned just too much.

Yale could win 20 games overall and may even sneak away with an NIT bid. But, in the Ivy League, the Bulldogs will have to settle for second place.

1990-91 YALE SCHEDULE		
Nov.	23-24	#Stanford Invitational
	29	Connecticut
Dec.	1	@Bucknell
	4	@Wagner
	7	Lafayette
	8	Swarthmore (PA)
	29	@Fairleigh Dickinson
Jan.	3	@Fairfield
	5	@Colgate
	11	@Princeton
	12	@Pennsylvania
	15	Brooklyn College (NY)
	19	Brown
	22	New Hampshire
	26	@Brown
Feb.	1	Columbia
	2	Cornell
Feb.	8	@Dartmouth
	9	@Harvard
	15	Pennsylvania
	16	Princeton
	22	Harvard
	23	Dartmouth
Mar.	1	@Cornell
	2	@Columbia

@ Road Games
# Palo Alto, CA (Rider, St. Mary's & Stanford)

LATE BREAKING NEWS

Alabama Birmingham - Center Doug Turner will not return to the team.

Appalachian State - 6-4 swingman Tony Thompson has been ruled in eligible for his freshman season. 6-6 senior Pat Lyons has announced he will transfer, but not play basketball.

Auburn - Freshman signee Aaron Swinson is academically ineligible. Another freshman recruit, Robert Shannon, chose to attend Odessa (Tex.) JC.

Cincinnati - The Bearcat coaching staff expects immediate help of the bench from late signee Terrell Holcomb, a 6-2½ freshman point guard from Linden-McKinley HS in Columbus, Ohio. Holcomb, who was twice an All-Columbus selection and is from the alma mater of heavyweight champion Buster Douglas, was not on Cincinnati's pre-season roster.

Duquesne - Freshman forward Sean Rooney (St. Anthony's HS/Jersey City, N.J.) has been ruled academically ineligible. He will not play this year.

Eastern Kentucky - Forward Eric Butler transferred in from Robert Morris, and is eligible immediately. He is a sophomore.

Florida - Sophomore forward Travis Schintzius left for St. Petersburg (Fla.) JC.

Fullerton State - Junior pointguard Wayne Williams, one of the nation's top assist men, returned to the Titans after indicating he would leave the program. Junior College transfers Kim Kemp and Aaron Sunderland are ineligible. Joe Betrand opted to attend Compton (Calif.) JC.

George Washington - Coleman Scott transferred to Champlain (Vt.) JC.

Illinois State - Forward Derek Stokes is academically ineligible.

Jacksonville - Sean Byrd has given up his effort to return to the team. The Sun Belt Conference freshman of the year in 1987-88 missed the last two seasons with knee problems.

Loyola Marymount - Assistant coach Jay Hillock was elevated to head coach, replacing Paul Westhead who went to the Denver Nuggets. Hillock previously served as the head coach at Gonzaga. In four years at Gonzaga, Hillock was 60-50.

Marshall - Guard Brett Vincent transferred in from Robert Morris and is eligible immediately. The Thundering Herd also announced the signing of two late junior college transfers, 6-10 Wesley Cornish of Hagerstown (Md.) JC and 6-6 junior Eric Clay of Imperial Valley (Calif.) College. Neither Shawn Clifton, a JC transfer, or freshman signee Chris Patterson are eligible.

Maryland - 6-8 junior Walt Williams, who announced he would transfer after the announcement of NCAA sanctions, will remain with the Terrapins and play pointguard.

Massachusetts - Freshman Ted Cotrrell will attend Maine Central Institute in Pittsfield, Maine, this year instead of enrolling at Massachusetts.

Miami of Florida - Three-year starter Thomas Hocker has withdrawn from school.

Missouri - All-America guard Anthony Peeler is academically ineligible for the first semester. Reportedly, he could miss up to 14 games.

New Orleans - Guard Leonard Bennett returned to school after previously declaring his intention to transfer to Southern Mississippi.

Oregon State - Freshman guard Kareem Anderson is academically ineligible. Starting center Scott Haskin underwent back surgery and is expected to miss the entire season.

Pennsylvania - Starting center Hassan Duncombe, a 6-8 senior, was ruled academically ineligible. Under Ivy League rules, he would have to win a special appeal to be granted an extra year of eligibility in 1991-92.

Pepperdine - Mark Georgeson, still recovering from a broken left hip suffered in a February auto accident, probably will not play again. Two major operations left Georgeson with 15 screws in his hip.

Robert Morris - Senior guard Brett Vincent transferred to Marshall after NCAA sanctions were announced. Forward Eric Butler transferred to Eastern Kentucky.

St. Francis - Freshman forward Leo Nadal is academically ineligible.

St. Mary's - Junior College transfer Brian Brazier will be in a brace for more than two months after suffering a broken neck in an auto accident. He will miss the entire season.

South Carolina - Freshman forward Maurio Hanson was ruled academically ineligible. He will attend Spartanburg Methodist (S.C.) JC.

Tennessee Chattanooga - 6-3 senior Tommy Bankston transferred to Le-Moyne Owen. 6-4 senior Ben Wiley left the team for personal reasons.

Tennessee State - Forward Darryl Brooks, the seventh-leading scorer in Division I last season, was ruled academically ineligible.

Texas A&M - Prized freshman guard Ed Wheeler enrolled at Paris (Tex.) JC.

Texas-Pan American - Fred Young, the Broncos' leading returning scorer and rebounder, will forego his final season of eligibility. He chose to join the police academy in Houston, his hometown.

Virginia Military Institute -6-4 freshman Jamie Lee, originally a VMI signee, enrolled at Campbell (N.C.) College. Larry Jefferies, a 6-5 forward, left school.

Washington - Guard Steve Hall transferred to Virginia Tech.

Weber State - Forward Kevin Williams left for Henry Ford (Mich.) JC.

Western Carolina - 6-2 sophomore Bo Greenwood transferred to Tennessee Tech, but will not play basketball.

Wisconsin - Freshman guard Tracy Webster is not eligible to play this season.

Xavier - Senior forward David Minor left the team.

KEY TO ABBREVIATIONS

FR—freshman	F—forward	apg—assists per game	Mil—military
SO—sophomore	C—center	stpg—steals per game	JC—junior college
JR—junior	G—guard	blpg—blocks per game	CC—community college
SR—senior	ppg—points per game	Acad—academy	HS—high school

COLLEGE ROUNDUP

* **For the Record**
* **1990 NBA Draft**
* **1989-90 Conference Records**
* **Newcomer of the Year & Other Newcomers of Impact**
* **NCAA Division I Women's All-America Team & Top 25**
* **Junior College All-America Team & Top 30**
* **J.D. Hinkle, Jr. NAIA All-America Team & Top 20**
* **NCAA Division II All America Team & Top 20**

FOR THE RECORD

1989-90 TOP 20 — DIVISION I INDIVIDUAL LEADERS
(NOTE: *Returning in 1990-91)

SCORING

	FG	FT	PTS	AVG
1. Bo Kimble, Loyola Marymount	404	231	1131	35.3
2. *Devin Bradshaw, US International	291	221	875	31.3
3. Dave Jamerson, Ohio University	297	149	874	31.2
4. *Alphonzo Ford, Mississippi Valley	289	126	808	29.9
5. *Steve Rogers, Alabama State	286	213	831	29.7
6. Hank Gathers, Loyola Marymount	314	126	754	29.0
7. *Daryl Brooks, Tennessee State	258	79	690	28.8
8. Chris jackson, LSU	305	191	889	27.8
9. Dennis Scott, Georgia Tech	336	161	970	27.2
10. Mark Stevenson, Duquesne	297	160	788	26.5
11. Lionel Simmons, LaSalle	335	146	847	26.3
12. *Keith Gailes, Loyola (IL)	272	148	762	26.0
13. Kurk Lee, Towson State	285	172	805	25.7
14. Gary Payton, Oregon State	288	118	746	25.5
15. Bailey Alston, Liberty	266	141	714	25.5
16. Sydney Grider, Southwestern Louisiana	251	106	739	25.3
17. Vernell Coles, Virginia Tech	280	158	785	24.1
18. Travis Mays, Texas	240	197	772	24.1
19. Gerald Glass, Mississippi	284	109	723	23.8
20. Tony Smith, Marquette	240	173	689	23.8

FREE-THROW PERCENTAGE

	FT	FTA	PCT
1. *Rob Robbins, New Mexico	101	108	93.5
2. Mike Joseph, Bucknell	144	155	92.9
3. Chris Jackson, LSU	191	210	91.0
4. *Andy Kennedy, Alabama Birmingham	111	123	90.2
5. Steve Henson, Kansas State	101	112	90.2
6. *Jason Matthews, Pittsburgh	141	158	89.2
7. *Scott Sheffler, Evansville	84	95	88.4
8. Eldridge Recasner, Washington	99	112	88.4
9. *Clint Venable, Bowling Green	114	129	88.4
10. *Kevin Franklin, Nevada-Reno	68	77	88.3
11. *Keith Jennings, East Tennessee State	107	122	87.7
12. *Matt O'Brien, Georgia State	113	129	87.6
13. *William Lewis, Monmouth	69	79	87.3
14. *Greg Gary, Tulane	95	109	87.2
15. *Mike Iuzzolino, St. Francis (PA)	135	155	87.1
16. Keith Robinson, Notre Dame	107	123	87.0
17. *Scott Draud, Vanderbilt	100	115	87.0
18. *Steve Watson, Bowling Green	73	84	86.9
19. Joel Debortoli, San Francisco	73	84	86.9
20. *Frank Allen, Murray State	112	129	86.8

REBOUNDING

	G	NO	AVG
1. Anthony Bonner, St. Louis	33	456	13.8
2. Eric McArthur, California-Santa Barbara	29	377	13.0
3. Tyrone Hill, Xavier	32	402	12.6
4. Lee Campbell, Southwest Missouri	29	363	12.5
5. Cedric Ceballos, California-Fullerton	29	362	12.5
6. Hakim Shahid, South Florida	31	383	12.4
7. Ron Draper, American University	29	354	12.2
8. Derrick Coleman, Syracuse	33	398	12.1
9. Shaquille O'Neal, LSU	32	385	12.0
10. *C. Weatherspoon, Southern Mississippi	32	371	11.6
11. *Larry Johnson, UNLV	40	457	11.4
12. *Reggie Slater, Wyoming	29	328	11.3
13. *Dale Davis, Clemson	35	395	11.3
14. *Shaun Vandiver, Colorado	30	336	11.2
15. *Popeye Jones, Murray State	30	336	11.2
16. *Steve Stevenson, Prairie View	27	302	11.2
17. *Larry Stewart, Coppin State	33	369	11.2
18. Loy Vaught, Michigan	31	346	11.2
19. Lionel Simmons, LaSalle	32	356	11.1
20. Kenny Green, Rhode Island	26	284	10.9

ASSISTS

	G	NO	AVG
1. Todd Lehmann, Drexel	28	260	9.3
2. *Aaron Mitchell, Southwestern Louisiana	29	264	9.1
3. *Keith Jennings, East Tennessee State	34	297	8.7
4. Otis Livingston, Idaho	31	262	8.5
5. *Kenny Anderson, Georgia Tech	35	285	8.1
6. Gary Payton, Oregon State	29	235	8.1
7. Tony Edmond, Texas Christian	29	234	8.1
8. *Chris Corchiani, North Carolina State	30	238	7.9
9. *Darelle Porter, Pittsburgh	29	229	7.9
10. Lamar Holt, Prairie View	27	213	7.9
11. Gary Herer, Massachusetts	31	238	7.7
12. Steven Key, Boston University	30	228	7.6
13. *Bobby Hurley, Duke	38	288	7.6
14. Steve Smith, U.S. International	28	209	7.5
15. *Greg Anthony, UNLV	39	289	7.4
16. *Larry Yarbray, Coppin State	31	225	7.3
17. *Wayne Williams, California-Fullerton	29	209	7.2
18. *Tony Walker, Loyola Marymount	32	227	7.1
19. Jeff Bowling, Air Force	32	224	7.0
20. Carlton Screen, Providence	29	202	7.0

FIELD-GOAL PERCENTAGE

	FG	FGA	PCT
1. Lee Campbell, Southwest Missouri State	192	275	69.82
2. Stephen Scheffler, Purdue	173	248	69.76
3. Felton Spencer, Louisville	188	276	68.1
4. Brian Parker, Cleveland State	155	236	65.7
5. Brian Hill, Evansville	180	278	64.7
6. *Larry Stewart, Coppin State	233	361	64.5
7. Hakim Shahid, South Florida	201	314	64.0
8. *Tommy French, Hardin-Simmons	212	338	62.7
9. *Adam Keefe, Stanford	210	335	62.7
10. *Dale Davis, Clemson	205	328	62.5
11. *Larry Johnson, UNLV	304	487	62.4
12. Les Jepsen, Iowa	155	249	62.2
13. Mike Curry, Georgia Southern	164	264	62.1
14. Alaa Abdelnaby, Duke	217	350	62.0
15. *Robert Dykes, George Mason	169	273	61.9
16. Riley Smith, Idaho	270	441	61.2
17. *Sean Hammonds, Wright State	160	263	60.8
18. Ed Fogell, Penn State	191	314	60.8
19. Keith Robinson, Notre Dame	159	262	60.7
20. *C. Weatherspoon, Southern Mississippi	205	339	60.5

BLOCKED SHOTS

	G	NO	AVG
1. Kenny Green, Rhode Island	26	124	4.8
2. *Dikembe Mutombo, Georgetown	31	128	4.1
3. *Kevin Roberson, Vermont	30	114	3.8
4. *Lorenzo Williams, Stetson	32	121	3.8
5. *Omar Roland, Marshall	28	101	3.6
6. *Shaquille O'Neal, LSU	32	115	3.6
7. *Steve Stevenson, Prairie View	27	97	3.6
8. *David Harris, Texas A&M	31	108	3.5
9. *Luc Longley, New Mexico	34	117	3.4
10. Walter Palmer, Dartmouth	25	85	3.4
11. Stanley Wormely, Stanford	28	91	3.3
12. Eric McArthur, California-Santa Barbara	29	91	3.1
13. Alan Ogg, Alabama-Birmingham	31	91	2.9
14. *Derek Stewart, Augusta	28	82	2.9
15. *Damon Lopez, Fordham	32	91	2.8
16. Eldon Campbell, Clemson	35	97	2.8
17. *Robert Carter, Jackson State	28	76	2.7
18. *Daron Jenkins, Southern Mississippi	32	86	2.7
19. *Dane Holmes, Columbia	24	61	2.5
20. *Jeff Roulston, South Carolina	27	68	2.5

DIVISION I — TEAM TOP 12

WON-LOST PERCENTAGE

	W-L	PCT
1. LaSalle	30-2	.938
2. UNLV	35-5	.875
3. Arkansas	30-5	.857
3. Kansas	30-5	.857
5. Xavier (Ohio)	28-5	.848
6. Oklahoma	27.5	.844
7. New Mexico State	26-5	.839
8. Connecticut	31-6	.838
9. Michigan State	28-6	.824
10. Loyola Marymount	26-6	.813
10. Missouri	26-6	.813
12. Idaho	25-6	.806
12. Southern Baton-Rouge	25-6	.806

FIELD-GOAL PERCENTAGE

	FG	FGA	PCT
1. Kansas	1204	2258	53.3
2. Louisville	1097	2078	52.8
3. Princeton	592	1133	52.3
4. Purdue	778	1491	52.2
5. Loyola Marymount	1456	2808	51.9
6. Evansville	816	1577	51.7
7. Indiana	824	1603	51.4
8. Monmouth	699	1361	51.4
9. Michigan State	967	1884	51.3
10. Michigan	1035	2018	51.3
11. Notre Dame	847	1653	51.2
12. Southern Mississippi	981	1928	50.9

REBOUND MARGIN

	OFF	DEF	MAR
1. Georgetown	44.8	34.0	10.8
2. Xavier (Ohio)	40.4	30.0	10.4
3. Ball State	39.5	30.9	8.6
4. Michigan tate	38.1	29.8	8.4
5. Notre Dame	37.9	29.6	8.2
6. Northeastern	40.6	32.7	8.0
7. California-Santa Barbara	42.3	34.8	7.5
8. LSU	45.5	38.2	7.3
9. Minnesota	37.4	30.3	7.1
10. Eastern Kentucky	39.9	33.0	6.9
11. Penn State	36.3	29.6	6.7
12. Georgia Southern	41.1	34.5	6.7

SCORING OFFENSE

	G	PTS	AVG
1. Loyola Marymount	32	3918	122.4
2. Oklahoma	32	3243	101.3
3. Southern Baton-Rouge	31	3078	99.3
4. U.S. International	28	2738	97.8
5. Centenary	30	2877	95.9
6. Arkansas	35	3345	95.6
7. Texas	33	3091	93.7
8. UNLV	40	3739	93.5
9. Kansas	35	3223	92.1
10. LSU	32	2921	91.3
11. Alabama State	28	2553	91.2
12. Wright State			

SCORING DEFENSE

	G	PTS	AVG
1. Princeton	27	1378	51.0
2. Ball State	33	1935	58.6
3. Colorado State	30	1778	59.3
4. Wisconsin-Green Bay	32	1913	59.8
5. Northern Illinois	28	1710	61.1
6. Yale	26	1588	61.1
7. Alabama	35	2151	61.5
8. Boise State	27	1683	62.3
9. Monmouth	29	181	62.7
10. Fairfield	29	1833	63.2
11. Stanford	30	1910	63.7
12. Penn State	34	2172	63.9

SCORING MARGIN

	OFF	DEF	MAR
1. Oklahoma	101.3	80.4	21.0
2. Kansas	92.1	72.3	19.7
3. Georgetown	81.5	64.8	16.7
4. Arkansas	95.6	79.8	15.8
5. Southern Baton-Rouge	99.3	84.1	15.2
6. UNLV	93.5	78.4	15.0
7. LaSalle	86.1	71.3	14.7
8. Loyola Marymount	122.4	108.1	14.4
9. Connecticut	79.1	66.1	13.0
10. Ball State	71.5	58.6	12.9
11. Duke	89.1	76.6	12.5
12. Arizona	78.9	66.9	12.0

3-POINT FIELD GOALS

	G	NO	AVG		G	NO	AVG		G	NO	AVG
1. Kentucky	28	281	10.0	5. Dayton	32	261	8.2	9. Central Michigan	30	238	7.9
2. Loyola Marymount	32	298	9.3	6. Southern Baton-Rouge	31	251	8.1	10. Southwest Texas State	28	218	7.8
3. Southwestern Louisiana	29	251	8.7	7. LaSalle	32	258	8.1	11. Tennessee State	28	217	7.8
4. East Tennessee State	34	285	8.4	8. St. Francis (PA)	28	223	8.0	12. Princeton	27	208	7.7

1990 NBA DRAFT SELECTION

FIRST ROUND

TEAM	NAME	COLLEGE	HT.
1. New Jersey	Derrick Coleman	Syracuse	6-10
2. Seattle	Gary Payton	Oregon State	6-4½
3. Denver (from Miami)	Chris Jackson	LSU	6-1
4. Orlando	Dennis Scott	Georgia Tech	6-8
5. Charlotte	Kendall Gill	Illinois	6-5
6. Minnesota	Felton Spencer	Louisville	7-0
7. Sacramento	Lionel Simmons	LaSalle	6-8
8. LA Clippers	Bo Kimble	Loyola Marymount	6-3½
9. Miami (from Washington via Dallas and Denver)	Willie Burton	Minnesota	6-6½
10. Atlanta (from Golden State)	Rumeal Robinson	Michigan	6-2
11. Golden State (from Atlanta)	Tyrone Hill	Xavier	6-10
12. Houston (1)	Alec Kessler	Georgia	6-11
13. LA Clippers (from Cleveland)	Loy Vaught	Michigan	6-9
14. Sacramento (from Indiana via Dallas)	Travis Mays	Texas	6-2
15. Miami (from Denver) (2)	Dave Jamerson	Ohio	6-5
16. Milwaukee (3)	Terry Mills	Michigan	6-10
17. New York	Jerrod Mustaf	Maryland	6-10
18. Sacramento (from Dallas)	Duane Causwell	Temple	7-0
19. Boston	Dee Brown	Jacksonville	6-1
20. Minnesota (from Philadelphia)	Gerald Glass	Mississippi	6-5
21. Phoenix	Jayson Williams	St. John's	6-8½
22. New Jersey (from Chicago)	Tate George	Connecticut	6-5
23. Sacramento (from Utah)	Anthony Bonner	St. Louis	6-8
24. San Antonio	Dwayne Schintzius	Florida	7-1
25. Portland	Alaa Abedelnaby	Duke	6-10
26. Detroit	Lance Blanks	Texas	6-4
27. LA Lakers	Elden Campbell	Clemson	6-11

SECOND ROUND

TEAM	NAME	COLLEGE	HT.
28. Golden State (from New Jersey via Atlanta)	Les Jepsen	Iowa	7-0
29. Chicago (from Orlando)	Toni Kukoc	Juguplastika Split (Yug.)	6-9
30. Miami (2)	Carl Herrera	Houston	6-9
31. Phoenix (from Charlotte)	Negele Knight	Dayton	6-1½
32. Philadelphia (from Minnesota)	Brian Oliver	Georgia Tech	6-4
33. Utah (from Sacramento)	Walter Palmer	Dartmouth	7-2
34. Golden State (from LA Clippers)	Kevin Pritchard	Kansas	6-3
35. Washington	Greg Foster	UTEP	7-0
36. Atlanta (from Golden State)	Trevor Wilson	UCLA	6-7
37. Washington (from Atlanta)	A.J. English	Virginia Union	6-5
38. Seattle (4)	Jud Buechler	Arizona	6-6
39. Charlotte (from Houston)	Steve Scheffler	Purdue	6-9
40. Sacramento (from Indiana) (1)	Bimbo Coles	Virginia Tech	6-1½
41. Atlanta (from Cleveland via Miami & Golden State)	Steve Bardo	Illinois	6-5
42. Denver	Marcus Liberty	Illinois	6-8
43. San Antonio (from Milwaukee)	Tony Massenburg	Maryland	6-9
44. Milwaukee (from New York via Seattle)	Steve Henson	Kansas State	6-1
45. Indiana (from Dallas)	Antonio Davis	UTEP	6-9½
46. Indiana (from Boston)	Kenny Williams	Elizabeth City State	6-9
47. Philadelphia	Derek Strong	Xavier	6-8
48. Phoenix	Cedric Ceballos	Fullerton State	6-6½
49. Dallas (from Utah via Sacramento)	Phil Henderson	Duke	6-4
50. Phoenix (from Chicago)	Milos Babic	Tennessee Tech	7-0
51. LA Lakers (from San Antonio)	Tony Smith	Marquette	6-3½
52. Cleveland (from Detroit via Philadelphia)	Stefano Rusconi	Ranger Varese (Italy)	6-9
53. Seattle (from Portland)	Abdul Shamsid-Deen	Providence	6-10
54. San Antonio (from LA Lakers)	Sean Higgins	Michigan	6-9

Key:

(1) Traded to the Miami Heat   (2) Traded to the Houston Rockets   (3) Traded to the Denver Nuggets   (4) Traded to the New Jersey Nets

★ AMERICAN SOUTH ★

	CONFERENCE W	L	ALL GAMES W	L
1. *New Orleans	8	2	21	11
2. Louisiana Tech	8	2	20	8
3. Pan American	7	3	21	9
4. Southwestern Louisiana	4	6	20	9
5. Arkansas State	2	8	15	13
6. Lamar	1	9	7	21

★ ATLANTIC COAST ★

	W	L	W	L
1. Clemson	10	4	26	9
2. Duke	9	5	29	9
3. *Georgia Tech	8	6	27	7
3. North Carolina	8	6	21	13
5. Virginia	6	8	20	11
5. North Carolina State	6	8	18	12
5. Maryland	6	8	19	14
8. Wake Forest	3	11	12	16

★ ATLANTIC 10 ★

	W	L	W	L
1. *Temple	15	3	20	11
2. Penn State	13	5	25	9
3. West Virginia	11	7	16	12
3. Rhode Island	11	7	15	13
3. Rutgers	11	7	18	17
6. Massachusetts	10	8	17	14
7. George Washington	6	12	14	17
8. St. Joseph's	5	13	7	21
8. Duquesne	5	13	7	22
10. St. Bonaventure	3	15	8	20

★ BIG EAST ★

	W	L	W	L
1. Syracuse	12	4	26	6
2. *Connecticut	12	4	30	6
3. Georgetown	11	5	24	7
4. St. John's	10	6	24	10
5. Providence	8	8	17	12
5. Villanova	8	8	18	15
7. Seton Hall	5	11	12	16
7. Pittsburgh	5	11	12	17
9. Boston College	1	15	8	20

★ BIG EIGHT ★

	W	L	W	L
1. Missouri	12	2	26	6
2. Kansas	11	3	30	5
2. *Oklahoma	11	3	26	5
4. Kansas State	7	7	17	15
5. Oklahoma State	6	8	17	14
6. Iowa State	4	10	10	18
7. Nebraska	3	11	10	18
8. Colorado	2	12	12	17

★ BIG SKY ★

	W	L	W	L
1. *Idaho	13	3	25	6
2. Eastern Washington	11	5	18	11
3. Montana	10	6	18	11
4. Nevada-Reno	9	7	15	13
5. Montana State	8	8	17	12
5. Weber State	8	8	14	15
7. Boise State	7	9	12	15
8. Northern Arizona	3	13	8	20
8. Idaho State	3	13	6	21

★ BIG SOUTH ★

	CONFERENCE W	L	ALL GAMES W	L
1. *Coastal Carolina	11	1	23	6
2. North Carolina-Asheville	7	5	18	12
2. Campbell	7	5	15	13
4. Winthrop	6	6	19	10
5. Baptist	4	8	9	19
5. Augusta	4	8	8	20
7. Radford	3	9	7	22

★ BIG TEN ★

	W	L	W	L
1. Michigan State	14	3	27	6
2. Purdue	13	4	22	7
3. Michigan	12	6	23	8
3. Minnesota	11	7	23	9
5. Illinois	10	7	20	8
6. Ohio State	10	8	17	13
7. Indiana	8	9	18	10
8. Wisconsin	4	14	14	17
8. Iowa	4	14	12	16
10. Northwestern	2	16	9	19

★ BIG WEST ★

	W	L	W	L
1. New Mexico State	16	2	26	5
2. *UNLV	16	2	34	5
3. California-Santa Barbara	13	5	21	9
4. Long Beach State	12	6	23	8
5. Utah State	8	10	14	16
6. Pacific	7	11	15	14
7. Fullerton State	6	12	13	16
8. San Jose State	5	13	8	20
9. Fresno State	4	14	10	19
10. California-Irvine	3	15	5	23

★ COLONIAL ATHLETIC ASSOCIATION ★

	W	L	W	L
1. James Madison	11	3	20	11
2. *Richmond	10	4	22	10
2. American	10	4	20	9
2. George Mason	10	4	20	12
5. East Carolina	6	8	13	18
6. Navy	4	10	5	23
7. North Carolina-Wilmington	3	11	8	20
8. William & Mary	2	12	6	22

★ EAST COAST ★

	W	L	W	L
1. *Towson State	8	6	18	13
2. Lehigh	8	6	18	12
2. Hofstra	8	6	13	15
4. Delaware	7	7	16	13
4. Lafayette	7	7	15	13
4. Drexel	7	7	13	15
7. Bucknell	6	8	15	14
8. Rider	5	9	10	18

★ ECAC NORTH ATLANTIC ★

	W	L	W	L
1. Northeastern	9	3	16	12
2. *Boston University	9	3	17	12
3. Hartford	8	4	17	10
4. Maine	6	6	11	16
5. Vermont	4	8	12	17
6. Colgate	3	9	7	21
6. New Hampshire	3	9	5	22

★ IVY ★

	CONFERENCE W	L	ALL GAMES W	L
1. Princeton	11	3	20	7
2. Yale	10	4	19	7
3. Dartmouth	7	7	12	14
3. Harvard	7	7	12	14
3. Pennsylvania	7	7	12	14
3. Brown	7	7	10	16
7. Cornell	5	9	12	17
8. Columbia	2	12	4	22

★ METRO ★

	W	L	W	L
1. *Louisville	12	2	27	8
2. Southern Mississippi	9	5	20	12
2. Cincinnati	9	5	20	14
4. Memphis State	8	6	18	12
5. Florida State	6	8	16	15
5. South Carolina	6	8	14	14
7. Virginia Tech	5	9	13	18
8. Tulane	1	13	4	24

★ METRO ATLANTIC ★

NORTH

	W	L	W	L
1. Holy Cross	14	2	24	6
2. Siena	11	5	16	13
3. Fordham	10	6	20	13
4. Canisius	5	11	11	18
4. Army	5	11	10	19
4. Niagara	5	11	6	22

SOUTH

	W	L	W	L
1. *LaSalle	16	0	30	2
2. Iona	8	8	13	15
3. St. Peter's	7	9	14	14
3. Manhattan	7	9	11	17
5. Fairfield	6	10	10	19
6. Loyola (MD)	2	14	4	24

★ MID-AMERICAN ★

	W	L	W	L
1. *Ball State	13	3	25	7
2. Kent State	12	4	21	8
3. Bowling Green	9	7	18	11
3. Miami	9	7	14	15
5. Eastern Michigan	8	8	19	13
6. Toledo	7	9	12	16
7. Central Michigan	6	10	13	16
8. Ohio University	5	11	12	16
9. Western Michigan	3	13	9	18

★ MID-CONTINENT ★

	W	L	W	L
1. Southwestern Missouri	11	1	22	6
2. Wisconsin-Green Bay	9	3	22	8
3. *Northern Iowa	6	6	21	9
3. Illinois-Chicago	6	6	16	11
3. Western Illinois	6	6	15	12
6. Eastern Illinois	3	9	10	17
7. Valparaiso	1	11	4	23
8. Cleveland State	0	0	15	13

(NOTE: *Denotes winner of Conference Tournament)

★ MID-EASTERN ★

	Conf W	Conf L	All W	All L
1. *Coppin State	15	1	26	7
2. Florida A&M	13	3	18	11
3. Delaware State	9	7	14	14
4. South Carolina State	8	8	13	16
4. Bethune-Cookman	8	8	10	18
6. North Carolina A&T	6	10	13	16
7. Howard	5	11	8	20
8. Maryland-Eastern Shore	4	12	10	17
8. Morgan State	4	12	8	20

★ MIDWESTERN COLLEGIATE ★

	Conf W	Conf L	All W	All L
1. Xavier	12	2	28	5
2. *Dayton	10	4	22	10
3. St. Louis	9	5	21	12
3. Marquette	9	5	15	14
5. Evansville	8	6	17	15
6. Detroit	3	11	10	18
6. Loyola	3	11	7	22
8. Butler	2	12	6	22

★ MISSOURI VALLEY ★

	Conf W	Conf L	All W	All L
1. Southern Illinois	10	4	26	8
2. Creighton	9	5	21	12
2. *Illinois State	9	5	18	13
2. Tulsa	9	5	17	13
5. Bradley	6	8	11	20
5. Wichita State	6	8	10	19
7. Drake	5	9	13	18
8. Indiana State	2	12	8	20

★ NORTHEAST ★

	Conf W	Conf L	All W	All L
1. *Robert Morris	12	4	22	8
2. Monmouth	11	5	17	12
3. Marist	10	6	17	11
3. St. Francis (PA)	10	6	17	11
3. Mt. St. Mary's	10	6	16	12
6. Fairleigh Dickinson	8	8	16	13
7. Wagner	6	10	11	17
8. St. Francis (NY)	4	12	9	18
9. Long Island	1	15	3	23

★ OHIO VALLEY ★

	Conf W	Conf L	All W	All L
1. *Murray State	10	2	21	9
2. Tennessee Tech	9	3	19	9
3. Morehead State	7	5	16	13
3. Eastern Kentucky	7	5	13	17
5. Middle Tennessee	5	7	12	16
6. Austin Peay	2	10	10	19
6. Tennessee State	2	10	7	21

★ PACIFIC 10 ★

	Conf W	Conf L	All W	All L
1. Oregon State	15	3	22	7
2. *Arizona	15	3	24	7
3. California	12	6	22	10
4. UCLA	11	7	22	10
5. Oregon	10	8	15	14
6. Stanford	9	9	18	12
7. Arizona State	6	12	15	16
7. Southern California	6	12	12	16
9. Washington	5	13	12	17
10. Washington State	1	17	6	22

★ SOUTHEASTERN ★

	Conf W	Conf L	All W	All L
1. Georgia	13	5	20	9
2. *Alabama	12	6	25	9
2. LSU	12	6	23	9
4. Tennessee	10	8	16	14
4. Kentucky	10	8	14	14
6. Mississippi	8	10	13	16
6. Auburn	8	10	13	18
8. Mississippi State	7	11	16	14
8. Vanderbilt	7	11	21	14
10. Florida	3	15	7	21

★ SOUTHERN ★

	Conf W	Conf L	All W	All L
1. *East Tennessee State	12	2	27	8
2. Marshall	9	5	15	13
3. Appalachian State	8	6	19	11
4. Tennessee Chattanooga	7	7	14	14
4. VMI	7	7	14	15
6. Furman	5	9	15	16
6. Citadel	5	9	12	16
8. Western Carolina	3	11	10	18

★ SOUTHLAND ★

	Conf W	Conf L	All W	All L
1. *Northeast Louisiana	13	1	21	8
2. McNeese State	11	3	14	13
3. Southwest Texas State	9	5	13	15
4. Sam Houston	8	6	10	18
5. Texas-Arlington	6	8	13	15
6. Northwestern Louisiana	5	9	10	18
7. North Texas State	3	11	4	25
8. Stephen F. Austin	1	13	2	25

★ SOUTHWEST ★

	Conf W	Conf L	All W	All L
1. *Arkansas	14	2	29	5
2. Houston	13	3	25	7
3. Texas	12	4	24	9
4. Texas Christian	9	7	16	13
5. Baylor	7	9	16	14
5. Texas A&M	7	9	14	17
7. Rice	5	11	11	17
7. Southern Methodist	5	11	10	18
9. Texas Tech	0	16	5	22

★ SOUTHWESTERN ATHLETIC ★

	Conf W	Conf L	All W	All L
1. Southern University	12	2	25	5
2. *Texas Southern	10	4	18	12
3. Alabama State	7	7	15	13
3. Mississippi Valley	7	7	11	18
5. Alcorn State	6	8	7	22
6. Prairie View	5	9	9	18
6. Grambling	5	9	9	19
8. Jackson State	4	10	9	19

★ SUN BELT ★

	Conf W	Conf L	All W	All L
1. Alabama-Birmingham	12	2	22	9
2. *South Florida	9	5	20	11
3. Old Dominion	7	7	14	14
3. Western Kentucky	7	7	13	17
5. North Carolina-Charlotte	6	8	16	14
6. Jacksonville	5	9	13	16
6. South Alabama	5	9	11	17
6. Virginia Commonwealth	5	9	11	17

★ TRANSAMERICA ATHLETIC ★

	Conf W	Conf L	All W	All L
1. Centenary	14	2	22	8
2. Texas-San Antonio	13	3	21	7
3. *Arkansas-Little Rock	12	4	19	10
4. Georgia Southern	11	5	17	10
5. Stetson	8	8	14	17
6. Hardin-Simmons	5	11	9	18
7. Samford	4	12	6	21
8. Georgia State	3	13	5	22
9. Mercer	2	14	7	20

★ WEST COAST ATHLETIC ★

	Conf W	Conf L	All W	All L
1. *Loyola Marymount	13	1	26	6
2. Pepperdine	10	4	17	11
3. San Diego	9	5	16	12
4. Portland	7	7	11	17
5. Santa Clara	6	8	9	19
6. San Francisco	4	10	8	20
6. St. Mary's	4	10	7	20
8. Gonzaga	3	11	8	20

★ WESTERN ATHLETIC ★

	Conf W	Conf L	All W	All L
1. Colorado State	11	5	21	9
1. Brigham Young	11	5	21	9
3. Hawaii	10	6	25	10
3. *UTEP	10	6	21	11
5. New Mexico	9	7	20	14
6. Utah	7	9	16	14
6. Wyoming	7	9	15	14
8. San Diego State	4	12	13	18
9. Air Force	3	13	12	20

★ INDEPENDENTS ★

	All W	All L
Wright State	21	7
Northern Illinois	17	11
Akron	16	12
Notre Dame	16	13
DePaul	18	15
Miami (FL)	13	15
Missouri-Kansas City	13	15
Southern Utah	13	15
MD-Baltimore County	12	16
U.S. International	12	16
Liberty	11	17
Youngstown State	8	20
Brooklyn	7	21
Central Florida	7	21
Florida International	7	21
Chicago State	6	22
Central Connecticut	5	22
Nicholls State	4	23
Davidson	4	24

*(NOTE: *Denotes winner of Conference Tournament)*

NEWCOMERS OF IMPACT

NEWCOMER OF THE YEAR

ED O'BANNON
6-8   FR   Artesia HS/Lakewood, CA   UCLA

When O'Bannon decided not to go to UNLV —he had committed to the Runnin' Rebels but had not signed a binding national letter of intent —and switched to UCLA in August, it was like Christmas in the summertime at Pauley Pavilion on the UCLA campus in the upscale Los Angeles neighborhood of Westwood. Not since Bill Walton signed to play for coach John Wooden in 1970 has UCLA landed a player of this magnitude. O'Bannon is considered one of the five best prospects ever from southern California and his arrival in Westwood shows that UCLA is well on its way back to becoming a national power.

"How good can O'Bannon be? In the same class with Jordan, Byrd, Magic, and as Isiah? Think I'm crazy, well he has the same kind of work ethic and natural ability. . .," said Clark Francis of *Hoop Scoop*.

OTHER NEWCOMERS OF IMPACT

Adrain Autrey	6-4	FR	Bronx, NY	Syracuse
Damon Bailey	6-3	FR	Heltonville, IN	Indiana
Barnard Blunt	6-3	FR	Syracuse, NY	St. Joseph's
Shawn Bradley	7-5	FR	Castle Dale, UT	Brigham Young
Dexter Cambridge	6-8	JR	Lon Morris, TX JC	Texas
Bill Curley	6-9	FR	Duxbury, MA	Boston College
Anthony Douglas	6-7	SO	Memphis, TN	Memphis State
Doug Edwards	6-9	SO	Miami, FL	Florida State
Erik Edwards	6-8	FR	Wilmington, DE	Xavier
Matt Geiger	7-0	JR	Transfer from Auburn	Georgia Tech
Mike Hanson	6-0	SO	Transfer from Tennessee-Martin	LSU
Johnathan Haynes	6-3	FR	Philadelphia, PA	Temple
Grant Hill	6-8	FR	Reston, VA	Duke
Herbert Jones	6-5	JR	Butler County, KS CC	Cincinnati
Ray Kelley	5-11	SO	Transfer from TCU	Calif.-Santa Barbara
Tony Lang	6-8	FR	Mobile, AL	Duke
Terrence Lewis	6-4	JR	Howard County, TX JC	Washington State
Jamal Mashburn	6-8	FR	Bronx, NY	Kentucky
Joe McNall	6-10	FR	Spring Valley, CA	San Diego State
Eric Montross	7-0	FR	Indianapolis, IN	North Carolina
Isiah Morris	6-9	JR	San Jacinton, TX JC	Arkansas
Cornell Parker	6-7	FR	Norfolk, VA	Virginia
Andy Pennick	6-2	FR	Louisville, KY	Michigan State
Wesley Person	6-5	FR	Brantley, AL	Auburn
Brent Price	6-0	JR	Transfer from South Carolina	Oklahoma
Brian Reese	6-6	FR	Bronx, NY	North Carolina
Khalid Reeves	6-3	FR	Queens, NY	Arizona
James Robinson	6-2	FR	Jackson, MS	Alabama
Rodney Rogers	6-7	SR	Durham, NC	Wake Forest
Clifford Rozier	6-10	FR	Bradenton, FL	North Carolina
Melvin Simon	6-8	FR	Marrero, LA	New Orleans
Stevin Smith	6-2	FR	Dallas, TX	Arizona State
Elmore Spencer	7-0	JR	Connors State, OK JC	UNLV

DIVISION I WOMEN'S
ALL-AMERICAS AND TOP 25

By: Joseph C. Smith: Director of Women's Basketball News Service

1st Team

Edna Campbell	5-7	G	SR	Texas
Daedra Charles	6-2	C	SR	Tennessee
Beth Hunt	6-0	F	SR	South Carolina
Carolyn Jones	5-8	G	SR	Auburn
MaChelle Joseph	5-7	G	JR	Purdue
Tammi Reiss	5-5	G	JR	Virginia
Michelle Savage	6-1	F	JR	Northwestern
Wendy Scholtens	6-3	C	SR	Vanderbilt
Trish Stevens	6-3	C/F	SR	Stanford
Andrea Stinson	5-9	F/G	SR	North Carolina State

2nd Team

Rachel Bouchard	6-1	C/F	SR	Maine
Dana Chatman	5-6	G	SR	LSU
Delmonica DeHorney	6-4	C	SR	Arkansas
Laurie Merlino	5-8	G	SR	Washington
Gena Miller	6-3	C	SR	Fullerton State
Angela Moorehead	5-11	F	SR	Tennessee Tech
Francis Savage	5-9	G	SR	Miami (Fla.)
Steph Schueler	5-3	G	SR	Iowa
Dawn Staley	5-5	G	JR	Virginia
Rehema Stephens	5-11	F/G	JR	UCLA

3rd Team

Shannon Cate	6-1	F	JR	Montana
Beth Davis	5-9	G/F	JR	Wake Forest
Karen Deden	6-4	C	SR	Washington
Lisa Foss	5-7	G	SR	Northern Illinois
Sonja Henning	5-6	G	SR	Stanford
Tracy Lis	5-9	G/F	JR	Providence
Amber Nicholas	5-4	G	JR	Arkansas
Susan Robinson	6-1	F	JR	Penn State
Val Whiting	6-2	C	SO	Stanford
Dana Wilkerson	5-4	G	SR	Long Beach State

Honorable Mention

Jody Adams	5-6	G	SO	Tennessee
Cindy Anderson	5-6	G	JR	St. Joseph's
Kerry Bascom	6-0	F/C	SR	Connecticut
Sarah Behn	5-0	G	SO	Boston College
Kerry Boyatt	5-10	G	SO	Clemson
Tammy Brown	6-0	F	SR	Campbell College (N.C.)
Cami Cass	5-6	G	JR	Fordham
Sheila Ethridge	5-7	G	SR	Louisiana Tech
Denise Dove	5-4	G	SR	Northern Illinois
Dana Eikenberg	5-7	G	JR	Penn State
Shanya Evans	5-2	G	SR	Providence
Vicki Hall	6-0	G	JR	Texas
Tanya Hanson	6-2	C	JR	Rutgers
Lady Hardmon	5-9	G	JR	Georgia
Shantel Hardison	5-9	G	SR	Louisiana Tech

Cinietra Henderson	6-4	C	SO	Texas
Joy Holmes	5-10	F	SR	Purdue
Tammye Jenkins	6-4	C	SR	Georgia
Jen Jensen	5-10	F	SR	Drake
Rosemary Kosiorek	5-5	G	JR	West Virginia
Misty Lamb	6-2	C/F	SO	Vanderbilt
Camille Lowe	5-10	C/F	SO	Georgia
Cindy Makowski	5-6	G	JR	North Carolina Wilmington
Vicky Picott	6-0	F	SR	Rutgers
Mitzi Rice	5-11	F	SO	Tennessee Tech
Karen Robinson	5-6	G	SR	Notre Dame
Jennifer Shasky	5-10	F	SO	George Washington
Chantel Tremitiere	5-5	G	SR	Auburn
Julie VonDielingen	6-0	F	SO	Butler
Julie Zielstra	6-4	F/C	SR	Stanford

TOP 25

1. Virginia
2. Louisiana Tech
3. Auburn
4. Georgia
5. Texas
6. Tennessee
7. Stanford
8. Northwestern
9. North Carolina State
10. Long Beach State
11. Iowa
12. Penn State
13. Vanderbilt
14. Purdue
15. Mississippi
16. Arkansas
17. LSU
18. Western Kentucky
19. Washington
20. UNLV
21. Tennessee Tech
22. Clemson
23. Southern Mississippi
24. Montana
25. Stephen F. Austin

JUNIOR COLLEGE ALL-AMERICA TEAM AND TOP 30

By Rick Ball

★ FIRST TEAM ★

6-3	SO	Sam Cassell	San Jacinto, TX
6-5	SO	J. R. Rider	Antelope Valley, CA
6-7	SO	Michael Hughes	Southeastern, IA
6-9	FR	Anthony Cade	Connors, OK
6-10	SO	Frazier Johnson	Garden City, KS

★ SECOND TEAM ★

6-3	SO	Keith Wood	Hagerstown, MD
6-5	SO	Johnny McDowell	Howard, TX
6-6	FR	Darrin Hancock	Garden City, KS
6-7	SO	Matt Greene	Pensacola, FL
6-9	SO	Corie Blount	Rancho Santiago, CA

HONORABLE MENTION

5-7	SO	Mark Morris	Western, AZ
5-8	SO	Mark Bell	Barton County, KS
5-9	SO	Jackie Crawford	Indian Hills, IA
5-9	SO	Paul Johnson	Western, TX
5-9	SO	Ed Rivera	Central, FL
5-10	FR	Corey Baker	Chowan, NC
6-0	SO	Robert Shepard	Westark, AR
6-0	SO	Dwayne Hackett	Polk, FL
6-0	SO	Ron Johnson	Cowley County, KS
6-0	SO	Tim Brooks	Sullivan, KY
6-0	SO	Derrick Sharp	Brevard, FL
6-0	SO	Dennis Miller	Kankakee, IL
6-1	SO	Juriad Hughes	Casper, WY
6-1	SO	Alfredo Porter	Barton County, KS
6-1	SO	David Anderson	Southern, ID
6-2	SO	Alex Wright	Navarro, TX
6-2	SO	Ric Van Scoyce	Golden West, CA
6-2	SO	Nicky Van Exel	Trinity Valley, TX
6-2	FR	Randy Rutherford	Bacone, OK
6-2	SO	Ron Bayless	Kilgore, TX
6-2	SO	Brian Walker	Western, AZ
6-2	SO	Tony Amundsen	Chabot, CA
6-3	SO	Vincent Jackson	Moberly, MO
6-3	SO	Dale Brown	Gulf Coast, MS
6-3	SO	Ron Kirkhom	Murray, OK
6-3	SO	Jim Weathersby	Chemeketa, OR
6-3	SO	Gaylon Nickerson	Butler County, KS
6-3	SO	Les Shepard	Chaffey, CA
6-3	FR	Mark White	Northeastern, OK
6-4	SO	Donald Jenkins	Hutchinson, KS
6-4	FR	Terry Bynum	Anderson, SC
6-4	SO	Steve Worthy	Vincennes, IN
6-4	SO	Marcus Cohen	Florida C.C., FL
6-4	SO	John Portis	Coffeyville, KS
6-4	FR	Kevin Washington	Odessa, TX
6-4	SO	Joel Davis	Angelina, TX
6-4	SO	Cliff Reed	Dixie, UT
6-5	SO	Steve Rankin	Fresno, CA
6-5	FR	Cleveland Jackson	Butler County, KS
6-5	SO	Angelo Hamilton	Connors, OK
6-5	FR	Mark Atkins	Kankakee, IL
6-5	SO	James Dennis	Pensacola, FL
6-5	SO	Eric Gill	Central, FL
6-5	SO	John Staggers	Columbia, CA
6-5	SO	Juvon McGarry	Kankakee, IL
6-5	SO	Mario Bailey	Kankakee, IL
6-6	FR	Trasel Rone	Allen County, KS
6-6	SO	Harvey Petty	Howard, TX
6-6	SO	Steve Fitch	Lincoln, IL
6-6	SO	Robert Smith	Mississippi County, AR
6-6	SO	Rico McClean	Herkimer, NY
6-6	FR	Kent Bennett	Butler County, KS
6-6	SO	Cecil Pittman	Howard, TX
6-6	SO	Anthony Allen	Pasadena, CA
6-6	SO	Corey Wallace	Allegany, MD
6-6	SO	Eric Coates	Independence, KS
6-6	SO	William Paige	Mott, MI
6-6	SO	Willis Johnson	N. Greenville, SC
6-7	SO	Jonathan Triplett	Westark, AR
6-7	SO	Andre Duke	Independence, KS
6-7	FR	Jeff Belmer	Connors, OK
6-7	SO	Damon Ashley	Barton County, KS
6-7	SO	Banastreus Wingfield	Seward County, KS
6-7	SO	Sean Walker	Bacone, OK
6-7	SO	Malcolm Leak	Navarro, TX
6-7	SO	Tony Graves	Northeastern, OK
6-7	SO	Johnny Walker	Chipola, FL
6-7	SO	Corey Warner	Odessa, TX
6-7	FR	Fred Burley	Seminole, OK
6-7	SO	Charles Outlaw	South Plains, TX
6-7	SO	Paul Carter	Allegany, MD
6-7	SO	Corey Allen	Aquinas, TN
6-7	FR	Kelly Greer	Allen County, KS
6-7	SO	Jerry Preiskein	Oakland, MI
6-8	SO	Mike Green	Polk, FL
6-8	SO	Chandler Nairn	Garden City, KS
6-8	FR	Donald Ford	Alvin, TX
6-8	SO	Mitchell Foster	Western, AZ
6-8	SO	Charles Craine	Midland, TX
6-8	SO	Michael James	East Central, MS
6-8	SO	Derrick Gullien	Gulf Coast, MS
6-8	FR	Dwight Stewart	South Plains, TX
6-8	SO	Nate Jackson	Southern, ID
6-8	SO	Kenneth Williams	Kankakee, IL
6-8	SO	Darrell Mims	Northern, OK
6-8	FR	Robert Shannon	Odessa, TX
6-9	SO	Lorenzo Lockett	Indian River, FL
6-9	SO	Kevin Nixon	Valley, UT
6-9	SO	Eric Bellamy	San Jose, CA
6-9	SO	Carlito DaSilva	Southern, ID
6-9	SO	Derrick Chandler	Alvin, TX
6-9	FR	Carroll Boudreaux	Midland, TX
6-10	SO	Eric Pauley	Cypress, CA
6-10	SO	LaMarr Williams	Northeastern, OK
6-10	SO	Rodney Dent	Odessa, TX
6-11	FR	Rodney Odom	San Jacinto, TX
7-0	SO	Jim Waikle	Cypress, CA
7-1	SO	Ricky Lopes	Champlain, VT
7-1	SO	Gerry Holmes	Independence, KS
7-2	SO	Ken Nielsen	Palm Beach, FL

The mid-80s, thanks to Keith Smart's shot, saw an explosion in the recruiting of junior college players. Suddenly the top five conferences began seeking that JC "athlete" to fill an immediate need in their program. Young men that would have gotten Big Sky/Southland/Southern Conference type of offers in the '70s began to visit places like: Providence, Oklahoma, Indiana, Clemson and Virginia. The young men hadn't improved, but their image and marketability had.

As junior college basketball enters the '90s, I see more juco teams that are loaded with talent. Propositions 48 and 42 (plus the improved JC image) has made jucoland the most viable port of entry for many players. The Division II and NAIA entrance requirements have been realigned so many can no longer choose that as an alternative. So many of the Prop. 48 "redshirts" have not seemed to recover their skills after the year of not practicing, so that direction seems less popular every year. Larry Johnson and many other high school stars have shown that one can go to a junior college and actually improve one's game. The small campus and class size will enhance the young man's chances of improving his basic academic skills.

Junior college squads are now so stocked with players that often a ten minute per game sophomore will get several solid low major college offers! This past summer I knew of more good high school players that wanted to go to junior college and couldn't get in, because the JCs were overbooked. These players weren't 5-10 guards, but decent 6-5 types that were left out due to their own indecision.

If you want good entertainment value, go to a junior college game. So often, I see a game that has 8-12 future major college players for an admission price of $3.00 and I can sit within ten feet of the floor! Welcome to jucoland. — *Rick Ball*

TOP 30

Nearly 600 junior colleges play men's basketball, here is a preseason look:

1. Garden City, KS		16. Gulf Coast, MS
2. Kankakee, IL		17. Mott, MI
3. Southern, ID		18. Northeastern A&M, OK
4. Connors, OK		19. Barton County, KS
5. Howard, TX		20. Allegany, MD
6. Independence, KS		21. Southeastern, IA
7. Polk, FL		22. North Greenville, SC
8. San Jacinto, TX		23. South Plains, TX
9. Butler County, KS		24. Vincennes, IN
10. Western, AZ		25. Antelope Valley, CA
11. Rancho Santiago, CA		26. Central, FL
12. Pensacola, FL		27. Allen County, KS
13. Odessa, TX		28. Logan, IL
14. Westark, AR		29. Three Rivers, MO
15. Champlain, VT		30. Navarro, TX

J.D. HINKLE, JR.
NAIA ALL-AMERICA TEAM AND TOP 20

NOTE: This NAIA All-America Team and Top 20 is named in honor of J.D. Hinkle, Jr., who died in 1986. Hinkle, the former mayor of Buckhannon, W.Va., and a West Virginia State Senator, was one of the greatest supporters of small college athletics. He attended 29 straight NAIA national basketball tournaments, occupying the same seat location every year — Box 41 at the Municipal Auditorium and Section 139 at Kemper Arena.

FIRST TEAM

Howard Bonser	6-11	SR	Emporia State (Kan.)	Johnnie Hilliard	6-4	SR	Eastern Oregon
Willie Davis	6-8	SR	Alderson-Broaddus (W.Va.)	Edgar Leon	6-8	SR	Georgia Southwestern
Mike Glitz	6-6	SR	Holy Family (Pa.)	Greg Sutton	6-2	SR	Oral Roberts (Okla.)
Jay Guidinger	6-9	SR	Minnesota-Duluth	Dave Wilson	6-11	JR	George Fox (Ore.)
Jeff Pinder	6-6	SR	Pfeiffer (N.C.)	Ivan Wineglass	6-5	SR	Bellevue (Neb.)

HONORABLE MENTION

John Baskin	SR	Mesa State (Colo.)	Julius Lockett	SR	Concord (W.Va.)
Russell Blackman	SR	Lander (S.C.)	Rick Miller	JR	Manchester (Ind.)
Ray Boyd	SR	St. Joseph's (Vt.)	Bill Pilgram	JR	Carroll College (Mont.)
Lawrence Buell	SR	Lincoln Memorial (Tenn.)	Richard Rutland	SR	Indiana Tech
Duane Bushman	SR	Wisconsin-Eau Claire	John Smith	SR	Baker (Kan.)
Devin Egelant	SR	Western Montana	Tony Smith	JR	Pfeiffer (N.C.)
Terrance Gaines	SR	Oklahoma Christian	Scott Speedy	SR	Belmont (Tenn.)
Pat Giller	SR	Benedictine (Kan.)	Vic Wells	SR	Lewis & Clark State (Ore.)
Hannes Haid	JR	Hawaii-Pacific	Del Willis	JR	Alaska-Pacific
Mike Johnson	SR	Wisconsin-Eau Claire	Floyd Wilson	SR	Langston (Okla.)
Scott Kenney	SR	Central Washington			

TOP 20 (1989-90 record in parenthesis)

1. Wisconsin-Eau Claire (30-4)
2. Oral Roberts, Okla. (29-3)
3. Central Washington (31-5)
4. Pfeiffer, N.C. (22-11)
5. Columbia, Mo. (30-8)
6. Minnesota-Duluth (27-6)
7. Birmingham Southern, Ala. (31-3)
8. Georgia Southwestern (30-3)
9. George Fox, Ore. (29-5)
10. Emporia State, Kan. (23-8)
11. Central Arkansas (24-11)
12. Grand Canyon, Ariz. (26-10)
13. Alderson-Broaddus, W.Va. (26-11)
14. Drury, Mo. (28-5)
15. Belmont, Tenn. (27-6)
16. Holy Family, Pa. (24-7)
17. Hawaii-Pacific (19-15)
18. Mesa State, Colo. (19-9)
19. St. Thomas Aquinas, N.Y. (25-11)
20. Oklahoma City (17-13)

DIVISION II ALL AMERICA TEAM AND TOP 20

By Chuck Mistovich

FIRST TEAM

Armando Becker	6-5	SR	Central Missouri State
Myron Brown	6-3	SR	Slippery Rock State (Pa.)
Corey Crowder	6-5	SR	Kentucky Wesleyan
Harold Ellis	6-5	JR	Morehead (Ga.)
Willard Mack	6-3	SR	C.W. Post (N.Y.)
Lambert Shell	6-4	JR	Bridgeport (Conn.)
Glenn Stanley	6-4	JR	Southwest Baptist (Mo.)
Dave Vonesh	6-8	SR	North Dakota
Dwight Walton	6-5	SR	Florida Tech
Ulysses Hacket	6-3	JR	South Carolina-Spartanburg

HONORABLE MENTION

Gary Battle	SR	New Haven (Conn.)	Charlie McDonald	SR	Troy State (Ala.)
Jeff Birchard	SR	Morningside (Iowa)	Jeff Meyers	SR	West Georgia
Phil Cartwright	JR	Nebraska-Omaha	Jason Mims	SR	Eastern Montana
Antonio Chambers	SR	Kentucky State	Vincent Mitchell	SR	Kentucky Wesleyan
Miles Clark	SR	North Carolina Central	Mike Monroe	SR	Millersville (Pa.)
Jerome Coles	SR	Norfolk State (Va.)	Pat Morris	SR	Bridgeport (Conn.)
Mike Cornelius	SR	Missouri Western	Ilo Mutombo	SR	Southern Indiana
Jon Cronin	JR	Stonehill (Mass.)	Paul Neal	SR	Merrimack (Mass.)
Jeff Delaveaga	JR	California-Lutheran	Trent Neal	JR	Nebraska-Omaha
Drexel Deveaux	SR	Tampa (Fla.)	Sheldon Owens	JR	Shaw (N.C.)
Malcolm Dowdy	SR	Adelphi (N.Y.)	Craig Phillips	SR	Bloomsburg (Pa.)
Lamar Fair	SR	Cheyney State (Pa.)	Ralph Rivers	JR	Metropolitan State (Colo.)
Darryl Freeman	SR	Gannon (Pa.)	Terry Ross	SR	Cal Poly Pomona
Julius Fritz	SR	Fort Valley State (Ga.)	Darren Sanderlin	SR	Norfolk State
Dan Goheski	JR	Northern Michigan	Tom Schurfranz	JR	Bellarmine (Ky.)
Truman Greene	SR	Lock Haven (Pa.)	Astley Smith	SR	Florida Tech
LaKeith Humphrey	JR	Central Missouri State	Randy Stover	JR	Philadelphia Textile (Pa.)
Todd Jenks	SR	Grand Valley State (Mich.)	Brett Szabo	SR	Augustana (S.D.)
Robby Jeter	SR	Wisconsin-Platteville	Eric Taylor	JR	Oakland (Mich.)
Chris Kuhlmann	JR	Morningside (Iowa)	Thomas Thames	SR	Southeast Missouri State
Leon Larthridge	SR	Ferris State (Mich.)	Brian Williams	SR	Tampa (Fla.)
Pat Madden	SR	Jacksonville State (Ala.)			

TOP 20 (1989-90 record in parenthesis)

1. Central Missouri State (27-6)
2. Florida Tech (26-4)
3. Kentucky Wesleyan (31-2)
4. Southeast Missouri State (26-5)
5. Tampa, Fla. (26-5)
6. C.W. Post, N.Y. (26-5)
7. North Dakota (29-9)
8. Bridgeport, Conn. (23-9)
9. Florida Southern (22-8)
10. Ashland, Ohio (22-8)
11. Bakersfield, Calif. (29-5)
12. Gannon, Pa. (24-8)
13. Slippery Rock State, Pa. (23-6)
14. Norfolk State, Va. (27-4)
15. Morehouse, Ga. (26-7)
16. Southwest Baptist, Mo. (25-6)
17. Virginia Union (27-3)
18. South Carolina-Spartansburg (29-3)
19. Millersville, Pa. (20-9)
20. Nebraska-Omaha (21-9)

★ ★ ★

HIGH SCHOOL SECTION

* **Girls High School All-America Team**

* **Ben Wilson High School**
* **Top 44**
* **100 More Stars of the Future**

* **Honorable Mention All-America Team**

* **Top 44 Profiles**

GIRLS HIGH SCHOOL ALL-AMERICA TEAM

by
Russ Walbrun, Publisher
Midwest/National Girls Basketball

★ **FIRST TEAM** ★

Michelle Marciniak	5-7	SR	Central Catholic, Allentown, PA
Rebecca Lobo	6-4	SR	Southwick, MA
Niesa Johnson	5-9	SR	Clinton, MS
Samantha Williams	6-1	SR	Manual, Louisville, KY
Bobbie Kelsey	6-0	SR	Morrow, GA

★ **SECOND TEAM** ★

Tiffany Woosley	5-6	SR	Central, Shelbyville, TN
Anita Kaplan	6-5	SR	Bethleham Central, Delmar, NY
Yolanda Watkins	6-2	JR	Decatur, AL
Jennifer Jacoby	5-7	SR	Rossville, IN
Dana Johnson	6-2	SR	Western, Baltimore, MD

★ **FIFTH TEAM** ★

Kerri Reeves	6-0	SR	Cuyahoga Falls, OH
LaToya Weavor	6-1	JR	Starkville, MS
Shelly Sheetz	5-8	SR	Kennedy, Cedar Rapids, IA
Katie Smith	6-0	JR	Logan, OH
Debbie Hemery	5-8	SR	Christ the King, Middle Vill., NY

★ **THIRD TEAM** ★

Vonda Ward	6-5	SR	Trinity, Garfield Heights, OH
Markita Aldridge	5-10	SR	M.L. King, Detroit, MI
Amy Lofstedt	6-1	SR	Mason City, IA
Audrey Gomez	5-7	SR	St. John Vianney, Holmdel, NJ
Angela Aycock	6-2	SR	Lincoln, Dallas, TX

★ **FOURTH TEAM** ★

Vickie Johnson	5-9	SR	Coushatta, LA
Jackie Williams	5-11	SR	West, Joliet, IL
Tara Cosby	6-3	SR	Kenton Ridge, Springfield, OH
Kellie Cook	5-9	SR	Nevada Union, Grass City, CA
Rachel Hemmer	6-1	SR	Westlake, Austin, TX

HONORABLE MENTION

★ **SOUTH** ★

Stephenie Lawrence	6-0	SR	Morrow, GA
Stephenie Wheeler	6-0	SR	Stephens County, Toccoa, GA
Joskeen Garner	5-11	JR	Florien, LA
Vickie Inman	5-7	SR	Pisgah, Canton, NC
Lisa Gerton	5-8	SR	Pleasure Ridge, Louisville, KY
Racquel Spurlock	6-3	SR	Donaldsonville, LA
Patricia Nash	5-8	SR	Neshoba Central, Philadelphia, MS
Rochone Dilligard	6-1	SR	Lebanon, TN
Zeki Blanding	6-3	SR	Lee, Arlington, VA
Konecka Drakeford	5-11	SO	Prividence Day, Charlotte, NC
Mara Cunningham	6-3	SR	Fairfax, VA
Tera Sheriff	6-1	SR	Murrah, Jackson, MS
Charleata Beale	6-0	SR	Garfield, Woodbridge, VA
Keeta Matthews	6-0	JR	Mitchell, Memphis, TN
LaKisha Frett	6-2	SO	Phoebus, Newport News, VA

★ **WEST** ★

Etta Maytubby	5-10	SR	Del City, OK
Twylana Harrison	5-10	SR	Levelland, TX
Tanda Rucker	5-10	SR	Berkeley, CA
Judy Holcomb	5-6	SR	Midway, Waco, TX
Charisse Sampson	5-10	SR	Washington, Los Angeles, CA
Gwen Hobbs	5-8	SR	Navajo Academy, Farmington, NM
Jama Holman	5-5	SR	Lamar, AR
Janet Davis	6-4	JR	Morningside, Inglewood, CA
Rita Banks	5-8	JR	Southeast, Oklahoma City, OK
Cherilyn Morris	5-8	SR	El Dorado, Albuquerque, NM
Nikki Manzo	6-4	SR	Lompoc, CA
Jacinda Sweet	5-9	SR	North Hollywood, Los Angeles, CA
Shawntay Chadwick	5-6	SR	Longview, TX
Laura Gonsalves	6-3	SR	Reed, Sparks, NV
Melissa Wuschnig	6-0	JR	Monta Vista, Cupertino, CA

★ **MIDWEST** ★

Rhonda Blades	5-7	SR	Parkview, Springfield, MO
LaShawn Brown	6-4	SR	Cleveland Heights, OH
Letitia Bowen	6-0	SR	Buchanan, MI
Jenny Reimer	6-0	SR	Southeast, Lincoln, NE
Holly Skeen	6-2	SR	Canal Winchester, OH
Jenny Jacobson	5-11	SR	Regis, Cedar Rapids, IA
Kris Dupps	5-10	SR	Heath, OH
Arneda Yarbrough	5-5	SR	Horlick, Racine, WI
Nattasha Woddle	6-2	SR	Indian Creek, Trafalgar, IN
Kina Brown	5-11	SR	Washington, Chicago, IL
Lori Lawler	5-11	SR	Lourdes, Rochester, MN
Caryn Shinn	5-10	SR	Murray-Wright, Detroit, MI
Kim Williams	5-6	SO	Marshall, Chicago, IL
Kelly Fergus	6-3	JR	Brunswick, OH
Robbyn Preacely	5-4	JR	Morgan Park, Chicago, IL

★ **EAST** ★

Kristen Somogyi	5-5	JR	St. Peter, New Brunswick, NJ
Falisha Wright	5-4	SR	Kennedy, Paterson, NJ
Nikki Hill	6-3	JR	Christ the King, Middle Vill., NY
Darlene Saar	6-2	SR	Christ the King, Middle Vill., NY
Pam Webber	5-7	SR	Holidaysburg, PA
Michelle Thornton	5-6	SR	Prendergast, Upper Darby, PA
Tabitha Chambers	6-4	JR	Walbrook, Baltimore, MD
Allegra Schell	5-6	SR	Central, Providence, RI
Lakeysha Wright	5-4	SR	Kennedy, Paterson, NJ
Amy Sherry	5-9	SR	Cortland, NY
Malaika Stewart	6-1	SR	Albany, NY
Kendra Nelson	5-9	JR	Robeson, Brooklyn, NY
Mia Lewis	5-7	SR	Dunbar, WV
Tina Nicholson	5-3	JR	Downington, PA
Kisha Gwyn	5-7	JR	Holton-Arms, Bethesda, MD

BEN WILSON
★ HIGH SCHOOL ★
TOP 44

NOTE: Ben Wilson was Blue Ribbon's 1984-85 Co-High School Player of the Year. He led Chicago Simeon HS to the Illinois state title as a junior and was ranked as the No. 1 senior in the nation entering his senior year. Just a few days before the first game of his senior year, Wilson was tragically shot to death in front of a store adjacent to the Simeon campus. We dedicate our High School Top 44 in the name of this great young athlete who would have been one of the all-time greats ever out of Chicago.

FIRST TEAM

Juwan Howard	6-9	SR	Chicago Vocational	Chicago, IL
Jason Kidd	6-4	JR	St. Joseph Notre Dame	Alameda, CA
Glenn Robinson	6-9	SR	Roosevelt	Gary, IN
David Vaughn	6-10	SR	Whites Creek	Whites Creek, TN
Chris Webber	6-9½	SR	Detroit Country Day	Birmingham, MI

SECOND TEAM

Thomas Burrough	6-8	SR	Oak Hill Academy	Mouth of Wilson, VA
James Forrest	6-7	SR	Southside	Atlanta, GA
Alan Henderson	6-9	SR	Brebeuf Prep	Indianapolis, IN
Cherokee Parks	6-11	SR	Marina	Huntington Beach, CA
Roderick Rhodes	6-7	JR	St. Anthony's	Jersey City, NJ

THIRD TEAM

Tom Kleinschmidt	6-5½	SR	Gordon Tech	Chicago, IL
Jalen Rose	6-7	SR	Southwestern	Detroit, MI
Donald Williams	6-3	SR	Garner	Garner, NC
Bubba Wilson	6-11	SR	Stone County	Wiggins, MS
Sharone Wright	6-10	SR	Southwest	Macon, GA

OTHER TOP 44 MEMBERS

Cory Alexander	6-2	SR	Oak Hill Academy	Mouth of Wilson, VA
Matt Alosa	6-2	SR	Pembroke Academy	Pembroke, NH
Yuri Barnes	6-8	SR	Manchester	Richmond, VA
Travis Best	5-11	SR	Springfield Central	Springfield, MA
Jason Caffey	6-8	SR	Davidson	Mobile, AL
Derrick Carroll	6-6½	SR	Eau Claire	Columbia, SC
John Carter	6-9	SR	Star Spencer	Oklahoma City, OK
Ben Davis	6-9	SR	Oak Hill Academy	Mouth of Wilson, VA
Steve Edwards	6-6	JR	Miami Senior	Miami, FL
Othello Harrington	6-8	JR	Murrah	Jackson, MS
Anthony Harris	6-2	SR	Danbury	Danbury, CT
Alonzo Johnson	7-0	SR	Francis Marion	Marion, AL
Rudy Johnson	6-7	SR	Ribault Senior	Jacksonville, FL
Jimmy King	6-4	SR	Plano East	Plano, TX
Keith LeGree	6-2	SR	Statesboro	Statesboro, GA
Voshon Lenard	6-4	SR	Southwestern	Detroit, MI
Donyell Marshall	6-8	SR	Reading	Reading, PA
Erik Meek	6-10	SR	San Pasqual	Escondido, CA
Loren Meyer	6-10	SR	Ruthven-Ayrshire	Ruthven, IA
Silas Mills	6-7	SR	Washington	Milwaukee, WI
Tim Moore	6-6½	SR	Milby	Houston, TX
Howard Nathan	5-11	SR	Manual	Peoria, IL
Calvin Rayford	5-9	SR	Washington	Milwaukee, WI
James Scott	6-5	SR	Eastside	Paterson, NJ
John Smith	6-8	SR	A.C. Flora	Columbia, SC
Damon Stoudamire	5-11	SR	Wilson	Portland, OR
Carlos Strong	6-8	JR	Cedar Shoals	Athens, GA
Antonio Watson	6-8	SR	Eastmoor	Columbus, OH
Glen Whisby	6-8	SR	Brookhaven	Brookhaven, MS

100 MORE STARS OF THE FUTURE

Jerome Allen	SR	6-3	Merion Station, PA/Episcopal
Orlando Antigua	SR	6-7	Bronx, NY/St. Raymonds
Mario Bennett	SR	6-8	Denton, TX/Denton
Robert Bennett	SR	6-7	Chicago, IL/Julian
Daimon Bethea	SR	6-7	Elkhart, IN/Memorial
Etdrick Bohannon	SR	6-9	San Bernardino, CA/San Bernardino
Ira Bowman	SR	6-4	West Orange, NJ/Seton Hall Prep
Chris Brand	SR	6-2	Bloomington, IN/South
Donta Bright	JR	6-5	Baltimore, MD/Dunbar
Jermaine Brown	SR	6-3	Fairdale, KY/Fairdale
Eric Brunson	SR	6-4	Salem, MA/Salem
Dan Buie	SR	6-8	Harrisburg, PA/Harrisburg
Clarence Ceasar	SR	6-7	Iowa, LA/Iowa
Patrick Craft	SR	6-10	Atmore, AL/Escambia County
William Davis	SR	7-0	Brooklyn, NY/Boys and Girls
Andrew Declercq	SR	6-9	Clearwater, FL/Countryside
Kevin Dempsey	SR	6-6	San Jose, CA/Santa Teresa
Ray Donald	SR	6-8	Pensacola, FL/Booker T. Washington
Percy Eberhart	JR	6-8	Athens, GA/Clarke Central
Tyus Edney	SR	5-10	Long Beach, CA/Poly
Doug Etzler	SR	6-0	Convoy, OH/Crestview
Malik Evans	SR	6-7	Sugarland, TX/Willowridge
Michael Evans	JR	6-0	Norfolk, VA/Booker T. Washington
Brian Fair	SR	6-3	Phoenix, AZ/South Mountain
Sherell Ford	SR	6-6	Maywood, IL/Proviso East
Chris Gant	SR	6-7	Houston, TX/Smiley
Michael Gardner	SR	5-11	Fredericksburg, VA/James Monroe
William Gates	SR	6-1	Westchester, IL/St. Joseph
Nathan Gilmore	SR	6-9	San Marcos, TX/San Marcos
Devin Gray	SR	6-6	Baltimore, MD/St. Frances
Rashard Griffith	SO	6-11	Chicago, IL/Martin Luther King
David Grim	SR	6-7	Massillon, OH/Washington
Greg Gurley	SR	6-5	Shawnee Mission, KS/South
Chip Hare	SR	6-9	Massillon, OH/Perry
Mike Hawkins	SR	6-1	Canton, OH/McKinley
Brian Henson	SR	6-1	McPherson, KS/McPherson
Fred Hoiberg	SR	6-5	Ames, IA/Ames
Deon Jackson	SR	6-7	South River, NJ/South River
Luke Jackson	SR	6-6	Beaumont, TX/Westbrook
Ray Jackson	SR	6-5	Austin, TX/L. B. Johnson
Jamal Johnson	SR	6-8	Kirkwood, MO/Kirkwood
Bernard Jones	SR	6-6	Philadelphia, PA/Roman Catholic
Willie Jones	SR	6-7	Sylacauga, AL/B. B. Comer
Wilfred Kirkaldy	SR	6-9	Mouth of Wilson, VA/Oak Hill
Charles Kornegay	JR	6-8	Dudley, NC/Southern Wayne
Lavon Lamb	JR	6-7	Youngstown, OH/Rayen
Todd Lindeman	SR	7-0	Iron Mountain, MI/North Dickinson
Michael Lloyd	JR	6-1	Baltimore, MD/Dunbar
Charles Macon	JR	6-7	Michigan City, IN/Elston
Will Macon	SR	6-7	Pittsburgh, PA/Perry
Reginald Manuel	SR	6-3	Macon, GA/Southwest
James Marshall	SR	6-6	Washington, DC/Dunbar
Paul Marshall	SR	6-2	Shreveport, LA/Southwood
Dean Marshman	SR	6-2	Mount Vernon, NY/Mount Vernon
Jerry McCullough	SR	6-0	New York, NY/Rice
Russ Millard	SR	6-8	Cedar Rapids, IA/Washington
Martice Moore	JR	6-7	Atlanta, GA/North Fulton
Isaac Morgan	SR	6-5	Elizabeth, NJ/Elizabeth
Lamond Murray	SR	6-7	Fremont, CA/J. F. Kennedy
Ike Nwankwo	JR	6-10	Houston, TX/Cy-Creek
Kevin Ollie	SR	6-2	Los Angeles, CA/Crenshaw
Greg Ostertag	SR	7-1	Duncanville, TX/Duncanville
Ray Owes	SR	6-8	San Bernardino, CA/San Bernardino
Bryan Passink	SR	6-4	Savannah, GA/Benedictine
Derrick Patterson	SR	6-5	Chicago, IL/Dunbar
Sean Pearson	SR	6-5	LaGrange Park, IL/Nazareth
Al Pinkins	SR	6-6	Camilla, GA/Mitchell Baker
Mark Pope	SR	6-9	Bellevue, WA/Newport
Johnnie Reece	SR	6-2	Denver, CO/Manual
Terrence Rencher	SR	6-3	Bronx, NY/St. Raymonds
Johnny Rhodes	SR	6-4	Washington, DC/Dunbar
Andre Riddick	SR	6-9	Brooklyn, NY/Bishop Loughlin
K. J. Roberts	SR	6-1	Kent, WA/Kent-Meridian
Louis Roe	SR	6-7	Atlantic City, NJ/Atlantic City
Ray Ross	SR	6-3	Portland, OR/Parkrose
Rasul Salahuddin	SR	6-2	Mount Vernon, NY/Mount Vernon
Al Segova	SR	6-7	Auburn, AL/Auburn
Shun Sheffield	SR	6-9	Albany, GA/Westover
Greg Simpson	JR	6-0	Lima, OH/Senior
Lazarus Sims	SR	6-4	Syracuse, NY/Henninger
Eric Snow	SR	6-2	Canton, OH/McKinley
Eugenio Soto	SR	6-8	Teaneck, NJ/Teaneck
Duane Spencer	JR	6-10	New Orleans, LA/Cohen
Jerry Stackhouse	SO	6-7	Kinston, NC/Kinston
Damon Stoudamire	SR	5-11	Portland, OR/Wilson
Billy Taylor	SR	6-6	Aurora, IL/West Aurora
Bill Teal	SR	6-4	St. Petersburg, FL/Gibbs
Aminu Timberlake	SR	6-8	Chicago, IL/DeLaSalle
Marcus Timmons	SR	6-8	Sikeston, MO/Scott County
Kareem Townes	SR	6-3	Philadelphia, PA/Southern
Jacque Vaughn	SO	6-0	Pasadena, CA/Muir
Rasheed Wallace	SO	6-8	Philadelphia, PA/Simon Gratz
Jayson Walton	SR	6-6	Dallas, TX/Kimball
Tes Whitlock	SR	6-1	Anaheim, CA/Loara
Pointer Williams	SR	6-0	New Orleans, LA/St. Augustine
Corliss Williamson	JR	6-7	Russellville, AR/Russellville
Jason Williford	SR	6-6	Richmond, VA/John Marshall
Avis Willis	SR	6-0	Alexandria, VA/West Potomac
Frank Wilson	SR	6-10	Lake Charles, LA/Washington-Marion
Julian Winfield	SR	6-3	St. Louis, MO/Cardinal Ritter

★   ★   ★

HIGH SCHOOL HONORABLE MENTION ALL-AMERICA TEAM

Compiled By

NAME	CL	HEIGHT	CITY/HIGH SCHOOL
ALABAMA			
Jimmy Bearden	JR	6-8	Gardendale/Gardendale
George Brooks	SR	6-8	Lafayette/Lafayette
Carlos Browning	SR	6-8	Selma/Selma
Bennie Daniels	SR	5-10	Elba/Elba
Frankie Davidson	SR	6-2	New Market/Buckhorn
Antonio Dixon	SR	6-2	Phenix City/Central
Derrick Flowers	SR	6-8	Dothan/Northview
Scott Friedman	SO	6-7	Tuscaloosa/Academy
Rodney Griggs	SO	6-8	Hueytown/Hueytown
Greg Grimsley	SO	6-4	Abbeville/Abbeville
George Hill	SR	6-8	Fairhope/Fairhope
Corey Jackson	SR	6-2	Auburn/Auburn
Wade Kaiser	JR	6-8	Vestavia Hills/Vestavia
David Kilgore	SO	6-5	Jasper/Walker
Sedrick Martin	SR	6-5	Dothan/Dothan
Tony McGinnis	SR	6-4	Huntsville/Butler
Cedric Neloms	SR	6-7	Leighton/Colbert County
Victor Newman	SR	6-4	Dothan/Houston Academy
Belvin Nolan	SR	6-2	Northport/Tuscaloosa County
Danny Pearson	SR	6-2	Mobile/B. C. Rain
Romeo Penn	SR	6-4	Birmingham/Wenonah
Jimmy Pincheon	SR	6-4	New Market/Buckhorn
Tracy Posey	SR	6-5	Vincent/Vincent
Roy Rogers	SR	6-9	Linden/Linden
Hassan Sanders	JR	6-1	Tuscaloosa/Central
George Scott	SR	6-4	Enterprise/Enterprise
Frederick Spencer	SR	6-5	Butler/Choctaw County
Marcus Starks	SR	6-4	Midfield/Midfield
Kendall Weaver	SR	6-3	Birmingham/Ramsay
Franklin Williams	SO	6-5	Headland/Headland
Norman Williams	SO	6-6	Birmingham/West End
ALASKA			
Travis Allam	SR	6-5	Houston/Houston
Jason Kaiser	SR	6-3	Anchorage/Service
Reid Kornstad	SR	5-11	Nikiksi/Nikiski
Trajan Langdon	FR	5-11	Anchorage/East
Jeff Lentfer	SR	6-7	Anchorage/Service
Butch Lincoln	JR	5-8	Kotzebue/Kotzebue
Rommie Wheeler	SR	5-10	Eielson AFB/Ben Eielson
Archie Young	SR	6-4	Wrangell/Wrangell
ARIZONA			
Carlos Artis	SR	6-3	Phoenix/Washington
George Banks	SR	6-6	Tucson/Marana
Dave Brown	SR	6-6	Phoenix/South Mountain
Sean Flannery	SO	6-6	Tucson/Salpointe
Brian Gilliam	SR	6-3	Phoenix/North
Damion Gosa	SR	6-7	Phoenix/Carl Hayden
Dennis Griffin	SR	6-8	Thatcher/Thatcher
Jimmy Kolyszko	SR	6-6	Scottsdale/Saguaro
Tabari Johnson	JR	6-7	Phoenix/South Mountain
Johnny Tapaha	SR	5-10	Holbrook/Holbrook
ARKANSAS			
Kevin Bright	SR	6-8	Horatio/Horatio
Marcus Brown	JR	6-2	West Memphis/West Memphis
Walter Camper	JR	6-0	Brinkley/Brinkley
Diaon Cross	JR	6-2	Little Rock/Parkview
Anthony Edwards	SR	6-1	Little Rock/Parkview
Lucky Holman	SR	6-5	Pine Bluff/Pine Bluff
Maurice Robinson	JR	6-7	Little Rock/Parkview
Patrick Schueck	SR	6-7	Little Rock/Catholic
Karoma Smith	SR	6-3	Jacksonville/Jacksonville
Jason Stewart	SR	6-0	Saratoga/Saratoga

NAME	CL	HEIGHT	CITY/HIGH SCHOOL
Keith Stricklen	SR	5-10	Morrilton/Morrilton
J. B. Suffridge	JR	6-6	North Little Rock/North Little Rock
Clint Thomas	SR	6-6	Little Rock/Parkview
CALIFORNIA			
Sam Allen	SR	6-7	Sacramento/Rio Americano
Deandre Austin	SR	6-2	Lakewood/Artesia
Drew Barry	SR	6-2	Concord/DeLaSalle
Shaun Battle	JR	6-5	San Bernardino/Cajon
Kevin Beal	SR	6-4	Los Angeles/Manual Arts
Brian Bell	SR	6-5	San Jose/Yerba Buena
Sonny Benjamin	SO	6-5	Riverside/North
Stacy Boseman	SO	6-4	Inglewood/Morningside
Dwain Bradberry	SR	6-2	Los Angeles/Manual Arts
Eric Brown	SR	6-5	City of Industry/Workman
Monte Buckley	SR	6-6	Sacramento/Christian Brothers
Darnell Cherry	SR	6-8	San Diego/Morse
Chris Davis	SR	6-7	Manhattan Beach/Mira Costa
Eric Fischer	SR	6-10	Walnut Creek/Los Lomas
Mark Flick	SR	6-7	Cerritos/Cerritos
Chris Ford	SR	6-2	Los Angeles/Fremont
Kevin Fricka	JR	6-7	Chino/Don Lugo
Reggie Geary	SR	6-2	Santa Ana/Mater Dei
Darren Greene	SR	6-5	Pasadena/Muir
David Harbour	SR	6-2	Camarillo/Camarillo
Juaquin Hawkins	SR	6-5	Lynwood/Lynwood
Roger Hendrix	SR	6-6	Rolling Hills/Rolling Hills
John Hines	SR	6-9	Dos Palos/Dos Palos
Trent Jackson	JR	6-3	Santa Monica/Santa Monica
Barnabas James	SR	6-6	Los Angeles/Washington
Brandon Jesse	JR	6-5	Huntington Beach/Edison
Clay Johnson	SR	6-5	Stockton/Stagg
Reggie Johnson	SR	6-9	San Francisco/Mission
Rob Johnson	SR	6-5	El Toro/El Toro
Avondre Jones	SO	6-10	Lakewood/Artesia
Wyking Jones	SR	6-6	Playa del Rey/St. Bernard
Robin Kirksey	SR	6-6	Gardena/Gardena
Elzie Love	SR	6-5	Perris/Perris
Rodney Malloy	SO	6-4	Lynwood/Lynwood
Brandon Martin	JR	6-4	Reseda/Cleveland
Troy Matthews	SO	6-3	Lawndale/Leuzinger
Johnny McWilliams	SR	6-5	Pomona/Pomona
Eric Mobley	SR	6-1	Santa Monica/Crossroads
John Molle	SR	6-5	Irvine/Irvine
Mark Moneypenny	SR	6-10	Santa Ana/Mater Dei
Doug Muse	SR	6-9	Hayward/Moreau
Kevin Nanney	SR	6-8	Fremont/Mission San Jose
Landers Nolley	JR	6-7	Santa Monica/St. Monica
Charles O'Bannon	SO	6-5	Lakewood/Artesia
Curtis Parker	JR	6-4	El Cerrito/El Cerrito
Darryl Parker	SR	6-5	Vista/Rancho Buena Vista
Matt Purdy	SR	6-7	Santa Barbara/Santa Barbara
Rick Price	FR	6-3	Long Beach/St. Anthony
Darnell Robinson	JR	6-8	Emeryville/Emery
Marcus Rogers	SR	6-0	Redlands/Redlands
Joel Rosborough	SR	6-3	Long Beach/Jordan
Scott Saber	SR	6-8	Sacramento/Kennedy
Manjue Sampson	SR	6-6	San Bernardino/Cajon
Arthur Savage	SR	6-6	Inglewood/Morningside
Enid Scott	SR	6-7	Pasadena/Muir
Deandre Smith	JR	6-6	Long Beach/Jordan
Khary Stanley	JR	6-9	Carson/Carson
Michael Tate	SR	6-4	Los Angeles/Fremont
Pat Thacker	SR	6-6	Long Beach/Millikan
Nathan Ware	SO	6-6	Lynwood/Lynwood
Rudy Washington	JR	6-3	Carson/Carson

HIGH SCHOOL HONORABLE MENTION ALL-AMERICA TEAM

NAME	CL	HEIGHT	CITY/HIGH SCHOOL
Earl Williams	SR	6-6	Fresno/Roosevelt
Frank Willis	SR	6-8	Lawndale/Leuzinger
Jaha Wilson	SR	6-6	San Francisco/Riordan
COLORADO			
Tremayne Anchrum	SR	6-5	Denver/Montebello
Justin Armour	SR	6-6	Manitou Springs/Manitou Springs
Josh Baird	SR	6-3	Collbran/Plateau Valley
Anthony Barrett	JR	6-6	Steamboat Springs/Steamboat Springs
Randy Brewer	SR	6-3	Denver/Thomas Jefferson
Sean Coleman	SR	6-0	Denver/North
Ron Fines	SR	6-4	Arvada/West Arvada
Jeff Foster	SR	6-4	Littleton/Araphoe
Jon Gaines	SR	6-3	Aurora/Central
Sande Golgart	SR	6-5	Arvada/Arvada
Peter Hefty	JR	5-11	Wheat Ridge/Wheat Ridge
Kamanti Hoard	SR	6-3	Denver/Montebello
Robert Johnson	FR	6-1	La Veta/La Veta
Doug Price	JR	6-9	Littleton/Araphoe
Tom Purfield	SR	6-4	Pueblo/Centennial
Kurt Schneider	SR	6-7	Fruita/Monument
Terrence Scott	JR	6-6	Denver/Academy
Matt Sherman	JR	6-3	Colorado Springs/Roy Wasson
Myron Simms	SR	6-2	Denver/Montebello
Chris Stock	SR	6-4	Boulder/Fairview
Mike Worley	SR	6-2	Swink/Swink
CONNECTICUT			
Shaman Antrum	JR	5-11	
Brian Anzellotti	SR	6-0	New Haven/Hillhouse
Jeff Calhoun	SR	6-1	Torrington/Torrington
Emanuel Christophe	JR	6-5	Storrs/E. O. Smith
Mike Donnelly	SO	5-11	Bridgeport/Harding
Kyle Geer	SR	6-3	Trumbull/St. Joseph
Matt Gras	SR	6-9	Bridgeport/Bassick
Novich Hunter	SR	6-5	Trumbull/St. Joseph
Tebucky Jones	SO	6-3	Stamford/Western Hills
Hank Majersky	SR	6-7	New Britain/New Britain
Jerome Malloy	SR	6-4	Bristol/Eastern
Brendan McCarthy	SR	6-3	Waterbury/John F. Kennedy
Skip Metz	JR	6-9	Waterbury/Sacred Heart
P. J. Monohan	JR	6-3	Richfield/Richfield
J. J. Moore	JR	6-3	Manchester/East Catholic
Jo Jo Outlaw	SR	5-11	Bridgeport/Bassick
Garnett Pettaway	JR	6-1	Cheshire/Cheshire Academy
Harun Ramey	SR	6-6	Waterbury/John F. Kennedy
Kareem Robinson	SR	6-6	Waterbury/Crosby
Terry Rountree	SR	6-2	Stratford/Stratford
Terrance Spain	SO	6-1	New Haven/Wilbur Cross
Harley Sullivan	SR	6-1	Trumbull/St. Joseph
Malik Williams	SR	6-3	New Britain/New Britain
Manny Williamson	SR	6-2	Waterbury/John F. Kennedy
			New Haven/Wilbur Cross
DELAWARE			
Troy Boyer	JR	6-0	
Monte Christopher	JR	6-7	Wilmington/Dickinson
Chris Demascio	SO	6-5	Wilmington/Wilmington
Clarence Jarrett	SR	6-2	Bear/Caravel
Elliot Loper	SR	6-5	Greenville/A.I. DuPont
Andrew Miles	SR	6-1	Newark/Glasgow
Steve Pierce	SR	6-6	Hockessin/Sanford
Lovett Purnell	SR	6-2	Smyrna/Smyrna
Chris Makos	SR	6-5	Seaford/Seaford
Antonio Stapleton	JR	6-6	Wilmington/Salesianum
Rodney Robinson	JR	6-1	Wilmington/Wilmington
			Frankford/Indian River
FLORIDA			
Dwayne Ansley	SR	6-7	Suwanee/Live Oak
Ben Bellamy	SR	6-5	Wildwood/Wildwood
Alvin Braddock	JR	6-7	Ocala/Vanguard

NAME	CL	HEIGHT	CITY/HIGH SCHOOL
Dwight Brown	SR	6-4	St. Petersburg/Gibbs
Ray Carter	SR	6-2	Tallahassee/Leon
Todd Catron	SR	6-6	Orlando/Boone
Lonnie Chester	JR	6-4	Inverness/Citrus
Chris Davis	JR	6-7	Lakeland/Kathleen
Thomas Demps	JR	6-5	Winter Park/Lake Howell
Terry Edwards	SR	5-10	Bronson/Bronson
Reggie Elliott	SR	6-3	Seminole/Seminole
Russell Evans	SR	6-4	Plant City/Plant City
Craig Flowers	SR	6-5	Orlando/Oak Ridge
Tim Ford	SR	6-3	Jacksonville/Ribault
Patrick Gordon	SR	6-4	Orlando/Oak Ridge
Terry Hanks	SR	6-8	Miami/Edison
Dametri Hill	JR	6-6	St. Petersburg/Dixie Hollins
Johnny Ingram	SR	6-4	Orlando/Oak Ridge
Pepper Johnson	SR	5-9	Daytona/Seabreeze
Ivan Jones	JR	6-4	Orlando/Boone
Dennis Kon	JR	6-10	Plantation/Plantation
Pat Lawrence	SR	6-7	St. Petersburg/Gibbs
Albert Legette	SR	6-4	Gainesville/Buchholtz
Donda Lett	SR	6-1	Pensacola/Escambia County
Donald Lockhart	JR	6-7	Palatka/Palatka
Donnie Mathews	SO	6-3	Gainesville/Eastside
Dan Middleton	SR	6-6	Sarasota/Cardinal Mooney
Vern Mitchell	JR	6-3	Sarasota/Sarasota
Dan Moore	SR	6-6	Orlando/Jones
Howard Porter	SR	6-4	Bradenton/Manatee
Steve Rich	JR	6-9	Ft. Lauderdale/Cardinal Gibbons
Tim Richert	JR	6-2	St. Petersburg/Catholic
David Ritchie	SR	6-6	Tampa/Jesuit
Dankey Roberson	SR	6-2	Sarasota/Riverview
Donzel Rush	JR	6-7	Miami/Carol City
Antwon Smith	JR	6-5	St. Petersburg/Gibbs
Donahue Smith	SR	6-3	Seminole/Osceola
Trey Thomas	SO	6-6	Deland/Deland
Kevin Williams	JR	6-6	Hallandale/Hallandale
GEORGIA			
Marlon Allen	SR	6-5	Columbus/Shaw
Greg Anderson	SR	6-6	Albany/Westover
Shandon Anderson	JR	6-5	Atlanta/Crim
Anthony Battle	SR	6-9	Talbotton/Central
Johnny Bell	JR	6-9	Athens/Cedar Shoals
Dathon Brown	SR	6-6	Atlanta/Douglass
Ray Carruth	SR	6-3	Commerce/Commerce
Kevin Cato	JR	6-9	Decatur/Cedar Grove
Robert Childs	SR	6-1	Atlanta/Riverwood
Marzell Clayton	SR	6-7	Atlanta/George
Jimmy Costner	SR	6-10	Fort Oglethorpe/Lakeview
Randy Cuffs	SR	5-11	Albany/Albany
Melvin Drake	SO	6-5	Albany/Albany
Darrell Dunham	JR	6-1	Woodberry/Woodberry
Lonnie Edwards	SO	5-10	Decatur/Southwest DeKalb
Scott Farley	SR	6-7	Powder Springs/McEachern
Marcus Grant	SR	6-4	Macon/Central
Melvin Hartry	SR	6-2	Irwinton/Wilkinson County
Conara Hill	SR	6-7	Atlanta/Douglass
Joven Johnson	SO	6-1	Savannah/Savannah
Dell Lewis Jones	SR	6-2	Atlanta/Westlake
Steve Jones	SR	6-5	Lithonia/Lithonia
Brian Kelley	SR	6-6	Decatur/Towers
John Kerner	JR	6-9	Atlanta/St. Pius
Ashley Landers	SR	6-8	Monroe/Monroe Area
Michael Locklear	SR	5-11	Marietta/Sprayberry
Jimmy Lunsford	SR	6-7	Cordele/Crisp County
Costa Malone	SR	6-9	Atlanta/Fulton
Robert Martin	SR	6-5	Atlanta/Tri-Cities
Lakista McKuller	SR	6-3	Americus/Sumter County
Robert Mikell	SR	6-7	Richmond Hill/Richmond Hill
Maurice Mincey	SR	6-6	Sandersville/Washington County
Cory Mitchell	SO	6-6	Atlanta/Douglass

HIGH SCHOOL HONORABLE MENTION ALL-AMERICA TEAM

NAME	CL	HEIGHT	CITY/HIGH SCHOOL
Kris Nordholz	SR	5-11	Gainesville/Gainesville
Kevin O'Brien	SR	6-7	Marietta/Pope
Myron Pace	JR	6-2	Cedartown/Cedartown
Derrick Parker	JR	6-9	Decatur/Columbia
Pertha Robinson	JR	5-10	Albany/Dougherty
Octavius Thomas	JR	6-0	Atlanta/George
Brian Thompson	JR	6-4	Atlanta/Douglass
Chris Tiger	JR	6-8	Atlanta/Crestwood
Darrell Walls	SR	6-0	Savannah/Windsor Forest
Cinwon Whitehead	FR	5-11	Atlanta/West Fulton
Craig Wilcox	SR	6-4	Eastman/Dodge County
Natambu Willingham	SR	6-10	Atlanta/North Fulton
Dontonia Winfield	SO	6-7	Albany/Westover
David Winslow	SR	6-8	Atlanta/Southside
Marcus Woods	SR	6-2	Atlanta/Southside

HAWAII

NAME	CL	HEIGHT	CITY/HIGH SCHOOL
Kainoa Bray	SR	6-6	Honolulu/Merryknoll
Gurney Holley	SR	6-4	Kailua/Kalaheo
Phil Jackson	JR	6-4	Honolulu/Merryknoll
Kalia McGee	SR	6-0	Honolulu/University
Brad Nueku	SR	5-9	Honolulu/Damien Memorial
Josh Smith	SR	6-1	Kailua/Kalaheo

IDAHO

NAME	CL	HEIGHT	CITY/HIGH SCHOOL
Eric Cotton	SR	6-6	Pocatello/Pocatello
Stan Hales	SR	6-0	Pocatello/Pocatello
Justin Jones	JR	6-1	Malad/Malad
Jared Mercer	SO	5-11	Kamiah/Kamiah
Jim Potter	SR	6-8	Boise/Bishop Kelly

ILLINOIS

NAME	CL	HEIGHT	CITY/HIGH SCHOOL
Chad Altadonna	SR	6-2	Centralia/Centralia
Tony Baker	SR	6-5	Pittsfield/Pittsfield
Jason Bey	SR	6-1	Chicago/Gordon Tech
Donnie Boyce	SR	6-4	Maywood/Proviso East
Chris Collins	JR	6-3	Northbrook/Glenbrook North
Terry Collins	SR	6-5	Joliet/Joliet West
Dan Cross	SR	6-3	Carbondale/Carbondale
Marc Davidson	SR	6-6	Aurora/Christian
Lenneal Denman	SR	6-7	Midlothian/Bremen
Nate Driggers	SR	6-4	Chicago/Corliss
Gerald Eaker	JR	6-9	Westchester/St. Joseph
Chris Ellis	SR	6-0	Olympia Fields/Rich Central
Rob Feaster	SR	6-5	Wilmette/Loyola Academy
Mike Finley	SR	6-6	Maywood/Proviso East
Walter Graham	SR	6-8	Champaign/Champaign
Ryan Grant	SR	6-7	Effingham/Effingham
Rod Harrison	SR	6-2	Chicago Heights/Marian Catholic
Rick Hielscher	SR	6-8	Winnetka/New Trier
Ryan Hoover	JR	6-1	Rockton/Hononegah
Reed Jackson	SR	6-5	Norris City/Omaha-Enfield
Lamarr Justice	SR	6-2	Batavia/Batavia
Richard Keene	JR	6-5	Collinsville/Collinsville
Brian Kern	SR	6-8	Vandalia/Vandalia
Andy Kilbride	SR	6-3	Kankakee/Kankakee
Mike Kirksey	SR	6-0	Peoria/Central
Derrick Landrus	SR	6-1	Charleston/Charleston
Jon Litwiller	JR	6-5	Morton/Morton
Gregory Logan	SR	6-7	Chicago/South Shore
Amal McCaskill	SR	6-9	Westchester/St. Joseph
Nick Newlin	SR	6-4	Hinsdale/Hinsdale Central
Mike Odumuyiwa	SR	6-5	Aurora/West
Belefia Parks	SR	6-0	Chicago/Simeon
Stephen Payne	SR	6-7	Palos Heights/Shepard
Anthony Pulliam	SR	6-3	Rock Island/Rock Island
Caleb Rath	SR	7-0	Pinckneyville/Pinckneyville
Kevin Rhodes	SR	6-1	Canton/Canton
Edward Richardson	SR	6-7	Chicago/Simeon
Kareem Richardson	JR	5-11	Rantoul/Rantoul
David Robinson	SR	6-6	Rock Island/Rock Island
Jamal Robinson	JR	6-3	Westchester/St. Joseph
Jamar Sanders	SR	6-5	Mount Vernon/Mount Vernon
Eric Sauceda	SR	6-2	Elgin/St. Edward
Johnelle Slone	SR	6-5	Richton Park/Rich South
Scott Syrzynski	JR	6-7	Sesser/Sesser-Valier
Eric Thomas	SR	6-1	Peoria/Richwoods
Joe Weaver	SR	6-2	Chicago/Vocational
Corey Williams	JR	6-7	Batavia/Batabia
Wayne Williams	SR	6-7	Olympia Fields/Rich Central
Kenyatta Wilson	SR	6-1	Chicago/Robeson
Arturo Witcher	SR	6-1	Harvey/Thornwood

INDIANA

NAME	CL	HEIGHT	CITY/HIGH SCHOOL
Lance Barker	SR	6-1	Columbus/East
Brandon Brantley	SR	6-7	Merrillville/Andrean
Michael Bush	SR	6-4	LaPorte/LaPorte
Neil Coyle	SR	6-8	Campbellsburg/New Washington
Erik Coyne	SR	6-6	Bloomington/South
Derrick Cross	SR	5-11	Bloomington/North
Mike Cunningham	JR	5-11	Evansville/Bosse
Cliff Daniels	SR	6-4	Newburgh/Castle
Ron Darrett	SR	6-4	Evansville/Central
Matt Dellinger	JR	6-7	Ft. Wayne/Concordia
Herb Dove	SR	6-4	Indianapolis/Perry Meridian
Andy Elkins	SR	6-6	Evansville/Bosse
Brian Evans	SR	6-8	Terre Haute/South
Marlon Fleming	SR	6-4	Indianapolis/Southport
Carlos Floyd	SR	6-5	Gary/Roosevelt
David Foskuhl	JR	6-10	Anderson/Highland
Jerry Freshwater	SR	5-10	Marion/Marion
Chad Gilbert	SR	6-8	Charlestown/Charleston
Brian Gilpin	JR	6-10	Fortville/Mount Vernon
Richie Hammel	JR	5-11	Lafayette/Jefferson
Byron Jones	SR	6-0	Indianapolis/Ben Davis
Brent Kell	SR	6-1	Evansville/Harrison
Jason Lambrecht	SR	6-3	Bedford/North Lawrence
Walter McCarthy	JR	6-9	Evansville/Harrison
Lee McGregor	SR	6-2	Vincennes/...
Andre Owens	SR	5-10	South Be...
Daryl Peterson	SR	6-6	Clayton/...
Charles Ricks	SR	6-0	East Chica...
Fred Scott	SR	6-6	Indianapolis/P...
Scott Shepherd	JR	6-0	Indianap...
Andre Smith	SR	6-0	Indiana...
Earl Smith	SR	6-1	Gary/L...
Mike Swanson	SR	6-2	El...
Lasalle Thompson	SR	5-11	Indi...
Chris Wilburn	SR	6-2	Martinsvil...
Dewey Williams	SR	6-9	Indianapolis...
Jason Williams	SR	6-3	In...
Ryan Wolf	SR	6-4	Martinsv...

IOWA

NAME	CL	HEIGHT	CITY/HIGH SCHOOL
Terry Anderson	SR	6-4	
Hurl Beecham	SR	6-6	
Kelby Bender	SR	6-4	Cedar Falls/...
Tucker Else	JR	6-0	Emmet...
Pat Joyce	SR	6-8	
Rob Kain	SR	6-6	Orange City/...
Jason Kleis	SR	6-3	
Carson Landsgard	SR	6-5	
Kevin Larsen	SR	5-10	
Troy Larsen	SR	6-1	Elk Ho...
Josh Nelsen	JR	6-1	
Eric Pothoven	SR	6-4	
Brendan Reilly	SR	6-7	
Sean Rice	SR	6-0	
Brian Schofield			

338

HIGH SCHOOL HONORABLE MENTION ALL-AMERICA TEAM

KANSAS

NAME	CL	HEIGHT	CITY/HIGH SCHOOL
Michael Blackwell	SR	6-3	Topeka/Topeka
Andre Burnside	SR	6-7	Kansas City/Harmon
Jason Carter	SR	6-3	Valley Center/Valley Center
Demetrius Floyd	SR	6-3	Kansas City/Schlagle
Adrian Griffin	JR	6-5	Wichita/East
Brian Jackson	JR	6-1	Wichita/Wichita Heights
Johnny Murdock	SR	6-1	Wichita/South
John Ontjes	SR	5-11	Nickerson/Nickerson
Adam Peakes	SR	6-4	Stilwell/Blue Valley
Lucas Wagler	SR	5-11	Junction City/Junction City
Vince Watkins	SR	6-5	Olathe/North
Darren Webber	JR	6-6	Ellsworth/Ellsworth

KENTUCKY

NAME	CL	HEIGHT	CITY/HIGH SCHOOL
Darrin Allaway	JR	6-7	Hopkinsville/University Heights
Corey Beard	SR	6-3	Louisville/Ballard
Earnest Bell	SR	6-5	Louisville/Western
Charles Broughton	SR	6-2	London/Laurel County
Greg Butler	SR	6-4	Mayfield/Graves County
Marty Cline	JR	6-1	Hopkinsville/University Heights
Joey Davenport	JR	6-0	Dixon/Webster County
Kevin Eilers	SR	6-6	Covington/Holmes
Mike Fraliex	JR	6-0	Princeton/Caldwell County
Robert Hammons	SR	6-6	Lexington/Bryan Station
Chris Harrison	SR	6-3	Tollesboro/Tollesboro
Chris Haynes	JR	6-5	Covington/Scott
Darrin Horn	SR	6-5	Lexington/Tates Creek
Shannon Hoskins	JR	6-1	Hazard/M.C. Napier
J.J. Hylton	JR	6-1	Belfry/Belfry
Chris Martin	SR	5-11	Morehead/Rowan County
Bryan Milburn	SR	6-7	Russell Springs/Russell County
Maurice Morris	SR	6-2	Fairdale/Fairdale
Jason Osborne	SO	6-6	Louisville/Male
Corey Pouncy	SR	5-10	Covington/Holmes
Bo Roadin	SR	6-5	Corbin/Corbin
Kris Robinson	JR	6-8	Henderson/Henderson County
Jody Salisbury	SR	6-10	Paintsville/Johnson Central
Victor Saunders	SR	6-6	Louisville/Waggener
Demond Thomas	SR	6-2	Elizabethtown/Elizabethtown
Carlos Turner	JR	6-5	Fairdale/Fairdale
Todd Tyler	SR	6-6	Bardwell/Carlisle County
James White	SR	6-2	Hopkinsville/University Heights
Keith Willard	SR	6-1	Lexington/Tates Creek
Corey Williams	JR	6-7	Paris/Bourbon County

LOUISIANA

NAME	CL	HEIGHT	CITY/HIGH SCHOOL
ayshard Allen	SO	6-4	Marreno/Ehret
oug Annison	SR	6-6	Baton Rouge/Bishop Sullivan
dre Brown	SO	6-5	Houma/Vanderbilt Catholic
ny Cutright	SR	6-4	Zwolle/Zwolle
nk Cypress	SR	6-6	West Jefferson/West Jefferson
tt Cyprian	SR	6-0	Covington/St. Paul
on Fobbs	SR	6-7	Lake Charles/Washington-Marion
ard Gardner	JR	6-7	Many/Many
am Grant	SR	6-5	New Orleans/St. Augustine
Hayward	JR	6-8	Alexandria/Peabody
ie Hill	SR	6-3	Kilbourne/Kilbourne
my Hodges	SR	6-4	Baton Rouge/Redemptorist
Honeycutt	SO	6-8	Grambling/Grambling
n Hurst	SR	6-2	River Ridge/John Curtis Christian
s Jones	SR	5-10	Sunset/Sunset
Livingston	SO	6-2	New Orleans/Newman
McMillion	SR	6-0	Logansport/Stanley
Minniefield	SR	6-3	Shongaloo/Shongaloo
n Rollins	JR	6-6	Mandeville/Mandeville
Savoy	SR	6-8	Thibodaux/Thibodaux
Smith	SR	5-11	New Orleans/St. Augustine
ykes	SR	6-3	Dry Prong/Grant
Taylor	SR	6-2	Marrero/Archbishop Shaw
aylor	SO	6-4	Walker/Walker
Scotty Thurman	JR	6-6	Ruston/Ruston

MAINE

NAME	CL	HEIGHT	CITY/HIGH SCHOOL
George Butler	SR	6-2	Pittsfield/Maine Central Institute
Len Cole	SR	6-7	Lawrence/Lawrence
Dana Duran	SR	6-9	Oakland/Messalonski
Matt Gaudet	SR	6-0	Rumford/Mountain Valley
Dennis Leonard	SR	5-10	Pittsfield/Maine Central Institute
Aaron McDonald	SR	6-5	Millinocket/Stearns
Chris Morere	JR	6-7	Jackman/Jackman
Scott Sawyer	SR	6-5	South Portland/South Portland

MARYLAND

NAME	CL	HEIGHT	CITY/HIGH SCHOOL
Terrance Alexander	SR	6-3	Baltimore/Dunbar
Kenny Avent	SO	6-4	Beltsville/High Point
Tony Bishop	JR	6-7	Towson/Towson Catholic
John Blackmon	SR	5-10	Potomac/Bullis
Keith Booth	SO	6-5	Baltimore/Dunbar
Wayne Bristol	SR	6-1	Beltsville/High Point
Abdul Brown	SO	6-6	Baltimore/Southern
David Cason	SR	5-10	Baltimore/Southern
Phil Chenier, Jr.	SR	6-6	Columbia/Wilde Lake
Tony Dantzler	SR	6-0	Baltimore/Southern
Jeremy Dean	JR	6-7	Potomac/Harker Prep
Billy Drayton	JR	6-5	Temple Hills/Crossland
Ted Ellis	SR	6-2	Hyattsville/DeMatha
Derrick Ford	SR	6-8	Forestville/Suitland
Rob Garner	SR	6-2	Oxon Hill/Potomac
Marvin Gross	SR	6-4	Baltimore/Dunbar
Kevin Hockady	SR	6-5	Joppa/Joppatowne
Obadiah Johnson	SR	6-2	Largo/Largo
Vaughn Jones	JR	6-4	Hyattsville/DeMatha
Marvin Kosh	JR	6-0	Baltimore/Walbrook
Chris McGuthrie	JR	5-10	Silver Spring/Springbrook
Alexander Mobley	FR	6-6	Baltimore/Dunbar
Tony Moore	JR	6-7	Kensington/Newport Prep
Jelani Nix	SR	6-7	Bladensburg/Bladensburg
Kevin Norris	SO	5-9	Baltimore/Lake Clifton
Larry Osborne	JR	6-9	Forestville/Suitland
Jermaine Porter	JR	6-6	Baltimore/Walbrook
Don Reid	SR	6-8	Largo/Largo
Nii Nelson Richards	SR	6-3	Wheaton/Good Counsel
Stacy Robinson	JR	6-5	Lanham/Duval
John Salley	SR	6-7	Baltimore/Southern
Sidney Shelton	SR	6-7	Potomac/Harper Prep
Sam Short	SR	6-2	Potomac/Harper Prep
Duane Simpkins	JR	6-0	Hyattsville/DeMatha
Kurt Small	SR	6-2	Wheaton/Good Counsel
John Spann	SR	6-5	Forestville/Suitland
Steve Thomas	SR	6-6	Baltimore/Walbrook

MASSACHUSETTS

NAME	CL	HEIGHT	CITY/HIGH SCHOOL
Shannon Bowman	FR	6-4	Dorchester/Dorchester
Roney Eford	SR	6-5	Sheffield/Berkshire School
Jiechael Henderson	JR	6-6	Boston/East Boston
Desi Jackson	JR	6-6	Springfield/Central
Jamal Jackson	JR	6-7	Boston/East Boston
Derek Kellogg	SR	6-1	Springfield/Cathedral
Danny Marshall	SR	6-10	Amesbury/Amesbury
Larry Merritt	SR	5-9	Boston/Cathedral
Asa Palmer	SO	6-7	Belmont/Belmont
Steve Purpura	SR	6-9	Shrewsbury/St. Johns
Patrick Richardson	SR	6-6	North Easton/Oliver Ames
John Sagarino	SR	5-11	Everett/Everett
Fred Smith	JR	6-2	Springfield/Central
Keith Spencer	JR	6-4	Northfield/Mt. Hermon
Bevan Thomas	SR	6-6	Boston/Catholic Memorial
Shawn Williams	SR	6-1	Boston/East Boston

HIGH SCHOOL HONORABLE MENTION ALL-AMERICA TEAM

NAME	CL	HEIGHT	CITY/HIGH SCHOOL	NAME	CL	HEIGHT	CITY/HIGH SCHOOL
MICHIGAN				Brian Sand	SR	6-8	Brooklyn Park/Park Center
Tim Alderink	SR	6-2	Holland/Christian	Steve Seawright	SR	6-5	Minneapolis/South
David Amos	SR	6-5	Ann Arbor/Huron	Jason Sims	SR	6-6	Minneapolis/South
Ibn Bakari	JR	6-9	Detroit/Southwestern	Jeff Timonen	SR	5-10	Plymouth/Armstrong
Jake Baker	SR	6-6	Plymouth/Salem	Jeff Van Someren	SR	6-6	Edina/Edina
Christ Bakos	SR	6-5	Birmingham/Detroit Country Day	Craig Wacholz	SR	6-8	Mayer/Lutheran
Javon Basnight	SR	6-5	Detroit/Mackenzie	Dan Ward	SR	5-10	Mankato/Loyola
Randy Bennett	SR	6-9	Jenison/Jenison				
Emmanuel Bibb	SR	6-2	Detroit/Denby	**MISSISSIPPI**			
Larry Bolden	JR	6-1	Detroit/Cody	Fredrick Ashley	SR	6-8	McComb/McComb
Derrick Boles	SR	6-6	Belleville/Belleville	Eric Dampier	SO	6-9	Monticello/Lawrence County
Quincy Bowens	SR	5-10	Detroit/Southwestern	Mark Davis	SR	6-4	Utica/Utica
Lakeith Boyd	JR	6-2	Detroit/Henry Ford	Luther Dilworth	SR	6-7	Corinth/Corinth
Dayle Cates	SR	6-1	Mount Clemens/Mount Clemens	Marion Dorsey	JR	6-2	Shelby/Broad Street
Chris Daniels	SR	6-8	Albion/Albion	Reginald Garrett	SR	6-5	Brandon/Northwest Rankin
Larry Daniels	SR	6-7	Detroit/Cooley	Greg Gillom	SR	6-7	Oxford/Lafayette
Jesse Drain	SR	6-6	Saginaw/Saginaw	Shawn Hadley	SR	6-4	Laurel/Northeast Jones
Deshanti Foreman	SR	6-7	Detroit/Murray-Wright	Ronnie Henderson	SO	6-4	Jackson/Murrah
Joel Frakes	SR	6-1	Stevensville/Lakeshore	Wayne Hereford	SR	6-4	Moorville/Moorville
Darrius Hall	SR	6-7	Detroit/Northwestern	Glover Jackson	SR	6-8	Vicksburg/Warren Central
Michael Hamilton	SR	6-5	Detroit/Southwestern	Keith Killins	SR	6-4	Meridian/Meridian
Tim Hawkins	SR	6-6	Detroit/Central	Marcus Mann	JR	6-6	Walnut Grove/South Leake
Marcus Hughes	SO	6-8	Detroit/St. Martin De Porres	Kwane Moore	SR	6-4	Greenwood/Amanda Elzy
Ron Hunter	SR	6-4	Belleville/Belleville	Marcus Moore	SR	6-0	Corinth/Corinth
Scott Hunter	SR	6-5	Vicksburg/Vicksburg	Corey Norwood	SR	6-4	Tupelo/Tupelo
Shawn Jackson	SR	5-10	Saginaw/Buena Vista	Marcus Pittman	SR	6-8	McComb/McComb
Stefan Knul	SR	6-10	Manchester/Manchester	Jerrell Roberson	JR	6-8	Greenville/Weston
Bob Kummer	JR	6-7	Redford/Catholic Central	John Stokes	JR	6-9	Collins/Collins
Mike Lake	SR	5-11	Berrien Springs/Berrien Springs	James Taylor	FR	6-7	Flora/East Flora
Tarik Lester	SR	5-10	Grosse Point/University Leggett	Sanchez Turner	SR	6-1	Vancleave/Vancleave
Derek Lowe	SR	6-5	Dearborn/Edsel Ford	Lorenzo Vasser	FR	6-7	Oxford/Lafayette
Craig Martin	SR	5-11	Oakland/Oakland Christian	Russell Walters	SR	6-9	Laurel/Northeast Jones
Iyapo Montgomery	SR	6-3	Birmingham/Detroit Country Day	Jay Walton	SR	6-7	Pascagoula/Pascagoula
John Nichols	SR	6-6	Jackson/Jackson	Dewayne Whitfield	SR	6-7	Aberdeen/Aberdeen
Kenneth Patterson	JR	6-5	Detroit/Northern				
Steve Polonoski	JR	6-9	Rockford/Rockford	**MISSOURI**			
Andy Poppink	SR	6-5	Tecumseh/Tecumseh	Lyle Beckemeyer	SR	6-5	Wellington/Napoleon
Antonio Ragland	JR	6-4	Detroit/Chadsey	Eric Bickel	SR	6-10	Overland/Ritenour
Alan Rainge	SR	6-3	Pontiac/Central	Brent Blevins	SR	6-2	Forsyth/Forsyth
Rashad Reeves	JR	6-1	Detroit/Mackenzie	Billy Brent	SR	6-3	Springfield/Kickapoo
Desmond Rice	SR	6-5	Detroit/Cass Tech	Andrew Evans	SR	6-3	St. Louis/Cardinal Ritter
Jay Riemersma	SR	6-5	Zeeland/Zeeland	Brian Frey	SR	6-8	Kansas City/Rockhurst
Andy Smith	SR	6-2	Farmington/Harrison	Brian Gavin	JR	6-1	Chesterfield/Parkway Central
Matt Stuck	JR	6-4	Manton/Manton	Ronald Golden	SR	6-5	St. Louis/University City
Matthew Thompson	SR	6-9	Flint/Southwestern	Scott Highmark	SR	6-4	Ballwin/Parkway West
John Tillery	JR	6-4	Royal Oak/Shrine	Steve Horton	SR	6-8	Jefferson City/Jefferson City
Matthew Timme	SR	6-8	Muskegon/Reeths Puffer	Eric Howard	SR	6-7	St. Louis/DeSmet
Charles Turner	JR	6-7	Southfield/Southfield	Derrick Johnson	SR	6-1	Jefferson City/Jefferson City
Jason Wade	SR	5-10	Ann Arbor/Pioneer	Chris Jordan	JR	6-4	Mokane/South Calloway
Michael Walker	SR	6-10	Oscoda/Oscoda	Lavon Kincaid	SR	6-1	Kirkwood/Kirkwood
David Washington	SR	6-8	Albion/Albion	Mike Lawson	SR	6-5	Pattonsburg/Pattonsburg
Omar Wedlow	SR	6-8	Detroit/Chadsey	Dan Mahurin	SR	6-6	Macks Creek/Macks Creek
Daniel West	SR	6-1	Saginaw/Saginaw	Mark Matthews	SR	6-4	Springfield/Hillcrest
Theron Wilson	SR	6-8	Royal Oak/Dondero	Mike McClain	SR	6-0	Springfield/Glendale
Wes Wood	SR	6-2	Saginaw/Valley Lutheran	Jason Mills	SR	6-4	Warrensburg/Warrensburg
				Les Saunders	SR	5-10	Raytown/South
MINNESOTA				Brandon Shelby	JR	5-9	Osceola/Osceola
Mike Amos	SR	6-9	Minnetonka/Hopkins	Dallas Spears	SR	6-8	St. Louis/Hazelwood
Todd Bauman	SR	6-3	Tyler/Russell-Tyler	Ryan Stepp	SR	6-4	Kansas City/Park Hills
Rich Buck	SR	6-3	Red Wing/Red Wing	Kelly Thames	SO	6-5	Jennings/Jennings
Rich Frandeen	JR	6-8	Edina/Edina	Tim Tolliver	SR	6-4	St. Louis/Cleveland
Aaron Hungerholt	SR	6-0	Rushford/Rushford	Scott Welsh	JR	6-3	Willard/Willard
Sly Johnson	JR	6-4	St. Paul/Central	Chris Woods	SR	6-10	St. Charles/Francis Howell
Kory Kettner	SR	6-8	Nicollet/Nicollet				
Ramon Kopper	SR	6-8	Woodbury/Woodbury	**MONTANA**			
Beau Lynch	SR	6-7	Edina/Edina	Matt Garrison	JR	6-7	Billings/Senior
Joel McDonald	SR	6-4	Chisolm/Chisolm	John Giles	SR	6-5	Twin Bridges/Twin Bridges
Patrice Nzigamasbo	SR	6-6	Mound/Mound-Westonka	Gerald Gilham	JR	6-2	Browning/Browning
Don Phillips	SR	6-5	Minneapolis/Roosevelt	Mark Gilman	SR	6-4	Kalispell/Flathead
Matt Robinson	SR	6-9	Columbia Heights/Columbia Heights	Scott Hatler	SR	6-2	Great Falls/Great Falls
Dave Ruda	SR	6-8	Long Prairie/Long Prairie	Shane Lord	SR	5-11	Cascade/Cascade

HIGH SCHOOL HONORABLE MENTION ALL-AMERICA TEAM

NAME	CL	HEIGHT	CITY/HIGH SCHOOL
Todd Redd	JR	6-6	Helena/Helena Capital
Tom Reynolds	SR	6-7	Havre/Havre

NEBRASKA

NAME	CL	HEIGHT	CITY/HIGH SCHOOL
Terrance Badgett	SR	6-6	Omaha/South
Tom Burt	SR	6-6	Lincoln/Pius X
Darin Engelbart	SR	5-11	Lincoln/Northeast
Jason Glock	SR	6-5	Wahoo/Wahoo
John Haugh	SR	6-2	Omaha/Westside
Curtis Johnson	SR	6-6	Lincoln/Southeast
Curtis Marshall	SR	6-0	Omaha/Creighton Prep
Erick Strickland	JR	6-3	Bellevue/Bellevue West
Joe Vogel	JR	6-9	North Platte/North Platte
Andy Woolridge	JR	6-2	Omaha/Benson

NEVADA

NAME	CL	HEIGHT	CITY/HIGH SCHOOL
Sean Allen	SR	6-8	Las Vegas/Western
Daryl Christopher	SR	6-0	Las Vegas/Western
Harold Foster	SR	6-8	Las Vegas/Valley
Damien Smith	JR	6-2	Las Vegas/Chaparral
Mark Sterbens	SR	6-2	Las Vegas/Bishop Borman
Booker Washington	JR	6-6	Las Vegas/Western

NEW HAMPSHIRE

NAME	CL	HEIGHT	CITY/HIGH SCHOOL
David Brown	SR	6-5	Derry/Pinkerton Academy
Daryl Collette	SR	6-11	Merrimack/Merrimack
Scott Drapeau	SR	6-8	Penacook/Merrimack Valley
Ryan Gatchell	JR	6-5	Epping/Epping
T.J. Gondek	SR	6-5	Nashua/Nashua
Matt Guyer	JR	5-10	Laconia/Laconia
Neil Hood	JR	6-8	Derry/Pinkerton Academy
Mike McMurray	SR	6-3	Wilton/Wilton-Lyndenbrough
Matt Smith	SR	6-1	Concord/Concord

NEW JERSEY

NAME	CL	HEIGHT	CITY/HIGH SCHOOL
Halim Abdullah	SO	5-7	Jersey City/St. Anthony's
Chris Alexander	SR	6-9	Long Branch/Long Branch
Ethan Alexander	SR	6-5	Paterson/Eastside
Luis Ayala	JR	6-5	Teaneck/Teaneck
Mark Bass	SR	5-10	Trenton/McCorristin
Kareem Brown	SR	6-6	Voorhees/Eastern
Tyrone Brown	SR	6-3	Elizabeth/Elizabeth
Rakiim Burgess	SR	6-7	Jersey City/Snyder
Keith Carmichael	SR	6-2	Camden/Camden
Alcides Catanho	SR	6-5	Elizabeth/Elizabeth
Kent Culuko	SR	6-3	Mahwah/Mahwah
Antwan Dasher	SR	6-0	Bayonne/Marist
Waliyy Dixon	JR	6-3	Linden/Linden
Danny Earl	SO	6-0	Medford/Shawnee
Jason Fichter	SR	6-7	Lincroft/Christian Brothers
Jamie Gregg	JR	6-7	Leonia/Leonia
Roy Hairston	SR	6-4	Jersey City/Snyder
Deon Hames	JR	5-9	Princeton/Hun School
Roscoe Harris	JR	6-4	Bayonne/Marist
Romaine Haywood	JR	6-6	Atlantic City/Altantic City
Randy Holmes	SR	6-2	Lakewood/Lakewood
Danny Hurley	SR	6-1	Jersey City/St. Anthony's
Lance Jackson	SR	6-1	Newark/Westside
Robin James	SR	6-4	Oradell/Bergen Catholic
Keith Kurowski	JR	6-1	Lincroft/Christian Brothers
Quincy Lee	JR	6-2	Paulsboro/Paulsboro
Ray Lucas	SR	6-3	Harrison/Harrison
Jamal Marshall	SR	6-6	Bayonne/Marist
Jermain Mathis	JR	6-3	East Orange/Clifford Scott
Vince McCaffrey	FR	6-3	Pennsauken/Bishop Eustace
Dave Meiselman	SR	6-8	Wayne/Wayne Valley
Mike Melchionni	JR	6-5	Pennsauken/Bishop Eustace
Zeffie Penn	JR	6-5	Jersey City/Snyder
Justin Phoenix	JR	6-6	Cherry Hill/Camden Catholic
Demetrius Poles	SR	6-7	Franklinville/Selsea Regional
Jalil Roberts	SO	6-5	Jersey City/St. Anthony's

NAME	CL	HEIGHT	CITY/HIGH SCHOOL
Steve Rogers	SR	6-5	Camden/Woodrow Wilson
Glenn Sekunda	SR	6-7	Parsippany/Parsippany Hills
Michael Stout	SR	6-3	Pennington/Pennington School
Matt Tchir	SR	5-9	Toms River/East
Lawrence Thomas	JR	6-0	Elizabeth/Elizabeth
Tom Tomaczak	FR	6-9	Lincroft/Christian Brothers
Rob Tyson	SR	6-7	East Orange/East Orange
Reggie Welch	JR	6-5	Camden/Woodrow Wilson
Curtis Whiting	SR	6-0	Hackensack/Hackensack
Donnell Williams	SO	6-5	Bayonne/Marist
Emeka Wilson	SR	6-7	East Orange/Clifford Scott
James Wright	SR	6-1	Jersey City/St. Anthony's

NEW MEXICO

NAME	CL	HEIGHT	CITY/HIGH SCHOOL
Troy Brewer	JR	6-0	Hobbs/Hobbs
Nathan Erdmann	JR	6-4	Portales/Portales
Joel Koplik	SR	6-4	Albuquerque/Academy
Chris McCall	SR	6-8	Lovington/Lovington
Marc Soto	JR	6-6	Belen/Belen
Chris Spull	SR	6-5	Clovis/Clovis
David Strong	SR	6-6	Albuquerque/Sandia
Jeremy Trujillo	SO	6-7	Albuquerque/West Mesa
Doug Tydeman	SR	6-3	Albuquerque/Highland

NEW YORK

NAME	CL	HEIGHT	CITY/HIGH SCHOOL
Shawn Abercrombie	SR	6-1	Manhasset/Manhasset
Lance Anderson	JR	6-6	Brooklyn/Westinghouse
Sherwin Anderson	SO	5-10	Brooklyn/Bishop Loughlin
Dwayne Archibold	JR	6-7	Staten Island/Curtis
Lamont Austin	SO	6-1	New York/LaSalle
Terrence Bethel	SR	5-11	Bronx/Tolentine
John Brennan	SR	6-8	Huntington Station/Walt Whitman
Derek Brown	SR	6-3	Franklin Square/Carey
Maurice Brown	JR	5-10	Brooklyn/Grady
Tyler Brown	SO	6-3	Bronx/St. Raymonds
Craig Caldwell	SR	5-10	Syracuse/Nottingham
Stacey Castle	JR	6-1	Far Rockaway/Far Rockaway
Willie Cauley	SR	6-6	Niagara Falls/Niagara Falls
James Ceresier	SR	6-6	Brooklyn/Abraham Lincoln
Mike Chaplin	SR	6-6	East Elmhurst/Monsignor McClancy
Maurice Cox	SR	5-10	Niagara Falls/LaSalle
Lateef Duncan	SR	6-0	Rensselaer/Rensselaer
Eric Eberz	JR	6-6	Buffalo/St. Joseph's Institute
Dean Edwards	SR	6-7	Olean/Olean
Crafton Ferguson	SR	6-7	Cambria Heights/Andrew Jackson
George Finney	SR	6-5	Elmsford/Alexander Hamilton
Bobby Fitzgibbons	JR	6-8	Buffalo/Nichols
Clyde Fraser	SR	6-7	Brooklyn/Brooklyn Tech
Steve Frazier	SR	6-8	Rochester/East
Winston Gordon	SO	6-6	Brooklyn/Bishop Ford
Raul Hagins	JR	6-2	Rochester/Wilson
Frank Harris	SR	6-2	Bronx/Riverdale Country Day
Otis Hill	JR	6-8	Pleasantville/Pleasantville
Darnell Hidges	JR	6-2	Bronx/Tolentine
Derek Jackson	SR	6-2	Syracuse/Corcoran
Colin Johnson	SR	6-3	Mount Vernon/Mount Vernon
Sherman Jones	JR	5-11	New York/Manhattan Center
Joe Joyner	JR	6-5	Amityville/Amityville
Avery Lamb	SR	6-8	Auburn/Auburn
Jared Leake	SR	6-1	New York/Dalton
Jeremy Livingston	SR	5-11	Jamaica/Archbishop Molloy
Arthur Long	SR	6-8	Rochester/East
Felipe Lopez	FR	6-5	New York/Rice
Ray Lynch	SR	6-4	Bronx/All Hallows
David Mascia	SR	6-2	Lynbrook/Lynbrook
Jason McKinney	SR	6-9	Rochester/McQuaid Jesuit
Shandu McNeil	SO	5-7	Jamaica/Archbishop Molloy
Floyd Miller	SR	6-5	Brooklyn/Van Arsdale
Cornelius Overby	JR	6-2	Bronx/Lehman
Jamal Phillips	SR	6-7	Brooklyn/Grady

HIGH SCHOOL HONORABLE MENTION ALL-AMERICA TEAM

NAME	CL	HEIGHT	CITY/HIGH SCHOOL
Kareem Porter	SO	6-5	Bronx/Tolentine
Ed Posey	SO	6-6	Hempstead/Hempstead
Tracy Pringle	SR	6-4	New York/Mabel Dean Bacon
Ken Robinson	SR	6-5	Buffalo/Grover Cleveland
Malik Russell	SR	6-7	Brooklyn/Poly Prep
Damon Santiago	SR	5-11	Bronx/Adlai Stevenson
Maurice Brown	JR	6-4	New York/LaSalle
Jimmy Shaffer	SR	6-2	Brooklyn/Xaverian
Kevin Shaw	SO	6-8	Middle Village/Christ The King
Tchaka Shipp	JR	6-6	Brooklyn/Abraham Lincoln
Jermaine Smoak	SR	6-2	Brooklyn/Van Arsdale
Keith Spencer	JR	6-5	Springfield Gardens/Springfield Gardens
William Sydnor	SR	6-7	New York/Martin L. King
Rashawn Thompson	SO	6-3	Bronx/St. Raymonds
Rich Vetere	JR	6-4	Middle Village/Christ The King
John Wallace	JR	6-8	Rochester/Greece-Athena
Nehru Wilkins	JR	6-3	Bronx/Cardinal Hayes
Jayson Williams	SR	6-6	Brookville/Long Island Lutheran
Jerel Williams	SR	6-7	Buffalo/McKinley
Eric Wyatt	SR	5-11	Henrietta/Rush-Henrietta

NORTH CAROLINA

NAME	CL	HEIGHT	CITY/HIGH SCHOOL
Scooter Banks	SR	6-5	Clinton/Clinton
William Bethea	SO	6-0	Greensboro/Page
Melvin Branham	SR	6-7	Durham/Jordon
Barry Canty	JR	6-3	Charlotte/Independence
Jeff Capel	SO	6-3	Fayetteville/Reid Ross
Wes Collins	SR	6-5	Kinston/Kinston
Antoine Dalton	SR	6-8	Lexington/Lexington
James Daniels	SR	6-6	Shallotte/West Brunswick
Andre Davis	JR	6-2	Charlotte/Independence
Daniel Everette	SR	6-0	Elizabeth City/Northeastern
Junior Floyd	SR	6-6	Gastonia/Hunter Huss
Brian Frazier	SR	6-3	Roanoke Rapids/Roanoke Rapids
Victor Hamilton	SR	6-7	Forest City/East Rutherford
Donald Hartsfield	SR	6-4	Wake Forest/Wake Forest-Rolesville
Sean Hope	SR	6-8	Graham/Graham
Roderick Howard	SO	5-10	Gastonia/Ashbrook
Jon Hunter	JR	6-9	Graham/Graham
John Jacques	SR	6-5	Delco/Acme-Delco
Billy Kretzer	JR	6-8	Greensboro/Page
Pearce Landry	SR	6-2	Greensboro/Page
Rusty Larue	JR	6-2	Greensboro/Northwest Guilford
Brian Lewis	SR	6-5	Rutherfordton/R.S. Central
Travis Littles	JR	5-10	Charlotte/Providence Day
Habib Maiga	SR	6-11	Raleigh/Cardinal Gibbons
Andre McCollum	SR	6-1	Durham/Hillside
Chase Metheney	SO	7-1	Charlotte/East Mecklenburg
Adam Miller	JR	6-3	Pineville/South Mecklenburg
Darren Moore	JR	6-8	Marion/McDowell
Freddie Pate	SR	6-3	High Point/Central
Phillip Powe	SR	6-6	Raleigh/Broughton
Geoffrey Richards	SR	6-8	Charlotte/Latin
Tyrone Satterfield	SR	6-5	Mebane/Eastern Alamance
Lewis Sims	SR	6-7	Claremont/Bunker Hill
Jason Smith	SR	6-5	Washington/Washington
Shawn Smith	SO	6-5	Gastonia/Hunter Huss
Tim Stokes	SR	6-5	Charlotte/Harding
Jason Stowe	SR	6-5	Concord/Concord
Era Vaughn	SR	6-4	Kings Mountain/Kings Mountain
Derrick Wall	SR	6-5	Durham/Northern
Bratton White	SR	6-7	Charlotte/Myers Park
Mike White	SR	6-7	Spencer/North Rowan
Marcus Wilson	JR	6-7	Monroe/Monroe
Corwin Woodard	SR	6-2	Wilson/Fike
Prentice Woods	JR	6-6	Statesville/West Iredell

NORTH DAKOTA

NAME	CL	HEIGHT	CITY/HIGH SCHOOL
Trenton Bean	SR	6-3	West Fargo/West Fargo
Eric Buckeye	SR	6-0	Edgeley/Edgeley
Chipper Hanson	SR	6-3	Hillsboro/Hillsboro
Marty McDonald	JR	6-2	Munich/Munich
Bart Manson	SR	6-0	Minot/Minot
Brett Inniger	SR	6-3	Fargo/South
Mike Wieser	SR	6-5	Fargo/South

OHIO

NAME	CL	HEIGHT	CITY/HIGH SCHOOL
Steve Belter	SR	6-8	Cincinnati/Oak Hills
Bryant Bowden	JR	6-8	Canton/McKinley
Gerry Branner	SR	6-7	Cincinnati/Woodward
Quinton Brooks	JR	6-8	Akron/Firestone
Antwuan Brown	SR	6-4	Cincinnati/Withrow
Richard Brown	JR	6-3	Dayton/Dunbar
Sean Clarke	JR	6-6	Kettering/Alter
Orlando Donaldson	JR	6-6	Cincinnati/Aiken
Lazelle Durden	SR	6-3	Rossford/Rossford
Paul Edwards	SR	6-8	Malvern/Malvern
Robbie Eggars	SO	6-8	Cuyahoga Falls/Cuyahoga Falls
Steve Ehretsman	SR	6-7	Cleveland/St. Ignatius
Jeff Elder	SR	6-7	Dayton/Colonel White
Chico Feagin	SR	6-6	Mansfield/Mansfield
Tommy Feagin	SO	6-2	Columbus/Briggs
Damon Flint	SO	6-2	Cincinnati/Woodward
Keith Gregor	JR	6-7	West Chester/Lakota
Andy Hawkins	JR	6-8	London/London
Brian Hocevar	SO	6-7	Cleveland/St. Joseph
Deon Jackson	JR	6-5	Dayton/Patterson Co-Op
John Jacobs	SR	6-7	Lockland/Lockland
Jermaine Jelks	JR	6-5	Sidney/Sidney
Ed Jenkins	SO	6-6	Columbus/Centennial
Kevin Johnson	SO	6-7	Columbus/Mifflin
Andy Karazim	SR	6-3	Cincinnati/St. Xavier
Ron Kenley	SR	6-5	Columbus/West
Jason Kent	JR	6-3	Columbus/East
Chris Kingsbury	SO	6-3	Hamilton/Hamilton
Shane Komives	SR	6-4	Toledo/St. John's
Jay Larranaga	SO	6-3	Toledo/St. John's
Andy Meyer	JR	6-6	Kettering/Alter
Chris Mikola	SR	6-6	Warren/Howland
Tony Miller	SR	5-11	Cleveland/St. Joseph
Marc Molinsky	SR	6-4	Kettering/Alter
David Naber	SR	6-5	Cincinnati/Elder
Chuck Perry	SR	6-5	Columbus/Wehrle
Marco Pikaar	SR	6-10	Beavercreek/Beavercreek
Shawn Pugsley	SR	6-0	Lima/Senior
Jeff Quackenbush	SR	6-7	Newark/Newark
J.B. Reafsnyder	SR	6-10	West Chester/Lakota
Terry Roberts	SO	6-7	Toledo/Scott
Ryan Schrand	SR	5-10	Cincinnati/LaSalle
Verdel Sears	SR	6-4	Cleveland/St. Joseph
Malcolm Sims	JR	6-5	Shaker Heights/Shaker Heights
Doug Speelman	SR	6-8	Wooster/Wooster
Larry Sykes	SR	6-8	Toledo/St. Francis De Sales
Jason Terry	JR	7-0	Sparta/Highland-Morrow
Anthony Walker	JR	6-1	Columbus/Linden McKinley
Mike West	JR	6-3	North Bend/Taylor
Tom West	JR	6-5	North Bend/Taylor
Nate Wilbourne	JR	6-10	Columbus/Upper Arlington
Dan Williams	SR	6-3	Akron/Garfield
Brian Wolf	SO	6-5	Youngstown/Liberty
Jon Wooley	JR	6-9	Elida/Elida

OKLAHOMA

NAME	CL	HEIGHT	CITY/HIGH SCHOOL
Shon Alexander	SR	6-5	Preston/Preston
Freddie Barnes	SR	6-0	Taft/Taft
Chris Hayes	JR	6-4	Tulsa/Union
William Henderson	SR	5-11	Oklahoma City/Millwood
Jeremy Hicks	SR	6-8	Enid/Oklahoma Bible Academy
Tarrence Huddleston	SR	6-7	Okmulgee/Okmulgee
Chris Leblanc	JR	6-7	Edmond/Edmond
Jay Malham	SR	6-6	Broken Arrow/Broken Arrow
Ryan Minor	JR	6-5	Hammon/Hammon

HIGH SCHOOL HONORABLE MENTION ALL-AMERICA TEAM

NAME	CL	HEIGHT	CITY/HIGH SCHOOL
Eric Moore	SR	6-7	Tulsa/Booker T. Washington
Bryant Reeves	SR	7-0	Gans/Gans
Bryan Rieke	JR	6-3	Dale/Dale
Terry Rollins	JR	6-4	Tuttle/Tuttle
Ramon Smith	SR	6-4	Tulsa/Rogers
Syii Tucker	SR	6-6	Oklahoma City/Douglas
Jason Turk	SO	6-0	Collinsville/Collinsville
Mike Walker	SR	6-3	Midwest City/Midwest City
Travis Washington	SR	6-0	Broken Arrow/Broken Arrow
Junior Whitaker	SR	6-5	Beggs/Beggs
Marlow White	SR	6-4	Haskell/Haskell
Eric Wiens	SR	6-4	Oologah/Oologah
Henry Winston	JR	6-1	Boynton/Boynton
Jason Yanish	SR	6-8	Glenpool/Glenpool

OREGON

NAME	CL	HEIGHT	CITY/HIGH SCHOOL
Rick Brainard	SR	6-5	Eugene/North Eugene
Matt Brunetti	SR	6-4	Cottage Grove/Cottage Grove
Matt Droege	SR	6-7	Cottage Grove/Cottage Grove
Lorin Fields	SR	6-6	Beaverton/Beaverton
Alan Fish	SO	6-4	Salem/South Salem
Casey Flicker	JR	6-0	Keizer/McNary
Walter Gintz	SR	6-4	Portland/Grant
Nico Harrison	SR	6-4	Tigard/Tigard
Eric Heinle	SR	6-4	Sheldon/Sheldon
Todd Manley	SR	6-9	Portland/Adventist Academy
Taj McFarlane	SR	6-7	Salem/North Salem
Miguel McKelvey	JR	6-7	Eugene/South Eugene
Brendon Pocock	SR	6-7	Eugene/South Eugene
Craig Stinnett	SR	6-7	Sutherlin/Sutherlin
Travis Sydow	SR	6-5	Salem/South Salem
Chris Thanos	SO	6-8	Corvallis/Crescent Valley

PENNSYLVANIA

NAME	CL	HEIGHT	CITY/HIGH SCHOOL
Leon Agnew	SR	6-9	Greensburg/Hempfield
Levan Alston	SR	6-3	Philadelphia/Simon Gratz
Jeff Balistree	JR	6-2	Waynesboro/Waynesboro
Grant Berges	SR	6-7	Malvern/Great Valley
Brook Bright	SO	6-8	Meadville/Meadville
Paul Burke	SR	6-0	Philadelphia/Chestnut Hill Academy
Dante Calabria	JR	6-3	Beaver Falls/Blackhawk
Damien Delts	SO	6-6	West Mifflin/West Mifflin
Ryan Dennis	SO	6-7	Grove City/George Junior Republic
Carlos Dixon	SR	6-3	Pittsburgh/Woodland Hills
Mark Dudley	SR	6-3	Stroudsburg/Stroudsburg
Danny Fortson	FR	6-5	Altoona/Altoona
Greg Gilbert	SO	6-2	Abington/Abington
Alonzo Goldston	SR	6-7	Concordville/Glen Mills
Andre Griffin	SR	6-3	Philadelphia/Simon Gratz
Jim Hamilton	SR	6-4	Erie/Cathedral Prep
Faron Hand	JR	6-5	Philadelphia/Franklin Learning Ctr.
Steve Hauer	JR	6-3	Shamokin/Our Lady of Lourdes
Malik Hightower	SR	6-2	Pittsburgh/Oliver(?)
Khyl Horton	JR	6-5	Erie/Mercyhurst Prep
Antoine Hubbard	SO	5-9	Allentown/Salisbury
Gabe Jackson	SR	6-4	New Brighton/New Brighton
Gerald Jordan	SR	6-8	Philadelphia/West Philadelphia
Russell Kelley	SR	6-4	West Middlesex/West Middlesex
Kevin Kosak	SR	6-4	Mt. Pleasant/Mt. Pleasant
Jason Lawson	SO	6-7	Philadelphia/Olney
Kyle Locke	JR	6-4	Philadelphia/Roman Catholic
James McDonald	SR	6-10	Erie/Academy
Jeremy Metzger	JR	6-8	Erie/McDowell
Brian Miller	SR	5-11	Monongahela/Ringgold
Kobie Morgan	SR	6-2	Mercersburg/Mercersburg Academy
Shawn Morris	SR	6-1	Pittsburgh/Penn Hills
Bruce Patterson	SR	6-3	Pittsburgh/Langley
Brian Pearl	SR	6-1	York/York Catholic
Tom Pipkins	SO	6-2	New Kensington/Valley
Jamahal Redmond	SO	6-5	Philadelphia/Simon Gratz
Todd Robinson	SR	6-1	New Hope/Solebury Academy
Del Savage	SR	6-5	Pottstown/Pottstown
Geoff Schoeneck	SR	6-8	Easton/Area
Andy Seigle	SR	6-9	Carbondale/Carbondale
Wilbur Shaw	SR	6-4	Chester/Chester
Shawn Smith	FR	5-10	Philadelphia/Simon Gratz
Bob Sura	SR	6-4	Wilkes-Barre/G.A.R. Memorial
Robert Tate	SR	6-2	Harrisburg/Harrisburg
Frank Tomera	JR	6-10	Johnstown/Greater Johnstown
David Wallace	SR	5-11	Jenkintown/Abington Friends
Alvin Williams	SO	6-3	Ft. Washington/Germantown Academy
Craig Wise	SR	6-4	Philadelphia/Central

RHODE ISLAND

NAME	CL	HEIGHT	CITY/HIGH SCHOOL
Jason Costa	SR	6-2	Warwick/Hendricken
Mike Hassett	SR	6-2	Providence/LaSalle Academy
Curtis McCants	SO	5-10	Pawtucket/St. Raphael Academy
Brian McGovern	JR	6-2	Coventry/Coventry
Tim Reed	SO	6-0	Newport/Rogers

SOUTH CAROLINA

NAME	CL	HEIGHT	CITY/HIGH SCHOOL
Phil Allen	SR	5-11	Georgetown/Georgetown
Jason Bell	JR	6-7	Duncan/James Byrnes
Michael Blassingame	SR	6-8	Seneca/Seneca
Andy Bostick	SR	6-5	Florence/South Florence
Marion Busby	SR	6-0	Columbia/Eau Claire
Larry Davis	SR	6-2	Denmark/Denmark-Olar
Steve Davis	SR	6-2	Manning/Manning
Rashaan Douglas	JR	6-5	Myrtle Beach/Socastee
Henry Hammond	SO	6-7	Iva/Crescent
Robbie Johnson	JR	6-2	Barnwell/Barnwell
George Kelada	SR	6-7	Greer/Riverside
Patrick Marshall	SR	6-4	Irmo/Irmo
William Massey	SR	6-5	Rock Hill/Northwestern
Tyrone McCoy	SR	6-3	Bethune/Bethune
Desi McQueen	SR	6-8	Bennettsville/Marlboro County
Chuck Robinson	SR	6-7	Charleston/James Island
Scott Sanders	JR	6-4	Mount Pleasant/Wando
Jason Scott	SR	6-9	Charleston Heights/Northside Christian
George Spain	SR	6-8	Columbia/Spring Valley
Sigmund Tucker	SR	6-5	Hopkins/Lower Richland
George Ward	SR	6-7	Columbia/W.J. Keenan
Tyrone Wilson	SR	6-2	Hopkins/Lower Richland
Casey Witherspoon	SR	6-5	Columbia/Dreher

SOUTH DAKOTA

NAME	CL	HEIGHT	CITY/HIGH SCHOOL
Jesse Dana	SO	5-10	Rapid City/Central
Chuck Dejean	SR	6-5	Huron/Huron
Steve Diekmann	SR	6-3	Yankton/Yankton
Eric Kline	SR	6-0	Aberdeen/Aberdeen
Bo Lintz	JR	6-6	Rapid City/Central
Cory Louder	SR	6-2	Elkton/Elkton
Lance Luitjens	JR	6-2	Custer/Custer
Sean Piatkowski	SO	6-2	Rapid City/Rapid City
Jay Steele	JR	6-6	Custer/Custer

TENNESSEE

NAME	CL	HEIGHT	CITY/HIGH SCHOOL
Demetrius Alexander	SR	6-5	Chattanooga/Brainerd
Al Allen	SR	6-6	Nashville/Brentwood Academy
Brice Bloodworth	SR	6-4	Hendersonville/Beech
Leslie Brunn	SR	6-7	Elizabethton/Elizabethton
Stanley Caldwell	JR	6-6	Union City/Union City
Gilbert Campbell	JR	6-8	Maryville/Maryville
Billy Crouch	SR	6-6	Clarkrange/Clarkrange
Marc Davis	SR	5-11	Englewood/McMinn Central
Jabari Dial	SO	6-1	Jefferson City/Jefferson County
Kevin Dixon	SR	6-2	Fayetteville/Lincoln County
Chris Elliott	SR	6-2	Memphis/Central
Sylvester Ford, Jr.	SO	6-5	Memphis/Fairley
Kyle Freeman	SR	6-2	Pulaski/Giles County
Jesse Gilbert	JR	6-2	Knoxville/Fulton
Lemarcus Golden	JR	6-2	Memphis/Treadwell

HIGH SCHOOL HONORABLE MENTION ALL-AMERICA TEAM

NAME	CL	HEIGHT	CITY/HIGH SCHOOL
Steve Hamer	JR	6-10	Middleton/Middleton
Chris Haynes	SR	6-4	Memphis/Briarcrest
Trevor Head	SR	6-7	Kingsport/Dobyns-Bennett
Tshombe High	JR	6-3	Chattanooga/Brainerd
Darrell Hodge	JR	6-4	Chattanooga/Howard
Dewayne Jackson	JR	6-7	Somerville/Fayette-Ware
Chuck Johnson	JR	6-5	Greeneville/North Greene
Chris Jones	SO	6-4	Somerville/Fayette-Ware
Fredrick Kinnie	JR	6-4	Denmark/West
Otis Lawson	SR	6-4	Memphis/Fairley
Erwin Lewis	SO	6-2	Kingsport/Dobyns-Bennett
Jeff Marshall	SR	6-6	Kingsport/Sullivan North
Ara Matthews	SR	6-5	Chattanooga/Chattanooga
Justin McClellan	SR	6-5	Cookeville/Cookeville
Chad McClendon	SR	6-6	Madisonville/Madisonville
Ron McCrary	SR	6-5	Memphis/Bartlett
Ron McMahan	SR	6-4	Athens/McMinn County
Andy McQueen	SR	6-5	Clarksville/Northeast
Jason Meadows	SO	6-5	Byrdstown/Pickett County
Kevin Millen	SR	6-6	Memphis/Raleigh-Egypt
Mark Newman	SR	6-7	Sevierville/Sevier County
Wade Parsons	JR	6-0	Crossville/Cumberland County
Victor Payne	SR	6-10	Memphis/Southside
Andy Pennington	JR	6-3	Madisonville/Madisonville
Scotty Redmond	SR	6-3	Oak Ridge/Oak Ridge
Will Rowland	SR	6-2	Murfreesboro/Oakland
Jeff Sexton	SR	6-7	Memphis/Christian Brothers
Marlin Simms	SR	6-5	Whites Creek/Whites Creek
Paxton Smith	SR	6-7	Jamestown/York Institute
Kevin Sparks	SO	5-11	Memphis/Harding Academy
Jeff Van Demark	SR	6-9	Knoxville/Doyle
Kenny Washington	SR	6-4	Memphis/Westwood
Shane Williams	JR	6-1	Johnson City/Science Hill
Michael Wilson	SR	6-6	Memphis/Melrose

TEXAS

NAME	CL	HEIGHT	CITY/HIGH SCHOOL
Darrin Anderson	SR	6-8	Fort Worth/Eastern Hills
Kevin Barker	SR	6-8	Longview/Pine Tree
Dion Barnes	SR	6-0	Houston/Madison
Todd Barton	SR	6-9	Columbus/Columbus
Derrick Battie	JR	6-9	Dallas/South Oak Cliff
Ali Bell	SR	6-4	Austin/Bowie
Marvin Bell	SR	6-4	Duncanville/Duncanville
Rodney Bell	SR	6-3	Garland/South Garland
Joe Blair	JR	6-7	Houston/C.E. King
Mario Bogle	SR	6-5	Fort Worth/Southwest
Aundre Branch	SR	6-2	Kingwood/Kingwood
Shannon Brantley	SR	6-6	Houston/Booker T. Washington
Jason Brassow	SR	6-1	Alief/Alief-Elsik
Marco Bristo	SR	6-8	Houston/Kashmere
Jacob Capps	JR	6-5	Houston/Westfield
Bryan Collins	SR	6-8	San Antonio/Sam Houston
Chad Collins	SR	5-11	San Antonio/MacArthur
Bobby Crawford	SO	6-2	Houston/Eisenhower
Calvin Crawford	SR	6-6	Dallas/Skyline
Otis Evans	SR	5-6	Fort Worth/Dunbar
Steve Frazier	SR	6-5	Kingwood/Kingwood
Alfred Grigsby	SR	6-7	Houston/Yates
Chris Hall	JR	6-6	Houston/Cy-Fair
Michael Harris	SR	6-7	Dallas/Lincoln
Richard Hastings	SR	6-5	Liberty Hill/Liberty Hill
Kelon Haynie	SR	6-4	Dallas/J.F. Kimball
Corey Henderson	SR	6-5	Houston/Lee
Craig Hernadi	SR	6-7	Kingwood/Kingwood
Brian Hightower	SR	6-3	Burkburnett/Burkburnett
William Howze	SR	6-7	Houston/Northbrook
Lance Hughes	SR	6-4	Georgetown/Georgetown
Ryan Hunter	SR	6-4	Beaumont/Monsignor Kelly
Damon Johnson	SR	6-5	Converse/Judson
Jarvis Kelley	SO	6-7	Houston/Milby
Ken Kerley	SR	6-3	San Antonio/John Jay

NAME	HT	CLASS	CITY/HIGH SCHOOL
Joel Lafleur	JR	6-1	Port Neches Grove/Port Neches Grove
Fred Lillie	SR	6-7	Humble/Humble
Cordell Love	JR	6-3	Dallas/South Oak Cliff
Larry Matthews	SR	6-6	Houston/Milby
Jason Mayo	JR	5-9	Dallas/Skyline
Kelvin Mclyer	SR	6-5	Port Arthur/Lincoln
Chris McKinney	SR	6-8	Waco/Waco
Kevin Miles	JR	6-8	Dallas/W.W. Samuell
Keith Murray	SR	6-8	Dallas/Lincoln
Dameon Page	JR	6-5	Burkburnett/Burkburnett
Barry Pruitt	JR	6-0	Dayton/Dayton
Sheldon Quarles	JR	6-9	Fort Worth/Tremble Tech
Eric Redeaux	JR	6-7	Beaumont/Central
Jeff Reno	JR	6-6	Port Arthur/Lincoln
Darrell Sadler	JR	6-4	Waco/University
Jesse Sandstad	JR	6-7	Dallas/Highland Park
Carl Simpson	SR	6-7	Galveston/Ball
Jeurel Sims	SR	6-3	Houston/Booker T. Washington
Rick Steele	SO	6-4	Livingston/Livingston
Joe Stephens	SR	6-5	Houston/North Shore
Des Stewart	JR	6-5	Waco/Waco
Shawn Stewart	SR	6-1	Farwell/Farwell
L.D. Swanson	SR	6-2	Garland/South Garland
Garrick Thomas	JR	6-4	Houston/MacArthur
Hershel Wafer	SR	6-6	Galveston/Ball
Terry Wallace	SR	6-5	Dallas/Bryan Adams
Michael Williams	SR	6-8	Dallas/Spruce
Tony Williams	SR	6-5	Wichita Falls/Hirschi

UTAH

NAME	HT	CLASS	CITY/HIGH SCHOOL
Justin Barlow	SR	6-6	Sandy/Alta
Bret Barton	SR	6-1	Kaysville/Davis
Richard Jackson	SR	6-6	Provo/Timpview
Ryan Nebeker	SR	6-6	Ogden/Ben Lomond
Robbie Reid	SO	5-11	Spanish Fork/Spanish Fork
Rick Robbins	SR	6-3	Fillmore/Millard
Scott Sexton	SR	6-5	Sandy/Alta
Ken Wamsley	JR	5-9	Salt Lake City/West Jordan
Tramayne Watson	SR	6-5	Ogden/Ogden
Justin Weidauer	SR	6-7	Salt Lake City/Cottonwood

VERMONT

NAME	HT	CLASS	CITY/HIGH SCHOOL
David Christie	SR	6-5	Bennington/Mt. Anthony Union
Bernie Cieplicki	SR	6-3	South Burlington/Rice Memorial
Joshua Farnsworth	JR	6-2	Windsor/Windsor
William Patno	SR	6-2	Montpelier/Montpelier
Scott Reed	SR	6-2	Fair Haven/Fair Haven Union
T.J. Sabotka	SR	6-2	Rutland/Rutland
Dean Selby	SR	6-2	Hyde Park/Lamoille Union
Jonathan Young	SR	6-0	Newport/North Country Union

VIRGINIA

NAME	HT	CLASS	CITY/HIGH SCHOOL
Chad Anderson	SR	6-3	Woodbridge/Woodbridge
Eric Baker	SR	6-11	Chatham/Hargrave Military Academy
Luther Bates	SR	6-6	Palmyra/Fluvanna County
Joey Beard	SO	6-9	Reston/South Lakes
Steven Birchette	SR	6-5	Lawrenceville/Brunswick
Leon Blakeney	SR	6-3	Alexandria/Mount Vernon
David Blizzard	SR	6-5	Hampton/Hampton
Brian Brickhouse	SR	6-5	Norfolk/Maury
Tyson Brooks	SR	6-5	Front Royal/Warren County
Jojo Chambers	SR	6-6	Highland Springs/Highland Springs
Kevin Connors	SR	6-5	Richmond/Hermitage
Theron Curry	SR	6-6	Reston/South Lakes
Delwin Dillard	JR	6-5	Sussex/Central
Donnie Douglas	JR	6-10	Arlington/Bishop O'Connell
Versham Eley	JR	6-8	Williamsburg/Bruton
Joe Fitzgerald	SR	6-6	Roanoke/William Fleming
Patrick Flynn	JR	6-7	Manassas/Osbourn
Dwayne Forte	SR	6-5	Mouth of Wilson/Oak Hill
Ed Geth	JR	6-9	Norfolk/Granby

HIGH SCHOOL HONORABLE MENTION ALL-AMERICA TEAM

NAME	CL	HEIGHT	CITY/HIGH SCHOOL
Jason Gilliam	SR	5-11	Mouth of Wilson/Oak Hill
Odell Hodge	JR	6-8	Martinsville/Laurel Park
Robbie Howard	SR	6-5	Waynesboro/Waynesboro
Henry Jamison	JR	6-8	Mouth of Wilson/Oak Hill
Mario Joyner	SR	6-6	Virginia Beach/Salem
Jackson Julson	SO	6-7	Blacksburg/Blacksburg
Luteke Kalombo	SR	6-7	Herndon/Herndon
Bart Lammerson	SR	6-9	Vienna/James Madison
Mark Mayer	SR	6-1	Arlington/Bishop O'Connell
Aaron Messelrodt	SO	6-5	Chantilly/Chantilly
Mario Mullen	SR	6-6	Virginia Beach/Bayside
Jabe O'Neill	SR	6-10	Chatham/Hargrave Military Academy
Rashaan Parker	JR	6-7	Richmond/Armstrong-Kennedy
Michael Petin	JR	6-8	Richmond/Meadowbrook
Kevin Ross	JR	6-5	Richmond/John Marshall
Antonio Saunders	JR	6-2	Richmond/Armstrong-Kennedy
Keith Scott	SR	6-2	Staunton/Robert E. Lee
Paul Sessoms	SR	6-6	Portsmouth/Craddock
Edmund Sherod	SO	6-3	Richmond/John Marshall
Jerome Spellman	JR	6-7	Richmond/George Wythe
Greg Taylor	SR	6-3	Chesapeake/Deep Creek
Stanley Taylor	SR	6-3	Prince George/Prince George
Simpson Tolliver	SR	6-8	Richmond/George Wythe
Jamie Warren	SR	6-2	Springfield/West Springfield
Chris White	SR	6-1	Ettrick/Matoaca
Greg Williams	SO	6-3	Fairfax/W.T. Woodson
Joe Williams	SR	6-7	Alexandria/Mount Vernon
Ronell Williams	JR	6-5	Virginia Beach/Bayside

WASHINGTON

NAME	CL	HEIGHT	CITY/HIGH SCHOOL
Tom Ackerman	SR	6-3	Nooksack/Nooksack Valley
Matt Bollinger	SR	6-1	Seattle/O'Dea
Jason Bond	SR	6-8	Seattle/Lakeside
Bryant Boston	SR	6-2	Seattle/Garfield
Fred Brown	JR	6-2	Mercer Island/Mercer Island
Derric Croft	SR	6-5	Lynden/Lynden
Scott Didrickson	SR	6-7	Mercer Island/Mercer Island
David Hawken	SR	6-5	Tahoma/Maple Valley
Damon Hoard	SR	6-4	Puyallup/Puyallup
Paul Jarrett	SR	6-7	Ilwaco/Ilwaco
Lenard Jones	JR	6-6	Seattle/Kings
Nate Linman	SR	6-6	Seattle/Christian
Donny Marshall	SR	6-7	Federal Way/Federal Way
Deforest Phelps	SR	6-6	Bremerton/Bremerton
Jeff Potter	SR	6-8	Redmond/Redmond
David Puliot	SR	6-8	Grandview/Grandview
Jason Sherrill	SR	6-6	East Wenatchee/Eastmont
Scott Tharp	JR	6-8	Battleground/Battleground
Greg Wickstrand	JR	6-5	Seattle/Blanchet
Andre Winston	JR	6-1	Seattle/Cleveland

WASHINGTON, DC

NAME	CL	HEIGHT	CITY/HIGH SCHOOL
Jason Aber	SR	6-6	Washington/Gonzaga
Kenayatta Carmichael	JR	6-8	Washington/Dunbar
David Cox	SR	5-11	Washington/St. John's
Leon Cunningham	JR	6-6	Washington/Archbishop Carroll
Micah Edwards	SR	6-6	Washington/Woodrow Wilson
Andre Logan	JR	6-7	Washington/Wilson
Joel Ortiz	SR	6-6	Washington/Coolidge
Eric Pratt	SR	6-3	Washington/Coolidge
Romeo Roach	SR	5-5	Washington/Dunbar
Damon Singletary	SR	6-2	Washington/Dunbar
Eric Singletary	SO	6-0	Washington/Sidwell Friends
John Stuckey	SR	6-5	Washington/Coolidge
Kobie Taylor	SR	6-2	Washington/Coolidge
Curt Thomas	SR	6-4	Washington/McKinley Tech
James Washington	SR	6-8	Washington/Dunbar
Eric White	JR	6-2	Washington/Coolidge
Warren Williams	SR	6-4	Washington/St. John's

WEST VIRGINIA

NAME	HT	CLASS	CITY/HIGH SCHOOL
Thomas Burgoyne	SR	6-5	Wheeling/Central Catholic
Matt Gaudio	SR	6-7	Wellsburg/Brooke
James Hall	SR	6-4	Smithers/Valley
Scott Hartzell	SR	6-0	Bridgeport/Bridgeport
Romel Lynch	SR	6-1	Oak Hill/Oak Hill
Chris Meighen	SR	6-4	Clarksburg/Washington Irving
Jeff Miller	SR	6-3	Logan/Logan
Deaundra Murphy	SR	6-5	Logan/Logan
Jared Prickett	JR	6-8	Fairmont/West Fairmont
Dan Rush	SR	6-7	Logan/Logan
Andy Scott	SR	6-10	Ridgeley/Frankfort
Glenn Staples	SR	6-5	Beckley/Woodrow Wilson
Brian Thaxton	SR	6-7	South Charleston/South Charleston
Scott Yahnke	SR	6-7	Glen Dale/John Marshall

WISCONSIN

NAME	HT	CLASS	CITY/HIGH SCHOOL
Craig Aamot	SR	6-1	Waukesha/South
Glen Allen	SR	6-5	Greenfield/Whitnall
Brian Currie	JR	6-6	Milwaukee/Rufus King
Tony Giombetti	SR	6-4	Madison/LaFollett
Myron Glass	SR	5-11	Kenosha/St. Joseph
Tracy Gross	SR	6-2	Milwaukee/Custer
Dale Hanford	SR	6-6	Milwaukee/Marshall
Preston Johnson	SR	6-2	Wauwatosa/East
Ryan Marifke	JR	6-1	Racine/Prairie
Otto McDuffie	JR	6-4	Milwaukee/Rufus King
Thomas Metcalf	SR	6-3	Milwaukee/Custer
Terry Preston	JR	6-0	Mequon/Homestead
Freddie Lee Riley	JR	5-9	Milwaukee/Hamilton
Craig Smith	JR	5-11	Milwaukee/University
Shannon Smith	SR	6-4	Whitefish Bay/Dominican
Greg Timmerman	JR	6-8	Cuba City/Cuba City
Jamal Turrentine	SR	6-2	Milwaukee/Washington

WYOMING

NAME	HT	CLASS	CITY/HIGH SCHOOL
Mark Bebout	SR	6-2	Riverton/Riverton
Demetrius Drew	SR	6-5	Cheyenne/Central
Matt Haertzen	SR	6-3	Newcastle/Newcastle
Brian Marso	SR	5-11	Gillette/Campbell
Willie Noseep	SR	5-9	Riverton/Riverton

FIRST TEAM

JUWAN HOWARD

(6-9, 230 lbs., SR, C/F, 23.5 ppg, 10.0 rpg, 3.0 apg, 3.0 blpg, Chicago Vocational HS/Chicago, Ill.) Howard was sensational over the summer, especially at the Nike/ABCD Camp at Princeton University, and vaulted into the national Top Five. Howard was both the leading scorer (15.1 ppg) and a leading rebounder (6.8 rpg) for the week at the Nike/ABCD Camp. *Hoop Scoop* named Howard the winner of its Ben Wilson Memorial award which is annually given to the Most Valuable Player at the Nike/ABCD Camp in honor the late Ben Wilson, who was the top player at the camp in 1984.

"This overachieving intimidating big man simply overpowers and outworks his opponents. He can step out to 12' and score on the turnaround jumper or hit the baby hook in close. Howard plays tough physical defense and he rebounds with the best," wrote Allen Rubin in *Hoop Scoop*.

"He's a super player and more importantly, a super person," said coach Wayne Merino of Artesia HS in Lakewood, Calif., who coached Howard at the Nike/ABCD Camp. He's like a Larry Johnson with two more inches. He beats his man down the floor and he's so tough to stop inside. If he adds the jumphook to his repertoire, it may be all over."

Howard was an Illinois Class AA all-state selection and a member of the All-Chicago team as a junior. His high school coach, Dick Cook, said that Howard "has tremendous pride and plays hard all the time."

This solid student finished his junior year with a 3.2 grade point average and plans on majoring in television/radio communications in college. His college shopping list includes Michigan, Michigan State, Arizona, UNLV, Dayton, Georgetown, Marquette, DePaul, Indiana and Kentucky.

JASON KIDD

(6-4, 195 lbs., JR, G, 18.0 ppg, 7.0 rpg, 10.0 apg, 5.0 stpg, St. Joseph Notre Dame HS/Alameda, Calif.) Kidd enters the 1990-91 season as the unanimous choice by all scouts and talent evaluators as the No. 1 junior in the country. He was terrific all summer long. Kidd was rated the No. 3 player at the Nike/ABCD Camp by *Hoop Scoop* and was unanimously considered the top point guard at the talent-packed camp.

"Kidd plays with incredible intensity at all times. He's a workaholic on both ends. Combining his size and speed with his ability to get the ball and push it up court hard every time is lethal. One Eastern coach best summed up Kidd when he said that he never takes a bad shot. When Kidd is open he'll take a flatfooted jumpshot a la Michael Cooper and usually convert," wrote Garth Franklin of *Hoop Scoop*.

He possesses the heart of a lion and wears opposing guards down with his physical play. Kidd is the rare player who doesn't have to score to be effective and dominate a game. He is an uncanny defensive ballhawk who came up with 11 steals in a game at the Nike/Boo Williams Invitational tournament last April in Norfolk, Va.

West Coast scout Frank Burlison of the *Long Beach Press-Telegram* calls Kidd "probably the most polished player ever from northern California."

All Star Sports ranked Kidd as the top player at the Nike/ABCD Camp. "He understands the game better, and plays at a higher level than any other junior we have observed. He could start today for virtually every Division I program, and he still has two years of high school eligibility remaining. Some compare him to Walt Frazier. Others say he is more advanced than Kenny Anderson at the same stage. He has a fabulous basketball body (6-4, 195 lbs.), and is a tremendous, hard-nosed competitor. His greatest ability is his incredible savvy and knowledge of the game. He seems to have a 'sixth sense' of anticipation and being in the right place. Some West Coast college coaches believe Kidd will bypass college and go directly to the NBA," wrote *All Star Sports* publisher Bob Gibbons.

GLENN ROBINSON

(6-9, 208 lbs., SR, F, 21.5 ppg, 13.0 rpg, 5.0 blpg, Roosevelt HS/Gary, Ind.) Robinson will duel with second-team *Blue Ribbon* All-America Alan Henderson for the Indiana's coveted Mr. Basketball award. They don't take summer play into consideration in the Mr. Basketball balloting in Indiana, but Robinson had a better summer than Henderson. The Gary Roosevelt product was spectacular at several venues. *All Star Sports* ranked him as the No. 2 senior at the Nike/ABCD Camp and all evaluators placed him among the Top Three prospects at that camp.

"(Robinson) is one of the most consistent and efficient players we've observed. Robinson is a composed, 'no frills' blue-collar worker with the best drop-step move for a high school player that we've ever seen," said Bob Gibbons of *All Star Sports*.

Robinson was a first-team All-Indiana selection last year. He was named to the all-tournament team at the Las Vegas Invitational and at the conclusion of his junior season *Parade Magazine* picked him for its prestigious All-America team.

"Glenn 'The Chosen One' Robinson is all business. Robinson would have been MVP of the Nike Camp if Juwan Howard hadn't out-dueled him in their head-to-head confrontation," said Garth Franklin of *Hoop Scoop*.

Purdue coach Gene Keady usually does not beat Bob Knight in head-to-head battles for the premier players in Indiana. However, the combative Keady may win the battle for Robinson as Purdue was considered the favorite in the fall. Robinson is also considering Kentucky, Indiana, Michigan State, DePaul, Kansas, Miami (Fla.) and Syracuse.

DAVID VAUGHN

(6-10, 220 lbs., SR, C/F, 20.6 ppg, 12.5 rpg, 3.7 blpg, Whites Creek HS/Whites Creek, Tenn.) The Grand Ole Opry isn't the only attraction in the Nashville area this year as 6-10 David Vaughn has emerged as a first-team All-America player after an excellent summer. Vaughn comes from a strong basketball lineage. His father was a star at Oral Roberts and played in the ABA. He is also a nephew of Memphis State coach Larry Finch.

Vaughn is a very active, quick, fluid big man with great speed for his size. He can consistently hit the outside shot out to 20 feet. Vaughn was named Mr. Basketball in Tennessee's Class AAA last year. The Tennessee Coaches Association named Vaughn their 1990 Player of the Year. Last spring against the Soviet Junior National team, he made 10-of-13 shots and finished the game with 25 points, 15 rebounds and six blocks. Some recruiters have even gone as far to say Vaughn reminds them of a "young David Robinson."

He is a good student who plans to major in Business Administration in college. With Finch's family ties to Vaughn, Memphis State is considered a lock. "If David Vaughn does not go to Memphis State look for the Mississippi River to start flowing northward," said Bob Gibbons of *All Star Sports*.

CHRIS WEBBER

(6-9 1/2, 230 lbs., FR, C, 24.0 ppg, 13.0 rpg, 4.0 blpg, Detroit Country Day HS/Birmingham, Mich.) Prior to the summer Webber was the unanimous choice as the No. 1 player in the Class of 1991. Webber was not as impressive over the summer as Robinson and Howard as he simply tried to do too much by himself. However, we have seen other big time high school players get bored with the summer circuit in the past such as John Williams, Dennis Scott and Kenny Anderson. True talent generally rises to the top and that will happen with Chris Webber.

"Webber is the most physically impressive, the most athletic gifted, and probably has the most potential of any player in this class," said Bob Gibbons of *All Star Sports*.

Webber was a first-team *Parade Magazine* All-America last year. He was named to the Michigan Dream Team and is a three-time all-state selection. He has all the prerequisite tools to become a major league power forward in the future. Most long time observers of Michigan high school basketball believe that Webber and former Syracuse All-America Derrick Coleman are the most gifted players to come out of the state since Magic Johnson.

Webber attends a prestigious private school in the Detroit suburbs. He is a member of the Chess Club and Young Leaders of America at Detroit Country Day HS. His favorite subject is English and he hopes to become a writer. Webber was featured on Deborah Norville's special "Kids and Sports" on NBC.

Some college coach is going to be estatic when Webber takes out his pen and puts his signature on his school's national letter of intent. Webber reportedly favors playing in the Big Ten. At the end of the summer Michigan State was considered the leader with Kentucky, Duke, Michigan, Syracuse and Detroit all in the picture.

SECOND TEAM

THOMAS BURROUGH

(6-8, 230 lbs., SR, F/C, 22.4 ppg, 12.2 rpg, Oak Hill Academy/Mouth of Wilson, Va.) Burrough is another reason why this is the year of the power forward in high school basketball. He is one of numerous big time power forward prospects who have college coaches lined up in a deep crowd at their doors.

Burrough played last year at West Charlotte (N.C.) HS and transferred to Oak Hill Academy for his senior year. He was a dominant force at the AAU Junior Boys Championship in July at Jonesboro, Ark. He is so powerful under the boards that Burrough reminds many of Wake Forest freshman Rodney Rogers who was the most physically imposing player in the Class of '90. He is not only powerful and a terrific physical specimen but also plays hard.

North Carolina Charlotte, Wake Forest, North Carolina State, Indiana, Kentucky, and South Carolina are all heavily involved with Burrough.

JAMES FORREST

(6-7, 240 lbs., SR, F, 29.0 ppg, 11.0 rpg, 2.8 blpg, Southside HS/Atlanta, Ga.) Forrest was a monster as a junior. He led Southside HS to a 30-2 record and the Georgia state title. In the Georgia state tournament, Forrest hit 51-of-84 shots (61 percent) in four games.

He was named Mr. Basketball in Georgia and was the Gatorade player of the year in the state. Some scouts believe Forrest could be the "next Larry Johnson." He has extreme quickness for his size, the physique of an NFL linebacker, and also possesses great speed. His turnaround jumper is money in the bank.

Forrest is solid in the classroom and plans on studying Business Management in college. His hometown school, Georgia Tech, is far out ahead of the pack and should sign Forrest.

ALAN HENDERSON

(6-9, 200 lbs., SR, F, 29.7 ppg, 14.0 rpg, 4.0 blpg, Brebeuf Prep/Indianapolis, Ind.) Henderson has been a hot name on the national scene since his freshman year. He was rated as the No. 2 underclassman at the Nike/ABCD Camp. He also had a 32-point, 15-rebound performance against 7-0 Eric Montross, one of the top three high school players in the country last year who is expected to be an immediate impact player as a freshman at North Carolina.

Henderson is more of a finesse than a power player and would like to play small forward in college. He does have a versatile, multi-dimensional game and has been a "do it all" player in high school.

"Henderson owns a turn-around jumper which is as smooth as silk along the baseline and wings. In addition, he is capable of going to war in the paint. . ." wrote Roy Schmidt of *Hoop Scoop*.

His father is a cardiologist and Henderson plans to study medicine, law or business in college. He is an honor student with a 3.7 GPA and has scored 1,300 on his SAT test. "I'm looking for the best possible combination —a winning team and outstanding academics," he told *Big East Briefs*.

Henderson is considering Indiana, Purdue, Michigan, Duke, Northwestern, Stanford, Notre Dame, Georgetown and Minnesota. Indiana is considered the leader for Henderson.

CHEROKEE PARKS

(6-11, 205 lbs., SR, C, 22.1 ppg, 13.2 rpg, 3.8 apg, 3.5 blpg, Marina HS/Huntington Beach, Calif.) Parks is one of three Top 44 members who were first-team *Parade Magazine* All-Americas as a junior. His play has drawn comparisons to former UCLA great Bill Walton.

"He's got the chance to be a very special player. It would be foolish to say he's going to be as good —or even nearly as good —as Walton was. But some of his actions and skills remind one of the former UCLA star who led the Portland Trail Blazers to their only NBA championship.

"However, even to be mentioned in the same breath is noteworthy. I haven't seen any other prep center since Walton who inspires such a comparison," wrote Mitch Chortkoff in *Basketball Weekly*.

California prep expert Frank Burlison calls Parks, "the most skilled big man from California in the past 15 years."

He possesses an excellent shooting touch out to the middle distances and shot 59 percent from the floor and 79 percent from the foul line as a junior. He's an extremely gifted outlook passer with excellent mobility.

Parks was the player of the year in Southern California's Orange County. He is a fine student and plans on studying pre-law in college. Parks is expected to choose from Arizona State, UCLA, Arizona, Duke, Kentucky and Syracuse.

RODERICK RHODES

(6-7, 195 lbs., JR, F, 17.0 ppg, 8.0 rpg, 4.0 apg, 3.5 stpg, St. Anthony's HS/Jersey City, N.J.) Rhodes is the premier junior in the East this year and one of the nation's two finest junior prospects. He started as a freshman on a St. Anthony's team, led by Duke point guard Bobby Hurley, that was ranked No. 1 in the nation. St. Anthony's has one of the premier high school programs in the country and has put numerous players in the Division I ranks. Rhodes is the most talented player to come through coach Bob Hurley's St. Anthony's program.

"He can score 15 or 40 and still dominate a game. Roderick doesn't always need the ball to have a great impact on a game," said Ed Broderick of the Nike/ABCD camp.

Rhodes is extremely versatile and performs at a high level when the game is on the line. He is a slashing scorer and only needs to develop a more consistent outside shot to reach greatness.

He was a fourth-team *Parade Magazine* All-America selection as a sophomore and was an All-New Jersey pick as well. Hurley is as good a coach as there is in high school basketball. He has a strong sense of discipline at St. Anthony's and his players work very hard. There is no doubt that he will continue to develop Rhodes' vast potential.

THIRD TEAM

TOM KLEINSCHMIDT

(6-5 1/2, 295 lbs., SR, F, 28.3 ppg, 8.2 rpg, 4.3 apg, 3.0 stpg, Gordon Tech HS/Chicago, Ill.) Kleinschmidt is a proven winner who led Gordon Tech HS to a 30-2 record and the Illinois state championship game. He averaged 32 points per game in the Illinois Class AA tournament, including 27 in the title game against the No. 1 rated team in the country, Chicago Martin Luther King HS. He is a terrific competitor and has been called "the toughest kid on the block," by Bob Gibbons of *All Star Sports*.

He trimmed down as a result of an exhaustive weight training conditioning program in the off-season. Kleinschmidt is extremely smart and makes the big plays under pressure. He is not an extremely explosive athlete but gets everything out of his ability and has never had problems with quicker players.

He was ranked as the No. 4 small forward at the Nike/ABCD Camp by *Hoop Scoop*. "Kleinschmidt grows on you as you keep watching him. He does a superlative job of taking care of the little things and outhustling his opponents. He's also one of the smarter players I've seen . . . He knows how to get the defender off balance and has a fantastic touch when he casts from outside the key. Wherever he chooses, that team will pick up more W's. He's a Winner who rubs off on his teammates," said Garth Franklin of *Hoop Scoop*.

His father was a high school teammate of Duke coach Mike Krzyzewski. His father is also a basketball official at the college and high school level. Kleinschmidt's top three schools are DePaul, Michigan and Michigan State. Others involved are Kansas, Virginia, Marquette, Arizona and Purdue.

JALEN ROSE

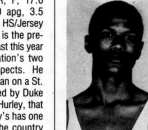

(6-7, 190 lbs., SR, G/F, 18.0 ppg, 9.0 rpg, 4.0 apg, Southwestern HS/Detroit, Mich.) Rose was a key figure in Southwestern's 27-0 record and first-ever state title for coach Perry Watson. Rose was honored on the All-Michigan Dream Team and is a two-time all-state selection.

He is a hot shooting swingman who was very adept last season at hitting three-pointers off the dribble. Rose is also fundamentally sound and very well coached by Watson. He was rated as the No. 2 small forward at the Nike/ABCD Camp by *Hoop Scoop*.

"Besides his tremendous scoring ability, Rose can really run the court and is tough on the boards when he puts his mind to it. Several college coaches said if they could have just one small forward in camp,

Rose would be their man,'' said Roy Schmidt of *Hoop Scoop*.

A good student who plans to study communications in college, Rose may be headed for Syracuse. He also likes UNLV, Michigan State and Michigan.

DONALD WILLIAMS

(6-3, 177 lbs., SR, G, 29.2 ppg, 5.0 rpg, 2.0 apg, 2.0 stpg, Garner HS/Garner, N.C.) Williams was not only the top senior in the state of North Carolina last year but he is also one of the most proficient long range shooters in the country.

''Williams has unlimited range and reminds us of N.C. State 'shooting star' Rodney Monroe, said Bob Gibbons of *All Star Sports*.

The release on his shot is extremely quick and Williams hit nearly 50 percent of his three-point attempts last year. He also has a great work ethic, is a better than average defender and an exciting performer.

''Williams was the most exciting perimeter player at this camp (Nike/ABCD). He has the ability to break your back with one of his long distance bombs. While your first impression is to criticize him for his selfishness in taking an outside shot at any chance, you soon are rooting for him to take the shot every time after watching him kiss the nylons from downtown. With the 3-point shot in college basketball, Donald Williams is one of the most important recruits for high profile college programs,'' wrote Garth Franklin of *Hoop Scoop*.

This scoring machine is also a good student and works with young people in elementary schools in his area. Supposedly, North Carolina is his top choice, but Arkansas, James Madison, North Carolina State, South Carolina, Virginia and Wake Forest are also involved.

BUBBA WILSON

(6-11, 220 lbs., SR, C, 23.0 ppg, 12.5 rpg, 5.2 blpg, Stone County HS/Wiggins, Miss.) Wilson left the Nike/ABCD Camp with a major reputation. He was ranked as the No. 6 senior in the camp by *All Star Sports*. ''(Wilson) is the most mobile and best runner of all the big men. This lithe left-hander is also an excellent shooter,'' said Bob Gibbons of *All Star Sports*.

He can also knock down the outside jumper out to 17 feet and has terrific shotblocking ability. Wilson has twice been a first-team All-Mississippi selection. He truly could be a ''star of the future'' for whatever program is fortunate enough to land him.

Kentucky coach Rick Pitino is in the lead for Wilson. Duke, Florida State and Mississippi State are also in there pitching.

SHARONE WRIGHT

(6-10, 215 lbs., SR, C, 15.0 ppg, 9.0 rpg, 3.0 blpg, Southwest HS/Macon, Ga.) Wright plays in one of the most prestigious programs in the country for legendary coach Don Richardson. He has improved as much in the last year as any big man in the country.

Wright showed his improvement in June when he was named MVP of the prestigious Boston Shootout, scoring 27 points in the championship game while leading the Georgia team to the title. He can score with his back to the basket or facing the hoop. At times, Wright is a virtual offensive machine.

''A strong methodical paint player who uses his strength and body to the limit. He's also a tough rebounder and a very physical defensive player. Wright comes from one of the nation's top programs —he's a good student (3.5 GPA) and a winner,'' said Allen Rubin of *Hoop Scoop*.

Clemson, DePaul, Florida, Florida State, Georgia Tech, Miami (Fla.) and Virginia are all trying to land Wright.

OTHER TOP 44 MEMBERS

CORY ALEXANDER

(6-2, 175 lbs., SR, G, 18.6 ppg, 4.8 rpg, 5.8 apg, Oak Hill Academy/Mouth of Wilson, Va.) Alexander will enroll his third school for his senior year. The Waynesboro, Va., native transferred to prestigious Flint Hill Prep in Falls Church, Va., for his junior season but left that school after coach Stu Vetter resigned. He is now playing for coach Steve Smith at Oak Hill Academy on what should be the nation's strongest prep team.

''He can drill the 3-pointer from downtown, he has an exceptional handle and he runs the show like P.T. Barnum. Alexander always finds the open man due to his outstanding court vision, as he is always looking up-court. He'd make an excellent spokesman against drunk driving, because he's always under control. He has awesome spin moves coming off the dribble and is quite similar to Chris Jackson, because he can stop on a dime and free himself to create his own shot,'' said Roy Schmidt of *Hoop Scoop*.

Alexander is an offensive minded point guard who can dunk in traffic and has great physical tools. This brilliant passer can play either backcourt spot. He's an excellent student with over a 90 GPA and plans to study architecture in college.

Alexander has narrowed his college choices down to Georgia Tech, James Madison, Louisville and Virginia.

MATT ALOSA

(6-2, 187 lbs., SR, G, 35.0 ppg, 7.0 rpg, 10.0 apg, 3.0 stpg, Pembroke Academy/Pembroke, N.H.) The Concord, N.H., native is the most heralded player from New Hampshire in decades. He was named the Gatorade player of the year in New Hampshire last year and is a three-time all-state selection. He is also a three-time team MVP at Pembroke Academy.

Alosa is a pure point guard with remarkable court vision. He has a great attitude, is a big league three-point shooter and a true student of the game.

An honor student with an 91.2 GPA, Alosa plans to study finance or business in college. Providence coach Rick Barnes accepted a verbal commitment from Alosa last spring.

YURI BARNES

(6-8, 230 lbs., SR, C/F, 19.0 ppg, 12.0 rpg, 5.0 blpg, Manchester HS/Richmond, Va.) Barnes is one of a multitude of outstanding power players in the Class of '91. He led Manchester to a 20-7 season and a trip to the Virginia AAA state tournament. He has strong hands, a great attitude and can block shots. Barnes needs to refine his offensive game but he has a great desire to improve.

A fine student with a high GPA, Barnes was a second-team All-Virginia selection last year. He is looking at several Big East and ACC schools as well as some prominent out of his region schools programs such as Minnesota.

TRAVIS BEST

(5-11, 175 lbs., SR, G, 24.0 ppg, 7.2 rpg, 8.9 apg, 5.0 stpg, Springfield Central HS/Springfield, Mass.) One of the top point guard prospects in the nation, Best was the player of the year in Western Massachusetts last season and a first-team all-state selection. He is a terrific penetrator and passer, very creative with the ball and has a scorer's mentality. Best can also put strong pressure on opposing ballhandlers and has three-point range. His work habits are first rate and he loves the transition game.

Best poured in 51 points and led Springfield Central HS to the finals of the Massachusetts state tournament as a sophomore.

''There are players who have more natural basketball ability and better skills than he has,'' said Tom Konchalski of the *HSBI Report*. ''But the thing that sets him apart from the others is he's such a fierce competitor. He plays the game at a very high level of intensity at both ends of the floor.

''He really pushes the ball up the court and is a very good passer in transition. He scores mainly on penetration, but he's a kid who's willing to give the ball up, too. He's also a terrific defender.''

Konchalski also is impressed with Best's ability to make his shots when the game is on the line.

Best is down to three schools —Connecticut, Georgia Tech and Virginia.

JASON CAFFEY

(6-8, 220 lbs., SR, F, Davidson HS/Mobile, Ala.) Last year one of the bluest of the blue chip prospects was Mobile native Tony Lang of LeFlore HS. Lang signed with Duke and he is expected to see considerable playing time as a freshman. Caffey has not received as much publicity as Lang, but veteran Alabama observers believe he could be even be a better prospect.

Caffey plays all over the court on his Davidson HS team. He shoots from the outside, brings the ball up against the press and has shown a vast array of perimeter skills. Caffey has been described as a Danny Manning type. He has extremely long arms, blocks shots and oozes potential.

He did not attend any of the highly rated competition camps but the word is getting out on Caffey. He is the best prospect in Alabama. Recruiters from Alabama and Auburn consider Caffey the one prospect in the state of Alabama they have to land. Hometown South Alabama is also going to be in the hunt.

DERRICK CARROLL

(6-6 1/2, 200 lbs., SR, F, 21.0 ppg, 10.0 rpg, 2.0 apg, 2.0 stpg, Eau Claire HS/Columbia, S.C.) Columbia, S.C., has produced its share of big time players over the years. Alex English, of the Dallas Mavericks, is one of the all-time scorers in NBA history and a Columbia native. So are Xavier McDaniel of the Seattle SuperSonics and Tyrone Corbin of the Minnesota Timberwolves. Carroll is one of two Columbia natives in the Ben Wilson Top 44.

He led Eau Claire HS to a 31-2 record and a second consecutive South Carolina AAA title last season. Eau Claire coach George Glymph called Carroll "a superb offensive player with a terrific attitude." He is an excellent three-point shooter and an outstanding passer.

Named the South Carolina player of the year in Class AAAA last season, Carroll is a solid student who plans to study Business Management in college. Clemson, Georgia Tech and North Carolina State are after Carroll, but it is believed he will eventually sign with the hometown South Carolina Gamecocks.

JOHN CARTER

(6-9, 210 lbs., SR, C, 14.5 ppg, 11.0 rpg, 4.0 blpg, Star Spencer HS/Oklahoma City, Okla.) Potential is the key word concerning John Carter. He has unlimited athletic ability, is a big time shotblocker and rebounder but has not come close to tapping his potential. He is a quick leaper with a reported 36-inch vertical jump.

"A relentless competitor who runs the court extremely well, Carter plays hard at both ends and he's an excellent rebounder. Offensively he can pop out to 17' and he has a nice turnaround jumper from within 12'. Carter gets off his feet quick. Thus, he's a very good rebounder and shotblocker. The star is born," said Allen Rubin of Hoop Scoop.

Arkansas is expected to land Carter. Kansas, UNLV, DePaul, Kentucky, UCLA, Rice and Georgetown also are after Carter.

BEN DAVIS

(6-9, 240 lbs., SR, C, 10.8 ppg, 10.6 rpg, 3.0 blpg, Oak Hill Academy/Mouth of Wilson, Va.) One of three Oak Hill Academy starters in our Top 44, Davis is a native of Fort Pierce, Fla., and one of the nation's premier rebounders. His power on the boards and inside play helped Oak Hill post a 29-0 record last year. Davis was named to the all-tournament team at the Iolani Prep Classic in Hawaii. Eastern Basketball rated him the No. 4 junior in the east last season.

Oak Hill coach Steve Smith is impressed with Davis' work habits, intensity, attitude and "determination to get better every time he plays."

"Charles Oakley-type player. Although he has limited offensive moves, Davis has the strength and physical ability to be an effective interior player," said Greg Schemitz of Big East Briefs.

St. John's could be the frontrunner for Davis. He also is considering Connecticut, Florida State, Georgetown, Oklahoma, Pitt, Virginia and Wake Forest.

STEVE EDWARDS

(6-6, 180 lbs., JR, G/F, 17.2 ppg, 7.2 rpg, 5.9 apg, 4.0 stpg, Miami Senior HS/Miami, Fla.) Edwards is the second member of his family to be a member of Blue Ribbon's Ben Wilson High School Top 44. His older brother, Doug Edwards, was a unanimous first-team high school All-America two years ago, most talent evaluators ranked him second in the nation behind Kenny Anderson, and he will be eligible this year at Florida State. Steve Edwards has stepped out of his brother's shadow and is making his own mark in the game.

Edwards and Kentucky freshman Gimel Martinez led Miami Senior to a 33-3 record and a second consecutive Florida 4A state title last season. Edwards is an outstanding shooter who made 84 three-pointers last season. He is expected to grow to 6-8 plus and has tremendous potential.

"He's the most exciting off guard I've seen in awhile. Fantastic to watch . . . if he's taking it to the basket, he hangs if it's suspended in mid-air and converts at an amazing rate. He can dribble, shoot, and has tons of confidence," said Garth Franklin of Hoop Scoop.

"He's everything Anfernee Hardaway was supposed to be," said West Coast Prep expert Frank Burlison.

His high school coach, "Shakey" Rodriguez calls Edwards "a Magic Johnson-type guard." Edwards was a Florida all-state selection last year. His brother, Doug, was a non-predictor coming out of high school and Steve is already paying serious attention to his academics and wants to make sure he is eligible as a college freshman.

OTHELLO HARRINGTON

(6-8, 200 lbs, JR, F/C, 26.6 ppg, 16.0 rpg, Murrah HS/Jackson, Miss.) The high school talent in Mississippi has received more national publicity than ever in the last few years. The publicity surge was because of some great guards such as Chris Jackson (LSU), Litterial Green (Georgia) and James Robinson, who will be eligible as a freshman at Alabama this year. If Othello Harrington continues to develop, he can be as good at his respective position as those talented trio of Mississippi guards are at theirs.

He will turn 16 in January and is ranked as the No. 3 junior in the country by Bob Gibbons. Gibbons also considers Harrington the top junior big man. As a sophomore he had high games of 39 points, 16 rebounds and 14 blocked shots. His sophomore scoring average was the highest in Murrah history and this program has had many college prospects. He also set a Murrah rebounding record with 576 last year and his 226 blocked shots (6.3 blpg) also established a school single-season record.

"I look for Othello to grow two more inches. Othello can be as good as he wants to be," Murrah coach Orsmond Jordan told the Jackson Clarion-Ledger newspaper.

Harrington was the player of the year in the Jackson Metro Area as a sophomore.

"Similar to a young Wayman Tisdale at this stage. He relies on his athletic ability to dunk on you around hoop and has quicks to fill a lane. Future franchise if he works on skills," wrote Van Coleman in Basketball Times.

ANTHONY HARRIS

(6-2, 183 lbs., SR, G, 29.0 ppg, 8.0 rpg, 6.0 apg, Danbury HS/Danbury, Conn.) Harris is considered the top prospect in Connecticut this year. He was named to the all-tournament team at the Las Vegas Invitational and Eastern Basketball selected Harris as one of the Top 10 juniors in the east.

"He's John Williams (former New Mexico state star and NBA player from Connecticut) revisited," said Tom Konchalski of the HSBI Report. "Anthony is very strong physically. He can take the ball into the lane, pull up, and score. He has the ability to stop on a dime and can really elevate into his shot. He's a great scorer."

He has been used as a point guard for most of his career but played mainly at the wing guard spot last season. "He's a balanced player," said Danbury coach Ken Smith. "He sees the floor very well, is a very good ballhandler, and can shoot the three-pointer without any problem."

This versatile combination guard committed to Syracuse last spring.

ALONZO JOHNSON

(7-0, 225 lbs., SR, C, 10.2 ppg, 9.0 rpg, 6.0 blpg, Marion HS/Marion, Ala.) Johnson grew two inches over the spring and is a legitimate seven-footer with excellent shotblocking and rebounding skills. He has all the offensive tools a big man needs, including power moves, full and half hooks and drop steps. Despite his vast potential and size, Johnson must become aggressive as he has not always been a dominant force in high school.

"This seven-footer has risen to the occasion. He's very aggressive around the basket, but his defense is ahead of his offense —he's a good shot blocker and intimidator. Rebounding is his main forte —he has good hands," said Allen Rubin of *Hoop Scoop.*

A solid student, Johnson plans to study Criminal Justice in college. He's a recruiting target of such southern powers as Alabama, Auburn, Georgia Tech, LSU and Tennessee. Don't look for Johnson to get out of the region.

RUDY JOHNSON

(6-7, 190 lbs., SR, F, 14.8 ppg, 11.1 rpg, 5.0 blpg, 3.2 stpg, Ribault Senior HS/Jacksonville, Fla.) As a junior, Johnson led Ribault HS to a 32-1 record and the Florida AAA state title. He was the MVP in the state tournament and a first-team All-Florida pick.

Johnson is a gifted athlete with an excellent first step to the basket. He is a super quick, slasher in the lane who scores well on drives both in the half court setting and the fast break. He's also an exceptionally quick leaper with outstanding timing. He blocked over 100 shots as a junior. Johnson also has 18-foot shooting range but his perimeter game needs to be fully developed.

"One of the more athletic wingmen in camp (Nike/ABCD), Johnson fit 59% from the field and didn't take a bad shot. Johnson is probably more comfortable playing around the basket in high school, but could be excellent playing for a run and gun team," said Garth Franklin of *Hoop Scoop.*

He is a solid student who wants to become a computer analyst. Johnson will likely choose between Alabama, Auburn, Florida, Loyola Marymount and Mississippi.

JIMMY KING

(6-4, 185 lbs., SR, G, Plano East HS/Plano, Tex.) King was outstanding over the summer at the Five-Star Camp and the Las Vegas Invitational. He is now considered the best prospect in the senior class in the state of Texas.

King has good skills and a feel for the game and breathtaking athletic ability. He took off from around the free throw line, a la Michael Jordan, several times this summer and threw down thundering slam dunks. He also is a tremendous press player who can play the 94-foot game due to his quickness and long arms.

"Immensely talented guard who's unstoppable when inspired. . ." wrote Van Coleman in *Basketball Times.*

Prime time programs from across the country are involved with King like Arkansas, Georgetown, Kansas, Kentucky, Notre Dame, Oklahoma, Syracuse, Texas and UCLA. Georgetown may be the leader for Texas' No. 1 senior prospect.

KEITH LeGREE

(6-2, 200 lbs., SR, G, 28.3 ppg, 11.4 rpg, 8.0 apg, 3.0 stpg, Statesboro HS/Statesboro, Ga.) A first-team All-Georgia selection as a junior, LeGree is the best guard in the state. He is extremely strong and powerful, so much so that he has been compared to some other great power guards like Quinn Buckner and Rumeal Robinson. In high school LeGree overpowers most offenders and he is an exceptional backcourt rebounder. He also has a strong set of offensive moves and is a true three-point threat.

"This bull of a point guard muscled his way inside for a staggering 21-24 free throws (#2 in camp) and 30 rebounds, tops for a guard . . . he plays the position calm and strong and is one of the top points available in this class," said Garth Franklin of *Hoop Scoop* after watching LeGree at the Nike/ABCD Camp.

He also has a great attitude and work habits. LeGree led Statesboro HS to a 22-4 record and a regional championship last year.

He is closely considering Cincinnati, Georgia, Georgia Tech, Kentucky, Louisville, Minnesota and South Carolina.

VOSHON LENARD

(6-4, 185 lbs., SR, G, 19.2 ppg, 8.0 rpg, 4.0 apg, 2.0 stpg, Southwestern HS/Detroit, Mich.) Lenard is one of two players from coach Perry Watson's Southwestern HS program in the *Blue Ribbon* Ben Wilson High School Top 44. Lenard's play last year was a big reason why Southwestern gave Watson his first ever state championship.

Some Michigan observers believe Lenard could one day be better than teammate Jalen Rose, although Rose is rated higher at this point. Lenard has a great work ethic and desire. He can shoot three-pointers, shuts big scorers down on defense and can play a power or finesse game. He was excellent over the summer at the Nike/ABCD Camp and the AAU Junior Boys National Championship tournament at Jonesboro, Ark.

"When talking about the top 2-guards in the country, Lenard seems to be the name many forget. He doesn't do anything that immediately catches the eye, but when you look at his stats you can see that he consistently gets the job. Lenard has to be the best defensive guard in the country, as he's around the ball and makes things happen. Offensively, he has good shooting to 3-point land and a quick first step that enables him to blow by defenders. He's a great athlete who loves to play above the rim," wrote Roy Schmidt of *Hoop Scoop.*

Hoop Scoop ranked Lenard the No. 2 off-guard at the Nike/ABCD Camp. He is expected to choose between two Big Ten schools —Michigan and Minnesota.

DONYELL MARSHALL

(6-8, 175 lbs., SR, F, 20.4 ppg, 12.0 rpg, 6.0 blpg, Reading HS/Reading, Pa.) Prior to the Nike/ABCD Camp, Marshall was an unheralded player. He jumped into the national Top 20 after his performance at the camp. Marshall is extremely thin and has been called the "Splendid Splinter." He is a springy leaper, a dead-eye three-point shooter and has great quickness going to the basket. Marshall is also an excellent shotblocker with great timing and long arms. He literally glides up and down the court. Marshall also passes well and can play facing the basket or posting up. He definitely needs some strength and bulk, but the physical tools are there for Marshall to become a big timer.

Marshall is likely to stay close to his Reading, Pa., home. He is being recruited by Connecticut, Kansas, Kentucky, La Salle, Maryland, Pitt, Rutgers, St. Joseph's, South Carolina and Villanova.

ERIK MEEK

(6-10, 230 lbs., SR, C, San Pasqual HS/Escondido, Calif.) Unlike many of his fellow Top 44 members, Meek is not a great athlete with big time leaping and running ability. However, Meek gets the most out of his ability and is a plugger who just keeps pounding away.

"There are big men with better athletic abilities, but few understand post play as well as Meek," said Frank Burlison of the *Long Beach Press-Telegram.*

Meek is very strong, boxes out well under the boards, has a big wide body, is an excellent passer and sets tough picks. He is not a dominating offensive player but is very functional.

He is a fine student who is a prime recruiting target of all the top western programs.

LOREN MEYER

(6-10, 220 lbs., SR, C, 31.0 ppg, 18.0 rpg, 6.0 blpg, Ruthven-Ayrshire HS/Ruthven, Iowa) Meyer has dominated Iowa Class A competition. Some evaluators wondered how well Meyer would do outside of Iowa this summer and he performed well. Meyer played well at the 19 and Under National AAU/USA Junior Men's Basketball Championship in Jacksonville, Fla., and the Nike/ABCD Camp.

During the summer, Meyer showed exceptional passing skills for his size. He also runs well and has good mobility and possesses impressive outside shooting ability. Meyer is also an extremely hard worker with a great attitude. He needs to work more on his defense and get stronger but that should come.

Meyer has made every possible all-star team in the state of Iowa the past two years. He verbally committed before the end of his junior year to Iowa State.

SILAS MILLS

(6-7, 190 lbs., SR, F, 14.0 ppg, 10.0 rpg, Washington HS/Milwaukee, Wisc.) Mills is another player who had excelled at the local level but was unknown nationally prior to this summer. He quickly proved early in the summer that he belonged among the elite in the country. Mills is a marvelous athlete with great physical ability. He can play above the rim and is an awesome power dunker. He is also a strong rebounder.

"An electrifying, high-wire big-time player with awesome talent!! . . . played tremendous in state tourney and is on skyrocketing climb as a player," said Russ Walburn of the *M&M Report*.

"Silas 'Come Fly With Me' Mills put on the top aerial display at the camp (Nike/ABCD) . . . he's clearly top 25 in the country when he's playing with this kind of enthusiasm. He was the 8th leading scorer with the fifth best field goal percentage (63%)," said Garth Franklin of *Hoop Scoop*.

Reportedly, Mills' mother would like to see him attend hometown Marquette. Kansas, Kentucky, Michigan, Utah and others are all working on Mills.

TIM MOORE

(6-6 1/2, 210 lbs., SR, F, Milby HS/Houston, Tex.) It usually takes a while for the word to get out on Texas players. That is the case with Tim Moore as he was not a nationally known player until this summer after a spectacular performance at the AAU Junior Boys National Championship tournament at Arkansas State in Jonesboro, Ark. He played well enough to be considered the No. 2 prospect in Texas behind Jimmy King.

Moore drew comparisons to Clyde Drexler of the Portland Trail Blazers (a Houston native) because of his astonishing dunking ability. Moore was so spectacular on the break this summer that he has to be considered as athletically talented a small forward as there is in the entire country. He also shot the ball well.

All Star Sports ranks Moore as the No. 39 prospect, regardless of class, in the country. He is expected to stay local with and sign with the Houston Cougars. However, Arkansas, Kansas, Kansas State, Oklahoma, Southern California and Texas are all still after Moore.

HOWARD NATHAN

(5-11, 170 lbs., SR, G, 24.0 ppg, 5.0 rpg, 8.0 apg, 4.0 stpg, Manual HS/Peoria, Ill.) Nathan is the top point guard prospect in the state of Illinois and a player who did well over the summer. *All Star Sports* ranks Nathan as the best point guard in the Class of 1991. Last season he quarterbacked Manual HS to a 28-3 record.

The slick and creative ballhandling Nathan is a terrific penetrator with great speed, quickness and acceleration. He also showed over the summer he can hit consistently from the perimeter.

"He has the complete package, including an incredible first step, outstanding penetration and playmaking ability and relentless hustle and defense," said Roy Schmidt of *Hoop Scoop*. Nathan was ranked as the No. 3 point guard at the Nike/ABCD Camp by *Hoop Scoop*.

Nathan's top schools are DePaul, Kansas, Illinois, Kentucky and Michigan.

CALVIN RAYFORD

(5-9, 165 lbs., SR, G, 15.0 ppg, 2.5 rpg, 10.0 apg, 5.0 stpg, Washington HS/Milwaukee, Wisc.) Rayford is one of two Milwaukee Washington HS players in the Ben Wilson High School Top 44. He teamed with fellow Top 44 member, Silas Mills, to lead Washington to a 26-1 record and the Wisconsin state championship last year. He may be the quickest player nationally in the senior class.

Rayford is so quick he is literally a blur. He is a tremendous playmaker, a dangerous three-point shooter and an outstanding penetrator and defensive ballhawk.

"Possibly best guard ever out of the state! Blessed with blazing speed and quickness. Lone junior named to all-state first team after leading the team to state crown . . . great young man who wants to go to a place that runs," said Russ Walburn of *M&M Report*.

Despite being only 5-9, Rayford wears a size 11 shoe and could grow more. He led the Nike/ABCD Camp in assists (4.2 apg) and many believe he is the top senior point guard in the country. Marquette may be the team to beat. UNLV, Michigan, Michigan State, Kansas, Georgia Tech and Louisville are also pursuing Rayford.

JAMES SCOTT

(6-5, 185 lbs., SR, F, 24.0 ppg, 12.0 rpg, Eastside HS/Patterson, N.J.) Scott recently underwent arthroscopic knee surgery but is expected to be ready to play by Christmas at Eastside HS in Patterson, N.J. As a junior he was a first-team All-New Jersey selection in Group I. Last spring he was the MVP of the McDonald's tournament in Charlotte, N.C. He also played well in June at the Five-Star Camp at Honesdale, Pa.

"Scott is a phenomenal athlete with strong post up moves and great hands. Scott also has a good enough handle and enough range to be an outstanding wing guard in college," said Clark Francis of *Hoop Scoop*.

Most Eastern experts believe Scott is definitely the top senior in New Jersey this year. He is a slashing, high grade athletic type scorer who has been unstoppable in high school offensively from 15 feet on in.

He is a hot prospect for Big East schools like Boston College, Providence and Seton Hall, plus a few SEC programs and ACC teams like Georgia Tech.

JOHN SMITH

(6-8, 215 lbs., SR, F, 16.9 ppg, 9.3 rpg, 4.0 blpg, A.C. Flora HS/Columbia, S.C.) Smith and his Columbia rival, Derrick Carroll, are the top two prospects in South Carolina this year. Smith is also one of the finest power forwards in the country. He was named to the All-America team at the 17 and Under AAU tournament prior to his junior year, was team MVP at A.C. Flora HS last season and an all-state selection.

Smith is an outstanding competitor who is a very aggressive rebounder and rejector. He has gotten bigger and stronger in the last year.

"Smith plays hard and is a warrior," said Roy Schmidt of *Hoop Scoop*.

He plays in one of the premier programs in South Carolina for nationally recognized coach Carl Williams. A.C. Flora is also the alma mater of NBA players Xavier McDaniel and Tyrone Corbin.

He is expected to sign late next spring. South Carolina and most of the ACC are heavily involved with Smith.

DAMON STOUDAMIRE

(5-11, 160 lbs., SR, G, 23.8 ppg, 4.0 rpg, 6.2 apg, Wilson HS/Portland, Ore.) The top prospect out of the Pacific Northwest this year, Stoudamire is also one of the premier point guards in the country. He is an excellent passer and ballhandler with shooting range that extends well beyond the three-point line. Stoudamire is also an outstanding competitor and works extremely hard at both ends of the court. He has exceptional defensive anticipation as well.

"Probably the smartest and quickest point guard under pressure (along with Calvin Rayford)," said Garth Franklin of *Hoop Scoop* after watching Stoudamire at the Nike/ABCD Camp.

"Knows his job and does a good job of creating in half-court game or can push it in the open court," wrote Van Coleman in *Basketball Times*.

He is also an outstanding student athlete and a member of the DECA Junior Achievement organization at Wilson HS. Stoudamire plans to study business in college. He is related to Georgetown Hoya guard Antoine Stoudamire. This big time point guard prospect is a prime recruiting target of virtually the entire Pacific-10 Conference.

CARLOS STRONG

(6-8, 205 lbs., JR, C/F, 16.8 ppg, 10.0 rpg, 2.6 apg, 3.0 stpg, Cedar Shoals HS/Athens, Ga.) Strong is a versatile combination forward who is a terrific rebounder and can score from the inside or on the perimeter.

The All-Georgia pick was impressive over the summer at the Nike/ABCD Camp at Princeton University. "Carlos truly lived up to his name in that he is strong in the middle. He had a solid shooting percentage from the field (26-of-49) . . . Likely to be a combination 3/4 forward in college and top 10 senior at this time next year,'' wrote Garth Franklin of *Hoop Scoop*.

"Strong post up type power forward who just explodes to hole on the blocks, but can also go out and stick 17-foot jumper,'' wrote Van Coleman in *Basketball Times*.

Strong is not the only big time junior in Athens, Ga. He has a rival, 6-8 Percy Eberhardt of Clarke Central HS, and their duels over the next two seasons should be something to behold.

ANTONIO WATSON

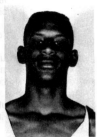

(6-8, 195 lbs., SR, F, 23.0 ppg, 16.0 rpg, Eastmoor HS/Columbus, Ohio) Watson is considered the top senior prospect in the state of Ohio this season. He is an excellent shooter and ballhandler for his size, very quick to the ball on the boards and rebounds well. He needs to get stronger and heavier, but the ability is there for Watson to become an excellent power forward.

"One look at his body and his footwork and you think you're dealing with one of the five best forwards around (and very likely you are) He's a high major . . . fluid big man who makes it look easy around the basket. Should be a top 25 All-America,'' said Garth Franklin of *Hoop Scoop*.

It will be hard to keep Watson away from the clutches of Ohio State coach Randy Ayers. However, Cincinnati, Arizona State, Michigan, Michigan State, Notre Dame, Pitt and Purdue are all trying to take Watson out of Columbus and away from the Buckeyes.

GLEN WHISBY

(6-8, 230 lbs., SR, F, 20.0 ppg, 10.0 rpg, 4.0 blpg, Brookhaven HS/Brookhaven, Miss.) Whisby is a third of three players from Mississippi in the *Blue Ribbon* Ben Wilson High School Top 44. He is one of the strongest inside performers in the south and a very physical post player. In high school, Whisby overpowers almost everyone he faces.

"Most of time at camp (Nike/ABCD) Whisby truly looked liked a man among boys. Along with David Vaughn, he was one of the most intimidating shot blockers in camp . . . he has a very strong body and is athletic enough to make an impact in the SEC in years to come,'' wrote Garth Franklin of *Hoop Scoop*.

Brookhaven HS coach Dale Kimbal believes Whisby needs to improve his passing and ballhandling and to learn to consistently block out under the boards. He so easily outjumps most opponents that Whisby does not have to block out in high school.

"Athletically, he could take you to blocks and dunk on you or step out and drill 18-foot jumper. Has lots of room to improve, especially on the perimeter,'' wrote Van Coleman in *Basketball Times*.

The Mississippi schools, plus DePaul, Michigan and others are very interested in landing Whisby.

NCAA MEN'S TOURNAMENT INFORMATION

EAST REGIONAL

First-Second Rounds
March 14 & 16: Cole Fieldhouse, College Park, Maryland
March 15, 17: Carrier Dome, Syracuse, New York

FINALS
March 22, 24: Meadowlands Arena, East Rutherford, New Jersey

SOUTHEAST REGIONAL

First-Second Rounds
March 14, 16: Freedom Hall, Louisville, Kentucky
March 15, 17: The Omni, Atlanta, Georgia

FINALS
March 21, 23: Charlotte Coliseum, Charlotte, North Carolina

MIDWEST REGIONALS

First-Second Rounds
March 14, 16: Hubert H. Humphrey Metrodome, Minneapolis, Minnesota
March 15, 17: Univ. of Dayton Arena, Dayton, Ohio

FINALS
March 22, 24: Pontiac Silverdome, Pontiac, Michigan

WEST REGIONALS

First-Second Rounds
March 14, 16: Jon M. Huntsman Center, Salt Lake City, Utah
March 15, 17: McKale Center, Tucson, Arizona

FINALS
March 21, 23: Kingdome, Seattle, Washington

FINAL FOUR
Indiana Hoosier Dome, Indianapolis, Indiana

SEMI-FINALS
March 30: East vs. Midwest
West vs. Southeast

CHAMPIONSHIP GAME
April 1

FUTURE FINAL FOUR SITES
1992: Hubert H. Humphrey Metrodome, Minneapolis, Minnesota; April 4, 6
1993: Louisiana Superdome, New Orleans, Louisiana; April 3, 5
1994: Charlotte Coliseum, Charlotte, North Carolina; April 2, 4

NCAA WOMEN'S TOURNAMENT INFORMATION

First Round
March 13: On the campus of one of the participating institutions

Second Round
March 15-17: On the campus of one of the participating institutions

EAST REGIONAL FINALS
March 21, 23: St. Joseph's University, Philadelphia, Pennsylvania

MIDEAST REGIONAL FINALS
March 21, 23: University of Tennessee, Knoxville, Tennessee

MIDWEST REGIONAL FINALS
March 21, 23: University of Texas, Austin, Texas

WEST REGIONAL FINALS
March 21, 23: University of Nevada, Las Vegas, Nevada

FINAL FOUR
March 30, 31: Lakefront Arena, University of New Orleans, Louisiana